FALCONER
OF
HALKERTON

VIVE UT VIVAS

LORD FALCONER OF HALKERTON

FALCONER OF HALKERTON

A Genealogy of a Scottish Family and Its
Branches in England, the United States, and
Jamaica, Including Those Spelled
"Falconar" and "Faulkner"

by

Paul McKee Gifford

With a Chapter by Paul Beresford Weller

Heraldic Illustrations by Richard M. Crossett

HERITAGE BOOKS, INC.

Published 1997 by

HERITAGE BOOKS, INC.
1540E Pointer Ridge Place
Bowie, Maryland 20716
1-800-398-7709

ISBN 0-7884-0615-9

A Complete Catalog Listing Hundreds of Titles
On History, Genealogy, and Americana
Available Free Upon Request

To the memory of my grandmother
Mabel Grace Faulkner McKee,
whose memories started this off

Contents

Illustrations and Charts

Preface

The ancient Scottish family of Falconer of Halkerton and its cadet lines have needed a published genealogy for many years. This became especially apparent in 1966, when the Arthur George Keith-Falconer, 10th Earl of Kintore and 12th and last Lord Falconer of Halkerton, died without any identified heirs-male, meaning, in Scottish legal terminology, descendants or other relatives in the male line. His sister inherited the Kintore title, which passed to her son, but the Halkerton title, which, since 1778, had been a lesser and almost forgotten title, now became dormant. Until and unless a claimant petitions the Lyon King of Arms for a matriculation of arms (meaning that the claimant proves that he is the senior male-line heir, using evidence which not only documents his own line, but the extinctions of all senior lines and individual males), the title will remain dormant.

Whether or not the title is ever successfully claimed, the family has provided many worthy individuals, played prominent roles at times in Scottish government, and as the British Empire developed, sought their fortunes in distant colonies. Some were successful and some not, and in America, in any case, their descendants multiplied and prospered.

This genealogy attempts to trace all male lines from the lairds of Halkerton. The earliest ancestor from whom descents can be proved is Alexander Falconer of Halkerton, who died about 1499. However, the cadet lines listed here nearly all descend from his great-grandson, Alexander Falconer of Halkerton, who died in 1587. The various branches, arranged by chapter, are carried down to the present or to the extinction of the male line. Children of Falconer daughters are also listed. Some branches of this family have seen their genealogies in print, but most have not. This is thus a first attempt at a comprehensive history of this family.

This volume had its origins in a not unusual way. I began looking into my Faulkner ancestors about 1964, when I was thirteen. My grandmother, Mabel G. (Faulkner) McKee, had earlier taken me, as a boy of ten, to the Grand Point Cemetery, in Irvington, Illinois, to see the graves of her ancestors, and I recall helping her copy some of the inscriptions. Later on, I traced our line back a generation from what my grandmother knew to Alexander Faulkner, who fought in the American Revolution from Pennsylvania. In 1971,

I got in touch with Ann Faulkner, of Mount Clemens, Michigan, who had been busy for several years comprehensively tracing this branch of her husband's family. She had discovered a possible ancestor in Alexander Falconar (c.1693-after 1758), the Maryland merchant.

Alexander gave his sons the same names which were used a few generations later in my own branch, and, although the documentation was weak, many other mitigating factors, described in the text, suggested that Alexander was indeed the immigrant ancestor. Further, it looked like Alexander had a brother Gilbert, a merchant in Kent County, Maryland. In 1979 I located the record of Gilbert's marriage, in the Philadelphia Monthly Meeting of Friends register, which named his father as David Falconar, merchant of Edinburgh. I immediately looked in the Scottish sources available to me and learned of the Falconers of Halkerton. The names chosen by this family certainly resembled those used by the American family. But where did David, the Quaker merchant, fit in? In 1979 and 1980, using the vast resources of the Genealogical Society of Utah, I was able to place David, hitherto all but omitted from the published genealogies. The lack of an adequate genealogy, as well as the discovery that the title was dormant, led me to pursue the project whose results lay before you.

In 1982, I spent several days in Maryland, tracing what I could of the families of the immigrants Gilbert and Alexander. For several years afterwards, due to other circumstances, I was inactive. Then in 1987, George E. Spaulding, Jr., who had traced his line to Alexander, the immigrant, began to correspond. When Major Paul B. Weller, then of Cirencester, Gloucestershire, got in touch with me in 1988, the impetus for comprehensively tracing the family began. I had carried on some correspondence with his father-in-law, Peter Serrell Falconer, the representative of the family long established in Gloucestershire, who had earlier done some investigation into the genealogy of the family. It became clear to Paul and me that by pooling research on both sides of the Atlantic, some progress towards determining the heir might be made, and it was indeed. I set my goal on tracing all male lines down to the present, as well as attempting to determine the identity of the heir to the title. Although the search to determine the heir to the title was ultimately unsuccessful, I was able to trace most lines.

The research for this book was of necessity done in several countries and states. I went to Jamaica for a week in 1989 and followed up with another trip in 1994. In 1991, I spent a productive five weeks in Great Britain, approximately two in England and three in Scotland. Between 1988 and 1994 I made several trips, some repeated, to Maryland, Pennsylvania, New York, Kentucky, Ohio, Indiana, Illinois, Missouri, looking at courthouse records, libraries, and cemeteries.

Correspondence began in earnest by responding to queries placed several years before in different publications. Billie Hart, of Austin, Texas, and Marguerite Leander, of Sioux Falls, South Dakota, were both very kind to send copious materials on their branches. Ann Faulkner was extremely generous in allowing me copies of her extensive research and I want to thank her for that. Other correspondence followed.

Trying to locate living descendants proved at first to be as difficult as genealogists have described. The most recent available indexed census was 1910 or even 1900 for many states. I tried mass blanket mailings, with mixed results. Then the fortuitous appearance of the digital Social Security Death Benefits Index and the fully indexed 1920 census greatly facilitated the search. By searching for obituaries in local papers, I could identify living descendants. Having found their names in telephone directories, I wrote to over two hundred and twenty. Of those, some had invalid addresses, some were the wrong individuals, and others did not care to respond. But the majority did, and many spent much time gathering the information for me.

I wish to acknowledge the help of those named above, and to thank here the many descendants of this family who have responded to my inquiries, even though their names may not appear here: Mark R. Clark, Judy Critchlow, Shug Dickerson, Amy Falconer, John Stuart Falconer, Leonard Falconer, Marion Falconer, Norman R. Falconer, Paul R. Falconer, Barbara Wilkes Faulkner, Bertha Faulkner, Betty Faulkner, Charles C. Faulkner, Curtis L. Faulkner, David D. Faulkner, Edward C. Faulkner, Frank D. Faulkner, Fred J. Faulkner, Leonard R. Faulkner, Mary (Mrs. David) Faulkner, Raymond Faulkner, Rollin Faulkner, William E. Faulkner, Marion F. Honsinger, Jeroen van Iddekinge, Marilyn Ledford, Edward M. Nicholas, Claudia M. Rentrop, Paul H. Roske, Patricia J. Kirkman Sullivan, Robert W. Wagner, Alta Walsh, Rena Westbrook-Johnson, and Donald Whyte. Other correspondents are referenced in the sources. I would also like to acknowledge the help received from the librarians and town historians and others who were kind enough to provide information. Finally, I would like to thank the Earl of Kintore for permission to search the Kintore Papers and for allowing me to photograph and publish portraits from his collection.

All Scottish families such as the Falconers probably have left descendants of various branches in former British colonies and other countries, but this family may be unusual in that no male lines of descent traceable to the senior line survive in Scotland. By the beginning of this century, only three Falconer lines existed in Great Britain: the Keith-Falconers, the Falconar-Stewarts of Feddal, and the Falconers of Gloucestershire. Members of these branches went to such distant parts of the empire as India, Malaya, South Africa, Khartoum, Aden, Burma, and Australia. They served gallantly in the Crimean War, Boer War, and World Wars I and II, some fatally. Others were prominent judges, physicians, and architects. Only one other three-generation male line developed after the 18th century, due in part to deaths in action, but perhaps also due to the difficulty some younger sons had in establishing themselves.

The Americans, meanwhile, had developed new identities. Two or three strains formed. One managed to retain the life, which the original immigrant Gilbert sought to attain, as merchants and slave-owning planters, raising tobacco and cotton. Strong Confederates, their way of life ended with the Civil War. The descendants of the merchant Patrick Falconar, who came to New Jersey in 1684, included some merchants, but mostly consisted of yeoman, Yankee farmers in New York. Similarly, those of Alexander, who came to Maryland before 1719, if they stayed east, became Methodist carpenters and blacksmiths, or, if they went west, were Baptist or Methodist farmers and invariably supported the cause of the Union, many with their lives.

Most of these American descendants have forgotten their distant Scottish heritage, as they married spouses of different origins. As the United States became urbanized at the beginning of this century, so did this family's members, although they tend to live in smaller cities, rather than in large metropolitan areas. Descendants in the male line of the immigrants Gilbert, Alexander, and Patrick have concentrated themselves in New York, Pennsylvania, Maryland, Kentucky, Ohio, Michigan, Indiana, Illinois, Arkansas, Missouri, Oklahoma, Texas, Nebraska, Iowa, California, Oregon, and Washington.

Like the Americans, the Jamaican descendants of the Falconers took on a different identity. Scottish adventurers who went to that island usually regarded it as a temporary stay, intending to return to Great Britain with a fortune. Due both to this feeling and to the lack of white women, men frequently made alliances with free women of color. They acknowledged their mixed-race offspring and provided for them by giving them land, apprenticeships, and cash. The Jamaican Falconers traced here mostly lived in a community established during slavery by other free people of color. In recent years, their descendants have emigrated to Great Britain, the United States, and Canada.

When I reached a point where further research on some lines became difficult or impossible, I realized that identification of the heir to the Lordship Falconer of Halkerton would not likely occur and that it would be better not to delay the publication of the genealogy any further. Various events have conspired to delay publication, and some information is apt to be out of date. This first attempt is likely to have a certain number of errors or incomplete information as well. I apologize for this, but with several thousand individuals named, information on people in the past being sometimes difficult to find and information on living people sometimes received third-hand, such problems are inevitable. Corrections and additions can be sent to me at 710 Avon St., Flint, Michigan 48503; perhaps a later edition may appear if enough interest warrants it.

Paul McKee Gifford
Flint, Michigan
1996

Explanatory Note

Organization

This genealogy is divided into chapters, arranged according to seniority, and each is assigned a letter. The descent of the lairds of Halkerton, Lords Falconer of Halkerton, and Earls of Kintore thus is given in Chapter A. Within each chapter, individual fathers are delineated in numerical order, prefaced by the letter of the chapter. The identifying number "A1" is given to Alexander Falconer (d. 1499/1500), the first from whom unbroken descent can be traced. The progenitor of a cadet line is assigned a chapter letter and the number "1", so, for example, Gilbert Falconar, the second son of David Falconar who settled in Maryland, is identified with the alphanumeric designation "J1." Gilbert's eldest son is "J2," and his second son is "J3," and so on. David's eldest son John is "G2," as he continued a cadet line, but his third son Alexander, who established a new line in Maryland, is "K1." The numbering system is, I hope, readily apparent to the reader and should not present problems in locating the ancestors or descendants of a particular person. The simplified pedigree which follows on pages viii-ix shows, in tabular form, the relationship of the different branches.

Terminology

Most of the readers of this book will be Americans, since a family's genealogy, by its nature, rarely attracts interest outside of its own descendants. At the same time, much of it concerns Scots living in Scotland. Despite American unfamiliarity with Scottish legal terminology, social conventions, as well as the Scots language, I have chosen, for the most part, not to attempt to "translate" these transactions and to limit the insertion of historical context.

Nevertheless, a few basic explanations of some of the Scottish conventions are probably in order. When a man owned land, he was a laird and was invariably designated by the name of his chief piece of property. Thus Alexander Falconar of Glenfarquhar was called so because Glenfarquhar was the name of his chief property. A tenant would be designated with the style "in [name of land]. Unless entailed in some other way, land was inherited by the eldest son.

Until the eighteenth century, the landed classes arranged marriages, especially of their heirs, through contracts. Spouses were chosen both to make alliances with influential families and to provide a substantial dowry, or tocher. In the Medieval period, younger sons often became priests, clerks, or merchants, although some also held land in feudal tenure. Ministers and lawyers (earlier clerks and notaries) in the sixteenth and seventeenth centuries were called "Master," or "Mr." By the end of the seventeenth century, the old feudal world was drawing to a close, and the younger sons began to find careers as lawyers, merchants, naval and army officers, clergymen, and physicians.

Forms of Names

This book follows the general practice of spelling personal names in the way the person spelled his or her name. "Falconer" was the usual spelling until the middle of the seventeenth century, when "Falconar" became general. Some branches continued to use the latter form until this century, but are now all extinct. Three American branches adopted "Faulkner," two during the eighteenth century and one in the following century.

Individuals are listed by their full names. Occasionally nicknames or alternate given names are given in parentheses, but only where these differ substantially from the legal names. Scottish women kept their maiden names after marriage until the eighteenth and nineteenth centuries. Otherwise, married women's surnames are enclosed in parentheses.

Dates

Dates are presented in the form [day] [month] [year], hence 2 August 1843. Some factors complicate matters, however. England and her overseas colonies retained the Julian calendar until September 1752, while Scotland adopted the Gregorian calendar in 1600. The Julian calendar, which by 1752 was about twelve days behind the Gregorian calendar, began on Lady Day, March 25th. March was thus considered to be the first month of the year. A date such as 5 February 1740 in the Julian calendar was actually 16 February 1741 in the Gregorian calendar, so the practice here is to write the Julian year of the date falling after December 31 and before March 25 as 1740/1, for example.

Quaker practice was to number months, so that in the Julian calendar January was the tenth month and March the first month. Dates from Quaker records here are given in the form where the month is designated by a small-case roman numeral, e.g., 14 x 1726/7, would be 14 January 1726/7. Scottish Quakers before 1752 seem to have followed the English Julian calendar, although further evidence for this practice than I have seen would be desirable.

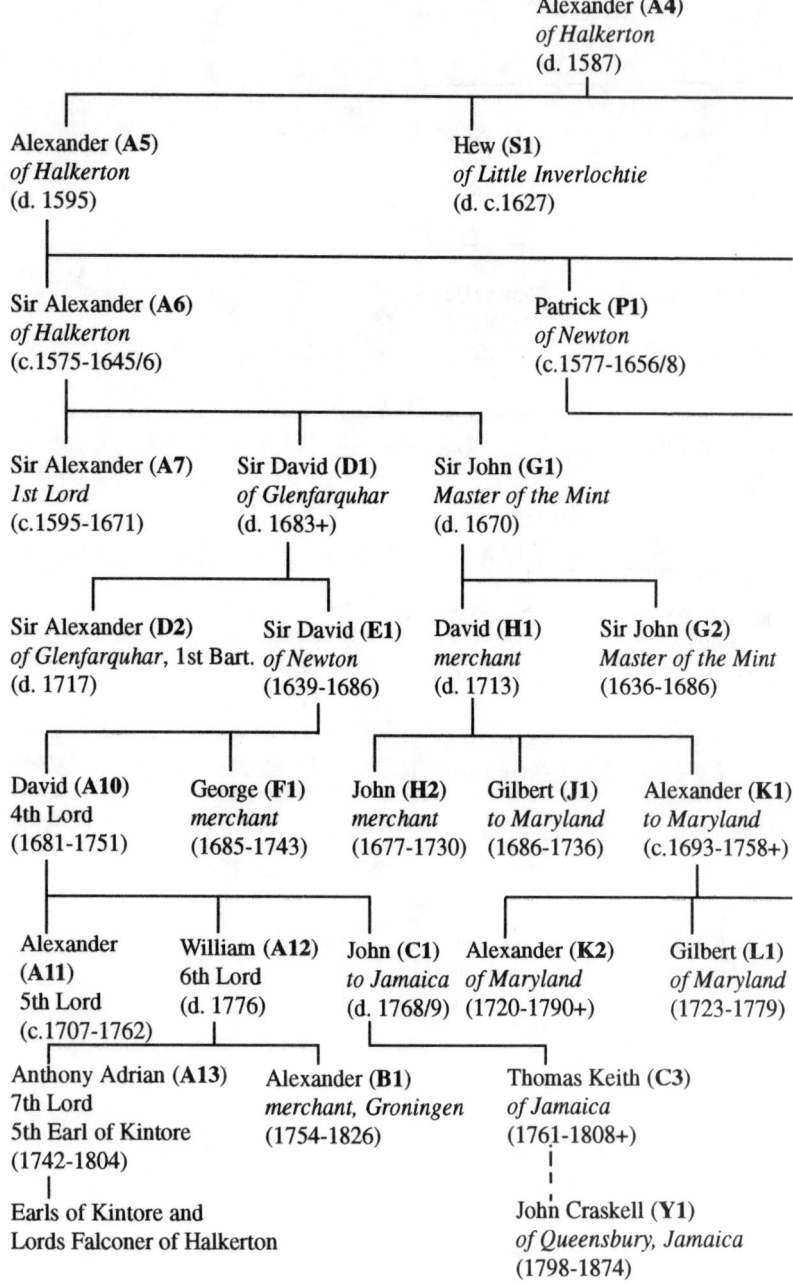

Alexander (**A4**)
of Halkerton
(d. 1587)

Alexander (**A5**)
of Halkerton
(d. 1595)

Hew (**S1**)
of Little Inverlochtie
(d. c.1627)

Sir Alexander (**A6**)
of Halkerton
(c.1575-1645/6)

Patrick (**P1**)
of Newton
(c.1577-1656/8)

Sir Alexander (**A7**)
1st Lord
(c.1595-1671)

Sir David (**D1**)
of Glenfarquhar
(d. 1683+)

Sir John (**G1**)
Master of the Mint
(d. 1670)

Sir Alexander (**D2**)
of Glenfarquhar, 1st Bart.
(d. 1717)

Sir David (**E1**)
of Newton
(1639-1686)

David (**H1**)
merchant
(d. 1713)

Sir John (**G2**)
Master of the Mint
(1636-1686)

David (**A10**)
4th Lord
(1681-1751)

George (**F1**)
merchant
(1685-1743)

John (**H2**)
merchant
(1677-1730)

Gilbert (**J1**)
to Maryland
(1686-1736)

Alexander (**K1**)
to Maryland
(c.1693-1758+)

Alexander
(**A11**)
5th Lord
(c.1707-1762)

William (**A12**)
6th Lord
(d. 1776)

John (**C1**)
to Jamaica
(d. 1768/9)

Alexander (**K2**)
of Maryland
(1720-1790+)

Gilbert (**L1**)
of Maryland
(1723-1779)

Anthony Adrian (**A13**)
7th Lord
5th Earl of Kintore
(1742-1804)

Alexander (**B1**)
merchant, Groningen
(1754-1826)

Thomas Keith (**C3**)
of Jamaica
(1761-1808+)

Earls of Kintore and
Lords Falconer of Halkerton

John Craskell (**Y1**)
of Queensbury, Jamaica
(1798-1874)

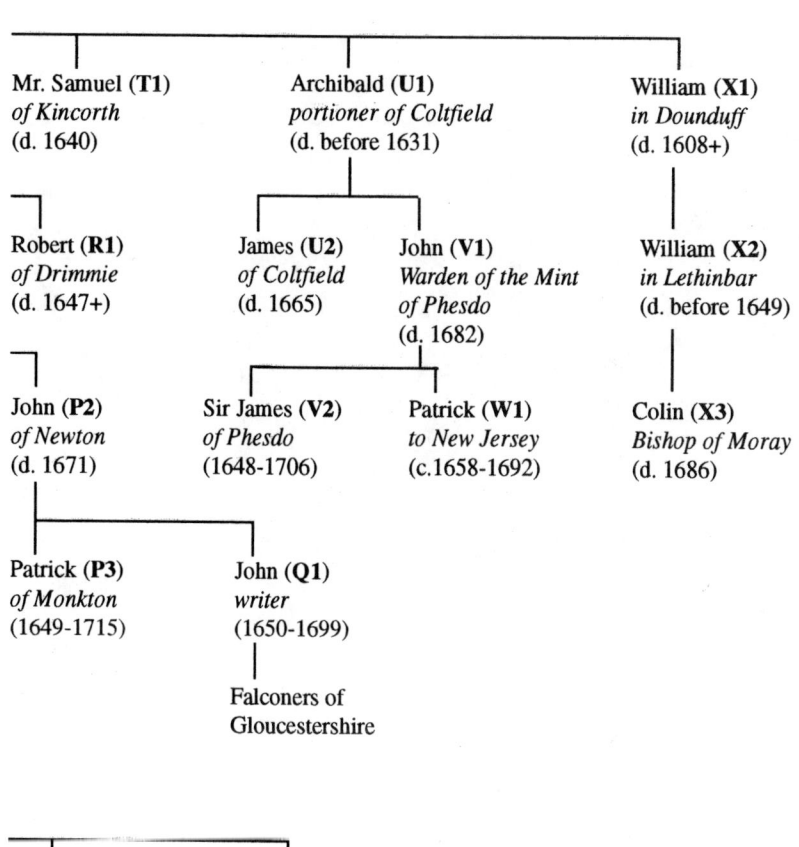

Mr. Samuel (**T1**)
of Kincorth
(d. 1640)

Archibald (**U1**)
portioner of Coltfield
(d. before 1631)

William (**X1**)
in Dounduff
(d. 1608+)

Robert (**R1**)
of Drimmie
(d. 1647+)

James (**U2**)
of Coltfield
(d. 1665)

John (**V1**)
Warden of the Mint
of Phesdo
(d. 1682)

William (**X2**)
in Lethinbar
(d. before 1649)

John (**P2**)
of Newton
(d. 1671)

Sir James (**V2**)
of Phesdo
(1648-1706)

Patrick (**W1**)
to New Jersey
(c.1658-1692)

Colin (**X3**)
Bishop of Moray
(d. 1686)

Patrick (**P3**)
of Monkton
(1649-1715)

John (**Q1**)
writer
(1650-1699)

Falconers of
Gloucestershire

David (**M1**)
to Kentucky
(1726-1787+)

Samuel (**N1**)
to Pennsylvania
(1732-1788)

PEDIGREE OF FALCONER OF HALKERTON
(Simplified)

Further generations are found
in the chapters designated
by the first code letter.

Lands owned by Falconers in Kincardineshire and Angus, 16th to 18th centuries.

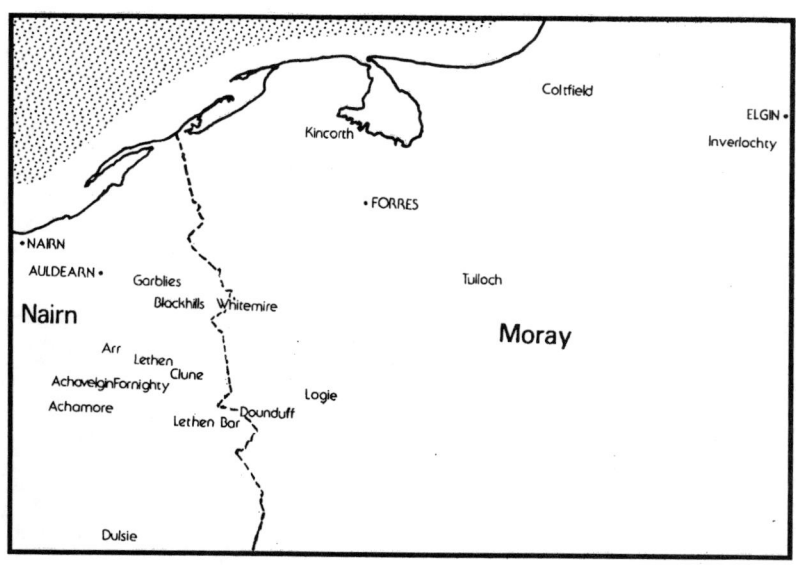

Lands in Nairnshire and Morayshire owned by Falconers, 16th to 18th centuries. The map of Scotland shows the locations of Nairnshire and Morayshire in the north and the Kincardineshire-Angus area in the east.

CHAPTER A

Falconer of Halkerton

Scotland in the twelfth century witnessed a transformation in its social system. Following the accession to the throne of Malcolm Canmore and his English queen Margaret in 1057, feudal relations gradually supplanted the bond of kinship between ruler and noble. This was part of a larger transformation, as Scotland was brought into the cultural realm of western Europe. Its unique religious and legal traditions, developed in isolation, gave way to Roman law and custom. The courts of David I (1124-1153) and his successors became increasingly Norman in character, through marriage alliances with the English royal family. Opportunities in Scotland opened up for great lords, their feudal dependents, and individual adventurers, from England, including Normandy, Brittany, and elsewhere in France. Some joined the royal retinue and received feudal grants in return for their service. The court, which did not have a permanent residence at this point in time, included all the high officers of the kingdom, such as the steward and the marischal, as well as the lesser individuals needed to run the court and the kingdom.

Falconry was the favored sport of medieval kings and nobility. Finding, training, and maintaining falcons was a full-time occupation, so that the position of Royal Falconer was, in some kingdoms, a high post.[1] The Howe of the Mearns, a well-watered, fertile area in the south of Kincardineshire, about ten miles northwest of the city of Montrose, in the vicinity of Halkerton, was a prime location for this sport and may well have been so since the tenth century. The royal mews may have been located there, as J. C. Watt suggested.[2] The ancestor of the Falconers of Halkerton was, we can assume, falconer to King William the Lion, and it is reasonable to suppose that king and court visited the Howe of the Mearns seasonally to enjoy the sport.

The family of Falconer of Halkerton claims descent from **Ranulf le Falconer**, eldest son of **Walter de Lowthorp**e (Loutorp), who obtained from William the Lion, King of Scotland, a charter, dated at Montrose, 2 June, between 1209 and 1211 (probably 1211). A copy and translation of this charter, made in 1656, reads as follows:

> William be the grace of God To all whom thir presents concernes Witt ye me to
> haue giwin and granted and be this my present charter confirmed To Ranolph

falconar eldest sone of Walter of Loutorp Kingower in Gowerin et in le Merne fyve dauchs of Land callit Balemacoy and Ackwendothan and Balebeggin et Lacherachgeigh Kenni and davoch of Endolach with the pertinents to him and his aires To be holdine of me and my aires in few and heretage frielie honorablie weill and in peace for the seruice of his owne body and if it sall happine that he cannot giue the seruice of awin bodie the seruice unius archarii in the armie before the witness' Arneass my chaplaine William Cuming my Justiciar Walter de Bosco and Hugh my clerks de Camera Walter de Wechterlis Richard Reuell Bric' iudice meo at Monross the second day of Junii.[3]

G. W. S. Barrow speculates that Balemacoy was Balmakewan, in the parish of Marykirk; Ackwendothan was Auchinzeoch, in Fordoun; Balebeggin was Balbegno, in Fettercairn; and Endolach was Bogendollo, in Fettercairn,[4] all in Kincardineshire. The lands of Halkerton, one mile north of present-day Laurencekirk, may have been Lacherachgeigh Kenni. The location of Kingower in Gowerin is uncertain, although not in the Mearns.

Ranulf, as eldest son, could have chosen to remain in Yorkshire to await his inheritance, but his skill as a falconer led to a grant of land held not as a sub-tenant, but directly from the crown. He was thus what Barrow, in describing the influx from England during the twelfth and thirteenth centuries, calls an adventurer, someone who came to Scotland seeking an opportunity, as a result of having some specialized skill, rather than as a dependent of a great lord.[5] Barrow furthermore believes that "Loutorp" mentioned in the grant was Lowthorpe, a parish in the East Riding of Yorkshire.

The family which held Lowthorpe during the twelfth and thirteenth centuries, as tenants of the Meinill family, does indeed appear to be the one to which Ranulf le Falconer belonged. References indicate there were perhaps as many as three generations of men named Walter de Lowthorpe. Walter de Loutorp witnessed a gift by Walter, Prior of Newburgh, to Henry de Botcherby, nephew of William, Archdeacon of Nottingham, of half a carrucate of land in Hooton Pagnell (sometime between 1199 and 1214).[6] Walter de Luuethorp was a witness to two earlier charters, one a feoffment by Clement, Abbot of St. Mary's, York, to Geoffrey de Stuteville, of three-and-one-half carrucates in Gilling-in-Ryedale, dated by Farrer to be between 1170 and 1175, and a grant by Abbot Clement in 1167 of the town of Normanby to Ralph Fraser.[7] Radulfus (Ralph) de Louthorp, his predecessor and perhaps father, made a grant of the lands of Sprohescroft and Ackeshales to the Cistercian Abbey of St. Mary of Sallay in Craven during the early years of the reign of Henry II (after 1154).[8] Peter, son of Walter of Louthorp by his wife Julian, daughter of Ralph Sakesper, who lived in the time of King Richard I, granted a moiety of two bovates in Pokethorp, which he had inherited from Ralph Sakesper, in 1252.[9]

Walter of Loutorp and Alice, his wife, held two bovates in the Feet of Fines in 1234.[10] This Walter appears to have earlier been married to Hawise, daughter of Roger de Neville, who died before 1227.[11] Thomas de Lowthorpe, son of Walter de Lowthorpe by Hawise de Neville, held the land in 1270. He was dead by 1279, leaving his two daughters, Cecily and Margery, as co-heirs. Cecily married Robert de Heslerton and Margery married his brother John de Heslerton before 1290/1291.[12] Cecily and Margery were also co-heirs of their brother Simon de Lowthorpe.[13] The evidence for this family is scant, yet it appears likely that the progenitor of the Falconers of Halkerton,

Ranulf (or Randle, Randolf) le Falconer, was the eldest son of the Walter de Loutorp (Lowthorpe) mentioned above.

The precise genealogy for the family during the next two hundred fifty years cannot be traced, unfortunately, since sources for this period are very limited and Falconers occur only intermittently. Approximately nine generations separate Ranulf from Alexander (A1), but of those, we can only document five or six at most.

Twelfth-century documentation is especially scarce and is clouded by traditions recorded centuries later. William *Auceps*, or William the falconer, granted certain lands to the kirk of Marington or Maryton sometime between 1218 and 1222.[14] A story related by a local eighteenth-century writer, John Napier, says that William the Lion's fowler was laird of Lumgair. This laird's son married the heiress of Luther and succeeded to the lands of Luther, which became known as Halkerton.[15] Walter de Lunkyrr witnessed a deed of vendition of the lands of Drumsleid, in the county of Kincardine, by Gregory, Bishop of Brechin, about 1250, and J. P. Wood suggested that he was a member of the family.[16]

We can only speculate here on the division of the English and Scottish lands about this time. Ranulf le Falconer, as eldest son of Walter de Lowthorpe, would have inherited the lands of Lowthorpe, and chronology would make it reasonable to assume that Ranulf's heir was Walter. However, it is also possible that the English lands went to a younger brother of Ranulf. One might assume that the more important Scottish lands succeeded to his eldest son, but it is impossible to learn the true answer. Chronology would suggest that Robert le Fauconer (born about 1270 or earlier) belonged to the same generation as Cecily and Margery, the heirs of Thomas de Lowthorpe, but the number of intervening generations is obscured by the lack of evidence.

Henry Fauconer, with consent of Robert, his son and heir, before 1291, granted the lands of Kynguthin to Randulph of Dundee.[17] Perhaps Kynguthin was Kingoodie in Longforgan and identical with the "Kingower in Gowerin" mentioned in the charter to Ranulf le Falconer.[18]

Robert le Fauconer was one of those called to estimate the valuation of the baronies of Kilravock and Easter Geddes in 1295.[19] These lands were in Nairnshire, in the north of Scotland, indicating that by this time the Falconers had probably acquired the lands of Lethen, in the parish of Auldearn, which would remain in the family's possession until 1605. He swore fealty to Edward I, King of England, on 14 March 1295/6 and again at Aberdeen, 17 December 1296.[20] He was one of the barons of the Mearns who swore fealty to Edward I in 1296.[21] His seal, with a rather vague impression, bears a falcon killing a small bird.[22]

Henry Falconer of Lethen, about 1350, witnessed a charter to John de Hay and Eufemia de St. Clair, with lands in Nairn and Sutherland as her dower.[23]

Andrew Falconer of Lethinvar was one of the barons who attended Alexander, Earl of Buchan, the King's Lieutenant, in a declaration which stated that the lands of the Bishop of Moray in le Badenach were not held by the laird of Badenach, 11 October 1380.[24] Andrew Fawconer was on an inquisition regarding the lands of Aldrochty, on 30 August 1393.[25]

Alexander Falconer was an accomplice, with Hugh Arbuthnot of that Ilk and other lairds of the Mearns, in the murder of John Melville of Glenbervie, sheriff of the Mearns. The barons invited Melville to a hunting party, then slew him, put him in a boiling cauldron and each took a spoonful of the broth. They were able to obtain pardons for their deed, at Falkland on 1 September 1421, from J. Johnston, steward of Fife and chief of the Clan Macduff, who invoked an archaic Celtic law. This law held that any "manslayer" who was within the ninth degree of kin and blood to Macduff, sometime Earl of Fife, on giving nine cows and a heifer calf at the Cross of Macduff, was free from "slaughter."[26]

According to a genealogy in a collection of genealogies of the barons of the Mearns compiled in 1578,[27] Alexander Falconer, earliest ancestor of the family named in this source, married the daughter of —— Strachan, laird of Thornton, and was the father of Alexander, who married a daughter of —— Ogilvy of Powrie.

This could be true if Alexander, who had succeeded to the lands by 1472, was the younger brother, rather than son, of David, below. However accurate this genealogy might be, this relationship cannot be independently verified and therefore must remain uncertain.

David Falconer of Halkerton was one of the jury at an inquisition held in presence of the sheriff of Kincardine on 1 April 1448, upon which a charter of confirmation was granted by King James II in favor of the Bishop of Brechin.[28]

A1 **Alexander Falconer** of Halkerton and of Lethen, said to be the son of Alexander Falconer, but perhaps the son of David Falconer, born perhaps about 1440, died after 10 May 1498 but before or during 1500.[29] He is the earliest in the line from whom a descent can be proved.

His wife was said to be a daughter of —— Ogilvy of Powrie.[30]

He had succeeded to the lands of Lethen by 1 March 1472, when he witnessed a sasine of Kilmalemak to Gilbert le Hay of Ury on a crown precept.[31] On 21 June 1482, he was one of the arbiters and arbitrators of the marriage contract between the daughter of William, Thane of Cawdor, and Huchone the Ros of Kilravock and Huchone the Ros, his son and heir-apparent.[32] He was a witness, with Robert Falconer, Duncan Falconer, and others, to a revocation to the sale of the lands of Ester Kyndes by Mariot Sutherland, spouse of William, Thane of Cawdor, on 13 July 1485.[33] He was elected to an assize in the Keith barony court, in the case of William Hog of Vigornshalch, on 14 October 1488,[34] and he, with others, was mentioned when the case went before the Lords Auditors of Causes and Complaints on 13 October 1489.[35] He witnessed a charter to the parish church of Abirluthnot, on 7 October 1490.[36] The Lords Auditors, on 11 October 1490, heard a cause pursued by Adam Auchinlek, executor to the deceased Mr. William Auchinlek, parson of Glenbervie, against Alexander Falconare of Halkertoun, for the "wrangwis withaldin" from him of the sum of forty marks of the teind-sheaves of the lands of Halkertoun.[37] He was one of the jury on the service of John Wishart of Pitarrow to his father, on 29 July 1491, concerning the lands of Balfeith and the mill of Conveth in the barony of Redehal.[38] On 25 February 1492, he was on an inquest against James Colisone in a cause regarding Sir John of Auchinleck of that Ilk of the lands of Glenbervie, Barras, and Kemnay.[39] He pursued an cause against David Falconer of Ballandro on 10 May 1498 for nonpayment of debt, and David was ordered to pay him ten merks.[40]

Issue of Alexander Falconer of Halkerton by a daughter of Ogilvy of

Powrie:[41]

A2   i.   George, his heir.

      ii.   daughter, who married David Falconer of Ballandro (Z2). She and the other daughters are named in the 1578 genealogy of barons of the Mearns; their placement in this generation is based on chronology.

      iii.   daughter, who married —— Lyell of Balmaledy.

      iv.   daughter, who married James Wishart of Pitarrow, and had issue, surname *Wishart*: a. *James*, his heir, who married the daughter of —— Lermond of Dairsie and was the father of Sir John Wishart of Pitarrow, who married Janet Falconer, below.[42]

A2 **George Falconer** of Halkerton and Lethen, born perhaps about 1465, was said to have died in 1511.[43]

His wife was Elizabeth Erskine, daughter of the laird of Dun,[44] probably John Erskine of Dun, by his wife Katharine Monypenny.[45]

As son and heir apparent of the laird of Haukartstone, he witnessed, on 3 February 1493/4, a charter of the lands of Troup given by the Earl Marischal to his son William.[46] In 1500, he was seised in the lands of Halkerton.[47] Styled "of Lethtyn," he witnessed a notarial instrument between William, Thane of Cawdor, and Huchone Ros of Kilravock, on 21 January 1501/2.[48] As "de Lething," he was a baillie in a precept of sasine to John Calder, precenter of Ross, of the Two Tulliglens, 23 February 1506.[49] On 25 February 1506/7, he received a crown charter of the lands of Lethen, namely Lethen, Lethenbar, Lichtnes, Auchmore, Auchinvalyn, le Ar, Dunnern, Litill Dulceis, and Mekill Dulceis, which were incorporated into a free barony of Lethen, in Nairnshire.[50] He discharged his "kynnisman" Robert Falconer, fiar of Ballandro, of the profit of the quarter of the mains of Ballandro, on 10 December 1507.[51] He and Robert "Falconare" received a precept of remission from the King, at Inverness 9 July 1510, for common oppression of subjects of the King and for all other actions, except treason, murder, arson, manslaying, thefts, receiving stolen property, mutilation, rape of women, receiving rebels, etc.[52] He was a baillie in a charter, from the Abbey of Arbroath to James Wishart, of the lands of Redhall, on 28 October 1510.[53] He was dead by 12 February 1512/3, when the gift of the ward of the lands of Halkertoun with the myln, in Kincardine, and of the lands and barony of Lathin, in Nairn, was made to Mr. Thomas Erskine.[54]

Issue of George Falconer of Halkerton and Elizabeth Erskine:[55]

      i.   Alexander Falconer, eldest son, who died during the lifetime of his father. He married Janet Arbuthnot, daughter of Robert Arbuthnot of that Ilk. She married, as her second husband, George Auchinleck of Over Kinnimouth.[56]

A3   ii.   David Falconer.

      iii.   George Falconer. On 25 February 1533/4, named as brother of David Falconer of Halkerton, he signed a petition for Sir Thomas Erskine of Brechin to the Lords of Council; among other "kynnismen, frendis and servandis" who signed were David Falconer of Halkerton, Alestar Falconar, John Falconar, Robert Falconar, and Walter Falconar, chaplain of Tantallon.[57] On 11 July 1544, he witnessed the instrument on a decree-arbitral regarding the lands of Pitskellie, in Kincardineshire.[58] Styled "in Fyndowray," with David Falconer of Halkerton, he witnessed a charter of lands of Ogill, in Forfarshire, to David Fentoun, on 15 June 1545.[59] He was on an assize on 8 March 1549/50,[60] and on one with Alexander Falconer of Halkerton, when "of Are," 12 January 1554,[61] and was styled "of Findowray" in 1561.[62] Conceivably George may have been the George Falconer in Faisdo who witnessed an instrument of sasine of the lands of Myddiltoun to Alexander Falconer of Halkerton and his spouse on 7 June 1555.[63]

? iv. Robert Falconer of Laik, who, on 10 February 1546, with David Falconer of Lethyn, was on a juror's inquisition over the estate of Sir John Campbell of Calder, at Elgin.[64] It was probably he who served with David Falconer on the assize in 1547, mentioned below.

v. daughter, who married Sir Alexander Dunbar of Cumnok, sheriff of Moray, and had issue, surname *Dunbar*: a. *Margaret*, married Robert Monro of Foulis.[65]

vi. Isobel, said to be the daughter of David Falconer of Halkerton, but chronologically more apt to be in this generation, married, as his second wife, Alexander Strachan of Thornton.[66]

A3 **David Falconer** of Halkerton and of Lethen, born about 1495, died between 20 May 1547 and 23 October 1549, was buried at the kirk of Auldearn.

He married Mariot Dunbar, said to be the daughter of the brother of Gavin Dunbar, Bishop of Aberdeen,[67] and thus probably the daughter of Alexander Dunbar of Conzie, by his wife Janet, daughter of John, 7th Earl of Sutherland.[68] The marriage probably took place not long before 8 August 1520, when David and Mariot (or Marjorie) Dunbar received a charter under the Great Seal of the lands of Lethenbar, Litle Fleenes, and half lands of Auchmoir.[69]

He was seised in the barony of Halkerton on 10 March 1515/6,[70] and in the lands of Lethen on 2 May 1516.[71] Literate, he signed a contract with Hugh Rose of Kilravock at Auldearn on 31 January 1523/4 agreeing to betroth his daughter Janet to the latter's son and heir, Hugh.[72] He had a charter of confirmation of the lands of Easter Kilravock on disposition by Hugh Rose of Kilravock, 4 October 1525,[73] a charter of the lands of Easter Middleton, in Kincardineshire, to himself and Mariot Dunbar, his spouse, from John Middleton of that Ilk, in excambion for the lands of Netherside of Halkerton and others, on 19 January 1539/40,[74] and a further charter of part of the same lands on 8 October 1546.[75] On 11 July 1544, he was one of the judges chosen to settle a dispute between Archibald Douglas of Glenbervy and James Wischart of Mekile Carnebogis over the lands of Petskellie.[76] On 10 February 1546/7, he and Robert Falconer of Laik were on a juror's inquisition in the estate of Sir John Campbell of Calder, at Elgin.[77] He and Robert Falconer were on an assize for the valuation of the lands of Locharroun, in Inverness, 20 May 1547, and on an assize over the lands of Lochelch.[78] These charters, assizes, contracts, and other writs demonstrate that he lived partly at Lethen and partly at Halkerton.

Issue of David Falconer of Halkerton and Mariot Dunbar:[79]

i. Janet Falconer, alive 31 January 1523/4, died 27 January 1580.[80] She married Sir John Wishart of Pitarrow, Comptroller of Scotland, but had no issue. Her testament-testamentar, dated 5 January 1580, makes bequests to her sisters Lady Kylrock and Lady Ballandro, to her niece Isobell Falconer, who was presently in service with her, and to other relatives and friends.

A4   ii. Alexander Falconer, his heir.

      iii. Katharine Falconer, died 24 July 1591.[81] She married Hugh Rose of Kilravock, according to the terms of the contract above, which provided that if her sister Janet failed to do so, another daughter would. He died 10 June 1597.[82] They had a charter from her brother Alexander of part of the lands of Halkerton, on 30 August 1557. To Mr. John Wood, they granted a charter of the lands of Forrenes and others, in the barony of Ardclach, on 1 June 1567.[83] According to Hew Rose, writing in 1683-1684, she was a "frugall and good manager, being verie assisting to her husband, particularly in paying the debt and burden upon his fortune."[84] Issue, surname *Rose*: a. *Janet*, married David Dunbar of Durris; b. *Marjorie*, married, by contract dated 1563, James Cuming of Drummynd; c. *Katharen*, married by contract dated 8 November 1569, William Urquhart of Burriezards; d. daughter, married, by contract dated 1 June 1571, John Hay of Lochloy; e. *Isabell*, married, by contract dated 14 June 1575, William Douglas of Earlsmilne; f. *Elizabeth*, married, by contract dated 31 August 1579, Walter Urquhart of Cromartie; g. *Agnes*, married first, by contract dated 6 May 1582, David Rose of Holme, and second, William Campbell; h. *Helen*, married, first, Robert Innes of Dryme, and, second, by contract dated 24 December 1585, John Rose of Holme; i. *William*, married, by contract dated 5 January 1571, Lilias Hay, sister to William Hay of Dalgatie.

      iv. Isobel Falconer. She married, as his first wife, John Middleton of that Ilk, and died between 26 March 1553 and 13 March 1557/8. Issue, surname *Middleton*:[85] a. *John*, his heir, married, firstly, Elizabeth Ramsay, and, secondly, Katherine Mortimer; b. *Marjorie*, died October 1608, married Gilbert Bisset of Pitmuckiston.

      v. Marjorie Falconer. She married Alexander Wishart of Carnebeg. On 2 October 1556, he received a precept of a royal charter confirming him in a third part of the lands of Halkerton, sold to him by Alexander Falconer of Halkerton.[86] Issue.

      vi. Elizabeth Falconer, died in September 1592.[87] She had a charter of the lands of Ballandro from Robert Falconer of Ballandro (Z5), as her future spouse, on 5 November 1552.[88] She later married him and had issue.

A4 Alexander Falconer of Halkerton, born probably about 1522, died 10 November 1587 at Lethen, was buried at Auldearn.[89]

He married, by a contract dated 1 June 1543,[90] Elizabeth Douglas, daughter of Archibald Douglas of Glenbervie by his wife Agnes, daughter of William Keith, 3rd Earl Marischal. This marriage to a member of the powerful Douglas family resulted in the incorporation of the three mollets and a heart to the Falconer arms.

He and Elizabeth Douglas, his spouse, were granted a charter of the Hill of Halkerton on 24 April 1544.[91] As son and heir of his late father David Falconer of Halkerton, he was seised in the Mains of Halkerton on 23 October 1549.[92] On 7 June 1555, he and Elizabeth Douglas were seised in the temple lands of Myddiltoun, in the parish of Conveth.[93] One of two stones, now on the offices attached to the farmhouse at the Mains of Halkerton, originally from Halkerton castle, has the date 1556 and has a female head carved on it. W. R. Fraser speculated that the stone indicated that Alexander and his lady had built the first part of the castle.[94] He may have been indeed responsible for renovations to the castle, since, unlike his father, grandfather, and great-grandfather, who were frequently styled "of Lethen," he normally bore the style "of Halkerton," although he died in the North.

Indeed, most evidence of his activities comes from records concerning Nairn and Moray. He was seised in the lands of Lethen on 5 November 1549.[95] He was granted a charter of the lands of Fernychtie and others in Nairnshire on 18 November 1556,[96] after he had received a charter, by Alexander Dunbar, Prior of the monastery of Pluscarden, of the lands of Fornychtie with its ale-house, on 8 November 1556.[97] Fornichtie had earlier been wadset to Falconer of Halkerton with the conditions that Falconer pay £6,13s.,4d., with the carriage of five horses and their leaders for leading peats, failing which, 6s.,8d. for each horse, and that he furnish one horseman to the King's wars.[98] On 18 August 1571, he was given the escheat of the goods of George Dunbar in Alves, who had been put to the horn at the instance of Mr. Alexander Dunbar, Dean of Moray, for non-payment of certain sums of money.[99] The Privy Seal issued, on 15 March 1573/4, a precept for a charter of confirmation on a charter by Alexander Falconar of Halkertoun to Elizabeth Douglas, his spouse, the life-rent of the lands and manor of Lethin, with its alehouse and alehouse croft, the towns and land of Ar and Newtoun, with the mill-town and mill-lands of Lethin and multures pertaining thereto, and Linmoir, in the barony of Lethin.[100] Alexander appears as a witness or a party to various writs in the muniments of the Roses of Kilravock between 1559 and 1577.[101]

Alexander was given the ward of the barony of Borrowfeild, half of Newbigging, in Angus, the lands of Ovir Craugnestoun and Drummolze, in Kincardineshire, and all other heritage of the deceased —— Gardin of Borrowfeild, on 28 January 1574/5, until the entry of the heir.[102]

In his testament-testamentar, dated 2 November 1587, he requested that he be buried in the choir of the parish kirk of Auldearn, beside his father and others. He left a legacy to his youngest son William. He appointed his eldest son Alexander, David Dunbar of Durris, and his spouse Elizabeth Douglas his executors. Witnesses were John Ross of Bellewat, Hugh Falconer, Mr. Samuel Falconer, Archibald Falconer, his lawful sons; Robert Falconer in Bar, and David Falconer in Auchinan.[103]

Issue of Alexander Falconer of Halkerton and Elizabeth Douglas, his spouse:[104]

A5   i.   Alexander Falconer.
      ii.   daughter, who married, as his first wife, John Rose of Bellivat, and had issue, surname *Rose*:[105] a. *John* of Bellivat; b. *Hugh*, married Katharine Ord; c. *David*.
      iii. Agnes Falconer, died May 1590.[106] She married, by a contract dated 15 April 1567, Alexander Guthrie of that Ilk, who died 10 June 1597, and had issue, surname *Guthrie*:[107] a. *Rebecca*; b. *Magdalene*; c. *Martha*; d. *Sarah*; e. *Alexander*; f. *James*; g. *William*; h. *Samuel*; i. *Harry*; j. *Hercules*.
      iv.   Christian Falconer. She first married David Dunbar of Durris, who died in 1592. That same year she married, as his second wife, Patrick Dunbar of Blairie, later of Conzie, as on 2 June 1592, he gave a charter of the lands of Miln to her in life-rent.[108] In 1597, she received a bequest of five merks from Hugh Rose of Kilravock.[109] On 30 June 1602, Patrick Dunbar of Conzie was cautioner for Mark Dunbar of Durris, Hew Falconer of Innerlochtie, and Mr. Samuel Falconer of Ar; Mark Dunbar of Durris was cautioner for Archibald Falconer in Farnichtie and William Falconer in Lethinbar, not to reset or

intercommune with Alexander McRanald of Gargavach and others.[110]   She was living on 6 November 1630, when she was given life-rent in a sasine to Alexander Brodye, portioner of Kynloss, with a precept of sasine from Patrick Dunbar of Kilboyack.[111]

v.   Magdalen Falconer. She married, as his second wife, James Sutherland of Kinstearie, born 1561, probably died in 1623. She seems to have been married secondly to William Innes of Mayne, named in a sasine dated 15 March 1631.[112] A tablet in the Auldearn church calls her "daughter of the Laird of Halcartown."[113]

S1   vi.   Hew Falconer of Little Inverlochtie.

T1   vii.   Samuel Falconer of Kincorth.

viii.   Isobel Falconer.[114] In 1580, she was in service with her aunt Janet, widow of Sir John Wishart of Pitarrow. She was the spouse of Mark Dunbar of Grangehill, son and heir of David Dunbar of Durris. They were living 2 June 1636.[115] A fragment of a tablet in the church at Essil, Morayshire, bears two shields charged with the Dunbar and Falconer arms with the initials "M.D.: I.F."[116] Issue, surname *Dunbar*: a. *Ninian* of Grangehill, married Mary Ogilvy.

U1   ix.   Archibald Falconer, portioner of Coltfield.

X1   x.   William Falconer in Dounduff, youngest son.

A5 **Alexander Falconer** of Halkerton was probably born about 1545 and died in December 1595.[117]

He married Isabel Gray, widow of David Strachan of Carmylie and daughter of Patrick, 4th Lord Gray, by his wife Marion, daughter of James, 4th Lord Ogilvy of Airlie. By her first husband, she had a son Patrick and a daughter Isobel. She died 20 October 1589, leaving her whole moveable estate to her husband.[118]

On 16 June 1573, the Privy Seal issued a precept for a charter of confirmation on a charter by Alexander Falconer of Halcartoun to Alexander Falconer, his son and heir apparent, and Isobel Gray, Lady Carmylie, his spouse, of the Manis of Myddletoun, now occupied by Alexander the elder and his tenants, and one-third of the lands of Drumquharbir.[119] He was seised as heir of his father in the barony of Halkerton and lands of Lethen in 1588.[120] He had a charter to himself and his son Alexander of the lands and baronies of Lethen and Halkerton and the lands of Middiltoun, Eister Middiltoun, Drumforbes, and Husbandtoun, on 12 October 1593.[121]

Issue of Alexander Falconer of Halkerton and Isabel Gray:

A6   i.   Sir Alexander Falconer.

P1   ii.   Patrick Falconer of Newton.

iii.   Marjorie Falconer. She married, shortly after 27 November 1598, Angus mac William Mackintosh (known as Williamson) of Termett.[122] Issue, surname *Mackintosh*:[123] a. *Lachlan*.

R1   iv.   Robert Falconer of Drimmie.

v.   Jean Falconer. She married, by a contract dated 12 September 1620, John Fullarton, younger, of Kinnaber.[124] Issue, surname *Fullarton*:[125] a. *Alexander*, baptized 17 July 1621; b. *John*, baptized 23 December 1623; c. *Janet*, baptized 28 February 1624; d. *Nans*, baptized 30 December 1626; e. *Margaret*, baptized 1 March 1628; f. son, baptized 30 December 1632.

Alexander Falconer of Halkerton also had a natural daughter:[126]

> vi. Isobel Falconer. She married, by contract dated 15 February 1615, Dr. Francis Strathauchin, called Apparisiis, of Elgin. She and William Falconer, merchant burgess of Elgin, were parties to a contract with Mr. David Falconer of Glenfarquhar, at Elgin, 1 May 1638.[127]

A6 Sir Alexander Falconer of Halkerton was born probably about 1575 and died between 12 June 1645 and 24 June 1646.[128]

He married, by contract dated 18 or 28 November 1594,[129] Agnes Carnegie, eldest daughter of Sir David Carnegie of Colluthie, member of the Privy Council, by his wife Euphame Wemyss, and sister of the 1st Earls of Southesk and Northesk.[130] She died 8 December 1634.[131]

He had a charter of the barony of Halkerton and of the lands of Lethen to himself and Agnes Carnegie, his spouse, on 27 January 1594/5,[132] and again to himself 28 July 1612, at which time his lands were erected into a free barony of Halkerton, he being styled "D[ominus] Alexandrus" [Sir Alexander].[133] They resigned the lands of Lethen, held in the family since the thirteenth century, to John Grant of Freuchie, on 12 November 1605.[134]

The sale of Lethen may have resulted from a desire to rid himself of the problems associated with numerous feuds with other Nairnshire and Morayshire families. Soon after receiving his inheritance, the Falconers became embroiled in a violent dispute with their cousins, the Roses of Ballivat. On 27 May 1596, he, his uncle Hew Falconer of Flenis, and others complained to the Privy Council that John Rose of Ballivat and others of that family had troubled them by "soirning, herreing and wraking" of their tenants and "dinging" and pursuing them sometimes for their lives, in particular having violently snatched certain horses and cattle from Robert Falconer in Lethenbar. For not appearing before them, the Council denounced the Roses as rebels.[135] Rose and others of his family came in a band one night in September, armed with bows, swords, hagbuts, and pistols, to Falconer's lands of Meikle Dulsie, where his tenants were taking their night's rest, and broke open the doors of the houses and carried away their corn and goods with carts and sledges which they had brought with them.[136] Further feuding continued in 1598 with the Roses and the Dunbars, but eventually John Rose of Bellivat sold his lands west of the Spey to Falconer of Halkerton in 1605.[137]

As chief of the family, he sometimes had to come to the defense of Falconers in need. On 9 January 1616, a Commission under the Signet was issued to Sir Alexander Falconer of Halkerton, Hew, Mr. Samuell, Archibald, and William Falconner, his uncles, Patrik Dunbar of Blairie, Patrik Falconer of Newtoun, Duncan McIntoshe of Abererarder, and James Sutherland of Kingstaire, to apprehend and keep in custody till trial Mr. John Oschell, Doctor of Medicine, who was put to the horn on 22 December 1615 at the instance of Harie Falkonner in Blakbalk, as "near" kinsman, and others as kinsmen of the late David Falconer, to the charge of having murdered the said David Falconer.[138]

Leaving the North for relatively peaceful Kincardineshire unfortunately did not mean an end to feuds. One was developing between Halkerton and his tenants and George Keith, Earl Marischal and his tenants in 1616. Andro Barclay, in the Stane of Benholm, complained to the Privy Council on 9 Sep-

tember 1618 that Sir Alexander Falconer of Halkerton had conceived a hatred against Barclay. Testimony was given that, in August 1616, Andro went,
by the Earl Marischal's command, to the laird to ask the "maills" (rents) of
certain lands possessed by Falconer of Halkerton. Halkerton first "menaced"
Barclay within his own house and afterwards, "training him furth to the bak
of his awne yard," assaulted him and severely wounded him, saying "tak yow
that for your maisteris sak." Halkerton denied the charge, and the Council
assoilzied (acquitted) him.[139]

Whether by design or circumstance, the Privy Council seemed to favor
Halkerton in his dispute with Andro Barclay, apparently the Earl Marischal's
proxy. Barclay complained that Halkerton ordered sixty of his tenants to
remove a millstone from a quarry, in the Stane of Benholm, owned by the
Earl Marischal. Halkerton's tenants were met, on the night of 7 July 1618,
by some of the Earl Marischal's tenants, armed with long staves, halberds,
and swords, who attacked them and severely wounded one of them. The
Council felt the pursuers had not proved their case and assoilzied Halkerton
and his tenants.[140] Soon afterwards, Andrew Gelly, miller at Halkerton mill,
John Kirk in Sporrehillok, and Robert Falconer, servitor to Halkerton, came
before the Council, complaining that Barclay and others, armed with "swords,
long staves, forks, etc.," had surprised them early one morning while they
were bringing a millstone home to the mill of Halkerton, and took and detained Gelly. Later, according to Gelly, Barclay and others went, by order of
George Keith, Earl Marischal, to Robert Falconer and assaulted and detained
him. The Council ruled in Halkerton's favor, fining Barclay £20.[141]

Whether associated with the feud or seizing an opportunity, Andrew Wood
in Syde, with two accomplices, came to Halkerton at one night in October
1618 and killed thirty wild geese, eleven "brissell" fowls [Brazil fowls, perhaps
turkeys], and twenty-five ducks, and left with them. Wood and two others,
later that month, came to Halkerton with staves and nets, and took two bee-
hives, thirty "brissell" fowls, sixty wild geese, and twenty-five ducks.[142]

Finally, on 18 November 1634, John Cowie in Ruidmyre complained before the Council against Halkerton and his son Alexander, that they conceived a grudge against him and conspired to do him some affront "under
colour of law." On the same date, Alexander Chrystie in Pitgarvie complained
against Halkerton, his son Alexander, and his brother Patrick, that "out of a
deadly hatred and malice against him and having resolved to take his life,
[they] have for long vexed and troubled him with pleas both before the Lords
of Session and his Majesty's Justice."[143] What twenty years earlier might have
been accompanied by violence was now being accomplished through legalis-
tic schemes and settled by legal appeals, indicating how far feuding, if not
disputes, had declined.

The Privy Council cases involving him display a contentious side to his
nature, although the nature of Scottish law and society in his age probably
required contentiousness from a laird who was rising in influence. Letters to
other lairds which survive show that he raised greyhounds and kept bees,[144]
surely interests which gave him more pleasure.

Issue of Sir Alexander Falconer of Halkerton by Agnes Carnegie:

A7   i.   Sir Alexander Falconer, created Lord Falconer of Halkerton in 1646, his heir.
D1   ii.   Sir David Falconar of Glenfarquhar, second son.

G1   iii.   Sir John Falconer, Master of the Mint, third son.

      iv.   Marjorie Falconer, eldest daughter, living in 1630, when she borrowed 2000
             merks from her brother Sir Alexander.[145]

      v.   Agnes Falconer. She married, first, Alexander Keith of Benholm. She had a
             charter as his future wife, 19 September 1633.[146] He died between 20 and 25
             February 1634, and she married, as her second husband, in 1634, John,
             Master of Forrester.[147] No issue.

      vi.   Jean Falconer. She married, in 1637, John Grant of Logie and Moyness,
             sheriff of Moray. They had a charter of the lands of Moyness and Golfuirde,
             in Auldearn, Nairn, confirmed 25 June 1642.[148]

      vii.   Margaret Falconer. She died, unmarried, shortly before 19 February 1659,
             when Sir Patrick Falconer was served heir to Margaret, his "immediat elder
             sister."[149] David Falconar, merchant-burgess of Edinbrugh (H1), was served
             heir-conquest to her on 18 November 1676.[150]

      viii. Sir Patrick Falconar. He was admitted Advocate on 23 February 1642.[151] On
             8 September 1652, he was admitted a burgess of Aberdeen.[152] On 1 January
             1664, he, "youngest lawfull sone to the deceast Sir Alexander," discharged all
             debts granted by him to his father preceding 3 March 1620.[153]

Sir Alexander Falconer also had, by Margaret Jamieson, daughter of John
Jamieson in Tullienessil, two natural sons:[154]

      ix.   James Falconer, living 29 July 1640, when Margaret Jamieson was seised in
             the croft of land called Diracroft for her sons James and George Falconer,[155] but
             probably died young.

      x.   George Falconer, born probably about 1638, buried 23 April 1693 in Trotter
             tomb, Greyfriars, Edinburgh.[156] By
             a sasine dated 2 June 1645, he was
             to receive an annualrent of 160
             merks on the lands of Newton.[157]
             On 23 February 1656, his curators
             sued Patrick Falconer of Newton to
             recover the annualrent due him on
             the lands of Newton.[158] A letter from George Falconer to Sir John Falconar of
             1683 addresses him as "cousin."[159] He was a merchant burgess of Edinburgh,
             when, on 2 March 1685, through the patronage of Sir David Falconar of
             Newton, he was elected Keeper of the Parliament House and Session House,
             sharing the office from 10 February 1686.[160] He seems to have been married
             twice. By an unknown first wife, he had a child who was buried 4 April 1671
             at Edinburgh.[161] He married, as his second wife, on 12 November 1686, Rachel
             Gines.[162]

A7 Sir Alexander, first Lord Falconer of Halkerton, born about 1595, died
1 October 1671, aged seventy-seven, at Halkerton, Kincardineshire, was buried
at Conveth (now Laurencekirk).[163]

    He married, by contract dated 2 and other days of April 1619,[164] Anna
Lindsay, only child of John, 9th Lord Lindsay of the Byres. They were separated in 1627, when both appeared before the Privy Council. As they were
"so farre distractit and alienat in heartie love and affectioun," they requested
separation. The Council ordered him to pay her 1000 merks annually, but
2000 the first year. He responded by accusing her of libel, and she was made
to pay 1000 merks.[165]

He had a charter of the barony of Halkerton to himself and Anna Lindsay, his future wife, dated 21 April 1619.[166] On 31 May 1643, he was admitted to the burgess roll of Aberdeen.[167] On 24 June 1646, the King ratified a charter by the deceased Sir Alexander Falconer of Halkertoun, with the consent of Mr. Patrick Falconer, his son, to Sir Alexander Falconer, fiar of Halkertoun, of the lands of Diracroft, in Conveth.[168] He was granted a charter on 22 February 1667 of the lands of Barnhill, Henstoun, and West Culrado, in the parish of Garvock.[169]

He was appointed Lord of Session on 9 July 1639 in place of Lord Woodhall of Balmanno, whom he paid 7000 merks to demit.[170]　According to

Fountainhall, he was the "creature" of Lord Traquair, the Treasurer, who influenced the King to accept the demission.[171] The King granted him a yearly pension of £200 for his "abilitie, integratie, and affectioun for administratioun of Justice," on 12 December 1643, and it was renewed in 1661.[172] His rise and influence in the Scottish government was recognized on 20 December 1646, when he was created Lord Falconer of Halkerton, with destination to himself and his heirs-male whatsoever.[173] He was member of Parliament for Kincardineshire, in 1643-1644, 1644-1645, and 1645-1647; a Commissioner of Treasury, 1 February 1645, and a Commissioner for the Plantation of Kirks in 1644. In 1649 he was superseded as a Lord of Session.

A stone on the offices at the Mains of Halkerton bears the initials "LA." and the year 1648; W. R. Fraser speculated that that may have indicated an addition to Halkerton castle.[174] The old wing of Gallery House, south of Marykirk, has a stone with the year 1650, the initials "LAF," indicating that he probably built the original wing of the house.

The court poet William Drummond of Hawthornden lamented his sacrifices for the cause of the King:

> I feare to me such fortune be assign'd
> As was to thee, who did so well deserue,
> Braue Halkertone! even suffred here to sterue
> Amidst base-minded freinds, nor true, nor kind.
> Why were the Fates and Furies thus combined
> Such worths for such disasters to reserue?
> Yet all those euills neuer made thee swerue
> From what became a well resolued mind:
> For swelling greatnesse neuer made thee smyle,
> Despising greatnesse in extreames of want;
> O happy thrice whom no distresse could dant!
> Yet thou exclaimed, O Time! O age! O Isle!
> Where flatterers, fooles, baudes, fidlers are rewarded,
> Whilst Vertue sterues vnpitied, vnregarded![175]

By his testament-testamentar, dated 1 October 1671, he appointed Alexander, Master of Halkerton, to be his only executor and universal legator of all his personal property.[176]

Issue of Alexander, first Lord Falconer of Halkerton, by Anna Lindsay:[177]

A8   i.   Alexander, second Lord, baptized 17 June 1620.

      ii.   Thomas Falconer.[178]

      iii.   Agnes Falconer, baptized 29 January 1626, died 4 January 1711, aged 85, at Forglen, Banff.[179] She married, on 2 September 1648, by contract of marriage dated 17 August and 2 September 1648,[180] George Ogilvy, 2nd Lord Banff. Her tocher was 20,000 merks. They had issue, surname *Ogilvy*: a. *George*, 3rd Lord; b. *Sir Alexander* of Forglen; c. *Jeane*, baptized 5 January 1651; d. *Agnes*, baptized 29 December 1651, married Francis Gordon of Craig of Auchindoir; e. *Margaret*, baptized 8 October 1654, unmarried; f. *Helen*, died 9 January 1714, married, 25 April 1694, Sir Robert Lauder of Blelmouth; g. *Mary*, married (contract dated 1 June 1680) John Forbes of Balilugg; h. *Isobel*; i. *Marjory*; j. *Janet*, born 1668.

A8 **Alexander, second Lord Falconer of Halkerton**, baptized 17 June 1620 at Montrose, died 4 March 1684.

J. Falconer Syme

He married, in 1666,[181] Margaret Ogilvy, second daughter of James, second Earl of Airlie. She married, as her second husband,[182] Patrick Lyell of Balhall and died shortly before 11 February 1715.[183]

When Master of Halkerton, he was appointed a justice of the peace for Kincardineshire on 13 January 1670.[184] He was served heir to his father in the lands and barony of Halkerton on 30 April 1672.[185] In 1675, he alienated the lands of Middleton in favor of Sir Alexander Falconar of Glenfarquhar, Bart.[186] In November 1679, his house of Halkerton suffered a fire,[187]unfortunately destroying the family's muniments. In 1680 and 1681 a new roof was added to the house, as well as mortar and slate, although in 1685 more slate was needed to finish the house.[188]

By a bond of provision, dated at Stonehaven 7 February 1684, he provided for his younger children. He gave to his eldest daughter Jean 5000 merks; to his second daughter Helen 4000 merks; to his third daughter Euphan 3000 merks; and to his youngest daughter Elisabeth he gave 3000 merks. To Alexander Falconar, his youngest son, he gave 5000 merks. These sums were to be paid when each of the daughters reached the age of sixteen or at their marriage between the ages of sixteen and twenty-one. The daughters and son were to be "alimented" at schools until they reached the age of sixteen.[189]

Issue of Alexander, second Lord Falconer of Halkerton, by Margaret Ogilvy:

A9   i.   David, 3rd Lord Falconer of Halkerton.

       ii.   James Falconer.[190]

       iii.   Alexander Falconer, died August 1708, unmarried. Tacksman of the lands of Halkerton,[191] his brother David was served heir to him on 22 November 1712.[192]

       iv.   Jean Falconer. She married, first, 27 October 1706, at Marykirk,[193] as his second wife, James Forbes of Thornton, who died 4 June 1713, and had issue, surname *Forbes*:[194] a. *James*, baptized 20 September 1707, died young; b. *John*, baptized 19 March 1710, died young. On 11 May 1722, at Montrose,[195] she married, as her second husband, James Ouchterlony, baillie of Montrose. She was served co-heir of provision general to her brother Alexander Falconar on 9 September 1729.[196]

       v.   Helen Falconer. She died, unmarried, before 10 June 1714, when her brother David was served heir to her.[197]

       vi.   Euphame Falconer. She married, 24 February 1706, at Edinburgh,[198] John Row of Bandeath. On 12 August 1727, she was served heir-portioner general to her brother David.[199] Her testament was confirmed 23 January 1728. Issue, surname *Row*:[200] a. *John*; b. *Euphame*.

       vii.   Elizabeth Falconer. She married, on 18 January 1711, at Montrose,[201] by a contract dated 19 January 1711,[202] Walter Porterfield of Comestoun.

Natural son of Alexander, 2nd Lord Falconer of Halkerton:[203]

       viii.   Andrew Falconar, wright in Kirktown of Conveth (now Laurencekirk). Having been useful to his father "both by his bodily service and his mechanick imployment," his father gave him a bond of 500 merks on 8 February 1684.[204] In August 1689, General Mackay's troops stayed overnight in Conveth on their way north, and Andrew and other tenants there suffered losses of crops. They petitioned the Privy Council for reimbursement, Andrew claiming the loss of six bolls of corn and two firlots of oats and fodder.[205] On 19 May 1692, he sold the "Bell Acre" in Kirktown of Conveth, intending to move.[206] Nothing further is known of him.

A9 David Falconer, third Lord Falconer of Halkerton, born probably about 1668, died, unmarried, in February 1724.[207]

In 1680 he was sent to Edinburgh to be educated by Rev. John Falconer, later minister at Carnbie, Fifeshire, and an Episcopal Bishop.[208] David was served heir to his father in the barony of Halkerton on 27 March 1690.[209]

Unfortunately, he had already seemed to develop a mental illness by this time. John Napier, later in the eighteenth century, referred to a local tradition that either the proprietor of Halkerton or the tenants of the Mains of Halkerton had had "a taint of insanity," resulting from a case in which one of Halkerton's heirs (probably David, if true) had killed the son of the miller of Halkerton in a scuffle, the tenant of the Mains then perjuring himself by claiming that the heir was insane, in order to free him from punishment.[210] In any case, on 23 February 1710, the Lord was found to be *incompos mentis fatuus idiota seu furiosus* and to have been so for the previous twenty years.[211]

Prior to this legal determination of his mental condition, his brother Alexander was made tacksman of his estate so that he could collect rents and pay debts. When Alexander died in 1708, rents became neglected, and the estate's creditors, led by Sir Alexander Falconar of Glenfarquhar, went to court so that Glenfarquhar could take the administration of Halkerton's estate. The Lord's mother, however, opposed these actions. Sir Alexander petitioned the Court of Session on 17 February 1710 to appoint, in the meantime, James Ferguson of Pitfour as factor of the Lord's estate.[212] On the same date, David Falconar of Newton and Marjory Irvine, relict of Alexander Strachan, writer in Edinburgh, petitioned for payment of the debts from Lord Halkerton. Newton's share was one year's annualrent at 5½ percent of the principal amount of £18,694,14s.,8d.[213]

Despite repairs made to Halkerton Castle after its 1679 fire, it continued to decline during the lifetime of this lord, who was the last to live there. W. R. Fraser remarked that it gradually fell into ruins, until about 1790, when its walls were demolished, the stones being used in building dikes and the parish church. Traces of the castle could still be seen in 1888 in the Wood of Halkerton.[214]

A10   David Falconar, fourth Lord Falconer of Halkerton, eldest son of Sir David Falconer of Newton (E1) and great-grandson of Sir Alexander Falconer of Halkerton (A6), was born 27 May 1681 in Edinburgh and died 24 September 1751 at Inglismaldie, parish of Marykirk, Kincardineshire.

He married, on 23 December 1703 at Marykirk, by a contract dated 27 November 1703,[215] Katharine Margaret Keith, eldest daughter of William, second Earl of Kintore, baptized 29 June 1690, died 1

March 1762 in Edinburgh.[216]

He was served heir to his father on 23 February 1693 in the lands and barony of Dulapple and its mill, and shortly afterwards in the lands of Craighaugh, of Nether Perth and Cononies with the mill of Perth, and lands of Over Perth, Balachies, and Banks, and fishing rights on the Northesk, all united with lands in Kincardineshire into the barony of Newtoun.[217] In 1702, he was appointed one of the commissioners for Kincardineshire, and in 1704 for Forfarshire.[218] He was served heir-male general to his uncle, Sir Alexander Falconer of Glenfarquhar, on 3 March 1718, in the lands of Tibbarties, Auchinblae, Midletown, and Houston, in Kincardineshire. He was served heir male special to his cousin, David, third Lord, in the barony of Haulkertoun, including the lands of Diracroft, Barnhill, etc., on 3 August 1724.[219] On 4 July 1743, he executed a bond of tailzie on the lands of Halkerton and other lands.[220] On 16 March 1749, he took sasine of a house on the south side of the Lawn Market, in Edinburgh, which he had bought in 1737.[221]

In 1730, he commissioned an artist with the initials "W. R.," who was no doubt William Robertson, a favorite of Jacobite patrons,[222] to paint a series of portraits of him and his wife and children. The artist also painted portraits of Alexander, first Lord, and of Sir David Falconer of Glenfarquhar, though whether these were copied from contemporary portraits or "ancestor" portraits based on verbal descriptions, we shall never know. These are now in the collection of the Earl of Kintore.

He gave the following amounts of money to his younger children by bonds of provision on 31 July 1746: to William, he gave £18,000 Scots; to Jean, £16,000, which, on her marriage, would be changed to 20,000 merks given to her husband; to John, £6000; to Mary, 20,000 merks; to George, £18,000; and to May, 20,000 merks.[223] Lord Halkerton had earlier advanced to his son David £1500, and on 2 March 1745 the latter exonered his claim.[224]

In her widowhood, Lady Halkerton disputed her estate with her eldest son Alexander and some of her other children. As a result of her dissatisfaction with some of her children, she left some out of her testament of 2 March 1762. She appointed her son-in-law George Norvell of Boghall to be her executor and assigned to him all sums of money which were due to her as well as any personal estate not specified in the testament. The only bequests to her children or grandchildren were a diamond-encrusted ring with a miniature of her late husband, which she gave to her son John; her silver dressing plate to son John's wife, which after her death would go to John's daughter Katharine [sic]; to David, son of John, she gave a ring with one large diamond set with two smaller diamonds and four diamond sparks; to John's son Keith she gave a ring set with a large ruby and ten diamond sparks, which had belonged to her mother; to her son Captain George Falconer she gave a gold watch and £300 sterling, he to pay his sister Mary one-third of that amount, but if he obtained the command of a warship by the time of her death, he would receive £200, £100 going to daughter Mary; to her granddaughter Katharine, daughter of James Falconar of Monkton, her diamond shoe buckles; to her unmarried daughter Mary all the furniture in her Edinburgh house and six tablecloths and a dozen napkins from her country house of Canterland Lodge, as well as £300 sterling. She made other bequests to friends, servants, and Keith relatives.[225]

Whether she disinherited some of her children out of spite or not, there

David, 4th Lord Falconer of Halkerton (A10)
The following group of ten portraits was painted by "W. R.," probably William Robertson, in 1730.
Collection of the Earl of Kintore.

Katharine Margaret Keith, wife of David, 4th Lord Falconer of Halkerton.

David Falconer (A13)

Jean Falconer, second daughter of David, 4th Lord Falconer of Halkerton, later spouse of James Falconar of Monkton (P4)

John Falconer (C1)

**Mary Falconer, daughter of
David, 4th Lord Falconer of
Halkerton**

George Falconer,
later Captain, R.N. (A14)

Marion (May) Falconer,
daughter of David, 4th Lord
Falconer of Halkerton, later
spouse of George Norvell of
Boghall and Deans

can be no doubt that both she and her husband caused some to resent their influence over their lives. Lord Halkerton refused to permit his daughter Katharine to marry and cut off his second son William after he married a Dutch woman, although he later reconciled. Perhaps the parents had difficulty accepting marriages which were not arranged by the families involved, which had always been the custom among the aristocracy.

Issue of David, fourth Lord Falconer of Halkerton, by Katharine Margaret Keith:

A11   i.   Alexander, fifth Lord, born about 1707.

      ii.   Katharine Falconer, died, unmarried, in Edinburgh 1 December 1748, buried at Greyfriars.[226] The Earl of Kellie was interested in marrying her and in 1731 sent a third-person inquiry to her father, but her father responded negatively.[227]

A12 iii. William, sixth Lord.

A13 iv. David Falconer, merchant and insurance broker of London, born about 1716, died 4 September 1775 at Bury Court, St. Mary Axe. On 19 February 1739/40,[228] he married Frances Lamplugh, of St. Mary Savoy, spinster, baptized 6 May 1710 in Bridekirk, Cumberland,[229] died before 1764, daughter of Robert Lamplugh, of Dovenby, Cumberland, by his wife Jane Lamplugh. A portrait at Dovenby Hall, labeled "Elizabeth Falconer," is undoubtedly of her mother Frances.[230] David was apprenticed, 17 April 1732, to Alexander Dick, of London, merchant, for a term of five years.[231] He was a wine merchant in 1748;[232] in the 1750s he was a partner with James Farquhar. By his will, dated 7 September 1775, he made his nephew David sole heir to his estate.[233] Issue of David and Frances (Lamplugh) Falconer:[234]

        a. Jane Falconer, buried 11 December 1741.

        b. Katharine Falconer, baptized 20 December 1740, buried 4 May 1742.

        c. Frances Falconer, baptized 9 November 1742, buried 29 March 1743.

        d. Jane Falconer, baptized 13 December 1743, buried 23 December 1743.[235]

        e. David Falconer, baptized 25 May 1745, died without issue before 1768.

        f. Theresa Falconer, baptized 11 November 1746, buried 2 December 1752.

        g. Elizabeth Falconer, baptized 9 January 1748, died, unmarried, in 1768, having inherited in 1764 Dovenby Hall from her uncle Richard Lamplugh. Following her death, the property passed to Peter Brougham Lamplugh, indicating that Elizabeth was the last surviving child of this marriage.[236]

        h. Charles Falconer, baptized 10 October 1749, died without issue before 1768.

        i. Frances Falconer, baptized 31 October 1750, buried 19 November 1751.

        j. John Falconer, baptized January 1753, buried 22 August 1754.

C1   v.   John Falconer, planter of Clarendon, Jamaica, born about 1718.

      vi. Jean Falconer, died 16 February 1797 in Edinburgh.[237] She married, 16 December 1750, at Edinburgh,[238] James Falconar of Monkton (P4), son and heir of Patrick Falconar of Monkton, Midlothian, and Balnakettle, Kincardine, who died December 1779, and had issue.

A14   vii. George Falconer of Phesdo, Captain, Royal Navy, born about 1722, died 3 May 1780, aged 58, at Liphook, Hampshire,[239] was buried at Westminster Abbey.[240] He married, probably about 1767,[241] Hannah Ivie, daughter of —— Ivie of Ireland and widow of Lieutenant —— Hardy, R.N. She married, as her third husband, on 23 September 1786 in Edinburgh, John Mill of Fearn, Angus.[242] He was commissioned lieutenant 12 February 1744/5; commander, 10 November 1756; and captain, 27 April 1762.[243] He was in command of the *Captain*, 1762; the frigate *Juno*, 1762 to 1764; the *Essex*, in 1764, which sailed to Africa; the *Crescent*, in 1771; and, in 1775, the *Mars*. Commanding the last-named ship in October 1777, he captured an American merchant brig.[244] At the time of his death he commanded H.M.S. *Invincible*. He was admitted to the burgess roll of Edinburgh on 10 October 1759, gratis, as "for good services he has done his king and country in the discharge of the dutys of that station at this interesting juncture."[245] He was served heir to John Falconer of Phesdo in that property on 10 September 1766,[246] and afterwards spent most of his time ashore there. Their son and heir was:[247]

a. George Gordon Falconer, born about 1780,[248] died 24 June 1856,[249] probably at his residence in Turnham Green, Middlesex. He was an extra clerk, beginning in 1816, and an established clerk, from 1821, in the Examiner's Office, His Majesty's East India Company, until his retirement in 1836. This department, which also at that period employed James Mill and his son John Stuart Mill, was responsible for communications with the company's officers in India. He married, on 20 December 1806, at St. Pancras, Middlesex, Mary Anne Holbrook.[250] Probably the daughter of John and Elizabeth Holbrook, baptized 21 May 1780 at St. Botolph without Aldgate, London, she died 24 January 1863[251] in Brighton.

viii. Mary Falconer, died, unmarried, 27 September 1775 in Edinburgh. In her testament, dated 31 March 1775, she appointed her sister Jean, spouse of James Falconer of Monkton, to be her executrix; she gave money to her brother David; she asked Rev. John Allen, an Episcopal clergyman, to pay £400 sterling to the children of her deceased brother John. She made other bequests to non-relatives.[252]

ix. Marion (May) Falconer, died 18 November 1787 at Deans. She married, at Inglismaldie, 31 April 1759, George Norvell of Boghall and Deans,[253] and had issue, surname Norvell:[254] a. *Catherine Margaret*, baptized 30 December 1765, married, 10 January 1791, Cosby Swindell, Captain, 55th Foot; b. *Elizabeth*, baptized 28 January 1768.

A11   **Alexander, fifth Lord Falconer of Halkerton**, born about 1707, died 5 November 1762 in Edinburgh.[255]

He married, at St. George's, Hanover Square, 25 June 1757, Frances Mackworth, daughter of Herbert Mackworth, of the Gnoll, Glamorganshire, born 28 August 1731, died 3 March 1814, but had no issue. She married, as her second husband, 19 July 1765,[256] at South Audley Street Chapel, Anthony Joseph Browne, 7th Viscount Montagu, who died 9 April 1787.

He went abroad in early youth and attached himself to George, Earl Marischal and his brother, General (later Field-Marshal) James Keith, and served in Russia and Germany. He returned to Scotland when he succeeded to the title in 1751. At the end of 1752, in company with James Allardice of

Allardice, he set off for a ship docked in Aberdeen in a coach drawn by six black mares.[257] Lord Halkerton spent 1753, 1754, and most of 1755 in France, mainly in Orleans, Paris, and Caen. Returning home in 1756, after a stay in London, he went to Bath in January, 1757. He returned to Inglismaldie with his bride in 1758.[258]

A12 **William, sixth Lord Falconer of Halkerton**, born perhaps about 1712, buried 11 December 1776 in Groningen, Holland.[259]

    On 24 August 1735, at Waalse kerk, Groningen, he married Rembertina

Maria van Iddekinge, daughter of Pieter Rembt van Iddekinge, burgomaster of Groningen, by his wife Beerta Johanna Gerlacius,[260] born 24 August 1713 in Groningen, died 22 October 1799 in Groningen.

He went to Groningen to study. His parents did not approve of this marriage, and they refused to countenance or assist him or his family,[261] undoubtedly motivating him to remain in Holland the rest of his life. He was a merchant in Groningen and *kwartier-schout* [bailiff of the quarter] in 1765 in 's Hertogenbosch. He succeeded his brother in 1762 and was served heir 21 November 1768. Letters to John Mackenzie of Delvine, his attorney in Scotland, reveal that he was greatly concerned with providing education and incomes for his children. According to John Napier, he paid off the debts on his brother's estate, even though he did not risk losing his real estate, since it was entailed.[262] After he succeeded to the title, he visited Scotland only once, in 1767[263]——an indication how estranged from his family he had become. He and his children had by now become thoroughly Dutch. He lived in a house on Oosterstraat in Groningen, as did his father-in-law and brother-in-law Anton Adriaan van Iddekinge.[264]

Issue of William, 6th Lord Falconer of Halkerton, by Rembertina Maria van Iddekinge:[265]

i. David Falconer, born 24 August 1735, baptized 28 August 1735, died young.

ii. Pieter Rembt Falconer, baptized 23 September 1736. His father's "unlucky son,"[266] he died at Groningen 3 February 1773,[267] without issue. Although the eldest son, circumstances evidently prevented him from being his father's heir.

iii. Barta Johanna Falconer, baptized 31 January 1738, died, unmarried, 16 January 1809 in Groningen. She and her sister Susanna made a joint will in 1787, bequeathing all property to the children of their brother Alexander. The sisters lived on the west side of the Boteringestraat in Groningen at the time of their deaths.[268]

iv. Catharina Margrieta Falconer, baptized 19 June 1739, died in infancy.

v. Wibbina Sophia Falconer, baptized 30 September 1740, died 11 May 1803 in Groningen. She married, by license at Groningen dated 22 August 1761, Dr. Wilhelm Andries Baurmeester (or Baumeister), son of Andreas Frederik Baurmeester, baptized at Groningen 13 January 1734, buried there 4 November 1781, secretary of the municipality of Selwerd, and had issue, surname *Baurmeester*:[269] a. *Remdina Maria*, baptized 26 May 1762 at Groningen, died 28 March 1785 at Finsterwolde; married, 11 May 1782 at Finsterwolde, John Hendrik de Sitter; b. *Siberdina Johanna*, baptized 5 June 1763; c. *Barta Susanna*, baptized 13 May 1766; d. *Willem Frederik Buntinga*, baptized 19 February 1768; e. *Barta Susanna Alexandra*, baptized 6 April 1774, married, 8 February 1794, Antony Boon; f. *Anna Kedurg Sophia*, baptized 24 January 1777.

A15 vi. Anthony Adrian, 7th Lord Falconer of Halkerton, baptized 2 February 1742.

vii. Susanna Helena Wilhelmina Falconer, baptized 17 July 1744, died in infancy.

viii. Susanna Helena Wilhelmina Falconer, baptized 18 September 1746, died, unmarried, 13 December 1808 in Groningen.

ix. Catharina Margaretha Falconer, baptized 21 March 1749.

B1 x. Alexander Falconer, baptized 23 August 1754.

xi. William Falconer,[270] Lieutenant, 15th Regiment of Foot, baptized 29 April 1757, killed 11 September 1777 at the Battle of Brandywine, in Pennsylvania.[271] He was commissioned ensign, 15 August 1775; promoted to lieutenant, 25 November 1776.[272] He died without leaving issue, as he or any heirs were not named in proceedings, 11 May and 12 July 1782, which sought to collect cash in lieu of annuities for the benefit of the younger children of William, 6th Lord, per an agreement dated 11 July 1765.[273]

A15   Anthony Adrian Keith-Falconer, fifth Earl of Kintore and seventh Lord Falconer of Halkerton, was baptized 2 February 1742 at Martinikirk, Groningen, Holland, and died 30 August 1804 at Keith Hall, Kintore, Aberdeenshire.

Keith Hall, near Inverurie. Built in the 17th century, it was the home of the Earls of Kintore.

On 9 March 1766, at Academiekerk, Groningen, he married Christina Elisabeth Sichterman, daughter of Jan Albert Sichterman, intendant-general in the Dutch East India Company, by his wife Sibilla Volckera Sadelijn,[274] born 26 November 1738 at Hooghly, Bengal, India, baptized 5 February 1739 at the Anglican Church in Calcutta,[275] died 26 March 1809.

He was matriculated at Groningen University on 20 December 1759 and acquired further education at Leiden, where he lived with a governor in 1763.[276]

He seems to have neglected his duties in Leiden, however, running up debts, and went off to London without his governor (tutor), which displeased his father.[277] The errant young man returned home, however, and made amends with him. Upon his marriage, his father gave him the house and lands of Inglismaldie, with an annual income of £100.[278] On 23 April 1766, he released to his brothers and sisters his interest in the estates in Holland of Lord Halkerton and Rembt van Iddekinge,[279] and went to Scotland, so that his children would be British subjects by virtue of their place of birth,[280] a necessary step to ensure his heir's right to inherit the title and lands of the Earl of Kintore.

Arriving in August, 1766, at Inglismaldie, from which Falconers had been absent for most of the previous fifteen years, he found the servants "thieves and rascals" and fell into a dispute with his factor, Stair Baillie, who left him in 1769.[281] He soon began improving his estates in such ways as pruning birch trees, planting 10,000 fir trees, buying cows, and developing a quarry.[282] His lands included Halkerton, Powburn, Burnton, Inglismaldie, Newton, one-third of Balmakelly, Canterland, Smiddyhill, Shiels, Barnhill, Collardoe, Glensaugh, Glenfarquhar, Corsbite, Drumhendry, Capoch, all in Kincardineshire; and Dunlappie, in Angus. The value of his father's lands in Scotland, about 1770, was £9836,2s.,2d.[283]

He was admitted a burgess of Montrose in 1765, of Aberdeen in 1767, and of Brechin in 1774.[284]   He succeeded George, Earl Marischal, to the Earldom of Kintore, on 28 May 1778.

Fraser relates a number of stories about him and his eccentricities.[285] He describes his interest in firearms and shooting barn fowl, for which he would compensate his tenants' losses. He even shot a bird which had flown into the Logie Pert church during services. His correspondence with his eldest son certainly shows this interest in firearms, as in one letter, Lord Inverury promised to buy him one at Regensburg (Ratisbon) in 1787.[286]

Issue of Anthony Adrian, 5th Earl of Kintore and 7th Lord Falconer of Halkerton, by Christina Elisabeth Sichterman, baptized at Marykirk:[287]

A16   i.   William, 8th Lord Falconer of Halkerton and 6th Earl of Kintore, baptized 11 December 1766.

      ii. Sibilla Keith-Falconer, born 9 January 1768, died 23 April 1792.

      iii. Maria Rembertina Keith-Falconer, baptized 8 February 1769, died at Bath 24 August 1851.

      iv. Catharine Margaret Keith-Falconer, baptized 3 June 1770, died 10 December 1849.

      v.   Francina Constantia Keith-Falconer, born 9 June 1771, died 4 December 1779.

      vi. Jean Keith-Falconer, baptized 3 June 1772, died young.

      vii. Christina Elizabeth Keith-Falconer, baptized 31 December 1774, died December 1826.

      viii. Susanna Helen Keith-Falconer, baptized 30 August 1777, died young.

William, 6th Earl of Kintore, attributed to Sir Henry Raeburn.

Collection of the Earl of Kintore.

A16   **William Keith-Falconer, sixth Earl of Kintore and eighth Lord Falconer of Halkerton**, was baptized 11 December 1766 at Marykirk, Kincardineshire, and died 6 October 1812 at Keith Hall.

He married, on 18 June 1793, at Aberdeen,[288] Maria Bannerman, daughter of Sir Alexander Bannerman of Kirkhill, Bart., and his wife Mary Gordon, born 29 February 1771[289] at Aberdeen, died 30 June 1826 at Green Park Place, Bath, buried on 13 July 1826 at Bath Abbey.

He was educated by private tutors in Edinburgh, from 1778 to 1781, and then at Scorton Academy in Lancashire. Accompanied by his governor William Ritchie, he spent the years between 1782 and 1787 on the Grand Tour, living for periods in Lausanne, Mainz, Rüsselsheim, Jena, and Basel. He received a commission in the Scots Greys on 7 February 1787. His chief passions in life were fox hunting and raising horses.[290]

Issue of William, sixth Earl of Kintore and eighth Lord Falconer of Halkerton, by Maria Bannerman:

A17   i.   Anthony Adrian, 9th Lord Falconer of Halkerton and 7th Earl of Kintore, born 20 April 1794.

      ii. Alexander Keith-Falconer, born 11 October 1798 at Philorth, died 5 June 1821, unmarried.[291]

A18   iii. William Keith-Falconer, born 11 December 1799, died 5 January 1846 at Monkrigg, Haddingtonshire. He married, on 24 June 1830, Louisa Grant, daughter of William Grant of Congalton. She died at Boulogne on 12 February 1862.[292] He entered the Royal Navy on 14 February 1812, as a first-class volunteer, on board the *Invincible*. He was attached, in April 1814, to the *Royal Oak*, and served in expeditions against Baltimore and New Orleans. He was commissioned a lieutenant on 10 November 1819 and was promoted to the rank of commander on 14 August 1827 and to the command of the *Philomel*. Although this ship was one of the vessels present at the battle of Navarin on 20 October 1827, he was compelled to perform lieutenant's duty on board the *Dartmouth* during that battle. He was made captain on 18 August 1828 and remained from that time on half-pay.[293] Issue of William and Louisa (Grant) Keith-Falconer:[294]

         a. Dora Keith-Falconer, born 1831, died 1856. She married, at Tor, Torquay, Devonshire, 20 January 1856,[295] Henry John Arthur Lockwood, son of Robert Manners Lockwood by his wife Lady Julia Lockwood.

         b. Adrian William Keith-Falconer, born 12 February 1837 in Edinburgh,[296] died 10 February 1887 in Herne Bay, Kent, buried in Herne Cemetery.[297] He attended Harrow for three or four years, until 1853, then took private instruction in preparation for entrance to Haileybury College.[298] In 1855, he resided at Torquay, Devonshire, and was a cornet in the 1st Royal Devon Yeomanry Cavalry. The administration on his meager estate was granted to his cousin Charles James Keith-Falconer.[299]

      iv. Mary Keith-Falconer, born 2 May 1795, died at Bath, 5 July 1864.

A17   Anthony Adrian Keith-Falconer, seventh Earl of Kintore and ninth Lord Falconer of Halkerton, was born 20 April 1794 and died, at Keith Hall, 11 July 1844.

He married, as his first wife, on 8 June 1817, at Montrose, Juliet Renny, fourth daughter of Robert Renny of Borrowfield and Elizabeth Jean Tailyour, born 6 January 1785 at Montrose, died 9 July 1819 at Inglismaldie, without issue.

He married, as his second wife, on 27 August 1821, at Dunnichen, Angus, Louisa Hawkins, youngest daughter of Francis Hawkins, Senior Judge of Circuit and Appeal at Bareilly, in the Bengal Presidency, born 28 August 1802, died 1 November 1841. She divorced him on 3 March 1840, and married, as her second husband, on 2 April 1840, B. North Arnold, M.D., of Millo and Langho, Lancashire.

He matriculated at St. Mary Hall, Oxford, on 7 December 1812.[300] He was created Baron Kintore of Kintore, in the Peerage of the United Kingdom, on 5 July 1838. His fondness for fox hunting can be seen from a painting by John Ferneley which he commissioned, now on exhibit at the Aberdeen Museum, which depicts a hunt at Kintore.

Issue of Anthony Adrian, seventh Earl of Kintore and ninth Lord Falconer of Halkerton, by Louisa Hawkins:

i. William Adrian, Lord Inverurie, born 2 September 1822, killed while fox hunting, unmarried, 17 December 1843, at Winwick Warrens, Northamptonshire, buried at Brixworth, Northamptonshire.[301] He was a Lieutenant in the 17th Light Dragoons.

A19 ii. Francis Alexander, 10th Lord Falconer of Halkerton and 8th Earl of Kintore, born 7 June 1828.

A20 iii. Charles James Keith-Falconer, born 1 July 1832, died 7 January 1889 at Brighton, Surrey. He was a major in the 4th Light Dragoons and 10th Hussars and served in the Crimean War. In his retirement he lived in South Kensington. He married, on 24 January 1857, Caroline Diana Aldridge, third daughter of Robert and Caroline Anne (Beauclerk) Aldridge of St. Leonard's Forest, Sussex. She died 24 February 1920 at Hampton Court Palace. Issue:

a. Diana Mary Keith-Falconer, born 8 November 1858, died, unmarried, 2 April 1952.

b. Cecil Edwards Keith-Falconer, Lieutenant-Colonel, Northumberland Fusiliers, born 11 October 1860, killed in action 10 November 1899 near Orange River, South Africa. He served in the Egyptian expedition at Dongola, in 1896; the Nile expedition, 1897; at Khartoum, in 1898. He married, 24 June 1899, Georgina Sarah Blagrave, daughter of John Henry Blagrave of Calcot Park, Berkshire, who died 4 March 1929. No issue.

A22 c. Charles Adrian Keith-Falconer, born 12 December 1861, died 23 February 1920 at The Garth, Bicester, Oxfordshire, where he settled in 1892 and was a follower of the Bicester Hounds.[302] He married, 11 June 1887, Williamina Emily Hume-Dick, daughter of the Right Hon. William Wentworth Fitzwilliam Hume-Dick of Humewood, Co. Wicklow, Ireland. She died 17 August 1945. Only child:[303]

1. Adrian Wentworth Keith-Falconer, of Brunswick Gardens, London, and Inglismaldie Castle, born 17 June 1888, died 19 February 1959.[304] Educated at Eton and New College, Oxford, he served as Captain in the Oxfordshire Yeomanry and Major, D.A.Q.M.G. A member of the British Armistice Commission, 1919-1920, he was parliamentary private secretary to the Secretary of State for Foreign Affairs, 1921-1922.[305] He married, on 25 November 1925, Phyllis Messervy, daughter of Ernest Francis Messervy, of St. Martin, Jersey, but had no issue.

d. Florence Keith-Falconer, born 18 May 1864, died 13 November 1939. She married, 5 August 1893, Rev. Hesketh France-Hayhurst, vicar of Middlewich, Chester, son of Rev. Thomas William Hamilton France-Hayhurst, born 15 November 1866, died 7 January 1925, and had issue, surname *France-Hayhurst*:[306] a. *Kenneth*, born 1894, died 1895; b. *Reginald Geoffrey*, born 7 May 1896, died 22 December 1970, married 10 May 1919 Gladys Violet Claremont; c. *Marion*, born 2 June 1898, died 5 October 1969, married, 24 October 1931, Henry Beauclerk Howe; d. *Cecily*, born 2 June 1901, died 9 February 1970, married, 27 January 1927, Cecil Petvin Porter, M.B.

e. Ida Madeleine Keith-Falconer, born 2 March 1868, died, unmarried, 2 January 1955.

  f. Victor Francis Alexander Keith-Falconer, born 27 October 1869, killed in action at Colenso, Natal, 21 February 1900. Captain, Prince Albert's (Somerset) Light Infantry.

  g. Evelyn Millicent Keith-Falconer, born 20 May 1872, died, unmarried, 20 August 1914.

  h. Violet Katherine Keith-Falconer, born 21 July 1875, died 2 September 1881.

  i. Sybil Blanche Keith-Falconer, born 9 September 1878, died 15 April 1966. She married, on 7 February 1911, Col. Eden Bernard Powell, H.S.O., late the Rifle Brigade, who died 10 November 1964, son of Henry Pryor Powll, of Ockley.[307]

 iv. Isabella Catherine Keith-Falconer, born 5 June 1824, died 8 February 1870. She married, 4 August 1847, Henry Grant of Congalton.

A19 **Francis Alexander Keith-Falconer, eighth Earl of Kintore and tenth Lord Falconer of Halkerton**, was born 7 June 1828 at Wadley House, Farringdon, Berkshire, and died 18 July 1880, at 22 Mansfield St., Marylebone.

  He married, 24 June 1851, at St. George, Hanover Square, his cousin, Louisa Madeleine Hawkins, second daughter of Francis Hawkins, of Cairnbank, Scotland. She died 6 February 1916.

  He was Lord-Lieutenant of Kincardineshire from 1856 to 1864 and of Aberdeenshire from 1864 to 1880. Known as the "preaching earl" in the North of Scotland, he was an elder in the Free Church of Scotland and a member of its General Assembly.[308]

  Issue of Francis Alexander, eighth Earl of Kintore and tenth Lord Falconer of Halkerton, by Louisa Madeleine Hawkins:[309]

A21 i. Algernon Hawkins Thomand, 11th Lord Falconer of Halkerton and 9th Earl of Kintore, born 12 August 1852.

  ii. Dudley Metcalfe Courtenay Keith-Falconer, born 19 January 1854, died 27 November 1873.

  iii. Ion Grant Neville Keith-Falconer, born 5 July 1856, died 11 May 1887 at Sheikh Othman, near Aden, Arabia.[310] He married, 4 March 1884, in Cannes, France, Gwendolen Bevan, daughter of Robert Cooper Lee Bevan of Fosbury House, Wiltshire. She died 24 October 1937. They had no issue. She married, as her second husband, 15 December 1894, Major Frederick Ewart Bradshaw, I.S.C. He was a student at Harrow from 1869 to 1873, during which time he felt a religious calling. He entered Trinity College, Cambridge, from which he received the degrees of B.A. in 1878 and M.A. in 1882. He studied Hebrew, Syriac, and Arabic, and lectured in Hebrew as well; in 1886 he accepted the post of Lord Almoner's Professor of Arabic. He wrote *Kalilah and Dimnah: Or, the Fables of Bidpai* (Cambridge: University Press, 1885), a translation of a Syriac manuscript. In Cambridge, he helped raise money to purchase buildings for use as missions. Besides his interest in Semitic languages, he was well known as a bicyclist, having participated in numerous races and a pioneering trip from Land's End to John O'Groats, and served as president of the London Bicycle Club. He was also interested in shorthand and wrote an article on the subject for the *Encyclopedia Britannica*. Having received authorization from the Free Church of Scotland, he and his wife traveled to Arabia in November 1886. They established a mission at Sheikh Othman, a village in the hills near Aden, but he soon was overcome by illness. His widow and mother afterwards provided stipends for two missionaries, and the mission, which included a medical dispensary, had developed into a forty-five-bed hospital by the time of Aden's independence in 1967.[311]

iv. Madeleine Dora Keith-Falconer, born 27 June 1858, died 11 December 1925. She married, 12 July 1889, Francis Henry Tonge, Captain, 62nd Regiment, Lord of the Manor of Highway, Wiltshire, born 8 June 1855 at Walcot Hall, Northamptonshire, died 6 March 1936. They had no issue.[312]

v. Blanche Catherine Keith-Falconer, born 15 September 1859, died 15 September 1922. She married, 4 December 1883, Colonel Granville Roland Francis Smith, C.V.O., C.B., Coldstream Guards, son of Roland and Constance Henrietta Sophia Louisa (Somerset) Smith, born 24 December 1860, died 4 March 1917, and had issue, surname *Smith:*[313] a. *Granville Keith-Falconer*, Lieutenant, Coldstream Guards, born 26 February 1886, died in action at Ypres, 29 October 1914, married, 2 March 1910, Lady Kathleen Clements; b. *Roland Audley*, born 31 January 1887, died 1946, married, 23 June 1913 Margaret Halcro Erskine Hill; c. Sir *Arthur Francis*, K.C.B., Lieutenant-General, Coldstream Guards, born 9 December 1890, died 1977, married, 19 September 1918, Hon. Monica Victoria Crossley; d. *Geoffrey Leveson Ion*, Lieutenant, Coldstream Guards, born 12 November 1893, died in action at Loos, September 1915.

vi. Arthur Keith-Falconer, born 27 August 1863, died 9 December 1877.

vii. Maude Keith-Falconer, born 20 July 1869.

A21 **Algernon Hawkins Thomand Keith-Falconer, ninth Earl of Kintore and eleventh Lord Falconer of Halkerton**, was born 12 August 1852 and died 3 March 1930 at Lixmount House, near Edinburgh.

He married, 14 August 1873, Sydney Charlotte Montagu, second daughter of George, 6th Duke of Manchester by Harriet Sydney Dobbs, born 14 October 1851, died 21 September 1932.

He was educated, from 1866 to 1868, at Eton, and then Trinity College, Cambridge, receiving the degrees of B.A. in 1874, M.A. in 1877, and Ll.D. in 1894. He received the following honors: Knight Grand Cross of the Order of St. Michael and St. George, 4 February 1889; Grand Cordon of the Crown of Italy; first class Red Eagle of Prussia; Grand Cross Military Order of Christ of Portugal; and Grand Cross of the North Star of Sweden.

He served as Lord-in-Waiting to Queen Victoria, from 1885 to 1886 and from 1895 to 1901 and to King Edward VII, from 1901 to 1906. He was appointed aide-de-camp to the King on 2 January 1903. He served as Captain of Yeomen of the Guard from 1886 to 1889 and Governor and Commander-in-chief of South Australia from 1889 to 1895. The *Times* called him a "strong and successful" governor, liked by the Australians for his approachability.[314] As Colonel, he commanded the 3rd battalion of Gordon Highlanders in 1903, retiring from military service on 19 May 1906. He was chief Conservative whip and in 1913 was elected deputy speaker of the House of Lords. Chairman of Committees in 1918-1919 and 1927-1928, he presided over a number of private bill committees.

Issue of Algernon Hawkins Thomand, ninth Earl of Kintore and eleventh Lord Falconer of Halkerton, by Sydney Charlotte Montagu:[315]

i. Ethel Sydney Keith-Falconer, Countess of Kintore (after 1966), born 20 September 1874, died 1974. She married, 16 February 1905, Sir John Lawrence Baird, 2nd Bart., eldest son of Sir Alexander Baird, Bart., created Baron Stonehaven of Ury in 1925 and Viscount Stonehaven, in the peerage of the United Kingdom, in 1938, born 27 April 1874, died 20 August 1941. He served as Governor-General of Australia. Issue, surname *Baird* (*Keith* after 1974): a. *Annette Sydney*, born 1905, died 1 February 1950, married Michael Henry Mason, of Eynsham Park, Oxfordshire; b. *James Ian*, 12th Earl of Kintore and 3rd Baronet, born 25 July 1908, died 10 January 1989, married, in 1935, Delia, daughter of William Lewis Brownlow Loyd, and had issue, including *Michael Canning William John Keith*, 13th and present Earl of Kintore, born 22 February 1939; b. *Robert Alexander Greville*, Squadron Leader, R.A.F., born 1910, killed in action 1943, married, 1939, Dorviegelda Malvina MacGregor; c. *Ariel Olivia Winifred*, born 1916, married, 1946 (dissolved 1958), Sir Kenneth Alexander Keith; d. *Hilda Ava Fiona Nancy*, born 1919, married, 1945, Lieutenant-Colonel Ronald Fulton Lucas Chance.

ii. Hilda Madaleine Keith-Falconer, born 5 November 1875, died 1967.

iii. Ian Douglas Montagu Keith-Falconer, Lord Inverurie, born 5 April 1877, died 26 August 1897 in London, Lieutenant, 3rd Battalion of Gordon Highlanders.

A23   iv. Arthur George, 10th Earl of Kintore and 12th Lord Falconer of Halkerton, born 5 January 1879.

A23   **Arthur George Keith-Falconer, 10th Earl of Kintore and 12th Lord Falconer of Halkerton**, was born 5 January 1879 and died 25 May 1966.[316]

He married, on 23 November 1937, at Edinburgh, Helena Zimmerman, former wife of William Angus Drogo Montagu, 9th Duke of Manchester, and daughter of Eugene and Marietta (Evans) Zimmerman, of Cincinnati, Ohio, born 1879 in Cincinnati, Ohio, died 15 December 1971 at Keith Hall.[317]

Educated at Eton between 1892 and 1895, he joined the Scots Guards in 1899. He was a lieutenant, serving between 1900 and 1902 in the South African War. He was promoted to the rank of captain in 1914 and served in World War I. He was attaché to the British legation to Buenos Aires in 1907.

They had no issue, and his titles, except that of Lord Falconer of Halkerton, passed to his sister and then to her eldest son.

NOTES

[1] John Cummins, *The Hound and the Hawk: the Art of Medieval Hunting* (New York: St. Martin's Press, 1988), p. 217.

[2] James Crabb Watt, *The Mearns of Old* (Edinburgh: William Hodge & Co., 1914), pp. 200f.

[3] Scotland, King, *The Acts of William I, King of Scots 1165-1214*, G. W. S. Barrow, ed., Regesta Regum Scottorum 2 (Edinburgh: at the University Press, 1971), p. 452f. This is Barrow's transcription of a copy in the British Library, Add. 24,276, f. 53. If the original charter had survived, it probably was destroyed in the fire at Halkerton in 1679. A *Genealogical Deduction of the Family of Rose of Kilravock*, written in 1683-4 by Mr. Hew Rose, Minister of Nairne, later edited by Cosmo Innes (Aberdeen: for the Spalding Club, 1848) includes a segment of Latin text from what must have been another separately preserved copy: "Ranulpho Falconer, filio Walteri Falconer in lie Carse de Gourie, terras de Halkertoune et Balbegno, propter servitium corporis sui, et si facere non possit, unum idoneum archarium, etc." (p. 74).

[4] Scotland, King, *The Acts of William I, King of Scots 1165-1214*, p. 452f.

[5] G. W. S. Barrow, *The Anglo-Norman Era in Scottish History* (Oxford: Clarendon Press, 1980), pp. 92, 116.

[6] *Early Yorkshire Charters*, Volume VI: *The Paynel Fee*, ed. Charles Travis Clay, Yorkshire Archaeological Society. Record Series, Extra Series 3 (1939), p. 238f.

[7] *Early Yorkshire Charters*, 1: 325; 3: 489.

[8] *Chartulary of the Cistercian Abbey of St. Mary of Sallay in Craven*, ed. Joseph McNulty, *Vol. 1 (nos. 1-388)*, Yorkshire Archaeological Society. Record Series 87 (1933), p. 82.

[9] *Feet of Fines for the County of York, from 1246 to 1272*, ed. Col. John Parker, Yorkshire Archaeological Society. Record Series 82 (for the Society, 1932), p. 89.

[10] *Feet of Fines for the County of York, from 1232 to 1246*, ed. Col. John Parker, Yorkshire Archaeological Society. Record Series 67 (for the Society, 1925), p. 19.

[11] *A History of the County of York: East Riding*, vol. 2, ed. K. J. Allison, Victoria History of the Counties of England, ed. R. B. Pugh (Oxford: for the Institute of Historical Research by Oxford University Press, 1974), p. 96.

[12] Ibid., 2: 273.

[13] *Early Yorkshire Charters*, 2: 465.

[14] Andrew Jervise, *The History and Traditions of the Land of the Lindsays* (Edinburgh: David Douglas, 1882), p. 403n., citing *Registrum Vetus de Aberbrothoc* (Edinburgh: for the Bannatyne Club, 1848), p. 100.

[15] J. R. N. Macphail, ed., *Papers from the Collection of Sir William Fraser, K.C.B., LL.D.* Publications of the Scottish History Society, 3rd ser., vol. 5 (Edinburgh: at the University Press by T. and A. Constable for the Scottish History Society, 1924), p. 70. William Ruxton Fraser, in *History of the Parish and Burgh of Laurencekirk* (Edinburgh: William Blackwood & Sons, 1888), p. 36, wrote that the lands of Luthra belonged to the Abbey of Arbroath, until 1246, when it conferred Luthra, Conveth, and Scotston, to Sir John Wishart, and speculated that Wishart transferred Luthra, later Halkerton, to Robert le Falconer, living in 1296. The fact that the charter was retained by the family so long, however, would seem to indicate that possession of the lands later called Halkerton was a right under this charter.

[16] Sir Robert Douglas, *The Peerage of Scotland: Containing an Historical and Genealogical Account of the Nobility of That Kingdom, from Their Origin to the Present Generation*, 2nd ed. rev. and corr. by John Philip Wood (Edinburgh: G. Ramsay, 1813), 2: 54, citing the chartulary of Arbroath, *penes* [belonging to] Macfarlane. Jervise, in *History and Tradition of the Land of the Lindsays*, p. 403n., cites *Registrum Episcopatus Brechinensis* (Edinburgh: for the Bannatyne Club, 1856), 2: 272, and gives the date as 1218-1222.

[17] Sir James Balfour Paul, *The Scots Peerage: founded on Wood's Edition of Sir Robert Douglas's Peerage of Scotland* (Edinburgh: David Douglas, 1908), 5: 242 (hereafter cited as: *Scots Peerage*). The author cites information from J. R. N. Macphail, but I have been unable to verify this reference. Elsewhere in this chapter, where the text is not otherwise referenced, it can be assumed that *The Scots Peerage* is the source of the information.

[18] See *The Acts of William I, King of Scots 1165-1214*, p. 453n. for Geoffrey Barrow's discussion of this land.

[19] Cosmo Innes, ed., *A Genealogical Deduction of the Family of Rose of Kilravock, with Illustrative Documents from the Family Papers, and Notes*, Spalding Club Publications, vol. 18 (Edinburgh: for the Spalding Club, 1848), p. 30. Afterwards as Innes, *Family of Rose of Kilravock*.

[20] Great Britain, Public Record Office, *Calendar of Documents Relating to Scotland*, ed. Joseph Bain (London: H. M. General Register House, 1884), vol. 2 (1272-1307), nos. 730, 782.

[21] *Instrumenta publica sive processus super fidelitatibus et homagiis scotorum domino regi angliae factis A.D. MCCXCI-MCCXCVI* (Edinburgh, the Bannatyne Club, 1834), p. 157.

[22] E39/99/8, Public Record Office.

[23] *Ane Account of the Families of Innes*, compiled by Duncan Forbes of Culloden in 1698, ed. Cosmo Innes (Aberdeen: for the Spalding Club, 1864), p. 60.

[24] *Registrum Episcopatus Moraviensis*, (Edinburgh: for the Bannatyne Club, 1837), p. 187.

[25] Ibid., p. 205.

[26] A transcript of this document, cited as MS 31.6.15 in the Advocates' Library, appears in Macphail, ed., *Papers from the Collection of Sir William Fraser*, p. 64n.

[27]"Copy of a Manuscript Entitled 'A Genealogie of the Barons of the Mearns of Late Memory Descending Lineally unto the Year of God 1578'," *Miscellany of the Third Spalding Club* (Aberdeen: for the Third Spalding Club, 1950), 2: 216f. Hereafter as "1578 Manuscript Genealogy."

[28]Scotland, *Registrum Magni Sigilli Regum Scotorum: The Register of the Great Seal of Scotland, 1424-1513*, ed. J. B. Paul (Edinburgh: H. M. Stationery Office, 1882), no. 495, p. 112. Hereafter as: *Register of the Great Seal.*

[29]His son George got sasine of Halkerton in 1500 (see below). The approximate year of birth is derived from the claim in the Arbuthnot genealogy that his son George had a son and heir Alexander who had married and died prior to 1511.

[30]"1578 Manuscript Genealogy," p. 216f. Powrie was held by the Ogilvies of that Ilk.

[31]Forbes, *Families of Innes*, p. 90.

[32]Cosmo Innes, ed., *The Book of the Thanes of Cawdor* (Aberdeen: for the Spalding Club, 1859), p. 65.

[33]Ibid., pp. 68-69.

[34]Gordon Donaldson, ed., *Protocol Book of James Young, 1485-1515* (Edinburgh: for the Scottish Record Society by J. Skinner, 1950), p. 29.

[35]Scotland, Lord Auditors, *The Acts of the Lords Auditors of Causes and Complaints 1466-1494* (Edinburgh: H. M. Stationery Office, 1828), 1: 137. Hereafter as *Acts of the Lords Auditors.*

[36]*Register of the Great Seal of Scotland, 1424-1513*, no. 1987, p. 417.

[37]*Acts of the Lords Auditors*, 2: 146.

[38]*Liber S. Thome de Aberbrothoc*, Publications of the Bannatyne Club, v. 86 (Edinburgh: for the Club, 1848), p. 269.

[39]*Acts of the Lords Auditors*, 2: 292.

[40]Scotland, Lords of Council, *Acts of the Lords of Council in Civil Causes*, vol. 2: *1496-1501*, ed. George Neilson and Henry Paton (Edinburgh: H. M. Stationery Office, 1918), p. 203f. A merk was not a coin, but a unit of value, worth 13s.,6d.

[41]That George was the son and heir of Alexander can be proved by references in the text; the daughters are named in the "1578 Manuscript Genealogy" and placed here on the basis of chronology.

[42]"1578 Manuscript Genealogy," pp. 216-217; these daughters are named only as daughters of "the Laird of Halkerton Falconar," so the generation is estimated.

[43]George Crawfurd, *The Peerage of Scotland* (Edinburgh: for the author by George Stewart, 1716), pp. 183-184.

[44]"1578 Manuscript Genealogy," p. 216.

[45]Violet Jacob, *The Lairds of Dun* (London: J. Murray, 1931), pp. 31-32. Thomas Erskine of Brechin, who held the wardship of the lands of Halkerton, was probably her brother.

[46]*Register of the Great Seal, 1424-1513*, no. 2208, p. 466.

[47]Scotland, Exchequer, *Rotuli Scaccarii Regum Scotorum: The Exchequer Rolls of Scotland* (Edinburgh: H. M. Stationery Office, 1897), 11: 463. Hereafter as *Exchequer Rolls.*

[48]Innes, *Book of the Thanes of Cawdor*, p. 113.

[49]William Fraser, *The Chiefs of Grant* (Edinburgh: n.p., 1883), 3: 45.

[50]*Register of the Great Seal, 1424-1513*, no. 3068, p. 655.

[51]Donaldson, ed., *Protocol Book of James Young*, p. 68.

[52]*Register of the Privy Seal of Scotland*, vol. 1: *1488-1529*, no. 2091, p. 320.

[53]*Liber S. Thome de Aberbrothoc*, p. 399.

[54]*Registrum Secreti Sigilli Regum Scotorum: The Register of the Privy Seal of Scotland*, vol. A.D. 1488-1529, ed. M. Livingstone (Edinburgh: H. M. General Register House, 1908), p. 378. Hereafter as *Register of the Privy Seal.* This indicates that David, the heir, was under legal age in 1512.

[55]The parentage of Alexander, David, and George is proven by references in the text. The parentage of Robert is tentative and unproven. The wife of Alexander Dunbar of Cumnock is placed here on chronological grounds.

[56]Mrs. P. S.-M. Arbuthnot, *Memories of the Arbuthnots of Kincardineshire and Aberdeenshire* (London: George Allen & Unwin, 1920), p. 40. Hugh Arbuthnot's 16th-century genealogy of the Arbuthnot family, in the National Library of Scotland, is the source for the information on the son Alexander.

[57]Scotland, Lords of Council, *Acts of the Lords of Council in Public Affairs, 1501-1554*, ed. Robert Kerr Hannay (Edinburgh: H. M. General Register House, 1932), p. 420.

[58]Macphail, *Papers from the Collection of Sir William Fraser*, p. 155.

[59]*Register of the Great Seal, 1513-1546*, no. 3123, p. 734.

[60]Robert Pitcairn, *Criminal Trials in Scotland* (Edinburgh: William Tait, 1833), vol. 1, part 1, p. 347.

[61]*Register of the Great Seal, 1546-1580*, no. 993, p. 223.

[62]Gordon Donaldson, ed., *Accounts of the Collectors of Thirds of Benefices, 1561-1572*, Publications of the Scottish History Society, 3rd ser., 42 (Edinburgh: by T. and A. Constable for the Scottish History Society, 1949), pp. 105, 139.

[63]Calendar of Charters, RH6/1648, Scottish Record Office (hereafter SRO).

[64]Innes, *Book of the Thanes of Cawdor*, p. 171. He might have been a son of George, but no proof exists.

[65] Walter MacFarlane, *Genealogical Collections...made by Walter MacFarlane 1750-1751*, ed. J. M. Clark (Edinburgh: for the Scottish History Society, 1900), 1: 38.

[66] Ibid., 2: 668, citing "Mr. Strachan's Manuscript History of the House of Thornton."

[67] "1578 Manuscript Genealogy," p. 217. According to Hew Rose, writing in 1683 or 1684, she was "of the familie of Conzie and Kilboyack" (Innes, *Family of Rose of Kilravock*, p. 72).

[68] See *Scots Peerage*; in Gerald Paget, *The Lineage and Ancestry of H.R.H. Prince Charles, Prince of Wales* (Edinburgh: Charles Skilton, 1977), 2: 246, the parents are given as James Dunbar of Conzie (eldest son of Alexander) and (incorrectly) Ellen Innis. The latter was the wife of Sir James Dunbar of Cumnok.

[69] Inventory of writs of lands of Lethen, John C. Brodie Papers, GD247/71, SRO.

[70] *Exchequer Rolls*, 14: 581.

[71] Ibid., 14: 583.

[72] Innes, *Family of Rose of Kilravock*, pp. 197-199.

[73] *Register of the Great Seal, 1513-1546*, no. 336, p. 75.

[74] Ibid., *1513-1546*, no. 2075, no. 2076, p. 466.

[75] Ibid., *1546-1580*, no. 18, p. 4.

[76] Macphail, *Papers from the Collection of Sir William Fraser*, p. 154.

[77] Innes, *Book of the Thanes of Cawdor*, p. 171.

[78] *Register of the Great Seal, 1546-1580*, no. 203, p. 48f.

[79] *Scots Peerage*; according to Macfarlane, in his *Genealogical Collections*, 2: 269, David's daughter Isobell married Alexander Strachan of Thornton. Possibly, however, she belonged to an earlier generation.

[80] Testament, Commissariot of Edinburgh, confirmed 11 Nov. 1583, CC8, SRO.

[81] Innes, *Family of Rose of Kilravock*, p. 74.

[82] Ibid., p. 286.

[83] *Registrum Episcopatus Moraviensis*, p. 405.

[84] Innes, *Family of Rose of Kilravock*, p. 74.

[85] *Scots Peerage*, 6: 173f. According to the 1579 genealogy, however, Isobell, daughter of David Falconer of Halkerton, married, as his first wife, John Strachan of Thornton.

[86] *Register of the Great Seal, 1546-1580*, no. 1209, p. 270.

[87] Testament, Commissariot of Edinburgh, CC8/8/37.

[88] She seems to have married Alexander Lindsay of Broadland, and they received a charter of Broadland and Phesdo on 25 October 1562 (*Register of the Great Seal, 1546-1580*, no. 1432, p. 324f.), yet she was described as the relict of Robert Falconer of Ballandro in 1585 and at her death.

[89] Testament, Commissariot of Edinburgh, CC8/8/24, SRO.

[90] *Register of the Great Seal, 1546-1580*, no. 719, p. 159f.

[91] *Register of the Great Seal, 1513-1546*, no. 3010, p. 706.

[92] *Exchequer Rolls*, 18: 482.

[93] Calendar of Charters, RH6/1648, SRO.

[94] W. R. Fraser, *History of the Parish and Burgh of Laurencekirk*, p. 38f.

[95] *Exchequer Rolls*, 18: 485.

[96] *Register of the Great Seal, 1580-1593*, no. 977, p. 318.

[97] Inventory of writs of lands of Fornichtie, John C. Brodie Papers, GD/247/71, p. 4, SRO.

[98] George Bain, *History of Nairnshire* (Nairn: "Telegraph" Office, 1928), p. 102.

[99] *Register of the Privy Seal*, 6: 237.

[100] Ibid., 6: 444.

[101] Innes, *Family of Rose of Kilravock*, pp. 229, 237, 242, 251, 269.

[102] *Register of the Privy Seal*, 7: 4f.

[103] Testament, Commissariot of Edinburgh, CC8/8/24, SRO.

[104] Ibid., CC8/8/24, unless where noted.

[105] MacFarlane, *Genealogical Collections*, 2: 488; Innes, *Family of Rose of Kilravock*, p. 523f.

[106] Testament, Commissariot of Edinburgh, CC8; transcription at Society of Genealogists Library.

[107] Testament, Commissariot of Edinburgh, CC8, SRO.

[108] Inventory of writs of lands of Lethen, John C. Brodie Papers, GD247/71, SRO.

[109] Innes, *Family of Rose of Kilravock*, p. 284.

[110] Scotland, Privy Council, *The Register of the Privy Council of Scotland*, ed. John Hill Burton, (Edinburgh: H. M. Stationery Office, 1882), 6: 735. Hereafter as *Register of the Privy Council*.

[111] Particular Register of Sasines for Elgin, Forres, and Nairn, RS28/3, p. 271, SRO.

[112] Ibid., RS28/3, p. 331, SRO.

[113] George Bain, *History of the Parish of Auldearn* (Nairn: "Telegraph" Office, 1898), p. 63. "Madeline Falconer, daughter to the Laird of Halcartown."

[114] Testament of Janet Falconer, widow of Sir John Wishart of Pittarow, Commissariot of Edinburgh, CC8, SRO.

[115] Particular Register of Sasines for Elgin, Forres, and Nairn, RS28/4, f. 92, SRO.

[116] Andrew Jervise, *Epitaphs and Inscriptions from Burial Grounds and Old Buildings in the North East of Scotland* (Edinburgh: David Douglas, 1879), 1: 264.

[117] Testament, Commissariot of Edinburgh, CC8/8/43, SRO.

[118] Testament, 23 March 1589/90, Commissariot of Edinburgh, CC8, SRO.

[119] *Register of the Privy Seal*, 6: 378.

[120] *Exchequer Rolls*, 21: 541, 542.

[121] *Register of the Great Seal, 1593-1609*, no. 9, p. 4.

[122] Register of Deeds, 272: 145, cited in: *Scots Peerage*, 9: 123n.

[123] Alexander Mackintosh Shaw, *Historical Memoirs of the House and Clan of Mackintosh and of the Clan Chattan* (London: for the author by R. Clay's Sons and Taylor, 1880), p. 314.

[124] Register of Deeds, 301: 3 and 254: 180, cited in: *Scots Peerage*, 5: 246n.

[125] Montrose Parish Register.

[126] Forfar Inhibitions, DI57/22, 12 April 1615, SRO.

[127] Bundle 314, Kintore Papers, Aberdeen University Library. William was perhaps another illegitimate child.

[128] *Register of the Great Seal, 1634-1651*, no. 1668, p. 629.

[129] Register of Deeds, 48: 216, 18 Nov. 1594, cited in: *Scots Peerage*, 5: 246n. Not verified.

[130] See William Fraser, *History of the Carnegies Earls of Southesk, and of Their Kindred*, 2 vols. (Edinburgh: n.p., 1867).

[131] Testament, Commissariot of St. Andrews, CC20, SRO.

[132] *Register of the Great Seal*, vol. 6: *1593-1609*, no. 208, p. 70.

[133] *Register of the Great Seal*, vol. 7: *1609-1620*, no. 718, p. 267f.

[134] Inventory of writs of Lethen, John C. Brodie Papers, GD247/71, SRO. Lethen was sold to Alexander Brodie in 1621, in whose family it has remained until the present century.

[135] *Register of the Privy Council*, 5: 291.

[136] George Bain, *History of Nairnshire*, 2nd ed. (Nairn: "Telegraph" Office, 1928), p. 183.

[137] Innes, *Family of Rose of Kilravock*, pp. 289-291, 524.

[138] *Register of the Privy Council*, 10: 490f.

[139] Ibid., 11: 435.

[140] Ibid., 12: 435f.

[141] Ibid., 12: 437f.

[142] Ibid., 12: 1620.

[143] Ibid., (2nd ser.), 5: 412.

[144] Jacob, pp. 170-171; Alexander Falconer of Halkerton to John Grant of Freuchie, 24 Dec. 1601, in: Fraser, *Chiefs of Grant*, 2: 39.

[145] Bond, Kintore Papers, Bundle 292, Aberdeen University Library. It may be that she and Margaret are identical.

[146] General Register of Sasines, RS1/38, f. 98, SRO.

[147] General Register of Inhibitions, DI5/1, 8 Oct. 1634; DI15/2, 1 Dec. 1634, SRO.

[148] Register of the Great Seal, 1634-1651, no. 1146, p. 431.

[149] Scotland, *Inquisitionum ad Capellam Domini Regis Retornatarum, quae in Publicis Archivis Scotiae Adhuc Servantur, Abbreviatio*, vol. 2: *Inquisitiones Generales*, ed. Thomas Thomson (Edinburgh: H. M. Stationery Office, 1811-1816), no. 4426, 19 Feb. 1659. Hereafter as *Inquisitiones Generales*.

[150] *Inquisitiones Generales*, 2: no. 5649.

[151] Sir Francis J. Grant, ed., *The Faculty of Advocates in Scotland, 1532-1943: with Genealogical Notes* (Edinburgh: Scottish Record Society, 1944), p. 69.

[152] Alexander M. Munro, ed., "Aberdeen Burgess Register, 1631-1700," *Miscellany of the New Spalding Club*, vol. 2 (Aberdeen: for the New Spalding Club, 1908), p. 402.

[153] Register of Deeds, RD3/432, SRO.

[154] Particular Register of Sasines for the Sheriffdom of Kincardine, RS7/4, f. 121ff., SRO.

[155] Ibid.

[156] Henry Paton, ed., *Register of Interments in the Greyfriars Burying-Ground, Edinburgh, 1658-1700* (Edinburgh: for the Scottish Record Society, 1900), p. 212.

[157] Particular Register of Sasines for the Sheriffdom of Kincardine, RS7/4, f. 230, SRO.

[158] Court of Session Processes, CS138/1806, SRO.

[159] George Falconar to Sir John Falconar, Moses Bundle 254/7793a, Edinburgh District Archives.

[160] Marguerite Wood and Helen Armet, *Extracts from the Records of the Burgh of Edinburgh: 1681 to 1689* (Edinburgh: Oliver & Boyd, 1954), pp. 138, 167.

[161] Paton, ed., *Register of Interments in Greyfriars Burying-Ground*, p. 212.

[162] Henry Paton, ed., *Register of Marriages for the Parish of Edinburgh, 1595-1700* (Edinburgh: for the Scottish Record Society by James Skinner, 1905), p. 224.

[163] Donald Crawford, ed., *Journals of Sir John Lauder, Lord Fountainhall, with His Observations on Public Affairs and Other Memoranda, 1665-1676*, Publications of the Scottish History Society, vol. 36 (Edinburgh: at the University Press by T. & A. Constable for the Society, 1900), p. 215; testament, Commissariot of St. Andrews, CC20/4/13.

[164] *Register of the Great Seal*, vol. 7: 1609-1620, no. 2022, p. 731f.

[165] *Register of the Privy Council*, 2nd ser., 1: 540-542, 548-550.

[166] *Register of the Great Seal*, vol. 7: 1609-1620, no. 2022, p. 731f.

[167] Munro, "Aberdeen Burgess Register," p. 33.

[168] *Register of the Great Seal, 1634-1651*, no. 1668, p. 629

[169] *Register of the Great Seal, 1660-1668*, no. 1026, p. 511.

[170] Crawford, ed., *Journals of Sir John Lauder, Lord Fountainhall*, p. 215.

[171] Ibid., p. 216.

[172] Register of the Privy Seal, PS3/1, f. 70, SRO.

[173] *Register of the Great Seal, 1634-1651*, no. 1733, p. 650.

[174] Fraser, *History of the Parish and Burgh of Laurencekirk*, p. 40.

[175] Quoted in W. R. Fraser, *History of the Parish and Burgh of Laurencekirk*, p. 41.

[176] Testament, Commissariot of St. Andrews, CC20, SRO.

[177] Baptisms in Montrose Old Parish Register.

[178] Court of Session. Register of Acts and Decreets, 391: 111, A.D. 1626, cited in: *Scots Peerage*, 9: 123n. Not verified.

[179] "Diary of John Row, Principal of King's College," *Scottish Notes and Queries*, 1st ser., 7 (1894): 183.

[180] Cavendish D. Abercromby, *The Ogilvies of Banff* (n.p., 1939), p. 61; inventory of Forglen Muniments, SRO

[181] Letter, David, Bishop of Brechin, to Rev. Thomas Small, 24 Apr. 1666, Airlie Muniments, GD16/35/9, SRO, which gives him warrant to approve of the marriage without open proclamation.

[182] *Index to Forfar Sasines*, p. 259 (referring to series 3, 3: 102, 9: 402).

[183] Decreet and precept, Kintore Papers, Bundle 92, Aberdeen University Library.

[184] *Register of the Privy Council*, 3rd ser., 3: 124.

[185] *Inquisitiones*, Kincardine, no. 119.

[186] Fraser, *History of the Parish and Burgh of Laurencekirk*, p. 42.

[187] Innes, *Family of Rose of Kilravock*, p. 74.

[188] Account between Lord Halkerton and Sir John Falconer, Kintore Papers, Bundle 92, Aberdeen University Library; Sir John Falconar to Barbara Jaffray, 11 Aug. 1685, Moses Bundle 254/7793a, Edinburgh District Archives.

[189] Bond of provision, Kintore Papers, Bundle 104, Aberdeen University Library.

[190] Court of the Lord Lyon. Funeral escutcheon, cited in *Scots Peerage*, 5: 249n.

[191] Court of Session Processes, CS236/H/1/43, SRO.

[192] Scotland, *Decennial Indexes to the Services of Heirs in Scotland*, vol. 1: 1700-1749 (Edinburgh: for H. M. Stationery Office by Murray and Gibb, 1863), 1: (1710-19), 9.

[193] Marykirk Parish Register; 5 November 1706 is the date in the Laurencekirk Register, according to IGI.

[194] Alistair and Henrietta Tayler, *The House of Forbes* (Aberdeen: for the Third Spalding Club, 1937), p. 423; Marykirk Parish Register.

[195] Montrose Parish Register.

[196] *Decennial Indexes to Services of Heirs*, 1: (1720-29), 3.

[197] Ibid., 1: (1720-29), 9.

[198] Henry Paton, ed., *The Register of Marriages for the Parish of Edinburgh, 1701-1750*, Scottish Record Society, pt. 43 (Edinburgh: for the Society by James Skinner, 1908), p. 178.

[199] *Decennial Indexes to Services of Heirs*, 1: (1720-29), 9.

[200] Inventory of writs, Kintore Papers, Bundle 104, Aberdeen University Library.

[201] Montrose Parish Register.

[202]Register of Deeds, RD4/114, SRO.

[203]Bond, Kintore Papers, Bundle 85, Aberdeen University Library.

[204]Ibid.

[205]Register of the Privy Council, 3rd ser., 14: 707-708; 15: 636. The amount was approximately 34 bushels of wheat and three bushels of oats and fodder.

[206]Disposition and assignation, Kintore Papers, Bundle 85; Declaration in favor of Andrew Falconer, Kintore Papers, Bundle 92, Aberdeen University Library.

[207]Decennial Indexes to Services of Heirs, 1: (1720-29), 9.

[208]Moses Bundle 254/7769, Edinburgh District Archives.

[209]Inquisitiones Spec., Kincardine, no. 157.

[200]Macphail, Papers from the Collection of Sir William Fraser, p. 71.

[211]Chancery, C22/53, f. 374, SRO.

[212]Court of Session Processes, CS/18/2203, SRO.

[213]Court of Session Processes, CS236/H/1/43, SRO.

[214]Fraser, History of the Parish and Burgh of Laurencekirk, p. 42.

[215]Marriage certificate, Kintore Papers, Bundle 47, Aberdeen University Library.

[216]Scots' Magazine, 24: 112.

[217]Inquisitiones Spec., Kincardine, no. 161.

[218]Scotland, Parliament, The Acts of the Parliaments of Scotland, ed. Thomas Thomson and Cosmo Innes (Edinburgh: H. M. Stationery Office, 1872), 2: 23, 149.

[219]Decennial Indexes to Services of Heirs, 1: (1710-19), 9; (1720-29), 9. Thus there was no Alexander, 4th Lord, as is stated in Scots Peerage, 5: 450.

[220]Register of Tailzies, RT1/10, ff. 181-190, SRO.

[221]Sasine, Kintore Papers, Bundle 107, Aberdeen University Library.

[222]This information is from James Holloway, Assistant Keeper, Scottish National Portrait Gallery.

[223]Obligation, Alexander, Lord Falconer of Halkerton, in favor of Katharine, Lady Halkerton, 1751, Kintore Papers, Bundle 105, Aberdeen University Library.

[224]Discharge of David Falconer, Kintore Papers, Bundle 107, Aberdeen University Library.

[225]Testament, Kintore Papers, Bundle 107, Aberdeen University Library.

[226]Brown, Epitaphs and Monumental Inscriptions in Greyfriars Churchyard, Edinburgh, p. 244.

[227]George Falconar to David, Lord Falconer of Halkerton, 16 June 1731; Lord Falconer to George Falconar, 23 June 1731, in Kintore Papers, Bundle 195, Aberdeen University Library.

[228]Bridewell Hospital Chapel: Marriages, 1671-1837, ed. C. Webb, City of London Marriages, vol. 2 (London: Society of Genealogists, n.d.), p. 286.

[229]S. Taylor, "The Lamplugh Family of Cumberland, Part 2," Transactions of the Cumberland & Westmorland Antiquarian & Archaeological Society, n.s., 39 (1939): 86.

[230]A. R. Jabez-Smith, "Some Portraits at Dovenby Hall," Transactions of the Cumberland and Westmorland Antiquarian and Archaeological Society, n.s., 44 (1964): 263.

[231]Inland Revenue Office, IR1/13, f. 50, Public Record Office.

[232]Bond, 14 Feb. 1748, Delvine Papers, MS 1268, f. 13, National Library of Scotland.

[233]Prerogative Court of Canterbury, PROB11/1011 (146 RH-147 LH), Public Record Office.

[234]Baptisms at St. Antholin Budge Row, London; burials at St. John the Baptist upon Wallbrook, London, except as noted.

[235]Register of St. Antholin Budge Row, London.

[236]Jabez-Smith, "Some Portraits at Dovenby Hall," p. 258.

[237]Testament, Commissariot of Edinburgh, 22 Nov. 1797, CC8, SRO.

[238]Paton, ed., Register of Marriages for the Parish of Edinburgh, 1701-1750, p. 178.

[239]Scots' Magazine, 42: 279.

[240]Joseph Lemuel Chester, ed., Burial Registers of Westminster Abbey (London: 1876), p. 430.

[241]William, 6th Lord Falconer of Halkerton, to John Mackenzie of Delvine, 20 Oct. 1767, Delvine Papers, MS 1265, f. 181, National Library of Scotland. He believed George "designs to marry."

[242]Scots' Magazine, 48: 464.

[243]Commissioned Sea Officers of the Royal Navy 1660-1815 ([National Maritime Museum], 1954?), vol. 1, unpaginated.

[244]John Charnock, Biographia Navalis (London: for R. Faulder, 1798), 6: 482.

[245]Charles B. Boog Watson, Roll of Edinburgh Burgesses and Guild-Brethren, 1701-1760, Scottish Record Society, pt. 122 (Edinburgh: for the Society by J. Skinner, 1929), p. 67.

[246] Decennial Indexes to Services of Heirs, 2: (1760-69), 13.

[247] William Maxwell Morison, Decisions of the Court of Session (Edinburgh: Constable, 1811), 37: 16380.

[248] Possibly baptized 5 February 1780 at St. Clement Danes, Westminster, London, but parents were not named.

[249] Gentleman's Magazine, 1 (n.s.): 258.

[250] East India Company, Regular Widow's Fund minutes, L/AG/23/3A/2, India Office Library.

[251] East India Company, Regular and elders widows' funds, L/AG/21/23/16, f. 60, India Office Library. The balance of her pension payment was payable to S. S. Ripsey, a widow.

[252] Testament, Commissariot of Edinburgh, CC8/8/123/1, SRO.

[253] Scots' Magazine, 21: 331; Marykirk Parish Register.

[254] Baptisms at Bathgate, West Lothian (IGI).

[255] Gentleman's Magazine, 32: 552.

[256] Ibid., 35: 346.

[257] Macphail, Papers from the Collection of Sir William Fraser, p. 71.

[258] Alexander, Lord Falconer of Halkerton, to John Mackenzie of Delvine, passim, Delvine Papers, MS 1264, National Library of Scotland.

[259] J. W. F. Baron van Wassenaer, "Falconer-Van Iddekinge-Sichterman," De Nederlandsche Leeuw 108, nr. 1-2 (Jan.-Feb. 1991): 117; Decennial Indexes to Services of Heirs, 2: (1770-79) 13, however, gives 12 December 1776 as his date of death..

[260] Genealogy, certified 6 April 1970, Centraal Bureau voor Genealogie, The Hague.

[261] Memorandum concerning succession of Halkerton, Kintore Papers, Bundle 90, Aberdeen University Library.

[262] Macphail, Papers from the Collection of Sir William Fraser, p. 71.

[263] William, 6th Lord Falconer of Halkerton, to John Mackenzie of Delvine, 20 Dec. 1763, 15 June 1767, 14 June 1768, Delvine Papers, MS 1265, ff. 164, 178, 187, National Library of Scotland.

[264] Jeroen van Iddeking, Markepad 8, 9462 RL, Gasselte, The Netherlands.

[265] The first two baptisms were recorded in Waalse kerk, Groningen; the remainder were recorded in register of Martini-Kerk, Groningen; deaths, from genealogy by Central Bureau voor Genealogie, and Wassenaer, "Falconer-Van Iddekinge-Sichterman," pp. 117-118.

[266] William, 6th Lord Falconer of Halkerton, to John Mackenzie of Delvine, 8 May 1773, Delvine Papers, MS 1265, National Library of Scotland.

[267] Anthony Adrian Falconer to John Mackenzie of Delvine, 26 Feb. 1773, Delvine Papers, MS 1267, National Library of Scotland.

[268] Research by Jeroen van Iddeking; Nederlands Patriciaat, 6 (1915): 334.

[269] Falconer archief, 552.165, Rijksarchief van Groningen, researched and translated by Jeroen van Iddeking.

[270] Baptized as Willem Arnold Hendrik Cornelis Falconer.

[271] R. J. Jones, History of the 15th East Yorkshire Regiment: 1685-1914.

[272] A List of the General and Field Officers...for the year 1777 (London: for J. Millan, 1777), p. 69 (inscribed copy at PRO).

[273] Protocol van Volmachten Procuraten, III gg 2: 34-36; 41ff., Groningen Rechterlijke Archieven, in Gemeente Archief in Groningen.

[274] Centraal Bureau voor Genealogie genealogy.

[275] Extract of baptism, Kintore Papers, Bundle 256, Aberdeen University Library.

[276] William, 6th Lord Falconer of Halkerton, to John Mackenzie of Delvine, 20 Dec. 1763, Delvine Papers, MS1265, f. 164, National Library of Scotland.

[277] William, 6th Lord Falconer of Halkerton, to John Mackenzie of Delvine, 13 Nov. 1764, Delvine Papers, MS1265, f. 168, National Library of Scotland.

[278] William, 6th Lord Falconer of Halkerton, to John Mackenzie of Delvine, 8 Mar. 1766, Delvine Papers, MS1265, ff. 171-172, National Library of Scotland.

[279] H. O. Feith, Register van het Archief van Groningen (Groningen: n.p., 1857), 5: 20.

[280] Memorial concerning entail of Boghall, Kintore Papers, Bundle 44, Aberdeen University Library.

[281] Anthony, 7th Lord Falconer of Halkerton, to John Mackenzie of Delvine, 19 Oct. 1766, 26 Oct. 1766, Delvine Papers, MS 1267, ff. 11, 13-14, National Library of Scotland.

[282] Ibid., 2 Sept. 1767, 26 Jan. 1768, 11 Feb. 1768, Delvine Papers, MS 1267, ff. 36, 49, 51, National Library of Scotland.

[283] Loretta R. Timperley, ed., A Directory of Landownership in Scotland c.1770 (Scottish Record Society, New Series 5) (Edinburgh: for the Society by Econoprint Ltd., 1976), pp. 19, 181-183.

[284] Burgess tickets, Kintore Papers, Bundle 59, Aberdeen University Library.

[285] Fraser, History of the Parish and Burgh of Laurencekirk, p. 45f.

[286] William, Lord Inverury, to Anthony Adrian, Earl of Kintore, 22 Jan. 1787, Kintore Papers, Bundle 197, Aber-

deen University Library.

[287] Marykirk Parish Register; in Wood, *The Peerage of Scotland*, the baptismal dates are incorrectly listed as dates of birth.

[288] *Gentleman's Magazine*, 63/1: 575.

[289] Alexander Emslie Smith, "Register of S. Paul's Episcopal Chapel, Aberdeen," *The Miscellany of the New Spalding Club*, vol. 2, Aberdeen University Studies, no. 31 (Aberdeen: for the University, 1908), p. 194.

[290] William Ritchie to Anthony Adrian, Earl of Kintore, various letters; William, Lord Inverury, to the Earl of Kintore, correspondence, in Kintore Papers, Aberdeen University Library.

[291] Lady Kintore to Hugh Gordon, 3 July 1821, Kintore Papers, Aberdeen University Library, implies that he was unmarried.

[292] *Gentleman's Magazine*, 12 (n.s.): 515.

[293] William R. O'Byrne, *A Naval Biographical Dictionary* (London: John Murray, 1849), p. 600.

[294] *Decennial Indexes to Services of Heirs*, 1850-1859, p. 52.

[295] *Gentleman's Magazine*, 45: 180.

[296] Ibid., 7: 314.

[297] E. Dwelly, *Dwelly's Parish Records*, vol. 3: *Kent M.I.* (Herne Bay: by the Author, 1914), p. 110.

[298] J. H. Stogdon, *The Harrow School Register, 1845-1925*, 2nd ed. (London: Longmans, Green, 1925), 1: 241; East India Company, Haileybury College Petitions, J/1/87/24, India Office Library. He never attended Haileybury College, however.

[299] Will index, Somerset House.

[300] Joseph Foster, *Alumni Oxonienses: The Members of the University of Oxford, 1715-1886* (Oxford: Parker, 1886), vol. *E-K*, p. 446.

[301] The circumstances of his death are described in: Fraser, *History of the Parish and Burgh of Laurencekirk*, p. 46f.

[302] *London Times*, 26 Feb. 1920.

[303] Ibid.

[304] Ibid., 20 Feb. 1959.

[305] Great Britain, Foreign Office, Foreign Office List (1937).

[306] *Burke's Genealogical and Heraldic History of the Landed Gentry* (London: Burke's Peerage Ltd., 1972), p. 166.

[307] *London Times*, 1 Mar. 1920.

[308] Marcus L. Loane, *They Were Pilgrims* (Sydney: Angus and Robertson, 1970), p. 145, citing Lady Hilda Keith-Falconer, "Keiths of Long Ago," manuscript at Keith Hall, 1967.

[309] *Scots Peerage*, 5: 253-254.

[310] Will index, Somerset House.

[311] Loane, *They Were Pilgrims*, pp. 143-190, where a fuller biography can be found. Sources for Loane's study included Robert Sinker, *Memorials of the Hon. Ion Keith-Falconer: Late Lord Almoner's Professor of Arabic in the University of Cambridge, and Missionary to the Mohammedans of Southern Arabia*, 5th ed. (Cambridge: Deighton, Bell and Co., 1888) and James Robson, *Ion Keith-Falconer of Arabia*, Master Missionary Series (New York: Doran, 19—).

[312] *Burke's Genealogical and Heraldic History of the Landed Gentry*, (London: Burke's Peerage, Ltd., 1939), p. 2261.

[313] *Burke's Genealogical and Heraldic History of the Landed Gentry* (London: Burke's Peerage Ltd., 1952), p. 2335; *Who Was Who, 1916-1928*, p. 972; *London Times*, 6 March 1917.

[314] *London Times*, 4 March 1930.

[315] *Scots Peerage*, 5: 255f.

[316] *London Times*, 27 May 1966.

[317] Marian Fowler, *In a Gilded Cage: from Heiress to Duchess* (New York: St. Martin's Press, 1993), pp. 203-254.

CHAPTER B

Falconer of Groningen

B1 Alexander Falconer, younger son of William, 6th Lord Falconer of Halkerton, baptized 23 August 1754 in Groningen, Holland, died 27 September 1826 in Groningen.[1]

He married, in Groningen, 15 August 1784, Margaretha Clementia Keiser, daughter of Dr. Jan Harman Keiser by his wife Johanna Clara Quintus, born 8 June 1759 in Groningen, died 26 November 1826 in Groningen.

He and his brother William were sent to Scotland at the beginning of 1770, in order to learn the language and customs of Scotland, indicating how thoroughly Dutch they were. They attended school in St. Andrews and at Perth Academy. In 1775 he returned to Holland, where he intended to begin a mercantile career.[2] It seems doubtful that he was successful in this objective, but he did secure a post as master of artillery at Groningen. In the 1790s, he suffered from financial insolvency, and in 1799 it was ordered that furniture of his be sold in order to pay off debts amounting to 2151 Caroly guilders.[3] He lived on Hardingestraat at the time of the birth of his first child, then by 1789 the family lived on Turfstraat.[4]

Issue of Alexander and Margaretha Clementia (Keiser) Falconer:[5]

    i.   Rembertina Maria Falconer, baptized 1 July 1785, died young.

B2   ii. Antoon Adriaan Falconer, baptized 10 September 1786.

    iii. Jan Herman Falconer, baptized 11 February 1789, died, unmarried, 17 November 1815 in Groningen.

    iv. William Falconer, merchant, baptized 4 August 1790, died 11 May 1862 in Groningen, leaving no issue. He married, in Groningen on 17 November 1831, Janna Wessels, daughter of Lammert Wessels Kuipers by his wife Pietertien Bonnes, baptized 22 May 1796 in Groningen, died 13 September 1860 in Groningen.

    v. Johannes Clarus Falconer, baptized 18 March 1792, died 22 August 1792 in Groningen.

    vi. Johan Hendrik Falconer, baptized 15 May 1793 in Groningen, died, unmarried, 1 January 1828 at Wildervank.

vii. Rembertina Maria Falconer, baptized 6 March 1795, died 28 February 1867 in Groningen. She married, in Groningen on 12 June 1828, Evert Tammes, son of Tamme Jans by his wife Harmtje Roelfs, baptized 20 May 1798 in Groningen, died 22 January 1864 in Groningen, a bargeman. Issue, surname *Tammes*: a. *Wilhelmina*, born 30 January 1816, died 25 May 1869, married Abraham Karp;[6] b. *Berend*, born 31 December 1825, died 14 September 1826.

viii. Johanna Clara Falconer, baptized 21 June 1797, died 18 April 1856 in Groningen. She married, as her first husband, in Groningen, 2 September 1827, Jacob Kramer, son of Johannes Jacobs Kramer by his wife Pietertje Gozens, baptized 14 January 1801 in Groningen, died 19 May 1836 in Groningen. She married, as her second husband, in Groningen on 20 April 1837, Goossen Kramer, his brother, baptized 4 November 1803 in Groningen, died 11 September 1867 in Haren, a soldier and later a cabinet maker.

B2 **Antoon Adriaan Falconer**, baptized 10 September 1786 in Groningen, died 5 May 1853 at Wildervank.

He married, as his first wife, in Groningen, 15 December 1813, Margaretha Blink, daughter of Meinardus Blink by his wife Trijntje van der Veen and widow of Willem Jan Gersonius, baptized 26 December 1779 at Veendam, died 29 June 1833 at Veendam.

He married, as his second wife, 18 June 1834 at Veendam, Tamke Dieterds Smit, daughter of Dieterd Jans Smit by his wife Grietje Jans, born 16 November 1786 at Bellingwolderschans, died 27 January 1848 at Wildervank.

In 1817, he was a wine seller and grocer, living on Damsterdiep in Groningen.[7]

Only child, by his first wife:

i. Margaretha Clementia Falconer, born 9 November 1815 in Groningen, died 4 February 1816 in Groningen.

NOTES

[1] This is based on research compiled and certified 6 April 1970 by the Centraal Bureau voor Genealogie, The Hague, and also J. W. F. Baron van Wassenaer, "Falconer-Van Iddekinge-Sichterman," *De Nederlandsche Leeuw* 108, nr. 1-2 (Jan.-Feb. 1991): 118-119..

[2] William, Lord Falconer of Halkerton, to John Mackenzie of Delvine, 16 Dec. 1769, 26 Jan. 1773, 22 Mar. 1774, 1 Apr. 1775, MS 1265, National Library of Scotland.

[3] III n 17/212, 213, 216, 223, 224, 228, Gemeente Archief van Groningen, researched by Jeroen van Iddeking.

[4] Jeroen van Iddeking.

[5] Only the records of the baptisms of the two daughters named Rembertina Maria were found in the register of Martini-Kirk. The others must have been baptized in another church in Groningen.

[6] *Gens Nostra* 23 (1968): 332. It is apparent that she and Evert lived together for a number of years without benefit of marriage.

[7] Jeroen van Iddeking, citing a Groningen city directory.

CHAPTER C

John Falconer of Jamaica

The line of succession to the title goes through the following branch. Unfortunately, research has failed to determine conclusively whether the legitimate male lines of this branch became extinct after the second generation. However, it appears that they may indeed have become extinct, because the last known wills of members of this branch, dating from 1822 and 1838, do not mention any male Falconer heirs and seem to indicate that none existed then. Nevertheless, unless firm proof of extinction of all the sons or their legitimate male issue can be found, the line of succession will likely remain lost within this branch.

C1 **John Falconer**, fourth son of David, 4th Lord Falconer of Halkerton (A10), by his wife Katharine Margaret Keith, was born about 1718 in Inglismaldie, Kincardineshire, Scotland, and died between 20 November 1768 and 21 July 1769, probably in Clarendon Parish, Jamaica.

He married, 31 January 1748/9, in St. Andrews Parish, Jamaica,[1] Frances (Nairn) Lindsay, born about 1728, died 1786, widow of Richard Lindsay of St. Andrews and daughter of Hon. John and Frances Nairn.[2] She married, as her third husband, by 5 September 1771, John Reid, of St. Catherine Parish.[3]

Apprenticed on 17 April 1734 to John Stevenson of Edinburgh, merchant,[4] John did not stay in that city. He arrived in Jamaica, perhaps in 1746, and soon formed a mercantile partnership with James Wyatt. They bought, on 1 January 1747, a lot in Kingston, but John sold out a year later.[5] Like most others of his class who went to Jamaica, he intended to stay only long enough, perhaps ten years, in order to develop a sugar plantation to the point where it could provide him with £1000 or £1500 annually and then return to Britain.[6] Through his marriage, he become owner of lands and slaves in St. Andrew's parish, which had belonged to his wife's first husband,

and of a sugar works in Clarendon Parish, "Fort Nairn," which she had inherited from her father. Both properties, however, were encumbered with debts. John mortgaged "Fort Nairn," a property which consisted of 623 acres and 93 slaves, to Thomas Straton, a Kingston merchant, on 20 March 1752.[7] On 9 March 1752, John Falconer, then of Kingston, assigned a power of attorney to Charles Bowles, of North Ashton, Oxfordshire, to collect whatever he stood to inherit from his father in order to pay off the Nairn estate's debts to Bowles.[8] On 3 June 1760, he paid off the mortgage on the sugar works held by Charles Bowles, of New Windsor, Berkshire. It is clear, however, that he never found his fortune on this island.

His will, dated 20 November 1768, gave £5 each to his children John, David, Alexander, William, George, Thomas Keith, Nairn Lindsay, Shickle, Frances Elizabeth, and Elizabeth. The remainder of his estate went to his wife Frances. He appointed his wife and John Shickle executrix and executor.[9] Frances Falconer, of Clarendon Parish, widow, sold, on 21 July 1769, to John Bryan, of Clarendon Parish, for £1000, a 155½-acre tract at Dry River in Clarendon Parish.[10] The will of Frances Reid, of Clarendon Parish, dated 20 February 1786, gave her entire estate to her son Alexander Falconer, mentioning no other children.[11]

Issue of John and Frances (Nairn) Falconer:[12]

i. John Falconer, born 29 December 1749. On 25 July 1755, Frances Nairn, of Clarendon Parish, Jamaica, widow of Hon. John Nairn, sold 300 acres in Clarendon Parish to him for £5.[13] He was a mariner of Kingston, Jamaica, on 6 March 1777, when he sold this land to Charles Chisholme of London, mariner, and James Chisholme of Clarendon Parish, practitioner in physick and surgery, for £300.[14] The course of his life after this date is uncertain. There was a John Falconer, gentleman, of Kingston, who in 1792, with Thomas Cumming, of Kingston, merchant, sold a slave named Clitus to Alexander Innes of Kingston, cooper, for £80.[15] John Falconer, a merchant of Kingston, was alive in 1802,[16] and John Falconer, a planter of St. Elizabeth Parish, who died in 1804, who had a recently deceased brother William.[17] On the other hand, since his mother Frances gave her entire estate to her son Alexander, it is possible that both John and David were dead by 1786.

ii. David Falconer, baptized 26 November 1751, heir to his uncle David in 1775, presumably the David Falconer buried 21 March 1802 at Vere Parish, Jamaica.[18] He seems to be otherwise absent from Jamaican records, so this identification is somewhat doubtful. He presumably lived in London.

C2 iii. Alexander Falconer, born probably in 1752.[19]

iv. Frances Elizabeth Falconer, baptized 10 April 1755, buried 12 July 1812 in Clarendon Parish, Jamaica, unmarried.[20] By her will, dated 17 February 1797, she bequeathed to her brother Alexander a large silver bell and two solid silver eggs, bequeathed to her by her grandmother Lady Halkerton, and a diamond ring containing a picture of her grandfather; to her brother William she gave £100, the money coming from the sale of her slaves; and she gave the rest of her real and personal property to her sister Elizabeth.[21]

v. William Falconer, baptized 9 September 1757. He was alive on 3 June 1804, when his brother Alexander bequeathed him an annuity of £20 sterling. Although he has not been identified, it would seem that he either left Jamaica early, as the William Falconers in Jamaican records from 1787 to 1838/9 refer to others, or perhaps, as the bequest of an annuity might indicate, was incompetent or infirm.[22]

vi. Elizabeth Falconer, baptized 28 September 1758, buried 10 August 1839 at the family burial ground at the Falconer Tavern, Clarendon Parish, Jamaica, unmarried.[23] She bequeathed, by her will dated 25 July 1838, money to her "friend" (and maternal cousin) Mary Williams Fearon of Clarendon Parish, widow of Rowland Williams Fearon; land, "Bullard's Savanna," which had been bequeathed to her by her brother Shickle, to Rev. George Crawford Ricketts Fearon; and further money to other members of the Fearon family.[24]

vii. George Falconer, baptized 2 December 1759, living 3 June 1804. On 2 January 1797, he and Robert Davis, both planters of Vere Parish, Jamaica, mortgaged 32 slaves to Alexander Falconer.[25] On 2 August 1798, he and Shickle Falconer mortgaged property to Alexander Falconer, and they still owed him the principal and annual interest on 6 July 1804.[26] George's identity after that date is uncertain, although perhaps he was the George Falconer, overseer of Coldham and Lloyd's estates, who was buried 15 June 1817 at Swamp Estate in St. David.[27] On 2 July 1817 an inventory of his estate was made by James Mackintosh of Vere Parish.[28] This person had a daughter Ann, born 18 August 1816.[29]

C3 viii. Thomas Keith Falconer, baptized 26 June 1761.

ix. Nairn Lindsay Falconer, born about 1763, died in 1791.[30] On 8 Dec. 1782, he was commissioned a lieutenant in the Royal Navy.[31] He was assigned to the sloop *Savage*, which was stationed in North America, on 23 April 1783,[32] but was placed on half-pay 1 January 1784.[33]

C4 x. Shickle Falconer, born probably about 1765.

C2 **Alexander Falconer**, born 1752, died 5 June 1804 in Clarendon Parish, Jamaica.[34]

He married, on 2 April 1798 in Clarendon Parish,[35] Sarah Bryan, probably the daughter of William Bryan, a planter of Clarendon Parish, and Mary (Smith) Bryan. Their marriage contract, dated 31 March 1798, provided a yearly sum of £300 to her if she survived him.[36] After his death, she and her daughters lived in London and was there on 25 June 1818, when she sold Montrose, a Negro slave, to William Bryan of Clarendon Parish.[37]

The sole heir to his mother's considerable estate, he was a successful sugar planter in Clarendon Parish and acted as attorney for Lord Penrhyn's estates there. His activities in this sphere are described in a detailed letter by Rowland Williams Fearon, his successor, to Lord Penrhyn (see Appendix 3).

At the time of his death, his personal estate included 117 slaves and was appraised at £22,702, 16s., 3½d.[38] His will, dated 3 June 1804, confirmed the annuity due his wife and bequeathed her £500, his household furniture, plate, post chaise, the choice of two horses, and two Negroes, John Hulona and Montrose. He gave his sisters Frances and Elizabeth each an annuity of £50. He ordered his executors to place William Sanderson and Edward Sanderson, "mulatto sons of a free Black woman named Margaret Bryan," to be apprenticed to a trade and to each receive £50 sterling as an apprentice fee, £30 annually, and £200 at the expiration of their apprenticeships. Richard Sanderson, "quadroon son of Ann Lovemore, a mulatto," was to be apprenticed with the same provisions. His brother William was to receive an annuity of £20. He asked that any debts from his sisters Frances and Elizabeth and from his brothers George, Shickle, William, and Tom Falconer be regarded as satisfied. He bequeathed a pen[39] in St. Catherine Parish, "Alexandria," to Margaret Bryan, as well as slaves Kintore alias John Nairne, Present

Bristol, and a mulatto man, McFarlane. He requested his executors to purchase the rights of "Alexandria" from the brother of Booth Clarke and give the land to Margaret Bryan's mulatto daughters Elizabeth Sanderson and Laura Sanderson, with slaves their mother's slaves, and bequeathed the daughters £100 each. The executors were to sell 600 acres, called "Hayes and Siddons Run," adjacent to Mr. Dawkins's "Bog Hole." They were to continue his "jobbing" going and to maintain the number of slaves, by buying six or eight slaves annually. His land "Hopewell" was to be sold. The profits from the sales were to collect interest which would maintain his daughters Sarah and Mary Ann. When they became twenty-one they would receive the rest of his estate. He appointed Francis Smith, of Spanish Town, and Rowland Williams Fearon to be his executors.[40]

Issue of Alexander and Sarah (Bryan) Falconer:

i.　Mary Frances Falconer, born 5 January 1799, died young, probably on 11 December 1801, was buried at Rules Penn, Clarendon Parish.[41]

ii.　Sarah Falconer, baptized on 19 July 1800 and/or 24 February 1801.[42] On 2 November 1823, she and Mary Ann Falconer, both of Devonshire Street, Portland Place, Middlesex, acknowledged their father's bequests to them to his executors.[43] She seems to have died without heirs by 1843.

iii.　Susanna Bryan Falconer, born 20 May 1801, died 4 February 1804.

iv.　Mary Ann Falconer, born 10 November 1802. She was a spinster living in England on 5 April 1843, when she, Mary Williams (Bryan) Fearon, widow, of St. Catherine Parish, Mary Williams Fearon, George Fearon, of England, and Eliza Oakes Fearon released their interest in 125 acres to Walter Sinclair, of Clarendon Parish.[44]

Mulatto children of Margaret Bryan, a free black woman, presumably by Alexander Falconer:

v.　Laura Sanderson. She purchased a slave named Rebecca, alias Quashiba, from John Creighton of St. Catherine Parish, for £120 on 7 October 1809.[45] She appears to have been Creighton's mistress, since on 18 October 1814, she received a male slave name George, alias Rodney, from Creighton's executor, noting that the slave was to be given to her in lieu of a house which was to be built for her.[46] She consigned slaves in 1818.[47]

vi.　William Sanderson, born about 1786.[48] On 24 September 1810, he and Edward Sanderson, both of St. Catherine Parish, free persons of color, received their bequests and the same day purchased a 50-acre pen in the parish of St. Catherine from Elizabeth Rodon, of London, widow, for £680.[49]

vii.　Edward Sanderson, born about 1788, buried 15 November 1817 in St. Catherine Parish, Jamaica.[50]

viii.　Elizabeth Sanderson. On 25 February 1812, an agreement was signed between Jane Rodon Christian of Vere Parish, a widow, John Hewitt Smith and Jane Rodon his wife, of Kingston, Margaret Bryan of Clarendon Parish, Elizabeth Sanderson and Laura Sanderson of Clarendon Parish, and Francis Smith of St. Catherine Parish and Rowland Williams Fearon, the executors of Alexander Falconer's estate, in which Alexandria Pen was purchased for £42.[51]

Ann Lovemore, a free mulatto who lived in Kingston and St. Catherine Parish, was his mistress before his marriage. On 1 February 1798, Alexander

Falconer gave her, for the token sum of five shillings, a female Negro slave named Jesse.[52] Quadroon[53] children of Alexander Falconer by Ann Lovemore:[54]

   ix. Richard Sanderson, born about 1794. On 8 November 1815, his father's executors fully paid his bequest to Richard Sanderson, of St. Catherine Parish.[55]

   x. Hugh Sanderson, born 1 November 1796, baptized 14 December 1797, died young.

   xi. Mary Frances Sanderson, born 26 October 1798, baptized 11 November 1798, died young.

C3 Thomas Keith Falconer was baptized 26 June 1761 in Clarendon Parish, Jamaica, was living on 3 July 1807.

He was a coffee and cotton planter in St. Elizabeth Parish, Jamaica. On 9 April 1804, Thomas Keith Falconer gave to Sarah Powell fifty acres, bounded by the fifty acres which was John Craskell Falconer's settlement. She was to have forty acres planted in coffee and ten acres in provisions, to dig a pond, and build a coffee house, barbecues, and a mill house, for which Thomas Keith Falconer was to contribute £100. The land was to devolve, on her death, to her "reputed" children by Nicholas Bent.[56] Having failed to pay off a mortgage of £1200 to William Rowe, of St. Elizabeth, on 3 July 1807, he disposed of a cotton plantation, "Gibraltar," of 550 acres, and a coffee plantation, "Keith Hall," in the Brownshill Mountains in St. Elizabeth, through a defeasance.[57] Although the St. Elizabeth Parish register may be deficient in recording the number of burials in this period, his estate does not appear in the Jamaica series of inventories, administration accounts, letters testamentary, or wills, so we must presume that, having become financially ruined, he left Jamaica about this time.

The mother of his first two children has not been identified, although she would have been a quadroon (one-quarter African). Perhaps she died soon after John's birth, and the settlement of land to Sarah Powell was to provide her the means to raise the children. Since Sarah Powell's land was to devolve, after her death, to her children by Nicholas Bent, it would seem unlikely that she was the children's mother. Thomas Keith Falconer, by a quadroon woman, was the father of the following "mestee" children:[58]

   i. George Ann Falconer, born before 1798.

Y1 ii. John Craskell Falconer, born 1798.

His second mistress was Susannah Eleanor Bent, the free quadroon daughter of John Bent and Anne Rochester, born 14 April 1785 in St. Elizabeth, died there in 1837. She was the owner of 16 slaves in 1817.[59] By her will, dated 13 January 1831, she bequeathed most of her estate, including three slaves, to the six "reputed" children of John Craskell Falconer by Dorothy Bent, namely Aaron Sheckle Falconer, Cornelius Keith Falconer, Maria Anne Falconer, Susannah Eleanor Falconer, Thomas Keith Falconer, Jr., and Catherine Keith Falconer. She also left a slave to Dorothy Bent. The residue of the estate was to go her sons and daughters, Thomas Keith Falconer, Joseph Christopher Falconer, Richard Ashman Falconer, Ann Frances Gordon, and Mary Caroline Ebanks.[60]

Issue of Thomas Keith Falconer by Susannah Eleanor Bent:[61]

    iii.   Thomas Keith [baptized as Thomas Mullings] Falconer, born 1 October 1802. He married, on 27 August 1840, Mary Palmer, of Rainsberry, St. Elizabeth.[62]

    iv.   Ann Frances Falconer, born about 1805, baptized 23 August 1820. She married Larckin Gordon, a free person of color and planter of Happy Retreat, St. Elizabeth, and had issue, surname *Gordon:*[63] a. *John,* born 22 December 1823; b. *Catalina Amelia,* born 1 May 1825; c. *Julius Frederick,* born 23 January 1837; d. *Herbert,* born 8 April 1838; e. *Ferguson,* born 14 July 1840; f. *Amaritta Ann,* born 20 February 1843, married Richard H. Falconer (Y9).

    v.   Joseph Christopher Falconer, born about 1805, baptized 20 March 1823.

    vi.   Richard Ashman Falconer, born about 1808, baptized 20 March 1823. He may have been the Richard Falconer who on 10 July 1845 purchased a one-acre plot in Endeavor, in St. Ann's parish.[64] This person was probably the Richard Falconer who married, on 31 January 1845, in St. Thomas in the Vale parish, Harriett Henriques.[65]

C4 Shickle Falconer, born probably about 1765, was buried 28 January 1827 in Clarendon Parish, Jamaica.[66]

He was a "practitioner of physic." In 1820 he owned a plantation, called "Shickleton," and fourteen slaves.[67]

By his will, dated 8 August 1822, he bequeathed to his nieces Sarah and Mary Ann Falconer £10 each. He gave his unnamed sister (Elizabeth) all his real and personal property. To each of his "natural" children, Jane Shickleson, Susannah Dalas, and Elizabeth Jeanet, he gave £20 each. He appointed William Henry Dicke to be executor.[68] His children were possibly by Mary Copple, a free person of color, to whom he sold, for £41, an eight-acre tract bordering "Shickleston" on 27 August 1821.[69]

Issue of Shickle Falconer by a woman of color:

    i.   Jane Shickleson.

    ii.   Susannah Dalas. "Dalas" was presumably her married name.

    iii.   Elizabeth Jeanet. It is uncertain whether "Jeanet" was her surname or married name.

NOTES

[1] St. Andrew Parish Register.

[2] John Falconer to Alexander, Lord Falconer of Halkerton, 23 Feb. 1752, Delvine Papers, MS 1265, f. 234, National Library of Scotland.

[3] Jamaica Inventories, 52: 215, Jamaica Archives, Spanish Town.

[4] Charles B. Boog Watson, *Register of Edinburgh Apprentices, 1701-1755* (Edinburgh: for the Scottish Record Society by James Skinner, 1929), p. 30.

[5] Jamaica Deeds, 132: 116; 133: 158, Island Record Office, Spanish Town.

[6] John Falconer to Alexander, Lord Falconer of Halkerton, 23 Feb. 1752, in Delvine Papers, MS 1265, f. 234, National Library of Scotland.

[7] Jamaica Deeds, 147: 150, Island Record Office.

[8] Bundle 108, Kintore Papers, Aberdeen University Library.

[9] Jamaica Wills, 40: 20, Island Record Office.

[10] Jamaica Deeds, 236: 50.

[11] Jamaica Wills, 51: 197.

[12] St. Andrew Parish Register, 1749-1751; Clarendon Parish Register, 1755-1839; Jamaica Wills, 40: 20; 30: 150.

[13] Jamaica Deeds, 280: 188.

[14] Ibid., 283: 53; 280: 188.

[15] Ibid., 405: 107.

[16] Jamaica Chancery, 175: 24, Jamaica Archives.

[17] Jamaica Inventories, 102: 230. As the inventory was entered 13 September 1804, it is possible that this person was the same, since his brother William could have died after 3 June 1804, when mentioned in Alexander's will.

[18] Vere Parish Register. Since there is no record of proceedings of his estate in Jamaica, there is some doubt as to his identity.

[19] John Falconer to Alexander, Lord Falconer of Halkerton, 23 Feb. 1752, Delvine Papers, MS 1265, f. 234, National Library of Scotland.

[20] Clarendon Parish Register, 3: 320.

[21] Jamaica Wills, 86: 143.

[22] He was not the William Falconer, of Hanover, cooper, whose estate was proved 17 July 1802 (Jamaica Letters of Administration, 29: 86), and he was not William Falconer, a planter of St. Catherine Parish, who married Christian Mackintosh in 1805 and purchased Brightmony, in Auldearn, Nairn, where he had several children. This person was the son of Mrs. Magdalen Falconer, widow of the laird of Blackhill, and younger brother of Aeneas Falconer of Blackhill (Auldearn Parish Register).

[23] Clarendon Parish Register, Burials, 1826-71, p. 157.

[24] Prerogative Court of Canterbury, PROB11/1922, PRO.

[25] Jamaica Deeds, 440: 154.

[26] Jamaica Inventories, 104: 82, Jamaica Archives.

[27] St. David Parish Register, 1: 89.

[28] Jamaica Inventories, 131: 109, Jamaica Archives.

[29] St. David Parish Register, 1: 77.

[30] He appears in the half-pay registers in the first half of 1791, but not in the second half of the year, or thereafter, ADM25/120, ADM25/121, PRO.

[31] *Commissioned Sea Officers of the Royal Navy 1660-1815*, vol. 1.

[32] ADM11/65/2, p. 339, PRO.

[33] ADM25/106, p. 128, PRO.

[34] Clarendon Parish Register.

[35] Ibid.

[36] Jamaica Deeds, 161: 03.

[37] Ibid., 671: 226.

[38] Jamaica Inventories, 104: 82, Jamaica Archives.

[39] An enclosed pasture.

[40] Jamaica Wills, 72: 169.

[41] Clarendon Parish Register.

[42] Ibid., 1: 241, 242.

[43] Jamaica Deeds, 728: 267.

[44] Ibid., 858: 226.

[45] Ibid., 645: 89.

[46] Ibid., 652: 2.

[47] Ibid., 645: 89; 674: 248.

[48] St. Catherine Parish Register, 2: 326. He, aged 23, and his brother Edward, 21, were baptized 25 October 1809.

[49] Jamaica Deeds, 604: 100; 603: 1.

[50] St. Catherine Parish Register, 2: 397.

[51] Jamaica Deeds, 622: 3.

[52] Ibid., 456: 157.

[53] A person of three-quarters European and one-quarter African ancestry.

[54] The baptisms of the two younger children were recorded in the Kingston Parish Register.

[55] Jamaica Deeds, 652: 214.

[56] Ibid., 558: 244.

[57] Ibid., 559: 218.

[58] Ibid., 457: 230.

[59] Slave Registration Lists, Jamaica, T 71/164/111, PRO.

[60] Jamaica Wills, 118: 60.

[61] St. Elizabeth Parish Register, 1: 130, 2: 21, 189, 190. Thomas Keith was named as the father only in the baptism of Thomas Mullings; no parents were named in the baptismal register for the others, who were only described as "mustees" (one-eighth African).

[62] Ibid., Marriages,

[63] St. Elizabeth Parish Register, 2: 299, 317; 3: 107, 175; 4: 54, 154. There certainly must have been more children.

[64] Jamaica Deeds, 888: 102.

[65] St. Thomas in the Vale Parish Register, 4: 544.

[66] Clarendon Parish Register, vol. 22, no. 3.

[67] *The Jamaica Almanack for the Year 1820* (Kingston: Alexander Aikman, 1820), p. 25.

[68] Jamaica Wills, 108: 89.

[69] Jamaica Deeds, 718: 51.

CHAPTER D

Falconar of Glenfarquhar

D1 **Sir David Falconar** of Glenfarquhar, in the parish of Fordoun, Kincardineshire, second son of Sir Alexander Falconer of Halkerton (A6) and Agnes Carnegie, born probably about 1598, died after 20 September 1683, was buried in St. Paladius Chapel in Fordoun.[1]

He married, as his first wife, Margaret Hepburn, daughter of Sir Robert Hepburn of Bearford.[2]

His second wife was Elizabeth Douglas,[3] widow of Captain Robert Irvine of Monboddo, and daughter of Sir William Douglas of Glenbervie.[4]

He and his brother John renounced any claim to the lands and barony of Halkerton, on 1 November 1626.[5] He had a charter of the mains of Balbegno, in Fettercairn, 2 August 1627.[6] Admitted Advocate in 1629, he was appointed Commissary of Edinburgh on 24 October 1642. He was admitted to the burgess roll of Aberdeen on 31 May 1643.[7] As Deputy for Kincardineshire, he consented to the Union with England, 27 February 1652;[8] was a member for that county in the united parliament in 1652;[9] and in the Scottish parliament in 1667. Despite having participated in Cromwell's government, he and his son David were conjunctly granted the office of Commissary of Edinburgh on 23 September 1661.[10] On 20 September 1683, he made his son Alexander cessioner in the sum of 1000 merks.[11]

In 1629 he acquired the lands of Glenfarquhar, originally granted to his father in 1619, which included the privilege of the right to hold a fair, known as Paldy Fair, annually, during one week in July. When William Douglas of Glenbervie began holding a fair on the nearby lands of Dillivard during the week immediately preceeding the Paldy Fair, it interfered with Paldy Fair's smooth operation. Thus began a dispute between the two lairds. John Napier remarked, a century later, that, on one occasion, the laird of Glenfarquhar invited Earl Marischal and about forty noblemen and gentlemen to dine in a specially prepared tent at the market, after which they walked to the Dillivard fair with colors flying and drums beating. The people from the other fair reacted by cutting up the drum heads.[12] The dispute was settled after Falconar pursued an action concerning this fair against the laird of Glenbervie before the Lords of Session on 24 June 1642.[13] The Lords ruled that Glenbervie had to schedule his fair at least one month from the date of the Paldy Fair.

Issue of Sir David Falconar of Glenfarquhar and Margaret Hepburn:

	i.	Margaret Falconer, born 19 April 1634,[14] probably died young.
D2	ii.	Sir Alexander Falconar of Glenfarquhar.
	iii.	Sir David Falconar (or Falconer) of Newton, born 1639.
	iv.	Agnes Falconar, "eldest daughter." By a contract dated 16 November 1665, she married James Scott, son of James Scott of Logie, Provost of Montrose.[15] Issue, surname *Scott*[16] a. *Margaret*, baptized 25 February 1667; b. *James*, baptized 18 January 1671; c. *David*, baptized 23 October 1673; d. *Elizabeth*, baptized 3 December 1674; e. *Katharine*, baptized 13 April 1676; f. *Isobel*, baptized 6 March 1679; g. *Helen*, baptized 26 June 1682.

D2 **Sir Alexander Falconar** of Glenfarquhar, 1st Baronet, born perhaps about 1635, died 17 March 1717[17] and was buried at Fordoun.

He married, as his first wife, Marjory Irvine, eldest daughter of Captain Robert Irvine of Monboddo by his wife Elizabeth Douglas, who died, of childbirth, before Easter, 1661. They took sasine of Glenfarquhar on 1 December 1659.[18] Her executors brought an action against his daughter and executor, Lady Balmain, with reference to her share in Sir Alexander's estate in 1719.[19]

Many years later, Helen Burnet recorded some doggerel about Marjory Irvine:

From Monboddo there flew a Swan
And lighted on Glenfarquhar—
She laid an egg, and then she died,
And that was all her laughter.

He married, as his second wife, Helen Graham, daughter of John Graham of Crigie, who died in March 1720 in Edinburgh.[20] They had no issue.

He was created a Baronet, 20 March 1670, with remainder to the heirs-male of his body. He was appointed a justice of the peace for Kincardineshire on 13 January 1670.[21] He was served heir to his mother, Margaret Hepburn, 2 August 1673.[22] A Member of Parliament for Kincardineshire in 1678, he was Commissioner of Justiciary for the Highlands in 1682 and 1701.[23] On 24 December 1684, Sir John Falconar of Balmakelly disponed to him the lands and barony of Scotston and the lands of Shiells. On 3 September 1686 he and his wife received a grant for a new barony of Scotston, with the lands of Haddo and Shiells united with those of Scotston.[24] Between 1688 and 1702 he was in a legal dispute with Sir David Carnegie over Carnegie's claim to a right of thirlage over the lands of Scotstoun and Powburne.[25] Violence resulted, as he pursued a cause against Sir David Carnegie of Pitarrow before the Court of Session on 13 November 1695, charging that Carnegie had assaulted him with a drawn sword.[26] He was a Commissioner for Kincardineshire in 1704.[27]

The Kincardineshire writer John Napier had many kind words to say about him. In his eyes, Glenfarquhar was the model laird, always treating his friends with good ale and advising country people to settle disputes among themselves without getting lawyers involved. He instructed his butler always to provide dinner and drink to any person having occasion to visit Glenfarquhar and would invite his tenants, when they paid their rents, to dine with him, presenting them with fruit and sweetmeats for their wives and children. If a tenant was unable to manage a large farm, Glenfarquhar let the tenant have one more to his ability.[28]

Napier, however, felt differently towards Dame Helen Graham. He related a story about a widow of one of the baronet's tenants who accosted him one day while he and his lady were in a carriage on the way to Glenbervie. The widow asked, "Sir Alexander I mun hae a yocking from you the morn" [I must have a yoking (plow team) from you tomorrow]. Dame Helen, apparently a rather jealous person, misinterpreted the request and threatened a separation, until his close friend the Earl Marischal calmed her down. Another time, the lady discovered the following chalked on the coach house door:

Souple Sandy Falconer and dirten Helen Grahame
God bless the good man and Deil confound the Dame.

Upset, Dame Helen blamed Sir Alexander for his apparent laxness towards his servants. He answered, "Eh, my dear, 'tis just the flock of cairds in revenge for scolding them the other day and being set off without a drink." They soon discovered that one "Jockie the herd" had written the doggerel and Sir Alexander asked him to leave Glenfarquhar. However, the boy's poetic talent impressed the laird and he provided for his education, the boy ultimately becoming a schoolmaster.[29]

He founded four bursaries in King's College, Aberdeen, for boys of the name of Falconer, on 7 August 1716.[30] Legacies from his estate went to David, 4th Lord Falconer of Halkerton, to his grandson Sir Alexander Ramsay, to Alexander Falconer, brother of John Falconer of Phesdo, and to Captain Ogilvy.[31]

Issue of Sir Alexander Falconar and Marjory Irvine:[32]

    i.   Elizabeth Falconar. She married, by contract dated 1678,[33] as his second wife, Sir Charles Ramsay of Balmain, 3rd Bart., who died in 1695, and had issue, surname *Ramsay*:[34] a. *Sir David*, 4th Bart., died s.p. September 1710; b. *Sir Alexander*, 5th Bart., died, unmarried, 27 January 1754; c. *Charles*, died 1727, merchant in Montrose, married Catherine Milne, daughter of James Milne, provost of Montrose; d. *Helen*, married, in 1707, Hercules Scott of Brotherton, born 1659, died 1747; e. daughter, married John Fullarton of Kinnaber; f. *Betty*, unmarried.

NOTES

[1]Macphail, *Papers from the Collection of Sir William Fraser*, p. 86.

[2]Lyon Court, Funeral escutcheon, cited in: *Scots Peerage*, 5: 247n.

[3]Register of Deeds, RD2/38, p. 354, SRO.

[4]Jonathan Forbes Leslie, *The Irvines of Drum and Collateral Branches* (Aberdeen: n.p., 1909), p. 208.

[5]Register of Deeds, RD3/20, p. 20f., SRO.

[6]*Register of the Great Seal*, 1620-1633, p. 396.

[7]Munro, "Aberdeen Burgess Register, 1631-1700," p. 33.

[8]C. Sanford Terry, ed., *The Cromwellian Union: Papers relating to the Negotiations for an Incorporating Nation between England and Scotland, 1651-1652*, Publications of the Scottish History Society, no. 40 (Edinburgh: for the Scottish History Society, 1902), p. 48.

[9]Ibid., p. 183.

[10]Register of the Privy Seal, PS3/1, p. 154, SRO.

[11]Assignation, Kintore Papers, Bundle 89, Aberdeen University Library.

[12]Macphail, *Papers from the Collection of Sir William Fraser*, pp. 67-68, 84, 117-123.

[13]Morison, *Decisions of the Court of Session*, 9: 4146.

[14]Wood, *The Peerage of Scotland*, 2: 56.

[15]Marriage contract, Kintore Papers, Bundle 102, Aberdeen University Library.

[16]Montrose Parish Register.

[17]Testament, Commissariot of St. Andrews, CC20.

[18]Sasine, Kintore Papers, Bundle 44, Aberdeen University Library.

[19]Sheriff Court Records of Kincardineshire, from information of Dr. Macnaughton, Stonehaven, cited in: *Scots Peerage*, 5: 247n.

[20]Testament, Commissariot of Edinburgh, CC8/8/87, SRO; the testament appears in full in: Macphail, *Papers from the Collection of Sir William Fraser*, pp. 163-167.

[21]*Register of the Privy Council*, 3rd ser., 3: 124.

[22]*Inquisitiones Generales*, no. 5649, 2 Aug. 1673.

[23]Register of the Great Seal, GS /10/294, GS /15/36, SRO.

[24]Register of the Great Seal, GS /70/87, SRO; Fraser, *History of the Parish and Burgh of Laurencekirk*, p. 63.

[25]Kintore Papers, Bundle 156, Aberdeen University Library.

[26] *Decisions of the Court of Session*, 3: 1370.

[27] *Acts of the Parliaments of Scotland*, 6: 145.

[28] Macphail, *Papers from the Collection of Sir William Fraser*, pp. 66-69.

[29] Ibid., pp. 66-67.

[30] Peter John Anderson, ed., *Fasti Academiae Mariscallanae Aberdonensis: Selections from the Records of the Marischal College and University, 1543-1860*, volume 1, Publications of the New Spalding Club, no. 4 (Aberdeen: for the New Spalding Club, 1889), p. 204.

[31] Alexander, 5th Lord Falconer of Halkerton, to John Mackenzie of Delvine, 30 Jan. 1752, 13 Feb. 1752, Delvine Papers, MS1264, ff. 36, 40, National Library of Scotland.

[32] If Alexander Falconer of Glenfarquhar had a son Alexander, who, according to Douglas and Wood, and repeated by Paul in his *Scots Peerage*, though corrected in the last volume, succeeded David as the fourth Lord, we have no record. David Falconer of Newton succeeded Alexander of Glenfarquhar as his heir male, and he succeeded the third Lord as his heir.

[33] *Scots Peerage*, 9: 123.

[34] "1578 Manuscript Genealogy," p. 214ff.; *Burke's Peerage*, 1921 ed., p. 1811.

CHAPTER E

Sir David Falconar of Newton

E1 **Sir David Falconar** (or Falconer) of Newton, second son of Sir David Falconer of Glenfarquhar (D1) and Margaret Hepburn, born 1639, died 15 December 1685 in Edinburgh, aged forty-six, and was buried at Greyfriars, where a monument in his memory exists.[1]

He married, as his first wife, by contract dated 1662,[2] Elizabeth Nairn, daughter of Robert Nairn of Muckersy and sister of Robert, 1st Lord Nairn. She was buried in Greyfriars 20 January 1676.

He married, as his second wife, on 16 February 1678, at Edinburgh,[3] Mary Norvell, daughter of George Norvell of Boghall, Linlithgowshire, by Margaret Elphinstone, baptized 21 September 1654 in Edinburgh. She survived him, and was married, secondly, to John Home of Ninewells.[4] By the second marriage, she was the mother of a daughter Mary, who married —— Edgar of Weatherlieland,[5] and also a son John, born May 1692, died May 1693, and a son Michael.

He was admitted an advocate on 29 June 1661 and conjunct Commissary of Edinburgh 23 September 1661. On 14 July 1668, he pursued an action against Sir James Keith of Caddome before the Court of Session; Keith was fined and imprisoned for reviling and threatening an advocate in the exercise of his office and sent to the tolbooth.[6] He was appointed a justice of the peace for Kincardineshire on 13 January 1670.[7] He was appointed a Lord of Session on 12 June 1676 and a Commissioner of Justiciary on 17 October 1678. He was admitted to the burgess roll of Edinburgh on 24 September 1679.[8] He was appointed an Ordinary Lord of Session, 14 October 1681;[9] President of the College of Justice (i.e., Lord President of the Court of

Session) on 5 June 1682;[10] Commissioner of Exchequer, 15 July 1682; Auditor of Treasury, 21 January 1684; a Privy Councillor, 13 June 1684 and 3 March 1685;[11] and was a Member of Parliament for Forfarshire in 1685-1686. He compiled the decisions of the Court of Session from November 1681 to 9 December 1685, the last day on which he sat in court. We must assume that his judicial integrity was held in high regard, as he was free from political controversy during his life.

He bought, on 28 January 1663, the lands of Newton. On 1 February 1678, he received a grant of the lands of Newtoun and others, and on 25 February 1682, he received a further grant of the lands of Barnes, Newton, and Smiddiehill, erecting them into a barony, and erecting the town and lands of Brigend into the burgh of the barony of Inglismaldie.[12] On 10 July 1685, he was granted the lands of Neather Pearth.[13] He also purchased the house of Inglismaldie, which remained in the family until this century.

He registered the following blazon: Or, a falcon's head crowned with an antique crown issuing out of a man's heart all proper betwixt three mollets azure.[14]

By his testament, dated 14 December 1685, he made his eldest son David his executor and intromitter of his estate and debts, leaving him the burden of his debts and provisions for the other children. He reserved for his wife the dwelling house in Edinburgh and the house of Inglismaldie. He nominated three tutors for his children and asked that his wife would maintain each of them until they reached the age of eleven.[15] His funeral in Edinburgh was full of the pomp and ceremony reserved for high government officials.

Issue of Sir David Falconar and Elizabeth Nairn:[16]

i.　　Alexander Falconar, baptized 6 August 1663, died young.

Issue of Sir David Falconar and Mary Norvell:[17]

ii.　　Margaret Falconar, born 13 February 1679, died, unmarried, 1 December 1747.[18] She or one of her sisters was the unnamed daughter of President Falconer with whom David Erskine was involved in marriage negotiations in 1706. Erskine needed the post of clerkship to the Privy Council in order to clinch the marriage and, in a letter, requested consideration from the Earl of Mar.[19] The negotiations were unsuccessful. Margaret's testament gave property to her niece Mary Falconer, Lady "Mountain," and to James Falconer of Mountain; £50 to her brother George; £250 sterling and all her clothes and furniture to her nieces Mary and Margaret Edgar, and £50 to their mother.[20]

iii.　　Mary Falconar, born 26 May 1680 in Edinburgh. She married John Fullarton of Dudwick and had issue, surname *Fullarton*:[21] i. *John*; ii. *Agnes*, who married John Forbes of Boyndlie, and one son and two daughters.

A10　　iv.　　David Falconar, 4th Lord Falconer of Halkerton, born 27 May 1681.

v.　　Alexander Falconer alias Hay of Delgaty, born 1 June 1682, died July 1745.[22] Admitted Advocate, 23 February 1705.[23] He assumed the named of Hay on succeeding to the estate of Delgaty.[24] He was married for 27 years[25] to Mary Hay, daughter of John Hay, 11th Earl of Erroll, and Countess of Erroll in her own right. She died without issue 19 August 1758. He had an intellectual bent, the National Library of Scotland owning a translation done by him, prior to his marriage, of writings of Savonarola.[26] James Boswell, in a visit to the Earl of Erroll in 1773, remarked that his "valuable and numerous" library was "chiefly made" by Mr. Falconer.[27] The Earl of Erroll possesses his portrait.

vi. Katharine Falconar, born 3 October 1683, died 1745. She married, 4 January 1708, Joseph Home of Ninewells, son of John Home of Ninewells, born 10 February 1681, died August 1713, and had issue, surname *Home (Hume)*:[28]
a. *John* of Ninewells, baptized 6 March 1709, died 1786, married Agnes Carre;
b. *Katherine*, born 1710, died 1790; c. *David*, the philosopher, born 26 April 1711, died 25 August 1776.

vii. Elizabeth Falconar, born 28 September 1684, died unmarried.

F1   viii. George Falconar, merchant of Edinburgh, born 19 November 1685.

NOTES

[1] James Brown, *The Epitaphs and Monumental Inscriptions in Greyfriars Churchyard, Edinburgh* (Edinburgh: J. Moodie Miller, 1867), p. 244.

[2] Kintore Papers, Bundle 102, Aberdeen University Library.

[3] Paton, ed., *Register of Marriages for the Parish of Edinburgh, 1595-1700*, p. 224.

[4] Privy Council Decreets, 11 Aug. 1691 and 19 Aug. 1696, cited in *Scots Peerage*, 5: 249.

[5] Moses Bundle 163/6304, Edinburgh District Archives.

[6] Morison, *Decisions of the Court of Session*, 1: 344; Crawford, ed., *Journals of Sir John Lauder, Lord Fountainhall*, p. 213.

[7] *Register of the Privy Council*, 3rd ser., 3: 124.

[8] Charles B. Boog Watson, ed., *Roll of Edinburgh Burgesses, 1406-1700* (Edinburgh: for the Scottish Record Society by James Skinner, 1926), p. 177.

[9] Register of the Great Seal, C2/10/74, p. 240, SRO.

[10] Register of the Privy Seal, PS3/1, p. 423, SRO

[11] Register of the Great Seal, C2/10/281, p. 373; C2/11/2, p. 80, SRO.

[12] *Calendar of State Papers, Domestic Series*, 1682, ed. F. H. Blackburne Daniell (London: Her Majesty's Stationery Office, 1932), p. 98.

[13] Register of the Great Seal, GS /66/34, GS /68/109, GS /70/16, SRO.

[14] Scotland, Lord Lyon, Public Register of All Arms and Bearings, 1: 150.

[15] Draft of testament, Kintore Papers, Bundle 104, Aberdeen University Library.

[16] Edinburgh Parish Register.

[17] Dates of birth from notation on petition of John Home of Ninewells, Kintore Papers, Bundle 44, Aberdeen University Library.

[18] Testament, Commissariot of Edinburgh, CC8/8/111/2, SRO.

[19] David Erskine to the Earl of Mar, 19 June 1706, in Mar and Kellie Muniments, GD124/15/444, SRO.

[20] Testament, Commissariot of Edinburgh, CC8/8/111/2, SRO.

[21] Alistair and Henrietta Taylor, *Jacobites of Aberdeenshire and Banffshire in the Rising of 1715* (Edinburgh: Oliver and Boyd, 1934), p. 93f; idem, ed., *The Jacobite Cess Roll for the County of Aberdeen in 1715* (Aberdeen: for the Third Spalding Club, 1932), p. 55.

[22] Grant, *The Faculty of Advocates in Scotland, 1532-1943*, p. 68.

[23] Ibid.

[24] *Scots Peerage*, 6: 247.

[25] Jervise, *Epitaphs and Inscriptions from Burial Grounds and Old Buildings in the North East of Scotland*, 2: 246.

[26] MS 3859, purchased in 1950.

[27] R. W. Chapman, ed., *Johnson's Journey to the Western Islands of Scotland and Boswell's Journal of a Tour to the Hebrides with Samuel Johnson, LL.D.* (London: Oxford University Press, 1924), p. 224.

[28] Ernest Campbell Mossner, *The Life of David Hume* (Austin: University of Texas Press, 1954), pp. 6, 13, 16, 19; Patrick W. Montague-Smith, "Ancestry of David Hume the Philosopher," *Genealogists' Magazine* 13 (Mar. 1961): 278-279.

CHAPTER F

Falconar of Carlowrie

F1 **George Falconar**,[1] fourth son of Sir David Falconer of Newton (E1) by his second wife Mary Norvell, was born 19 November 1685 at Edinburgh and died 21 May 1743.[2]

He married Janet Marjoribanks, daughter of John Marjoribanks of Leuchie, and sister of Major General Alexander Marjoribanks of the Dutch service.

Twelve-pound banknote issued by the Bank of Scotland, with the signature of George Falconar, Accountant. ©Trustees of the National Museum of Scotland.

Apprenticed to an Edinburgh merchant, Patrick Couts, he was admitted to the burgess roll of Edinburgh on 17 July 1706.[3] His mercantile business soon enjoyed success. His skill was such that in 1716, he was appointed to the office of Accountant of the Bank of Scotland, which he held until his death.[4] His signature appears on some of the earliest banknotes issued by the Bank of Scotland.

Issue of George Falconar and Janet Marjoribanks:

i.   George Falconar of Carlowrie, born 13 December 1713 at Edinburgh,[5] died, without issue,[6] 19 December 1789 at Edinburgh.[7] He was heir to his uncle, Major General Alexander Marjoribanks, from whom he inherited Carlowrie, in West Lothian.[8] A wine merchant at Cadiz and then Edinburgh, in 1786 he was chosen to be a Director of the Bank of Scotland.[9]

ii.   Alexander Falconar, died, without issue, 8 May 1767 at Edinburgh.[10] He was Secretary (i.e., accountant) at the Bank of Scotland.

F2   iii.   David Falconar.

iv.   Mary Falconar. She, presumably then the only surviving sister of George, was "dangerously ill" on 10 August 1773.[11] Her testament was confirmed 28 January 1797.[12]

v.   daughter.[13]

F2 David Falconar, born perhaps about 1725, died 8 July 1777, probably in London.

He married, 8 August 1776, at St. Clement Danes, London,[14] Margaret Honey, who died in 1786.

Although sparse records of him indicate that he lived in London, he may have been the D. Falconer who, in 1773, was clerk-deputy of the weigh-house in Edinburgh.[15]

Issue of David and Margaret (Honey) Falconar:

F3   i.   David Falconar of Carlowrie, baptized 26 January 1770.[16]

ii.   Anna Falconar, died unmarried.

iii.   Mary Falconar, died unmarried.

F3 David Falconar of Carlowrie was baptized on 26 January 1770 at St. Martin in the Fields, Middlesex, and died 14 June 1842.

He married Jane Stewart, daughter of Robert Stewart of Binny by his wife Magdalen Menteith. She died in 1837.

Educated at Edinburgh High School, he inherited Carlowrie, in Kirkliston parish, West Lothian, and lived the life of a country squire.

Issue of David and Jane (Stewart) Falconar:

i.   Magdalen Falconar, born 11 April 1797, died unmarried.

ii.   Jane Falconar, born 12 August 1798, died 9 December 1844. She married, on 29 April 1822, at Bowden, Roxburghshire, William Currie of Linthill, Roxburghshire, and left issue.

F4   iii.   George Falconar of Carlowrie, born 27 January 1800.

iv.   David Falconar, born 1801, died, without issue, 22 May 1827, at Coates Crescent, Edinburgh.[17]

    v.   Helen Robina Falconar, born 12 October 1802, died 1882. She married John Tulloch, R.N., and left issue.

    vi.   Mary Stewart Falconar, born 11 April 1805, died, unmarried, July 1843.

    vii.   Joanna Falconar, born 9 April 1807, died, unmarried, April 1857.

    viii.   Robert Stewart Falconar, born January 1810, died 16 August 1812.[18]

F4 George Falconar of Carlowrie was born 27 January 1800 and died 20 August 1870.

He married, as his first wife, on 2 July 1827,[19] Isabella Christian Goldie, daughter of Lieutenant-General Alexander John Goldie, of The Nunnery, Isle of Man. She died in 1831, leaving no issue.

He married, as his second wife, 14 March 1842, Frances Georgina Mercer, daughter of George Mercer of Gorthy, Perthshire, D.L. She died in December 1891.

He served in the Rifle Brigade and as a captain in the 80th Regiment of Foot.

Issue of George and Frances Georgina (Mercer) Falconar:

    i.   John Stewart Falconar, born 12 April 1843, died, unmarried, 27 May 1874, and was buried at Perth. He was incumbent of St. John's, Aberdeen.

F5   ii.   George Mercer Falconar-Stewart, born 10 June 1844.

    iii.   William David Falconar, born 15 July 1845, drowned in Johore Straits (now Singapore), without issue, in 1876.

    iv.   Frances Henrietta Falconar, born 30 September 1846.

    v.   Helen Jane Falconar, born 8 July 1848, died 12 May 1919. She married, 30 September 1869, John Monsey Collyer, of Gimingham, Norfolk, born 28 April 1840, died 2 December 1924, and had issue, surname *Collyer*:[20] a. *John Johnston*, Brig.-General, born 21 September 1870, married, 1 July 1903, Hilda Rochford; b. *George Falconar*, born 1 August 1872, married, 29 October 1904, Guendolyne Thorbury; c. *Roger Messenger Monsey*, born 28 April 1874, married, 30 November 1909, Maud Winifred Noel; d. *William Bedingfield*, born 5 October 1875, died in infancy; e. *Hugh Nathaniel*, born 6 May 1877, married, 20 November 1918, Lillian Margaret Watkin-Williams; f. *Alexander*, born 26 March 1880, died in infancy; g. *Charles Alexander Stewart*, born 1 July 1881, married, 27 July 1920, Ethel Georgina Wright.

    vi.   Charles Louis Currie Falconar, born 16 October 1856, died, without issue, in 1881.

F5 George Mercer Falconar-Stewart of Binny was born 10 June 1844 and died 16 October 1921.

He married, 8 September 1881, Louise Victoria Emanuella Bartolucci, daughter of Vincenzo Bartolucci, of Cantiano Marche, by his wife Clementina Dundas. She died 10 November 1936.

Educated at Glenalmond, he served as Justice of the Peace and Secretary of the Local Government Board for Scotland.

Issue of George Mercer and Louise Victoria Emanuella (Bartolucci) Falconar-Stewart:

    i.   Ronald Dundas Falconar-Stewart, D.S.O., Lieutenant-Colonel, Argyll and Sutherland Highlanders, born 4 July 1882, killed in action in Macedonia, 19

September 1918. Educated at Durham School. Unmarried.

F6   ii.   Cyril Falconar-Stewart, born 14 May 1884.

       iii.   Percy George Falconar-Stewart, born 24 November 1886, died at Rangoon, unmarried, 6 May 1924. Educated at Glenalmond.

       iv.   Ian Stewart Falconar-Stewart, Lieutenant, Argyll and Sutherland Highlanders, born 18 May 1892, died of wounds at Rouen, 1917, unmarried.

       v.   Charles Falconar-Stewart, died in infancy.

F6 **Cyril Falconar-Stewart** of Feddal, in Braco, Perthshire, was born 14 May 1884 and died 18 December 1962.

He married, 15 September 1915, Nita Allan, daughter of Bryce Allan, of Wemyss Bay, Renfrewshire.

Educated at Malvern and Edinburgh Academy, he served as a Major, Royal Scots, in World War I and in the Intelligence Corps in World War II. He was a member of The King's Bodyguard for Scotland (The Royal Company of Archers), and in 1916 received an M.C. He was appointed Justice of the Peace for Perthshire in 1933.

With his death, the male line of this branch of the family became extinct. Issue of Cyril and Nita (Allan) Falconar-Stewart:

       i.   Grizel Anne Falconar-Stewart, born 9 January 1917, lives in Edinburgh. She married, 1944, Wladyslaw Chlebowski, and has issue, surname *Chlebowski*: a. *Jan Ronald Stewart*, born 1945; b. *Ewa Stewart*, born 1948, married, in 1975, Dr. William David Smith, of Edinburgh; c. *Victor Tadeusz Stewart*, born 1953.[21]

       ii.   Ronald George Falconar-Stewart, Squadron Leader, Royal Air Force, born 2 April 1920, killed in action, 2 January 1943.

NOTES

[1] Unless cited otherwise, the source for the statements in this section is: *Burke's Genealogical and Heraldic History of the Landed Gentry*, L. G. Pine, ed. (London: Burke's, 1952), p. 2418.

[2] Testament, Commissariot of Edinburgh, CC3/5/105, SRO.

[3] Watson, *Roll of Edinburgh Burgesses, 1701-1760*, p. 67.

[4] Charles A. Malcolm, *The Bank of Scotland, 1695-1945* (Edinburgh: R. & R. Clark, n.d.), p. 243.

[5] Edinburgh Parish Register.

[6] Memorial concerning entail of Boghall, Kintore Papers, Bundle 44, Aberdeen University Library.

[7] *Scots' Magazine*, 51: 622.

[8] Delvine Papers, MS 1264, National Library of Scotland.

[9] *London Times*, 4 April 1786.

[10] *Scots' Magazine*, 29: 334.

[11] George Falconar of Carlowrie to John Mackenzie of Delvine, 10 Aug. 1773, Delvine Papers, MS 1264, National Library of Scotland.

[12] Grant, *Commissariot Record of Edinburgh*, part 3, p. 89.

[13] Wood, *Peerage of Scotland*, 2: 56.

[14] St. Clement Danes, London, Parish Register (IGI). According to Scots law, children are legitimated by the subsequent marriage of their parents and have all the rights of lawful children (*Encyclopedia of the Laws of Scotland*, Rt. Hon. Viscount Dundee, ed., Edinburgh: W. Green & Son, 1930, 9: 140).

[15] *Williamson's Directory for the City of Edinburgh, Canongate, Leith, and Suburbs: from the 25th May 1773, to 25th May 1774* (Edinburgh: William Brown, 1889), p. 25.

[16] Register of St. Martin in the Fields, London (IGI).

[17] *Blackwood's Edinburgh Magazine*, 22: 265.

[18] *Scots' Magazine*, 74: 728.

[19] *Blackwood's Edinburgh Magazine*, 22: 557.

[20] *Burke's Genealogical and Heraldic History of the Landed Gentry* (London: Burke's Peerage Ltd., 1939), p. 455.

[21] *Debrett's Illustrated Peerage*, 1980, p. P449.

CHAPTER G

Masters of the Scottish Mint

G1 Sir John Falconer, Master of the Mint in Scotland, third son of Sir Alexander Falconer of Halkerton (A6), born perhaps as early as 1600, was buried 21 June 1670 at Greyfriars, Edinburgh.[1]

He married, as his first wife, Sibilla Ogilvy, whose origin is unknown, but which appears to have been rather closely related to James, first Earl of Airlie.[2] She died 4 December 1634.[3]

He married, as his second wife, Esther Briot, daughter of Nicolas Briot by his wife Esther Pintaut.

We know little of his life before his appointment to the mint. He may have been the same John Falconer who, on 11 December 1627, pursued an action before the Lords of Session against the heirs of Robert Beatie, burgess in Montrose, who had assigned a bond of 1000 merks to Andrew Wilson, a resident of Germany.[4]

Following his marriage, he became servitor to his father-in-law Nicolas Briot, a French medallist who had developed a new type of coinage press while in the employ of the King of France, but who had later gone into the service of the English King. Briot must have taught him the skills necessary for managing the Scottish mint. The Privy Council chose, on 3 August 1637, Nicolas Briot to be Master of the Mint in Edinburgh, and John Falconer was joined with him in this office.[5] The Master of the Mint was the day-to-day superintendent of the mint. His duties consisted of receiving and giving out bullion, according to the provisions of the acts of Parliament, and determining that it was of just standard; paying the salaries of the workmen; and keeping accounts of the coinages. He also had custody of one of the keys to the chests in which the money was kept.[6]

Warrants were soon issued for the coinage of silver, gold, and copper.[7] Briot returned to England in 1642[8] and Sir John was the sole bearer of the office. A warrant was issued to him in 1650 to strike sixty stone of copper,[9] but the mint was otherwise inactive during the Interregnum, even though he was ordered in 1651 to set up the mint in a house in Dundee.[10]   He retired to the country instead.

He had a charter, dated 30 November 1643, of the lands of Bruntoune, in Kincardineshire, from William, Earl Marischal.[11]   In April 1648, he was named a Commissioner for War for Kincardineshire.[12]   Under Cromwell, he "suffered great losses by the insolencies of the rebells;"[13] he later pleaded before the Privy Council that during this period he met with unspecified "troubles and sufferings."[14]   On 14 June 1652, he alienated the lands of Bruntoune to Mr. David Falconar of Glenfarquhar.[15]   One Mademoiselle Oliver pursued an action against him on 11 July 1657.[16]   On 4 August 1658, was released from the Tolbooth at Edinburgh, having been imprisoned for debt to David Boyll of Kelburne.[17]   With the restoration of the King imminent, he petitioned Parliament on 2 February 1660 for authority to coin a quantity of copper money.[18]

Crowns minted at the Scottish mint under the direction of Sir John Falconer, father (left) and son (right.) Note the "F" marks over the bust of Charles I (left) and under that of Charles II (right.) Collections of the Hunterian Museum, University of Glasgow.

The shortage of copper coins was a serious problem, especially for the country's poor. But he faced a number of obstacles before he could resolve the situation. First of all, his eldest son David, who had been joined with him in his office since 1646, became a Quaker in this year, rendering him unable to hold the office. This was settled on 31 December 1660, when the Privy Council ratified Sir John and his son John as conjunct Masters of the Mint, with an annual salary of £100.[19]   Sir John had gone to London during the summer of 1660, in order to receive the stamps with the likeness of the new king, but faced delays. A warrant for £100 was issued on 20 March 1661, to pay the costs of transporting him, his family, his workmen, and tools.[20]   Meanwhile, the Scottish Parliament passed an act on 12 June 1661 ordering the General and Master of the Mint to coin 3000 stone of turners (copper twopence pieces), and, on the same day, passed another act requiring the General and Master to each provide 20,000 merks on their own credit towards purchasing gold and silver bullion for the minthouse.[21]   On 2 October the General of the Mint, Charles Maitland of Halton, petitioned the Privy Council to write a letter to the Secretary of State for Scotland to expedite the production of the stamps.[22]   Finally, at the end of the year, Sir John received the standards for gold and silver coinage and a nest and two piles of weights.[23]   But his eighteen-month stay in London had now left him penniless. In order to have an income to support the transport of workmen and tools back to Scotland, he procured a warrant for a baronetcy for Richard Cocks, of Dumbleton, Gloucestershire, and on 21 January 1662, petitioned the King to be made a baronet[24] but was unsuccessful.

Returning to Scotland, he found that Maitland (who was brother of the Earl of Lauderdale, Chancellor of Scotland, the single most powerful individual in Scotland) had taken over his lodgings in the minthouse. This was the only the beginning of a long animosity between Maitland and the Falconers, father and son. In June 1662, the Privy Council appointed a commission to settle their differences.[25] Sir John pleaded that the Master's office required a residence in the minthouse and this had been confirmed by Charles I; that the Masters could not have control over the money and bullion if they did not have command of the gates night and day; that the Master's office required daily contact with the nation's subjects, which the General's office did not; that the Masters needed to provide accommodation for the workmen and their families; and that both he and his father-in-law had provided the funds for construction of the workhouses but had not yet been reimbursed. Sir John also protested that the General should not disburse money to the workmen and that the General should not have the profits resulting from the coinage of copper.[26] On 10 July 1662, the commission determined which rooms in the minthouse would be used for Sir John's accommodation and which would be vacant.[27]

Finally, the coining of 3000 stone of turners began on 31 July 1663, two years after Parliament ordered it. The issuing period was extended for two years after 12 June 1664.[28] Sir John seems to have transferred his official duties to his son John during this period.

He died in debt. His personal estate, inventoried on 19 July 1673, was appraised at £430, but the sum of his debts, with the value of his personal estate deducted, was £1300.[29]

Issue of Sir John Falconer and Sibilla Ogilvy:[30]

J1 i. David Falconar.

Issue of Sir John Falconer and Esther Briot:[31]

G2 ii. Sir John Falconar of Balmakellie, Master of the Mint, baptized 3 October 1636.

iii. Catharine Falconer, baptized 19 December 1638.

iv. James Falconer, baptized 29 June 1640. Not further traced. He and the other sons of Sir John, except David, John, and Robert, all probably died young, as their names do not appear in the papers of the younger Sir John or in other contemporary records.

v. child, baptized 18 August 1641.

vi. Patrick Falconer, baptized 20 September or 3 October 1642, probably died young.

G3 vii. Robert Falconar, merchant in London, baptized 26 July 1644.

viii. Charles Falconer, baptized 11 November 1646, probably died young.

ix. William Falconer, baptized 23 January 1649, probably died young.

xi. Andrew Falconer, baptized 13 July 1652, probably died young.

xii. Esther Falconer, baptized 12 February 1654.

G2 **Sir John Falconar** of Balmakellie, Master of the Mint, baptized 3 October 1636 in Edinburgh, died 1 February 1686[32] at London, and was buried in St. Margaret, Westminster.

He married, 6 April 1665, at Edinburgh, Barbara Jaffray, eldest daughter of George Jaffray, merchant burgess of Edinburgh, and Bessie Johnston.[33] She was still living in 1721. Her tocher consisted of 12,000 merks, with property in Aberdeen worth 6,000 merks, which she was to have in life-rent.[34]

He joined his father as conjunct Master of the Mint on 31 December 1660, the Privy Seal recognizing the "panes and care" the father having taken in educating the son in "the knowledge of the said office" and also of his "proficiencie and qualificatiouns attained fitt to discharge" the office.[35] John appears to have taken over from his father about 1665, after the mint had been coining for two years. In that year he presented a supplication to the Privy Council, asking that merchants holding scrap copper be allowed to sell it to the mint, because the supply of bullion was interrupted by war at sea.[36] On 13 June 1666, a royal warrant was issued to the General and Master of the Mint to coin copper for two years. At the end of this period, on 16 July 1668, the King exonerated the General and Master in the coinage of this copper.[37]

Following the death of his father in 1670, he assumed the knighthood and sole office. On 5 February 1672, his elder half-brother David renounced any claims to the office, and Sir John paid him £600 sterling.[38] He and his brother Robert were admitted burgesses of Aberdeen on 23 August 1673. Sir John was not made a burgess of Edinburgh until 19 July 1676.[39]

He seems to have prospered financially in the 1670s, investing his profits in lands in Kincardineshire, Angus, and elsewhere. He acquired the lands and mansion house of Wallyford, near Musselburgh, by 1672, but sold them for 56,000 merks in March 1675 to Sir William Binning, Provost of Edinburgh.[39A] On 4 April 1677, he purchased from Sir James Keith of Powburn, Bart., the lands and barony of Scotston.[40] His seat was at Galraw (or Gallery, as it is spelled today) in the parish of Logie Montrose, Angus. In 1677, he contracted with Thomas Wilkie, a mason of Edinburgh who had made alterations to the minthouse, to build a house on this property. This house, which still stands, consisted of three storeys and an attic and was attached to a smaller house built perhaps in 1650. The upper dining room was to have "fruit work" in the plaster of the ceiling.[41]   On 21 August 1679, a warrant for a charter of new infeftment was issued to him and his heirs male of the lands and barony of Galleraw and the lands and barony of Scotstoun, with an erection of the premises into the barony of Balmakelly.[42]   He sat in Parliament as Commissioner for Kincardineshire in 1678, 1681-1682, and 1685.

His arms were: Or, a falcon's head issuing out of an heart proper betwixt three mollets azure on a chief of the second alse many bezants.[43]

Sir John's house at Gallery, built in 1677 or shortly after. The original wing, to the left, is not visible.

Sir John was responsible for carrying out a warrant issued on 27 February 1677 for the coining of 3000 stone of copper in twopence and sixpence pieces.[44]   On 31 March 1677, he contracted with John Hall of Graycruik and George Galbraith, merchant burgesses of Edinburgh, to import 1500 stone of Swedish copper.[45]   He contracted in 1678 with David Moodie, merchant of Montrose, for two tons of pure rose copper to be imported from Stockholm or Trandem, and on 28 January 1679, he contracted with John Coutts, provost of Montrose, Robert Rennald and James Milne, merchants of Montrose, for 10,000 pounds of goare copper from Stockholm or Trandem.[46]

His office was contested, sometime between 1679 and 1681, by certain friends of his half-brother David. They felt that David had not received his fair share from the profits of the office and went before the Duke of York with an appeal.[47]   This dispute was resolved on 10 January 1682, when the King issued a warrant for a gift ratifying to Sir John Falconar of Balmakellie the former gift to him of the office of Master of the Mint.[48]   On the same day, the King issued a warrant for a gift to Sir John's unnamed son of a yearly pension investigate the mint.[50]   Maitland of Halton and his son Richard, having received advance information about the formation of the commission, suddenly left for England, taking with them most of the mint's records.[51] This commission spent the next three months going over the mint's registers, daybooks, and papers, sealed up the pix, and questioned the mint's officers daily.[52] Sir John felt abandoned by the General, having to suffer the brunt of the commission's accusations. When Maitland did return to Scotland, he refused to testify before the commission, sending a representative instead.

It issued a report on 4 August. This charged the General and Master with melting down old coins, rather than importing bullion, for the purchase of which they were provided an annual sum; that silver of substandard fineness was minted, without assay; that 29,600 stone of copper had been minted, rather than the 6,000 stone allowed by law; that the General had taken half of the five-percent profit allowed from the bullion intended for the King; that the General had forced the Master to give him a bribe of £600 to balance the accounts preceding 1674 and that the General had received a salary between 1660 and 1664, when no money was coined; that the General, who had power to hold court against the other officers of the mint, did not, despite the evidence of their malversation; and that the General had forced the Warden to lend to him, but in the name of Alexander Maitland, counterwarden, the sum of 11,000 merks.[53]

The King received the commission's report, and on 25 August, ordered the removal of the mint's officers and ordered Sir George Mackenzie of Rosehaugh, the King's Advocate, to prosecute them.[54] In the meantime, Robert Barclay of Urie, the Quaker apologist and brother-in-law of Sir John's brother David, went to London to appeal on Sir John's behalf before the Scottish Council and the Duke of York.[55] Sir John, in a letter presented by Barclay to the Duke, attempted to distance himself from Maitland of Halton, claiming that he had tried to cooperate with the commission's investigation. He declared in his petition that if "I went along in anything which was irregular, it was with a great reluctancy," but had little choice, having been under the "power & influence of a great man to whose advantadge and humor as a captive under deck."[56] Barclay reported from London that, although the Register had represented his case favorably before the Council, Richard Maitland, the Justice-Clerk, pressured the English on the Council to disallow the petition as "not sufficient." Barclay personally presented the petition to the Duke, but the latter was "displeased" with his petition and told him that only an "absolute submission" to the King would resolve his situation.[57]

On 2 October, the King issued a warrant to prosecute the General (now Earl of Lauderdale, having succeeded his brother, who died in August) and other officers of the mint.[58] The King's letter was read on 7 November before the Privy Council, which ordered the Treasurer, William, Marquess of Queensberry, and the King's Advocate, Sir George Mackenzie of Rosehaugh, to try them before the Lords of Session.[59] The mint was now suspended, which created fear among the people.[60] Mackenzie issued a summons on 25 November to the Earl of Lauderdale, Sir John, and the other officers of the mint, for coining copper in excess of the authorized amount.[61]

The Lords of Session heard the case on 19 and 23-26 January 1683, trying the officers on the points raised by the commission. During the case and in subsequent appeals, Sir John repeatedly tried to absolve himself of any responsibility for the alleged malversations. He stressed that the Lords made no attempt to distinguish his office and its duties from the others. Among other responses, he denied that any bullion was substandard, that melting down foreign coins was against the law, that Scottish weight standards were different from English standards, and that in 1679 he retired to the country after coining the authorized amount of copper, only to return to Edinburgh on the General's orders. Since the General was "a person of great influence," Sir John felt he had little choice but to comply with his orders or else risk incurring "his highest resentment, of which the greatest in the kingdom then stood in awe of."[62]

On 20 March, the Lords found that the officers were liable *in solidum* to the King in the sum of £72,000. The final sentence was decreed on 10 May. The Earl of Lauderdale was to pay £20,000, of which £16,000 was to go to the Chancellor and £4,000 to Sir John Graham of Claverhouse. Sir John was fined in four and a half years' full rent of his personal and real estate, besides the bullion he had in hand. The fine was lowered, because they had privately forced him to give his brother David a bond of 9,000 merks. Mr. James Falconer, son of the warden, and Alexander Maitland, the former counterwarden, were fined in six years' rent of their estates. The efforts of Sir John's cousins, Lady Erroll and Sir David Falconar of Newton, and his uncle Sir David Falconer of Glenfarquhar, Sir John's cautioners in the office, allowed the Earl of Lauderdale to discharge any relief he claimed against Sir John——because, as Fountainhall noted, they "feared it might at the long run land upon them."[63]

Sir John's plan now was to attempt to build political support on his behalf from the "great men" in government. He requested support from Graham of Claverhouse in a letter on 22 March, remarking that "if I must be made a sacresty, I would wish to be only to the King's own pleasure and will and not to the humor, cruelty, or severity of any particular person who perhaps cannot make any distinction betwixt the King's friends and the greatest enemy he has [Lauderdale]."[64] At the urging of the Treasurer, the Earl of Perth, Sir John avoided Lauderdale—a strategy which ultimately worked against him. Fountainhall wrote, after his death, that "many thought Sir John justly rewarded, for prostituting so low in deponing and loading my Lord Lauderdale, the Generall, with a prospect therby to keep himselfe in his place."[65] Sir John complained in a letter to the Earl of Perth on 11 January 1684 that his "express promises and positive assurances [of help] has been totally violated."[66]

He went to London in July 1683 on his own initiative, incurring the wrath of the Treasurer and Chancellor, who did not approve of the visit.[67] Returning to Scotland, he stayed out of the political fray for the rest of the year. At the beginning of 1684, his mother-in-law, Bessie Johnston, passed the word that he had "gone over the water," while he actually stayed in Edinburgh at the house of Mary Auchmuty.[68] Sir John's fine was set at £3000, to be divided between him and James Falconer of Phesdo.[69] Now the Earl of Perth finally delivered on his promises to help Sir John, offering to plead in his behalf before the Duke of York.[70] The Duke assured Perth that he would show Sir John favor, "the way & method behoved to be left to himselfe."[71]

Sir John had, in the meantime, begun the arduous process of collecting money from his debtors. He registered no fewer than 35 deeds from November 1682 to 1686. He sold the lands and barony of Scotston and the lands of Shiells to Sir Alexander Falconar of Glenfarquhar on 24 December 1684.[72] Although the exact nature of his accounts with his brother David is unclear, they were complex. David provided Sir John with a loan of 10,000 merks on 7 May 1682.[73] Sir John's fine passed in 1683 required him to pay David 9,000 merks, which would seem to be the amount necessary to pay back the loan. Finally they settled their accounts through arbitration on 6 August 1685.[74]

The Duke of York, although consumed by other issues, did mitigate Sir John's fine. On 4 April 1685, he was exonered, quitclaimed, and forever discharged of the sums discerned in relation to the bullion.[75] The King issued a warrant on 30 July 1685 concerning his fines. Sir John's fine was determined at £1,500 sterling; James Falconer of Phesdo's was set at £1,000 sterling.[76]

Sir John went to London in September 1685 to appeal for his reinstatement as Master of the Mint. The Duke of York had succeeded his brother Charles II and his court was full of intrigue. Sir John had little choice but to wait patiently until the King could find the time for an audience with him. He wrote his wife on 7 November that he was "very wearie of the place, especially in being idle, although I pass my tyme in the best of company and the most learned, curious and famous men this place affords." Sir William Sharp of Scotscraig was appointed General, and it appeared that the opening of the mint was imminent. Unfortunately, Sir John never had the opportunity to present his case before the King, as he fell ill and died on 1 February 1686. Fountainhall records the contemporary rumor of the cause of his death as "heart-break."[77]

Willing to compromise on the location of an appointment, Sir John refused to do so on his religion, a condition reportedly offered to him.[78] His widow then went to London to redress her sad financial condition. Robert cautioned her on 18 March not to be "surprized at any thing you have or shall meet wth for there's little Charity or Generosity to bee mett wth nowadayes."[79] Barbara went before the King and obtained a recommendatory letter to the Lords of Treasury of Scotland to do her justice and to retain the grant of escheat and life-rent of her husband, the benefit of which to be used for herself and her children. In order to raise funds with which to pay his fine, Sir John had mortgaged his lands and baronies with David Falconar of Newton, Sir Alexander Falconar of Glenfarquhar, James Milne of Hatton, and James Scott of Logie.

Barbara and her daughters attempted to recover some of Sir John's losses between 1713 and 1718, in cases against James Scott of Logie, David Falconar of Newton, Sir Alexander Falconar of Glenfarquhar, and Alexander Milne of Hatton. Her son-in-law Charles Menzies of Kinmundy, writer to the Signet, acted as her attorney. The survival of the papers of Sir John and his family in the Edinburgh District Archives has enabled us to recreate the details of this unfortunate case and see the private lives and character of its principals.

Sir John and Barbara held steadfast to each other during his troubles. While he was in Edinburgh, Barbara stayed at Gallery, overseeing financial and legal affairs in the country. Some of her letters give details about her and her children's lives there. Their daughter Elizabeth played the viol, for example.[80] Sir John showed concern for the spiritual education of his children, reminding his wife to "teach [them] to know him & cause them to read the Scriptures much. And above all I beseech you lett constant family worship be at least once every night."[81] Sir John bought a gown for Esther, two "littel dixionaries, verry propper" for his son John and also a copybook of a "hand write which I would have John learne and the rest of the children, after it is the only properest and most legible vsed hand now."[82]

Other letters describe items purchased in Edinburgh for the family. Barbara requested Mary Auchmuty to get her a "new fashion gase [gauze] hoode and a gase guise if they be in fashone"[83] Her mother, Bessie Johnston, sent her in January 1684 four ells of linen for aprons, four ells of serge for a petticoat, two pairs of shoes, and wondered if Isabel, Barbara's servant, had anything to spin.[84] Sir John wrote her that he was sending four gallons of "seck" [wine] and was hoping to find scarce olives and olive oil.[85] Her mother followed with a letter announcing the shipment at Leith of three gallons of sack, twelve choppin bottles, twelve mutchkin bottles, a ham, linens, a blue satin petticoat, a flowered gown, silver saltfats and dishes, a suit and pair of stockings for Sir John, and a gown for her granddaughter Nicholas, but had difficulty finding a silver spoon, a pearled apron, and other items.[86]

Issue of Sir John Falconar and Barbara Jaffray:[87]

i.   child, buried 25 May 1665.[88]

ii.   John Falconar, baptized 13 July 1666, probably buried 21 January 1668.[89]

iii. Charles Falconar, baptized 20 December 1667, died young.

iv.   Elizabeth Falconar, baptized 15 December 1668. She was unmarried and living as late as 1714.

v.   Esther Falconar, baptized 14 June 1670, died 1724 in Edinburgh, at which time she was married to a man who her sister Barbara thought was "nether solid as to his principalls, nether qualified with good manners."[90]

vi.   John Falconar, baptized 27 September 1671, probably buried 10 February 1673.

vii. Barbara Falconar, baptized 28 October 1673. On 13 April 1718, she married, as his second wife, Charles Menzies of Kinmundy, writer to the Signet.[91] Sir John's papers, now in the Edinburgh District Archives, were preserved by her.

viii. Mary Falconar, baptized 5 December 1674.

ix.   John Falconar, baptized 25 March 1676, died May 1702 at Edinburgh.[92] Sir John's heir, he was educated in Montrose and from 1690 to 1694 at King's College, Aberdeen. He was "at the lateran" in Edinburgh at the time of his death.[93]

x.   Nicholas Falconar [daughter], baptized 26 March 1678.

xi.   Alexander Falconar, baptized 2 May 1679, died in 1702.[94]

VI ET INDUSTRIA

G3   **Robert Falconar**, merchant in London, baptized 26 July 1644 in Edinburgh, Scotland, died after 1689, when in London, England.

He married, on 20 June 1678, at St. Bride Fleet Street, London,[95] by license dated 18 June 1678,[96] Mary Bridgeman, of St. Katherine Creechurch, London, perhaps the daughter of James and Prothesa Bridgeman, baptized 29 July 1657 at St. Helen Bishopsgate, London.[97]

He was apprenticed to George Robinson, of London, merchant, in 1660, and served him for seven years.[98] With his brother John, he was admitted a burgess of Aberdeen, 23 August 1673.[99] On 17 April 1680, he had an agreement with his brother Sir John to supply the Scottish Mint with bullion, to the value of £5,000, for one year.[100] In 1683, he was detained as bankrupt, writing to Sir John on 3 March 1682/3 that he did not have forty shillings at his command.[101] His creditors continued to pursue him. The last records of him in England seem to be in a Chancery suit on 9 July 1689, when he complained that his old master, George Robinson, had intended to defraud him,[102] and his daughter Mary's baptism on 25 October 1689. It would appear that he then may have fled the country in order to avoid jail or his creditors, although, in that year of revolution, politics may have played a role as well.[103]   He was not listed in a census of London inhabitants made in 1695.[104]

His arms were: Or, a falcon's head issuing out of a heart proper betwixt three mollets azure on a chief wavy of the second alse many bezants.[105]

Issue of Robert and Mary (Bridgeman) Falconar:[106]

   i.   John Falconar, baptized 5 June 1679. He nor his other brothers have not been traced. There is some reason to believe, however, that John (d. 1749) of Kent County, Delaware, and Robert Falconar (d. 1753) of Kent County, Maryland, may have belonged to this branch of the family, as they lived near the family of Gilbert Falconar (J1).

   ii.   Robert Falconar, buried 17 January 1680/1.

   iii.   Robert Falconar, born 2 March 1682/3. He or another unnamed child was "like to die," 3 April 1683.[107]   A Robert Falconer was commissioned a 2nd Lieutenant in the Royal Navy on 5 November 1703 and assigned to H.M.S. *Pendennis*.[108]   Captain Robert Falkner was buried 4 January 1716/7 in St. Bride Fleet Street.[109]

   iv.   William Falconar, baptized 28 June 1685.

   v.   James Falconar, baptized 16 May 1687, buried 31 May 1687.

   vi.   Mary Falconar, baptized 25 October 1689.

NOTES

[1] Paton, ed., *Register of Interments in the Greyfriars Burying-Ground, Edinburgh, 1658-1700*, p. 213.

[2] Moses Bundle 254/7734, Edinburgh District Archives.

[3] Testament dative, Commissariot of Brechin, CC3, SRO.

[4] Morison, *Decisions of the Court of Session*, 11: 4501.

[5] *Register of the Privy Council*, 2nd ser., 6: 239, 542.

[6] R. W. Cochran-Patrick, *Records of the Coinage of Scotland from the Earliest Period to the Union* (Edinburgh: Edmonston and Douglas, 1876), 1: xxiii.

[7] *Register of the Privy Council*, 2nd ser., 6: 240, 244; 8: 23, 32.

[8] Helen Farquhar, "Nicholas Briot and the Civil War," *Numismatic Chronicle and Journal of the Royal Numismatic Society*, 4th ser., 14 (1914): 176-185.

[9] *Acts of the Parliaments of Scotland*, vol. 6, pt. 2, p. 602, 618.

[10] Sir James Balfour, *The Historical Works of Sir James Balfour, Lord Lyon King of Arms to Charles I and Charles II* (Edinburgh: 1725), 4: 280.

[11] Bundle 141, Kintore Papers, Aberdeen University Library.

[12] *Acts of the Parliaments of Scotland*, vol. 6 (new ed.), pt. 2, p. 34.

[13] Memorial, Moses Bundle 254/7761, Edinburgh District Archives.

[14] *Register of the Privy Council*, 3rd ser., 1: 205.

[15] Bundle 141, Kintore Papers, Aberdeen University Library.

[16] *Decisions of the English Judges, During the Usurpation, from the Year 1655 to his Majesty's Restoration...in June 1661* (Edinburgh: for Hamilton and Barbour, 1762), p. 65f.

[17] "The Old Tolbooth with Extracts from the Original Records," *Book of the Old Edinburgh Club* (Edinburgh: the Club, 1911), 4: 128.

[18] MS La. III 354, Lauderdale Papers, University of Edinburgh Library.

[19] Register of the Privy Seal, RS3/1, f. 19f., SRO.

[20] Great Britain, *Calendar of Treasury Books, 1660-1667* (London: for His Majesty's Stationery Office by Mackie & Co., 1904), p. 228.

[21] *Acts of the Parliaments of Scotland*, 7: 254.

[22] *Register of the Privy Council*, 3rd ser., 1: 45.

[23] *Calendar of Treasury Books, 1660-1667*, pp. 293, 317.

[24] State Papers, Domestic Series, SP 29/49, PRO.

[25] *Register of the Privy Council*, 3rd ser., 1: 235.

[26] Cochran-Patrick, *Records of the Coinage of Scotland*, 2: 176-178.

[27] *Register of the Privy Council*, 3rd ser., 1: 204f.

[28] Ibid., 3rd ser., 1: 367.

[29] Testament dative, Commissariot of Edinburgh, CC8, SRO.

[30] Testament dative, Commissariot of Brechin, CC3, SRO.

[31] Edinburgh Parish Register.

[32] Barbara Jaffray to Elizabeth Falconar, 9 Nov. 1714, Moses Bundle 254/7793a, Edinburgh District Archives.

[33] Edinburgh Parish Register.

[34] Helen Armet, "Sir John Falconer of Balmakellie, Master of the Scottish Mint," *The Scottish Genealogist* 14 (April 1967): 1-2. That article is based on his papers in Moses Bundle 254, Edinburgh District Archives.

[35] Register of the Privy Seal, PS3/1, f. 171, SRO.

[36] *Register of the Privy Council*, 3rd ser., 2: 32.

[37] *Register of the Privy Council*, 1667-1673, p. 99.

[38] Moses Bundle 254/7731, Edinburgh District Archives.

[39] Watson, *Roll of Edinburgh Burgesses, 1406-1700*, p. 177.

[39A] John A. Inglis, "Edinburgh during the Provostship of Sir William Binning, 1675-1677," *Scottish Historical Review* 12 (1915): 370.

[40] Fraser, *History of the Parish and Burgh of Laurencekirk*, p. 62.

[41] Moses Bundle 254/7772, Edinburgh District Archives.

[42] Great Britain, *Calendar of State Papers (Domestic Series), Jan. 1, 1679 to Aug. 31, 1681*, ed. F. H. Blackburne Daneill (London: for H.M. Stationery Office, 1915), p. 223.

[43] Scotland, Lord Lyon, Public Register of All Arms and Bearings in Scotland, 1: 150.

[41] Moses Bundle 254/7772, Edinburgh District Archives.

[42] Great Britain, *Calendar of State Papers (Domestic Series), Jan. 1, 1679 to Aug. 31, 1681*, ed. F. H. Blackburne Daneill (London: for H.M. Stationery Office, 1915), p. 223.

[43] Scotland, Lord Lyon, Public Register of All Arms and Bearings in Scotland, 1: 150.

[44] Moses Bundle 254/7736, Edinburgh District Archives.

[45] Cochran-Patrick, *Records of the Coinage of Scotland*, 2: 178-180.

[46] Ibid., 2: 180-182.

[47] Moses Bundle 254/7734, Edinburgh District Archives.

[48] *Calendar of State Papers, Domestic Series, 1679-1681*, p. 21.

[49] Ibid., p. 21.

[50] Memorial, Moses Bundle 254/7761, Edinburgh District Archives.

[51] Cochran-Patrick, *Records of the Coinage of Scotland*, 2: 187.

[52] Sir John Falconer to Richard, Lord Maitland, undated, Moses Bundle 254/7793a/72, Edinburgh District Archives.

[53] Cochran-Patrick, *Records of the Coinage of Scotland*, 2: 186-197.

[54] *Register of the Privy Council*, 2nd series, 7: 543f.

[55] Robert Barclay of Urie to Sir John Falconar, 27 Aug. 1682, Moses Bundle 254/7793a, Edinburgh District Archives.

[56] Draft letter, Sir John Falconer to James, Duke of Albany and York, Moses Bundle 254/7757, Edinburgh District Archives.

[57] Robert Barclay of Urie to Sir John Falconar, 27 vi [Aug.] 1682, Moses Bundle 254/7793a, Edinburgh District Archives.

[58] *Calendar of State Papers (Domestic Series), 1682*, p. 451.

[59] *Register of the Privy Council*, 2nd ser., 7: 563.

[60] Sir John Falconer to Barbara Jaffray, 4 Nov. 1682, Moses Bundle 254/7793a, Edinburgh District Archives.

[61] *Register of the Privy Council*, 2nd ser., 7: 544.

[62] Moses Bundle 254/7739, Edinburgh District Archives.

[63] Sir John Lauder of Fountainhall, *Historical Notices of Scottish Affairs* (Edinburgh: Bannatyne Club, 1848), 1: 397-406, 438-440.

[64] Draft letter, Sir John Falconar to Sir John Graham of Claverhouse, 22 Mar. 1683, Moses Bundle 254/7793a, Edinburgh District Archives.

[65] Lauder, *Historical Notices of Scottish Affairs*, 2: 698.

[66] Draft letter, Sir John Falconar to the Earl of Perth, 11 Jan. 1684, Moses Bundle 254/7757, Edinburgh District Archives.

[67] Robert Urquhart to Sir John Falconar, 17 July 1683, Moses Bundle 254/7793a, Edinburgh District Archives.

[68] Sir John Falconar to Barbara Jaffray, 25 Feb. 1684, Moses Bundle 254/7793a, Edinburgh District Archives.

[69] Sir John Falconar to Barbara Jaffray, 11 Jan. 1684, Moses Bundle 254/7793a, Edinburgh District Archives.

[70] Sir John Falconar to Barbara Jaffray, 25 Feb. 1684, Moses Bundle 254/7793a, Edinburgh District Archives.

[71] Sir John Falconar to Barbara Jaffray, 20 Mar. 1684, Moses Bundle 254/7793a, Edinburgh District Archives.

[72] Fraser, *History of the Parish and Burgh of Laurencekirk*, p. 63.

[73] Register of Deeds, RD4161, f. 1103, SRO.

[74] Sir John Falconar to Barbara Jaffray, 6 Aug. 1685, Moses Bundle 254/7793a, Edinburgh District Archives.

[75] Register of the Privy Seal, PS3/3, SRO.

[76] Moses Bundle 254/7753, Edinburgh District Archives.

[77] Lauder, *Historical Notices of Scottish Affairs*, 2: 698.

[78] Ibid., 2: 698; Memorial, Moses Bundle 254/7793a/59, Edinburgh District Archives.

[79] Robert Falconar to Barbara Jaffray, 18 Mar. 1685/6, Moses Bundle 254/7793a, Edinburgh District Archives.

[80] Barbara Jaffray to Sir John Falconar, 16 Dec. 1683, Moses Bundle 254/7793a, Edinburgh District Archives.

[81] Sir John Falconar to Barbara Jaffray, 15 Aug. 1685, Moses Bundle 254/7793a, Edinburgh District Archives.

[82] Sir John Falconar to Barbara Jaffray, 8 Aug. 1685, Moses Bundle 254/7793a, Edinburgh District Archives.

[83] Barbara Jaffray to Sir John Falconer, 16 Dec. 1683, Moses Bundle 254/7793a, Edinburgh District Archives.

[84] Bessie Johnston to Barbara Jaffray, 22 Jan. 1684, Moses Bundle 254/7793a, Edinburgh District Archives.

[85] Sir John Falconar to Barbara Jaffray, 20 Mar. 1684, Moses Bundle 254/7793a, Edinburgh District Archives.

[86] Bessie Johnston to Barbara Jaffray, 5 Apr. 1684, Moses Bundle 254/7793a, Edinburgh District Archives.

[87] Edinburgh Parish Register.

[88] Paton, *Register of Interments in the Greyfriars Burying-Ground*, p. 213.

[89] Ibid., p. 213.

[90] Barbara Menzies to Charles Menzies of Kinmundy, 16 July 1724, Moses Bundle 254/7793a, Edinburgh District Archives.

[91] Paton, ed., *The Register of Marriages for the Parish of Edinburgh, 1701-1750*, p. 178,

[92] Barbara Jaffray to Elizabeth Falconar, 9 Nov. 1714, in Moses Bundle 254/7793a, Edinburgh District Archives.

[93] Deposition of David Falconar of Newtoun, 19 Jan. 1715, in process of Barbara Jaffray v. Alexander Milne of Hatton, Moses Bundle 254/7792, Edinburgh District Archives. A lateran is a lectern, the clerk's desk in a church. *Roll of Alumni in Arts of the University and King's College of Aberdeen, 1596-1860*, ed. P. J. Anderson, Aberdeen University Studies 1 (Aberdeen: for the University, 1900), p.

[94] Within four days of the death of his only brother John. Memorial for Barbara Jaffray, 4 Dec. 1717, Moses Bundle 254/7793a, Edinburgh District Archives.

[95] St. Bride Fleet Street Parish Register.

[96] Diocese of London, Marriage Licence Allegations, Guildhall Library.

[97] A Robert Bridgeman, merchant, paid his own way to New Jersey in 1685 and was in Perth Amboy in 1688. One might suspect that he was her brother.

[98] Falconer v. Robinson, Chancery, C10/277/27, PRO.

[99] Munro, ed., "Aberdeen Burgess Register, 1631-1700," p. 439.

[100] Moses Bundle 254/7754, Edinburgh District Archives.

[101] Robert Falconar to Sir John Falconar, 3 Mar. 1682/3, Moses Bundle 254/7793a.

[102] Falconer v. Robinson, Chancery, C10/277/27, PRO.

[103] An unidentified Robert Falconer wrote an "introduction to geography" and a large part of the descriptive text on Europe in part one of *A System of Geography; Or, a New and Accurate Description of the Earth in All Its Empires, Kingdoms, and States* by Herman Moll (London: printed for A. and J. Churchill, 1701). Perhaps this person was he.

[104] *London Inhabitants within the Walls 1695* (London: London Record Society, 1966).

[105] Scotland, Lord Lyon, Public Register of All Arms, 1: 300.

[106] St. Andrew Undershaft (London) Parish Register; William's baptism recorded at St. Katherine Creechurch, London.

[107] Robert Falconar to Sir John Falconar, 3 Mar. 1682/3, 3 Apr. 1683, Moses Bundle 254/7793a, Edinburgh District Archives.

[108] Index to Commissions and Warrants, ADM6/8, f. 23, PRO.

[109] St. Bride Fleet Street Parish Register, FHS microfilm no. 380,156.

CHAPTER H

Quaker Falconars

H1 **David Falconar**, eldest son[1] of Sir John Falconer, Master of the Mint (G1), by his first wife Sibilla Ogilvy, born probably about 1632, died 18 iv [June][2] 1713 at Kingswells, near Aberdeen, and was buried 20 iv 1713 at Urie, Kincardineshire.[3]

He married, 7 iii [May] 1672, in a Quaker ceremony at Aberdeen,[4] Margaret Molleson, daughter of Gilbert Molleson, of Aberdeen, merchant, by his wife Margaret Smith. She was born 26 August[5] and was baptized 28 August 1653 at St. Nicholas, Aberdeen,[6] and died 22 vii [September] 1697 at Springhall, near Urie, Kincardineshire, and was buried at Urie. Her sister Christian was the wife of Robert Barclay of Urie, the Quaker apologist.[7]

It was customary for office holders to join their eldest sons to their offices. The recently deceased Nicolas Briot, however, wished that his own grandson John Falconar would be made conjunct Master. This became a political problem for Sir John, as kinship still formed the dominant social structure in Scotland, since he owed his office, in no small part, to his marriage to Briot's daughter. Through the influence of David's "friends," presumably his mother's relatives, including James Ogilvy, Earl of Airlie, Sir John joined David to the office of Master of the Cunziehouse [mint] on 10 August 1646. The father had been "verie cairfull and painefull to educat and instruct" his son David in the "knowledge and exercise" of the office.[8] In 1647, David testified in a case involving a riot at the mint.[9] The following year and "otherways," Sir John sent his eldest son to France, England, and Utrecht for an education, which "cost him more than all his Children besides," according to a petition made by the younger Sir John, in a dispute between the two over the office presented before James, Duke of York (later James II), between 1679 and 1681. Referring to his conversion to the heretical Quaker sect, Sir John claimed that "some mistakes falling out, betwixt David & his father, to a high degree, made him declare many times his breach of promise to his father in law was punished by ye disobedience of his son."[10]

David would have received a classical education, probably by private tutors, as he did not matriculate at the University of Utrecht, and was probably conversant in French and Dutch. Unlike his younger brother John, who retained a form of the older secretary hand, David adopted the newer italic style of handwriting. We have little information on him during the Interregnum. He probably lived in Kincardineshire, like his father. In 1658, he was factor to Mr. Patrick Falconer, eldest son of Patrick Falconer of Newton.[11] No doubt he was consumed with personal religious questions during this period.

The Restoration in 1660 brought his father a new opportunity to reaffirm his right to the office of Master of the Mint. Sir John was accompanied on his visit to London by his son John. Already estranged from his father, David became convinced of Quaker beliefs that year while his father was in London. Sir John, "out of much anger and grief," went to the King and begged him to cancel the gift of conjunct Master to David and have his son John's name placed instead. The younger John, however, pleaded that the substitution be kept blank, even meeting with the Earl of Airlie and Sir James Ogilvy, "who were the only Mother's friends David had at London," to urge them to discuss the matter with his father. The substitution of the office remained open for some time.[12]

David renounced all claims to the office in a discharge dated 5 February 1672, Sir John giving him £600 sterling "out of meer Affection." This was probably necessary in order for him to be admitted a burgess of Edinburgh, which occurred on 1 March 1672.[13] Several years later, certain parties unsuccessfully advanced a claim to the Duke of York (who, as a Catholic, was known to be sympathetic to Quakers) that David's religious beliefs had rendered him unable to hold the office, and that David, "having suffered for his Ma[jes]ty, and not being in such good condition in his fortune as his brother,"[14] should share in a part of Sir John's income.

For ten years following his conversion, David's professional options were limited. In any case, his religious activities were probably paramount. He was several times imprisoned at Edinburgh.[15] He and one Mackenzie were freed from prison by the Privy Council on 19 April 1664, on the condition that they refrain from keeping Quaker meetings.[16] Denied the opportunity of a position in the Scottish government, he acted as factor, or estate agent, to Quaker lairds. In 1666 he was factor to the imprisoned Anthony Haig of Bemersyde.[17] On 25 x [December] 1666, he was appointed factor to David Barclay of Urie.[18] He and Urie's son Robert Barclay organized Quaker meetings around Aberdeen beginning the following year.[19] The Council ordered, on 3 December 1667, that he be prosecuted for performing marriages in violation of the act of Parliament against clandestine marriages.[20] He and a number of others were convicted of holding meetings and conventicles at the house of Alexander Gellie, burgess of Aberdeen, and ordered to prison for a month in 1670.[21]

He was admitted a burgess of Aberdeen on 2 September 1671[22] and began to establish a mercantile business there, as he appears in the Friends' records as being mostly in Aberdeen in 1672 and 1673.[23] Apparently, out of religious conviction, he withheld his payment of tax to Aberdeen authorities from April 1673 to April 1674.[24] He then established his business in Edinburgh, where he remained from 1674 to 1689. During this period, he collected letters relating to the "sufferings" of Friends in Scotland and maintained the financial accounts of the Edinburgh Meeting. He purchased the

land for the Quaker cemetery in Edinburgh, known as Pleasants.[25]   The
Edinburgh Meeting appointed him and Maurice Trent, the Quaker merchant
in Leith who also was associated with the Falconers of Phesdo, on xi [January] 1681 to contract with a mason to build a large meeting house at the end
of the burial ground.[26]   His religious convictions seem not to have affected
his relations with his relatives, which were cordial. For example, in 1680 he
advanced £433 for Lord Halkerton's parliament robes and clothing for the
Lord and his son, the Master of Halkerton, and supplied the Master with
most of his living expenses while he was being educated in Edinburgh that
year.[27]

When his half-brother Sir John faced prosecution for malversation in
office in 1682, Robert Barclay, having influence with the Duke of York and
regarding Sir John a brother, pleaded before the Duke on Sir John's behalf.[28]

David's social position was secure enough, despite his religious views, to
have Sir George Mackenzie of Rosehaugh, the Lord's Advocate, issue a summons against Charles, Earl of Lauderdale, General of the Mint, on 8 March
1683, charging that Lauderdale had forged documents.[29]   David's financial
affairs became complicated by the troubles of Sir John. The full extent of his
trade can only be learned from a thorough examination of the many deeds
registered in those in which he was involved, which I unfortunately have not
done. On 7 May 1682, Sir John borrowed 10,000 merks from him, and in the
ensuing years attempted to preserve whatever estate he could claim from the
demands of his many creditors. David's and Sir John's accounts were put
through arbitration, and on 26 August 1685, their accountants determined
that David owed Sir John £299, 8s., 2d. sterling. David assigned his brother
a debt of 829 livres, 5 sous, due to him by Stephen Ernault, factor in Rouen,
and 5410 merks, 8 shillings, 8 pennies, in Scots money were then due to
David. In a complex contract, dated 7 May 1686, between David, on behalf of
himself and his children, and James Milne of Hatton, the former settled this
debt by selling the lands of Easter and Wester Balmannes and Wench Farm
to Milne. David wished to protect his children "procreat or to be procreat"
from the claims of any future creditors. Gawin Lawrie, the assistant governor of East New Jersey, was mentioned as one who might act as Falconar's
factor.[30]

He became a proprietor (or, more properly, a "fractioner") of the Scottish
Quaker colony of East New Jersey. William Penn had acquired it from the
Duke of York and made Robert Barclay governor, and the land was divided
into twenty-four shares. Each proprietor could divide his share further into
"fractions." David Falconar first bought ten acres on Ambo Point, for £15, for
his son John, on 23 November 1682. On 20 February 1682/3, Robert Barclay
of Urie sold him, for the nominal sum of five shillings, one twenty-fourth
share of his one twenty-fourth share, or 500 acres. This purchase indicates
the regard Barclay had for his brother-in-law, since David at that time needed
to help Sir John and his bankrupt brother Robert. David purchased from Sir
John Gordon for an undisclosed sum, on 11 April 1685, one-twentieth of his
one forty-eighth share. He bought, from the Proprietors, on 22 January 1689/
90, 250 acres in Monmouth County. On 17 June 1690, Robert Barclay, by
his attorney John Reid of Hortensie, sold David Falconar a lot at Barnegat
and ten acres in Perth Amboy. Finally, on 25 March 1701, Robert Barclay of
Urie, son and heir of the Apologist, sold him, for £100 received by his father,

500 acres on the Manalpan River.[31]   In addition to these purchases, David
Falconar also advanced £50 of goods on the *Exchange of Stockton*, a ship
bound for New Jersey in 1683, and was a partner in a consignment of goods
on a ship bound for New Jersey in 1686.[32]   He never went to New Jersey,
although he probably encouraged Patrick Falconar (W1), the younger son of
John Falconer of Tulloch, warden of the Mint, whose estate was also troubled
by the machinations of the authorities, to emigrate there.

David Falconar may have played a larger role in the East New Jersey
colonization scheme than his share in the proprietorship indicates.   A number of the proprietors seem to have been merchants in Montrose, like David
Mudie and Gawin Lawrie, the former of whom had been part of the bullion
trading network which included, besides David in Edinburgh, his half-brother
Robert in London, and some of the sons of John Falconer of Phesdo, the
warden.[33]   Robert and Thomas Fullarton, younger brothers of David's second
cousin John Fullarton of Kinnaber, were both proprietors, as was William
Haig, younger brother of Anthony Haig of Bemersyde, the Quaker laird for
whom David had acted as factor.   David Lyell, a London goldsmith and a
proprietor, probably belonged to the Montrose family which included Patrick
Lyell of Balhall, who married the widow of Alexander, 2nd Lord Falconer of
Halkerton.   Patrick Sandilands, an Aberdeen merchant with whom Sir John
Falconar was acquainted,[34] was also a proprietor.   Perhaps Barclay's gift of
land to David Falconar was as much recognition for the latter's assistance in
enlisting support for the venture as for his loyal personal service.

In 1689, he retired to Kirktonhill, in Marykirk, Kincardineshire.[35]   Gilbert Mollesone, citizen and draper of London, made David, then styled "of
Kirktonhill," his "entire friend and brother," his factor, on 29 October 1691.[36]
On 9 May 1695, styled "merchant in Edinburgh now in Springhall near Urrie,"
he bought, from Hercules Scott of Brotherton, for 260 merks, the lands of Hill
of Halkerton and part of the Glenns.   He sold this to Robert Barclay of Urie on
10 May 1699.[37]   He was designated "in Springhall" on 1 June 1699.[38]   The
last years of his life seem to have been spent in the neighborhood of Aberdeen, at Kingswells, the seat of the Quaker Andrew Jaffray.

Issue of David Falconar by his wife Margaret Molleson:[39]

	i.	Margaret Falconar, born 12 vii [September] 1673, died 28 ii [April] 1676.
	ii.	Christian Falconar, born 5 vii [September] 1674, died 16 ix [November] 1675.
H2	iii.	John Falconar, born 11 i [March] 1677.
	iv.	David Falconar, born 15 ii [April] 1678, died 20 ii [April] 1689.
	v.	Margaret Falconar, born 16 iii [May] 1679, living 14 v [July] 1697, when she and her mother signed an epistle from women Friends in Aberdeen.[40]
	vi.	Robina Falconar, born 15 i [March] 1682, died 16 v [July] 1683.
	vii.	Robert Falconar, born 16 xii [February] 1683, died ix [November] 1685 in the Mearns.
J1	viii.	Gilbert Falconar, merchant of Kent County, Maryland, born 30 iv [June] 1686.
	ix.	Helen Falconar, born 14 iv [June] 1688.
	x.	Jane Falconar, born about 1690. She, "son [sic] of David Falconer, merchant of Aberdeen," was apprenticed in the Drapers Company to her uncle Gilbert Molleson, citizen draper of London, on 16 February 1703, for seven years.[41] She received a certificate of clearness for Pennsylvania on 12 i [March] 1710/

11.[42]   She was appointed executrix of the will of William Smeaton, mariner, whose will was proved in Anne Arundel County, Maryland, in 1730.[43]   She married,[44] as his second wife, after 1730, Simon Wilmer of Kent County, Maryland, son of Simon and Rebecca (Tilghman) Wilmer, born 25 September 1686, died 1737.

K1   xi.   Alexander Falconar, born about 1693.

J2   **John Falconar** was born 11 i [March] 1677 in Edinburgh, Scotland, and died 2 xi [January] 1729/30 at his house in St. Martin's Lane, Cannon Street, London.[45]

He married, 6 September 1705, in London,[46] Anna Quare, daughter of Daniel Quare, clockmaker of London, by his wife Mary Steevens. She was born 18 ix [November] 1686 in St. Mary Woolnooth, London, and died 3 v [July] 1711 in St. Dunstans in the East, London. Her father was a noted watch and clock maker, with professional connections to the Court. As a result, the wedding guests included not only eminent Quakers such as William Penn and George Whitehead, but also diplomats, merchants, and noblemen, from Venice, Florence, Hanover, Portugal, the Holy Roman Empire, Sweden, and Prussia.

John Falconar was apprenticed to his uncle Gilbert Molleson, citizen and draper of London, on 1 July 1691, for a term of seven years.[47]   Receiving his freedom of the company in 1698, he set out for Maryland. His father gave him power of attorney on 27 July 1699 to sell his tracts in New Jersey. He was already styled "of Maryland" on 20 January 1699/1700, when he, Robert Burnet, of New Jersey, gentleman, and Rip van Dam, of New York, merchant, received a power of attorney from Gilbert Molleson and Francis Palmer of London, factor, to collect debts from George Willoks. As attorney for his father, he sold 250 acres on the Manalpan River to Eliphalet Frazie, of Elizabeth Town, yeoman, for £50 sterling, on 9 May 1700. His cousin Robert Barclay of Urie gave a power of attorney on 1 September 1701 to him, then styled "of Sasifrax Merch[an]t in Maryland," and John Reid, of East New Jersey, to have 1000 acres in East Jersey, 120 acres at Barnegat, and 2 1/2 acres at Perth Amboy surveyed for his uncle John Molleson.[48]

As the proprietors surrendered political control of the colony of East New Jersey to the Crown in 1702, they appeared anxious to sell their property, and John Falconar acted in their behalf on several occasions. On 1 December 1702, he and John Molleson, the latter of Piscataqua, sold to John Reid of Hortencie, Monmouth County, 500 acres on Milstone Brook in Monmouth County. He acknowledged, as his father's attorney, a 500-acre tract on the Manalpan River, to be deducted out of Robert Barclay's proportion due him as a proprietor, on 15 January 1702/3. On 20 January 1702/3, he was attorney in two transactions: for Andrew Jaffray (Jeffry), "late of Kingswells, Scotland," he sold to John Johnston of East New Jersey, Esquire, for £82, 10s., New York currency, all his one-sixteenth interest in East New Jersey; and, with John Molleson of Piscataqua, for Robert Barclay of Urie, Esquire, he sold to John Johnston, for five shillings, his whole undivided one-twenty-fourth share, except one-tenth of the one-twenty-fourth share due him as a proprietor. The following day Falconar and Molleson sold Barclay's same share to Johnston for £1222, 4s., 6d., New York currency. On 26 January 1702/3, he, with John Molleson, was attorney for Robert Barclay of Urie, of the first part, and sole attorney for David Falconer, of the second part, as well as being a party of the third part, sold to Miles Forster, of Perth Amboy, merchant, ten acres on Ambo Point, for £25 in New York currency. He received powers of attorney on 16 xii [February] 1702/3 from Andrew Jaffray of Kingswells to sell his one-sixteenth interest, and, on 18 February 1702/3, from Alexander Galloway, merchant in Aberdeen, to recover all debts due his deceased father Andrew Galloway, merchant in Aberdeen.[49]

He first appears in the minutes of Cecil Monthly Meeting on 13 iii [May] 1702, when he and Philip Reason were appointed to make an inquiry concerning the clearness of William Makett, who desired a certificate for England. The Quaker traveler Samuel Bownas visiting Maryland in August 1702, was entertained by Falconar. The young factor, who Bownas called "John Faulkner, a young man from Scotland, who was then storekeeper in B. Bains and Co's. employ," urged Bownas to respond to a letter from the former Quaker George Keith, who was then in Maryland, preaching against his former beliefs. Falconar told Bownas "Keith would call the country together, and make much noise about it, as if we were afraid, etc., and it was best to nip his expectation in the bud."[50] At the Cecil meeting on 8 v [July] 1703, John Falconar requested a certificate, as he "intended for England."[51] His return, however, was delayed.

Anne Warner authorized him on 6 August 1703 as attorney to acknowledge a conveyance from her and George Warner, her husband, to Nicholas Waterman. On 24 February 1703/4, Andrew Toulson, of Cecil County, Maryland, planter, and Mary, his wife, sold to John Falconar, for 3120 pounds of tobacco, 40 acres on the south side of the Sassafras River, part of a tract called "Taylor's Neck." Thomas Howell, of Cecil County, gentleman, sold to John Falconar, "late of London but now resident in Cecil County," on 3 July 1704, "Williamston," a tract of 500 acres on Stoolepone Bay, and "The Pond," a 200-acre tract on Chesapeake Bay.[52]

He returned to London before 25 v [July] 1705, when he appeared at Peel Monthly Meeting with a certificate of clearness for marriage from Cecil Monthly Meeting.[53] With his brother Gilbert acting as his factor in Maryland, he now could build up his business with planters in that colony. He owned or hired a ship, *Falconar*, with Samuel Richardson, master, which, on 5 March 1708/9, was docked on the Severn River.[54] In 1709 he testified before Parliament about the growing season in "Virginia" and, with other leading merchants, petitioned to ease export duties on tobacco to France.[55] As France purchased all its British tobacco through a single London agent, it controlled the price of the commodity. The ledgers of those agents show his name as a source of their tobacco.[56] His was one of the larger houses; in 1719, he imported 913,272 pounds of tobacco.[57]   John Falconar could depend on a ready credit line from his kinsmen: on 6 October 1710, Sir Alexander Falconar of Glenfarquhar, Baronet, lent him £3000.[58]

He also attended to official business on behalf of Quakers in Scotland, Pennsylvania, and Maryland. He and other London Quakers, including Gilbert Molleson and David Barclay, wrote Friends at Aberdeen on 3 i 1712, informing them that William Penn delivered a petition to the Queen asking to rescind Aberdeen's law requiring burgesses to make oaths.[59]   Falconar and David Barclay wrote them on 20 vii 1713, asking requesting to be excused as correspondents, as they disagreed with them over an unspecified issue.[60] When the proprietorship of Maryland was returned to Lord Baltimore in 1715, London Friends appointed him, Theodore Eccleston, John Field, and Joseph Wyeth to present the application of Maryland Quakers to have "their antient priviledges."[61]   On 4 and 5 iii 1715, John Falconar, Samuel Waldenfield, William Armstead, and Daniel Phillips were appointed to be correspondents for Aberdeen Friends.[62]   James Steel, Secretary of Pennsylvania, requested him in 1719 and 1720 to settle with London residents holding titles to land in that colony.[63]   Aberdeen Friends resolved, in 1727, to limit their London correspondents, feeling they would be better served by restricting them to David Barclay and John Falconar.[64]

Surviving letters and account books of American merchants and planters reveal that his trade went beyond Maryland tobacco. James Alexander, of Perth Amboy, dealt with him,[65] as did James Logan, of Philadelphia, who exported animal skins to him between 1715 and 1722.[66]   Falconar worked with his cousin David Barclay in exporting cloth and clothing, as the papers of these merchants show. He also insured voyages between Philadelphia, the West Indies, and London. Robert "King" Carter, of Virginia, writing him that "you grow into my esteem,"[67] shipped him tobacco between 1727 and 1729. The Philadelphia merchant Samuel Powel felt that Falconar "was a man I had a great Value for."[68]

Although his business generally was successful, problems did arise. He was one of the many investors duped by the fraudulent scheme of the directors of the South Sea Company,[69] and when the bubble burst in 1720, transatlantic trade suffered. James Logan wrote to him on 27 July 1720 that "trade here has in general taken such an unhappy turn" and that "about one half of those [goods] thou shipt to me last year remain unsold."[70]   The market in tobacco was depressed through the following decade, and the Maryland legislature considered at various times laws which would improve the quality and regulate the quantity of the crop.[71]   In London, the merchants blamed the depression on the monopoly of the French agent as well as the irregular quality of the leaf. Falconar and Henry Darnall, the Maryland planter and member of the colony's council who was then in London, took an initiative in 1727 and 1728 to form a cartel of tobacco merchants which would fight the control of the French monopoly and lobby Parliament for favorable laws.[72] The following year planters exhibited their disunity towards this proposal in the columns of the *Maryland Gazette*.[73]   Although the wide open competition among the planters may have hampered such an attempt at organization, Falconar's untimely death at the beginning of 1730 removed the principal organizer of this scheme, and nothing more came of it.

His Quaker plainness apparently did not negate his need to assert his gentility. He received a grant of arms, on 13 August 1720, from the Lord Lyon, King of Arms, as "eldest lawfull son of David Falconer who was eldest lawfull son of Sr John Falconer Knight Master of the Mint at Edinb[urgh] who was third lawfull son of Sir Alexander Falconer of Halkerton baronet & brother german to Alexander Falconer first Lord Halkerton," as follows: Or, a hawk's head issuing from a heart proper betwixt three mollets azur on a bordure vert four bezants (for difference).[74]

His will, dated 14 August 1729, probated 2 January 1729/30, divided his estate equally among his four children, in accordance with Quaker fashion, giving 20 guineas each to his cousin David Barclay and friend Daniel Philips, "Doctor of Physick," and appointing them and his eldest son John executors and ordering them to collect his debts.[75] In 1738, John Falconar, Jr., stated that the net value of his father's estate was £9000 "and upwards,"[76] but it may have been as high as £24,000.[77]

Issue of John and Anna (Quare) Falconar:[78]

i.   Mary Falconar, born 13 i [March] 1706[/7], living in 1750. She married, on 24 February 1732/3, at St. Pancras, London, Thomas Gould, a banker (whose firm was the predecessor to Barclay's Bank) who had been declared bankrupt the month before.[79] They originally intended to be married in 1728.[80] She and John "Falkner" were witnesses at the marriage of William Penn III to their cousin Christian Forbes, 7 x [December] 1732, at Wandsworth, Surrey.[81] Issue, surname *Gould*: a. child, buried 19 March 1746/7 at St. Pancras; b. *Thomas*, baptized 2 April 1748 at Wandsworth, Surrey, living in 1776, as he received a bequest from his aunt Margaret.

ii. Margaret Falconar, born 13 xii [February] 1707[/8], died, testate, 13 iv [April] 1777 at St. Botolph Bishopsgate, London, was buried 22 iv [April] 1777 in Bunhill Fields Burial Ground.[82] On 17 xii [February] 1742/3,[83] she, "an agreeable Lady with a Fortune of £6000,"[84] married Robert Bell of London, hosier, citizen and long-bow string maker, son of Reynold and Jane Bell of Gill, Cumberland. Prior to her marriage, she had resided at Swarthmore, Lancashire.[85] From 1758, she was active as a Quaker minister.[86] Issue, surname *Bell*: a. *Robert*, born 27 xii [February] 1743/4, who married Mariam ——; b. *John*, born 15 xi [January] 1746/7, in America at the time she wrote her will on 21 November 1776; c. *Reynold*, born 5 iv [June] 1748, died young.

iii. John Falconar, born 17 i [March] 1708[/9], living 21 November 1776, probably the the "Mr. John Faulkner from Cheapside" buried 7 May 1783 in Bunhill Fields Burial Ground.[87] In 1726 he was probably in Maryland. He sailed to America in the Fall of 1729, staying in Philadelphia in September 1730,[88] but soon returned to London to collect debts due to his father's estate and to continue his mercantile business. He consigned one ship, *William and Katherine*, which was moored in the South River in Maryland on 22 May 1731. He hired another ship, the *John and Benjamin*, which was in the South River on 16 May 1732.[89] On 8 August 1733 he was declared bankrupt,[90] so after the ship returned to London, on 25 August 1733, its owners, James Taylor, a shipbuilder, and Henry Voght, sued Falconar and became assignees of his estate.[91] He clearly had already been in financial trouble by 28 May 1733, when James Alexander announced that he had received a power of attorney to sell a 500-acre tract on the Manalpan River in New Jersey which had been granted to David Falconar; it was sold at public auction on 15 November 1733.[92] Falconar petitioned the Treasury for remission of interest on tobacco bonds on 24 March 1735/6, and on 21 September 1736, his petition was granted.[93] In 1736/7, he sold property in Maryland which he had inherited from his father: on 20 February, he, David Barclay, and Daniel Phillips sold to Richard Bennett, of Wye River, Maryland, for £30, lot number 15 in New Town on the Chester River, Kent County, Maryland; and on 25 February, he alone sold the same property to Bennett for five shillings.[94] In October 1738, he and the other executors of his father's estate sued Abraham Falconar for £500 sterling, which Abraham's father Gilbert had bound to John Falconar, Sr., on 31 October 1721. They lost the case on appeal, on 17 October 1738.[95] John Falconar, Jr., does not appear in any of the London directories, and the course of his life after this date, including marriages or children, is uncertain. His sister Margaret Bell did bequeath him an annuity of £25 per annum for life, by her will dated 21 November 1776.[96]

The name of his wife, if any, has not been found. However, it may be appropriate here to introduce a complicating issue. Katharine (Barclay) Forbes, of Dublin, John's father's first cousin, made a bequest to her "cousin" David Falconer, by her will, dated 15 February 1758.[97] David Barclay, of Bush Hill, Middlesex, brother of Katharine Forbes and the executor of John Falconar, Sr.'s estate, bequeathed, by a codicil to his will, dated 2 December 1767, to a David Falconer, among many other bequests to friends and relatives, twenty guineas.[98] Since John's brother David had died without issue in 1752, we have to account for these one or two David Falconers. Perhaps Katharine was unaware that David had died earlier, or perhaps she confused him for his brother John. Other possibilities are that the intended legatee was David Falconer (A13), the London merchant, or even, especially in the second case, of David Falconar (F2), who lived in London in 1770. Thus the first impression offered by these two wills, that the David Falconer mentioned was part of this branch, seems to be wrong. If he were, he is somewhat of a phantom, as Quaker registers do not indicate that John married or had children. Moreover, Church of England parish registers do show marriages in London and its environs which may refer to this John Falconar, but the same sources, as indexed in the International Genealogical Index, do not show possible children, a David Falconar in particular. Finally, Margaret Bell's 1777 will remembers many relatives on both sides of her family, but does not mention a David Falconer. If we can accept the explanations for their identities offered above, then it is easier to assume that John died childless and unmarried, as evidence seems to imply.

iv.   David Falconar, merchant of London, born 8 vi [August] 1710, died unmarried, shortly before 25 June 1752. At the time of his father's death he was in Newfoundland,[99] and likely had spent some of his youth in Philadelphia.[100] He became a merchant in the Levant Company. For some time before 1750, he lived at Constantinople, trading manufactured "bagatelles" from Britain for cotton from Smyrna.[101] In 1750, he was in London, associated in the insurance business with Richard Glover, whom he appointed executor of his will on 19 October 1750. In the will, which was proved 25 June 1752, he gave all his estate to his unnamed "Brother and Sisters."[102] In 1751, he travelled to Acre, Jaffa, and Jerusalem, and following his death, the journal of his trip was published. In it, he commented: "'Tis altogether the very worst country I ever saw."[103]

NOTES

[1] That he was the eldest can be proved by: Scotland, Lord Lyon, Public Register of All Arms and Bearings in Scotland, 1: 305; Watson, *Roll of Edinburgh Burgesses, 1406-1700*, p. 177; and Sibilla Ogilvy's testament.

[2] Quakers numbered their months rather than calling them by their names; although Scotland used the Gregorian calendar at that time, Scottish Quakers appear to have numbered months as if they used the Julian calendar, as in England, where March was the first month.

[3] W. F. Miller, "The Record Book of Friends of the Monethly Meeting at Urie," *Journal of the Friends Historical Society* 9 (Sept. 1910): 92.

[4] Society of Friends in Scotland, Quarterly Meeting, Digests of Births, Marriages, and Deaths, Friends Historical Library, London.

[5] Quarterings of the Molleson family, Barclay of Bury Hill Mss, Friends Historical Society Library, London.

[6] St. Nicholas Parish Register.

[7] Miller, "The Record Book of Friends of the Monethly Meeting at Urie," 9 (Dec. 1910): 186. For the Mollesons, see Donald Whyte and Paul M. Gifford, "Early Mollisons in Aberdeen," *Aberdeen & North East Scotland Family History Society Journal* 32 (Autumn 1989): 3-9; 34 (Spring 1990): 2-11.

[8] Discharge of David Falconar, Moses Bundle 254/7731, Edinburgh District Archives; Register of the Privy Seal, PS1/114, f. 9, SRO.

[9] Cochran-Patrick, *Records of the Coinage of Scotland*, 2: 130f.

[10] Case between David Falconar and Sir John Falconar, Moses Bundle 254/7734, Edinburgh District Archives.

[11] Register of Deeds, RD2/3, p. 402, SRO.

[12] Case between David Falconar and Sir John Falconar, Moses Bundle 254/7734, Edinburgh District Archives.

[13] Watson, *Roll of Edinburgh Burgesses, 1406-1700*, p. 177.

[14] Moses Bundle 254/7731, Edinburgh District Archives.

[15] W. F. Miller, "A Dictionary of All Names of Persons Mentioned in the Meeting Books belonging to Edinburgh Yearly Meeting of the Society of Friends," f. 81, MS., Friends Historical Library, London.

[16] *Register of the Privy Council of Scotland*, 3rd ser., 1: 528f.

[17] John Russell, *The Haigs of Bemersyde: A Family History* (Edinburgh: William Blackwood, 1881), p. 278n.

[18] Kincardine Sheriff Court Books, cited in: *Scots Peerage*, 9: 123n.

[19] Miller, "Record Book of Friends of the Monethly Meeting at Urie," p. 92.

[20] *Register of the Privy Council of Scotland*, 3rd ser., 2: 376.

[21] Louise B. Taylor, ed., *Aberdeen Council Letters*, (London: Oxford Univ. Press, 1957), 5: 6f.

[22] Munro, "Aberdeen Burgess Register," p. 435.

[23] Miller, "Dictionary of All Names of Persons Mentioned in the Meeting Books belonging to Edinburgh Yearly Meeting of the Society of Friends," f. 81, Friends Historical Library.

[24] Taylor, *Aberdeen Council Letters*, 6: 30, 48.

[25] Miller, "Dictionary of All Names of Persons Mentioned in the Meeting Books belonging to Edinburgh Yearly Meeting of the Society of Friends," f. 81f., Friends Historical Library.

[26] "Notes on Edinburgh Meeting Houses," *Journal of the Friends Historical Society* 6 (Jan. 1909): 30.

[27] Accounts between Sir John Falconar and Lord Halkerton, Moses Bundle 254/7769, Edinburgh District Archives.

[28] Robert Barclay to Sir John Falconar, 25 v 1682, 27 vi 1682, Moses Bundle 254/7793a, Edinburgh District Archives.

[29] Court of Session Processes, CS181/2043, SRO.

[30] Register of Deeds, RD4161, fol. 1103ff., SRO.

[31] East Jersey Deeds, A: 105, 106, 230; D: 124, 324; H: 2.

[32] *Documents Relating to the Colonial History of the State of New Jersey*, William Nelson, ed. (Archives of the State of New Jersey, 1st ser., vol. 1), pp. 466f., 508ff. Hereafter as *Archives of the State of New Jersey*.

[33] There was a Robert Bridgeman, merchant, who went to New Jersey, in 1685; James, William, and Maurice Trent, sons of Maurice Trent, the Leith merchant and father-in-law of Sir James Falconer of Phesdo (V2), settled in New Jersey and Pennsylvania.

[34] Patrick Sandilands to Sir John Falconer, 29 Aug. 1683, Moses Bundle 254, Edinburgh District Archives.

[35] Miller, "Dictionary," f. 82.

[36] Register of Deeds, RD4/74, p. 1314, SRO.

[37] Register of Deeds, RD 4/113, SRO.

[38] Register of Deeds, RD4/85, f. 394, SRO.

[39] Society of Friends in Scotland, Quarterly Meeting, Digests of Births, Marriages, and Deaths, Friends Historical Library. The Quaker wedding was considered illegal, as a clandestine marriage. But under Scots law, this was a marriage by declaration *de praesenti*, and thus the children would be legitimate. See Patrick Fraser, *Treatise on Husband and Wife, according to the Law of Scotland*, 2nd ed. (Edinburgh: T. & T. Clark, 1876), 1: 294.

[40] Box Meeting MSS, 1671-1753, f. 47, Friends Historical Library.

[41] Register of Royal Company of Drapers; "son" was probably a mistranslation of the Latin *fil.*, an abbreviation for *filia*, or daughter.

[42] London Two-weeks Meeting minutes, Friends Historical Library.

[43] Maryland Testamentary Proceedings, 29: 158.

[44] Maryland Inventories, 21: 423.

[45] Society of Friends in England, Quarterly Meeting Digests, Friends Historical Library; *The Political State of Great Britain* 39 (1730): 106.

[46] Society of Friends in England, Devonshire House Meeting minutes.

[47] Records of the Drapers' Company, London.

[48] East Jersey Deeds, G: 65, 64, 103; H: 95.

[49] Ibid., H: 90, 73, 23, 51, 53, 173, 33, 35.

[50] "An Account of the Life, Travels, and Christian Experiences of Samuel Bownas," *Friends' Library: Comprising Journals, Doctrinal Treatises and Other Writings*, vol. 8 (Philadelphia: Joseph Rakestraw, 1839), pp. 21f.

[51] Cecil Monthly Meeting minutes, 2: 130, 138, photostatic copy at Maryland Historical Society.

[52] Cecil Co. (Md.) Deeds, I: 308, 351, 421.

[53] Society of Friends in England, Peel Monthly Meeting minutes, Friends Historical Library.

[54] John M. Hemphill, "Freight Rates in the Maryland Tobacco Trade: Appendix," *Maryland Historical Magazine* 54 (June 1959): 154f.

[55] Leo F. Stock, ed., *Proceedings and Debates of the British Parliament Respecting North America*, vol. 3: 1702-1727, (Washington: Carnegie Institution, 1930), p. 310.

[56] Jacob M. Price, *France and the Chesapeake: A History of the French Tobacco Monopoly, 1674-1791, and of Its Relationship to the British and American Tobacco Trades* (Ann Arbor: University of Michigan Press, 1973), 1: 533f.

[57] Information from Jacob M. Price, Professor of History, University of Michigan.

[58] Bond, given in 8 Jan. 1720, Bundle 90, Kintore Papers, Aberdeen University Library.

[59] Aberdeen Monthly Meeting records, CH10/3/64, SRO.

[60] Ibid., CH10/3/65, SRO.

[61] Minutes of Meeting for Suffering, 21: 390, 397, quoted by Kenneth L. Carroll, "Quaker Opposition to the Establishment of a State Church in Maryland," *Maryland Historical Magazine* 65 (Summer 1970): 169.

[62] Aberdeen Monthly Meeting records, CH10/3/65, SRO.

[63] James Steel, Letter Books, 10 iii 1719; 22 iv 1720, Historical Society of Pennsylvania.

[64] W. F. Miller, "Gleanings from the Records of Aberdeen Yearly Meeting, 1672-1786," *Journal of the Friends Historical Society*, 8 (June 1911): 66n.

[65] James Alexander, Account Book, 1: 214, 248, New Jersey Historical Society.

[66] James Logan, Parchment Letter Book, 1712-15, p. 290; Letter Books, 4; 12, 14, 17, 24, 26, 39, 43, 52, 74; Letter Book, 1717-31, pp. 14, 22, 26, 33, 34, 48, 52, 57, 59, 62, 74, 78, 104, 139, 201, 271, Historical Society of Pennsylvania.

[67] Carter Letter Books, 24 July 1727; 22 Aug. 1727; 9 July 1728; 23 July 1728; 27 June 1729; 14 July 1729, Virginia Historical Society.

[68] Samuel Powel to Thomas Hyam, 20 iii 1730, Samuel Powel Letterbook, 1727-1739, Historical Society of Pennsylvania.

[69] Chancery, C11/1731/21, PRO.

[70] Logan, Letter Book, 1717-31, p. 139, Historical Society of Pennsylvania.

[71] Vertrees J. Wyckoff, *Tobacco Regulation in Colonial Maryland*, Johns Hopkins University Studies in Historical and Political Science, n.s., 22 (Baltimore: Johns Hopkins Press, 1936), pp. 127-147.

[72] Henry Darnall, *A Just and Impartial Account of the Transactions of the Merchants in London, for the Advancement and Price of Tobacco, about the Latter End of the Year 1727, and Beginning of 1728* (Annapolis, Md.: W. Parks, 1728), most material in this pamphlet being written by Falconar.

[73] Wyckoff, *Tobacco Regulation in Colonial Maryland*, pp. 138-139.

[74] Scotland, Lord Lyon, Public Register of All Arms and Bearings in Scotland, 1: 305.

[75] Prerogative Court of Canterbury Wills.

[76] Chancery, C11/2459/29, PRO.

[77] His daughter Margaret was described as having a fortune of £6000, according to a news clipping dated 1743 in "Corrigenda to the Cambridge Edition of 'The Journal of George Fox'," *Journal of the Friends Historical Society* 10

(1911):: 50.

[78]Society of Friends in England, Devonshire House meeting minutes, Friends Historical Library.

[79]*Gentleman's Magazine,* 3 (Jan. 1733).

[80]William Rolfe to Samuel Powel, 20 Apr. 1728, John Taylor to Samuel Powel, 14 Aug. 1728, Powel Family Papers, Historical Society of Pennsylvania.

[81]Howard M. Jenkins, "The Family of William Penn," *Pennsylvania Magazine of History and Biography* 22 (1898): 172.

[82]Testimony concerning Margaret Bell, Devonshire House Monthly Meeting, Temp MSS 4/20, Friends Historical Library.

[83]Ratcliff Monthly Meeting, English Quarterly Meeting digests, Friends Historical Library.

[84]*Journal of the Friends Historical Society,* 10 (1913): 50.

[85]Swarthmore Monthly Meeting register, Friends Historical Library.

[86]Testimony, Temp MSS 4/20, Friends Historical Library.

[87]Bunhill Fields Burial Ground Register, RG4/3986, PRO. Bunhill Fields was the Non-conformist burying ground for London; the residence of David Barclay was in Cheapside.

[88]Samuel Powel to John Falconar, 16 May 1729; Samuel Powel to David Barclay, 20 iii 1730, in Samuel Powel Letterbook, 1727-1739, Historical Society of Pennsylvania.

[89]Hemphill, "Freight Rates in the Maryland Colonial Trade," pp. 170f., 172f.

[90]Bankrupts Docket Book, B/4/7, f. 254, PRO; also Anne Arundel Co. (Md.) Deeds, RD#2: 282.

[91]Taylor and Voght v. Falconar, Chancery C11/1891/39, PRO.

[92]*Archives of the State of New Jersey,* 1st ser., 11: 315, 328.

[93]Great Britain, Treasury, *Calendar of Treasury Books and Papers, 1735-1738,* prepared by William A. Shaw (London: H.M. Stationery Office, 1900), pp. 213, 232.

[94]Kent Co. (Md.) Deeds, JS#18: 439, 436.

[95]Maryland Provincial Court, EJ#5: 4f.

[96]Will of Margaret Bell, P.C.C., PROB 11/1030/148, PRO.

[97]Irish Prerogative Court, in: R. Burnham Moffat, *The Barclays of New York* (New York: n.p., 1904), p. 25. The original will was presumably lost in the 1921 fire.

[98]Copy of will, Gurney of Bawdeswell Collection, Norfolk and Norwich Record Office.

[99]John Taylor to Samuel Powel, 27 Mar. 1729, Powel Family Papers, Historical Society of Pennsylvania.

[100]David Falconar to Charles Norris, 1 May 1750, Norris Papers, Historical Society of Pennsylvania, where he greets Norris's sister "Debby."

[101]Ibid. This letter establishes his identity, as he sent greetings to his "cousin Sanny" [Alexander] Barclay at Philadelphia, and mentioned Richard Glover.

[102]Prerogative Court of Canterbury, PROB 11/795, 1752.

[103]David Falconar, *A Journey from Joppa to Jerusalem in 1751* (London: E. Comyns, 1753), p. 36.

CHAPTER J

Gilbert Falconar of Maryland

J1 **Gilbert Falconar**, second son of David Falconar, Quaker merchant of Aberdeen and Edinburgh (H1), by his wife Margaret Molleson, born 30 iv [June] 1686 in Edinburgh,[1] died intestate shortly before 24 April 1736, when Hannah Falconar was bound to Simon Wilmer and James Calder to administer his estate, in Kent County, Maryland.[2]

He married, on 12 xi [January] 1709/10, in Philadelphia, Pennsylvania, Hannah Hardiman, daughter of Abraham and Diana (Thomas) Hardiman of Philadelphia.[3] She died 12 x [December] 1748.[4] This marriage connected him to such prominent Philadelphia merchants as Samuel Carpenter (Hannah's aunt's husband), George Fitzwater, and George Claypoole (husbands of Hannah's sisters).[5]

Gilbert was apprenticed, on 25 June 1702, to his uncle Gilbert Molleson, citizen draper of London, for a term of seven years.[6] He witnessed Gilbert Molleson's signature on 15 April 1702, as one of the proprietors of East New Jersey, of the surrender of the government of that colony to the Crown.[7] He broke the terms of his apprenticeship, however, and followed his brother to America. On 24 February 1703/4, he witnessed a deed from Andrew Toulson of Cecil County, Maryland, and Mary, his wife, to John Falconar.[8]

When John Falconar returned to London for his marriage in 1705, Gilbert stayed behind in Maryland. He was of "Sassafrax" River, Maryland, on 23 September 1707, when he received a power of attorney from Gilbert Molleson.[9] On 20 October 1707, he quitclaimed, on behalf of Gilbert Molleson, 140 ares to his other uncle John Molleson, of Piscataqua, Middlesex County, East New Jersey, planter.[10] He lived in Kent County, Maryland, on 29 May 1709, when he acted as attorney for John Falconar in the sale of "Exchange," a tract of 100 acres on the south side of the Sassafras River, for which the latter had received a patent on 10 July 1704, to Richard Scaggs, of Kent County, for 3000 pounds of tobacco.[11] Gilbert applied to Cecil Monthly Meeting on 14 vii [September] 1709 for a certificate, as he intended to move to Philadelphia and marry.[12]

His stay in Philadelphia was short. He requested a certificate on 27 viii

[October] 1710, as he was to go to Great Britain,[13] but he returned to the city by 9 v [July] 1712, when he and his wife, Samuel Carpenter, George Fitzwater and Mary, his wife, Deborah Hardiman, all of Philadelphia, heirs of Abraham Hardiman, late of Philadelphia, weaver, sold property to William Fishbourne of Philadelphia, merchant.[14] On 26 xii [February] 1713/4, Hannah Falconar requested a certificate with her husband, as they were about to move again, and, on 26 iv [June] 1714, they received a certificate from Philadelphia Yearly Meeting to Kennett Monthly Meeting.[15] While a resident of the region of Pennsylvania covered by the Kennett Monthly Meeting, he sold, on 2 August 1714, by a power of attorney from his brother John dated 22 September 1707, to William Clay, of Kent County, Maryland, "Williamston," of 500 acres, and "The Pond."[16]

Gilbert's next residence was in the bustling port of New Castle, Delaware. He had received powers of attorney in 1713 and 1714 from Elizabeth Hilton and Samuel Arnold to buy and sell land there. On 8 iv [June] 1715, he and Jasper Yeats petitioned the Board of Property of Pennsylvania for a grant of the marsh at the southwest end of the town of New Castle, which they agreed to drain as a public health measure.[17] A warrant was issued to them ten days later and on 2 May 1717, a survey of the marsh was made for Gilbert Falconar and platted into six lots, consisting of ten acres. He had 330 acres on Blackbird Creek surveyed for his heirs, on 14 February 1714/5, and received a warrant for 40 acres on the branches of Appoquinimink Creek on 28 March 1715 and a survey for two tracts of 176 acres and 50 acres on 29 April 1715.[18] Isaac Norris, the wealthy Quaker merchant of Philadelphia, sold Gilbert a house and lot in New Castle facing the Delaware River, on 16 October 1716.[19] He did not remain there long, although he clearly intended to conduct much of his trade from New Castle.

He purchased "Henberry," a 900-acre tract on the north side of the head of the Chester River in Kent County, Maryland, from Andrew Hamilton, who had accepted the appointment of Attorney General of Pennsylvania, on 16 September 1717.[20] This was to be his home until his death. He acquired two patents, "Edinburgh," a 1074-acre tract in Queen Anne's County near the Delaware border, in 1722; and "The Hope," of 210 acres, in Kent County, in 1725.[21] His brother John sold him, for the token sum of two shillings, on 21 December 1722, a 40-acre tract on the south side of the Sassafras River, part of "Terson's Neck," which John had purchased in 1703.[22] From these regular purchases of land, some being on navigable coastal rivers and hence valuable, we can conclude that his business between 1714 and 1725 was profitable.

We can get some idea of his commercial endeavors from the letter books of James Logan, the Quaker Secretary of Pennsylvania and merchant, and from the accounts between him and Richard Bennett, of Wye River, Maryland's richest merchant-planter. Between 1717 and 1719, Logan and Gilbert Falconar formed partnerships for the export of skins from the Indian trade to England. In 1717, Gilbert purchased over £100 of Indian goods from Bennett. John Falconar was one of Logan's chief correspondents between 1717 and 1720, insuring his cargo on voyages between Philadelphia, Jamaica, and England, and shipping cloth, clothing, iron, and nails to Philadelphia.[23]

Logan complained to John Falconar about the quality of the goods, urging him to deal with other drapers than "D[avid] B[arclay] & company," about whom, he remarked, Gilbert "had no very good opinion."[24] Gilbert's imports were probably much the same, but he probably sold them to shopkeepers in New Castle and planters in Maryland. The partnerships ended in 1719, when Gilbert disputed the finances of a particular venture; thereafter Logan and Gilbert Falconar remained on bad terms.[25]

Richard Bennett traded extensively with Gilbert Falconar. Between 1715 and 1726, Gilbert sold him such items as gloves, satin and linen, beer, and barrels of herring, paying Bennett for goods both in cash and bills of exchange on John Falconar. On 31 March 1721, Gilbert Falconar agreed to purchase from Bennett three parcels of land at the head of Chester River: "Goosehaven," of 500 acres; part of "Partnership," of 300 acres; and part of "London Bridge," of 650 acres.[26] The price was £156 sterling and a 40-acre parcel on the Sassafras River, "Terson's Neck." Bennett sold the land to Gilbert on 19 November 1724 for £150 sterling and Gilbert sold "Terson's Neck" to Bennett on 4 January 1724/5.[27] The ownership of these tracts remained contested for two further generations, as Gilbert became indebted even more to Bennett.

Although the balance of trade between the two men stayed in Bennett's favor after 1720, Bennett continued to do business with Falconar. Perhaps the latter's family connections mitigated any doubts Bennett had regarding Falconar's ultimate ability to pay. They halted business in 1726, but in 1730 resumed their association as partners in the sale of a "cargo" of slaves. On 22 October, Gilbert Falconar, in a letter to Bennett, thanked him for advancing his share of the debt due to the London merchants.[28] Falconar, one year later, had not paid this substantial debt, and, on 11 January 1731/2, he acknowledged a debt to Bennett of £178, 15s., 1d. sterling; £186, 3s., 10d. current money; and 1305 pounds of tobacco.[29] Bennett never received any payment while Gilbert was alive, and the debt increased at an annual interest rate of six percent. Considering the size of the debt, it is rather curious that on 20 August 1733, Alexander Falconar mortgaged land to Gilbert Falconar and Richard Bennett (see below).

In the declining years of his life, his land transactions reveal his attempts to reverse his losses, despite his failure to pay his debts to Bennett. On 7 March 1726/7, he sold, to Sarah Holt, of New Castle County, Delaware, widow, a tract of 104 acres in Reddyon Hundred in New Castle County.[30] He sold 110 acres of "The Hope" to Benjamin Parsons, of Kent County, carpenter, for £29, on 20 June 1728. On 19 June 1730, he sold a house and lot, bounded on the Delaware River, in New Castle, to Joseph Parker, of New Castle, yeoman, for £78. To Richard Grafton, of New Castle, merchant, he sold two parcels of marshland at the south end of the town of New Castle, for 5 shillings and £15, on 1 and 2 May 1731.[31] He mortgaged a moiety of "London Bridge" on 25 May 1734 to Benjamin Tasker, of Annapolis, Esquire, for £53, 15s., 5½d.[32] Finally, on 15 January 1735/6, he sold to Francis Spearman, of Kent County, for 15,000 pounds of tobacco, 300 acres of "Partnership."[33]

As one might expect, Gilbert Falconar strongly supported the Penns in the dispute with the recent Scotch-Irish settlers over the proprietorship of Delaware. From Dover, on 19 January 1735/6, he urged Thomas Penn to "oblige the people and assert thy own just rights" by removing the locally appointed Prothonotary Hugh Durbrow.[34]

Gilbert never left the Society of Friends, but his participation declined after he moved to Maryland. In the minutes of Cecil Monthly Meeting, he appears as a witness to weddings, but otherwise his presence is scant. The presence of three "old" wigs in the inventory of his estate certainly would indicate a lack of commitment to plainness.

He died intestate. On 17 May 1736, Giden Pearse and Jerves Spencer took an inventory of his personal estate, appraising it at £399, 17s., 11d. It included eleven slaves, silver plate, and two old Bibles and "sundry old Books," and listed "nearest of kin" as Jane Wilmer and "A. Falconer."[35] Hannah then paid part of her late husband's debts to Richard Bennett, although the latter, convinced of Gilbert's son Abraham's "villainy,"[36] eventually brought suit against Abraham in Maryland Provincial Court. At the New Castle County (Delaware) Orphan's Court, on 21 February, in the 17th year of George II's reign [1743/4], Abraham and John Falconar and James Whittington and Christian, his wife, prayed for an order for the sale of Gilbert Falconar's real estate to discharge his debts.[37]

Issue of Gilbert and Hannah (Hardiman) Falconar:

J2   i.   Abraham Falconar, eldest son.

     ii. Margaret Falconar. She and her mother Hannah were witnesses at the marriage of William Frew and Hannah Bodien, 28 ix [November] 1730, at the Cecil Monthly Meeting.[38] In her will, dated 18 May 1738, proved 1 June 1738 in Kent County, Maryland, she bequeathed to her mother Hannah Falconar a Negro woman named Sue, a Negro man named Will, and a Negro boy Ishmal; to her brother Abraham, one shilling sterling; to her brother John, one pair of gold sleeve buttons and a silver seal; to her mother she gave all her moveable estate, except one riding mare, which she gave to her sister Christian Falconar. She named her mother to be her executrix. Her will was sealed with Falconer of Halkerton arms.[39]

J3 iii. John Falconar.

    iv. Christian Falconar, died before 1 December 1767 in Kent County, Maryland.[40] She married James Whittington, who died before 13 July 1767 in Kent County, Maryland.[41] Her next of kin were listed as Gilbert Whittington and Jane Whittington; the administrator of her estate was John Whittington.

J2 Abraham Falconar, born perhaps about 1715, died intestate shortly before 29 July 1754 in Kent County, Maryland.[42]

He married Elizabeth Barnes, daughter of William and Ann Barnes of Kent County, Delaware. She died intestate shortly before 26 July 1765, when Gilbert Falconar was bound to administer her estate.[43]

In order to protect the inheritance of his father's lands from the claims of Richard Bennett, he, rather deviously, sold to his father-in-law William Barnes, on 26 February 1741[/2], "Henberry," "Goosehaven," "Partnership," and part of "London Bridge," with a combined acreage of 1725 acres, for the sum of £30 in Maryland currency.[44] Bennett sued Falconar in Maryland Provincial Court in September 1744 for recovery of the debt owed to him by Abraham as heir to his father Gilbert. Bennett had heard that Falconar would offer a forged receipt from Bennett and was gossiping that Bennett was a "very riged cruell man to debtors" and had taken almost everything from his mother, including "twelve Negroes, all her houshold goods and cattle, and hardly prevail'd with to leave her a bed to lye on and cow to give milk."[45] The Provincial Court in 1747 ordered the sheriff of Kent County to sell the lands, but he found no buyers, and on 5 October 1748 he sold them to Abraham for the debt to Bennett and court costs. On 6 October 1748 Falconar and William Barnes mortgaged these lands to Bennett for the original debt. By his will, written in 1751, William Barnes bequeathed the lands to Abraham, with a consideration that if Abraham paid Barnes's four youngest daughters £300, he should have the whole of the lands. Edward Lloyd, executor of the Bennett estate, brought a bill in Maryland Chancery Court in 1752 to foreclose the mortgage, and in February 1753, the court granted a decree of foreclosure against Falconar. Falconar died without paying his debt.[46]

Abraham served in the Lower House of the Maryland legislature from 1751 to 1754. He was styled "gentleman."[47]

Issue of Abraham and Elizabeth (Barnes) Falconar, born in Shrewsbury Parish, Kent County, Maryland:[48]

J4   i.   Gilbert Falconar, born 20 March 1741[/2].

      ii.   Sarah Falconar, born 6 July 1743. She married Robert Evans,[49] probably of Cecil County, Maryland.

      iii.   Hannah Falconar, born 17 January 1744/5, died about 1791-1793 in Kent County, Maryland. She married Jacob Comegys, son of Cornelius Comegys, born about 1736 in Kent County, Maryland, died 1805 in Berkeley County, (West) Virginia and had issue, surname *Comegys*:[50] a. *William*, born 1772, died 1844, married, 21 June 1800, Sarah Morgan; b. *Charlotte*, married, 18 January 1798, Wilson Athey; c. *Nancy*, married, 3 August 1803, Joseph Cross; d. *Deborah*, married, 12 February 1807, John Cross; e. *John*, born 29 December 1784, married, 26 April 1810, Elizabeth Marshall; f. *Hannah*, born 8 November 1786, died 21 June 1865 in Seneca County, Ohio, married, 23 March 1810, in Berkeley County, Virginia, William Warner; g. *Benjamin*, died 1856, married, 8 April 1811, Demaris V. Thompson.

      iv.   Ann Falconar, born 5 September 1746.

      v.   Priscilla Falconar, born 26 December 1747. She married William King.[51]

J5   vi.   Abraham Falconar, born 14 August 1749.

      vii.   Elizabeth Falconar, born 7 July 1752.

J3 **John Falconar**, born perhaps about 1720, probably in Kent County, Maryland, died between 14 March and 5 November 1767 in Queen Anne's County, Maryland.

He married Catharine Barnes, daughter of William and Ann Barnes and sister of Elizabeth, wife of his brother Abraham.[52] She died shortly before 8 March 1768 in Queen Anne's County.[53]

He was an innkeeper and planter. He acquired, between 1747 and 1754, several patents for land in Kent County: "London Derry," of 70 acres; "Falconer's Adventure," of 995 acres; and "Falconer's Lott," of 35 acres.[54]

In his will, dated 14 March 1767, he gave to his wife Catharine all his real and personal estate, except the tenement where Sarah Massey lived, with two acres of land, as long as she remained his widow. When she died or married again, the estate would go to his two eldest (unnamed) daughters and to his son William, if he were of legal age, and they were to divide the estate equally among all his children. He gave to his son John, after his mother's death or marriage, 102 acres he bought from Christopher Spry, also 55 acres, part of "Friendship," which he had bought from Thomas Spry, and 24 acres he bought from Samuel Keene, part of two tracts, "Haybid" and "Addition." He gave to his son William, after his mother's death or marriage, all the remainder of his lands, except the above tenement with two acres of land, which was to be rented out for eighteen years for not less than £5 a year, the rents to pay for buildings to be built on his son John's land. He ordered that when John came of age, three vestrymen or churchwardens would appraise the buildings to see if the rents had been honestly made use of, for which the son William would pay them twenty shillings each. After eighteen years the tenement would pass to William, providing he had fulfilled this request. He gave to his daughters equal right and privilege in all his land as long as they were single. He ordered his sons to pay a yearly rent of £6 on all his lands equally to each of his daughters during their lives. He also authorized his wife to sell 204 acres to Christian Smith. Finally, he appointed his wife executrix of his will. The will was proved in court on 6 November 1767.[55]

Issue of John and Catharine (Barnes) Falconar, born in Shrewsbury Parish, Kent County, Maryland:[56]

	i.	Deborah Falconar, born 1 November 1746, died between 11 and 25 June 1794 in New Castle County, Delaware.[57] She married, as her first husband, George Blackshare, son of Randal and Eve Blackshare, of Kent County, Delaware. He died shortly before 23 January 1772, in Kent County, Delaware.[58] Issue, surname *Blackshare*: a. daughter, married George Ward, who later married Anna Falconer. Her second husband was —— White, whom she survived.
	ii.	Martha Falconar, born 25 December 1748. Not further traced.
J6	iii.	William Falconar, born 28 January 1753.
	iv.	Ann Falconar, born 28 June 1755. She received a bequest by the will of James Smith, of Worton, Kent County, Maryland, dated 29 April 1775. She was unmarried in 1796, when named as a debtor to John Vansant.[59]
	v.	Margaret Falconar, born 20 November 1757, died before 4 February 1769.
	vi.	Anna Falconar, born 14 September 1759. She married, as her first husband, Charles White, of New Castle County, Delaware, who died shortly before 4 November 1793.[60] Issue, surname *White*: a. *William.* She married, as her second husband by bond dated 20 November 1795, George Ward, who administered Charles White's estate.[61]
	vii.	John Falconar. He died between 14 March 1767 and 4 February 1769 without issue.

J4 Gilbert Falconar, born 20 March 1741[/2] in Shrewsbury Parish, Kent County, Maryland, died March 1788 in Kent County, Maryland.[62]

His first wife was Mary Hazel, daughter of Benjamin and Sarah Hazel, born 27 January 1746, in Shrewsbury Parish, Kent County, Maryland.[63]

His second wife was Mary ——, niece of Charlotte Griffith. She was alive

23 July 1823, though a "lunatic" since about 1784.[64]

He received a license for an ordinary (i.e., tavern) in Kent County, on 31 August 1770. In 1771, Gilbert recovered the lands "Henberry," "Goosehaven," "Partnership," and part of "London Bridge," which had been disputed for almost 40 years. Gilbert was styled "gentleman" or "farmer" in deeds. He served as a captain of militia on the colonial side during the Revolution.[65]

Issue of Gilbert and Mary (Hazel) Falconar, born in Kent County, Maryland:[66]

    i.   Abraham Falconar. He survived his father, but by 15 July 1794, had died "beyond sea intestate and without issue."[67]

    ii.   Benjamin Falconar,[68] died without issue.[69]

    iii. Priscilla Falconar. She was living on 15 July 1794, unmarried.[70]

Issue of Gilbert and Mary (——) Falconar, born in Kent County, Maryland:[71]

    iv.   Charlotte Falconar, born about 1773, died before 23 July 1825. She married Richard Moffett, son of Richard and Mary Moffett, born 17 March 1762 in Shrewsbury Parish, Kent County, Maryland.[72]

    v.   Mary Falconar, born about 1775, living in Delaware in 1794.[73] She married David Webb. Webb petitioned in 1825 to be made trustee of the estate of Mary's mother, in the place of Richard Moffett, who he called "intemperate" and "unfit" to take care of the duties.[74]

    vi.   Juliana Falconar, born about 1788. She died before 23 July 1825, without leaving issue.

J5 Abraham Falconar, born 14 August 1749 in Shrewsbury Parish, Kent County, Maryland, died 31 January 1804 in Georgetown, Kent County, Maryland.[75]

On 27 October 1782,[76] he married Sarah Hall, daughter of Jonathan and Elizabeth (Seale) Hall, born 17 May 1760 in St. Luke's Parish, Queen Anne's County, Maryland.[77]

Abraham was a merchant in Baltimore and a planter in Kent County. He served as a captain of militia during the Revolution,[78] and as justice of the peace in 1788, in Queen Anne's County.[79] After independence, Baltimore's importance as a port increased, and his trade must have been prosperous. He was an original member of the Library Company of Baltimore, founded 8 January 1796.[80] His brig *Patriot*, on a voyage from Baltimore to Trinidad in 1796, with a cargo of flour, dry goods, and other merchandise, was captured by a French privateer, *La Fileuse*, commanded by Jean Valet, and sold as a prize by the French Prize Tribunal in the Windward Islands.[81] The loss he sustained must have almost ruined him, for his heirs petitioned the United States Congress for restitution twice, until finally receiving a settlement in 1888.

Issue of Abraham and Sarah (Hall) Falconar:[82]

 i. Elizabeth Falconar, born 8 August 1783, died, unmarried, 8 February 1858, "late of 83 Sharp St.," in Baltimore, Maryland.[83]

 ii. Sarah Falconar, born 15 October 1785, died shortly before 18 July 1859 in Baltimore, unmarried.[84]

 iii. Anna Falconar, born 17 December 1787, died shortly before 8 April 1842 in Baltimore, unmarried.[85]

 iv. Jonathan Hall Falconar, born 22 May 1790, died 11 March 1865 in Baltimore, Maryland.[86] From 19 August to 30 November 1814, he served as Quarter Master in Charles Pennington's Company, First Artillery Regiment. He also served as a lieutenant in that war.[87] From 1849 he worked as a clerk for the Baltimore & Ohio Railroad.[88] He apparently never married.

J7 v. Abraham Hall Falconar, born 29 January 1793.

 vi. Catharine Falconar, born 11 September 1795, died, unmarried, 6 April 1861 in Baltimore, Maryland.[89]

 vii. Caroline Falconar, born 10 February 1801, died, unmarried, 23 July 1863 in Baltimore, Maryland.[90]

J6 William Falconar, born 28 January 1753 in Shrewsbury Parish, Kent County, Maryland, died July 1790 in Queen Anne's County, Maryland.[91]

He married, as his first wife, Jane Massey, daughter of James and Jane (Spry) Massey of Kent County, Maryland, born 29 October 1751 in St. Luke's Parish, Queen Anne's County, Maryland.[92]

He married, as his second wife, after 14 April 1789, Jerusha, widow of Eleazar Massey. On 18 August 1791, she married William Miers.[93]

William was a substantial landowner in Queen Anne's and Kent Counties, styled "gentleman" and "planter." He signed an oath of fidelity to the American cause in 1778.[94] In 1790, Jerusha Falconer's property included 18 slaves.[95] William died, however, leaving an insufficient amount of personal property to cover a debt to Benjamin Comegys.[96]

Issue of William and Jane (Massey) Falconar, who spelled their name "Falconer," born in Queen Anne's County, Maryland:[97]

J8 i. Peregrine Falconer, born about 1776.

 ii. John Stuart Falconer, born 17 August 1777,[98] died 30 June 1854 in Montgomery, Alabama, buried in the Oakwood Cemetery.[99] He moved to South Carolina with his brother William in 1804. In 1817 he came to Montgomery; he held a quarter share in the plat of the town and built the first house there. Postmaster for many years, he later was a planter. He never married.[100] At the time of his death, he owned 1873 acres and 47 slaves.[101]

J9 iii. William Falconer, born 17 October 1780.

J10 iv. Joshua Falconer, born 8 September 1785.

 v. Ann Falconer, born 1786, buried 11 May 1806 at St. Paul's, Baltimore.

J7 **Abraham Hall Falconar**, born 29 January 1793 in Baltimore, Maryland, died intestate before 9 October 1848 in Baltimore, Maryland.[102]

He married, on 15 October 1818, at the Associate Reformed Church in Baltimore, Catharine Goff Cantwell, daughter of —— and Sarah Cantwell.[103] She died 16 February 1842 in Baltimore.[104]

He served as a private in Richard B. Magruder's Company, First Artillery Regiment, from 19 August to 30 November 1814.[105] He was a clerk, merchant, and owner of a textile mill. From 1815 to 1819 he was Grand Master of Corinthian Lodge of Masons.

Issue of Abraham Hall and Catharine Goff (Cantwell) Falconar, born in Baltimore, Maryland:[106]

J11   i.   John Henry Falconar, born 22 July 1819.

     ii.   Caroline Elizabeth Falconar, born 30 January 1822, died, unmarried, between 22 June and 6 July 1867 in Baltimore, Maryland.[107]

     iii.   Abraham Smith Falconar, born 1 September 1829,[108] died 15 April 1886 in Baltimore, Maryland, was buried in Greenmount Cemetery.[109] He married, on 12 November 1863,[110] Nancy Thomas Poultney, daughter of Samuel and Ellin Moale (Curson) Poultney, born 27 April 1837, died 22 July 1893.[111] He was an accountant and clerk for Thomas Poultney and Sons, a mercantile firm.[112] He and his wife had no issue.[113]

     iv.   Edward White Falconar, born 23 December 1831. John H. Falconar was appointed his guardian in 1848. During the Civil War, he served on the Confederate side as a private in Company C, 1st Maryland Infantry, and/or the Maryland American Rifles.[114] He was a clerk and was listed in Baltimore city directories up to 1870 as residing at 152 N. Eutaw St. He was single in 1860.[115] Not further traced, although the index to the 1870 census of Baltimore does not show him or a widow or family, and it appears probable that he died without issue.

J8 **Peregrine Falconer**, born about 1776 in Queen Anne's County, Maryland, died 24 February 1817 in Baltimore, Maryland.[116]

He married, on 1 November 1808 at St. Paul's Church, Baltimore, Elizabeth Levy, daughter of Levy Andrew and Susan (Scott) (Magruder) Levy, the former a Jewish merchant in the Indian fur trade who converted to Christianity.[117] She was born 3 October 1775 in Lancaster, Pennsylvania, and died 23 November 1856 in York, Pennsylvania.[118]

A merchant, Peregrine formed partnerships with Cornelius Comegys of Philadelphia, John Gleaves Comegys of Baltimore, and David Olden of Baltimore, among others. He was in St. Louis and Ste. Genevieve, Missouri, prior to 1808, to head a branch of the house of Pierce, Comegys, and Falconer. That year, they offered for sale to the Secretary of War 175,000 pounds of lead. He had a commercial office in Huntsville under his brother Joshua's direction.[119] He also purchased, about 1800, the Mammoth Spring Tract in northern Alabama, which was patented 24 September 1814. Peregrine served as a private in the War of 1812.[120]

Issue of Peregrine and Elizabeth (Levy) Falconer, born in Baltimore, Maryland:[121]

J12   i.   William Andrew Falconer, born 14 October 1809.

      ii.   Susanna Jane Falconer, born 8 November 1810, buried 10 March 1817 at St. Paul's, Baltimore.

     iii.   George Falconer, born 20 March 1812, died, unmarried, 23 October 1852 in Baltimore, Maryland.[122]

     iv.   Comegys Falconer, born 3 July 1815, died in "early manhood" without marrying.[123]

      v.   Charles Falconer, born 20 September 1816, buried 18 February 1819 at St. Paul's, Baltimore.

J9 **William Falconer**, born 17 October 1780[124] in Queen Anne's County, Maryland, died 7 June 1840 in Montgomery County, Alabama, was buried in the Falconer Cemetery, near Sprague, Alabama.

On 24 December 1805, he married, as his first wife, Ann Singleton, daughter of Joseph and Elizabeth (Rembert) Singleton of Manchester, South Carolina, born 31 August 1782, died 27 August 1815 in Manchester, South Carolina, buried in the Singleton Cemetery.[125]

He married, as his second wife, Nancy Wilder, daughter of William S. and Sarah Wilder, born 4 October 1794 in Virginia,[126] died 25 June 1859 in Montgomery, Alabama, buried in the Falconer Cemetery.

In 1804, he moved to Richland Fork, near Manchester, Sumter District, South Carolina. Urged by his brother Peregrine, in 1817 he and his brother John first came to Alabama,[127] although he did not settle permanently until 1826. His plantation, "Buck Hill," was near Montgomery. He bequeathed 48 slaves and a considerable amount of property to his children.[128]

Issue of William and Ann (Singleton) Falconer, born in Sumter District, South Carolina:[129]

      i.   Elizabeth Jane Falconer, born 29 November 1806, died 16 August 1826. She married, 18 March 1824, James Edwin Belser, son of William and —— (Yvervant) Belser, born 22 December 1805 in Charleston, South Carolina.[130] He was a lawyer. Issue, surname *Belser*: a. *Martha Elizabeth*, born 27 November 1824, died 16 March 1825.[131] He married, as his second wife, Adeline Jane Stokes.

     ii.   Sarah Ann Falconer, born 13 September 1808, died 29 September 1810 in Sumter District, South Carolina.

     iii.   Martha Falconer, born 31 May 1811, died 15 April 1876 in Montgomery, Alabama. She married, on 7 February 1828, Hugh William Henry, a physician and planter, son of Michael and Abigail (Hazard) Henry, born 29 April 1791 Westford, New York, died 6 February 1870 Baltimore, Maryland. Issue, surname *Henry*:[132] a. *John Hazard*, born 3 January 1829, died 19 June 1906 Montgomery, Alabama, married 15 April 1863, at Selma, Alabama, Mary Jane McCurdy; b. *Catherine Elizabeth*, born 17 January 1830, died June 1833; c. *Hugh William*, born 8 September 1831, married, 2 November 1865, Louisa Benson; d. *Michael*, born 27 November 1834, died at three months; e. *DeWitt Clinton*, born 3 April 1836, died 18 March 1844; f. son, born and died 31 July

1838; g. *Michael*, born 29 September 1839, died 29 March 1844; h. *Clift Falconer*, born 6 January 1845, died 3 September 1857; i. *Martha Anne Singleton*, born 2 July 1850, married, 6 December 1870, George Oscar Robinson, of Baltimore.

iv. Ann (Nancy) Singleton Falconer, born 20 January 1813, died 25 April 1868 in Montgomery, Alabama, buried in the Falconer Cemetery. She married, 25 April 1833, in Montgomery County, Alabama,[133] Benjamin Hart, son of Benjamin and Mary (Salley) Hart, of Columbia, South Carolina, born 11 June 1811, died 23 December 1849, and had issue, surname *Hart*: a. *William R.*, born about 1836; b. *Derrill N.*, born about 1841; c. *Robert Singleton*, born 9 January 1843, died 21 March 1916 in Woodford County, Kentucky; d. *John S.*, born about 1845.

J13   v.   William Joseph Falconer, born 13 October 1814.

Issue of William and Nancy (Wilder) Falconer, the first four born in Sumter District, South Carolina, the rest in Montgomery County, Alabama:[134]

vi. Sarah Ann Falconer, born 16 February 1819, died 1871. She married, on 7 October 1841,[135] James Richard Dillard, son of James Reuben and Delilah (Ponder) Dillard, born 2 October 1818 in Lexington, Virginia. He was a planter in Montgomery County, member of the state legislature, and captain of a militia company during the Civil War. Issue, surname *Dillard*:[136] a. *Reuben*, died at the age of two; b. *Susan Oliver*, born about 1843, married, 1866, Dr. James Buckner Luckie; c. *James Dabney*, born about 1845; d. *Sarah H.*, married Frank Smith; e. *Caroline F.*, born about 1847, died at the age of eighteen; f. *Delilah Ponder*, born about 1851; g. *Nancy*, born about 1853, married, first, John Arrington, second, H. A. C. Howze; h. *Mary T.*, born about 1858, married Dr. J. P. Ellshenz; i. *William Richard*, married —— Chandler.

vii. Henrietta Eleanor Falconer, born 28 December 1820, died a few months after the family's removal to Alabama.[137]

viii. Caroline (Cad) Eliza Falconer, born 15 February 1823, died, unmarried, testate, 29 November 1855 in Montgomery, Alabama, buried in the Falconer Cemetery.

ix. John Peregrine Falconer, born 14 August 1825, died 24 October 1843, buried in the Falconer Cemetery.

x. Jane Elizabeth Falconer, born 21 September 1827, was living in Lexington, Kentucky, about 1900. She married, 20 October 1854,[138] Dr. Charles McEachern (McEachin), born about 1825 in South Carolina. She moved to Woodford County, Kentucky, about 1869. Issue, surname *McEachern*:[139] a. *Sarah M.*, born about 1854; b. *Mary*, born about 1858.

xi. Stewart Wilder Falconer, born July 1830, died 28 September 1840, buried in the Falconer Cemetery.

J14   xii.   Joshua Abram Falconer, born 7 November 1835.

xiii. Henrietta Eleanor Falconer, born in 1839, died between 1880 and 1900 in Woodford County, Kentucky. She married, 14 February 1855,[140] Peter George Powell, born January 1836 in Alabama, living in 1900 in Woodford County, Kentucky. Issue, surname *Powell* (they had eight children[141]): a. *Bettie*, born about 1861; b. *Robert M.*, born about 1866; c. *Charles McEachin*, born about 1868, married Emma ——; d. *Peter George*, born August 1870, married Mary Agnes ——.

J10   **Joshua Falconer**, born 8 September 1785[142] in Queen Anne's County,

Maryland, died 8 March 1831 in Montgomery, Alabama.[143]

He married, by license dated 23 September 1818,[144] Lucy Irby, born about 1800 in Virginia, died in 1868 in Montgomery, Alabama.[145]

He went West as a young man, first to St. Louis, Missouri, where he worked in his brother Peregrine's mercantile house. He was later a merchant in Huntsville, Alabama, in partnership with Edward F. Comegys. Joshua moved to Montgomery about 1826. He and his brother John built the first house in Montgomery, which was torn down in 1898, floating it on rafts down the Alabama River.[146]

Issue of Joshua and Lucy (Irby) Falconer:[147]

    i.   Frances C. Falconer, born 16 June 1821 in Huntsville, Alabama, died February 1875 in Montgomery, Alabama.[148] She married, on 15 November 1837,[149] Elisha Denison Ledyard, son of Nathaniel and Elizabeth (Denison) Ledyard, born 27 March 1813 in New London, Connecticut, died June 1882 in Montgomery, Alabama, and had issue, surname *Ledyard*:[150] a. *Edward Tyler*, born 25 October 1838, married Bettie Lathrop; b. *Elisha Denison*, born 25 September 1840, married, 5 September 1861, Olivia Smith Hall; c. *John*, born 11 September 1842; d. *William Falconer*, born 16 January 1846, died 21 September 1910, married, 2 December 1869, Mary M. Gilmer; e. *Eisrine Mason*, born 2 October 1851, died 16 November 1854.

J15   ii.   William J. Falconer, born 1827.

J11   John Henry Falconar, born 22 July 1819 in Baltimore, Maryland, was buried 30 September 1889 in Oak Hill Cemetery, Washington, D. C.[151]

He married first, on 24 June 1851, at Christ Church, Baltimore, Angelina M. Griffith, daughter of Richard H. and Mary Ann (Magruder) Griffith, born October 1831 in Montgomery County, Maryland.[152] She received a divorce from him, by a decree dated 10 December 1857,[153] and was living in Baltimore in 1864 and 1870, unmarried.[154]

He married, as his second wife, on 3 December 1870 in Baltimore,[155] Pauline M. Haller, born about 1846 in Wurttemberg, Germany,[156] died 14 July 1910 in Washington, D.C., buried in Oak Hill Cemetery. She married, as her second husband, on 8 June 1892, in Washington,[157] Joseph Sirvent y Roig.

John H. Falconar was a lawyer, a dry goods commission merchant,[158] a teacher, and a clerk in the U. S. Post Office Department. He enlisted at Harrisburg, Pennsylvania, on 1 April 1862, as a private in Captain Knapp's Pennsylvania Battery E, and was discharged 25 March 1863.[159] His will, dated 16 May 1888, filed 18 February 1890, gave all personal property to his wife Pauline, including any share of claims under the French Spoliation Claims Act.[160] He presumably was the last survivor of his family, as the French Spoliation Claims case mentioned no other living family member.[161]

Issue of John Henry and Angelina M. (Griffith) Falconar, born in Baltimore, Maryland:[162]

    i.   Gilbert Henry Falconar, born 1852, baptized 7 June 1853 at Christ Church, Baltimore. He was alive on 16 February 1857,[163] but has not been traced further, although he presumably had died without issue by 1870 and certainly by the date of his father's will.

Issue of John Henry and Pauline M. (Haller) Falconar, born in Washington, D.C.:[164]

    ii.   Pauline C. Falconar, born about 1871, buried 16 January 1889, aged 17, at Oak Hill Cemetery, Washington, D. C.[165]

J12   **William Andrew Falconer**, born 14 October 1809 in Baltimore, Maryland, died 29 August 1848 near Fort Smith, then in Crawford County, Arkansas,[166] was buried at the Falconer Cemetery in Fort Smith, a small graveyard on the south edge of the city.

He married, on 16 June 1835, in Crawford County, Arkansas,[167] Mary Ellen Titchenal (or Tichenal), daughter of John R. and Rebecca (Harbert) Titchenal, born 23 August 1815 near Clarksburg, Harrison County, [West] Virginia,[168] died 27 November 1878 in Upper Township, Sebastian County, Arkansas.[169] In 1855, she married, as her second husband, Thomas McCarron.

He was a planter and self-taught physician. Following family tradition, in 1829 he arrived at Skullyville, in Indian Territory, to work as a clerk for the Du Val brothers, who had a mercantile establishment there. He took a grant of land in 1838, at Massard Prairie near Fort Smith and purchased thousands of acres more, the property being known as the Falconer Ranch. He organized Masonic services at Belle Point in the 1830s and brought Bermuda grass, American elms, and an Episcopal minister from Maryland.[170] Letters from him to his mother, aunt, and brothers are held at St. John's Church, Fort Smith.

Issue of William Andrew and Mary Ellen (Titchenal) Falconer, the first born in Skullyville, Indiana Territory, the rest born in Sebastian County, Arkansas:[171]

J16   i.   Henry Irvine Falconer, born 2 November 1836.

    ii.   Susan Eliza Falconer, born 25 February 1838, died 11 June 1841.

J17   iii.   William Charles Falconer, born 14 October 1839.

J18   iv.   George Comegys Falconer, born 21 July 1843.

J19   v.   John Peregrine Falconer, born 21 May 1845.

    vi.   Septimus Andrew (Doc) Falconer, born 27 February 1847, died 8 September 1871, buried in the Falconer Cemetery.[172] He married, on 2 March 1869, in Sebastian County, Arkansas,[173] Emma Louisa Warren, daughter of Abel and Mary A. (—) Warren,[174] born about 1852. By 1881, Emma Louisa had married Rufus Caldwell.

    vii.   Margaret A. Falconer, born January 1849, died 1932 in Fort Smith, Arkansas. She married, on 31 January 1878, in Sebastian County, Arkansas,[175] Charles Dudley McKinney, son of Robert W. and Elizabeth (Cretchfield) McKinney, born 24 March 1843 in Fayetteville, Tennessee, died 9 January 1892 in Fort Smith, Arkansas, buried at the Falconer Cemetery.[176] Issue, surname *McKinney*: a. *Mary Elizabeth*, born 15 March 1879, unmarried; b. *Perry Falconer*, born 20 March 1881; c. *Kate Williams*, born 1 February 1883, married William Luce; d. *Fannie Armistead*, born 29 May 1885, died, unmarried, 27 January 1977 Fort Smith, Arkansas; e. *Charles Comegys*, born 1 January 1888.

J13   William Joseph Falconer, born 13 October 1814 near Manchester, Sumter District, South Carolina, died 27 August 1866, probably in Montgomery County, Alabama.[177]

He married, 7 February 1836, Mary E. Wilder, born about 1821 in South Carolina, living in 1860 in Montgomery County, Alabama.[178]

He owned a relatively modest plantation in Montgomery County. He may be the W. J. Falconer who served as a private in Company G, 17th Alabama Infantry, during the Civil War, though this record could have also referred to his cousin William (J15).[179]

Issue of William Joseph and Mary E. (Wilder) Falconer, born in Montgomery County, Alabama:[180]

J20   i.   Joseph S. Falconer, born about 1837.
      ii.   Elizabeth Falconer, born about 1841. She married, 10 July 1861, in Montgomery County, Alabama,[181] John D. Wall.
      iii. Emma V. Falconer, born about 1845.
      iv.   Matilda A. Falconer, born about 1854.

J14   Joshua Abram Falconer, born 7 November 1835 in Montgomery County, Alabama, died 20 November 1926 in Pisgah, Woodford County, Kentucky, was buried in Pisgah Cemetery.

He married, on 17 July 1867,[182] Sarah (Sally) Malloy Bunting, half-sister of his brother-in-law Charles McEachern, born 1840 in South Carolina, died 16 November 1908 in Pisgah, Kentucky, buried in Pisgah Cemetery.

He served as a private in Goldthwaite's Battery, Alabama Light Artillery,[183] and in Semple's Battery, Cleburne's Division,[184] during the Civil War. After the war, he moved to Kentucky, and bought a farm in Fayette County. He and his family belonged to the Pisgah Presbyterian Church.

Issue of Joshua Abram and Sarah Malloy (Bunting) Falconer, born in Woodford County, Kentucky:[185]

      i.   Jane Elizabeth (Bessie) Falconer, born 11 April 1869, died 15 August 1944, buried in Pisgah Cemetery. She married, 2 February 1899, James Taylor Cox, born 25 August 1864, died 13 July 1950, and had no issue.[186]
      ii.   Katherine Bunting Falconer, born 15 October 1870, died, unmarried, 22 October 1911 in Woodford County, Kentucky, buried in Pisgah Cemetery.[187]
J21   iii. John Rutherford Falconer, born 31 July 1875.

J15   William J. Falconer, born 1827 in Montgomery, Alabama, died 17 February 1899 in Calvert, Texas, was buried in Bryan City Cemetery, Bryan, Texas.[188]

He married, on 30 April 1850, in Montgomery County, Alabama,[189] Caroline Gray,[190] born about 1825 in Alabama, living in 1860 in Montgomery County, Alabama.

The will of his uncle John gives to William J. Falconer, son of Joshua, $1000.[191]   He was a newspaper editor, lawyer and planter. From 1846 to 1849, he lived in Shreveport, Louisiana, where he was in the employ of a newspaper. Perhaps he also read law there, as he was back in Montgomery in 1850, when the census reported his occupation as that of a lawyer. In

1860, he lived at "Snowdoun," his plantation in Montgomery County, Alabama, and reported the value of his real estate at $40,000, and his personal estate at $50,000.[192] It is uncertain whether he served as a soldier during the Civil War, although he was an ardent Confederate. He was a tax collector after the war, also built a large store and helped establish an Episcopal church.[193] He wrote *Bloom and Brier; Or, As I Saw It, Long Ago: A Southern Romance* (Philadelphia: Claxton, Remsen and Haffelfinger, 1870), a novel belonging to the apologist genre of Virginius Dabney and other former Confederates. Sometime between 1870 and 1873, in his role as tax collector, he seems to have discovered a way to recuperate the losses he doubtlessly incurred during the war: He absconded, or at least was accused of doing so, with $19,000 of Montgomery County's funds, and, in order to escape a requisition, fled to Florida.[194] In 1873, he lived in Oakfield, near Pensacola, Florida.

About 1874 he and his family moved to Texas,[195] where he edited or published a number of newspapers. He purchased the *Ellis County News* of Waxahachie and moved the plant to Ennis, where he published the *Ennis News* until 1875.[196] He was the editor of the Bryan (Texas) *Appeal and Post*, from March, 1875 to October, 1876.[197] He also worked for the *Brazos Pilot* in Bryan.[198] In 1876 he was named Secretary of the Board of Trustees of the Agricultural and Mechanical College of Texas in Bryan (now Texas A & M University).[199] At the time of his daughter's wedding in 1877, he lived in Florida. Returning to Texas, he was chairman of the Democratic caucus held in Millican in 1882 and chairman of the Democratic executive committee of Brazos County in 1884.[200] In 1895, he started a new newspaper in Bryan, *The People*.[201] He moved to Evergreen, Alabama, in 1896, but returned to Texas in 1897, where he purchased a half-interest in the Navasota *Tablet*.[202] His last place of residence was Calvert, Texas.

Issue of William J. and Caroline (Gray) Falconer, born in Montgomery County, Alabama:[203]

J22   i.   Frank Falconer, born 1851.

ii.   Lucy C. Falconer, born about 1855, buried 11 July 1881 in Bryan City Cemetery. She married, on 28 June 1877, in Bryan, Texas, Guy M. Bryan, Jr., son of William Joel Bryan, born 25 January 1843 in Brazoria County, Texas, died 3 September 1921 in Santa Barbara, California, and had issue, surname *Bryan*:[204] a. *Lucy*, born about 1878, married Frank H. Hervey, who died 6 July 1939 in San Antonio, Texas.

iii.   William Falconer, born 1857, was buried 24 January 1891 in Bryan, Texas, City Cemetery.

iv.   daughter,[205] who died young.

J16   **Henry Irvine Falconer**, born 2 November 1836 at the Choctaw Agency, Indian Territory (now Oklahoma), died 21 December 1885 in Fort Smith, Arkansas, was buried in the Falconer family cemetery.

He married, on 27 February 1879, in Sebastian County, Arkansas,[206] Sarah (Sallie) Price Wilson, daughter of Thomas Edmiston and Mary Ann (Dillard) Wilson,[207] born May 1862 in Upper Township, Sebastian County, Arkansas,[208] living in 1917 in Cincinnati, Ohio. She attended the Medical School of the University of Michigan in 1889-1890 and 1891-1893.[209] In Cincinnati, she was matron of the Hamilton County Jail.

When a young man, he went to prospect in the gold fields in California. He had moved back to Fort Smith by 1870, when he was an unmarried retail merchant.[210]   He served as Sheriff of Sebastian County from 1874 to 1884.[211]

Issue of Henry Irvine and Sarah Price (Wilson) Falconer (they also adopted a daughter, Henri Irvine Ysuelta Falconer, born June 1885,[212] who became a physician and lived in Washington, D.C.[213]):[214]

    i.   Neosho Legrande Falconer [daughter], born 1880, died 3 April 1882 Fort Smith, Arkansas.[215]

J17   **William Charles Falconer**, born 14 October 1839 near Fort Smith, Arkansas, died 22 April 1899 near Spiro, Oklahoma, then Choctaw Nation, Indian Territory. He was buried in the Old Cache Cemetery near Cartersville, Oklahoma.

He married, as his first wife, on 26 November 1868, in Sebastian County, Arkansas,[216] Julia Vermelle Hawkins, daughter of Erasmus Bryant and Sarah Ann (Moncrief) Hawkins, born 29 June 1849 in Choctaw Nation, Indian Territory, died at the age of 36.[217] Her mother was one-quarter Choctaw Indian, brought by her parents to Indian Territory in 1830.[218]

He married, as his second wife, Fannie May Fuller, born 10 October 1861, died 8 January 1948 in Henryetta, Oklahoma, buried in Elmwood Cemetery, Hartshorne.

He served as a private in Company A, Gordon's Regiment of Arkansas Cavalry, and in Company B, Clarkson's Battalion of Confederate Cavalry, Independent Rangers (Missouri).[219] He operated a store at Skullyville, Choctaw Nation, Indian Territory.[220]

Issue of William Charles and Julia Vermelle (Hawkins) Falconer, born in Skullyville, Indian Territory:[221]

J23   i.   Henry Irving Falconer, born 18 November 1870.

    ii.   Mary Belle Falconer, born 23 February 1872, lived at Spiro, Oklahoma. She married John Fannin. Issue, surname *Fannin*: a. *Hamilton*, of Fort Smith; b. *Hugh W.*, born 2 August 1898, died January 1971 in Spiro, Oklahoma; c. *Harlan J.*, of Huntsville, Texas.

    iii.   Susan Eliza Falconer, born 30 March 1874, died 25 March 1899 in Cowlington, Oklahoma, buried at Old Cache Cemetery. She married Andrew J. Stacy and had issue.

J24   iv.   William Charles Falconer, born 11 December 1875.

    v.   Samuel E. Falconer, born about December 1877, died 22 October 1879, aged 1 year, 10 months.[222]

    vi.   Julia Vermelle Falconer, born 14 March 1880, died by 1961.[223] She married John J. Underwood and lived in Oklahoma City, Oklahoma.[224] Issue, surname *Underwood*: a. *Vermelle*, born 30 April 1903, died June 1986 in Oklahoma City, Oklahoma, married P. B. Robberson; b. *John J.*

    vii.   Erasmus Bryant Falconer, born 22 May 1882, died about 1892.

Issue of William Charles and Fannie May (Fuller) Falconer:[225]

J25   viii.   Charles Andrew Falconer, born September 1890.

ix. Allie M. Falconer, born 25 June 1893, died January 1981 in Henryetta, Oklahoma. She married, on 25 December 1914, Andrew Hunter Patterson, born 4 February 1891, died 26 August 1972 in Henryetta, Oklahoma. Issue, surname *Patterson*: a. *Christina H.*, born 6 November 1915, married James Hosmer Hays; b. *Katherine Charlotte*, born 13 December 1916, lives in Englewood, Colorado, married, 21 January 1936, William Thomas Newman; c. *Vermelle*, born 15 February 1918, lives in Henryetta, Oklahoma, married Rayfe Gilreath; d. *Andrew Hunter*, born 1 March 1920, lives in Henryetta, Oklahoma, married Mary Katherine Brennan.

x. Oran Earl Falconer, born 10 March 1898, died October 1966 in Carlsbad, New Mexico. He married Della B. McGilberry, born 9 October 1900, died January 1984 in Carlsbad, New Mexico, but had no children.

J18 **George Comegys Falconer**, born 21 July 1843 near Fort Smith, Arkansas, died 1 November 1890 in Fort Smith, Arkansas,[226] was buried in the Falconer family cemetery.

He married, on 9 March 1874, in Sebastian County, Arkansas,[227] Lucy Helen Beavers, daughter of William E. and Margaret E. (Brown) Beavers, born 21 February 1854 in Saline County, Arkansas,[228] living 1910 in Fort Smith, Arkansas.

He served as a private in Company A, Gordon's Regiment, Arkansas Cavalry, and as a private in Company B, Clarkson's Battalion, Confederate Cavalry, Independent Rangers (Missouri),[229] and in Thompson's Regiment of Cavalry.[230]

Issue of George Comegys and Lucy Helen (Beavers) Falconer, born in Fort Smith, Arkansas:[231]

i. Georgie Ellen Falconer, born 31 December 1875, died, unmarried, 28 June 1894 in Fort Smith, Arkansas, buried in the Falconer Cemetery.

ii. Mabel Falconer, born 16 July 1876, died 27 December 1895 in Fort Smith, Arkansas.[232]

iii. Lucy Lenore Falconer, born 1 February 1882, died 13 May 1971 in Pine Bluff, Arkansas. On 15 December 1907, in Fort Smith, Arkansas, she married William Winston Richmond, of Little Rock, Arkansas.[233] Issue, surname *Richmond*: a. *Lucy Helen Falconer*, born 13 September 1908, died 13 May 1971, married 7 October 1936, at Pine Bluff, Arkansas, Andrew J. Hamilton, Jr.

iv. Helen Beauford Falconer, born 11 January 1889,[234] died 3 May 1988 in Pine Bluff, Arkansas. She married, on 2 June 1910, in Fort Smith, Arkansas, Howell Lane Westbrook, of Pine Bluff, Arkansas. Issue, surname *Westbrook*: a. *Howell Falconer*, born 31 August 1918, died 14 August 1974, married 5 February 1946, at Pine Bluff, Arkansas, Sara Elizabeth Dearing; b. *William George*, born 29 June 1923, married, 7 June 1953, at Little Rock, Arkansas, Angie Lee Carson.

J19 **John Peregrine Falconer**, born 21 May 1845 near Fort Smith, Arkansas, died 5 December 1915 in Fort Smith, Arkansas, buried at Burke Cemetery, Charleston, Arkansas.[235]

He married, on 3 September 1868, in Charleston, Arkansas,[236] Fannie Taliaferro Armistead, daughter of John Carter and Anne Sarah Armistead, born January 1844 in Fauquier County, Virginia, living in 1927 in Fayetteville, Arkansas.

He served as a private in the Second Texas Cavalry.[237] Known as "Colonel," a title which may have come from an office in the militia, he played an active role in subduing criminals. He was a merchant in Charleston, Arkansas, after 1867, active in the city's development.[238]

Issue of John Peregrine and Fannie Taliaferro (Armistead) Falconer, born in Charleston, Arkansas:[239]

   i.   William Armistead Falconer, born 16 June 1869, died 1927 in Fayetteville, Arkansas, was buried in Forest Park Cemetery, Fort Smith.[240] On 24 October 1894, at Charlottesville, Virginia, he married Annie Lyons Gilmore, daughter of James H. Gilmore of Charlottesville.[241] They had no issue. He was a lawyer and classicist. Educated at the University of Virginia, he received the degrees of D.C.L. (University of the South, 1922) and Ll.D. (University of Arkansas, 1925). He served as Judge of the County and Probate Court, Sebastian County, Arkansas, from 1902 to 1908; was appointed in 1909 to the Arkansas Board of Railroad Commissioners; Chancellor of the 10th Circuit Court, 1913-1919; and Professor of Law, University of Arkansas, 1925-1927. His translations of Cicero's *De Senectute, De Amicitia,* and *De Divinatione,* originally published in 1923, were reprinted several times later in the century.[242]

   ii. Roberta Lee Falconer, born about 1872, died 7 November 1948 in Dallas, Texas. She married[243] ―― Ware but was divorced by 1910. She had issue, surname *Falconer:* a. *Falconer A.,* born 22 January 1900, died April 1966 in Dallas, Texas.

   iii. Margaret Harrison Falconer, born 5 August 1873,[244] died 9 September 1955 in Dallas, Texas.

J20   Joseph S. Falconer, born about 1837 in Montgomery County, Alabama, died 15 January 1863 in New Market, Tennessee.

He married, on 22 January 1860, in Montgomery County, Alabama, Sarah M. Merritt, daughter of Joshua H. Merritt, born about 1838 in Alabama, living in 1880 in Montgomery County, Alabama. She married, as her second husband, on 17 November 1866, in Montgomery County, Alabama,[245] William Turner, born about 1836 in North Carolina, living in 1880.

He was a farmer living near the Ramah Post Office when he enlisted, on 9 May 1862, at Dublin, Alabama, as a private in Company C, 60th Alabama Infantry Regiment. At the time of his death, he belonged to Company D, 3rd Battalion, Hilliard's Legion.[246]

Issue of Joseph S. and Sarah M. (Merritt) Falconer, born in Montgomery County, Alabama:[247]

   i.   Willie Falconer, born about 1862, living in 1870, but probably died by 1880.

J21   John Rutherford Falconer, born 31 July 1875 in Pisgah, Woodford County, Kentucky, died 11 October 1933 in Louisville, Kentucky, was buried in Pisgah Cemetery.

He married, on 27 June 1907, Alice Cary Price, daughter of Daniel B. and Alice (Cary) Price,[248] born 14 September 1875 in Woodford County, Kentucky, died 22 October 1971 in Louisville, Kentucky, buried in Pisgah Cemetery.[249]

They lived in St. Louis, Missouri, from 1907 to about 1923, when they moved Anchorage, Kentucky. He was manager of the accident and liability department of Aetna Life Insurance Company at the time of his death.

Issue of John Rutherford and Alice Cary (Price) Falconer, born in St. Louis, Missouri:[250]

    i.   Alice Cary Falconer, born 18 December 1910, lives in Louisville, Kentucky. She married, 23 May 1936, Eugene Freeman Farmer, born 14 October 1904. Issue, surname *Farmer*: a. *Alice Cary*, born 22 March 1937, married William Lee Lyons; b. *Elizabeth Pendleton*, born 1 April 1940, married Douglas Henry Owen, Jr.

J26 ii. John Stuart Falconer, born 29 December 1914.

J22   **Frank Falconer**, born 1851 in Montgomery County, Alabama, died 12 December 1894 in Austin, Texas, was buried in Bryan City Cemetery.[251]

He was married twice. The name of his first wife has not been learned. He married, as his second wife, on 23 December 1893, in Travis County, Texas,[252] P. Alice Wilson.

In 1890 he purchased the "Wilkes place," near Bryan, Texas.[253] At the time of his death, he was a laborer at a cottonseed oil mill in Austin, where he had moved in 1893. He was a member of the Ancient Order of United Workmen.[254]

Issue of Frank and his first wife, born in Bryan, Texas:[255]

J27 i. Guy Bryan Falconer, born 12 April 1883.

Issue of Frank and P. Alice (Wilson) Falconer:[256]

    ii. child, probably born in 1894.

J23   **Henry Irving Falconer**, born 18 November 1870 near Cedars, Choctaw Nation, Indian Territory (now Oklahoma), died 10 February 1947 in Fort Smith, Arkansas.

He married, on 8 September 1903 at Fort Smith, Arkansas,[257] Ida Lucretia (Taylor) McGinty, daughter of John and Lucretia (Gary) Taylor, also partly of Choctaw descent, born 30 September 1874 on Ring Prairie, near Oak Lodge, in what is now LeFlore County, Oklahoma, living 1937.[258]

He served as U.S. Deputy Marshal of the Western District of Arkansas, during the 1890s, and as Deputy Sheriff of Skullyville County and Sans Bois County, Indian Territory. After statehood in 1906, he "made and lost fortunes in the real estate business."[259]

Issue of Henry Irving and Ida Lucretia (Taylor) Falconer:[260]

J28 i. John Henry Falconer, born 21 December 1904.

    ii. Clara Belle Falconer, born 4 April 1907, died 27 July 1981 in Anaheim, California. She married, as her first husband, in March 1927, Earl Frye, who died in 1961. Issue, three sons; she married, as her second husband, in 1945, Lester T. Cutshall; and she was married a third time.

J29 iii. Joe D. Falconer, born 1 May 1908.

J30 iv. Wyatt Byrd Falconer, born 31 October 1909.

    v. Vermelle Lucretia (Babe) Falconer, born 23 December 1911, died 24 July 1989 in Spiro, Oklahoma, buried in the Spiro City Cemetery. She married, on 21 May 1932, Robert Lee Redwine and had one daughter.

vi. Ida Taylor (Shug) Falconer, born 2 November 1913. She married, as her first husband, on 6 August 1936 at McAlester, Oklahoma, Herbert Lee Bailey (divorced 5 May 1942); as her second husband, she married, on 16 July 1945 at Fort Smith, Arkansas, Harold Hardy Dickerson (divorced September 1947); and, as her third husband, on 17 April 1948, Preston Leon Dickerson. She lives in Spiro, Oklahoma. She has, by her third husband, three daughters and one son.

J24   William Charles Falconer, born 11 December 1875 near Cedars, Choctaw Nation, Indian Territory (now Oklahoma), died 3 January 1935 in Poteau Township, LeFlore County, Oklahoma.

He married, on 7 January 1910, in LeFlore County, Oklahoma,[261] Dora Brown, born about 1889.

He was a rancher and farmer at Cowlington. In his early years he was a U.S. Deputy Marshal in Indian Territory.

Issue of William Charles and Dora (Brown) Falconer:[262]

J31 i.   Leard Tillman Falconer, born 4 October 1910.

ii. Addie Vermelle Falconer, born 24 March 1912, lives on a farm south of Spiro, Oklahoma. She married, on 10 March 1936, Henry Doyle Rhodes, born 9 September 1904, died 31 August 1982 in Spiro, Oklahoma, and had issue, surname *Rhodes*: a. *Joe Columbus*, born 23 October 1937; b. *Elizabeth Ann*, born 21 October 1939; c. *Raymond Doyle*, born 10 September 1941.

iii. Marguerite Falconer, born 27 November 1913, died 28 November 1969. She married, in 1933, Jewerl W. Nelson, who died about 1986 in Tulsa, Oklahoma, and had issue, surname *Nelson*: a. *Dora Gene*, born 1936; b. *Patsy Lou*, born November 1941; c. *Treva Nell*, born January 1944.

iv. Dora Nell Falconer, born 4 February 1917, lives in Diamond Bar, California. She married, on 4 January 1941, Bolling Holmes Lund, born 12 December 1918, died 23 March 1989, and had issue, surname *Lund*: a. *Carole*, born 1942, died 13 January 1991.

J32 v.   Charles Bill Falconer, born January 1921.

vi. Perry Brown Falconer, born June 1926, lives in Keota, Oklahoma. He married Helen Hatley of McCurtain, Oklahoma, and adopted her two sons by a previous marriage. He is a retired rural mail carrier.

J25   Charles Andrew Falconer, born September 1890 in Skullyville, Choctaw Nation, Indian Territory (now Oklahoma), died 4 March 1945 in Los Angeles County, California.

He married Alice Glasson.

He and his family lived in El Centro, California, about 1941.

Issue of Charles Andrew and Alice (Glasson) Falconer:

i.   Leona Falconer. She married Jack Cox and had issue. They lived in El Centro, California, about 1941.

ii. Mildred Falconer.

iii. Charles Andrew Falconer, born 22 July 1921, died 2 March 1970 in Orange County, California. He married C—— B——.

iv. Walter Falconer. Not further traced.

J26 **John Stuart Falconer**, born 29 December 1914 in St. Louis, Missouri, lives in Lancaster, Pennsylvania.

He married, on 3 February 1940 in Lancaster, Pennsylvania, Isabel Groff Raub, born 15 April 1915.

He was an executive of the Armstrong Cork Company.

Issue of John Stuart and Isabel Groff (Raub) Falconer:

    i.   Alice Cary Falconer, born 13 March 1942. She married, in 1964, Guy F. Driver, Jr., born 13 March 1940, but divorced. Issue, surname *Driver*: a. *Edith Elizabeth*, born 24 February 1973; b. *Cary Falconer*, born 8 September 1974.

J33   ii.   John Stuart Falconer, born 21 September 1943.

    iii.   Edith Raub Falconer, born 20 July 1946, lives in Elmira, New York. She married Frederic Parkhurst Skinner, M.D., and has issue, surname *Skinner*: a. *Frederic Parkhurst*, born 13 May 1967; b. *Cary Falconer*, born 2 February 1972.

    iv.   Isabel Hamilton Falconer, born 15 May 1951.

    v.   David Price Falconer, born 22 September 1952.

J27 **Guy Bryan Falconer**, born 12 April 1883 in Bryan, Texas, died 31 January 1973 in Seattle, Washington.

He married Marie C. ——, born 25 March 1899, died August 1972 in Seattle, Washington.

In 1900, he lived in Republic Precinct, Ferry County, Washington.[263] He served as a lieutenant in the U.S. Navy. He was an officer of the Washington Title Insurance Company, an executive of the National Title Insurance Company, and served on the board of the Pioneer National Title Insurance Company.

Issue of Guy Bryan and Marie C. Falconer:[264]

    i.   Marjorie Falconer, living in Painesville, Ohio, in 1973. She married Jack Sanderson.

    ii.   Marie Falconer, living in Kalapane, Hawaii, in 1973. She married William Cox.

    iii.   Fay Falconer, lives in Seattle, Washington. She married Kenneth Tourtellot.

    iv.   John Bryan Falconer, died before 1973.

J28 **John Henry (Ching) Falconer**, born 21 December 1904 in Panama, Oklahoma, died 16 January 1983 in Long Beach, California, buried in Forest Lawn Memorial Park, Cypress.

He married, on 9 October 1927, at Poteau, Oklahoma, Gladys Carlile, born 5 June 1906 in Bonanza, Arkansas, died 16 April 1975 in Long Beach, California.

He worked as a cowboy, oil field worker, and owner-operator of riding stables.

Issue of John Henry and Gladys (Carlile) Falconer:

    i.   Nancy Evelyn Falconer, born 5 December 1933, lives in Huntington Beach, California. She married Otho Elmer. They have three children.

ii.   John Stacy Falconer, born 13 December 1935, died 15 May 1936 in Spiro, Oklahoma.

iii. Mary Elizabeth Falconer, born 2 October 1941. She married William Timothy Bartlett, born 24 March 1938, died 1 June 1982 in Long Beach, California. Two children.

J29   Joe D. Falconer, born 1 May 1908[265] in Spiro, Oklahoma, died 13 June 1980 in Oklahoma City, Oklahoma, was buried at Sayre, Oklahoma.

He married, on 23 January 1932, Georgia Edwin Perrin, born May 1914, living in Sayre, Oklahoma. After his death, she married Fladger Martin.

Only child of Joe D. and Georgia Edwin (Perrin) Falconer:

i.   a daughter, who lived one hour and ten minutes.[266]

J30   Wyatt Byrd Falconer, born 31 October 1909[267] in Spiro, Oklahoma, died 5 April 1981 in Sacramento, California.

He married Edna Margaret Poe, born 20 August 1917 in Planada, California, died 10 May 1977 in Sacramento, California.

He was a machinist, millwright, and an avid hunter and fisherman.

Issue of Wyatt Byrd and Edna Margaret (Poe) Falconer, born in Trona, California:

i.   Linda Ann Falconer, born 16 April 1940, died 17 March 1989, buried at Sacramento, California. She married, on 25 June 1961, in Sacramento, California, George Michael McClarrinon, and had issue, two children. He lives in Sacramento.

J34   ii.   Henry Irving Falconer, born 12 August 1942.

iii. Bonnie Gay Falconer, born 26 April 1955, lives in Tendoy, Idaho. She married, on 24 June 1978 in Salmon, Idaho, Kelly William Anglin, and has three sons.

J31   Leard Tillman Falconer, born 4 October 1910 near Cowlington, Oklahoma, died 4 May 1993 in Kinta, Oklahoma, was buried in Keota Cemetery.

He married, in April 1933, Alva Eva Tom, daughter of Albert Tom (a full-blood Choctaw) and Tessie (Stevens) Tom, born 20 October 1916 in LeFlore County, Oklahoma, died 27 May 1988 in Kinta, Oklahoma.

Soon after their marriage they moved onto land north of Keota, Oklahoma, that had been allotted to Albert Tom.

Issue of Leard Tillman and Alva Eva (Tom) Falconer:[268]

J35   i.   Norman Ray Falconer, born 12 March 1934.

ii.   Betty Sue Falconer, born May 1935, lives in Keota, Oklahoma. She married Andrew W. Johnnie and has issue, surname *Johnnie*: a. *William Andrew*, born April 1953; b. *Raymond Michael*, born April 1956, died October 1980 near Stillwater, Oklahoma.

J36   iii. David Lee Falconer, born 28 August 1936.

iv.   Freda Joyce Falconer, born 2 January 1940, lives in Prague, Oklahoma. She married Hershel Wayne Parker and has issue, surname *Parker*: a. *John Wesley*, born 3 December 1959; b. *Terri Lynn*, born 6 December 1961, lives in Seminole, Oklahoma, married —— Prichard.

J37   v.   Donald Stacy Falconer, born 8 August 1941.

J38   vi.   Ronald Simpson Falconer, born 8 August 1941.

J32   **Charles Bill Falconer**, born January 1921, lives in Keota, Oklahoma.
He married Thelma Irene Green, but later divorced. She lives in Spokane, Washington.

He was an Aerial Gunnery Instructor in the U.S. Air Force, spending most of his time in the service at Fairchild Air Force Base near Spokane, Washington.

Issue of Charles Bill and Thelma Irene (Green) Falconer:

   i.   daughter.

   ii.   Charles Bill Falconer, lives in Keota, Oklahoma.

J33   **John Stuart Falconer**, born 21 September 1943 in Lancaster, Pennsylvania, lives in Carrollton, Texas.

He married, in October 1963 in Chicago, Illinois, Carol Ann Weeks, born 9 May 1944.

He is a furniture company representative.

Issue of John Stuart and Carol Ann (Weeks) Falconer:

   i.   John Stuart Falconer, born 17 June 1964, lives in Lewisville, Texas. He married, in 1986, Tracy Lynn Mehaffey, born 21 August 1965.

J34   **Henry Irving Falconer**, born 12 August 1942 in Trona, California, lives in Stockton, California.

On 31 January 1965, in Reno, Nevada, he married Laura Elaine Williams, born 29 June 1945. They were divorced on 3 February 1969.

He has worked as a singer-guitarist, construction worker, machinist, and actor in television commercials.

Only child of Henry Irving and Laura Elaine (Williams) Falconer:

   i.   Deborah Lynn Falconer, born 11 August 1965. She is a model.

J35   **Norman Ray Falconer**, born 12 March 1934 in Keota, Oklahoma, lives in Midwest City, Oklahoma.

He married, as his first wife, in February 1954, Mary Anne King, daughter of Ralph Hugh and Sarah (Million) King. They were divorced in May 1967 at Sacramento, California.

He married, as his second wife, on 26 May 1967 in Midwest City, Oklahoma, Barbara Ann (Vaughan) Bear.

He entered the U.S. Air Force in 1954 as an enlisted man and retired in 1981 with the rank of Lieutenant Colonel. He served in southeast Asia between 1965 and 1971. He received a B.S. (Industrial Engineering), Oklahoma State University, 1962; M.B.A., Auburn University, 1976; M.Ed. (Science), Central State University, 1984. Currently he teaches school and is studying toward ordination as a Deacon in the Episcopal Church of Oklahoma.

Issue of Norman Ray and Mary Anne (King) Falconer:

J39   i.   Ralph Tillman Falconer, born 9 July 1956.
       ii.   Perry Ray Falconer, born 15 April 1958, died 23 December 1971 in Bangkok, Thailand.

Issue of Norman Ray and Barbara Ann (Vaughan) Falconer:

       iii. Joseph Alaric Falconer, born 10 August 1968, lives in Dallas, Texas.

J36   **David Lee Falconer**, born 28 August 1936 in Keota, Oklahoma, lives in Prague, Oklahoma.
He married, as his first wife, Beverly J. Petty. This marriage ended in divorce.
He married, as his second wife, Florence Melson.
He is a truck driver.
Issue of David Lee and Beverly J. (Petty) Falconer (they also adopted her son born before her marriage, David Robert Petty, born 17 July 1954):

       i.   Eva Marie Falconer, born 18 February 1956, lives in Denver, Colorado. She married —— Kirokas.
       ii.   Ronald Wayne Falconer, born 5 May 1959, lives in Tampa, Florida.

J37   **Donald Stacy Falconer**, born 8 August 1941 in Keota, Oklahoma, lives in Moore, Oklahoma.
He married Katherine Lee Burge of Stigler, Oklahoma.
He works for Trans-Con Trucking Company of Oklahoma City.
Issue of Donald Stacy and Katherine Lee (Burge) Falconer:

       i.   Stephen Stacy Falconer, born 3 March 1963, lives in Moore, Oklahoma.
       ii.   Michael Scott Falconer, born 19 May 1964, is stationed at Luke Air Force Base, Arizona. He has a daughter.
       iii. Kristi Dawn Falconer, born 29 September 1972.

J38   **Ronald Simpson Falconer**, born 8 August 1941 in Keota, Oklahoma, lives in Kinta, Oklahoma.
He married Martha Jane Gilstrap of Keota, Oklahoma, but was divorced.
Issue of Ronald Simpson and Martha Jane (Gilstrap) Falconer:

       i.   Rhonda Kaye Falconer, lives in Poteau, Oklahoma.
       ii.   Renee Falconer.

J39   **Ralph Tillman Falconer**, born 9 July 1956, lives in Oklahoma City, Oklahoma.
He married, 15 March 1975, Deborah Lynn VanWinkle.
He is a Captain, U.S. Air Force, stationed at Tinker Air Force Base.
Issue of Ralph Tillman and Deborah Lynn (VanWinkle) Falconer:

    i.   Jason Ray Falconer, born 31 May 1977.

    ii.   Jeremy Michael Falconer, born 12 January 1982.

    iii. Jessica Dawn Falconer, born 9 February 1985.

NOTES

[1] Society of Friends Meeting of Scotland, Abstracts of Minutes, Friends Historical Library, London.

[2] Kent Co. (Md.) Administration Accounts, 3: 124.

[3] Records of Philadelphia Monthly Meeting, in William Wade Hinshaw, *Encyclopedia of American Quaker Genealogy* (Ann Arbor: Edwards Bros., 1937) 2: 520. For her family, see: Ernestine Parke Moss, *Cornelius Comegys of Kent County, Maryland* (Memphis, Tenn.: the author, 1982), pp. 148-149.

[4] Hinshaw, *Encyclopedia of American Quaker Genealogy*, 2: 302.

[5] Edward Carpenter and L. H. Carpenter, *Samuel Carpenter and His Descendants* (Philadelphia: Lippincott, 1912), p. 9f.

[6] Records of the Drapers' Company, London.

[7] *Archives of the State of New Jersey*, 1st ser., 2: 460.

[8] Cecil Co. (Md.) Deeds, 1: 351.

[9] East Jersey Deeds, I: 205.

[10] Original deed, New Jersey Historical Society.

[11] Kent Co. (Md.) Deeds, J.S.#N: 188.

[12] Cecil Monthly Meeting minutes, 2: 138, photostatic copy, Maryland Historical Society.

[13] Philadelphia Monthly Meeting minutes, in Hinshaw, *Encyclopedia of American Quaker Genealogy*, 2: 520.

[14] Philadelphia Co. (Pa.) Deeds, E7#8: 191.

[15] Kennett Monthly Meeting minutes.

[16] Kent Co. Deeds, BC#1: 35.

[17] Minutes of the Board of Property of the Province of Pennsylvania, *Pennsylvania Archives*, 2nd ser., 19: 669, 712, 594.

[18] New Castle Co. (Del.) Warrants and Surveys, folders Y1#3, F2#10, F2#41, F1#13, F2#9.

[19] New Castle Co. (Del.) Deeds, I#1: 338.

[20] Kent Co. (Md.) Deeds, BC1: 285.

[21] Maryland Patents, FF#7: 333; PL#6: 42.

[22] Kent Co. (Md.) Deeds, J.S.#W: 307; Cecil Co. (Md.) Deeds, I: 351. .

[23] James Logan to John Falconar, 10 v. 1717; 26 vi. 1717, 24 Sept. 1717, Logan MSS, Historical Society of Pennsylvania.

[24] James Logan to John Falconar, 2 iv. 1718, Logan MSS, Historical Society of Pennsylvania.

[25] James Logan to John Falconar, 25 vi. 1719, 18 Oct. 1721, 8 Nov. 1722, Logan MSS, Historical Society of Pennsylvania.

[26] Accounts between Richard Bennett and Gilbert Falconar, Lloyd Papers, Maryland Historical Society.

[27] Kent Co. (Md.) Deeds, J.S.#W: 380, 383.

[28] Gilbert Falconar to Richard Bennett, 22 Oct. 1730, Lloyd Papers, Maryland Historical Society.

[29] Memorandum, Lloyd Papers, Maryland Historical Society.

[30] New Castle Co. (Del.) Deeds, H1: 200.

[31] Kent Co. (Md.) Deeds, J.S.#X: 238, I#1: 338, Y-2: 737; B-2: 247.

[32] Maryland Provincial Court, P.L.#8: 270.

[33] Kent Co. (Md.) Deeds, J.S.#18: 222.

[34] Gilbert Falconar to Thomas Penn, Penn Papers, Historical Society of Pennsylvania.

[35] Maryland Inventories, 21: 423.

[36] Richard Bennett to Daniel Dulany, 8 Nov. 1745, Lloyd Papers, Maryland Historical Society.

[37] New Castle Co. (Del.) Orphan's Court Book, C1: 34.

[38] Cecil Monthly Meeting minutes, p. 66, Maryland Historical Society.

[39]Kent Co. (Md.) Original Wills, no. 411; Harry Wright Newman, *Heraldic Marylandiana* (Washington: the author, 1968), p. 67.

[40]Maryland Inventories, 97: 198.

[41]Ibid., 94: 337; he was the son of John Whittington, of Queen Anne's County, Maryland, whose will, dated 3 October 1721, proved 15 May 1722, gave him "Honest Dealing" on Cypress Branch in Kent County.

[42]Kent Co. (Md.) Administration Accounts, 5: 97.

[43]Ibid., 5: 435.

[44]Kent Co. (Md.) Deeds, ES#23: 439.

[45]Richard Bennett to Daniel Dulany, 7 Sept. 1745, 8 Nov. 1745; Richard Bennett to Ira Hall, 18 Nov. 1745; Richard Bennett to James Calder, 7 Apr. 1746, Lloyd Papers, Maryland Historical Society.

[46]Cadwallader Collection, Gen. John Cadwallader section, third party correspondence, bills, receipts, Historical Society of Pennsylvania.

[47]Edward C. Papenfuse, et al., *A Biographical Dictionary of the Maryland Legislature, 1635-1789*, Vol. 1: *A-H* (Baltimore and London: 1979), p. 316.

[48]Shrewsbury Parish register.

[49]Kent Co. (Md.) Inventories, 6: 81.

[50]Moss, *Cornelius Comegys of Kent County, Maryland*, pp. 88-92; Poeter, p. 64f.

[51]Queen Anne's Co. (Md.) Inventories, AB1: 304; Kent Co. (Md.) Inventories, 6: 137.

[52]Will of William Barnes, Delaware Wills.

[53]Maryland Inventories, 97: 335; Kent Co. (Del.) Orphan's Court Book, B: 174.

[54]Maryland Patents, BT & BY #3: 154; BC & GS #3: 11; certificate no. 88.

[55]Queen Anne's Co. (Md.) Wills, 2: 203.

[56]Shrewsbury Parish register.

[57]New Castle Co. (Del.) Wills, N: 442, in: *A Calendar of Delaware Wills*, p. 132.

[58]Kent Co. (Del.) Register of Wills, L: 106.

[59]Maryland Chancery Court Records, 114: 93.

[60]New Castle Co. (Del.) Administrations.

[61]Kent Co. (Del.) Marriage Bonds, 3: 65; Kent Co. (Del.) Register of Wills, A54: 173-175.

[62]Maryland Chancery Court Records, 34: 209.

[63]Shrewsbury Parish register.

[64]Maryland Chancery Paper 2044.

[65]Army Accounts 1: 52.

[66]Maryland Chancery Court Records, 34: 209; Chancery Paper 2044.

[67]Maryland Chancery Paper 2044.

[68]Kent Co. (Md.) Wills, 40: 61.

[69]Maryland Chancery Court Records, 34: 209.

[70]Ibid.

[71]Ibid.; Chancery Paper 2044.

[72]Shrewsbury Parish register.

[73]Maryland Chancery Court Records, 34: 209.

[74]Chancery Paper 2044, Maryland State Archives.

[75]*Baltimore Federal Gazette*, 9 Feb. 1804, in: Robert Barnes, *Marriages and Deaths from Baltimore Newspapers, 1796-1816* (Baltimore: Genealogical Pub. Co., 1978), p. 108.

[76]Deposition of John H. Falconar, in Walter De C. Poultney, administrator de bonis non of Abraham Falconer, deceased, v. The United States, French Spoliation case no. 2786, U.S. Court of Claims, National Archives.

[77]Register of St. Luke's Parish; her identity is proven by the will of John Seale, of Queen Anne's County, her uncle, who died in 1797, leaving her a legacy; see Maryland Chancery Paper 1840, Maryland State Archives.

[78]Maryland, *Calendar of Maryland State Papers*, Number 4, Part 2: *The Red Books*, Hall of Records Commission Publications, no. 8 (Annapolis: Maryland Hall of Records, 1953), pp. 34, 237.

[79]Papenfuse, *A Biographical Dictionary of the Maryland Legislature, 1635-1789*, 1: 316.

[80]"The Library Company of Baltimore," *Maryland Historical Magazine* 12 (Dec. 1917): 310.

[81]Petition, 27 Dec. 1886, Poultney v. United States.

[82]Deposition of John H. Falconar, 1 Oct. 1888, Poultney v. United States.

[83]*Baltimore Sun*, 9 Feb. 1858.

[84]Baltimore City (Md.) Inventories, 77: 187.

[85]Ibid., 52: 149.

[86] *Baltimore Sun*, 13 March 1865.

[87] F. Edward Wright, p. 47; William Mathew Marine, *The British Invasion of Maryland, 1812-1815*, ed. Louis Henry Dielman (Baltimore: Society of the War of 1812 in Maryland, 1913), p. 282.

[88] Edna Kanely, "Baltimore and Ohio Railroad Employees," *Maryland Genealogical Society Bulletin*, 22 (Spr. 1981): 113.

[89] Joseph C. Maguire, *Index of Obituaries and Marriages in the (Baltimore) Sun, 1861-1865* ([Baltimore]: Maryland Historical Society Library, 1991), p. 140.

[90] Ibid., p. 140.

[91] Maryland Chancery Court Records, 30: 378.

[92] Register of St. Luke's Parish; Massey, p. 62.

[93] "Record of Marriages in Maryland and Delaware, by Rev. George Moore, 1789-1810," in Gaius Marcus Brumbaugh, *Maryland Records: Colonial, Revolutionary, Court and Church from Original Sources* (reprint ed., Baltimore: Genealogical Pub. Co., 1985), 2: 596.

[94] Card file, Maryland State Archives.

[95] 1790 census.

[96] Maryland Chancery Court Records, 30: 378f.

[97] Ibid.

[98] Bible record possessed by John Stuart Falconer, 1275 Meadowbrook Rd., Lancaster, PA 17603..

[99] Mary Elizabeth (Stay) Buckner Papers, Tennessee State Library.

[100] T. M. Owen, *History of Alabama and Dictionary of Alabama Biography* (Chicago: S. J. Clarke, 1921), 3: 558.

[101] Schedule of estate, in Buckner Papers, Tennessee State Library.

[102] Baltimore Co. (Md.) Guardianship Accounts, 22: 338, 339.

[103] Falconar Papers, Maryland Historical Society.

[104] *Baltimore Sun*, 22 Feb. 1842, in: Thomas L. Hollowak, *Index of Marriages and Deaths in the (Baltimore) Sun, 1837-1850* (Baltimore: Genealogical Pub. Co., 1978), p. 187.

[105] F. Edward Wright, *Maryland Militia*, Vol. 2 (Baltimore: n.p., 1979), p. 50.

[106] Register of Associate Reformed Church, pp. 123, 128, 129.

[107] Baltimore City (Md.) Wills, IPC#34: 188.

[108] Register of Associate Reformed Church, p. 128; his gravestone, at Greenmount Cemetery, Baltimore, says 1828.

[109] Gravestone, Greenmount Cemetery; Kent Co. (Md.) Letters of Administration.

[110] J. Hall Pleasants, *The Curzon Family of New York and Baltimore* (Baltimore: n.p., 1919), p. 51; license issued 7 November 1863, Baltimore City (Md.) Marriage Licenses, Issue Book LSN 1851-65, p. 196, Maryland State Archives.

[111] Gravestone, Greenmount Cemetery; *Curzon Family of New York and Baltimore*, p. 51.

[112] 1880 census, Baltimore, Baltimore Co., Md., 1-88-31.

[113] Pleasants, *Curzon Family of New York and Baltimore*, p. 51.

[114] Consolidated Index to Confederate Records; Daniel D. Hartzler, *Marylanders in the Confederacy* (Silver Spring, Md.: Family Line Publications, 1986), p. 142.

[115] 1860 census, Baltimore, Baltimore Co., Md., 15th ward, p. 158.

[116] Register of St. Paul's Church, Maryland Historical Society.

[117] Stern, *First American Jewish Families: 600 Genealogies* (Cincinnati: American Jewish Archives, 1977), p. 170.

[118] *Baltimore Sun*, 26 Nov. 1856, in: Walter E. Arps, Jr., *Departed This Life: Death Notices from the (Baltimore) Sun* (Silver Spring, Md.: Family Line, 1986), 2: 54.

[119] Nancy Moler Poeter, *The Comegys Family: Descendants of Cornelius Comegys and Willimentje Gysbert of the Eastern Shore of Maryland 1630-1981* (Baltimore: Gateway Press, 1981), p. 37; Buckner Papers, Tennessee State Library.

[120] Marine, *The British Invasion of Maryland, 1812-1815*, p. 282.

[121] Register of St. Paul's Church, Maryland Historical Society.

[122] *Baltimore Sun*, 26 Oct. 1852; Buckner Papers, Tennessee State Library.

[123] Buckner Papers, Tennessee State Library.

[124] Bible record, gravestone inscription.

[125] Genealogy, in Buckner Papers, Tennessee State Library.

[126] Information from John Stuart Falconer.

[127] John Falconer to Abraham H. Falconar, 26 March 1817, Falconar Papers, Maryland Historical Society.

[128] Will, in Buckner Papers, Tennessee State Library; Montgomery Co. (Ala.) Wills, 2: 224.

[129] Montgomery Co. (Ala.) Wills, 2: 224ff.; 4: 16; Bible record.

[130] Owen, *History of Alabama*, 3: 132.

[131] Bible record.

[132] Buckner Papers, Tennessee State Library.

[133] Bible record.

[134] Bible record; Montgomery Co. (Ala.) Wills, 2: 224ff.

[135] Montgomery Co. (Ala.) Marriage Records, E: 111.

[136] Owen, *History of Alabama*, 3: 492.

[137] Buckner Papers, Tennessee State Library.

[138] Montgomery Co. (Ala.) Marriage Record, 2: 47.

[139] 1860 census, Montgomery Co., Ala., p. 125.

[140] Montgomery Co. (Ala.) Marriage Record, 2: 96.

[141] Buckner Papers, Tennessee State Library.

[142] Baltimore Co. (Md.) Orphan's Court Book, 2: 262.

[143] *Southern Advocate*, 26 March 1831, in Pauline Jones Gandrud, *Marriage, Death and Legal Notices from Early Alabama Newspapers, 1819-1893* (Easley, S. C.: Southern Historical Press, 1981), p. 472.

[144] Madison Co. (Ala.) Marriage Records, 2: 262.

[145] Owen, *History of Alabama*, 3: 559.

[146] *Montgomery Advertiser*, 14 Aug. 1898.

[147] Owen, *History of Alabama*, 3: 557; genealogy in Buckner Papers, Tennessee State Library.

[148] Dates here are from the Ledyard Bible, in Alabama Department of History and Archives.

[149] Montgomery Co. (Ala.) Marriage Records, C: no. 784.

[150] Ledyard Bible, Alabama Department of History and Archives.

[151] Parish Register of Grace Protestant Episcopal Church, Washington, D.C., typescript by Rose Trexler Mitchell, p. 43, D.A.R. Library.

[152] Howard Griffith Stevenson, *Griffith Family: A Few of the Descendants of William and Sarah Muccubbin Griffith* (N.p.: 1927), p. 148.

[153] Baltimore City (Md.) Equity Papers, Box 233.

[154] Montgomery Co. (Ala.) Land Records, EBP2: 2; 1870 census, Baltimore, Baltimore Co., Md., 11th ward, p. 44..

[155] Baltimore City (Md.) Marriage Licenses, Book 3-1-F-R, p. 150.

[156] 1880 census, D.C.; perhaps she was the Marie Pauline Haller, born 19 September 1850 in Freudenstadt, Wuerttemberg, who emigrated with her family in September 1854, Trudy Schenk and Ruth Froelke, *The Wuerttemberg Emigration Index*, vol. 3 (Salt Lake City: Ancestry, 1987), p. 73.

[157] D.C. Superior Court, Marriage Record, 31: 320.

[158] *Williams' Baltimore Directory for 1860.*

[159] Civil War pensions, application no. 659,151, National Archives.

[160] Superior Court of the District of Columbia, Register of Wills, file no. 3845.

[161] Poultney v. U.S., French Spoliation case no. 2786, U.S. Court of Claims.

[162] Register of Christ Church, Baltimore.

[163] Baltimore City (Md.) Equity Papers, Box 233, Bill of Complaint, Maryland State Archives.

[164] 1880 census, Washington, D.C., 2-20-44-36.

[165] Parish Register of Grace Protestant Episcopal Church, Washington, D.C., typescript by Rose Trexler Mitchell, p. 43, D.A.R. Library.

[166] *Baltimore Sun*, 28 Sept. 1848, in Thomas L. Hollowak, *Index to Marriages and Deaths in the (Baltimore) Sun, 1837-1850*, p. 187.

[167] *Arkansas Gazette*, 7 July 1835.

[168] William A. Falconer to Eliza Falconer, 10 May 1848, in William A. Falconer Papers, St. John's Church, Fort Smith, Ark.; typescript copy at Fort Smith Public Library.

[169] Gravestone, Falconer Cemetery, Fort Smith.

[170] John Luce, "Falconer Family Cemetery," letter to Norman R. Falconer; Cole.

[171] William A. Falconer to Eliza Falconer, 10 May 1848.

[172] Register of St. John's Church.

[173] Sebastian Co. (Ark.) Record of Marriages, A: 113.

[174] Sebastian Co. (Ark.) Record of Wills and Testaments, A: 21, 128.

[175] Sebastian Co. (Ark.) Record of Marriages, B: 254.

[176] Register of St. John's Church.

[177] Falconer Bible record; however, Virginia (Mrs. C. H.) Whitaker, of Monroe, Louisiana, to the Alabama Depart-

ment of Archives and History, 1981, says that Bible records show that he died 23 July 1860. However, since the 1860 census shows his wife to be the head of her household, perhaps he died in 1856.

[178] 1860 census, Montgomery Co., Ala., p. 1.

[179] Consolidated Index to Confederate Records, National Archives.

[180] 1860 census, Montgomery Co., Ala., p. 1.

[181] Montgomery Co. (Ala.) Marriage Records, 3: 80.

[182] John Stuart Falconer is the source for the information on the descendants of Joshua A. Falconer.

[183] Consolidated Index to Confederate Records.

[184] Confederate Veteran Association of Kentucky certificate, owned by John Stuart Falconer.

[185] John Stuart Falconer records.

[186] Michael I. Ward, *Pisgah 1784-1984: Woodford County, Kentucky*, pp. 169, 278.

[187] Ibid.

[188] *Bryan Eagle*, 23 Feb. 1899; *Bryan City Cemetery, Brazos County, Texas, Books 1, 2, 3, & 4*, transcribed by Mary Collie-Cooper (Bryan, Tex.: 1987), pp. 126-127.

[189] Montgomery Co. (Ala.) Marriage Records, 2A: 3.

[190] Or Graves, according to genealogy in Buckner Papers, Tennessee State Library.

[191] Montgomery Co. (Ala.) Wills, 4: 16f.

[192] 1860 census, Montgomery Co., Ala., p. 44.

[193] Genealogy; S. E. McEachern to Martha Henry, 5 Dec. 1874; Edna B. Triplett to Mary E. Buckner, 29 June 1938, in Buckner Papers, Tennessee State Library.

[194] (Austin) *Daily Democratic Statesman*, 28 Apr. 1875. I am grateful to Bill Page, who found and e-mailed these Texas newspaper references to me.

[195] Buckner Papers, Tennessee State Library.

[196] *History of Ellis County, Texas* (n.p.: 1972), p. 63.

[197] *Brenham Daily Banner*, 17 Oct. 1876.

[198] *Bryan Eagle*, 2 Oct. 1890.

[199] (Austin) *Daily Democratic Statesman*, 18 July 1876.

[200] *Weekly Brazos Pilot*, 1 Sept. 1882; *Galveston Daily News*, 16 Apr. 1884.

[201] *Galveston Daily News*, 24 Aug. 1895.

[202] *Bryan Eagle*, 20 May 1897.

[203] 1860 census, Montgomery Co., Ala., p. 44.

[204] 1880 census, Brazos Co., Tex., 334c-22-15.

[205] Genealogy in Buckner Papers, Tennessee State Library.

[206] Sebastian Co. (Ark.) Record of Marriages, B: 285.

[207] LDS Ancestral File.

[208] 1900 census, Cincinnati, Hamilton Co., Ohio, 62-74-3-37.

[209] *University of Michigan, Catalogue of Graduates, Non-graduates, Officers and Members of the Faculties, 1837-1921* (Ann Arbor: by the University, 1923), p. 845.

[210] 1870 census, Sebastian Co., Ark., p. 225.

[211] *History of Benton, Washington, Carroll, Madison, Crawford, Franklin, and Sebastian Counties, Arkansas*, p. 708.

[212] 1900 census, Cincinnati, Hamilton Co., Ohio, 62-74-3-35.

[213] This information from Bernice Cole, who learned this from John Luce.

[214] 1880 census, Sebastian Co., Ark., 12-178-25-12; Sebastian Co. (Ark.) Letters of Administration, p. 346; she reported in the 1910 census that she had one child, not then living.

[215] Fort Smith Record of Deaths, vol. 1.

[216] Sebastian Co. (Ark.) Record of Marriages, A: 95.

[217] Ibid.

[218] Reminiscences of Sarah Ann Harlan, in Works Projects Administration Indian-Pioneer History Collection, 28: 92, Oklahoma Historical Society; also in Muriel H. Wright, "Sarah Ann Harlan: From Her Memoirs of Life in the Indian Territory," *The Chronicles of Oklahoma* 39 (Summer and Autumn 1961):   .

[219] Consolidated Index to Confederate Records.

[220] Henry I. and Ida L. Falconer, interview with Gomer Gower, 15 July 1937, WPA Indian-Pioneer History Collection, 64: 110, Oklahoma Historical Society.

[221] Reminiscences of Sarah Ann Harlan, 28: 92; birth dates from Norman Falconer.

[222] Falconer Cemetery record.

[223] Muriel Wright, 39: 158.

[224] Julia V. Underwood, questionnaire, WPA Indian-Pioneer History Collection, 73: 256.

[225] 1900 census, Choctaw Nation, Indian Territory, 13-96-2-59.

[226] Register of St. John's Church.

[227] Sebastian Co. (Ark.) Record of Marriages, B: 149.

[228] Register of St. John's Church.

[229] Consolidated Index to Confederate Records.

[230] Arkansas Confederate Pensions.

[231] Register of St. John's Church, 2: 164; much information on this family comes from Rena Westbrook-Johnson, 103 N. 16th St., Fort Smith, AR 72901.

[232] Fort Smith Record of Deaths, 2: 50.

[233] Register of St. John's Church, 2: 414.

[234] Ibid.; 1887 is probably correct.

[235] Register of St. John's Church, 2: 456.

[236] Ibid., 1: 220.

[237] Consolidated Index to Confederate Records.

[238] Fay Hempstead, *Historical Review of Arkansas* (Chicago: Lewis, 1911), 2: 914.

[239] Ibid.; 1880 census, Sebastian Co., Ark., 37-126-2-87.

[240] Clipping from Fort Smith newspaper.

[241] Hempstead, *Historical Review of Arkansas*, 2: 914.

[242] Cicero, *De Senectute, De Amicitia, De Divinatione*, with an English translation by William Armistead Falconer (New York: G. P. Putnam's Sons, 1923), later was published by Harvard University Press in 1953, 1964, and 1971.

[243] Sebastian Co. (Ark.) Record of Marriages, E: 537, not seen.

[244] Register of St. John's Church.

[245] Montgomery Co. (Ala.) Marriages, 4: 56.

[246] Confederate Military Record card, Alabama Department of Archives and History.

[247] 1870 census, Montgomery Co., Ala., p. 104.

[248] William E. Railey, "Railey-Randolph History and Genealogy," *Register of the Kentucky Historical Society* 9 (Sept. 1911): 74f.

[249] Ibid., pp. 169, 278.

[250] John Stuart Falconer.

[251] *Austin Daily Statesman*, 13 Dec. 1894.

[252] Travis Co. (Tex.) Marriage Records, 8: 315. His name is written as "Fal," as if the transcriber was unable to decipher the rest of the name on the original record.

[253] *Bryan Eagle*, 10 April 1890.

[254] *Austin Daily Statesman*, 13 Dec. 1894.

[255] *Bryan Eagle*, 20 Dec. 1894.

[256] *Austin Daily Statesman*, 13 Dec. 1894.

[257] Sebastian Co. (Ark.) Record of Marriages, H: 389.

[258] Henry I. and Ida L. Falconer, interview with Gomer Gower, 15 July 1937.

[259] Ibid.

[260] Ida (Shug) Dickerson, 647 N. Columbus, Spiro, OK 74959, is the source for the information on Henry I.'s descendants.

[261] *LeFlore County, Oklahoma: Marriages, Vol. 4, 1907-1910.*

[262] Dora Lund, 1273 N. Diamond Bar Blvd., Diamond Bar, CA 91765.

[263] 1900 census, Ferry Co., Wash., 4-15-2-17.

[264] *Seattle Daily Times*, 2 Feb. 1973.

[265] Delayed certificate of birth, Oklahoma State Department of Health.

[266] Ida (Shug) Dickerson.

[267] Ibid.

[268] Norman R. Falconer, 6724 Donna Lane, Midwest City, OK 73150.

CHAPTER K

Alexander Falconar of Maryland

K1 **Alexander Falconar**, third surviving son of David Falconar (G1) and his wife Margaret Molleson, born about 1693,[1] probably at Kirktonhill, parish of Marykirk, Kincardineshire, Scotland, was living as late as 28 February 1758, in Prince Georges County, Maryland.[2]

A note attached to the inventory of the estate of Francis Phubert, of Queen Anne's County, Maryland, dated 19 August 1728, in which Gilbert Falconar signs on behalf of "my brother" Alexander Falconar, whom he believed to be the estate's largest creditor, provides unequivocal, albeit indirect, evidence that Alexander was the son of David Falconar.[3] This identification is also supported by a careful study of his legal transactions, as shown below, and by traditions passed among descendants. One nineteenth-century account even names the father of Alexander as "Lord David Falconer of Monckton" and adds that his sister Jane came to the Colonies[4] (see Appendix 4).

Alexander first appears in Maryland records on 9 February 1718/9, when at Queen Anne's Parish, Prince Georges County, he married Susannah Duvall, daughter of Samuel and Elizabeth (Iiams) Duvall. She was born 3 September 1699 in All Hallows Parish, Anne Arundel County, Maryland,[5] and was living as late as 12 May 1756.[6]

Alexander came to Maryland as a merchant, probably acting as a local agent on the Western Shore for his brother John. In 1719, he was in a list of taxables in Patuxent Hundred, in Prince Georges County.[7] On 10 August 1721, Samuel Duvall, for "natural love and affections," deeded his daughter Susannah Falconar "Samuel's Choice," consisting of 100 acres.[8] Alexander received a patent on "Darnall's Grove," of 100 acres, before 1723.[9] On 3 June 1724, he bought from Ann Tyler, of Prince Georges County, widow, a 50-acre tract called "Dutchman's Imployment," for £50 sterling.[10] He was listed as a creditor, for John Falconar, on the estate of Thomas Swearingen, of Prince Georges County, in 1726.[11] He bought "Ryley's Neglect" of 96 acres for £120 from Thomas Jones of Anne Arundel County on 29 June 1726; John Falconar was a witness.[12] His land at this time amounted, then, to 350 acres.

His subsequent financial history closely parallels those of Gilbert and especially of John Falconar, Senior and Junior. Because he had come to

America more recently and during worse economic times, he was perhaps more dependent on John Falconar for credit than Gilbert was. Kent County land records indicate desperate attempts, from 1730 to 1733, to pay his creditors. His troubles in the last year may have been related to the failed voyage of the *John and Benjamin* in 1731. The ship was in Maryland in May 1732, precisely at the time residents of Prince Georges County, despairing of the low price of tobacco, wantonly cut up plants on a number of plantations.[13] In a deed dated 3 November 1730, styled "gentleman," he sold "Darnall Grove" and "Dutchman's Employment" to Elizabeth Hepburn of Prince Georges County, widow, for £54, 2s. sterling.[14] On 15 June 1731, he sold a slave named Peter, for £12, 9d. sterling due to Samuel Storke per the sum of £14, 7s., 10d. sterling due of John Poole, merchants of London, to Storke and Poole.[15] He mortgaged, for £24, 15s., on 31 January 1732/3, four horses, six cows, three heifers, four yearlings, twelve ewes and one plow, to Turner Wootton.[16] On 3 August 1733, he sold various household furniture and utensils, including a walnut desk, an oval table, and five feather beds, to Maj. Edward Sprigg, for £12, 17s., 7d.[17] On 20 August 1733, he mortgaged "Samuel's Choice," of 100 acres, to Richard Bennett of Queen Anne's County and Gilbert Falconar of Kent County, for £68.[18] His social status declined as a result of his near-bankruptcy. Styled "merchant" or "gentleman" in deeds from 1724 to 1733, he was "planter" in 1748 and 1756.[19]

Susannah was a member of the Church of England and their children were presumably baptized in that church. Alexander would have been "disowned" for marrying someone outside the Quaker community, yet he seems to have retained his identity as a Quaker. For example, following Quaker practice, he affirmed in court, rather than swearing on oath, that he witnessed the will of Henry Odell, of Prince Georges County, dated 19 May 1738.[20]

He managed to acquire two further tracts, "Ridles Purchase," consisting of 110 acres, and "Roper's Range"; deeds for these purchases, however, have not been found. But debts continued to plague him. On 16 June 1742, he mortgaged livestock and other personalty to his wife's brother-in-law Edward Tyler, for £29,18s.,10d.[21] He sold "Ridles Purchase" to Christopher Lowndes of Prince Georges County, merchant, for £25, on 23 February 1748/9.[22] On 5 August 1749, for the sum of a debt of £24 due to John Hepburn, Alexander sold to his son Gilbert Falconer, of Prince Georges County, six cows, three heifers, five two-year-old steers, and four calves.[23] On 12 September 1754, he and Alexander Falconer, Jr., and Gilbert Falconer, of Prince Georges County, confessed judgment of 302 pounds of tobacco to Jacob Iglehart.[24] On 12 May 1756, he sold "Roper's Range" to Richard Snowden, of Anne Arundel County, for £17, 13s.[25] Alexander Falconar and Gilbert Falconar, "Jr." witnessed the will of Elizabeth Simmons of Prince Georges County on 10 March 1757.[26]

Alexander Falconar redeemed "Darnall's Grove," for he or his eldest son and heir Alexander owed quit rents on it from 1753 to 1768.[27] The father was certainly dead by 1769, when Gilbert became owner of that property, and probably dead by 26 October 1765, when Samuel Chase sued Alexander Falconar in the deed described below. This Alexander was probably the son, because under primogeniture, as his father's eldest son, he was his sole heir and would have inherited the land. Another clue to his identity is the fact that his wife Charity released her right of dower. Although the father could have had a second marriage to a woman named Charity, this woman seems more likely to have been the son's wife, since he had a daughter Charity. No proceedings relative to the estate of the father have been found.

Harry Wright Newman thought it odd that, of their eleven children, he could only locate two (Alexander and Gilbert) in later records.[28] The subsequent history of Alexander's daughters still remains obscure.

Issue of Alexander and Susannah (Duvall) Falconar, born in Queen Anne's Parish, Prince Georges County, Maryland:[29]

K2   i.   Alexander Falconar, born 11 February 1719/20.

      ii.   John Falconar, born 13 August 1721. He may have been the otherwise unidentified John "Falkner" who served in Capt. Joshua Beall's Company as a private from 9 October 1757 to 8 November 1758.[30] This person died as a soldier, as on 16 October 1759, Joshua Beall was bound to administer the estate of John Falkner in common with others.[31] Whether he was the soldier or not, I have not been able to identify him in contemporary records. He may have died as a child.

M1   iii.   Gilbert Falconar, born 15 January 1722/3.

      iv.   Margaret Falconar, born 20 August 1724. She witnessed the will of Samuel Waters, of Anne Arundel County, dated 10 October 1747, but had moved out of Maryland by 16 September 1749, when the will was probated.[32]

N1   v.   David Falconar, born 22 April 1726.

      vi.   Eleanor Falconar, born 26 November 1727.

      vii.   Jane Falconar, born 31 July 1729.

      viii.   Lucy Falconar, born 15 January 1730/1.

P1   ix.   Samuel Falconer, born 25 October 1732.

      x.   Sarah Falconar, born 7 January 1735/6.

      xi.   Rachel Falconar, born 25 April 1737.[33]

K2 **Alexander Falconar**, born 11 February 1719/20 Queen Anne's Parish, Prince Georges County, Maryland, was living in 1790 in Frederick County, Maryland.[34]

He married Charity ——. In a deed to Edward Hall, dated 26 October 1765, mentioned below, Charity, wife of Alexander Falconar, released her right of dower.

With his father and brother Gilbert, he confessed judgment of 302 pounds of tobacco to Jacob Iglehart on 12 September 1754.[35] On 28 February 1758, Alexander Falconar, "Senr.," for £28, 6s., sold to "my son" Alexander Falconar his share of tobacco then in the warehouse, two black horses, a bay mare, a sow and four pigs, a gilt and four shoats, ten shoats, and two ewes.[36]

On 20 September 1765, Samuel Chase sued Alexander Falconar on a writ of seisin for the recovery of "Samuel's Choice," and the court ordered him to deliver to Samuel Chase full seisin of the land by the second Tuesday of April, 1766.[37] On 26 October 1765, he mortgaged "Samuel's Choice" to Edward Hall, son of Henry Hall, of Prince Georges County, planter, for £150.[38] He had presumably inherited "Darnall's Grove" by this time, as well.

Sometime later he moved to Frederick County, Maryland. He witnessed the will of Thomas Powell, Sr., of Frederick County, on 26 October 1775,[39] and signed an oath of allegiance to the American cause in 1776, when a resident of what later became Washington County, Maryland. He witnessed, on 27 March 1780, the testimony of Samuel Trenter and Charity Trenter in a slander suit against John Shaw of Washington County.[40] He witnessed the will of George Cley, of Frederick County, on 30 October 1784.[41] In 1790, he was listed in the census as a resident of Frederick County, with two males over 16, one male under 16, and three females. He was probably dead by 1800, as he does not appear in the census taken that year.

Issue of Alexander and Charity Falconar:[42]

    i.   Mary Falconar. She married, on 17 February 1779, at the Evangelical Lutheran Church, Frederick, Maryland, Robert Byfield.

    ii.   Charity Falconar. She married, on 11 July 1790, at the Evangelical Lutheran Church, Frederick, Maryland, Elisha Barnes, living in 1800 in Washington County, Maryland.[43] Both parents died of typhoid fever four days apart.[44] Issue: surname *Barnes*: a. *Nancy*; b. *Alexander*.

   iii.   Margaret Falconer. There is no proof that she was Alexander's daughter, but her descendants said that she was from Prince Georges County, Maryland. She married Alexander Wilson, and moved to Morgantown, (now West) Virginia, before 1800. Their son *David S.*, born 1800, died 1839 in Newark, Ohio, was the father of James Falconer Wilson (1828-1895), of Fairfield, Iowa, U.S. Congressman and Senator from that state.[45]

   iv.   Susan Falconer. She married —— Wilson and moved to Virginia and probably later to the Zanesville, Ohio, area. Issue, surname *Wilson*:[46] a. *Alexander*; b. *George A. J.*, born 1 January 1807 in Virginia, died 20 February 1884 in Springfield, Kentucky, a Catholic priest of the Dominican order; c. *Amy*; d. *May*. Father Wilson was the first native-born American Dominican, the first to visit Rome, and Provincial of the American order in 1843. He was very interested in the genealogy of the Falconers and in the story of the Scottish inheritance. In 1871 he received permission to visit Scotland,[47] presumably to investigate the family's history, since there would have been little Dominican business there. Unfortunately, his papers, which undoubtedly would have contained valuable genealogical information, do not seem to have survived.

K3   v.   John Barclay Falconar, born probably about 1774.

K4   vi.   George Washington Falconar, born in 1777.

K3 John Barclay Falconar, born probably about 1774, died shortly before 10 August 1802, while he was said to have been on a voyage to Scotland.[48] His estate was probated in Frederick County, Maryland.[49]

He married, by license dated 9 April 1798 in Frederick County, Maryland, Ann Maria Shane.[50] She lived in Baltimore after his death and there married, as her second husband, on 3 December 1810, Joshua Knight, a merchant of Montgomery County, and had issue by him.[51]

He was a blacksmith, with a shop in Frederick.[52] He was an early member of Hiram Lodge, Ancient Free and Accepted Masons, of Frederick, which was organized in 1799.[53] In 1800, he lived in Frederick County, with a household consisting of one male under 10, two males 16 to 26, one male 26 to 45, one female under 10, and one female 16 to 26.[54]

Only surviving child of John Barclay and Ann Maria (Shane) Falconar:[55]

i.   Susan Falconar. She married Dr. —— (perhaps Rogers) Hoffman, of Baltimore, Maryland. She possibly married, as her first husband, by a license dated 19 December 1831, in Baltimore, Stephen Curren.

K4 George Washington Falconar, born in 1777 in Frederick County, Maryland, died 6 January 1856 in Macon County, Illinois, was buried in Mount Zion Presbyterian Cemetery.[56]

He married, by a license dated 9 April 1800 in Frederick County, Maryland, Mary Boyd. She was born 28 February 1777 [calculated] and died 21 December 1842 and was buried in the Mount Zion Presbyterian Cemetery.[57]

He was a blacksmith and lived in New Market, Frederick County. In 1839, he, with John Falconer, came to Macon County, Illinois,[58] traveling on the National Road. He was president at the organization of Mount Gilead Methodist Episcopal Church, his son-in-law John "Falconar" being a trustee, in 1845.[59]

In his will, dated 5 December 1855, he ordered that as much of his personal property as was necessary to pay his debts be sold, the remainder to be divided among his unnamed children. He gave to his daughter Mary twenty acres off the north end and of the east half of the southwest quarter of section two, township fifteen north, range two east. This portion would have been in lieu of a wedding present presumably given to each of his other children. He appointed his son Enoch G. Falconar to be executor. The will was proved on 4 February 1856.[60]

Issue of George Washington and Mary (Boyd) Falconar, born in Frederick County, Maryland:[61]

K5   i.   Jeremiah Falconer, born 24 February 1801 [calculated].

ii.   Anna Falconer, born 6 September 1803 [calculated]. His "eldest daughter," she married, on 5 June 1832, in Frederick County, Maryland,[62] John Falconer (L4), son of Elisha Falconer.

iii. Eliza Falconar, born about 1806, living in 1860 in Decatur, Illinois. She married, on 26 July 1842, in Macon County, Illinois,[63] John Patterson, born about 1812 in Ireland, living in 1860. Issue, surname *Patterson*:[64] a. *George W.*, born about 1843.

K6   iv.   Enoch G. Falconar, born about 1810.

v.   Mary Falconar, born 8 June 1812, died, unmarried, 8 June 1891 in Brownwood, Texas, buried in Greenleaf Cemetery.[65]

K5 Jeremiah Falconer, born 24 February 1801 [calculated] in Frederick County, Maryland, died 17 May 1872 in Macon County, Illinois, was buried in Greenwood Cemetery, Decatur.[66]

He, by a license dated 29 November 1826, in Montgomery County, Maryland,[67] married Mary Prather, born 15 October 1806 [calculated] in Maryland, died 30 November 1850 in Macon District, Macon County, Illinois, buried in Greenwood Cemetery.

He married, as his second wife, on 23 June 1857, in Macon County, Illinois,[68] Mary A. Doak. She married, as her second husband, on 27 September 1877, in Macon County, Illinois,[69] Robert N. Davis.

He was a blacksmith. His farm was located on the present site of the Pittsburgh Glass Company in Decatur.

Issue of Jeremiah and Mary (Prather) Falconer, the first five born in Frederick County, Maryland, the rest born in Macon County, Illinois:[70]

K7 i.   William W. Falconer, born 7 October 1827.

    ii.   Mary E. Falconer, born about 1830, living in 1873 in Minneapolis, Kansas, buried in Highland Cemetery. On 7 March 1850, in Macon County, Illinois,[71] she married Stephen M. Whitehouse, born 8 February 1821 in Washington County, Virginia, died 6 December 1875 in Kansas. He served as sheriff of Macon County from 1854 to 1856, and moved to Kansas in 1869.[72]

    iii. Eliza L. Falconer, born 31 October 1833 [calculated], died, unmarried, 22 January 1854, buried in Greenwood Cemetery.

    iv.   Frances Emeline Falconer, born about 1836. On 14 May 1857, in Macon County, Illinois,[73] she married James J. Jordan, son of Henry and Kesiah (Hall) Jordan, born about 1832 in Menard County, Illinois, died about 1904 in Blue Mound, Illinois. Issue, surname Jordan:[74] a. Mary E., born about 1858; b. Elizabeth; c. Emma; d. Ida; e. Fanny.

K8 v.   George Bartley Falconer, born 6 September 1838.

K9 vi.   Jeremiah Milton Falconer, born about 1840.

    vii. Thomas H. Falconer, born about 1843. In 1873, his residence was unknown to his family, although thought to be in "one of the western territories." Perhaps he was the T. H. Falconer who died 15 January 1907 in Umatilla County, Oregon.

K10 viii. Prather Singleton Falconer,[75] born 23 January 1846.

    ix.   Bradford Mortimer Falconer, born 27 September 1847 [calculated], died 4 July 1868, buried in Greenwood Cemetery.

    x.   Amanda P. Falconer, born 2 May 1851 [calculated], died 9 October 1852, buried in Greenwood Cemetery.

K6 Enoch G. Falconar, born about 1810 in Frederick County, Maryland, died not long before 12 May 1873 in Decatur, Macon County, Illinois,[76] was buried in Greenwood Cemetery.

His wife was Alice Webb, born about 1817 in England, living in 1885 in Decatur, Illinois. In her widowhood she worked as a seamstress.

Probably named for Enoch George, an early Methodist Bishop of Baltimore, he was a Methodist clergyman and came to Illinois as a young man. He served in 1834 and 1835 as pastor of the Methodist church in Carlinville, Illinois, and also pastor of the Chesterfield church in Macoupin County, Illinois.[77] He was appointed to be preacher for the Petersburg, Illinois, circuit in 1841. In 1842, he was admitted to Deacon's orders in the Illinois Annual Conference of the Methodist Episcopal Church.[78] He was appointed preacher for the Waterloo, Illinois, circuit, in 1845, and for that of Mt. Carmel, Illinois, in 1847, and, in 1851, he was "superannuated."[79] In 1857 he was commissioned Justice of the Peace.[80] During the Civil War he served as a chaplain in Companies F and S, 8th Illinois Infantry. In the last years of his life he was active as a "local" preacher.

Issue of Enoch G. and Alice (Webb) Falconar:[81]

i. George S. Falconar, born about 1844, died before 1860.

ii. Mary Ellen Falconar, born about 1847, living in 1917 in Lakeland, Florida. She married, on 14 September 1875, in Macon County, Illinois,[82] John McDonald. Issue, surname *McDonald* (there were five, all living in 1910):[83] a. *Anna V.*, born 5 May 1881, died December 1974 in Davenport, Florida, married Lee Trammell.

iii. Francis (Frank) A[sbury] Falconar, born 1 October 1849, died 24 November 1894 in Chicago, Illinois,[84] buried in Greenwood Cemetery, Decatur. He married Laura ——, born March 1851 in Ohio, living in 1900 in Chicago, Illinois, but had no issue.[85] He was a railroad conductor.

iv. Anna M. C. Falconar, born 10 September 1856, died 6 May 1917 in Decatur, Illinois, buried in Greenwood Cemetery. She married, on 10 March 1891, Walter M. Bishop. Issue, surname *Bishop*:[86] a. *Bessie.*

v. Ruth B. Falconar, born about 1858, died before 1873.

vi. Elizabeth Falconar.

K7 William W. Falconer, born 7 October 1827 in New Market, Frederick County, Maryland, died 7 October 1890 in South Wheatland Township, Macon County, Illinois, was buried in Mount Gilead Cemetery.

On 3 February 1853, in Macon County, Illinois,[87] he married Euphemia A. Foley, born 6 May 1831 in Kentucky, died 18 November 1912 in Mount Zion, Macon County, Illinois, who was buried in Mount Gilead Cemetery.

Issue of William W. and Euphemia A. (Foley) Falconer, born in Macon County, Illinois:[88]

K11 i. Stephen Falconer, born about 1853.

ii. Mary (Mayme) N. Falconer, born 2 September 1855, died, unmarried, 20 June 1944, buried in Mount Gilead Cemetery.

iii. Thirza Falconer, born about 1857, died young.

K12 iv. William Milton Falconer, born about 1862.

K13 v. Frank D. Falconer, born November 1864.

vi. John Melvin Falconer, born 16 August 1866, died, unmarried, 23 September 1930 in Mount Zion, Macon County, Illinois, buried in Mount Gilead Cemetery.

vii. Florence Anna Falconer, born July 1871, died 1942, buried in Mount Zion Cemetery. She married, on 2 February 1893, in Macon County, Illinois,[89] Irby C. Britton, born March 1868 in Tennessee, died 1944. Issue, surname *Britton*:[90] a. *Nobel F.*, born 21 October 1895, died December 1976 in Springfield, Illinois; b. *Millard W.*, born August 1898; c. *Ethel T.*, born about 1902; d. *Melvin*, born 8 December 1903, died December 1969 in Los Angeles, California; e. *Huly R.*, born about 1907; f. *Florence*, born about 1909.

K8 George Bartley Falconer,[91] born 6 September 1838 in Frederick County, Maryland, died 12 July 1923 in Denver, Colorado.

He married, on 17 October 1875, in Lincoln County, Kansas, Mary Elizabeth Thompson, born about 1854 in Illinois.

He was a blacksmith. He served as a corporal in Company B, 8th Illinois Infantry, enlisting 16 April 1861 at Decatur, Illinois, and being discharged 25

July 1861. In 1865, he moved to the Platte River, Nebraska. From 1870 to 1904, he lived in Anter Township (near Minneapolis), Ottawa County, Kansas. In 1904, he moved to Hennessey, Kingfisher County, Oklahoma. He was in Fairview, Major County, Oklahoma, in 1912.

Issue of George Bartley and Mary Elizabeth (Thompson) Falconer, born in Ottawa County, Kansas:[92]

K14   i.   Arthur M. Falconer, born 1 September 1876.

     ii.   Fannie F. Falconer, born 31 July 1879, living in 1959 in Denver, Colorado. She married Elmer F. Warren, born about 1879 in Illinois, and had issue, surname *Warren:*[93] a. *Mary D.*, born about 1908; b. *Herbert C.*, born about 1910; c. *George F.*, born about 1913.

    iii.   son, born and died 15 October 1885, buried in Highland Cemetery.

K9 Jeremiah Milton Falconer, born about 1840 in Macon County, Illinois, was living in 1893 in Decatur, Illinois.

He married, as his first wife, on 7 March 1866, in Macon County, Illinois,[94] Ellen Ready, born 5 December 1844 [calculated] in Illinois, died 31 October 1880, buried in New Hope Cemetery, Marrowbone Township, Moultrie County, Illinois.

He married, as his second wife, on 30 September 1885, in Moultrie County, Illinois, Sarah E. Riggin, of Dalton City, Illinois, born about 1851 in Illinois.

He was a farmer in Dora Township, Moultrie County, Illinois, during his first marriage. In 1893, he was a "trader."

Issue of Jeremiah Milton and Ellen (Ready) Falconer:[95]

    i.   George R. Falconer, born October 1866, living in 1928 in Alton, Illinois. In 1900, he was living in St. Louis, Missouri, with a wife Maggie, born November 1874.[96] He married, as his second wife, by 1906, Martha Elizabeth (Crozier) Nichols, daughter of William and Martha Elizabeth (Elkinson) Crozier, born 10 October 1866 in Marion County, Illinois, died 7 April 1928 in Alton, Illinois, buried in Oakwood Cemetery.[97] In 1920, he worked as a watchman on Federal property.[98]

    ii.   daughter, died 21 May 1870, buried in the New Hope Cemetery.

    iii.   Mary (Mollie) Falconer, born about 1871. She married, on 2 December 1890, in Macon County, Illinois,[99] Elsberry Hoggatt.

K10   Prather Singleton Falconer, born 23 January 1846 in Macon County, Illinois, died 17 September 1924 in Blue Mound, Macon County, Illinois, was buried in Brown Cemetery.

He married, on 18 September 1874, in Macon County, Illinois, Nancy Catherine Warnick, daughter of Ira Griffin and Priscilla Juliette (Burke) Warnick,[100] born 18 September 1853 in Macon County, Illinois, died 28 December 1925 in Blue Mound, Illinois, buried in Brown Cemetery.

He served in the Civil War. He and his family were living in 1880 in Sheridan Township, Ottawa County, Kansas. They returned to Illinois by 1887 and lived thereafter in the village of Blue Mound.

Issue of Prather Singleton and Nancy Katherine (Warnick) Falconer, born in Macon County, Illinois:[101]

   i.   Della Falconer, born 1874, died 1877, buried in Brown Cemetery.

   ii.   Bradford Falconer, born 1876, died 1877, buried in Brown Cemetery.

   iii.   Ollie Falconer, born about 1878, living in 1926 in Blue Mound, Illinois. She married —— Moss. Issue, surname *Moss*: a. *Eloda*, married —— Harbarger.

   iv.   Thomas Alfred Falconer, born February 1887, died, unmarried, 16 July 1942 in Blue Mound, Illinois, buried in the Brown Cemetery. He served as a private in the 339th MG Battalion, 88th Division, during World War I. He was a grocer and stock buyer; during the Depression, he was employed by the Works Projects Administration.[102]

   v.   Esten W. Falconer, born 30 September 1888, died 17 July 1971 in Taylorville, Illinois, buried in the Hall Cemetery, near Blue Mound, Illinois. He married, on 12 September 1928, in Decatur, Illinois, Mrs. Opal (Christison) Varvel, born 28 August 1900, died October 1984, but had no children of his own. He lived in Blue Mound.[103]

K11   **Stephen Falconer**, born about 1853 in Macon County, Illinois, died before 1900, probably in Douglas, Alaska.

He married Frances M. ——, born June 1862 in California, living in 1900 in Douglas, Alaska.

Issue of Stephen and Frances M. Falconer, born in Washington State:[104]

   i.   Mabel Falconer, born February 1882, living in 1930 in Oakland, California. She married —— Fleming, as her first husband, and, by 1920, Everett F. Gainor, as her second husband.

   ii.   Guy S. Falconer, born September 1883, died 13 February 1920 in Oakland, California. He married Mabel ——, but had no issue.[105] He worked as an oiler for the Oakland Gas, Light, and Heat Company.

K12   **William Milton Falconer**, born about 1862 in Macon County, Illinois, died 11 April 1936 in Walla Walla County, Washington.[106]

He married, on 16 September 1891, Martha Ann Berryman, daughter of James Emanuel and Mary (Berryman) Berrymam, born about 1870 in Walla Walla County, Washington.

He was a wheat rancher near Lowden, Washington.

Issue of William Milton and Martha Ann (Berryman) Falconer:[107]

   i.   William Emanuel Falconer, born 3 November 1908, lives in Walla Walla, Washington. He married, on 25 May 1932, in Walla Walla, Washington, Mary Gwendolyn Bishop, born 19 April 1910 White Salmon, Washington. They have no children. He was a wheat and pea farmer near Lowden until his retirement.

K13   **Frank D. Falconer**, born November 1864 in Macon County, Illinois, died 24 May 1926 in South Wheatland Township, Macon County, Illinois, was buried in Mount Zion Cemetery.

He married, on 13 March 1890 in Macon County, Illinois,[108] Eva M. Ward, daughter of Hiram and Clara E. (Odor) Ward, born May 1867 in Illinois, died 2 June 1946 in Moweaqua, Illinois, who was buried in Mount Zion Cemetery.

Issue of Frank D. and Eva M. (Ward) Falconer, born in Macon County, Illinois:[109]

K15   i.   Lester William Falconer, born 29 March 1891.

       ii.   William Boyd Falconer, born 16 April 1895, died, unmarried, 9 September 1969 in Macon, Illinois.[110]

      iii.   Eva May Falconer, born 24 August 1897, died, unmarried, 28 September 1921, in South Wheatland Township, Macon County, Illinois, buried in Mount Zion Cemetery.

K14   Arthur M. Falconer, born 1 September 1876 in Anter Township, Ottawa County, Kansas, died 20 October 1959 in Fontana, San Bernardino County, California.

He married Wilma A. Tyler, born about 1897 in Missouri, died 15 August 1973 in Fontana, California.[111]

He served as master sergeant, in the 20th Kansas Infantry Regiment, during the Spanish-American War. In 1920, he was unmarried, living in Kansas City, Missouri.[112] From 1924 he was a poultry rancher in Fontana.

Issue of Arthur M. and Wilma A. (Tyler) Falconer, born in San Bernardino County, California:[113]

       i.   Billy K. Falconer, living in 1959 in Lee Vining, California, and in 1973 in June Lake, California. He had three children.

K15   Lester William Falconer, born 29 March 1891 in Macon County, Illinois, died 14 July 1971 in Mount Zion, Macon County, Illinois.

He married Ethel I. Caldwell, daughter of Charles B. and Hilie Jane (McCaffree) Caldwell,[114] born 18 August 1895 in Macon County, Illinois, died October 1986 in Macon, Illinois.

Issue of Lester William and Ethel I. (Caldwell) Falconer:

       i.   Helen Pauline Falconer, died 5 May 1920, buried in Mount Zion Cemetery.

      ii.   Mildred M. Falconer, lives in Macon, Illinois. She married George William Wells and has issue.

K16   iii.   Robert William Falconer, born 29 March 1924.

K16   Robert William Falconer, born 29 March 1924 in Decatur, Illinois, lives in Vista, California.

He married, on 9 February 1946, Lois Aileen Tomlinson, born 22 April 1924, of Macon, Illinois.

He served as a fighter pilot in World War II. He graduated from the University of Illinois with a degree in aeronautical engineering and subsequently worked in St. Louis, Missouri. In 1954, the family moved to the Los Angeles area and in 1971, he lived in Santa Maria, California.

Issue of Robert William and Lois Aileen (Tomlinson) Falconer:[115]

       i.   Carol Falconer, lives in Bonita, California. She married Capt. Robert Thomas, U.S.N.

      ii.   daughter.

     iii.   daughter.

NOTES

[1] He testified on 2 November 1744, aged 51, regarding the boundaries of the Glebe. Prince Georges Co. (Md.) Deeds, BB: 323.

[2] Prince Georges Co. (Md.) Deeds, PP: 101.

[3] Maryland Inventories, 13: 299.

[4] Statement by W. H. Barnes regarding his family's ancestry, copied by Mrs. George Leasure of Delphos, Ohio, in 1917 and sent to Harry Willson Falconer, now possessed by Harry W. Falconer II, 270 Riverside Dr., Rossford, OH 43460. See Appendix 4. Barnes (the grandson of Elisha and Charity Falconer Barnes) wrote that "Lady" Jane Falconer, of Edinburgh, Scotland, only daughter of David "Lord" Falconer, never married and came to the "Colonies" to see her brother but later returned to Scotland. Alexander, "only son" of this David, settled at Williamsport, Maryland. "Moukton" was a transcriber's error for "Monkton," property held by a branch of the Falconers in the 18th century. Father George Wilson's name is at the bottom of the page, indicating that he may have been the source of some or all of the information.

[5] Harry Wright Newman, *Mareen Duvall of Middle Plantation* (Washington: 1952), pp. 148-151.

[6] Prince Georges Co. (Md.) Deeds, NN: 455.

[7] *Calendar of Maryland State Papers.* No. 1: *The Black Books* (Baltimore: new ed., 1967), p. 23.

[8] Prince Georges Co. (Md.) Deeds, J: 166.

[9] Patent index, Maryland State Archives, citing "#4: 335" as source.

[10] Prince Georges Co. (Md.) Deeds, M: 128.

[11] Maryland Inventories, 11: 434.

[12] Prince Georges Co. (Md.) Deeds, M: 14.

[13] Wyckoff, *Tobacco Regulation in Colonial Maryland*, p. 154.

[14] Prince Georges Co. (Md.) Deeds, Q: 129.

[15] Ibid., Q: 277.

[16] Ibid., Q: 596.

[17] Ibid., Q: 675.

[18] Ibid., Q: 701.

[19] Ibid., Q: 128, 596; EE: 618; NN: 455.

[20] Prince Georges Co. (Md.) Wills, 21: 889-890.

[21] Prince Georges Co. (Md.) Deeds, Y: 479.

[22] Ibid., EE: 618.

[23] Ibid., EE: 699.

[24] Ibid., NN: 292.

[25] Ibid., NN: 455.

[26] Maryland Wills, 30: 385.

[27] Prince Georges Co. (Md.) Debt Books.

[28] Harry Wright Newman, *Mareen Duvall of Middle Plantation*, pp. 148-151.

[29] Queen Anne's Parish register.

[30] *Maryland Historical Magazine* 70: 108.

[31] Maryland Testamentary Proceedings, 77: 303.

[32] Maryland Wills, 27: 48.

[33] Or 7 January 1735, according to St. Paul's register.

[34] 1790 census.

[35] Prince Georges Co. (Md.) Deeds, NN: 292.

[36] Ibid., PP: 101.

[37] Maryland Provincial Court, lib. DD#10: 538.

[38] Prince Georges Co. (Md.) Deeds, TT: 541-3; Bowie Family Papers, folder 17, Maryland State Archives.

[39] James M. Magruder, *Magruder's Maryland Colonial Abstracts* (Baltimore: Genealogical Pub. Co., 1968), 1: 14.

[40] Washington Co. (Md.) Land Records, B: 320-321.

[41] Frederick Co. (Md.) Wills, GM2: 125.

[42] Statement by W. H. Barnes (see note 4). This includes brief sketches of John B. Falconer; Susan Falconer, who married Mr. Wilson; Charity; and the children of "Uncle Washington."

[43] 1800 census, Frederick Co., Md., p. 163.

[44] Statement by W. H. Barnes (see note 4); he wrote "typhus fever."

[45] *American Historical Register* 2 (June 1895): 1128; *History of Jefferson County, Iowa.*

[46] Statement of W. H. Barnes (see note 4).

[47] V. F. O'Daniel's notes of a letter from Jandel to Wilson, 4 Feb. 1871, Provincial Archives, Providence College.

[48] Statement of W. H. Barnes (see note 4).

[49] Frederick Co. (Md.) Orphans Court Proceedings, lib. GM3, n.p.

[50] Frederick Co. (Md.) Marriage Licenses.

[51] *Baltimore American,* 5 Dec. 1810; statement of W. H. Barnes.

[52] *Bartgis's Republican Gazette,* 31 March 1802, in: F. Edward Wright, *Western Maryland Newspaper Abstracts,* vol. 2, *1799-1805* (Silver Spring, Md.: Family Line, 1986), p. 107.

[53] T. J. C. Williams and Folger McKinsey, *History of Frederick County, Maryland* (Baltimore: 1910), p. 536.

[54] 1800 census, Frederick Co., Md., p. 161.

[55] Statement of W. H. Barnes (see note 4).

[56] Cemetery inscription; John W. Smith, *History of Macon County, Illinois, from Its Organization to 1876* (Springfield, Ill.: Rokker's Printing House, 1876), p. 261.

[57] Georgia Thompson, "Earliest Legible Tombstones in the Mt. Zion Presbyterian Cemetery," *Central Illinois Genealogical Quarterly* 5 (1969): 108.

[58] Smith, *History of Macon County,* p. 261.

[59] *Central Illinois Genealogical Quarterly* 27 (Winter 1981): 99.

[60] Macon Co. (Ill.) Circuit Court, file 280.

[61] Smith, *History of Macon County,* p. 261; will.

[62] *Frederick Times,* 14 June 1832.

[63] Macon Co., Ill., Marriage Record, 1: 10.

[64] 1850 census, Macon Co., Ill., p. 167.

[65] Bob Day, *Greenleaf Cemetery, Brownwood, Texas* (Bangs, Tex.: the author, 1988), p. 77.

[66] Gravestone inscription.

[67] Janet Thompson Manuel, *Marriage Licenses: Montgomery County, Maryland: 1798-1898* (Silver Spring, Md.: Family Line, 1987), p. 107.

[68] Macon Co. (Ill.) Marriages, 1: 33.

[69] Ibid., 2: 69.

[70] 1850 census, Macon Co., Ill., p. 141; Macon Co. Circuit Court, file 832.

[71] Macon Co. (Ill.) Marriages, 1: 17.

[72] Smith, *History of Macon County,* p. 53.

[73] Macon Co. (Ill.) Marriages, 1: 32.

[74] *Car-Del Scribe* (May 1984).

[75] His name may have been Singleton Prather Falconer.

[76] Macon Co. (Ill.) Mortgages, 37: 197.

[77] *History of Macoupin County, Illinois* (Philadelphia: Brink, McDonough & Co., 1879), p. 75.

[78] Illinois Conference of the Methodist Episcopal Church. Minutes, 18 Aug. 1842, in Illinois Wesleyan University Archives.

[79] *Illinois State Journal,* 22 Oct. 1841, 2 Oct. 1845, 21 Oct. 1847, 30 Sept. 1851.

[80] Illinois Executive Record 1856-60, 7: 246.

[81] 1850 census, Macon Co., Ill., p. 167; 1860 census, Macon Co., Ill., p. 639.

[82] Macon Co. (Ill.) Marriages, 2: 50.

[83] 1910 census, Hillsborough Co., Fla., 18-49-7.

[84] Cook Co. (Ill.) Death Records Index, 1871-1916.

[85] 1900 census, Cook Co., Ill., 30-302-13-30.

[86] *Decatur Herald,* 7 May 1917.

[87] Macon Co. (Ill.) Marriages, 1: 21.

[88] Estate files of William W. and Euphemia A. Falconer, Macon Co. (Ill.) Circuit Court, files 1714 and 4401; 1880

census, Macon Co., Ill., 36-164-7-37.

89 Macon Co. (Ill.) Marriages, 2: 201.

90 1900 census, Macon Co., Ill., 119-63-5-25; 1910 census, Macon Co., Ill., 159-129-54.

91 His middle name, the source for which is the 1860 census, might have actually been "Barclay."

92 Pension file (certificate no. 866,010), National Archives.

93 1920 census, Denver, Colo., 16-297-1-23.

94 Macon Co. (Ill.) Marriages, 1: 118.

95 1870 census, Moultrie Co., Ill., p. 17; 1880 census, Moultrie Co., Ill., 42-166-9-46.

96 1900 census, St. Louis Co., Mo., 86-48-3-30.

97 Death certificate, Illinois State Archives.

98 1920 census, Madison Co., Ill., 187-36-3-81.

99 Macon Co. (Ill.) Marriage Record, 2: 124.

100 Doris Roney Bowers, "Warnick Family Genealogical Lines," *Central Illinois Genealogical Quarterly* 23 (1987): 190.

101 1880 census, Ottawa Co., Kans., 15-221-1-1; 1900 census, Macon Co., Ill., 119-66-3-47; *Blue Mound Leader*, 25 Sept. 1924.

102 *Decatur Herald and Review*, 19 July 1942, p. 3.

103 Ibid., 18 July 1971.

104 Estates of Euphemia A. Falconer and John M. Falconer, Macon Co. (Ill.) Circuit Court, files 4401 and 8247; 1900 census, Alaska, 4-6-28-18.

105 *San Francisco Examiner*, 14 Feb. 1920.

106 Washington State Death Index.

107 1910 census, Walla Walla Co., Wash., 2-239-3; William E. Falconer, Walla Walla, WA.

108 Macon Co. (Ill.) Marriages, 2: 102.

109 Estate of John M. Falconer; 1900 census, 119-68-1-65.

110 Macon Co. Circuit Court, file 69P329.

111 *San Bernardino Evening Telegram*, 17 Aug. 1973.

112 1920 census, Jackson Co., Mo., 53-245-11-81.

113 *San Bernardino Evening Telegram*, 21 Oct. 1959.

114 Adair Co. (Ky.) Deeds, 48: 133.

115 Carol Thomas.

CHAPTER L

Gilbert Falconar, Son of Alexander

L1 **Gilbert Falconar**, third son of Alexander (K1) and Susannah (Duvall) Falconar, born 15 January 1722/3 in Queen Anne's Parish, Prince Georges County, Maryland, died testate between 10 July and 11 August 1779 in Frederick County, Maryland.[1]

He married, before 27 March 1754, Margery Miles (or Mills), daughter of Thomas and Mary Miles,[2] born 31 December 1731 in Prince Georges County, Maryland.[3] She married, as her second husband, by a license dated 13 December 1783 in Frederick County, Maryland, John Maddon.

He first appears in the records, as an adult, in 1749. With Nicholas Digges and Richard Duckett, he confessed judgment to John Hepburn of the sum of £48, 14s., and 380 pounds of tobacco.[4] On 7 August 1749, Gilbert Falconar sold to Digges and Duckett, for £16, one horse, a red cow and calf, one bed and bed clothes, three pewter plates, and a dish.[5]

Gilbert Falconar probably lived on his father's property. The Debt Books of Prince Georges County list him as owing a quitclaim tax on "Darnall's Grove" from 1769 to 1772, having succeeded Alexander, his brother. On 26 August 1775, he redeemed "Samuel's Choice," which had belonged to his father and maternal grandfather, from Edward Hall, son of Henry, for £150.[6] He sold this land on 21 November 1778 to Walter Bowie for £1000.[7] By this date he had already moved to Frederick County. In 1778, when living there, he made an oath of fidelity to the American cause.[8] On 29 April 1778, he purchased, for £2000, "Resurvey on Wild Cat Hill," consisting of 319 acres, "Meadows," of 462 acres, and "Convenience," of 219 acres, all adjoining tracts, from Thomas Neill, of Frederick Town, merchant.[9] On 8 January 1779, he presented his qualification as deputy sheriff.[10]

In his will, dated 10 July 1779, Gilbert Falconar gave to his wife Margery the tract "The Meadow," which would pass to his "youngest" son Elisha after her decease. His personal estate went to his wife, the profits arising from the produce of the plantation to support Elisha until he reached the age of eighteen. To his son Gilbert he gave the tract "Convenience." He asked that "Resurvey on Wild Cat Hill" be sold at public vendue, the profits to pay his debts. He appointed his son Gilbert executor and his wife Margery executrix. Witnesses were Thomas Beatty, William Brashear, Jr., and Samuel Duvall.[11]

His personal estate was appraised on 20 November 1779 at £7703, 10s.,

10d.; "kindred" were listed as Elizabeth Falconer and "Sasanner" Falconer.[12]

Issue of Gilbert and Margery (Miles) Falconar, born in Prince Georges County, Maryland:

   i.   Gilbert Falconer, born perhaps about 1752, was living as late as 27 November 1794, in Frederick County, Maryland. In 1778, when a resident of Prince Georges County, he signed an oath of allegiance to the American side.[13] On 17 September 1779, he sold "Convenience," a tract of 219 acres he inherited from his father, to John Benson of Frederick County, for £1250.[14] On 30 May 1780, he and Margery Falconer, as ordered by the will of Gilbert Falconar, Sr., sold "Resurvey on Wild Cat Hill" to William Worthington of Frederick County for £2080, but on the same day he purchased the same tract back from Worthington.[15] On 27 November 1794, he sold to David Funk of Washington County, Maryland, a Negro woman slave named Henny, aged 17 in April 1795, who had been sold to him by Margery Falconer, executrix of his father's estate.[16] In the 1790 census, he was recorded with two males over 16, four females, and two slaves. Gilbert may have left Maryland after this date; he does not appear in the 1798 assessment list of Frederick County nor in any of the indexes to the 1800 census. There is no evidence he married or had children.[17]

   ii.   Elizabeth Falconer. Since Gilbert, Sr., had no sister with this name, Elizabeth, as "kindred," must be his daughter, although she is not named in his will. Although on 28 November 1779 her name was listed as Falconer, she may have been the otherwise unidentified "Eliza." Falconer who married, on 23 February 1779 in Montgomery County, Maryland, James Deakin.[18]

   iii.   Susannah Falconer.[19]

   iv.   Eleanor Falconer, born 17 July 1763.[20]

   v.   Martha Falconer, born 4 February 1766.[21]

L2   vi.   Elisha Falconer, born about 1772.

L2 Elisha Falconer, born about 1772 in Prince Georges County, Maryland, died 21 June 1847 in New Market, Frederick County, Maryland.[22]

He married first, by a license dated 30 April 1794 in Frederick County, Maryland, Sarah Davis. Her family has not been identified.

He married, as his second wife, by a license dated 6 January 1810 in Frederick County, Maryland, Eleanor Norwood, daughter of Belt and Sarah (Gaither) Norwood,[23] born 27 August 1787.[24]

He was a master carpenter, as were each of his sons, and lived on "The Meadow," a tract of 462 acres he inherited from his father, which lay near New Market, Maryland. By 1798, his mother had transferred 132 acres of this tract to Nicholas Hall, John Iiams, and William Wood.[25] Between 1810 and 1821 he sold off parts of this tract.[26] He was turned out of his office as constable in 1802, along with many other public officials.[27] He served in the militia during the War of 1812.[28] In religion, he was a Methodist,[29] which flourished in Maryland during his lifetime.

Issue of Elisha and Sarah (Davis) Falconer, born in Frederick County, Maryland:[30]

   i.   Maria Falconer, born about 1795, died 25 July 1879 in Frederick County, Maryland, buried in Liberty Chapel Cemetery.[31] She married, by a license dated 23 April 1813 in Frederick County, Jonathan Browning, Jr., born 4

December 1790 in Washington County, Maryland,[32] living in 1850. Issue, surname *Browning:*[33] a. *John L.*; b. *Rachel,* married Henry Brogen; c. *Eliza,* married David Echie; d. *Sarah,* married Daniel Biddinger; e. *Ellen,* married John Hiter; f. *Miranda,* born about 1817, married Jesse Penn; g. *Elizabeth,* married John W. Crum.

L3   ii.   Reuben Falconer, born about 1801.

L4   iii.   John Falconer, born 21 January 1803.

L5   iv.   Mahlon Falconer, born about 1805.

Issue of Elisha and Eleanor (Norwood) Falconer, born in Frederick County, Maryland:[34]

L6   v.   Ralph James Falconer, born about 1812.

vi.   Sarah Falconer. The order of births of this family is unknown, as is the identity of her mother. She may have been the Sarah "Fortner" who married, by license dated 1 June 1837 in Frederick County,[35] Hugh Brennan.

L7   vii.   Elisha Falconer, born 28 February 1815.

L8   viii.   Nelson Faulkner, born 28 February 1815.

ix.   Eden Falconer, born 9 December 1818, died 30 October 1848, buried in Glade Reformed Cemetery, Walkersville, Maryland.[36] He married, by a license dated 16 March 1842, in Frederick County, Maryland, Sophia Barrick, daughter of Frederick and Catharine (Cramer) Barrick, born 2 April 1820 Frederick County, Maryland.[37] No issue. She married, as her second husband, by a license dated 28 November 1850, in Frederick County, Maryland, Richard B. Brown.

L9   x.   William Hamilton Falconer, born 3 April 1820.

xi.   Elizabeth Falconer, born about 1820, living in 1850 in New Market, Maryland. She married, by license dated 4 October 1835, in Frederick County, Maryland, Alexander Hamilton Thom[p]son, born about 1817, and had issue, surname *Thomson:*[38] a. *Sarah E.,* born about 1838; b. *Eliza A.,* born about 1840; c. *Charles A.,* born about 1841; d. *Mary E.,* born about 1845; e. *Margaret J.,* born about 1848.

L10   xii.   Alfred Falconer, born 1 January 1823.

xiii.   Joshua Falconer, perhaps died young, as he has not been further traced.

xiv.   Susan Falconer, born about 1826, buried 10 April 1873 in Glenwood Cemetery, Washington, D.C. She married, in June 1848,[39] James G. Ellis, son of John and Sarah (Norwood) Ellis, born about 1822 in Washington, D.C., buried 4 February 1872 in Glenwood Cemetery, and had issue, surname *Ellis:*[40] a. *James W.,* born about 1847; b. *Sarah Helen,* born about 1849, married, 14 February 1871, Edmund T. Ryan; c. *John A.,* born about 1851, buried 23 May 1890; d. *George G.,* born about 1853; e. *Harry C.,* buried 31 March 1859; f. *William K.,* born about 1858.

xv.   Ellen Falconer. She married, on 22 November 1852 in Washington, D.C., Henry Eckardt.[41]

L3 Reuben Falconer, born about 1801 in Frederick County, Maryland, died shortly before 13 March 1871 in New Market, Frederick County, Maryland.[42]

He married first, by license dated 13 December 1830 in Frederick County, Maryland, Lucinda Prather, born 1812, died 9 October 1845, "in her 34th year," buried in the Methodist Cemetery, New Market, Maryland.

He married, as his second wife, by license dated 29 March 1848 in Frederick County, Maryland, Sarah (Miles) Swamley, widow of Mahlon

Swamley, born about 1800 in Maryland, died between 1850 and 1860.

Like his father and his brothers, Reuben was a carpenter. He also specialized in making furniture.

Issue of Reuben and Lucinda (Prather) Falconer, born in Frederick County, Maryland:[43]

    i.   Eliza Ann Falconer,[44] born about 1829, living in 1850 in Buckeye District, Frederick County, Maryland. She married, by license dated 13 January 1847, in Frederick County, Richard T. Dixon. Issue, surname *Dixon*:[45] a. *Georgean S.*, born about 1847; b. *Manszella C.*, born about 1849.

L11 ii.   Oliver L. Falconer, born 10 October 1831.

L12 iii.   Eldred S. Falconer, born 8 December 1833.

    iv.   E. Virginia Falconer, born about 1836, buried 2 April 1869 in Glenwood Cemetery, Washington, D.C. She married, by license dated 26 May 1864 in Frederick County, Maryland, Robert B. Ferguson, born 30 September 1837 [calculated], died 25 September 1889 in Washington, D.C., buried Glenwood Cemetery. Issue. He married, as his second wife, Sarah A. ——.

    v.   Mortimer Falconer, born 1 July 1843 [calculated], died, unmarried, 15 August 1924 in Maple Wood Farms, Maryland, buried in Glenwood Cemetery.[46] He was a clerk and a druggist in Washington.

    vi.   Lucien Falconer, born about 1844, died, of congestive fever, February 1850 in New Market, Frederick County, Maryland.[47]

L4 John Falconer, born 21 January 1803[48] in Frederick County, Maryland, died 31 August 1880, aged 77 years, 7 months, and 9 days, in South Wheatland Township, Macon County, Illinois, was buried in Mount Gilead Cemetery.

He married, on 5 June 1832, in Frederick County, Maryland,[49] Anna Falconar, daughter of George Washington (K4) and Mary (Boyd) Falconar, born 6 September 1803 [calculated] in Frederick County, Maryland, died 8 August 1875 in South Wheatland Township, Macon County, Illinois, buried in Mount Gilead Cemetery.

He came to Illinois in 1839 and purchased land in South Wheatland Township. He attended a temperance convention in Macon County, as secretary of the Mount Gilead Washington Temperance Society.[50]

Issue of John and Anna (Falconar) Falconer, the first three born in Frederick County, Maryland, the rest in Macon County, Illinois:[51]

    i.   George W[ashington] Falconer, born 25 September 1833 [calculated], died 31 August 1839 in Zanesville, Ohio, buried in Mount Gilead Cemetery.

L13 ii.   Emory Vinton Falconer, born 19 March 1835.

    iii.   Anna Mary Falconer, born about 1838, died 31 March 1921 in Brownwood, Texas, buried in Greenleaf Cemetery.[52] She married Leonidas Bair, born 26 September 1840 in Indiana, died 2 January 1912 in Brownwood, Texas, buried in Greenleaf Cemetery. They were in Brown County, Texas, by 1881. Issue, surname *Bair*: a. *Lonnie*, born 1875, died, unmarried, 1940; b. *Ollie B.*, born 19 January 1879, died 19 August 1882.

    iv.   Sarah N. J. Falconer, born about 1841. On 26 May 1862, in Macon County, Illinois,[53] she married Francis M. DeMaranville. She died soon after and he was married again to Lilla J. ——. In 1880, he lived in Knox County, Nebraska.

    v.   Enoch McL. Falconer, born 9 May 1843 [calculated]. He, of Cerro Gordo, Illinois, enlisted as a private in Company A, 116th Illinois Infantry, on 6 August 1862, died 18 April 1863 at Milliken's Bend, Louisiana,[54] and was buried in Mount Gilead Cemetery.

L14 vi.   Charles B. Falconer, born January 1848.

L5 Mahlon Falconer, born about 1805 in Frederick County, Maryland, died 25 August 1870 in Washington, D.C.,[55] was buried in Glenwood Cemetery.[56]

He married, by a license dated 18 November 1839, in Frederick County, Maryland, Jane Dorson Brown, born about 1815 in Maryland, died 11 August 1864 in Washington, D.C., buried in Glenwood Cemetery.

He was a carpenter. In 1850, they lived in Ellicott City, Maryland. They moved to Washington, D.C. by 1864.

Issue of Mahlon and Jane Dorson (Brown) Falconer:[57]

    i.   James W. B. Falconer, born August 1842 [calculated], died 12 May 1844, aged 1 year, 9 months, buried in the Methodist Cemetery, New Market, Maryland.

    ii.   William George Falconer, born 4 October 1844, died 17 December 1850, buried in the Quaker Hill Graveyard, Ellicott City, Maryland.

L15 iii.   Richard T. J. Falconer, born December 1846.

    iv.   Albert B. Falconer, buried 6 September 1868 in Glenwood Cemetery, in Mahlon's plot.[58]

L6 Ralph James Falconer, born about 1812 in Frederick County, Maryland, died in 1871 in Washington, D.C., was buried in Glenwood Cemetery.

He married, on 5 May 1840, Susan Ellis,[59] daughter of John and Sarah (Norwood) Ellis, born March 1823 [calculated] in Washington, D.C., buried 18 May 1883, aged 60 years, one month, and 20 days, in Glenwood Cemetery, Washington, D.C.

He was a master carpenter. He had settled in Washington by 1840. In 1846, he was a grocer.

Issue of Ralph James and Susan (Ellis) Falconer, born in Washington, D.C.:[60]

L16 i.   George E. Falconer, born about 1841.

    ii.   Emma W. Falconer, born about 1845, buried 19 October 1882 in Glenwood Cemetery. She married, on 31 January 1871, at the Fourth Presbyterian Church, in Washington, D.C., James Campbell, probably the son of Mason and Mary S. (Chaddock) Campbell, born 9 November 1837 in New York, died 4 April 1899 in Washington, D.C., buried in Glenwood Cemetery. Issue, surname *Campbell*:[61] a. *Jessie F.*, born 4 November 1871, died 23 January 1946. He married, as his second wife, Mary S. ——.

    iii.   Susan Falconer, born about 1851, probably the Susan A. Falcanor buried in Mount Olivet Cemetery, Washington, D.C., on 23 March 1882.

    iv.   Jessie E. Falconer, born about 1853.

    v.   James A. Falconer, born October 1855, buried 3 November 1878 in Glenwood Cemetery, aged 23 years, 17 days.

    vi.   DeWitt C. Falconer, born about 1859, died between 1860 and 1870.

L7 Elisha Falconer, born 28 February 1815 in New Market, Frederick County, Maryland, was buried 21 November 1889 in Glenwood Cemetery, Washington, D.C.[62]

He married, on 1 December 1840, in Ellicott City (then Ellicott's Mills), Maryland,[63] Sarah McCausland, of Ellicott's Mills, born 1819 in Maryland, buried 4 January 1889, aged 69 years, 10 months, and 2 days, in Glenwood Cemetery.[64]

A carpenter, he was in Ellicott City, Maryland, by 1840, but moved to Washington in the 1850s. He was a wood and coal dealer in 1870.

Issue of Elisha and Sarah (McCausland) Falconer:[65]

i.   John W. Falconer, born about 1841, died 10 February 1893, aged 53, buried in Glenwood Cemetery. He married, on 5 June 1866, Matilda Kain.[66] She died, or they were separated, by 1870.

ii.   Theodore Falconer, born December 1843, buried 27 December 1881, aged 38 years and 1 day, in Glenwood Cemetery.

iii. Mary Almira Falconer, born about 1845, buried 2 January 1892 in Glenwood Cemetery. She married, on 15 November 1869 in Washington, D.C., Jerome Lee, born about 1843, buried 11 October 1887 in Glenwood Cemetery. Issue, surname *Lee*:[67] a. *Joyce*, born about 1874 in Ohio; b. *Owen*, born about 1877; c. daughter, born 1880; d. *Myron J.*, born 1882, buried 26 April 1898.

iv.   Sally Falconer, born about 1849, died before 1860.

v.   Charles E. Falconer, born August 1853, buried 10 September 1873, aged 20 years, 12 days, in Glenwood Cemetery.

vi.   Letitia Falconer, born about 1855, buried 4 October 1892 in Glenwood Cemetery, unmarried.

vii. Georgia Falconer, born 19 July 1858,[68] died, unmarried, 16 March 1919, buried in Glenwood Cemetery.

viii. Ella Falconer, born 10 September 1861,[69] buried in Glenwood Cemetery.

L8 Nelson Faulkner, born 28 February 1815 in New Market, Frederick County, Maryland, died 25 February 1896 in Urbana, Ohio, was buried in Kingscreek Baptist Church Cemetery, Kingscreek, Ohio.

He married Anna Neer, daughter of David and Hannah (Russell) Neer of Loudoun County, Virginia, born 17 January 1820 in Loudoun County, Virginia, died 1 April 1901 in Westville, Ohio.

Like his brothers, he was a carpenter. He moved from Harpers Ferry, Virginia, to Concord Township, Champaign County, Ohio, between 1846 and 1850, where the remainder of his children was born.

Issue of Nelson and Anna (Neer) Faulkner (she gave birth to ten children):[70]

L17 i.   Charles W. Faulkner, born 3 November 1843.

ii.   James W. Faulkner, born about 1846, died before 1900, possibly in Washington, D.C., presumably unmarried. He enlisted 5 February 1864 in the 113th Ohio Volunteer Infantry, and was discharged 27 February 1864.

iii. Emma Virginia Faulkner, born 30 May 1850, died 29 December 1916 in Columbus, Ohio, buried in Kingscreek Cemetery. On 31 March 1870, in Urbana, Ohio, she married David Osborn Taylor, son of Thomas and Lucy (Chamberlin) Taylor, born 1 August 1844 in Salem Township, Champaign County, Ohio,

Twins Elisha Falconer and Nelson Faulkner, c. 1885.

died 28 October 1915 in Kingscreek, Ohio. Issue, surname *Taylor:*[71] a. *Ralph Eugene,* born 19 January 1871; b. *Grace Luretta,* born 31 July 1872, died 12 November 1962 in Columbus, Ohio, married 9 December 1891 Lucien Oliver Coleman; c. *Anna Lucy,* born 20 May 1875, died 15 March 1917 in Columbus, Ohio, married 31 May 1894 George H. Ream; d. *Edna Maud,* born 20 November 1876, died after 1943 in Columbus, Ohio, married Bert Sutton; e. *Earl,* born 21 February 1879, died 3 August 1879 in Knightstown, Indiana; f. *Letha Elizabeth,* born 27 November 1880, married Fred J. Akorborg; g. *Ethel Estella,* born 11 July 1883, married Charles N. Cranford; h. infant, born and died 27 August 1886; i. *Charles Nelson,* born 7 October 1888, died 8 August 1943 in Columbus, Ohio, married (1) 9 October 1905 Pearl Benner, (2) 20 April 1916 Gladys Jessie Derr; j. *Enos Roy,* born 26 April 1891, died 21 September 1891.

iv. Susan (Sudie) Ann Faulkner, born 16 January 1851, died 5 November 1931 in Westville, Ohio. She married, on 23 November 1876, in Urbana, Ohio, Charles Hunter Walters, born 21 April 1842 in Martinsburg, West Virginia, died 12 December 1908 in Kingscreek, Ohio, and had issue, surname *Walters:* a. *Earl,* born 10 August 1881, died 8 October 1938 in Urbana, Ohio, married 16 March 1909 Elizabeth Vitula Elwell.

v. Sarah Elizabeth Faulkner, born 14 October 1854, died 2 October 1901 in Toledo, Ohio, buried in Woodlawn Cemetery, Toledo. She married, on 13 September 1877, in Urbana, Ohio, Richard Millard McKee, son of James and Eliza (Moore) McKee, born 26 July 1844 in Auburn Township, Waynesburgh,

Ohio, died 25 March 1907 in Toledo, Ohio a lawyer, who settled in Toledo, Ohio. Issue, surname *McKee*: a. *Albert Pearl*, born 6 September 1878, died September 1960 in Toledo, Ohio, married Marian Weigtman; b. *Clara Mabelle*, born 16 July 1881, died 27 May 1970 in Toledo, Ohio, married, in 1906, Jay Andrew Popp; c. *Dora Blanche*, born 27 July 1887, died 8 March 1926 in Montclair, New Jersey, married Clarence Arthur Popp; d. *Florence Annette*, born 8 December 1892, died 12 January 1974 in Toledo, Ohio, married 7 June 1916 George Edgar Spaulding.[72]

vi.   Frank F. Faulkner, born about 1857, probably died between 1860, when listed in the census, and 1865, when his siblings were christened.

vii. Hannah Francis Faulkner, born 1858, died, unmarried, 20 July 1895 in Urbana, Ohio, buried in Kingscreek Baptist Church Cemetery.

viii. Clara Jane Faulkner, born 28 May 1860, died, unmarried, 29 November 1948 in Dayton, Ohio, buried in Kingscreek Baptist Church Cemetery. She was a registered nurse who worked for many years at Dayton State Hospital.

L18   ix.   Edward Franklin Faulkner, born 14 October 1864.

L9 **William Hamilton Falconer**, born 3 April 1820 in Frederick County, Maryland, died 11 April 1890 in Baltimore, Maryland, aged 71 years,[73] was buried in Lorraine Park Cemetery.

He married first, on 4 May 1846, in Washington, D.C.,[74] Mary Elizabeth Bryan, born about 1824, buried 8 September 1854, aged 30, in Glenwood Cemetery, Washington, D.C.[75]

He married, 7 January 1856, in Washington, D.C., Mary Ann Jemima Boteler, daughter of Charles Wesley and Mary (Moriarity) Boteler, born 10 February 1826 in Washington, D.C., died 14 June 1912.[76]

He was a prominent building contractor and architect. He lived in Washington from the 1840s to 1863. While there, he was responsible for the construction of the Louise Home, the original Corcoran Art Gallery, and many other buildings. In 1863 he and his family moved to Frederick, Maryland.[77] He later lived in Baltimore. He served on the Executive Committee of the Maryland Deaf and Dumb Institution in 1882.[78]

Issue of William Hamilton and Mary Elizabeth (Bryan) Falconer, born in Washington, D.C.:[79]

L19   i.   Joseph H. Falconer, born about 1847.

ii.   Emily Ellen Falconer, born April 1849 [calculated], buried 3 December 1849, aged 7 months, 21 days, in Glenwood Cemetery.

iii. Marion O. Falconer, born about 1852, buried 15 September 1925 in Glenwood Cemetery. She married John W. Lane, who was buried 6 September 1914, aged 63 years, 5 months, 15 days, in Glenwood Cemetery.[80] No issue. She was in a sanitarium in Philadelphia for many years.

Issue of William Hamilton and Mary Ann Jemima (Boteler) Falconer, the first three born in Washington, D.C.:[81]

iv.   William Falconer, buried 1858, aged 1 year, 6 months, in Glenwood Cemetery.

L20   v.   Charles E. Falconer, born 5 June 1859.

L21   vi.   Henry (Harry) Willson Falconer, born 22 July 1862.

vii. Fannie Falconer, born 1865 in Frederick, Maryland. She married, in 1887, William Rodgers, born 1860, died 1933, a grain exporter and broker of Baltimore, Maryland. Issue, surname *Rodgers*:[82] a. *Maurice Falconer*, born 5 October 1888, died September 1968 in Baltimore, Maryland, married, 8 June 1921, Mary Katharine Taylor; b. *George William*, born 1893, died 1940, married Margaret Wright; c. *Evans*, born 1895, died 1896; d. *John Kirkwood*, born 1897, died 1898.

viii. Mary Falconer, born July 1868 in Maryland, living in Baltimore, Maryland, in 1926. She married Charles E. Bristor, born May 1855 in Maryland, living in 1900, and had issue, surname *Bristor*:[83] a. *Allen F.*, born July 1892; b. *Charles E.*, born June 1897.

L10 Alfred Falconer, born 1 January 1823 in New Market, Frederick County, Maryland, died 5 February 1885 in Washington, D.C., was buried in Glenwood Cemetery.[84]

He married, on 27 June 1866, Sarah (Sallie) Anne Clocker, daughter of John and Emeline (Henning) Clocker, born 6 August 1836 in St. Mary's County, Maryland, died 5 May 1920 in Washington, D.C, buried in Glenwood Cemetery.

He was a carpenter and had settled in Washington by 1860.

Issue of Alfred and Sarah Anne (Clocker) Falconer, born in Washington, D.C.:[85]

i. John Bennett Falconer, born 18 April 1867, died 25 September 1868, buried in Glenwood Cemetery.

ii. Mary Lee Falconer, born 10 February 1869, died 28 August 1894 in Washington, D.C., buried in Glenwood Cemetery. She married, on 24 April 1889, James Henry Bessling, born 11 October 1853 New York, N.Y., died 12 December 1931 Washington, D.C. Issue, surname *Bessling*: a. *Edward Norwood*, born 14 June 1894, died 12 September 1972, married 16 May 1927, Washington, D.C., Ruth Jones.

L22 iii. Frank Norwood Falconer, born April 1871.

L11 Oliver L. Falconer, born 10 October 1831 in New Market, Frederick County, Maryland, probably died before 1860 in New Market, Frederick County, Maryland.

By a license dated 16 October 1852, in Frederick County, Maryland, he married Clementine E. Barbour, daughter of Johnsey and Catherine (Longsworth) Barbour, born 16 August 1831 in New Market, Frederick County, Maryland, died 9 August 1857, buried in the Methodist Cemetery, New Market.[86]

A carpenter, Oliver was living with his father in 1850, but seems to have disappeared by 1860. The son Lucian was raised by his grandfather Reuben and uncle Eldred; the daughter Clementine was raised by her maternal aunt Harriet C. (Barbour) Murdock and her husband John Murdock, of Boonsboro, Maryland, who also helped raise Lucian.

Issue of Oliver L. and Clementine E. (Barbour) Falconer, born in Frederick County, Maryland:[87]

L23 i. Lucian Edward Falconer, born 5 August 1853.

    ii.   Clementine Lucinda Katherine (Katie) Falconer, born 20 December 1855. She married, on 13 April 1881, in Boonsboro, Maryland, Francis E. Storm, born 31 October 1855 in Boonsboro, Maryland, a tinner and stove dealer, and had issue, surname *Storm:*[88] a. *Hattie*, born 10 March 1882, died 17 September 1882; b. *Alice C.*, born 5 August 1883; c. *Pauline S.*, born 31 March 1888; d. *John F.*, born 20 January 1890, died October 1970 in Washington, D.C.; e. *Harriet C.*, born 30 June 1892; f. *Frances M.*, born 16 April 1894.

L12 Eldred S. Falconer, born 8 December 1833 in New Market, Frederick County, Maryland, died 8 August 1892 in New Market, Maryland, was buried in the New Market Methodist Episcopal Church Cemetery.[89]

He married, as his first wife, Alice ——, born about 1836 in Maryland, living in 1860.[90]

He married, as his second wife, on 3 May 1869, in Frederick County, Maryland,[91] Mary Frances Penn, daughter of Jesse and Miranda (Browning) Penn and granddaughter of Jonathan and Maria (Falconer) Browning, born 18 May 1839 in New Market, Frederick County, Maryland, died 20 December 1901, buried in the Methodist Cemetery in New Market, Maryland.

Issue of Eldred S. and Alice (——) Falconer:[92]

    i.   Jesse L. Falconer, born 9 June 1861, died 25 July 1867.

Issue of Eldred S. and Mary Frances (Penn) Falconer, born in Frederick County, Maryland:[93]

L24   ii.   William E. Falconer, born February 1869.
L25   iii.   John Lucian Falconer, born 24 July 1871.

L13 Emory Vinton Falconer, born 19 March 1835 in Baltimore, Maryland, died 26 January 1917 in Decatur, Illinois, was buried in Greenwood Cemetery.

He married, on 12 January 1869 in Macon County, Illinois,[94] Mary Elizabeth Carter, daughter of James K. and Mary Carter, born March 1840 in Illinois, died 13 April 1927 in Decatur, Illinois.

They left the farm in the 1870s and moved to Decatur, where he worked as a machinist for Roberts, Lytle, and Company and cabinetmaker. He was employed by the Decatur Coffin Company for nineteen years and then for sixteen years by the H. Mueller Manufacturing Company. He was a member of the First Christian Church in Decatur.[95]

Issue of Emory Vinton and Mary Elizabeth (Carter) Falconer, born in Macon County, Illinois:[96]

    i.   Howard J. Falconer, born 19 June 1869, died 18 July 1871, buried in Mount Gilead Cemetery.
    ii.   Emma V. Falconer, born [19 June] 1869, living in 1917 in Stanton, Nebraska. She married, 23 February 1910, in Macon County, Illinois,[97] Harry E. Tutin. Issue, surname *Tutin:* a. *Mary Lois.*
    iii.   son, born 1 January 1875, died 28 February 1875, buried in Mount Gilead Cemetery.

iv. Hattie J. Falconer, born [1] January 1875, died prior to 1917 in Oklahoma City, Oklahoma. She married C. E. Molesworth, M.D., but had no issue.

L14 Charles B. Falconer, born January 1848 in Macon County, Illinois, died between 1900 and 1910 in Mitchell County, Texas, or Lubbock County, Texas.

He married, as his first wife, on 10 July 1876, in Macon County, Illinois,[98] Ella T. Hamilton, born 18 September 1857, died 17 January 187-, buried in Mount Gilead Cemetery, Mount Zion Township, Macon County, Illinois.[99]

He married, as his second wife, Nellie Green, born August 1871 in Arkansas, living in 1910 in Colorado City, Texas. She married, as her second husband, Samuel L. Gamble.

He was a cigar manufacturer in Decatur in 1881, but probably moved to Brownwood, Texas, soon thereafter. He lived in Ballinger, Texas, in 1893. His occupation in 1900, when he lived in Mitchell County, Texas, was that of a carpenter.

Issue of Charles B. and Nellie (Green) Falconer:[100]

L26 i. Charles Bingly Falconer, born 14 October 1893 in Ballinger, Texas.

ii. Frances Falconer, born 25 December 1894, died December 1986 in Fort Worth, Texas. She married M. H. Johnson.

iii. Anna Cleone Falconer, born November 1896, lives in Loveland, Colorado. She married R. E. Anderson and had issue, surname *Anderson*: a. daughter, lives in Fort Collins, Colorado, married R. A. Sullivan; b. *M. H.*, lives in Santa Ana, California.

L27 iv. John Edward Falconer, born 12 December 1901.

v. Martha B. Falconer, born 10 December 1903 in Lubbock County, Texas,[101] lives in Wichita Falls, Texas. She married —— Myers, and had issue, surname *Myers*: a. *Dexter H.*, lives in Metuchen, New Jersey.

L15 Richard T. J. Falconer, born December 1846 in Ellicott City, Maryland, died 5 December 1911 in Washington, D.C., was buried in Glenwood Cemetery.

He married, on 20 January 1869,[102] Emma E. Flenner, born 1847 in Washington, D.C., died 22 November 1921 in Washington, D.C., buried in Glenwood Cemetery.

He was a telegraph operator.

Issue of Richard T. J. and Emma E. (Flenner) Falconer, born in Washington, D.C.:[103]

i. William Alfred Falconer, born 22 November 1872, died 24 April 1950 in Washington, D.C., was buried in Glenwood Cemetery. He married, in February 1916, Winifred Mary Putland, born about 1875 in Canada, died 18 October 1965 in Washington, D.C., buried in Glenwood Cemetery. They had no issue. He worked in various departments of the Federal government from 1894 to 1946. He was first an engraver for the U. S. Department of Commerce, then an employee of the Post Office Department and the U. S. Geological Survey. About 1906 he began working for the Coast and Geodetic Survey. He was a member of the Washington and the Federal Writers' Leagues and the Washington Readers' Club. He was also a charter member of the men's bible class of Calvary Methodist Church.[104]

L16 George E. Falconer, born about 1841 in Washington, D.C., was buried 23 March 1868 in Glenwood Cemetery, Washington, D.C.

He married, on 11 May 1864,[105] Margaret Culverwell, born about 1842 in Washington, D.C., living in 1880 with her mother-in-law, Mrs. Susan Falconer. In 1870 she worked at the U.S. Treasury Department.

Issue of George E. and Margaret (Culverwell) Falconer, born in Washington, D.C.:[106]

  i.   Susan Falconer, born about 1867.

L17 Charles W. Faulkner, born 3 November 1843 in Harpers Ferry, (now West) Virginia, died 30 June 1909 in Dayton, Ohio, was buried in Woodland Cemetery.

He married, on 25 November 1868, Sarah Corwin Jones, daughter of Rev. Muncier and Sarah (Corwin) Jones, born 6 June 1848 in Lebanon, Ohio, died 15 September 1929 in Dayton, Ohio, buried in Woodland Cemetery.

He enlisted for three years as a private on 14 December 1863 in Company B, 66th Ohio Volunteer Infantry and was discharged near Louisville, Kentucky, on 15 July 1865. He was a carpenter.

Issue of Charles W. and Sarah Corwin (Jones) Faulkner, born in Urbana, Ohio:[107]

	i.	Carrie K. Faulkner, born 7 August 1872, died, unmarried, 19 September 1952 in Dayton, Ohio, buried in Woodland Cemetery. She was a schoolteacher.
	ii.	Earl Faulkner, born 21 February 1873, died 3 August 1873, buried in Kingscreek Cemetery.
	iii.	Blanche Faulkner, born 21 February 1873, died 17 October 1896 in Dayton, Ohio, buried in Woodland Cemetery.
L28	iii.	Carl J. Faulkner, born 15 November 1877.
	iv.	Roy M. Faulkner, born 17 July 1881 in Dayton, Ohio, died, unmarried, 27 February 1941 in Dayton, Ohio, buried in Woodland Cemetery. He was a clerk and salesman.

L18 Edward Franklin Faulkner, born 14 October 1864 in Urbana, Ohio, died 14 September 1929 in LaPorte, Indiana, was buried in Pine Lake Cemetery.

He married Caroline A. Smith, born 24 December 1864 in Greenville, Pennsylvania, died 22 February 1929 in LaPorte, Indiana, buried in Pine Lake Cemetery.

He was a painter.

Issue of Edward Franklin and Caroline A. (Smith) Faulkner:

L29 i.   Earl William Faulkner, born 5 August 1896.

L19 Joseph H. Falconer, born about 1847 in Washington, D.C., was living in 1880 in Washington, D.C.

His wife was Sarah Catherine Johnson, daughter of Walter C. and

Catherine Johnson, born November 1848 in Washington, D.C., died 13 April 1931 in Sykesville, Maryland, buried in Glenwood Cemetery.

He was a grocer and then a commodities broker in Washington. He deserted his wife and family in 1881 and they never knew for certain where he went, although they heard reports of him being seen about 1900 in Chicago, Illinois, and later in San Francisco.[108] If he did live in those places, he probably used another name.

Issue of Joseph H. and Sarah Catherine (Johnson) Falconer, born in Washington, D.C.:[109]

    i.   Walter J. Falconer, born July 1874, living in 1920 in Bronx, New York. He married, about 1903, Annie ——, born about 1860 in Maryland, and in 1910, they lived in New York, New York, where he worked as a clerk in a cigar store.[110] In 1920, he was married to Sallie K. ——, born about 1864 in Maryland. No issue.

    ii.   Edna May Falconer, born 1 July 1879, living in 1920 in Richmond, Virginia. She married Samuel T. Atkinson.

    iii.   Joseph H. Falconer, born February 1883, living in 1915 in Washington, D.C. Not further traced.

L20 Charles E. Falconer, born 5 June 1859 in Washington, D.C., died 1 July 1937 at his summer home, Gibson Island, Maryland.[111]

He married, on 12 June 1883, at St. Paul's Episcopal Church in Baltimore, Alice Markell, daughter of Charles and Charlotte (Traill) Markell, born January 1859 in Maryland, died 28 April 1943 in Baltimore, Maryland.

He was educated at Frederick College and moved to Baltimore in 1878. In 1879 he bought an interest in a stationery manufacturing company, which in 1892 became known as the Falconer Company. He also built an edifice known as the Falconer Building.

Issue of Charles E. and Alice (Markell) Falconer, born in Baltimore, Maryland:[112]

L30   i.   Charles Markell Falconer, born 27 September 1884.

        ii.   Mary Falconer, born 26 January 1887, died, unmarried, May 1984, in England.

L31   iii.   Norwood Boteler Falconer, born 27 December 1894.

L21 Henry (Harry) Willson Falconer, born 22 July 1862 in Washington, D.C., died 15 June 1947 in Perrysburg Township, Wood County, Ohio, was buried in Lorraine Park Cemetery, Baltimore, Maryland.

He married, on 12 October 1904, in Toledo, Ohio, Mabel Virginia Daniels, born 2 June 1869 in Toledo, Ohio, died 8 May 1952 in Perrysburg Township, Wood County, Ohio, buried in Lorraine Park Cemetery.

He moved to Toledo in 1898, where he established an insurance business, later known as Falconer, Dunbar, and Picton, Inc. He was a junior warden of Trinity Episcopal Church, president of Toledo City Mission, vice-president of Flower Hospital, and a member of the Toledo Club, Toledo Chamber of Commerce, the Young Men's Christian Association, the Elks, Masons, and historical and patriotic organizations.[113]

Issue of Harry Willson and Mabel Virginia (Daniels) Falconer, born in Rossford, Ohio:[114]

L32   i.   Robert Daniels Falconer, born 22 November 1905.
      ii. Mary Virginia Falconer, born 22 November 1905.

L22 Frank Norwood Falconer, born April 1871 in Washington, D.C., died March 1941 in Florida, was buried in Arlington National Cemetery.

He married Cora Peterson, daughter of Andrew and Lydia Ann (Hamilton) Peterson, born 1876, died January 1945 in Newark, New Jersey, buried in Arlington National Cemetery.

He was a printer in Washington, D.C., in 1894. He served as a private in Company B, 9th New York Infantry, and in Company H, 28th Volunteer Infantry, during the Spanish-American War. He moved to Brooklyn, New York, prior to 1900,[115] and lived there the rest of his life.

Issue of Frank Norwood and Cora (Peterson) Falconer, born in Brooklyn, New York:[116]

      i.   Cecil Gilbert[117] Falconer, born 11 November 1905, died August 1982 in New Jersey. She married, in 1930 in New York, New York, George Welsh. They had no children.
L33   ii. Alfred Frank Falconer, born 25 September 1908.

L23 Lucian Edward Falconer, born 5 August 1853 in New Market, Maryland, died 9 August 1904 in Cairo, Illinois, was buried in Thistlewood Cemetery.

He married, on 8 June 1882, in Louisville, Kentucky,[118] Catherine Elizabeth Lucas, born September 1853 in Indiana, died 31 October 1940 in Cairo, Illinois.

In 1860 and 1870, he lived in the household of Reuben Falconer in New Market, Maryland. He learned cabinet making from Capt. John C. Brinning, in Boonsboro, Maryland, then, by 1881, went to Louisville, where he worked as a cabinetmaker. He came to Cairo in 1885 and opened an undertaking business. He was a Mason, Odd Fellow, and Modern Woodman.[119]

Issue of Lucian Edward and Catherine Elizabeth (Lucas) Falconer, born in Cairo, Illinois:[120]

      i.   Virginia Falconer, born 7 May 1886, died, unmarried, September 1966 in Cairo, Illinois.
L34   ii. Murray Lucian Falconer, born 6 June 1888.

L24 William E. Falconer, born February 1869 in New Market, Frederick County, Maryland, died before 16 June 1958, probably in New Market, Maryland.

He married, as his first wife, Annie E. Koogle, born 22 May 1877, died 10 May 1912, buried in the Methodist Cemetery, New Market, Maryland.

He married, as his second wife, by 1920, Elizabeth (Coughlin) Carson, daughter of Michael and Mary (Newton) Coughlin, born 22 February 1874 in

Leesburg, Virginia, died 11 July 1955 in Frederick, Maryland, buried in Mount Olivet Cemetery.

Issue of William E. and Annie E. (Koogle) Falconer, born in New Market, Maryland:[121]

    i.   Charles Eldred Falconer, born April 1898, died 12 August 1964 in Baltimore, Maryland. He married Mary C. Kefauver.[122] They had no issue. He served in World War I as a pharmacist's mate in the U.S. Navy. He worked as a commerce agent for the Baltimore and Ohio Railroad.

    ii.   Frances A. Falconer, born 1900, died 1918, buried in the Methodist Cemetery, New Market.[123]

L35 iii.   Lucian Koogle Falconer, born about 1902.

    iv.   Charlotte A. Falconer, born about 1906, living in 1964 in Lanham, Maryland. She married J. William Howser.

L25 John Lucian Falconer, born 24 July 1871 in New Market, Frederick County, Maryland, died 29 July 1941 in Baltimore, Maryland.

He married, in May 1902, in New Market, Maryland, Minnie May Crebs, daughter of Francis and Louise Crebs.

He was a carpenter, like his forefathers.

Issue of John Lucian and Minnie May (Crebs) Falconer, born in New Market, Maryland:[124]

L36 i.   Ralph Singleton Falconer, born 13 July 1903.

    ii.   Mary Catherine Falconer, born 16 March 1905, lives in Baltimore, Maryland. She married William N. Hogarth, and had issue, surname *Hogarth*: a. *Don Falconer*.

    iii.   M. Evelyn Falconer, born 3 December 1909, lives in Baltimore, Maryland. She married Walter C. Hickman.

L37 iv.   Elmer Francis Falconer, born 3 March 1914.

L38 v.   Howard H. Falconer, born 3 March 1914.

L26 Charles Bingly Falconer, born 14 October 1893 in Ballinger, Texas, died 2 August 1957 in Oklahoma City, Oklahoma, was buried in Rose Hill Cemetery.[125]

He married, as his second wife, Thelma Pierce, born 28 February 1902 in Texas, living in San Diego, California. They later divorced; she lived in Dallas, Texas, until 1979, when she moved to San Diego.

He married, as his third wife, Martha ——, living in 1957 in Oklahoma City.

A veteran of World War I, he moved from Fort Worth, Texas, to Oklahoma City about 1926, where he worked as a tailor.

Issue of Charles Bingly and Thelma (Pierce) Falconer:[126]

    i.   Charlsie Cleone (Jacquie) Falconer, born 2 July 1920 in Fort Worth, Texas, lives in San Diego, California. She married, on 30 October 1940, in Dallas, Texas, John Wesley Hayn, born 10 September 1918 in Dallas, Texas, living in San Diego, and has issue, surname *Hayn*: a. *Janet*, born 17 May 1942, died 19 August 1969 in Dallas, Texas, married Adrian Glenn Sanders, divorced; b.

Joan, born 9 April 1945, lives in San Diego, California; c. *John Wesley*, born 5 August 1948, lives in Bolivar, Missouri, married, 16 June 1973, Phyllis Jean Russell; d. *James Joseph*, born 10 October 1952, lives in Charlottesville, Virginia, married, 19 December 1976 Grace Fielder.

L27 John Edward Falconer, born 12 December 1901 in Mitchell County, Texas.

He married, as his first wife, Mary Shannon.

He married, as his second wife, Nelly Chisholm.

He married, as his third wife, Martha ——.

Issue of John Edward and ?Mary (Shannon) Falconer:[127]

    i.   Leon Falconer, born 22 December 1921, lives in Whittier, California.

    ii.   Gladys Falconer, lives in Oklahoma City, Oklahoma. She married Claude R. Hall.

    iii. Olie Falconer, lives in San Antonio, Texas. She married George Dawson.

    iv. Ed Falconer, died 1964. She married Phillip Greene and lived in South West City, Missouri.

L28 Carl J. Faulkner, born 15 November 1877 in Dayton, Ohio, died 17 September 1938 in Dayton, Ohio, was buried in Aley's Cemetery, Beaver Creek, Ohio.

He married Elizabeth Kundert, daughter of Adam and Regina Kundert, born 27 August 1879 in Ohio, died 28 October 1980 in Dayton, Ohio, buried in Aley's Cemetery, Beaver Creek, Ohio.

He served as a private in Company G, 3rd Ohio Infantry, during the 1898 Spanish-American War. Later he was a metal worker.

Issue of Carl J. and Elizabeth (Kundert) Faulkner, born in Dayton, Ohio:[128]

L39   i.   Corwin K. Faulkner, born 4 May 1904.

      ii.   Regina A. Faulkner, born about 1907, lives in Centralia, Washington. She married Lester E. Zwiefel and had issue, surname *Zwiefel*: a. *Suzanne Elizabeth*, married first, 3 August 1957, in Wausau, Wisconsin, Joseph Alex McGuire, and, second, Alan James.

L29 Earl William Faulkner, born 5 August 1896 in LaPorte, Indiana, died 20 January 1983 in LaPorte, Indiana, was buried in Pine Lake Cemetery.

He married Vada Leona Collins, born 16 June 1897, died 22 April 1986 in LaPorte, Indiana, buried in Pine Lake Cemetery.

He was a tinner and a clerk.

Issue of Earl William and Vada Leona (Collins) Faulkner:[129]

    i.   Belvie Faulkner, born 1916, living in 1988 in Benton Harbor, Michigan. She married — Siegel.

L30 Charles Markell Falconer, born 27 September 1884 in Baltimore, Maryland, died 4 February 1957 in Baltimore, Maryland.

He married Ida Schumacher, born 6 September 1881, died July 1975 in

Baltimore, Maryland.

He was vice-president and treasurer of Falconer Company and president of the Automobile Club of Maryland. He graduated in 1902 from City College of Baltimore.

Issue of Charles Markell and Ida (Schumacher) Falconer:[130]

    i.   Mary Anne Falconer, born 1919. She or her unnamed sister married Hugh Brent III and in 1957 lived in Jackson, Mississippi.

    ii.   Alice Falconer, lived in Baltimore, Maryland. She married, as her first husband, Carl F. Treadway, but divorced.

    iii.   daughter. She or her sister Mary Anne married Jerome Kemp Travers and lived in Baltimore, Maryland.

L31 Norwood Boteler Falconer, born 27 December 1894 in Baltimore, Maryland, died 13 October 1970 in Baltimore, Maryland, was buried in Loudon Park Cemetery.

He married Dorothy Hymes, born 7 March 1897, died 15 December 1976 in Baltimore, Maryland, buried in Loudon Park Cemetery.

A realtor, he was a veteran of World War I.

Issue of Norwood Boteler and Dorothy (Hymes) Falconer:[131]

L40   i.   Ralph Falconer, born 25 May 1923.

    ii.   Patricia Falconer, living in 1978 in Live Oak, Florida. She married —— Weldon.

    iii.   John T. Falconer, living in 1978 in Baltimore.

L32 Robert Daniels Falconer, born 22 November 1905 in Perrysburg Township, Wood County, Ohio, died 13 August 1985 in Wood County, Ohio.

He married Gertrude Poast, daughter of William G. and Jennie Belle (Clawson) Poast, born 29 July 1910 in Jennings Township, Putnam County, Ohio, died October 1976 in Toledo, Ohio.

Issue of Robert Daniels and Gertrude (Poast) Falconer:[132]

L41   i.   Harry Willson Falconer, born 26 November 1937.

L42   ii.   Robert Daniels Falconer, born 14 November 1940.

L33 Alfred Frank Falconer, born 25 September 1908 in Brooklyn, New York, died 20 November 1973 in Oceanside, Long Island, New York.

He married, on 20 October 1933, in Elkton, Maryland, Lillian Roslyn Spinks, daughter of Charles and Matilda (Baker) Spinks, born 19 February 1912, living in Oceanside, New York.

He worked as a salesman.

Issue of Alfred Frank and Lillian Roslyn (Spinks) Falconer:[133]

    i.   Patricia Constance Falconer, born 15 January 1942, lives in Rockaway, New Jersey. She married Sheldon Barris and has issue, surname *Barris*: a. *Jeffrey David*; b. *Lyn Mai*.

    ii.   Marion Joyce Falconer, born 22 May 1946, lives in Lynbrook, New York. She married Richard Davies (divorced in 1978) and has issue, surname *Davies*:

a. *Denise Leah*, born 9 April 1971.

L34 Murray Lucian Falconer, born 6 June 1888 in Cairo, Illinois, died 10 June 1972 in Cairo, Illinois, was buried in Thistlewood Cemetery, Mounds, Illinois.

He married Grace Sells, born 12 June 1892, died October 1979 in Covington, Louisiana.

He was office manager for the Thistlewood Grain Company.

Issue of Murray Lucian and Grace (Sells) Falconer:[134]

   i.   Miriam Falconer, born 24 September 1919, living in 1972 in Covington, Louisiana. She married —— O'Leary and had four children.

L35 Lucian Koogle Falconer, born about 1902 in New Market, Maryland, died 18 September 1962 in New Market, Maryland.

He married Alverta Comer.

Issue of Lucian Koogle and Alverta (Comer) Falconer:[135]

L43   i.   Lucian Koogle Falconer.

   ii.   William C. Falconer, lives in Silver Spring, Maryland. He married Ruth E. Ramsburg.

   iii.   Robert P. Falconer. He married Sandra L. Shockley.

L36 Ralph Singleton Falconer, born 13 July 1903 in New Market, Frederick County, Maryland, died 9 November 1985 in Thurmont, Maryland, was buried in St. Joseph's Cemetery, Emmitsburg, Maryland.

He married Alice Elizabeth (Miller) Byard, former wife of Benjamin Byard, born 14 July 1903 in Emmitsburg, Maryland, died January 1994 in Thurmont, Maryland.

He was Executive Director of the Maryland Department of Parole and Probation.

Issue of Ralph Singleton and Alice Elizabeth (Miller) Falconer:[136]

L44   i.   Paul Richard Falconer, born 27 December 1930.

L45   ii.   John Robert Falconer, born 28 October 1932.

L46   iii.   Ralph Thomas Falconer, born 22 July 1934.

   iv.   Marcianna Falconer, born 26 October 1941. She married, as her first husband, —— Kedzierski; as her second husband, —— Wooten; and, as her third husband, —— Woods.

   v.   Bruce Alan Falconer, born 7 December 1945. He married Kathy Lawler.

L37 Elmer Francis Falconer, born 3 March 1914 in New Market, Frederick County, Maryland, died 4 October 1974 in Baltimore, Maryland, was buried in Lorraine Park Cemetery.

He married, on 17 January 1944, in Ellicott City, Maryland, May K. Schaefer, born 7 May 1921 in Baltimore, Maryland. She lives in Baltimore.

He was a route salesman.

Issue of Elmer Francis and May K. (Schaefer) Falconer, born in Baltimore, Maryland:[137]

    i.   Dolores May Falconer, born 25 February 1945, lives in Parker, Colorado. She married, on 15 December 1967, Paul A. Page, and has issue, surname *Page*: a. *Brian Paul*, born 19 October 1974.

    ii.   John Lucien Falconer, born 2 August 1946, Professor of Engineering at the University of Colorado, Boulder.

    iii.   Elmer Francis Falconer, born 31 May 1948, lives in Baltimore, Maryland. He married, on 7 June 1986, in the Philippines, Suzy Angelos.

    iv.   Nancy Ann Falconer, born 22 January 1953, lives in Forest Hill, Maryland. She married, on 13 May 1978, Francis Gilbert Regan, and has issue, surname *Regan*: a. *Kimberly Elizabeth*, born 19 October 1983; b. *Andrew Gilbert*, born 17 July 1987.

    v.   Betty Sue Falconer, born 17 July 1955, lives in Baltimore, Maryland. Issue, surname *Falconer*: a. *Gary Wayne*, born 5 May 1989.

    vi.   Charlotte Marie Falconer, born 6 February 1962, lives in Baltimore, Maryland. She married, on 17 May 1986, Norman William Rogers, and has issue, surname *Rogers*: a. *Norman William*, born 4 November 1988.

L38 Howard H. Falconer, born 3 March 1914 in New Market, Maryland, died 25 October 1976 in Frederick, Maryland.

He married Lucille Wachter, daughter of William and Helen (Kreps) Wachter, born 25 August 1916 in Frederick, Maryland, died 26 March 1976 in Frederick, Maryland.

They owned a beauty shop in the 1940s; he later worked for a retail business in Frederick.

Issue of Howard H. and Lucille (Wachter) Falconer:[138]

    i.   Dale Falconer, born 25 July 1938, died 12 September 1938, buried in Mount Olivet Cemetery, Frederick, Maryland.

    ii.   Carole Falconer, born 23 July 1939, died 29 October 1941, buried in Mount Olivet Cemetery.

L39 Corwin K. Faulkner, born 4 May 1904 in Dayton, Ohio, died 21 May 1988 in Kettering, Ohio, was buried in David Cemetery.

He married, 4 June 1932, in Newport, Kentucky, Dorothy Barbeau, daughter of Charles and Florence Barbeau, born 29 November 1905 in Circleville, Ohio, died 20 August 1994 in Kettering, Ohio.

He was a purchasing agent employed by the U. S. government.

Issue of Corwin K. and Dorothy (Barbeau) Faulkner:[139]

    i.   Thomas C. Faulkner, born 2 January 1941 in Celina, Ohio, lives in Pullman, Washington. He married, as his first wife, Judith A. Van Ry. He married, as his second wife, on 28 August 1977, in Cheyenne, Wyoming, Rhonda Lynn Blair. He is Professor of English Literature at Washington State University.

L40 Ralph Falconer, born 25 May 1923 in Baltimore, Maryland, died 8 May 1978 in Baltimore, Maryland.

He married Emily McFerren.

He was a graduate of Principia College.

Issue of Ralph and Emily (McFerren) Falconer:[140]

    i.   David N. Falconer, living in 1978 in Traverse City, Michigan.

L41 Harry Willson Falconer, born 26 November 1937 in Perrysburg, Ohio, lives in Rossford, Ohio.

He married, on 20 June 1987, in Rossford, Ohio, Amy Cotton Custer, daughter of William Robert and Annabel (Beam) Custer, born 19 October 1956 in Cleveland, Ohio.

He is president of Picton, Cavanaugh, Inc., an insurance firm.

Issue of Harry Willson and Amy Cotton (Custer) Falconer:[141]

    i.   Robert Daniels Falconer, born 27 January 1988.
    ii.   Abigail Beam Falconer, born 1 March 1990.

L42 Robert Daniels Falconer, born 14 November 1940 in Perrysburg, Ohio, died 4 August 1981 in North Troy, Vermont.

He married, on 19 November 1966, in Baltimore, Maryland, Helen Mawer Bergland, born 30 August 1944 in Baltimore, Maryland. She married, as her second husband, on 13 April 1985, Thomas Reilly, born 30 July 1938.

He was the owner of House of Troy-Light Logic, a camping equipment manufacturer.

Issue of Robert Daniels and Helen Mawer (Bergland) Falconer:[142]

    i.   Sarah Daniels Falconer, born 29 January 1969.
    ii.   Lloyd Alexander Falconer [daughter], born 26 November 1971.

L43 Lucian Koogle Falconer, lives in Frederick, Maryland.

His wife is Neeta D. ——.

Issue of Lucian Koogle Falconer:[143]

    i.   Gina M. Falconer, born about 1958. She married, on 20 September 1980, in Frederick, Maryland, Clarence S. Hagelin, Jr.
    ii.   Lucian Koogle Falconer, born about 1959. He married, as his first wife, on 25 October 1981, in Frederick, Maryland, Debra Marlene Pitman. He married, as his second wife, on 22 November 1986, in Frederick, Maryland, Penny Waine Hobbs.
    iii.   Philip E. Falconer, born about 1966. He married, on 5 August 1989, in Frederick, Maryland, Patricia A. Meitzler.
    iv.   Kenneth Michael Falconer. He married, on 24 June 1992, in Frederick, Maryland, Roxanne Cunningham.

L44 Paul Richard Falconer, born 27 December 1930 in Emmitsburg, Maryland, lives in Westminster, Maryland.

He married, on 11 October 1952, in Glyndon, Maryland, Katharine May Loose, born 3 May 1931 in Glyndon, Maryland.

He was Chief of the United States Probation Department for Maryland. They lived in Owings Mills and Baltimore, as well as Westminster, Maryland.

Issue of Paul Richard and Katharine May (Loose) Falconer:[144]

i. Donald Richard Falconer, born 10 December 1956, lives in Cookeville, Tennessee. He married, on 7 June 1983, Linda (Pickle) Jones.

ii. Belinda Alison Falconer, born 16 April 1960.

L45 **John Robert Falconer**, born 28 October 1932 in Baltimore, Maryland, died 8 October 1961 in Baltimore, Maryland, was buried in Veterans' Cemetery.

He married, on 20 June 1952, in Baltimore, Maryland, Dorothy Ellen White, born 8 January 1935 in Baltimore County, Maryland. She married, as her second husband, Anthony F. Zaukus, and they live in Glen Burnie, Maryland.

He was a Baltimore police officer.

Issue of John Robert and Dorothy Ellen (White) Falconer:[145]

i. Elisa Marie Falconer, born 26 November 1953, lives in Glen Burnie, Maryland. She married, on 30 December 1971, Bruce Gregory Colburn.

ii. Kathy Ellen Falconer, born 20 November 1955, lives in Glen Burnie, Maryland. She married, on 12 September 1975, Glenn Edward Bennett, Jr.

iii. John Robert Falconer, born 10 January 1958. He married Kathy Paul.

iv. Kenneth Richard Falconer, born 8 July 1961. He married, on 20 August 1982, Julia Marie Frank.

L46 **Ralph Thomas Falconer**, born 15 July 1934 in Baltimore, Maryland, has lived in Baltimore and Waldorf, Maryland.

He married, as his first wife, Wallis Machen.

He married, as his second wife, Wanda ——.

He is a plumber and pipefitter in Virginia Beach, Virginia.

Issue of Ralph Thomas and Wallis (Machen) Falconer:[146]

i. Thomas Falconer.

ii. Timothy Falconer.

iii. Susan Falconer.

iv. Rebecca Falconer.

NOTES

[1] Frederick Co. (Md.) Wills, GM 1: 142-144.

[2] Administration Accounts, 36: 346.

[3] Queen Anne's Parish Register.

[4] Prince Georges Co. (Md.) Deeds, EE: 690.

[5] Ibid., EE: 698.

[6] Ibid., CC#2: 596.

[7] Ibid., TT: 425; original deed in Bowie Family Papers, Maryland State Archives.

[8] Oaths of Fidelity, Box 4, folder 25, Maryland State Archives.

[9] Frederick Co. (Md.) Deeds, RP1: 361.

[10] Ibid., RP1: 263.

[11] Frederick Co. (Md.) Wills, GM 1: 142-144.

[12] Frederick Co. (Md.) Inventories, GM1: 212.

[13] Oaths of Fidelity, Box 4, folder 25, Maryland State Archives.

[14] Frederick Co. (Md.) Deeds, WP2: 223.

[15] Ibid., WP2: 627, 626.

[16] Washington Co. (Md.) Deeds, I: 9.

[17] Ibid.; if he had been married in 1794, his wife would have released her dower interest, but the deed shows no such release.

[18] Montgomery Co. (Md.) Marriages.

[19] It is also possible that the "Sasanner" named as next of kin in the inventory of Gilbert's estate was his mother Susannah (Duvall) Falconar.

[20] St. Paul's and Queen Anne's parish registers.

[21] Ibid.

[22] Society of Colonial Wars in the State of Maryland, *Genealogies of the Members and Record of Services of Ancestors* (Baltimore: Williams & Wilkins for the Society, 1940), 2: 69; Frederick Adams Virkus, ed., *The Compendium of American Genealogy* (orig. 1942; repr. Baltimore: Genealogical Pub., 1987), 7: 368.

[23] *History of Frederick County, Maryland*, p. 1216.

[24] Society of Colonial Wars, 2: 69.

[25] "1798 Frederick County Assessment: Sugar Loaf and Lingamore Hundred," *Western Maryland Genealogy* 7 (Jan. 1991): 1, 60.

[26] Frederick Co. (Md.) Deeds, 38: 381, 384; 41: 531; 14: 71.

[27] *Frederick-Town Herald*, 24 July 1802, in: Wright, *Western Maryland Newspaper Abstracts*, p. 107.

[28] Marine, *British Invasion of Maryland*, p. 282.

[29] Draft letter from Nelson Faulkner to a child of Elisha, reported by George Spaulding (see Appendix 4).

[30] Ibid.

[31] Jacob Mehrling Holdcraft, *Names in Stone* (Baltimore: Genealogical Publishing Co., 1985), 1: 394.

[32] IGI.

[33] Frederick Co. (Md.) Wills, JRR1: 427.

[34] Nelson Faulkner letter (see note 29).

[35] Frederick Co. (Md.) Marriages.

[36] Holdcraft, *Names in Stone*, 1: 394.

[37] Eloise Barrick Weller, *Barrick (Berg) Families of Frederick County, Maryland* (Evansville, Ind.: Evansville Bindery, 1989), p. 96.

[38] 1850 census, Frederick Co., Md., p. 244.

[39] Records of Harry W. Falconer, in possession of Harry W. Falconer II, 270 Riverside Dr., Rossford, OH 43460.

[40] 1860 census, Washington, D.C., 4th ward, p. 143.

[41] *Baltimore Sun*, 1 Dec. 1852.

[42] Frederick Co. (Md.) Estate Docket, SGC1: 91.

[43] 1850 census, Frederick Co., Md., p. 238; 1860 census, Frederick Co., Md., p. 931.

[44] No proof of her parentage exists, but this is the most likely supposition.

[45] 1850 census, Frederick Co., Md., p. 210.

[46] *Washington Post*, 16 Aug. 1924.

[47] 1850 census, mortality schedule.

[48] "1830," a typographical error, in Smith, *History of Macon County*, p. 261; but the age on his gravestone would indicate 22 January 1803.

[49] *Frederick Times*, 14 June 1832, according to card in Dielman-Hayward File, Maryland Historical Society.

[50] *Illinois State Journal*, 27 March 1845.

[51] 1850 census, Macon Co., Ill., p. 140; 1860 census, Macon Co., Ill., p. 297.

[52] Day, *Greenleaf Cemetery*, p. 77, the source for the dates in this family.

[53] Macon Co. (Ill.) Marriages, 1: 70.

[54] Illinois, Adjutant General, *Adjutant General's Report*, 6: 250.

[55] *Frederick Examiner*, 31 Aug. 1870.

[56] Glenwood Cemetery records, typescript, D.A.R. Library; Washington Death Records, Box 85, #6370.

[57] 1850 census, Anne Arundel Co., Md., p. 458.

[58] His identity is uncertain.

[59] *Baltimore Sun*, 11 May 1840, in: Hollowak, p. 187.

[60] 1860 census, Washington, D.C., 3rd ward, p. 815.

[61] 1880 census, D.C., 4-100-9-3.

[62] Records of Glenwood Cemetery, D.A.R. Library.

[63] *Baltimore American*, 5 Dec. 1840.

[64] Records of Glenwood Cemetery, D.A.R. Library.

[65] 1850 census, Anne Arundel Co., Md., p. 422; 1860 census, D.C., 3rd ward, p. 721.

[66] Notes of Harry W. Falcoer, in possession of Harry W. Falcoer II.

[67] 1880 census, D.C., 1-9-1-17.

[68] Register of Church of the Epiphany, Washington, D.C., typescript copy, D.A.R. Library.

[69] Ibid.

[70] George E. Spaulding, Jr., 3227 Lake Dr., S.E., Grand Rapids, MI 49506, is the chief source for this family and for its descendants.

[71] 1880 census, Champaign Co., Ohio, 7-28-31-37.

[72] George E. Spaulding, Jr.

[73] *Democrat Advertiser*, 19 April 1890.

[74] D.C. Marriage Records, in D.A.R. Library.

[75] Records of Glenwood Cemetery.

[76] Society of Colonial Wars in Maryland, *Genealogies of the Members and Record of Services of Ancestors* (Baltimore: Williams & Wilkins for the Society, 1940), 2: 69.

[77] Biographical information from a sketch by his son Harry, possessed by Harry W. Falcoer II.

[78] J. Thomas Scharf, *History of Western Maryland* (Philadelphia: 1882), p. 501.

[79] Petition to sell lunatic's estate, Falcoer Papers, MS 2290, Maryland Historical Society.

[80] Records of Glenwood Cemetery.

[81] Falcoer Papers, MS 2290, Maryland Historical Society.

[82] Virkus, *Compendium of American Genealogy*, 7: 368.

[83] 1900 census, Baltimore Co., Md., 16-153-14-54.

[84] Letter from E. Norwood Bessling, Washington, D.C., to Harry W. Falcoer, 18 Nov. 1932, in possession of Harry W. Falcoer II.

[85] Ibid.

[86] Holdcraft, *Names in Stone*, 1: 394.

[87] Murdock family Bible, in *Bible Records of Washington County, Maryland* (Westminster, Md.; Family Line Publications, 1992), p. 52-54; Will of Johnsey Barbour, Frederick Co. (Md.) Register of Wills, TLMc1: 639.

[88] Murdock family Bible.

[89] Holdcraft, *Names in Stone*, 1: 394.

[90] 1860 census, Frederick Co., Md., p. 931.

[91] Frederick Co. (Md.) Marriage Record (1865-1880), p. 154.

[92] Paul R. Falcoer, 369 Jasontown Rd., Westminster, MD 21158.

[93] 1880 census, Frederick Co., Md., 13-80-19-4.

[94] Macon Co. (Ill.) Marriages, 1: 172.

[95] *Decatur Herald*, 27 Jan. 1917.

[96] 1900 census, Macon Co., Ill., 118-55-24-69; 1880 census, Macon Co., Ill., 36-150-70-1.

[97] Macon Co. (Ill.) Marriages, 2: 263.

[98] Ibid., 2: 58.

[99] *Macon County Gravestone Inscriptions*. The date is transcribed as 1876, which must be wrong.

[100] Jacquie Hayn, San Diego, CA; 1900 census, Mitchell Co., Tex., 80-115-15-61; 1910 census, Mitchell Co., Tex., 104-167-313.

[101] Index to Texas birth records.

[102] Records of Wesley Methodist Church, Washington, D.C., at D.A.R. Library.

[103] 1880, D.C., 6-50-39-50; Wesley Methodist Church records.

[104] *Washington Post*, 26 April 1950.

[105] Notes of Harry W. Falconer, in possession of Harry W. Falconer II.

[106] 1880 census, D.C., 4-100-9-3.

[107] 1900 census, Montgomery Co., Ohio, 44-17-11. The information on Charles W. Faulkner and his family was provided by George E. Spaulding, Jr.

[108] Falconer Papers, MS 2290, Maryland Historical Society.

[109] 1880 census, D.C., 2-94-5-12.

[110] 1910 census, New York Co., N.Y., 728-22-59.

[111] Clipping in Dielman-Hayward File, Maryland Historical Society.

[112] 1900 census, Baltimore Co., Md.,   ; St. Paul's Episcopal Church register.

[113] Statement of Harry W. Falconer, in possession of Harry W. Falconer II.

[114] Records of Harry W. Falconer II.

[115] 1900 census, Kings Co., N.Y., 63-30-3-72.

[116] Letter, E. Norwood Bessling to Harry W. Falconer, 18 Nov. 1932.

[117] Name legally changed from Mildred Cecil.

CHAPTER M

David Faulkner, Son of Alexander

M1 **David Falconar** (Faulkner), fourth son of Alexander (K1) and Susannah (Duvall) Falconar, born 22 April 1726 in Queen Anne's Parish, Prince Georges County, Maryland, was living in 1787 in Franklin Township, Fayette County, Pennsylvania.[1] He was said to have died in Kentucky.[2]

His wife has not been identified. She may have been the Betsy Faulkner living in a household in Washington County, Kentucky, in 1810, aged over 45.[3]

Since legally acceptable proof for his identity or children has failed to surface, it is necessary here to put forward the argument in favor of his identity as the son of Alexander (K1) and as the father of Alexander, Samuel, and John. Apart from his birth record, his name has not been located in contemporary Maryland records, yet evidence is probably sufficient to suggest that he was the David "Falknor," "Falconer," "Forkner," "Folkner," and "Faulkner" living in Pennsylvania in the 1780s.

1. We know that Alexander Faulkner (M2), came to Kentucky from Pennsylvania. The only man of this name listed in the comprehensive post-Revolutionary Pennsylvania tax lists was recorded, along with David, in Franklin Township, Fayette County (Westmoreland County in 1783), Pennsylvania, in 1783, 1785, and 1786, and 1787.[4] In this sparsely populated, frontier area, one would assume a relationship between the two.

2. An account of the family of Samuel Falconer (N1) (see Appendix 4), written about 1855, says that Samuel removed from Maryland to Berkeley County, Virginia (now West Virginia), in company with his brother David, and that David later moved to Kentucky.[5] Samuel's home in Pennsylvania, on Pigeon Creek in Washington County, was across the Monongahela River from David's home in Franklin Township, Fayette County. This account lends further support to David's identity as the son of Alexander, since it identifies two brothers from Maryland named Samuel and David.

3. We also know that Alexander had a brother Samuel (M3). This is based on Jane (Faulkner) Faulkner's (daughter of Samuel, M5) description of her late husband Samuel (M14) as a "2nd cousin,"[6] on a letter written by David Faulkner (M6) mentioning "uncle," and on residence of the two families near each other both in Kentucky and Illinois.

4. Alexander's brother Samuel (M3), in 1850, reported the place of his birth as Maryland.[7] His mother, then, lived in that colony in 1769. Given the limited number of Faulkner and Falconer families in Maryland, this would imply that the father was probably a son of Alexander (K1).

5. Alexander (M2) gave his sons the names Samuel, David, John, and Gilbert. Samuel's (M3) second son was named David; others included Alexander, Samuel, and John. This combination of names, especially with the less common "Gilbert," suggests a relationship to the family of Alexander, the immigrant (K1).

6. Family traditions and stories, not always the best of sources, confirm this identification. Alexander's grandson David (M21) said that the family was "Scotch" in origin.[8] In a genealogy which he sketched out about 1896, he identified the immigrant as John Faulkner, a native of Scotland; he named David, son of John, as the father of Mark, who he said was the father of Alexander. He said that the family settled in Virginia but that the father of Alexander died in Madison County, Kentucky.[9] Research shows that he confused the names and number of generations, but he did state that the family's origin was Scottish and that the son of the immigrant was named David. Certainly there must be a kernel of truth in his traditional account made at an elderly age.

7. Charles Baldwin, a great-great-grandson Alexander (M2), wrote in 1950 that Civil War-era relatives told him that the family was of Scottish origin and that "the original Faulkner held some kind of grant from the Scottish Crown."[10] My grandmother, Mabel G. (Faulkner) McKee, told me that her grandmother had told her that the family originally lived in a castle in Scotland and that at some point received an inheritance but never claimed it, because of the distances or difficulties involved. My second cousin Ann (Faulkner) McKinney confirms those stories and adds that she was told that the original spelling of the name was "Falconer." Such distant stories, passed down through many generations, deserve a healthy skepticism. Yet in this particular case, they tend to ring true.

The argument connecting this prolific branch with the Falconers of Halkerton thus relies on a particular combination of circumstances—residence, proved by tax lists and personal papers; given names; oral and written traditional accounts, which point to a Scottish landed family; and the absence of any conflicting evidence. A skeptic might argue that the lack of positive evidence, whether going forward from David or backward from Alexander and Samuel, renders this line unknown. However, the preponderance of evidence can only lead to this interpretation. I welcome any attempt to disprove this line.

A David "Faulkner" received a survey warrant on 100 acres in Lancaster County, Pennsylvania, on 23 August 1750.[11] He disappears thereafter from the Lancaster County land records. This may not be the same person as our subject. In any event, he presumably moved to Berkeley County, West Virginia (then Frederick County, Virginia), prior to 1756, as David's (M21) account states that Alexander was born in Virginia in that year. Diligent search has, unfortunately, failed to find a record of him or his brother Samuel in contemporary Virginia records,[12] yet there can be little doubt that Samuel lived there, since his wife Elizabeth's family can be documented there. We must infer that David and Samuel rented or squatted on the frontier land.

David moved to western Pennsylvania with his brother Samuel in 1772, according to the account of Samuel's family, mentioned above.

He may have been the David who was in Hamiltonbann Township, York County, Pennsylvania, in 1781 and 1782.[13] He certainly then was in Franklin Township, Fayette County (Westmoreland County in 1783), Pennsylvania, where he was taxed in 1783, 1785, and 1786.[14] In 1783, he was taxed on 100 acres, one horse, two cattle, nine sheep, and five white inhabitants. He may be the one listed in the 1790 census as a resident of Allegheny County, in the portion taken from Washington County, with one male of sixteen and over, three males under sixteen, and five females, although this may be another man of his name. However, two different traditional accounts say that he went to Kentucky.

Presumed children of David Falconar (there may have been several daughters):

M2   i.   Alexander Faulkner, born about 1756 in Virginia.[15]

?   ii.   David Faulkner. He was taxed as a resident of Union Township, Fayette County, Pennsylvania, in 1786. His assessment of eightpence was smaller than the four shillings assessed to David, living in nearby Franklin Township, which might imply that one was older than the other. Since the name was not common and both lived near each other, it is hard to believe that they were not related——if they were two different people. Since this is the only reference to him I have found, it might be possible that the tax assessment refers to his father, in which case he did not exist. Not further traced.

M3   iii.   John Faulkner.

M4   iv.   Samuel Faulkner, born about 1769 in Maryland.

M2 Alexander Faulkner, born about 1756, probably in Berkeley County, West Virginia (then Frederick County, Virginia),[16] died testate shortly before 21 October 1833 in Metcalfe (then Barren) County, Kentucky.[17] He spelled his name "Falkner" in an autograph signature giving his consent for his daughter Elizabeth's marriage.[18]

He married, about 1786, Margaret Conyers, daughter of Samuel and Keziah (Sparks) Conyers,[19] born 30 December 1755 in Fauquier County, Virginia, died in early July, 1836 in Metcalfe (then Barren) County, Kentucky.[20] Her father lived in Washington Township, Fayette County, Pennsylvania, at the time of her marriage.[21]

He served as a sergeant in Lt. Col. Butler's Company, Fourth Pennsylvania Regiment, from 28 May 1777 to the expiration of his term on 28 May 1780, but continued in the service, at the request of Col. Butler, until 7 November 1780, and was discharged at Camp Totowa. He had originally enlisted on 1 January 1777 in the Third Pennsylvania Regiment.[22] As Alexander "Falconer," he received depreciation pay for his service in the Fourth Regiment.[23] After the war, he settled in Franklin Township, Fayette County, Pennsylvania, where he was taxed as a single man in 1783, 1785, and 1786.[24]

Like many others living on the western Pennsylvania frontier at that time, he contemplated moving to Kentucky. He first made a scouting trip, going down the Allegheny and Ohio Rivers and landing at Limestone (now Maysville), Kentucky, on 31 March 1786. Four men in his party had been killed by Indians en route. One of the group reminisced many years later that "Faulkner was a reel-footed man; dreadfully lazy; wouldn't work a stroke; and we had like to have left him behind on his way."[25]

He returned to Pennsylvania, married, then settled in Kentucky permanently. He was listed in the 1789 tax list of Fayette County and the 1790 and 1791 lists of Bourbon County. From 1794 to 1812 he was taxed as a resident of Washington (later Marion) County, Kentucky, with 100 acres on the west side of Hardin's Creek. On 3 March 1802, Benjamin Caulk and Elinor, his wife, sold to Alexander Faulkner, for £33, 100 acres on the north side of Harding's Creek.[26] In 1812, Alexander sold further land to Benedict Spaulding,[27] and moved to Barren County. On 15 February 1813, Henry Cook and Elizabeth, his wife, of Barren County, Kentucky, sold to Alexander Faulkner, for $1200, a tract of 498 acres.[28] On 25 August 1814, Alexander "Fortner" and Margarett, his wife, sold to Henry Cook, for $50, 2 acres and 86 poles.[29]

In his will, dated 16 July 1829, he bequeathed all his property to his wife Margaret. After her death, his son Gilbert would be given $100 in horses or other property; to the heirs of his son Samuel, he gave $1; to the heirs of his daughter Elizabeth, $1; to his son John he gave $1; to his son David he gave the balance of all the property including all the land. Witnesses were William, Felix, and Isaac Faulkner, his nephews.[30] An inventory of his personal estate, made by David Faulkner on 8 November 1833, revealed a value of $373.[31]

Issue of Alexander and Margaret (Conyers) Faulkner:

M5   i.   Samuel Faulkner, born probably about 1787.

M6   ii.   David Faulkner, born 2 September 1789.[32]

M7   iii. John Faulkner, born 30 March 1791 [calculated].

M8   iv.   Gilbert Faulkner, born 10 February 1793.[33]

      v.   Enoch Faulkner. He died as an infant.[34]

      vi.   Aaron Faulkner, born about 1800. He drowned on the Mississippi River about 1821.[35]

      vii. Elizabeth Faulkner, born about 1802, died between 2 September 1822 and 16 July 1829. She married, with the consent of Alexander Faulkner, on 7 January 1819, in Barren County, Kentucky, John Edwards.[36] They had two children.

M3 **John Faulkner**, born perhaps about 1765, probably in Berkeley (then Frederick) County, West Virginia, died after 1791, when in Bourbon County, Kentucky.

Perhaps his wife was the Betsy Faulkner listed in the 1810 census in Washington County, Kentucky.

The 1790 tax list of Fayette County, Kentucky, shows John "Folker," along with Alexander and Samuel "Folker;" in 1791, the three were in Bourbon County, their names spelled "Faulkler." In 1790, John and Alexander "Forkner" and other inhabitants of Bourbon County petitioned the General Assembly of Virginia to protest the county court's granting permission for the establishment of mills on Stoner's Fork of the Licking River, which would obstruct navigation on Stoner's Fork and Bramblet's Lick, necessary for the transportation of their tobacco to the Ohio River.[37] John Faulkner was paid 25 pounds of tobacco, as was Samuel Faulkner, for one day's attendance in court as a witness in a lawsuit by James Chatham against Joseph Case in March 1791 and 50 pounds for two days in May 1791.[38] It seems likely that the John Faulkner listed below was a nephew of Alexander and Samuel Faulkner, since he lived near them; in any case, he was born to a father living in Kentucky.

Possible son of John Faulkner:

M9   i.   John Faulkner, born about 1792.

M4 Samuel Faulkner, born about 1769 in Maryland,[39] died shortly before 16 May 1853 in Green County, Kentucky.[40]

He married, on 3 February 1791, in Bourbon County, Kentucky, Mary Wilson. She had the consent of William Wilson, her father.

He was listed in the tax lists of Bourbon County from 1790 to 1792. He settled on Russell Creek, Green County, in 1793.[41] On 7 December 1798, he received a grant of 200 acres on Russell Creek in Green County,[42] selling this in December 1818 to John Stringer.[43] He purchased 100 acres on the Greasy Creek waters of the Little Barren River, in Green County, from Nicholas and Mary Burks in February 1800,[44] which he sold in August 1804 to Aaron Blakeman.[45] On 10 November 1838, he received another grant of 42 acres on the East Fork of Little Barren River in Green County.[46] He bought 50 acres on the Knob Lick Knob in Barren (now Metcalfe) County from Henry Cook in 1814 but sold this in 1817 to Abner Jolliff.[47]

Samuel was appointed a justice of the peace on 16 December 1822.[48] He was sheriff of Green County as late as 1842.[49] He and most of his family had become Cumberland Presbyterians by 1832.[50]

In his will, dated 8 May 1852, he bequeathed to his unmarried daughter Sarah her bed and furniture, a horse, ten sheep, and cattle, and 75 acres of the land on which he lived (a tract of 150 acres), the remaining half to his son John; they would share his house. To his daughter Mary Smith, he gave $50; to his son Felix $100; to his son Alexander $100; to his son Isaac he gave either the deed to 50 acres of land taken off his home property or $1; to his son William he gave $1 and discharged all debts held against him; and to his son David he gave $10. He asked that all the remainder of his real and personal property be sold, with the consideration that his son John be able to purchase "my boy" Tom at the appraised price "if he chooses to take him."[51] The proceeds of the sale would be divided equally among his children Mary Smith, Sarah, Isaac, and John. He explained that, in order to quell any misunderstanding about the bequests, he was generous with Mary, Felix, and Alexander in order to make their shares equal. The will was proved on 16 May 1853.[52]

Issue of Samuel and Mary (Wilson) Faulkner, born in Green County, Kentucky:

M10   i.   William Faulkner, born 7 March 1793.

      ii.   Mary Faulkner, born about 1795, died after 1880, when she was living in Metcalfe County, Kentucky. She married, by license dated 7 October 1822 in

Green County, Kentucky, David R. Smith, son of Isaac Smith. Issue, surname *Smith*: a. *Lucy Ann*, born about 1823, married William Malone; b.
Louisa, born about 1828, married Benjamin Malone.

M11 iii. David Faulkner, born about 1798.

    iv. Joseph Faulkner,[53] born perhaps about 1800, died, without issue, after 1836.

M12 v. Alexander Faulkner, born 1802.

M13 vi. Felix Faulkner, born about 1804.

M14 vii. Samuel Faulkner, born about 1807.

M15 viii. Isaac Faulkner, born about 1808.

M16 x. John Faulkner, born about 1814.

    xi. Sarah Faulkner, born about 1817. She married, on 4 October 1857, in Green
County, Kentucky, as his second wife, Young Hughart. In 1858, they lived in
Adair County, Kentucky.

M5 Samuel Faulkner, born about 1787, probably in Fayette County, Pennsylvania, died shortly before 3 October 1825 in Adair County, Kentucky.

He married, on 21 May 1808, in Washington County, Kentucky, Elizabeth (Betsy) Grayham, daughter of Marcus Grayham of Washington (later
Marion) County.

They probably moved to Barren (later Metcalfe) County, Kentucky, but
by 1815 had settled in Adair County. He was appointed a constable there for
two-year terms in 1818, 1820, 1822, and 1824.[54] He was also a tax commissioner, taking in lists of taxable property in Capt. Samson Casky's District, in
1819 and 1820.[55] On 20 May 1824, he received a grant of 35 acres on
Casey's Creek in Adair County.[56]

On 3 October 1825, David Faulkner and Sampson Casky were appointed
administrators of his estate. The appraisal of his estate revealed an estimate
of $514.60.[57] In July 1826, Marcus Faulkner, "orphan son" of Samuel
Faulkner, chose John Faulkner as his guardian.[58] In October 1826, the
Barren County Court ordered that Alexander Faulkner be appointed guardian of James, Margarett, Samuel, and William Faulkner, all orphans of Samuel
Faulkner under 14.[59]

Issue of Samuel and Elizabeth (Grayham) Faulkner:

M17 i. Marcus Grayham Faulkner, born 9 August 1809 [calculated].

    ii. Jane Faulkner, born 3 July 1810 [calculated], died 26 January 1893, aged 82
years, 7 months, 23 days, in Irvington, Illinois, buried in Grand Point Cemetery. On 23 September 1830, in Barren County, Kentucky, she married
Samuel Faulkner (M14). She married secondly, on 17 December 1848, in
Washington County, Illinois,[60] James Armstrong, born 17 March 1801 [cal-
culated], died 18 January 1852, buried in Grand Point Cemetery.

    iii. Catherine Faulkner. She married, on 29 May 1829 in Barren County, Ken-
tucky, James Dale. She died about two years before 15 January 1832, by
which time James Dale had remarried.[61]

    iv. James Faulkner, born about 1815, died after 1860, when living in the house-
hold of Elizabeth (Jolliff) Faulkner in Washington County, Illinois.[62] He lived
in Troop County, Georgia, with his uncle Gilbert, in 1841.[63] There is no
indication that he ever married.

    v. Margaret Faulkner, born 22 September 1819, died 15 November 1873 in
Jefferson County, Illinois, buried in Little Grove Cemetery, Walnut Hill, Illi-

nois. On 19 November 1837, in Jefferson County, Illinois,[64] she married Owen Breeze, born 20 November 1817 in Orange County, Indiana, died 19 January 1886. Issue, surname *Breeze* (there were five):[65] a. *Martha Jane*, born 7 January 1839, died 10 March 1913, buried in Little Grove Cemetery, married John Sanders; b. *Sidney*, born 5 February 1842, died 1 July 1889, buried in Little Grove Cemetery, married Maria ——; c. *Harriet*, born about July 1846, died 11 January 1911, married, 1865, Joseph A. Boles; d. *Hannah*, died young.

M18   vi.   Samuel P. Faulkner, born about 1822.

M19   vii.   William Faulkner, born about 1825.

M6 David Faulkner, born 2 September 1789 in Bourbon County, Kentucky, died 19 July 1849 in Metcalfe (then Barren) County, Kentucky.[66]

He married first, 6 November 1815 in Barren County, Kentucky, Mary (Polly) Antridge, daughter of John Antridge.[67]

He married, as his second wife, on 29 June 1825, Permelia Shirley, daughter of James and Mary Shirley,[68] born 14 February 1793[69] in Metcalfe (then Barren) County, Kentucky, died 10 October 1855 in Metcalfe (then Barren) County, Kentucky.[70]

David served an apprenticeship to a blacksmith for five years, starting at the age of fifteen.[71] He inherited most of his father's land, but continued to work at the blacksmith's trade. His personal estate was appraised on 24 October 1849 at $105.[72] On 21 July 1839, all five daughters and two sons lived with him; "eldest son" Alexander lived nearby.[73] They were Baptists.

Issue of David and Mary (Antridge) Faulkner, born in Metcalfe (then Barren) County, Kentucky:[74]

M20   i.   Alexander Faulkner, born 14 January 1817.

     ii.   John Faulkner, born 26 September 1820, died in 1846 or before.[75]

Issue of David and Permelia (Shirley) Faulkner, born in Metcalfe (then Barren) County, Kentucky:

    iii   Mary Faulkner, born about 1826. On 7 July 1842, in Barren County, Kentucky, she had a bond to marry David Parker, son of Moses Parker of Green County; David Faulkner was surety.[76] Issue, surname *Parker*:[77] a. *Miriam*, born about 1842; b. *Margaret*, born about 1844; c. *Julia*, born about 1846; d. *Elizabeth*, born about 1849.

    iv.   Nancy Faulkner, born about 1826. On 22 December 1845, in Barren County, Kentucky, she married William Smith, born about 1815 in Tennessee. She had the consent of David Faulkner. Issue, surname *Smith*:[78] a. *Malinda J.*, born about 1849; b. *Elizabeth S.*, born about 1852; c. *Isaac F.*, born about 1855; d. *Albert V.*, born 1859.

M21   v.   David Faulkner, born 10 September 1828.

    vi.   Letha Faulkner, born 11 March 1832. She married, on 2 November 1855 in Green County, Kentucky,[79] as his second wife, Nicholas McCubbin, born 6 August 1806, died 6 September 1869 Green County, Kentucky. Issue, surname *McCubbin*:[80] a. *Amelia*, born 18 September 1856, died 21 February 1936, married Porter Crump; b. *Nicholas D.*, born 10 September 1859, died 3 September 1940, married, 21 June 1883, Letha Milby; c. *Marion Waller*, born 25 March 1861, died 16 July 1951, married, 7 March 1883, Sarah Cobb; d.

Malissia, born 28 September 1866, died 9 May 1948, married, May 1903, Tom Quisenberry.

M7 John Faulkner, born 30 March 1791 [calculated] in Bourbon County, Kentucky, died 16 April 1851, "aged 60 yrs. 17 ds.," in Irvington Township, Washington County, Illinois, was buried in Grand Point Cemetery.

He married, on 1 January 1817 in Barren County, Kentucky,[81] Elizabeth Jolliff, daughter of James and Elizabeth (Norris) Jolliff, born 1793 in Kentucky, died 18 August 1884 in Irvington Township, Washington County, Illinois.[82] She was buried in Grand Point Cemetery.

Tax lists show him to be in Adair County, Kentucky, in 1815 and 1816. Between 1822 and 1827 he purchased a total of over 229 acres on the "barrens," in Barren County, Kentucky, from William and John Edwards.[83] The tax list of 1829 shows him to have been the owner of four slaves. On 1 October 1830, he sold 220 acres near Buck Hill to William M. Edwards for $700.[84] He and his family moved the next year to Washington County, Illinois, where he soon erected a horse mill.[85] He purchased 120 acres of Federal land in sections 23 and 26 of township 1 south, range 1 west (later Irvington Township) on 7 September 1836, and another 120 acres in sections 23 and 27 in 1839.[86] They were devout Baptists and in 1849 he donated the land for the Grand Point Baptist Church and cemetery. At the time of his death, he owned 240 acres.[87]

By his will, dated 1 December 1846, he appointed his son Richard to be his executor to sell as much real estate as needed to pay off his debts. He gave to his wife Elizabeth the remainder of his estate, as long as she remained his widow. If she remarried, the property would be equally divided among his children. The will was proved on 5 May 1851.[88]

Issue of John and Elizabeth (Jolliff) Faulkner, the first eight born in Metcalfe (then Barren) County, Kentucky, the rest born in Washington County, Illinois:[89]

M22   i.   John Bear Faulkner, born 11 November 1815.[90]

ii.   Catherine Faulkner, born 16 December 1817, died 10 October 1867 near Richview, Illinois. She married, on 22 October 1835, in Washington County, Illinois,[91] Matthew Pate, son of Matthew and Polly Pate, born 9 August 1818 in Saline County, Illinois, died 8 September 1893 in Round Rock, Williamson County, Texas. He married, as his second wife, on 4 March 1869, in Washington County, Illinois, Mrs. Sarah Maria (Underwood) Livesay. Issue, surname *Pate*:[92] a. *John*, born 25 October 1836, died 5 October 1889 in Mount Vernon, Illinois, married, 6 September 1868, Eliza J. Walker; b. *Mary Elizabeth*, born 8 July 1838, died 8 March 1839; c. *Malinda A.*, born 9 June 1840, died 27 October 1855; d. *Martha*, born 27 February 1843, died 7 November 1928 in Vera, Knox County, Texas, married, 3 May 1876, Louis Philip Meinzer; e. *Eliza A.*, born 15 October 1845, married, 27 April 1865, David Taylor; f. *Alexander*, born 15 March 1848, died 19 June 1917, buried in Round Rock Cemetery; g. *Simeon W.*, born 24 June 1850; h. *Melissa C.*, born 27 August 1852, died 12 March 1876, married, 13 April 1873, John W. Page; i. *Charles A.*, born 18 February 1855, married Bettie ——; j. *Richard*, born 7 December 1857.

M23   iii.   Richard Faulkner, born 24 February 1820 [calculated].

M24   iv.   Aaron Faulkner, born 17 December 1821 [calculated].

v. Elizabeth Faulkner, born 5 January 1824, died 11 December 1894 Irvington, Illinois, buried in Grand Point Cemetery. On 16 February 1843, in Washington County, Illinois,[93] she married Littleberry B. Baldwin, son of Greenberry B. Baldwin, born 26 February 1817 Kentucky, died 6 January 1900 in Centralia, Illinois. Issue, surname *Baldwin*: a. *Eliza*, born 8 January 1844, died 10 August 1923, married, 23 February 1860, David Breeze; b. *Richard D.*, born 8 February 1845, died 6 August 1923, married, 22 October 1874, Mary E. Kerr; c. *Jackson C.*, born about 1846, died 3 June 1900, married, 18 May 1873, Mary C. Curtis; d. *Angeline*, born about 1849; e. *Peggy J.*, born about 1852; f. *Wiley J.*, born about 1854; g. *Polly A.*, born about 1856; h. *Mabury*, born about 1858; i. *Almira*, born about 1865; j. *Mary*, born about 1869.

M25 vi. Gilbert Faulkner, born 31 December 1825.

vii. James F. Faulkner, born 1 November 1827, died 20 November 1855 in Irvington Township, Washington County, Illinois, buried in Grand Point Cemetery. He married, on 11 December 1851 in Washington County, Illinois, Nancy Earls. She married, as her second husband, on 3 July 1856 in Washington County, Illinois,[94] Wilson Taylor. He was of "large stature, as were all of the Faulkner and Jolliff families."[95]

M26 viii. Abner Faulkner, born 11 September 1830.

ix. Margaret Faulkner, born about 1832, living in Carlyle, Clinton County, Illinois, in 1880. On 14 March 1850, in Washington County, Illinois,[96] she married William Marion (Meg) Taylor, son of William Preston and Jane Taylor, born about 1830 in Illinois. They moved to Kansas after 1880. Issue, surname *Taylor*:[97] a. *Elizabeth*, born about 1851; b. son, born about 1853; c. *Malinda C.*, born 21 September 1855 [calculated]; d. *Clarinda Jane*, born 24 August 1858 [calculated]; e. *Charles*, born about 1861; f. *Leona*, born about 1864; g. *John Wilson*, born about 1866; h. *Alva*, born about 1869; i. *Lydia*, born about 1873.

M27 x. Alexander Faulkner, born 13 January 1836.

xi. Angeline Faulkner, born 9 March 1838, died 24 August 1906 Irvington Township, Washington County, Illinois, buried in Grand Point Cemetery. She married, on 20 January 1853, in Washington County, Illinois,[98] Clark Wallace Mitchell, son of James H. Mitchell, born 4 July 1834 Kentucky, died 27 November 1909, probably at the Soldier's Home, Danville, Illinois. Issue, surname *Mitchell*: a. *John L.*, born 13 September 1854 [calculated], died 8 February 1882, buried in Grant Point Cemetery; b. *Mary A.*, born 15 August 1857, married —— White; c. *Marion George*, born 19 January 1860; d. *Charles N.*, born 4 May 1862 [calculated], died 21 August 1890, buried in Grand Point Cemetery; e. *Pearley G.*, born 17 February 1881.

M28 xii. Charles J. Faulkner, born about June 1840.

xiii. Mary Caroline Faulkner, born about 1843, died 6 March 1877 Irvington Township, Washington County, Illinois.[99] On 2 May 1867, in Washington County, Illinois, she married Jackson Trout, born 28 February 1841 in Ohio, died 26 January 1902 in Irvington, Illinois, buried in Grand Point Cemetery. Issue, surname *Trout*: a. *Ensign E.*, born 9 March 1869, died 1958 in Centralia, Illinois, married Flora Ann Wilburn.

M8 Gilbert Faulkner, born 10 February 1793, probably in Bourbon County, Kentucky, died 5 October 1861 in Marion County, Kentucky.[100]

He married, on 17 May 1842, in Marion County, Kentucky, Louisa D. (Purdy) England, daughter of Henry Purdy and widow of Joseph England, born 22 October 1807 in Marion County, Kentucky, died 8 February 1875 in

Marion County, Kentucky.[101] By her first husband she had five children.

Gilbert lived in LaGrangeville, Troup County, Georgia, in 1839, but lived most of his life in Marion County, Kentucky.

Issue of Gilbert and Louisa D. (Purdy) Faulkner, born in Marion County, Kentucky:[102]

    i.   Georgia Ann Florida Faulkner, born 7 July 1843, died 7 February 1921 in Louisville, Kentucky. She married, on 2 July 1863, Francis (Frank) M. Hawkins, born about 1838 in Kentucky. Issue, surname *Hawkins:*[103] a. *Mary L.,* born about 1865, married William C. Carroll; b. *John W.,* born about 1867. They lived in Lebanon, Kentucky.

M29 ii.   John Ellington Morgan Faulkner, born 11 November 1848.

M9 John Faulkner, born about 1792 in Kentucky, died after 1850, when living in Barren County, Kentucky.[104]

He married, on 13 December 1825, in Barren County, Kentucky, Rachel Hiser, daughter of John and Sarah (Fancher) Hiser. She was dead by 1850.

He was listed in tax lists of Barren County from 1816 to 1829. In order to distinguish him from John Faulkner (M7), the tax lists call him John "Red" Faulkner.

Issue of John and Rachel (Hiser) Faulkner:[105]

    i.   Elizabeth A. Faulkner, born about 1827. She married, in 1853 in Barren County, Kentucky, Isaac N. Brown, a Methodist clergyman and shoemaker, born 10 July 1810 Kentucky, died 2 July 1896, buried in Little Hope Cemetery, Barren County.[106] Issue, surname *Brown:*[107] a. *Rachel,* born about 1854; b. *Emily,* born about 1857; c. *Margaret,* born about 1860; d. *George J.,* born about 1862; e. *William G.,* born about 1864.

    ii.   Catherine A. Faulkner, born about 1829. She married, in 1854 in Barren County, Kentucky, William B. Parker.

M30 iii.   William R. Faulkner, born about 1832.

M10   William Faulkner, born 7 March 1793 in Green County, Kentucky, died 18 November 1858 in Southeast Township, Orange County, Indiana, was buried in the Harned Family Cemetery.[108]

On 18 November 1818, in Orange County, Indiana, he married Anna Harned, daughter of William Harned,[109] born about 1800 in Loudoun County, Virginia, died 3 May 1883 Orange County, Indiana, buried in the Old Town Cemetery, Paoli, Indiana.

He served during the War of 1812 in Jo Davis Company of Kentucky Mounted Infantry.[110] He went to Indiana, but returned to Kentucky in the 1820s. He and Anna were mentioned in the records of Little Barren Church between 1829 and 1841.[111] He served one term as Deputy Sheriff of Green County, Kentucky. They moved back to Indiana by 1841.

Issue of William and Anna (Harned) Faulkner, the first two born in Orange County, Indiana, the rest in Green County, Kentucky:[112]

M31 i.   Warren Faulkner, born 14 May 1820.

    ii.   Elizabeth Jane Faulkner, born 26 November 1826, died 1 September 1853, buried in the Harned Cemetery. On 15 October 1846, in Orange County,

Indiana, she married Levi Long.[113]

iii. Margaret Malinda Faulkner, born 22 September 1828, died 31 August 1891 in Wayne County, Illinois, buried in the Bruce Cemetery, Four Mile Township. She married, on 12 October 1848, in Orange County, Indiana,[114] Richard Sanders, born 15 December 1824 in Orange County, Indiana, died 29 August 1873 Wayne County, Illinois, buried in the Bruce Cemetery. In 1860, they lived in Jefferson County, Illinois.[115] Issue, surname *Sanders:*[116] a. *Mary A.*, born about 1850; b. *Elizabeth C.*, born about 1852, married 31 December 1887, in Wayne County, Illinois, John Keene, Jr.; c. *Martha*, born about 1854; d. *Margaret*, born about 1856; e. *Josephine*, born about 1857; f. *Delilah*, born about 1858; g. *Effie*, born about 1866, married, 11 December 1890, in Wayne County, Illinois, Charles Mandrell.

iv. Sarah (Sally) C. Faulkner, born about 1830, died 27 March 1865, buried in the Harned Cemetery. On 14 November 1854 in Orange County, Indiana, she married Levi Long.[117]

M32 v. Alfred Faulkner, born 2 August 1832.

M33 vi. Joseph Franklin Faulkner, born 2 March 1834.

vii. Martha Louisa Faulkner, born about 1838. She was single in 1883.

viii. Amanda Faulkner, born 20 February 1840, died 31 May 1841, buried in the Harned Cemetery.

M34 ix. James Thomas Faulkner, born about 1841.

x. John Samuel Faulkner, born about 1844. In 1883, he lived in Dubois County, Indiana.

M11 **David Faulkner**, born about 1798 in Green County, Kentucky and died during the Civil War, in Carroll County, Arkansas.[118]

He married first, by a bond dated 27 November 1823 in Barren County, Kentucky, Emma Corbet Slaughter, daughter of Thomas Keen and Catherine Taliaferro (Slaughter) Slaughter. David deserted her and she married John Perkins, by whom she had three sons and five daughters.[119]

He married, as his second wife, by a license dated 10 October 1829, in Morgan County, Illinois,[120] Sarah Ann Taber, born about 1808 in Tennessee or Kentucky, living 1880 in Eureka Springs, Arkansas.[121] She was, no doubt, related to Russell, William, and Henry Taber, three brothers who came from Tennessee and settled in Macoupin County, Illinois, in 1830. They later moved to Missouri and subsequently settled along the White River, in Arkansas. The Tabers (and this might be said of David Faulkner as well), according to one writer, "appeared to be rovers and could not bear the influence of civilization."[122]

By 1829, he had settled in Macoupin County, Illinois, as he was listed in a poll book for an election held that year.[123] He and his family moved to Taney County, Missouri, prior to 1839. They settled in Carroll County, Arkansas, by 1860.

Issue of David and Emma Corbet (Slaughter) Faulkner:[124]

i. Thomas Keen (Kay) Faulkner. Probably died young.

Issue of David and Sarah Ann (Taber) Faulkner, the first six born in Macoupin County, Illinois, the rest in Taney County, Missouri:[125]

    ii. Mary Ann Faulkner, born about 1831, living in 1875 in Taney County, Missouri. She married, as her first husband, J. Barber, and had issue, surname *Barber*:[126] a. *Elizabeth*, born about 1850; b. *Sarah A.*, born about 1852; c. *John M.*, born about 1854; d. *Mary A.*, born about 1859; e. *Columbia J.*, born about 1862. She married, as her second husband, William White, born about 1848 in Arkansas, and had issue, surname *White*:[127] f. *George W.*, born about 1867; g. *Harriet D.*, born about 1869.

M35 iii. Albert Faulkner, born about 1832.

    iv. Nancy Faulkner, born 26 October 1833, died 21 June 1915 in Carroll County, Arkansas. She married William B. Brasswell. Issue, surname *Brasswell*:[128] a. *Martha Ann*, born about 1856; b. *Sarah J.*, born about 1857; c. *Phebe*, born about 1859; d. *William Frank*, born about 1862; e. *Caldonia*, born about 1870; f. *Emsly Edmond*, born about 1872; g. *Anda*, born about 1874.

M36 v. Felix Grundy Faulkner, born about 1835.

    vi. Wiley Faulkner, born about 1837, probably died before 1875. He married, on 9 February 1871 in Carroll County, Arkansas, Catherine Mickles, born about 1850 in Pennsylvania.

M37 vii. James Faulkner, born 27 September 1839.

    viii. Sarah Faulkner, born about 1841, living in 1911 in Guthrie, Oklahoma. She married Robert B. Logue, born about 1843 in Illinois, living in 1910 in Lincoln County, Oklahoma. In 1880 they lived in Denton County, Texas. Issue, surname *Logue*:[129] a. *David*, born about 1864 in Missouri; b. *Sarah E.*, born about 1867 in Arkansas; c. *Joanna*, born about 1870; d. *Thomas*, born about 1873; e. *Mary*, born about 1874; f. *Willis*, born about 1876; g. *Elbert*, born about 1879 in Texas; h. *Jesse*, born about 1885.

    ix. Isaac Faulkner, born about 1844, probably died before 1875.

M38 x. Samuel Faulkner, born 2 December 1848.

M39 xi. David Faulkner, born 2 December 1848.

M12   **Alexander Faulkner**, born 1802 in Green County, Kentucky, died shortly before 1 December 1880 in Perry Township, Boone County, Indiana.

He married first, on 6 October 1825 in Barren County, Kentucky, Nancy Dale, probably the daughter of William and Jane (Shirley) Dale.

He married, as his second wife, on 16 May 1831 in Barren County, Kentucky, Mary (Polly) Dale, daughter of William and Jane (Shirley) Dale, born about 1802 in Barren County, Kentucky, died February 1879, buried in Mount Tabor Cemetery, Perry Township, Boone County, Indiana.

Alexander settled in Boone County in 1834. He was a Democrat.[130]

Issue of Alexander and Nancy (Dale) Faulkner:

    i. Francis M. Faulkner, born 13 February 1829 [calculated], died, without issue, 17 September 1849, buried in Mount Tabor Cemetery.

Issue of Alexander and Mary (Dale) Faulkner, born in Boone County, Indiana:[131]

    ii. Mary Jane Faulkner, born about 1834. She married, on 6 April 1854 in Boone County, Indiana,[132] Tasville Guilliams.

    iii. Angeline Faulkner, born 23 April 1834 [calculated], died 21 July 1895, aged 61 years, 2 months, 28 days, buried in Mount Tabor Cemetery. She married, on 23 December 1860, in Boone County, Indiana,[133] Jacob Goodman, born about 1833 in Baden, living in 1880. Issue, surname *Goodman*:[134]   a. *Mary J.*, born about 1862, married, 18 December 1884, Stephen E. Ross; b. *Henry V.*, born about 1865; c. *Ila P.*, born about 1867, married, 23 April 1897, Elmer Debruler; d. *Nannie M.*, born about 1870, married, 9 October 1895, Charles Burdette; e. *Charles M.*, born about 1873, died 4 April 1887; f. *William Franklin*, born about 1876, married, 10 August 1902, Clara E. Dale.

    iv.   Joseph Faulkner, born about 1838. He was living at White Lick about 1866,[135] but died without heirs before the date of his father's will.

    v.   Martha A. Faulkner, born October 1840 [sic; 1839?], died, unmarried, 2 October 1924 Lebanon, Indiana, buried in Oak Hill Cemetery.

M40 vi.   William Faulkner, born 11 November 1840.

    vii. America Faulkner, born about 1844, living in 1880 in Perry Township, Boone County, Indiana. She married, on 15 December 1861, in Boone County, Indiana,[136] Benjamin Franklin Slagle, born about 1830 in Ohio. Issue, surname *Slagle*:[137] a. *Ida E.*, born about 1863, married, 9 October 1882, Thomas J. Schank; b. *William S.*, born about 1866, married 15 March 1894 Mary Jones; c. *Mallissa A.*, born about 1868, married 11 August 1888 C. H. Mavel; d. *James O.*, born about 1872, married 2 March 1893 Della Harsin; e. *Ora*, born 1874, died 1958, married 23 March 1898 Nellie E. Halk.

    viii. Nancy Faulkner, born 2 March 1846 [calculated], died, unmarried, 6 September 1867, buried in Mount Tabor Cemetery.

M41 ix.   Albert Faulkner, born 1 January 1848 [calculated].

M13 **Felix Faulkner**, born about 1804 in Green County, Kentucky, died shortly before 18 February 1859 in Washington County, Illinois.[138]

He married first, by a license dated 25 April 1836 in Macoupin County, Illinois,[139] Rebecca Hunt, born 8 January 1819 in Kentucky, died 9 April 1853 in Washington County, Illinois, buried in Grand Point Cemetery.

He married, as his second wife, on 11 July 1853 in Washington County, Illinois,[140] Margaret Whittenburg, born 17 December 1804, died 9 January 1855 in Washington County, Illinois, buried in Grand Point Cemetery.

He married, as his third wife, on 20 February 1855 in Washington County, Illinois,[141] Rhoda (Smith) Moore, daughter of James B. Smith and widow of Samuel W. Moore, born 18 February 1820 in Wayne County, Tennessee, died 15 March 1909 in Richview, Illinois, buried in Richview Cemetery. She married, on 31 July 1860, in Washington County, Illinois,[142] James H. Arnold.

He was of Bond County, Illinois, when he purchased 80 acres of Federal land in section 14, township 11 north, range 8 west, in Macoupin County, Illinois, on 3 November 1835.[143] He moved to Washington County, Illinois, prior to 1850. On 19 August 1854, he purchased 40 acres of Federal land in section 22, Irvington Township.[144] At the time of his death, he was a partner with D. W. Lowe and George Lowe, under the name of D. W. Lowe and Company, apparently makers of fence rails.

Issue of Felix and Rebecca (Hunt) Faulkner, the first five born in Macoupin County, Illinois, the rest in Washington County, Illinois:[145]

    i.   Louisa Faulkner, born about 1839.

    ii. Laban A[rnold] Faulkner, born about 1841, died 23 September 1867 in Carlinville, Illinois. On 19 October 1865, in Macoupin County, Illinois, he married Susan Jarvis. No issue. He served for three years in Company C, 14th Illinois Infantry, then in Company F, Veteran Battalion of the 14th Illinois Infantry.[146]

M42　iii.　Robert Ross Faulkner, born 6 March 1845.

　　　iv.　Elizabeth N. Faulkner, born about 1845.

　　　v.　Martha C. Faulkner, born about 1847, living in 1880 in Irvington, Illinois. On 21 August 1870, in Washington County, Illinois,[147] she married Enoch H. Hewett, born about 1848 in Illinois, and had issue, surname *Hewett:*[148] a. *Haden,* born about 1871; b. *Elza,* born about 1873; c. *Eugene,* born about 1874; d. *Burton,* born about 1877; e. *Charles,* born about 1879; f. *Mabel,* born 28 December 1880, died 25 July 1888, buried in Grand Point Cemetery.

M43　vi.　Samuel Wilson Faulkner, born 27 December 1849.

　　　vii.　Mary Ann Faulkner, born about 1852, living in 1880 in Nilwood, Macoupin County, Illinois. She married, on 30 April 1872, in Macoupin County, Illinois,[149] George W. Roberts, born about 1851 in Kentucky. Issue, surname *Roberts:*[150] a. *Walter,* born about 1873; b. *Eva,* born about 1877; c. *Anna,* born 1879.

Issue of Felix and Rhoda (Smith) Faulkner, born in Washington County, Illinois:[151]

M44　viii.　George P. Faulkner, born 7 April 1857.

M14　Samuel Faulkner, born about 1807 in Green County, Kentucky, died 18 November 1846 at San Antonio, Texas, while in military service.

He married, on 23 September 1830 in Barren County, Kentucky, his cousin Jane Faulkner, daughter of Samuel and Elizabeth (Grayham) Faulkner, born 3 June 1810 [calculated], died 26 January 1893 in Irvington, Illinois, buried in Grand Point Cemetery. She married secondly, on 17 December 1848, in Washington County, Illinois, James Armstrong, born 17 March 1801 [calculated] in Kentucky, died 18 January 1852, aged 50 years, 10 months, 1 day, buried in Grand Point Cemetery.

They probably came to Illinois in company with his cousin John. He purchased 80 acres of Federal land in section 22, township 1 south, range 1 west, in Washington County, Illinois, on 25 November 1837.[152] He enlisted, in June 1846, as a private in Capt. Coffee's Company, 2nd Regiment of Illinois Volunteers.

Issue of Samuel and Jane (Faulkner) Faulkner, born in Washington County, Illinois:[153]

　　i.　Elizabeth Ann Faulkner, born 12 November 1831, died 11 November 1836.

　　ii.　Milford Graham Faulkner, born 25 March 1833, died shortly after 1 February 1864, and was buried in Grand Point Cemetery. He served in Company F, 49th Illinois Infantry, during the Civil War. As he died soon after he applied for a pension based on his service, it can be assumed that he died unmarried.

　　iii.　James Anderson Faulkner, born 22 November 1834, died 23 March 1838.

　　iv.　Mary Jane Faulkner, born 24 December 1836, died 18 August 1838.

　　v.　Caroline Faulkner, born 9 December 1838, died 25 June 1902 in Sprinkle, Travis County, Texas, buried in Fiskville Cemetery, North Austin. She married, on 1 January 1857, in Washington County, Illinois,[154] William Henry West, born 15 March 1837 in Illinois, died 13 June 1905, buried in Fiskville Cemetery. They lived in Washington County, Illinois, in 1870, but moved to Blanco County, Texas, soon after. William was said to have married again, in

Illinois. They had issue, surname *West*:[155] a. *Samuel W.*, born 22 September 1857, died 9 August 1905, buried in McKinney Cemetery, Blanco, Texas, married Mary Elizabeth Hinds; b. *Melissa J.*, born about 1861, married —— Ferguson; c. *Juliett*, born about 1863; d. *Albert S.*, born about 1866; e. *Frank H.*, born about 1869; f. *Mary E.*, born about 1869, probably died young; g. *Horace Emzy*, born 1877, died 1961, buried in Fiskville Cemetery, married Emma G. ——; h. *Clarence*, born 1881, died, unmarried, 1956, buried in Fiskville Cemetery.

    vi.   Margaret K. Faulkner, born 12 January 1840.

M45 vii. Francis M. Faulkner, born 30 July 1843.

    viii. Louisa Jane Faulkner, born 27 November 1845, living in 1900 in Irvington, Illinois. She married —— Tibbs and had issue, surname *Tibbs*: a. *Charles H.*, born about 1868; b. *S. C.* [dau.], born about 1874; c. *Martha E.*, born January 1877.[156]

M15 **Isaac Faulkner**, born about 1808 in Green County, Kentucky, was living on 7 January 1882 in Green County, Kentucky.[157]

He married first, on 21 January 1834 in Green County, Kentucky, Mary B. Abney, daughter of John Key and Tamer (Robinson) Abney, born about 1817 in Green County, Kentucky, died 10 June 1855, of dropsy, in Green County, Kentucky.[158]

He married, as his second wife, on 30 March 1856 in Green County, Kentucky, Nancy Jane Crail, daughter of James and Sarah (Greenstreet) Crail, born about 1832 in Green County, Kentucky, died 1909 in Green County, Kentucky.[159]

He inherited land on the Little Barren River, in the southern part of Green County. In the 1850s he was a slave owner. At the time of his death, he had fifteen children either living or who had died but had left children.[160]

Issue of Isaac and Mary B. (Abney) Faulkner, born in Green County, Kentucky:[161]

    i.   Cynthia E. Faulkner, born 17 June 1836, died 18 December 1901 in Green County, Kentucky. She married, by bond dated 21 September 1859,[162] as his second wife, Miles Houk, son of George and Susannah (Harper) Houk, born 20 September 1812 in Barren County, Kentucky. Issue, surname *Houk*:[163] a. *Laurice L.*, born 21 September 1860, married, 13 March 1882, James A. Shelton; b. *Florinda Burd*, born 15 June 1862, married, 28 February 1881, Marshall W. Judd; c. *Alfred Rush*, born 26 May 1864, married, 20 March 1882, Sarah E. Shelton; d. *Albert Eugene*, born 13 July 1867, married Elizabeth Lee; e. *Mary Wood*, born 8 June 1870, married, 20 September 1887, Woodson O. Judd; f. *Amanda Louisa*, born 22 October 1872, married, 1 May 1890, Robert Ervin; g. *Sarah Jane*, born 31 December 1876, married, 16 January 1894, Samuel Young.

    ii.   Sarah Amanda Faulkner, born 15 December 1838, died 17 January 1906 in Green County, Kentucky, buried in the Thompson Cemetery. She married, by bond dated 3 November 1860,[164] Elonzo Robert Thompson, son of Thomas Aried and Susan Ann (Keene) Thompson, born 28 December 1838 in Green County, Kentucky, died 23 January 1909, buried in the Thompson Cemetery in the community of Little Barren. Issue, surname *Thompson*:[165] a. *Samuel H.*, born 26 October 1861, died 11 August 1905, married Lena M. ——; b. *Mary S.*, born about 1863; c. *Charlie T.*, born 21 July 1866, died 20 June 1867; d. *William A.*, born 15 June 1869, died 25 October 1871; e. *Martha W.*, born 6 September 1871, died 11 September 1871; f. *Nancy L.*, born 2 November 1872, died 19 September 1876; g. *Emelona A.*, born 2 February 1874, died 20 August 1876; h. *Aried Roy*, born 19 December 1877, died 22 June 1948 in Green County, Kentucky.

M46   iii.   Samuel Alexander Faulkner, born about 1841.

M47   iv.   John M. Faulkner, born July 1842.

      v.   Mary J. Faulkner, born about 1844, died, unmarried, after 1860.

     vi.   Narcissa Helen Faulkner, born 16 July 1846, died 8 May 1921 in Emma Township, White County, Illinois, buried in Big Prairie Cemetery. She married first, on 31 December 1874, in White County, Illinois, Henry C. Munsey. She married, as her second husband, Rev. William D. Walker. No issue.

   vii.   Aletha S. Faulkner, born about 1848. She married, on 12 December 1869, in Green County, Kentucky,[166] William C. McGlasson.

  viii.   daughter, born 1850, died young.

M48   ix.   Levi Ulysses Faulkner, born 28 July 1850 [calculated].

M49   x.   James Robert Faulkner, born 6 July 1853.

   xi.   Hugh K. Faulkner, born 1 June 1855,[167] living in 1900 in White County, Illinois, unmarried.[168] He probably married Fannie Elizabeth ——, born 12 October 1859 [calculated] in Kentucky, died 28 August 1881 in Emma Township, White County, Illinois.[169] Not further traced.

Issue of Isaac and Nancy Jane (Crail) Faulkner, born in Green County, Kentucky:[170]

   xii.   Lamira Josephine Faulkner, born 6 February 1857,[171] died February 1929, buried in Hiser Cemetery, Green County, Kentucky. She married, on 6 July 1893, in Green County, Kentucky,[172] as his second wife, Creed Warf, son of Larkin and Sarah Warf, born about 1832 in Virginia, died December 1921 in Green County, Kentucky. Issue, surname *Warf:*[173] a. *Iva Belle*, born 5 June 1892, died 21 September 1973 in Taylor County, Kentucky, married (1) Bennie Hiser, (2) Arvin Bibb; b. *Nancy Lera*, born 9 July 1894, died in Washington County, Kentucky, married (1) Jim Arnett, (2) Malcum Stump; c. *Omie*, born 14 June 1896, married Ira Hiser; d. *Goble O.*, born 8 May 1897, died 3 March 1965 in Green County, Kentucky, married Betty (Simpson) Judd; e. *Teddy Veachel*, born 7 March 1900, died 21 November 1977 in Gradyville, Kentucky, married, 8 November 1928, Susan Elizabeth Finn; f. *Aud*, died in infancy.

  xiii.   William J. Faulkner, born about 1859, died before 1870.

  xiv.   Ellen Belle Faulkner, born 19 February 1861,[174] died probably in 1900. She married, on 10 February 1894, in Green County, Kentucky,[175] John G. Jeffreys, born March 1865 in Green County, Kentucky. Issue, surname *Jeffreys:*[176] a. *William E.*, born January 1897. He married, as his second wife, on 18 August 1901, in Green County, Kentucky,[177] Polnia Jeffreys, born about 1863.

   xv.   Edmona Allen Bird Faulkner, born 17 September 1863, died 15 June 1937 in Green County, Kentucky, buried in Bethel Cemetery, Metcalfe County. She married, on 12 August 1880, in Green County, Kentucky,[178] William Morgan Forbes, born 22 May 1856 in Green County, Kentucky, died 15 June 1928, buried in Bethel Cemetery. Issue, surname *Forbes:*[179] a. *James Worth*, born 25 December 1881, died 12 December 1961, married Florence J. ——; b. *Charles Finley*, born 3 June 1884, died 17 March 1967; c. *George William*, born 28 August 1889; d. *Edna Earl*, born 30 April 1890, died 13 November 1962; e. *Jeannette*, born 7 March 1897, died 13 June 1977; f. *Edgar*, born 10 June 1904, died 6 January 1910.

xvi. Anna C. Faulkner, born about 1866, died 1 August 1913 in Green County, Kentucky.[180] She married, on 23 August 1894, in Green County, Kentucky,[181] as his first wife, James Henry Warf, son of Creed and Cenia Newell (Neagles) Warf, born about 1866 in Green County, Kentucky. Issue, surname *Warf:*[182] a. *Vida M.,* born 10 May 1895, married, 23 December 1916, C. C. Robertson; b. *Laura B.,* born 4 March 1896; c. *Louis B.,* born 10 May 1897, died May 1977 in Sadorus, Illinois; d. *Lura Dove,* born 15 July 1899, died 21 April 1969 in Green County, Kentucky, married, 17 February 1916, Daniel Edward Judd; e. *Henry;* f. *Walbert,* born 1904, died 20 February 1965, married Nancy Compton; g. *Martha,* born 26 March 1907, died 25 January 1982 in Cave City, Kentucky, married Ed Compton. James Henry Warf married, as his second wife, Sudie (Curry) Whitlock.

xvii. Emma F. Faulkner, born September 1869, living in 1900 in Carrier Mills Township, Saline County, Illinois. She married, on 24 February 1891, at Carmi, Illinois,[183] Thomas B. Kelton, son of Samuel and Frances (Travelstrait) Kelton, born October 1869, living in 1920 in Carrier Mills Township, Saline County, Illinois. Issue, surname *Kelton:*[184] a. *Nettie,* born August 1893; b. *Dovie,* born March 1894; c. *Jewell* [son], born May 1898; d. *Olive,* born about 1904.

M50 xviii. Isaac C. Faulkner, born April 1873.

M51 xix. Louis V. Faulkner, born 22 September 1874.

M16 **John Faulkner**, born about 1814 in Green County, Kentucky, was living on 10 July 1890 in Metcalfe County, Kentucky.[185]

He married first, on 22 June 1837, in Green County, Kentucky, Sarah Cook, daughter of Jarrot W. and E. Cook, born about 1820 in Virginia, died 20 July 1854 in Green County, Kentucky.[186]

He married, as his second wife, on 12 July 1855, in Adair County, Kentucky,[187] Amanda F. Kinnaird, daughter of David Harbert and Mary (Yates) Kinnaird, born about 1818 in Adair County, Kentucky.

He and his sister Sarah inherited land from his father on the waters of the East Fork of the Little Barren River. On 28 May 1858, Young Hughart and Sarah, his wife, of Adair County, Kentucky, sold him 75 acres of land at the mouth of Caney Fork, a branch of the East Fork of the Little Barren River, which she had inherited from her father Samuel Faulkner.[188] John was a slaveowner in 1857.

Issue of John and Sarah (Cook) Faulkner, born in Green County, Kentucky:[189]

i. Mary E. Faulkner, born 8 April 1838, died 4 May 1900, buried in the Kinnaird Cemetery, Red Lick, Adair County, Kentucky.[190] She married, on 21 October 1858, in Green County, Kentucky, John David Kinnaird, born 5 November 1836 in Adair County, Kentucky, died 20 December 1878. Issue, surname *Kinnaird:*[191] a. *John S.,* born about 1860, married, 3 February 1887, Hibernia V. Woodward; b. *Henry L.,* born about 1860; c. *Fantly T.,* born 1 May 1865, died 2 May 1882; d. *James W.,* born about 1868; e. *Cordie H.,* married, 15 October 1889, R. H. Walker; f. *Edward B.,* born 10 June 1873, died 1 January 1943 in Metcalfe County, Kentucky.

ii. Louisa M. Faulkner, born 31 October 1841, died 27 October 1902, buried in the Kinnaird Cemetery, Adair County, Kentucky.[192] She married Napoleon W. Kinnaird, born 13 February 1839 in Adair County, Kentucky, died 7 April 1917, buried in the Kinnaird Cemetery. Issue, surname *Kinnaird:*[193] a. *Charles*

C., born about 1862, married, 10 February 1887, N. G. Marrs; b. *William D.*, born about 1864; c. *Sarah S.*, born about 1867, married 5 October 1886, R. L. Bell; d. *Olevia E.*, born 18 December 1870, died 15 March 1948, unmarried; e. *Ida*, born about 1877.

Issue of John and Amanda F. (Kinnaird) Faulkner, born in Metcalfe (then Barren) County, Kentucky:[194]

M52   iii.   Charles L. Faulkner, born 26 June 1856.

       iv.   Lamira K. Faulkner, born 6 March 1857,[195] living in 1910 in Metcalfe County, Kentucky. She married, on 10 July 1890, in Metcalfe County, Kentucky, William T. Clark, born November 1866 in Tennessee. Issue, surname *Clark*:[196] a. *Elbert*, born 11 May 1891, died 22 February 1978 in Glasgow, Kentucky; b. *Carrie*, born May 1893; c. *Frederick*, born February 1896; d. *Willie*, born December 1898; e. *Wesley K.*, born about 1902, died 29 January 1977 in Glasgow, Kentucky; f. *Chesley*, born about 1902, died 13 September 1968 in Christian County, Kentucky.

       v.   Bettie Faulkner, born 10 February 1861.[197]

M17   **Marcus Grayham Faulkner**, born 9 August 1809 [calculated] in Washington (now Marion) County, Kentucky and died 30 November 1884, "aged 75 ys., 3 mo., 21 ds.," in Irvington Township, Washington County, Illinois, was buried in Fouts Cemetery, Walnut Hill Township, Jefferson County, Illinois.

He married first, on 9 February 1830 in Barren County, Kentucky, Elizabeth Williams, daughter of James and Nancy (James) Williams of Green County, Kentucky,[198] born 1805 in Virginia, died August 1841 in Washington County, Illinois.

He married, as his second wife, on 9 December 1841 in Jefferson County, Illinois,[199] Eliza Railey, daughter of Isaac Railey, born in St. Clair County, Illinois, died August 1853 in Washington County, Illinois.

He married, as his third wife, on 24 November 1853 in Washington County, Illinois, Sally W. (Lowe) Dennis, widow of Josiah Dennis, and daughter of George and Nancy (Whittenburg) Lowe, born in St. Clair County, Illinois, died 14 April 1859 in Washington County, Illinois.

He married, as his fourth wife, on 6 November 1859 in Washington County, Illinois, Letha (Reed) Boles, widow of Hugh A. Boles, born 10 March 1817 [calculated] in Maryland, died 17 February 1903, "aged 85 ys., 11 ms., 7 ds.," buried in Fouts Cemetery.

He served for many years as justice of the peace, hence his common title "Squire," being commissioned so in 1839, 1843, 1849, 1853, and 1858.[200] He was commissioned captain of the 2nd battalion, 41st Illinois Regiment, on 24 November 1845.[201] According to Charley Baldwin, he was active as a vigilante. In the 1840s, gangs of horse and cattle thieves were common in southern Illinois, and such activity was thought necessary for justice on the frontier. In an unfortunate example of what the abolitionist newspapers considered enforcement of the Illinois "Slave Law," Marcus G. Faulkner on 20 June 1853 bought the service of a black man who had been released from the county jail after being held there for six weeks, for $4.75 for one month. After one month, unless he left the state, the man would again be arrested and sold to the highest bidder.[202] He purchased 77 acres of Federal land in section 16, township 1 south, range 1 west, on 8 March 1849, and acquired by warrant, which he received due to his military service, 160 acres in section 15, in Irvington Township, on 25 July 1850, and 40 acres, in section 7, township 3 south, range 5 east, in Wayne County, Illinois, on 6 April 1852.[203] A school was located on his land.

Issue of Marcus Grayham and Elizabeth (Williams) Faulkner, the first in Hart County, Kentucky, the rest in Washington County, Illinois:[204]

 i. Emily Faulkner, born about 1830. In 1887, the executor of her father's estate believed that she, her brother Azariah and sister Eliza resided outside of Illinois, but could not learn where.

 ii. Azariah W. Faulkner, born about 1836, living in 1887, but the administrators of his father's estate could not learn his residence, nor that of his brother William or sisters Emily, Eliza, and Belle. He married first, on 3 December 1857 in Jefferson County, Illinois,[205] Martha Daniels; second, by license dated 21 December 1870 in Jefferson County, Illinois, Mary Jolliff; third, on 17 June 1872, Mrs. Mary Clark. He served as a private in Company C, 11th Illinois Infantry, during the Civil War. Since no one applied for a pension based on his military service, it is likely that he died outside of Illinois, after 1872, without issue.

 iii. Levi W. Faulkner, born about 1838, died, unmarried, 31 December 1862 at Stone River, while in service in Company F, 44th Illinois Infantry.[206]

Issue of Marcus Grayham and Eliza (Railey) Faulkner, born in Washington County, Illinois:[207]

 iv. Isaac N. Faulkner, born about 1843, living in 1870 in Irvington Township, Washington County, Illinois, unmarried,[208] was buried in the George Cemetery, Irvington Township, Washington County, Illinois.[209] He served in Company F, 44th Illinois Infantry.[210]

 v. Zachary Taylor Faulkner, born about 1846, living in 1860, but had died by the time of his father's death.

 vi. Maria M. Faulkner, born about 1846, probably died in 1879 or 1880. She married on 14 July 1865, in Washington County, Illinois, Henry Taylor. Issue, surname *Taylor*: a. *Charles*, born about 1867; b. *Frank*; c. *Mary J.*, born about 1869; d. *Augusta*, born about 1873; e. *Marcus G.*, born about 1874; f. *J. Vernon*, born about 1877.

 vii. William R. Faulkner, born about 1849, living in 1887.

M53 viii. Simeon W[alker] Faulkner, born 11 November 1850.

Issue of Marcus Grayham and Sally W. (Lowe) Faulkner, born in Washington County, Illinois:[211]

M54 ix. James Hamilton Faulkner, born 5 August 1856.

 x. Eliza Faulkner, born about 1857, living in 1887 outside of Illinois.

 xi. Isabella (Belle) Faulkner, born about 1859, living in 1887. She married —— Taylor. Her husband may have been Robert Taylor, who died before 1885 and had issue, surname *Taylor*: a. *Laura*, born 7 September 1873; b. *Samuel*, born 22 February 1875.[212]

Issue of Marcus Grayham and Letha (Reed) Faulkner, born in Washington County, Illinois:[213]

   xii.   Cynthia Melvina Faulkner, born 29 April 1862, died 18 April 1957. She married Isaac N. Railey. Issue.

M18   Samuel P. Faulkner, born about 1822 in Adair County, Kentucky, was living in 1881 in Linn County, Missouri.

He married, as his first wife, Martha ——, born about 1825 in Kentucky, living in 1850 in Macon County, Missouri.[214]

He married, as his second wife, on 24 August 1860, in Linn County, Missouri,[215] Elizabeth Fulton, daughter of —— and Lucy (——) Fulton, born about 1828 in Missouri, living in 1880.

In 1850, he was a wheelwright and lived in Macon County, Missouri, without land. He came to Linn County by 1859 and owned part of the plat of the village of New Boston.

Issue of Samuel P. and Martha Faulkner, born in Macon County, Missouri:[216]

M55   i.   John A. Faulkner, born 26 February 1846.
M56   ii.   William R. Faulkner, born August 1847.
      iii. Isaac Newton Faulkner, born about 1849, living in 1870. Not further traced.
      iv.   James H. Faulkner, born about 1850, living in 1870. Not further traced.
M57   v.   David Washington Faulkner, born 1851.
      vi.   Samuel J. Faulkner, born about 1854, living in 1870. Not further traced.
      vii. Mary J. Faulkner, born about 1856.

Issue of Samuel P. and Elizabeth (Fulton) Faulkner, born in Linn County, Missouri:[217]

      viii. Lena Faulkner, born about 1861.
      ix.   Marcus Faulkner, born about 1862, living in 1880. Not further traced.
      x.   Charles A. Faulkner, born 4 June 1868, died, unmarried, at Leavenworth, Kansas, after 1910.
M58   xi.   George Ware Faulkner, born 4 June 1868.

M19   William Faulkner, born about 1825 in Adair County, Kentucky, was buried 17 July 1895 in the Eastern Cemetery, Louisville, Kentucky.[218]

He married, on 28 August 1851, in Jefferson County, Kentucky,[219] Harriet Ann Browning, daughter of Louis Browning, born about 1830 in Kentucky, buried 23 March 1888 in the Eastern Cemetery, Louisville, Kentucky.

He seems to have been raised by his uncle Gilbert and lived in Lebanon, Kentucky, until he moved to Louisville. There he worked as a watchman and engineer for Ray, Richards, and Company.

Issue of William and Harriet Ann (Browning) Faulkner, born in Louisville, Kentucky:[220]

      i.   William Faulkner, born about 1856. Not further traced.

M59 ii. Samuel Faulkner, born about 1857.

iii. Stephen A. Douglas Faulkner, born September 1860,[221] died, unmarried, 17 April 1923 at Louisville, Kentucky.[222] He worked as a watchman and policeman.

M20 **Alexander Faulkner**, born 14 January 1817 in Metcalfe (then Barren) County, Kentucky, died intestate shortly before 15 January 1844 in Barren County, Kentucky.[223]

He married, on 21 May 1838, in Barren County, Kentucky, Charlotte Ford, born about 1818 in Kentucky. On 7 January 1847, in Barren County, Kentucky, she married, as her second husband, Stephen R. Edwards.

Issue of Alexander and Charlotte (Ford) Faulkner, born in Metcalfe (then Barren) County, Kentucky:[224]

i. Mary Ann Faulkner, born about 1839. She married, on 15 August 1861, in Metcalfe County, Kentucky, James Greer.

ii. Susanna (Susan) M. Faulkner, born November 1842, died 29 June 1915 in Barren County, Kentucky. She married Thomas P. Arnold and had issue, surname *Arnold*:[225] a. *Minnie B.*, born about 1861; b. *John R.*, born about 1863; c. *Merritt S.*, born about 1865; d. *Oscar*, born March 1872; e. *Lula B.*, born about 1876; f. *Hattie*, born July 1878; g. *William T.*, born August 1889.

M21 **David Faulkner**, born 10 September 1828 in Metcalfe (then Barren) County, Kentucky, died between 23 September and 15 October 1904 in Metcalfe County, Kentucky,[226] was buried in Shannon Cemetery, Knob Lick, Kentucky.

He married, on 31 October 1850, in Barren County, Kentucky, Nancy Jane Hiser, daughter of Aaron and Sallie (Jewell) Hiser, born 17 February 1832 in Metcalfe (then Barren) County, Kentucky,[227] died about 1896.

As well as being a farmer, he taught school for eighteen terms, beginning in 1857. He served as deputy sheriff of Metcalfe County from 1870 to 1872 and 1875 to 1876 and was appointed deputy collector in 1873. After serving as a constable for two years, he was elected county judge of Metcalfe County in 1878 and served until 1886. He was a captain in the state militia. He was a Republican and a member of the Missionary Baptist Church. A Free and Accepted Masons lodge, number 816, in Knob Lick, was named after him, he having served the Masonic fraternity in various positions.[228]

Issue of David and Nancy Jane (Hiser) Faulkner, born in Metcalfe County, Kentucky:[229]

M60 i. John Franklin Faulkner, born 21 September 1851.

M61 ii. William Alexander Faulkner, born 8 January 1854.

iii. Sarah Permelia Catherine Faulkner, born 17 March 1856.

M62 iv. James Aaron Faulkner, born 1 May 1858.

M63 v. Benjamin Marion Grider Faulkner, born 25 May 1860.

vi. David Newton Faulkner, born 31 July 1862. Alive in 1886, but not further traced.

vii. Martha Jane Elizabeth Faulkner, born 3 August 1865, living in 1886.

viii. Letha Evaline Faulkner, born 30 June 1867, died by 1870.

ix.   Samuel Emmett Faulkner, born 15 September 1870, died by 1880.

x.   Lewis Franklin Faulkner, born 1 August 1871, died by 1880.

M22   John Bear Faulkner, born 11 November 1815 in Adair or Barren County, Kentucky, died 3 April 1857 in Vandalia, Illinois, was buried in Grand Point Cemetery.

He married, on 4 July 1838, in Clinton County, Illinois,[230] Mary Ann Collins, born 29 December 1816 in Virginia, died 18 February 1891, buried in Grand Point Cemetery.

He served as pastor of various Baptist churches, including the Grand Point Church, the Bethel Missionary Baptist Church in Clinton County, and the Baptist Church of Christ at Elkton, Illinois. His meager estate consisted mostly of books.

Issue of John Bear and Mary Ann (Collins) Faulkner:[231]

i.   Frances E. Faulkner, born 20 September 1839, died 10 April 1857, buried in Grand Point Cemetery.

M64   ii.   Thomas Richard Faulkner, born 16 March 1841.

M65   iii. Michael Collins Faulkner, born 30 June 1843.

iv.   Harriet Katherine Faulkner, born 8 May 1846, died 30 October 1855, buried in Grand Point Cemetery.

v.   Margaret J. Faulkner, born August 1848. On 12 March 1876, in Washington County, Illinois, she married Joseph P. Carpenter, born March 1852 in Connecticut, and in 1900, lived in Forrest, Livingston County, Illinois.[232]

vi.   John B. Faulkner, born about 1851, living in 1870 in Irvington Township, Washington County, Illinois. Not further traced.

vii. Germina A. Faulkner, born about 1852, living in 1870.

viii. Samuel M. Faulkner, born about 1853, probably died between 1860 and 1870.

ix.   Gilbert Faulkner, born about 1855, living in 1870 in Irvington Township, Washington County, Illinois. Not further traced.

x.   Amanda C. Faulkner, born about 1856, living in 1870.

M23   Richard Faulkner, born 24 February 1820 [calculated] in Metcalfe (then Barren) County, Kentucky, died 2 February 1859, "aged 38 Yrs., 11 Mo. & 9 D's," in Irvington Township, Washington County, Illinois, was buried in Grand Point Cemetery.

He married first, on 16 January 1845, in Washington County, Illinois,[233] Orpha Julie (McMurphy) Jolliff, widow of his cousin Richard Jolliff, born about 1820 in New York.

He married, as his second wife, on 4 December 1851 in Washington County, Illinois,[234] Mary Rebecca Hewett, daughter of Miles Hewett. She married, as her second husband, on 18 July 1859 in Washington County, Illinois, James Dyer, born about 1820 in New York. They were divorced in 1863.

He may have seen military service during the Mexican War, as he purchased land in Irvington Township by warrant. In two transactions on 4 October 1852 and 23 March 1853, he acquired 120 acres in section 23. He also acquired 160 acres in section 8 on 27 November 1854.[235] He was commissioned Public Administrator on 3 January 1857.[236]

Issue of Richard and Orpha Julie (McMurphy) Faulkner, born in Washington County, Illinois:[237]

i. Elizabeth N. Faulkner, born about 1847. She married, by license dated 23 November 1871 in Washington County, Illinois, Charles S. LeRoy.

ii. Caroline Faulkner, born February 1848, living 1900 in Jackson Township, Carter County, Missouri.[238] In May 1866, in Washington County, Illinois, she married Eli H. Harvey, a Civil War veteran, born February 1844 Illinois, living in 1900. Issue, surname *Harvey*: a. *John*, born September 1879; b. *Richard*, born April 1881; c. *Howard*, born January 1884; d. *Sarah*, born August 1887; e. *June*, born March 1889; f. *McKinley*, born March 1894.

iii. Richard Faulkner, born 1850, died young.

Issue of Richard and Mary Rebecca (Hewett) Faulkner, born in Washington County, Illinois:

iv. James Faulkner, born 2 February 1853, died 1 October 1882 in Bloomfield, California. He received a Certificate in Agriculture from Illinois Industrial University (now University of Illinois) in 1875. He taught school at Ringwood, Illinois, 1875-1876; then in California. He was Republican candidate for County Superintendent of Schools at the time of his death.[239]

M66 v. Richard Douglas Faulkner, born 27 August 1858.

M24 **Aaron Faulkner**, born 17 December 1821 [calculated] in Metcalfe (then Barren) County, Kentucky, died 12 April 1869, "aged 47 years, 3 months, 26 days" in Irvington Township, Washington County, Illinois, was buried in Grand Point Cemetery.

He married, on 2 July 1845, in Washington County, Illinois,[240] Emeline Taylor, daughter of William Preston and Jane Taylor, born about 1824 in Illinois, died 17 December 1873 in Washington County, Illinois.[241]

Aaron purchased, between 1847 and 1853, about 160 acres of Federal land in sections 16 and 17 in Irvington Township.[242]

Issue of Aaron and Emeline (Taylor) Faulkner, born in Washington County, Illinois:[243]

i. Riley Faulkner, born 1846, died 12 September 1864 at Pine Bluff, Arkansas, in service in Company B, 62nd Illinois Infantry.[244]

ii. Marion Faulkner, born about 1848, died, unmarried, 5 October 1918 in Redlands, California.

iii. Elizabeth Jane Faulkner, born about 1849, died before 1873. On 12 April 1866, in Washington County, Illinois, she married Elisha Holland, a Civil War veteran. Issue, surname *Holland*: a. *Martha S.*; b. *James N.*, born about 1871, died 19 May 1923 in Centralia, Illinois.

iv. Catharine Faulkner, born 15 September 1852 [calculated], died 28 September 1870, buried in Grand Point Cemetery. She married, on 3 October 1869, in Washington County, Illinois, Zacharias Rethard. Issue, surname *Rethard*: a. *Riley*, died 1870.

v. Mary Caroline Faulkner, born about 1854. She married, on 8 January 1874 in Washington County, Illinois, Gilbert Skinner.

vi. Margaret E. Faulkner, born 26 March 1861, died 8 November 1895 in Illinois.

On 23 November 1882, in Washington County, Illinois, she married Richard A. Baldridge, son of Joseph and Polly Mira (West) Baldridge, born 16 March 1862 in Jefferson County, Illinois, died 30 September 1939 in Illinois. Issue, surname *Baldridge*:[245] a. *Emmett Joseph*, born 28 July 1883, died 23 September 1890; b. *Berthold E.*, born 30 May 1885; c. daughter, born and died 8 September 1886; d. *Mira May*, born 17 April 1888; e. *R. O.*, born 11 January 1890.

vii. Martha A. Faulkner, born about 1862, living in Redlands, California, in 1910.[246] She married —— Smallwood.

Gilbert Faulkner   **Angeline (Armstrong) Faulkner**

M25   **Gilbert Faulkner**, born 31 December 1825 in Metcalfe (then Barren) County, Kentucky, died 27 February 1891 in Elkville, Jackson County, Illinois, was buried in Grand Point Cemetery.

He married, on 29 November 1849, in Washington County, Illinois,[247] Angeline Armstrong, born 11 July 1833 in Barren County, Kentucky, died 30 December 1901 in Elkville, Illinois, buried in Grand Point Cemetery.

He served as a private in Company A, 2nd Regiment of Illinois Volunteers, from 20 June 1846 until 18 June 1847, when he was discharged at Camargo, Mexico. With a land warrant due to him because of his military service, he entered 80 acres of Federal land in section 23, on 25 February 1853. He must have lived briefly in Sangamon County, Illinois, for on 23 April 1856, as a resident of that county, he purchased 40 acres of Federal land in section 21 in Irvington Township.[248] He lived at Irvington until 1886, when he moved to Elkville.

Issue of Gilbert and Angeline (Armstrong) Faulkner, born in Washington County, Illinois:[249]

i. Mary Elizabeth Faulkner, born 25 November 1850, died 24 November 1874 in Irvington, Illinois, buried in Grand Point Cemetery. On 4 April 1871, in Washington County, Illinois, she married Louis Philip Meinzer, son of Philip Wiman Meinzer, born 2 November 1848 in Ashley, Washington County, Illinois, died 2 September 1895 in Seymour, Baylor County, Texas, buried in Vera, Texas, and had issue, surname *Meinzer*:[250] a. *Wiman*, born 1 January 1872, died 7 October 1946, married, 12 September 1912, Myrtle Agnes Coody; b. *Anna Ethelian (Effie)*, born September 1874, married W. W. Ballard. Louis married, as his second wife, on 3 May 1876, in Texas, Martha Pate, daughter of Matthew and Catherine (Faulkner) Pate.

ii. Susan L. Faulkner, born probably on 25 November 1850, died 1856, buried in Grand Point Cemetery.

iii. Arra Ann Faulkner, born 1852, died 1922, buried in Elkville Cemetery.[251] On 24 April 1873, in Washington County, Illinois, she married Jacob Reece Williams, son of Reece and Martha (Jolliff) Williams,[252] born 21 February 1851 Washington County, Illinois, died 3 September 1926 in Elkville, Illinois.

iv. Idurnia E. Faulkner, born 10 November 1856, died 16 January 1864, buried in Grand Point Cemetery.

v. Ellen Caroline Faulkner, born in December 1859, living in 1900 in Vergennes Township, Jackson County, Illinois. She married, on 11 September 1892, in Jackson County, Illinois,[253] William Shingleton, son of Thomas and Catherine (House) Shingleton, born August 1866 in Illinois, living in 1900. Issue, surname *Shingleton*: a. *Wyman*, born September 1894; b. *Angeline*, born October 1896.

vi. Fannie J. Faulkner, born 6 March 1862, died 7 June 1871, buried in Grant Point Cemetery.

vii. Christina (Tena) Faulkner, born October 1866, died 1949, buried in Elkville Cemetery. She married, on 3 September 1891, in Jackson County, Illinois, Edward Leek, born 26 September 1867, died 18 May 1919, and secondly, on 21 January 1923, at Eldorado, Illinois, W. J. Harrell, M.D., but divorced.

viii. Julie Etta Faulkner, born April 1869, died 1942, buried in Elkville Cemetery. She married, on 26 June 1894, in Jackson County, Illinois,[254] William F. Williams, son of J. F. and Frances (Bryant) Williams, born November 1873 in Illinois, died 1950, and lived at DuQuoin and Eldorado, Illinois.

ix. Lillie E. Faulkner, born 20 February 1871, died 23 September 1876, buried in Grand Point Cemetery.

x. Ximenus Q. Faulkner, born 3 November 1874, died, unmarried, 3 August 1911, buried in Grand Point Cemetery.

M26 **Abner Faulkner**, born 11 September 1830 in Metcalfe (then Barren) County, Kentucky, died 4 November 1896 in Irvington Township, Washington County, Illinois, was buried in Grand Point Cemetery.

He married, on 18 November 1852, in Washington County, Illinois,[255] Maria (Railey) Copple, daughter of Isaac Railey and widow of James Samuel Copple, born 27 November 1829 in Kentucky, died 22 April 1898, buried in Grand Point Cemetery.

Abner served as a private and corporal in Company B, 62nd Illinois Infantry, from 15 January 1862 to 2 May 1865. His farm was in Irvington Township.

Issue of Abner and Maria (Railey) Faulkner, born in Washington County, Illinois:[256]

i.   Elizabeth N. Faulkner, born 8 October 1853, died 26 June 1937 in Edna, Kansas, buried in Edna Cemetery.[257] She married, on 31 December 1876, in Washington County, Illinois, Henry Clay McCullough, born 24 January 1852, died 20 May 1917, buried in Edna Cemetery. Children, surname *McCullough*:[258] a. *Leonard A.*, born 21 March 1878, died 9 December 1904; b. *Charles J.*, born 1881, died 1961; c. *Richard E.*, born 31 October 1881, died 5 October 1952, married Ines Mae ——; d. *Herbert C.*, born 1 June 1882, died 6 December 1954, married Jessie Mae ——; e. *Grover C.*, born 1884, died 1960; f. *Reta*, born 9 September 1891, died 23 November 1904; g. *Belle*, born 28 November 1894, died 19 March 1976.

ii.   Orpha Faulkner, born 21 May 1855, died 7 September 1939 in Edna, Kansas, buried in Edna Cemetery.[259] She married, on 14 March 1878 in DeWitt County, Illinois,[260] Oliver P. Brooks.

M67 iii. Charles J. Faulkner, born 10 August 1856.

iv.   Richard Marion Faulkner, born 6 May 1859, died 2 June 1930 in Irvington, Illinois. He married, on 24 February 1901, in Washington County, Illinois, Leona Hattie Beal, born 30 May 1868, died 5 November 1945. They were buried in Fouts Cemetery, Walnut Hill. They had no children.

v.   Armitta Caroline Faulkner, born 19 March 1861, died 12 February 1930 in Heyworth, McLean County, Illinois. She married, on 12 February 1882, in DeWitt County, Illinois,[261] Stephen Douglas Earls, and had issue, surname *Earls*:[262] a. *Clarence*, born July 1883; b. *Iona*, born July 1884; c. *Bennie*, born September 1886; d. *Laurie*, born February 1888; e. *Frank*, born February 1895.

vi.   Clarinda J. Faulkner, born 14 March 1865, died 16 September 1884, buried in Grand Point Cemetery.

vii. Jacob Alexander Faulkner, born 1868, died 24 October 1953 in Belleville, Illinois, buried in Hillcrest Memorial Park, in Marion County, Illinois. He married, on 25 December 1890, in Washington County, Illinois, Christina Belle Stilley, born February 1871 in Missouri, died 1959. They had an adopted daughter, Evelyn, born 1917, who married, in 1935, in Marion County, Illinois, Ray Sheldon.

M27 **Alexander Faulkner**, born 13 January 1836 in Washington County, Illinois, died 24 June 1908 in Richview, Washington County, Illinois, was buried in Grand Point Cemetery.

He married, on 26 March 1857 in Washington County, Illinois,[263] Rachel Caroline Wayman, daughter of Asa and Mary (Carr) Wayman, born 17 February 1838 Jefferson County, Illinois, died 8 May 1925 South Jacksonville, Florida. She married, as her second husband, on 16 October 1912 at Nashville, Illinois, John W. Pitchford. They are buried in Grand Point Cemetery.

He seems to have taught school in his younger days. He served as first sergeant and second lieutenant in Company B, 62nd Illinois Infantry, from 15 January 1862 to 2 May 1865, mostly on recruiting duty in Illinois. After the war, he returned to farming in Irvington, until about 1889, when he bought a farm in Richview. He served as commander of the Simeon Walker Post, Grand Army of the Republic.

Issue of Alexander and Rachel Caroline (Wayman) Faulkner, born in Washington County, Illinois:[264]

i.   John Faulkner, born 1860, died in 1861, buried in Grand Point Cemetery.

ii. Loretta Faulkner, born 8 June 1861 [calculated], died 18 August 1862, buried in Grand Point Cemetery.

iii. James H. Faulkner, born 1865, died 27 July 1866, buried in Grand Point Cemetery.

M68 iv. Enoch Armstrong Faulkner, born 24 December 1866.

M69 v.   Richard Wilson Faulkner, born 31 July 1868.

M70 vi. Charles Willis Faulkner, born 28 February 1870.

M71 vii. Alva Jerold Faulkner, born 19 October 1871.

M72 viii. Norris Alexander Faulkner, born 1 July 1873.

Alexander (M27) Faulkner family at Bartow, Florida, 25 December 1894. In back, left to right: Enoch A. (M68), Anna (Coffel) Faulkner, Anna M. (Martin) Faulkner, Richard W. (M69), Norris A. (M72), Jessie (Taylor) Faulkner, Alva J. (M71); seated: Alexander (M27), Rachel C. (Wayman) Faulkner, holding Mabel G. Faulkner; in foreground: William A. Martin, Blanche Faulkner, Beulah Faulkner, Sue (Gaskins) Faulkner holding Norris A., Jr.

M28   **Charles J. Faulkner**, born about June 1840 in Irvington Township, Washington County, Illinois, died 6 March 1873, "aged 32 years, 9 months,"[265] in Irvington Township, Washington County, Illinois, was buried in an unmarked grave in Grand Point Cemetery.

He married, on 19 July 1859 in Washington County, Illinois,[266] Melinda Ann Bryant, born about 1842 in Tennessee, died 19 August 1911 in Irvington, Illinois. She married, as her second husband, on 3 May 1876 in Washington County, Illinois,[267] Elijah Jolliff, born 9 September 1825 in Jefferson County, Illinois, died 26 August 1900.

He served as private and corporal in Company F, 44th Illinois Infantry, from 13 September 1861 to 15 September 1864, suffering a facial wound at the battle of Mission Wound in 1863.[268]   On 22 January 1864, he purchased 39 acres of Federal land in section 30, township 1 north, range 1 west, in Washington County.[269]   After the war, he was a sharpshooter in a Wild West show, possibly that of Wild Bill Hickok.

Issue of Charles J. and Melinda Ann (Bryant) Faulkner, born in Washington County, Illinois:

  i.   Alpharetta R. Faulkner, born July 1860, died 1923 in Oregon County, Missouri, buried in the Jolliff Cemetery. On 20 October 1879, she married Elijah S. Jolliff, son of William N. and Margaret (Pace) Jolliff, born October 1860 in Washington County, Illinois, died 27 February 1911 in Oregon County, Missouri. Issue, surname *Jolliff:*[270] a. *Alva Claude*, born 16 January 1881, died 11 May 1927, married, 2 October 1902, Maudie Bales; b. *Emma Lula*, born August 1884, died 1930, married, 20 June 1901, Martin Redburn; c. *Charles L.*, born January 1891, died 1956, married, 17 December 1907, Clara Redburn; d. *Rufus H.*, born 17 December 1895, died September 1973 in Coffeyville, Kansas, married, 1921, Marie Perkins; e. *Adolph L.*, born September 1897, died 1962; married 1918 Meda Blackburn.

 ii.   Emeline M. Faulkner, born 23 September 1866, died 22 January 1957. On 14 August 1886, in Washington County, Illinois, she married Lewis Benjamin Jolliff, son of Elijah and Sarah (Forbes) Jolliff, born about 1866, died 1946. They were divorced before 1909. Issue, surname *Jolliff:*[271] a. *Clarence William*, born 30 May 1887, died 9 July 1974 in Central City, Illinois, married, 1909, Maude Miller; b. *Emma*, born 22 April 1893, died 21 January 1982, married, first, 25 December 1909, Frank Howard, second, 16 January 1926 John Behling.

iii.   Adeline (Addie) Delana Faulkner, born November 1871, buried 18 May 1907 in Elmwood Cemetery, Centralia, Illinois. She married, on 4 November 1892, Robert M. Hatfield, born July 1866, died 1921, buried in Elmwood Cemetery. Issue, surname *Hatfield:*[272] a. *Lawrence N.*, born 30 April 1893, died 3 December 1968 in Centralia, Illinois, married, in 1915, Marguerite Johnson; b. *Leo F.*, born 30 May 1895, died 17 July 1969 in Zeigler, Illinois.

M29   **John Ellington Morgan Faulkner**, born 11 November 1848 in Marion County, Kentucky, died 10 April 1941 in Louisville, Kentucky. He and his family were buried in Cave Hill Cemetery, Louisville.

He married, on 23 January 1896, Ida Bell Purdy, who died 10 January 1939, in Louisville, Kentucky.

He lived in Lebanon until 1907, when he moved to Louisville, and was known locally as a raconteur of local history. He taught school in 1873 for three terms. Later he entered the service of the United States Revenue Service as a gauger and storekeeper. He read extensively, one interest being the life of Napoleon. He secured for Lucas Moore the nomination for Kentucky Commissioner of Agriculture; following Moore's election, he became his chief deputy.[273]

Issue of John Ellington Morgan and Ida Bell (Purdy) Faulkner, born in Lebanon, Kentucky:[274]

    i.   Byron Macaulay Faulkner, born 29 October 1896, died 20 December 1913 in Louisville, Kentucky, buried in Cave Hill Cemetery.

M73 ii.   Carroll Purdy Faulkner, born 22 May 1898.

M30 **William R. Faulkner**, born about 1832, probably in Obion County, Tennessee, died 6 February 1864, of consumption, at Glasgow, Kentucky.[275]

He married, on 10 January 1860, in Green County, Kentucky, Almira E. Sidebottom. She died in 1870 at the house of F. G. Dyer, probably in Green County, Kentucky.

In 1860, he lived in Hart County, Kentucky. On 16 September 1863, he enlisted as a private in Company E, 37th Regiment of Kentucky Mounted Infantry, for one year, but died while in service.[276]

Issue of William R. and Almira E. (Sidebottom) Faulkner:[277]

    i.   Margaret A. H. Faulkner. She married, on 17 September 1883, in Larue County, Kentucky, Thomas B. Braden.

M31 **Warren Faulkner**, born 14 May 1820 in Orange County, Indiana, died 27 December 1914 in Keenes, Four Mile Township, Wayne County, Illinois, was buried in the Thomason Cemetery.

He married, as his first wife, on 24 October 1844, in Orange County, Indiana, Elizabeth Sanders, daughter of Thomas and Hannah (Copple) Sanders, born 10 October 1826 in Orange County, Indiana, died 19 December 1899 in Keene's Station, buried in the Thomason Cemetery.[278]

He married, as his second wife, in 1901 in Jefferson County, Illinois, Mrs. Margaret (Dulaney) Burge.

He bought, on 9 February 1859, land in section 19, Walnut Hill Township, Jefferson County, Illinois, selling it on 22 February 1864.[279] He and his family then moved to Wayne County.

Issue of Warren and Elizabeth (Sanders) Faulkner, the first four born in Orange County, Indiana, the fifth in Jefferson County, Illinois (they also adopted a daughter, Nancy Johnson, born about 1863):[280]

    i.   Robert D. O. Faulkner, born 12 September 1845, died on or about 22 November 1862, of measles, at Munfordville, Hart County, Kentucky, while in Company H, 80th Illinois Infantry. He was buried in the National Cemetery, Louisville, Kentucky.

M74 ii.   William Thomas Faulkner, born 17 June 1847.

    iii.   Rhoda Ellen Faulkner, born 3 November 1849, died shortly before 3 October 1878 in Four Mile Township, Wayne County, Illinois.[281] She married, as her first husband, Andrew Bullard and had issue, surname *Bullard*: a. *Robert*

W., born about 1872, married, 11 March 1893, in Wayne County, Illinois, Louisa Jones; b. *John*, born about 1874. She married, as her second husband, —— Walker.

M75   iv.   John Sanders Faulkner, born 9 July 1852.

M76   v.   Joseph L. Faulkner, born 23 November 1862.

    vi.   Margaret A. Faulkner, born 5 April 1865, died 10 December 1865, buried in Bruce Cemetery, Four Mile Township.[282]

M32   Alfred Faulkner, born 2 August 1832 in Green County, Kentucky, died 2 June 1911 in Danville, Illinois, was buried at the Danville Home for Disabled Veterans. His home had been in Centràlia Township, Marion County, Illinois.

He married, on 20 March 1859, in Marion County, Illinois,[283] Amanda Caroline Grubb, daughter of Virgil and Delilah (Sanders) Grubb, born 3 March 1838 in Southeast Township, Orange County, Indiana, died 1 July 1908 in Marion County, Illinois, buried in Little Grove Cemetery, Walnut Hill.

He moved to Grand Prairie Township, Jefferson County, Illinois, in 1854. He served in Company H, 80th Illinois Infantry, until his discharge 19 June 1865. After the war, he lived in Orange County, Indiana, but in March 1868, he returned to Illinois. He was a member of the Christian Church and a Republican.[284]

Issue of Alfred and Amanda Caroline (Grubb) Faulkner:[285]

    i.   Martha Ellen Faulkner, born 1860. She married, as her first husband, on 26 May 1878, in Marion County, Illinois, William Parker; and, as her second husband, Hickman Willis.

M77   ii.   Thomas Marion Faulkner, born December 1862.

M78   iii.   Virgil Franklin Faulkner, born 6 May 1866.

    iv.   Joel Harvey Faulkner, born about 1868. In 1922, he lived in Bond County, Illinois.

    v.   John Albert Faulkner, born about 1871. He died between 1900 and 1911.

    vi.   William Sherman Faulkner, born about 1878, died November 1917 in Union County, Illinois. He married, on 15 June 1899, at Salem, Marion County, Illinois,[286] Rosa R. Bingham, daughter of Marion and Mary (Christ) Bingham, born about 1882 in Illinois.

M33   Joseph Franklin Faulkner, born 2 March 1834 in Green County, Kentucky, died 4 February 1898 in French Lick, Indiana, was buried in the Old Town Cemetery, Paoli, Indiana.

He married, on 19 October 1863, in Orange County, Indiana,[287] Sarah Catharine Long, daughter of Charles and Anne (Elliott) Long, born 19 December 1845 Harrison County, Indiana, died 14 March 1917 in French Lick, Indiana, buried in Old Town Cemetery.

He enlisted, on 18 December 1861 at Richview, Illinois, in the 49th Illinois Volunteer Infantry, and was discharged 15 August 1862 at Jackson, Tennessee. He taught school, farmed, and practiced homeopathic medicine, in Valeene, Indiana, until 1872; Dubois County, Indiana, 1872 to 1884; Birdseye, Indiana, 1884 to 1893; and in French Lick, Indiana, from 1893.[288] The medical practice required a stable with six horses.[289] He was a Baptist, a Republican, a Freemason, and a member of the Grand Army of the Republic.[290]

Issue of Joseph Franklin and Sarah Catharine (Long) Faulkner, the first four born in Orange County, Indiana, the rest in Dubois County, Indiana:[291]

    i.   Emma Faulkner, born 23 April 1865. She married, 6 April 1886, in Dubois County, Indiana, Anthony F. Dickey.

M79 ii. Charles L. Faulkner, born about 1867.

    iii. John S. Faulkner, born about 1869. He was convicted of assault and battery with intent to murder in 1892 and served a two-year term in the Southern Indiana State Prison.[292] He lived in Arkansas at the time he accidentally killed his brother Charles, but later disappeared. He may have gone to California.[293]

    iv. Thomas Faulkner, died in infancy.

    v. William C. Faulkner, born 17 April 1873. He married, on 11 January 1912, in Marion County, Indiana,[294] Elizabeth Wynn, born 8 March 1870. He was a floor layer and finisher and was living as late as 1930 in Indianapolis, Indiana.

    vi. Anna Belle Faulkner, born 30 September 1877, died about 1969 in Iowa. On 12 July 1907, in Orange County, Indiana,[295] she married Lewis S. Horsey, born 17 July 1839.

    vii. Marion Marcus Faulkner, born 12 April 1884, died 22 August 1968 in Louisville, Kentucky, buried in the Old Town Cemetery, Paoli, Indiana. He was married and divorced, but had no issue.[296]

    viii. Charlotte J. Faulkner, born 1 March 1888, died in the early 1960s in Cedar Falls, Iowa. She married, 29 August 1916, Charles O. Todd,[297] professor of psychology at Iowa State University (or University of Iowa). Issue, surname *Todd*: a. *Charles*; b. *Kathleen*.

M34 **James Thomas Faulkner**, born about 1841 in Green County, Kentucky, died 11 December 1908 in Cedar Hill, San Juan County, New Mexico.[298]

He married, on 12 October 1876, in Cañon City, Fremont County, Colorado, Mary Jane Gray, daughter of Benjamin S. Gray, born 1856, died 7 August 1934 in Cedar Hill, San Juan County, New Mexico, buried in Cedar Hill Cemetery.

He served in Company F, 59th Indiana Infantry, during the Civil War. He was a farmer, moving to Colorado after the war and later to New Mexico.

Issue of James Thomas and Mary Jane (Gray) Faulkner:[299]

    i. Viola May Faulkner, born 5 August 1877 in Colorado, lived in Durango, Colorado. She married Fred E. Pierce, born about 1876 in Iowa. Issue, surname *Pierce*:[300] a. *Veva*, born about 1904; b. *Margaret*, born about 1905; c. *Frances*, born 1915.

    ii. Maude Faulkner, born 30 July 1880.

    iii. Thomas Franklin Faulkner, born 23 October 1883 in New Mexico, died 1916, buried in Cedar Hill Cemetery.

    iv. Josephine F. Faulkner, born 10 February 1885 in New Mexico, died 1938, buried in Aztec Cemetery. She married John I. Sumner.

    v. Olive Faulkner, born 9 May 1898 in Colorado, died 9 March 1959, buried in Aztec Cemetery. She married, 7 October 1915, Isaac M. Nixon, born about 1890 in Wyoming. Issue, surname *Nixon*:[301] a. *Merna*, born 1917.

M35   **Albert Faulkner**, born about 1832 in Macoupin County, Illinois, died 21 March 1863, of typhoid fever, at the Fayetteville Regimental Hospital, Fayetteville, Washington County, Arkansas, was buried in the National Cemetery there.[302]

He married, on 23 August 1855, in Benton County, Arkansas, Eliza J. Ellington, daughter of —— and Sarah (——) Ellington, born about 1839, living in 1877 in Stone County, Missouri. She married, as her second husband, on 5 September 1868, in Stone County, Missouri,[303] James H. Ragsdale.

In 1860, he and his family lived in Hickory Township, Carroll County, Arkansas. He enlisted 14 May 1862 at Benton County, Arkansas, and mustered in on 3 July 1862 at Springfield, Missouri, as a private in Company A, 1st Regiment of Arkansas Cavalry Volunteers, a Union unit.

Issue of Albert and Eliza J. (Ellington) Faulkner, born in Carroll County, Arkansas:[304]

    i.   Sarah C. Faulkner, born 28 September 1857, died 8 March 1910 in Stone County, Missouri, buried in Charity Cemetery, near Bradfield. She married, on 21 April 1878, in Greene County, Missouri, George Cornell, born January 1856 in Illinois, and had issue, surname *Cornell:*[305] a. *Joe*, married Vinnie Robinson; b. *John L.*, born December 1885; c. *Rosa B.*, born October 1889, married George Dobyns.

    ii.   Mary Ann Faulkner, born 16 February 1860, died 16 August 1949 in Stone County, Missouri, buried in Charity Cemetery. She married, on 21 April 1878, in Greene County, Missouri, James Marion Branstetter, born 10 March 1853 in Missouri, died 6 October 1949, buried in Charity Cemetery, and had issue, surname *Branstetter:*[306] a. *Daniel Pennington*, born 27 January 1879, died 24 August 1930 in Bradfield, Missouri, married Nettie Smith; b. *Sara Rhoda*, born 2 January 1881, died 12 September 1951, married Ben Brown; c. *Eliza Jane*, born 29 January 1883, died 15 September 1963 in Kansas, married Randall Dahlman; d. *John William*, born 16 April 1885, died 16 January 1948 in Tulsa, Oklahoma, married Maud Cornett; e. *James Pleasant*, born 28 October 1887, died 14 June 1964, married Frances McGinnis; f. *Wessie Mable*, born 16 May 1891, married Tom Austin; g. *Mary Lois Helen*, born 13 February 1894, died, unmarried, February 1981 in Tulsa, Oklahoma; h. *Edna Iris Pearl*, born 17 December 1896, married Bert Wrinkle.

M80 iii.   John William Henry David Elbert Penelton Faulkner, born 12 July 1862.

    iv.   Avery Faulkner, died young, buried in Charity Cemetery.

M36   **Felix Grundy Faulkner**, born about 1835 in Macoupin County, Illinois, died 21 June 1911 in Siloam Springs, Benton County, Arkansas.[307]

He married first, in May 1860, Clementine Fitzpatrick, born about 1845 in Missouri, died 6 June 1895.

He married, as his second wife, on 14 January 1897, in Washington County, Arkansas,[308] Jane Cook, born about 1834, died 14 April 1897.

He married, as his third wife, on 13 July 1897, in Washington County, Arkansas,[309] Margaret Cook, of Siloam Springs, Arkansas, born about 1837 in Tennessee, died 11 January 1924 at Wheeler, Washington County, Arkansas.

Felix Grundy Faulkner was named after a prominent Kentucky politician. He enlisted 12 August 1862, at O'Fallon, St. Clair County, Illinois, in

Company I, 117th Illinois Infantry. His right arm was amputated following a wound at the Battle of Nashville, 15 December 1864.[310]   After his discharge, on 5 August 1865, he resided at Springfield, Linn County, Kansas. In 1870, he lived in Hickory Township, Carroll County, Arkansas; in 1880, in Eureka Springs, Arkansas. In 1910, he lived in Jefferson County, Oklahoma.

Issue of Felix Grundy and Clementine (Fitzpatrick) Faulkner:[311]

i. Samuel Faulkner, born about 1863-1864, died, of diphtheria, before 1870.

ii. John Tyler Faulkner, born about 1865 in Kansas, died at the age of 25, while working in a lumber camp, probably in Texas. He was said to have left issue.

M81 iii. Thomas Marion Faulkner, born 24 September 1867.

iv. Alice Marie Faulkner, born 15 February 1869, died 16 September 1940 in Portland, Oregon, buried in Riverview Cemetery.[312] She married, as her first husband, —— Richardson, and had a son, a. *William H.* She married, as her second husband, Bright Harless, and had issue, surname *Harless*: b. *Della Maude*, born 22 March 1900 in Arkansas, died 16 December 1943 in Portland, Oregon, married Merle R. Hill; c. *Gene Elmer*. She married, as her third husband, James A. Kennedy.

M82 v. Felix Grundy Faulkner, born about 1873.

M83 vi. James Otis Faulkner, born 17 December 1876.

vii. Ada Gertrude Faulkner, born 6 August 1888, died 3 February 1973 in Portland, Oregon, buried in Riverview Cemetery. She married, on 11 November 1908, in Dawson, Oklahoma, Amos Russell Hogue, born 6 January 1888 in Arkansas, died 22 July 1931 and buried at Rush Springs, Oklahoma. After his death she came to Oregon, where she raised her family and worked as a caterer, housekeeper, and seamstress. They had issue, surname *Hogue*: a. *Amos*, born 2 June 1912 in Hastings, Oklahoma, married Margaret Irene Baker; b. *Almareene Gertrude*, born 13 July 1914 in Hastings, Oklahoma, married Warren Mesick; c. daughter, died soon after birth; d. *Ardelle*, born 6 June 1921, married, 26 June 1937, in Portland, Oregon, Theodore Baden; e. *Alice Marie*, born 19 October 1923 in Wirt, Oklahoma, died 23 August 1965 in Shakopee, Minnesota, married, first, Robert Victor Hamilton, second, John Jerald Mongelli, third, Walter H. Nelson; f. *Arthur Roy*, born 19 February 1926 in Healdon, Oklahoma, died 5 August 1970 in Ridgefield, Washington, married, first, Elizabeth ——, second, Elsie ——.

M37 **James Faulkner**, born 27 September 1839 in Taney County, Missouri, died 2 April 1888 at Eagle Rock, Barry County, Missouri, was buried in Munsey Cemetery.

He married, on 7 July 1861 in Taney County, Missouri, Rachel S. Reed, born 4 April 1840 in Indiana, died 17 March 1910 in Barry County, Missouri, buried in Munsey Cemetery.

He served on the Union side in the Civil War in Company I, 24th Missouri Infantry. In 1880, he and his family lived in Prairie Township, Carroll County, Arkansas.

Issue of James and Rachel S. (Reed) Faulkner, born in Carroll County, Arkansas:[313]

i. Sarah E. Faulkner, born 26 January 1866 in Missouri, died 28 December 1945, buried in Munsey Cemetery. She married, 2 December 1884, James Elbert A. Ball, born 16 January 1863, died 14 July 1943, buried in Munsey Cemetery. Issue, surname *Ball*:[314] a. *Arthur*, born 25 April 1886, died 9

December 1933; b. *Minnie L.*, born October 1888; c. *William A.*, born May 1891; d. *Dorah E.*, born June 1895.

ii. Vandora A. Faulkner, born about 1868 in Arkansas. She married, as her first husband, on 24 September 1888, Ulysses B. Pyatt; and as her second husband, on 6 December 1892, R. S. Goddard.

iii. Lanora Faulkner, born about 1871. She suffered from paralysis and epilepsy.

iv. Mary M. Faulkner, born 5 August 1875.

M84 v.   George D. Faulkner, born 6 October 1878.

vi. Alla E. Faulkner, born 21 July 1883.

M38   Samuel Faulkner, born 2 December 1848 in Taney County, Missouri, died 26 November 1928 in Prairie Township, Washington County, Arkansas, was buried in Parker Cemetery, Madison County, Arkansas.[315]

He married, in September 1876, Catharine J. Bailey, daughter of William Tandy and Maria (Wilcox) Bailey, born 10 May 1860 in Missouri, died 17 December 1928 in Washington County, Arkansas, buried in Parker Cemetery.

In 1880, they lived in Prairie Township, Carroll County, Arkansas.[316] They lived in 1900 in Richland Township, Madison County, Arkansas.[317]

Issue of Samuel and Catharine J. (Bailey) Faulkner, born in Carroll County and Madison County, Arkansas:[318]

i.   Sarah Mildred Palestine Faulkner, born 3 May 1877, died 21 August 1938 in Asher, Madison County, Arkansas, buried in Dunaway Cemetery. She married, 1895, George W. Dunaway, and had issue, surname *Dunaway*: a. *Nola*; b. *Arla*; c. *Agnes*; d. *Erma*, born 4 January 1904, died 1 August 1992 in Elkins, Arkansas, married Earl Hankins; e. *Elfie L.*; f. *Emery*.

ii. Jeannette Myrtle Faulkner, born 1 July 1878, died 1 April 1963 in Haskell, Muskogee County, Oklahoma. She married M. LaRue Drain, and had issue, surname *Drain*: a. *Emily*; b. *Ivy*; c. *Olen*, born 28 February 1903, died May 1978 in Muskogee, Oklahoma.

M85 iii. William Elvis Faulkner, born 4 September 1880.

M86 iv. David Ellis Faulkner, born 1 June 1883.

v.   Augusta (Gussie) Faulkner, born 28 December 1885, died 4 January 1980 in Elkins, Arkansas, buried in Mount Olive Cemetery. She married, as her first husband, on 9 December 1907, in Riverside County, California, Lester Lollar, who died 12 January 1954 in Oakland, California, and had issue, surname *Lollar*: a. *Raymond*; b. *Everett Carroll*, born 3 May 1923, died 30 December 1988 in Fayetteville, Arkansas, married Rema ——. She married, as her second husband, Ernest Hill, who died 27 August 1944 and was buried at Mount Liberty, Arkansas.

M87 vi. Roscoe Conklin Faulkner, born 2 May 1888.

vii. Lillie Mae Faulkner, born 27 August 1890, died 9 March 1970, buried in Mount Olive Cemetery. She married, as her first husband, John Wesley Hill, born 2 September 1885 in Arkansas, died 26 December 1955 at Mount Liberty, Arkansas, and had issue, surname *Hill*: a. *Goldie*, married Marvin Scarls Eubanks; b. *Helen*, married —— Rodgers; c. *Vird Ray*, born 26 May 1919, died 26 October 1971 in Fayetteville, Arkansas, married Blanche ——; d. *Void*. She married, as her second husband, William H. Lacy.

M88 viii. Samuel Faulkner, born 22 January 1893.

ix. Katy Faulkner, born 7 May 1895, died 29 September 1979 in Fayetteville, Arkansas, buried in Mount Olive Cemetery. She married Oliver Milton (Bud) O'Neal, son of Thomas R. and Elvira Lucinda (Jones) O'Neal, born 7 January 1886 in Joplin, Missouri, died 8 December 1958 in Washington County, Arkansas. Issue, surname *O'Neal*:[319] a. *George Washington*, born 22 December 1912, married Lucy McChristian; b. *Mary*, born 6 September 1914, married, 8 April 1934, Clayton Bell; c. *Chester*, born 16 November 1916, died 22 March 1972 in Elkins, Arkansas, married, 1950, Wilma Scranton; d. *Frances Lorene*, born 30 April 1920, married, October 1939, Elmer Haskel Ledford; e. *Carl*, married Mabel ——; f. *Oliver Milton*, died in infancy; g. *Ruby Marie*, married William Flavis Lawson; h. *Barbara Jean*, married Johnny Mack Canfield; i. *Donald Norris*, born 14 October 1937, died 20 February 19——, married Rose Kimble.

M89　x. Fred Faulkner, born 22 December 1897.

xi. infant, born 16 May 1901, died 31 May 1901, buried in Parker Cemetery.

xii. John Nolen Faulkner, born 30 June 1904, died, unmarried, 30 November 1973 in Bentonville, Arkansas, buried in Mount Olive Cemetery.

M39　**David Faulkner**, born 2 December 1848 in Taney County, Missouri, died 26 June 1923 in Kansas City, Kansas, was buried in Maple Hill Cemetery.[320]

He married, on 23 January 1870 at Berryville, Carroll County, Arkansas, Harriet Reed, probably the daughter of Alfred and Elizabeth (Briscoe) Reed,[321] born February 1850 in Barry County, Missouri, living in 1920 in Rosedale, Kansas.

In 1900, he and his family lived in Prairie Township, Carroll County, Arkansas.[322] In 1910, he was a teamster in Shawnee Township, Wyandotte County, Kansas.[323] They lived in Rosedale (later annexed to Kansas City), Kansas, in 1920.[324]

Issue of David and Harriet (Reed) Faulkner, born in Carroll County, Arkansas (they had eight children, all living in 1910):[325]

i. Minerva Cordelia Faulkner, born 5 December 1871, died 30 October 1960 in Muskogee, Oklahoma, buried in Green Hill Cemetery. On 6 January 1889, in Carroll County, Arkansas, she married William Oliver Miller, son of James G. Miller, born 31 October 1868 in Berryville, Arkansas, died 2 January 1950 in Muskogee, Oklahoma, buried in Green Hill Cemetery. Issue, surname *Miller*:[326] a. *Lena*, born August 1890, married Jim Painter; b. *Woody*, born 21 August 1893, died July 1976 in Richmond, California, married Fanny Jones; c. *Stella May*, born 12 May 1897, married, 11 August 1914, Bayliss McKinly Rowland; d. *Daisy*, born 1900, died 1902; e. *Charlie*, born 1902, died 1907; f. *Homer*, born 1904, died 1909; g. *Vivian*, born 12 January 1905, died 14 December 1989 California, married "Bullet" Fields; h. *Bessie*, born 1908, married Charley Humes; i. *John Jacob Astor*, born 2 August 1914, married Maud Rose.

ii. Sallisias I. Faulkner, born about 1872. Not further traced.

iii. Samuel Faulkner, born about 1875. Not further traced.

iv. Sarah E. Faulkner, born 1879.

M90　v. Charles Cicero Faulkner, born 10 June 1883.

vi. Lillian B. Faulkner, born July 1885, lived in Kansas City, Missouri, in 1964. She married —— Cramer.

vii. James A. Faulkner, born May 1890, died 22 September 1938 in Kansas City,

Kansas, was buried in Maple Hill Cemetery.[327]

viii.   Rosetta Faulkner, born July 1893.   She married George ——.

M40   William Faulkner, born 11 November 1840 in Perry Township, Boone County, Indiana, died 5 September 1923 in Boone County, Indiana,[328] was buried in Mount Tabor Cemetery.

He married, on 20 December 1866, in Boone County, Indiana,[329] Elizabeth Boyd, born January 1839 in Virginia, died 27 December 1915 in Fayette, Boone County, Indiana.[330]   She was divorced in 1865 from Levi Spicklemire.

He enlisted 21 August 1862 as a private in Company G, 79th Indiana Regiment, of the Army of the Cumberland, and was discharged as a corporal on 17 June 1865.

Issue of William and Elizabeth (Boyd) Faulkner, born in Perry Township, Boone County, Indiana:[331]

i.   Laura E. Faulkner, born 27 June 1868, died 12 November 1904, buried in Mount Tabor Cemetery. She married, 25 March 1886,[332] Wilson T. Johnson, born July 1862 in Indiana, and had issue, surname *Johnson:*[333] a. *Grace A.*, born May 1887, married, 20 August 1905, Harry C. Pedigo; b. *Maud*, born 4 January 1889, died April 1980 in Elkhart, Indiana, married, 20 November 1909, Truman Good; c. *Pleasant M.*, born August 1890, married, 30 December 1909, Ruth Smock; d. *Ermin H.* [son], born October 1892; e. *Hobart M.*, born November 1896; f. daughter, born 24 December 1902.

M91   ii.   John Alexander Faulkner, born 14 February 1870.

M92   iii.   Joseph Monroe Faulkner, born 4 January 1872.

iv.   Luvina A. Faulkner, born 21 October 1877, died 14 June 1902, buried in Mount Tabor Cemetery. She married, 28 October 1896,[334] Isaac N. Johnson, son of James F. and V. (Jordan) Johnson, and had issue, surname *Johnson:*[335] a. *Wilma O.*, born 15 May 1899.

v.   Mary A. Faulkner, born 16 May 1880, died November 1882, buried in Mount Tabor Cemetery.

M41   Albert Faulkner, born 1 January 1848 [calculated] in Perry Township, Boone County, Indiana, died 26 February 1876, was buried in Mount Tabor Cemetery.

He married Lucinda Smith. She married, as her second husband, on 22 October 1877,[336] John Rodgers.

Issue of Albert and Lucinda (Smith) Faulkner, born in Hendricks County, Indiana:[337]

i.   Ora Faulkner, living in 1879.

M93   ii.   Alva F. Faulkner, born about 1873.

iii.   Louella Faulkner, born about 1875. She married, 19 May 1889, in Hendricks County, Indiana,[338] John A. Riggins.

M42   Robert Ross Faulkner, born 25 December 1845 in North Palmyra Township, Macoupin County, Illinois, died 6 March 1893 in Gifford, Champaign County, Illinois.

He married first, on 25 August 1865 in Jefferson County, Illinois,[339] Nancy Elizabeth (Moore) Jolliff, widow of Richard Allen Jolliff and daughter of Samuel

W. and Rhoda (Smith) Moore, born 1 June 1842 in Missouri, died 28 January 1881 in Washington County, Illinois. She was buried in Grand Point Cemetery.

He married, as his second wife, on 28 January 1886 in Washington County, Illinois, Martha Ellen Broom, daughter of William and Parthena A. (Smith) Broom, born 11 March 1868 in White County, Illinois, died after 1943, when living in Chicago, Illinois. She resided in Vermilion County, Illinois, in 1896, and married, as her second husband, John H. Clement, on 16 October 1900 in Cook County, Illinois.

He served in Company F, 49th Illinois Infantry. He later worked as a railroad employee.

Issue of Robert Ross and Nancy Elizabeth (Moore) Faulkner, born in Washington County, Illinois:[340]

    i.   Ida H. Faulkner, born 8 September 1866 [calculated], died 9 October 1868, buried in Grand Point Cemetery.

    ii.   Ila M. Faulkner, born 30 July 1869 [calculated], died 12 May 1871, buried in Grand Point Cemetery.

    iii.   Iona Rhoda Faulkner, born 21 March 1871, died 19 January 1948 in Milford, Iowa. She married, on 22 May 1890, in Champaign County, Illinois,[341] as her first husband, Thomas Edward DeSpain, and had issue, surname *DeSpain*: a. *Durward E.*, born 26 April 1893, died 22 October 1912; b. *Lloyde L.*, born 1 April 1896, died 18 May 1961, married, first, Rose Shaffer, and, second, Ruth Elberta Duncan; c. *Bessie F.*, born 5 May 1898, died 7 June 1916, married Earl Rukes; d. *Howard J.*, born 24 April 1901, died, unmarried, 11 May 1981; e. *Russell H.*, born 28 October 1903, died December 1985 in Omaha, Nebraska, married, first, Wilda Belknap, and second, Eula ——; f. *Inez*, born 8 January 1907, married, A. I. Shaffer. Iona married, as her second husband, —— Sparra.

    iv.   Idella Rebecca Faulkner, born 1 March 1873, died 17 March 1957. She married James Harvey Hall and issue, surname *Hall*: a. *Ethel*, born 31 July 1894, died, unmarried, 22 November 1989.

Issue of Robert Ross and Martha Ellen (Broom) Faulkner:[342]

    v.   Georgia May Broom Faulkner, born 16 May 1883, living in 1943.[343]

M94 vi.   Chester Corrington Faulkner, born 14 March 1887.

    vii.   Valeria Verea Faulkner, born 17 September 1888, lived in Illinois. She married Harry Fisher and had issue, surname *Fisher*: a. *Bobby*, married Dorothy ——.

M95 viii. Ross R. Faulkner, born 1 March 1891.

M96 viii. Robert Raymond Faulkner, born 18 September 1893.

M43   **Samuel Wilson Faulkner**, born 27 December 1849 in Washington County, Illinois, died 24 December 1898 in Danville, Vermilion County, Illinois, was buried in Springhill Cemetery.

He married, as his first wife, Martha Ann Loyd, born about 1851 in Alabama, died in 1889 in Palmyra Township, Macoupin County, Illinois, buried in North Palmyra Cemetery.[344]

He married, as his second wife, on 20 January 1891, in Rossville, Illinois,[345] Mamie E. Cole, daughter of Robert and Anna (Darling) Cole, born

February 1872 in Williamsport, Indiana, living 1920 in Indianapolis, Indiana former wife of William Potts. She married, as her third husband, Frank Cotton.

He was a farmer as late as 1887 in Palmyra, Macoupin County, Illinois,[346] but by the time of his second marriage was a railroad employee, living in Alvin, Illinois. He also worked as a painter.

Issue of Samuel Wilson and Martha Ann (Loyd) Faulkner, born in Palmyra Township, Macoupin County, Illinois:[347]

    i.   Ruth Faulkner.

    ii.   Pelina Faulkner, born about 1872. She married Fred J. Draper, born December 1861 in Illinois, and was buried prior to 1898 in the North Palmyra Cemetery.[348] He married, as his second wife, Emma ——, born May 1878.[349]

    iii. Bertha Faulkner, born about 1874, buried in North Palmyra Cemetery.

M97 iv. Wilbur (born Wilburn) Wilson Faulkner, born 12 November 1878.

    v.   Octavia Elizabeth Faulkner, born 5 January 1882, was living in 1933 in Lafayette, Indiana. She married Walter Henry Ripley and had issue, surname *Ripley:*[350] a. *Martha Carmen*, born 22 June 1902 in Decatur, Illinois.

Issue of Samuel Wilson and Mamie E. (Cole) Faulkner, born in Danville, Illinois:[351]

    vi. Mamie A. Faulkner, born 3 December 1891, died 7 May 1972 in Indianapolis, Indiana. She married —— Baker and had issue, surname *Baker:* a. *Chester A.*; b. *Floyd D.*

M98 vii. Charles E. Faulkner, born 2 February 1896.

M44   **George P. Faulkner**, born 7 April 1857 in Washington County, Illinois, died 13 May 1887 in Meagher County, Montana.

He married, on 11 October 1877, in Marion County, Illinois, Melisha Catherine Deadmond, daughter of Thomas Nun and Rachel (McClelland) Deadmond, born 20 June 1855 in Illinois, died 8 November 1921 in Marion County, Illinois.

They moved to Montana about 1882.

Issue of George P. and Melisha Catherine (Deadmond) Faulkner, the first two born in Washington County, Illinois:[352]

    i.   Drusilla Faulkner, born 2 August 1875, died 18 March 1963 in Wilson, Park County, Montana, buried in Mt. View Cemetery, Livingston, Montana. She married, on 25 December 1895 in Livingston, Montana, John Bruckert, who died 24 November 1934, and had issue, surname *Bruckert:*[353] a. *Ely S.*, born May 1894; b. *Alice M.*, born November 1897; c. *Albert*, born 24 May 1898, died September 1978 in Cody, Wyoming; d. *Frank*, born 1900; e. *Earl*, born 1909; f. *Everett*, born 1912; g. *John*, born 1916.

    ii.   Felix Faulkner, born 12 September 1878, died 2 May 1879, buried in Grand Point Cemetery.

    iii. Elsie Faulkner, born 18 February 1882, died 20 February 1882, buried in Grand Point Cemetery.

    iv. Rachel Rhoda (Maud) Faulkner, born 11 August 1884 in Tostan, Broadwater County, Montana, died 29 May 1968, buried in the Deadmond Cemetery.

She married, on 26 February 1906 in Paducah, Kentucky, Jesse Everette Deadmond, and had a daughter.

    v.   Lulu Faulkner. She drowned as a small child in an irrigation ditch in Montana.

M45   **Francis M. Faulkner**, born 30 July 1843 in Washington County, Illinois, died 18 January 1881 in Louisville, Kentucky.

He married, on 18 August 1869, in Louisville, Kentucky, Maggie L. Long. She married, as her second husband, on 1 April 1885,[354] Jacob Krauth, Jr., and had a child, Charles O. Krauth, born July 1887.

He enlisted, on 1 July 1861 at Ashley, Illinois, as a private in Company F, 44th Illinois Infantry, and received a gunshot wound during his service. He settled in Louisville by 1874, where he worked as a sawyer and as a machinist, laborer, and carpenter for the Louisville, Cincinnati, and Lexington Railroad. About 1889, Jacob and Maggie L. (Long) Krauth moved to Denver, Colorado.

Issue of Francis M. and Maggie L. (Long) Faulkner, born in Louisville, Kentucky:[355]

    i.   Gertrude F. Faulkner, born 24 November 1870.

    ii.   Freeman H. Faulkner, born 18 October 1872. He married, by 1900, Anna —— —, born December 1878 in Canada.[356] In 1904, he was a clerk in Denver, Colorado. Not further traced.

    iii.   Carrie K. Faulkner, born 13 February 1875. She married, on 21 December 1892, in Arapahoe County, Colorado,[357] Joseph W. Wiswell, born May 1859 in Illinois. In 1900, they lived in Barr Precinct, Arapahoe County, Colorado. Issue, surname *Wiswell:*[358] a. *Lorena A.*, born October 1894; b. *Margaret L.*, born May 1900.

M46   **Samuel Alexander Faulkner**, born about 1841 in Green County, Kentucky, died 25 October 1884 in Emma Township, White County, Illinois,[359] was buried in Logan Cemetery.

He married, on 8 March 1876, in White County, Illinois, Malinda Goggin Logan, daughter of William R. and Fanny Logan, born 1 December 1848 in Emma Township, White County, Illinois, died 3 October 1883, buried in Logan Cemetery.

He served as a private and corporal in Company F, 87th Illinois Infantry.

Issue of Samuel Alexander and Malinda Goggin (Logan) Faulkner, born in Emma Township, White County, Illinois:[360]

M99 i.   Samuel Logan Faulkner, born 17 September 1877.

    ii.   Milton K. Faulkner, born 4 February 1879, died July 1884, buried in Logan Cemetery.

M47   **John M. Faulkner**, born July 1842 in Green County, Kentucky, died 19 March 1908 in Heralds Prairie Township, White County, Illinois, was buried in Union Ridge Cemetery.[361]

He married, by bond dated 8 January 1863, in Green County, Kentucky, Mary Elizabeth Houk, daughter of Miles and Susan P. (Handy) Houk, born 23

March 1834 in Green County, Kentucky,[362] died 26 March 1914 in Heralds Prairie Township, White County, Illinois.

He enlisted on 25 September 1861 in Company A, 13th Kentucky Infantry, during the Civil War, but deserted 20 March 1863 at Munfordsville, Kentucky. He went to Illinois soon thereafter.

Issue of John M. and Mary Elizabeth (Houk) Faulkner, born in White County, Illinois:[363]

M100 i.   Erskine B. Faulkner, born March 1864.

M48   **Levi Ulysses Faulkner**, born 28 July 1850 [calculated] in Green County, Kentucky, died 9 May 1891 in Emma Township, White County, Illinois,[364] was buried in Big Prairie Cemetery.

He married, as his first wife, on 12 January 1875, at G. B. McGlasson's, in Green County, Kentucky,[365] Sarah Jane McGlasson, born about 1850 in Green County, Kentucky, buried in Big Prairie Cemetery.

He married, as his second wife, on 10 November 1890, at Carmi, Illinois,[366] Susan J. Brooks, daughter of Bartley and S. (Sumpter) Brooks, born about 1859. She married, as her second husband, on 7 July 1892, in Posey County, Indiana,[367] William Chastain, born 15 January 1840, died 1 September 1908, buried in Concord Cemtery, Emma Township, White County, Illinois.

Levi U. Faulkner was a farmer in Emma Township, owning 141 acres at his death.

Issue of Levi Ulysses and Sarah Jane (McGlasson) Faulkner, born in Emma Township, White County, Illinois:[368]

      i.   Donald Calvern Faulkner, died young, buried in Big Prairie Cemetery.
      ii.   Maud Faulkner, born 24 July 1879, died 15 October 1879, buried in Big Prairie (also known as Hawthorne) Cemetery.[369]
      iii.   Minnie Helen Faulkner, born 2 October 1880, living in 1920 in Almyra, Arkansas. She married Samuel Rhein, born about 1872 in Illinois. Issue, surname *Rhein*:[370] a. *Gladys*, born about 1901; b. *Jesse F.*, born 29 October 1905, died August 1979 in Warren, Arkansas; c. *Lois*, born about 1908; d. *Gail H.*, born 1916, lives in Stuttgart, Arkansas, married John D. Roth.
M101 iv.   Clay Cash Faulkner, born 13 July 1882.
M102 v.   Claude L. Faulkner, born 2 June 1886.

M49   **James Robert Faulkner**, born 6 July 1853 in Green County, Kentucky, died 2 August 1923 in Emma Township, White County, Illinois, was buried in Emma Cemetery.

He married, as his first wife, on 26 October 1880 in Green County, Kentucky, Elzadie (Ella) McCandless, born about 1859, died in childbirth.

He married, as his second wife, on 15 August 1889, in White County, Illinois,[371] Winnie Alma Absher, daughter of William and Nancy (Walker) Absher, born 12 December 1863 near Vienna, Johnson County, Illinois, died January 1942 in Grayville, Illinois, buried 27 January 1942 in the Concord Cemetery.[372]

He was a farmer in Emma Township.

Issue of James Robert and Elzadie (McCandless) Faulkner:

    i.   son, who died in infancy.

Issue of James Robert and Winnie Alma (Absher) Faulkner, born in Emma Township, White County, Illinois:[373]

    ii.   Eula Marie Faulkner, born 1 April 1896, died 6 February 1984, buried in Emma Cemetery. She married, on 16 April 1911, Ben H. Coston, born 1889, died 1980. Issue, surname *Coston*: a. *Donald D.*; b. *Helen*, married Howard W. Carstensen.

    iii.   Lura Helen Faulkner, born 1 December 1899, living in 1942 in Grayville, Illinois. She married James Modest Lomas, born 1899, died 1925, buried Oak Grove Cemetery, Grayville, Illinois.

M50   **Isaac C. Faulkner**, born in April 1873 in Green County, Kentucky, died 1 April 1908 in Metcalfe County, Kentucky.[374]

He married, as his first wife, on 7 February 1897, in Green County, Kentucky, Louisa T. Jeffries, daughter of William Alexander Jeffries, born June 1871 in Kentucky, a deaf person. She was granted a divorce in June 1901.[375]

He married, as his second wife, on 4 December 1902, in Metcalfe County, Kentucky,[376] Anna Belle Jewell, daughter of David and Margaret Jewell, born about 1881 in Metcalfe County, Kentucky.

Issue of Isaac C. and Louisa T. (Jeffries) Faulkner, born in Green County, Kentucky:

    i.   Melvina Grace Faulkner, born February 1898.

M51   **Louis V. Faulkner**, born 22 September 1874 Green County, Kentucky, died 24 September 1956 at the Masonic Home, Shelbyville, Kentucky, was buried in Bethel Cemetery, Metcalfe County, Kentucky.

He married, as his first wife, on 8 December 1899, in Green County, Kentucky, Betty Myers, daughter of John Hulet and Sarah Elizabeth (Tolley) Myers,[377] who died 6 September, probably in 1903, in Green County, Kentucky.[378] Her baby also died on this date.

He married, as his second wife, on 1 December 1904, in Metcalfe County, Kentucky,[379] Nannie Price, daughter of Charles J. and Bettie (Thompson) Price, born about 1886 in Metcalfe County, Kentucky, died 25 November 1942 in Metcalfe County, Kentucky. She was granted a divorce on 4 January 1907 and given custody of her child.[380]

He lived on a farm on the waters of the East Fork of the Little Barren River, which he sold in 1922.

Issue of Louis V. and Nannie (Price) Faulkner, born in Metcalfe County, Kentucky:

    i.   Betty Lee Price, born 22 July 1906, died January 1985 in Fresno, California. She married, on 2 October 1925 in Green County, Kentucky, Monte Murrell.

M52   **Charles L. Faulkner**, born 26 June 1856 in Green County, Kentucky, was living on 1 January 1909 in Metcalfe County, Kentucky.[381]

He married, as his first wife, on 28 December 1876, in Columbia, Kentucky,[382] Amanda Belle Wilson, daughter of H. W. and Agnes A. Wilson, born 25 June 1856 in Columbia, Kentucky, died 2 January 1897, buried in Columbia City Cemetery.

He married, as his second wife, on 28 October 1901, at Columbia, Adair County, Kentucky,[383] Mollie Moran.

His wife in 1909 had the initials "V. L."

Issue of Charles L. and Amanda Belle (Wilson) Faulkner, born in Metcalfe County, Kentucky:[384]

     i.   Sarah (Sally) L. Faulkner, born August 1878, living in 1920 in Childress, Texas. She married, on 27 October 1898, in Metcalfe County, Kentucky, Elza N. Mitchell, born about 1873 in Green County, Kentucky. Issue, surname *Mitchell*:[385] a. *Harry*, born 11 August 1899, died October 1974 in Childress, Texas; b. *Anna Belle*, born about 1901; c. *Naylor*, born about 1903; d. *Grace*, born about 1908.

M103 ii.   John Thomas Faulkner, born 15 March 1880.

M104 iii. William Russell Faulkner, born 20 November 1883.

M105 iv. George H. Faulkner, born July 1887.

M106 v.   David Edward Faulkner, born 15 May 1889.

    vi.   Olie H. Faulkner, born November 1891, living in Columbus, Georgia, in 1940. In 1920, he was a sergeant in the U. S. Army, stationed at Fort Benning, Georgia. Not further traced.

    vii. Annie Faulkner, born about 1896, living in 1970. She married, on 18 February 1920, in Childress, Texas, Richard Clarence Bellah, son of Henry and Catherine (Cunningham) Bellah, born 1893 in Childress County, Texas. She came to Childress first in 1910, then returned to Kentucky, but went back to Texas in 1919. Issue, surname *Bellah*: a. *Richard Arvene*, born 22 March 1921, died 9 May 1989 in Childress, Texas; married 16 February 1947 Peggy ____.[386]

M53   **Simeon W[alker] Faulkner**, born 11 November 1850 in Washington County, Illinois, died 27 February 1878 in Washington County, Illinois, was buried in Grand Point Cemetery.

He married, on 2 January 1873, in Washington County, Illinois, Mary E. George, daughter of James and Katherine (Willard) George. She married, as her second husband, on 2 September 1880 in Washington County, Illinois, William Corvus.

Issue of Simeon W. and Mary E. (George) Faulkner, born in Washington County, Illinois:[387]

M107 i.   Franklin L. Faulkner, born April 1874.

    ii.   daughter, born 5 August 1877, died 7 August 1877, buried in Grand Point Cemetery.

    iii. Caty Belle Faulkner, born 1 February 1878, died 2 September 1878, buried in Grand Point.

M54   **James Hamilton Faulkner**, born 5 August 1856 in Washington County, Illinois, died 5 September 1940 in Centralia, Illinois, was buried in Fouts Cemetery.

He married, on 23 September 1879, in Washington County, Illinois, Rachel Melissa Trout, daughter of Samuel and Malinda A. (Earls) Trout, born 1 September 1860 in Washington County, Illinois, died 3 February 1936 in Centralia, buried in Fouts Cemetery.

He worked for the Illinois Central Railroad as a section laborer from 1901 to 1924, as well as a truck farmer. They lived in Irvington, Illinois.

Issue of James Hamilton and Rachel Melissa (Trout) Faulkner, born in Washington County, Illinois:[388]

M108 i.   Eldore Bert Faulkner, born 29 August 1880.

    ii.   Alma Ora Faulkner, born 5 November 1881, lived in Valley Park, Missouri. She married Eula Zimmerman.

    iii.   Myrtle Nina Faulkner, born 29 June 1885, died 21 August 1967 in San Pedro, California. She married Lewis Kline and lived in Centralia, Illinois.

M109 iv.   Eugene Willard Faulkner, born 15 June 1890.

    v.   Pearl Irvine Faulkner, born 8 December 1892, died in 1951 in Centralia, Illinois, buried in Elmwood Cemetery. She married, in 1912 in Irvington, Illinois, William LeRoy Grimes, son of William Martin and Mary (Brown) Grimes, who died 25 May 1973 in Centralia, Illinois. Issue, surname *Grimes*: a. *Leroy*, of North Hollywood, California; b. *Georgia Mae*, married —— Houssens, lived in Seattle, Washington; c. *Evelyn*, married —— Todd, lived in Centralia, Illinois; d. *Ida Rose*, married —— Knight, lived in Centralia, Illinois.

M110 vi.   Leonard E. Faulkner, born 23 March 1894.

M111 vii.   Manley E. Faulkner, born 7 February 1896.

    viii.   Clarence C. Faulkner, born 24 March 1900, lived in Manteno, Illinois.

M55   **John A. Faulkner**, born 26 February 1846 in Macon County, Missouri, died 24 August 1926 in LaPlata, Macon County, Missouri, was buried in LaPlata Cemetery.[389]

He married, on 3 January 1871, in Macon County, Missouri,[390] Armilda F. Griffin, born April 1846 in Missouri, died 1921 in LaPlata, Missouri, buried in LaPlata Cemetery.

Up through 1880, he lived in North Salem Township, Linn County, Misouri. In 1900 and 1910, he was in LaPlata.[391]

Issue of John A. and Armilda F. (Griffin) Faulkner, born in Linn County, Missouri:[392]

    i.   Norah F. Faulkner, born about 1872. She married, on 21 July 1890, in Macon County, Missouri,[393] Fred G. Forrest, of Richland Township, Macon County, Missouri.

    ii.   Daniel N. Faulkner, born December 1873, died, unmarried, 27 February 1924 in St. Joseph, Missouri,[394] buried in LaPlata Cemetery.

    iii.   John S. Faulkner, born about 1875, died 24 September 1892, buried in LaPlata Cemetery.

    iv.   Tabitha Ina Faulkner, born June 1878, living in 1926 in Neosho, Missouri.

She married, as her first husband, on 21 October 1896, at LaPlata, Missouri,[395] James Trail. She married again, on 16 November 1907, at Macon, Missouri,[396] John F. Barr, of Sedalia, Missouri.

    v.   James D. Faulkner, born October 1879, living in 1926 in Moberly, Missouri. Not further traced.

    vi.   Charles C. Faulkner, born May 1882, died, unmarried, 21 December 1936 in Hudson Township, Macon County, Missouri, buried in LaPlata Cemetery.

    vii.   George Faulkner, born February 1886, died 1917, buried in LaPlata Cemetery.

M56   **William R. Faulkner**, born August 1847 in Macon County, Missouri,[397] was living in 1904 in Clarence, Macon County, Missouri.

He married, as his first wife, Charlotte Jane ——, born about 1844 in Kentucky, living in 1880 in Wilson Township, Gentry County, Missouri. She died soon thereafter.

He married, as his second (or later) wife, on 10 April 1904, in Clarence, Missouri,[398] Hattie Saunders, of Clarence, Missouri. She married, as her second husband, on 4 September 1905 in Macon County, Missouri,[399] Dennis Sweet.

Issue of William R. and Charlotte Jane Faulkner, born in Missouri:[400]

    i.   William O. Faulkner, born about 1872. He and his sisters and brother, like his sister Mary, were probably adopted and may have assumed new surnames. None have been further traced.

    ii.   Beatrice Faulkner, born about 1875.

    iii.   Isaac N. Faulkner, born about 1876.

    iv.   Ida A. Faulkner, born about 1878.

    v.   Mary Faulkner, born about 1880, died 15 December 1889, in Macon County, Missouri. She was then the adopted daughter of Dr. E. A. and Martha E. Merifield.[401]

M57   **David Washington Faulkner**, born 1851 in Macon County, Missouri, died 1899 in Marceline, Missouri, was buried in Mount Olivet Cemetery.[402]

He married Margaret Jane (Garton) Sutton, daughter of William and Emaline Garton, born 28 September 1858 in New Boston, Linn County, Missouri, died 29 November 1932 in Marceline, Missouri, buried in Mount Olivet Cemetery.[403]

They moved from New Boston, Missouri, to Marceline, Missouri, about December 1892. In 1900, she was living in Kansas City, Missouri, but returned to Marceline, where she kept her own home until 1917.[404] She was a member of the Christian Church.

Issue of David Washington and Margaret Jane (Garton) Faulkner, born in Linn County, Missouri:[405]

    i.   Thomas Homer Faulkner, born 7 December 1883, died, unmarried, 14 September 1949, was buried in Mount Olivet Cemetery.[406] In 1933, he lived in St. Augustine, Illinois.

M112 ii.   Edward W. Faulkner, born October 1885.

    iii.   Nettie Florence Faulkner, born March 1888, living in 1959 in Marceline, Missouri. She married Edward C. Hettic, born about 1881 in Kansas, lived in

Marceline, and had issue, surname *Hettic*: a. *Edward*, born 20 October 1907, died May 1974 in Oak Grove, Missouri; b. *Margaret*; c. son, born 29 September 1920, died 2 October 1920; d. *Charles Eugene*, born 18 June 1924, died 16 March 1947 in Marceline, Missouri.

M113 iv. Asa (Acie) Faulkner, born 7 December 1889.

M114 v. Ralph Faulkner, born 1 June 1892.

vi. Harry B. Faulkner, born 24 June 1896, died, unmarried, 20 November 1959 in Marceline, Missouri, was buried in Mount Olivet Cemetery. He was a sergeant in the 9201st Technical Service Unit during World War I, decorated for service at St. Mihiel, Meuse, and Argonne, serving until 1920. He then worked for the Santa Fe Railroad, and lived in Marceline, where he was in 1933, but moved to Fitchburg, Massachusetts, where he worked for the Simons Saw Works. He also served in World War II. He resided in Fitchburg most of the remainder of his life.[407]

M58 **George Ware Faulkner**, born 4 June 1868 in Linn County, Missouri, died 11 June 1916 in Baker Township, Linn County, Missouri, was buried in Nester Cemetery, near New Boston.[408]

He married, on 5 September 1892, at Linneus, Missouri, Ida Belle Phillips, daughter of Eldredge Cross and Maggie (Kent) Phillips,[409] born 9 April 1873 in Linn County, Missouri, died 29 July 1955 in Brookfield, Missouri, buried in Nester Cemetery.

He was a farmer.

Issue of George Ware and Ida Belle (Phillips) Faulkner, born in Linn County, Missouri:[410]

i. DeWayne P. Faulkner, born 27 May 1896, died, unmarried, 7 December 1918 in Linn County, Missouri.

M115 ii. George Guy Faulkner, born 13 March 1900.

iii. Bessie Ellen Faulkner, born 4 August 1902, died, unmarried, 1 September 1988 in Linn County, Missouri.

iv. Anna Marie Faulkner, born 9 September 1905, died 2 February 1967 in Polo, Missouri. She married, in August 1925, —— Carmack.

M116 v. Samuel Eldridge Faulkner, born 1 October 1907.

vi. Virgil L. Faulkner, born 30 January 1911, died 22 March 1993 in Newton, Kansas. He married, on 23 December 1933, in Linn County, Missouri, Mabel Bradley, born 10 October 1915, died October 1982.

M59 **Samuel Faulkner**, born about 1857, or March 1859, in Louisville, Kentucky, was living in Jeffersonville Township, Clark County, Indiana, in 1900.[411]

He married, on 14 October 1890, in Clark County, Indiana,[412] Nellie L. (Dickey) Seigle, born April 1868 in Indiana, living in 1900.

He seems to have left Jeffersonville after 1900, but may have been the Samuel Faulkner living there in 1941, with a wife Mattie.

Issue of Samuel and Nellie L. (Dickey) Faulkner, born in Clark County, Indiana:[413]

i. Harriet E. Faulkner, born 3 January 1894, living in Jeffersonville, Indiana, in 1913.[414]

M60   John Franklin Faulkner, born 21 September 1851 in Metcalfe (then Barren) County, Kentucky, died 30 April 1929 in Waco, McLennan County, Texas, buried in Post Oak Cemetery, near Oglesby.

He married Sylvia Hawkins (Libbie) Redford, born December 1866 in Texas, died 24 March 1951 in Marion County, Texas, buried in Post Oak Cemetery.

They lived in San Antonio, Texas, in the early 1890s; in 1900, the family was living in Milam County, Texas, and in Coryell County in 1910.[415] He was a farmer.

Issue of John Franklin and Sylvia Hawkins (Redford) Faulkner:[416]

> i.   Birdie Mae Faulkner, born 12 April 1887, died 9 April 1969, buried in Post Oak Cemetery.[417] She married John Wesley Warren, born 5 July 1886, died 23 January 1943, buried in Post Oak Cemetery.
>
> ii. Modest Clyde Faulkner, born 18 April 1891 in Bexar County, Texas, died February 1977 in Waco, Texas, buried in Post Oak Cemetery. She married Edgar Armine Overby, born 26 May 1888, died 18 December 1953, buried in Post Oak Cemetery.
>
> iii. Floyd Evans (Jack) Faulkner, born 6 August 1893 in San Antonio, Texas, died 20 September 1961 in Waco, Texas, buried in Rest-Ever Memorial Park, Bryan, Texas. His wife was Ruby (———) Holland. They had no issue. He was buried with Nona Belle Faulkner, born 1900, buried 31 July 1967, who was probably an earlier wife. In 1917, he moved to Waco, where he worked as a traveling salesman, for V. Kemendo Company; for the Pollock Paper Company, from 1943 to 1951; and for the Monarch Food Company, from 1951 to 1961.[418]
>
> iv. Mary Helen Faulkner, born December 1895. She or her sister Rosa was married in 1961 to O. R. Jones of Waco; the other was married to Roy Brown of Houston, Texas.
>
> v.   Rosa L. Faulkner, born January 1898.
>
> vi. Minnie L. Faulkner, born 1904, died 7 September 1912 in Coryell County, Texas,[419] buried in Post Oak Cemetery.

M61   William Alexander Faulkner, born 8 January 1854 in Metcalfe (then Barren) County, Kentucky, died 3 April 1935 in Coats, Pratt County, Kansas.

He married, on 18 December 1887, Sarah (Sadie) Caroline Evans, born 11 October 1870 Missouri, died 20 March 1904 in Johnson Township, Polk County, Missouri.

In Missouri by 1883, he lived in Johnson Township, Polk County, Missouri, in 1900 and 1910, near Humansville.

Issue of William Alexander and Sarah Caroline (Evans) Faulkner, born in Johnson Township, Polk County, Missouri:[420]

> i.   son, born 12 September 1888, died 13 September 1888.
>
> ii.   David Benjamin Faulkner, born 17 September 1889. He went West and disappeared.
>
> M117 iii. Emmett William Faulkner, born 28 December 1891.
>
> M118 iv.   Marion Alexander Faulkner, born 26 April 1894.
>
> v.   Nannie Belle Faulkner, born 21 August 1896 in Missouri, lives in Richland, Missouri. She married ——— Tinsley.

M119 vi. Ira Gordon Faulkner, born 23 August 1899.

     vii. Charles J. Faulkner, born 8 August 1901, died 18 October 1902.

    viii. Frank W. Faulkner, born 18 February 1904, died 31 July 1904.

M62   **James Aaron Faulkner**, born 1 May 1858 in Metcalfe (then Barren) County, Kentucky, was living in 1910 in Archer County, Texas.[421] He possibly died 18 July 1928 in McLennan County, Texas.[422]

He married, on 23 November 1881, in Metcalfe County, Kentucky,[423] Mariah Elizabeth Renick, born December 1858 in Metcalfe County, Kentucky, died 9 July 1929 in Bellevue, Clay County, Texas, buried in Holliday Cemetery, Holliday, Texas.[424]

In 1900, they lived in Collin County, Texas.

Issue of James Aaron and Mariah Elizabeth (Renick) Faulkner, the first four born in Metcalfe County, Kentucky; the fifth and sixth in Johnson Township, Polk County, Missouri; the rest in Texas:[425]

     i. Flora Faulkner, born October 1882, living 1961 in Bellevue, Texas. She married —— Stephenson.

    ii. Dora E. Faulkner, born November 1883.

   iii. Mary Essie Faulkner, born 13 January 1885, died 1 August 1956 in Henrietta, Texas. She married, on 6 April 1907, Charles Lee Elmore, son of J. W. Elmore, born 22 February 1883 in Rutherford County, Tennessee, died 1 June 1953 in Henrietta, Texas. He was a farmer. Issue, surname *Elmore*:[426] a. *Monie*, died at the age of three and a half; b. *Frank Stanley*, born 31 July 1924 in Halsell, Texas, died 11 June 1983 in Gainesville, Texas, married, 5 April 1958, Betty Ruth Hayman, of Sylvania, Alabama, born 22 February 1931.

    iv. Viola Faulkner, born April 1886. She or Dora married J. T. Myers and lived in Bowie, Texas, in 1951.

M120 v. George David Faulkner, born 24 August 1887.

     vi. Hattie J. Faulkner, born February 1890, living in 1961 in Bowie, Texas. She married —— Cantrell.

    vii. Nora Elizabeth (Lizzie) Faulkner, born 21 February 1892, died 2 March 1979 in Henrietta, Texas. She lived in Joy, Texas. She married, by license dated 27 November 1920, in Clay County, Texas, J. Aston Howell.

M121 viii. James Franklin Faulkner, born June 1893.

M122 ix. Frederic S. Faulkner, born 5 November 1898.

M63   **Benjamin Marion Grider Faulkner**, born 25 May 1860 in Pleasant Valley, Metcalfe County, Kentucky, died 19 October 1930 in Wisdom, Metcalfe County, Kentucky, was buried in New Liberty Cemetery.

He married, on 17 February 1892, in Metcalfe County, Kentucky,[427] Henrietta Simmons, daughter of D. H. and Bettie (Flink) Simmons, born 22 October 1873 in Metcalfe County, Kentucky, died 2 October 1942, buried in New Liberty Cemetery.

Issue of Benjamin Marion Grider and Henrietta (Simmons) Faulkner, born in Metcalfe County, Kentucky:[428]

     i. Nanie Gertie Faulkner, born 11 August 1892, died 14 October 1896.

    ii. Lucy J. Faulkner, born 10 January 1894, died 10 September 1970, buried at New Holland, Illinois. She married, on 15 February 1914, at Alane,[429] Metcalfe

County, Kentucky, Dan B. Tibbs, and had issue, surname *Tibbs*: a. *Homer*, married Gerry ——; b. *May Katherine*, married James Biggs, then Bud Gaddy; c. *Henry Paul*, married Ann ——; d. *Rollin Dean*, married Peggy ——, then Gwyn ——; e. *Jimmy Bill*, married Flora ——; f. *Dale Wayne*, died young.

iii. Martha (Mattie) A. Faulkner, born 22 August 1895, died 20 October 1976 in Glasgow, Kentucky, buried in Randolph Cemetery, Metcalfe County, Kentucky. She married, on 25 January 1918, in Knob Lick, Kentucky,[430] Herman G. Gilley, born about 1898, died 28 October 1978 in Metcalfe County, Kentucky, son of Isaac and Rena (Page) Gilley, and had issue, surname *Gilley*: a. *Paul*, married Kathelene Emerson; b. *Junior*, married Dorothy Reece; c. *Wilbur*, married Maxine Compton, lives in Edmonton, Kentucky; d. *H. G.*, married Drucella Gray.

M123 iv. David Roy Faulkner, born 21 January 1897.

M124 v. Henry Loyd Faulkner, born 25 August 1901.

M125 vi. James R. Faulkner, born 29 July 1904.

vii. Harry Faulkner, born 21 November 1909, died 6 November 1965 in Metcalfe County, Kentucky, buried in New Liberty Cemetery. He married Magdalene Hurt, born 1913. They had no issue.

M64   Thomas Richard Faulkner, born 16 March 1841 in Vandalia, Fayette County, Illinois, died 16 May 1922 in Baxter Springs, Cherokee County, Kansas.

He married first, on 17 May 1866 in Washington County, Illinois, Talitha (Baldwin) Bower, born 12 July 1834 in Indiana, died 17 May 1910[431] in Baxter Springs, Cherokee County, Kansas. She had married first, on 19 February 1854, Calvin Griffith; and second, on 25 December 1858, Stephen Bower.

He married, as his second wife, on 18 May 1911, Nellie Hall. They were divorced in 1912 at Columbus, Kansas.

He served as a private in Company F, 48th Illinois Infantry, from 12 September 1861 to 15 August 1865. In 1880, he lived in Salt Creek Township, Lincoln County, Kansas, and in 1900, was in Baxter Springs.

Issue of Thomas Richard and Talitha (Baldwin) Faulkner, the first six born in Washington County, Illinois (they also adopted a daughter, Alta Faulkner, born 18 October 1884, died 30 October 1902, married I. S. Dixon):[432]

i. Minnie J. Faulkner, born 28 February 1867, died 20 February 1958, buried in Baxter Springs Cemetery. She married John R. Archer, born 27 February 1864, died 5 October 1950, buried in Baxter Springs Cemetery.

ii. Isaac M. Faulkner, born 28 March 1868 [calculated], died 8 December 1869, buried in Grand Point Cemetery, near Irvington, Illinois.

iii. Mattie Faulkner, died young.

iv. Frank P. Faulkner, died 27 April 1872, buried in Grand Point Cemetery.

v. Ida Faulkner, born 5 September 1872 [calculated], died 19 January 1873, buried in Grand Point Cemetery.

M126 vi. Thomas Richard Faulkner, born 3 February 1874.

M127 vii. Elmer Almon Faulkner, born 8 August 1877.

M65   Michael Collins Faulkner, born 30 June, probably in 1843, probably in Washington County, Illinois, died 18 February 1880 in Irvington Township, Washington County, Illinois, was buried in Grand Point Cemetery.

He married, on 1 August 1872, in Washington County, Illinois, Martha (Russell) Taylor, daughter of Edward and Elizabeth (Jolliff) Russell and widow of James W. Taylor. She was born 13 or 14 September 1841 in Washington County, Illinois, and died 19 January 1922.[433] She married, as her third husband, 4 July 1885 at Clarisville, Missouri, George Workman. They were later divorced.

Michael C. Faulkner served as private and corporal in Company F, 44th Illinois Infantry, from 13 September 1861 to 18 June 1865, receiving wounds.

Issue of Michael Collins and Martha (Russell) Faulkner, born in Washington County, Illinois:[434]

    i.   Eddie Faulkner, born about 1874. He and his brother both died young, after 1880.[435]

    ii.   Eugene Faulkner, born 18 August 1876.

M66   **Richard Douglas Faulkner**, born 27 August 1858 in Irvington Township, Washington County, Illinois, died 20 March 1935 in San Francisco, California.[436]

He married, on 29 January 1884, in Ophir, Placer County, California,[437] Kate Higgins, born December 1864 in Ophir, Placer County, California, died 3 January 1932 in San Francisco, California.

He graduated from Illinois Industrial University in 1877; in 1895, he received the degree of Bachelor of Laws in Agriculture. He taught school at Iristown, Illinois, in 1877-1878. In 1878, he went to California, and, at the time of his marriage, was principal of the school in Ophir. He went to San Francisco, where he was principal of the Parental School, Hancock and Lincoln Grammar Schools (from 1888), and of Horace Mann Junior High School, retiring in 1928. His country home was in Fetters Springs, Sonoma County, California. He established a scholarship at the University of California.

Issue of Richard Douglas and Kate (Higgins) Faulkner:[438]

    i.   James Faulkner, born August 1885, probably the James J. Faulkner who died, unmarried, 10 October 1944 in Napa County, California.[439]

    ii.   Frances Edna Faulkner, born March 1887, died, unmarried, 12 April 1961 in Craven County, California. In 1932, she was a mental patient at Napa State Hospital. Her father set up a trust to provide for her care; it expired in 1961.

M67   **Charles J. (Tobe) Faulkner**, born 10 August 1856 in Irvington Township, Washington County, Illinois, died 6 December 1950 in Grand Prairie Township, Jefferson County, Illinois, was buried in Fouts Cemetery.

He married, on 24 November 1880 in Washington County, Illinois, Rachel M. Armstrong, daughter of Garrett Armstrong, born 1859 in Irvington Township, Washington County, Illinois, died 6 February 1927 in Grand Prairie Township, Jefferson County, Illinois, buried in Fouts Cemetery.

He was a farmer in Grand Prairie Township most of his life, primarily raising fruit. In later years, he often spent winters with his daughter Maud in Pomona, Florida.

Issue of Charles J. and Rachel M. (Armstrong) Faulkner, born in Washington County, Illinois:[440]

i.   Ivy May Faulkner, born 4 February 1883, died 25 April 1883, buried in Grand
      Point Cemetery.

ii.   Paul Otto Faulkner, born 8 November 1885, died 8 February 1889, buried in
      Grand Point Cemetery.

iii. Maud Ethel Faulkner, born 22 November 1887, died 29 October 1937 in
      Centralia, Illinois, buried in Fouts Cemetery. She married, in 1907 in Jefferson
      County, Illinois, Rufus Arnold Willoughby, born 27 February 1876 in Jefferson
      County, Illinois, died 1954 in Centralia, Illinois, buried in Fouts Cemetery.
      He was a fruit farmer near Cravat, living part of the year in Pomona, Florida.
      Issue, surname *Willoughby*: a. *Pansy Gladys*, born 1907, died 1909; b.
      Evelyn Ada, born 4 April 1909, lives in Central City, Illinois; b. *Charles
      Hershel*, born 10 August 1910, died 10 December 1975 in Centralia, Illinois,
      married Ferne Ferguson.

iv.   Pansy E. Faulkner, born 1889, died 23 May 1973 in Centralia, Illinois, buried
      in Hillcrest Memorial Park. She married, in 1910 in Jefferson County, Illi-
      nois, Benjamin H. Tuttle, born 1888, died 1944, buried in Hillcrest Memorial
      Park. Issue, surname *Tuttle*: a. *Blaine*, died 1992; b. *Harold*, born 1914,
      died 1942.

v.   Tena A. Faulkner, born 16 May 1896, died 7 September 1905.

vi.   Gladys Faulkner, born and died 29 January 1901.

M68   Enoch Armstrong Faulkner, born 24 December 1866 in Irvington
Township, Washington County, Illinois, died 12 September 1912 in Valley
Junction (now West Des Moines), Polk County, Iowa, was buried in Richview
Cemetery, Richview, Illinois.

He married, on 28 June 1886 in Richview, Illinois,[441] Anna Rebecca Coffel,
daughter of Jesse and Permelia (Cameron) Coffel, born December 1865 in
Illinois, died September 1933 in Valley Junction, Iowa.

In 1886, he went to work as a brakeman on the Plant System at Maitland,
Florida. In 1908, he lived in Las Vegas, New Mexico. During the Mexican
Revolution (about 1910) he had to smuggle himself out of Mexico inside a
locomotive. He was a train dispatcher at the time of his death.

Issue of Enoch Armstrong and Anna Rebecca (Coffel) Faulkner:

i.   Beulah Cameron Faulkner, born 7 July 1887 in Winter Park, Florida, died 19
      September 1932 in Iowa. She married Abraham Frank Ackerman, born 31
      January 1889 in Whitney, Texas, died 26 May 1925 in Council Bluffs, Iowa,
      and had issue, surname *Ackerman*: a. *Merwyn Frank*, born 21 July 1911,
      died 26 September 1984 Des Moines, Iowa; b. *Jesse Alexander*, born 3 May
      1913, died 23 April 1975 Imperial Beach, California; c. *Norris Edward*, born
      4 January 1915, died 12 September 1984 Albuquerque, New Mexico; d. *Mar-
      garet Elizabeth Ann (Betty)*, born 5 January 1920, died 28 October 1994 Nash-
      ville, Tennessee, married Howard Wilson Stolp, then Charles Roudabush.

ii.   Blanche N. Faulkner, born 11 October 1889 in Orlando, Florida, died 1951 in
      Valley Junction, Iowa. She married Victor Wolff, born 7 July 1888, died May
      1964. Issue, surname *Wolff*: a. *Gertrude*, born about 1910, married Byron
      Crow; b. *Alex Jesse*, born about 1913; c. *Richard G.*; d. *Dorothy*, married
      William Pritchard.

iii. Alexander Coffel Faulkner, born 17 October 1892 in Arcadia, Florida, died 12
      August 1960 in San Diego County, California. He married Louise ——, born
      4 June 1896, died May 1984 in West Des Moines, Iowa, where they lived most

of their lives. They had two adopted children.

    iv.   Emma Faye Faulkner, born 7 March 1895 in Port Tampa, Florida, died, unmarried, 4 November 1976 in Imperial Beach, California. She was a schoolteacher.

M128 v.   Jesse Richard Faulkner, born 19 July 1898.

    vi.   Robert Faulkner, born 1902, died at birth.

M129 vii.   Arthur Glenn Faulkner, born 7 August 1904.

M69   **Richard Wilson Faulkner**, born 31 July 1868 in Irvington Township, Washington County, Illinois, died 25 November 1900 in Bartow, Florida, was buried in the New Cemetery.

He married, on 25 December 1890 in Irvington, Illinois,[442] Anna May Martin, daughter of Philip M. and Cloe Catharine (Welty) Martin, born 8 April 1872 in Perry County, Illinois, died 29 September 1958 in Webster Groves, Missouri, buried in the New Cemetery, Bartow, Florida.

He went to Maitland, Florida, in 1887, and to Bartow, Florida, after his marriage, where he worked as a telegraph operator and dispatcher for the Plant System.

Issue of Richard Wilson and Anna May (Martin) Faulkner, born in Bartow, Florida:

    i.   Mabel Grace Faulkner, born 7 October 1891 in Bartow, Florida, died 31 October 1987 in Madison, Wisconsin. She married, on 7 September 1921 in Tampa, Florida, Amos Franklin McKee, son of Thomas Jefferson and Anna Matilda (Huthmacher) McKee, born 20 October 1889 in Centralia, Illinois, died 20 August 1972 in St. Louis, Missouri. Issue, surname *McKee*: a. *Anne Grace*, born 3 August 1922, lives in Springfield, Missouri, married, 10 March 1951, Richard Davis Niles; b. *Edna Ruth*, born 20 July 1923, lives in Madison Heights, Michigan, married, 11 July 1946, Norman Augustus Gifford. The compiler, Paul Gifford, is the latter's son.

    ii.   Clarence Albert Faulkner, born 11 February 1895, died 13 July 1895 in Bartow, Florida, buried in the New Cemetery.

M70   **Charles Willis Faulkner**, born 28 February 1870 in Irvington Township, Washington County, Illinois, died 7 January 1932 in East St. Louis, Illinois.

He married, on 15 August 1889 in Irvington, Illinois,[443] Sarah Waddell, daughter of John and Malissa (Ohar) Waddell, born 1868 in Okawville, Illinois, died 1947 in Fairfield, Illinois. She was granted a divorce from him on 8 December 1906 in St. Clair County, Illinois.[444] About 1908 she married William G. Moore, born 1871, died 1947 in Fairfield, Illinois. They were buried in Maple Hill Cemetery. In 1910, they lived in East St. Louis, Illinois.[445]

By 1902, he had become a chronic alcoholic, working sporadically at manual labor. In 1908, he lived in French Village, Illinois.

Issue of Charles Willis and Sarah (Waddell) Faulkner, born in Washington County, Illinois:

M130 i.   Orval F. Faulkner, born 28 January 1891.

    ii.   Caroline F. Faulkner, born March 1893.

M131 iii.   Charles Oscar Faulkner, born 28 September 1895.

M71   Alva Jerold Faulkner, born 19 October 1871 in Irvington Township, Washington County, Illinois, died 1899 in Sanford, Florida.

He married Jessie Taylor, born February 1876 in South Carolina or Florida, died 1911, probably in Atlanta, Georgia. She was living in 1900 in Bartow, Florida.[446]

He was employed by the Plant System railroad, living at Winter Park, Tampa, Ortega, and Bartow, Florida.

Issue of Alva Jerold and Jessie (Taylor) Faulkner:

i.   Gertrude Faulkner, born 23 October 1895, died 22 November 1973 in Tampa, Florida. She married Lonnie Lee Adams. They divorced about 1930. Issue, surname *Adams*: a. *Oscar*; b. *Lonnie Lee*, born 5 October 1920, lives in Plant City, Florida.

M132 ii.   Alva Jerold Faulkner, born 21 February 1897.

iii.   Wilbur M. Faulkner, born March 1899, died August 1974 in Magnolia, Arkansas. He married Bernice ——. No issue. He served in the U.S. Navy, then lived in Fort Worth and Belleaire, Texas.

M72   Norris Alexander (Doc) Faulkner, born 1 July 1873 in Irvington Township, Washington County, Illinois, was found dead on 4 April 1930 in Jacksonville, Florida.

He married, as his first wife, Sue Gaskins, born February 1877 in North Carolina, living 1910 in Arcadia, Florida. They were later divorced.

He married, as his second wife, Jean Riens, born about 1888 in Washington.

He was a railroad employee when he came to Florida in the 1890s. He lived in Tampa in 1900 and in Arcadia, Florida, in 1910. He was a produce broker in Jacksonville from 1912.

Issue of Norris Alexander and Sue (Gaskins) Faulkner:

i.   Norris Faulkner, born 1894, died young.

ii.   Sadie L. Faulkner, born May 1900, died about 1980.

Issue of Norris Alexander and Jean (Riens) Faulkner, born in Jacksonville, Florida:

iii.   Norman Albert Faulkner, born about 1920, lives in Tucson, Arizona. He married, as his first wife, Helen Louise Proetz. They adopted children. He married, as his second wife, Lila C. Scheel. He was a colonel in the U. S. Air Force and practiced law. He lived for many years in Tallahassee and Gainesville, Florida.

iv.   Jean Marie Faulkner, born 17 July 1920, died August 1983 in Lakeland, Florida. She married Hugh W. Smith and issue, surname *Smith*: a. *Sterling*.

v.   Bonnie May Faulkner, lives in Weynett, Oklahoma. She married Robert W. McCowan. They lived in Iowa and Washington.

M73 **Carroll Purdy Faulkner**, born 22 May 1898 in Frankfort, Kentucky, died 28 April 1990 in Naples, Florida, was buried in Cave Hill Cemetery, Louisville, Kentucky.

He married, on 21 June 1930, in Indianapolis, Indiana, Lila Madeline Brown, daughter of William H. and Ollie (Cecil) Brown, born about 1909 in Bardstown, Kentucky, who lives in Naples, Florida.

Issue of Carroll Purdy and Lila Madeline (Brown) Faulkner, born in Louisville, Kentucky:[447]

  i. Marilyn Louise Faulkner, born 23 July 1931. She married Glenn Burchett and then John Hunter Peak.

  ii. Juanita Faulkner, born 1 November 1935, lives in Plantation, Florida. She married, as her first husband, John Hunter Peak, and had one son. She married, as her second husband, Paul Darden. She married, as her third husband, David Max.

M74 **William Thomas Faulkner**, born 17 June 1847 in Orange County, Indiana, died 1 August 1928 in Chatham Township, Sangamon County, Illinois, was buried in the Thomason Cemetery, Wayne County, Illinois.

He married, on 7 November 1879, in Jefferson County, Illinois,[448] Mary Josephine Klinker, born 19 December 1854 in Ohio, died 1 April 1928 in Wayne City, Illinois.[449]

He and his family lived in 1900 in Wayne City, Wayne County, Illinois, where he worked as a salesman.

Issue of William Thomas and Mary Josephine (Klinker) Faulkner, born in Wayne City, Illinois:[450]

  i. Alice Emma Faulkner, born February 1880, living in 1928 in Bonnie, Illinois. She married —— Bennett.

  ii. Bertha E. Faulkner, born August 1884, died 1940 in Auburn, Illinois, buried in Old Chatham Community Cemetery.[451] She married James H. Irwin, born about 1876 in Illinois. Issue, surname *Irwin*:[452] a. *Thomas E.*, born about 1904; b. *Charles H.*, born about 1906; c. *Harry S.*, born about 1908; d. *James F.*, born about 1914; e. *Carl F.*, born about 1916; f. *Jess A.*, born 1919.

  iii. Lena Alma Faulkner, born 5 March 1888, living in 1928 in Orchardville, Illinois. She married, on 18 December 1904, in Wayne County, Illinois,[453] James W. Austin, born about 1873 in Illinois. Issue, surname *Austin*:[454] a. *Earna* [son], born about 1909; b. *Eldo* [son], born about 1911; c. *Noama* [daughter], born about 1917.

  iv. Zona L. Faulkner, born 19 February 1891, died 1916, buried in the Thomason Cemetery. She married —— Sloan and had issue, surname *Sloan*:[455] a. *Lesbia A.*, born 1914; b. *James F.*, born 1916.

  v. Dorsa M. Faulkner, born 3 November 1895, died April 1973 in Georgetown, Indiana. She married Arthur D. Avery, born about 1875 in Indiana. They lived in 1928 in Wayne City, Illinois.

M75 **John Sanders Faulkner**, born 9 July 1852 in Orange County, Indiana, died 8 December 1914 in Wayne County, Illinois, buried in the Thomason Cemetery.[456]

He married, on 3 April 1881 in Wayne County, Illinois, India Belle Harlan, daughter of Nathaniel and Maria (Kenshalo) Harlan,[457] born 31 July 1857 in Wayne County, Illinois, died 22 January 1923, buried in the Thomason Cemetery.

Issue of John Sanders and India Belle (Harlan) Faulkner, born in Four Mile Township, Wayne County, Illinois:[458]

M133 i.   Frederick Elvis Faulkner, born 15 March 1883.

      ii.   Clara Ruth Faulkner, born 10 February 1886, died 6 January 1962, unmarried, buried in the Thomason Cemetery.

M134 iii.   Frank Leslie Faulkner, born 25 April 1890.

      iv.   Stella V. Faulkner, born 23 July 1894, died 9 February 1978 in Richmond, California. She married Edward Keene and lived in Keenes, Illinois.

      v.   Gussa Marie Faulkner, born 16 August 1901. She married, in 1920 in Marion County, Illinois, William L. Anderson, and had four children. They lived in Windsor, Illinois.

M76   Joseph L. Faulkner, born 23 November 1862 in Walnut Hill Township, Jefferson County, Illinois, died 1915 in Wayne County, Illinois, was buried in the Thomason Cemetery.

He married, 25 December 1887, in Wayne County, Illinois, Rosa E. Esmon, daughter of B. D. and S. A. (Patterson) Esmon, born July 1870 in Jefferson County, Illinois, died 1948, buried Thomason Cemetery.

Their farm was in Four Mile Township, Wayne County, Illinois.

Issue of Joseph L. and Rosa E. (Esmon) Faulkner, born in Wayne County, Illinois:[459]

      i.   Charles E. Faulkner, born 1889, died 1891, buried in the Thomason Cemetery.

M135 ii.   Samuel David Faulkner, born 22 February 1892.

M136 iii.   Homer Warren Faulkner, born 30 September 1895.

M137 iv.   William Ray Faulkner, born 27 March 1901.

      v.   Arch Lee (Jim) Faulkner, born 15 September 1905, died February 1971 in Chicago, Illinois. He married, as his first wife, Wanda ——, born 1906, died 18 December 1955, buried at Cypress, Illinois. He married, as his second wife, Helen Peltz. He had no children.[460]

      vi.   Alma D. Faulkner, born about 1908. She married Cephas Kelly and had issue, surname *Kelly*: a. *Cephas Lee*.

M77   Thomas Marion Faulkner, born December 1862 in Marion County, Illinois, was living in 1920 in Centralia Township, Marion County, Illinois.[461]

He married, by license dated 16 September 1886 in Marion County, Illinois,[462] Rosa B. Dobbs, daughter of William Henry and Barbara Ann (Rush) Dobbs, born 1 November 1869 in Jefferson County, Illinois, died 17 April 1925 in Centralia, Illinois, buried in Elmwood Cemetery.

Issue of Thomas Marion and Rosa B. (Dobbs) Faulkner, born in Marion County, Illinois:[463]

      i.   Lilla A. Faulkner, born 8 January 1887, died 13 January 1954 in Centralia, Illinois, buried in Hillcrest Memorial Park. She married, in 1905 in Marion

County, Illinois, Aquilla Leroy Corners, born 21 October 1882, died 5 May 1946, buried in Hillcrest Memorial Park. Issue, surname *Corners*: a. *Randall L.*, born 31 December 1905, died 25 October 1986; b. *Harold L.*, born 21 July 1907, died 25 November 1957.

ii. Ida Faulkner, born May 1889.

iii. Mable F. Faulkner, born 21 January 1891, died 18 December 1978 in Nashville, Illinois, buried in Elmwood Cemetery, Centralia. She married, on 28 February 1915, in Marion County, Illinois, Paul H. Larsh, born 24 February 1891, died July 1978 in Centralia, Illinois.

iv. Maude Faulkner, born January 1893, living in 1954 in St. Louis, Missouri. She married, in 1917 in Marion County, Illinois, Maynard M. Johnson.

v. Pearl Faulkner, born 26 July 1896, died April 1974 in San Bernardino, California. She married —— Cox.

vi. Blanche Faulkner, born 20 January 1899, died September 1975 in St. Louis, Missouri. She married —— McMullen.

M138 vii. Charles Edward Faulkner, born 18 April 1902.

M139 viii. Ray L. Faulkner, born 20 January 1904.

ix. Helen L. Faulkner, born 29 October 1905, died 16 November 1992 in Odin, Illinois, buried in Hillcrest Memorial Park. She married, as her first husband, Ralph Sloat, and had issue, surname *Sloat*: a. *Ralph*, of Antioch, California. She married, in 1932, Julius O. Caudle, born 21 December 1903, died 21 September 1957. Issue, surname *Caudle*:[464] b. *J. O.*, of Miami, Florida.

M140 x. Allen Leroy Faulkner, born 4 June 1906.

xi. Dorothy J. Faulkner, born about 1909, living in 1954 in St. Louis, Missouri. She married —— Perry.

xii. Ruth Faulkner, born about 1913. She married —— Molnar and in 1978, lived in St. Louis, Missouri.

M78 **Virgil Franklin Faulkner**, born 6 May 1866 in Southeast Township, Orange County, Indiana, died 5 August 1934 in Impola, Napa County, California, where he was buried.

He married, on 13 April 1892, in Jefferson County, Illinois,[465] Minnie Elizabeth Scudamore, daughter of James A. and Mercy (Partridge) Scudamore, born 10 December 1871 near Mount Vernon, Illinois, died 16 March 1948 in Osceola, Mississippi County, Arkansas, buried in Garden Point Cemetery, Etowah, Arkansas.

He was a farmer in Centralia Township, Marion County, Illinois, and in Jefferson County, Illinois, and a member of the Christian Church.

Issue of Virgil Franklin and Minnie Elizabeth (Scudamore) Faulkner:[466]

i. Myrtle May Faulkner, born 8 March 1893, died in childbirth 9 December 1914 in Etowah, Mississippi County, Arkansas, buried in Garden Point Cemetery. She married, on 20 January 1914, in Etowah, Arkansas, Robert Henry Wilmoth.

ii. Ethel LeVena Faulkner, born 13 March 1896. She married, on 18 May 1915, in Etowah, Arkansas, Emmett Dee Strawn.

iii. Marie Olive Faulkner, born 25 March 1901. She married, on 12 January 1928, in Kansas City, Missouri, Erce Ernest Eggert.

M141 iv. Earl Virgil Faulkner, born 14 May 1903.

M142 v.   Berthel Alfred Faulkner, born 25 October 1905.

M79   Charles L. Faulkner, born about 1867 in Dubois County, Indiana, accidentally shot and killed by his brother John in a tavern in Arkansas in 1899 or 1900.

He married Carrie E. Higginbottom, who died 21 March 1900 in De Vall's Bluff, Prairie County, Arkansas, and was buried in Orange County, Indiana.

He was a lumberman in Arkansas.

Issue of Charles L. and Carrie E. (Higginbottom) Faulkner:[467]

    i.   Carrie Kathleen Faulkner, born 21 April 1893 in Cairo, Illinois, died 8 April 1967 in Louisville, Kentucky. She married, on 19 October 1912 in Orange County, Indiana, Clarence Kay Dixon, born about 1889, died 12 March 1983 in Louisville, Kentucky. Issue, surname *Dixon:* a. *Clarence Kay;* b. *Jane,* died 1965; another son and two more daughters.

    ii.   Lucille Faulkner, born 6 May 1897 in Pine Bluff, Arkansas. She married, on 31 July 1915 in Orange County, Indiana, Russell Agan.

    iii.   Charles E. Faulkner, born 5 March 1900, died young.

M80   John William Henry David Elbert Penelton Faulkner, born 12 July 1862 in Hickory Township, Carroll County, Arkansas, died 12 July 1899 in Bradfield, Stone County, Missouri, was buried in Charity Cemetery.

He married, on 15 March 1893, in Stone County, Missouri, Rosa Ann Points, born 26 April 1874 in Bradfield, Stone County, Missouri, died 7 December 1951 in Oklahoma City, Oklahoma, buried in Maple Park Cemetery, Aurora, Missouri. She married, as her second husband, on 22 April 1908, in Aurora, Missouri, George Byron Killey, who died 6 July 1936 in Aurora, Missouri. She married, as her third husband, on 30 September 1937, in Oklahoma City, Oklahoma, Walter L. Snuffer.

He purchased 160 acres in township 23, range 22, in Stone County, Missouri, in 1897.

Issue of John William Henry David Elbert Penelton and Rosa Ann (Points) Faulkner, born in Stone County, Missouri:[468]

M143 i.   James Hillyard Faulkner, born 28 April 1894.

    ii.   Zelmar Faulkner [daughter], born 28 January 1896, died 23 January 1899, buried in Bradfield Cemetery.

M81   Thomas Marion Faulkner, born 27 September 1867 in Arkansas, died 9 July 1935 in Steelville, Crawford County, Missouri.

He married Margaret Elizabeth Marley, born 14 September 1872 in Kansas, died 8 May 1915 in Waurika, Oklahama.

In 1900, they lived at Shawnee, Pottawatomie County, Kansas, in 1910 in Jefferson County, Oklahoma, and in 1920 at Waurika, Jefferson County, Oklahoma.[469] He worked as a farmer and barber. As a youth, he raced horses, and with his parents' encouragement, became a jockey.

Issue of Thomas Marion and Margaret Elizabeth (Marley) Faulkner:[470]

    i.   Bertha Delle Faulkner, born 29 October 1893 in Arkansas, died 8 August

1973 in Rolla, Missouri. She married, on 26 November 1918, as his second wife, James Herkley Sanders, born 28 January 1891 in Huzzah, Crawford County, Missouri, died 24 January 1972 at Steelville, Missouri, and had issue, surname *Sanders*: a. *Lois Elizabeth*, born 23 February 1920, died 13 March 1920 in Waurika, Oklahoma; b. *James Herkley*, born 16 February 1921, married, 11 June 1949, Delores Helen Nagle; c. *Lenna Opal*, born 12 Septmeber 1922, married, 10 August 1940, Harold Clinton Doss; d. *Pearl Anita*, born 18 February 1924 at Huzzah, Missouri, married first, 16 February 1946, Orville L. Cain, second, 7 December 1962, Arthur A. Krueger; e. *Thomas Otis*, born 1 June 1926, married first, Doris Johnson, second, Aline Smith; f. *Bertha May*, born 20 July 1928, died 2 July 1931 Steelville, Missouri; g. *Gloria Lee*, born 25 August 1930, married, 28 February 1953, William Ernest Coffman; g. *Joshua J. T.*, born 24 April 1933, died 10 April 1989 in St. Louis, Missouri, married, 28 March 1933, Lila Claire Krueger.

ii. Felix Otis Faulkner, born 22 July 1895 in Arkansas, died, unmarried, 4 December 1954 in Stockton, California, was buried in Golden Gate National Cemetery, San Bruno, California. He served in World War I.[471] He married Leota London, who did not survive him. No issue.

iii. Guy Ralph Faulkner, born 15 December 1898 in Oklahoma, died November 1983, then a resident of Casper, Wyoming. He had earlier lived in California. He married, as his first wife, Peggy ——, and had a son who died in infancy. He married, as his second wife, Charlette ——.

iv. Harry LeRoy Faulkner, born 28 March 1900 in Oklahoma, died, without issue, 18 January 1983 in Long Beach, California, buried All Souls Cemetery.[472] In 1954, he lived in Compton, California. He married Stance ——, but had no issue.

v. Mary Opal Faulkner, born 19 October 1906, died 26 May 1979 in Roswell, New Mexico. In 1954, she lived in Gallup, New Mexico. She married Alex Hopkins and had five children.

vi. Pearl Abigail Faulkner, born 5 March 1910, living in 1954 in Santa Barbara, California. She married Richard Gaunt, and had issue, surname *Gaunt*: a. *Richard.*

M82   Felix Grundy Faulkner, born about 1873, probably in Washington County, Illinois, was living in 1920 in Tulsa County, Oklahoma.

He married, on 23 September 1894, in Benton County, Arkansas,[473] Lizzie O'Brien, born about 1880 in Arkansas, living in 1920.

Issue of Felix Grundy and Lizzie (O'Brien) Faulkner, born in Oklahoma:[474]

i. Joseph Faulkner, possibly born 27 February 1902, died February 1973 in San Diego, California.

ii. Goldie Faulkner, born about 1904.

iii. Felix Faulkner, born about 1906. He married Montess —— and in 1933, lived in Tulsa, Oklahoma.

iv. Lizzie Faulkner, born about 1908.

v. Bertha Faulkner, born about 1911.

M83   James Otis Faulkner, born 17 December 1876 in Carroll County, Arkansas, died 5 February 1962 in Weiser, Idaho, was buried in Weiser Cemetery.

He married, on 23 February 1902, Shirley Arvilla Irelan, daughter of

Silas Oliver and Marian (Marlin) Irelan, born 24 February 1884 or 1885 in Taney County, Missouri, died 5 November 1962 in Weiser, Idaho, buried in Weiser Cemetery.

By 1903, they were in Wagner, Oklahoma. After a stay in Everett, Washington, they returned to Dawson, Tulsa County, Oklahoma, where they lived in 1910. By 1913, they returned to Everett, Washington, but by 1916 were living near Gleed, Yakima County, Washington, where they were at the time of the 1920 census.[475]

Issue of James Otis and Shirley Arvilla (Irelan) Faulkner:[476]

> i. Cora Gladys Faulkner, born 3 January 1903 in Wagner, Oklahoma. She married Mervel Lewis, and had issue, surname *Lewis*: a. *Betty*, married —— Bethune.
>
> ii.
> Marian Opal Clementine Faulkner, born 10 April 1905 in Everett, Washington, died 5 October 1987 in Pendleton, Oregon. She married Ernest Young. They had no issue.
>
> iii. Alice Maude Faulkner, born 2 April 1909 in Dawson, Oklahoma, died in Utah. She married Ernest Holloway. They had no issue.
>
> iv. Margaret Claudeen Faulkner, born 27 May 1913 in Everett, Washington, died probably in California. She married Tom Onstott. They had no issue.
>
> M144 v. James Oliver Faulkner, born 4 April 1916.
>
> M145 vi. Thomas Lynne Faulkner, born 23 February 1919.
>
> M146 vii. Fred Otis Faulkner, born 16 June 1922.

M84 **George D. Faulkner**, born 6 October 1878 in Prairie Township, Carroll County, Arkansas, died 1942 in Eagle Rock, Missouri, was buried in Maplewood Cemetery, near Exeter, Missouri.

He married, on 2 June 1901, Mary (Steve) Easley, daughter of Christopher Columbus and Susan (Cotner) Easley, born 4 June 1878 in Barry County, Missouri, died 1975, buried in Maplewood Cemetery.

Issue of George D. and Mary (Easley) Faulkner, born in Barry County, Missouri:[477]

> i. Norman William Faulkner, born 14 May 1902, died 16 September 1977 in Eureka Springs, Arkansas, was buried in Maplewood Cemetery. He married Betty McHainy. They had no issue. He was a policeman in Eureka Springs.
>
> ii. James Edward Faulkner, born 15 May 1905, died 30 July 1939, buried in Maplewood Cemetery. He married Frances McKee.
>
> M147 iii. Alton Faulkner, born 4 March 1908.
>
> iv. Clifford Faulkner, born 8 October 1909, died 1935, buried near Columbus, Kansas.
>
> v. Faye Faulkner, born 4 April 1916, died 1970, buried in Maplewood Cemetery. She married Norman May, born 1922.
>
> vi. Emma Mae Faulkner, born 25 September 1919, lived at Cassville, Missouri. She married, on 8 November 1945, Onel E. Deal.

M85 **William Elvis Faulkner**, born 4 September 1880 in Prairie Township, Carroll County, Arkansas, died 1 July 1931 in Fullerton, Orange County, California, was buried in Loma Vista Cemetery.

He married, on 28 October 1903, in Madison County, Arkansas,[478] Erin Logue, born July 1883 in Washington County, Arkansas, died 11 August 1961 in Fullerton, California, buried in Loma Vista Cemetery.

Issue of William Elvis and Erin (Logue) Faulkner, born in Wesley, Madison County, Arkansas:[479]

M148 i.   William Hayden Faulkner, born 21 April 1904.

     ii.   Oren Samuel Faulkner, born 13 February 1907, died 12 August 1970 in Fullerton, California, buried in Loma Vista Cemetery. He married, as his first wife, on 17 February 1927,[480] Sarah Dunaway. He married, as his second wife, Millie ——. They had no children. He was a farmer and laborer.

     iii.   Lucy Faulkner, born and died in 1907, aged 3 days, buried in the Thomas Cemetery, near Wesley, Arkansas.

     iv.   Elsie Marie Faulkner, born 1908, lives in Brea, California. She married, as her first husband, at Fullerton, California, Allison Boyd, born 1885 in Madison County, Arkansas, died 1967 in Fullerton, California, and had issue, surname *Boyd*: a. *Terry E.*, born 1933; b. *Thomas A.*, born 1933. She married, as her second husband, Frank Shockley.

M149 v.   Clyde Clifford Faulkner, born 16 October 1914.

M150 vi.   Lloyd Daniel Faulkner, born 24 March 1918.

M151 vii.   Frederic Joseph Faulkner, born 15 April 1921.

M86   David Ellis Faulkner, born 1 June 1883 in Wesley, Madison County, Arkansas, died 14 July 1955 in Lincoln, Washington County, Arkansas, was buried in Lincoln Cemetery.

He married, on 24 September 1909, in Huntsville, Madison County, Arkansas,[481] Emma Lucretia Wood, daughter of Isaac M. and Alice A. (Coley) Wood, born 22 February 1891 in Hilton, Scott County, Virginia, died 28 November 1966 in Lincoln, Arkansas, buried in Lincoln Cemetery.

Issue of David Ellis and Emma Lucretia (Wood) Faulkner:[482]

M152 i.   Elton Ellis Faulkner, born 17 April 1911.

     ii.   Virgil Edmon Faulkner, born 26 March 1913, died 12 January 1977 in Langdon, Reno County, Kansas. He married, on 27 August 1937, in Bentonville, Arkansas, Florence Norwood.

     iii.   Hazel Faulkner, born 4 February 1915, died 19 July 1980 at Midpines, California. She married first, on 14 April 1942, Harris Young, divorced in 1956; second, in April 1966, Lewis Smith.

     iv.   Isaac Bud Faulkner, born 30 September 1917, lives in Hutchinson, Kansas. He married, on 27 August 1937, in Bentonville, Arkansas, Juanita R. Litle.

     v.   George Faulkner, died young, buried in the Thomas Cemetery.

M153 vi.   James Orville Faulkner, born 1 March 1921.

     vii.   Claude Elvis Faulkner, born 6 April 1925, died 27 April 1983 at Hutchinson, Kansas. He married Mary Lou Woodall.

M87   Roscoe Conklin Faulkner, born 2 May 1888 in Madison County, Arkansas, died 9 April 1936 in Madison County, Arkansas, was buried in Parker Cemetery.

He married, on 6 August 1910, in Madison County, Arkansas,[483] Nannie

Viola (Wood) Evans, daughter of Isaac M. and Alice A. (Coley) Wood,[484] born 22 November 1890 in Indiana, died 8 October 1967 in Huntsville, Arkansas, buried in Drakes Creek Cemetery.

Issue of Roscoe Conklin and Nannie Viola (Wood) Faulkner, born in Madison County, Arkansas:[485]

M154 i.   Clarence Faulkner, born 31 May 1910.

M155 ii.   Gordon Ezry Faulkner, born 26 June 1912.

M156 iii.   Garland Faulkner, born 2 June 1915.

    iv.   Theron Faulkner, born about 1917, lives in Littleton, Colorado. He married Floy Lee Corbit.

    v.   Virgie Faulkner, lives in Texas. She married, as her first husband, J. Jackson, and, as her second husband, —— Wood.

M157 vi.   Hollis Afton Faulkner, born 2 May 1921.

M158 vii.   Alvin Faulkner, born 15 January 1926.

    viii.   Rosie Faulkner, born 24 July 1929. She married, on 15 March 1948, Ervin Edens, born 15 May 1924, died 4 June 1988, buried in the Ledbetter Cemetery, Madison County, Arkansas.[486]

M88   **Samuel Faulkner**, born 22 January 1893 in Asher, Madison County, Arkansas, died 9 July 1964 in Thorney, Madison County, Arkansas, buried in Mount Olive Cemetery, north of Elkins.

He married, on 10 September 1916, at Thorney, Arkansas,[487] Frances Evelyn Dill, daughter of Frank and Ruth (Hankins) Dill, born 30 May 1896 in Enterprise, Madison County, Arkansas, died 25 July 1979 in Elkins, Arkansas, buried in Mount Olive Cemetery.

Issue of Samuel and Frances Evelyn (Dill) Faulkner, born in Madison County, Arkansas:[488]

    i.   Lola Isbelle Faulkner, born 9 March 1917. She married James Clyde Jestice, born 8 April 1913 in Piney, Yell County, Arkansas, and has issue, surname *Jestice*: a. *Sammie Jo*; b. *Billie Ruth*.

M159 ii.   Raymond Dill Faulkner, born 20 November 1918.

M160 iii.   Eugene Clifford Faulkner, born 2 October 1920.

M161 iv.   Amos Euel Faulkner, born 29 May 1925.

M162 v.   Samuel Faulkner, born 15 December 1927.

    vi.   William Franklin Faulkner, born 24 April 1935, lives in Elkins, Arkansas. He married, on 4 October 1982, in Miami, Oklahoma, Velda Jean King, born 18 June 1936 at Thorney, Arkansas.

M89   **Fred Faulkner**, born 22 December 1897 in Asher, Madison County, Arkansas, died 30 October 1977 in Lawton, Oklahoma, was buried in Sunset Memorial Gardens.

He married, as his first wife, on 27 March 1917, in Madison County, Arkansas,[489] Viola Haskins.

He married, as his second wife, on 3 July 1922,[490] in Thorney, Arkansas, Nola Homesley, born 21 March 1899, died 1 September 1994 in Lawton, Oklahoma.

He was a businessman, moving from Fayetteville, Arkansas, to Lawton in

1941.

Issue of Fred and Nola (Homesley) Faulkner, born in Madison County and Fayetteville, Arkansas:[491]

M163 i.   Herman Douglas Faulkner, born 5 June 1923.

ii.   Allen H. Faulkner, born 9 June 1924, died, unmarried, 5 July 1992 in Lawton, Oklahoma. He worked as an oil derrick operator, policeman, and tree surgeon.

iii.   Cecil Herbert Faulkner, living near Lawton, Oklahoma, in 1992.

iv.   Max Ralph Faulkner, living in Apache, Oklahoma, in 1992.

v.   Billy Bruce Faulkner, born 28 April 1931, died 9 March 1967, drowned in Colorado River, near Glenwood Springs, Colorado.

M164 vi.   Terry Tex Faulkner, born 5 October 1937.

M90   **Charles Cicero Faulkner**, born 10 June 1883 in Berryville, Carroll County, Arkansas, died 22 February 1964 in Kansas City, Kansas, was buried in Monticello Cemetery, Johnson County, Kansas.

He married, in Kansas, Emma O'Connors, who died 30 December 1919 in Silver Bow, Montana.

He came to Kansas City, Kansas, at the age of 21. In the teens he went to Butte, Montana, where he worked as a copper miner. He and his children returned about 1923 to Shawnee, Kansas. He worked as a powder man for List and Clark Construction Company and was known as a good baseball player.

Issue of Charles Cicero and Emma (O'Connors) Faulkner, born in Silver Bow, Montana:[492]

i.   Earl O. Faulkner, born 1911, died, unmarried, March 1965 in Shawnee, Kansas, buried in Monticello Cemetery.

ii.   Alfred Joseph Faulkner, born 18 December 1915 and died 27 November 1986 in Independence, Missouri, buried in the U.S. Cemetery, Leavenworth, Kansas. He married, as his first wife, Beatrice ——, and, as his second wife, Shirley   . He had no issue. In 1964, he lived in Camdenton, Missouri.

M165 iii.   Archie Ball Faulkner, born 11 October 1919.

M91   **John Alexander Faulkner**, born 14 February 1870 in Perry Township, Boone County, Indiana, died 3 April 1950 in Fayette Township, Boone County, Indiana, was buried in Mount Tabor Cemetery.

He married, as his first wife, on 30 May 1891, in Boone County, Indiana,[493] Rosetta Smith, daughter of Henry and Rebecca (Whaley) Smith, born January 1874 in Indiana, died 15 October 1919 in Boone County, Indiana.[494]

He married, as his second wife, in 1923 in Fayette, Indiana, Mrs. Ionia Howard.

He was a farmer in Boone County all his life. He was a member of Mount Tabor Baptist Church.

Issue of John Alexander and Rosetta (Smith) Faulkner, born in Boone County, Indiana:[495]

i.   Lulu E. Faulkner, born 4 March 1892, died August 1969 Lebanon, Indiana, buried in Mount Tabor Cemetery. On 28 March 1912,[496] she married Newton K. Brownlee, born 1886, died 1942, buried in Mount Tabor Cemetery.

ii. Byron Lester Faulkner, born 16 August 1899, died 14 January 1975 in Indianapolis, Indiana, was buried in Mount Tabor Cemetery. He married Mrs. Margaret Gallaway, but had no children. He lived in Indianapolis from 1935, working for fifteen years as a carpenter for Cornelius Printing Company.[497]

iii. daughter, born 2 December 1902, died young.

iv. Mozella D. Faulkner, born 24 June 1905. She married —— Wilson and in 1950, lived in Sheridan, Indiana.

M92 **Joseph Monroe Faulkner**, born 4 January 1872 in Perry Township, Boone County, Indiana, died 31 January 1928 in Marion County, Indiana, was buried in Mount Tabor Cemetery.

He married, 25 September 1894,[498] Elizabeth Ellen Brandenburg, daughter of David and Jane (Davis) Brandenburg, born January 1874, died 17 February 1942 in Indianapolis, Indiana, buried in Mount Tabor Cemetery.

He left Boone County before 1919 and lived thereafter in Marion County, Indiana.

Issue of Joseph Monroe and Elizabeth Ellen (Brandenburg) Faulkner:[499]

i. Willie E. Faulkner, born 1 July 1895, died January 1963. At the time of his death, he resided in Clay Township, Hendricks County, Indiana. He married, on 23 September 1916, Thelma L. (——) Johnson.

M166 ii. Claud Ester Faulkner, born 25 June 1898.

M167 iii. Chester E. Faulkner, born 14 July 1901.

M168 iv. Charlie Vestal Faulkner, born 1 October 1903.

v. Leottia Mae Faulkner, born 5 April 1908, died 2 July 1961 in Brownsburg, Indiana, buried in Mount Tabor Cemetery. She married, on 14 August 1925 in Indianapolis, Indiana, Ernest A. Wheeler, son of Glenn D. and Gertrude (Kempker) Wheeler, born 19 August 1904 in Muskegon, Michigan, died 14 October 1980 in Indianapolis, Indiana, and had issue, surname *Wheeler*: a. *Bettie Joan*, born 5 June 1933, lives in Las Vegas, Nevada, married, 27 June 1969, Arthur L. Thomas, Jr.; b. *Barbara Mae*, born 22 May 1935, lives in Carmel, Indiana, married, 31 December 1951, Charles A. Pittman; c. *Joseph Ernest*, born 4 January 1940, lives in Roachdale, Indiana, married, 13 December 1957, Linda L. Lynch; d. *Beverlie Leottia*, born 13 November 1941, married, 1959, Nicholas Peter Dirkx; e. *Beatrice Leottia*, born 13 November 1941, lives in Las Vegas, Nevada, married, 1967, Donald E. Koehler.

M169 vi. Noble Harrison Faulkner, born 20 October 1917.

M93 **Alva F. Faulkner**, born about 1873 in Hendricks County, Indiana, died before 1937 in Clermont, Marion County, Indiana.

He married, 4 November 1896, in Hendricks County, Indiana,[500] Noretta Ann Myers, daughter of Marion and Millie Myers, who died 18 June 1957, aged 81, in Clermont, Indiana, and was buried in Greenlawn Cemetery, Brownsburg, Indiana.[501]

He was a farmer and later an employee of the Prest-O-Lite Company. He was also a member of the Clermont Volunteer Fire Department.

Issue of Alva F. and Noretta Ann (Myers) Faulkner, born respectively in Boone, Hendricks, and Marion Counties, Indiana:[502]

i. Opal L. Faulkner, born 10 September 1898, died 14 February 1980 in Indianapolis, Indiana. She married, on 30 August 1918, in Marion County, Indiana, Dwight L. Bilbee. In 1964, she lived in Speedway, Indiana. Issue, surname *Bilbee*: a. *Dwight L.*, born 26 February 1919, died May 1984 Brownsburg, Indiana, buried in Greenlawn Cemetery, married Marianna ——.

M170 ii. Willie F. Faulkner, born 26 July 1904.

iii. Lucille Faulkner, born 18 July 1911, died about 1985. She married Sherman C. Cossell and lived in Indianapolis, Indiana.

M94 Chester Corrington Faulkner, born 14 March 1887 in Richview, Washington County, Illinois, died 26 March 1967 in Storm Lake, Iowa, was buried in Marathon Cemetery.

He married, on 1 March 1914 in Amo, Minnesota, Jennie Melvina MacRunnels, daughter of E. C. MacRunnels, born 16 October 1894 in Delaware County, Iowa, died 5 February 1931 in Sioux City, Iowa.

He was a farmer and a Methodist.

Issue of Chester Corrington and Jennie Melvina (MacRunnels) Faulkner, born in Marathon, Iowa:[503]

i. Iona Fern Faulkner, born 1 December 1914, died 6 January 1991. She married George Urving Christopher, born 16 April 1909. In 1967 they lived in Redwood City, California. Issue, surname *Christopher*: a. *Donald G.*, born 29 January 1934, married Sara Mae Howser; b. *Vanita F.*, born 2 December 1938, married, first, Charles Dwayne Snodgrass, and, second, William Ronald Cochran; c. *Danny G.*, born 29 April 1952, married, first, Mary Rose Wallace, and, second, Janice Marie Convirs.

ii. Vera Mildred Faulkner, born 23 November 1915, died 6 November 1955. She married, as her first husband, Jim Binning, and had issue, surname *Binning* (also one adopted son): a. *Roger L.*, married Diane Kay Johnson. They divorced and she then married Homer DeWitt, who died in 1962.

iii. Viola Leona Faulkner, born 17 August 1917, lives in Laurens, Iowa. She married Charles L. Blake, born 23 January 1917, and had issue, surname *Blake*: a. *Karen K.*, born 10 January 1940, married James Albert Baumunk; b. *Sonja M.*, born 16 July 1946, married Larry John Perkins.

M171 iv. Chester Lyle Faulkner, born 29 March 1919.

v. Millie Melvina Faulkner, born 2 November 1920, lives in Warsaw, Missouri. She married John William Parr, born 18 July 1918, died 9 October 1980, and had issue, surname *Parr*: a. *William C.*, born 7 August 1941, married Beverly June Stull; b. *Joan M.*, born 11 September 1946, married, first, Doyal Melton Jones, and, second, Walter R. Purevich; c. *Lee H.*, born 14 June 1953.

M172 vi.
Robert Eugene Faulkner, born 16 March 1923.

M173 vii. Darold Dean Faulkner, born 21 February 1926.

viii. LaVonne Ardell Faulkner, born 12 January 1931, lives in Spirit Lake, Iowa. In 1967, she lived in Belleaire Beach, Florida.

M95 Ross R. Faulkner, born 1 March 1891 in Gifford, Illinois, died 17 June 1957 in Springfield, Illinois.

He married Ellen McGill, daughter of —— and Anna McGill, born 25 April 1895 in Illinois, living in 1991 in Springfield, Illinois.

He was a laborer for an electric company in Springfield in 1920.

Issue of Ross R. and Ellen (McGill) Faulkner, born in Springfield, Illinois:[504]

M174 i.   Ross R. Faulkner, born 11 September 1915.

    ii.   Harvey C. Faulkner, born 2 April 1918, died 28 October 1918.

    iii. Ellen May Faulkner, born 22 May 1922, lives in Brookfield, Illinois. She married Edwin Arthur Voss, born 18 July 1926. Issue, surname *Voss*: a. *Ronald A.*, born 3 September 1950; b. *Randy*, born 18 March 1956; c. *Ricky*, born 23 July 1958.

M175 iv. Jerome L. Faulkner, born 3 July 1925.

    v.   Ethel D. Faulkner, born 1 July 1927. She married Ira Gibson, born 28 April 1926, died 11 October 1973. Issue, surname *Gibson*: a. *Mary E.*, born 20 October 1957; b. *Ira*, born 30 October 1958, died 31 May 1975.

    vi. Daniel J. Faulkner, born 27 November 1929. He married Juanita Marie Thompson, born 28 January 1931.

M176 vii. Donald A. Faulkner, born 23 May 1933.

M96 **Robert Raymond Faulkner**, born 18 September 1893 in Gifford, Illinois, died 5 January 1975 in Washington, D.C., was buried in Fort Lincoln Cemetery.

He married Helen Marguerite Pelton, born 28 March 1892 in Illinois, died 1 November 1965 in Washington, D.C.

He was a lawyer with his own firm in Washington.

Issue of Robert Raymond and Helen Marguerite (Pelton) Faulkner:[505]

    i.   Joann R. Faulkner, born 23 November 1917, died 27 November 1981. She married Charles Frank (Buddy) King, born 8 June 1916, died 27 June 1979. They lived in Arlington, Virginia, and had issue, surname *King*: a. *Helen I.*, born 16 October 1940, lives in Falls Church, Virginia, married James Wellington Anderson.

    ii. Barbara A. Faulkner, born 9 October 1923, lives in Bowie, Maryland. She married Robert Joseph O'Neill, born 10 December 1921, and has issue, surname *O'Neill*: a. *Robert J.*, born 1 August 1947, married Dana Francis Spellman, divorced; b. *Michael T.*, born 17 October 1950, married Ruth Ellen Lancaster; c. *Kevin P.*, born 6 May 1954, married Leslie Ann McKee; d. *Stephen D.*, born 23 September 1957; e. *Barbara A.*, born 29 October 1960.

M97 **Wilbur Wilson Faulkner**, born 21 November 1878 in Palmyra, Macoupin County, Illinois, died 12 June 1933 in Fort Wayne, Allen County, Indiana, was buried in United Brethren Cemetery, Colburn, Indiana.

He married, on 22 September 1901,[506] Alice Mae Holmes, born 22 January 1880 in Lafayette, Tippecanoe County, Indiana, died 12 July 1966 in Fort Wayne, Allen County, Indiana.

They lived in Lafayette, Indiana, until 1924, when they moved to Fort Wayne, where he was employed as a solicitor in the circulation department of the Fort Wayne News-Sentinel.

Issue of Wilbur Wilson and Alice Mae (Holmes) Faulkner, born in Lafayette, Indiana:[507]

    i.   Cleo Arvilla Faulkner, born 17 August 1902, died September 1987 in Fort Wayne, Indiana. She married, on 20 June 1923, in Tippecanoe County, Indiana,[508] Eric Ansil Scott. They had no issue.

    ii.   Dorothy Elizabeth Faulkner (Sister M. Clare Frances), born 1904, lives in Fort Wayne, Indiana.

   iii.   Ruby Mae Faulkner, born 12 November 1906, died 1985 in Pittsburgh, Pennsylvania. She married Charles A. Woods and had issue, surname *Woods*: a. *Charles A.*, born 1929; b. *Patricia*, born 1933, married Robert Hagaman; c. *Milton Cullen*, born 1946, died 1993.

   iv.   Lillian Hope Faulkner, born 12 September 1908, died, unmarried, 10 January 1974 in Fort Wayne, Indiana, buried in Catholic Cemetery. She worked as a bookkeeper and comptroller.

M177 v.   Wilbur Wilson Faulkner, born 1910.

M178 vi.   James Elwood Faulkner, born 24 August 1912.

M179 vii.   Robert Clarence Faulkner, born 27 November 1914.

M180 viii.   George King Faulkner, born 26 May 1920.

M98 **Charles E. Faulkner**, born 2 February 1896 in Danville, Vermilion County, Illinois, died 7 April 1964 in Indianapolis, Indiana.

    He married, on 1 October 1919, in Indianapolis, Indiana,[509] Lena Craig, born 14 November 1895.

    He was a Pentecostalist minister.

    Issue of Charles E. and Lena (Craig) Faulkner:[510]

    i.   Jewel Faulkner, living in 1964 in Vandalia, Ohio.

    ii.   Emerald Faulkner.

   iii.   Ralph Faulkner.

   iv.   Charles C. Faulkner, lives in Indianapolis, Indiana.

M99 **Samuel Logan Faulkner**, born 17 September 1877 in Emma Township, White County, Illinois, died 15 September 1960 in Poseyville, Indiana, was buried in Bellefontaine Cemetery.

    He married, 1 March 1899, in Gallatin County, Illinois, Ella Clarkson, born 15 June 1879 in Gallatin County, Illinois, died 17 October 1979 in Mount Vernon, Indiana, buried in Bellefontaine Cemetery.

    He was a farmer in White County, later moving to Evansville and Mount Vernon, Indiana.

    Issue of Samuel Logan and Ella (Clarkson) Faulkner, born in White County, Illinois:[511]

M181 i.   John S. Faulkner, born 5 June 1901.

    ii.   Ruby Faulkner, born 19 April 1903, lives in Naples, Florida. She married, in 1939, Edward Ashworth. They had no issue. They lived at Mount Vernon, Indiana for many years.

M182 iii.   Raymond E. Faulkner, born 10 June 1908.

M183 iv.   Freeman E. Faulkner, born 4 August 1910.

    v.   Kenneth E. Faulkner, born 2 January 1915, died 5 February 1982 in Evansville, Indiana, buried in St. Joseph Cemetery. He married, in 1940, Martha A. Keown. They had no issue.

M184 vi.   Powell S. Faulkner, born 3 October 1918.

M100   Erskine B. Faulkner, born March 1864 in White County, Illinois, died after 1900 but before 1903, presumably in Asbury Township, Gallatin County, Illinois.

He married, on 17 March 1887, in White County, Illinois,[512] Lou Anna Taylor, daughter of George W. and Mary Taylor, born about 1865 in White County, Illinois. She married, as her second husband, on 8 August 1903, in Shawneetown, Illinois,[513] Thomas W. Smith.

At the time of his marriage, he was a teacher. They lived on a 40-acre farm in Asbury Township, Gallatin County, Illinois, which adjoined the farm of his father John.

Issue of Erskine B. and Lou Anna (Taylor) Faulkner, born in Gallatin County, Illinois:[514]

M185 i.   Fred Lee Faulkner, born 15 December 1887.

ii.   Leslie E. Faulkner, born 11 September 1897, living in 1951 in Chicago, Illinois. He married Sarah E. ——. He served in World War I. Not further traced.

iii.   Harland Erskine Faulkner, born 15 May 1900, living in 1951 in Chicago, Illinois. He married Ruth McCullough, daughter of Allan and Mary J. McCullough of Chicago, by 1920.[515] Not further traced.

M101   Clay Cash Faulkner, born 13 July 1882 in Emma Township, White County, Illinois, died in 1943 or 1944 in Wagner, South Dakota.

He married Olive Almeda Jones, born 27 February 1892 in South Dakota, died November 1969 in Platte, South Dakota. She married, as her second husband, Julius Thomson.

They moved to South Dakota between 1900 and 1910.

Issue of Clay Cash and Olive Almeda (Jones) Faulkner, born in Dante, South Dakota:[516]

i.   Nia M. Faulkner, born 6 November 1912, lives in Des Moines, Iowa. She married Joe W. Doherty.

M186 ii.   Dale Calvern Faulkner, born 27 August 1915.

M102   Claude L. Faulkner, born 2 June 1886 in Emma Township, White County, Illinois, died 1949 in Platte, South Dakota, was buried in Platte City Cemetery.[517]

He married Ellen ——, born 1887 in Illinois, died 1962, buried in Platte City Cemetery.

Issue of Claude L. and Ellen Faulkner, born in Platte, South Dakota:[518]

i.   Mabel Faulkner, born about 1906 in South Dakota.

ii.   Marie Faulkner, born about 1908.

iii.   Ruth Faulkner, born about 1910.

M103 John Thomas Faulkner, born 15 March 1880 in Sulphur Well, Metcalfe County, Kentucky, died 30 November 1940 in Greensburg, Green County, Kentucky, was buried in Greensburg Cemetery.[519]

He married, on 10 February 1901, Ida Pearl Wilcoxson, daughter of James A. and Therissa Louise (Dills) Wilcoxson, born 14 July 1884 in Green County, Kentucky, died 22 November 1968 in Greensburg, Kentucky, buried in Greensburg Cemetery.[520]

He was a farmer and, from 1933, a policeman.

Issue of John Thomas and Ida Pearl (Wilcoxson) Faulkner, born in Green County, Kentucky:[521]

M187 i.   Carl Freeman Faulkner, born 19 July 1902.

     ii.   Pauline Faulkner, born about 1907. She married Raymond Franklin and, in 1940, lived in Liletown, Kentucky, and, in 1982, Greensburg, Kentucky.

    iii.   Violet Christine Faulkner, born 28 December 1914, living in 1982 in Louisville, Kentucky. She married, on 15 July 1948, Paul Curry, son of W. A. and Emma (Wilcoxson) Curry, born 12 May 1914.[522]

    iv.   Maple V. Faulkner, born 10 November 1919, died 8 July 1922, buried in the Archie Curry Cemetery, Green County, Kentucky.

     v.   Pansy Faulkner, born 14 September 1923. She married Edward Tucker, and in 1940, lived in Liletown, Kentucky, and, in 1982, Indianapolis, Indiana.

M104 William (Willie) Russell Faulkner, born 20 November 1883 in Metcalfe County, Kentucky, died 27 September 1960 in Glasgow, Kentucky, was buried in Maple Hill Cemetery, near Mell, Green County, Kentucky.

He married, on 27 October 1907, in Metcalfe County, Kentucky,[523] Sallie Mae Finn, daughter of John Wesley and Mary Jane (Dowell) Finn,[524] born 22 March 1885 in Green County, Kentucky, died 8 July 1964 in Glasgow, Kentucky, buried in Maple Hill Cemetery.

His farm was in Metcalfe County, near the Green County community of Mell.

Issue of William Russell and Sallie Mae (Finn) Faulkner, born in Metcalfe County, Kentucky:[525]

     i.   Luella Grace Faulkner, born about 1909, living in 1964 in Scottsburg, Indiana. She married —— Matney.

     ii.   Vernell Faulkner, born 21 September 1911, died 10 September 1927 in Metcalfe County, Kentucky.

    iii.   Laverne Faulkner [daughter], born 3 October 1913, living in 1964 in Wanamaker, Indiana. In 1960, her husband was —— Abbott; in 1964, it was —— Caplinger.

M188 iv.   Clyde S. Faulkner, born about 1917.

     v.   Annie R. Faulkner, born 1919.

    vi.   Mae Belle Faulkner, living in 1964 in Scottsburg, Indiana. She married —— Bagby.

    vii.   Cloia A. Faulkner, lives in Paris Crossing, Indiana. She married Ralph D. Kessler.

M189 viii. Henry Clay Faulkner.

M105   George H. Faulkner, born July 1887 in Metcalfe County, Kentucky, was living in Childress, Texas, in 1940.

He married Daisy ——, presumably the one born 21 October 1888, died March 1977.

He was a railroad employee.

Issue of George H. and Daisy Faulkner, born in Childress, Texas:[526]

    i.   Mary Faulkner, born about 1912, lives in Lubbock, Texas. She married Edward Crews.

    ii. Zona Beth Faulkner, born about 1914.

    iii. George Scott Faulkner, born 20 January 1927.

M106   David Edward Faulkner, born 15 May 1889 in Metcalfe County, Kentucky, died 24 November 1965 in Springfield, Illinois.

He married Helen E. Murrell, born 16 November 1896 in Green County, Kentucky, died 16 November 1972 in Springfield, Illinois, buried in Roselawn Cemetery.

He left Kentucky not long after 1919 and in Springfield was employed, until 1960, by Allis Chalmers Manufacturing Company.

Issue of David Edward and Helen E. (Murrell) Faulkner, the first three born in Green County, Kentucky, the rest in Springfield, Illinois:[527]

M190 i.   David Earl Faulkner, born 9 October 1914.

    ii. Charles Faulkner, born 17 December 1916 in Metcalfe County, died young.

    iii. Ruth Faulkner, born 14 November 1919, living in 1991 in Springfield, Illinois. She married Herbert Rigney and had issue, surname *Rigney:* a. *Herbert,* born 29 August 1945; b. *Richard,* born 13 July 1950, died 29 June 1986 in Springfield, Illinois.

    iv. Robert Lee Faulkner, died October 1971 in Phoenix, Arizona.

    v. Harold E. Faulkner, born 7 August 1930, died, unmarried, 30 January 1976 in Springfield, Illinois.

M107   Franklin L. Faulkner, born April 1874 in Irvington Township, Washington County, Illinois, died in 1953 in Centralia, Illinois.

He married, as his first wife, on 15 July 1894 in Washington County, Illinois, Lulu E. Sweckard, daughter of Erastus M. and Sarah E. (Boles) Sweckard, born 28 December 1877 in Illinois, died 14 September 1958 in Missouri, buried in Ozarks Memorial Cemetery, Branson, Missouri. They divorced after 1926.

He married, as his second wife, Iva E. ——, born 20 September 1896, died April 1969 in Centralia, Illinois.

He was a conductor and yardmaster on the Illinois Central Railroad. In 1900, the family lived at 2618 S. Broadway, St. Louis, Missouri.

Issue of Franklin L. and Lulu E. (Sweckard) Faulkner:[528]

    i.   Lattie B. Faulkner, born 4 May 1895, died 12 May 1975 in St. Louis, Missouri, buried in Ozarks Memorial Cemetery. In 1912, in Marion County, Illinois, she married Wilburn Sherman. She married, as her second husband, Cameron Lee Quillman, born 6 October 1896, died 12 December 1958.

M191 ii. Lloyd Weldon (Jack) Faulkner, born 13 April 1897.

M192 iii. Virgil Braden Faulkner, born 26 March 1899.

    iv. Ferne Faulkner [daughter], born about 1904.

    v. Cynthia Faulkner, born 1914, living in 1973 in Tulsa, Oklahoma. She married Eldridge Bogan, and had issue, surname *Bogan*: a. *Douglas*.

    vi. Nadine Faulkner, born 1916, living in 1973 in Garland, Texas. She married —— Prater.

M108 Eldore Bert Faulkner, born 29 August 1880 in Irvington Township, Washington County, Illinois, died 17 May 1949 in Foyil, Rogers County, Oklahoma, was buried in Woodlawn Cemetery, Claremore.

He married, in May 1921, Macy Bernice (Carrell) Tate, daughter of John and Mary Carrell, born 3 April 1888 in Effingham, Illinois, died 31 January 1980 in Claremore, Oklahoma, buried in Woodlawn Cemetery. She had issue by her first husband. They divorced in 1939 but remarried in 1944. She worked as a nurse.

In 1910, he was in Altus, Jackson County, Oklahoma. He was in Tulsa, Oklahoma, from 1924 to 1948, then moving to Foyil. He worked as a self-employed plasterer.

Issue of Eldore Bert and Macy Bernice (Carrell) Faulkner:

    i. Velma Ilene Faulkner, born 1922, lives in Claremore, Oklahoma. She married Albert F. Gambel.

M109 Eugene Willard Faulkner, born 15 June 1890 in Irvington Township, Washington County, Illinois, died 21 November 1946 in Centralia, Illinois, was buried in Hillcrest Memorial Park.

He married, in 1917 in Harlingen (or Arlington), Texas, Iva M. Matherne, born 20 September 1896 in Louisiana, died April 1969 in Marion County, Illinois.

He worked as a brakeman and flagman for the Illinois Central Railroad.

Issue of Eugene Willard and Iva M. (Matherne) Faulkner, born in Centralia, Illinois:

M193 i. Richard James Faulkner, born 12 October 1924.

    ii. Ruth Faulkner.

M110 Leonard E. Faulkner, born 23 March 1894 in Irvington Township, Washington County, Illinois, died 15 October 1939 in Hines, Illinois, was buried in Fouts Cemetery.

He married, on 24 December 1917 in Centralia, Illinois, Etta Mae Timmons, daughter of James Timmons, born 1900, died 1954 in Washington County, Illinois, buried in Fouts Cemetery.

He served in World War I and worked for the Illinois Central Railroad.

Issue of Leonard E. and Etta Mae (Timmons) Faulkner:

    i. Howard Faulkner, born 22 August 1924, died 4 November 1980 in Hampton, Georgia. He worked as a policeman and used car dealer in Atlanta. He married Virginia ——, who lives in Atlanta, Georgia. They had no issue.

ii.   James E. Faulkner, born 1926, died 1926, buried in Fouts Cemetery.

M111   Manley E. Faulkner, born 7 February 1896 in Irvington Township, Washington County, Illinois, lived in East St. Louis, Illinois, and Caseyville, Illinois.

He married Mary ———, born 22 February 1898, died in November 1985 in Caseyville, Illinois.

Issue of Manley E. and Mary Faulkner:

i.   Ellen E. (Betty) Faulkner, born 1915, lives in Lebanon, Illinois. She married George Martin.

ii.   Irene Faulkner, born about 1916.

iii. Doris Faulkner, lives in Caseyville, Illinois. She married Robert Woodside.

M112   Edward W. Faulkner, born October 1885 in New Boston, Linn County, Missouri, was living in St. Augustine, Illinois, in 1933, but died before 1953.

He married, by 1920, Mary K. Dwyer, daughter of John A. Dwyer, born about 1892 in Illinois.[529]

Probable children of Edward W. and Mary K. (Dwyer) Faulkner:[530]

i.   Ed Faulkner, living in Rock Island, Illinois, in 1953.

ii.   Shirley Faulkner, living in Bushnell, Illinois, in 1953. She married ——— Sullivan.

iii. John Faulkner, living in Chicago, Illinois, in 1953.

iv.   Ralph Faulkner, living in Bushnell, Illinois, in 1953.

M113   Asa (Acie) Faulkner, born 7 December 1889 in New Boston, Linn County, Missouri, died 1 November 1953 in Quincy, Illinois, was buried in Mount Olivet Cemetery, Marceline, Missouri.

The name of his first wife is not known, but they probably divorced.

He married, as his second wife, on 17 January 1953, Alice Calhoun.

He served as a private in a medical detachment of the 364th Infantry during World War I, entering the service on 7 May 1918 and being discharged on 13 May 1919. In 1932, he moved to Quincy, Illinois, where he lived in the soldiers' home and worked as a special deputy sheriff. He was murdered by a gunman with a pistol.[531]

Issue of Asa Faulkner:[532]

i.   Leona E. Faulkner, born and died in 1913, buried in Mount Olivet Cemetery.

M114   Ralph Faulkner, born 1 June 1892 in New Boston, Linn County, Missouri, died 22 December 1933 in Kansas City, Missouri, was buried in Mount Olivet Cemetery, Marceline, Missouri.[533]

He married, on 15 December 1914,[534] Sarah (Burton) Moore, widow of Isaac Moore and daughter of James Noah and Lea (Craig) Burton, born 3 January 1888 near Lingo, Missouri, died 15 January 1968 in Brookfield, Missouri, buried in Mount Olivet Cemetery, Marceline.[535]   By her first husband, she had four children.

He was a switchman on the Santa Fe Railroad. He served on the Marceline

City Council for six years; he was chairman of the police committee for two years.

Issue of Ralph and Sarah (Burton) Faulkner, born in Marceline, Missouri:[536]

    i.   Pearl Faulkner, born about 1915, lives in Brookfield, Missouri. She married Joe Richards.

    ii.   Vina Lee Faulkner, born about 1917. She married —— Buckley.

M115 George Guy Faulkner, born 13 March 1900 in New Boston, Linn County, Missouri, died 23 August 1947 in New Boston, Linn County, Missouri, was buried in Rose Hill Cemetery, Brookfield, Missouri.

He married, on 5 December 1931, at Linneus, Missouri, Alice Isabelle Burns, born 27 July 1906 in Brookfield, Linn County, Missouri, died 23 July 1979 in Brookfield, Missouri, buried in Rose Hill Cemetery.

He was a farmer.

Issue of George Guy and Alice Isabelle (Burns) Faulkner, born in Linn County, Missouri:[537]

M194 i.   Lowell Burns Faulkner, born 3 September 1932.

    ii.   Alice Roselee Faulkner, born 31 December 1935, died 8 April 1964 Sterling, Colorado. She married, on 10 April 1954, in Brookfield, Missouri, Laurel Eugene Reid, who lives in Springfield, Missouri, and had issue, surname *Reid:* a. *Virginia Sue*, born 6 January 1955, lives Warrenton, Missouri, married Bart Kieffer; b. *James Dean*, born 5 January 1957.

M195 iii.   Charles Curtis Faulkner, born 26 May 1937.

M196 iv.   George Leslie Faulkner, born 3 March 1939.

M116 Samuel Eldridge Faulkner, born 1 October 1907 in New Boston, Linn County, Missouri, died 2 December 1980 in Sullivan County, Missouri, was buried in Hoover Cemetery.

He married, on 27 January 1933, at Linneus, Missouri, Alberta Virginia Johnson, born 28 January 1906 in Browning, Sullivan County, Missouri, died 2 December 1960 in Harris, Missouri, buried in Hoover Cemetery.

He was a farmer, a logger, and a sawmiller.

Issue of Samuel Eldridge and Alberta Virginia (Johnson) Faulkner:[538]

M197 i.   Ronald Keith Faulkner, born 3 December 1939.

M117 Emmett William Faulkner, born 28 December 1891 in Missouri, died July 1972 in Haviland, Kansas.

He married Jessie ——, born 25 March 1901 in Kansas, died February 1980 in Coffeyville, Kansas.

Issue of Emmett William and Jessie Faulkner:

    i.   Nina Faulkner, born 1918.

M198 ii.   Clifford J. Faulkner, born 18 November 1921.

M118 Marion Alexander Faulkner, born 26 April 1894 in Indian Territory (now Oklahoma), died 2 November 1958 in Severy, Kansas.

He married, in 1914, Bertha Ellanora Pfandler, born 17 October 1890 in West Virginia, died December 1971 in Severy, Kansas.

He was a garage mechanic and owned an automobile garage and dealership.

Issue of Marion Alexander and Bertha Ellanora (Pfandler) Faulkner, born near Humansville, Missouri:[539]

M199 i. Frank David Faulkner, born 6 April 1915.

    ii. Helen Wilma Faulkner, born 29 April 1917. She married William Boone.

M200 iii. Gordon Ernest Faulkner, born 9 February 1919.

    iv. Mary Lois Faulkner, born 25 July 1924, lives in Midland, Texas. She married Charles K. Bruton.

M119 **Ira Gordon Faulkner**, born 23 August 1899 in Metcalfe County, Kentucky, died 9 June 1990 in Coats, Kansas.

He married, on 20 July 1921, Vinice Lucille Schooley, born 25 April 1902, died January 1993 in Coats, Kansas.

Issue of Ira Gordon and Vinice Lucille (Schooley) Faulkner:[540]

    i. Dorine Vinice Faulkner, born 25 April 1922, lives in Coats, Kansas. She married, on 30 August 1940, Maurice Calvin Allphin, born 14 June 1919, and had issue, surname *Allphin*: a. *Paul Michael*, born 7 September 1946, married, 2 February 1965, Jo Ann Hughes; b. *Deana Irene*, born 21 October 1952.

M201 ii. Harold Lloyd Faulkner, born 2 August 1925.

M120 **George David Faulkner**, born 24 August 1887 in Humansville, Polk County, Missouri, died 6 July 1950 in Bowie, Texas, was buried in Friendship Cemetery, Bellevue, Texas.

He married, on 11 December 1910, in Archer City, Texas,[541] Martha (Mattie) Sophronia McDonald, daughter of Edward Armor and Mary Frances (McCall) McDonald, born 30 December 1885 in Bynum, Hill County, Texas, died 24 January 1966 in Baton Rouge, Louisiana.

He was living in 1910 in Collin County, Texas.[542] They lived in Lindale, Texas, before moving to Bowie in 1936, where he was employed by the Evans Motor Company.[543]

Issue of George David and Martha Sophronia (McDonald) Faulkner:[544]

    i. Frances Elizabeth (Bessie) Faulkner, born 3 November 1911 in Lake Creek, Archer County, Texas, died 20 March 1970 in Fort Worth, Texas, buried in Rose Hill Cemetery. She married, as her first husband, in 1933, Floyd Matthew Segler, born 1 January 1912, and had issue, surname *Segler*: a. *Margaret Louise*, born 1 April 1935, married, 27 January 1957, in Baton Rouge, Louisiana, Harold Eugene Wilkes; b. *Florence Jane*, born 3 November 1936, married, 3 February 1968, in Baton Rouge, Louisiana, Ferrell Thomas Morales. They divorced in 1937, and she married, as her second husband, in 1945 in Wichita Falls, Texas, John Franklin Gilliland, and had issue, surname *Gilliland*: c. *John David*, born 25 March 1947, died 25 May 1968 Fort Worth, Texas.

    ii. Mary Belle Faulkner, born 13 September 1914 in Lake Creek, Archer County,

Texas, lives in Jacksonville, Alabama. She married, on 19 October 1935, Riley Elijah Griffith, born 11 December 1915 in Archer County, Texas, died 30 June 1955 in Gainesville, Texas, and had issue, surname *Griffith*: a. *James Riley*, born 17 November 1936, married Myrita Jean Smith; b. *Raymond Lee*, born 11 November 1938, died 9 June 1985; c. *Patsy Laverne*, born 29 September 1940, married, 6 November 1965, Rodney Freeman Lambert.

iii. Jessie Lois Faulkner, born 26 September 1916 in Clay County, Texas, lives in Gainesville, Texas. She married, on 3 August 1935, in Bellevue, Texas, Claude Lee Griffith, born 6 January 1914, died 12 November 1972, buried in Oak Grove Cemetery, Gainesville, and had issue, surname *Griffith*: a. *Claude Lee*, born 3 August 1936, married Ethel L. Skinner; b. *Billy Joe*, born 26 July 1938, married Jean O'Brian; c. *Elijah George*, born 30 October 1940, married Karen Threadgill; d. *Gerald Wayne*, born 19 May 1942; e. *Jessie Lee*, born 31 May 1944, died 18 May 1987 f. *Van Gordon*, born 22 December 1946, married Linda Glen, divorced, then Frankie Ralston; g. *Sandra Kay*, born 7 January 1950, married Lloyd Vaughn, divorced, then Dean Carrigan; h. *Paul Ray*, born 30 March 1953, married Connie Perkins; i. *Shirley Fay*, born 4 January 1955, married Steve Payne; j. *Matthew Freddy*, born 5 January 1957, married Joanna Stockwell.

M202 iv. James Edward Faulkner, born 14 November 1918.

v. Nora Katherine Faulkner, born 6 May 1921 in Bellevue, Texas, lives in Denham Springs, Louisiana. She married, on 15 April 1948, in Baton Rouge, Louisiana, Charles Gervis Crum, born 20 August 1922 in Baton Rouge, Louisiana, and had issue, surname *Crum*: a. *Charles Gervis*, born 18 March 1950, married Carol Ann White, divorced; b. *Madeline Marie*, born 29 November 1951, married, 6 August 1981, Milton Hugo Arias; c. *Elizabeth June*, born 14 November 1954, married, 25 August 1979, Richard Steven Bello.

M203 vi. George Franklin Faulkner, born 17 April 1924.

M204 vii. Robert Lee Faulkner, born 13 December 1926.

viii. Peggy Joyce Faulkner, born 21 November 1930 in Bellevue, Texas, lives in Colleyville, Texas. She married Raymus Bridgwater, born 2 January 1929 in Chopin, Louisiana, and had issue, surname *Bridgwater*: a. *Raymus*, born 22 June 1949; b. *Raymond Sydney*, born 29 July 1950, died 5 December 1950; c. *Katherine Faye*, born 23 June 1953, married, January 1974, Steve Holmes; d. *Laura Lea*, born 26 February 1955, married, 25 February 1971, William David Harden; e. *David William*, born 7 April 1957, married Grace Pollard, divorced, then Gayle Lynn Brown, divorced, then Denise Bullett; f. *Melody Lyn*, born 21 November 1965.

M121 **James Franklin Faulkner**, born June 1893 in Collin County, Texas, was living in 1951 in Bellevue, Texas.

He married Vera Etta Davis, born 27 February 1898 in Texas, died 30 April 1992 in Gainesville, Texas.

Issue of James Franklin and Vera Etta (Davis) Faulkner (there were perhaps others):[545]

i. Jack Franklin Faulkner, born 13 November 1920 in Bellevue, Texas, lives in Gainesville, Texas.

M122 **Frederic S. Faulkner**, born 5 November 1898 in Collin County, Texas, died 17 July 1961 in Wichita Falls, Texas, was buried in Holliday Cemetery.[546]

He married, by license dated 26 October 1920, in Clay County, Texas,

Katy Seaberry, born 13 December 1898, died 6 May 1957, buried in Holliday Cemetery.

He was a druggist and lived in Wichita Falls from 1939.

Issue of Frederic S. and Katy (Seaberry) Faulkner:[547]

    i.   Bette Faulkner, lived in Denver, Colorado, in 1961. She married —— Rutledge.

    ii.   Christine Faulkner, lived in Kamay, Texas, in 1961. She married —— Dewell.

    iii.   Sue Faulkner, lived in Fort Worth, Texas, in 1961. She married —— Meadows.

    iv.   Neil Faulkner, lived in Farmington, New Mexico, in 1961.

M123 **David Roy Faulkner**, born 21 January 1897 in Metcalfe County, Kentucky, died 22 September 1973 in Glasgow, Kentucky, was buried in New Liberty Cemetery, Metcalfe County, Kentucky.

He married, on 13 September 1920, in Jeffersonville, Indiana, Evelyn May Clark, daughter of Harlin and Dora (Wilcoxson) Clark, born 13 January 1906 in Barren County, Kentucky.[548]

He was a farmer in Metcalfe County, Kentucky.

Issue of David Roy and Evelyn May (Clark) Faulkner:[549]

M205 i.   Roy Gilbert Faulkner, born 4 February 1922.

M206 ii.   James Dalton Faulkner, born 18 October 1923.

M207 iii.   Rollin Thomas Faulkner, born 15 January 1929.

M124 **Henry Loyd Faulkner**, born 25 August 1901 in Metcalfe County, Kentucky, died 5 July 1974 in Edmonton, Kentucky, was buried in New Liberty Cemetery.

He married, on 24 December 1927, in Edmonton, Kentucky,[550] Beatrice Barton, daughter of Ed and Myrtie Barton, born 30 September 1909.

Issue of Henry Loyd and Beatrice (Barton) Faulkner:[551]

M208 i.   Henry Harold Faulkner, born 23 September 1928.

M125 **James R. Faulkner**, born 29 July 1904 in Metcalfe County, Kentucky, died 21 December 1980 in Edmonton, Kentucky, was buried in New Liberty Cemetery.

He married, on 16 September 1923, in Wisdom, Metcalfe County, Kentucky,[552] Emma Richard DeVore, daughter of James Buchanan and Blakey A. (Forrest) DeVore, born 2 February 1902 in Metcalfe County, Kentucky, died 9 December 1985 in Edmonton, Kentucky, buried in New Liberty Cemetery.

Issue of James R. and Emma Richard (DeVore) Faulkner:

    i.   Shelby R. Faulkner, born 21 June 1924, died 30 March 1950, buried in New Liberty Cemetery. He served in World War II.

    ii.   Wallace Powell Faulkner, born 30 May 1932, died 11 June 1934, buried in New Liberty Cemetery.

M126 Thomas Richard Faulkner, born 3 February 1874 in Irvington Township, Washington County, Illinois, died 1944, was buried in Baxter Springs (Kansas) Cemetery.

His wife was Mabel Mae ——, born 17 February 1876 in Oklahoma, died 14 January 1959 in Vinita, Oklahoma, buried in Sixkiller Cemetery, Delaware County, Oklahoma. Her home had been in Afton, Oklahoma.[553]

In 1910 they lived in Rogers County, Oklahoma, and ten years later, in Craig County, Oklahoma. They appear to have been separated for many years, although not legally divorced.

Issue of Thomas Richard and Mabel Mae Faulkner:[554]

    i.   Thomas R. Faulkner, born 27 October 1914, died 21 July 1960 in Sacramento, California, was buried in Sixkiller Cemetery, Delaware County, Oklahoma. His wife was Virginia ——. No issue. He worked as an operating engineer.[555] He served as a staff sergeant in the 507th Coast Artillery during World War II.[556]

M127 Elmer Almon Faulkner, born 8 August 1877 in Salt Creek Township, Lincoln County, Kansas, died 1951 in Baxter Springs, Kansas, buried in Baxter Springs Cemetery.

He married Lena M. Wade, born 1875 in Kentucky, died 1948, buried in Baxter Springs Cemetery.

Issue of Elmer Almon and Lena M. (Wade) Faulkner:[557]

    i.   Olive Jane Faulkner, born 3 July 1896, died 22 March 1988 in Tulsa, Oklahoma. Educated at Kansas State Teachers College (M.S., 1936), Colorado University School of Nursing (B. S., 1939), Western Reserve University (M. S., 1939), she held nursing positions in Wyoming and, after 1945, in Richmond, Virginia.[558]

    ii. Earl M. Faulkner, born 12 March 1901 in Colorado, died 27 September 1919, buried in Baxter Springs Cemetery.

    iii. John Faulkner, born May 1902, died 31 October 1902, age 5 months, in Baxter Springs, buried in Baxter Springs Cemetery.

M209 iv. Paul Revere Faulkner, born 23 January 1904 in Oklahoma.

    v. Frances Faulkner, born about 1906 in Oklahoma.

    vi. Chester L. Faulkner, born 10 August 1908 in Oklahoma, died 5 March 1974, buried in Baxter Springs Cemetery. He married Adena M. ——, born 8 February 1911, died 25 November 1957, buried in Baxter Springs Cemetery. He married, as his second wife, Lula ——.

    vii. Claude Faulkner, born 1910, died 1910, buried in Baxter Springs Cemetery.

    viii. Donald W. Faulkner, born 1914 in Oklahoma, died 1957, buried in Baxter Springs Cemetery.

M128 Jesse Richard Faulkner, born 17 July 1898 in Richview, Illinois, died March 1974 in Maxwell, Iowa.

He married, in 1920, Josephine Mary Allen, born 7 January 1900, died 13 April 1988 in Cocoa, Florida.

They lived in Valley Junction, Iowa, after their marriage, but moved to Maxwell, Iowa, where they lived for many years.

Issue of Jesse Richard and Josephine Mary (Allen) Faulkner:[559]

    i.   Virginia Ann Faulkner, born 2 November 1921, lives in Merritt Island, Florida. She married first, on 15 February 1942 in Bondurant, Iowa, John David Tingley, born 12 March 1918 in Dallas County, Iowa, died June 1978 in Florida,[560] by whom she had issue, surname *Tingley*: a. *Diane Jo*, born 18 August 1946, married Artis Dunn; b. *Debra Ann*, born 5 April 1958. She married, as her second husband, about 1987, Jack McKinney. They operate a marina.

M210 ii.   Dwight Owen Faulkner, born 20 May 1926.

    iii.   Eileen Ruth Faulkner.

M211 iv.   Donald Richard Faulkner, born 1940.

M129   Arthur Glenn Faulkner, born 7 August 1904 in Cairo, Illinois, died 22 July 1985 in Des Moines, Iowa, was buried in Resthaven Cemetery, West Des Moines.

    He married, on 2 May 1921, in Newton, Iowa, Thelma Bowman, born 24 August 1902 in Des Moines, Iowa, died 22 July 1989 in Des Moines, Iowa.

    He worked as a railroad machinist and lived in Minneapolis, Minnesota, and Ankeny, Iowa, most of his life.

    Issue of Arthur Glenn and Thelma (Bowman) Faulkner:[561]

M212 i.   John McCoy Faulkner, born 13 October 1922.

    ii.   Glenn E. Faulkner, born 28 June 1925, lives in New Jersey. He married, in 1946, Louise Allen.

M130   Orval F. Faulkner, born 28 January 1891 in Okawville, Illinois, died 4 May 1955 in Fairfield, Illinois, was buried in Maple Hill Cemetery.

    He married, as his first wife, Josephine ——, born about 1898 in California, living in 1920 in San Francisco, California. They probably divorced soon after 1920.

    He married, as his second wife, Lulu Blanche Runyon, daughter of Henry and Mary (Myers) Runyon, born 20 January 1888, died 10 February 1954 in Fairfield, Illinois. There appear to have been no children.

    He served as a corporal in the U. S. Army Quartermaster Corps during World War I. He worked as a painter in East St. Louis, San Francisco, St. Louis, and, from about 1930, Fairfield.

    Issue of Orval F. and Josephine Faulkner:[562]

    i.   Howard G. Faulkner, born 1918. Not further traced.

M131   Charles Oscar Faulkner, born 28 September 1895 in Okawville, Illinois, died 7 June 1957 in Fairfield, Illinois, was buried in Maple Hill Cemetery.

    He married, as his first wife, on 18 June 1913, in East St. Louis, Illinois, Lillian Smith. She divorced him on 2 October 1920.[563]

    He married, as his second and third wife, on 8 November 1920, and on 19 September 1948, in Fairfield, Illinois, Belle Adams, daughter of A. W. and Rebecca (Tice) Adams, born 13 August 1898, died 6 April 1994.

He worked as a painter and carpenter, moving to Fairfield from East St. Louis in 1922.

Issue of Charles Oscar and Lillian (Smith) Faulkner, born in East St. Louis, Illinois:

    i.   Velma Rae Faulkner, born about 1914, living in 1971 in East St. Louis, Illinois. She married —— Randolph and had three children.

    ii.   Paul Albertis Faulkner, born 5 September 1915, died 18 January 1935 at Jefferson Barracks, south of St. Louis, Missouri, buried in Hope Cemetery, East St. Louis, Illinois. At the time of his death he was a worker for the Civilian Conservation Corps.[564]

M213 iii.   Gerald Reece Faulkner, born 19 January 1917.

M132 **Alva Jerold Faulkner**, born 21 February 1897 in Tampa, Florida, died 9 February 1975 in Winter Haven, Florida, was buried in Oaklawn Cemetery.

He married, on 9 December 1918, Van Esther ——, born 21 September 1898 in Florida, died July 1978 in Albany, Georgia.

He served in the U. S. Navy during World War I. He lived in Jacksonville, where he owned a grocery store, and in Orange Park and Winter Haven, Florida.

Issue of Alva Jerold and Van Esther Faulkner, born in Jacksonville, Florida:

M214 i.   Alva Jerold Faulkner, born about 1920.

M215 ii.   Jack Faulkner, born about 1922.

    iii.   Aileen Faulkner, lived in Homewood, Illinois. She married Jack McNeil and had four or five children.

    iv.   Anne Esther Faulkner. She married George Mordecai and had issue, surname *Mordecai*: a. *Page*; b. *Scott*, born 1960; c. son.

M133 **Frederick Elvis Faulkner**, born 15 March 1883 in Wayne County, Illinois, died 12 August 1929 in Mount Vernon, Illinois, was buried in the Thomason Cemetery.

He married, on 23 August 1911, in Wayne County, Illinois,[565] Oma Lee Rainwater, daughter of Henry C. and Mary E. (Lanc) Rainwater, born 30 November 1893 in Wayne County, Illinois, died 18 March 1973 in Rockford, Illinois, buried in the Thomason Cemetery.

He was a merchant, farmer, and owned and operated a threshing machine.

Issue of Frederick Elvis and Oma Lee (Rainwater) Faulkner, born in Four Mile Township, Wayne County, Illinois:[566]

M216 i.   Berlyn Eugene Faulkner, born 13 February 1914.

M217 ii.   Harlan Euil Faulkner, born 13 June 1916.

    iii.   Helen Lucille Faulkner, born 11 October 1920, lives in Rockford, Illinois. She married, as her first husband, on 29 April 1938, Kenneth Mace, who died 19 August 1953, and had issue, surname *Mace*: a. *Roger Norman*; b. *Ronald K.*; c. *Raymond Paul*; d. *Randall*. She married, as her second husband, on 16 November 1957, Claude W. Hawkes.

M134 **Frank Leslie Faulkner**, born 25 April 1890 in Wayne County, Illinois, died 23 February 1942 in Field Township, Jefferson County, Illinois, was buried in Mt. Zion Cemetery.

He married, as his first wife, on 23 August 1911, in Wayne County, Illinois, Oma Eva Luke, born 1892 in Ohio, died 25 April 1926, buried in Mt. Zion Cemetery.

He married, as his second wife, in 1927 in Jefferson County, Illinois, Ruby Pearl Green, born 1888, died 17 December 1933 in Webber Township, Jefferson County, Illinois, buried in Mt. Zion Cemetery.

He married, as his third wife, Lydia Ruth Cummings, daughter of Calvin and Margaret (Smith) Cummings, born 28 February 1892 in Nevada, Missouri, died 2 April 1961 in Fairfield, Illinois.

He taught in schools in Jefferson County.

Issue of Frank Leslie and Oma Eva (Luke) Faulkner, the first five born in Four Mile Township, Wayne County, Illinois, the rest in Jefferson County, Illinois:

M218 i. Kenneth Leslie Faulkner, born 8 June 1912.

M219 ii. Keith C. Faulkner, born 12 November 1914.

iii. Mable I. Faulkner, born 21 January 1916, lives in Chicago, Illinois. She married Oscar E. Williams.

M220 iv. Harry A. Faulkner, born 2 December 1918.

M221 v. Charles A. Faulkner, born 3 December 1922.

M222 vi. Frank Evans Faulkner, born 27 October 1924.

vii. Hilda F. Rollman (born Grace Indiabelle Faulkner but adopted), born 25 April 1926. She married, in 1950, J. O. Blair, and has issue. She lives in Springfield, Illinois.

Issue of Frank Leslie and Lydia Ruth (Cummings) Faulkner, born in Jefferson County, Illinois:

viii. Virginia Ruth Faulkner, born and died 28 December 1935.

ix. Clara Joyce Faulkner, born 6 April 1940. She married Charles Lovin.

M135 **Samuel David Faulkner**, born 22 February 1892 in Four Mile Township, Wayne County, Illinois, died 23 August 1973 in Mount Vernon, Illinois, was buried in the Thomason Cemetery.

He married, on 3 July 1920, in Mount Vernon, Illinois, Ruth Leona Pasley, daughter of George and Elsie (Boswell) Pasley, born 27 April 1901 in Belle Rive, Illinois, died 5 January 1981 in Bucklin, Kansas, buried in the Thomason Cemetery.

He served in the U. S. Army during World War I. He was a fireman in the Mount Vernon Fire Department until his retirement in 1956.

Issue of Samuel David and Ruth Leona (Pasley) Faulkner, born in Mount Vernon, Illinois:[567]

i. Doris Mae Faulkner, born 25 May 1921, died 1 March 1993 in Bucklin, Kansas, buried in Bucklin Cemetery. She married, on 24 March 1940, in Mount Vernon, Illinois, Edward H. Christopher, born 7 March 1915 in Bucklin, Kansas, a farmer, and had issue, surname *Christopher*:[568] a. *David Leo*, born 4 June 1946; b. *Gary Edward*, born 8 April 1949.

M223 ii.   Harold Lee Faulkner, born 13 March 1923.

iii.   Betty Faulkner, born 8 December 1928, died before 1981. She married M. M. McDonald and lived in Mount Vernon, Illinois.

M136   **Homer Warren Faulkner**, born 30 September 1895 in Four Mile Township, Wayne County, Illinois, died 10 May 1969 in Mount Vernon, Illinois, was buried in Oakwood Cemetery.

He married, on 30 June 1915, in Wayne County, Illinois, Golda Samantha Keen, born 10 August 1899 near Keens, Illinois, died March 1969 in Mount Vernon, Illinois, buried in Oakwood Cemetery.

He was a manufacturer of an artificial sweetener and lived in Mount Vernon.

Issue of Homer Warren and Golda Samantha (Keen) Faulkner, born in Mount Vernon, Illinois:[569]

i.   Jeanetta May Faulkner, born 19 September 1916, lives in Vero Beach, Florida. She married, on 22 July 1939, W. L. Settlemire and in 1969, lived in Mount Vernon, Illinois.

M224 ii.   Homer Warren Faulkner, born 27 November 1922.

M137   **William Ray Faulkner**, born 27 March 1901 in Four Mile Township, Wayne County, Illinois, died 1 May 1971 in Bloomington, Illinois, was buried in Oakwood Cemetery, Mount Vernon, Illinois.

He married, in 1919 in Jefferson County, Illinois, Hermenia Lengfelder, born 21 March 1900, died May 1983, buried in Oakwood Cemetery.

He was an oil field worker and carpenter.

Issue of William Ray and Hermenia (Lengfelder) Faulkner:[570]

M225 i.   Ray Wadsworth Faulkner, born 26 July 1921.

M138   **Charles Edward Faulkner**, born 18 April 1902 in Marion County, Illinois, died 7 February 1934 in Centralia Township, Marion County, Illinois, was buried in Elmwood Cemetery.

He married, in 1924 in Marion County, Illinois, Anna Gladies Sloan, born 16 February 1902, died 24 January 1985. She married, as her second husband, Louie Edwin Tate, and lived in St. Louis, Missouri.

He worked as a truck driver.

Issue of Charles Edward and Anna Gladies (Sloan) Faulkner:

i.   Melvin Lyle Faulkner, born about 1925, died, unmarried, 7 November 1954 near Centralia, Illinois, buried in Hillcrest Memorial Park.

M226 ii.   Hubert Duane Faulkner, born 25 March 1928.

M139   **Ray L. Faulkner**, born 20 January 1904 in Marion County, Illinois, died 30 July 1974 in St. Louis, Missouri, was buried at Calvary Mausoleum.

He married Ann Toeben, born 4 August 1913, died March 1981 St. Louis, Missouri.

He lived in St. Louis, Missouri, where he worked as a clerk for Chevrolet Motor Division.

Issue of Ray L. and Ann (Toeben) Faulkner:[571]

    i.   Mary Rae Faulkner. She married —— Jacobs and had issue.

M140 Allen Leroy Faulkner, born 4 June 1906 in Marion County, Illinois, died 14 January 1952 in Baltimore, Maryland, was buried in Elmwood Cemetery, Centralia, Illinois.

He married, in 1928 in Salem, Illinois, Sylvia Claybourne. They later divorced.

He worked in Baltimore as a dry cleaner from 1943 until his death.

Issue of Allen Leroy and Sylvia (Claybourne) Faulkner:[572]

    i.   Leta Rose Faulkner.
    ii.   Betty Joyce Faulkner.

M141 Earl Virgil Faulkner, born 14 May 1903 in Grand Prairie Township, Jefferson County, Illinois, died 21 July 1969 in Osceola, Mississippi County, Arkansas.

He married Mildred Heard, born 11 June 1912 in Hayti, Missouri.

Issue of Earl Virgil and Mildred (Heard) Faulkner:

M227 i.   Sharon LeRoy Faulkner, born 18 January 1938.

M142 Berthel Alfred Faulkner, born 25 October 1905 in Grand Prairie Township, Jefferson County, Illinois, died 18 July 1969 in Mount Clemens, Michigan, and was buried in Romeo Cemetery.

He married, on 19 March 1938, in Marion, Arkansas, Lilah Mae Morris, daughter of William Alexander and Mamie Ellen (Ingram) Morris, born 11 May 1914 near Trenton, Tennessee, died 13 March 1993 in Romeo, Michigan.

He was a surveyor and mechanic and she was a teacher.

Issue of Berthel Alfred and Lilah Mae (Morris) Faulkner:

M228 i.   Joseph Douglass Faulkner, born 2 November 1941.
    ii.   John Wayne Faulkner, born 4 January 1943, lives in Springfield, Virginia. He married first, on 19 June 1965 at Lansing, Michigan, Marie Josephine Warn; and second, Sandra Reinman.
M229 iii.   Paul Morris Faulkner, born 23 August 1945.

M143 James Hillyard Faulkner, born 28 April 1894 in Verona, Barry County, Missouri, died 4 February 1978 in Midwest City, Oklahoma, was buried in Maple Park Cemetery, Aurora, Missouri.

He married, on 31 August 1912, in Mount Vernon, Missouri, Ethel Winnie Cook, daughter of Judson Dean and Nora Virginia (Bailey) Cook, born 2 April 1895 in Aurora, Missouri, died 26 July 1971 in Aurora, Missouri, buried in Maple Park Cemetery.

He married, as his second wife, in 1972, Beulah N. Green, born 21 June 1888 in Jonas, Texas.

He worked as a mailer for the Oklahoma City *Times*.

Issue of James Hillyard and Ethel Winnie (Cook) Faulkner:[573]

M230	i.	James Byron Faulkner, born 1 September 1913.
	ii.	Lovel F. Faulkner, born 1 July 1915, died 4 July 1915.
	iii.	Rosa Ethel Mae Faulkner, born 25 May 1916. She married, on 30 August 1936, in Oklahoma City, Oklahoma, James Allen Thompson, born 23 October 1916. They have no issue.
M231	iv.	Walter Richard Faulkner, born 21 September 1919.
M232	v.	Raymond Dean Faulkner, born 10 December 1921.
M233	vi.	Charles Howard Faulkner, born 13 June 1924.
M234	vii.	Cecil Avery Faulkner, born 26 April 1926.

M144 James Oliver Faulkner, born 4 April 1916 near Gleed, Yakima County, Washington, died 17 November 1988 in Long Creek, Oregon, was buried in Long Creek Cemetery.

He married, on 1 October 1935, in Weiser, Idaho, Cleora Louisa Holloway, daughter of Benjamin Lafayette and Mary Lucetta (Peck) Holloway, born 3 June 1916 in Fargo Precinct, Canyon County, Idaho, died 4 January 1994 in Long Creek, Oregon.

Issue of James Oliver and Cleora Louisa (Holloway) Faulkner:[574]

	i.	Mary Shirley Faulkner, born 4 September 1938 in Weiser, Idaho. She married, on 27 December 1961, Gordon Powell, and had issue, surname *Powell*: a. *David*, born 16 September 1964; b. *William*, born 23 December 1967.
M235	ii.	James Bruce Faulkner, born 4 December 1944.
	iii.	Margaret Elizabeth Faulkner, born 10 November 1946 in Caldwell, Idaho, lives in Stanfield, Oregon. She married, on 29 January 1965, Allen K. Aichele, and had issue, surname *Aichele*: a. *Benny*, born 15 November 1965, died 27 July 1971; b. son; c. *Samantha Ann*, born 5 June 1969.

M145 Thomas Lynne Faulkner, born 23 February 1919 in Yakima County, Washington, died 4 February 1992 in Olalla, Washington.

He married, on 6 June 1942, Betty Hay. She lives in Olalla, Washington.

Issue of Thomas Lynne and Betty (Hay) Faulkner:[575]

	i.	Lynne Faulkner, born 1 August 1941.

M146 Fred Otis Faulkner, born 16 June 1922 in Yakima County, Washington, died 22 August 1973 in Portland, Oregon, was buried in Willamette National Cemetery.

He married Alpha E. ——, born 1 March 1921, died 14 September 1992.

Issue of Fred Otis and Alpha E. Faulkner:[576]

	i.	Suzanne Kathleen Faulkner, born 24 April 1951 in Butte, Montana.

M147   Alton Faulkner, born 4 March 1908, perhaps in Cassville, Missouri, lives in Eureka Springs, Arkansas.

He married Leona Ames.

Issue of Alton and Leona (Ames) Faulkner:[577]

    i.   Harley Faulkner, born 8 August 1941, lives in Eureka Springs, Arkansas.

M148   William Hayden Faulkner, born 21 April 1904 in Madison County, Arkansas, died 25 December 1973 in Fayetteville, Arkansas, was buried at Elkins, Arkansas.

He married, in 1927, at Wesley, Arkansas, Edith King, born 1906 in Madison County, Arkansas. She lives in Fayetteville, Arkansas.

He was a farmer. He lived late in life at Redding, California.

Issue of William Hayden and Edith (King) Faulkner:[578]

    i.   Wilma Ruth Faulkner, born 1928. She married Patrick Gardner.

M149   Clyde Clifford Faulkner, born 16 October 1914 in Wesley, Madison County, Arkansas, died 7 February 1988 in Oroville, California, was buried in Memorial Park Cemetery there.

He married, in 1940 at Brea, California, Elsie Born, born 1919 in Brea, California.

He was employed for 25 years by the La Habra, California, Police Department, retiring as Chief of Police.

Issue of Clyde Clifford and Elsie (Born) Faulkner:[579]

    i.   Robert Faulkner, born 1942, living in Oroville, California.
    ii.   Hayden Faulkner.
    iii. Oran Faulkner.

M150   Lloyd Daniel Faulkner, born 24 March 1918 in Wesley, Arkansas, died 28 March 1992 in Santa Clara, California, was buried in Elkins, Arkansas.

He married, in 1937 in Elkins, Arkansas, Bessie King, born 1919 in Wesley, Arkansas.

He was a manager for the Ford Motor Company.

Issue of Lloyd Daniel and Bessie (King) Faulkner:[580]

    i.   Wanda Faulkner.
    ii.   Carol Faulkner.

M151   Frederic Joseph Faulkner, born 15 April 1921 in Wesley, Arkansas, lives in Riverside, California.

He married, as his first wife, on 19 June 1941, in Fullerton, California, Betty Lorraine Waller, born 14 July 1923 in Anaheim, California. They divorced, and she married Ronald Wilkerson.

He married, as his second wife, Carol Ann Wasserburger.

He is an operation and maintenance supervisor.

Issue of Frederic Joseph and Betty Lorraine (Waller) Faulkner:

i.   Charlene Louise Faulkner, born 14 April 1941, lives in Concord, California. She married, on 22 December 1961, in Riverside County, California, James N. Walsh.

ii. Frederic LeRoy Faulkner, born 10 November 1943, lives in Morristown, New Jersey. He married Cindy McKinnon.

iii. Roxanne Lee Faulkner, born 10 February 1948. She married, on 15 February 1985, in Riverside County, California, Stanley O. Orrock.

iv. Loren Ray Faulkner, born 5 September 1949. He married, on 17 December 1977, in Riverside County, California, Linda M. Corn.

v.   George Frederic Faulkner, born 30 January 1951. He married Debbie ——.

M152 Elton Ellis Faulkner, born 17 April 1911 in Drakes Creek, Madison County, Arkansas, died 18 April 1981 in Fayetteville, Arkansas, was buried in Drakes Creek Cemetery.

He married, on 16 July 1935, in Johnson, Arkansas, Ruby Mildred Denton, born 11 March 1914 in Braily, Arkansas, died 13 April 1992 in Prairie Grove, Arkansas, buried in Drakes Creek Cemetery.

They lived in Kansas, Colorado, but most of Elton's life they lived in Cane Hill, Arkansas, where he repaired John Deere vehicles.

Issue of Elton Ellis and Ruby Mildred (Denton) Faulkner:[581]

i.   Emily Dee Faulkner, born 8 April 1938. She married, on 30 October 1959, Roy Layton Austin.

M236 ii. Ivan Ray Faulkner, born 22 March 1940.

iii.   Sherry Ann Faulkner, born 8 February 1952. She married Richard Lee Rodgers.

M153 James Orville Faulkner, born 1 March 1921 in Nelogoney, Osage County, Oklahoma, lives at Hutchinson, Kansas.

He married, on 18 January 1946, in Hutchinson, Kansas, Auda Ruth Litle, daughter of James A. and Fannie (Wilson) Litle, born 1 February 1924 in Cane Hill, Washington County, Arkansas.

He served in the U.S. Army Air Force during World War II.

Issue of James Orville and Auda Ruth (Litle) Faulkner:

i.   James David Faulkner, born 14 November 1946. He married, in May 1969 in Oklahoma, Cyntha J. Brown.

ii. Wanda Lee Faulkner, born 10 October 1948, lives in Hutchinson, Kansas. She married, on 14 June 1969 in Hutchinson, Kansas, Elsworth A. Lindbloom.

iii. Larry Dale Faulkner, born 8 October 1949. He married, on 10 March 1974 in Hutchinson, Kansas, Terri Lynn Green.

iv. Claude Anderson Faulkner, born 19 October 1951, lives in Wichita, Kansas. He married, on 22 February 1980, in Oklahoma, Vicki Ann Chisholm.

M154 Clarence Faulkner, born 31 May 1910 in Madison County, Arkansas, lives in Huntsville, Arkansas.

He married, as his first wife, Edna Avis McCarver, born 20 March 1915, died 22 July 1978 in Huntsville, Arkansas.

He married, as his second wife, Thelma Brown.

Issue of Clarence and Edna Avis (McCarver) Faulkner:[582]

    i.   Clevas A. Faulkner, born 31 May 1931, lives in Bentonville, Arkansas. He married, on 28 June 19—, in Bentonville, Arkansas, Wilma (Holcomb) Walls, daughter of Robert E. and Roxie (Farmer) Holcomb, born 24 August 1927 in Bentonville, Arkansas. He works as a truck driver. No issue.

M237 ii.   Conley Ottis Faulkner, born 1 May 1935.

    iii.   Clayton Faulkner, lives in Springdale, Arkansas.

    iv.   Clifford Faulkner, lives in Huntsville, Arkansas.

    v.   Mildred Faulkner, lives in Springdale, Arkansas. She married Troy Litterell, and has issue, surname *Litterell*: a. *Terry*; b. *Tim*; c. *Sharon*, married Jim Napier.

    vi.   Glenda Faulkner, lives in Huntsville, Arkansas. She married Bob Thompson and has issue, surname *Thompson*: a. *Bobby Wayne*; b. *Ronnie*; c. *Brenda*; d. *Gail.*

M155 **Gordon Ezry Faulkner**, born 26 June 1912 in Asher, Madison County, Arkansas, lives near Huntsville, Arkansas.

He married, on 11 January 1944, at Fayetteville, Arkansas, Mary Vassie Eubanks, daughter of Japtha Albert and Martha (Glenn) Eubanks, born 20 November 1921 in Japton, Madison County, Arkansas.

Issue of Gordon Ezry and Mary Vassie (Eubanks) Faulkner (they also have an adopted granddaughter, Laura Lynn Faulkner, born 6 November 1970, who married Scott Hensley and has two sons):[583]

M238 i.   Leary Alan Faulkner, born 1 February 1947.

    ii.   Lynice Faye Faulkner, born 19 January 1952. She has married two or three times and has children.

M156 **Garland Faulkner,** born 2 June 1915 Drakes Creek, Madison County, Arkansas, lives near Huntsville, Arkansas.

He married, on 22 July 1942, at Drakes Creek, Arkansas, Geneva Hazel Davis, born 28 May 1921 at Drakes Creek, Arkansas.

Issue of Garland and Geneva Hazel (Davis) Faulkner:[584]

M239 i.   Glendon Dwight Faulkner, born 29 May 1943.

    ii.   Gary Lynn Faulkner, born 4 October 1946. On 29 August 1965, he married Wanda Ingraham.

    iii.   Bobby Paul Faulkner, born and died 23 November 1955.

    iv.   Betty Joyce Faulkner, born 23 November 1955, lives near Huntsville, Arkansas. She married, on 14 February 1981, Rick Gifford.

M157 **Hollis Afton Faulkner**, born 2 May 1921 in Madison County, Arkansas, died 28 May 1980 in Fayetteville, Arkansas, was buried in Drakes Creek Cemetery.

He married, as his first wife, Christle Ester Sisemore.

He married, as his third wife, Cecil Hankins.

He lived in Huntsville, Arkansas.

Issue of Hollis Afton and Christle Ester (Sisemore) Faulkner:[585]

   i. Lorene Faulkner, lives in West Fork, Arkansas. She married, on 29 May 1965, Charles Ronald Lewis, and has issue, surname *Lewis*: a. *Russell Keith*, born 21 December 1965, married 4 June 1988 Melissa Kay Blew; b. *Ronald Kevin*, born 15 April 1968, married 13 April 1991 Laurel Townsend.

M240 ii. Laymon Faulkner, born 1 April 1951.

M241 iii. David Ray Faulkner, born 8 July 1961.

   iv. Aneta Kay Faulkner, lives in West Fork, Arkansas. She married —— Volgamore.

M158 Alvin Faulkner, born 15 January 1926 in Madison County, Arkansas, lives near Wesley, Arkansas.

He married, as her second husband, Imogene (Parker) Keller, former wife of Bobby Dean Keller and daughter of Ollie Orlena and Claudie (Ewell) Parker, born 2 August 1927 in Japton, Arkansas.

Issue of Alvin and Imogene (Parker) Faulkner:[586]

   i. Tracy Ann Faulkner, born 14 August 1959. She married Ron Redding and has two children, born in Huntsville, Arkansas.

M242 ii. Johnnie Lee Faulkner, born 12 July 1961.

M159 Raymond Dill Faulkner, born 20 November 1918 in Thorney, Arkansas, died 14 August 1991 in Fullerton, California.

He married Mary Lou Wheeler, born 21 May 1930 in Thorney, Arkansas.

Issue of Raymond Dill and Mary Lou (Wheeler) Faulkner:

   i. Phyllis Faye Faulkner

   ii. Philip Ray Faulkner, died unmarried.

M160 Eugene Clifford Faulkner, born 2 October 1920 in Thorney, Arkansas, lives in Sapulpa, Oklahoma.

He married Betty Jean Jestice, born 21 January 1926 in Fayetteville, Arkansas.

Issue of Eugene Clifford and Betty Jean (Jestice) Faulkner:

   i. Carol Jean Faulkner.

   ii. Thomas Eugene Faulkner, died young.

   iii. Joe David Faulkner.

   iv. Robert Eugene Faulkner.

M161 Amos Euel Faulkner, born 29 May 1925 in Thorney, Arkansas, lives in Springfield, Missouri.

He married Rosemary Wheeler, born 27 June 1933 in Thorney, Arkansas.

Issue of Amos Euel and Rosemary (Wheeler) Faulkner:

   i. James Lee Faulkner.

   ii. Geneva Faulkner.

   iii. Franklin Joe Faulkner.

M162   Samuel Faulkner, born 15 December 1927 in Thorney, Arkansas, lives in Fullerton, California.

He married Geraldine Hill, born 31 July 1927 in Thorney, Arkansas.

Issue of Samuel and Geraldine (Hill) Faulkner:

    i.   Ronald Ray Faulkner.

    ii. Randall Jay Faulkner.

    iii. Jackie Faulkner.

    iv. Cheryl Rae Faulkner.

M163   Herman Douglas Faulkner, born 5 June 1923 in Thorney, Arkansas, lives in Lawton, Oklahoma.

He married, on 18 August 1939, at Fayetteville, Arkansas, Edna G. Boone. He was a businessman in Lawton.

Issue of Herman Douglas and Edna G. (Boone) Faulkner:

    i.   Shirley June Faulkner, born 6 September 1940. She married, on 8 September 1958, Patrick O'Dell.

    ii. Elizabeth Shirlene Faulkner, born 5 August 1943, lives in Dallas, Texas. She married, on 8 February 1964, Nicholas Garrett.

    iii. Judy D. Faulkner, born 3 October 1944. She married, on 24 June 1961, Alfred Brown.

M164   Terry Tex Faulkner, born 5 October 1937 in Fayetteville, Arkansas, lives in Eagle, Colorado.

He married, as his first wife, on 16 September 1960, in Eagle, Colorado, Rose Marie Harris.

He married, as his second wife, on 23 April 1970, in Eagle, Colorado, LaVerle Marie Cooper, daughter of Lebert Larkin and Marion Virginia (Randall) Faulkner, born 2 February 1944 in Glenwood Springs, Colorado.

He has worked as a businessman, state patrolman, restaurant owner, and in communications, and lived in Lawton, Oklahoma, Montana, South Dakota, Missouri, Texas, and Eagle, Colorado.

Issue of Terry Tex and Rose Marie (Harris) Faulkner:

    i.   Sonja Jo Faulkner, born 14 October 1961, lives in Eagle, Colorado. She married, on 2 May 1982, William Frank Beasley, and has issue, surname *Beasley*: a. *Lyndsay Ree*, born 1 December 1983; b. *Whitney Lee*, born 27 February 1987.

    ii. Michael Scott Faulkner, born 18 October 1963, died 19 October 1963.

M243 iii. Fredric Blake Faulkner, born 20 February 1965.

    iv. Kelli Ann Faulkner, born 18 June 1968, lives in Walden, Colorado. She married, on 26 March 1986, Victor Satterfield, and has issue, surname *Satterfield*: a. *Alacia Rae*, born 27 August 1986; b. *Chad Jamie*, born 27 March 1989; c. *Justin Cole*, born 3 September 1990.

Issue of Terry Tex and LaVerle Marie (Cooper) Faulkner (they also adopted her child, Tyler James Cooper, born 22 June 1968):

v. Stephanie Lynn Faulkner, born 4 October 1971, lives in Gypsum, Colorado. She married, on 17 February 1990, Jimmy Jordan, and has issue, surname *Jordan*: a. *Logan Dean*, born 18 June 1992.

vi. Mindy Marie Faulkner, born 28 August 1974, lives in Telluride, Colorado. She married, on 31 December 1993, Dale Young.

vii. Holly Sue Faulkner, born 30 October 1980.

M165 Archie Ball Faulkner, born 11 October 1919 in Vat, Montana, died 9 January 1968 in Kansas City, Missouri, was buried in Monticello Cemetery.

He married, in 1939 in Kansas City, Missouri, Seeta Joyce Williams, daughter of Benny and Seeta Jane (Harmon) Williams, born 17 June 1919 in Indenpendence, Missouri. She married, as her second husband, Alex Coffee.

He worked as a switchman for the Missouri Pacific Railroad.

Issue of Archie Ball and Seeta Jane (Williams) Faulkner:

i. Avis Geraldine Faulkner, born 21 February 1940, lives in Gardner, Kansas. She married, as her first husband, on 30 September 1960, in Hagerstown, Maryland, Harold Dean McDaniel, born 21 January 1939, and had issue, surname *McDaniel*: a. *Bradley Lynn*, born 7 January 1962; b. *Scott LaDeane*, born 1 October 1963; c. *David Layne*, born 22 June 1965, married, 22 April 1965, Janette Lynn Dailey. Avis was divorced in 1968 and married, as her second husband, 15 June 1979, in Olathe, Kansas, Emmett Otto Watkins, born 13 March 1938.

ii. Gloria Joyce Faulkner, born 30 December 1941. She married, as her first husband, Donald A. Peterson, and, as her second husband, Charles Carpenter.

iii. Sharyn Rose Faulkner, born 17 February 1945. She married, as her first husband, Earl Robinson, and, as her second husband, Gary Dean Vanderpool.

M244 iv. George Garilee Faulkner, born 29 September 1948.

M166 Claud Ester Faulkner, born 25 June 1898 in Perry Township, Boone County, Indiana, died 16 April 1952 in Indianapolis, Indiana, was buried in Washington Park Cemetery.

He married, on 9 August 1923, in Marion County, Indiana, Mary Thelma McCoun, born 12 August 1905 in Hendricks County, Indiana, died 6 August 1972. By 1956, she had married again to Joseph R. Rangel.

He was a factory worker and a "jack of all trades" and lived in Indianapolis.

Issue of Claud Ester and Mary Thelma (McCoun) Faulkner:[587]

i. Paula Joe Faulkner, born 26 August 1925, lives in Montpelier, Indiana. She married, on 29 November 1943, John Robert Carfield, and has issue, surname *Carfield*: a. *Jerry R.*, born 1947; b. *James Ryding*, born 1951.

ii. Phyllis Lee Faulkner, born 11 April 1933, lives in Plainfield, Indiana. She married John E. Dingman and has three children.

M167 Chester E. Faulkner, born 14 July 1901 in Perry Township, Boone County, Indiana.

He married, on 3 November 1923, in Marion County, Indiana, Sophia Wybenga. She lived in Plainfield, Indiana, in 1959.

He was a millwright who resided in Indianapolis as late as 1947.
Issue of Chester E. and Sophia (Wybenga) Faulkner:

    i.   William R. Faulkner. He lives in Plainfield, Indiana.

    ii.   Dorothy Faulkner, lives in Coatesville, Indiana. She married —— Curtis.

M168 Charlie Vestal Faulkner, born 1 October 1903 in Perry Township, Boone County, Indiana, died 2 May 1962 in Indianapolis, Indiana, was buried in Floral Park Cemetery.

He married, as his first wife, Ruth Cavit.

He married, as his second wife, on 31 August 1935, in Indianapolis, Indiana, Kitty Ellen Clark, born 18 May 1909, who lives in Indianapolis, Indiana. She married, as her second husband, George Dewey Whitlow, who died in 1976.

He worked as an inspector for the Chevrolet Motor Company.

Issue of Charlie Vestal and Kitty Ellen (Clark) Faulkner:

M245 i.   Stanley Monroe Faulkner, born 10 July 1942.

    ii.   Kenneth Clark Faulkner, born 22 May 1946, lives in Brooklyn Park, Minnesota. He married, on 12 August 1967.

    iii.   Patricia Ellen Faulkner, born 2 January 1951. She married, on 21 February 1970, Bradford Hendrickson. They divorced in 1988.

M169 Noble Harrison Faulkner, born 20 October 1917 in Perry Township, Boone County, Indiana, died 10 February 1981 in Marion County, Indiana, was buried in Floral Park Cemetery.

He married, on 31 March 1939, in Marion County, Indiana, Adelaide Virginia Wilkes, born 3 October 1922 in Marion County, Indiana. She lives in Indianapolis.

He was a maintenance worker.

Issue of Noble Harrison and Adelaide Virginia (Wilkes) Faulkner:[588]

M246 i.   Charles Lee Faulkner, born 14 January 1947.

    ii.   Todd Robert Faulkner, born 5 July 1951, died 7 July 1951.

    iii.   Noble Alan Faulkner, born 28 June 1955, died 28 June 1955.

M170 Willie F. Faulkner, born 26 July 1904 in Hendricks County, Indiana, died 13 June 1985 in Clermont, Indiana.

He married Flora M. Bedwell, born 5 February 1914, died November 1994 in Indianapolis, Indiana.

He made his home in Clermont from 1914.

Issue of Willie F. and Flora M. (Bedwell) Faulkner:

M247 i.   John David Faulkner, born 5 September 1940.

M171 Chester Lyle (Bud) Faulkner, born 29 March 1919 in Marathon, Iowa, died 8 February 1989 in Aurora, Colorado.

He married, as his first wife, Mary Ida Burris, born 9 June 1924, died 6 March 1956.

He married, as his second wife, Leona May (Clark) Skinner, born 13 November 1913, but divorced.

He married, as his third wife, Hannah F. Long, born 3 October 1910.

Issue of Chester Lyle and Mary Ida (Burris) Faulkner:[589]

    i.   Judy K. Faulkner, born 19 February 1945. She married, as her first husband, Alvin Roger Dickerson, but divorced. She married, as her second husband, Laymond Eugene Percival, and had issue, surname *Percival*: a. *Ida C.*, born 1 January 1973.

    ii.   Floria L. Faulkner, born 16 June 1946. She married Robert Clarence Smith, born 15 May 1937, and has issue, surname *Smith*: a. *Robert J.*, born 2 April 1967; b. *Margaret A.*, born 18 December 1973.

M248 iii.   Chester Lyle Faulkner, born 15 August 1954.

M172 **Robert Eugene Faulkner**, born 16 March 1923 in Marathon, Iowa, lives in Arnolds Park, Iowa.

He married, on 22 June 1943, in Jackson, Minnesota, Evelyn A. Rubel, born 25 December 1924 in Laurens, Iowa.

He was owner of a plumbing and heating business until his retirement in 1990.

Issue of Robert Eugene and Evelyn A. (Rubel) Faulkner:[590]

    i.   Connie R. Faulkner, born 24 June 1947.

    ii.   Sherry A. Faulkner, born 6 August 1950. She married Robert Lee Tiede, and has issue, surname *Tiede*: a. *William R.*, born 1 April 1971; b. *Christy A.*, born 26 January 1973; c. *Rebecca D.*, born 11 March 1977.

    iii.   Vickie L. Faulkner, born 3 May 1952. She married William Bernard Kane, and has issue, surname *Kane*: a. *Nicole L.*, born 20 February 1974; b. *Traci A.*, born 22 March 1975; c. *Tara B.*, born 3 September 1977.

M249 iv.   Robert LeRoy Faulkner, born 9 August 1954.

M173 **Darold Dean Faulkner**, born 21 February 1926 in Marathon, Iowa, died 17 August 1991 in Sumner, Iowa, was buried in Union Mound Cemetery.

He married, on 27 April 1947, in Laurens, Iowa, Violetta Elizabeth MacKie, born 13 April 1927 in Laurens, Iowa.

He was an industrial arts teacher and coach in Sumner for 39 years.

Issue of Darold Dean and Violetta Elizabeth (MacKie) Faulkner:

    i.   Diana Lyn Faulkner, born 29 April 1948.

M250 ii.   David Dean Faulkner, born 28 May 1950.

    iii.   Debbie Ann Faulkner, born 14 August 1954. She married, on 18 January 1975, William Roger Sieck, born 3 March 1953, and has issue, surname *Sieck*: a. *Dwayne W.*, born 23 July 1975; b. *Deidra E.*, born 29 February 1991.

    iv.   Denise Eileen Faulkner, born 31 October 1960.

    v.   Donald Alan Faulkner, born 21 March 1968.

M174 **Ross R. Faulkner**, born 11 September 1915 in Springfield, Illinois, died 8 December 1988 in Huntington Park, California.

He married Naomi Winiford (Doris) Ewen, born 9 March 1920, died 24 January 1989 in Huntington Park, California.

Issue of Ross R. and Naomi Winiford (Ewen) Faulkner:

    i.   Patricia A. Faulkner, born 18 November 1941. She married, as her second husband, Patrick Daggerty, and has issue, surname *Daggerty*: a. *Danielle P.*

M175   **Jerome L. Faulkner**, born 3 July 1925 in Springfield, Illinois, lives in Springfield, Illinois.

He married Shirley Dean Cummins, born 23 November 1936.

Issue of Jerome L. and Shirley Dean (Cummins) Faulkner:

    i.   Jerome L. Faulkner, born 31 December 1954, lives in Springfield, Illinois. He married Jennifer Marie Dahlhauser, born 18 February 1953.

    ii.   Reva E. Faulkner, born 7 June 1956, lives in Springfield, Illinois. She married Terry Lee Montalbano, born 25 May 1957, and has issue, surname *Montalbano*: a. *Heather R.*, born 15 October 1981.

M251 iii. Thomas Joseph Faulkner, born 27 September 1957.

M176   **Donald A. Faulkner**, born 23 May 1933 in Springfield, Illinois, lives in Springfield, Illinois.

He married, as his first wife, Thelma Duran. She died 9 March 1963.

He married, as his second wife, Delores Cooke, born 16 August 1931.

Issue of Donald A. and Thelma (Duran) Faulkner:

M252 i.   Michael R. Faulkner, born 3 August 1955.

    ii.   Constance M. Faulkner, born 10 July 1956. Issue, surname *Faulkner*: a. *Sean M.*, born 26 October 1974.

    iii. Laura D. Faulkner, born 24 February 1958.

    iv. Lois L. Faulkner, born 19 April 1960. Issue, surname *Faulkner*: a. *Eric P.*, born 14 May 1980.

M177   **Wilbur Wilson Faulkner**, born 1910 in Lafayette, Indiana, died 1960.

He married, on 16 May 1931, in Fort Wayne, Indiana, Dorothy Doris Tholen, born 1916, died 1989.

Issue of Wilbur Wilson and Dorothy Doris (Tholen) Faulkner:

    i.   JoAnn May Faulkner, born 1931. She married, as her first husband, Millard Meldeson Williams, Jr., and had issue, surname *Williams*: a. *Dwayne Millard*, born 1962; b. *Deborah Mildred*, born 1963. She married, as her second husband, Terry Panas, born 1930.

    ii.   Barbara Faulkner, born 1933. She married, as her first husband, Jesse Joseph Michel, born 1934, and had issue, surname *Michel*: a. *Jesse Joseph*. She married, as her second husband, John Preston Vernon, born 1932, and had issue, surname *Vernon*: a. *Janet*, born 1954; b. *John Preston*, born 1956; c. *Judi Lynn*, born 1964.

M253 iii. William Michael Faulkner, born 1937.

M254 iv. Patrick Joseph Faulkner, born 1943.

M178 James Elwood Faulkner, born 24 August 1912 in Lafayette, Tippecanoe County, Indiana, died 15 May 1993 in Apple Valley, California.

He married, as his first wife, on 20 November 1937, in Fort Wayne, Indiana, Helen Irene Smith, born 30 May 1921 in Huntington, Indiana, who lives in Terre Haute, Indiana. They later divorced.

He married, as his second wife, Barbara Alice Sturges, born 1919.

Issue of James Elwood and Helen Irene (Smith) Faulkner:

i. Janice Duane Faulkner, born 1938, lives in South Bend, Indiana. She married Douglas Ira Cowen, born 1934, and has issue, surname *Cowen*: a. *Douglas Anthony*, born 1960, married Dawn Florey; b. *Juliana*, born 1961, married Robert Freske; c. *Ann Jeanette*, born 1965, married Jason Derek Palmer; d. *James Aaron*, born 1969.

ii. Saundra Mae Faulkner, born 1939. She married, as her first husband, Edward George Shotkowski, born 1936, died 1981, and had issue, surname *Shotkowski*: a. *Diane Mary*, born 1962, married Bradley Don Capshaw; b. *Susan Ann*, born 1966, married Ritchey Paul Jordan; c. *Amy Lynn*, born 1968, married Wayne Walker; d. *Jennifer Kay*, born 1974. Saundra married, as her second husband, Jack Doy Willey, born 1942.

iii. Judith Ann Faulkner, born 25 December 1943, lives in Terre Haute, Indiana. She married Rex Charles Critchlow, born 1940, and has issue, surname *Critchlow*: a. *Teresa Ann*, born 1964, married Timothy David Nering; b. *Rex Alan*, born 1965, married Michele Lynn McQueen; c. *Helen Jean Marie*, born 1969, married Marvin Lee Eugene Manning.

M179 Robert Clarence Faulkner, born 27 November 1914 in Lafayette, Tippecanoe County, Indiana, died 3 December 1994, possibly in Syracuse, New York, where he lived before his death.

He married Mildred Mary Price.

Issue of Robert Clarence and Mildred Mary (Price) Faulkner:

i. Robert Clarence Faulkner, born 1940.
ii. Douglas Faulkner, born 1942.
iii. Stephen Faulkner, born 1945.
iv. Michael Faulkner, born 1946.

M180 George King Faulkner, born 26 May 1920 in Lafayette, Tippecanoe County, Indiana, died 5 April 1974 in Lancaster, California.

He married Marilyn Dolores Wilson, born 1920.

He was a physician.

Issue of George King and Marilyn Dolores (Wilson) Faulkner:

i. Kristen May Faulkner, born 1953.
ii. Kevin Faulkner, born 1954.
iii. Deborah Faulkner, born 1957. She married Patrick Edwin Farrant, born 1951.

M181 John S. Faulkner, born 5 June 1901 in White County, Illinois, died 16 June 1962 in Evansville, Indiana, was buried in Locust Hill Cemetery,

Evansville.

He married Lavayden Hall, born 1900, died 1970.

Issue of John S. and Lavayden (Hall) Faulkner:

    i.   Ella Viola Faulkner, born 7 January 1930, died 18 August 1971 Evansville, Indiana, buried in Locust Hill Cemetery. She married —— Klaus and had issue, surname *Klaus*: a. *Robbie*.

M182   Raymond E. Faulkner, born 10 June 1908 in White County, Illinois, lives in Naples, Florida.

He married, on 30 August 1933 at Carmi, Illinois, Esther M. Stein, born 11 August 1912, died June 1985 in Mount Vernon, Indiana.

He was a building contractor in Evansville, Indiana, most of his life.

Issue of Raymond E. and Esther M. (Stein) Faulkner:

    i.   Donna Raye Faulkner, born November 1946.

M183   Freeman E. Faulkner, born 4 August 1910 in White County, Illinois, died 9 December 1976 in Evansville, Indiana, was buried in Oak Hill Cemetery.

He married, in August 1946, in Evansville, Indiana, Ruby Borum, born 11 December 1912, died August 1993 in Evansville, Indiana.

Issue of Freeman E. and Ruby (Borum) Faulkner:

    i.   Brenda Faulkner, born 31 January 1953.

M184   Powell S. Faulkner, born 3 October 1918 in White County, Illinois, died 15 January 1971 in Evansville, Indiana, was buried in Parklawn Cemetery.

He married Marie Webb, born 1 July 1919, died 17 October 1994 in Evansville, Indiana.

Issue of Powell S. and Marie (Webb) Faulkner:

    i.   Nancy Jo Faulkner, born December 1946.
    ii.   Jane A. Faulkner, born October 1948.
    iii. Janet V. Faulkner, born October 1948, died 1951, buried in Parklawn Cemetery.
    iv. Jeanne M. Faulkner, born October 1948.

M185   Fred Lee Faulkner, born 15 December 1887 in Asbury Township, Gallatin County, Illinois, died 15 July 1961 in Geneva, Illinois, was buried in Mount Emblem Cemetery, Elmhurst, Illinois.

He married, as his first wife, Pearl Stratton, who died 25 November 1938 in Chicago, Illinois. They had divorced.

He married, as his second wife, Runa ——, born 30 April 1900, died April 1982 in Geneva, Illinois.

In 1908, he lived in East St. Louis, Illinois. He moved to Chicago from Oklahoma City, Oklahoma. He worked for Morris and Company and then Armour Company as a food testing technician.

Issue of Fred Lee and Pearl (Stratton) Faulkner:[591]

M255 i.   Fred Lee Faulkner, born 7 October 1914.

M186   **Dale C. Faulkner**, born 27 August 1915 in Dante, South Dakota, died 9 March 1984 in Omaha, Nebraska, was buried in Forest Lawn Cemetery.

He married, on 27 November 1942, in Hot Springs, Arkansas, Bertha Irene Satterfield, born 5 August 1921 in Collins, Arkansas, living in Omaha, Nebraska.

He was property manager in the Omaha Division of Safeway Stores, Inc.

Issue of Dale C. and Bertha Irene (Satterfield) Faulkner:

   i.   Janis Kay Faulkner, born 5 March 1951 in Norton, Kansas, lives in Omaha, Nebraska. She married, on 5 January 1973, Mark F. Enenbach, and has issue, surname *Enenbach*: a. *Matthew Mark*, born 26 May 1979; b. *Jonathan David*, born 19 March 1984; c. *Jacob Andrew*, born 26 June 1987.

   ii.   Vicki Dale Faulkner, born 6 May 1955 in Omaha, Nebraska, lives there.

M187   **Carl Freeman Faulkner**, born 19 July 1902 in Liletown, Green County, Kentucky, died 28 September 1982 in Greensburg, Kentucky, was buried in Greensburg Cemetery.

He married, on 20 July 1924, Beulah Robertson, born 1 September 1899, died 8 February 1975 in Greensburg, Kentucky.

Moving to Greensburg in 1930, he operated various businesses there. At different times he owned four groceries, four restaurants, a bowling alley, and a pool room. He owned a total of eight different farms at various times. He also worked as a postal carrier for eight years.

Issue of Carl Freeman and Beulah (Robertson) Faulkner:[592]

   i.   Mary Maxine Faulkner, born 17 April 1925, died, unmarried, 15 July 1984 in Louisville, Kentucky.

M188   **Clyde S. Faulkner**, born about 1917 in Metcalfe County, Kentucky, lives in Edmonton, Kentucky.

He married Elizabeth Buchanan.

Issue of Clyde S. and Elizabeth (Buchanan) Faulkner:[593]

   i.   Ronald B. Faulkner, born 22 December 1942.

M189   **Henry Clay Faulkner**, lives in Edmonton, Kentucky.

He married Lanora Matney.

Issue of Henry Clay and Lanora (Matney) Faulkner:

   i.   Patrick M. Faulkner, born 16 February 1962. He married, on 2 April 1985, in Edmonton, Kentucky, Teresa J. (Davis) McAllister, born 15 September 1957. They were divorced 19 November 1989 in Green County, Kentucky.

M190   David Earl Faulkner, born 9 October 1914 in Green County, Kentucky, lives in Springfield, Illinois.

He married, as his first wife, Eileen Sumpter. She was buried at Divernon, Illinois.

He married, as his second wife, Marjorie (Fry) Moose, born 28 June 1917 at Pawnee, Illinois, living in Springfield, Illinois.

He worked as a mechanic.

Issue of David Earl and Eileen (Sumpter) Faulkner:

M256 i.   Donald Faulkner, born 12 February 1939.

M257 ii.   Walter Leroy Faulkner, born 31 December 1940.

M258 iii. Ronald George Faulkner, born 12 August 1943.

M259 iv.   James Richman Faulkner, born 13 September 1944.

M191   Lloyd Weldon (Jack) Faulkner, born 13 April 1897 in Irvington, Illinois, died 9 February 1973 in Greeley, Colorado, was buried in Sunset Memorial Gardens.[594]

He married, as his first wife, in 1919 in Marion County, Illinois, Lulu Mae Kepner.

He married, as his second wife, Mary Margaret Merritt, born 12 March 1904 in Fancyfarm, Kentucky, died 8 September 1952 in Baltimore, Maryland.

He married, as his third wife, Patricia Williams. She lives in Greeley, Colorado.

He served as a warrant officer in the U.S. Navy during World War I aboard the U.S.S. *Michigan*. He was also a champion heavyweight boxer. From about 1940, he was a division manager for the Electrolux Corporation, assigned to various points in the United States, including Baltimore, Buffalo, Sarasota, St. Petersburg, and Daytona Beach, Florida, and California. He came to Greeley about 1970.

Issue of Lloyd Weldon and Mary Margaret (Merritt) Faulkner:[595]

     i.   Peggy Jean Faulkner, born 22 March 1927, lives in Huntsville, Alabama. She married Montague X. Shanahan.

M260 ii.   Franklin Faulkner, born 17 May 1931.

     iii. Mary Patricia Faulkner, born 1 September 1939, lives in Columbia, Maryland. She married, on 12 August 1961, John P. Finnegan.

     iv.   Elizabeth Ann Faulkner, born 2 August 1941, lives in Annandale, Virginia. She married, on 2 February 1963, Cecil O. Trump.

Issue of Lloyd Weldon and Patricia (Williams) Faulkner:

     v.   Lloyd Weldon (Jack) Faulkner, born September 1951 in Buffalo, New York, lives in Havelock, North Carolina. He has three sons and one daughter.

M192   Virgil Braden Faulkner, born 26 March 1899 in St. Louis, Missouri, died 18 December 1972 in Forsyth, Missouri, was buried in Ozarks Memorial Cemetery, Branson, Missouri.

He married, as his first wife, on 15 July 1919, in Centralia, Illinois, Gladys

E. Talbott.

He was married, again, to Evelyn ——, who survived him.

After his first marriage, he lived in Centralia, where he worked as a switch-man for the Illinois Central Railroad. In later years, he was a salesman for the Electrolux Corporation.

Issue of Virgil Braden and Gladys E. (Talbott) Faulkner:[596]

    i.   Franklin Talbott Faulkner, born 22 September 1921, died 9 January 1922 in Centralia, Illinois, buried in Hillcrest Memorial Park.

Issue of Virgil Braden Faulkner:

    ii.   Franklin Faulkner.

M193 Richard James Faulkner, born 12 October 1924 in Centralia, Illinois, died 24 March 1981 in Centralia, Illinois, was buried in Hillcrest Memorial Park.

He married, on 21 November 1945, in Centralia, Illinois, Isabell Ruth Cottrell.

He was a veteran of World War II and the Korean War had an insurance agency.

Issue of Richard James and Isabell Ruth (Cottrell) Faulkner:

M261 i.   William E. Faulkner, born 10 November 1948.

M194 Lowell Burns Faulkner, born 3 September 1932 in Linn County, Missouri, died 5 January 1976 in Linn County, Missouri, was buried in Rose Hill Cemetery, Brookfield, Missouri.

He married, on 15 October 1950, in Linn County, Missouri, Bette Jo Owens, born 5 June 1933 in Hale, Missouri. She married, as her second husband, Bill Bussman, of Marceline, Missouri.

Issue of Lowell Burns and Bette Jo (Owens) Faulkner:

M262 i.   Lowell Roger Faulkner, born 28 October 1951.

    ii.   Bette Catherine Faulkner, born 9 March 1954, lives in New Booton, Missouri. She married Steven Witt.

M195 Charles Curtis Faulkner, born 26 May 1937 in Linn County, Missouri, lives in Brookfield, Missouri.

He married, on 10 November 1957, in Brookfield, Missouri, Virginia Kathryn Peery, born 10 February 1939 in Jefferson City, Missouri.

He is a foreman.

Issue of Charles Curtis and Virginia Kathryn (Peery) Faulkner, the first two born in Brookfield, Missouri:[597]

M263 i.   Guy Lawrence Faulkner, born 26 October 1958.

    ii.   Kathryn Therese Faulkner, born 9 January 1960. She married, on 9 April 1983, in Brookfield, Missouri, Charles Morrison, born 18 November 1955, in Salisbury, Missouri, and has issue, surname *Morrison*: a. *Brian Charles*, born 1 September 1984; b. *Mathew Michael*, born 25 April 1987.

iii. Melinda Anne Faulkner, born 19 August 1961 in Holyoke, Colorado. She married, on 3 December 1982 in Brookfield, Missouri, Larry Bradley, but divorced, and had issue, surname *Bradley*: a. *Tyler Ryan*, born 19 October 1987.

iv. Charlene Renee Faulkner, born 19 March 1965 in Macon, Missouri. She married, on 19 November 1988 in Lees Summit, Missouri, David Buenger, born 18 February 1966, and has issue, surname *Buenger*: a. *Christine Renee*, born 1 August 1989. She is an accountant.

M196 George Leslie Faulkner, born 3 March 1939 in Linn County, Missouri, lives in Brookfield, Missouri.

He married, on 8 October 1966, in Brookfield, Missouri, Bonnie Jean York, born 10 June 1946, died 10 March 1979 in Brookfield, Missouri, buried in Rose Hill Cemetery.

He has been a farmer and factory worker.

Issue of George Leslie and Bonnie Jean (York) Faulkner:

i. Leigh Ann Faulkner, born 10 September 1967. She married, on 6 October 1989, David Simarz.

ii. George Lance Faulkner, born 5 July 1970.

M197 Ronald Keith Faulkner, born 3 December 1939 at Princeton, Mercer County, Missouri, lives at Harris, Missouri.

He married, on 27 September 1963, at Cainsville, Missouri, Wilma Lorene Francis, born 4 December 1945 at Cainsville, Missouri.

He is a farmer, logger, and sawmiller.

Issue of Ronald Keith and Wilma Lorene (Francis) Faulkner:[598]

i. Kelly Brian Faulkner, born 23 April 1964.

ii. Kurtis Dean Faulkner, born 14 August 1965.

iii. Ronald Kris Faulkner, born 3 December 1966.

iv. Samuel Douglas Faulkner, born 31 August 1968. He married, on 20 October 1990, at Princeton, Missouri, Tamme Gene Wright.

M198 Clifford J. Faulkner, born 18 November 1921, died 18 February 1990 in Nickerson, Kansas.

He married Helen ———, who lives in Nickerson, Kansas.

Issue of Clifford J. Faulkner:

i. David Faulkner, lives in Dallas, Texas.

ii. Stephen Faulkner, lives in Mount Hope, Kansas.

M199 Frank David Faulkner, born 6 April 1915 near Humansville (Johnson Township), Polk County, Missouri, lives in Carmel, California.

He married, on 5 January 1941, in Emporia, Kansas, Theresa Alice Hellmer, born 17 October 1917 near Olpe, Kansas, died 18 July 1978 in Grants Pass, Oregon.

He was educated at Kansas State Teachers College (B.A., 1940), Kansas State College (M.S., 1942), and the University of Michigan (Ph.D., 1969). He was junior physicist at the Applied Physics Laboratory, Johns Hopkins University, from 1944 to 1946; research mathematician at the Engineering Research Institute, University of Michigan, from 1946 to 1950. He was From 1950 to 1981, he was on the mathematics faculty of the United States Naval Postgraduate School, leaving with the rank of Distinguished Professor of Mathematics.

Issue of Frank David and Theresa Alice (Hellmer) Faulkner:[599]

M264 i.   Frank David Faulkner, born 14 July 1943.

     ii.   Harold George Faulkner, born 3 January 1945 in Bethesda, Maryland, lives in Minneapolis, Minnesota. He married Cheryl Perry, but divorced.

    iii.   Mary Alice Faulkner, born 23 June 1949 in Ann Arbor, Michigan, lives in Memphis, Tennessee. She married Charles Martin Kirk, Jr., and has two children.

M265 iv.   William Marion Faulkner, born 26 April 1951.

     v.   Robert Gordon Faulkner, born 31 December 1957 in Carmel, California, lives in San Diego, California. He married Sandra Rexing.

    vi.   Andrew Wayne Faulkner, born 6 October 1959 in Carmel, California. He lives in Sherman Oaks, California.

M200 Gordon Ernest (Jack) Faulkner, born 9 February 1919 near Humansville (Johnson Township), Polk County, Missouri, died March 1987 in Howard, Kansas, was buried at Severy, Kansas.

He married, as his first wife, Maxine Barnes, but was later divorced.
He married, as his second wife, Hazel ——.
Issue of Gordon Ernest and Maxine (Barnes) Faulkner:

     i.   James Gordon Faulkner, lives in Midland, Texas. He has two sons.

M266 ii.   Gregory Lee Faulkner.

M201 Harold Lloyd Faulkner, born 2 August 1925, died 25 February 1964, probably in Coats, Kansas.

He married, on 1 December 1946, Gladys Marie Cox.
Issue of Harold Lloyd and Gladys Marie (Cox) Faulkner:[600]

     i.   Terry Lynn Faulkner, born 20 October 1947.

     ii.   Jerry Gordon Faulkner, born 31 December 1949.

    iii.   Mark Jay Faulkner, born 26 January 1954.

    iv.   Vinice Ann Faulkner, born 2 March 1958.

M202 James Edward Faulkner, born 14 November 1918 in Clay County, Texas, died 1960, was buried in the National Cemetery, San Antonio, Texas.

He married, in 1949, Gladys Pauline Woodall, born September 1919 in Blair, Oklahoma. They divorced in 1954.
Issue of James Edward and Gladys Pauline (Woodall) Faulkner:

     i.   Debra Kay Faulkner, born 9 November 1951, lives in Wichita Falls, Texas. She married, as her first husband, on 16 December 1968, Carl W. Kestler, and had issue, surname *Kestler:* a. *Rodney Clyde*, born 1 February 1970, died 19 January 1983; b. *Mark Edward*, born 14 July 1971; c. *Tiffany Kay*, born 20 November 1975; d. *Brandon West*, born 10 November 1977; e. *Kimberly Brook*, born 2 February 1983. They divorced, and she married, as her second husband, on 26 April 1985, Gary Lee Humphrey, born 19 April 1985.

M203   George Franklin Faulkner, born 17 April 1924 in Clay County, Texas, died 8 June 1989 in Wichita Falls, Texas, was buried in Friendship Cemetery, Bellevue, Texas.

He married, on 21 October 1946, Louie Annabelle Rowe, born 29 November 1925 in Kansas.

Issue of George Franklin and Louie Annabelle (Rowe) Faulkner:

M267 i.   George Arthur Faulkner, born 19 June 1947.
M268 ii. James David Faulkner, born 14 January 1950.
M269 iii. Robert Edward Faulkner, born 1 June 1953.
     iv. Frank Lee Faulkner, born 20 January 1961, lives in Wichita Falls, Texas.

M204   Robert Lee Faulkner, born 13 December 1926 in Lake Creek, Archer County, Texas, lives in Copperas Cove, Texas.

He married, on 16 March 1955, in Sapporo, Japan, Michiyo Hirabayashi, daughter of Matsumi and Sumiko Hirabayashi, born 27 November 1930 in Nagano Prefecture, Japan.

He served in the U. S. Army.

Issue of Robert Lee and Michiyo (Hirabayashi) Faulkner:

i.   Alan T. Faulkner, died July 1966 in Baton Rouge, Louisiana, buried at Port Hudson, Louisiana.
ii. Alfred Lee Faulkner, born 25 November 1958, lives in Temple, Texas.
iii. Rebecca N. Faulkner, born 5 November 1964.

M205   Roy Gilbert Faulkner, born 4 February 1922 in Knob Lick, Metcalfe County, Kentucky, died 24 August 1995 in Louisville, Kentucky.

He married, on 1 June 1946, Marcus Josephine Monday.

Issue of Roy Gilbert and Marcus Josephine (Monday) Faulkner, the first born in Barren County, Kentucky, the rest in Jefferson County, Kentucky:[601]

i.   Rebecca Ann Faulkner, born 7 August 1948. She married James Kennett.
ii. Roy Gilbert Faulkner, born 8 October 1953. He married, on 16 August 1980, in Jefferson County, Kentucky, Sharon K. Rogers.
iii. Emily J. Faulkner, born 1959. She married, on 1 January 1983, in Jefferson County, Kentucky, James D. Campbell.
iv. Richard Mark Faulkner.

M206   James Dalton Faulkner, born 18 October 1923 in Knob Lick, Metcalfe County, Kentucky, died 1 March 1955 in Barren County, Kentucky, buried in Neals Chapel Cemetery, Barren County, Kentucky.

He married, on 24 December 1949, Reba Erlene Lohden. She married again.

Issue of James Dalton and Reba Erlene (Lohden) Faulkner:[602]

M270 i. James Delbert Faulkner, born 2 November 1950.

M207 Rollin Thomas Faulkner, born 15 January 1929 in Metcalfe County, Kentucky, lives in Glasgow, Kentucky.

He married, on 14 August 1948, Martha Ella Veluzat, born 22 January 1932 in Barren County, Kentucky.

He is a banker.

Issue of Rollin Thomas and Martha Ella (Veluzat) Faulkner:[603]

    i. Sheroline Faulkner, born 12 September 1952, lives in Cave City, Kentucky. She married, as her first husband, Laymon Shaw, son of Fred and Nancy (Sneed) Shaw, and had issue, surname *Shaw*: a. *Kendall*, born 30 March 1972, married 4 April 1990 Marie Houchens. She married, as her second husband, Marshall Rouse, and had issue, surname *Rouse*: b. *Thomas Matthew*, born 15 March 1975, died 16 March 1975; c. *Bobby Neal*, born 28 February 1978; d. *Shon Timothy*, born 1 April 1980. She married, as her third husband, Marshall E. Byrd.

    ii. Jackie Lee Faulkner, born 22 January 1955. She married, on 22 March 1974, in Barren County, Kentucky, Phillip H. Tracy, son of Barney and Edith Tracy, and has issue, surname *Tracy*: a. *Tena Marie*, born 21 December 1977; b. *Bradley Joe*, born 3 April 1981.

M208 Henry Harold Faulkner, born 25 September 1928 in Metcalfe County, Kentucky, died 18 December 1982, was buried in New Liberty Cemetery.

He married Doris Shirley.

He served as a corporal in the U. S. Army during the Korean War.

Issue of Henry Harold and Doris (Shirley) Faulkner:

M271 i. Danny Faulkner, born 29 November 1950.

    ii. Vickie Faulkner. She married Johnny Jackers.

M209 Paul Revere Faulkner, born 23 January 1904 in Oklahoma, died 17 May 1986 in Norman, Oklahoma, was buried in Washington, Oklahoma.

The name of his wife is not known.

He worked as a barber for 50 years. He lived in Miami, Oklahoma, for many years; in Edmond, Oklahoma, for seven years; and from 1983 in Washington, Oklahoma. He served in the U. S. Army and Marine Corps.

Issue of Paul Revere Faulkner:[604]

M272 i. Don W. Faulkner.

M210 Dwight Owen Faulkner, born 20 May 1926 in Maxwell, Iowa, lives in Ankeny, Iowa.

He married, on 13 June 1948, Patricia Ann Scott.

Issue of Dwight Owen and Patricia Ann (Scott) Faulkner:

M273 i. Scott Richard Faulkner, born 4 July 1950.

    ii. Patrice Marie Faulkner, born 31 May 1952. She married —— Fayers.

    iii. Cynthia Lee Faulkner, born 24 July 1954, lives in Cylinder, Iowa.

    iv.   Melinda Ann Faulkner, born 4 October 1956, lives in Japan.

M211   **Donald Richard Faulkner**, born 1940 in Maxwell, Iowa, lives in Spring Valley, California.

He married Geneva ——.

Issue of Donald Richard and Geneva Faulkner (they also adopted a son, Jason):

    i.   Dwight Faulkner.

M212   **John McCoy Faulkner**, born 13 October 1922 in Des Moines, Iowa, lives in Ankeny, Iowa.

He married, on 25 January 1947, in Des Moines, Iowa, Phyllis Elvick, born 31 August 1927 in Battle Creek, Iowa.

He worked as a welding engineer.

Issue of John McCoy and Phyllis (Elvick) Faulkner:[605]

    i.   Saundra Diane Faulkner, born 29 December 1947, lives in Ankeny, Iowa. She married, as her first husband, in June 1968, John Kovac, and, as her second husband, on 21 March 1986, Ray Thomas, and has issue.

    ii.   John Matthew Faulkner, born 18 August 1957. He married, on 8 June 1980, Judith Kopczynski.

    iii.   Jacquelyn Leigh Faulkner, born 3 June 1961. She married, on 3 August 1986, Eric Komplin.

M213   **Gerald Reece Faulkner**, born 19 January 1917 in East St. Louis, Illinois, died 4 January 1971 in Marion, Illinois, was buried in Veterans Memorial Cemetery, Fairfield, Illinois.[606]

He married, on 25 June 1938, in Fairfield, Illinois, Nigel F. Brown, daughter of P. R. and Bonnie (White) Brown, born about 1917 in Karval, California. They later divorced.

He worked as a painter and carpenter in Fairfield. He served as a specialist, first class, in the U. S. Navy during World War II.

Issue of Gerald Reece and Nigel F. (Brown) Faulkner:

    i.   Carolyn Joyce Faulkner, born 8 April 1939, living in 1971 in Golt, California. She married —— Romero.

    ii.   Franklin Reece Faulkner, born 17 May 1942, living in 1971 in Joliet, Illinois.

    iii.   LaDonna Rae Faulkner, born 11 March 1947, living in 1971 in Fairfield, Illinois. She married Carl Ewing, and had issue, surname *Ewing*: a. *Radonna Sue*; b. *Evan Allen*; c. *Kevin Reece*.

    iv.   Charles Lee Faulkner, born 9 August 1948.

M214   **Alva Jerold Faulkner**, born 1920 in Jacksonville, Florida, died about 1989 in St. George Island, Florida.

He married Reggie ——, who lives in Albany, Georgia.

He lived most of his life in Albany, Georgia.

Issue of Alva Jerold and Reggie Faulkner:

    i.   John Faulkner.

    ii.   son.

    iii.   daughter. She married about 1973.

M215 Jack Faulkner, born in Jacksonville, Florida, lives in Cummins, Georgia.

    He was a horticulturalist in Naples, Florida.

    Issue of Jack Faulkner:

    i.   Diane Faulkner. She was married, had a son and a daughter, and lived in Tampa, Florida, in 1977.

    ii.   Jay Faulkner.

M216 Berlyn Eugene Faulkner, born 13 February 1914 in Keenes (Four Mile Township), Wayne County, Illinois, lives in Jamestown, Kansas.

    He married, on 8 September 1939, in Clinton, Iowa, Zella Roberta Livesay, born 9 March 1920 near Mount Vernon, Illinois.

    He was self-employed and a Methodist minister and lived in Mount Vernon, Illinois; Bluford, Illinois; Valeda, Kansas; St. John, Kansas; and Douglass, Kansas.

    Issue of Berlyn Eugene and Zella Roberta (Livesay) Faulkner:[607]

M274 i.   Philip Eugene Faulkner, born 19 February 1940.

    ii.   Kathryn Lucille Faulkner, born 7 February 1941. She married, as her first husband, on 10 July 1960, David M. Hill. She married, as her second husband, on 25 November 1968, James Dunbar.

M217 Harlan Euil Faulkner, born 13 June 1916 in Keenes (Four Mile Township), Wayne County, Illinois, died 8 December 1973 in Dallas, Texas, was buried in Laurel Lane Cemetery, Dallas.

    He married, as his first wife, on 26 April 1938, Beulah Alberta Bozarth, born about 1920. They divorced.

    He married, as his second wife, on 1 January 1948, Marjorie Keppen. They divorced.

    He married, as his third wife, Frances Juanita Blackwood, born 27 November 1925. She lives in Dallas, Texas.

    Issue of Harlan Euil and Beulah Alberta (Bozarth) Faulkner:

    i.   Loretta June Faulkner, born 1 November 1938.

    ii.   Effie Corvine Faulkner, born 3 July 1940.

    Issue of Harlan Euil and Marjorie (Keppen) Faulkner:

    iii.   Doris Elaine Faulkner.

    iv.   David Warren Faulkner.

    Issue of Harlan Euil and Frances Juanita (Blackwood) Faulkner:[608]

    v.   Linda Kay Faulkner, born 28 November 1953. She married, in September

1973, Tommy Holman, and has four sons.

M275 vi.   Robert Gary Faulkner, born 25 February 1956.

vii.   Patsy Ruth Faulkner, born 22 June 1957, lives in Dallas, Texas.

M276 viii.   Richard Warren Faulkner, born 15 November 1959.

M277 ix.   Randy Thomas Faulkner, born 8 January 1962.

x.   Lisa G. Faulkner, born 8 May 1964, lives in Dallas, Texas. She married, on 2 July 1987, Dale Elsik.

M218   Kenneth Leslie Faulkner, born 8 June 1912 in Keenes (Four Mile Township), Wayne County, Illinois, died 14 July 1971 in Steward, Illinois.

He married, on 26 September 1938, in Mount Vernon, Illinois, Pansy Imogene Alexander, born 26 September 1920 in Mount Vernon, Illinois.

Issue of Kenneth Leslie and Pansy Imogene (Alexander) Faulkner:

i.   Barbara Faulkner, born 26 December 1940.

ii.   Sharon Kay Faulkner, born 14 December 1942, died 4 January 1943 Field Township, Jefferson County, Illinois, buried in the Union Chapel Cemetery.

iii.   Virginia Faulkner, born 18 July 1944.

iv.   Marge Faulkner, born 23 January 1947.

M219   Keith C. Faulkner, born 12 November 1914 in Keenes (Four Mile Township), Wayne County, Illinois, lives near Mount Vernon, Illinois.

He married, as his first wife, in 1936, Ethel M. Ficken, born 19 January 1917, died 7 February 1987 in Germantown Hills, Illinois.

He married, as his second wife, on 29 June 1989, Dorthea M. Walker.

Issue of Keith C. and Ethel M. (Ficken) Faulkner:[609]

M278 i.   Arnold K. Faulkner, born 18 December 1936.

ii.   Everett E. Faulkner, born 14 September 1938, lives at Chillicothe, Illinois. He married Donna ———.

iii.   Marjorie Elaine Faulkner, born 10 November 1940, lives in Peoria Heights, Illinois. She married, as her first husband, Ron Frenzel, and had issue, surname *Frenzel*: a. *Jeff*, lives in Houston, Texas. She married, as her second husband, in 1978, Roland Geidat.

iv.   Judith A. Faulkner, born 26 January 1942, lives in Peoria, Illinois. She married William Hauser, but divorced. Issue, surname *Hauser*: a. *Don*, of Huntsville, Arkansas; b. *Mark*, of Little Rock, Arkansas.

v.   Linda Jane Faulkner, born 19 June 1945, lives in Peoria Heights, Illinois. She married Charles F. Hire, and has no children.

vi.   Kathleen Kay Faulkner, born 25 September 1949, lives in Washington, Illinois. She married Richard Dravis and has issue, surname *Dravis*: a. *Christopher*, born 1977; b. *Matthew*, born 1980.

M220   Harry A. Faulkner, born 2 December 1918 in Keenes (Four Mile Township), Wayne County, Illinois, lives in Indianapolis, Indiana.

He married, on 14 April 1944, in Gainesville, Texas, Alda Eileen Kibler, born 24 September 1922 in Jasper County, Illinois.

He worked as a die setter.

Issue of Harry A. and Alda Eileen (Kibler) Faulkner:[610]

i.   Jonell E. Faulkner, born 14 November 1948, lives in Indianapolis, Indiana. She married Tim Kennedy.

ii. Sandra K. Faulkner, born 19 March 1951, lives in Indianapolis, Indiana. She married Frank Shirley.

iii. Harry A. Faulkner, born 14 November 1959, lives in Houston, Texas. He married, in 1982, Jan Collins.

M221   Charles A. Faulkner, born 3 December 1922 in Keenes (Four Mile Township), Wayne County, Illinois, lives in Neptune, New Jersey.

He married, on 29 January 1944, in Frederick, Oklahoma, Peggy Doris Sweazy, born 12 August 1924 in Effingham, Illinois.

He worked as a pilot and engineer.

Issue of Charles A. and Peggy Doris (Sweazy) Faulkner:[611]

i.   Susan Lynn Faulkner, born 9 July 1946, lives in Belmar, New Jersey. She married, on 16 September 1972, Thomas Rea.

ii. Paul Arthur Faulkner, born 31 June 1955.

M222   Frank Evans Faulkner, born 27 October 1924 in Jefferson County, Illinois, lives in Mount Vernon, Illinois.

He married, on 24 December 1942, in Cape Girardeau, Missouri, Dorothy A. Johnson, born 13 February 1926 in Bonnie, Illinois.

Issue of Frank Evans and Dorothy A. (Johnson) Faulkner:[612]

i.   Jerry Evans Faulkner, born 6 October 1943, died 23 September 1957 Mount Vernon, Illinois, buried in Bethel Cemetery.

ii. Elaine Kaye Faulkner, born 20 October 1946, lives in Silverthorne, Colorado. She married, on 29 June 1979, Hugh H. Albritton, Jr.

iii. Steven Jon Faulkner, born 17 November 1959, lives in Mount Vernon, Illinois. He married, on 15 March 1989, Jodi Rogers.

iv. Valerie Dawn Faulkner, born 20 October 1961, lives in Mount Vernon, Illinois. She married, 8 August 1980, Darrell R. Champ, and has issue, surname *Champ*: a. *Cody Rae*, born 4 October 1985; b. *Kaylee*, born 13 November 1986.

M223   Harold Lee Faulkner, born 13 March 1923 in Mount Vernon, Illinois, lives in Augusta, Georgia.

He married Edna Marie McKowen, daughter of George Oscar and Leona Hazel (Smith) McKowen, born 20 November 1925 in Mount Vernon, Illinois. They divorced, and she married, in 1954, as her second husband, Ronald E. Chambliss.[613]

Issue of Harold Lee and Edna Marie (McKowen) Faulkner, born in Mount Vernon, Illinois:

i.   Jo Carol Faulkner, born 11 May 1946.

M224   Homer Warren (Bud) Faulkner, born 27 November 1922 in Mount

Vernon, Illinois, lives in Vero Beach, Florida.

He married, on 3 September 1949, in Sikeston, Missouri, Betty Ann Waldman, born 21 October 1930 in Sikeston, Missouri, living in Vero Beach, Florida.

He worked as an airline captain. He and his wife lived for many years in Fort Lauderdale, Florida.

Issue of Homer Warren and Betty Ann (Waldman) Faulkner:[614]

    i.   Bruce Warren Faulkner, born 21 November 1950, died 8 August 1952.

    ii.   Blake Edward Faulkner, born 24 August 1952, lives in Stuart, Florida. He married, on 3 October 1986, Constance (Bogue) Brown.

    iii.   James Warren Faulkner, born 20 August 1955, lives in Vero Beach, Florida. He married, on 1 May 1979, Mina Pak.

M225   Ray Wadsworth Faulkner, born 26 July 1921 in Mount Vernon, Illinois, died 16 January 1991 in Bloomington, Illinois, was buried in Oakwood Cemetery, Mount Vernon, Illinois.

He married, on 20 October 1946 in Mount Vernon, Illinois, Ruth Verdene Krone, born 5 February 1924 in Tamaroa, Illinois.

He worked as a builder in the construction of homes and lived for many years in Normal, Illinois.

Issue of Ray Wadsworth and Ruth Verdene (Krone) Faulkner, born in Mount Vernon, Illinois:[615]

    i.   Suzanne Christine Faulkner, born 6 December 1947. She married, on 19 April 1977, Charles Francis Albarelli. They have two children.

    ii.   Marilyn Renee Faulkner, born 28 October 1952. She married, on 21 October 1983, Michael Mulvaney. Issue, surname *Mulvaney*: a. *Collin Faulkner*, born 23 June 1985; b. *Leah Rose*, born 17 March 1987.

    iii.   Brent Alan Faulkner, born 30 October 1955. He married, on 4 October 1986, Michel Devon Henry.

M226   Hubert Duane Faulkner, born 25 March 1928 in Centralia, Illinois, lives in Sandoval, Illinois.

He married, as his first wife, in 1955 in Marion County, Illinois, Barbara Ann Needham.

He married, as his second wife, Pat Endicott.

Issue of Hubert Duane and Barbara Ann (Needham) Faulkner:[616]

    i.   Norman Duane Faulkner, born 23 May 1956, lives in Wamac, Illinois, where he is chief of police. He married, in 1975 in Marion County, Illinois, Terry Lee Brothers.

M279 ii.   Glen Edward Faulkner, born 8 January 1958.

    iii.   David Bruce Faulkner, born 27 February 1959.

    iv.   Sherry Lynn Faulkner, born 13 October 1960. She married, in 1976, John Alvin Vaughn, but divorced.

    v.   Lori Jean Faulkner, born 18 November 1962.

Issue of Hubert Duane and Pat (Endicott) Faulkner:

vi.   Steven Lyn Faulkner, born 25 June 1968, lives in Seminole, Florida.

M227   Sharon LeRoy Faulkner, born 18 January 1938, lives in Marshall, Texas.

He married Joyce ——.

Issue of Sharon LeRoy and Joyce Faulkner:

i.   Darrin Faulkner.

ii.   Melinda Faulkner.

iii.   Tamela Faulkner.

M228   Joseph Douglass Faulkner, born 2 November 1941 in Etowah, Arkansas, lives in Mount Clemens, Michigan.

He married, on 4 September 1965 in Presque Isle, Michigan, Ann Louise Freiberg, daughter of Edwin Herman and Celia Marie (Cowham) Freiberg, born 10 March 1941 Wyandotte, Michigan.

He was in the U. S. Army and works for Michigan Rivet; Ann is a teacher and secretary and has compiled many of the genealogies in this section.

Issue of Joseph Douglass and Ann Louise (Freiberg) Faulkner:

i.   Joseph Edwin Faulkner, born 5 May 1966.

ii.   James Douglass Faulkner, born 8 July 1967.

M229   Paul Morris Faulkner, born 23 August 1945 in Etowah, Arkansas, lives in Huntington Woods, Michigan.

He married, as his first wife, on 26 October 1966 in Pontiac, Michigan, Leslie Barbara Schlafer, daughter of Milton and Evelyn (Novitz) Schlafer, born 20 August 1945 in Detroit, Michigan.

Issue of Paul Morris and Leslie Barbara (Schlafer) Faulkner:

i.   Robert Shayle Faulkner, born 26 September 1974.

ii.   Corey David Faulkner, born 13 February 1977.

iii.   Jonathan Adam Faulkner, born 13 February 1977.

M230   James Byron Faulkner, born 1 September 1913 in Aurora, Missouri, died 15 February 1983 in Oklahoma City, Oklahoma, was buried in Chapel Hill Cemetery.

He married, as his first wife, Sylvia Rose Coulter, born 24 April 1914, died 7 March 1987 in Oklahoma City, Oklahoma. They divorced and she later married —— Pribyi.

He married, as his second wife, Captola Roberts.

He married, as his third wife, Fleta Ivone Miles.

He worked as a crane operator for a steel manufacturing company and served in the U.S. Navy during World War II.

Issue of James Byron and Sylvia Rose (Coulter) Faulkner:

M280 i.   George Byran Faulkner, born 27 March 1939.

ii.   Delbert Eugene Faulkner, born 24 July 1940.

    iii.   Tommie Jay Faulkner, born 8 January 1943. He works as a home builder.

Issue of James Byron and Fleta Ivone (Miles) Faulkner:

    iv.   Leslie Hilliard Faulkner, born 12 April 1947.

M231 Walter Richard Faulkner, born 21 September 1919 in Oklahoma City, Oklahoma, died 29 April 1976 in Lawton, Oklahoma, was buried in Post Cemetery, Fort Sill, Oklahoma.

He married, as his first wife, on 21 September 1938, in Oklahoma City, Oklahoma, Marie Owczarzak, born 14 July 1921 in Harrah, Oklahoma. They later divorced.

He married, as his second wife, Fuji Tonegawa, born 22 December 1928 in Tokyo, Japan, died 8 December 1979 in Lawton, Oklahoma, buried in the Post Cemetery, Fort Sill.

He was a career soldier, serving as a sergeant first class in the U.S. Army in World War II and the Korean War.

Issue of Walter Richard and Marie (Owczarzak) Faulkner:

M281 i.   James Richard Faulkner, born 14 August 1939.

M282 ii.   Buddy Joe Faulkner, born 6 November 1940.

Issue of Walter Richard and Fuji (Tonegawa) Faulkner:

    iii.   Marjorie Ann Faulkner, born 4 July 1955 in Japan. She married, on 1 June 1975, in Lawton, Oklahoma, Randy Mitchell Tardiff, and has issue, surname *Tardiff*: a. *Melissa Lynn*, born 20 September 1977; b. *Michelle Marie*, born 9 September 1980; c. *Misty Nichole*, born 27 October 1984.

    iv.   Joyce Norma Faulkner, born 17 April 1958 in El Paso, Texas. She married, on 28 August 1986, Rickey Don Bolles, born 3 November 1956 in Wichita Falls, Texas, and has issue, surname *Bolles*: a. *Ashley Nicole*, born 1 June 1988; b. *Andrea Somer*, born 11 July 1990.

M232 Raymond Dean Faulkner, born 10 December 1921 in Oklahoma City, Oklahoma, lives in Oklahoma City, Oklahoma.

He married on 7 June 1945, in Oklahoma City, Oklahoma, Mava Elois Yoachum, daughter of Alva Marrion and Iva May (McCann) Yoachum, born 13 October 1926 in Moore, Oklahoma.

He worked as a supervisor in a commercial warehouse and as a computer programmer analyst. During World War II, he served as a private first class in the Third Marine Division in action in the Pacific Theater and was awarded the Purple Heart and Bronze Star medals.

Issue of Raymond Dean and Mava Elois (Yoachum) Faulkner:

    i.   Barbara Jeanette Faulkner, born 24 April 1946, died 22 April 1966 in Stillwater, Oklahoma, buried in Resthaven Cemetery, Cleveland County, Oklahoma.

    ii.   son, born 31 January 1949, died 31 January 1949 in Oklahoma City, Oklahoma, buried in Sunny Lane Cemetery.

M283 iii. Chris Allen Faulkner, born 25 March 1951.

    iv.   Donald Ray Faulkner, born 17 November 1964, lives in Scottsdale, Arizona.

He is an accountant.

M233 Charles Howard Faulkner, born 13 June 1924 in Oklahoma City, Oklahoma, lives in Edmond, Oklahoma.

He married, as his first wife, Alice Mae Scott Brown. They divorced.

He married, as his second wife, on 10 November 1952, in Oklahoma City, Oklahoma, Anna Zichanowich, born 1 October 1926 in Minsk, Belarus.

He worked as a supervisor in a candy manufacturing company.

Issue of Charles Howard and Alice Mae (Scott) Faulkner:

    i.   Charlette Ann Faulkner, born 2 October 1945.

    ii. Billy Howard Faulkner, born 2 October 1950.

Issue of Charles Howard and Anna (Zichanowich) Faulkner:

    iii. Gregory Howard Faulkner, born 18 April 1958, lives in Oklahoma City, Oklahoma. He married, on 17 September 1983, in Oklahoma City, Oklahoma, Cynthia Marie Earls, born 14 January 1959 in Oklahoma City, Oklahoma. He works as a mail carrier.

M234 Cecil Avery Faulkner, born 26 April 1926 in Oklahoma City, Oklahoma, lives in Oklahoma City, Oklahoma.

He married, on 28 April 1951, in Oklahoma City, Oklahoma, Geneal Rosa Lumley, born 22 July 1926 in Cashion, Kingfisher County, Oklahoma. By her first husband, Preston Wilford Barber, she had a daughter, Vivian Lee Barber, born 26 July 1948, whom Cecil adopted.

He worked as a computer console operator for the Oklahoma Department of Highways.

Issue of Cecil Avery and Geneal Rosa (Lumley) Faulkner, born in Oklahoma City, Oklahoma:

M284 i.   Cecil David Faulkner, born 11 May 1952.

    ii. son Faulkner, born 11 October 1957, died 11 October 1957 in Oklahoma City, Oklahoma.

    iii. Angela Gaylene Faulkner, born 25 June 1960. She married, as her first husband, on 17 November 1976, in Oklahoma City, Oklahoma, Walter Bickerstaff, and had issue, surname *Bickerstaff*: a. *Angel Marie*, born 22 November 1977, married, 1 May 1993, Thomas Newton Ragsdale; b. *Bonnie Jean*, born 5 August 1979; c. *John Thomas*, born 20 November 1981. She married, as her second husband, Willis Thomas Moore, and has issue, surname *Moore*: d. *Willis Thomas*, born 30 September 1985. Her second marriage ended in divorce.

    iv. Valerie Ann Faulkner, born 30 August 1964. She married, on 16 September 1983, in Oklahoma City, Oklahoma, Bobby Dale Griffey, born 23 April 1959 in Wichita, Kansas, and has issue, surname *Griffey*: a. *Lea Ann*, born 20 January 1984.

M235 James Bruce Faulkner, born 4 December 1944 in Weiser, Idaho, died 2 October 1964.

Issue of James Bruce Faulkner:

i. Gina Marie Faulkner, born 31 May 1965.

M236 Ivan Ray Faulkner, born 22 March 1940 in Pueblo, Colorado, lives near Fayetteville, Arkansas.

He married, on 21 May 1960, in Lincoln, Arkansas, Judith Ann Reed, born 26 September 1942 in Clovis, New Mexico.

He is an engineer; she is a teacher.

Issue of Ivan Ray and Judith Ann (Reed) Faulkner, born in Fayetteville, Arkansas (they also have an adopted daughter Veda Elizabeth, born 21 September 1966 in Idaho Falls, Idaho):[617]

i. Emery Joe Faulkner, born 23 September 1965. He married, on 30 December 1988, Young Young Kim.

M237 Conley Ottis Faulkner, born 1 May 1935 in Huntsville, Arkansas, lives in Huntsville, Arkansas.

He married, on 7 April 1956, at Cobb Creek, Arkansas, Betty Lou Gardner, born 8 January 1938 in Wesley, Arkansas.

Issue of Conley Ottis and Betty Lou (Gardner) Faulkner:[618]

i. Judy Ann Faulkner, born 9 May 1958. She married, on 26 August 1978, Tim Seigal.

ii. Connie Faye Faulkner, born 22 July 1959. She married, on 15 April 1987, Loyd Bennett.

M238 Leary Alan Faulkner, born 1 February 1947 in Fayetteville, Arkansas, lives in Fayetteville.

He married Terri Muir, born in California, but divorced in 1981.

He works as a lineman for American Air Filter Company.

Issue of Leary Alan and Terri (Muir) Faulkner:[619]

i. David Faulkner, born 19 September 1976.

ii. Mark Faulkner, born 26 July 1978.

M239 Glendon Dwight Faulkner, born 29 May 1943 in Wesley, Arkansas, lives in Prairie Grove, Arkansas.

He married, on 1 July 1966, at Wesley, Arkansas, Judy Rhea Howard, born 25 January 1948 at Rudd, Arkansas.

He is an inspector for the Arkansas Highway Department and a Freewill Baptist minister.

Issue of Glendon Dwight and Judy Rhea (Howard) Faulkner:[620]

i. Angela Lynn Faulkner, born 14 January 1967.

ii. Stephen Glen Faulkner, born 24 December 1970.

iii. Anthony Dwight Faulkner, born 7 June 1977.

M240 Laymon Faulkner, born 1 April 1951 in Fayetteville, Arkansas, lives in Springdale, Arkansas.

He married, as his first wife, on 12 June 1971, at Wesley, Arkansas, Betty Ann Lossing, born 20 March 1955.

He married, as his second wife, Linda Arlene Ivey, daughter of Clarence Edward and Phoenix (Skaggs) Ivey and former wife of Ricky Joe Smith.

He is a sheet metal worker.

Issue of Laymon and Betty Ann (Lossing) Faulkner:[621]

    i.   Brian Lee Faulkner, born 3 June 1973.

    ii.   Tina Rene Faulkner, born 26 June 1979.

M241 **David Ray Faulkner**, born 8 July 1961 in Huntsville, Arkansas, lives in Fayetteville, Arkansas.

He married, as his first wife, Angela Hernandez. They divorced.

He married, as his second wife, on 30 March 1985, in Fayetteville, Arkansas, Wanaleta Falkner, born 16 February 1957 in Fayetteville, Arkansas.

He manages a store.

Issue of David Ray and Angela (Hernandez) Faulkner:

    i.   Brent Allen Faulkner, born 15 October 1979.

    ii.   Brenda Kristina Faulkner, born 4 November 1983.

Issue of David Ray and Wanaleta (Falkner) Faulkner:[622]

    iii.   Talley Ray Faulkner, born 7 November 1985.

    iv.   Shawna Latrelle Faulkner, born 17 January 1991.

M242 **Johnnie Lee Faulkner**, born 12 July 1961 in Huntsville, Arkansas, lives in Huntsville, Arkansas.

He married Linnette Middleton, daughter of Bob and Lorene (Carter) Middleton, born April 1963.

Issue of Johnnie Lee and Linnette (Middleton) Faulkner:[623]

    i.   Shelly Lynn Faulkner, born 27 March 1985.

    ii.   Cory Michael Faulkner, born 5 November 1987.

M243 **Fredric Blake Faulkner**, born 20 February 1965 in Eagle, Colorado, lives in Rapid City, South Dakota.

He married, as his first wife, on 27 July 1986, Tammy Eddings.

He married, as his second wife, on 18 July 1992, in Rapid City, South Dakota, Gina Ketchum.

Issue of Fredric Blake and Gina (Ketchum) Faulkner:

    i.   Taylor Lynn Faulkner, born 26 December 1993.

M244 **George Garilee Faulkner**, born 29 September 1948 in Independence, Missouri, lives in Independence, Missouri.

He married, on 21 June 1968, in Independence, Missouri, Candice Louise Upham, daughter of Homer L. and Alice Grace (Teitz) Upham, born 27 September 1952 in Boicourt, Linn County, Kansas.

He works as a truck driver.

Issue of George Garilee and Candice Louise (Upham) Faulkner:

    i.   Tina Louise Faulkner, born 30 June 1969, lives in Independence, Missouri. She has issue, surname *Faulkner*: a. *Nichelle Louise*, born 27 January 1990.

    ii.   Vance Garilee Faulkner, born 3 July 1974.

M245 **Stanley Monroe Faulkner**, born 10 July 1942 in Indianapolis, Indiana, lives in Greenfield, Indiana.

He married, on 9 October 1965, in Indianapolis, Indiana, Christy Ann Burleson, daughter of Howard C. and Mildred R. (Kimbler) Burleson, born 9 December 1945 in Indianapolis, Indiana.

Issue of Stanley Monroe and Christy Ann (Burleson) Faulkner:[624]

    i.   Michael Todd Faulkner, born 12 May 1967, lives in Columbus, Ohio.

    ii.   Scott Christopher Faulkner, born 28 September 1970.

M246 **Charles Lee Faulkner**, born 14 January 1947 in Marion County, Indiana, lives in Indianapolis, Indiana.

He married, on 4 November 1966 in Marion County, Indiana, Stephanie Jo Farmer, born 27 January 1947 in Putnam County, Indiana.

He is an officer in the Indianapolis Police Department, assigned to its horse patrol.

Issue of Charles Lee and Stephanie Jo (Farmer) Faulkner:[625]

    i.   Brian Wesley Faulkner, born 29 October 1968.

    ii.   Craig Allen Faulkner, born 30 May 1971.

M247 **John David Faulkner**, born 5 September 1940 in Lebanon, Indiana, lives in Clermont, Indiana.

He married, on 4 April 1960, in Pike Township, Marion County, Indiana, Sara R. Wooten, born 25 September 1939 in Pike Township, Marion County, Indiana. They divorced, and she married Charles L. Bell.

Issue of John David and Sara R. (Wooten) Faulkner:[626]

M285 i.   Kenneth Dean Faulkner, born 29 October 1960.

    ii.   Alan Lee Faulkner, born 7 April 1969.

    iii. John Darrin Faulkner, born 18 January 1972.

M248 **Chester Lyle (Butch) Faulkner**, born 15 August 1954, lives in San Diego, California.

He married Caroline A. Bautista, born 3 January 1954.

He is in the U.S. Navy.

Issue of Chester Lyle and Caroline A. (Bautista) Faulkner:

    i.   David Allen Faulkner, born 1 February 1978.

    ii.   Charles Corrington Faulkner, born 30 July 1979.

iii.   Caroline Angelica Faulkner, born 2 October 1981.

M249   Robert LeRoy Faulkner, born 9 August 1954 in Arnolds Park, Iowa, lives in Arnolds Park, Iowa.
He married Debra Wolterman, born 15 August 1954.
Issue of Robert LeRoy and Debra (Wolterman) Faulkner:

i.   Heather M. Faulkner, born 26 June 1975.
ii.   Amber L. Faulkner, born 5 December 1980.

M250   David Dean Faulkner, born 28 May 1950 in Cherokee, Iowa, lives in Onalaska, Wisconsin.
He married, on 20 January 1973, in Rockwell, Iowa, Teresa Jean Mabie, born 3 July 1951 in Marshalltown, Iowa.   She is a curriculum specialist at the University of Wisconsin-LaCrosse.
He has lived in Tipton, Iowa, and Macomb, Illinois, and has worked as a teacher of vocational education.   He is currently in the Academic Computing Center of the University of Wisconsin-LaCrosse.
Issue of David Dean and Teresa Jean (Mabie) Faulkner, born in Cedar Rapids, Iowa:

i.   Jaime Ann Faulkner, born 2 March 1977.
ii.   Jennie Lynn Faulkner, born 1 March 1982.
iii.   Julie Renee Faulkner, born 27 September 1983.

M251   Thomas Joseph Faulkner, born 27 September 1957, lives in Springfield, Illinois.
He married, on 21 June 1986, in Bronson, Michigan, Trudy Kay Szafranski, born 1 December 1957.
Issue of Thomas Joseph Faulkner, born out of wedlock:

i.   Aaron Joseph Faulkner, born 2 October 1978.

Issue of Thomas Joseph and Trudy Kay (Szafranski) Faulkner:

ii.   Trisha Kay Faulkner.

M252   Michael R. Faulkner, born 3 August 1955.
He married Dina ——.
Issue of Michael R. and Dina Faulkner:

i.   Bradley D. Faulkner, born 24 February 1980.

M253   William Michael Faulkner, born 1937, lives in Slidell, Louisiana.
He married Rita May Zeringue, born 1937.
Issue of William Michael and Rita May (Zeringue) Faulkner:

    i.   Steven Michael Faulkner, born 1961.
    ii.   Sharon Kelly Faulkner, born 1963.
   iii.   Saundra Lynn Faulkner, born 1964.
   iv.   Benjamin Wilson Faulkner, born 1967.
    v.   Angela Marie Faulkner, born 1972.
   vi.   Heather Michelle Faulkner, born 1982.

M254 **Patrick Joseph Faulkner**, born 1942, lives in Kenner, Louisiana. He married Emmajean Bremmermann, born 1945.
Issue of Patrick Joseph and Emmajean (Bremmermann) Faulkner:

    i.   Keith Patrick Faulkner, born 1965.
    ii.   Vickie Lynn Faulkner, born 1972.

M255 **Fred Lee Faulkner**, born 7 October 1914, died 24 August 1986 in Elmhurst, Illinois, was buried in Mount Emblem Cemetery.
    He married, on 12 February 1939 or 1940, in Oak Park, Illinois, Alice Esther Rennels, born 12 May 1913 in Canada, lives in Batavia, Illinois. She was from Park Falls, Wisconsin.
    He served in the Pacific Theater during World War II. He worked as a research technician for Armour Foods and lived in Lombard, Illinois for many years. They lived in Arizona from 1974 to 1981.
    Issue of Fred Lee and Alice Esther (Rennels) Faulkner:

M286 i.   Lee Rennels Faulkner, born 27 October 1942.

M256 **Donald Faulkner**, born 12 February 1939 in Springfield, Illinois, lives in Springfield, Illinois.
    He married Vicky Hazlett.
    Issue of Donald and Vicky (Hazlett) Faulkner:[627]

    i.   David Faulkner, born 24 August 1964.

M257 **Walter Leroy Faulkner**, born 31 December 1940 in Springfield, Illinois, lives in Springfield, Illinois.
    He married Carol Kamees.
    Issue of Walter Leroy and Carol (Kamees) Faulkner:

    i.   Todd Faulkner, born 12 May 1964.

M258 **Ronald George Faulkner**, born 12 August 1943 in Springfield, Illinois, lives in Springfield, Illinois.
    He married Lynda Cox.
    Issue of Ronald George and Lynda (Cox) Faulkner:

    i.   Ronda Faulkner, born 2 November 1965.
    ii.   Aaron Faulkner, born 3 June 1968.

M259 James Richman Faulkner, born 13 September 1944 in Springfield, Illinois, lives in Springfield, Illinois.

He married Carolin Easton.

Issue of James Richman and Carolin (Easton) Faulkner:

  i.   Nicholas Faulkner, born 24 July 1971.
  ii. Jacob Faulkner, born 21 December 1973.

M260 Franklin Faulkner, born 17 May 1931 in Baltimore, Maryland, lives in Huntsville, Alabama.

He married Shirley Roden.

In 1973, he lived in New Castle, Delaware.

Issue of Franklin and Shirley (Roden) Faulkner:

  i.   Amy Faulkner.
  ii. Eric Faulkner, born 14 March 1962 in Washington, D.C.

M261 William E. Faulkner, born 10 November 1948 in Centralia, Illinois, lives in Lake Mary, Florida.

He married, on 26 February 1971, in Chicago, Illinois, Catherine A. Broten, born 21 September 1951 in Chicago, Illinois.

He moved from Centralia to Sanford, Florida, in 1978, where he works as a respiratory therapist. In 1990 the family moved to Lake Mary.

Issue of William E. and Catherine A. (Broten) Faulkner:

  i.   Gregory James Faulkner, born 31 July 1972.
  ii.   Laurie Ann Faulkner, born 20 June 1974.
  iii. Michael Eugene Faulkner, born 11 June 1975.
  iv.   Christopher Allen Faulkner, born 21 July 1977.

M262 Lowell Roger Faulkner, born 28 October 1951 in Brookfield, Missouri, lives in Springfield, Missouri.

He married Nancy Ashton, born 1 July 1951.

Issue of Lowell Roger and Nancy (Ashton) Faulkner:[028]

  i.   Johnny Roger Faulkner, born 22 November 1970.
  ii.   Amy Lee Faulkner, born 30 October 1972.
  iii. Becky Lee Faulkner, born 24 October 1976.
  iv.   Ricky Roger Faulkner, born 28 March 1978.
  v.   Andy Roger Faulkner, born 3 December 1979.
  vi.   Katy Lee Faulkner, born 6 November 1980.

M263 Guy Lawrence Faulkner, born 26 October 1958 in Brookfield, Missouri, lives in Lees Summit, Missouri.

He married, as his first wife, on 10 December 1977, in Chillicothe, Missouri, Candace Marie Jones. They later divorced.

He married, as his second wife, Nanci Meyers.
He works as a tool and die maker.
Issue of Guy Lawrence and Candace Marie (Jones) Faulkner, born in Brookfield, Missouri:

    i.   George Lawrence Faulkner, born 12 July 1978.

Issue of Guy Lawrence and Nanci (Meyers) Faulkner, born in Kansas City, Missouri:

    ii.   Guy Charles Faulkner, born 22 July 1982.
    iii.   Jimi Marshal Faulkner, born 14 October 1984.
    iv.   Alyssa Karin Faulkner, born 11 October 1987.

M264 **Frank David Faulkner**, born 14 July 1943 in Ann Arbor, Michigan, lives in Ukiah, California.
He married Cynthia Llanos.
Issue of Frank David and Cynthia (Llanos) Faulkner:

    i.   Joaquin Faulkner.

M265 **William Marion Faulkner**, born 26 April 1951 in Annapolis, Maryland, lives in Carmel, California.
He married Norma Linda Nava.
Issue of William Marion and Norma Linda (Nava) Faulkner:

    i.   Deanna Faulkner, born 13 November 1984.
    ii.   Marianne Faulkner, born 15 June 1987.

M266 **Gregory Lee Faulkner** lives in Severy, Kansas. He has the following children:

    i.   Christopher Faulkner, born 4 July 1971.
    ii.   Polly Faulkner, born 7 January 1974.

M267 **George Arthur Faulkner**, born 19 June 1947 in Gainesville, Texas, lives in Petaluma, California.
He married Diana Lawson, daughter of Doyle and Billy Lawson, born 30 July 1948.
Issue of George Arthur and Diana (Lawson) Faulkner:

    i.   Darrin Faulkner, born 29 June 1972.
    ii.   Matthew Faulkner, born 1 January 1978, died 1978.

M268 **James David Faulkner**, born 14 January 1950 in Gainesville, Texas, lives in Wichita Falls, Texas.
He married, on 3 March 1975, in Wichita Falls, Texas, Betty Louella Carlisle, daughter of Willie Forest and Dora Louise (Culverhouse) Carlisle,

born 10 July 1945 in Bowie, Texas.

Issue of James David and Betty Louella (Carlisle) Faulkner:

    i.   David Scott Faulkner, born 31 August 1975.

M269   **Robert Edward Faulkner**, born 1 June 1953 in Wichita Falls, Texas, lives in Wichita Falls, Texas.

He married, on 19 July 1974, Patricia Diane Howard, born 27 January 1956 in Bermuda.

Issue of Robert Edward and Patricia Diane (Howard) Faulkner:

    i.   Julie Diane Faulkner, born 25 January 1977.
    ii.   Robert Eugene Faulkner, born 4 January 1981.

M270   **James Delbert Faulkner**, born 2 November 1950 in Glasgow, Kentucky, lives in Jefferson County, Kentucky.

He married, as his first wife, Connie Lindsey.

He married, as his second wife, on 5 April 1974, in Jefferson County, Kentucky, Judith A. Ernst. They were divorced 17 April 1990.

He married, as his third wife, on 8 February 1992, in Oldham County, Kentucky, Dawn M. Shelburne.

Issue of James Delbert and Connie (Lindsey) Faulkner:

    i.   April Dawn Faulkner, born and died 8 April 1969, buried in Neals Chapel Cemetery, Barren County, Kentucky.

Issue of James Delbert and Judith A. (Ernst) Faulkner:

    ii.   Sarah Faulkner.
    iii. Kami Faulkner.

M271   **Danny Faulkner**, born 29 November 1950 in Barren County, Kentucky, lives in Hopkinsville, Kentucky.

He married Judy ——.

Issue of Danny Faulkner:

    i.   Jason Faulkner, born 9 September 1975.

M272   **Don W. Faulkner** lives in Washington, Oklahoma.

Issue of Don W. Faulkner:[629]

    i.   Don W. Faulkner, living in 1986 in Norman, Oklahoma.

M273   **Scott Richard Faulkner**, born 30 August 1950 in Des Moines, Iowa, lives in Ankeny, Iowa.

He married, on 4 July 1989, Leslie Ball.

He is a veterinarian.

Issue of Scott Richard Faulkner and Becky Hunnell:

    i.   Andrew Caleb Faulkner, born 23 September 1985.

M274 **Philip Eugene Faulkner**, born 19 February 1940 in Mount Vernon, Illinois, lives in Emporia, Kansas.
    He married, as his first wife, on 1 October 1959, Anita Beck.
    He married, as his second wife, on 4 June 1983, Jennie Lou Benton.
    He married, as his third wife, on 25 August 1988, Bernadine ——.
    Issue of Philip Eugene and Anita (Beck) Faulkner:

    i.   Sandra Kay Faulkner, born 18 February 1961.

Issue of Philip Eugene and Bernadine Faulkner:

    ii.   Evan Robert Faulkner, born 17 March 1989.

M275 **Robert Gary Faulkner**, born 25 February 1956 in Dallas, Texas, lives in Cedar Hill, Texas.
    He married, on 22 November 1974, Linda Gail ——.
    Issue of Robert Gary and Linda Gail Faulkner:

    i.   Curtis Lee Faulkner, born 3 August 1976.
    ii.   Daniel Wayne Faulkner, born 17 October 1983.
    iii.   daughter.
    iv.   daughter.

M276 **Richard Warren Faulkner**, born 15 November 1959 in Dallas, Texas, lives in Dallas.
    He married, in April 1983, —— ——. They later divorced.
    Issue of Richard Warren Faulkner:

    i.   Matthew Warren Faulkner, born 6 March 1986.

M277 **Randy Thomas Faulkner**, born 8 January 1962 in Dallas, Texas, lives in Lancaster, Texas.
    He married, on 13 June 1981, Mona ——.
    Issue of Randy Thomas and Mona Faulkner:

    i.   daughter.

M278 **Arnold K. Faulkner**, born 18 December 1936 in Benson, Illinois, lives in Canton, Illinois.
    He married Edna ——.
    Issue of Arnold K. Faulkner:

    i.   Scott Faulkner.
    ii.   Brian Faulkner.

M279 **Glen Edward Faulkner**, born 8 January 1958 in Centralia, Illinois, lives in San Francisco, California.

He married and divorced.

Issue of Glen Edward Faulkner:

    i.   Zachary Faulkner.

M280 **George Byran Faulkner**, born 27 March 1939 in Oklahoma City, Oklahoma, lives in Oklahoma City, Oklahoma.

He married, on 8 July 1961, in Oklahoma City, Oklahoma, Dottie Dee Swadley, born 16 December 1942 in Checotah, Oklahoma.

He works as a diesel mechanic.

Issue of George Byran and Dottie Dee (Swadley) Faulkner:

    i.   Gary Byran Faulkner, born 24 August 1962.

M281 **James Richard Faulkner**, born 14 August 1939 in Oklahoma City, Oklahoma, lives in Oklahoma City, Oklahoma.

He married, on 26 May 1961, in Enid, Oklahoma, Sharon Kay Erickson, born 13 June 1942 in Waukomis, Oklahoma.

He was a career U.S. Air Force officer, retiring as colonel. He now a civilian flight trainer for the Air Force.

Issue of James Richard and Sharon Kay (Erickson) Faulkner:

    i.   Eric Todd Faulkner, born 13 August 1966 in Altus, Oklahoma.

    ii. Jayme Jo Faulkner [daughter], born 22 January 1971 in Big Springs, Texas.

M282 **Buddy Joe Faulkner**, born 6 November 1940 in Oklahoma City, Oklahoma, died 20 October 1970.

He married, on 24 June 1964, in Enid, Oklahoma, Toni Gau.

Issue of Buddy Joe and Toni (Gau) Faulkner:

    i.   Curt James Faulkner.

    ii. Julie Faulkner.

M283 **Chris Allen Faulkner**, born 25 March 1951 in Oklahoma City, Oklahoma, lives in Dallas, Texas.

He married, as his first wife, on 13 August 1971, in Oklahoma City, Oklahoma, Diana Ruth Semrad, born 23 August 1951 in Oklahoma City, Oklahoma. They divorced.

He married, as his second wife, on 4 January 1980, in Dallas, Texas, Mary Ann (Peak) Nichols, born 26 July 1948 in Oklahoma City, Oklahoma.

He married, as his third wife, on 29 December 1990, in Dallas, Texas, Robin Maxine Standley, born 26 June 1962 in Fort Worth, Texas.

He is president and chief executive officer of the Lehndorff USA Companies.

Issue of Chris Allen and Robin Maxine (Standley) Faulkner:

    i.   Clayton Patrick Faulkner, born 23 March 1993.

M284   **Cecil David Faulkner**, born 11 May 1952 in Oklahoma City, Oklahoma.

He married, on 12 July 1974, in Oklahoma City, Oklahoma, Vickie Marie Phillips, born 24 January 1955. They later divorced.

He works as a mailer for the U.S. Federal Reserve Bank.

Issue of Cecil David and Vickie Marie (Phillips) Faulkner:

    i.   Staci Marie Faulkner, born 17 February 1975 in Moore, Oklahoma.
    ii.   Misti Dawn Faulkner, born 12 July 1977 in Moore, Oklahoma.
    iii. Crystal Kay Faulkner, born 4 October 1978 in Oklahoma City, Oklahoma.

M285   **Kenneth Dean Faulkner**, born 29 October 1960 in Lebanon, Indiana, lives in Edwards, California.

He married, in August 1982 in Okinawa, Japan, Tammy Baker.

Issue of Kenneth Dean and Tammy (Baker) Faulkner:

    i.   Brandon Robert Faulkner, born 21 February 1984.
    ii.   Trisha Faulkner, born 21 January 1987.

M286   **Lee Rennels Faulkner**, born 27 October 1942 in Illinois, lives in Geneva, Illinois.

He married, on 2 June 1967, B. Janice Miller, born 29 April 1942 in Chicago, Illinois, lives in Geneva, Illinois.

He is a residential designer and contractor with his own business and Janice is a registered nurse and educator.

Issue of Lee Rennels and B. Janice (Miller) Faulkner:

    i.   Andrew Miller Faulkner, born 12 September 1969 in Geneva, Illinois, died there 14 August 1986.
    ii.   Michael Adam Faulkner, born 31 August 1971 in Geneva, Illinois.

NOTES

[1] *Pennsylvania Archives*, 3rd ser., 22: 597.

[2] David Faulkner (M21) wrote in 1896 that the father of Alexander Faulkner died in Madison County, Kentucky. A memorandum, presumably copied about 1906 by Samuel D. Fitton or Mary W. (Falconer) Fitton from information written about 1855 sent by a daughter of Elizabeth (Smedley) (Falconer) Hetherington to Cyrus Falconer (N13), says that David, brother of Samuel, went to Kentucky.

[3] 1810 census, Washington Co., Ky., p. 322.

[4] *Pennsylvania Archives*, 3rd ser., 22: 383, 545, 597.

[5] Memorandum, about 1906, written by Samuel D. Fitton or Mary W. (Falconer) Fitton, probably copied from a note Cyrus Falconer (N13) received from a daughter of Elizabeth (Smedley) (Falconer) Hetherington.

[6] Pension file for Samuel Faulkner, National Archives.

[7] 1850 census, Ky., Green Co., p. 101.

[8] W. H. Perrin et al., *Kentucky: A History of the State* (Louisville: F. A. Battey, 1886), p. 801.

[9] Mrs. Glenn Burchett, "Bible Records of the Faulkner Family of Marion County, Kentucky," *Kentucky Ancestors* 4 (1966): 60.

[10] Charles Baldwin to Mabel G. (Faulkner) McKee, 21 November 1950, in possession of Anne G. Niles, Springfield, Mo. He assumed the grant was "south of the grant made to George Rogers Clark, taking in part of Virginia and Tennessee," a characteristically oral tradition, confusing geography.

[11] *Pennsylvania Archives*, 3rd ser., 24: 409.

[12] There was a David Faulkner in Hopewell, Virginia, after 1770, but this person was a Quaker, the son of Jesse Falkner, who moved from Bethlehem, Berks County, Pennsylvania.

[13] *Pennsylvania Archives*, 3rd ser., 21: 383, 601.

[14] Ibid., 3rd ser., 22: 383, 545, 597.

[15] Burchett, "Bible Records of the Faulkner Family of Marion County, Kentucky," *Kentucky Ancestors* 4 (1966): 60.

[16] Ibid. This is now West Virginia.

[17] Barren Co. (Ky.) Order Book, 5: 204.

[18] Barren Co. (Ky.) Marriage Bonds.

[19] Her parents, date of birth, and spouse are named in a pedigree, "Family of Conyers," Genealogical Society of Utah microfilm no. 1597807 .

[20] Burchett, "Bible Records of the Faulkner Family of Marion County, Kentucky," *Kentucky Ancestors* 4 (1966): 60.

[21] *Pennsylvania Archives*, 3rd ser., 22: 592.

[22] Ibid., 5th ser., 2: 1063, 1078.

[23] Ibid., 5th ser., 4: 134; *Minutes of the Supreme Executive Council of Pennsylvania*, vol. 14 (Harrisburg: Theo. Fenn & Co., 1853), p. 63.

[24] *Pennsylvania Archives*, 3rd ser., 22: 383, 545, 597.

[25] Robert Jones, interviewed by Lyman Draper, in Kentucky Papers of the Draper Collection, MS 13CC 151-165, in State Historical Society of Wisconsin.

[26] Washington Co. (Ky.) Deeds, B: 544.

[27] Ibid., D: 82.

[28] Barren Co. (Ky.) Deeds, B: 469.

[29] Ibid., D: 247.

[30] Barren Co. (Ky.) Wills, 3: 41.

[31] Barren Co. (Ky.) Inventories, : 345.

[32] David Faulkner Bible record, in possession of May K. (Mrs. James) Biggs, 520 E. Pine, Mason City, IL 62664, about 1975.

[33] Burchett, "Bible Records of the Faulkner Family of Marion County, Kentucky," *Kentucky Ancestors* 4 (1966): 60.

[34] David Faulkner to J. M. Faulkner, 30 Oct. 1883, in possession of Juanita Max.

[35] Ibid.

[36] Barren Co. (Ky.) Marriage Bonds. John Edwards (if this is the same person as John W. Edwards, born 1799, son of Alexander Edwards) married secondly, Polly Hardy, and moved to Madison County, Illinois. See Cyrus Edwards, *The Edwards Family of Barren County, Kentucky: History and Traditions* (Horse Cave, Ky.: the author, 1924), p. 87.

[37] James Rood Robertson, *Petitions of the Early Inhabitants of Kentucky*, Filson Club Publications, no. 27 (Louisville, Ky.: John P. Morton & Co., 1914), p. 145f., 202.

[38] Bourbon Co. (Ky.) Order Book, A: 383, 399.

[39] 1850 census, Green Co., Ky., p. 101.

[40] Green Co. (Ky.) Death Records; Wills, 3: 180-182.

[41] Brents-Standard-Wake v. David and Robert Forbis, Green Co. (Ky.) Circuit Court, no. 5519.

[42] W. C. Jillson, *The Kentucky Land Grants* (Louisville: Filson Club, 1925), p. 314.

[43] Green Co. (Ky.) Deeds, 8: 479.

[44] Ibid., 2: 43.

[45] Ibid., 4: 123.

[46] Ibid., p. 548.

[47] Barren Co. (Ky.) Deeds, D; 121; E: 519.

[48] Green Co. (Ky.) Order Book, 7: 165, 208.

[49] Green Co. (Ky.) tax list, 1842.

[50] David Faulkner to Gilbert Faulkner, 15 January 1832.

[51] He was probably the Thomas Faulkner, a black aged 47 in the 1880 census in Metcalfe County. Bub, son of Thos. and Everline Faulkner, born 4 March 1874, died 16 September 1890, was buried in the McGlasson Cemetery

in southwestern Green County. Green County birth records indicate that a slave of John Faulkner (M16) gave birth to a child on 3 October 1857.

[52] Green Co. (Ky.) Wills, 3: 180-182.

[53] Deposition of Warren Faulkner, Green Co. (Ky.) Circuit Court, no. 1175.

[54] Adair Co. (Ky.) Court Minute Book, D: 48, 154, 293, 420.

[55] Ibid., D: 40, 115, 161, 189.

[56] Grants South of Green River, Q: 32, cited in Jillson, *The Kentucky Land Grants*, p.548.

[57] Adair Co. (Ky.) Court Minute Book, E: 25; Adair Co. (Ky.) Will Book, C: 358.

[58] Barren Co. (Ky.) Order Book 4B: 543.

[59] Ibid., 4B: 464.

[60] Washington Co. (Ill.) Marriages, A: 25.

[61] David Faulkner to Gilbert Faulkner, 15 January 1832, typescript copy at Metcalfe County Library, Edmonton, Ky.

[62] 1860 census, Washington Co., Ill., p. 721.

[63] Warren Faulkner to Gilbert and James Faulkner, 16 Sept. 1841, original in possession of Juanita Max; information from Ann Faulkner.

[64] Jefferson Co. (Ill.) Marriages, 1: 29; 2: 12.

[65] J. H. G. Brinkerhoff, *Brinkerhoff's History of Marion County, Illinois* (Indianapolis: B. F. Bowen, 1909), p. 749.

[66] Perrin, *Kentucky: A History of the State*, p. 801.

[67] Martha Powell Reneau, *Marriage Bonds of Barren County, Kentucky 1799-1849* (n.p.: 1984).

[68] Perrin, *Kentucky: A History of the State*, p. 801.

[69] David Faulkner Bible record, owned by May K. (Tibbs) (Mrs. James) Biggs about 1975.

[70] Death certificate, in *Kentucky Register* 43 (1945): 211; the Bible record says 25 November 1855.

[71] Perrin, *Kentucky: A History of the State*, p. 801.

[72] Barren Co. (Ky.) Inventories, 6: 74.

[73] David Faulkner to Gilbert Faulkner, 21 July 1839, in possession of Juanita Max, information from Ann Faulkner.

[74] The David Faulkner Bible record proves the births of all except Mary and Nancy. The letter shows that there were two other daughters not named in the record.

[75] Eva Coe Peden and Gladys Benedict Wilson, *Little Barren Church (formerly Tramels Creek), Metcalfe County, Kentucky 1815-1849* (Glasgow, Ky.: 1976), pp. 5, 7, 10, 18.

[76] Ibid.

[77] 1850 census, Green Co., Ky., p. 152.

[78] 1860 census, Metcalfe Co., Ky., no. 457.

[79] Ruth Perkins and Judy Froggett, *Old Marriage Certificates: Box C, 1836-1861: Green County, Kentucky* (Greensburg, Ky.: Green County Library, 1984).

[80] Information from N. B. McCubbin, via Ann Faulkner.

[81] Barren Co. (Ky.) Marriage Bonds.

[82] See Elizabeth Dill Hartline, *A Jolliff Family History: with Rheas, Faulkners, Holstlaws, Alexanders* ([Anna, Ill.]: the author, 1982), pp. 23-39; 87-100.

[83] Barren Co. (Ky.) Deeds, I: 440; J: 408; K: 321; L: 176.

[84] Ibid., M: 181.

[85] John Reynolds, *The Pioneer History of Illinois*, 2nd ed. (Chicago: 1887), p. 265n.

[86] Illinois, Archives Division, Public domain sales land tract record listing.

[87] Tax receipt for 1851, in Washington Co. (Ill.) Circuit Court, Box 26.

[88] Washington Co. (Ill.) Circuit Court, Box 26.

[89] Reynolds, *Pioneer History of Illinois*, p. 265n.

[90] Date from his gravestone, in Grand Point Cemetery. Since the sketch in *The Pioneer History of Illinois* calls him son of John and Elizabeth and he was regarded as a full brother, he was obviously born illegitimate, but legitimized by marriage of the parents.

[91] Washington Co. (Ill.) Marriages, A: 3.

[92] Brunette Collier, Odessa, TX.

[93] Washington Co. (Ill.) Marriages, A: 13.

[94] Ibid., A: 47.

[95] Reynolds, *Pioneer History of Illinois*, p. 265n.

[96] Washington Co. (Ill.) Marriages, A: 29.

[97] 1880 census, Clinton Co., Ill., 5-84-27-5.

[98] Washington Co. (Ill.) Marriages, A: 35.

[99] Pension file of Jackson Trout, National Archives.

[100] Burchett, "Bible Records of the Faulkner Family of Marion County, Kentucky," *Kentucky Ancestors* 4 (1966): 59.

[101] Ibid.

[102] Ibid.

[103] 1870 census, Marion Co., Ky., p. 43.

[104] 1850 census, Barren Co., Ky., p. 439a.

[105] Barren Co. (Ky.) Circuit Court, Suit no. 2390; 1850 census, Barren Co., Ky., p. 439a.

[106] Peden, *Barren County, Kentucky, Cemetery Records*, p. 132.

[107] 1870 census, Barren Co., Ky., p. 634.

[108] Ann Faulkner.

[109] Arthur L. Keith, "The Harned Family," *New York Genealogical and Biographical Record* 61 (Jan. 1930): 33.

[110] *Portrait and Biographical Record of Clinton, Washington, Marion and Jefferson Counties, Illinois* (Chicago: Chapman, 1894), p. 239f.

[111] Peden and Wilson, *Little Barren Church (formerly Tramels Creek), Metcalfe County, Kentucky 1815-1849*, p.

[112] *Portrait and Biographical Record of Clinton, Washington, Marion and Jefferson Counties, Illinois*, p. 239f.

[113] Orange Co. (Ind.) Marriage Records, C-2: 157.

[114] Ibid., C-3: 207.

[115] 1860 census, Jefferson Co., Ill., p. 737.

[116] Ibid., p. 737.

[117] Orange Co. (Ind.) Marriage Records, C-4: 29.

[118] Testimony of Warren Faulkner, in John Faulkner estate, 1886, Green Co., Ky.

[119] James Young, Glasgow, Ky., to Ann Faulkner, 10 Jan. 1979.

[120] Morgan Co. (Ill.) Marriages, A: 6.

[121] 1880 census, Carroll Co., Ark., 2-226-1-5.

[122] *History of Macoupin County, Illinois*, p. 215; Cleora Faulkner wrote to me that James Otis Faulkner believed her name to be Walker, which may indicate that she was actually a widow of one of the Taber brothers.

[123] Ibid., p. 27; 1830 census, Macoupin Co., Ill., p. 214.

[124] James Young, Glasgow, KY, to Ann Faulkner.

[125] 1850 census, Taney Co., Mo., p. 351; 1860 census, Carroll Co., Ark., p. 815.

[126] 1860 census, Carroll Co., Ark., p. 819.

[127] 1870 census, Taney Co., Mo., p. 336.

[128] 1860 census, Carroll Co., Ark., p. 812.

[129] 1880 census, Denton Co., Tex., 10-108-60-29; 1910 census, Lincoln Co., Okla., 35-101-165.

[130] Cline and McHaffie, *The People's Guide...Directory of Boone County, Indiana* (Indianapolis: 1874), p. 382.

[131] Boone Co. (Ind.) Wills, 2: 38; 1850 census, Boone Co., Ind., p. 137.

[132] Boone Co. (Ind.) Marriage Record, C-2: 359.

[133] Ibid., C-3: 538.

[134] 1880 census, Boone Co., Ind., 14-130-32-46.

[135] Deposition of Warren Faulkner, Green Co. (Ky.) Circuit Court, no. 1175.

[136] Boone Co. (Ind.) Marriage Record, C-4: 21.

[137] 1880 census, Boone Co., Ind., 3-123-5-23; Boone Co. (Ind.) Marriage Records, WPA compilation.

[138] Authorization to appraise real estate, Washington Co. (Ill.) Circuit Court, file.

[139] Macoupin Co. (Ill.) Marriages, 1, no. 237.

[140] Washington Co. (Ill.) Marriages, A: 36.

[141] Ibid., A: 43.

[142] Ibid., B: 221.

[143] Illinois, Archives Division, Public Domain Sales Land Tract Record Listing.

[144] Ibid.

[145] 1850 census, Washington Co., Ill., p. 143; 1860 census, Washington Co., Ill., p. 726.; Washington Co. (Ill.) Circuit Court, drawer 25.

[146] Pension file (WC 117-348), National Archives.

[147] Washington Co. (Ill.) Marriages, C: 52.

[148] 1880 census, Washington Co., Ill., 55-126-6-32.

[149] Macoupin Co. (Ill.) Marriages, 5: 83.

[150] 1880 census, Macoupin Co., Ill., 38-119-26-13.

[151] 1860 census, Washington Co., Ill., p. 726.

[152] Illinois, Archives Division, Public Domain Sales Land Tract Record Listing.

[153] Pension file of Samuel Faulkner, National Archives.

[154] Washington Co. (Ill.) Marriages, A: 25.

[155] Information from David Surles, PO Box 684488, Austin, TX 78767; 1870 census, Jefferson Co., Ill., p. 406. He also cited *Heritage of Blanco County, Texas*.

[156] 1880 census, Washington Co., Ill., 55-126-2-8; 1900 census, Washington Co., Ill., 153-136-15-32.

[157] Green Co. (Ky.) Deeds, 31: 311.

[158] Frances Terry Ingmire, *Green County, Kentucky, Deaths* (St. Louis: Ingmire Publications, 1984), p. 10.

[159] "Slinker-Bishop Little Record Book," *Green County Review* 6 (July 1983): 40.

[160] Green Co. (Ky.) Deeds, 47: 590.

[161] 1850 census, Green Co., Ky., p. ; 1860 census, Green Co., Ky., p. 578.

[162] Green Co. (Ky.) Marriage Bonds, 1853-63: 48.

[163] Record in Jeffries file, Green County Library.

[164] Green Co. (Ky.) Marriage Bonds, 1854-64: 115.

[165] 1880 census, Green Co., Ky., 10-59-25-45; *Green County, Kentucky, Cemeteries*, 2: 92.

[166] Green Co. (Ky.) Marriage Bonds, 1868-71: 176.

[167] Frances Terry Ingmire, *Green County, Kentucky, Births* (St. Louis: Ingmire Publications, 1984), p. 63.

[168] 1900 census, White Co., Ill., 56-111-18-33.

[169] White Co. (Ill.) Register of Deaths, 1: 95. She was married, but her husband was not identified.

[170] 1860 census, Green Co., Ky., p. 578; 1870 census, Green Co., Ky., f. 475v.-476r.; 1880 census, Green Co., Ky., enum. dist. 59, sheet 25.

[171] Ingmire, *Green County, Kentucky, Births*.

[172] Green Co. (Ky.) Marriages, 1890-93, 594f.

[173] Information provided by Odiellia Curry, 1225 Charlie Rhea Rd., Greensburg, KY 42743.

[174] Ingmire, *Green County Births*.

[175] Green Co. (Ky.) Marriage Bonds, 1893-97: 134f.

[176] 1900 census, Green Co., Ky., 26-37-9-73.

[177] Green Co. (Ky.) Marriage Bonds, 1899-1903, 134.

[178] Ibid., 1879-82: 44f.

[179] LDS ordinance entry form by Floyd Dalton Erwin, 1610 Edgerton St., Goldsboro, NC 27530; Bible record once in possession of George Forbis, Sulphur Well, KY, is the source.

[180] Index to Kentucky Vital Records.

[181] Green Co. (Ky.) Marriages, 1893-97: 194f.

[182] Information provided by Odiellia Curry.

[183] White Co. (Ill.) Marriages, A: 285, no. 45.

[184] 1900 census, Saline Co., Ill., 143-77-3-42.

[185] Green Co. (Ky.) Deeds, 32: 578.

[186] Frances Terry Ingmire, *Green County, Kentucky, Deaths* (St. Louis: Ingmire Publications, 1984), p. 10.

[187] Adair Co. (Ky.) Marriage Returns, no. 1819.

[188] Green Co. (Ky.) Deeds, 24: 534.

[189] 1850 census, Green Co., Ky., p. 101; 1860 census, Metcalfe Co., p. 6.

[190] *Metcalfe County, Kentucky, Cemetery Records: Volume 1* (n.p.: Metcalfe County Historical Society, 1983).

[191] 1870 census, Metcalfe Co. (Ky.), f. 55v.; Metcalfe Co. (Ky.) Marriage Register.

[192] *Metcalfe County, Kentucky, Cemetery Records: Volume 1*.

[193] 1870 census, Metcalfe Co. (Ky.), f. 19r.;1880 census, Metcalfe Co., 22-195-9-6.

[194] Adair Co. (Ky.) Vital Records, typescript at Kentucky Historical Society.

[195] Ingmire, *Green County, Kentucky, Births*.

[196] 1900 census, Metcalfe Co., Ky., 57-57-10-20; 1910 census, Metcalfe Co., Ky., 68-70-138.

[197] Metcalfe Co. (Ky.) Vital Records, IGI.

[198] Query by Thomas E. Williams, 25 Ryswick Lane, Frankfort, KY 40601, in: *Kentucky Ancestors* 23 (Spr. 1988).

[199] Jefferson Co. (Ill.) Marriages, 2: 84.

[200] Illinois Executive Record, 3: 99; 5: 118, 291; 6: 177; 7: 307.

[201] Ibid., 4: 359.

[202] *Illinois State Journal,* 30 June 1853.

[203] Illinois, Archives Division, Public Domain Sales Land Tract Record Listing.

[204] 1850 census, Washington Co., Ill., p. 143; Washington Co. (Ill.) Circuit Court file, box 149.

[205] Jefferson Co. (Ill.) Marriages, 2: 85.

[206] Illinois, Adjutant General, *Adjutant General's Report,* 3: 312.

[207] 1850 census, Washington Co., Ill., p. 143; Washington Co. (Ill.) Circuit Court file, box 149.

[208] 1870 census, Washington Co., Ill., f. 321.

[209] Illinois, Veterans' Commission, *Honor Roll,* 1956. The graves in this cemetery must have been later transferred to Grand Point Cemetery, where members of the George family now lie.

[210] *Adjutant General's Report,* 3: 312.

[211] 1860 census, Washington Co., Ill., p. 726; Washington Co. (Ill.) Circuit Court file, box 149.

[212] Washington Co. (Ill.) Petition Record, B: 347. The children had a claim against the estate of Marcus G. Faulkner for $60; Belle Taylor was listed as a child of Marcus G. Faulkner in his estate file.

[213] 1870 census, Washington Co., Ill., p. 314.

[214] 1850 census, Macon Co., Mo., p. 129.

[215] Linn Co. (Mo.) Marriage Certificates, 2A: 59.

[216] 1850 census, Macon Co., Mo., p. 129; 1860 census, Linn Co., Mo., p. 623.

[217] 1870 census, Linn Co., Mo., f. 343; 1880 census, Linn Co., Mo., 3-178-17-30.

[218] Records of Eastern Cemetery.

[219] Jefferson Co. (Ky.) Marriage Register, 5: 105.

[220] 1870 census, Jefferson Co., Ky., p. 5.

[221] 1900 census, Jefferson Co., Ky., 34-1-7-37.

[222] Index to Kentucky death records; Jefferson Co. (Ky.) Inventory Book, 135: 451.

[223] Barren Co. (Ky.) Order Book, 7: 223.

[224] Cyrus Edwards, *The Edwards Family of Barren County, Kentucky,* p. 61.

[225] 1900 census, Barren Co., Ky., 3-18-10-20.

[226] Metcalfe Co. (Ky.) Deeds, 22: 136; Metcalfe Co. (Ky.) Inventories, 3: 345.

[227] Perrin, *Kentucky: A History of the State,* p. 801.

[228] Ibid., p. 801.

[229] Ibid., p. 801; David Faulkner Bible record.

[230] Clinton Co. (Ill.) Marriages, 1: 67.

[231] 1850 census, Washington Co., Ill., p. 141. The parentage for the children born after 1850 is not proven. In 1860, John B., Germina (or Jemima), Samuel, and Gilbert were listed in the household of Elizabeth (Jolliff) Faulkner. Mary Ann Faulkner was not listed there, but may have been missed by the census taker. In 1870, John B. Faulkner was a laborer on the farm of Lawrence Gigliart; Amanda was a servant in the household of Jeremiah Lister; while Germina and Gilbert (and Mary A., aged 55) lived with Elizabeth (Jolliff) Faulkner (p. 313r.). Although James Faulkner (son of Samuel Faulkner), a laborer on Elizabeth Faulkner's farm in 1860 and 1870, could be the father, he does not seem to have ever married, nor does he appear listed as the head of a subsidiary household.

[232] 1900 census, Livingston Co., Ill., 111-101-8-98.

[233] Washington Co. (Ill.) Marriages, A: 16.

[234] Ibid., A: 33.

[235] Illinois, Archives Division, Public Domain Sales Land Tract Record Listing.

[236] Illinois , Archives Division, Executive Record, 7: 60.

[237] 1850 census, Washington Co., Ill., p. 145.

[238] 1900 census, Carter Co., Mo., 15-36-13-57.

[239] *University of Illinois Alumni Directory,* 1918.

[240] Washington Co. (Ill.) Marriages, A: 18.

[241] Washington Co. Petition Record, A: 166.

[242] Illinois, Archives Division, Public Domain Sales Land Tract Record Listing.

[243] 1850 census, Washington Co., Ill., p. 144; 1860 census, Washington Co., Ill., p. 863; 1870 census, Washington Co., Ill., p. 319; Washington Co. (Ill.) Circuit Court file, box 71.

[244] Illinois, Adjutant General, *Adjutant General's Report,* 3: 249.

[245] LDS ordinance forms by Evelyn P. Anderson, 305 N. 600 East, Brigham City, UT 84302.

[246] 1910 census, San Bernardino Co., Cal., 75-108-217.

[247] Washington Co. (Ill.) Marriages, A: 28.

[248] Illinois, Archives Division, Public Domain Sales Land Tract Record Listing.

[249] 1850 census, Washington Co., Ill., p. 143; 1860 census, Washington Co., Ill., p. 721; 1870 census, Washington Co., Ill., p. 312.

[250] Claudia Meinzer Rentrop, R. 4, Box 5410, San Augustine, TX 75972.

[251] W. G. Richison, *Cemeteries of Jackson County, Illinois*, Vol. 3: *Elk Township* (Murphysboro, Ill.: Jackson County Historical Society, 1980), p. 7, which is the source for the other burials in Elkville.

[252] Hartline, *A Jolliff Family History*, p. 143.

[253] Jackson Co. (Ill.) Marriages, 2: 63.

[254] Ibid., 2: 111.

[255] Washington Co., (Ill.) Marriages, A: 35.

[256] 1860 census, Washington Co., Ill., p. 851; 1870 census, Washington Co., Ill., p. 328.

[255] Tina Rice and Wanda Houts, *Tombstone Inscriptions: Labette County, Kansas* (n.p.: 1981), 1: 198.

[258] Ibid.

[259] Ibid., 1: 46.

[260] DeWitt Co. (Ill.) Marriages, D: 1.

[261] Ibid., 1: 52.

[262] 1900 census, McLean Co., Ill., 107-119-3-86.

[263] Washington Co. (Ill.) Marriages, A: 51.

[264] Pension file (certificate no. 643,959), National Archives.

[265] *Centralia Sentinel*, 13 March 1873. The death date given in the newspaper is 7 March 1873, but the pension file says 6 March.

[266] Washington Co. (Ill.) Marriages, B: 145.

[267] Ibid., C: 108.

[268] Hartline, *A Jolliff Family History*, p. 98.

[269] Illinois, Archives Division, Public Domain Sales Land Tract Record Listing.

[270] Hartline, *A Jolliff Family History*, p. 153.

[271] Ibid., p. 154.

[272] 1900 census, Marion Co., Ill., 123-20-6-20.

[273] Typescript of Sam J. Boldrick's letter to the editor of the *Hardin County Enterprise*, 11 April 1941, Filson Club.

[274] Burchett, "Bible Records of the Faulkner Family of Marion County, Kentucky," *Kentucky Ancestors* 4 (1966): 59-61.

[275] Pension file, National Archives.

[276] Ibid.

[277] Ibid.

[278] Betty A. Butler Beeson, *Wayne County, Illinois, Death Records: 1886-1910* (Goff, Ill.: the author, 1984), p. 40.

[279] Jefferson Co. (Ill.) Deeds, L: 23, P: 99.

[280] Pension file for Robert Faulkner (certificate no. 502,468), National Archives; 1860 census, Jefferson Co., Ill., p. 232; 1880 census, Wayne Co., Ill., 56-140-35-7.

[281] Doris E. Witter Bland, *Wayne County, Illinois, Newspaper Gleanings, 1876-1879* (Fairfield, Ill.: Bland Books, 1989), p. 60.

[282] Doris Ellen Bland, *Wayne County, Illinois, Cemetery Inscriptions*, vol. 4 (Fairfield, Ill.: Bland Books, 1973).

[283] Marion Co. (Ill.) Marriage Record, C: 285.

[284] *Portrait and Biographical Record of Clinton, Washington, Marion, and Jefferson Counties, Illinois*, p. 239f.

[285] Ibid., p. 239f.

[286] Marion Co. (Ill.) Marriage Record, E: 69.

[287] Orange Co. (Ind.) Marriage Record, C-5: 75.

[288] Pension file (certificate no. 473,645), National Archives.

[289] Letter, C. K. Dixon, Jr., M.D., Louisville, KY, to Ann Faulkner, 29 Apr. 1971.

[290] *History of Pike and Dubois Counties, Indiana* (Boston: Goodspeed, 1885), p. 722f.

[291] Pension file; 1880 census, Dubois Co., Ind., 9-160-21-6; *Paoli Republican*, 21 Mar. 1917.

[292] Descriptive List of Convicts in the Indiana State Prison South, 1891-1895, p. 162, Indiana State Archives.

[293] C. K. Dixon, Jr.

[294] Marion Co. (Ind.) Marriage Record, 64: 471.

[295] Orange Co. (Ind.) Marriage Record, C-12: 44.

[296] C. K. Dixon, Jr., Louisville, KY.

[297] Ibid.

[298] Pension file (certificate no. 681, 886), National Archives.

[299] Ibid.; Ann Faulkner read the inscriptions on the gravestones and the research in the pension and marriage records.

[300] 1920 census, LaPlata Co., Colo., 22-64-10-14.

[301] 1920 census, San Juan Co., N.M., 7-117-2-1.

[302] Pension file (certificate no. 180,011), National Archives.

[303] Stone Co. (Mo.) Marriages, C: 169.

[304] Pension file, National Archives.

[305] 1900 census, Stone Co., Mo., 107-123-4-17.

[306] 1900 census, Stone Co., Mo., 107-123-10-28.

[307] LDS family sheets by Bessie T. Rowland, 514 W. Olive, Rogers, AR 72756.

[308] Washington Co. (Ark.) Marriage Record, K: 309.

[309] Ibid., K: 385.

[310] Service record, National Archives.

[311] 1870 census, Carroll Co., Ark., p. 16; 1880 census, Carroll Co., Ark., 2-226-1-5; Alta Walsh, 6003 SE Firwood St., Milwaukie, OR 97222, provided much information on this branch, especially the families of the daughters and the son Thomas M.

[312] Her given name was probably originally Mary Alice, as indicated by the 1870 census.

[313] Pension file (certificate no. 326,977), National Archives; IGI; 1880 census, 2-29-3-20.

[314] 1900 census, Barry Co., Mo., 4-13-6-51.

[315] Gravestone inscription, "Parker Cemetery, on Lower Lollar Creek, Madison County, Arkansas," *Madison County Musings* 1: 17.

[316] 1880 census, Carroll Co., 2-29-12-29.

[317] 1900 census, Madison Co., Ark., 24-73-6-33.

[318] Marilyn Ledford, HCR 61 596, Elkins, AR 72727; Wanda Lindbloom, 4814 E. 69th St., Hutchinson, KS 67502.

[319] Marilyn Ledford.

[320] *Kansas City Star*, 27 June 1923.

[321] According to Bessie Rowland's information.

[322] 1900 census, Carroll Co., Ark., 4-44-9-21.

[323] 1910 census, Wyandotte Co., Kans., 80-202-244.

[324] 1920 census, Wyandotte Co., Kans., 67-200-7-1.

[325] Bessie Rowland; 1880 census, Carroll Co., Ark., 2-29-3-27; 1900 census, Carroll Co., Ark., 4-44-9-21; 1910 census, Wyandotte Co., Kans., 80-202-244.

[326] Bessie Rowland.

[327] *Kansas City Star*, 27 Sept. 1938.

[328] Boone Co. (Ind.) Order Book, 35: 510.

[329] Boone Co. (Ind.) Marriage Record, C-4: 566.

[330] Boone Co. (Ind.) Death Record, R-23: 39.

[331] Pension file (certificate no. 1,136,962), National Archives.

[332] Boone Co. (Ind.) Marriage Record, C-9: 173.

[333] 1900 census, Boone Co., Ind., 6-18-7-21.

[334] Boone Co. (Ind.) Marriage Record, C-11: 338.

[335] 1900 census, Hendricks Co., Ind., 28-26-1-98; Hendricks Co. Birth Record, A-8: 20.

[336] Boone Co. (Ind.) Marriage Record, C-7: 147.

[337] Will of Alexander Faulkner.

[338] Hendricks Co. (Ind.) Marriage Record, 26: 33.

[339] Jefferson Co. (Ill.) Marriages, vol. 3.

[340] Pension file (certificate no. 524,841), National Archives; David D. Faulkner, 1000 Oak Ave., Onalaska, WI 54650, provided almost all of the information on his descendants.

[341] Champaign Co. (Ill.) Marriages, license no. 4294.

[342] David D. Faulkner; Georgia was apparently adopted by Robert.

[343] Her delayed birth certificate indicates that she was the child of Robert and Martha.

[344]*Tombstone Revelations in Macoupin County, Illinois* (N.p.: Macoupin County Historical Society Committee, n.d.).

[345]Vermilion Co. (Ill.) Marriage Register, 2: 189.

[346]Macoupin Co. (Ill.) Release Record, DK: 99.

[347]1880 census, Macoupin Co., Ill., 38-121-8-15; Macoupin Co. (Ill.) Births, 1: 61, 228; Judy Critchlow, 8100 Bono Rd., Terre Haute, IN 47802, provided much information about this branch.

[348]*Tombstone Revelations in Macoupin County, Illinois*, p.

[349]1900 census, Macoupin Co., Ill., 119-55-11-33.

[350]IGI.

[351]1900 census, Vermilion Co., Ill., 151-70-7-98.

[352]Mary Lyons, Dorothy Lindbloom, to Ann Faulkner.

[353]1900 census, Park Co., Mont., 7-78-3-29; 1920 census, Park Co., Mont., 15-101-6-94.

[354]Jefferson Co. (Ky.) Marriage Register, 14: 21.

[355]Pension file (certificate no. 215,697), National Archives.

[356]1900 census, Denver Co., Colo., 1-24-6-2.

[357]Arapahoe Co. (Colo.) Marriages, 900: 175.

[358]1900 census, Arapahoe Co., Colo., 5-151-6-32.

[359]Pension file (certificate no. 415,365), National Archives.

[360]Ibid.; White Co. (Ill.) Record of Births, 1: 68.

[361]White Co. (Ill.) Circuit Court, box 556; Death Register, 2: 349.

[362]Jeffries file, Green County Library, Greensburg, Ky.

[363]White Co. (Ill.) Circuit Court: estate files of John M. Faulkner, box 556; Mary E. Faulkner, box 536.

[364]White Co. (Ill.) Death Register, 1: 182.

[365]Green Co. (Ky.) Marriage Record, Book 1873-1876, p. 198.

[366]White Co. (Ill.) Marriages, A: 278.

[367]Posey Co. (Ind.) Marriages, C-11: 47.

[368]White Co. (Ill.) Circuit Court, estate of Levi U. Faulkner, box 396; White Co. Record of Births, 1: 87, 154, no. 3154; 2: 113.

[369]White Co. (Ill.) Record of Deaths, 1: 51.

[370]1920 census, Arkansas Co., Ark., 1-2-11-2.

[371]White Co. (Ill.) Marriages, A: 250.

[372]Obituary, from Helen Carstensen.

[373]White Co. (Ill.) Record of Births, 3: 42, 108.

[374]"Slinker-Bishop Little Record Book," *Green County Review* 6 (July 1983): 40.

[375]Green Co. (Ky.) Circuit Court, case no. 1560.

[376]Metcalfe Co. (Ky.) Marriage Bonds, 1902-1906, p. 104.

[377]Genealogy of Myers family by Kathy Turner, Green County Library, Greensburg, Ky.

[378]"Slinker-Bishop Little Record Book," p. 40.

[379]Metcalfe Co. (Ky.) Marriage Bonds, 1902-1904.

[380]Metcalfe Co. (Ky.) Circuit Court Orders, 12: 404.

[381]Metcalfe Co. (Ky.) Deeds, 20: 187. A Charlie L. Faulkner died 18 December 1923 in Cumberland County, Kentucky. It is uncertain whether this is the same man.

[382]Adair Co. (Ky.) Marriage Bonds, 8: 378.

[383]Metcalfe Co. (Ky.) Marriages.

[384]1880 census, Metcalfe Co., Ky., 22-196-15-44; 1900 census, Adair Co., Ky.

[385]1920 census, Childress Co., Tex., 27-19-3-37.

[386]*They Followed the Rails: In Retrospect: A History of Childress County* (Childress, Tex.: Childress Reporter, 1970), pp. 52-53.

[387]1880 census, Washington Co., Ill., 55-126-18-27; Washington Co. (Ill.) Births, for the second two.

[388]Family record in possession of William E. Faulkner.

[389]Death certificate; Elizabeth P. Ellsberry, *Cemetery Records of Macon County, Missouri* (Chillicothe, Mo.: the author, 1963), vol. 7. This is the source for the other burials there.

[390]Macon Co. (Mo.) Marriages, E: 143.

[391]1910 census, Macon Co., Mo., 62-83-97.

[392]Ibid.; 1880 census, Linn Co., Mo., 20-179-12-10; 1900 census, Macon Co., Mo., 60-77-2-90.

[393] Macon Co. (Mo.) Marriages, 4: 126.

[394] Phyllis E. Mears, *Macon County, Missouri, Obituaries 1921-1933* (Decorah, Ia.: Anundsen Pub. Co., 1992), p. 89.

[395] Macon Co. (Mo.) Marriages, 6: 148.

[396] Ibid., 10: 310.

[397] 1900 census, Shelby Co., Mo., 107-157-2-35.

[398] Macon Co. (Mo.) Marriages, 8: 345.

[399] Ibid., 9: 25.

[400] 1880 census, Gentry Co., Mo., 12-271-2-25.

[401] *Macon County Republican*, in: Phyllis E. Meers, *Macon County Obituaries 1889-1903* (Decorah, Ia.: Anundsen Pub. Co., 1987), p. 11.

[402] Robert Couch, *Cemeteries of Marceline Township, Linn County, Missouri* (Marceline, Mo.: the author, 1986), p. 84.

[403] May Couch, *McLaughlin Funeral Home Records* ([Marceline, Mo.]: n.p., 1986), 1: 94.

[404] *Marceline News*, 9 Dec. 1932.

[405] 1880 census, Linn Co., Mo., 20-179-11-35; 1900 census, Jackson Co., Mo., 45-104-5-13.

[406] Couch, *McLaughlin Funeral Home Records*, 2: 201.

[407] *Marceline* (Mo.) *News and Bucklin* (Mo.) *Herald*, 26 Nov. 1959.

[408] Information on him and his descendants is from Charles Curtis Faulkner, 647 Brookfield Ave., Brookfield, MO 64628.

[409] *History of Macon County, Missouri* (N.p.: Macon County Historical Society, 1987), p. 612.

[410] Charles C. Faulkner, Brookfield, MO.

[411] 1900 census, Clark Co., Ind., 9-3-10-89.

[412] Clark Co. (Ind.) Marriage Record, O: 491.

[413] Clark Co. (Ind.) Record of Births, 44: 27.

[414] Jeffersonville City Directory for 1913-1914.

[415] 1900 census, Milam Co., Tex., 79-64-9-74; 1910 census, Coryell Co., Tex., 41-5-32.

[416] 1900 census, Milam Co., Tex., 79-64-9-74.

[417] "Post Oak Cemetery, Oglesby, Coryell County, Texas, " *Heart of Texas Records* 24 (Fall 1981): 90, the source for the gravestone records of other members of this family.

[418] *Waco Times-Herald*, Sept. 1961.

[419] Coryell Co. (Tex.) Death Records, 1: no. 992.

[420] 1900 census, Polk Co., Mo., 95-127-19-6; 1910 census, Polk Co., Mo., 66-148-286; most information on this family comes from Frank David Faulkner, Box 3835, Carmel, CA 93921.

[421] 1910 census, Archer Co., Tex., 4-12-3.

[422] Index to Texas death records.

[423] Metcalfe Co. (Ky.) Marriage Bonds, 1881-1884, p. 50.

[424] Clay Co. (Tex.) Death Record, 2: 19; Mr. and Mrs. O. V. Hampton, *Archer County, Texas, Cemeteries* (Wichita Falls, Tex.: North Texas Genealogical and Historical Association, 1970), p. 31.

[425] 1900 census, Collin Co., Tex., 20-4-14-1.

[426] Polly Elmore James, 900 N. Howeth, Gainesville, TX 76240.

[427] Metcalfe Co. (Ky.) Marriage Bonds, 1891-94, p. 182.

[428] 1910 census, Metcalfe Co., Ky., 68-69-18; records of Rollin Faulkner, 206 Marmak Dr., Glasgow, KY 42141, and Wilbur Gilley, 374 Wisdom Rd., Edmonton, KY 42129.

[429] Metcalfe Co. (Ky.) Marriage Bonds, 15, no. 14.

[430] Ibid., 17, no. 41.

[431] Pension file, National Archives, read by Ann Faulkner. Her gravestone says 26 May 1909; the source for the gravestone inscriptions in the Baxter Springs Cemetery is Marilyn Schmitt, *Baxter and Spring Valley Township Cemeteries* ([Baxter Springs, Kans.]: Cherokee County Genealogical Society of Southeast Kansas, 1983).

[432] Pension file (certificate no. 154,371), National Archives.

[433] Hartline, *A Jolliff Family History*, pp. 61, 143.

[434] 1880 census, Washington Co., Ill., 55-126-14-6.

[435] Pension file of Michael C. Faulkner/Martha Workman (certificate no. 869,742), National Archives.

[436] *San Francisco Examiner*, 21 Mar. 1935.

[437] *San Francisco Call*, 3 Feb. 1884.

[438] 1900 census, San Francisco Co., Cal., 31-132-1-56; Will, San Francisco Co. (Cal.) Probate Court.

[439] 1920 census, Monterey Co., Cal., 22-18-5-53.

[440] Hartline, *A Jolliff Family History*, p. 149.

[441] Washington Co. (Ill.) Marriages, D: 111.

[442] Ibid., D: 171.

[443] Ibid., D: 153.

[444] St. Clair Co. (Ill.) Circuit Court, Chancery file no. 1263.

[445] 1910 census, St. Clair Co., Ill., 187-116-5.

[446] 1900 census, Polk Co., Fla., 15-132-7-95.

[447] Burchett, "Bible Records of the Faulkner Family of Marion County, Kentucky," *Kentucky Ancestors* 4 (1966): 59-61.

[448] Jefferson Co. (Ill.) Marriages, 6: 33.

[449] Wayne Co. (Ill.) Death Record, 4: 360.

[450] 1900 census, Wayne Co., Ill., 155-106-1-80; *Wayne City Journal*, 5 Apr. 1928, 2 Aug. 1928.

[451] *Chatham Township Cemeteries* (n.p.: for the Sangamon County Genealogical Society, n.d.).

[452] 1920 census, Sangamon Co., Ill., 224-129-5-1.

[453] Wayne Co. (Ill.) Marriage Record, D: 5.

[454] 1920 census, Wayne Co., Ill., 235-164-13-81.

[455] 1920 census, Wayne Co., Ill., 235-166-4-57.

[456] Betty A. Butler Beeson, *Wayne County, Illinois Death Records: 1910-1916* (Goff, Ill.: the author, 1984), p. 38.

[457] *History of Wayne County, Illinois* (Chicago: 1884), p. 50f.

[458] 1900 census, Wayne Co., Ill., 155-97-15-81.

[459] 1900 census, Wayne Co., Ill., 155-97-9-69; 1910 census, Wayne Co., Ill., 208-121-151.

[460] *Chicago Tribune*, 17 Feb. 1971.

[461] 1920 census, Marion Co., Ill., 191-168-5-69.

[462] Marion Co. (Ill.) Marriages, D: 187.

[463] Ibid.; 1900 census, Marion Co., Ill., 123-18-4-69.

[464] *Centralia Sentinel*, 19 Nov. 1992.

[465] Jefferson Co. (Ill.) Marriages, 6: 37.

[466] Ann Faulkner.

[467] Information from C. K. Dixon, M. D., via Ann Faulkner.

[468] *History of Stone County, Missouri* (Marionville, Mo.: Stone County Historical Society, 1989), pp. 415-417, where Raymond D. Faulkner writes of the family.

[469] 1900 census, Pottawatomie Co., Kans., 15-202-2-100; 1910 census, Jefferson Co., Okla., 25-149-306; 1920 census, Jefferson Co., Okla., 31-213-16-21.

[470] Alta Walsh, 6003 SE Firwood St., Milwaukie, OR 97222; census and other sources.

[471] *Stockton Record*, 9 Dec. 1954.

[472] *Long Beach Press-Telegram*, 20 Jan. 1983.

[473] Benton Co. (Ark.) Marriage Record, D: 72.

[474] 1910 census, Rogers Co., Okla., 64-177-72; 1920 census, Tulsa Co., Okla., 92-181-3-44.

[475] 1920 census, Yakima Co., Wash., 52-204-13-98.

[476] 1910 census,   Okla., 67-216-255; Cleora Faulkner provided most of the information on this branch.

[477] Bessie Rowland.

[478] Madison Co. (Ark.) Marriage Record, G: 203.

[479] 1910 census, Madison Co., Ark., 39-79-96; Fred J. Faulkner, 3680 Monroe #601, Riverside, CA 92504.

[480] Madison Co. (Ark.) Marriage Record, J: 455.

[481] Madison Co. (Ark.) Marriage Record, H: 213.

[482] Wanda Lindbloom via Ann Faulkner.

[483] Madison Co. (Ark.) Marriage Record, H: 281.

[484] *History of Washington County, Arkansas* (Springdale, Ark.: Shiloh Museum, 1989), p. 1508.

[485] Geneva Faulkner.

[486] *Madison County Musings* 10 (Spring 1991):   .

[487] Madison Co. (Ark.) Marriage Record, I: 287.

[488] Betty (Mrs. Eugene) Faulkner, Sapulpa, OK.

[489] Madison Co. (Ark.) Marriage Record, I: 328.

[490] Ibid., J: 173.

[491] *Lawton Constitution*, 31 Oct. 1977.

[492] George Garllee Faulkner provided most of the information on this branch; *Kansas City (Mo.) Times*, 22 Feb. 1964.

[493] Boone Co. (Ind.) Marriage Record, C-10: 297.

[494] Boone Co. (Ind.) Death Record, R-23: 130.

[495] 1900 census, Boone Co., Ind., 6-18-4-59; 1910 census, Boone Co., Ind., 19-4; *Lebanon Reporter*, 4 Apr. 1950.

[496] Boone Co. (Ind.) Marriage Record, C-16: 126.

[497] *Indianapolis Star*, 15 Jan. 1975, p. 48.

[498] Boone Co. (Ind.) Marriage Record, C-11: 90.

[499] Hendricks Co. (Ind.) Birth Record, 31: 25; Boone Co. (Ind.) Birth Record, R-7: 31, R-9: 31, R-13: 11, H-2: 56.

[500] Hendricks Co. (Ind.) Marriage Record, 28: 5.

[501] *Indianapolis News*, 20 June 1957.

[502] Boone Co. (Ind.) Birth Record, R-7: 36; Hendricks Co. (Ind.) Birth Record, 11: 496; Marion Co. (Ind.) Birth Record, E-11: 155.

[503] David D. Faulkner provided all the information on all the descendants of Robert R. Faulkner, Sr.

[504] Ibid.

[505] Ibid.

[506] Tippecanoe Co. (Ind.) Marriages, S20: 145.

[507] Judy Critchlow is the chief source for information on this family; birth dates from Tippecanoe Co. (Ind.) Birth Records, CH-3: 28; CH-5: 10, 85; CH-7: 74.

[508] Tippecanoe Co. (Ind.) Marriages, M-39: 98.

[509] Marion Co. (Ind.) Marriages, 105: 470.

[510] *Indianapolis Star*, 9 April 1964.

[511] Martha A. Faulkner, 1123 Regency Ct., Evansville, IN 47710.

[512] White Co. (Ill.) Marriages, A: 195.

[513] Gallatin Co. (Ill.) Marriages, 11: 116.

[514] 1900 census, Gallatin Co., Ill., 82-36-4-43; White Co. (Ill.) Circuit Court, estates of John M. and Mary E. Faulkner, boxes 556 and 573.

[515] 1920 census, Cook Co., Ill., 30-366-3-94.

[516] Bertha I. (Satterfield) Faulkner, 12412 Shamrock Rd., Omaha, NE 68154.

[517] "Platte City Cemetery, Charles Mix County, South Dakota," *South Dakota Genealogical Society Quarterly* 8 (Oct. 1989): 50.

[518] 1920 census, Charles Mix Co., S.D., 8-49-5-40.

[519] Greensburg *Record-Herald*, 6 Dec. 1940.

[520] Ibid., 28 Nov. 1968.

[521] 1910 census, Green Co., Ky., 34-44-143; Index to Kentucky Birth Records.

[522] Dorothy Ford Wulfeck, *Wilcoxson and Allied Families* (Waterbury, Conn.: Commercial Service, 1958, printers), p. 194.

[523] Metcalfe Co. (Ky.) Marriage Bonds, 13: 253.

[524] Patricia Finn Hunter, *A Finn Genealogy 1750-1985: Some Ancestors and Descendants of Colman Finn, 1823-1916, Grandson of Richard Finn, 1750-1833, of Adair County, Kentucky* (Knoxville, Tenn.: the author, 1986), p. 37.

[525] 1920 census, Metcalfe Co., Ky., 70-83-2-11; Index to Kentucky Birth Records; *Greensburg Record-Herald*, 30 Sept. 1960, 10 July 1964.

[526] 1920 census, Childress Co., Tex., 27-21-3-49.

[527] David Earl Faulkner, 1828 S. College, Springfield, IL 62704; *Illinois State Journal*, 25 Nov. 1965, 17 Nov. 1972.

[528] Elizabeth A. (Faulkner) Trump, 4108 Turkey Creek Ct., Annandale, VA 22003.

[529] 1920 census, Knox Co., Ill., 169-179-8-57.

[530] *Marceline News and Bucklin Herald*, 13 Nov. 1953.

[531] Ibid., 6 Nov. 1953, 13 Nov. 1953.

[532] Robert Couch, *Cemeteries of Marceline Township, Linn County, Missouri* (Marceline, Mo.: the author, 1986), p. 84.

[533] *Marceline News*, 29 Dec. 1933.

[534] Linn Co. (Mo.) Marriages, vol. 2.

[535] *Brookfield (Mo.) Daily News-Bulletin*, 15 Jan. 1968.

[536] Charles C. Faulkner.

[537] Ibid.

[538] Ronald K. Faulkner, R. 1, Harris, MO 64645.

[539] Frank D. Faulkner.

[540] Evelyn Faulkner, via Ann Faulkner.

[541] Archer Co. (Tex.) Record of Marriage Licenses, 3: 83.

[542] 1910 census, Collin Co., Tex., 24-1-27.

[543] *Bowie News*, 14 July 1950.

[544] Marlene Jackson, *McDonald Family Catalog* (Santa Fe, N.M.: the author, n.d.). This is the source for the information on all of their descendants.

[545] Clay Co. (Tex.) Birth Record, 5: 36.

[546] O. V. Hampton, *Archer County, Texas, Cemeteries* (Wichita Falls, Tex.: North Texas Genealogical and Historical Association, 1970), p. 31.

[547] *Wichita Falls Times Record*, 19 July 1961. One of his children was born 26 July 1923 in Clay County (Index to Texas Births).

[548] Wulfeck, *Wilcoxson and Allied Families*, p. 281.

[549] Ibid.; Wilbur Gilley, Edmonton, KY.

[550] Metcalfe Co. (Ky.) Marriage Bonds, 1927-29, p. 26.

[551] Wilbur Gilley.

[552] Metcalfe Co. (Ky.) Marriage Bonds, 21: 76.

[553] Death certificate no. 00231, Oklahoma Department of Health.

[554] 1920 census, Rogers Co., Okla., 14-7-14-72.

[555] *Sacramento Bee*, 22 July 1960.

[556] Ruth Lee Oakley Geouge, *Sixkiller Cemetery: Our Loved Ones at Rest* (Miami, Okla.: Timbercreek Ltd., 1987), p. 15.

[557] 1910 census, Cherokee Co., Kans., 10-13-434; Don Ford, *Cemetery Inscriptions: Cherokee County, Kansas* (Bowie, Md.: Heritage Books, 1988), p. 115.

[558] *Who's Who of American Women*, 6th ed., p. 386f.

[559] Patricia (Scott) Faulkner, 2209 N.E. 102nd Ave., Ankeny, IA 50021.

[560] Marian McCauley Frye, *The Tingley Family Revised* (n.p., 1980), 5: 153.

[561] John McCoy Faulkner, 1402 N.W. Beechwood St., Ankeny, IA 50021.

[562] 1920 census, San Francisco Co., Cal., 111-327-1-36.

[563] St. Clair Co. (Ill.) Circuit Court, Chancery file no. 4992.

[564] *Wayne County Record*, 24 Jan. 1935.

[565] Wayne Co. (Ill.) Marriage Record, E: 77.

[566] Berlyn E. Faulkner, 414 Chestnut St., Jamestown, KS 66948.

[567] *Mt. Vernon Register-News*, 24 Aug. 1973, 6 Jan. 1981.

[568] Edward H. Christopher, Box 64, Bucklin, KS 67834.

[569] Betty A. Faulkner, 400 18th St., Villa #2, Vero Beach, FL 32960.

[570] Information on his descendants from Ruth Faulkner, 401 Bradley Lane, Normal, IL 61761.

[571] *St. Louis Post-Dispatch*, 1 Aug. 1974.

[572] *Centralia Sentinel*, 17 Jan. 1952.

[573] *History of Stone County, Missouri*, p. 416; information from Raymond D. Faulkner, 4905 NW 62nd St., Oklahoma City, OK 73122.

[574] Cleora Faulkner, Box 218, Long Creek, OR 97856.

[575] Cleora Faulkner.

[576] *Portland Oregonian*, 22 Aug. 1973.

[577] Bessie Rowland and Ann Faulkner.

[578] Fred J. Faulkner.

[579] *Oroville Mercury-Register*, 8 Feb. 1988.

[580] Fred J. Faulkner.

[581] Judy Faulkner, 3000 Adams Rd., Fayetteville, AR 72703.

[582] Wilma Faulkner, Apt. 1020C Meadow Wood Lane, Bentonville, AR 72712.

[583] Mary Vassie Faulkner, R. 6, Huntsville, AR 72740.

[584] Geneva Faulkner, R. 2, Box 84, Huntsville, AR 72740.

[585] Lorene Lewis, P.O. Box 297, West Fork, AR 72774.

[586]"The James William and Malissa A. Protsman Rogers Family in Madison Co., Arkansas," *Madison County Musings* 7 (Spring 1983): 28.

[587]Paula Carfield, 306 S. Main, Montpelier, IN 47359.

[588]Adelaide V. Faulkner, 315 Welcome Way, Apt. 208B, Indianapolis, IN 46241.

[589]David D. Faulkner.

[590]Evelyn Faulkner, 70 Gingles Dr., Arnolds Park, IA 51331.

[591]B. Janice (Miller) Faulkner, 810 Dow Ave., Geneva, IL 60134.

[592]*Greensburg Record-Herald*, 7 Oct. 1982.

[593]Index to Kentucky birth records.

[594]*Greeley Tribune and Republican*, 9 Feb. 1973.

[595]Elizabeth A. (Faulkner) Trump.

[596]Death certificate, Illinois State Archives.

[597]Charles C. Faulkner.

[598]Ronald K. Faulkner.

[599]Frank D. Faulkner.

[600]Records of Evelyn Faulkner, through Ann Faulkner.

[601]Wulfeck, *Wilcoxson and Allied Families*, p. 345.

[602]Ibid., p. 345.

[603]Ibid., p. 346.

[604]*Norman Transcript*, 18 May 1986.

[605]John M. Faulkner.

[606]Doris Ellen Bland, *Wayne County, Illinois, Cemetery Inscriptions*, 5: 201.

[607]Berlyn E. Faulkner.

[608]Frances Faulkner, 8912 Beckleycrest, Dallas, TX 75232.

[609]Keith C. Faulkner, R.R. 4, Box 30, Mt. Vernon, IL 62864.

[610]Harry A. Faulkner, 5233 Daniel Dr., Indianapolis, IN 46226.

[611]Charles A. Faulkner, 219 Victor Pl., Neptune, NJ 07753.

[612]Frank Evans Faulkner, 602 S. 22nd St., Mt. Vernon, IL 62864.

[613]*Facts and Follies: A History of Jefferson County, Illinois* (Dallas: Taylor Publishing Co., 1978), p. 240.

[614]Homer W. Faulkner, Jr., 400 18th St., Villa #2, Vero Beach, FL 32960.

[615]Ruth V. (Krone) Faulkner.

[616]H. Duane Faulkner, R.R. 1, Sandoval, IL 62886.

[617]Judy Faulkner.

[618]Conley O. Faulkner, 210 Missouri, Huntsville, AR 72740.

[619]Mary Vassie Faulkner.

[620]Glendon D. Faulkner, 905 Dogwood Lane, Prairie Grove, AR 72753.

[621]Laymon Faulkner, 4109 Broken Arrow Cove, Springdale, AR 72764.

[622]Wanaleta (Falkner) Faulkner, 12 E. Sycamore, Fayetteville, AR 72703.

[623]"The James William and Malissa A. Protsman Rogers Family in Madison Co., Arkansas," p. 28.

[624]Stanley M. Faulkner, 2562 N. 300 E., Greenfield, IN 46140.

[625]Adelaide V. Faulkner.

[626]J. David Faulkner, 3010 Mabel St., Clermont, IN 46234.

[627]David Earl Faulkner, the source for all his descendants.

[628]Charles C. Faulkner.

[629]*Norman Transcript*, 18 May 1986.

CHAPTER N

Samuel Falconer, Son of Alexander

N1 **Samuel Falconer,** fifth son of Alexander (K1) and Susannah (Duvall) Falconar, born 25 October 1732 in Queen Anne's Parish, Prince Georges County, Maryland, died, of smallpox, before 15 October 1788 in Washington County, Pennsylvania, when letters of administration were granted to his widow Elizabeth.[1] He was treated by Dr. John Knight.

An important and seemingly reliable account, apparently written about 1855 by Elizabeth (Falconer) Freeman, from information supplied at that time by her mother Elizabeth (Smedley) (Falconer) Hetherington, was sent to her cousin Cyrus Falconer and has been preserved by his descendants.[2] This states that Samuel, from Queen Ann [sic] County, Maryland, moved to Berkeley County, Virginia (now West Virginia) with his brother David and, in 1772, settled on Pigeon Creek, near the present village of Bentleysville, in Washington County, Pennsylvania. The account provides much other information about him and his family, some of which can be substantiated by contemporary records, but otherwise it fills major gaps.

Other older statements lend further support to his identity as Alexander's son. In 1875 it was written that his sons Henry and Samuel came from Maryland.[3] Cyrus Falconer affirmed that his grandfather was born in Maryland.[4] A tradition in the branch which settled in Barry County, Michigan, holds that three brothers came from England, one becoming a slaveholder on a large plantation in the Shenandoah Valley of Virginia, another moving to Spencer County [sic], Ohio (the ancestor of this branch), the third becoming a cattleman in the West.[5] This story may refer to John, Gilbert, and Alexander Falconar, although it is too vague to mean much. The account described above does say that Samuel was accompanied in his removal to Virginia by his brother David, who later moved to Kentucky. This and the statements that he was from Maryland are the strongest proof of his identity as Alexander's son.

Samuel Falconer married Elizabeth Newkirk, daughter of Abraham and Keziah (Shipman) Newkirk.[6] She died 15 August 1809.[7]

He signed a petition, dated 27 October 1778, requesting that Yohogania County, Virginia (which at that time was the political division in which he lived) be divided by the Monongahela River.[8] During the American Revolution, he was a ranger on the frontier, in Eleazer Williamson's Company from

Westmoreland County, Pennsylvania.[9]   He and his brother-in-law Isaac Newkirk escaped without a wound from Gen. William Crawford's defeat in 1782 at the hands of an allied force of Indians, at what is now Little Sandusky, Ohio.[10] Dr. Knight, who treated him at his final illness, was captured there and wrote a famous account of it. He was taxed in 1781, living in Washington County, on 100 acres of land, two horses and two cows.[11]

On 23 September 1790, John Wallace and his wife Mary sold 185 acres of land on Pigeon Creek in Somerset Township, Washington County, bordered by land of Seshbazzar Bently and others, for £100, to Elizabeth Falconer and her sons Henry and Abraham.[12]   On 23 March 1807, Elizabeth sold her interest in this land to her son Abraham for $500, with the stipulation that Abraham was to care for her during her natural life and to compensate his brothers and sisters for their share of the real and personal estate that had belonged to their father.[13]

Like many others in newly settled areas about 1800, the second Great Awakening affected Elizabeth and her family. She and her children Henry, Margaret, and Samuel were members of what later became the Speers Church of Christ and the Maple Grove Baptist Church.[14]

Issue of Samuel and Elizabeth (Newkirk) Falconer, the first four born in Berkeley County, West Virginia, the remainder born in Washington County, Pennsylvania:[15]

N2   i.   Henry Falconer, born 2 August 1763.

    ii.   Keziah Falconer, twin of Henry, born 2 August 1763, died August 1830 near Rossville, Butler County, Ohio. She married —— Van Horn (probably Bernard Van Horn, who was of Fallowfield Township in 1790 and 1793) and had issue.

N3   iii. Abraham (Abram) Falconer.

    iv.   Susannah Falconer, who died after 1830, when in Wadsworth Township, Medina County, Ohio. She married James Gifford, born about 1755, died 6 October 1829 in Wadsworth Township, Medina County, Ohio, a Revolutionary War veteran from Maryland, and had issue.

N4   v.   Samuel Falconer, born perhaps about 1773.

    vi.   Elizabeth (Betsy) Falconer, twin of Samuel, born perhaps about 1773. She married Moses Knox. They lived in Butler County, Ohio, and had a large family.

    vii. Margaret Falconer, born 1775, died 15 October 1831, aged 55 years, buried in Pigeon Creek Presbyterian Church cemetery, Somerset Township, Washington County, Pennsylvania. She seems to have married, as her first husband, —— Morton, by whom she had a daughter, surname *Morton*: a. *Nancy*, born 30 September 1798 [calculated], died, unmarried 6 August 1850. She married, as her second husband, on 5 December 1804, Sampson Nichol, born 1752 County Tyrone, Ireland, died 24 April 1817 Washington County, Pennsylvania. He served for seven years as an ensign during the American Revolution.[16] Issue, surname *Nichol* (*Nicholl*): b. *Margaret Barcas*, born about 1805, married William Burke; c. *Eleanor*, born about 1806, married Samuel Ramsay; d. *Cynthia*, born 24 December 1808, died, unmarried, 20 February 1854; e. *Bathsheba*, born 16 November 1810, died 10 February 1892 in Iowa, married Thomas Sturgis; f. *Elizabeth*, born 15 August 1812, married Thomas M. Falconer (N16); g. *Minerva*, born about 1814, married William Bell; f. *Samuel Falconer*, born 24 May 1816, died 1 April 1889, married Rachel Downey.[17]

viii. Eleanor Falconer, born 22 April 1777 [calculated], died 15 October 1831, aged "64 [but must be 54] days, 4 months, 23 days," buried in Jacobsburg Cemetery, Smith Township, Belmont County, Ohio. She married Thomas Ramsay (Ramsey), born 2 May 1772 [calculated], County Tyrone, Ireland, died 10 July 1839 in Smith Township, Belmont County, Ohio.[18] Issue, surname *Ramsay:*[19] a. *Samuel,* born about 1803, married, 1835, Eleanor Nichol; b. *David;* c. *Abram,* born 1807, died 1886, married Sarah Maloney; d. *John,* born about 1807; e. *Allen,* born 28 May 1811, died 19 July 1887, buried in Jacobsburg Cemetery, married, 22 December 1836, Mary Thornborough; f. *Aaron F.,* born 27 March 1813, died 14 May 1890 in Belmont County, Ohio, married, 11 June 1844, Nancy Thornborough; g. *Eleanor,* born 9 April 1816, married Samuel Falconer (N15); h. *Margaret;* i. *Nancy,* married —— Taylor; j. *Jennie;* k. *Elizabeth,* married —— Riley.

ix. Jane Falconer, who never married.

N5   x. Isaac Falconer, born 22 September 1781.[20]

xi. Ann Falconer. She married George J. Smedley and had issue. They lived in Meigs Township, Adams County, Ohio, in 1820; Elizabeth Township, Lawrence County, Ohio, in 1830; and, in 1840, Green Township, Scioto County, Ohio.

N6   xii. Reuben Falconer, born 12 March 1789 [calculated].[21]

N2 Henry Falconer, born 2 August 1763 in Berkeley County, now in West Virginia, died 28 November [calculated] 1836, aged 73 years, three months, and 26 days, in Wadsworth Township, Medina County, Ohio.[22]

He married Frances (Fannie) Throckmorton, born 1774, died 1827.[23] Said to be of French descent,[24] she was probably the daughter of Daniel Throckmorton, who died in Hampshire County, Virginia, prior to 1782.[25] Her mother may have been a daughter of William Demoss of Hampshire County, two of whose children are known to have married a brother and sister of Daniel Throckmorton. The name Demoss has been carried down in this branch and might account for the statement that she was of French descent.

In 1800, he lived in Fallowfield Township, Washington County, Pennsylvania.[26] On 8 May 1800, he and his wife Frances sold their interest in the 185-acre tract on Pigeon Creek to his brother Abraham for $266.66.[27] By 1801, he had settled in Canfield Township, Trumbull County, Ohio. In 1803, he purchased 125 acres in Canfield Township from Herman Canfield, half of which Henry and Frances sold to his brother Samuel for $145 in 1805. On 8 October 1807 Henry entered an agreement with his brother Abraham, to purchase 600 acres of land in Canfield Township, together with a gristmill, to be paid by 1812. When Abraham died, litigation was necessary to resolve this contract. In 1810 he had 120 acres.[28] By 1818 he was in Wadsworth.

Issue of Henry and Frances (Throckmorton) Falconer:[29]

N7   i. Samuel Alexander Falconer, born 20 October 1797.

ii. Esther Falconer, born 14 October 1800, died April 1874. She married, on 1 September 1821, in Medina County, Ohio, Henry Baughman, and had issue, surname *Baughman:*[30] a. *Seth,* born about 1826; b. *Joel,* born about 1837.

iii. William Falconer, born 19 April 1803, probably died young.

iv. Keziah Falconer, born 1 June 1805, probably died young.

v. Abraham Falconer, born 5 February 1807, died 7 April 1818. His was said to have been the second burial in the Wadsworth Cemetery.[31]

N8   vi.   Daniel Throckmorton Falconer, born 13 November 1809.

vii.   Frances Falconer, born 22 July 1812, living in 1860 in Vermontville Township, Eaton County, Michigan. She married, on 20 December 1832, in Lorain County, Ohio, David Erastus Bissett, born about 1812 in Ohio, living in 1860. Issue, surname *Bissett:*[32] a. *Henry*, born about 1833; b. *Alexander S.*, born about 1835, maried Miranda J. ——; c. *Gershon Eurotus*, born about 1835; d. *Electa*, born about 1839; e. *David Erastus*, born about 1842; f. *Julia E.*, born about 1846; g. *James E.*, born about 1854.

viii.   Belinda Falconer, born 15 August 1814, died 1891 in Jackson County, Wisconsin. She married, on 10 May 1835, in Lorain County, Ohio, Daniel Braman, son of Otis and Lydia (Felt) Braman, born 31 January 1809 in Bethany, New York, died 8 December 1882 in Garden Valley, Wisconsin.[33] They moved in 1851 to Allamakee County, Iowa, then in 1856 to Jackson County, Wisconsin. Issue, surname *Braman:*[34] a. *G. J.*, born 1839, married 25 December 1864, at Grafton, Ohio, Belle M. Crittenden.

N9   ix.   Gilbert DeMoss Falconer, born 25 July 1816.

N10   x.   Reuben Falconer, born 9 May 1818.

N3   **Abraham (Abram) Falconer**, born perhaps about 1765 in Berkeley County, now in West Virginia, died in April 1809 in Washington County, Pennsylvania.

His wife was Elizabeth Smedley, daughter of George Frederick and —— (Hurst) Smedley,[35] born 1778 in Maryland, died 4 May 1860, "in her 83rd year," in West Bethlehem Township, Washington County, Pennsylvania, buried in Beallsville Cemetery. On 19 March 1812, Elizabeth married Hugh Hetherington.[36] Her grandfather was John Smedley, born 1732 in Baden, Germany, who died in Flemingsburg, Kentucky, coming from Washington County, Pennsylvania, leaving a family of seven children.[37]

In 1800, he lived in Somerset Township, Washington County. He bought out his brother Henry's share of 185 acres on Pigeon Creek on 8 May 1800.[38] Administration on his estate was granted to Isaac Newkirk and Elizabeth Falconer, his widow. On 25 Nov. 1813, his administrators sued Henry Falconer, of Canfield, to collect on notes signed in payment of land.[39]

Issue of Abraham and Elizabeth (Smedley) Falconer:[40]

i.   George Falconer, probably died young.[41]

ii.   Hannah Falconer, probably died young.

N11   iii.   Samuel Falconer.

iv.   Christiana Falconer, born 1803,[42] died 31 July 1890 in Chrisman, Edgar County, Illinois. She married, on 3 June 1824,[43] as his second wife, John E. Mitchell, son of Robert and Ellen (Brady) Mitchell, born 1 August 1784, died 11 September 1843. They had issue, surname *Mitchell:*[44] a. *Mary*, born 21 October 1825, married James Dalrymple; b. *Elizabeth*, born 1 September 1828, died 16 May 1928, married John B. Galway; c. *Barsheba*, born 18 January 1831, married Thomas Carson; d. *Freeman*, born 24 June 1833, died young; e. *Abraham Faulkner*, born 30 August 1835, married Emily Clarke; f. *Damaris*, born 1838, died 9 June 1860, married Obadiah Spowls; g. *Alexander Campbell*, born 21 September 1840, married Rachel Hardy; h. *John*, born 12 October 1843.

v.   Elizabeth (Eliza) Falconer, born 1805, died 30 August 1878 in West Bethlehem Township, Washington County, Pennsylvania, "in the 74th year of her age," buried in Beallsville Cemetery. She married, on 10 March 1825,[45] John Freeman, then of Fayette County, Pennsylvania, born 1801, died 27 January 1864, "in the 64 Year of his age," buried in Beallsville Cemetery. They had no issue.

vi. Rhoda Falconer, born about December 1808, died 18 July 1839, "aged 30 years, 7 months," buried in Pigeon Creek Presbyterian Church cemetery. She married, on 15 September 1824,[46] as his third wife, Samuel Davis, son of Walter and Eliza (Minor) Davis of Chambersburg, Franklin County, Pennsylvania, born 7 March 1786, died 16 October 1836, buried in Pigeon Creek cemetery, and had issue, surname *Davis:*[47] a. *Abraham Falconer*, born 12 October 1825, died 10 September 1876 in Pittsburgh, Pennsylvania, married Bridget Maguire; b. *Joseph Harrison*, born 24 November 1827, died 4 February 1892, married Jemima Ann McClure; c. *Mary Elizabeth*, born 11 October 1829, died 7 November 1884, married Henry M. Crawford; d. *Rhoda Elmira*, born 11 December 1831, died 31 October 1854, married William Fisher; e. *Harriet Caroline*, born 11 February 1834, died 15 June 1852, married Gideon Hankins; f. *Emily Mariah*, born 18 March 1836, married, 15 February 1855, J. Holmes Taylor.

N4 Samuel Falconer, born perhaps about 1773 in Washington County, Pennsylvania, was living in 1830 in Wadsworth, Medina County, Ohio.[48]

He married, as his first wife, Nancy ——, who died 27 January 1812, aged 40, in Canfield, Mahoning County, Ohio.[49]

He married, as his second wife, Jane ——, who died in 1814.[50]

He and his wife lived in Somerset Township, Washington County, Pennsylvania, in 1800, without children.[51] He moved to Ohio and, in 1810, he was taxed on 62 acres in Canfield Township, Mahoning (then Trumbull) County, Ohio. After the death of his first wife, his children were raised by others.[52]

Issue of Samuel and Nancy Falconer:[53]

i. Samuel Falconer, born probably about 1800, was living in Sharon, Medina County, Ohio, in 1840,[54] but was probably dead by 1850. He probably married, as his first wife, on 30 October 1823 in Wayne County, Ohio, Isabella Wheeler, although this record may refer to his father. He married, 20 February 1834, in Wayne County, Ohio, Mary (Polly) Livingstone, born about 1794 in Vermont, living in 1850 in Westfield Township, Medina County, Ohio.[55] They probably had no issue.

ii. Jane Falconer, born about 1802. She married, 4 April 1821, in Wayne County, Ohio, Benjamin Simcox, son of Samuel Simcox. He died 30 December 1855 in Harrisville Township, Medina County, Ohio. Issue, surname *Simcox:*[56] a. *Eli*, born 6 February 1822; b. *Sherman*, born about 1826; c. *Benjamin*, born about 1832; d. *Abraham*, born about 1834; e. *Rachel*, born about 1839; f. *Demariah*, born about 1841; g. *Malessia*, born about 1843. She may have married, as her second husband, —— Vestel.

iii. Anna Falconer. She married, 30 August 1825, in Trumbull County, Ohio, James Reed, born 1799, son of James Reed of Canfield. He moved to Michigan. She apparently married, as her second husband, William Bean.

iv. Sarah Falconer, born 31 August 1806, died 3 June 1899 in Shell Rock, Iowa.[57] She married, on 2 August 1824, Samuel Hunt, of Canfield, Ohio, born 25 February 1801 in Brooke County, (West) Virginia, died 26 December 1879. They lived in Champion District, Trumbull County, Ohio, and had issue, surname *Hunt:*[58] a. *William*, born 31 December 1824, died 17 March 1905 in Bristol, Ohio; married, 1 January 1850, Sarah Ann Weiss; b. *Thomas*, born about 1832; c. *Sarah*, born about 1835; d. *Mary*, born about 1838; e. *James*, born about 1840; f. *Chauncey F.*, born about 1842; g. *Minerva*, born about 1845; h. *Elizabeth*, born 1849.

N12   v.   Abram Falconer, born 22 April 1808.

vi.   Nancy Falconer. She married, on 21 December 1830 in Trumbull County, Ohio, Nicholas Crum, born about 1805 in Pennsylvania, living in 1850 in Youngstown Township, Mahoning County, Ohio. Issue, surname *Crum*: a. *John W.*, born about 1831; b. *Nancy A.*, born about 1834; c. *Sarah*, born about 1836; d. *Mary*, born about 1839; e. *Emeline*, born about 1842; f. *Samuel*, born about 1844. He married second, on 3 May 1844, in Trumbull County, Ohio, Sally Dickey. He married third, Agnes ——, born about 1828.

vii.   Elizabeth (Eliza) Falconer, born about 1812. She married, on 3 December 1847, in Medina County, Ohio,[59] James Clark. Issue, surname *Clark*: a. *Emily*, born about 1849. She married, as her second husband, —— Davis.

N5 **Isaac Falconer**, born 22 September 1781 in Washington County, Pennsylvania, died 27 November 1840 in St. Clair Township, Butler County, Ohio, was buried in Rossville Cemetery, but reinterred in 1854 in Greenwood Cemetery, Hamilton.

He married Nancy Wilkins, daughter of Samuel and Agnes (Smedley) Wilkins, born 24 July 1789 in Washington County, Pennsylvania, died 17 November 1854, buried in Greenwood Cemetery. Samuel Wilkins's father was John Wilkins, who came from near London to America "in easy circumstances."[60] Agnes Smedley was the sister of George F. Smedley, the father of Elizabeth, wife of Abraham Falconer. Nancy (Wilkins) Falconer was a Presbyterian.[61]

He moved from Washington County, Pennsylvania, to Rossville (which later became part of Hamilton), Butler County, Ohio, in April 1812. He kept a tavern in a hewed log house and owned and operated a ferry until 1816. In that year he built a frame building, in which he operated a hotel, the "Falconer House," until 1838. He worked primarily as a cabinetmaker, having his own shop in Rossville from 1818 until his death. He was among the first to build flatboats on the Miami River and, in them, carried on trade down the Ohio and Mississippi Rivers, the last trip to New Orleans with a load of his furniture being in 1827. He also ran a sawmill and farmed. He was drafted in 1814 but peace was reached before he saw military action. He served afterwards as captain of a militia company.[62]

Issue of Isaac and Nancy (Wilkins) Falconer:[63]

N13   i.   Cyrus Falconer, born 21 January 1810.

ii.   Reasin B[eall] Falconer, died 1 December 1812 at Hamilton, Ohio.

N14   iii.   John Hall Falconer, born 1814.

iv.   Hiram R. Falconer, died 15 October 1823.

v.   Maria Louisa Falconer, born about 1824, died 11 February 1878 in Columbus, Ohio. On 5 May 1842, in Butler County, Ohio, she married John G. Deshler, a banker of Columbus, Ohio.

vi.   Jerome B[onaparte] Falconer, died 5 August 1843.

N6 **Reuben Falconer**, born 12 March 1789 [calculated] in Washington County,

Pennsylvania, died 20 November 1851, aged 62 years, 8 months, and 8 days, and was buried in Pipe Creek Cemetery, Mead Township, Belmont County, Ohio.

He married, as his first wife, Sarah Marshall, daughter of John C. and Elizabeth Marshall, born 25 October 1792 [calculated], died 22 July 1823, aged 30 years, 8 months, 27 days, buried in Pipe Creek Cemetery.

He married, as his second wife, on 7 June 1825, Jane Stewart, born about 1790 in Pennsylvania, whose parents have not been identified.[64]

Reuben, then of Washington County, Pennsylvania, received a certificate for a patent on land in section 1, township 6, range 4, in Belmont County, Ohio, on 17 November 1815.[65] On 6 November 1826, Reuben and his second wife Jane, together with Elizabeth, widow of John C. Marshall, Abraham Teters and Nancy his wife, Samuel Marshall and Mary his wife, Mahalah and Nathan Marshall, quitclaimed the northeast quarter of section 32, township 6, range 4, in Belmont County, to Thomas Marshall.[66]

On 19 November 1851, Reuben wrote his will. He gave to his daughter Elisabeth Daniels, wife of William Daniels, $10, in addition to two notes, each calling for $15, which he held of William Daniels, dated 2 May 1832; to his daughter Nancy Taylor, he gave $250; to his three sons, Samuel, Thomas M., and John, he gave each their respective receipts for $500; to his daughter Emily Shepherd, he gave a 42.4-acre tract in the northwest quarter of the southwest quarter of section 7, township 3, range 4, in Monroe County; to his son James, he gave the farm Reuben lived on in Smith Township; to his two daughters Penena and Mary Jane Falconer he gave each $300, a horse saddle and bridle, and bed and bedding, and to his infant grandson Reuben Brandon he gave $10 when he became 21. He appointed his son James executor.[67] On 2 August 1852, James Falconer and his mother Jane Falconer, of Belmont County, sold, for $3500, to John Falconer, of Monroe County, Ohio, the southeast quarter of section 1, township 6, range 4, consisting of 161.45 acres, free from all encumbrances except $850 which John agreed to pay to Peninah Falconer, $300 to Mary Jane Falconer, and $250 to Nancy Taylor.[68]

Issue of Reuben and Sarah (Marshall) Falconer:

    i.   Elizabeth Falconer. On 26 August 1826, in Belmont County, Ohio, she married William Daniels.

N15 ii.   Samuel Falconer, born 20 July 1814.[69]

N16 iii.   Thomas M. Falconer, born 11 November 1815 [calculated].

    iv.   Nancy Falconer, born 1818, died 1900, buried in Belmont Ridge Christian Church Cemetery, in Washington Township, Belmont County, Ohio.[70] On 16 February 1837, in Belmont County, Ohio, she married Frazier Taylor. Issue, surname Taylor:[71] a. Reuben, born 1838, died 1906; b. Nancy, born about 1840; c. Elizabeth, born about 1842; d. Sarah, born about 1845; e. Lavinia, born about 1847; f. Jesse, born about 1849.

N17 v.   John C. Marshall Falconer, born 20 December 1820.

    vi.   Emily Falconer, born about 1823, living in 1860 in Green Township, Monroe County, Ohio. She married, by a license dated 13 March 1840, in Athens County, Ohio,[72] Elza Shepherd, born about 1816 in Ohio. Issue, surname Shepherd:[73] a. Martha, born about 1842; b. John F., born about 1844; c. Aaron, born about 1845, died young; d. Amos, born about 1849, died young; e. Isaiah, born about 1852; f. Sarah A., born about 1854; g. Elizabeth, born about 1859.

Issue of Reuben and Jane (Stewart) Falconer:

vii.   Sarah Falconer, born about 1827, died in 1850 or 1851. She married, on 22 December 1849, in Belmont County, Ohio, James Brandon, by whom she had issue, surname *Brandon*: a. *Reuben*.

N18   viii.   James Falconer, born about 1828.

ix.   Peninnah Falconer, born 27 April 1833 [calculated], died 7 July 1880, buried in Centerville cemetery. On 9 September 1852, in Belmont County, Ohio, she married George Thornborough, son of William Thornborough, born 9 September 1822, died 18 October 1900. Issue, surname *Thornborough*: a. *Homer*, born 6 — 1857/8, died 18 May 1876; b. daughter, born 30 October 1872, died in infancy. They had one son and eight daughters.[74]

x.   Mary Jane Falconer, born about 1835.

N7 Samuel Alexander Falconer, born 20 October 1797 in Washington County, Pennsylvania, died 17 February 1873 in Castleton Township, Barry County, Michigan,[75] was buried in Woodland Cemetery.

He married, on 5 January 1828 in Lorain County, Ohio,[76] Margaret Bissett, born about 1810 in Ohio, living 1883, buried in Woodland Cemetery. She was probably the daughter of Ezekiel Bissett, born about 1773 in Pennsylvania, living in 1850 in Spencer Township, Medina County, Ohio, with whom the daughter "Delilah" (sic, Diantha) was living at the time of the census.

He was elected constable, in Spencer Township, in 1832.[77] In 1850, he lived in Carlisle Township, Lorain County, Ohio. They moved to Michigan after 1860.

Issue of Samuel Alexander and Margaret (Bissett) Falconer:[78]

i.   Fanny Elizabeth Falconer, born about 1840. She married, on 16 October 1859, in Medina County, Ohio,[79] William Ash.

ii.   Diantha P. Falconer, born about 1844. She married, on 6 February 1868, in Carlton Township, Barry County, Michigan,[80] James R. Meloy, born about 1846 at Roy, Macomb County, Michigan.

iii.   Eliza Falconer, born 19 March 1847 [calculated], died 14 October 1855, buried in Rockwood Cemetery, LaGrange Township, Lorain County, Ohio.[81]

iv.   Sarah Falconer, born about 1849.

N8 Daniel Throckmorton Falconer, born 13 November 1809 in Canfield Township, Mahoning (then Trumbull) County, Ohio, died 1873 in Vermontville Township, Eaton County, Michigan, was buried in Woodlawn Cemetery.

He married, on 14 November 1839, in Lorain County, Ohio,[82] Eleanor Monks, daughter of Michael and Eunice (Worden) Monks, born 2 June 1819 in New York, died 30 June 1898 Vermontville Township, Eaton County, Michigan,[83] buried in Woodlawn Cemetery.

Issue of Daniel Throckmorton and Eleanor (Monks) Falconer:[84]

i.   Celestia V. Falconer, born May 1843 in Ohio, living 1900 in Vermontville Township, Eaton County, Michigan, unmarried.[85]

N9 **Gilbert DeMoss Falconer**, born 25 July 1816 in Canfield Township, Mahoning (then Trumbull) County, Ohio, died in 1855,[86] probably in Lowell, Kent County, Michigan.

He married, on 2 January 1839 in Lorain County, Ohio,[87] Elizabeth Matthews, born 1825 [sic?], died 1848.

He was a wagon maker and lived in Spencer Township, Medina County, and Carlisle Township, Lorain County, Ohio, before coming to Michigan in 1851, settling in Lowell. He first saw Hastings on 20 November 1853, when he and Anson Willson came with a horse team from Eaton County, Michigan.[88]

Issue of Gilbert DeMoss and Elizabeth (Matthews) Falconer:[89]

N19 i. Martin DeMoss Falconer, born 29 June 1839.

ii. daughter (possibly). She was the mother of Maude Moe and Edith Cummings, who in 1937 lived in Valley City, North Dakota, and Kansas City, Missouri, respectively. They were nieces of Martin D. Falconer.[90]

N10 **Reuben Falconer**, born 9 May 1818 in Wadsworth Township, Medina County, Ohio, died 4 August 1891 in Spencer Township, Medina County, Ohio,[91] was buried in Spencer Cemetery.

He married, on 1 October 1840, in Medina County, Ohio, Lucinda May (Graves) Booth, widow of Daniel Booth and daughter of Lebbeus and Lucena (Graham) Graves, born 25 November 1814 in Leroy, Genesee County, New York, died 25 December 1893 in Spencer Township, Medina County, Ohio.

He was a farmer in Spencer Township. He served as a private in Company K, 8th Ohio Volunteer Infantry, from 27 April 1861 to 18 August 1861.[92]

Issue of Reuben and Lucinda May (Graves) Falconer, born in Spencer Township, Medina County, Ohio:[93]

N20 i. Reuben Henry Falconer, born 27 October 1841.

ii. Fanny Lucena Falconer, born 26 July 1843, died 16 February 1855, buried in Spencer Cemetery.

iii. Lucinda Matilda Falconer, born 14 August 1845, died 25 December 1893. She married, on 28 September 1865, in Medina County, Ohio, George W. Gallatin, son of John W. and Elizabeth Gallatin.

N21 iv. Archelaus Revier Falconer, born 21 September 1847.

N22 v. Amandus DeForest Falconer, born 27 September 1849.

N23 vi. Roswell Graham Falconer, born 5 April 1852.

vii. John Eugene Falconer, born 10 February 1855, living in 1920 in Medina County, Ohio, unmarried.

viii. son, born and died 12 March 1857.

N11 **Samuel Falconer**, born probably about 1800 in Somerset Township, Washington County, Pennsylvania, died before January 1825 in Washington County, Pennsylvania.

His wife was Elizabeth Horn, daughter of David and Nancy Horn.[94] She married, as her second husband, after January 1834, James Wilson.[95]

Issue of Samuel and Elizabeth (Horn) Falconer:[96]

    i.   George T. Falconer. He died, unmarried, prior to 30 September 1860.[97]

    ii.   Eliza Jane Falconer, born about 1824. She married Thomas H. Howden, born about 1818 in Washington County, Pennsylvania. Issue, surname *Howden:*[98] a. *Elizabeth,* born about 1844; b. *Margaret,* born about 1845; c. *James F.,* born about 1847; d. *Jerome,* born about 1853; e. *William,* born about 1858.

N12   **Abram (Abraham) Falconer,** born 22 April 1808 in Canfield, Mahoning (then Trumbull) County, Ohio, died 21 March 1886, near Wauseon, Fulton County, Ohio, was buried in Union Cemetery.[99]

    He married, as his first wife, on 28 March 1833, in Wadsworth, Medina County, Ohio, Barbara Smith. She died 19 January 1847.[100]

    He married, as his second wife, on 5 October 1847, Medina County, Ohio, Deborah (Shaw) Brigham, widow of Dexter Brigham, daughter of Thomas Shaw,[101] born about October 1812 in Plainfield, Massachusetts, died 27 June 1893, aged 80 years, 8 months, buried in Union Cemetery.

    They moved from Harrisville, in Medina County, to Fulton County in the spring of 1854. A devout Baptist, Abram joined the church in Wadsworth in 1838. He joined the Baptist church at West Barre, after moving to Fulton County, but transferred his membership in 1866 to the Wauseon Baptist Church, where he was deacon for many years.[102]

    Issue of Abram and Barbara (Smith) Falconer (besides these, there were also two who died before 1847):[103]

    i.   Leonard Falconer, born 12 October 1833, died 26 November 1862 at Pilot Knob (Sandersville), Tennessee, buried in Lena Cemetery. He served as a corporal in Company K, 38th Ohio Volunteer Infantry. He married, 25 March 1860, Elizabeth E. Bates, daughter of Abner C. and Laura W. (Baker) Bates, born 2 June 1842 Chester, Ohio. They had no issue. She married, 12 June 1866, in Grand Rapids, Michigan, Melville D. Ford.[104]

    ii.   Albert Falconer, born about 1835, died 1 September 1864, in the battle of Jonesboro, Georgia.[105] He served as a corporal, in Company K, 38th Ohio Volunteer Infantry. No issue.

    iii.   Susanna Falconer, born 9 February 1836, died 31 March 1893, buried in Union Cemetery, Wauseon, Ohio. She married Winfield Scott Brigham, born 30 December 1814 Otsego, New York, died 17 April 1906 Bowling Green, Ohio.[106] Issue, surname *Brigham:* a. *Elmina;* b. *Emma F.,* living in Paw Paw, Michigan, 1890, married, 26 November 1868, H. B. Taft; c. *Elizabeth F.,* married —— Ford.

    iv.   Elvira Falconer, born about 1837, died 25 August 1873, buried in Wauseon Union Cemetery. She married Linus Taft and had issue, surname *Taft:* a. *George Albert,* married, 24 December 1891, A. Georgiana Altman; b. *Edwin Linus,* married, 21 February 1891, Minnie M. Altman.

    v.   Sarah J. P. Falconer, born November 1840 [calculated], died 18 April 1856, buried in Lena Cemetery, southeast of Wauseon.

    vi.   Ellen Falconer, born about 1843. She married, 16 March 1865, in Fulton County, Ohio,[107] Warren C. Williams, and had issue, surname *Williams:* a. *Ernest Albert.* He married, as his second wife, on 24 October 1882, in Fulton County, Ohio, Jessie Britton.

Issue of Abram and Deborah (Shaw) Falconer:

vii. Etta Falconer, born 13 October 1851 [calculated], died 28 October 1862, buried in Lena Cemetery.

viii. Edwin W. Falconer, born about February 1859, died 1 April 1859, aged 4 weeks, buried in Lena Cemetery.

N13   **Cyrus Falconer**, born 21 January 1810 in Washington County, Pennsylvania, died 28 January 1895 in Hamilton, Ohio, was buried in Greenwood Cemetery.

On 8 October 1839, in Butler County, Ohio, he married Mary Woods, daughter of Hon. John and Sarah Ann (Lynch) Woods, born 3 June 1821 in Springborough, Warren County, Ohio, died 18 September 1870 in Hamilton, Ohio, buried in Greenwood Cemetery.

He married, as his second wife, on 1 February 1872, in Franklin County, Ohio, Margaret McKee, daughter of James McKee, of Wheeling, West Virginia, born 18 September 1825, died 15 September 1878, buried in Greenwood Cemetery.[108] They had no issue.

He married, as his third wife, on 20 May 1880, in Butler County, Ohio, Elinor (Ella) Elizabeth Crawford, daughter of David and Jeanette (Giffen) Crawford, of Hamilton, born 3 March 1841 in Hamilton, Ohio, died 13 January 1929 in Hamilton, Ohio, buried in Greenwood Cemetery. She was president of the Board of Managers of the Hamilton Children's Home and gave her house to the Home.

He was a student at Miami University from 1826 to the Fall of 1827. In that year, he accompanied his father to New Orleans, becoming firmly opposed to slavery after witnessing the system during the trip. He studied in 1830 and 1831 at the Ohio Medical College in Cincinnati, and was licensed to practice medicine in 1832. In 1838 he entered Cincinnati Medical College and received a degree in 1839.[109] Prominent in professional and civic affairs, he published in medical journals, helped found the Butler County Medical Society, and served as vice-president of the Ohio State Medical Association. He was on the board of directors of the Hamilton and Rossville Hydraulic Company, in 1859; one of the organizers in 1851 of the Hamilton union school system and was on the board of school examiners for nine years; a trustee of Ohio State Agricultural College (now Ohio State University) during the gubernatorial terms of R. B. Hayes and Noyes. He was a delegate to the Whig National Convention in 1839. He was a leading member of the First Presbyterian Church of Hamilton.[110]

Issue of Cyrus and Mary (Woods) Falconer:[111]

i. John Woods Falconer, born 30 September 1840, fatally wounded at the battle of Appomattox Court House, died 21 April 1865 at Farnham, Virginia. Educated at Miami University from 1859 to 1861, he served first as a private in Company F, 3rd Ohio Volunteer Infantry, in 1861. He was admitted to the bar in 1864. In 1864, he was appointed a captain in Company A, 41st U. S. Colored Troops. Unmarried.

ii. Jerome B[onaparte] Falconer, born 17 March 1844, wounded at the battle of Stone River, died 15 August 1863, at Hamilton, unmarried. In 1861 and 1862 he was a student at Miami University, whose library now holds a diary he wrote during this period. He served as a sergeant in Company C, 93rd

Ohio Volunteer Infantry.

iii. William Beckett Falconer, born 14 May 1847, died 15 September 1924 in Hamilton, Ohio, buried in Greenwood Cemetery. He may be the William Falconer who married, on 12 November 1872, in Delaware County, Ohio, Maggie Bailer. He did marry, on 7 October 1880, in Licking County, Ohio, Eva Woodbridge. He attended the School of Pharmacy of the University of Michigan in 1869-1870. He was in the express business and drug business in Hamilton and was an executive of the Hamilton Buggy Company, a carriage manufacturer in Hamilton. From 1901 to 1912, he lived in Pittsburgh, Pennsylvania, where he was associated with a steel company. In the latter year he returned to Hamilton, where he was an executive with the Hamilton Chamber of Commerce.[112] No issue.

iv. Mary Louisa (Louise) Falconer, born 15 February 1852, died 13 October 1931 in Montclair, New Jersey. On 8 October 1873, in Butler County, Ohio, she married Gen. Eugene Powell, son of Thomas Watkins and Elizabeth (Gordon) Powell, born 16 November 1834 in Delaware, Ohio, died 17 March 1907 in Columbus, Ohio, and had issue, surname *Powell:*[113] a. *Mary Louise,* born 10 November 1874, died 18 February 1950, married Alexander Thompson Ovenshine; b. *Elizabeth,* born 28 November 1878, died about 1906, married Hjalmar Erickson; c. *Frederick Falconer,* born 27 March 1888, died 23 September 1936.

v. Helen Falconer, born 9 December 1853, died 6 February 1887 at Fort D. A. Russell, Wyoming, buried in Greenwood Cemetery, Hamilton. She married, on 13 November 1877, Lyster Miller O'Brien, Colonel, U. S. Army, son of Rev. John and Charlotte (Tull) O'Brien, born 7 December 1836 Monroe, Michigan, and had issue, surname *O'Brien:*[114] a. *Charlotte Ide,* born 1 October 1878, married —— Nicholas; b. *Allen Falconer,* born 13 May 1880, died 21 May 1880; c. *Falconer,* born 14 April 1882; d. *Herbert Lyster,* born 30 January 1887, died 6 January 1892.

N24 vi. Cyrus Falconer, born 5 March 1856.

vii. Scott Falconer, born 12 May 1858, buried 21 October 1859 in Greenwood Cemetery.

viii. Mary W. Falconer, born 22 May 1863, died 10 August 1921 in Hamilton, Ohio, buried in Greenwood Cemetery. She was a pianist and patron of music. She married, on 7 June 1888, Samuel Dustin Fitton, a banker of Hamilton, born 1846, died 8 December 1919 in Hamilton, Ohio, and had issue, surname *Fitton:* a. *Cyrus James,* born 14 March 1889, died 26 May 1978, married Elaine Jones; b. *Donald Webster,* born 1890, died 1972, married Nannie V. ——.

Issue of Cyrus and Elinor Elizabeth (Crawford) Falconer:[115]

N25 ix. Robert Crawford Falconer, born 16 February 1882.

N14   **John Hall Falconer**, born 1814 in Butler County, Ohio,[116] died 25 September 1866 in Noble, Richland County, Illinois.[117]

He married, on 26 August 1835 in Butler County, Ohio, Charlotte Smith, born about 1815 in Ohio, died 4 October 1873 in Pawtucket, Rhode Island,[118] buried in Greenwood Cemetery, Hamilton, Ohio.

He operated, from 1838, a hotel, the "Falconer House," in Rossville and worked there as a tailor. In 1860, he moved to Noble, Richland County, Illinois, where he was a merchant and miller.[119]

Issue of John Hall and Charlotte (Smith) Falconer, born in Rossville, Butler County, Ohio:[120]

    i.   Catharine Falconer, born 5 August 1836, died 4 November 1904 in Pawtucket, Rhode Island. On 25 June 1856, in Hamilton, Ohio, she married Henry Augustus Stearns, son of Abner and Anne (Russell) Stearns, born 23 October 1825, died 1912, who became Lieutenant Governor of Rhode Island. Issue, surname *Stearns*:[121]   a. *Deshler Falconer*, born 7 August 1857; b. *George Russell*, born 19 January 1860; c. *Walter Henry*, born 3 January 1862, married, 5 June 1890, Abbie Harris Razee; d. *Kate Russell*, born 21 July 1864; e. *Charles Falconer*, born 27 July 1866; f. *Henry Foster*, born 3 March 1868; g. *Anna Russell*, born 4 January 1873, died 7 February 1874; h. *Caroline Cranston*, born 18 January 1875.

    ii.   Laura A. Falconer, born about 1839. On 10 November 1867, in Richland County, Illinois,[122] she married Andrew J. Mitchell. Issue, surname *Mitchell*: a. *Harry L.*, of Franklin County, Ohio, in 1908.

    iii.   Charles D. Falconer, born 15 April 1842, died 3 March 1918 in Napa, California. He served in the Navy during the Civil War, until mustered out in 1865 as a sergeant major of marines. In 1870, he moved to Salina, Kansas, where he served as under sheriff and superintendent of the county infirmary and then one of the officers in the Kansas State Penitentiary at Lansing. Prominent in Kansas politics, he must have been frequently confused with his distant cousin Charles Edward Faulkner (W36). He resided in Toledo, Ohio, from 1897 to 1899. In the latter year settled in Browns Valley, Napa County, California, where he purchased a ranch and raised French prunes. On 10 March 1878, in Wamego, Kansas, he married Rebecca Jane Vosburg, daughter of Henry J. and Sarah (Rockwell) Vosburg, born in Christian County, Illinois, died 17 May 1926. They had no children.[123]

N26 iv.   Henry (Harry) Clay Falconer, born 28 February 1846.

    v.   Frank Falconer, born 10 June 1848, died 2 September 1908, buried in Haven Hill Cemetery, Olney, Illinois. He served in the 11th Illinois Volunteer Infantry during the Civil War. He was judged insane in 1874 and spent the rest of his life in Illinois Southern Hospital for the Insane.[124]

    vi.   Jerome B[onaparte] Falconer, born 12 July 1851, died without heirs after 1873 and before 1908.[125]

    vii.   child.

N15 **Samuel Falconer**, born 20 July 1814 in Washington County, Pennsylvania, was living in 1886 in Bishopville, Homer Township, Morgan County, Ohio.

He married, on 24 September 1835, in Belmont County, Ohio,[126] his first cousin Eleanor Ramsay, daughter of Thomas and Eleanor (Falconer) Ramsay, born 9 April 1816 in Belmont County, Ohio, living in 1886.

He was a farmer in Homer Township.

Issue of Samuel and Eleanor (Ramsay) Falconer:[127]

    i.   Sarah Falconer, born 20 September 1836, died 28 December 1836.

N27 ii.   John Aaron Falconer, born 1 December 1837.

    iii.   Nancy Falconer, born 28 December 1839, died 28 December 1839, buried Cary-Lewis Cemetery, Homer Township.

    iv.   Elizabeth Falconer, born 19 February 1841,[128] died 11 November 1891, buried in Bishopville Cemetery. On 24 September 1863 in Morgan County, Ohio,[129] she married Jacob H. Lewis, born 21 March 1842, died 1 November 1887, buried in Bishopville Cemetery. Issue, surname *Lewis:*[130] a. *Samuel J.,* born about 1864; b. *Jesse H.,* born about 1869; c. *Thomas R.,* born about 1873; d. *Bertha J.,* born about 1875.

    v.   Penina Falconer, born 11 July 1844, died 20 October 1861, buried Cary-Lewis Cemetery.

    vi.   Margaret Eleanor Falconer, born 10 July 1846, died 9 February 1861, buried Cary-Lewis Cemetery.

N28   vii.   Reuben Thomas Falconer, born 6 July 1847.

    viii.   Mary Martha Falconer, born 17 May 1849. On 17 July 1873, in Morgan County, Ohio, she married John Strait.

N29   ix.   Samuel A. Falconer, born 11 August 1851.

    x.   Isaac Abraham Falconer, born 30 October 1854, died 12 October 1864, buried Cary-Lewis Cemetery.

    xi.   Jane Amanda Falconer, born 4 March 1859, died 16 July[131] 1861, buried Cary-Lewis Cemetery.

N16   **Thomas M[arshall] Falconer**, born 11 November 1815 [calculated] in Belmont County, Ohio, died 13 July 1875, aged 59 years, 8 months, 2 days, buried in Ridge Cemetery, Platte Township, Dodge County, Nebraska.

He married, as his first wife, on 3 November 1837, in Washington County, Pennsylvania,[132] his first cousin Elizabeth Nichol,[133] daughter of Sampson and Margaret (Falconer) Nichol, born 15 August 1812 in Washington County, Pennsylvania, died 20 June 1850, buried in the Cary-Lewis Cemetery, Homer Township, Morgan County, Ohio.

His second wife was Rebecca, a sister of the wife of Dr. H. I. Rogers, of Appanoose County, Iowa, born about 1820 in Pennsylvania, living in 1860 in Walnut Township, Wayne County, Iowa.[134]

Until about 1850, he lived in Trimble Township, Athens County, Ohio. He and his family lived eight miles southwest of Centerville, Appanoose County, Iowa, from about 1850 to about 1856; five miles south of Promise City, Wayne County, Iowa, from about 1856 to 1861.[135]

Issue of Thomas M. and Elizabeth (Nichol) Falconer:[136]

N30   i.   Reuben Falconer, born 12 January 1840.

    ii.   Sarah Ann Falconer, born about 1842, died 13 September 1877, buried in Hooper Cemetery, Dodge County, Nebraska. She married, on 1 June 1859, in Wayne County, Iowa,[137] Jesse Foglesong, son of Charles and Polly M. (Aldridge) Foglesong, born 8 April 1838 in Johnson County, Indiana, died 12 January 1915 in Washougal, Clark County, Washington, and had issue, surname *Foglesong:* a. *Thomas Charles,* born 3 May 1861, died June 1912 in Schuyler County, Missouri, married Julia Gardner first, then Della M. (Edwards) Hughes; b. *Louella,* born about 1863, married Peter W. Bush; c. *William,* born 22 May 1864, died in Pendleton, Oregon; d. *Mary,* born about 1872, died before 1892. Jesse married a second time.[138]

    iii.   Margaret Falconer, born September 1844, living in 1900 in Fremont, Nebraska.[139] She married, on 30 December 1858, in Wayne County, Iowa,[140] Henry Foglesong, son of George and Mary (Dutton) Foglesong, born 9 June 1838 in Indiana, living in 1900, and had issue, surname *Foglesong:*[141] a. *Sarah,* born 1859; b. *Mary J.,* born about 1862. They appear to have divorced, Henry marrying a woman named Imogene, and then they married each other again, and had: c. *John W.*, born June 1875; d. *Fred L.*, born October 1877; e. *Hattie L.*, born 31 January 1880 in Gentryville, Gentry County, Missouri, married —— Devore.

N31 iv. Samuel Falconer, born July 1848.

Issue of Thomas M. and Rebecca Falconer:[142]

    v. Eliza Falconer, born about 1855.

N32 vi. John T. Falconer, born about 1857.

N17 **John C. Marshall Falconer**, born 20 December 1820 in Belmont County, Ohio, died 14 October 1865 in Goshen Township, Belmont County, Ohio, and was buried in Centerville Cemetery.

He married, as his first wife, on 26 May 1840, in Belmont County, Ohio,[143] Margaret Hinds, but she must have died within a few years.

On 26 February 1846, in Belmont County, Ohio,[144] he married Harriet Matilda Thornborough, daughter of William and Matilda (Lazenby) Thornborough, born 15 February 1827 in Belmont County, Ohio, died 25 August 1905 in Adams County, Iowa, buried in Carl Cemetery. She married, as her second husband, 11 August 1871,[145] James Warnock, by whom she had a son, Welrose. They moved to Adams County, Iowa, shortly after their marriage.

John and Harriet were of Monroe County, Ohio, on 7 August 1852, when they sold the southeast quarter of section one in township six, range four in Belmont County, consisting of 161 acres, to Abram Ramsey.[146] George Thornborough, administrator of his estate, sold at public auction on 5 January 1867 to William Patterson the 164-acre farm in the northwest quarter of section 21, township 7, range 5, in Belmont County, on which John resided at the time of his death.[147]

Issue of John C. Marshall and Harriet Matilda (Thornborough) Falconer:[148]

    i. Reuben Falconer, born 29 November 1846, died 12 July 1847, buried in Centerville Cemetery.

    ii. Louisa Matilda Falconer, born 21 February 1848, died June 1920 in Adams County, Iowa, buried in Carl Cemetery. She married William F. Thompson, born 1848, died 1922, but had no issue. They lived at Ottumwa, Iowa.

N33 ii. Reuben Thomas Falconer, born 22 November 1849.

    iii. Sarah Jane (Jennie) Falconer, born 18 October 1851, died 8 May 1919 near Carbon, Adams County, Iowa, buried in Oakland Cemetery. She married, 4 March 1873, John W. Houck, son of John and Ernestine (Amdor) Houck, born 19 August 1844 in Dearborn County, Indiana, died 14 August 1934, buried in Oakland Cemetery. Issue, surname *Houck*:[149] a. *Harry R.*, born 27 February 1874, died 17 August 1918, married Lou Cooper; b. *Daisy*, born about 1875, died 28 November 1943, married Lewis Reese; c. *Nettie*, born about 1877, died 29 June 1948, married Ernest Neill; d. *Percy*, born 21 February 1880, died 14 January 1881; e. *Joye G.*, born 2 December 1891, died June 1986 in Corning, Iowa, married Thomas Hardisty and then John Brantley.

N34 iv. William George Falconer, born 1 July 1855.

    v. Martha Elizabeth Falconer, born 18 June 1857, died 4 October 1934 in Corning, Adams County, Iowa, buried in Quincy Cemetery. She married, as her first husband, on 30 January 1877, Thomas Jefferson Mooney. Issue, surname *Mooney* (there were four): a. *Elsie M.*, born February 1880; b. *Anna M.*, born October 1881; c. *Guy Raymond*, died 20 September 1901;. They divorced, and she married, as her second husband, on 3 January 1900, as his second wife, Isaac Thomas Homan (father of Minerva Belle Homan who married John Lincoln Falconer, no. N35), born 5 August 1838 in Indiana, died 4 October 1905.

    vi.   Hannah M. Falconer, born 27 June 1859, died 30 December 1937 in Manila, Mississippi County, Arkansas. She married, 1 September 1881, Benjamin Wilson Cowan, born 19 July 1854 in Harrison County, West Virginia, died 1937 in Manila, Arkansas.

    vii. John Brough Falconer, born 4 August 1862, died 14 February 1865,[150] buried in Centerville Cemetery.

N35   viii. John Lincoln Falconer, born 22 May 1865.

N18   **James Falconer**, born about 1828 in Belmont County, Ohio, died 29 May 1862, of typhoid fever, near Corinth, Mississippi.[151]

He married, on 1 September 1853,[152] Martha ——. She married, as her second husband, on 8 October 1874, in Champaign County, Illinois, Ephraim J. Hill.

He lived on land in Sunsbury Township, Monroe County, Ohio. He enlisted as a private, for three years, on 21 October 1861, in Company A, 77th Regiment of Ohio Volunteer Infantry.

Issue of James and Martha Falconer:[153]

    i.   Reuben Newkirk Falconer, born 24 July 1854. He was living in 1900 in Pilot Township, Vermilion County, Illinois, unmarried.[154] He may have had a widow who lived in Mount Vernon, Illinois.

    ii.   Margaret Jane Falconer, born 14 March 1857, died 1941 in Vermilion County, Illinois. She married, as his second wife, on 30 March 1884, in Vermilion County, Illinois,[155] Austin Juvinall, son of Andrew and Mary (James) Juvinall, born 1843 in Vermilion County, Illinois, died 1904 in Vermilion County, Illinois. Issue, surname *Juvinall:*[156] a. *Ora*, married —— Lane; b. *George Verne*, born 15 November 1884, died September 1963, married Nellie L. ——; c. *O. Glen*, born 1886, died 1956, married Mafra M. ——; d. *James.*

    iii. Mary Melissa Falconer, born 25 November 1858. She married —— Lehman and, in 1883, lived in Urbana, Illinois.

N36 iv. Cassius Millard Falconer, born 1 November 1860.

N19   **Martin DeMoss Falconer**, born 29 June 1839 in Spencer Township, Lorain County, Ohio, died 3 May 1937 in Carlton Township, Barry County, Michigan, was buried in Irving Cemetery.

He married, as his first wife, on 13 September 1870, in Lowell, Michigan,[157] Minnie R. Sawyer, born about 1848 in Lowell, Michigan. At that time, he resided in Frankfort, Benzie County, Michigan. They later divorced.

He married, as his second wife, on 15 March 1876 in Barry County, Michigan, Jennie Lind Engle, born 16 October 1857, died 18 May 1940, buried in Irving Cemetery.

He came to Eaton and then Barry County, Michigan, in 1853. Graduating from Charlotte High School, he taught at rural schools in Charlotte and

Lowell, Michigan, but went back to Ohio in 1860. Returning to Michigan, he sold cheese in Detroit, ran engines for the Sack and Blind factory in Traverse City, and worked on Great Lakes boats as an engineer in the winter. He came to Barry County in 1874, where he farmed and worked as a mason. Among his interests were playing the fiddle and reading the Bible, with which he liked to disagree.

Issue of Martin DeMoss and Jennie Lind (Engle) Falconer:[158]

N37   i.   LeRoy DeMoss Falconer, born 24 February 1877.

      ii.   Florence Adell Falconer, born 9 January 1879, died 19 September 1979 in Kalamazoo, Michigan. She married, as her first husband, Byron R. Pettit, born 1876, died 1933, buried in Irving Cemetery, and had issue, surname *Pettit*:[159] a. *Melvin L.*, born 24 March 1908, died 22 July 1989 in Dewitt, Michigan. She married, as her second husband, Charles Cooper.

      iii.   Grace Falconer, born 9 April 1881, died 10 August 1883 in Carlton Township, Barry County, Michigan.

N38   iv.   Benjamin Franklin Falconer, born 1 October 1885.

      v.   Mary Elizabeth Falconer, born 17 February 1889, died 29 September 1981 in Hastings, Michigan. On 24 June 1908, she married Charles Hicks Edwards, son of John Edwin and Elizabeth (McGregor) Edwards, born 6 September 1884, died 1 May 1954. Issue, surname *Edwards*:[160] a. *Thelma E.*, born about 1910; b. *Orton V.*, born about 1914.

      vi.   Ethel Maud Falconer, born 1 March 1892, died 24 December 1965 in Roxbury, Massachusetts. She married, on 26 November 1916, in Hastings, Michigan, John Calvin Vaughan, son of J. W. and Nora (Character) Vaughan (later divorced), and then Fred Gregg, followed by Loyd Koler.

N39   vii.   Forest Earl Falconer, born 17 May 1894.

N20   **Reuben Henry Falconer**, born 27 October 1841 in Spencer Township, Medina County, Ohio, died 9 May 1922 in Moline, Kansas.

He married, on 27 June 1865, in Medina County, Ohio, Mary Jane Auble, daughter of Jacob and Jane Margaret (Gallatin) Auble, born 23 February 1844 in Guilford Township, Medina County, Ohio, died 13 October 1916 in Moline, Kansas.

He served as a drummer in Company B, 42nd Ohio Volunteer Infantry, from 22 September 1861 to 30 September 1864. They lived at Nashville, Michigan, from about 1867 to 1880; in Triplett Township and Gravel Point, Chariton County, Missouri, 1880 to 1899; and in Moline thereafter.

Issue of Reuben Henry and Mary Jane (Auble) Falconer:[161]

N40   i.   William Eugene Falconer, born 6 April 1867.

      ii.   Cora Belle Falconer, born 18 March 1869. She married, on 10 April 1888, John Harrison Stone, son of William Jordan and Mary Ann (Foster) Stone, born 31 July 1863 in Mountain Grove, Missouri, died 16 December 1918 in Roswell, New Mexico, and had issue, surname *Stone* (born in Moline, Kansas): a. *Daisy Golden*, born 28 July 1889 in Mountain Grove Missouri; b. *Rodney Ray*, born 18 April 1891; c. *Mabel Lee*, born 2 January 1893; d. *Blanche Lora*, born 15 January 1895; e. *Maude Belle*, born 15 February 1897. She married, at Mountain Grove, Missouri, as her second husband, Harley Crowell.

      iii.   Lucinda Jane Falconer, born 18 November 1871, lived in Houston, Missouri.

She married John McCalla, who died in Cabool, Missouri, and had issue, surname *McCalla*: a. *Hobart L.*, born 24 August 1896; b. *Myrtle M.*, born 11 August 1899; c. *Earl F.*, born 29 January 1902, died October 1975 in Cabool, Missouri.

iv. Ida May Falconer, born 27 September 1873, lived at Mountain Grove, Missouri. She married Will Fry, and had issue, surname *Fry*: a. *Henry Austin*, born 31 March 1891; b. *Alice Odessa*, born 12 March 1893; c. *Chadey Hazel*, born 26 September 1895; d. *Pearl May*, born 23 August 1911; e. *Paul James*, born 22 December 1913.

v. Nellie Maude Falconer, born 7 June 1875, died July 1894, at Gravel Point, Missouri. She married George Ogle and had one son, *George*, who died at birth.

vi. Minnie Lee Falconer, born 15 April 1877, died May 1894 at Gravel Point, Missouri.

vii. Fannie Edith Falconer, born 9 June 1880, lived at Moline, Kansas; Homerville, Ohio; Sullivan, Ohio; and Weslaco, Texas. She married Harry Amsbaugh and had issue, surname *Amsbaugh*: a. *Jesse Lee*, born 22 March 1907; b. *Mary Edith*, born 15 April 1909; c. *Creta Arminta*, born 29 January 1911; d. *Kent Eugene*, born 8 March 1913, died February 1960.

N21 Archelaus Revier Falconer, born 21 September 1847 in Spencer Township, Medina County, Ohio, died 29 February 1928 in Harrisville Township, Medina County, Ohio, was buried in Woodlawn Cemetery.

He married, on 17 October 1872, Mary Magdalena Hoegner, daughter of J. W. and Maria Hoegner, born 7 March 1850 in Ohio, died 3 July 1926 in Harrisville Township, Medina County, Ohio, buried in Woodlawn Cemetery.

Issue of Archelaus Revier and Mary Magdalena (Hoegner) Falconer:[162]

N41 i. Frank Arthur Falconer, born 29 June 1874.

ii. Bertha Adell Falconer, born 9 April 1876, died September 1972 in Medina, Ohio, buried in Woodlawn Cemetery. She married, 16 October 1897, in Medina County, Ohio,[163] Frank W. Dague, and had issue, surname *Dague*: a. *Howard A.*, born 26 February 1899, died April 1986 in Westland, Michigan; b. *Maybelle P.*, born and died 1901; c. *Mary M.*, born and died 1904; d. *Mildred*, born about 1905, married —— Rock, lived in Cleveland, Ohio.

iii. Emma Maria Falconer, born 6 January 1879, died 30 November 1955 in Lodi, Ohio, buried in Woodlawn Cemetery. She married, 7 March 1900, in Medina County, Ohio,[164] William H. Kemery, born 1877, died 1956, and had issue, surname *Kemery*: a. *Gertrude Ellen*, born 6 November 1900, died February 1978, married Howard C. Handel; b. *Orville Elroy*; c. *Mary Belle*, born about 1905, married —— Mikesell.

N42 iv. Edward Leslie Falconer, born 20 September 1882.

N43 v. Herbert Allen Falconer, born 24 March 1892.

N22 Amandus DeForest Falconer, born 27 September 1849 in Spencer Township, Medina County, Ohio, died 4 July 1930, as a result of a car accident, in Hermanville, Ohio, was buried in Elmwood Cemetery, Lorain.

He married, on 26 May 1874, in Medina County, Ohio, Jennie A. Williams, born April 1851 in Lynchburg, Virginia, died 28 October 1918 in Lodi, Ohio, buried in Elmwood Cemetery.

In 1880, he lived in Spencer Township, Medina County, Ohio; in 1900 in

Lorain, Ohio; in 1910, in Cleveland; and, in 1920, in Lodi, Ohio. His obituary mentions that he was a Civil War veteran, but I have not been able to find any evidence of that.

Issue of Amandus DeForest and Jennie A. (Williams) Falconer:[165]

N44 i. Allen Eugene Falconer, born 16 June 1875.

N45 ii. Sherman DeForest Falconer, born 19 September 1878.

     iii. Maude M. Falconer, born 20 September 1881, died 2 February 1882 in Spencer Township, Medina County, Ohio.[166]

     iv. Mabel G. Falconer, born 22 March 1886 in Lorain, buried 16 April 1887 in Elmwood Cemetery.

     v. Grace A. Falconer, born 19 January 1888 in Lorain, buried the same day in Elmwood Cemetery.

     vi. Alta A. Falconer, born 22 February 1894, died 1918 in Lodi, Ohio. She married, 25 March 1915, in Medina County, Ohio,[167] George A. Lintern, born 1894, died 1958, buried in Spencer Cemetery.

     vii. Alma A. Falconer, born 23 March 1896, died young.

N23 **Roswell Graham Falconer**, born 5 April 1852 in Spencer Township, Medina County, Ohio, died 5 January 1919 in Spencer Township, Medina County, Ohio, was buried in Litchfield Burial Park.

He married, on 20 September 1876 in Medina County, Ohio, Cora M. Parent, daughter of V. W. and Lucy A. (Baldwin) Parent,[168] born 2 August 1858 in Ohio, died in 1945, buried in Litchfield Burial Park.

Issue of Roswell Graham and Cora M. (Parent) Falconer:[169]

     i. Lucy May Falconer, born 8 March 1879 in Spencer Township, Medina County, Ohio, died 24 May 1914 in Litchfield, Ohio. She married, 25 November 1896, in Medina County, Ohio, William A. Preston, born November 1874 in Ohio, living in 1920 in New London, Ohio, and had issue, surname *Preston*:[170] a. *Walter H.*, born March 1898; b. *Mabel V.*, born May 1900; c. *Letha M.*, born about 1902; d. *Paul*, born about 1909; e. *Perry*, born about 1909; f. *Blaine*, born about 1911.

     ii. Reuben Valentine Falconer, born 15 October 1880 in Homer Township, Medina County, Ohio, died 26 October 1961 in Creston, Ohio, unmarried, buried in Litchfield Burial Park.

     iii. Lina Elvira Falconer, born 2 July 1885, lived in Barberton, Ohio. She married, 30 May 1903, in Medina County, Ohio, Harry E. Saurer, born about 1883 in Ohio, and had issue, surname *Saurer*:[171] a. *Loyal V.*, born about 1904; b. *Arthur E.*, born 2 March 1906, died October 1979 in Wadsworth, Ohio; c. *Dorothy E.*, born 1917; d. *Lillian M.*, born 1919.

N46 iv. Budd Benjamin Falconer, born 2 February 1891.

N47 v. Ted Alonzo Falconer, born 13 February 1893.

N24 **Cyrus Falconer**, born 5 March 1856 in Hamilton, Ohio, died May 1930 in East Aurora, New York, was buried in Greenwood Cemetery, Hamilton, Ohio.

He married Martha Platt, daughter of Cyrus and Jeannette (Hulm) Platt, born about 1862 in Delaware, Ohio, died 26 November 1941 in East Aurora, New York. She was a prominent social worker. One of the first probation officers of the juvenile court in Chicago, in 1906 she took charge of the House of Refuge in Philadelphia, a penal institution for girls, where she received national attention for the reforms she instituted. She spoke at colleges and schools around the United States, as well as in Europe. She later was executive secretary of the Federation Caring for Protestants in New York City.[172]

After their marriage, they moved to Topeka, Kansas, where he was associated with the Santa Fe Railroad. In the early 1890s, they lived at Oak Park, Illinois. In the 1920s, he lived in Columbus, Ohio, where he was associated with the Hocking Valley Railroad.

Issue of Cyrus and Martha (Platt) Falconer:[173]

    i.   Helen F. Falconer, living unmarried in Wilkes-Barre, Pennsylvania, in 1969.

N48   ii.   Douglas Platt Falconer, born 21 April 1889.

N49   iii.   Cyrus Falconer, born 3 October 1893.

N25   **Robert Crawford Falconer**, born 16 February 1882 in Hamilton, Ohio, died 14 July 1978 in Columbus, North Carolina.

He married, as his first wife, on 22 October 1914, Dorothy Lesley Putnam, born about 1882 in New York, died 15 April 1939 in Nutley, New Jersey.

He married, as his second wife, on 30 June 1942, at Lake George, New York, Ida Patton. She died in 1943.

He married, as his third wife, on 17 January 1947, at Nutley, New Jersey, Edna Goelz, born 9 December 1895, who survived him.

He entered Dartmouth College in September 1900, graduating in June 1905, with a B.A. degree. He graduated from Union Theological Seminary in 1908 with a B.D. He was a Congregational minister, serving as Associate Minister of the Pilgrim Congregational Church in Seattle, Washington, from 1909 to 1911; as minister of the Church of Christ, at Dartmouth College, from 1912 to 1917; and as minister at St. Paul's Congregational Church in Nutley, New Jersey, from 1919 to 1947. He then retired to Tryon, North Carolina. During World War I, he was Y.M.C.A. secretary in France and later Divisional Secretary, 4th Division of Army of Occupation in Germany. He wrote *A Child's Ramble Through the Bible: The Old Testament* (New York: Fleming H. Revall, 1922). His last home was in Tryon, North Carolina.

Issue of Robert Crawford and Dorothy Lesley (Putnam) Falconer:[174]

N50   i.   Robert Haven Falconer, born 28 February 1918.

N26   **Henry (Harry) Clay Falconer**, born 28 July 1846 in Rossville (now Hamilton), Ohio, died 22 April 1917 in Olney, Illinois,[175] was buried in Haven Hill Cemetery.

He married, on 25 December 1884, in Richland County, Illinois,[176] Martha (Peed) Faesler, daughter of Washington and Elizabeth (Knight) Peed, born 8 July 1861 in Petersburg, Indiana, died 15 January 1939 in Olney, Illinois, buried in Haven Hill Cemetery.

In 1900, he lived in Noble, Illinois, and, in 1910, in Olney, Illinois. He was a farmer. He also served as Richland County Treasurer.

Issue of Henry Clay and Martha (Peed) Falconer:[177]

i. Kate Stearns Falconer, born 18 December 1886, died 17 March 1967 in Glencoe, Illinois. She married, on 8 June 1918, in Edinburgh, Scotland, Maurice Marwick. She was served in 1918 and 1919 in England, Scotland, France, Luxembourg, and Germany. She lived in Chicago, Illinois, in 1917, and later in Glencoe. Issue, surname *Marwick*: a. *Edward F.*; b. *Julia Falconer*, married Robert Fritz Rainer.

ii. Mary Elizabeth Falconer, born 4 October 1892, lived in Miami, Florida, in 1939. She married, on 16 August 1916, in Richland County, Illinois, John M. Ritter.

iii. Laura Margaret Falconer, born 21 June 1898, died before 1939. She married, in 1921 in Richland County, Illinois, Caleb Torrence, and had issue, surname *Torrence*: a. *Mary Elizabeth*; b. *John F.*

N27 **John Aaron Falconer**, born 1 December 1837 in Homer Township, Morgan County, Ohio, died 16 January 1913 in Windsor Township, Morgan County, Ohio, was buried in Fairview Cemetery.

He married, on 22 January 1865, in Morgan County, Ohio,[178] Susanna A. Steffy, daughter of George and Sarah Steffy, born 1845 in Homer Township, Morgan County, Ohio, died 29 August 1916 in Windsor Township, Morgan County, Ohio, buried in Fairview Cemetery.

He enlisted, on 2 May 1864, as a private in Company K, 161st Ohio Infantry, was discharged 2 September 1864, and received a pension for his services.[179]

Issue of John Aaron and Susanna A. (Steffy) Falconer:[180]

i. Samuel Aaron Falconer, born 6 December 1865, died 20 May 1890, buried in Fairview Cemetery. He married Elizabeth ——, born 6 April 1866 [calculated], died 2 March 1887.

ii. George Elmer Falconer, born 3 December 1867, died 22 May 1879, buried in Bishopville Cemetery, Homer Township, Morgan County, Ohio.

iii. Ramsey Merton Falconer, born 1 October 1869 in Homer Township, Morgan County, Ohio, died 3 April 1904 in Unionville, Pennsylvania,[181] buried in Mt. Olivet Cemetery. He married, 14 February 1899, in Morgan County, Ohio,[182] Maude A. Lyne, daughter of Theodoric and Philena (Mummey) Lyne.

iv. Sarah Eleanor Falconer, born 30 September 1873, died 5 September 1893, buried in Fairview Cemetery.

v. Hester Amanda Falconer, born 11 November 1877, died 5 February 1891, buried in Fairview Cemetery.

N51 vi. Jasper Emmett Falconer, born 2 October 1882.

N28 **Reuben Thomas Falconer**, born 6 July 1847 in Morgan County, Ohio, died 7 November 1895, probably in Linn County, Missouri.

On 9 February 1869, in Belmont County, Ohio,[183] he married Mary Matilda Gladden, daughter of William and Hannah (Thornborough) Gladden, born 28 December 1849 in Belmont County, Ohio, died 17 April 1925 in Linn County, Missouri.

In 1880, he and his family lived in Cheney's Grove Township, McLean County, Illinois.[184] Mary M. and her younger children were living in 1900 in Jackson Township, Linn County, Missouri.[185]

Issue of Reuben Thomas and Mary Matilda (Gladden) Falconer:[186]

i.   Mary Elizabeth Falconer, born 5 February 1871 in Ohio, died 5 January 1939 in Texico, New Mexico, or Leedy, Oklahoma. She married, 16 October 1890, Alexander Brown, born about 1852 in Missouri, living in 1910 in Trail, Oklahoma. Issue, surname *Brown*:[187] a. *Loyd*, born about 1895; b. *Everett*, born about 1896; c. *Ethel*, born 1898; d. *Gladys*, born about 1904; e. *Dalla*, born about 1904; f. *Mabel*, born about 1906.

ii.   Anna Falconer, born 6 July 1872 in Illinois, died 3 July 1982. She married, 3 July 1892, Joe Lorette, and had issue, surname *Lorette*: a. *Earl Michael*, born 29 November 1896 in Yale, Oklahoma, married Eva Jane Custer.

iii.   Dora Falconer, born 12 March 1874, died 20 August 1895.

N52   iv.   John Herman Falconer, born 7 November 1875.

v.   Hannah Eleanor Falconer, born 16 March 1877, died 7 September 1932 in Asher, Oklahoma. She married, 6 July 1897, Bun Wolford.

N53   vi.   Thomas William Falconer, born 4 December 1879.

vii.   Eva May Falconer, born 26 May 1881 in Illinois, died 12 February 1949 in Wheeling, Missouri. She married, on 3 December 1900, Louis Labor.

N54   viii.   Roy Bert Falconer, born 26 October 1883.

ix.   infant Falconer, born 22 October 1886, died October 1886.

N55   x.   Samuel Falconer, born 2 October 1888.

N56   xi.   Dallas A. Falconer, born 20 February 1890.

xii.   Bertha Viola Falconer, born 22 June 1892, died 2 February 1973 in Purdin, Missouri. She married, 16 February 1916, Lyell Cecil Harris, and had issue, surname *Harris*: a. *Nolan Lyell*, born 10 December 1917, died 25 February 1969; b. *Hazel Ruth*, born 18 November 1919; c. *Gerald Wayne*, born 9 December 1920, died May 1985 in Madrid, Iowa; d. *Harold Lee*, born 10 February 1922; e. *J. D.*, born 10 September 1923; f. *Cecil Ray*, born 26 December 1924.

N29   **Samuel A. Falconer**, born 11 August 1851 in Homer Township, Morgan County, Ohio, was said to have died in 1938, place unknown, but probably in Michigan.[188]

He married, as his first wife, by license dated 23 October 1878 in Athens County, Ohio,[189] Calla Conaway.

He probably married, as his second wife, Jantha G. ——, born 8 July 1849 [calculated], died 27 May 1887 in Homer Township, Morgan County, Ohio,[190] buried in Fairview Cemetery.

He married, as his third wife, on 12 May 1888 in Morgan County, Ohio,[191] Anna E. McElfresh, born April 1862, living 1900, in Marion Township, Morgan County, Ohio.

He and his first wife lived in Athens County, Ohio, until 1886, when his father sold him 163 acres in Homer Township, Morgan County, Ohio. He was an automobile worker in Flint, Michigan, for the Buick Motor Division of General Motors Corporation, from 1920 to 1929. He was living in 1923 in Santoy, Perry County, Ohio.[192]

Issue of Samuel A. and Calla (Conaway) Falconer, born in Homer Township, Morgan County, Ohio:[193]

i.   John H. Falconer, born 27 July 1880. Not traced further.

Issue of Samuel A. and Anna E. (McElfresh) Falconer, born in Homer Township, Morgan County, Ohio:[194]

    ii.   Cassius A. (Scotty) Falconer, born 30 December 1889, died, unmarried, 23 December 1958 in Eureka, California. He was in Flint, Michigan from 1910 to 1913. He served in World War I. In 1950, he moved to Eureka, where he worked as a custodian-manager of the Humboldt County Community Hospital.[195]

    iii. Charles Glenn Falconer, born 28 May 1893, living in 1958 in Detroit, Michigan. He was in Flint, Michigan from 1919 to 1927.

    iv. Anna Velma Falconer, born 4 October 1894, died 9 December 1971 in Grayling, Michigan. She married, on 3 December 1919, in Flint, Michigan,[196] Frank Rhoades, son of Levi and Rebecca (McAllister) Rhoades, born about 1885 in Northumberland, Pennsylvania. She worked as a practical nurse in Detroit.

    v.   Grace Falconer, born May 1897.

    vi. George W. Falconer, born June 1899 in Virginia, probably died young.

N30 **Reuben Falconer**, born 12 January 1840 in Athens County, Ohio, died 7 November 1908 in Fremont, Dodge County, Nebraska, buried in Ridge Cemetery.

He married, on 4 March 1873 in Jefferson County, Iowa, Maria Elizabeth Humphreys, born 20 March 1852 in Iowa, died 3 August 1913 in Fremont, Nebraska, buried in Ridge Cemetery.

In 1865 and 1866, he lived three-and-a-half miles southeast of Fairfield, Iowa. About 1869, he moved to Maple Precinct, later Maple Branch Township, Dodge County, Nebraska.

He enlisted as a private, on 11 August 1862, in Company I, 36th Iowa Infantry, and was discharged 24 August 1865 at DeValls Bluff, Arkansas.

Issue of Reuben and Maria Elizabeth (Humphreys) Falconer:[197]

N57 i.   Ernest Falconer, born 24 December 1873.

    ii. Louella (Lulu) Falconer, born 14 November 1875, lived around Newman Grove and Tilden, Nebraska. She married Charles H. Boschult, born April 1876 in Nebraska, living in 1920 in Pierce County, Nebraska, and had issue, surname, Boschult:[198] a. *Mildred*, born about 1900; b. *Trajan*, born 26 May 1902, died July 1977 in Fremont, Nebraska; c. *Charles R.*, born 9 January 1904, died November 1984 in Omaha, Nebraska; d. *Anona*, born about 1905; e. *Rollin*, born about 1907; f. *Margaret*, born about 1910.

N58 iii. George Falconer, born 12 August 1878.

    iv. Etta Falconer, born 17 March 1882, died 28 February 1971 in Fremont, Nebraska, buried in Ridge Cemetery. She married George Dufek. No issue.

    v.   Ruth Falconer, born 17 December 1883, died 2 June 1908, buried in Ridge Cemetery. She married —— Moore and had issue, surname, *Moore*: a. *Lois*, married —— Dooze.

    vi. Ruby Falconer, born 17 December 1883, buried in Schuyler, Nebraska. She married Chris Unkel.

    vii. Thayer Falconer, born 29 September 1886, died 1951, buried in Ridge Cemetery. He married, in 1910, Alma K. Post, born about 1891. They divorced and she married Dick Bartling and moved to Missouri.

    viii. Ethel Blanche Falconer, born 11 September 1889, died 13 September 1984 in

Fremont, Nebraska. She married William C. Post, born 7 May 1888, died 21 February 1955, and had issue, surname *Post:* a. *Virgil A.*, born 3 July 1927, lives in Fremont, Nebraska, married, 14 April 1955, Eleanor A. Granneman.

N31   **Samuel Falconer**, born July 1848 in Athens County, Ohio, died 1906, was buried in Inman Cemetery, Holt County, Nebraska.[199]

He married Matilda Keltner, born October 1848 in Maryland, living in 1900.

In 1880, they lived in Maple Precinct, Dodge County, Nebraska, and in 1900, in Ewing Township, Holt County, Nebraska. It is likely that his widow and family left Holt County, Nebraska, not long after 1906.

Issue of Samuel and Matilda (Keltner) Falconer:[200]

    i.   Eva Falconer, born November 1871 in Iowa, died 1939 in Inman or Inman Township, Holt County, Nebraska, was buried in Inman Cemetery. She married, on 28 June 1887, in Dodge County, Nebraska,[201] Gilbert Noring, born 1863 in Norway, died 1931, buried in Inman Cemetery. They had issue, surname *Noring:*[202] a. *Samuel*, born 22 January 1890, died 22 April 1956 in Hastings, Nebraska, married Margaret A. Nordyke; b. *Anna M.*, born November 1892; c. *Bertha*, born 15 September 1895, died November 1977 in Page, Nebraska, buried in Inman Cemetery, married —— Craig; d. *Edith*, born 21 April 1898, died 24 December 1985 in Page, Nebraska, buried in Inman Cemetery, married —— Grubbs;. e. *Carrie*, born 26 July 1901, died June 1983 in Ewing, Nebraska, married —— Meyer; f. *Gilbert (Dub)*, born 2 December 1905, died 24 April 1988 in Arco, Idaho; g. *Bill*, born 1909, died 1957.

    ii.   John T. Falconer, born May 1874 in Nebraska, living with his parents in 1900.

    iii.   Edward Falconer, born about 1877. Not traced further.

N59 iv.   Lafayette Falconer, born April 1879.

    v.   Nina Falconer, born about 1881, married, on 7 June 1899, in Ewing, Nebraska,[203] George Malone, son of Thomas and Emaline (Doke) Malone, born about 1875 in Kansas, died 17 May 1902 in O'Neill, Nebraska, a railroad section laborer. Issue, surname *Malone:* a. *Mabel M.*, born about 1900, living in Boulder, Colorado, in 1918.[204]

    vi.   Raymond Falconer, born April 1883. He or one of his brothers or sisters was the father of Josie Falconer, born about 1911 in Arkansas, who in 1920 lived with her uncle Lafayette.[205]

    vii.   Lizzie Falconer, born October 1886.

    viii.   Grace Falconer, born December 1888.

    ix.   Mable Falconer, born December 1890.

N32   **John T. Falconer**, born about 1857 in Wayne County, Iowa, died 23 December 1930 in San Diego County, California.

He married Mary E. ——, born about 1860 in California, died 7 August 1939 in San Diego County, California.

In 1910, they lived in Berkeley, California.

Issue of John T. and Mary E. Falconer:[206]

    i.   Helen R. Falconer, born about 1887 in California.

N33   **Reuben Thomas Falconer**, born 22 November 1849 in Smith Town-

ship, Belmont County, Ohio, died 29 October 1908 in Carl Township, Adams
County, Iowa, was buried in Forest Hill Cemetery, Carl, Iowa.

He married Nancy Jane Homan, daughter of Wesley and Melissa Homan,
born 22 May 1856 in Iowa, died 5 August 1930 in Wallowa County, Oregon.

In 1899, the family went by train to Enterprise, Oregon, to visit their two
sons, who had moved there in 1898. He and his family were living in 1900 on
the Crow Indian Reservation, Custer County, Montana.

Issue of Reuben Thomas and Nancy Jane (Homan) Falconer, born in Adams
County, Iowa:[207]

N60   i.   Fred Wesley Falconer, born 1879.
N61   ii. Ross R. Falconer, born 11 January 1881.
      iii. Robert Thurman Falconer, born 28 August 1888 [calculated], died 22 October
           1890, from drowning, was buried in Forest Hill Cemetery.
      iv. Evelyn Falconer, born 2 January 1892, died, unmarried, April 1986 in Enter-
           prise, Oregon.
      v.   Carrie Mabel Falconer, born 21 July 1895, died 16 October 1969 in Oregon,
           was buried in Walla Walla, Washington. She married, on 21 July 1919, in
           Enterprise, Oregon, Wayne Kenneth Wagner, son of Alonzo Monroe and Isabel
           (Long) Wagner, born February 1892 in Enterprise, Oregon, died August 1967
           in Walla Walla, Washington, an electrician, and had issue, surname *Wagner*:
           a. *Pauline E.*, born 6 January 1922, lives in Walla Walla, Washington, mar-
           ried, 1943, Kenneth Knowles; b. *Robert W.*, born 25 August 1925, lives in
           Boulder, Colorado, married, June 1950, Roberta Jean Kennedy.

N34   **William George Falconer**, born 1 July 1855 in Smith Township,
Belmont County, Ohio, died 24 January 1930 in Carl Township, Adams
County, Iowa, was buried in Carl Cemetery.[208]

He married, on 1 January 1877, in Adams County, Iowa, Florence Bell
Tucker, daughter of Ephrem and Elizabeth (Siddens) Tucker, born 30 May
1860 in Putnam County, Indiana, died 19 April 1919 in Carl Township, Adams
County, Iowa, buried in Carl Cemetery.

He was a farmer in Carl Township.

Issue of William George and Florence Bell (Tucker) Falconer:[209]

N62   i.   Roy John Falconer, born 18 December 1877.
      ii. Myrtle Maud Falconer, born 18 August 1879, died 18 September 1959 in
           Corning, Iowa, buried in Carl Cemetery. She married, on 28 February 1900
           in Adams County, Iowa, Frank Bertrum Cramer, son of W. P. and Adeline
           (Milley) Cramer, born 9 August 1876, died 1953.[210] Issue, surname *Cramer*:
           a. *Grace*, born about 1901; b. *Flora*, born about 1902, married ——
           Hetherington; c. *John*, born about 1903; d. *Dora*, born about 1908; e. *Mar-
           guerite*, born 1919, lives in Sioux Falls, South Dakota, married Richard B.
           Leander.
N63   iii. Earl Irwin Falconer, born 25 August 1881.
N64   iv. Clyde Raymond Falconer, born 26 March 1883.
      v.   Alta May Falconer, born 8 January 1885, died 6 July 1935, buried in Carl
           Cemetery. She married, on 5 February 1905, Frank Newton Lewellen, born
           10 August 1877 in Competine Township, Wapello County, Iowa, died 11 Janu-
           ary 1954. Issue, surname *Lewellen*:[211]   a. *Percy Newton*, born 3 March
           1910, died February 1978 in Des Moines, Iowa; b. *Dale W.*, born 1919.

    vi.   Mattie E. Falconer, born 8 April 1887, died 1969, buried in Carl Cemetery. She married, on 20 December 1905, Frank Packenham, born 19 July 1884, died June 1968 in Corning, Iowa.

    vii. Dolly Falconer, born 31 December 1888, died 22 August 1889.

    viii. George Blaine Falconer, 12 April 1892, died 3 December 1899.

    ix. Bessie Harriet Falconer, born 30 June 1895. She married Guy Allen DeVore, born 1890, and in 1984, lived in Charles City, Iowa. Issue, surname *DeVore*:[212] a. *Norville J.*, born about 1914; b. *Arlie G.*, born about 1915, lives in Dexter, Minnesota; c. *Lauren R.*, born about 1917, lives in Terril, Iowa; d. *Watson P.*, born 1919; g. *Max Eugene*, lives in Corning, Iowa.

N65 x. Paul Tucker Falconer, born 29 August 1897.

N35   **John Lincoln Falconer**, born 22 May 1865 in Smith Township, Belmont County, Ohio, died 25 September 1945 in Quincy Township, Adams County, Iowa, while visiting, and was buried in Carl Cemetery.

He married, on 23 February 1888, in Adams County, Iowa, Minerva Belle Homan, daughter of Isaac Thomas and Nancy E. (Wilson) Homan, born 28 August 1865 in Adams County, Iowa, died 5 March 1932 in Trona, Colorado, buried in Trona Cemetery.

He was a farmer in Adams County, Iowa, later a cattle rancher in Colorado.

Issue of John Lincoln and Minerva Belle (Homan) Falconer:[213]

    i. Lena Violet Falconer, born 12 February 1890, died 20 October 1976 in Albany, Oregon, buried in Twin Oaks Cemetery. She married, as her first husband, on 11 February 1908, Ivar Christian Jensen, son of Lars Peter and Anna Elizabeth (Iversen) Jensen, born 17 September 1886 Storehangen, Denmark, died 5 December 1978 Albany, Oregon, by whom she had issue, surname *Jensen*: a. *Genevieve Marie*, born 4 March 1909, died 5 May 1980, married, 16 June 1926, —— Ellis; b. *Anna Elizabeth*, born 3 March 1910, died 20 March 1910; c. *Kathleen Lenore*, born 6 May 1911; d. *Phillip Merril*, born 8 November 1913; e. *Ina May*, born 13 July 1915, lives in Albany, Oregon, married —— Chladek. They were divorced in April 1917, and she married, on 5 October 1920, Carl Reuben Alley, born 11 November 1892, died February 1980 in Pleasant Hill, Missouri, and had issue, surname *Alley*: f. *Carlena June*, born 22 March 1922; g. *Ernest Melvin*, born 11 May 1928. They divorced in November 1938, and she married, on 22 May 1943, Roy Marpel Morton, born 11 January 1881, died 8 November 1956. She married, as her fourth husband, on 21 June 1958, Ivar Christian Jensen.

N66 ii. John Mark Falconer, born 1 September 1902.

N36   **Cassius Millard Falconer**, born 1 November 1860 in Sunsbury Township, Monroe County, Ohio, was living in 1900 in Oakwood Township, Vermilion County, Illinois, but died within a few years after that date.

He married Anna Lincoln Mosher, born February 1864 in Illinois, died 14 June 1917 in Middlefork Township, Vermilion County, Illinois, buried in Partlow Cemetery, Armstrong, Illinois.

Issue of Cassius Millard and Anna Lincoln (Mosher) Falconer:[214]

N67 i. Robert Harrison Falconer, born 11 August 1888.

N68 ii. Charles M. Falconer, born 5 November 1894.

    iii.   John Edward Falconer, born 1 January 1898, died 21 October 1970 in Danville, Illinois. He married, on 15 August 1936, at Danville, Illinois, Frances Bernice Lamb, born 29 July 1909 in Rossville, Illinois. A veteran of World War I, he worked for Rossville Telephone Company and the F.M.C. Corporation. They had no children.

N69   iv.   Walter Clark Falconer, born 24 July 1899.

N70   v.   Marion Falconer, born 21 January 1901.

N37   **LeRoy DeMoss Falconer**, born 24 February 1877 in Carlton Township, Barry County, Michigan, died 22 August 1957 in Wichita, Kansas.

He married, as his first wife, on 12 December 1894, at Hastings, Michigan,[215] Maggie Slocum, daughter of Elisha D. and Orinda (Barnhart) Slocum, born December 1872 in Michigan, living in 1935 in Bigelow, Arkansas. They divorced, and she married, as her second husband, on 2 September 1905, at Hastings,[216] Joseph M. Harding, son of John and Catherine (Steenard) Harding, born about 1872 in Michigan. By 1935, she had married —— Underwood.

He married, as his second wife, Nina ——, born about 1888 in Nebraska, living in 1920 in Pawhuska, Oklahoma.

He seems to have married, as his third wife, Rose ——, with whom he lived from about 1925 to 1935 in Oakland, California.[217]

He married, as his fourth wife, by 1935, Margaret ——, born 14 August 1895, died February 1974 in Augusta, Kansas.

He lived in Hastings, Michigan, about 1900, where he worked as a laborer, but later moved. In 1920, he and his wife Nina lived in Pawhuska, Oklahoma. From 1922 to 1935, he was in Oakland, California, working as a teamster and then as a foreman for the Santa Fe Express Company. By 1935, he was in Kansas City, Missouri, where he worked as a painter for a car dealer. He and his wife Margaret moved to Wichita, Kansas, in 1940, where he operated an appliance repair shop.

Issue of LeRoy DeMoss and Maggie (Slocum) Falconer (their names were changed to Underwood):[218]

    i.   Leo DeMoss Underwood, born 15 October 1896, died 4 April 1983 in Bigelow, Arkansas, buried in Wye Cemetery, Pulaski County, Arkansas. He married Inis Hillis. He was a stock farmer.

    ii.   Benjamin S. Underwood, born July 1898, living in 1957 in Hoodsport, Washington.

Issue of LeRoy DeMoss and Nina (——) Falconer, born in Kansas:[219]

    iii.   Franklin M. Falconer, born about 1911, living in 1957 in Phoenix, Arizona. He married Ruby ——.

N38   **Benjamin Franklin Falconer**, born 1 October 1885 in Carlton Township, Barry County, Michigan, died 20 April 1975 in Hastings, Michigan, was buried in Irving Cemetery.

He married, as his first wife, on 29 December 1909 at Hastings, Michigan, Minnie Rose Woolston, daughter of Charles and Carrie (Jones) Woolston, born 11 April 1891 in Middleville, Michigan, died 29 December 1963, buried in Irving Cemetery.

He married, as his second wife, on 22 October 1966, Earea Ann (Edwards) Crook, born 18 December 1886, died 1 February 1975 in Hastings, Michigan.

He bought a farm in Irving Township, Barry County, in 1916, and worked as a farmer the rest of his life.

Issue of Benjamin Franklin and Minnie Rose (Woolston) Falconer:[220]

N71   i.   Bernard LeRoy Falconer, born 24 July 1911.

      ii. Reba Marie Falconer, born 11 July 1915. She married, on 18 May 1932, George Lydy.

N72   iii. Robert Lee Falconer, born 21 October 1922.

N39   Forest Earl Falconer, born 17 May 1894 in Carlton Township, Barry County, Michigan, died 6 May 1978 in Hastings, Michigan, was buried in Irving Cemetery.

On 30 May 1917, he married Elzora Marie Hynes, daughter of Elmer and Eliza (Coons) Hynes, born 18 November 1900 in Woodland Township, Barry County, Michigan, died 5 April 1979 in Hastings, Michigan, buried in Irving Cemetery.

They lived in Hastings until 1923, when they moved to a farm near Hastings. She worked for a manufacturing company and as a nurse's aide.

Issue of Forest Earl and Elzora Marie (Hynes) Falconer:[221]

      i.   Dorothy Alice Falconer, born 13 January 1918, lives in Hastings, Michigan. She married Raymond Preston.

N73   ii. Forrest Dale Falconer, born 1 August 1921.

      iii. Beverly Mae Falconer, born 5 May 1926, living 1979 in Hastings, Michigan. She married, as her first husband, on 20 June 1942, at Middleville, Michigan, William Theodore Miller, son of William T. and Marie (Chercat) Miller. Issue, surname *Miller*: a. *Linda Kay*, born 17 February 1944, married, 30 June 1962, Ronald Finch; b. *Carolyn*, born 11 August 1945, married James Arthur Gonzales; and two other daughters. She later married Harold Wortley.

N40   William Eugene Falconer, born 6 April 1867 in Nashville, Barry County, Michigan, died 7 September 1934 in Moline, Kansas.

He married Cora M. Long, born about 1878 in Illinois.

Issue of William Eugene and Cora M. (Long) Falconer:[222]

N74   i.   Ralph Eugene Falconer, born 2 November 1897.

      ii. Grace May Falconer, born 24 August 1899, died December 1978 in Moline, Kansas. She married Jess Davis.

N75   iii. Kemper Theodore Falconer, born 4 November 1912.

N41   Frank Arthur Falconer, born 29 June 1874 in Spencer Township, Medina County, Ohio, died 31 August 1951 in Lodi, Ohio, was buried in Woodlawn Cemetery.

He married Magdalena (Lana) M. Bennader, born November 1874 in Ohio, died 8 March 1971 in Medina, Ohio, buried in Woodlawn Cemetery.

They had a farm in Harrisville Township and later lived in Lodi, Ohio.

From 1909 to 1919, Frank operated a general store and grain elevator in Pawnee, Ohio, for the first two years in partnership with his brother Edward. They dealt mostly in hay.

Issue of Frank Arthur and Lana M. (Bennader) Falconer, born in Harrisville, Ohio:[223]

> i.   Esther M. Falconer, born 1 July 1897, living in 1951 in Ashland, Ohio. She married, on 15 January 1918, in Medina County, Ohio,[224] Glenn Warren Strenick, born 4 May 1896, died June 1965.
>
> ii.   Maye Belle Falconer, born 1 May 1903, died 19 August 1984 in Seville, Ohio, buried in Spring Grove Cemetery, Medina. She married, on 10 May 1922, at Medina, Ohio,[225] Harold Edwin Sprankle, born 1903, died 1962. Issue, surname *Sprankle*: a. *Robert*; b. *Marjorie*, married —— Smith; c. *Shirley*, married —— Graff.
>
> iii. Margarite Lillian Falconer, born 23 July 1905, living in 1984 in Lodi, Ohio. She married Roy H. Harris, born 1899, died 1978.

N42   **Edward Leslie Falconer**, born 23 September 1882 in Harrisville Township, Medina County, Ohio, died 1957, was buried in Woodlawn Cemetery, Harrisville Township, Medina County, Ohio.

He married Mary A. Hein, born 13 November 1888, died June 1972 in Medina, Ohio, buried in Woodlawn Cemetery.

Issue of Edward Leslie and Mary A. (Hein) Falconer:

> i.   A. Irene Falconer, born 23 October 1912, lives in Medina, Ohio. She married, on 21 June 1936, at Lodi, Ohio,[226] Harry E. Orr, born 9 August 1914 in Pittsburgh, Pennsylvania, died 1974, buried in Woodlawn Cemetery, a farmer of Burbank, Ohio.

N76 ii.   Clair E. Falconer, born 3 June 1915.

N43   **Herbert Allen Falconer**, born 22 March 1892 in Spencer Township, Medina County, Ohio, died 13 August 1955 in Akron, Ohio, was buried in Woodlawn Cemetery, Lodi.

He married LaVonne Mae Ewing, born 24 March 1894, died 14 November 1955 in Elyria, Ohio, buried in Woodlawn Cemetery.

He ran a mill in Lodi.

Issue of Herbert Allen and LaVonne Mae (Ewing) Falconer:

> i.   Eloise Phyllis Falconer, born 27 September 1916, lives in Medina, Ohio. She married, on 13 February 1938, at Lodi, Ohio, Walter Snell, born 1916, died 1941 in Huron, Ohio. She then married Joseph Cowden, by who she had two daughters. They lived in Akron, Ohio; Erie, Pennsylvania; and Elyria, Ohio.

N77 ii.   Leonard E. Falconer, born 29 November 1918.

N44   **Allen Eugene Falconer**, born 16 June 1875 in Spencer Township, Medina County, Ohio, was living in 1920 in Lodi, Ohio.

He married, in Alliance, Ohio, Osea M. Charles, born July 1877 in Ohio, living in 1920 in Lodi, Ohio.

He was an electrician and electrical contractor in Lorain. He and his brother moved to Lodi after 1915.

Issue of Allen Eugene and Osea M. (Charles) Falconer, born in Lorain, Ohio:[227]

    i.   Alta A. Falconer, born 31 January 1897, died January 1974 in Lorain, Ohio. She married, on 23 September 1915, Harvey Hellinger, born 29 April 1896, died March 1975 in Lorain, Ohio, and had issue, surname *Hellinger*: a. *Harvey Charles*; b. *Charles Allen*; c. *Iris*; d. *Barbara.*

    ii.   Alva Ameda Falconer, born 23 September 1899. She married B. C. Hutchins.

    iii. Olive O. Falconer, born 13 May 1901. She married, as her first husband, on 26 August 1918, in Lorain County, Ohio,[228] John Allen Maurer, son of Alfred and Barbara (Treuschel) Maurer, born 23 July 1897, died June 1981 in Troy, Ohio. She married, as her second husband, —— Stalzer.

N45   **Sherman DeForest Falconer**, born 19 September 1878 in Spencer Township, Medina County, Ohio, died 12 August 1949 in Santa Monica, Los Angeles County, California.

He married, as his first wife, on 20 July 1899, in Lorain County, Ohio,[229] Mary M. Homan, daughter of Charles and Rozetta (Lang) Hohmman, born 13 August 1879 in Amherst Township, Ohio, died 10 June 1902 in Lorain, Ohio, buried in Elmwood Cemetery.

He married, as his second wife, on 4 December 1904, in San Jose, California, Cora Crist, born 30 December 1875 in Tiffin, Ohio, died 2 April 1962 in Santa Monica, California.

He was a plumber in Lorain, then in Wellington, Ohio, and Gary, Indiana, returning to Lorain, but moved to Lodi, Ohio, between 1915 and 1920. The family went to California later.

Issue of Sherman DeForest and Mary M. (Homan) Falconer:[230]

N78 i.   Seymour DeForest Falconer, born 18 April 1900.

Issue of Sherman DeForest and Cora (Crist) Falconer:[231]

    ii.   Genevieve Falconer, born 4 February 1907, died 28 February 1989 in Long Beach, California. She married Harry Higgins, and had issue, surname *Higgins*: a. *Keith.*

N79 iii. Ralph Anthony Falconer, born 15 October 1909.

N46   **Budd Benjamin Falconer**, born 2 February 1891 in Penfield Township, Lorain County, Ohio, died 6 April 1953 in Akron, Ohio, was buried in Mount Hope Cemetery.

He married Leona L. (——) Huston, widow of H. Huston, who died in 1924, by whom she had seven children. She died 23 December 1960 and was buried at Millersburg, Ohio.

He worked as an electrician. He served in World War I.

Issue of Budd Benjamin and Leona L. Falconer:

    i.   Ruth V. Falconer, who died at Kent, Ohio. She married Anthony Fettler, by whom she had three daughters and two sons.

N80 ii.   Robert G. Falconer.

N47 **Ted Alonzo Falconer**, born 13 February 1893 in Penfield Township, Lorain County, Ohio, died 24 October 1961 in Lodi, Ohio, was buried in Litchfield Burial Park.

He married Nettie M. Scott, born 6 December 1894 in Camden, Ohio, died 31 December 1984 in Wellington, Ohio.

Issue of Ted Alonzo and Nettie M. (Scott) Falconer:[232]

    i. Lucile M. Falconer, born 31 July 1916 in Elyria, Ohio, lives in Palm Bay, Florida. On 11 December 1934,[233] at Litchfield, Ohio, she married Arleigh J. Broward, son of Joseph and Mary (Brouse) Broward, born 11 September 1911 in Penfield Township, died 29 November 1987 in Medina, Ohio. Issue, surname *Broward*: a. *Arlene Mae*, born 25 September 1936, married Thomas Huber, divorced; b. *Jean Ann*, born 10 September 1939, married Leonard Gehring, divorced; c. *Judith Elaine*, born 8 February 1943, died 18 April 1957.

N81   ii. Robert Edgar Falconer, born 22 July 1918.

   iii. Helen Ruth Falconer, born 21 November 1930 in Wadsworth, Ohio, lives in Marietta, Georgia. On 12 February 1949,[234] in Medina County, Ohio, she married Glenn Francis Dougherty, Jr., son of Glenn Francis and Arlene (Eby) Dougherty, born 25 November 1926 in Wadsworth, Ohio. Issue, surname *Dougherty*: a. *Gail Ann*, born 12 December 1950, married, 15 June 1973, Michael L. Rossano, lives in Marietta, Georgia.

N48 **Douglas Platt Falconer**, born 21 April 1889 in Oak Park, Illinois, died 15 October 1969, probably in Riverside, Connecticut.[235]

He married, as his first wife, in 1914, Margery Annesley Hoyt. She died in 1948.

He married, as his second wife, Mary Biddle Sinclair. She died in 1963.

He married, as his third wife, Judith Atwater, born 29 December 1895, died July 1982 in Gwynedd, Pennsylvania.

Educated at Haverford College (A.B., 1912), he was a social worker and charities executive. He was executive secretary of the Essex County Children's Air Society and Society for Prevention of Cruelty to Children, in Newark, New Jersey, from 1913 to 1917; executive director of the Erie County Children's Aid Society and Society for Prevention of Cruelty to Children, in Buffalo, New York, from 1917 to 1931; general secretary of the Brooklyn Bureau of Charities from 1932 to 1938; executive director of the Greater New York Fund from 1938 to 1942; national executive director of the United Seaman's Service, Inc., from 1942 to 1946; and executive director of the Wyoming Valley Community Chest, Wilkes-Barre, Pennsylvania. He was deputy director of the United Nations Rural Relief Agency in China in 1946.[236]

Issue of Douglas Platt and Margery Annesley (Hoyt) Falconer:[237]

    i. Douglas Platt Falconer, born about 1915, died 19 May 1940 in Brooklyn, New York, unmarried.[238]

   ii. George Hoyt Falconer, born about 1918, lives in Pocono Lake Preserve, Pennsylvania. For many years, he lived in Lexington, Massachusetts. He has daughters.

  iii. Margaret A. Falconer, born about 1921. She married Frank Anderson and in 1969 lived in Wilkes-Barre, Pennsylvania.

N49 **Cyrus Falconer**, born 3 October 1893 in Oak Park, Illinois, died September 1969 in Fitchburg, Massachusetts.

He married, on 12 September 1917, in Lunenburg, Massachusetts, Helen Cross, born 13 May 1890 in Fitchburg, Massachusetts, died January 1982 in Centerville, Massachusetts.

He was a teacher and life insurance agent, and lived most of his life in Lunenburg, Massachusetts. He also lived in Wichita, Kansas; East Aurora, New York; and Boonton, New Jersey.

Issue of Cyrus and Helen (Cross) Falconer:[239]

N82   i.   Cyrus Falconer, born 17 October 1918.

    ii.   Walter Cross Falconer, born 1 March 1920, died April 1980 off the coast of the Bahamas. He was a Philadelphia banker. He married Marcia Wheeler and had issue.

    iii.   Mary Louise Falconer, born 2 August 1921, lives in Anchorage, Kentucky. She married Herbert Bell.

    iv.   Martha Platt Falconer, born 1 April 1925. She married Charles Sherman.

N50   **Robert Haven Falconer**, born 28 February 1918 in Dartmouth, New Hampshire, died 22 November 1970.

He married, on 30 June 1942 at Lake George, New York, Vera Marion (Kalal) Brozofsky, born 11 May 1913, living in 1984 in Santa Cruz, California.

Issue of Robert Haven and Vera Marion (Kalal) Falconer:

    i.   Richard Haven Falconer, born 14 August 1946, died 9 August 1964.

    ii.   Robert Ross Falconer, born 4 April 1948, living in 1984 in Santa Cruz, California. He was married, but divorced.

N51   **Jasper Emmett Falconer**, born 2 October 1882 in Windsor Township, Morgan County, Ohio, died December 1971 in Newark, Ohio.

He married, on 1 February 1905, in Morgan County, Ohio,[240] Nellie Choral Hook, daughter of J. Warren and Elizabeth (McKibben) Hook, born 11 September 1883 in Ohio, living 1910.

He was a farmer in Windsor Township, Morgan County, Ohio.

Issue of Jasper Emmett and Nellie Choral (Hook) Falconer, born Windsor Township, Morgan County, Ohio:[241]

    i.   Alice Ruth Falconer, born 9 March 1906, lives in Newark, Ohio. She married Robert Knechtges and had issue, surname *Knechtges*: a. *John*; b. *Paul E.*

    ii.   Isabel Faith Falconer, born 20 July 1909, lives in Newark, Ohio. She married, 1 February 1928, in McConnellsville, Ohio, Des S. Van Horn, born 15 May 1906 Malta, Ohio, died 14 July 1976 Newark, Ohio, a grocer. No issue.

    iii.   Mary Hope Falconer, born 12 February 1916, died 6 September 1924 in Morgan Township, Morgan County, Ohio.

N52   **John Herman Falconer**, born 7 November 1875 in Cheneys Grove Township, McLean County, Illinois, died 5 December 1924 in Happy, Swisher County, Texas.

He married, on 14 June 1904 in Woodward County, Oklahoma, Jessie

Anstance Keithley, daughter of Charles Berzett and Nancy (Palmer) Keithley, born 18 October 1879 in Taylor Township, Sullivan County, Missouri, died 26 November 1934 in Mooreland, Oklahoma.

They were living in 1910 in Woodward County, Oklahoma.

Issue of John Herman and Jessie Anstance (Keithley) Falconer:[242]

  i. Mary Viola Falconer, born 25 June 1905, died 14 August 1980 in Redding, California. She married George Hutchens.

  ii. Charles Thomas Falconer, born 30 October 1906, died 9 July 1971 in Hurley, South Dakota. He married, in 1942, Emma Eckenstine, born 7 June 1902, died 14 January 1991 Viborg, South Dakota. No issue.

  iii. Violet May Falconer, born 1 May 1908, died 11 February 1986 in Amarillo, Texas. She married, as her first husband, William Henry Grayson, by whom she had a daughter. She married, as her second husband, Billy Lewis Hysmith.

  iv. Dallas Berzett Falconer, born 17 May 1910, died 15 February 1939 in Shardon, South Dakota. He married, 13 September 1938 in Viborg, South Dakota, Jeanne Boterman. No issue.

  v. Claude Falconer, died at the age of six months.

N83 vi. Harold John Falconer, born 30 March 1913.

  vii. Velma Bernice Falconer, born 2 October 1917. She married, on 8 December 1935 at Parker, South Dakota, Robert Girten.

  viii. Clifford Dixon Falconer, born and died in 1919.

N53 **Thomas William Falconer**, born 4 December 1879 in Cheneys Grove Township, McLean County, Illinois, died 22 March 1970 in Viborg, South Dakota, was buried in Rosehill Cemetery.

He married, as his first wife, on 9 September 1902, Florence Canada, but they later divorced.

He married, as his second wife, on 12 June 1925 in Parker, South Dakota, Della Bell (McCollum) Leeper.

Issue of Thomas William and Della Bell (McCollum) Falconer[243]

N84 i. Thomas Dale Falconer, born 2 February 1927.

N54 **Roy Bert Falconer**, born 26 October 1883 in Draymer, Carroll County, Missouri, died 2 January 1960 in Purdin, Linn County, Missouri, was buried in Mount Olive Cemetery.

He married, as his first wife, on 3 October 1906, Maude Thompson, born 9 June 1884 in Linn County, Missouri, died 9 October 1945 in Purdin, Missouri.

He married, as his second wife, on 9 May 1947, in Linn County, Missouri, Maryan Olive Head, born 13 September 1904. She lives in Louisiana, Missouri.

Issue of Roy Bert and Maude (Thompson) Falconer (the first born at Chula, Missouri; the second at Linneus, Missouri):[244]

  i. Lelia Pearl Falconer, born 8 February 1907, lives in Purdin, Missouri. She married, on 14 May 1931, at Brookfield, Missouri, Auron Brown, and has issue, surname *Brown*: a. *Louise*, born 10 September 1932, married Bertin White; b. *Harold*, born 29 October 1934 St. Catherine, Missouri, married first, 16 August 1959, in Marceline, Missouri, Sondra Louise Atkins, and, second, 20 August 1980, at Liberty, Missouri, Renee Duke Brooks; c. *Virginia Ruth*, born 12 August 1943, married, 10 May 1964, Lyle Wayne Baker.

ii.   Dorothy Fern Falconer, born 6 March 1921, died 28 October 1944 in Linneus, Missouri. She married, on 2 February 1939, in Brookfield, Missouri, Lawrence Tate, and had issue, surname *Tate*: a. *Larry*, born 21 December 1939, married Judy Clawson; b. *Janet*, born 2 December 1943, married Donald Meek.

N55   Samuel Falconer, born 2 October 1888 in Braymer, Carroll County, Missouri, died 6 March 1959 in Purdin, Missouri.

He married, on 7 January 1921 in Linn County, Missouri, Edna Sparks, born 11 July 1889, died May 1977 in Missouri.

In 1910, he lived in Woodward County, Oklahoma.

Issue of Samuel and Edna (Sparks) Falconer (the first born at Purdin, Missouri; the second at Linneus, Missouri):

i.   Livah Garnelle Falconer, born 7 October 1921, died 15 November 1963 in Columbia, Missouri. She married, on 20 October 1942, in Linneus, Missouri, Loren Welch, and had issue, surname *Welch*: a. *Joyce*, born 3 May 1947, died 4 July 1986; b. *Billy*, born 19 February 1958.

ii.   Helen Falconer, born 11 January 1924, lives in Brookfield, Missouri. She married, on 31 December 1944, in Kansas City, Missouri, Arlo Truitt, and had issue, surname *Truitt*: a. *Lana Jane*, born 21 November 1945, lives in Purdin, Missouri, married, 22 December 1963, Raymond Buswell; b. *Jeannine Ann*, born 9 October 1948, married, 31 December 1973, Rudy Head.

N56   Dallas A. Falconer, born 20 February 1890 in Braymer, Carroll County, Missouri, died 2 July 1963 in Purdin, Missouri.

He married, on 30 June 1915, in Linn County, Missouri, Hermia Lee Bowyer, born 26 November 1897, died January 1975 in Missouri.

Issue of Dallas A. and Hermia Lee (Bowyer) Falconer:

N85   i.   Edwin Dale Falconer, born 19 August 1917.

N86   ii.   Virgil Lee Falconer, born 28 August 1919.

N87   iii. Max Falconer, born 8 December 1921.

N57   Ernest Falconer, born 24 December 1873 in Dodge County, Nebraska, died 16 April 1949 in Fremont, Nebraska, buried in Ridge Cemetery.

He married Freelove Catron, born 30 March 1871 in Virginia, died 2 March 1929 in Fremont, Nebraska, buried in Ridge Cemetery.

In 1900, they lived in Leroy Township, Lake County, South Dakota, where their second and third children were born.

Issue of Ernest and Freelove (Catron) Falconer:[245]

i.   Laura E. Falconer, born May 1897 in Nebraska.

ii.   Irene Falconer, born 1906.

iii. Eugene H. Falconer, born 12 April 1907, died 23 September 1993 in Fremont, Nebraska, where he was a postal worker. He married Elsie ——.

N58   George Falconer, born 12 August 1878 in Dodge County, Nebraska, died 1941 in Fremont, Nebraska, was buried in Ridge Cemetery.

He married Emma Moore, daughter of James Russell Moore, born 1883 in Missouri, died 1922 in Fremont, Nebraska.

Issue of George and Emma (Moore) Falconer:[246]

N88   i.   James Russell Falconer, born 24 September 1906.

    ii.   Virginia Falconer, born 1908, lives in Beatrice, Nebraska. She married, as her first husband, Robert J. Kelgard, of Avoca, Iowa, by whom she had issue, surname *Kelgard*: a. *Joan*, lives in Beatrice, Nebraska; as her second husband, —— Lewis, and, as her third husband, —— Burt, and lived at Jamestown and Fremont, Nebraska, and Seattle, Washington.

N89   iii. Myrle Falconer, born 23 September 1909.

    iv.   Milo Raymond Falconer, born 9 December 1910, died October 1987 in Council Bluffs, Iowa. He was a retail meat cutter and had an adopted daughter, Patricia.

N90   v.   Paul Dale Falconer, born 1916.

N59   Lafayette Falconer, born April 1879 in Dodge County, Nebraska, died 1948, probably in Clinton, Custer County, Oklahoma.

He married Evelyn M. Van Alstine, daughter of Alphonso W. and Emily E. (Clark) Van Alstine, born 19 September 1874 in Ridgeway, Minnesota,[247] died 1956. She was named Oklahoma "Mother of the Year" in the 1940s, having raised over 30 foster children.

He served as a private, in Company M, 3rd Nebraska Infantry, during the Spanish-American War. He settled in Clinton about 1900.

Issue of Lafayette and Evelyn M. (Van Alstine) Falconer (they also had an adopted son James):[248]

    i.   Elizabeth A. Falconer, born 1901, died 1929.[249]

    ii.   Grace M. Falconer, born 10 October 1904. She married —— Meggert and had issue, surname *Meggert*: a. *Mary Elizabeth*, married —— Naylor.

N91   iii. Guy Falconer, born 10 October 1904.

    iv.   Helen Falconer, born 1908, died 1946.

N60   Fred Wesley Falconer, born 1879 in Adams County, Iowa, died 9 May 1944 in Enterprise, Wallowa County, Oregon.

He married Josephine Weidert, born 17 February 1885 in Oregon, died January 1985 in Spokane, Washington.

Issue of Fred Wesley and Josephine (Weidert) Falconer:

    i.   Fred Wesley Falconer, born 1918, died 4 August 1965 in Spokane, Washington. He had three daughters.

N61   Ross R. Falconer, born 11 January 1881 in Adams County, Iowa, died 29 July 1957 in Enterprise, Oregon.

He married, in 1904, Veronica Evans, born 17 February 1885 in Oregon, died November 1979 in Enterprise, Oregon.

Issue of Ross R. and Veronica (Evans) Falconer:

i.   Helen M. Falconer, born 4 February 1905, died, unmarried, 23 February 1994 in Enterprise, Oregon. She attended Stanford University and taught school in California for many years.

N62   Roy John Falconer, born 18 December 1877 in Carl Township, Adams County, Iowa, died 20 March 1904 in Adams County, Iowa, was buried in Carl Cemetery.

He married Lizzie ——, born 25 July 1885 [calculated], died 27 October 1903, buried in Carl Cemetery.

In 1900, he worked as a hired hand in Washington Township, Adair County, Iowa.

Issue of Roy John and Lizzie Falconer:

i.   Fay William Falconer, born 14 September 1903 [calculated], died 3 May 1904, buried in Carl Cemetery.

N63   Earl Irwin Falconer, born 25 August 1881 in Carl Township, Adams County, Iowa, died 15 June 1971 in Corning, Iowa, was buried in Oakland Cemetery, Quincy, Iowa.

On 20 January 1904, in Quincy, Iowa, he married, as his first wife, Elva May Hardisty, daughter of Solomon and Lettie (Walton) Hardisty, born 10 April 1882, died 1 December 1939 in Carl Township, Adams County, Iowa, buried in Oakland Cemetery.

He married, as his second wife, on 28 February 1942, Grace (Fulton) Knolla, born 28 July 1894, died 11 December 1980 in Corning, Iowa.

He was a farmer in Carl Township.

Issue of Earl Irwin and Elva May (Hardisty) Falconer:[250]

N92   i.   Charlie William Falconer, born 26 February 1905.

ii.   Dortha Irene Falconer, born 6 January 1907, was living in 1984 in Carl or Corning, Iowa. She married, on 20 January 1926, Donald Eugene Pearson, son of William and Lura (Smyth) Pearson, born 30 March 1904 near Bridgwater, Iowa. Issue, surname *Pearson*:[251] a. *Evelyn June*, born 1928, married Ed Chappell, lives in Logan, Iowa; b. *Marlin Dean*, born 25 October 1930, married, 22 February 1950, Elinor Wallace.

N64   Clyde Raymond Falconer, born 26 March 1883 in Carl Township, Adams County, Iowa, died 13 January 1966 in Atlantic, Iowa, was buried in Evergreen Cemetery, Anita, Iowa.

He married, on 29 September 1909, in Massena, Iowa, Martha Kerkmann, born 3 July 1887 in Massena, Iowa, died in December 1979 in Anita, Iowa, buried in Evergreen Cemetery.

He ran a dairy in Anita, Iowa, for several years.

Issue of Clyde Raymond and Martha (Kerkmann) Falconer:[252]

N93   i.   Roquel H. Falconer, born 7 May 1912.
N94   ii.   Boyd William Falconer, born 29 October 1923.
      iii. Max C. Falconer, born February 1925, died 22 June 1946, buried in Ever-

green Cemetery.

N65 **Paul Tucker Falconer**, born 29 August 1897 in Carl Township, Adams County, Iowa, died 5 June 1981 in Creston, Iowa.

He married, on 23 February 1921, in Massena, Cass County, Iowa, Ida Reichardt, born 7 January 1903, died March 1987 in Creston, Iowa.

Issue of Paul Tucker and Ida (Reichardt) Falconer:[253]

N95 i. Ray William Falconer, born 30 October 1923.

  ii. Lois Mae Falconer, born 24 May 1927. She married, on 14 October 1945, Russell Hardisty, born 2 December 1923.

  iii. Alice Pearl Falconer, born 12 September 1930, lives in Creston, Iowa. She married, on 8 October 1950, Orvin M. Bowers, born 6 August 1918.

N66 **John Mark Falconer**, born 1 September 1902 in Brooks, Iowa, died 25 February 1984 in Lincoln, Nebraska, was buried in Wyuka Cemetery.

He married, on 23 May 1924, Verena Rasmussen, born 24 January 1902 in Colorado, who lives in Lincoln.

He was a Baptist minister.

Issue of John Mark and Verena (Rasmussen) Falconer:

  i. Elizabeth Alice Falconer, born 30 May 1925, lives in Lincoln, Nebraska. She married, as her first husband, on 12 January 1945, Jack Clifford Dillon, born 14 August 1924, and had issue, surname *Dillon*: a. *Mark Ellsworth*, born 2 August 1947, married, 7 June 1969, Sidney Anita Willson; b. *Brian Eric*, born 7 March 1950, married, 11 June 1971, Carol Marie Varise. They divorced 12 January 1977. She married, as her second husband, on 25 October 1978, Jack Warren Peterson, born 30 June 1931.

  ii. Audrey Elaine Falconer, born 7 October 1926, died 4 November 1926.

  iii. Rosalie Jane Falconer, born 12 March 1931, lives in Pierre, South Dakota. She married, on 19 December 1949, Earl Harold Osterkamp and has issue, surname *Osterkamp*: a. *Nicholas*, married Renee ——; b. *Carl*, married Deb ——; c. *Steve*.

N67 **Robert Harrison (Harry) Falconer**, born 11 August 1888 in Collison, Oakwood Township, Vermilion County, Illinois, died 22 May 1922 in Potomac, Illinois, was buried in Partlow Cemetery, Armstrong, Illinois.

He married, on 3 June 1914, in Armstrong, Illinois, Eva Mae Kelley, born 10 February 1894 in Armstrong, Illinois, died 21 February 1970 in Danville, Illinois, buried in Sunset Memorial Cemetery, Danville. She married, as her second husband, Joseph Reeves; and, as her third husband, Farrell Parrish.

He worked as an automobile mechanic.

Issue of Robert Harrison and Eva Mae (Kelley) Falconer:[254]

  i. Wilma Eva Falconer, born 24 September 1915, died 24 September 1915.

  ii. Robert Floyd Falconer, born 17 December 1916, lives in Redmon, Illinois. He married, as his first wife, on 3 June 1937, Garnie Lathrop; as his second wife, Margery D. ——; and, as his third wife, on 23 December 1971, Rilda Lillian Ellis.

  iii. Norma Ruth Falconer, born 2 November 1922, died 14 February 1923.

N68   **Charles M. Falconer**, born 5 November 1894 in Collison, Vermilion County, Illinois, died 21 December 1966 in Hines, Illinois, was buried in Leland Cemetery, Leland, Illinois.

He married, on 8 July 1929, in Plano, Illinois, Gladys Jacobsen. She died 1 August 1964.

He served in World War I. He was an assembler in the crane department of Conco Engineering Works in Mendota, Illinois, from 1938 to 1961.

Issue of Charles M. and Gladys (Jacobsen) Falconer:[255]

    i.   Rosemary Falconer, living in Oklahoma City, Oklahoma, in 1966. She married David Sherman.
    ii.   Marvin Falconer, born 9 December 1934, died December 1981. He lived in Leland, Illinois.

N69   **Walter Clark Falconer**, born 24 July 1899 in Oakwood Township, Vermilion County, Illinois, died 14 March 1973 in San Francisco, California, was buried in Holy Cross Cemetery.

He married Nora Concannon, born in Ireland.

After serving in the U.S. Army in Hawaii during World War I, he moved to San Francisco, where he worked as a postal worker.

Issue of Walter Clark and Nora (Concannon) Falconer:[256]

N96   i.   Walter J. Falconer, born 24 August 1930.

N70   **Marion (Abe) Falconer**, born 21 January 1901 in Vermilion County, Illinois, died January 1966 in Rossville, Illinois.

He married Viva ——, born 23 April 1906, died 21 June 1992 in Rossville, Illinois.

Issue of Marion and Viva Falconer:

    i.   Thelbert M. Falconer, lives in Rossville, Illinois.
    ii.   Marcella Falconer, lives in Rossville, Illinois. She married Richard L. Strawser.

N71   **Bernard LeRoy Falconer**, born 24 July 1911 in Carlton Township, Barry County, Michigan, lives in Carlton Township, Barry County, Michigan.

He married, on 28 October 1933, Lois Elaine Neil, born 3 September 1914.

He was a farmer in Carlton Township.

Issue of Bernard LeRoy and Lois Elaine (Neil) Falconer:[257]

    i.   Darlene Joy Falconer, born 1 August 1936, lives near Hastings, Michigan. She married, 3 July 1953, William George Pickard, son of Orville Eugene and Mary Isabell (Converse) Pickard, born 17 November 1933.
    ii.   Doreen Joyce Falconer, born 2 August 1936, stillborn.
N97   iii. Donald Jay Falconer, born 1 January 1939.
    iv.   Ben LeRoy Falconer, born 6 April 1947. He married, as his first wife, in 1971, Sharon K. Tebo. She married, as her second husband, in 1977, Gerald Lyons. He married, as his second wife, in 1977, Bonnie Buehler.

N72   Robert Lee Falconer, born 21 October 1922 in Carlton Township, Barry County, Michigan, lives in White Cloud, Michigan.

He married, as his first wife, on 20 December 1942, at Hastings, Michigan, Leta Landon, daughter of Cleon and Nina (Root) Landon.

He married, as his second wife, on 9 February 1946, Myrtle Norton, daughter of Harold E. and Mabel (Service) Norton.

Issue of Robert Lee and Myrtle (Norton) Falconer:

    i.   Rosanna Marie Falconer, born 29 October 1946, died 29 October 1946 in the Fuller Cemetery, Barry County, Michigan.

    ii. Larry Robert Falconer, born 13 February 1948, died 11 May 1948, buried in the Fuller Cemetery.

    iii. Patricia Lee Falconer, born 22 November 1955, lives in Hastings, Michigan. She married, in 1974, Michael J. Darrow. They divorced in 1975. She married, as her second husband, on 23 June 1988, Robert Doezema.

N73   Forrest Dale Falconer, born 1 August 1921 in Hastings, Michigan, living in 1979 in Battle Creek, Michigan, died in Floral City, Florida, was buried in Irving Cemetery.

He married, on 24 February 1941, at Hastings, Michigan, Virginia (Jean) E. Weaver.

Issue of Forrest Dale and Virginia E. (Weaver) Falconer:[258]

    i.   Loretta A. Falconer, born 1942. She has been married twice, but has no children.

    ii. Terrie Jo Falconer. She married Charles Barker and has issue, surname *Barker*: a. *Dale Leroy*, born 29 November 1977; b. *Clinton Travis*, born 7 March 1980.

N74   Ralph Eugene Falconer, born 2 November 1897 in Gravel Point, Missouri, died 10 March 1972 in Bristow, Oklahoma, was buried in Magnolia Memorial Cemetery.

He married, as his first wife, on 15 December 1927, Wilda Holleen Thomson.

He married, as his second wife, on 10 December 1963, in Bristow, Oklahoma, Lillie A. (——) Hutson.

He came to Bristow from Drumright, Oklahoma, in 1940. He was an oil field worker for the Sinclair Oil Company.

Issue of Ralph Eugene and Wilda Holleen (Thomson) Falconer:

N98   i.   James Eugene Falconer, born 27 December 1928.

N75   Kemper Theodore Falconer, born 4 November 1912 in Moline, Kansas, died 16 October 1993 in Newport News, Virginia.

He married first, on 13 December 1938, Cecelia Lorene Eastre, born 8 December 1919. He was married several other times.

In 1972, he lived in Arroyo Grande, California.

Issue of Kemper Theodore and Cecelia Lorene (Eastre) Falconer:[259]

    i.   Cora Yvonne Falconer, born 24 May 1940.

    ii.   Marie Aliene Falconer, born 31 July 1941.

N76   **Clair E. Falconer**, born 3 June 1915 in Pawnee, Ohio, lives in Medina, Ohio.

He married, on 10 June 1944,[260] in Medina, Ohio, Ruth F. Patten, daughter of Francis D. and Edna (Ayers) Patten, born 7 September 1922 in Northville, South Dakota.

Issue of Clair E. and Ruth F. (Patten) Falconer (there are also two other daughters):

    i.   Frances Elaine Falconer, born 13 July 1945. She married, on 4 November 1967,[261] in Cincinnati, Ohio, Earl Kenneth Mack, born 1 August 1944 Ludlow, Kentucky.

    ii.   Gayle Marie Falconer, born 23 June 1959. She married, on 23 June 1986,[262] in Medina, Ohio, Kenneth Jerome Rogers, Jr.

N77   **Leonard E. Falconer**, born 29 November 1918 in Lodi, Ohio, lives in Akron, Ohio.

He married, on 27 May 1952, in Akron, Ohio, Audrey Ellen North.

He was educated at Hiram College and saw service in the Pacific during World War II.

Issue of Leonard E. and Audrey Ellen (North) Falconer:

    i.   Robin Falconer, born 21 September 1954.

N99 ii.   Chris Falconer, born 6 January 1957.

    iii. Paula Falconer, born 22 March 1959.

N78   **Seymour DeForest (Don) Falconer**, born 18 April 1900 in Lorain, Lorain County, Ohio, died 27 March 1963 in Portland, Oregon.

He married, as his first wife, Lucille Hine, born 1902 in Lorain, Ohio. They divorced about 1928.

He married, as his second wife, on 7 July 1931, in Ventura, California, Leota Adelaide Drummond, daughter of William Henry and Gertrude (Dyer) Drummond, born 29 October 1893 in Piedmont, Oregon, died 15 July 1984 in Boise, Idaho.

He went to the Los Angeles, California, area, where he worked as a clerk, until 1934, when they moved to Portland, Oregon. In 1944, they went to Boise, Idaho, where he was manager of the Crane Plumbing Company. In 1954 he returned to Portland and worked as a salesman for that company.

Issue of Seymour DeForest and Lucille (Hine) Falconer:[263]

N100 i.   Robert Kay Falconer, born 22 December 1922.

    ii.   Ronald Falconer, born 22 December 1922, died 22 December 1922.

    iii. Jack Seymour Falconer, born 20 May 1926, died 16 March 1976 in San Francisco, California. His first marriage ended in divorce. He married, as his second wife, Rena ——, born 28 October 1914, living in Dublin, California. He had no issue.

N79   Ralph Anthony Falconer, born 15 October 1909 in Gary, Indiana, died 10 January 1995 in Crockett, Virginia.
He married, on 5 May 1935, Ivy Henderson.
They lived in Santa Monica, California, for many years.
Issue of Ralph Anthony and Ivy (Henderson) Falconer:

N101   i.   Ralph Anthony Falconer, born 1937.
        ii.   Ivy May Falconer, born 1939. She married, on 2 November 1963, in Los Angeles County, California, James Van Antwerp, and had issue, surname *Van Antwerp*: a. *David*, born 1959; b. *Craig*, born 1961; c. *Duane*, born 1964; d. *Ginger*, born 1966.
N102 iii. Ryan A. Falconer, born 1941.
N103 iv.   Sherman D. Falconer, born 1944.
        v.   Seymour Falconer, born 1946.
N104 vi.   Byron Falconer, born 1949.

N80   Robert G. Falconer, lives in Akron, Ohio.
He married Mary Lou (Miller) Womack.
He served in the U. S. Air Force from 1954 to 1958.
Issue of Robert G. and Mary Lou (Miller) Falconer:[264]

        i.   Lillian Kay Falconer. She married Kris Esker, by whom she has one son.
        ii.   Kimberly J. Falconer. She married Loren Griswold, by whom she has one son.
        iii. Robert G. Falconer, lives in Akron, Ohio. He married Cathy Simmons.
        iv.   Mary S. L. Falconer, born 1981.

N81   Robert Edgar Falconer, born 22 July 1918 in Elyria, Ohio, lives in Ocala, Florida.
He married, on 5 August 1939, in Akron, Ohio, Marie May, daughter of John Jacob and Opal (Malson) Steiner, born 3 July 1918 in Akron, Ohio, living in Ocala, Florida.
They lived Akron and Stow, Ohio; Danville, Illinois; Fort Wayne, Indiana; Covington, Indiana; Ontario, California; Claremont, California; Ashcboro, North Carolina; Mount Gilead, North Carolina; and Huntsville, Alabama. He worked as a mechanical engineer and tool maker.
Issue of Robert Edgar and Marie May (Steiner) Falconer:

        i.   Sherry Rae Falconer, born 24 November 1942, lives in Ingleside, Illinois. She married, as her first husband, in 1965, Richard Berent, and had issue, surname *Berent*: a. *David Allen*, born 30 September 1967, lives in Fort Lauderdale, Florida; b. *Linda Marie*, born 27 February 1970, lives in Urbana, Illinois. She married, as her second husband, on 11 October 1986, William Linning.

N82   Cyrus Falconer, born 17 October 1918 in Wichita, Kansas, died January 1973.
He married Elinor Conly.

Issue of Cyrus and Elinor (Conly) Falconer:

N105 i.   Cyrus Michael Falconer, born 4 September 1947.

N83   Harold John Falconer, born 30 March 1913 in Woodward County, Oklahoma, lives in Merced, California.

He married Lucille Tice.

Issue of Harold John and Lucille (Tice) Falconer:[265]

    i.   Agnes Falconer.

    ii.   Betty Falconer.

    iii. Charlotte A. Falconer, born about 1944. She married, on 6 December 1963, in Merced County, California,[266] Stephen R. Teal.

    iv.   Delores Falconer.

N84   Thomas Dale Falconer, born 2 February 1927 in Viborg, Turner County, South Dakota, died 18 October 1981 in Sioux Falls, South Dakota, was buried in Rosehill Cemetery, Parker, South Dakota.

He married, on 8 March 1951, in Parker, South Dakota, Doris Marie Michael.

Issue of Thomas Dale and Doris Marie (Michael) Falconer (born in Sioux Falls, South Dakota, except the last, born in Viborg, South Dakota):[267]

    i.   Gail Marie Falconer, born 7 December 1951. She married, on 8 June 1971, in Piedmont, South Dakota, Robert G. Miller.

    ii.   Meredith Jean Falconer, born 6 June 1960, lives in Hurley, South Dakota. She married, on 8 January 1979, in Sioux Falls, South Dakota, Jeffrey O. Clark.

    iii. Mary Ellen Falconer, born 1 May 1963. She married, on 18 May 1984, in Parker, South Dakota, Jerry Heirigs.

    iv.   Gloria May Falconer, born 7 July 1966. She married, on 28 August 1989, in Hurley, South Dakota, Darin Anderson.

    v.   Helen Kay Falconer, born 4 June 1969.

    vi.   Thomas Duane Falconer, born 14 October 1970.

N85   Edwin Dale Falconer, born 19 August 1917 in Purdin, Missouri, lives in Slater, Missouri.

He married, as his first wife, on 6 June 1936, in Brookfield, Missouri, Vivian Garrett. They divorced in the 1950s.

He married, as his second wife, on 31 March 1953, in Linn County, Missouri, Helen Maxine Dixon.

He married, as his third wife, on 31 December 1957, in Slater, Missouri, Frances (Gilliam) Sherman.

Issue of Edwin Dale and Vivian (Garrett) Falconer, born in Purdin, Missouri:

N106 i.   Edwin Dale Falconer, born 25 July 1937.

    ii.   Judith Lee Falconer, born 18 October 1939, lives in the Kansas City, Missouri, area. She married, on 24 November 1957, in Browning, Missouri,

Marlin Kay Steele, born 5 August 1934, and has issue, surname *Steele* (born at North Kansas City, Missouri): a. *Marla Kay*, born 10 April 1966; b. *Karla Lee*, born 9 December 1968.

iii.   Carolyn Kay Falconer, born 18 August 1943, lives in Pollock, Missouri. She married, on 30 May 1961, in Unionville, Missouri, Gordon Dale Campbell, born 7 June 1938, and has issue, surname *Campbell*: a. *Martin Dale*, born 30 May 1961, married, 13 April 1985, at Browning, Missouri, Tonda Lyn Benskin; b. *Donald Dean*, born 18 August 1963, married Kathleen Sue Staples; c. *Steven Dane*, born 11 May 1969.

Issue of Edwin Dale and Frances (Gilliam) Falconer, born in Marshall, Missouri:

iv.   Gayle Ann Falconer, born 18 March 1960. She married, on 4 June 1983, in Lincoln, Nebraska, Jon Robert Peterson.

N86   **Virgil Lee Falconer**, born 28 August 1919 in Purdin, Missouri, lives in Purdin, Missouri.

He married, on 21 February 1940, in Linn County, Missouri, Virginia Lea Pulliam, daughter of Willard and Susan (McCollum) Pulliam, born 1 January 1922 in Purdin, Missouri, died 14 January 1986 in Brookfield, Missouri.

Issue of Virgil Lee and Virginia Lea (Pulliam) Falconer, born in Purdin, Missouri:

N107 i.   Stanley Falconer, born 23 September 1940.

N108 ii.   Stephen D. Falconer, born 23 March 1942.

N87   **Max Falconer**, born 8 December 1921 in Purdin, Missouri, lives in Purdin, Missouri.

He married, on 23 March 1946, in Troy, Kansas, Mary G. Gilmer, born 11 July 1924 in Purdin, Missouri, died 30 May 1987 in Columbia, Missouri.

Issue of Max and Mary G. (Gilmer) Falconer, the first and second born in Kirksville, Missouri, the third in Milan, Missouri:

i.   Margaret Ellen Falconer, born 25 August 1947. She married, on 10 September 1966, in Purdin, Missouri, Thomas Leroy Rollins, born 2 May 1943, and has issue, surname *Rollins*: a. *Robin Renee*, born 23 March 1968, married Greg Daniel Williams; b. *Ronda Rochelle*, born 24 April 1972.

N109 ii.   Eddie Falconer, born 25 August 1948.

iii.   Brenda Falconer, born 20 August 1953, lives in Brookfield, Missouri. She married, on 21 January 1973, in Purdin, Missouri, Robert Delane Techau, born 11 November 1952, and has issue, surname *Techau*: a. *Robert Daniel*, born 23 August 1973; b. *Bryan DeLane*, born 16 October 1975.

N88   **James Russell Falconer**, born 24 September 1906 in Fremont, Nebraska, died October 1986 in Omaha, Nebraska.

He married, in 1936, Esther Sun, born 30 November 1905, died March 1979 in Omaha, Nebraska.

He was retail meat cutter and lived in Fremont until 1947, when he and his family moved to Omaha.

Issue of James Russell and Esther (Sun) Falconer:[268]

N110 i.   James Russell Falconer, born 1937.

    ii.   Douglas M. Falconer, born 1942, lives in Omaha, Nebraska. He married Carol —— and has two adopted children, Kate Lynn and Russell.

N89   **Myrle Falconer**, born 23 September 1909 in Fremont, Nebraska, died April 1980 in West Point, Nebraska.
He was a retail meat cutter.
Son of Myrle Falconer:[269]

    i.   Jerry Falconer, born 1941, died, unmarried, in 1989.

N90   **Paul Dale Falconer**, born 1916 in Fremont, Nebraska, died 1966.
Issue of Paul Dale Falconer:

    i.   Nancy Falconer, lives in Norfolk, Nebraska. She married Larry J. Sanne.

N91   **Guy Falconer**, born 10 October 1904 in Clinton, Oklahoma, died May 1973 in Garnett, Kansas.
He married, on 1 November 1930 in Wellington, Kansas, Helen ——, who lives in Garnett, Kansas.
Issue of Guy and Helen Falconer:

    i.   Joanna J. Falconer, lives in Leavenworth, Kansas. She married —— White.

N92   **Charlie William Falconer**, born 26 February 1905 in Windyville, Iowa, died 8 February 1974 in Milton-Freewater, Oregon.
He married, on 5 June 1929, in Council Bluffs, Iowa, Velma Corbin, daughter of Richard and Edith Corbin of Mt. Etna, Iowa.
He was a farmer in Carl Township, Adams County, Iowa, until the early 1940s. He and his family then moved to Enterprise, Oregon, where he was a farmer and sheep raiser.
Issue of Charlie William and Velma (Corbin) Falconer, born in Corning, Iowa:[270]

    i.   Reba Delphine Falconer, born 22 December 1929, lives in Enterprise, Oregon. She married, on 9 September 1949, in LaGrande, Oregon, Elmer Wayne Storm, born 28 June 1927 in Enterprise, Oregon, and has issue, surname *Storm*: a. *David Allen*, born 30 January 1952; b. *William Curtis*, born 24 November 1954.

N111 ii.   Earl Wesley Falconer, born 23 June 1931.

N112 iii.   Otto LeRoy Falconer, born 21 January 1933.

    iv.   Norma Jean Falconer, born 7 October 1934, lives in Milton-Freewater, Oregon. She married, on 12 June 1953, Frank Clough, born 24 March 1926, and has issue, surname *Clough*: a. *Mildred*, born 6 March 1954; b. *Anna Marie*, born 14 May 1955; c. *Cynthia Ann*, born 16 July 1956; d. *Richard Frank*, born 19 October 1957; e. *Kathleen Elizabeth*, born 1 July 1960; f. *Carolyn Rose*, born 19 March 1962; g. *James A.*, born 19 February 1965.

N93 **Roquel H. Falconer**, born 7 May 1912 in Carl Township, Adams County, Iowa, died 18 November 1989 in Missouri Valley, Iowa.

He married, on 11 May 1935, in Papillion, Nebraska, Neva M. Turner, born 30 January 1908 in Anita, Iowa, died 3 March 1966 in Anita, Iowa, buried in Evergreen Cemetery.

Issue of Roquel H. and Neva M. (Turner) Falconer:[271]

N113 i.   Jack T. Falconer, born 30 April 1937.

N94 **Boyd William Falconer**, born 29 October 1923 in Carl Township, Adams County, Iowa, died March 1995 in Adair, Iowa.

He married Hilda M. Scholl, daughter of Roy and Hazel (Gissible) Scholl, born 18 December 1925 in Anita, Iowa.

Issue of Boyd William and Hilda M. (Scholl) Falconer:

   i.   Alan Falconer, born 30 January 1949.
   ii.   Julie Falconer, born 15 July 1952.
   iii.   Janilyn Falconer, born 6 November 1954.

N95 **Ray William Falconer**, born 30 October 1923 in Massena, Iowa, lives in Afton, Iowa.

He married, on 10 March 1946, Sarah Rundlett.

Issue of Ray William and Sarah (Rundlett) Falconer:

   i.   Carol Falconer, born 1 January 1947. She married, on 2 September 1967, in Creston, Iowa, John Knorr.
   ii.   Barbara Falconer, born 3 December 1951.

N96 **Walter J. Falconer**, born 24 August 1930 in San Francisco, California, lives in Walnut Valley, California.

He married, on 1 February 1953, in San Francisco, California, Margaret S. Tobin, daughter of George and Hazel (Davis) Tobin.

He was a Lieutenant Colonel in the U.S. Army.

Issue of Walter J. and Margaret S. (Tobin) Falconer:[272]

   i.   Virginia Marie Falconer, born 30 January 1959, lives in Titusville, Florida. She married Rex Wilson.
   ii.   Walter J. Falconer, born 3 April 1960, lives in Grapevine, Texas. He married Suzanne Kuklock.
   iii.   David George Falconer, born 4 January 1964, lives in Pleasant Hill, California. He married Christine Uruburu.

N97 **Donald Jay Falconer**, born 1 January 1939 in Hastings, Michigan, lives north of Hastings.

He married, on 8 October 1960, Connie C. Overholt, daughter of George W. and Marian (Miller) Overholt, born 6 November 1938.

He works as a farmer.

Issue of Donald Jay and Connie C. (Overholt) Falconer:[273]

N114　i.　Donald Jay Falconer, born 30 January 1962.

　　　　ii.　Brenda Kay Falconer, born 9 September 1964, lives near Hastings, Michigan. She married, on 11 July 1981, Milton (Skip) Buehler, born 29 December 1960. Issue.

　　　　iii.　David Lee Falconer, born 14 June 1966. He married, in 1988, Belinda Guernsey.

N98　**James Eugene Falconer**, born 27 December 1928 in Mangum, Oklahoma, lives in Newport News, Virginia.

　　He married, as his first wife, on 21 August 1950, in Leavenworth, Kansas, Patricia Anne Moore, born 3 February 1932 in Texarkana, Texas. She married, as her second husband, William Cantrell.

　　He married, as his second wife, on 29 May 1963, in Orlando, Florida, Dorene Elizabeth Ewan.

　　He married, as his third wife, on 3 March 1973, at Langley Air Force Base, Virginia, Patsy Jean Hatchett.

　　He was a Lieutenant Colonel in the U. S. Air Force.

　　Issue of James Eugene and Patricia Anne (Moore) Falconer (they also had two adopted children, William David, born 14 August 1957, and David Cletus, born 20 August 1959):[274]

　　　　i.　Pamela Dawn Falconer, born 18 June 1954.

　　　　ii.　Brenda Kaye Falconer, born 11 August 1956, lives in Virginia Beach, Virginia. She married, on 6 November 1983, Thomas Macedo Harris II.

　　Issue of James Eugene and Dorene Elizabeth (Ewan) Falconer:

　　　　iii.　Ralph Andrew Falconer, born 17 July 1964, lives in Hampton, Virginia. He married, on 26 October 1985, Tina Marie Harford.

　　　　iv.　Alice Holleen Falconer, born 21 October 1966. She married, on 26 May 1990, Paul Andrew McDonald.

N99　**Chris Falconer**, born 6 January 1957 in Akron, Ohio, lives in Akron, Ohio.

　　Issue of Chris Falconer:

　　　　i.　Christopher Falconer, born 1979.

　　　　ii.　Benjamin Falconer, born 1984.

　　　　iii.　Amanda Falconer, born 1988.

N100　**Robert Kay Falconer**, born 22 December 1922 in Lodi, Ohio, lives in Boise, Idaho.

　　He married, as his first wife, on 22 August 1941, in Stephenson, Washington, Violet May Young, daughter of Marion Lewis and Edith May (Young) Lewis. They divorced on 28 August 1946 in Portland, Oregon.

　　He married, as his second wife, on 27 June 1948, in Arco, Idaho, Joan Combe, daughter of Louis and Alta Mae (Mecham) Combe, born 7 November

1928 in Arco, Idaho.

He worked for Mountain Bell Telephone and Telegraph Company.

Issue of Robert Kay and Violet May (Young) Falconer:[275]

N115 i. Thomas Kay Falconer, born 7 March 1942.

ii. Mary Lou (Penny) Falconer, born 27 June 1945, lives in Mesa, Arizona. She married, on 2 April 1965, in Kuna, Idaho, Elbert Melvin Lowe, son of Ernest and Wanda Lowe, and has issue, surname *Lowe*: a. *Chad Nathan*, married Chris Heath; b. *Robert Ernest*; c. *Wendy Moriah*; d. *Joshua Paul*.

Issue of Robert Kay and Joan (Combe) Falconer:

N116 iii. Michael Lee Falconer, born 28 December 1949.

iv. Robert Mark Falconer, born 19 October 1952, lives in Boise, Idaho. He married, on 15 July 1979, in Donnelly, Idaho, Kay E. Lear, daughter of Harry E. and Bernice L. (Sneed) Lear, born 21 December 1946 in San Antonio, Texas. He is a manager for the Hewlett-Packard Company. They have two adopted children: Deanna Michelle, born 7 October 1974; and Erik Nathan, born 21 July 1985 in Oregon.

v. Melissa Falconer, born 30 June 1962, lives in Littleton, Colorado.

N101 **Ralph Anthony Falconer**, born 1937.

He married, on 23 June 1961, in Los Angeles County, California, Patricia A. Buckley.

Issue of Ralph Anthony and Patricia A. (Buckley) Falconer:

i. Robin Falconer, born 1962.

ii. Scott Falconer, born 1964.

N102 **Ryan A. Falconer**, born 1941, lives in Carmel Valley, California.

He married, on 28 September 1963, in Los Angeles County, California, Margaret C. Layerson.

Issue of Ryan A. and Margaret C. (Layerson) Falconer:

i. Erik Falconer, born 1967.

ii. Brandy Falconer, born 1971.

N103 **Sherman D. Falconer**, born 1944, lives in Oak Harbor, Washington.

He married, on 31 May 1968, in Los Angeles County, California, Robyn King.

Issue of Sherman D. and Robyn (King) Falconer:

i. Caryn Falconer, born 1966.

ii. Jeff Falconer, born 1968.

iii. Renata Falconer, born 1971.

N104 **Byron Falconer**, born 1949.

He married Margaret ——.

Issue of Byron and Margaret Falconer:

   i.   Bev Falconer, born 1977.

   ii.   Ron Falconer, born 1980.

   iii. Rick Falconer, born 1981.

N105 **Cyrus Michael Falconer**, born 4 September 1947 in Huntington, New York, lives in Framingham, Massachusetts.

He married, in November, 1969, in Plymouth, Massachusetts, Nancy Doll, daughter of Ellsworth and Joann (Wheaton) Doll, born August 1947 in Wareham, Massachusetts.

He works in restaurant management.

Issue of Cyrus Michael and Nancy (Doll) Falconer:[276]

   i.   Meghan Elissa Falconer, born 2 March 1976.

   ii.   Jacob Michael Falconer, born 27 November 1981.

   iii. Molly Elizabeth Falconer, born 10 July 1985.

N106 **Edwin Dale Falconer**, born 25 July 1937 in Purdin, Missouri, lives in Brookfield, Missouri.

He married, on 26 May 1958, in Brookfield, Missouri, Naomi Rojean Lambert, born 1 March 1940 in Shelby, Missouri.

Issue of Edwin Dale and Naomi Rojean (Lambert) Falconer:

   i.   Kevin Dale Falconer, born 22 July 1959, lives in Brookfield, Missouri.

   ii.   Gerald Lee Falconer, born 2 March 1961, lives in Brookfield, Missouri. He married, on 10 November 1985, in Brookfield, Missouri, Linda K. Mundell.

   iii. Karen Denise Falconer, born 2 February 1962. She married, as her first husband, on 14 June 1980, David Brundage, but divorced. She married, again, on 14 May 1988, Richard F. Bishop.

N107 **Stanley Falconer**, born 23 September 1940 in Purdin, Missouri, died 4 September 1962 in Kansas City, Missouri, was buried at Purdin, Missouri.

He married, in 1961, Mildred George.

Issue of Stanley and Mildred (George) Falconer:

   i.   Tauna Falconer, born 10 February 1962, lives in Purdin, Missouri. She married Tom Creason.

N108 **Stephen D. Falconer**, born 23 March 1942 in Purdin, Missouri, lives in Purdin, Missouri.

He married Rosemary Kinsella, born 8 January 1946.

Issue of Stephen D. and Rosemary (Kinsella) Falconer:

   i.   Kristin Falconer, born 27 May 1969, lives in Purdin, Missouri.

   ii.   Chad Falconer, born 14 October 1970, lives in Columbia, Missouri.

   iii. Heather Falconer, born 13 March 1975.

N109 **Eddie Falconer**, born 25 August 1948 in Kirksville, Missouri, lives in Purdin, Missouri.

He married, on 26 February 1972, Cathy Louise Almond, born 6 September 1953.

Issue of Eddie and Cathy Louise (Almond) Falconer:

    i.   Russell Allen Falconer, born 9 April 1973.
   ii.   Richard Aaron Falconer, born 6 June 1975.
  iii.   Raymond Edward Falconer, born 12 January 1979.

N110   **James Russell Falconer**, born 1937 in Fremont, Nebraska, lives in Omaha, Nebraska.

Issue of James Russell Falconer:

    i.   Amy Falconer.
   ii.   Jane Falconer.

N111   **Earl Wesley Falconer**, born 23 June 1931 in Adams County, Iowa, lives in Hermiston, Oregon.

He married, as his first wife, Arthene Rose, born 27 April 1932. They were divorced, and he married again.

Issue of Earl Wesley and Arthene (Rose) Falconer:

    i.   Melinda Ann Falconer, born 30 April 1952.
   ii.   Tersia Lee Falconer, born 13 April 1954.
  iii.   Bernard Dale Falconer, born 16 May 1958.

N112   **Otto LeRoy Falconer**, born 21 January 1933 in Adams County, Iowa, lives in the Enterprise or Milton-Freewater, Oregon, area.

He married, on 20 December 1954, Lou Mae Elliott, born 17 September 1933.

Issue of Otto LeRoy and Lou Mae (Elliott) Falconer:

    i.   Jenise Helen Falconer, born 8 April 1956.
   ii.   Otto Dale Falconer, born 30 July 1959, lives in Walla Walla, Washington.
  iii.   Robert Dean Falconer, born 3 July 1961.

N113   **Jack T. Falconer**, born 30 April 1937 in Anita, Iowa, lives in Missouri Valley, Iowa.

He married Marjorie N. Young, born 2 October 1937.

Issue of Jack T. and Marjorie N. (Young) Falconer:

    i.   Paula Beth Falconer, born 15 August 1963.

N114   **Donald Jay (Butch) Falconer**, born 30 January 1962 in Hastings, Michigan, lives there.

He married, on 26 June 1982, Linda Otis, born 19 April 1963.

Issue of Donald Jay and Linda (Otis) Falconer:

    i.   Megan Marie Falconer, born 20 February 1985.

    ii.   Jessica Falconer, born 1986.

    iii.   Donald Jay Falconer, born 1987.

N115   **Thomas Kay Falconer**, born 7 March 1942, lives in Corbett, Oregon.

He married, on 5 February 1964, in Kern County, California, Sharon L. Nugent, daughter of Jack Nugent. They divorced in 1983.

Issue of Thomas Kay and Sharon (Nugent) Falconer:

    i.   Moriha Lyn Falconer, born 4 April 1964 in California. She has issue, surname *Falconer:* a. *Teresa May,* born 21 December 1984 in Portland, Oregon.

    ii.   Jacqueline Kay Falconer, born 8 November 1967 in Portland, Oregon. She married, on 28 July 1990, in Portland, Oregon, Todd Redfern, but divorced.

    iii.   Troy Robert Falconer, born 30 May 1970 in Portland, Oregon. He married, on 12 September 1992, in Portland, Oregon, Teresa Marie ——.

    iv.   son, died at birth.

N116   **Michael Lee Falconer**, born 28 December 1949 in Boise, Idaho, lives in Boise, Idaho.

He married, on 11 July 1970, Jill Durell.

Issue of Michael Lee and Jill (Durell) Falconer:

N117 i.   Todd Scott Falconer, born 25 September 1972.

    ii.   Matthew Reid Falconer, born 16 September 1975.

N117   **Todd Scott Falconer**, born 25 September 1972 in Boise, Idaho.

Issue of Todd Scott Falconer and T. J. Pfenning:

    i.   Alexandra Whitney Falconer, born 26 January 1993 in Boise, Idaho.

NOTES

[1] "Intestate Records of Washington County, Pennsylvania," *Pennsylvania Genealogical Magazine,* 30 (1977): 47.

[2] Memorandum written by Samuel D. Fitton or his wife, of Hamilton, Ohio, about 1906, preserved by Robert Crawford Falconer, whose widow mailed a copy to Don Fitton, of Hamilton, Ohio, who mailed another copy to Edward Nicholas, P.O. Box 8470, Santa Fe, NM 87504. The content of this statement indicates that it was originally written about 1850 and sent to Cyrus Falconer. Hereafter described as Cyrus Falconer statement (see Appendix 4).

[3] Edward Brown, *Wadsworth Memorial* (Wadsworth, Ohio: Steam Printing House, 1875), p. 45.

[4] *Memorial Record of Butler County, Ohio* (Chicago: Record Pub. Co., 1893), p. 250. The author, or perhaps Cyrus Falconer, mistakenly called him "Abraham," however.

[5] *Barry County, Michigan History 1985* (Hastings, Mich.: Barry County Book Committee, 1985), p. 201.

[6] The Cyrus Falconer statement says she was the sister of Isaac Newkirk and a brother who moved to Lancaster, Ohio. She would thus be the daughter of Abraham. See *The van Nieuwkirk, Nieukirk, Newkirk Family,* Publications of the Genealogical Society of Pennsylvania: Special Number (Philadelphia: Hall of the Historical Society of Pennsylvania, 1934), pp. 41-44. In this work, Elizabeth's husband is given as —— Hall or Hull. Perhaps she married Mr. Hall after 1800; her son Isaac's son John Hall could have been named after him.

[7] Cyrus Falconer statement (see App. 4); Maple Grove Baptist Church register, in Iams Collection, Citizens Library, Washington, Pa.

[8] Raymond M. Ball, *Yohogania County, Virginia: A Short-Lived County* (n.p., n.d.).

[9] *Pennsylvania Archives*, 3rd ser., 23: 309.

[10] Cyrus Falconer statement (see App. 4).

[11] *Pennsylvania Archives*, 3rd ser., 22: 770.

[12] Washington Co. (Pa.) Deeds, 1J: 37.

[13] Ibid., 1T: 751.

[14] Speers Church of Christ records, Iams Collection, Citizens Library, Washington, Pa.

[15] Cyrus Falconer statement (see App. 4).

[16] Forrest, *History of Washington County, Pennsylvania* (Chicago: S. J. Clarke, 1926), vol. 3.

[17] Samuel Falconer Nichol Bible, belonging to Allene Bowen, 1251 Lakeview Dr., Winter Park, FL 32789, via Ann Faulkner.

[18] Aged "77 years, 2 months, 8 ds.," gravestone inscription, Jacobsburg Cemetery, although "74" could be "71."

[19] A. T. McKelvey, *Centennial History of Belmont County, Ohio, and Representative Citizens* (Chicago: Biographical Pub. Co., 1903), pp. 689, 767.

[20] Gravestone inscription, Greenwood Cemetery, Hamilton, Ohio.

[21] His age, as recorded on his gravestone, indicates 1789 as his year of birth, but Samuel, who according to the Cyrus Falconer statement was his father, could not have been his father if he were born in that year.

[22] Bible record in possession of Leonard Falconer, 915 Mull Ave., Akron, OH 44313, which says "Henry Falconer Was born August Second 1763 and Died 1836, Age Seventy three years Three Months & 26 Days"; *History of Medina County and Ohio* (Chicago: Baskin & Battey, 1881), p. 758.

[23] But the Leonard Falconer Bible record says born 1766, died 1828, aged 62.

[24] *History of Medina County and Ohio*, p. 758.

[25] Frances Grimes Sitherwood, *Throckmorton Family History* (Bloomington, Ill.: Pantagraph Printing and Stationery Co., 1929), pp. 81, 101, 368.

[26] 1800 census, Washington Co., Pa., p. 50.

[27] Washington Co. (Pa.) Deeds, 1P: 544.

[28] *Ohio Tax Returns*.

[29] Leonard Falconer Bible record; *History of Medina County and Ohio*, p. 758.

[30] 1850 census, Medina Co., Ohio, p. 874.

[31] *History of Medina County and Ohio*, p. 430.

[32] 1850 census, Lorain Co., Ohio, p. 889; 1860 census, Eaton Co., Mich., p. 857.

[33] John E. Morris, *The Felt Genealogy* (Hartford, Conn.: The Case, Lockwood and Brainard Co., 1893), p. 98.

[34] *Commemorative Biographical Record of the Counties of Huron and Lorain, Ohio* (Chicago: J. H. Barr, 1894) 2: 925.

[35] Washington Co. (Pa.) Orphan's Court Record, Wills.

[36] Washington Co. (Pa.) Estates, 1825, file 13.

[37] Cyrus Falconer statement (see App. 4).

[38] Washington Co. (Pa.) Deeds, 1P: 544.

[39] Grace Marvin Winnagle, *Abstracts of Probate Records: Trumbull County, Ohio: Nov. 1803-Aug 1843* (Trumbull County Chapter, Ohio Genealogical Society, 1986), p. 222.

[40] Cyrus Falconer statement; Washington Co. (Pa.) Orphan's Court Record, B: n.p.

[41] In Washington Co. Court house docket C, p. 212, the partition of the estate of Abraham Falconer in March 1825 lists his surviving heirs, which do not include George and Hannah or their heirs.

[42] Query by Mrs. A. S. Penniston, P. O. Box 7253, Arlington, VA 22207, in *Genealogical Helper* (Sept. 1974).

[43] "Reporter Records: Marriages and Deaths, 1808-1825, Washington, Pennsylvania," Iams Collection, Citizens Library, Washington, Pa.

[44] Isabelle Mitchell Sumney.

[45] "Reporter Records: Marriages and Deaths, 1808-1825, Washington, Pennsylvania".

[46] Ibid.

[47] Information from Isabelle (Mrs. C. Oliver) Sumney, via Ann Faulkner.

[48] 1830 census, Medina Co., Ohio, p. 186; he was aged 50 to 60.

[49] Elisha Whittlesey's and Frederick Wadsworth's history of Canfield, 1804-1831, manuscript in Western Reserve Historical Society, in: Margaret Miller Simon, *Canfield Township Cemetery and Death Records: Mahoning County, Ohio* (Youngstown: Mahoning County Chapter, Ohio Genealogical Society, 1983), p. 74.

[50] Trumbull Co. (Ohio) Deeds, L: 134, 252.

[51] 1800 census, Washington Co., Pa., p. 114.

[52] *Wauseon Republican*, 27 Mar. 1886.

[53] Trumbull Co. (Ohio) Deeds, L: 437; Medina Co. (Ohio) Deeds, M: 146, 635, 636, 637; information from Helen Hahn, 947 Spink St., Wooster, OH 44691, via Ann Faulkner.

[54] 1840 census, Medina Co., Ohio, p. 195.

[55] 1850 census, Medina Co., Ohio, p. 372.

[56] *History of Medina County and Ohio*, p. 880.

[57] Dates from Norman J. Ulam's chart in *Ancestor Charts of Members of the Ohio Genealogical Society* (Mansfield, Ohio: the Society, 1987), p. 1057.

[58] 1850 census, Trumbull Co., Ohio, p. 213; information from Helen Hahn.

[59] Medina Co. (Ohio) Marriages, B: 160.

[60] Cyrus Falconer statement (see App. 4).

[61] *Memorial Record of Butler County, Ohio*, p. 251.

[62] *A History and Biographical Cyclopaedia of Butler County, Ohio* (Cincinnati: Western Biographical Pub. Co., 1882), p. 318f.

[63] *Memorial Record of Butler County, Ohio*, p. 250; genealogy prepared by Robert Crawford Falconer about 1906-1907.

[64] Violette B. Magoon, formerly of Seattle, WA, who had access to a Bible record, via Ann Faulkner.

[65] Carol Willey Bell, *Ohio Lands: Steubenville Land Office, 1800-1820* (Youngstown, Ohio: 1983).

[66] Belmont Co. (Ohio) Deeds, N: 92.

[67] Belmont Co. (Ohio) Wills, H: 242.

[68] Belmont Co. (Ohio) Deeds, 36: 293.

[69] Family records of J. E. Falconer, via Billie Hart, 2411 Sanders Ln., Austin, TX 78748, who provided nearly all the information on his descendants.

[70] Esther Weygandt Powell, *Tombstone Inscriptions and Family Records of Belmont County, Ohio* (Akron: the author, 1969), p. 216.

[71] 1850 census, Belmont Co., Ohio, p. 11.

[72] Athens Co. (Ohio) Marriage Record, 1/2: 186.

[73] 1850 census, Monroe Co., Ohio, p. 192; 1860 census, Monroe Co., Ohio, p. 55.

[74] Powell, *Tombstone Inscriptions and Family Records of Belmont County, Ohio*, p. 163.

[75] Barry Co. (Mich.) Death Record, A: 50.

[76] Lorain Co. (Ohio) Marriages, 1: 12.

[77] *History of Medina County and Ohio*, p. 557.

[78] 1850 census, Lorain Co., Ohio, p. 888.

[79] Medina Co. (Ohio) Marriages, C: 223.

[80] Barry Co. (Mich.) Marriages, C: 6.

[81] *Cemetery Inscriptions of Lorain County, Ohio* (Elyria, Ohio: Genealogical Workshop of the Lorain County Historical Society, 1980), p. 342.

[82] Lorain Co. (Ohio) Marriages, 1: 307.

[83] Eaton Co. (Mich.) Deaths, 3: 74.

[84] 1850 census, Eaton Co., Mich., p. 168v.; 1860 census, Eaton Co., Mich., p. 857.

[85] 1900 census, Eaton Co., Mich., 19-79-13-55.

[86] *Barry County, Michigan History 1985*, p. 201.

[87] Lorain Co. (Ohio) Marriages, 1: 301.

[88] *Barry County, Michigan History 1985*, p. 201.

[89] Ibid.

[90] *Hastings Banner*, Apr. 1937.

[91] *History of Medina County and Ohio*, p. 758.

[92] Ibid.

[93] Ibid.; Bible records from Leonard Falconer.

[94] Washington Co. (Pa.) Orphan's Court Record, D: 134.

[95] Isabelle Mitchell Sumney.

[96] Washington Co. (Pa.) Orphan's Court Record, C: 194, 338; Estates, file no. 13, F 1825.

[97] Washington Co. (Pa.) Estates, file no. 13, F 1825.

[98] 1850 census, Washington Co., Pa., p. 196; 1860 census, Washington Co., Pa., p. 1113.

[99] *Tombstone Inscriptions: Fulton County, Ohio* (Swanton, Ohio: Fulton County Chapter of Ohio Genealogical Society, 1986), 1: 75.

[100] *Wauseon Republican*, 27 Mar. 1886.

[101] W. I. Tyler Brigham, *The History of the Brigham Family* (New York: Grafton Press, 1907), p. 386.

[102] *Wauseon Republican*, 27 Mar. 1886.

[103] 1850 census, Medina Co., Ohio, p. 341; Fulton Co. (Ohio) Probate Court, Wills, 5: 372; *Tombstone Inscriptions: Fulton County, Ohio*, 1: 18, 75.

[104] Charles H. Farnam, *History of the Descendants of John Whitman of Weymouth, Massachusetts* (New Haven: Tuttle, Morehouse, and Taylor, 1889), p. 252.

[105] *Official Roster of the State of Ohio in the War of the Rebellion, 1861-1866*, 4: 76.

[106] Brigham, *History of the Brigham Family*, p. 386.

[107] Fulton Co. (Ohio) Marriages, 3: 29.

[108] *Memorial Record of Butler County, Ohio*, pp. 250-252.

[109] *Centennial History of Butler County, Ohio*, p. 871.

[110] *A History and Biographical Cyclopaedia of Butler County, Ohio*, pp. 318-320.

[111] *Memorial Record of Butler County, Ohio*, pp. 250-252; genealogy prepared by Robert Crawford Falconer about 1906-1907.

[112] *Hamilton Evening Journal*, 16 Sept. 1924.

[113] Information compiled by Edna (Goelz) Falconer and communicated by Edward Nicholas, of Santa Fe, NM.

[114] Edward Nicholas.

[115] Ibid., 1900 census, Butler Co., Ohio, 13-14-18-79.

[116] 1860 census, Butler Co., Ohio, p. 331.

[117] Estate file of John H. Falconer, Richland Co. (Ill.) Circuit Court, box 20.

[118] Ibid.; Estate file of Charlotte Falconer, box 20.

[119] Tom Gregory, *History of Solano and Napa Counties, California* (Los Angeles: Historic Record Co., 1912), p. 274f.

[120] Estate files of John H. Falconer and Charlotte Falconer, Richland Co. (Ill.) Circuit Court, box 20.

[121] Avis Stearns Van Wagenen, *Genealogy and Memoirs and Isaac Stearns and His Descendants* (Syracuse, N. Y.: Courier Printing Co., 1901), p. 349f.

[122] Lola B. Taylor, *Early Marriages of Richland County, Illinois, 1840-1899*, (Olney, Ill.: Taylor Print Shop, 1970), 1: 62.

[123] Gregory, p. 274f.; pension file (certificate no. 892,238), National Archives.

[124] Conservatorship file and estate file of Frank Falconer, Richland Co. (Ill.) Circuit Court, boxes 81 and 118.

[125] Estate files of Charlotte Falconer and Frank Falconer, Richland Co. (Ill.) Circuit Court, boxes 20 and 118.

[126] Belmont Co. (Ohio) Marriage Record, 4: 119.

[127] Family records of J. E. Falconer, via Billie Hart.

[128] Gravestone says 9 March 1842.

[129] Morgan Co. (Ohio) Marriage Record, F: 129.

[130] 1880 census, Morgan Co., Ohio, 48-141-25-33.

[131] Gravestone says "August."

[132] Record of marriages by Rev. Charles Wheeler, Washington Co., Pa., 1815-1839, at Washington County Historical Society.

[133] Bible records from Allene Bowen.

[134] 1860 census, Wayne Co., Iowa, p. 788.

[135] Pension file (certificate no. 672,704), National Archives.

[136] 1850 census, Athens Co., Ohio, p. 395; 1860 census, Wayne Co., Iowa, p. 788.

[137] Wayne Co. (Iowa) Marriage Record, 1: no. 204.

[138] Information on this Foglesong family and that of Henry Foglesong was provided by Helen M. Buche, 3440 3rd St. A, East Moline, IL 61244.

[139] 1900 census, Dodge Co., Neb., 11-89-13-51. Her year of birth was probably 1843.

[140] Wayne Co. (Iowa) Marriage Record, 1: no. 173.

[141] 1900 census, Dodge Co., Neb., 11-89-13-51.

[142] 1860 census, Wayne Co., Ia., p. .

[143] Belmont Co. (Ohio) Marriages, 5: 151.

[144] Ibid., Marriages, 7: 151; the family Bible, however, says 28 February 1846.

[145] Belmont Co. (Ohio) Marriages, 11: 400.

[146] Belmont Co. (Ohio) Deeds, 36: 292.

[147] Ibid., 52: 448.

[148] Bible record, from Violette Bixler Magoon, via Marguerite C. Leander, 1437 Westward Ho Place, Sioux Falls, SD 57105; *History of Adams County, Iowa* (n.p.: Adams County History Book Committee, 1984), p. 211.

[149] *History of Adams County, Iowa,* p. 300f.

[150] Gravestone says 15 February 1865.

[151] *Official Roster of the State of Ohio in the War of the Rebellion, 1861-1866* (Akron: by Authority of the General Assembly, 1888), 6: 303.

[152] Pension file (certificate no. 300,728), National Archives.

[153] Ibid.

[154] 1900 census, Vermilion Co., Ill., 152-93-15-56.

[155] Vermilion Co. (Ill.) Marriage Licenses, no. 433.

[156] George R. Smith, "Juvenal-Juvinall Family of Vermilion County, Illinois," *Illiana Genealogist* 8 (Spring 1972): 68.

[157] Kent Co. (Mich.) Marriage Records, 6: 98.

[158] *Barry County, Michigan, History,* p. 201.

[159] 1920 census, Barry Co., Mich., 7-49-11-62.

[160] 1920 census, Barry Co., Mich., 7-46-3-73.

[161] Pension file (certificate no. 1,003,081, National Archives; nearly all the information on their children and grandchildren is from genealogical information from Fannie Amsbaugh, in possession of Leonard Falconer.

[162] Affidavit, Medina Co. (Ohio) Probate Court.

[163] Medina Co. (Ohio) Register of Marriages, G: 557.

[164] Ibid., I: 104.

[165] Medina Co. (Ohio) Register of Births, 1: 68, 93, 109; 2, rec. 6327; Lorain Co. (Ohio) Register of Births, 2: 102, 132; 3: 41.

[166] Medina Co. (Ohio) Register of Deaths, 1: 59.

[167] Medina Co. (Ohio) Register of Marriages, K: 420.

[168] *History of Medina County and Ohio,* p. 762.

[169] Medina Co. (Ohio) Register of Births, 1: 93, 114; Lorain Co. (Ohio) Register of Births, 3: 39, 40; 1880 census, Medina Co., Ohio, 44-190-15-32; 1900 census, Medina Co., Ohio, 105-46-7-59; Robert E. Falconer, Ocala, FL.

[170] 1900 census, Medina Co., Ohio, 105-46-3-13; 1910 census, Medina Co., Ohio, 111-136-71; 1920 census, Huron Co., Ohio, 109-180-15-28.

[171] 1920 census, Summit Co., Ohio, 198-257-3-46.

[172] *New York Times,* 28 Nov. 1941.

[173] *Memorial Record of Butler County, Ohio,* p. 252.

[174] Information compiled by Edna (Goelz) Falconer, via Don Fitton and Edward Nicholas, who was the source for the information about Robert Crawford Falconer.

[175] Richland Co. (Ill.) Deaths, 3: 125.

[176] Taylor, *Early Marriages of Richland County, Illinois,* 1: 151.

[177] Richland Co. (Ill.) Births, A: 95, 151; 1900 census, Richland Co., Ill., 138-124-1-18; 1910 census, Richland Co., Ill., 180-165-10; estate file of Harry C. Falconer, Richland Co. (Ill.) Circuit Court, box 94.

[178] Morgan Co. (Ohio) Marriage Record, D: 184.

[179] Pension file (certificate no. 757,731), National Archives.

[180] Family record of J. E. Falconer, via Billie Hart; Morgan Co. (Ohio) Birth Record, 1: 30, 228, 356.

[181] Morgan Co. (Ohio) Death Record, 2: 112.

[182] Morgan Co. (Ohio) Marriage Record, H: 5.

[183] Belmont Co. (Ohio) Marriage Record, 11: 200.

[184] 1880 census, McLean Co., Ill., 37-185-34-17.

[185] 1900 census, Linn Co., Mo., 151-77-4-185.

[186] Bible record of Mary M. (Gladden) Falconer, via Billie Hart; Billie Hart provided the information on the children and grandchildren.

[187] 1910 census, Dewey Co., Okla.

[188] Billie Hart.

[189] Athens Co. (Ohio) Marriage Record, 6: 389.

[190] Morgan Co. (Ohio) Death Record, 1: 204.

[191] Morgan Co. (Ohio) Marriage Record, F: 524.

[192] Perry Co. (Ohio) Deeds, 103: 45.

[193] Morgan Co. (Ohio) Birth Record, 1: 308.

[194] Ibid., 2: 57, 97; 1900 census, Morgan Co., Ohio, 116-33-9-12.

[195] *Humboldt Times,* 24 Dec. 1958.

[196] Genesee Co. (Mich.) Marriage Record, 9: 267.

[197] Pension file, National Archives; Virgil Post, 2124 N. Clarmar, Fremont, NE 68025.

[198] 1920 census, Pierce Co., Neb., 33-175-8-52.

[199] Research by Carol L. Keyes of the Holt County Historical Society.

[200] 1880 census, Dodge Co., Neb., 3-52-18-25; 1900 census, Holt Co., Neb., 22-114-7-7.

[201] Dodge Co. (Neb.) Marriage Record, 5: 240.

[202] Information from Carol L. Keyes; individual ordinance form 0508977, L.D.S., from Leonard A. Weddell, 924 Kennedy Dr., Capitola, CA 95010; .

[203] Holt Co. (Neb.) Marriage Record.

[204] Holt Co. (Neb.) Probate Court; research by Carol L. Keyes.

[205] 1920 census, Custer Co., Okla., 21-30-1-11.

[206] 1910 census, Alameda Co., Cal., 15-67-51.

[207] 1880 census, Adams Co., Ia., 1-11-5-37; 1900 census, Custer Co., Mont., 10-209C-50-34; information on this family comes from Robert W. Wagner, 880 Racquet Ln., Boulder, CO 80303.

[208] Bible and cemetery records, from Marguerite C. Leander; other material on his family is in *History of Adams County, Iowa*, p. 211f.

[209] Bible and cemetery records, from Marguerite C. Leander.

[210] *History of Adams County, Iowa*, p. 173.

[211] 1920 census, Adams Co., Iowa, 2-5-1-11.

[212] 1920 census, Cass Co., Iowa, 11-50-3-31.

[213] Ina Chladek, 2700 Hill St., S.E., Albany, OR 97321.

[214] 1900 census, Vermilion Co., Ill., 152-41-12-53; R. Floyd Falconer, P.O. Box 155, Redmon, IL 61949.

[215] Barry Co. (Mich.) Register of Marriages, D: 108.

[216] Ibid., D: 269.

[217] Oakland city directories.

[218] Barry Co. (Mich.) Register of Births, D: 11; 1900 census, Barry Co., Mich., 5-39-10-98; Dorothy Falconer Preston.

[219] *Wichita Beacon*, 23 Aug. 1957; 1920 census, Osage Co., Okla., 58-102-29-31.

[220] *Barry County, Michigan, History*, p. 200.

[221] *Hastings Banner*, 8 May 1978, 9 April 1979.

[222] Leonard Falconer Bible record.

[223] Medina Co. (Ohio) Birth Record, 2, no. 12201; 1-F: 21369, 3: no. 94.

[224] Medina Co. (Ohio) Marriages, L: 168.

[225] Ibid., M: 23.

[226] Ibid., O: 212.

[227] Lorain Co. (Ohio) Birth Record, vol. 4.

[228] Lorain Co. (Ohio) Marriage Record, 19: 91.

[229] Ibid., 9: 105.

[230] 1900 census, Lorain Co., Ohio, 93-68-5-35.

[231] Robert K. Falconer, 1918 N. Amber, Boise, ID 83706; 1920 census, Medina Co., Ohio, 147-289-4-71.

[232] Information from Robert E. Falconer, 3830 N.E. 22nd Ave., Ocala, FL 34479.

[233] Medina Co. (Ohio) Marriages, O: 79.

[234] Ibid., S: 122.

[235] *New York Times*, 17 Oct. 1969.

[236] *Who Was Who in America*, 4: 223.

[237] *New York Times*, 17 Oct. 1969.

[238] *New York Times*, 20 May 1940.

[239] Mary Falconer Bell, 809 Glenbrook Rd., Anchorage, KY 40223.

[240] Morgan Co. (Ohio) Marriages, I: 58.

[241] 1910 census, Morgan Co., Ohio, 140-52-250; Morgan Co. (Ohio) Birth Record, 3: 51; 4; 4, 47.

[242] Billie Hart.

[243] Billie Hart.

[244] Lelia Brown, Purdin, MO.

[245] 1900 census, Lake Co., S.D., 9-215-11-17; 1920 census, Dodge Co., Neb., 15-104-12-40.

[246] Douglas M. Falconer, 3031 Newport Ave., Omaha, NE 68112.

[247] Lester Van Alstine, *Van Alstyne-Van Alstine Family History*, vol. 2 (Provo, Utah: J. Grant Stevenson, 1974), p. 222.

[248] 1910 census, Okla., Custer Co., Okla., 17-119-68; Joanna White.

[249] Lester Van Alstine, *Van Alstyne-Van Alstine Family History*, vol. 2 (Provo, Utah: J. Grant Stevenson, 1978), p. 269.

[250] *History of Adams County, Iowa*, p. 211.

[251] Ibid., p. 435f.

[252] Marguerite C. Leander.

[253] Ibid.

[254] R. Floyd Falconer.

[255] *Mendota Reporter*, 29 Dec. 1966.

[256] *San Francisco Examiner*, 15 Mar. 1973.

[257] *Barry County, Michigan, History*, p. 200.

[258] Dorothy Falconer Preston, 725 E. Bond, Hastings, MI 49058.

[259] James E. Falconer, 85 Wendfield Circle, Newport News, VA 23601.

[260] Medina Co. (Ohio) Marriages, Q: 324.

[261] Ibid., 1: 357.

[262] Ibid.

[263] *Idaho Statesman*, 16 July 1984.

[264] Information from Robert G. Falconer, 1856 9th St. S.W., Akron, OH 44314.

[265] Billie Hart.

[266] Index to California Marriages.

[267] Meredith Clark, R. 2, Box 3A, Hurley, SD 57036.

[268] Douglas M. Falconer.

[269] Virginia Burt, 2200 Ella St., Beatrice, NE 68310.

[270] *History of Adams County, Iowa*, p. 211; Marguerite C. Leander.

[271] Jack T. Falconer.

[272] Walter J. Falconer.

[273] *Barry County, Michigan, History*, p. 200.

[274] James E. Falconer,

[275] Robert K. Falconer.

[276] Cyrus M. Falconer.

CHAPTER P

Falconer of Newton and Monkton

by Paul McKee Gifford and Paul Beresford Weller

P1 **Patrick Falconer** of Newton, second son of Alexander Falconer of Halkerton (A5), born probably about 1577, died between 5 August 1656 and 15 October 1658,[1] presumably at Newton, in the parish of Marykirk, Kincardineshire.

He married, as his first wife, prior to 8 June 1600,[2] Margaret Carnegie, daughter of James Carnegie of Balmachie, and first cousin of Agnes Carnegie, who married Patrick's brother Alexander. She died testate 26 September 1626 at Newton, leaving all her personal estate to her husband.[3]

He married, as his second wife, Grisel Blair, sister of Sir John Blair of Balgillo and relict of Patrick Blair of Ardblair.[4]

On 18 August 1601, Patrik Falconer of Kilhill served on an assize in a cause of Sir David Wood of Craig pursued by Mr. Thomas Hammiltoune, advocate, for obstructing the designing of the manse and glebe, for the kirk of Fordoun.[5] Patrick acquired, by charter from George, Earl Marischal dated 19 June 1609, to himself and his spouse Margaret Carnegie, the lands of Bruntoune, and further on 29 January 1612, and became seised of them 5 February 1610 and 31 December 1613.[6] In that same year, 5 June 1613, holding a charter of alienation from George Lamby of Duncany, he was seized also of the lands of Newton with the consent of Christine Fullerton, Lamby's mother, and Margaret Halyburton, his spouse.[7] Patrick was appointed a Commissioner for the Peace in Kincardineshire on 24 August 1614 and a Justice of the Peace on 20 August 1623.[8] Burnton passed by a charter he signed on 14 November 1625 to William Keith.[9] In April 1648, he was made a commissioner of war for the same county.[10]

When family security was dependent upon political power and that power rested upon the holding of landed estates, and increasingly upon high office in the law and offices of profit under the Crown, the fortunes of Patrick Falconer and his two sons were only unusual in one respect, which was the apparent disinheritance of Patrick the elder in favor of John the younger. In any case, within those two generations they lost their estates of Burnton and Newton, ultimately to their cousins, upon whom devolved in due course the peerage and estates of Halkerton.

The process in detail is hard to unravel in the documents of the period, but prudent marriage, often among cousins; the purchase of land, foreclosure on others; debt and ruin, disgrace and disinheritance; political ambition and religious division all played their part. All these, however, seemed to be survived by the bonds of kinship.

Issue of Patrick Falconer of Newton and Margaret Carnegie:

i.   Patrick Falconar, eldest son, buried in the College Wynd, Greyfriars, 20 May 1675.[11] On 15 October 1658, he renounced heirship to the deceased Patrick Falconer of Newton in favor of John Falconer of Newton.[12] He was Commissary of Inverness by 2 March 1658.[13] A grant of this office was made to him on 10 September 1660.[14] On 6 March 1661, he was appointed one of the keepers of His Majesty's Wardrobe.[15]

P2   ii. John Falconer of Newton.

iii. Lilias Falconer. She married, as his second wife, Allan Mackintosh, sixth son of Lauchlan Mackintosh of that Ilk, and had issue, surname *Mackintosh*:[16] a. Aeneas; and two daughters.

Issue of Patrick Falconer of Newton and Grisel Blair:[17]

iv. Grisel Falconer. She was probably the wife of Robert Gray, eldest son of Andrew Gray of Kingorme.[18]

P2 **John Falconer** of Newton, born probably between 1606 and 1610, died in December 1671 in the parish of Conveth (Laurencekirk), Kincardineshire.[19]

He married, on 27 January 1648, at Edinburgh,[20] by contract dated 17 December 1647, Elizabeth Cant, daughter of John Cant of Morton and Catherine Creich. Her testament was confirmed on 11 December 1713.[21] By the terms of the contract, her tocher was £8,000, which was claimed at his death to yield an annual income of £480.[22]

On 25 April 1637 he appeared in the Commissariot of Elgin for Jean Falconer, wife of John Grant of Moyness.[23] He appears from this to have possessed legal training, although no other record of his practice of law has been found.

In 1651, for whatever reason, the estate of Newton passed from his father to John by a charter, dated 3 December at Montrose, signed by his father and witnessed by his nephew Alexander, 1st Lord Falconer of Halkerton (A7), David Falconar (G1), and Walter Lyell, later clerk of Brechin. This was supported by a deed of disposition and a deed of sasine, both of the same date.

The charter was an instrument of regrant of land or could have been admitting John as a purchaser; the disposition was a unilateral instrument, by which heritable or moveable property could be alienated from an heir of line; and the sasine was by this time a legal instrument of right of possession of land with priority in accordance with the date of registration, which in this case was done at Montrose, 26 April 1652.[24]

He presumably lived at Newton between 1651 and 1658, as children were baptized in Montrose during those years. However, he had lived in Edinburgh in 1649 and 1650, and on 9 December 1657, he was admitted to the burgess roll of the city.[25]

John's father came under legal attack over Newton. On 23 February 1656, an action was brought against him by George Falconer, a natural son of the deceased Sir Alexander Falconer of Halkerton, for arrears of interest owing to him of 200 merks pern annum on an earlier loan to Patrick, secured by wadset, that is, a pledge of lands, on the Newton estate. John produced the sum required and appeared before the Commissariot Court at Edinburgh with answers on 8 November 1656.[26] On 16 October 1658, Robert Arbuthnot and Robert Barclay entered a writ of inhibition against John,[27] which prohibited him from burdening his heritage or parting with it to the detriment of the inhibiting creditors.

John acquired by purchase the farm of the Excise in Perthshire at about this time, but this produced problems and in 1662 he made supplication to the Privy Council for compensation for his losses caused by the unlawful brewing and retailing of drink by the soldiers of the Perth garrison.[28] At the end of that year his financial difficulties had overwhelmed him and, by a deed of disposition of 28 January 1663, he sold the lands of Newton together with a quantity of barley, all the fodder in the barns, twenty oxen, sixty steers, six horses and mares with carts, wagons, ploughs, and other instruments of husbandry, to Mr. David Falconar, younger, advocate (E1).[29]

Children of John Falconer of Newton and Elizabeth Cant:[30]

P3 i.   Patrick Falconar of Monkton, Writer to the Signet, baptized 26 January 1649.

R1 ii. John Falconer, writer, baptized 15 February 1650.

    iii. Charles Falconer, writer in Edinburgh, baptized 8 August 1651, living 7 March 1727. He was servitor to Lord Wintoun, when he witnessed a contract in 1678 between Sir John Falconar, Master of the Mint, and David Moodie, merchant in Montrose, for two tons of copper.[31] As servant to David Falconer of Newtoune, Charles Falconer was admitted a burgess of Aberdeen, 8 May 1679.[32] By 1696 he was a writer in Edinburgh and at Montrose on 21 July he drew and witnessed with his brother-german John Falconer a bond of his mother Elizabeth Cant.[33] Described as "brother german to the deceast Mr. Patrick Falconar of Mounton," he declared by affidavit on 15 July 1715 to have appeared to give evidence at Edinburgh in a civil suit of Barbara Jaffray against James Milne of Hatton.[34] George Falconar, writing to his brother David, 4th Lord Falconer of Halkerton, on 3 September 1725, commented that "our cousin Charles Falconar for some weeks has been complaining of a great weakness, and I believe is dying."[35] He overcame this ailment, however, as on 7 March 1727, he was cautioner in letters of incident diligence in the case of Alexander Hay alias Falconer of Dalgettie, and other heirs of Robert Norvell, advocate, against George Home of Ninewells.[36]

    iv. Grisel Falconer, baptized 9 August 1654, living 21 July 1696, unmarried.[37]

v.   Margaret Falconer, baptized 12 February 1656.

vi.   Elizabeth Falconer, baptized 28 June 1658. She married, 25 July 1701, at Montrose,[38] Lieutenant John Boyd, of Montrose. She was executrix of her mother's will at Brechin in December 1713.[39]

P3 **Patrick Falconar** of Monkton, baptized 26 January 1649 in Edinburgh, died 20 March 1715.[40]

He married, on 22 April 1711, at Edinburgh,[41] Mary Falconer, daughter of Sir James Falconer of Phesdo (V2), born 4 March 1687 in Edinburgh, died 26 March 1767 in Edinburgh.[42]

He was a writer and notary at Edinburgh. He was a writer there by 23 August 1673, when he was admitted a burgess of Aberdeen.[43] On 22 March 1680, "at the age of thirty or thereby," in the presence of his second cousin, Sir David Falconar of Newton, and Sir Alexander Seton of Pitmedden, two of the Senators of the College of Justice, and of his younger brother John as his cautioner, he was admitted notary. Each notary used a distinctive sign or rebus and also a motto, and these had to be recorded in the register. Patrick's rebus and his motto *Jacktiora p'stans'* appears above his signature in the margin at the end of the entry. The record throws an interesting light upon the normal, but to our ideas strange, seventeenth-century lack of concern about the spelling of family names. John appears to have first signed his name as he usually spelled it and then to have altered the 'e' to an 'a.' Patrick's signature is very ornate, while John's is in the copybook style, which, with its clarity, was gaining favor.[44]

The following year, in 1681, Patrick signed the Test Act and was listed amongst advocates' servants and others employed in writing and agenting in Edinburgh.[45] He had acquired, by the time of his marriage, the lands of Monkton, in Inveresk, Midlothianshire. On 9 December 1717, his testament was confirmed.

Issue of Patrick Falconar of Monkton and Mary Falconer:

P4   i.   James Falconar of Monkton, born about 1712.

ii.   Patrick Falconar of Balnakettle, born 25 December 1714,[46] died 26 October 1797 at Edinburgh.[47] In 1795, according to the provisions of the deed of entail of Dame Elizabeth Trent, relict of Sir James Falconer of Phesdo, upon the death of his elder brother without heirs male, he inherited the estate of Balnakettle.[48] John, Viscount of Arbuthnott, was served heir male of taillie and provision special in the lands of Balnakettle, Little Strath, Haulhaugh, etc., in the parish of Fettercairn, on 17 March 1798.[49] His personal estate was substantial, as the inventory mentions 80 shares of stock in the Bank of Scotland, equivalent to £80,000 sterling.[50] His niece Mary, wife of Sir James Colquhoun of Luss, Bart., was served heir portioner general to Patrick on 9 May 1798.[51]

P4 **James Falconar** of Monkton, born probably in 1712, died 18 December 1779.[52]

He married, 16 December 1750, at Edinburgh,[53] Jean Falconer, daughter of David, 4th Lord Falconer of Halkerton (A10), who died at Edinburgh 16 February 1797.[54]

He was appointed a director of the Bank of Scotland in 1761.[55]   About 1770, he owned Monkton, in Inveresk, Midlothianshire; Balnakettle and Little Strath in Fettercairn, Kincardineshire; and Miltonhaven and Bourtrielish, in St. Cyrus, Kincardineshire, for a total assessment of £2114,14s.,10d.[56]

Issue of James Falconar of Monkton and Jean Falconer, baptized at Edinburgh:

i.   Catharine Falconar, baptized 27 March 1754, died in 1790. She married, 21 March 1781, in Edinburgh, John Mackenzie of Allangrange, Writer to the Signet, Examiner of Customs in Edinburgh, and had issue, surname *Mackenzie*: a. *George Falconer*; b. *Jane Falconer*, who married John Gillanders of Highfield.[57] His wife's inheritance was such that it allowed him to "devote himself to his favourite agricultural pursuits, in which he was eminently successful in his day."[58]

ii.   Patrick Falconar, baptized 20 April 1755, died without issue prior to the date of his father's testament.

iii. Mary Falconar, baptized 27 June 1757, died 12 April 1833 at Annfield House, Kettle, Fifeshire. She married, 22 July 1773, Sir James Colquhoun of Luss, Baronet, born 28 July 1741, died 23 April 1805, and had issue, surname *Colquhoun*:[59] a. *Sir James*, born 28 September 1774, died 3 February 1836 in Edinburgh, married, June 1799, Janet Sinclair; b. *William*, died in infancy; c. *Patrick*, advocate, died, unmarried, before 1803; d. *Ludovic*, died in infancy; e. *John Campbell*, advocate, born 31 January 1785, died 21 August 1854 in Edinburgh; e. *Sutherland Morris*, captain, R.N., died, unmarried, February 1827 in Jamaica; f. *Roderick*, R.N., H.E.I.C., died, unmarried, in 1834 in Edinburgh; g. *Jane Falconer*, married, at Edinburgh, 8 September 1803, David Kemp of Balusney Lodge, Fife; h. *Helen Sutherland*, unmarried; i. *Wilhelmina*, married, at Rossdhu, 15 July 1808, John Campbell of Stonefield, Argyll; j. *Catharine Falconer*, married, 25 July 1815 Alexander Millar of Earnock, Lanarkshire.

NOTES

[1] He was referred to in a deed of assignation dated 5 August 1656, and described as "the deceased Patrick Falconer of Newton" in a legal statement of cause registered at Montrose 15 October 1658, RD2/3, f. 402, SRO.

[2] Particular Register of Sasines for Sheriffdom of Kincardineshire, RS6/1, p. 16, SRO.

[3] Testament, Commissariot of St. Andrew's, CC20/4/8, SRO.

[4] Scotland, Scottish Record Office, *Index to Particular Register of Sasines for Sheriffdom of Forfar*, vol. 1, *1620-1700*, Indexes no. 59 (Edinburgh: H. M. Stationery Office, 1965), p. 104.

[5] Robert Pitcairn, *Criminal Trials in Scotland*, 2: 362.

[6] Charter, Kintore Papers, Bundle 141, Aberdeen University Library.

[7] Sasine, Kintore Papers, Bundle 138; Fraser, *History of Laurencekirk*, p. 69f.

[8] *Register of the Privy Council*,   ; *Acts of the Parliaments of Scotland*, 6, pt. 2: 34.

[9] Charter, Kintore Papers, Bundle 141, Aberdeen University Library.

[10] *Acts of the Parliaments of Scotland*, 6, pt. 2: 34.

[11] Paton, *Register of Interments in the Greyfriars Burying-Ground*, p. 213.

[12] Register of Deeds, RD2/3, f. 402, SRO.

[13] Register of Deeds, RD3/8, f. 536, SRO.

[14] Register of the Privy Seal, RS3/1, p. 90.

[15] Register of the Privy Seal, RS3/1, p. 147.

[16] MacFarlane, *Genealogical Collections*, 1: 270; Alexander Mackintosh Shaw, *Historical Memoirs of the House and Clan of Mackintosh and of the Clan Chattan* (London: for the author by R. Clay's Sons and Taylor, 1880), p. 281, which calls the son Angus..

[17] General Register of Sasines, RS1/56, f. 240ff.

[18] Register of Deeds, RD3/24, f. 271, SRO.

[19] Testament, Commissariot of St. Andrews, CC20/4/13, f. 9r., SRO.

[20] Edinburgh Old Parish Register.

[21] Testament dative, Commissariot of Brechin, CC3, SRO.

[22] Testament, Commissariot of St. Andrews, CC20/4/13, f. 9r., SRO.

[23] Particular Register of Sasines for Elgin, Forres, and Nairn, RS28/4, f. 128v., SRO.

[24] Kintore Papers, Bundle 138, Aberdeen University Library.

[25] Watson, *Roll of Edinburgh Burgesses, 1701-1760*, p. 177.

[26] Scotland, Court of Session Processes, CS138/1806, SRO.

[27] Kintore Papers, Bundle 284, Aberdeen University Library.

[28] *Register of the Privy Council*, 3rd ser., 1: .

[29] Kintore Papers, Bundle 112, Aberdeen University Library.

[30] The first two baptized at Edinburgh; the rest baptized at Montrose.

[31] Cochran-Patrick, *Records of the Coinage of Scotland*, 2: 180f.

[32] Munro, Ed., "Aberdeen Burgess Register," p. 447.

[33] Register of Deeds, RD4/84, f. 1386, SRO.

[34] Moses Bundle 254/7792, Edinburgh District Archives.

[35] George Falconar to David, 4th Lord Falconer of Halkerton, 3 Sept. 1725, in Kintore Papers, Bundle 195, Aberdeen University Library.

[36] Moses Bundle 171/6717, Edinburgh District Archives.

[37] Register of Deeds, RD4/84, f. 1386, SRO.

[38] Montrose Parish Register.

[39] Testament, Commissariot of Brechin, CC3/3/9, SRO.

[40] Testament, Commissariot of Edinburgh, CC8/8/86, f. 393, SRO.

[41] Paton, ed., *The Register of Marriages for the Parish of Edinburgh, 1701-1750*, p. 178.

[42] *Scots' Magazine*, 29: 224.

[43] Munro, ed., "Aberdeen Burgess Register," p. 83.

[44] Register of Admissions of Notaries, vol. 12, Edinburgh; notes on entries by J. P. E. Falconer.

[45] *Register of the Privy Council*, 2nd series, 12: vii, 117.

[46] Edinburgh Parish Register.

[47] *Scots' Magazine*, 59: 783.

[48] Register of Tailzies, RT1/12, f. 40ff., SRO; *Decennial Index to Service of Heirs*, vol. 1790-1799, p. 16.

[49] *Decennial Index to Service of Heirs*, vol. 1790-1799, p. 16.

[50] Testament dative, Commissariot of Edinburgh, CC8/8/131/1, SRO.

[51] *Decennial Index to Service of Heirs*, vol. 1790-1799, p. 16.

[52] Testament, Commissariot of Edinburgh, CC8/8/125/2, SRO.

[53] Paton, ed., *Register of Marriages for the Parish of Edinburgh, 1701-1750*, p. 178.

[54] *Scots' Magazine*, 59: 144.

[55] Malcolm, *The Bank of Scotland, 1695-1945*, p. 296.

[56] Loretta R. Timperley, *A Directory of Landownership in Scotland*, pp. 181, 183, 229.

[57] Alexander Mackenzie, *History of the Mackenzies* (Inverness: A. and W. Mackenzie, 1894), p. 360f.

[58] Ibid., p. 360.

[59] Sir William Fraser, *The Chiefs of Colquhoun and Their Country* (Edinburgh: n.p., 1869), 1: 393.

CHAPTER Q

Falconer of Chester, Bath and Gloucestershire

by Paul Beresford Weller

Q1 **John Falconer**, second son of John Falconer of Newton (P2) and Elizabeth Cant, baptized 15 February 1650 at Edinburgh,[1] died 10 May 1699 in Chancery Lane, London, was buried 12 May 1699 at St. Dunstans in the West, Fleet Street.[2]

He married, on 14 February 1681, at St. Giles Cathedral, Edinburgh,[3] Mary Dalmahoy, daughter of John Dalmahoy of Dalmahoy, Captain in His Majesty's Lifeguard of Horse for Scotland, and Rachel Wilbraham. She was baptized 19 March 1663 at Edinburgh, died 12 January 1754 in Chester, and was buried 16 January 1754 at the Cathedral of Chester.[4]

On 22 March 1680, John Falconer appeared as cautioner for his elder brother Patrick on the admission of the latter at Edinburgh as a notary and is described as his brother-german.[5] The following year he prudently and quietly signed the Test Act and was listed with his elder brother amongst advocates' servants and others employed in writing and agenting in Edinburgh, at a time when it was being rigorously enforced by Graham of Claverhouse.[6] Another list, this one a legally authenticated extract, but with no original signatures, includes one, "Mr. John Falconer, servant in Mr. Roderick McKenzie, clerk, his chalmer,"[7] in other words, an assistant, roughly equivalent of today's articled clerk, in Mr. McKenzie's chambers.

At the end of the summer of 1680, now qualified as a writer, there is record of him borrowing money from a friend, Thomas Gordon, described as servitor to the Lord Chancellor of Scotland. He gave his bond for £115 sterling on the 7th of September, which was witnessed by Alexander Gordon, son to the laird of Straloch, and William Bisset, merchant.[8] Thomas and Alexander Gordon were useful friends to have. They were kinsmen of Sir George Gordon of Haddo, appointed President of the Court of Session the following year, and then Lord Chancellor as 1st Earl of Aberdeen in 1682. The funds may have been needed in preparation for his wedding, but, unfortunately no marriage contract has been found.

From the year of his marriage, 1681, John Falconer remains a shadowy figure, although closely related to numerous leading Jacobites of the period, and with a wife from a similar background of loyalty to the House of Stuart.[9] Separated for long periods by his travels, and his short imprisonment in 1690, their marriage is mainly illuminated in surviving records by the birth of children, notarized legal transactions to do with money, and occasional incidents of drama. We have no letters of his, and no references to him appear in known correspondence, although the possibility of these exists in French archives during the period of the Stuart court at Saint Germain-en-Laye, and no portrait. Known to his descendants as "the Jacobite spy," one has to confess that either by his own caution or that of his widow or sons, or by some deliberate or accidental destruction of the family papers that that generation subsequently, not a note or memorandum of this very literate and active man has survived; his personal security remains still to this day largely unpenetrated.

Already in 1681, that five years had begun in Scotland known as the "Killing Time," when old scores were being settled, when there and in London great men were ruthlessly jockeying for power, and much ordinary business and matters of civil and criminal justice turned on "interest." If a man lacked a powerful protector whose own gambles succeeded, or found himself linked with a political loser, not to say a villain found out, as was the unfortunate Sir John Falconer at the mint with Charles Maitland, Lord Haltoun, he faced ruin. The Falconer family was still in a position of considerable influence. John Falconer had ability and, on the surface of things it does seem that had he wished it, like his elder brother, he was exceptionally well placed to pursue a successful career in the law. There may have been an impediment, possibly financial, or perhaps political, which caused him to turn his back on Edinburgh, but it seems probable that he had in his character an element of the gambler, an ambition to restore his family's lost fortunes by a political adventure. It is certainly clear that he already possessed a most unusual interest, a quite remarkable intellectual and practical talent for cryptanalysis and cryptography, which he saw as an adjunct to government and which might serve his fortunes. London beckoned, but henceforth our information is scarce.

On 17 February 1682, a deed of translation (i.e., a deed of transfer) was signed between "Maria Dalmahoy and Mr. John Falconer, Writer in Edinburgh, now my husband."[10] Three months later, in May, three of his friends, Gideon Murray and John Crawford, both writers, and Thomas Gordon, now described as a merchant, stood as sponsors at the baptism in Edinburgh of John and Mary's first child, John.[11]   On 16 September 1682 he executed a deed of factory (i.e., a power of attorney) at Edinburgh, in which he is described as a "writer in Edinburgh" who is "intending to go to London." This too was witnessed by Gideon Murray and by William Davidstone, writer at Edinburgh.[12]

By the next summer, Falconer and Murray were both in London, because on 30 July 1683, John executed the registration of a deed of trust at London, in which he appears as "now resident in London...being of intention to go abroad for some short time off from His Maj[es]ties Dominions," which was witnessed by "Gideon Murray, Gent., son to the deceased Gideon Murray of

Pitkerie, and James Greer, tailor, living in Blackemoor Street, in the parish of St. Clement Dane's."[13] Possibly Greer was their landlord. On John Falconer's wax seal on the deed appears the impression of a falcon's head, issuing out of a man's heart, between seven or eight roundels. These arms resemble more closely those of his kinsman, Falconer of Phesdo, rather than those of Falconer of Halkerton, to whom he was more nearly related, but the latter did not in fact matriculate their own arms until 1733. However, either way, this incorrect use on his seal then, and no doubt on other occasions, gave rise to confusion in the mind of his widow years later.[14] At the time in London it was probably a genuine error and seemed in any case of little importance.

These were the years when John Falconer's interest in cryptography and covert communication was being developed and, no doubt, practiced. They led to his publication in London, late in 1685, of the first edition of *Cryptomenysis Patefacta: or the Art of Secret Information Disclosed without a Key, Containing Plain and Demonstrative Rules for Deciphering All Manner of Secret Writing* (London: for Daniel Brown at the Black Swan and Bible, without Temple Bar, 1685).[15] The newness of the subject in print must have contributed to the need felt for a lengthy title, but it was not unusual to be so prolix. The book was dedicated to the author's kinsman Charles, second Earl of Middleton, Secretary of State for England, and later, in exile, Jacobite Secretary of State at Saint Germain.

The six pages of the "Epistle Dedicatory" and indeed the four pages of the advice "To The Reader," notwithstanding the normal panegyric style of preliminaries of the period, have a curious syntax, a wild punctuation and a very odd selection of words in upper case. It seems more than possible that both contain coded messages, maybe of a political character, as a demonstration of the writer's skill, or even as a jest for the few. To identify himself closely with the Secretary, the author refers to the military exploits of the 1st Earl of Middleton for Charles I in the Scottish war, leaves out his gallantry and leadership at Worcester curiously enough, but returns to his distinction as the first Royal Commissioner in Scotland after the Restoration, although ignoring his removal, and ends by applauding his life as Governor of the backwater of Tangier. An odd and uneven performance, it must be admitted. He finishes:

> Nay there are plenty of WANTS: But I have an intire Inclination, to serve my King and Country; and if this small Tract, at this time, do in any Measure evidence it, I HAVE my aim, and let it remain upon record to my perpetual infamy, if I do not chearfully, and upon all occasions venture the last drop of my Blood in His Majesties Service; and according to the circumstances, Act or Suffer for one infinitely BETTER than the GOOD OLD CAUSE. And next to the Royal Interest, I declare That my great Ambition in particular, is to be,

> My Lord
>   Your Lordship's Most Humble, and
>   Most Obedient Servant,
>   JOHN FALCONER

Family tradition has long held that during these years John became a Roman Catholic, which led to estrangement between husband and wife. Such

Cryptomenyſis Pateſacta :

Or the α . 32. 52 ſeſ.

A   R   T

O F

SECRET INFORMATION

Diſcloſed without a *K E Y.*

Containing,

Plain and Demonſtrative Rules,

for Decyphering all Manner of S E C R E T
W R I T I N G. With Exact Methods, for Reſol
ving Secret Intimations by S I G N S or G E
S T U R E S, or in S P E E C H. As alſo an In-
quiry into the Secret ways of C O N V E Y I N G
Written Meſſages : And the ſeveral M Y S T E-
R I O U S P R O P O S A L S for Secret Informa
tion, mentioned by *Trithemius*, &c.

By *J. F.*

Et varias uſus meditando extunderet Artes.
*Virg.*G. 1.

L O N D O N,

Printed for *Daniel Brown*, at the black *Swan* and
Bible, without *Temple-Bar*, 1685.

Title page of John Falconer's *Cryptomenysis Patefacta*, 1685.

a course would have had violently felt social and political implications, as well
as exposing them both, with their children, to danger and penalties from the
law. The belief may rest upon no more than an obvious understanding of the
words in the dedication, "the Good Old Cause," to mean that of the House of
Stuart, and an only slightly less obvious reading of the words "one infinitely
Better" to mean the cause of the good old faith. What is certain is that such
an act would have been flying hard in the face of the family adherence to
Knox's Calvinism and the Presbyterian system of worship through previous
generations. It would also have been taking a step which Middleton himself

had constantly rejected without any loss of influence and which he continued to resist until after James's death in 1701.

In his advice "To The Reader," the author writes:

> You will find amongst the following Observations, that by means of Secret Intelligence, not only Armies, but Kingdoms and Crowns have been lost. Which Things had never otherways, perhaps been attempted, at least not effected. And particularly, That in the beginning of the late Troubles, of ever Cursed Memory, the Canting (I would say Covenanting) People of both Kingdoms, studied a part of this Black Art as their first degree in the MYSTERY of Rebellion, which ended not before the Faith's Defender was removed to make way for Religion, and the Laws of God and his Viceregent were overturned to secure property; In short untill there was nothing Consequential visible in some Mens actions, but only in providing Asses for the Pulpit, and sending Horses to Church.

He continues, writing after the execution of Argyll and as James faces successfully the first threat to his throne, the doomed West Country invasion by Monmouth:

> The learned Lord Verulam, in his Advancement of Learning, reports the Art of Decyphering as WANTING, and therefore I thought it worth the while to search after it. The Advantages, that may probably arise from the Knowledge of it, I leave to be Collected from the danger of Secret Practises, especially in this Juncture. And as the Late Earl of Argile's later Designs, against the Government (discovered in several of his Letters last year) determined me to undertake this troublesome Task, so the open Rebellion now on foot added new Motives for its speedy Publication.

In 1688, the nation was taken by surprise by the Revolution, the work of a small determined minority. The Whigs in short were efficient and the Jacobites were not. What brought about the downfall of James was his attempt to secure toleration, which was interpreted by his enemies as a circuitous method of securing the return of England to the Church of Rome. His first object was to repeal those provisions, such as the Test Act, which prevented anyone from holding a post, civil or military, or voting in Parliament, unless he took communion as a member of the Church of England and swore an oath denying transubstantiation. Had the King kept his head he might also have kept his throne, but, amidst a general feeling of apathy, he fled.

In Scotland in 1690, there was little enthusiasm for William of Orange. There was real fear of the return of oppression and the prevailing sentiment was for James II, who, with all his failings, was a Stuart and a Scot. But an immediate and serious matter of concern for John Falconer was his all too recent open and public avowal of loyalty to James and his political utterances three years earlier in his book in London. Men in Edinburgh would have been familiar with it. Also the way would now have been barred to him to return to his profession of the law, had he wished to, unless he was prepared to do what the non-juring clergy had at such cost refused, which was to break his oath to James and take new oaths of allegiance to William and Mary. Edinburgh, for the time being, was no place for him.

What John Falconer's intentions were that year we do not know, but it is certain that in October he left Scotland, probably from Edinburgh and sailing from Leith, for Holland in a Dutch dogger. On board with him was John, second Lord Bellenden of Broughton, a known Jacobite with a quick temper, who the previous year had shot outright a soldier, who at the wrong moment, declared himself for William and Mary. He was traveling incognito under the name of "Mr. Ker." On the fourteenth their vessel was intercepted. Bellenden was arrested and with him John Falconer. Both were conveyed to Edinburgh and there thrown into the tolbooth, from which Bellenden was shortly transferred to the Castle.[16]

John was not without resources, but family fortunes had been mixed. Just as when financial misfortune arose lost estates were to be subsequently found in the hands of more provident kinsmen who had taken mortgages upon them in return for monies lent, so when a lost cause was backed politically cousins were to be found on the winning side, who, out of self-interest as well as affection, would deflect the more extreme penalties awaiting the losers. However, the head of the family, Alexander, second Lord Falconer of Halkerton, had died in 1684, and his son, David, third Lord, was only named heir in 1690, and was of little account in affairs until his death twenty years later, when he was declared to have been insane for all that time.

However, Sir James Falconer, Lord Phesdo (V2), their second cousin and contemporary, was now a Senator of the College of Justice and a Lord of Session. It was possibly his influence which led to John's release and the dropping of charges two days before Christmas. In his petition, he claimed, with apparent success, to have been bound for Holland on his lawful affairs and, unaware of Bellenden's presence in the dogger, and now confident that his innocence would be plain to the Lords of His Majesty's Privy Council. Innocent or not, in those arbitrary and bloody times he was fortunate in his family, and one way or another an order was issued to the magistrates of Edinburgh and the Keeper of the Tollbooth for his release, which was served on 23 December 1690.[17]

John then seems to have disappeared and may well have been on the continent at the court at Saint Germain-en-Laye, which was lavish and welcoming and, thanks to the unparalleled hospitality of Louis XIV, possessed besides an elegance and more adequate funds than had ever been available at Whitehall. These years were a time of constant political uncertainty. William of Orange was vulnerable and the succession to the throne frighteningly unclear. Secret diplomatic activity between the court at Whitehall and the court at St. Germain was continuous.

The rule of William was far from draconian, but it seems extraordinary to our way of thinking that two years after his release from the tolbooth, John, now apparently widely believed to be dead, published a second edition of *Cryptomenysis Patefacta*, printed as before for Daniel Brown at the Black Swan and Bible, without Temple-Bar, but now joined by Samuel Manship at the Black Bull in Cornhill. Plainly reception of the first edition had been warm, but the timing of the issue of the second seems to have been to shew the author as apolitical. Gone was the verbosity of the original title, to be replaced with more practical wording, and the new edition had neither the now treasonable "Epistle Dedicatory" nor the politically partisan advice "To The Reader."

Wide recognition of the real importance of the work in its field, however, waited until the second half of the twentieth century, as a result of the concentrated effort made by the Allies to break codes in the Second World War. John Falconer described how his rules for deciphering were the fruits of practical experience after he first became intrigued by the theory. Today the work is held to be the product of an acute, practical and experienced mind, and in 1966 was said to give what seems to be the earliest examples of the most widely used modern French military, Japanese diplomatic and Soviet spy ciphers.[18]   No doubt it carried with it, three hundred years ago, the high political and material hopes of its author.

The long gap of eleven years between the birth of John and Mary's first child and that of the second indicates at least the possibility of separation during the intervening years, and then reconciliation in the autumn of 1692. The second birth was followed by two more, and it must have been at this time, if not earlier, that an Anglican upbringing was agreed for all three. If John's Roman Catholicism existed, which is doubtful, it may have been a purely political move to enable him to use Catholic resources in his work. The rearing of the children was in the event to be in Dalmahoy and Wilbraham hands anyway. The marked zeal with which Mary later recorded her elder, surviving sons' devotion to the Church of England on their monuments,[19] and both her own and their strict observation of its rites in an age when conformity was politic, may reflect her protective reaction to her husband's Popery or simply against the rumor of it.

In December 1692,[20] a passport was issued at Whitehall to Mary Falconer to travel to Harwich and Holland, in order, one may suppose, to join her husband, in the wake of the new edition of the book, at the Stuart court in exile. There a major division now existed between those advisors of James, known as Compounders, who were prepared to accept certain conditions for his restoration to the throne, and the Non-Compounders, who held that the royal dignity accepted no compromise. In 1693, the tolerant Protestant Middleton, at the head of the Compounders, once more became co-Secretary of State with the Non-Compounder Duke of Melfort, and his views were adopted.[21] In reality it mattered little by 1693 what declaration James put out. Middleton's role at the exiled court later diminished and John's prospects at the center of the Stuart cause must have been weakened.

In the spring, John and Mary were back in Scotland for the birth of their second son in July 1693, perhaps in Montrose in the household of John's mother, Elizabeth Cant, or in the Canongate or at Holyrood in the household of Mary's mother, Rachel Kennedy. The Edinburgh poll tax returns for 1694, which appear to have been made in the summer, record in the parish of Old Kirk and Tolbooth "Mr. John Falconer, Writer; wife; children: John, about 12 years, James about 1 year."[22] In the summer of 1696, John was at Montrose witnessing a bond of his elderly mother with his younger brother Charles.[23] Finally, in March 1699, their last child, another son, was born in England, possibly in London or Cheshire, barely seven weeks before the father's death in London left their mother a widow of thirty-six with three small children under the age of six.

It was with the family of her mother and under the protection of her uncle Roger Wilbraham of Townsend, Nantwich, Cheshire, that Mary Falconer henceforth sought refuge, until her uncle was in turn succeeded at Townsend in 1708 by his son Randle. Townsend was a household loyal to the Stuarts, which had emerged with estates burdened with debt after the Civil War.

No reference to financial support for his niece appears in Roger Wilbraham's papers. Her widow's income, though small, may, with occasional legacies,[24] have been adequate. As far as we know, it was neither large enough nor so small that she was either pressed or tempted to marry again. Finally, following the death of her third, unmarried, son Thomas, in 1730, Mary Falconer became a rich woman, able to enjoy to the full the society of her family, cousins, and friends in Cheshire, Staffordshire, Derbyshire, and London. Her remaining two sons' prospects were transformed.

Within a year of this access of fortune she settled £4,000 upon the youngest, William, on the occasion of his marriage to his second cousin, Rachel Wilbraham, of which she retained half until her own death. It is probable that at this time, Leighton Hall, a Wilbraham property near Nantwich, was given to William by Randle Wilbraham of Townsend as part of the marriage settlement. Less than four years later, £4,500 was settled upon James, the elder surviving brother, on his marriage, and although again two thousand was retained for her lifetime, this no doubt greatly relieved the straitened circumstances of that disappointed naval officer, as well as being a prudent arrangement to secure the lives of his future children.[25]

By June 1731, Mary was living at Whitchurch, ten miles from Nantwich. It was there she was visited by John Byrom. Aged thirty-nine, he was a contemporary of her three sons, poet, inventor of a successful shorthand system, Fellow of the Royal Society, Freemason, and cautious Jacobite. His daughter wrote in her journal

> We came next morning (June 9) to Whitchurch to Mrs. Falconer's where we had cider, mead, and cowslip wine: Miss Cook, Mr. Yates and Sons were there: Went with us to the Church which was like our new Church. Mrs. Falconer shewed us a letter from Thomas Falconer from some part in Ethiopia.

Cryptography, stenography, Freemasonry, and Jacobitism between 1715 and 1745 might have made a volatile plot. We shall never know. Discretion as well as hospitality from the prudent sixty-eight-year-old widow are all that are evident.

A truly marked reticence appears in Wilbraham family records about all matters political during the Jacobite period. This finds its echo in the later and final destruction of John and Mary Falconer's papers and letters at Chester, in 1792, by their grandson William Falconer. Possibly both reflect an acute awareness of the fearful penalties involved in backing the wrong dynasty in those years. Just as in 1742 Pulteney told George II that two thirds of the nation was Tory,[26] so as late as 1777 Samuel Johnson horrified Boswell with the remark, "if England were fairly polled, the present king would be turned out tonight and his adherents hanged tomorrow."[27] Johnson and Boswell each knew the family of Falconer in Lichfield and Chester. As the tragedy and drama of the '45 receded, however, whatever regrets lay in the hearts of private gentlemen throughout England, there was also relief.

Mary Falconer's will, made in her extreme old age in 1753, and the monuments she had erected to the memories of her second son James and her third son Thomas, as well as that erected later by his Wilbraham wife to her youngest son William are all a compelling testimony to the character of this remarkable woman. The skill and fortitude with which she reared her sons, the wisdom with which she undoubtedly protected them from overt Jacobite association, and the sense with which she embraced for them the rites of the Church of England are apparent. In her last years she saw her family risen from danger, poverty, and prosecution as Scottish Jacobites, to wealth and position in the law and the church in England.

Under the terms of the will, she left bequests to servants and charity, £100 each to her six Falconer grandchildren, and £20 each to the two Elizabeths, her daughters-in-law. The main provisions were confirmation of the two marriage settlements of 1731 and 1734, and the appointment as residuary legatees of James Falconer, son of James by then dead, and his uncle William Falconer who was also executor.

It seems that direct communication between this now English, gentry family, established and well-connected in Cheshire and elsewhere, and their many noble Scottish kin had ceased. Despite the survival of the Falconer peerage, a glance at the list of peerages attainted and estates forfeited, and of families fled abroad or with members executed, between 1688 and 1790, to so many of whom they were related, gives a clear indication of why this happened.[28]   Many families were torn apart by the times, and that of Patrick Falconer of Monkton (P3) had accepted the Glorious Revolution. It was not until the next generation that links were pleasantly, but with no great enthusiasm, sought, and in any case by the end of the century the male line of Monkton was extinct. In England, with the death of John, the pursuit of power, wealth, and influence through politics and royal patronage never again became the preoccupation of this branch of the Falconers. A marked talent for the law and medicine and very considerable intellectual and scholarly gifts remained.

Issue of John Falconer and Mary Dalmahoy:[29]

    i.   John Falconer, born 1 May 1682, baptized 5 May 1682 at Edinburgh, living in 1694, but died young.

Q2   ii.   James Falconer, lieutenant, R.N., born 3 July 1693.

    iii.   Thomas Falconer, born 23 March 1695, died, unmarried, 25 January 1729/30, buried 1 February 1729/30 in St. George's, Brunswick Square, London.

        It would be easy to conclude that, as a younger son, he was early destined for mercantile ventures; that his infant character was assessed and his lot cast by his determined mother deliberately. Whether this was the case or not, so it turned out. In 1702 Thomas was taken by Helen Dalmahoy, widow of Captain Arthur Innes, and his mother's childless sister, to live with her in her husband's family in London.[30] There was warm and lasting affection between aunt and nephew which, however, never weakened the strong bond between mother and son and betwixt him and his brothers.[31]

        William Innes, stationer and bookseller at the sign of the Pen and Ink in Paul's Churchyard in the City, was a substantial merchant. Master of the Stationer's Company and a Governor of Christ's Hospital, he may have been responsible for Thomas's election in 1708 as a writer in what became known as the Honourable East India Company. His sureties were his mother's first cousins, Ralph and Stephen Wilbraham, then of Dorfold Hall, Nantwich, Cheshire.[32] He began work in December that year at old East India House in Leadenhall Street, and in the summer of 1709 sailed for India, together with eight other covenanted servants of the company.

The seventeenth century had ended with the British in India established as merchants and landowners in the three Presidencies of Madras, Bombay and Bengal. For the Moghul Empire it had not been a century of progress or achievement and it was now in a state of rapid, if not always evident, decline. Aurangzebe had extended his dominions, but his intolerance had hastened the collapse of his dynasty. The English, however, might well have looked back with some complacency. One hundred years earlier they had been a colony of traders begging for the right to exist on sufferance, and in competition with the Portuguese. Now the Governors of Madras and Bombay lived in regal state with a navy, a standing army, a militia, judges, and a mint. Bengal was no less proud, but the servants of the Company were still mainly concerned with kerseys and calicoes; it was trade they were after. Already, however, they were learning to be administrators in a small way, and every man among them was an occasional soldier.[33]

Thomas arrived at Calcutta, the city recently created by the Company in Bengal, in the heart of the richest of the Moghul provinces, in January 1709/ 10. It was said "most gentlemen and ladies in Bengal live both splendidly and pleasantly, the forenoons being dedicated to business and after dinner to rest, and in the evening to recreate themselves in chaises or palankeens in the fields, or to gardens, or by water in their budgeroes, which is a convenient boat that goes swiftly by the force of oars. On the river sometimes there is the diversion of fishing or fowling, or both; and before night they make friendly visits to one another." This was a well because the same writer says, "One year I was there and there were reckoned in August about twelve hundred English...and before the beginning of January there were four hundred and sixty burials registered in the Clerk's book of mortality."[34]

The organization of the Company and promotion were carefully structured, but the latter was likely through disease and excess, to be swifter than the normal expectation, and an inducement to persevere for those freshly arrived from England. The young writer then had to look forward to three or four years drudgery, if he lived so long. He was forbidden, throughout his service, to take part in private trade outside India, but the rules about internal and coastal trade varied at different periods and were seldom observed. Whatever the rules, in his first years he probably lacked either the capital or the knowledge needed to venture greatly. On the other hand, he had no inevitable expenses. He ate and boarded free and he had no long list of servants to pay; for in addition to his salary he had an allowance from the Company meant to cover the outlay he must incur.

In Calcutta in the Secretary's office, under the paymaster, at a starting salary of £5 per annum, Thomas spent five years receiving steady advancement. A newcomer could expect to rise to factor, on £20, in three or four years, and to merchant in five. After two years in the Secretary's office, he and Edward Stephenson and one other young writer were singled out, in an official letter to the Court of Directors in London, for extraordinary praise. Thomas finally gained experience in the import warehouse before becoming a junior merchant in September 1717, at £30 a year. Then Stephenson returned from a protracted embassy to the Emperor at Delhi and, in August 1719, he and Falconer were promoted to the rank of senior merchant.[35]

Four hundred miles up the Ganges, northwest of Calcutta, was the Company's factory at Patna, a post of importance and trust because of its distance from the eyes of the Council. Rumor was strong that all was far from well there with Company affairs and Stephenson, as Chief Agent, and Falconer, as second in command, were dispatched to take over and report. Samuel Browne and Hugh Barker, their predecessors, were recalled. The manifest dishonesty of both men became soon apparent. They had used Company funds to trade on their own account and with which to bribe in furthering their own interests. Both were dismissed, after due enquiry, following Stephenson's and Falconer's report to Calcutta. The confidence of the Council in the latter was demonstrated, in August 1720, when both were themselves appointed Members of Council at Calcutta. Stephenson remained at Patna and a year later Thomas became export warehouse keeper and received further promotion in Council.

Hugh Barker meanwhile had returned to England and there made a vigorous complaint of injustice against Thomas Falconer and Edward Stephenson. The accusations were serious, but at this distance it is hard to see them as more dangerous than the ill-judged attempt at self-justification of a very arrogant and obviously corrupt young man. Thomas wrote on 4 October 1722 to the President, Governor, and Members of Council in London, defending Stephenson and himself from the "heavy and unjust charge" made by Barker. The matter dragged on until June 1724, when, at Thomas's request, the Council in Calcutta examined a former broker at Patna, one Peraun Sherma, in connection with Barker's complaint. As a result of his testimony, finally all the charges against both Stephenson and Falconer were dismissed, and later that year the Company's confidence in Thomas was again amply reflected in his appointment as accountant in Calcutta.[36]

This incident casts an interesting light on the moral standards of the period. Whereas it is undoubtedly true, and has been demonstrated many times, that vast fortunes were made in India in the 18th century by corrupt and dishonest means, it must also be remembered that for diligent and honest servants of the Company it was possible to make large sums legitimately, using their experience and access to market information. The difference between honourable conduct and villainy then, although in many ways different, was undoubtedly as clearly known as it is today. All the evidence we have, both factual and circumstantial, shows Thomas to have been a young man of rectitude and honor in all things. It is clear from bequests made to him and trusteeships he undertook for colleagues and friends in these years, that he was both liked and admired. He served in Calcutta as church warden of the company's church of St. Anne until 1726, when in August he took up the appointment of chief agent at Kasimbazar, one hundred miles from Calcutta. However, his health was now in decline and within six months, in January 1727, he resigned from the Company's service and sailed on 1 February in some style from Balasore for England, in the Company's ship *Craggs*.[37]

After a voyage that did little for his malady he was, on 5 September 1727, put ashore at Deal in Kent, whence he posted the same day to London. He had now returned to England, after seventeen years in Bengal, highly regarded by the Honourable East India Company, but an ailing, albeit relatively rich, respected and successful young man of thirty-two. During those years of Eastern experience it is probable that he made at least one trip home, but of this no evidence has been found. However, the letter shown, in 1731, by Mary Dalmahoy to John Byrom at Whitchurch, written by Thomas "from some part in Ethiopia," indicates that he had made an expedition to that mysterious and unknown part of Africa at least, some years or a year or two before. The log of the *Craggs* shows no such deviation from its direct route which would have been, indeed, a major and costly diversion for a great merchantman and not easily done within the known dates of Thomas's homeward voyage. The mystery is intriguing. Such a journey might have been made from India or from England.[38]

Thomas took a furnished house at £71 a year in Merman Street in the fashionable parish of St. George the Martyr and presented himself to the Court of Directors at New India House. His journal records his continuing active interest in Company affairs and correspondence with his friends in Bengal. Mary Dalmahoy came to London, where her three sons now were, and stayed with her sister, Helen Innes, and then independently in lodgings in The Strand. Thomas was able to ease the finances of his brothers, and from letters to Cheshire we have an attractive picture of him. In one letter Helen Innes wrote "...'tis no small adition to my pleasure to be favour'd with ye few lynes from you in expressing ye esteem you have of my dear Nephew wch you also can hear from some kind friend of ye unspotted character he hath brought from India wch I hope when he comes to Cheshiere better acquaintance will confirm it. He is no Courter rather inclined for business, ye want of that employ he spends his time in reading. This bad weather keeps him much in ye House that he caint have the exercise he loves riding out. For about a fortnight ye sun & moon seems to be eclipst it is so very dark & fogie very bad for me." Then in the winter of 1728/9 she died with, one may imagine, considerable pride in her successful foster child now come home.[39]

The family possesses a portrait of Thomas, which must have been painted between the end of 1727 and the time of his death. The identical cut of the coats, style of the full wigs and the linen, which nonetheless show three marked and separate tastes, do make it seem likely that this and the portrait of his elder brother James, who was with him in London in 1728 and 1729 and whose tailor's bill he paid, and the portrait of his younger brother William, who was a member of the Inner Temple about then, were all painted at this time by the same London artist. They appear to be by the same unknown hand, a present, no doubt, from her sons for Mary Dalmahoy in Cheshire. In the picture of Thomas we see a man in his thirties of medium height and sallow complexion, with strong nose and chin and a direct intelligent gaze from brown eyes. He wears a full silver gray wig with knots, a plain brownish gray silk coat with covered buttons open soberly to show an unbuttoned waistcoat of the same. Both are cut low without collars over an elaborately frilled white shirt and high tight white neck cloth, in the latest fashion.

Thomas, without doubt, was able to enjoy the company of both his brothers, James, unhappily seeking employment from the Admiralty, and William, the young barrister from the Inner Temple. Wilbraham cousins too were nearby. But the winters were hard and, in poor health, he found them wretched. Two visits to Tunbridge Wells for a cure were made; plans to visit Bath and Italy too, came to naught as his condition worsened. The opera and the theatre engaged him and once at least the bawdy house. He wrote in his journal of "evening which is the only time for mirth," but plainly life in London would not have held him since he wrote, "I am fully determined to retire into the country after I have recovered my health a little, for London is to me a most disagreeable place."[40]

However, in January of the severe winter of 1729/30 he made his will and then on the 25th he died, unmarried, at Warwick Court, Holborn, with, one likes to think, his two brothers and his mother by him. Over the vault, erected in April by his mother, was a sarcophagus, surmounted by a pyramidical inscribed monument. On it curiously were placed the arms of Falconer of Phesdo, a distinguished but junior branch of the family to this, the Newton descent, in terms of consanguinity to the Halkerton peerage. It is improbable that she was unaware of the need for her sons to matriculate their arms in the Lyon Court and more likely that Mary was once again distancing her children from their Jacobite past. In this she was consistent. Who in England would know the armorial difference?[41]

By his will, dated 30 January 1729/30 at London, and proved in the Prerogative Court of Canterbury, Thomas left in specific bequests the considerable sum of £18,750.[42] The modern equivalent is difficult and complex to calculate, but is probably in overall purchasing power and investment yield something in the order of £8,000,000 sterling in 1995. The interestingly large amount of £6,000 included in this as a bequest to the Honourable United

Company of Merchants Trading to the East Indies——the H.E.I.C.——was coupled with application to have remitted to England the balance of his estate left in Bengal. According to his great-nephew, Judge Thomas Falconer, between £30,000 and £40,000 was never recovered.[43]

Thomas was capable and successful to a remarkable degree and in his relatively short life served his family well. He appears in addition to have been respected and liked by those amongst whom he worked and was evidently admired by his friends. He was thoughtful, kind, and generous in his dealings alive, and in his dispositions at his early death. That a rumor should have survived, for rumor is all it was, that Thomas had been involved in dishonest dealings, during his time as a servant of the East India Company, is plainly a product of the malice of the delinquent Barker and his powerful friends after Thomas's death.

It is not at all curious that few families pride themselves upon a current jailbird or known swindler amongst their number. But it is a little odd that equally rarely do families, so often described by our Victorian forebears as "of the highest respectability," fail to cherish a legend of wrong doing, particularly if successful and on a grand scale, providing it is long enough ago. The half-remembered malice of the Barkers later became transformed by Thomas's collateral descendants into a legend of piratical virility and romance at a time when proof of what had actually happened in India would have been very difficult to come by. Now the two deadly euphemisms "there is no smoke without fire" and "best let sleeping dogs lie" can be vigorously dismissed and apology made to honest Tom Falconer, the young Bengal merchant.

The principal bequest of £10,000 to his mother played a significant part in re-establishing the fortunes of the family. James and William Falconer, their brother's executors, had a protracted and complex task, only slightly alleviated by their expectations as joint residuary beneficiaries. William, the survivor, on whom the labor devolved, appears finally to have concluded matters in 1740.[44]   Thomas Falconer left no lawful issue.[45]

Q3   iv.   William Falconer, born 20 March 1699.

Q2 James Falconer, Lieutenant, R.N., born 3 July 1693 in Scotland, died 8 November 1738, was buried in the Cathedral of Chester.

He married, 24 September 1734, at Thorpe Constantine, Staffordshire, Elizabeth Inge, daughter of William Inge, Esquire, of Thorp, Staffordshire. She died 14 February 1775, aged 70, and was buried in the Cathedral of Chester. At his marriage he received £500 of £4,500 then settled upon him by his mother, of which the balance came eventually to his estate after her death in 1754.

He was elected a Scholar of the King's School, Chester, in September 1702, on the nomination of Prebendary Lancaster,[46] and with the recommendation, no doubt, of Randle Wilbraham of Townsend.

James left Chester in September 1706 and entered the Royal Navy later that year or 1707. This was at a time when the English navy had yet to form itself into the professional force which gave it its fame. Its weakness, such as it was, lay not in the men, but some of its officers. It was a weakness which the great admirals who served Queen Anne, Rooke, Shovell, Byng, and Leake, were busy eradicating. They succeeded so well that posterity has difficulty in believing that the English naval officer under the later Stuarts was not on all occasions what he has been for two hundred and fifty years past. The politics of a country with an unsettled dynasty had something to do with the evil. In

William's reign, the Jacobites had correspondents in the navy and counted on disaffection among a section of the officers. Jacobite hopes were disappointed, but fear of ambivalent loyalties was present to lower morale. More important, however, was the friction between the tarpaulin captains who had spent their lives at sea and the gentlemen who owed their rank to solicitation at Court or in the lobbies of Parliament.[47]

We have no record of how James Falconer gained his place, but his family secured it and he thus joined a navy in the process of reform, when the day was not far distant in which every officer would be both a gentleman and a sailor, a man of education bred to the sea since he was a lad. Of these, almost certainly, he was an early example and he joined his first ship as English squadrons were constantly on guard, around England's shores and in the Atlantic, embattled with increasing success against first the French and the Pretender, and then the navy of Spain. His captain would have worn a blue coat and full-bottomed wig, his sailors no uniform, but a variety of sea slops.[48]

In 1712, James is found rated ordinary seaman in H.M.S. *Centurion* but must have become a midshipman shortly; and five years later, in January 1717, he is recorded in the passing records of lieutenants to have been at sea upwards of ten years.[49] On 31 July 1718 he saw action under Admiral Sir George Byng at the destruction of the Spanish fleet off Cape Passaro. When his Captain was killed, as senior lieutenant, he succeeded to command and brought his ship to England for refit. On 4 May 1725 he was appointed second lieutenant in HMS *Kinsale*, a second rater,[50] and in 1729 he is listed in HMS *Berwick*, another second rater.[51] Thenceforward, after some twenty-two years of service, he appears to have been unemployed, as so many officers often were, with all the disappointment and frustrated ambition that implied.

He spent time with his family in Chester and more in London, in the company of his two younger brothers. William was in chambers and Thomas, the Bengal merchant, had reached England in the earlier winter of 1727. Thomas was in a position to help his brothers financially, and undoubtedly did so, as they enjoyed in London together the society of their many cousins and acquaintances. With his death in January 1729/30, James and William in the Inner Temple would find themselves comfortably well off. They became executors of his will and considerable estate. But they were already receiving his help.[52] It is possibly William, but more probably James, who appears seven months earlier, in John Byrom's *Journal* on 3 June 1729 in London. He wrote:[53]

> Mr. Falconer paid me five guineas tonight at nine o'clock, calling at Richard's; and coming into the street I said I was engaged and it was late, and we would meet tomorrow if he pleased; he said he had got money now and offered it to me; I desired him to put himself at no inconvenience; he said it was none now and so he paid me.

The next day Byrom entered:

> Rose late——I went to Richard's; thence to Mr. Falconer's, where I had a dish of coffee with him, and we had a *contraction* lecture.

Byrom's entry is a shade dismissive; he is selling his skill, he is successful and knows his value; and he also knows his caller. Since he and James were probably familiar as schoolboys at Chester and both were now in London much in the company of the Leigh and Wilbraham cousins from Cheshire, what could be more natural than James's desire to learn also the useful and esoteric skill of Byrom's shorthand, so popular amongst men he admired.[54]

The family possesses a portrait of James Falconer, which, with those of his two brothers, was probably painted in London in 1728 or 1729. In each, the family likeness is very marked. We see an active, lightly built man with a high color and weathered complexion. The nose and chin are pronounced, the eyes brown and the gaze sharp. He wears a full wig with knots, a red velvet silk coat with covered buttons open negligently to show a rich blue silk waistcoat, itself latched only by the top button and richly trimmed with gold braid and gold buttons. Both are cut low without collars over an elaborately frilled white shirt under a high tight white neck cloth in the latest fashion. He carries a black, probably tricorne, hat laced with gold.

The City of Chester archives record that, without payment, he was, on 22 June 1733, with other members of his family and gentlemen of the neighborhood, made a freeman of the city.[55] This was undoubtedly a compliment, but also a common device at the time to swell the electoral roll with voters of the right persuasion.

James Falconer was buried 12 November 1738 in the south aisle of the choir in Chester Cathedral. There, on the south wall, facing the center of the eighteenth-century stone Masonic screen, is a monument with inscription, and, as in 1730 in London, the arms of Falconer of Phesdo, placed by his mother.[56] His retention of the style of a naval officer to the end and, indeed, in his will, indicates a pride in his profession and a determined loyalty to the King. But those were years when men in their hearts had to choose which king.

James's will, dated 7 May 1735 at Chester, has three codicils, dated 26 May 1737, 24 October 1738 (after the birth of his first son), and another one on the last date. Probate was granted at Chester 6 December 1738 to his executor William, his brother. Guardianship of the two infant children was granted to William and to the widow. Numerous legacies are detailed, including the Charity School for boys in Chester. Provision is made for his widow, who also received his plate and furniture and coach and coach horses; and for his son and his daughter with remainder, should the children die under the age of twenty-one, and upon the death or remarriage of the widow, to his brother William and his heirs. William also received his saddle horses.[57]

Issue of James and Elizabeth (Inge) Falconer:

i.   Elizabeth Falconer, buried June 1764 in St. Mary's Chapel, Chester. A portrait of her was sold at Christie's, 1 July 1938, for 30 guineas. It was included in the sale of portraits belonging to Viscount Fielding and removed from Newnham Paddox, Rugby, after his death. It was described as by J. Fellowes, a portrait painted in 1740 of her when a child, in white frock with a pet bird on her left hand. She married, as his first wife, Thomas Pennant, esquire, of Downing, Flintshire, the celebrated antiquary and naturalist. Issue, surname *Pennant*: a. *David*, died 1841, married, 12 December 1793, Louisa, daughter of Sir Henry Peyton, Bart.; b. *Arabella*, who married Edward Hanmer.

Q4   ii.   James Falconer, D.D., born between 26 May 1737 and October 1738.

Q3 **William Falconer**, of the Inner Temple, born 20 March 1699 in England, died 2 June 1764 at Chester, Cheshire, was buried 6 June 1764 in the chancel of the church of St. John Baptist, Chester.

· He married, on 7 January 1730/1, at Nantwich, Cheshire, Elizabeth Wilbraham, his second cousin, daughter of Randle Wilbraham (first cousin of his mother Mary Dalmahoy) and his wife Mary Brooke, daughter of Sir Richard Brooke, Bart., of Norton. She was born in 1702 or 1703 and died 27 June 1782, aged seventy-nine, and was buried in the Church of St. John Baptist, Chester.

He was brought up in Chester where, at the age of seven and a half, he entered the King's School as a scholar in the place of his elder brother James, in September, 1706.[58] In 1713 he was apprenticed to William Bridges of Chester, gentleman, a local attorney.[59]

The legal profession then, by comparison with today, was a very small one. The Lord Chancellor and the Master of the Rolls were the only two Chancery judges; there were twelve common law judges; there was one judge in Doctor's Commons: a total of fifteen. Fewer than three hundred and fifty men in all practiced at the Bar and were all members of one of the four Inns of Court. The majority of Benchers and Barristers lived in their Inn and most were bachelors. The proportion of Oxford or Cambridge men amongst them was lower than now; most were gentlemen, but many were not.

The modern system of reading in chambers with a barrister only appeared about 1770. Earlier in the century many students for the Bar appear to have begun by attending in an attorney's office and frequenting the courts to observe and be noticed. Nevertheless, the student had to spend seven years after gaining admission to his Inn until his call to the Bar. The books available to him were equally unsatisfactory and again most experience was to be gained by observation, discussion, and argument, loitering in Westminster Hall, as Johnson told Boswell in 1784, half a century later, "to show that you want business."[60]

We have no details of William's time devilling for William Bridges, the Chester attorney, or of his first years in London after about 1723, when he must have been admitted to the Inner Temple at the age of twenty-three or twenty-four. In 1730, a qualified barrister, William became joint executor, with James, of their brother Thomas's will and considerable estate. After James's death this task devolved on him alone and he and his nephew James became residuary legatees as previously described.[61]

There is, in the possession of the family, a portrait of William Falconer, most likely painted in London in 1728 or 1729 at the same time as those of his two brothers and by the same artist. The more one examines them the more strongly one receives this impression. One can equally suppose that the brothers shared the services of the same tailor, wig maker, and shirt and cravat maker too, but the rigors of the latest London fashion and the skill of the painter could equally be the cause. All three are skillfully executed studies of head and shoulders, cut off above the waist. We see a young man of about thirty of light build with high color and firm features. The eyebrows are marked and the nose and chin pronounced. The lips are full and red, and the gaze from brown eyes is direct and serious with a hint of humor. He wears a full wig with knots, a rich blue velvet silk coat with covered buttons open elegantly to show a glimpse of blue silk lining, and a similar unbuttoned blue waistcoat. Both are cut low without collars over an elaborately frilled white shirt and high tight white neck cloth.

There is another portrait of Elizabeth, which may also have been painted in 1728 or 1729. It shows a beautiful and self-possessed young woman of twenty-six or seven, dressed in the height of fashion. Her dark hair is worn long and drawn back behind the ears to fall lightly on the shoulders. A high forehead and finely arched brows sit above brown eyes and a long slender nose. The face is heart-shaped and there is a delicate color in the cheeks. Her neck is slender, rising from a white bosom and sloping shoulders. She has turned her head slightly to the right as she regards the viewer with a steady glance to the left. Her blue silk contouche hangs loosely from the shoulders and is open, with an air of charming negligence, to show its green silk lining and a frilled white muslin underdress cut very low on her breast. The painting is unsigned, but has recently been attributed to Michael Dahl, who was then the best patronized portrait painter in England after Kneller. This need not surprise us in a family which employed Van Dyk.

In 1730, William is found recorded as a barrister and Member of the Inner Temple,[62] and that year he became a joint executor with James of Thomas's will and considerable estate. After James's subsequent death this task devolved upon him alone and he and his nephew James became residuary legatees, as previously described. After his brother Thomas's death it is, possible William continued to practice at Westminster, or he may have returned to Chester. The judges from Westminster did not go on circuit in Wales. Special "Judges of the Great Sessions" sat at Chester and in Wales and these offices were filled by members of the Bar who could also still practice.[63] Normal barrister's work was to be had as on the circuits elsewhere, but probably the fees were fewer and the attraction was to men of means. William could now afford this life.

It is likely that, after their marriage, William and Elizabeth remained in possession of the property in Chester previously occupied by Mary, when she moved in 1730, or the first half of 1731, to Whitchurch. The Wilbraham property of Leighton Hall, three and a half miles from Nantwich, but twenty-one miles from Chester, which was part of their marriage settlement, later may have been their occasional residence and that of their eldest son, but plainly it was a little far in their early years of marriage from an active life in Chester. Although marked clearly on the ordnance survey map, of this property today no trace remains except the knoll on which the house stood and the nearby Leighton Hall Farm.[64]

During the fourteen years after his marriage, until his appointment to the office of recorder, William Falconer practiced law in Chester and established himself in the confidence of his neighbors and fellow citizens. His eight children were all born there and six baptized in the same church of St. John Baptist.

The Assembly books of the Corporation of the City of Chester show that on 22 June 1733 William, his brother James, his brother-in-law Roger Wilbraham, and other gentry were admitted to be freeman of the city.[65] At the Assembly on 31 May 1745, William Falconer, Esq., was unanimously chosen to be one of the Aldermen of Chester, in the room of Thomas Mather, Esq., deceased, and at the same time he was unanimously elected Recorder of the city.[66] This appointment to the Recordership was afterwards confirmed by the Lords Justices of the Kingdom in the absence abroad of the King, and the confirmation, dated 1 August 1745, was signed by the Archbishop of Canterbury, Lord Chancellor Hardwick, the Duke of Dorset, Earl Gower, the Duke of Devonshire, the Duke of Grafton, and the Duke of Bolton, all members of Pelham's new Whig ministry.[67]

The Recorder was the chief legal officer of the city and his duties were to preside with the mayor at Quarter Sessions, to act if required as attorney for the city in any lawsuits undertaken by the Corporation, and lastly to give advice on any legal matters concerning the Corporation. For these services an honorarium was paid in the early 17th century of £13,6,8d. From the time of William Falconer the city continued to exercise the right to choose its own Recorder without royal approval until the Corporation Act of 1835, since which appointments have been made by the Crown.[68]

Meanwhile, in July 1745, the Young Pretender had landed in Scotland, raised the Highlanders, scattered a loyalist army at Prestonpans, and occupied Edinburgh. The news of his landing brought George II back from Hanover and he arrived in England on 31 August, but only his supporters knew at that moment how little lay between the Stuarts and the throne. In the autumn Charles Edward invaded England and by December reached Derby. In that army served a number of Scottish relatives. But at Derby, only a few days march from London and under seventy miles from Chester, the Prince's luck turned. His army had not been increased by many English recruits, as England cautiously watched; and his advisors fatally lost heart. While George II was preparing to leave his capital, the Pretender reluctantly abandoned the idea of a dash upon London and returned to Scotland. Though he was able to win one more victory at Falkirk, he suffered a crushing defeat at Culloden in April 1746, which ended Jacobite hopes in this campaign and for all time.[69] Scottish Jacobites fled and suffered. In England, in contrast, Jacobites in high places were not arrested and only those who had joined the rebellion were hunted down. But it was plain that, henceforth, active loyalty to the House of Stuart had little to commend it to prudent men. In Chester William and Elizabeth Falconer and Elizabeth Inge, widow of James, were doubtless as reticent about their Scottish kin as was Mary Dalmahoy at Whitchurch.

There is, in 1996, in the possession of the family, a handsome silver two-handled cup and cover, with a London hallmark and date 1740, made by the distinguished Huguenot goldsmith, Peter Archambo, the elder. It is of the peculiarly English kind which continued to hold a special position until at least the end of the century, both as the standard form of decorative plate for the sideboard or table, and as an appropriate item for presentation.[70] It is inscribed on the side, between the applied decoration and engraving, with arms for Falconer, dexter, a falcon's head issuing from a man's heart between three mullets all within nine roundels semee impaling for Wilbraham sinister three bands wavy. The cup stands eleven and three quarter inches high, is one of a number made for the City of Chester at this period, and was, according to family tradition, presented to William on his appointment as Recorder. In this example the convex cover is engraved also with a falcon perching and hooded proper.

William continued in office as Alderman and principal legal officer of the city until, well into his fifty-fourth year, he was compelled to resign under the burden of ill health. Formal expressions of concern and appreciation were recorded in the Assembly books of the city on 12 November 1754.[71] During the following months his advice was sought by the Corporation in legal and financial affairs. He continued to act as Trustee of the Charity School of St. John.[72] In the Chester City Archives is a book of legal cases and precedents written by him whilst in office.[73]

Foote Gower wrote to Thomas Falconer, William and Elizabeth's elder son, in 1771, in a letter entitled "A Sketch of the Materials for a New History of Cheshire:"

> The last Collector I shall mention is a name, my dear friend, that is sacred to yourself, since it is the late worthy Recorder of the City of Chester who was a warm and zealous friend to all its corporate rights, and to the whole circle of its interests. Was I writing to any other than you I should certainly mention him in the character of a lawyer of great knowledge and ability in his profession, and who had besides a strong tincture of literary pursuits, with a leading passion for the elucidation of legal antiquities. Of this he has left behind him ample proofs in the collections your friendship has favoured me with.

What these collections were we do not know, but Gower does give a faint picture of the interests and character of William to support the customary expression of his virtues on his monument and the admirable portrait of him painted when young in London. His scholarly interests may have been shared by Elizabeth, but the coupled reference is probably to Roger Wilbraham of Townsend, her grandfather.

It is probable that William Falconer lived during his Recordership, reared his family, and passed his retirement in the same substantial house in St. John's Street until his death. There is no evidence of a life spent, even in part, at Leighton Hall near Nantwich. He was buried in the city of Chester on 6 June 1764, in the chancel of the parish church of St. John the Baptist. A handsome monument of the period inscribed piously with his virtues and qualities, and recording also the death of Elizabeth Wilbraham in the same manner, and the births and deaths of five of their children, is nearby in the north aisle. This record is a not atypical reminder of the anguish suffered in family life by our forebears, whatever their circumstances. On the wall of the south aisle is a small painted and gilded board recording, with their armorials, the Mayors and Recorders of Chester from the parish of St. John. William Falconer, Recorder, is shown above a shield bearing the arms of Falconer of Phesdo and Wilbraham.

William's will is dated 24 March 1764 and probate was granted at Chester, 30 September 1764. The widow survived her husband by eighteen years and appears to have continued to live with her elder son Thomas until her death in St. John's Street.[74]

Issue of William and Elizabeth (Wilbraham) Falconer, born at Chester:

i. Mary Falconer, born 26 October 1731, died September 1789. She married, 25 June 1754, at St. John the Baptist, Chester, Charles Mainwaring, Esq., of Bromborough, Cheshire, and had issue.

ii.   Elizabeth Falconer, born 4 December 1732, died 8 December 1733, buried at St. John the Baptist.

iii. Frances Falconer, born 13 February 1734, died 14 January 1748 at Chester, buried at St. John the Baptist.

iv.   Thomas Falconer, of Chester and Leighton Hall, Nantwich, Cheshire, Esquire, born 20 July 1736 at Chester, baptized 11 August 1736 at St. John the Baptist, Chester, died 4 September 1792 at Chester, was buried in the church of St. Michael. A monument in his memory exists in the church of St. John the Baptist.

He survived infancy to suffer from chronic ill health all his life. In October 1750, he was admitted late to Westminster School, together with his cousin, James Falconer (Q4).[75] After a year he was withdrawn, probably because he lacked the necessary physical robustness, and was then tutored at home. He matriculated on 12 March 1754 and briefly entered Brasenose College, Oxford (where he was followed in October by James, up from Westminster), but came down at once without taking his degree.[76] It is probable that college life also was too taxing for his constitution. However, on 24 August of the same year he was admitted to Lincoln's Inn, where he could choose to live less rigorously. There is good reason to suppose he enjoyed those years, and in due course, on 20 June 1760, he was called to the Bar and from his letters we know he at last believed a career beckoned.[77]

However, he was dogged by ill health and never practiced law, but returned to make a quiet life mostly of study, at Chester in his father's house in St. John Street until 1787. Thomas maintained a large correspondence, but his sedentary life included daily mounted exercise and long hacks for his health. It seems very probable that one of his problems may have been an irritable bowel. He had, for some reason, a marked distaste for field sports, which seems to have had its root in the invariable severe discomfort he suffered from any kind of conviviality. Outdoor men were often excessively convivial. He speaks a shade slightingly of the hearty outdoor entertainment offered at Wynnstay. He was unusual in this respect and it seems bad luck he could not enjoy fox hunting, because his lonely, daily hacks frequently filled him with a gloom that some robust good fellowship, two or three times a month in winter, might have allayed.

In 1770, he traveled to Habsburg Flanders, the north of France, and visited Paris and Versailles. He was no misogynist. His own hospitality was liberal and he relished the company of the children of his elder sister Mary and the families of his younger brother William, and of his naturalist cousin, Thomas Pennant at Bodfari. Above all he enjoyed his books, his pen, and the letters of his friends.

Thirty-four of Thomas Falconer's letters on government, politics, public affairs, and literary matters, from about the time he came down from Lincoln's Inn, and written between 1757 and 1776, to his kinsman, Charles Gray of Chelmsford, have been found.[78] Thomas's side of their correspondence on both American and domestic politics and on trade and politics is fascinating. His academic and philosophical inclinations encourage him in letters to Gray, to take a long view. The love of debate in the Commons, the regard for principle, the family rather than party character of politics, and the negligible amount of legislation of the time come over clearly, but this goes hand in hand with a constant apprehension that the Constitution is in danger and that the country will be economically ruined. Indeed the times were not tranquil. Gray's own replies, unfortunately, are missing.

Falconer never married. There is, in the possession of the family, a portrait of him when young, possibly painted in 1746 or 1747, by an unknown artist. We see a boy of ten or eleven, left hand on hip with a black tricorne hat trimmed with silver braid under the arm, and right hand holding lightly a silver-headed, malacca cane with a black tassel. He stands looking with a level gaze from brown eyes under well-marked brows and a high forehead. Brown, curling hair tied back with dark ribbon falls to the neck. The complexion is fresh and a small mouth with red lips under a half-formed child's nose sits above a soft childish chin. His blue coat with eight covered buttons is long and plain, worn open and slashed at the sleeves with two covered buttons, to show a froth of lace held with silver button, at each wrist. A long, rich, blue waistcoat, trimmed with a profusion of silver braid and seven silver buttons, with two pockets with more silver braid and three silver buttons aside on each lap, is displayed beneath the coat, and held only with the bottom two buttons. Both plain coat and rich waistcoat of matching silk are cut low without collars, and show a frilled white shirt, and high white soft cravat tied with a black silk ribbon. The total effect is of composure, elegance, and innocence.[79]

Although Thomas Falconer played no part in local or national affairs and lacked health, he did enjoy a wide circle of acquaintances, made frequent visits of some duration to the country houses of his cousins and friends, and in the process traveled extensively in England and Wales. His hosts in turn were welcomed at Chester, where at one period his mother ran his household, and later his widowed sister, Mary Mainwaring, lived with him until she finally settled in Bath. He possessed a particular gift for encouraging the young and was warmly welcomed at Oxford and Lincoln's Inn until his last years, where he not only enjoyed the company of the Fellows and Benchers, but often shared his classical, literary and antiquarian interests with others, during lengthy visits. It is probable that during all this time the Leighton Hall property was let to tenants.

Thomas Pennant, the famous naturalist and antiquary, had, in 1760, married Elizabeth Falconer, cousin of Thomas and sister of James who was at school with him. He wrote to Thomas Falconer at Chester a letter dated 31 March 1765, giving a vivid description of mid-eighteenth century Paris, through the eyes of an English visitor. It seems to be a rare survivor of a generation of lost family correspondence, which must be intensely regretted.[80] However, forty-two letters from Tom Falconer to Tom Pennant and the latter's son David, between 1760 and 1790, have also survived in the Pennant papers. They form, as in the Gray correspondence, one side of a relationship of friendship and ever increasing affection on the part of the bachelor for his cousins, and in particular for his dead cousin Elizabeth's son. He encourages David during his time at Oxford and begins to share his love for classical civilization and constitutional government with the young man as he enjoys the Grand Tour. His letters follow David through France, Switzerland, Italy, and Germany. Later they pursue him through France and into Spain and to Italy again.[81]

Between 1768 and 1773 Thomas maintained a correspondence on scientific and geographical matters with Sir Joseph Banks, both before his departure in the *Endeavour*, with James Cook on his first voyage, and during the period of Banks's travels to the Hebrides and Iceland. The letters are cordial, with much exchange of information and encouragement from Thomas who urged also the need for knowledge of Africa, as well as the polar regions and Pacific.[82]

At Downing, in March 1769, Tom Pennant dedicated his *British Zoology* to his kinsman Thomas, acknowledging "the many advantages [he had] reaped from making [Falconer] confidant to the productions of an idle and rural pen."

In June 1772 a further tribute to Thomas's power of warm friendship and encouragement, where he discovered ability and talent, came from John Reinhold Forster, who formed part of the formidable team of scientific observers who accompanied James Cook that year on his second great voyage to the South Seas. Forster was the *Resolution's* naturalist, a man of mixed Scottish-Prussian descent, and a tiresome, rather mean-spirited pedant and prude, held in contempt by the lower deck. Yet it is only fair to acknowledge the well-read, curious Forster as a pioneer in the anthropology of the Pacific. He dedicated his translation of Baron Reidsel's *Travels through Sicily and That Part of Italy Formerly Called Magna Graecia*, to Thomas Falconer.[83]

In the autumn of 1779 James Boswell spent a fortnight, or a little more, at Chester, of which he wrote in a letter on 23 December 1782, "...where I declare I passed my time more happily than I ever did in any place——I know not if I should even except London——for the same portion of time. The general hospitality of the people, the curiosity of the town itself and the beauty of its environs, and the animation of a military society gave me the most cheerful spirits."[84] Boswell wrote in a letter dated 4 January 1780, "I found at Chester Mr. Falconer, a gentleman of fortune and extraordinary learning and knowledge, who is preparing a new edition of Strabo at the desire of the University of Oxford; he was exceedingly obliging to me."[85] The Geography was, for Thomas, the cornerstone of his classical and scientific interests.[86] He records the dispatch of the first two books to Oxford for printing, but as illness sapped his vitality and limited his movement, his notes and the rest of his translation of the remaining fifteen books of a new, complete, annotated edition of Strabo were still not ready for the press at his death. They were amongst the papers carried safely south to Bath by Dr. William, his heir. They earned him a small memorial when published in 1807 by his nephew Thomas.

He published two other minor works in his lifetime. The first was *Devotions for the Sacrament of the Lord's Supper by a Layman* (Warrington, 1786), of which there was a second edition published in London in 1798; this today will fill many a Christian reader with respect and admiration. The second was a paper he read in 1791, before the Society of Antiquaries, "Observations on Pliny's Account of the Temple of Diana at Ephesus," which was published later that year. After his death a quarto edition of his *Chronological Tables from the Death of Solomon to the Reign of Alexander the Great* appeared from Oxford in 1796, edited by F. Hodson.[87] At the end of his life, in his fifties, one forms an impression of a contented and amiable, but scholarly bachelor, who has overcome, at least partly, his youthful ill health, which may be close to the mark.

Shortly after Thomas's death, Anna Seward wrote, early in 1793, an epitaph in her correspondence which is not unpleasing, and has a ring of truth in its conventional excess:

> Within the last few months the world has lost another of those few human beings whose virtues and abilities adorn human nature—— Mr. Falconer——the Maecenas of Chester. The generous patron and warm friend of talent and worth——he who delighted to draw them from the shades of obscurity. Careless as he was of the tinsel differences of rank and fortune——genius and worth were ever the unfailing passports to his kind attention and hospitable board. In himself he was "a scholar and a ripe and good one."[88]

Thomas's will is dated 9 November 1782, and has two codicils dated 22 May 1786 and 4 November 1791, all made at Chester. After sundry small or considerable legacies to other members of his family and to his friends, servants, and charities, the balance of his real and personal estate was left to his brother, William Falconer, Doctor of Physic, who was appointed sole executor. Probate was granted in October 1792 at Chester.[89]

iv. William Falconer, born 25 August 1738, baptized 15 September 1738, died 25 October 1738, buried at St. John the Baptist.

v.   Alexander Falconer, born 12 February 1739/40, baptized 3 March 1739/40, died 21 February 1739/40, buried at St. John the Baptist.

Q5 vi. William Falconer, born 2 February 1745.

vii. Elizabeth Falconer, born 8 May 1746, baptized 26 May 1746, died 18 January 1764, buried at St. John the Baptist, Chester.

Q4 James Falconer, D.D., born between 26 May 1737 and October 1738, died 17 April 1809 at The Close, Lichfield, was buried 22 April 1809 in Lichfield Cathedral.

He married Mary Hall, daughter of Thomas Hall, of Hermitage, Cranage, Cheshire. She died 11 July 1821, aged 81 years.

He was admitted to Westminster School in October 1750, and left at the end of four years. He matriculated 31 October 1754 and entered Brasenose College, Oxford, where he graduated B.A. in 1758 and M.A. in 1761. In 1772 he received from Oriel College, Oxford, the degree of Bachelor and Doctor of Divinity.[90] He was rector of Thorpe Constantine, Staffordshire, vicar of Lullington, Derbyshire; Prebendary of Lichfield from 22 November 1777; Archdeacon of Derby from 10 February 1795; and Justice of the Peace.[91]

James Falconer and his wife were, without doubt, well acquainted with all the families described in the letters of Samuel Johnson and James Boswell, including the Sewards, Gastrells, and Astons, and the family of David Garrick also, and who constituted local society in Derby and in Lichfield, where it centered on the Cathedral and its Close.[92]

On 30 March 1782, Dr. Johnson wrote from Bolt Court, Fleet Street, London, to Jane Gastrell and Elizabeth Ashton, two of his fervent and lifelong admirers in Lichfield, in reply to their concerned enquiries about his health:

> Dearest Ladies——When Dr. Falconer saw me, I was at home only by accident, for I lived much with Mrs. Thrale and had all the care from her that she could take or that could be taken. But I have never been ill enough to want attendance, my disorder has been rather tedious than violent, rather irksome than painful. He needed not have made such a tragical representation.[93]

Probably the astute future Archdeacon, a cousin, after all, of Dr. William Falconer (Q5), the by now well-known and to become eminent physician in Bath, was no mean judge of Johnson's condition, which he himself, in his letters throughout that summer and autumn, admitted to be "oppressive, irksome and severe."[94]

Issue of James and Mary (Hall) Falconer:

i.   Elizabeth Falconer, born about 1764, died 8 December 1856 in Hill Ridware, Staffordshire, aged 92. She married, 17 September 1787, at St. Mary, Lichfield, Rev. John Batteridge Pearson, Prebendary of Pipe Parva, who died 14 August 1808 at Croxall, and had issue, surname *Pearson*:[95] a. *George*, born 18

September 1791, died 13 May 1860, married, 17 September 1825, Catherine Humberston; b. *Lucy*, born 4 July 1793, married William Harwood, M.D.; c. *James*, R.N., born 4 January 1795, died at sea; d. *Henrietta*, born 2 October 1796, died 6 August 1884, married, 22 November 1822, Charles Berwick Curtis; e. *John*, Staff-Captain, H.E.I.C. Maritime Service, born 19 February 1798, died 1 December 1855; f. *Charles*, Colonel, 61st Regiment, born 4 October 1799, married, Jane Eccles; g. *Mary*, born 9 November 1801, died March 1866, married Edward Thornewill.

ii.   Mary Falconer, born about 1766, died 23 January 1797, aged 31.[96] She married, 5 January 1791, Rev. John George Norbury, Fellow of King's College, Cambridge, Prebendary of Lichfield and Rector of St. Alban's with St. Olave's, London, who died 6 October 1800, aged 42.[97] They had no issue.

iii.   Frances Falconer, born 14 March 1773, died 27 April 1860. She married, 16 January 1793, at St. Mary, Lichfield, Major, later Lieutenant Colonel, William Charles Madan, baptized 9 July 1762 in York, Yorkshire, died 16 February 1830, but had no issue.[98]

iv.   Maria Catherine Falconer, baptized 10 August 1781 at Lichfield Cathedral, died 24 May 1824, aged 44 years, buried at St. George's Cathedral, Madras, India.[99] She married, 9 October 1802, Col. Sir Edward Miles, C.B., 89th Foot, born March 1777 in Roach's Town, Co. Tipperary, Ireland. Issue, surname *Miles*:[100] i. *Maria*, baptized 18 January 1808 at Lichfield; ii. *Edward*, baptized 19 January 1809 at Lichfield; iii. *Falconer*, baptized 19 December 1812 at Fermory.

Q5 **William Falconer,** M.D., F.R.S., born 8 February 1743/4 in Chester, baptized 14 February 1743/4 in the parish church of St John the Baptist, Chester, died 31 August 1824 at his house, 29, Circus, Bath, and was buried just outside the city in the parish churchyard of All Saints, Weston.[101]

He married by licence, 15 January 1771, in the parish church of Saint Swithin, Walcot, Bath, Henrietta Edmunds, daughter of Thomas Edmunds of Worsborough Hall, Yorkshire, by his wife Elisabeth, daughter and heiress of Henry Carrington of Worsborough. She died 15 September 1803 and was buried at Weston.

William Falconer became one of the most distinguished physicians of his time and a medical writer and scientist whose work is regarded with respect and interest today. He numbered amongst his professional friends John Haygarth, John Fothergill, Joseph Priestley, and Caleb Hillier Parry. Amongst his patients were George Garrick, Queen Charlotte, Lord Nelson after he lost his arm, and William Pitt the younger shortly before his death. He corresponded with many of the leading figures of the day such as David Garrick and Edmund Burke and was held in the highest esteem by all who knew him.

After childhood and youth in Chester he studied medicine at Edinburgh, from 1763 until receiving his M.D. on 26 August 1766. His father's death whilst he was at Edinburgh left him independent but set upon his profession. After six months in London, where he was admitted a Licentiate of the Royal College of Physicians, he travelled to Holland. At Leiden he attended the lectures of Gaubius and Albinus, the foremost anatomist of the eighteenth century, and took a further doctorate on 28 May. Thence he returned, via Paris, Dieppe and Brighton, to Chester, where he commenced to establish a practice and made the acquaintance of Dr. John Haygarth and Dr. John Fothergill. Both men were to encourage his early career, and shortly he joined the staff of the newly established Chester Infirmary. After two years, however, concluding that his prospects there were limited, with Fothergill's encouragement he resigned and determined to move south.

For one reason or another William rejected the possibilities in London, where he had both friends and relations, and decided that Bath was to become his home. In the eighteenth century people flocked to the spa city for two main reasons: for relief from illness and the pleasure of society. There was no lack of patients of every kind, many were rich, and the place was congenial. Without delay he announced his arrival, by publishing in August, 1770, *An Essay on the Bath Waters*. This had an immediate success and was shortly republished in a revised two-volume edition: the first of 456 pages in 1772, and the second of 332 pages in 1774.

In the following years he was to write a further forty-nine major works and substantial pamphlets on scientific, geographical, and classical matters, of which most were medical. Some reflected the perplexities of the day; others were ahead of their time. These, together with his logical and inquiring mind, were to bring him distinction. Most went into subsequent editions and many were translated into German and Italian, so that his reputation became European. From the first he used London publishers. William's energy was prodigious. His practice flourished, and on 18 March 1773, he was elected a Fellow of the Royal Society. He and his brother Thomas had made, about this time, the acquaintance of David Garrick, the famous actor-manager and man of letters, and Garrick's brother, George, became his patient.[102]

Two of the fundamental questions that had exercised men's thoughts since the second half of the seventeenth century were those concerning the exact nature and composition of air and water. Both excited William's questioning mind. The evident importance of good ventilation for houses and public buildings was beginning increasingly to attract attention, but the reasons for the beneficial effects remained unknown. By a series of uniquely logical experiments on the alkalis and their relationship with carbon dioxide, recorded in 1756, James Black had showed that when mild lime was burned into quick lime, or when it was treated with an acid, it lost in weight by yielding up a gas. Previously it had been imagined that the lime gained in weight, acquiring a mysterious substance, "phlogiston." Black disproved this idea, noting also that the gas which he had discovered was a product of combustion and of fermentation, and that it was present in expired air. He named it "fixed air," which is familiar to us as carbon dioxide.

The next step was taken by Joseph Priestley. Priestley was a Calvinistic unitarian minister of scientific bent, who in an earlier age would have been born for martyrdom, but who is now remembered as one of the greatest experimental chemists and has, indeed, been called the father of modern chemistry. He himself admitted that his deductions were often unsound, but nevertheless remained a supporter of the phlogiston theory his experiments did much to discredit. William, some eleven years younger, at this time came to know him and admire his research.

The importance of Priestley's work was that chemistry could thence forward develop as a rational science based entirely on quantitative measurements. He showed that growing plants were able to "restore" air which had been vitiated by the effects of combustion or of respiration, and he actually prepared oxygen, which he called "dephlogisticated air" in 1774, but he had probably stumbled upon it without realizing in 1771, when he was also experimenting with "fixed air," the term coined by Joseph Black. However, it was Antoine Laurent Lavoisier who really discovered the nature of oxygen and its importance in respiration, and who proved that inspired air contained oxygen, while expired air contained carbon dioxide. It was he who replaced the phlogiston theory. Lavoisier's life was spent mostly in Paris, where it ended tragically under the blade of the guillotine.

William too had been conducting experiments at the same time as Priestley, but before they would have met, and early biographical references give him credit for discoveries "erroneously attributed to Dr. Priestley."[103] He used the term "fixible air" in the same sense as Black's "fixed air." In 1825 it was recorded that "[Falconer] was remarkable for the discovery of the properties of fixed air; and was the first who suggested its possessing acid properties (now called carbonic acid gas), a discovery attributed to Dr. Priestly, but which he had published sometime before Dr. P. noticed it."[104]

This statement was repeated in 1848. Both references are necessarily to an earlier paper than William's *Experiments and Observations in Three Parts*, which unfortunately we do not have. It is possible that it was not published. We now know too that, at that same time, between 1771 and 1773, experiments with gases were also being conducted elsewhere by the Swedish chemist Scheele, who, in 1777, independently of Priestley, showed that the atmosphere consists chiefly of two gases, one supporting combustion, the other preventing it.

In 1776, William had published in London possibly his most original work, a volume on the qualities of water and air: *Experiments and Observations in Three Parts: On the dissolvent power of water impregnated with fixible air, compared with simple water, relative to medicinal substances. II. On the dissolvent power of water, impregnated with fixible air, on the urinary calculus. III. On the antiseptic power of water impregnated with fixible air, and a comparison of several antiseptic substances with one another relative to this quality* (London: William Goldsmith, 1776, 136pp., octavo). He dedicated it to Joseph Priestley, "as a small Acknowledgement of his high Merit in this Branch of Science." The book went into a second edition in the following year. Today, however, the antiseptic quality of carbon dioxide is no longer accepted.

On 12 May 1784, William was elected Physician to the Bath General Hospital, becoming a governor three months later. Both positions were honorary and without remuneration, but a public step towards recognition in the profession. His association with the hospital, later to become the Royal Mineral Water Hospital, continued until his retirement in 1819, and the family connection was to be later revived by his grandson, Randle Wilbraham Falconer, who held the same post for twenty-five years from 1856.

Like his brother, Thomas Falconer, William was a keen patron of the arts, but favored fine art and literature at the expense of music, which for some reason appeared to hold little attraction for him. It is possible that he simply rejected the musical development of the period rather than being really unmusical, for he is alleged to have held old-fashioned views on the subject, in contrast to his approach to medical science.

In the years between 1780 and 1787 the young Thomas Lawrence lived with his family at Bath, growing from a boy of twelve to a youth of eighteen, his talent developing from skill with the pencil to facility with pastel, and then first essays in oil. Falconer was his early and generous patron at this time and retained his friendship. There is some evidence that Henrietta was particularly kind to the young man, of whom she may have seen more than the busy doctor. Lawrence, who was to become the most remarkable British portrait painter of his age, became a frequent visitor to the house in Bladud Buildings, and took portraits of William, Henrietta and Thomas sometime in 1783 or during the following two years, which must have been among his earliest commissions and are still in the possession of the family. On his departure for London he made a present of some sixteen drawings and a self-portrait to William. In 1830, Warner wrote, "I have in my possession a letter written by Lawrence on the day he left Bath for London, in which he thanks Dr. William Falconer for his help and kindness, and for the gift of £50."[105]

The family also still possesses a silver inkpot stand, presented to William by Lawrence in the first years after he arrived in London. A decade later, during the winter of 1795-96, by which time he was Painter in Ordinary to the King, Lawrence visited the Falconers at Bath and shortly after asked William for a loan of two hundred pounds. We do not know whether the request was granted, and in a letter dated 13 January 1796, William wrote to young Thomas, at Edinburgh, "I do not think Lawrence recollected much of you personally & indeed he remembered more of your mother than he did of me. He however inquired very kindly after you."[106]

Nevertheless, William's granddaughter Henrietta saw Sir Thomas Lawrence in London shortly before his death in 1830, and wrote, "He spoke gratefully of my grandfather."[107] The self-portrait of the artist when a boy, referred to above, has an inscription on the reverse written by J. F. Meehan, who had purchased the portrait and the drawings given to William, in 1900. The first part of the writing reads: "Portrait of himself done at Bath prior to his leaving for London in 1786. This drawing was given with sixteen others to the late Dr. Falconer of Bath, as some return for his help and assistance, especially for the aid he had from the doctor on his entering his London career, as without that help it would not have taken place so soon."[108]

Copies of the Lawrence portraits of William and Henrietta were taken in oil on board, by Thomas Redmond, soon before he died in 1785, and were probably destined as presents for Henrietta's family. There appears to be no record of a copy of the portrait of Thomas and today only the whereabouts of that of William, which is in the collection of the Victoria Art Gallery at Bath, is known. An interesting account of the portraits and Dr. William Falconer's early patronage of Sir Thomas Lawrence, by David and Gillian Falconer, was published privately in 1981.[109]

The small 12" x 9 1/2" oval portrait in pastel of William, by Thomas Lawrence in 1783, is a striking half-length likeness of a fresh complexioned clean-shaven man in the prime of life. His gaze is confident, the eyes separated by a straight well-formed nose, under thick eyebrows. The original has a hint of more determination than is shown in the technically competent copy. The forehead is broad and clear, beneath brown hair dressed to have two deep horizontal curls at each side and a small formal queue at the back, not unlike a barrister's wig seen in court today. William wears a white muslin cravat, wound several times round the neck, under a soft turned-down shirt collar, and folded to fall inside a buttoned-across, white waistcoat with broad lapels. This is worn under a plain blue serviceable coat with a deep turned-down collar, short in front with large silver-gilt buttons, hanging open to show the fashionable and immaculate linen and the top of the breeches. It is unquestionably the portrait of a man of intellect; the expression is serious, but there is also an air of common sense. The sitter inspires confidence.

Dr. William Falconer.   Pastel by Sir Thomas Lawrence.

The matching, small, oval portrait in pastel of Henrietta Falconer, taken by Lawrence at the same time, shows a woman in her mid-forties with a well-defined nose, pale coloring, a mild chin and gentle expression. In this portrait the expression is more clearly to be seen in a photograph of Redmond's copy than in the original, but this may be understood without difficulty when one considers the young Lawrence had yet to rise to the technical skill of his later achievements, whereas the lesser provincial painter was at the height of his powers. Henrietta's hair is dressed in the fantastic pseudo-pastoral style derived from the pre-revolutionary French Court, at Versailles. A mass of gray ringlets rises from her brow over the head, and falls to the side of the face and to the neck behind. All is surmounted with the lightest of mob caps of filmy lace, under which the backward curls escape. She wears a low gown of gray silk, with a bodice fashionably cut and buttoned in imitation of a man's coat, but this has broad satin ribbons, crossing and tied round each button to finish in a large bow beneath the bosom. White lace from high on the shoulders crosses below the neck and hangs over the bodice and bow. Her arms are concealed by the lace of a shawl under which her left wrist can be seen, with a dark ribbon round it, resting on her lap. The air is of frailty.

Henrietta Edmunds Falconer. Pastel by Sir Thomas Lawrence.

The French Revolution was not one great uprising on the part of what today would be called the underprivileged against their rich and powerful oppressors. Rather it was four separate revolutions, one after another, each with a different aim, and each carried out by different leaders. The France of Louis XVI was bankrupt. No government had gained access to more than sixty percent of the revenue the nation could have produced, without any increase in taxation, had it been free to reorganize the state's framework. The King was forced to summon the Estates-General. There followed first the Orleanist revolution of 1789, which was in effect the beginning of the end for the *ancien regime*, and it was in early summer of 1790, as Paris seethed with excitement and the parties intrigued, that William wrote, on the 22nd of May, an able attack on the course events were taking, which appeared in the *Bath Chronicle* of the 3rd of June.

Like all commentators of the day, he did not share the concerns and perspectives of the modern historian when viewing the events in France. Like them he had received a conventional classical education, which, it was assumed, would have produced an orderly and logical mind. He would have supplemented this with a working knowledge of current politics and political theory, which, in his case, was solidly Whig in allegiance. He would have read such authors as Montesquieu and Locke and his own kinsman, Hume, but not Rousseau, and he plainly was aware of the speeches and publications of Edmund Burke. He drew on the experience of Athens, and remarked of the French then, that which has been seen in all those seduced by Fascism and Communism in our own century: "They did not reflect on what the experience of ages has evinced, that extremes of every kind approach nearer to one another than might be imagined, and that moderation, not violence, is the best security against arbitrary power."[110]

In words which strike to the heart of one of today's problems, in former Communist states, and in third-world countries lacking a democratic tradition, he wrote:

> The French legislators having had no practical knowledge of liberty in their own country, seem to have deduced their notions from books only, and to have adopted ideas concerning it, too refined and too speculative to be reduced to practice in the present situation of their nation. Instead of intoxicating the people with a "large and racy draught of liberty",——it would have been more prudent to have inured them by degrees to the change.[111]

This is all very much in the style of William's objective medical comments, and markedly unlike the archaic and overblown style adopted by the *Times*, which took the view that the whole revolution was a well-deserved comeuppance for the recent French involvement in North America, and that a Frenchman's greatest misfortune was not to have been born a Briton. Perhaps that is why he did not write to the London paper. His views, although generally held a year later, as revolutionary excesses mounted, were not then common.

After the fall of the Bastille, in July, and the seizure of King Louis by the Paris mob in October, a correspondence with Edmund Burke, the eminent statesman, followed. Burke's *Reflections on the French Revolution* was being read all over Europe and strongly encouraged France's rulers to resist, despite his condemnation of the previous regime. His opposition to the excesses was already costing Burke the support of his fellow Whigs, when William wrote from Bath, in early November:

> I took a similar Liberty some Time ago in sending tho' without a name a Paper which was printed in the Bath Chronicle & am now happy to find the sentiments I there ventured deliver confirmed by so able & decided a Judge. Such ideas are not professional as you well observe to a Physician but a love for Letters & an aversion for fashionable amusements have prompted me to spend those Portions of Leisure which exist & fall to the lot of every man rather in sober & temperate Study & Reflection than in what the world calls good Company.[112]

To this Burke replied with a gem of eighteenth-century courtesy and intellectual expression, which is worth quoting in part: "I am proud in finding you in the same opinion. I am perfectly sensible of my obligation to you for the pains you have taken in the various extracts you have made for the support of our common principles, and for my instruction as well as satisfaction. If your business should ever permit you to visit London, I shall be very happy if you will add to the favour of your present communication, that of permitting me to cultivate a personal acquaintance with a gentleman to whom I am so highly obliged, and for whose learning and abilities, as well as for the use he makes of them, I have so sincere a respect."[113]

A further exchange followed, of which Burke's reply is lost, and then one more letter from William in December, sending "by the Coach some remarks on the very unjust Censure on y[ou]r Work in the Monthly review penned in haste but with good Intentions."[114] These certainly appear to be the essay in the *Public Advertiser* on the twenty-first of December entitled "A Short Defense of Mr Burke's Pamphlet. In Reply to the Monthly Reviewers," signed "Candour," and dated the seventeenth of December. Whether he ever made occasion to call upon Burke in London, as invited, we do not know.

In September, 1792, William became executor and residuary legatee of the personal estate of his brother Thomas, who died at Chester. He also came into the Leighton Hall estate, near Nantwich, which had been entailed and settled by their father. He faced the necessity of going to Chester and settling Thomas's affairs when probate was granted that October. There was much to do and he undoubtedly tackled the task with his customary vigor. Leighton Hall, was probably visited and arrangements reviewed; and the leasehold property belonging to Mr. Williams in Bridge Street, Chester, disposed of, which Thomas had occupied in his last years. The best of the furniture, the books and the plate, and the family portraits were dispatched to Bath by hired wagons with guards. Some papers William brought down with him. All required close supervision.

Today it is a matter of infinite regret that the library started by William Falconer, Recorder of Chester, and added to by successive generations of this outstandingly literate family was sold at auction over six days at Bath, in 1842, through what can only be termed accident, mismanagement and misfortune. The Recorder may have had, five hundred books when he died; possibly fewer. When his son, Thomas the classical scholar, died this would not have been less than two thousand; probably more. John Byrom with a much less tranquil life left more than three thousand, so Dr. William may have possibly had as many as four thousand volumes packed and sent south in the winter of 1792. In the middle of the nineteenth century, when they were dispersed the total very probably would have been some eight thousand volumes, reflecting the interests and personalities of four owners over one hundred and twenty years.

But in 1792, or earlier, there were other things, neither dispersed nor retained, but destroyed. Not a letter, not a memorandum, nor even an account or a bill has come down to us from John Falconer, the Jacobite; we have only his brilliant book. Save the odd fragment, there is nothing from his widow, Mary Dalmahoy. Of their son, William, the Recorder of Chester, there are neither letters nor journal to be found; nothing except a dull book of precedents in the Chester archives, and a stray legal Opinion. Nor has any trace been found of the letters to Thomas in Chester, between 1736 and 1792, from his kinsman young David Pennant as a schoolboy, as an undergraduate, or whilst on the Grand Tour; although forty-two of Thomas's to him and his father have survived in the Pennant papers. There are no letters from Charles Gray, husband of Thomas's cousin Mary Wilbraham, and M.P. for Colchester, although we have thirty-four of his own to Gray on political matters, between 1757 and 1776.[115] No letters have been found between Thomas and William himself, and very few of those of the many scientific figures, such as Joseph Banks, with whom Thomas corresponded. There must have been many, many hundreds of letters which contained answers to the questions he had endlessly posed and discussion of matters botanical and scientific, as well as others of political and social interest.

These were active, busy, literate people, yet for more than a century there is this gap without records, during which, latterly anyway, they lived in comfortable circumstances. What we know of Thomas's temperament——his passion for collecting, not destroying; a lack of decisiveness in his character, maybe; and latterly his ill health——all make it seem unlikely that he would have weeded and destroyed so much of varying character, unless just conceivably it happened at the time of his move from St. John's Street to the two successive houses in Bridge Street, Chester. If the loss was simply that of the seventeenth-century papers, one could suppose that Mary Dalmahoy was wholly responsible, but for the subsequent far more dangerous years, logic does seem to point to a bonfire of family records, and with them Thomas's scientific correspondence, made in haste by William in Bridge Street, Chester, one week in October or November, 1792. The matter was referred to subsequently as a matter of some kind of accident.

William was no romantic. He was a vigorous, pragmatic and decisive man in good health, and, at forty-eight, in the prime of life, possessing all the self-confidence of a successful career at its zenith. He was very busy professionally and undoubtedly his aim was to conclude the necessary arrangements in Chester, and return south to Bath as quickly as possible. Certain things could be delegated to others; but sorting his brother's papers and accounts, his father's and mother's letters or journals, and also, but barely possibly, his grandfather's and grandmother's letters and deeds, and documents from the time of the flight of James II in 1688, and the time of the Scottish invasions of 1715 and 1745, all this he had to do himself.

The great question is was there anything to conceal? Maybe not, but if there was any Jacobite material he would not at that time have wanted it accidently revealed to others. With France aflame in revolution, Jacobin riots in Birmingham, and political societies for and against reform responding with excitement to events across the Channel, and government alarm mounting weekly, William might very reasonably have felt, even then, that no risk of a hint of disloyalty to the crown by his family was worth contemplating. This was the year that had seen the publication of Thomas Paine's *Rights of Man*, then regarded as seditious, its author tried in absentia for treason, as the pamphlet was widely distributed by corresponding societies in favour of manhood suffrage and constitutional reform.

At Bath the electoral franchise was limited to thirty members of the Corporation, just 0.1% of the city's population, and, unsurprisingly, any suggestion of the franchise being given to the uneducated was regarded by the ruling class as madness and insurrectionary. However, local loyalism that year was more evident amongst all classes than sedition. Any kind of disorder was regarded with anxiety and a loyal declaration to the Corporation by 362 sedan chair porters must have been well received: "We are conscious that our livelihood and the happiness of our families and ourselves depends entirely upon the prosperity and peace of the kingdom in general and of this city in particular."[116] One hundred five Bath publicans resolved not to allow any radical meetings on their premises in December, and promised to suffer no seditious language without "immediately giving information thereof to the Civil Magistrates."[117] We know that after returning home that month, William subscribed to the Association for Preserving Liberty, Property, and the Constitution of Great Britain against Republicans and Levellers. As a physician, he knew better than most that conditions for many in England needed reform, and as a scientist he saw a future of improvement of all kinds; but as a man of property, he felt confident that his country was already happier and more just than any other, and as a Bath citizen he knew its prosperity depended absolutely on the civil tranquility the city's visitors required.

On the face of things it does seem extremely unlikely that the papers of John Falconer, the cryptographer, and his widow, Mary Dalmahoy, had survived her death, in 1754. Hers was doubtless the first burning of papers, probably around 1730, before she removed to Whitchurch, but possibly even as late as the frightening winter of 1745. Only something of the sort can explain William's subsequent apparent ignorance of his grandfather's precise origins as related by his own grandson Thomas. Even his surviving letters of advice to his son, Thomas, in Edinburgh only three and four years later, in 1795 and 1796, are singularly vague about exact family relationships in Scotland, at the very time he is commending to him their usefulness in society.

In Thomas's and William's childhood their parents were undoubtedly highly reticent about their dangerous Scottish connections. After all, William was nineteen and his brother eight years older when their father died in 1764. Both intelligent, William simply cannot have been devoid of normal curiosity about the family's past. Their Dalmahoy forebears might well have been more spoken of by their grandmother, who lived with them until her death ten years earlier, and this would have been natural amongst the Wilbraham cousinhood in Cheshire. Indeed, it is possible that the memory of John Falconer was not well regarded by the Wilbrahams; he may have been felt to be a perilous connection. What we can look at with sympathy and great interest, they might have deplored and not spoken of. It is impossible to say. If, all those years later, in 1792, William did destroy his father's and his brother's papers, he may have heightened the mystery as well as obscuring for another hundred years the origins of the family, but more certainly he deprived us of much real knowledge of his brother and their father.

William was now rich, successful in his career as a physician, respected for his medical and scientific writing, and esteemed in his adopted city of Bath. His access of fortune upon Thomas's death came as the financial crash of 1793 thrust Bath into depression. Banks broke and builders toppled, as one speculative venture after another ran out of capital. There was now a turning point in the city's fortunes, which had been created in all its eighteenth-century, classical, urban splendor in no more than seventy years. Just as it had been born of a social demand effectively served by enthusiastic capitalism, now it became slowly deserted by fashion, and in all its magnificence, which we now admire and revere, it seemed for a while to lose its original charm for the great. It has been said it became too big. Certainly its modern suburban sprawl did begin, and the lower town degenerated in part into slums. For all that, it was still a place of bustle and as time passed stone mellowed, trees grew, and the city's beauty increased. As a place to live for the cultivated and well-to-do it was incomparable, and their numbers grew.

During the autumn of 1796, Katherine Plymley, an unmarried Shropshire lady, was in Bath as a companion to her uncle and aunt, Mr. and Mrs. Robert Corbett of Longnor Hall. Miss Plymley and Mrs. Falconer attended balls together at the upper rooms, including one on 3 December 1796 attended by the Prince of Wales, the Duke and Duchess of York, and twelve hundred persons.[118] She wrote in her diary:

> *22 October,*——On Monday I was at Mrs Falconer's public day, where about forty persons, among them Miss [Mary] Williams of Boddlewydden, the particular friend of Miss Panton's——Her lodgings are at No. 8 Bennet St., at a Millener's——2 small drawing rooms opening to each other, the one not above half furnish'd, one bedchamber (her maid sleeps in her room) &, I think, a room in a garret to place boxes etc.; for this she pays £70.
>
> *5 November,*——Last Sunday——In the evening I go to prayers in the Octagon, being accomodated by Mrs Falconer in her seat. The usual hour for eveng. prayers in the chapels is 5 o'clock.

This elegant building at the bottom of Milsom Street was the most famous of Bath's proprietary chapels; it had been built in 1767 with funds raised by subscription, and a rent was paid for pews. The standard of comfort to be found in these chapels was high and reflected the attitudes of the day, which saw church-going as an integral part of the social round. In Bath the Anglican and non-conformist preachers attracted critical as well as devoted followers; but only if they could afford a pew, until the Free Church, now Christ Church, was built in 1798.

The greater background to these domestic affairs was the war with France and its cost. William Pitt, in the full knowledge that the whole of Europe had yielded to the aggressor, again explored the possibilities of peace that same summer, whilst far away in a bold, but disastrous night-attack on the mole at Teneriffe, England's greatest sailor, Sir Horatio Nelson, lost his right arm, but not yet his life, and soon was to become briefly William's patient. The ship's surgeon, Thomas Eshelby, entered in his medical log on 25 July 1797: "compound fracture of the right arm by a musket ball passing a little above the elbow, an artery divided, the arm was immediately amputated and opium afterwards given."[119]

In those days, before anesthetics, the amputation was agonizing and the cutting of the flesh with a cold knife worse than the sawing of the shattered bone. But despite this Nelson continued in command and continued to negotiate and to write dispatches, until all that could be done was done. A month later, hard upon the news of the action announced in the *Bath Chronicle*, the popular commander arrived by post-chaise at his wife's lodgings at 17, New King Street, in the late evening of the 3rd of September. The arm had been taken off high under the shoulder and required daily dressing of the still unhealed stump, mainly because of a silk ligature that remained tiresomely intact and in place. It appears to have trapped a nerve also. The patient was feverish and in continuing pain, but anxious to be at the Admiralty.

William was called upon to attend him and acquiesced in Nelson's inclination to seek a London surgeon's opinion, whence he could soonest proclaim his fitness to Their Lordships in Whitehall. He charged one guinea.[120] What was probably needed was a quiet rural convalescence, with fresh air and fruit and vegetables. However, a week later, London it was; the ligature in due course fell away; and Nelson shortly, by the grace of God and without antiseptics, was back in service.

In the following year, 1798, William had the pleasure of renewing his acquaintance with an old friend, John Haygarth, who had remained Physician to the Chester Infirmary for the last thirty years and was a Fellow of the Royal Societies of both Edinburgh and London. He had now come south to take up practice in Bath, He shortly made his home in an elegant house in the Royal Crescent, where houses then sold for about £3,000.

Haygarth held sound and advanced views on the treatment of infectious disease and his numerous medical publications were held in high regard, so that when he and William collaborated, it was in a partnership of two acute, scientific, medical minds. Perhaps this was just as well, because the lingering credulity of the eighteenth century in matters medical has since only been equalled by the lingering twentieth century lack of political realism in the post-colonial age. In America, Elisha Perkins of Connecticut deluded the public by his metallic tractors, which subsequently sold in England for the large sum of five guineas a pair, and which, "when applied to the skin with a stroking movement," were said to "draw out" any disease. Falconer and Haygarth were persuaded to investigate these claims in a scientific and practical manner, and without surprise found them to be devoid of merit.

Haygarth had kept meticulous records of over ten thousand consultations made during thirty-four years in practice. William, too, described a series of 895 rheumatic cases admitted to the Mineral Water Hospital between 1785 and 1793.[121] He regarded acute and chronic rheumatism as different stages of the same disease, distinguished from gout in as much as the joint pain was bearable and the joints themselves were never red. He regarded rheumatism as primarily a muscular disorder, though he accepted that the joints were commonly affected, even to the extent of becoming fixed. The reason he seldom records cases of gout among these is that few cases of true gout were likely to occur among the poor patients of the hospital, who would not have enjoyed the sort of rich diet necessary for the disease to manifest itself. The two men's shared interest in rheumatic disease and the prevention and treatment of infectious fevers, and William's experience in the treatment of gout, led to a fruitful interplay of ideas and joint consultation in many cases in the years following. In the final weeks of life of Prime Minister William Pitt before his death on 23 January 1806, William and Haygarth were consulted regarding his debilitated condition.

Grenville succeeded Pitt as prime minister, and at the end of March, 1807, William, 3rd Duke of Portland, Thomas's and James's old schoolfellow, headed a Whig administration for the second time. He was followed by Spencer Perceval and the Earl of Liverpool in 1812. These have been called the forgotten Prime Ministers of British history. Few people know who sent Wellington to the Peninsular, or who was prime minister at the time of Waterloo.

During that same year of 1807, Caleb Hillier Parry wrote in the preface of one of his own books "It is on occasions like these that I regret my distance from a University or the Capital; but I have the greatest pleasure in publicly expressing how much that want has been lessened by the free use of the valuable library of my excellent and learned friend Dr. Falconer."[122]

There must have been other doctors in Bath and elsewhere who possessed libraries, as Sholem Glaser has said,[123] but it is certain there can have been none who added more to those inherited books from his own experience and pen than William. Before public, specialist libraries were available, his ever growing medical collection was of the first importance, and it is certain he derived great pleasure from the use of it by his friends and colleagues. To many of them he dedicated his own works, and to others he gave copies of his books as they were published. Parry, two doors away from his colleague, was particularly fortunate.

Years later William's eldest granddaughter Henrietta, remembered him at this time and in the years following as being "a man of tall and handsome presence, of a singularly mild and equable temper, enlivened occasionally by flashes of sharp wit."[124] There is no doubt he was also a man of forceful character, a quality that seems not to have been developed in his only son. These were the years when his furious professional activity wound down in the wake of his wife's death. He continued, it is true, as Physician to the Bath General Hospital until 1819, when he was seventy-five years old, but there were no more assertive and far-seeing medical publications, and he probably saw fewer patients.

William now had more leisure. George Monkland, soldier and writer about Bath, who described him as a man of good presence, with a dignified manner and "ever ready with a retort, an epigram, or a witty rejoinder,"[125] recalled seeing him early in the new century at Bull's Library. This was one of the subscription libraries that opened in the latter part of the Georgian era, and which provided something of a club atmosphere as well as a whiff of the London coffee house:

> There was Harrington seated in his curule chair, in his full-bottomed wig and three-cornered hat, one leg crossed over the other, and holding his handkerchief to his mouth when speaking——and Falconer, pacing up and down, portly and erect of form, his nose with spectacles bestrid,——he was short-sighted——and his hand resting in the bosom of his waistcoat.[126]

In 1814, the year of the Allies occupation of Paris in April and of Napoleon's abdication and exile to Elba, William made the acquaintance of Hester Lynch Piozzi. She had incurred severe disapproval from Samuel Johnson by remarrying after the death, in 1781, of her first husband Henry Thrale. The story of the Thrales' long friendship with Johnson, who looked upon Streatham Park as his second home and regarded his hostess as "the first of womankind," has been well told in recent years. Gabriel Piozzi died in 1809, and his widow divided her time between Bath and Wales until 1814. Then she retired entirely to Bath until her death in 1821. William himself appears to have had reservations about Johnson. Warner recalled dining with the Falconers in a large party which included Dr. Samuel Parr, well known for his classical scholarship and contentious nature, and sometimes referred to as the "Whig Johnson":

> A discussion took place respecting Samuel Johnson's conversational powers. They were highly lauded by Parr. Dr. Falconer expressed no great esteem for them, and no envy at those who had had the opportunity (which never occurred to himself) of listening to them; for said he, "Johnson was quite a monopoliser of the conversation: he would let no one talk except himself." "And pray," returned Parr, "what would you have gone into Johnson's company for, but to hear him talk?" "No, Sir. Johnson talked for *victory*, and not for *truth*——and all such talk I *utterly abhor*!"[127]

It was observed that William possessed a regard for truth which was "severe and uncompromising."[128] On another occasion he responded *a propos* a person of whom, it was said, "he had defended the practise of maintaining the wrong side of a question as a display of skill and invention, by the authority of Dr. Johnson——as good and great a man as Dr. Falconer": "In *that respect* I consider myself to be a better man than Dr. Johnson, for I never in my life maintained the wrong side of an argument, knowing it to be so."[129]

In 1817, a year before she died, Queen Charlotte visited Bath. George III, now completely blind, was miserably incarcerated in the last years of his illness. William, who had by permission, earlier dedicated books to the King, attended her privately and subsequently presented his grand-daughter, Henrietta, at a Pump Room levee.

William died in his own bed in his eighty-first year. His last words were "Thy Kingdom come."[130] In that year, the British took Rangoon in the first Burma War, Europe was settled; Byron died at Missolonghi, Scott wrote *Redgauntlet*, Beethoven completed the Ninth Symphony; and a year later trades unions were recognized as legal, and the first steam locomotive railway was opened. Medical science too was on the march. Tributes were paid to William who had pushed that march forward, in the newspapers of the day and circulating magazines:

> Yesterday died at an advanced age, the learned and venerable Dr. Falconer, at his house in the Circus. He may truly be said to have been one of the most distinguished ornaments of our city, of which his age marked him as the father. His extensive store of profound erudition did honour to the university from whose fountain they were derived, and gave lustre to Bath, his chosen residence. His professional career was conspicuous for sagacity of investigation, for promptitude of aprehension, and firmness of decision. His practice displayed zeal, which knew no abatement; assiduity which made no partial distinction of persons; liberality which may have moderated his fortune, but will embalm his fame. It has been remarked by those who were enabled to make the comparison, that his manner and his sententiousness of pithy observation, especially in his later years, bore much resemblance to the familiar style and address of Dr. Samuel Johnson. Of our honoured fellow citizen it may be said peculiarly: professions have rarely boasted a practitioner so learned; learning has rarely produced a professor so practically useful. Science and Learning are indebted to his pen.[131]

A full bibliography of his writings cannot be given here, and the reader is referred to the forthcoming *A History of the Family of Falconer in England* for a more complete list. Nevertheless, a brief summary folows. His major works, in addition to *Experiments and Observations in Three Parts*, listed above, are: *An Essay on the Bath Waters in Four Parts: containing a Preparatory Introduction on the Study of Mineral Waters in general* (London: for T. Lowndes, 1770); *Observations on Dr. Cadogan's Dissertation on the Gout and all Chronic Diseases* (London: for F. Newbery, T. Lownds; Bath: for Tennent and Bally, 1772? and other editions); *Observations and Experiments on the Poison of Copper* (London: for Joseph Johnson, 1774); *An Essay on the Water Commonly Used in Diet at Bath* (London, 1776); *Remarks on the Influence of Climate, Situation, Nature of Country, Population, Nature of Food, and Way of Life, on the Disposition and Temper, Manners and Behaviour, Intellects, Laws and Customs, Form of Government and Religion of Mankind* (London: for C. Dilly, 1781); *An Account of the Efficacy of the Aqua Mephitica Alkalina or Solution of Fixed Alkaline Salt, Saturated with Fixible Air, in Calculous Disorders, and other complaints of the Urinary Passages* (London: for T. Cadell, 1789; also later editions); *A Dissertation on the Influence of the Passions upon the Disorders of the Body* (London: for C. Dilly and J. Phillips, 1788), awarded the Fothergillian Medal in 1787; *Essay on the Preservation of the Health of Persons employed in Agriculture, and on the Cure of the Diseases incident to that way of Life* (Bath, 1789; also later editions in Italian); *A Practical Dissertation on the Medicinal Effects of the Bath Waters* (Bath: by R. Cruttwell, etc., 1790; also later editions); *An Account of the Use, Application, and Success of the Bath Waters in Rheumatic Cases* (Bath: for W. Meyler, 1795); *Observations respecting the Pulse* (London: for T. Cadell and W. Davies, 1796; also other editions); (with his son Thomas) *Arrian's Voyage round the Euxine Sea, translated and accompanied with a Geographical Dissertation and Maps* (Oxford: J. Cook; London: Cadell and Davies, 1805). His medical and scientific papers appeared in *Memoirs of the Medical Society of London*, *Transactions of the Manchester Literary and Philosophical Society*, *Letters and Papers of the Bath and West of England Agricultuaral Society*, and other journals, and later in life he wrote on classical subjects in *Athenaeum* and *The Classical Journal.*

Issue of William and Henrietta (Edmunds) Falconer:

Q6   i.   Thomas Falconer, born 24 December 1772.

Q6 **Thomas Falconer**, A.M., M.D., born 24 December 1772 in the parish of St. James, Bath, and baptized there on 1 February 1773,[132] died 19 February 1839 at 29, The Circus, Bath, and was buried at All Saints, Weston, Somerset.[133]

He married, on 7 December 1797, at St. Mary's Chapel, Queen's Square, Bath, Frances Raitt, daughter and heir of Lieutenant Colonel Robert Raitt, of the 2nd Queen's Royal Regiment, by his second wife Sarah Neale, baptized 9 August 1771 at Gibraltar, died 14 July 1841 at Bath.[134]

Thomas received the first elements of a classical education from the Rev. Nathaniel Morgan, who tutored him at Bath. Then in January 1783, at the age of eleven, he was admitted to the Grammar School at Manchester, where his father's kinsman Sir Thomas Egerton was a feoffee and an "old boy." There he was under Charles Lawson, High Master from 1764 to 1807, for whose kindness and attention to him he remained grateful. Both the High Master and the Usher had houses in Long Millgate which were, as well as their residences, boarding houses for boys who came mostly from Lancashire and Cheshire. Each house had a garden or playground on Walkers Croft, although the High Master's appears subsequently to have suffered the lack of one. Both men taught their classes in the same spacious, well-lit upper room of the new school, built in 1776. The annual speech day was held to be of great importance.

Thomas Falconer. Pastel by Sir Thomas Lawrence.

Lawson must have been a man very much to the taste of Thomas Falconer in Chester and his brother William in Bath. He became a figure of importance in Manchester and, like his immediate predecessors, extolled widely the virtues of a classical education for men of action and great employments in commerce and state, not just academics. He held out the temptation of ambition. If children were educated at home, their natural desire to excel would lie dormant, yet the "sparks of this ardor are latent in their breasts, and they can be nowhere so effectually kindled into a flame as in a public school." Such a school was the best preparation "for business. Were we born

only to speculate idly, a private education might not incapacitate us for these
employments; but we are designed to act as well as to think, and a youth
spent in privacy and retirement has too often been found an obstacle to appearing afterwards to advantage in the busier scenes of life." In all he said
Lawson was obviously thinking not of the day-boy, but of the boarder, the son
of a country gentleman or parson who might well think the cost of the boarding fees worth the professional training which the school offered.[135] This was
a good early summary of a part of the emerging public school ethos.

Manchester's great Grammar School possesses almost no record of admissions before 1888, and there seems to be no record of Thomas's leaving
date.[136] He did spend three weeks of the 1786 Christmas holidays in Chester
with his uncle and godfather, and it is possible this was the point at which,
for some reason, he was withdrawn from Manchester and spent the next year
as a fee-paying day pupil at the King's School at Chester. There he was under
Thomas Bolland, under whom that school had gained a certain reputation.
He contributed a number of pieces to an anthology, Prolustones Poeticae, by
Bolland and some of his other pupils, published in 1788.[137] His uncle was a
valuable mentor, no doubt. Whilst at Chester, when he was just sixteen, he
was elected a scholar of Corpus Christi College, Oxford, on 18 January 1788,
and matriculated four days later.

Up a Oxford, he graduated B.A. in 1791, and in due course took his
degree of A.M. and became Fellow of Corpus Christi on 7 November 1795.[138]
He then went to Edinburgh and attended the medical classes at the College
for two terms. From this time, as already noted, a few examples remain in
letters to him of his father's dry humor and advice.[139] He returned briefly to
Bath in the spring of 1796 and took stock; perhaps William then recognized
that in his son there was not the practical activity of mind he himself possessed. Thomas again went up to Oxford, this time to read theology, and was
admitted deacon in Christ Church Cathedral on 18 December.[140] He was
there ordained a priest a year later on 11 June 1797. He published, also that
year, an annotated, octavo edition of The Voyage of Hanno, which, leaving
aside his Strabo and its later posthumously published translation, was the
first of some twenty-three miscellaneous pamphlets and sermons on classical and Christian themes, published throughout his life. He was much admired by Dr. Samuel Parr, the whig Johnson, and friend of Priestley, who was
a considerable Latinist and political polemicist of his day, although quite
unreadable in ours.[141]

After their marriage, Thomas and Frances took a short lease of Bathford
House, beyond the eastern outskirts of the city. After two years he again
determined to qualify in medicine, and in 1800, with his family, took up
residence once more in Edinburgh to resume attendance at medical lectures
at the College for a further two sessions. However, it seems that he may still
have lacked enthusiasm for the subject. Rather than among medical men,
his chief acquaintance there at this time appears to have lain amongst classical scholars and Scottish Presbyterian churchmen, whose company he enjoyed despite his own firmly held Episcopalian views.[142]

On their return south the following year, Thomas took a lease of Vicarage
House, Corston, five miles from Bath on the old Wells road, where he, Frances,
and now their three children remained from 1801 until the death of his mother,
Henrietta Falconer, in September 1803. Thereafter they lived with Dr. Will-

iam at 29, The Circus, until his death.

Thomas's principal occupation in the first years after returning south was to edit the Oxford edition of Strabo, the first books and notes of which had been prepared, but never published, by his uncle Thomas Falconer, of Chester. Subsequently a little more than the first two books had been edited by Dr. John Parsons of Balliol, and about 1791, the Rev. Henry Halliwell of Brasenose had taken over the editorship and edited another five. Finally, in 1802, the whole work was handed to Thomas, who, having overcome numerous difficulties, completed it, added a substantial preface,[143] and in 1807, saw to its publication in two large folio volumes by the Oxford University Press: *Strabonis Rerum Geographicarum Libri.xvii. Graece et Latine, cum Variorum animadversionibus, Codicum MSS. Collationem, Annotationes et Tabulas Geographicus adjecit Thomas Falconer, Subjiciuntur Chrestomathiae Graece et Latine.*

At the time and in the years following there was an intriguing display of academic infighting which arose from the handling both of the subject matter and the editorship, which is not lacking in human interest.[144]

On numerous occasions, Thomas was invited to preach before the University, and in 1810 he was appointed Bampton Lecturer, a considerable tribute to his classical and Christian scholarship.[145]   In 1822 and 1823, having returned to the idea of practicing medicine, he took at Oxford the degrees of B. and D.Med.,[146] but in the event did not turn these qualifications to practical account. It was said, however, that he was unremitting in imparting gratuitous medical advice to afflicted persons as well as being very liberal in his charitable giving. He possessed ample means and, except for one short period as curate as St. James's, Bath, does not appear to have performed any normal clerical duty and declined a living in Dorset when it was offered to him.

He matriculated at Corpus Christi, Oxford, on 22 January 1788 and received the degrees of B.A. in 1788, fellow, M.A., in 1795, and M.D., in 1822. He was Bampton lecturer there in 1810.[147]   He wrote on religious topics.

Issue of Thomas and Frances (Raitt) Falconer:

i.   Henrietta Falconer, born 14 September 1798 at Bathford House, died 19 April 1892 at Guilton House, Sevenoaks, Kent, was buried at St. James, Bushey, Hertfordshire.[148] She married, on 14 January 1834, at Walcot, Bath,[149] John Arthur Roebuck, P.C., Q.C., M.P. for Bath, elected 1832, 1835, and 1841, and Sheffield, elected 1849 and 1852, and had issue, surname *Roebuck*: a. son, stillborn 7 July 1835; b. *Henrietta Zipporah*, born 3 August 1837 at Hordle, Hampshire, died 18 January 1916 at Guilton House, Sevenoaks, Kent, buried at Bushey, Hertfordshire.

ii. Frances Falconer, born 3 November 1800 at Edinburgh, died, unmarried, 21 December 1872, at Usk, Gwent, buried at Llanbadoc, Gwent.

iii. William Falconer, M.A., born 27 December 1801 at Corston, Somerset, died 9 February 1885 Bushey, Hertfordshire, was buried at the parish church of St. James.[150] He married, probably in 1839 or 1840, Jane Isabella (Robinson) Douglas, daughter of Joseph Robinson, Esq., and widow of Walter Sholto Douglas. By her first husband she had a daughter, Adeline Douglas, died 31 March 1916, who married Sir Henry Drummond Wolff, K.C.M.G. Jane died in Italy at St. Alessi, Pistoia, on 7 February 1869 and was buried three days later in the Protestant burial ground called the English Cemetery at Florence, which stood in a lonely spot amongst widely scattered houses and gardens outside the walls at the à Pinti Gate. Today it stands, well maintained, behind its walls on what is an island in the busy traffic stream of the Viale Piazza Donatello.[151]

William was educated firstly at Manchester Grammar School, but appears to have been placed subsequently with the Rev. John Parson, who conducted a school at Clifton and Redland outside Bristol,[152] before he matriculated and was accepted by Oriel College, Oxford, on 10 December 1819. He took his B.A. from Oriel with a 3rd Class Honours in classics, but a 1st Class Honours in mathematics on 2 December 1823.[153] In 1825, he set out on a tour of the continent, visiting France, Germany, Switzerland, and Italy, the progress of which he recorded in regular letters to his family and friends in Bath, in the form of a journal. A total of thirty-nine letters has been preserved, although evidently there were many more.[154] He returned home during the autumn or winter of 1826, after having declared from Florence in July his intention to visit Vienna before doing so. In the year following his return, William went back to Oxford, where he took his M.A. in October 1827, and, meantime, on 30 June, had been elected from Oriel to a Fellowship of Exeter College.[155] There he was a mathematical lecturer and became a tutor in 1828, librarian in 1832, and bursar in 1833.[156] Between 1832 and 1838 he was the University of Oxford Public Examiner.[157] In the latter year he was then ordained priest and in 1839 was inducted into the living of Bushey, in Hertfordshire. Its early seventeenth-century rectory was given an elegant classical dining room and staircase about this time. To it he added a new Georgian brick front about 1845.[158] From Bushey William took in hand the publication of his father's completed translation of the *Geography* of Strabo. The printing of an octavo edition was begun but, after five sheets, comprising nearly the whole of the First Book, had been completed, a disastrous fire at the printer's consumed all the copies of the entire work. Then shortly after this daunting event a translation by H. C. Hamilton was announced. However, this was unfinished, and William was enabled to take it up and himself complete it for publication. It appeared in three volumes in Bohn's Classical Library: *The Geography of Strabo literally translated, with Notes: The first six Books by H. C. Hamilton Esq., and the remainder by William Falconer, M.A., late Fellow of Exeter College, Oxford. In three volumes* (London: Henry G. Bohn, York Street, Covent Garden, 1854, 1856, 1857). This was generally well received, although it met with some criticism, but in any case, because of the sequence of events, the work may have owed at the end little to the original labors of Thomas of Bath. William remained at Bushey until his death nearly sixteen years after his wife died in Italy. They left no issue.

iv. Elizabeth Falconer, born 4 January 1803 at Corston, Somerset, died 30 November 1803 at Bath, buried at All Saints, Weston.

v. Thomas Falconer, born 28 August 1805 at The Circus, Bath, died, unmarried, 25 June 1882 at Bath, was buried in Locksbrook Cemetery. He may be assumed to have been educated at home and privately in Bath for lack of any evidence to the contrary. In 1823, he was admitted a Member of Lincoln's Inn and was called to the Bar on 8 February 1830.[159] He practiced in London as an equity draftsman and conveyancer and from 1837 to 1840 held the post of revising barrister for the boroughs of Finsbury, Tower Hamlets and Marylebone. He subsequently spent more than two years traveling through North America before returning to England in December 1842. Those two years of travel, in the days of slavery, were when the United States had yet to complete its expansion south and west to the Pacific coast. Texas had seceded from Mexico, but, because of the increasingly strong political feeling over the slavery question, had not yet been accepted into the union. In the Northwest, the Oregon boundary issue between Britain and the United States had yet to be resolved. The times were wild on those frontiers and seem already strange and remote. Thomas's own record of his itinerary is worth recording:

> Sailed on the afternoon of the 20th of October, 1840, in the "Britannia" steamer, from Liverpool for Boston, Massachusetts, in the United States of America. At Halifax, Nova Scotia, 31st October; at Boston, November 2 (seven o'clock in the morning); at Niagara, 16th November; at Washington, 5th December; at Cincinnati, 22nd December; at Grand Cairo [Illinois], 25th December; Natchez, on the 29th, and landed at New Orleans 1st January, 1841; at Galveston, in Texas, in February; left San Antonio de Bexar for Santa Fe, in June; at Zacatecas, January 1, 1842; St. Louis Potosi, January 10; Celaya, January 22; Calera 24th; Queretaro, 25th; Tula, on the 30th; in the city of Mexico, February 3, 1842; at Real del Monte, February 19; on the 7th of March, at Vera Cruz; sailed thence in the "Atlantique," March 9th; arrived at Matanzas, in the island of Cuba, 31st of March; at Havannah, April 3; sailed from Havannah in the "Solway" steamer (since wrecked) for New Orleans, April 11. From New Orleans to Galveston, the second time, in April, and left Galveston on May 20, and arrived, the third time, at New Orleans on May 26; left New Orleans by the "Red Rover," June 5; at St. Louis, Missouri, June 12; at Chicago, June 17; Mackinaw, 19th June; Amhurtsburg, 21st June; at Niagara, the second time, 23rd June; Kingston, 27th June; Montreal, 1st July; Quebec, 26th July; Kingston, the second time, 15th September; at Saratoga, 19th October; Albany, the second time, 21st October; Boston, the second time, 29th October; at Providence, in Rhode Island, November 4; Philadelphia, the second time, November 14; sailed from New York to England, in the "Hendrick Hudson" (since wrecked), November 21, 1842; landed at Hastings, December 22, 1842.[160]

Back in England Thomas returned for some years to his practice at the London Bar and to writing, until, in December 1848, he was offered the appointment of Private Secretary to Sir Henry Barkly, K.C.B., newly appointed Governor of British Guiana. Barkly was a successful colonial administrator, who went on to govern Jamaica; Victoria, Australia; then Mauritius; and finally Cape Colony, with a G.C.M.G. Seven years of achievement in this last post led to his being High Commissioner for the adjacent territories. Thomas declined the original offer. Had he accepted the post, it is interesting to speculate whether he too might have developed a proconsular career; but it is also perfectly possible that British Guiana, with its endemic tropical fevers, might have killed him.

In public affairs, his contribution between 1845 and 1849 to the peaceful resolution of the conflicting Oregon Territory claims of Britain and the United States, was substantial. His pamphlet, *The Oregon Question*, ran into two London editions and another published in New York, all in 1845. At a time when the United States was belligerently expansionist on its own continent, the outcome of the dispute was in marked contrast to the development of the problems with Mexico, which resulted in war and the annexation of vast territories to the Union. Alexander Baring, 1st Lord Ashburton, who had been the British Commissioner in Washington for the settlement of the dispute, wrote to him in a letter dated 14 April 1845:

> Permit me to offer you my very best thanks for the publication your

were so good as to send me. I delayed doing so until I have found time to read it with care and attention, and I feel obliged to you for a very masterly summary, in the shortest possible compass, of the several facts and arguments upon which the solution of this vexed question depends.

The gross partiality and intemperance with which any questions of international differences are discussed by our relations in America, as by our neighbours in France, are generally a severe provocation to those who have to answer them——yet I really think you have performed this task with firmness and temper, as I am quite sure you have done with power and talent.

Thomas's influence was also considerable on the proposals for reform at home of the scandalous and dilatory probate system.

In 1850, due to his American experience, as well as his legal abilities, he was appointed one of the three British joint arbitrators to receive evidence and determine the boundary between the British provinces of Canada and New Brunswick. His contribution to the Canadian boundary settlement was one of notable value, and within twelve months he was nominated for and accepted the appointment of Colonial Secretary for Western Australia, to which he was gazetted on 29 July 1851.

Again, however, for reasons we do not know, or simply because, upon reflection, he decided that this commitment was too far removed from the tenor of a life he could look forward to in this country, Thomas resigned the appointment. He was at this time a remarkably good-looking man, whose Byronic mien in the earlier oil painting of him by George Frederick Watts, R.A., most likely executed about 1840 before he went to America, is most striking. Watts was then young and short of commissions, but is today best known for the penetrating portraits he painted of his famous contemporaries.[161] Now, ten years later, Thomas was at the height of his powers, and it is natural to wonder whether a romantic attachment and a hope of marriage held him in Britain. The record is silent.

He shortly accepted the post of Count Court Judge for Glamorgan and Brecknock, and the District of Rhyader in Radnorshire. He was appointed on 22 December 1851, and there he served with distinction for thirty years, until his retirement in December 1881. During this time he made his residence at Usk, with his elder unmarried sister, Frances, and their handicapped brother John, and then for the remaining eight months of his life at 18, Royal Crescent, Bath, with his bachelor brother Alexander.

Thomas's first courts on his circuit were held in January 1852. He sat for seven years at Rhyader, Builth, Hay, Crickhowell, Brecon, Merthyr, Cardiff, Bridgend, Neath, and Swansea. In Breconshire, comprising the courts at Crickhowell, Hay, Builth, and Rhyader, the traveling on circuit amounted to 1,584 miles in each year and all this distance was at that time posted, which was the most tedious, uncomfortable and tiring part of the work. On two occasions, snowdrifts in the mountains in winter made the roads impassible to coach or horse, and three courts were cancelled. These were the only courts he missed in the next twenty years. The traveling on the other part of the circuit was somewhat irregular in arrangement. It amounted to about 2,300 miles in the year. The total mileage within his circuit limits then exceeded 3,876 in the year. Nevertheless, the number of plaints heard that first year were 9,796.

The work increased steadily, so that in some courts, by 1857 and 1858, the business had doubled as the trade and population of Glamorgan, and access to legal remedies, increased, and the total number of plaints heard was 25,718. That is an average of 118 or 119 a day. The burden had become too great for one man, even with long sittings and had there been no travel-ing. A change was made at the end of 1858 and in 1859. Neath, Crickhowell, Builth, Hay, Rhyader, and Cardiff ceased to be in Circuit No. 30.

The circuit towns became instead, Brecknock, Aberdare, Merthyr, Swansea, Pontypridd, Cowbridge, and Bridgend; and the circuit had also Equity, Bank-ruptcy, and Admiralty jurisdiction. Thomas now traveled on circuit, from and to Usk, where he fixed his residence, upwards of 3,454 miles each year, which was little less than before. In 1859 the number of plaints was 16,846, and by 1875 this had fluctuated greatly but finally risen to 19,605, or an average, including many more cases of complexity and high value, of 134 or 135 plaints in a day, when sittings continued regularly to seven o'clock at night.

Thomas had Sundays and usually five or six other days a month at home, for studying papers, keeping up with legislation, and writing judgments. Par-liament allowed a county court judge a month's holiday, and financial allow-ances carefully calculated to fall short of incurred expenses. His stipend was modest. What he valued was his independence, his quiet life at Usk, and his actual work. Professionally, he wrote many legal opinions, and numerous papers on miscellaneous subjects. Privately, he also pursued inquiries into the early origins of his family and recorded items of information that would otherwise have been lost. In this he was hampered by the lack of surviving matter from the latter part of the 17th and the first half of the 18th centuries and by the limited research facilities of the day. For his collected notes, however, we can be genuinely grateful, and where he was at fault, we can suppose we might well have fared worse.

Nine years before his retirement from the bench, measures were pro-posed to reorganize the conduct of county court jurisdictions, which Thomas, who still presided over Circuit No. 30, considered to be ill-considered and harmful. The quality of his mind and human concern for the poorer classes of the people affected, is demonstrated in the long paper he wrote in July 1872 to the Lords of the Treasury, on the whole subject of the administration of justice under the county court system. His views are reflected in a speech he made at Swansea, four years later, in December 1876, when he said:

> The total number of cases entered on this Circuit since I came here have been 430,833; ——these figures are exclusive of the year 1876.— —I have myself been present in these courts on 293 months, and [in only] one month I was too ill to attend in 25 years.
>
> The annual travelling on this circuit from Usk exceeds 3,500 miles in the year. I sleep in six or seven different beds in a month, so that of continuous home there has been very little enjoyment.
>
> The County Court system is to be commended, and the proposals made to alter what has been an enormous benefit to the public ought to be denounced in the strongest terms. Keep suitors of all classes near to their own homes when an attendance on a court is necessary, even if judges suffer the privation of that domestic personal comfort which they may long for. Before the wishes or interests of Judges or of Lawyers are considered, let us always ascertain those of Suitors, and all arrangements ought to be conformable to their interests.

Concerned by one proposal he regarded as particularly pernicious, he continued:

> The success of the system has arisen from the absence of the formal pleadings of the superior courts. By the issue of writs from the supe-

rior courts an effort is made to bring such pleadings instead of mere particulars into those courts, and when this shall be done one or both of the litigants will be simply plundered for the sake of costs.

In a brief reply to one of many addresses of thanks he received in those years, Thomas remarked that during the whole time that he had presided over the court he had uniformly treated every person, whatever his condition in life, as respectfully as he possibly could. That is rather touching. It is far removed from the Victorian oppressiveness so frequently dwelled upon by writers of later years.

This was a man who was a Liberal in politics and, what is rarer, most truly liberal in his professional conduct and private beliefs. The advent of the railway latterly must have eased the burden of his nigh constant travel on circuit, but the record of his monthly progressions through the mountains of Wales, between the towns where he held his courts, and the sheer quantity of work resolutely done, year in and year out, remains remarkable.

Thomas Falconer's more important published works are as follows: *History, Opinions, and Present Legal Position, of the English Presbyterians.* First and second editions (London: under the direction of the English Presbyterian Association by Anon. Rowland Hunter, 1834); [with Edward H. Fitzherbert] *Cases of Controverted Elections determined in Committees of the House of Commons, in the Second Parliament of the Reign of Queen Victoria, being the Third Parliament since the passing of the Acts for the Amendment of the Representation of the People* (London: Saunders and Benning, 1839); *Expedition to Santa Fe: An Account of its Journey from Texas, through Mexico, with Particulars of its Capture* (New Orleans: Lumsden, Kendall & Co., Office of the Picayune, 1842); *On the Discovery of the Mississippi, and on the South-Western, Oregon, and North-Western Boundary of the United States; with a translation from the original MS. of Memoirs, &c. relating to the Discovery of the Mississippi by Robert Cavelier de la Salle, and the Chevalier Henry de Tonty* (London: S. Clarke, 1844); "Notes of a Journey through Texas and New Mexico, in the years 1841 and 1842." *Journal of the Royal Geographical Society* 13 (1843): 226-244; *The Oregon Question: or, a Statement of the British Claim to the Oregon Territory, in Opposition to the Pretensions of the Government of the United States of America.* First ed., (London: 1845); Another edition (New York: W. Taylor, 1845); Second edition with additions, 51pp. (London: S. Clarke, 1845); *On Probate Courts* (London: 1850); *Papers respecting the Boundary between the Provinces of Canada and New Brunswick* (London: by command of both Houses of Parliament, 1851); *On Surnames and the Rules of Law affecting their Change* (Cardiff: privately printed, 1862; 2nd ed., London: C. W. Reynell, 1862); *On County Courts, Local Courts of Record, and on the Changes proposed to be made in such Courts in the Second Report of the Judicature Commissioners* (London: Stevens, 1873). He also contributed articles to the *Westminster Review* and the *Colonial Magazine.*

Thomas Falconer did not marry, and, like his elder brother, left no issue.

vi.   Alexander Pytts Falconer, born 11 June 1806 at The Circus, Bath, died, unmarried, 1 June 1891 at Bath, and was buried in Locksbrook Cemetery. He lived at Becton, Hordle, Hampshire..

vii.   George Falconer, born 12 February 1808, died 17 October 1817 at The Circus, Bath, buried at All Saints, Weston.

viii.   John David Falconer, born 2 September 1809, died, unmarried, 10 December 1878 at Usk, Gwent, was buried at Llanbadoc, Gwent. He was born deaf and dumb.

ix.   Mary Wilbraham Falconer, born 13 December 1811, died 4 January 1813 at The Circus, Bath, buried at All Saints, Weston.

Q7   x.   Randle Wilbraham Falconer, born 24 September 1813.

    xi.   Elizabeth Falconer, died 30 April 1821.

Q7 Randle Wilbraham Falconer, M.D., born 24 September 1813 at The Circus, Bath, died 6 May 1881 in Bath.

He married, as his first wife, on 21 September 1842, at Oxwich, Glamorganshire,[162] Anna Maria Wood, daughter of John Wood, of Cwm and Brynhafod, Carmarthenshire, born 19 September 1821, died 24 December 1847, at Tenby, Pembrokeshire,[163] buried at Penally, near Tenby.

He married, as his second wife, on 4 September 1850, at Walcot, Bath, Gloucestershire,[164] Sophia Harriet Frances Howard-Vyse, daughter of Major General Richard William Howard-Vyse, Royal Horse Guards, of Stoke Place, Buckinghamshire, and Boughton, Northamptonshire, by his wife Frances (Hesketh) Howard-Vyse, born 18 December 1822.

He studied medicine at the College in Edinburgh, following his father and grandfather before him, and attended lectures from 1835 until graduating as M.D. in 1839.[165] During these years in Scotland he became a Freemason.[166] Thomas Falconer, his father, had died in Bath, in February of his last year up at Edinburgh, and although his mother Frances lived on in The Circus until she also died two years later, in the summer of 1841, Randle started in practice and settled at Tenby in Pembrokeshire, thus beginning a family connection with the counties of South Wales which continued for more than seventy years, until the end of the First World War. A sight of the wills of Thomas and Frances Falconer is needed to know a little more of Randle's circumstances at this time. His surviving four elder brothers and two elder sisters also needed suitable provision, and his portion as the youngest may not have been large.[167] At Tenby there existed no Masonic lodge and he became a member of the Manchester Unity of Oddfellows, whose Lodge No. 2207 met at the Ship and Castle Inn there, and of which he became Honourable Grand. Recognition of his charitable activities as an Oddfellow is shown by the laudatory inscription on the silver snuff box presented to him when he retired as their lodge physician in 1847.[168] He developed his botanical interests too, during these early years of medical practice. The death of his first wife caused Randle to return to Bath at the end of 1847.

He took up residence with the two remaining children at 18, Russell Street, in the parish of Walcot, on its corner with Bennet Street immediately opposite the Assembly Rooms, a handsome and spacious house not one hundred yards from where he was brought up in the Circus. There, well placed, he began to establish a new medical practice. In this he continued with success until his death. On 12 February 1849, he was elected Physician of the Bath United Hospital. He resumed his Masonic life by joining the Bath Lodge of Honour, No. 528, in 1850 and withdrew from his previous Scottish lodge. He was, on 28 February 1856, elected Physician to the Royal Mineral Water Hospital, so following his grandfather.[169] On 9 November 1857, he was elected Mayor of Bath and was re-elected for a second term on 9 November 1858.[170]

As Physician to the Bath General Hospital, or the Royal Mineral Water Hospital, as it continued to be known after its official change of name, Randle interested himself greatly in the curative properties of the baths and this is reflected in his medical publications. Soon after his appointment he wrote his useful pamphlet, *The Baths and Mineral Waters of Bath* (Bath: Hayward & Payne, 1849; London: Simpkin, Marshal & Co., 1849), and went into six subsequent editions between 1858 and 1880.[171]

On 2 April 1860, after ten years, he retired from Lodge No. 528 and was elected to membership of Royal Sussex Lodge No. 53, also in Bath, and there he remained a member until his death.[172]   Royal Sussex Lodge was much better supported than either of the other two Bath Masonic Lodges of the day. They met in the Old Orchard Street theatre, which had been built in 1750 and later was converted to other purposes. That year he also published another work entitled *The Bath General or Mineral Water Hospital* (Bath: Hayward & Payne, 1860). A third edtion of this small book, "continued to the present time" by A. B. Brabazon, was brought out in a 158-page, octavo edition, in 1888.   These and his other publications were useful works, but not to be compared with those of his grandfather.

In his later years, now a Fellow of the Royal College of Physicians, when the British Medical Association met at Bath in 1878, Randle was elected President.   The following year he received an honorary doctorate from Queen's University, Belfast, and honorary fellowships from both King's and Queen's Colleges, Dublin.   He became a Fellow of the Medico-Chirurgical Society, of London.[173]

Issue of Randle Wilbraham and Anna Maria (Wood) Falconer, born at Tenby, Pembrokeshire:

Q8   i.   John Egerton Falconer, born 12 August 1843.

ii.   Walter Wilbraham Falconer, born 19 May 1845, died, unmarried, 30 October 1864 at Bath, was buried in Locksbrook Cemetery.

iii.   Catherine Henrietta Falconer, born 23 September 1846, died 14 October 1846 at Tenby, buried at Penally.

iv.   Thomas Dalmahoy Falconer, born 14 November 1847, died there January 1848, buried at Reynoldstone, on the Gower, in Glamorganshire.

Issue of Randle Wilbraham and Sophia Harriett Frances (Howard-Vyse) Falconer, born in the parish of Walcot, Bath:

v.   Lucy Wentworth Falconer, born 10 July 1851 died, unmarried, 9 August 1910, in Bath, was buried in Locksbrook Cemetery.

vi.   Sophia Harriet Rachel Falconer, born 29 May 1853, died, unmarried, in 1938 in Bath.

vii.   George Thomas Wentworth Falconer, born 28 April 1856, died 7 March 1857 in Bath, was buried in Charlcombe Cemetery.

viii.   Thomas Wentworth Falconer, born 21 January 1858, died 10 June 1906 on his yacht at East Cowes, was buried at Charlcombe Cemetery, Bath.   He married, on 28 June 1898, at St. Mary Abbots, Kensington, London, Georgemma (Glossop) le Breton, widow of Lt. Col. E. H. le Breton and daughter of Lt. Col. John J. Glossop.   They had no issue.

ix.   George Howard Falconer, born 21 January 1858, died 12 February 1864 at Bath, was buried in Charlcombe Cemetery.

x.   Randle Wilbraham Falconer, born 9 March 1861, died 25 May 1861, was buried in Charlcombe Cemetery.

Q8 **John Egerton Falconer**, born 12 August 1843 at Croft House, Tenby, Pembrokeshire, died 16 August 1917 at Wykenhurst, Bagallay Street, Hereford, and was buried in Hereford Cemetery. He was educated at Sherborne School, Dorset, where he was in School House from 1858 to 1861.[174]

He came into property from his mother's family and married, on 24 October 1877, at St. Andrew's, Walcot, Bath, Isabella Charlotte Sheppard, daughter of Philip Charles and Mary (Markham) Sheppard, of Bathampton Manor, near Bath in Somerset. She died 17 December 1920 also at Wykenhurst.

After family visits their married life began at Clifton in Somerset and then at Church Stretton, south of Shrewsbury. From 1881 they lived at Leintwardine House, to the west of Ludlow, also in Shropshire. There they kept a hospitable table and a good stable and enjoyed travel in winter and the entertaining of their friends and relations. In 1884 Egerton purchased the Grange, Nailsworth, in Gloucestershire. There they hunted with the 9th Duke of Beaufort's foxhounds and enjoyed the social life of the county. The Grange was then let on a series of leases, and from 1893 to 1897 their home was at Conway House, Paignton, in South Devon. Then in 1898 they moved to London and lived in Hampstead until 1912. Thence their final move was made in 1913 to Hereford, which was their home until they died.[175]

Egerton Falconer was sworn as a Freeman of Chester in 1878. Like his father, Egerton Falconer was a Freemason. He became member of Sherborne Lodge, No. 702, which met at Stroud in Gloucestershire, and attended meetings from 1892 to 1912.[176]

Issue of John Egerton and Isabella Charlotte (Sheppard) Falconer:

	i.	son, twin, died some hours after birth, 6 July 1878.
	ii.	Isabella Mary Falconer, born 6 July 1878, died 16 July 1878..
Q9	iii.	Thomas Falconer, born 23 June 1879.
	iv.	Edward Alaric Falconer, Major, R.F.C. born 9 February 1881, died, by drowning near Saltford lock, on the Avon between Bath and Bristol, in 1956. He married, on 9 April 1912, at St. Mark, Marylebone Road, London, Florence Wade. He was a mechanical engineer. During World War I he served as a Lieut. Commander, R.N.V.R., as a British officer with the 1st Canadian Division and finally, having joined the Royal Flying Corps, retired after the war with the rank of Major. They had no issue.
	v.	Florentia Egerton Falconer, born 23 May 1882, died 30 March 1957 at Carisbrook, Isle of Wight.[177] She did not marry and became a member of the Roman Catholic Dominican Order of Preachers and served for many years in the Priory of St. Dominic at Carisbrook.
Q10	vi.	William Wilbraham Phillips Falconer, born 1 December 1883.
Q11	vii.	John Philip Egerton Falconer, born 1 December 1883.
	viii.	Isabel Mary Falconer, born 11 May 1885, died 1968 at Edgebaston, Birmingham. She married, on 1 June 1907, at St. Mary the Virgin, Primrose Hill, London, Ernest William Hart, born 1880, died 1957, and had issue, surname *Hart*: a. *Isabel Audrey*, born 1908, married, 1927, William Arthur Peachell, Lt., later Col., Royal Corps of Signals; b. *Gerald George Falconer*, born 1911; c. *Elizabeth Lascelles Falconer*, born 22 April 1915, married, 1940, Claude Huntley.

Q9 **Thomas Falconer**, F.R.I.B.A., born 23 June 1879 at Church Stretton,

Shropshire, died 8 December 1934 at Amberley, Gloucestershire, and was cremated in Bristol.

He married, on 27 September 1911, at All Saints, Margaret Street, London, Florence Edith Serrell, daughter of Henry Campbell and Emmeline Anne (Kerl) Serrell, of a Dorsetshire family, born 7 April 1879, died January 1944.

He was educated at Sherborne School, Dorset, where he was in School House from 1893 to 1897. A very talented architect, who trained in London, examples of his work are most notably to be found in Gloucestershire, where he settled after marriage. He was deeply interested in archaeology. Following the example of his father and grandfather, Thomas Falconer was a Freemason, a member of Royal York Lodge, No. 2709, which met at Nailsworth, Gloucestershire.

Issue of Thomas and Edith (Serrell) Falconer:

Q12 i.   Peter Serrell Falconer, born 7 March 1916.

ii.   Peggy Florentia Falconer, born 5 March 1918 at Warminster, Wiltshire, lives in Minchinhampton, Gloucestershire. She married, on 4 December 1941, at the church of The Holy Trity, Slad, near Stroud, Gloucestershire, Major Douglas Guest, Royal Artillery, later C.V.O., M.A., Mus.B. (Cantab. & Oxon.), Mus.D. (Cantuar.), F.R.C.M., F.R.C.O., Hon. R.A.M., F.R.S.C.M., Organist-Emeritus, Westminster Abbey, who was born 9 May 1916, the second son of Harold Guest, of Henley-on-Thames, Oxfordshire. He was Organist and Master of the Choristers, Westminster Abbey, from 1963 to 1985, now retired. and had issue, surname *Guest*: a. *Susan Jennifer*, born 13 October 1943 at Cheltenham, Gloucestershire, married, 26 November 1966, at Westminster Abbey, Martin Hayward Garrett-Cox; b. *Penelope Ann*, born 9 December 1946 at Uppingham, Leicestershire, married, 3 October 1970, at Westminster Abbey, Simon de Lange, Ph.D., M.B., B.S., F.F.A.R.C.S., now Professor of Anesthesiology at the University of Maastricht in Holland.

Q10 **William Wilbraham Phillips Falconer**, born 1 December 1883 at Leintwardine House, Herefordshire, died 2 November 1952 in London.

He married, on 19 October 1911, at St. John, Cardiff, Gladys Jones, daughter of David Howard Jones of Carmarthen, born 1885, died 1969.

Educated at Sherborne School, Dorset, from 1898 to 1902, William Falconer was a good athlete there and later became Superintendent of Mechanotherapy in the Physical Clinic of the Royal Society of Medicine in 1916, and at the British Red Cross Clinic in London from 1917 to 1919. He was a specialist in physical remedial treatment. At that time he lived in Richmond, Surrey.

Issue of William Wilbraham Philips and Gladys (Jones) Falconer:

i.   John Dalmahoy Falconer, born 9 December 1914 in London, died 17 November 1994 at Ramsgate. He married, in London in July 1956, Edna Johanna Brooks, daughter of Alfred Foulsham Brooks. No issue.

ii.   Elidure Wilbraham Falconer, born 2 September 1920 at Llandrindod Wells, Radnorshire, died August 1981 at King's Lynn, Norfolk. He married, in 1950, at Richmond, Surrey as his first wife, Pamela Dawes. This marriage was later dissolved. He married, as his second wife, in 1975, at Hunstanton, Norfolk, Elizabeth Robinson. No issue.

iii.   Joan Egerton Falconer, born 2 September 1920 at Llandrindod Wells,

Radnorshire, lives in Chippenham, Wiltshire. She married, as her first husband, on 9 February 1942 in London, Gerrit Carel Geel, surgeon and Major in the Royal Dutch Army, divorced in 1944, and has issue, surname *Geel*: a. *Marie Ann Falconer*, born 1943, married, first, in 1963, Edward Alexander Caudwell, and second, in 1988, Wing Cdr. Anthony E. P. Webb, R.A.F. She married, as her second husband, on 20 July 1945, in London, James Bouverie-Brine, Colonel, Royal Tank Regiment, and has issue, surname *Bouverie-Brine*: a. *Christopher James Falconer*, born 1946, married, 1968, Ellen Agnes Maria Verkroost; b. *Kathleen Joan*, born 1948, married, 1968, Fl. Lt. Alexander Frederick Paul Rhodes, R.A.F.; c. *Amelia Pusey*, born 1953, married first, 1974, Edward Alfred Funnell, divorced 1981, and second, 1982, Stephen Patrick Lacey; d. *Elizabeth*, born 1956, married first, 1978, Dudley James Cox, divorced 1984, and second, Michael McGaughrin; e. *Michael Pusey*, born 1959, married, 1 September 1981, at Bradenstoke, Wiltshire, Claire Andrée Henley.

Q11   **John Philip Egerton Falconer**, born 1 December 1883 at Leintwardine House, Herefordshire, died 17 March 1970 at Wells, Somerset, was cremated and his ashes buried at Haycombe Cemetery, Bath, on 20 March 1970.

He married, on 14 May 1931, at Bath, Florence Eleanor Attwood, daughter of Alfred and Emily Elbertha (Fawdry) Attwood, born 1895, died 1957.

Educated at Westminster School, 1898-1901, he became a solicitor who practiced in London and subsequently in the West Country. He matriculated arms on 18 November 1957, in the Court of the Lord Lyon.

Issue of John Philip Egerton and Florence Eleanor (Attwood) Falconer:

Q13   i.   David Dunbar Falconer, born 19 April 1934
      ii. John Falconer, born 5 March 1939 at Bath, died 9 March 1939.

Q12   **Peter Serrell Falconer**, F.R.I.B.A., born 7 March 1916 at Knightsbridge, London, lives in Minchinhampton, Gloucestershire.

He married, on 16 August 1941, at Uplands, near Stroud, Gloucestershire, Mary Hodson, eldest daughter of the Rev. Cyril Broadley and Jessie Muriel (Hughes) Hodson, born 25 May 1917 at High Wycombe, Buckinghamshire.

He was educated at Bloxham School, Oxfordshire. He is founder of the Falconer Partnership, Architects and Consultants, and of Handling Consultants Limited, of Stroud and Johannesburg, and is a specialist in materials handling and industrial architecture. As well as doing industrial work for many years, Peter Falconer has built churches in this country and overseas, and restored many old buildings. Numerous examples of his work are listed in Pevsner. Latterly he has devoted more of his time to restoring or extending large country houses of the first quality, such as Skelton Castle in Cleveland. He was architect to H.R.H. The Prince of Wales in the restoration in 1986 and 1987 of Highgrove House, Gloucestershire, which possesses an elegance it never had before the nineteenth-century fire. Indeed it is much better than Keck's original building. In his eighties he is remarkable in that his talents are ever in demand. His arms were matriculated on the 18 November 1957 in the Court of the Lord Lyon.

Following his father, grandfather, and great-grandfather, Peter Falconer became a Freemason, joining Sherborne Lodge, No. 702, of which he became

Master in 1955.
    Issue of Peter Serrell and Mary (Hodson) Falconer:

    i.   Caroline Elisabeth Falconer, born 25 December 1942 at Cheltenham, Gloucestershire, lives in Caudle Green, Cheltenham, Gloucestershire. She married, on 29 September 1973, at Stroud, Gloucestershire, as his second wife, Paul Beresford Weller, Major, late Somerset Light Infantry, and has issue, surname *Weller*: a. *Victoria Mary Henrietta*, born 21 May 1976; b. *Atalanta Catherine*, born 21 December 1978; c. *Pandora May*, born 24 May 1983.

Q14   ii.   Thomas Serrell Falconer, born 23 October 1946.

Q15   iii.   Richard Alaric Falconer, born 22 March 1949.

Q16   iv.   William John Falconer, born 17 February 1952.

Q13   David Dunbar Falconer, B.A., born 19 April 1934 at Yeovil, Somerset, lives in Trowbridge, Wiltshire.
    He married, on 12 September 1959, at Bath Abbey, Gillian Mary Owen, daughter of Wing Cdr. W. R. and Doris May (Rashleigh) Owen, born 25 June 1938 at Murree, India.
    Issue of David Dunbar and Gillian Mary (Owen) Falconer:

    i.   Jonathan Randle Falconer, B.A., born 23 May 1961. He married, on 20 June 1992, at Bath, Tracy Ann Gronow.

Q17   ii.   Patrick Markham Falconer, born 22 January 1964.

    iii.   Henrietta Frances Falconer, B.A., born 4 January 1970.

Q14   Thomas Serrell Falconer, B.A., Dip.Arch., born 23 October 1946 at Cheltenham, Gloucestershire, lives in Fairseat, Kent.
    He married, on 2 May 1981, at St. Mary the Virgin, Stansted, Kent, Philippa Mary Sheldon, daughter of Rodney Clifford and Pamela (Watney) Sheldon, of the Court House, Fairseat, Kent, born 9 January 1956 at Fairseat, Kent.
    Educated at Tonbridge School, Kent, and the University of Newcastle, he practiced architecture in Newcastle as a principal in the Stephenson Falconer Partnership from 1974 to 1981 and Falconer Associates from 1981 to 1985. He subsequently moved south when he became a prominent Chevrolet Corvette specialist in the British automobile industry, and is author of numerous books on the Corvette and another on the Cadillac. He is in business in Kent.
    Issue of Thomas Serrell and Philippa Mary (Sheldon) Falconer:

    i.   Venice Mary Falconer, born 30 October 1981 at Newcastle, died 9 November 1981 at Newcastle.

    ii.   Olivia Sienna Falconer, born 13 March 1983 at Newcastle.

    iii.   Katharine Daisy Falconer, born 13 September 1986 at Pembury, Kent.

    iv.   Alexander Peter Falconer, born 29 June 1989 at Maidstone, Kent.

Q15   Richard Alaric Falconer, R.I.B.A., born 22 March 1949 at Cheltenham, Gloucestershire, lives in Painswick, Gloucestershire.
    He married, on 18 September 1982, at St. Mary, Painswick, as her sec-

ond husband, Virginia Suzanne Rowell Jarrett, daughter of Richard Francis Jarrett, F.R.C.P., M.R.C.S., M.A., M.B., Bch (Camb), and Joyce Mary (Rowell) Jarrett.

He was educated at Tonbridge School, Kent, and at architectural school in Oxford. He is a practicing architect and author of books on car racing.

Issue of Richard Alaric and Virginia Suzanne Rowell (Jarrett) Falconer, born at Gloucester:

    i.   Holly Frances Falconer, born 15 January 1984.

    ii.   Rosanna Frances Falconer, born 31 August 1985.

    iii. Venetia Frances Falconer, born 21 September 1989.

Ǫ16   **William John Falconer**, B.A., Dip.Arch., born 17 February 1952 at Minchinhampton, Gloucestershire, lives in Clifton, Bristol.

He married, as his first wife, on 4 August 1975, at Holy Trinity, Minchinhampton, Jane Elizabeth Foster, daughter of Peter and Joan Foster of London Colney, Hertfordshire, but this marriage was dissolved by divorce on 18 December 1978.

He married, as his second wife, on 15 July 1983, at Poole, Susan Mary Bill, youngest daughter of Arthur and Joan (Hewstone) Bill, of Wimborne, Dorset.

Educated at Tonbridge School, Kent, and the Universities of Nottingham and Bristol, he is a practicing architect.

Issue of William John and Susan Mary (Bill) Falconer, born at Bristol:

    i.   Phoebe Margaret Falconer, born 16 June 1993.

    ii.   Alice Falconer, born 8 February 1995.

Ǫ17   **Patrick Markham Falconer**, B.A., born 22 January 1964.

He married, on 16 September 1989, at Bristol, Deborah Anne Helena Close, daughter of Terrence and Patricia (Farrell) Close.

Issue of Patrick Markham and Deborah Anne Helena (Close) Falconer:

    i.   Georgina Louise Falconer, born 24 September 1991.

    ii.   Philippa Jane Falconer, born 5 July 1993.

    iii. James Patrick Falconer, born 22 December 1994.

SOURCES

[1] Edinburgh Old Parish Register.

[2] St. Dunstans in the West, Fleet Street, Parish Register.

[3] Edinburgh Old Parish Register.

[4] See: Thomas Falconer, *Family of Dalmahoy, of Dalmahoy, Ratho, County Edinburgh* (n.p.: by the author, c.1876).

[5] Register of Admissions of Notaries, NP2/12, SRO.

[6] *Register of the Privy Council*, 2nd series, 12: vii, 117.

[7] *Register of the Privy Council*, 2nd series, 12: vii, 183.

[8] Register of Deeds, RD4/56/123, SRO.

[9] Thomas Falconer, *Family of Dalmahoy*.

[10] Register of Deeds, RD4/50/343.

[11] Edinburgh Old Parish Register.

[12] Register of Deeds, RD4/56/123.

[13] Original deed in possession of David Falconer of Trowbridge, Wilts.

[14] Letter from the Lyon Clerk, Court of the Lord Lyon, to David Falconer of Trowbridge, Wilts., 1991, after examining a copy of the deed in question: "This blazon resembles that of Sir [sic] John Falconer of Phesdo, Warden of the Mint...The seal impression lacks only the three mullets."

[15] John Falconer, _Cryptomenysis Patefacta: or, the Art of Secret Information Disclosed without a Key: Containing Plain and Demonstrative Rules for Deciphering All Manner of Secret Writing: With Exact Methods for Resolving Secret Intimations by Signs, or Gestures, or in Speech. As, also, an Inquiry into the Secret Ways of Conveying Written Messages. And the Several Mysterious Proposals for Secret Information Mentioned by Trithemius_ (London: printed for Daniel Brown, at the Black Swan and Bible, without Temple Bar, 1685). 8vo.

[16] _Register of the Privy Council._

[17] Ibid.

[18] David Kahn, _The Code Breakers: the Story of Secret Writing_ (London: Weidenfeld & Nicolson, 1966), pp. 155f. Certain errors of detail are obvious in Kahn's narrative. They do not detract from the judgments he makes in this context.

[19] Notably the monument to Thomas Falconer in 1730 in the new burial ground at St. George's Brunswick Square, London: "...with the same sound Church-of-England Principles in Religion that he took with him from home and in which he died..."

[20] David Falconer of Trowbridge, Wilts., 1991.

[21] Shortly after the death of James II, Middleton had a vision of the dead king and became an ardent Roman Catholic with much influence on the Queen Dowager, Mary of Modena.

[22] _Edinburgh Poll Tax Returns for 1694_, Scottish Record Society, pt. 148 (Dec. 1950) (Edinburgh: for the Society by J. Skinner, 1951), p. 44.

[23] Register of Deeds, RD4/84, f. 1386, SRO.

[24] Mary Dalmahoy received legacies from her father, John Dalmahoy, by his will probated in 1669; from her brother Thomas Dalmahoy, to whom she, among others, was served heir in 1695; from her sister Helen Dalmahoy, widow of Captain Arthur Innes, who, by her will probated in 1728/9, gave her £40 and the whole contents of her sister's chamber in Tarporley; from her son Thomas, whose will probated in 1730 left her with a bequest of £10,000; and from her son James, whose will probated in 1738 gave her £40 per annum for life.

[25] Will of Mary Dalmahoy, probated at Chester, 25 Jan. 1754.

[26] Sir Charles Petrie, _The Jacobite Movement: the Second Phase._

[27] Heineman, _Boswell in Extremes, 1776-1778: the Private Papers of James Boswell_ (New Haven: Yale University Press, 1970), pp. 156-157.

[28] Sir Charles Petrie, _The Jacobite Movement: the First Phase, 1688-1716_ (London: Eyre & Spottiswoode, 1948), App. II, pp. 228-230.

[29] Dates of birth from a note in the hand of Mary Dalmahoy, recorded by J. P. E. Falconer in 1949.

[30] David Falconer, _The Bengal Merchant_ (Bath: the author, 1982).

[31] Letters of Helen (Dalmahoy) Innes.

[32] David Falconer, _Bengal Merchant._

[33] Philip Woodruff, _The Men Who Ruled India: the Founders_ (London: Jonathan Cape, 1953), passim.

[34] David Falconer, _Bengal Merchant._

[35] Woodruff, _The Men Who Ruled India: the Founders_, p. 79.

[36] David Falconer, _Bengal Merchant._

[37] Ibid.

[38] Joel J. Gold, ed., _The Yale Edition of the Works of Samuel Johnson_, vol. 11, _A Voyage to Abyssinia_ (New Haven, Conn.: Yale University Press, 1985), xxvif; Alan Moorehead, _The Blue Nile_ (London: Hamish Hamilton, 1962).

[39] David Falconer, _Bengal Merchant._

[40] Ibid.

[41] Thomas Falconer, Falconer Papers. The inscription on the sarcophagus had become "utterly destroyed" by 1853, but the arms were still visible.

[42] Thomas Falconer, Falconer Papers.

[43] Ibid.

[44] Ibid.

[45] A fuller account of his life may be found in the admirable monograph, _The Bengal Merchant_, by David Falconer, published privately at Bath in 1982, which most ably began the restoration of Thomas's character. See also: J. P. E. Falconer, "Thomas Falconer of Bengal," _Bengal: Past and Present_ 5 (Jan.-June 1910): 47-51.

[46] Dalmahoy Papers, and David Falconer, of Trowbridge, Wilts.

[47] G. M. Trevelyan, _England under Queen Anne_ (London: Longman, 1932), vol. 1, passim.

[48] Ibid.

[49] Passing Records, Lieutenants, Royal Navy, 1712-1745, f. 59, PRO. January 1717. James Falconer had been at sea "upwards of ten years."

[50] The Commissioned Sea Officers of the Royal Navy 1660-1815, vol. 1; Passing Certificates, Lieutenants, Royal Navy, 1691-1832: B. J. Home.

[51] The Commissioned Sea Officers of the Royal Navy 1660-1815, vol. 1.

[52] David Falconer, ed., Letters of Helen Innes (Trowbridge, Wilts., 1990).

[53] Private Journal and Literary Remains of John Byrom, 1: 364. Byrom, the covert Jacobite, had invented a successful system of shorthand, which he taught widely for a fee. Richard's was a fashionable London coffee house much frequented by Byrom.

[54] Private Journal and Literary Remains of John Byrom, 1: 272, 444, 455; 2: 49.

[55] Freedom Register, Archives, City of Chester.

[56] Thomas Falconer, Falconer Papers.

[57] Will of James Falconer.

[58] Thomas Falconer, Falconer Papers.

[59] "Apprentices of Great Britain," citing C43/13 (PRO), at the Society of Genealogists Library.

[60] Sir F. D. Mackinnon, "The Law and the Lawyers," in: A. S. Turberville, ed., Johnson's England: an Account of the Life & Manners of His Age, vol. 2 (Oxford: Clarendon Press, 1933), pp. 287-309.

[61] Thomas Falconer, Falconer Papers.

[62] Rolls of the Inner Temple.

[63] Mackinnon, "The Law and the Lawyers," p. 294.

[64] James Hall, History of the Town and Parish of Nantwich, pp. 424ff.

[65] Assembly Books, A/B/4/50; A/B/4/52v., Chester City Archives.

[66] Assembly Books, A/B/4/112, Chester City Archives.

[67] Lord Chancellor. Records of Appointments.

[68] "The Recordership," Chester City Archives.

[69] See Sir Charles Petrie, The Jacobite Movement (London: Eyre & Spottiswoode, 1948), for a fuller treatment.

[70] Timothy Schroder, English Domestic Silver, 1500-1900 (New York: Viking Press, 1988), p. 152.

[71] Assembly Books, A/B/4/159-159v., Chester City Archives.

[72] Assembly Books, A/B/4/176v., Chester City Archives.

[73] Cases and Precedents written by William Falconer, Recorder of Chester, 1745-1759, C R 594/1, Accession 688, Chester City Archives.

[74] The Chester Guide (Chester: P. Broster, 1781), also 2nd ed., 1782.

[75] Barker and Stenning, Record of Old Westminsters (London: 1928), p. 818.

[76] Brasenose College Register, 1509-1909, vol. 1: List of Members (Oxford Historical Society 55) (Oxford: for the Oxford Historical Society, 1909), p. 348.

[77] Records of Lincoln's Inn, 1660-1775 (London: 1899).

[78] Gray (1696-1782), M.P. for Colchester, lawyer and antiquary, Recorder of Ipswich, married, as his second wife, Mary Wilbraham, first cousin of Thomas.

[79] The family also has a miniature of William Henry Cavendish-Bentinck, which has long been believed to have been given to Thomas.

[80] David Falconer, "A Recently Discovered Letter from Thomas Pennant, the Naturalist," Notes and Queries 32 (June 1985): 225-227.

[81] An edition of the surviving collected letters of Thomas Falconer is in course of preparation for publication.

[82] Warren R. Dawson, ed., The Banks Letters: a Calendar of the Manuscript Correspondence of Sir Joseph Banks preserved in the British Museum, the British Museum (Natural History) and other Collections in Great Britain (London: British Museum, 1958), pp. 368-369.

[83] Alan Moorehead, The Fatal Impact (London: Hamish Hamilton, 1966), pp. 50, 59-60.

[84] Joseph W. Reed and Frederick A. Pottle, Boswell: Laird of Auchinleck, 1778-1782 (New York: McGraw-Hill, 1977), pp. 147-148. Boswell kept a separate journal of his jaunt which, unfortunately, has been found unaccountably missing in the great research and publication of Boswell's papers, led by Pottle between 1950 and 1990. One would very much like to read a journal of Boswell's so characterized by himself, when he described it in a letter to Johnson, on 7 November 1779 as "truly a log book of felicity."

[85] Letters of James Boswell addressed to the Rev. W. J. Temple (London: R. Bentley, 1857); Chauncey Brewster Tinker, Letters of James Boswell (Oxford: Oxford University Press, 1924). It is to be hoped that the missing journal may one day turn up, which more than likely contains an account of his meeting and conversations with Thomas.

[86]Sir John Hale puts the value of Strabo in perspective when he says that Strabo's "influence was also great in helping Europeans to think of their continent, in spite of its smaller size, as superior to the others...Seeing Europe through pre-Christian eyes at a time of...intense respect for the authors of classical antiquity, encouraged a secular, pragmatic view of its human and natural resources. It was this that...encouraged the topographical, anthropological and historical "Discovery of Europe," which gave Europeans the high ground of information from which they surveyed the larger, but lesser known continents." See John Hale, *The Civilisation of Europe in the Renaissance* (London: Harper Collins, 1993).

[87]In the early years of the 19th century, the university was undergoing a vigorous assault from those opposed to the extreme emphasis placed in England on classical education. Falconer's Strabo was described by Payne Knight in 1809 as a "ponderous monument of operose ignorance and vain expense," and the author was charged with "inaccuracy, ungrammatical Latin and lack of genuine scholarship." Strabo was described by Knight as a "pile of rubbish heaped up with so much labour," harsh words and perhaps not totally disinterested and which is an attack upon Thomas the younger, rather than his uncle, Thomas, of Chester. See *History of University of Oxford*, vol. 5: *18th Century* (Sutherland and Mitchell, 1991).

[88]Frank Brady, *James Boswell: the Later Years* (London: Heineman, 1984), pp. 188-189. Anna Seward, poetess, "The Swan of Lichfield," was daughter of the Rev. Thomas Seward, Canon Residentiary of Lichfield, who lived there in the Bishop's Palace.

[89]Prerogative Court of Canterbury Wills, 1792 Oct. 510.

[90]Foster, *Alumni Oxoniensis*, vol. E-K, p. 445.

[91]*Gentleman's Magazine*, 65: 710.

[92]James Boswell to Dr. Johnson, 22 Oct. 1779, in R. W. Chapman, ed., *Letters of Samuel Johnson* (London: Oxford University Press, 1952), vol. 2, letter 776; G. B. Hill and L. F. Powell, *Boswell's Life of Johnson* (London: Oxford University Press, 1934); Reed and Pottle, *Boswell: Laird of Auchinleck, 1778-1782*, pp. 145-147.

[93]Chapman, ed., *Letters of Samuel Johnson*, vol. 2, letter 76.

[94]Ibid., vol. 2.

[95]Aleyn Lyell Reade, *Johnsonian Gleanings*, Part 1, *Notes on Dr. Johnson's Ancestors and Connexions and Illustrative of His Early Life* (n.p.: for the author, 1909), pp. 13-17.

[96]St. Mary's Lichfield Parish Register.

[97]Readem, *Johnsonian Gleanings*, Part 1: 15n.

[98]*Gentleman's Magazine*, 103: 90; see Falconer Madan, *The Madan Family and Maddens in Ireland and England: A Historical Account* (Oxford: for subscribers at the University Press by John Johnson, 1933), p. 140. Madan, son of the Rt. Rev. Spencer Madan, D.D., Bishop of Bristol, and later of Peterborough, by his wife Lady Charlotte Cornwallis, sister to Charles, 1st Marquess Cornwallis, who, sixteen years earlier, commanded Howe's attack round the American right flank at the Battle of Brandywine in Pennsylvania, on 11 September 1777, in which Frances's fifth cousin, Lieutenant the Hon. William Falconer, of the 15th Foot, was killed.

[99]Julian James Cotton, *List of Inscriptions on Tombs or Monuments in Madras* (Madras: Superintendent, Government Press, 1905), p. 87.

[100]Miss E. H. B. Fairbrother's Indexes and Lists, WO25/802, PRO.

[101]As this is a condensed version of Paul Beresford Weller's *A History of the Family of Falconer in England* (forthcoming), fuller references to statements in this section on William will be found there. Only direct quotations are cited here.

[102]David Garrick to William Falconer, 13 Dec. 1774, 8 Aug. 1775, in: David M. Little and G. M. Kahrl, ed., *The Letters of David Garrick*, vol. 3 (London: Oxford University Press, 1963).

[103]*The Annual Biography and Obituary, for the Year 1825*, vol. 9 (London: for Longman, Hurst, Rees, Orme, Brown, and Green, 1825), p. 413.

[104]Ibid.

[105]Richard Warner, *Literary Recollections* (London: for T. Beckett & P. A. DeHondt, 1830).

[106]Falconer family archives.

[107]J. P. E. Falconer, "Family Events," MS, c.1934.

[108]David and Gillian Falconer, *Dr William Falconer's Early Patronage of Sir Thomas Lawrence, P.R.A.* (Trowbridge, Glocs.: the authors, 1981).

[109]Ibid.

[110]"An Attack upon the French Revolution," dated 22 May 1790, *Bath Chronicle*, 3 June 1790. Unsigned, this was referred to in the contemporary correspondence between William Falconer and Edmund Burke. This article was of just under two thousand words. It appears to have been published on 3 June 1790, and not 2 June, as previously cited elsewhere.

[111]Ibid.

[112]William Falconer to Edmund Burke, Nov. 1790, in: *The Correspondence of Edmund Burke*, vol. 6 (Cambridge: University Press, 1978), pp. 158-160.

[113]Edmund Burke to William Falconer, 14 Nov. 1790.

[114]William Falconer to Edmund Burke, Dec. 1790, WWM Bk 1/2272, 2273, 2294, Sheffield City Archives.

[115]Round Papers, Essex Record Office. A collected edition of these letters by Paul Beresford Weller is in preparation.

[116] *Bath History*, vol. 3: *Radicalism, Loyalism and the 'Reign of Terror' in Bath, 1792-1804*, by S. Poole (Stroud, Glocs.: Alan Sutton, 1990).

[117] Falconer family archives.

[118] Katherine Plymley, *The Diary of Katherine Plymley of Longnor, Salop* (Bath, 1992), 12 Nov. 1796; 26 Nov. 1796; 3 Dec. 1796.

[119] Quoted in: Tom Pocock, *Horatio Nelson* (Bodley Head, London: 1987).

[120] Falconer family archives.

[121] William Falconer, *An Account of the Use, Application, and Success of the Bath Waters in Rheumatic Cases* (Bath: for W. Meyler, and sold by G. G.& J.Robinson, London, 1795).

[122] Quoted in: Sholem Glaser, *The Spirit of Enquiry: Caleb Hillier Parry, MD, FSC* (Stroud, Glocs.: Alan Sutton Pub., 1995), p. .

[123] Ibid.

[124] Falconer family archives.

[125] George Monkland, *The Literature and Literati of Bath* (Bath: R. E. Peach, 1854), p. .

[126] Ibid.

[127] Monkland, *Literature and Literati of Bath*.

[128] Ibid.

[129] Obituary, *Gentleman's Magazine* 94, pt. 2 (1824): 375.

[130] Falconer family archives.

[131] *Bath Chronicle*, 2 September 1824.

[132] St. James Duke Street Parish Register.

[133] All Saints, Weston, Somerset, Parish Register.

[134] *Gentleman's Magazine*, n.s., 16: 220.

[135] J. A. Graham and B. A. Phythian, ed., *The Manchester Grammar School, 1515-1696* (Manchester: University Press, 1965).

[136] Such a late date seems extraordinary, but is apparently correct.

[137] The antiquary George Ormerod was amongst its pupils. The boys occasionally performed plays, and published a collection of Greek and Latin exercises, *Prolusiones Poeticae*, written partly by themselves and partly by Bolland. Subsequently in the early 19th century the school changed in character and 'had become appropriated to the education of the lower orders.' Latin and Greek were no longer taught. See *History of the County of Chester*, Victoria County Histories (London: Oxford University Press, 1980), 3: 230-232.

[138] Foster, *Alumni Oxoniensis*, vol. E-K, p. 445.

[139] Thomas Falconer (1805-1882) Papers.

[140] *Dictionary of National Biography*, s.v. "Falconer, Thomas," by J. M. R.

[141] Ibid.

[142] *Bath & Cheltenham Gazette*, Feb. 1839.

[143] Ibid.

[144] *History of the University of Oxford*, 1980.

[145] *Bath & Cheltenham Gazette*, Feb. 1839.

[146] Foster, *Alumni Oxoniensis*, E-K, p. 446.

[147] Ibid., p. 446.

[148] Parish register of St. James, Bushey, Herts.

[149] *Gentleman's Magazine*, 1: 220.

[150] Parish register of St. James, Bushey, Herts.

[151] *Cimetario degli Allori, Via Senese, Firenze: Records of Deaths and Burials.* The cemetery was established in 1827 outside the à Pinti Gate of Florence on land acquired by the Swiss Evangelical Reformed Church, whose property it remains today. 1,409 burials took place between 1838 and its closure in 1877. Jane Isabella Falconer was interred in a stone-walled tomb, no. 1036, after a service taken by an English priest. She is recorded erroneously as "Isabella Robinson, nee Falconer," in the cemetery records, which were maintained in French (information from Victoria Weller, Florence, 1995).

[152] Manchester Grammar School possesses almost no record of admissions before 1888.

[153] Foster, *Alumni Oxoniensis*, E-K, p. 446.

[154] In the possession of David Falconer of Trowbridge, Wilts.

[155] *Dictionary of National Biography*, s.v. "Falconer, Thomas," by G. F. R. B.

[156] Foster, *Alumni Oxoniensis*, E-K, p. 446.

[157] *Dictionary of National Biography*, s.v. "Falconer, Thomas," by G. F. R. B.

[158] Sir Nikolaus Pevsner, *Buildings of England*, vol. 7: *Hertfordshire* (London: Penguin Books, 1953). The dating is Pevsner's; the initiative for the work is presumptive. William could afford it.

[159] *Dictionary of National Biography*, s.v. "Falconer, Thomas," by G. F. R. B.

[160] Thomas Falconer (1805-1882) Papers.

[161] The source of the attribution of the portrait to G. F. Watts is not known. However, the sitter could well be about thirty-five, when Watts would have been about twenty-three, and 1840 is a likely year for Thomas's likeness to have been taken. The attribution could thus be right.

[162] *Gentleman's Magazine*, n.s., 18 (1842): 536.

[163] Ibid., 29 (1848): 333.

[164] Ibid., 34 (1853): 542.

[165] Correspondence with University of Edinburgh Library.

[166] Grand Lodge, Freemasons Hall, London, List of Members. Randal Wilbraham Falconer joined Lodge of Honour, No. 528, Bath, in 1850, "from Scotland." This lodge was renumbered 379 in 1863.

[167] Wills untraced, 1996.

[168] A rectangular, silver snuff-box approximately three inches by two inches by one inch, heavily chased with scrolling foliage on all four sides and the lid; hallmarked Birmingham, 1847, and made by Nathaniel Mills. Inscribed on the lid, around a falcon perched within a bordure containing the motto *Vive ut Vivas*, the words: "This Box was presented by the Brothers of the Royal Ship & Castle Lodge Tenby No. 2207 of M U —— of the I O F to Randle Wilbraham —— Falconer Esq. M.D. Past Grand of—— the above Lodge for meritorious conduct as an Officer, and also as a token of esteem for his valuable services as Medical Attendant of the Lodge.' *Notes*: a) The spaces above mark the intrusion of the crest into the wording. b) M.U. = Manchester Unity. c) I.O.F. = Independent Order of Oddfellows. d) Past Grand = past chairman. The snuff box is very similar to that illustrated in Peter Waldron, *The Price Guide to Antique Silver*, 2nd ed. (Antique Collectors Club, 1982), pp. 34-35, item 71.

[169] *Dictionary of National Biography*, s.v. "Falconer, Randle Wilbraham," by J. D.

[170] Ibid.

[171] In 1880, an enlarged edition was published in London by Messrs. Churchill.

[172] Egbert Lewis, *History of Royal Sussex Lodge No. 53* (Bath: n.d.). This lodge was founded in 1812. "2 April 1860. Bros. C. J. Vigne and R. W. Falconer, both of The Lodge of Honour, No. 528, were proposed as joining members. A question was asked as to the motives of these brethren in retiring from No. 528. This seems to have been satisfactorily answered as they were elected at the next meeting.' There is no printed history of Lodge of Honour, No. 528. '17 May 1881. An Emergency Lodge was held to pass a vote of condolence on the death of Bro. Falconer, and to communicate the same to his family.'

[173] *Dictionary of National Biography*, s.v. "Falconer, Randle Wilbraham," by J. D.

[174] Register, 1550-1950, Sherborne School, 18 Monk's Park Ave., Bristol 7, which is the source for the records of the other family members who attended this school.

[175] Freemasonry Returns under Act of Parl. 39 Geo. III, Chap. 79, Gloucestershire County Record Office.

[176] Ibid.

[177] Obituary, *Daily Telegraph*, April 1957.

CHAPTER R

Falconar of Drimmie

R1 **Robert Falconar** of Drimmie, in Angus, third son of Alexander Falconer of Halkerton (A5) and Isobel Gray, born perhaps about 1585, was living in 1647.[1]

He married Isobel Rossie, daughter of Patrick Rossie, fiar of that Ilk.[2]

Robert was seised in the lands and barony of Kinnaber on 16 December 1641.[3] In 1643 he was appointed a commissioner for Forfar.[4]

Children of Robert Falconar of Drimmie and Isobel Rossie:

R2   i.   Robert Falconar of Tayock.

      ii.   Patrick Falconar, baptized 2 November 1636 at Montrose.[5]

R2 **Robert Falconar** of Tayock, Angus, born perhaps about 1615, died before 19 January 1670.[6]

He married Agnes Stratoune, relict of John Napier, merchant in Montrose.. On 10 February 1659, Robert Falconer in Tyock and Agnes Straittowne, his spouse, disponed to William Nepar, son to the deceased Johne Nepar, merchant burgess in Montrose, a liferent tack of all their lands lying within the burgh of Montrose.[7]

He seems to be the Robert Falconar who witnessed an obligation of Francis Apparisiis, doctor of physick, and Robert Keith, burgess of Montrose, to Sir Alexander Falconer, fiar of Halkerton, and Robert Falconar of Drimmie, dated 1639.[8] Although not identified as Drimmie's son, it seems probable that he was. On 3 iii [May] 1663, his daughters Sibilla and Elizabeth were seised equally in the lands and town of Tayock, with liferent to their father.[9]

Children of Robert Falconar of Tayock and Agnes Stratoune:[10]

i. Sibilla Falconar, eldest daughter, who married, in a Quaker ceremony on 19 xi [January] 1670, William Napier, merchant and skipper of Montrose,[11] presumably identical to the William Napier above.

ii. Elizabeth Falconar. She married William Ross of Cloak. They were seised in the lands of Cloak, in Lumphanan, Aberdeenshire, in 1672.[12] On 12 December 1685, as relict of William Ross, she was a creditor of the estate of Sir David Falconar of Newton in the annualrent of 3000 merks.[13]

NOTES

[1] Forfar Register of Hornings and Inhibitions, DI57/39, 16 Aug. 1647, SRO.

[2] Ibid., 8 March 1625, cited in: *Scots Peerage*, 5: 246. Not verified.

[3] General Register of Sasines, RS1/50, SRO.

[4] *Acts of Parliaments of Scotland.*

[5] Montrose Old Parish Register.

[6] He was listed as deceased in his daughter Sibilla's marriage record.

[7] Register of Deeds, RD2/7, f. 202, SRO.

[8] Kintore Papers, Bundle 292, Aberdeen University Library.

[9] Register of Sasines for Forfar, RS35/1, f. 262ff., SRO.

[10] Ibid.; Register of Deeds, RD2/7, f. 202, SRO.

[11] Society of Friends, Aberdeen Monthly Meeting records, 2: 7, SRO.

[12] Alistair and Henrietta Taylor, eds., *The Jacobite Cess Roll for the County of Aberdeen in 1715*, p. 55.

[13] Kintore Papers, Bundle 47.

CHAPTER S

Falconer of Little Inverlochtie

S1 **Hew Falconer** of Little Inverlochtie, near Elgin, Morayshire, second son of Alexander Falconer of Halkerton (A4) and Elizabeth Douglas, probably born about 1555, was living in 1624, but died not long before 6 July 1627.

He married, as his first wife, Margaret Falconer, whose family is unidentified. She died in August 1602.[1]

On 5 July 1603, in Elgin, he married, as his second wife, Elspet Hay, eldest daughter of William Hay of Mayne.[2]

In 1589 and 1596, he was styled "of Flenes,"[3] indicating that he probably held that land by wadset from his father. He received a bequest from his aunt (and perhaps godmother) Katharine Falconer, spouse of Hugh Rose of Kilravock, of six bolls of "victual," in 1591.[4] He was "in Innerlochtie" on 2 November 1598, when a bond by Robert Falcouner of Ballandro for Hew in the amount of £1000, not to harm Thomas Hepburn of Innerlochtie, was registered.[5] He and Thomas Hepburn were "landward elderis" of the kirk at Elgin for Mekill Interlochtie, on 24 November 1598; on 15 February 1601, he was a landward elder for Quhytfeild and his part of Mekill Innerlochtie.[6]

On 11 November 1617 in Elgin, Thomas Grant of Cardellis was wounded and Patrick Grant, his son, was killed. Hew Falconer of Innerlochtie, his son Hew, Francis and Alexander Hay, sons of William Hay of Mayne, and others were "dilaitit of airt and pairt" [accused of participation in a crime] by the Privy Coucil in their involvement with this violence.[7] On 12 May 1619, Thomas Grant of Cardaillis and John his son and heir, were under the pain of 3000 merks not to molest Hew Falconner of Innerlochtie, his son Hew, or their tenants and servants.[8] James Reoche shot Hew's servant Alexander Sandiesone with a "pistolett" in September 1618, while stealing a horse belonging to Hew. On 25 February 1620, Reoche was found guilty and ordered to be beheaded.[9] It would seem that this incident was associated with the feud taking place at that time in Kincardineshire between the tenants of the Earl Marischal and those of Sir Alexander Falconer of Halkerton.

He was elected an elder of the Elgin kirk in 1615. In 1621, the kirk elders granted to him to build his seat in the kirk between the choir door and the desk at the south window, to be set up close to the first "grie" [rank], because the Earl of Moray's loft had taken light away from his present seat.[10] Hew was Justice of the Peace for Elgin and Nairn in 1623,[11] and Commissary of Moray in 1624.[12]   He was succeeded in the latter office by Mr. John Hay, whose name was written over Hew Falconer's name in an execution before the Privy Council by Andro McKy on 6 July 1627 against the Commissary of Moray.[13]

Children of Hew Falconer and Margaret Falconer:[14]

S2   i.   Hugh Falconer of Little Inverlochtie.
      ii.   Elspeth Falconer. She perhaps was the wife of Alexander Stewart of Quhytmyre, and, secondly, by 1648, of John Dunbar of Haldoch.[15]
      iii. Jean Falconer. On 2 December 1614, she ratified a promise to marry Robert Fithie in Knokayndoche.[16]

Children of Hew Falconer and Elspet Hay:

      iv.   Alexander Falconer. On 30 June 1624, he was apprenticed to Alexander Muir, skinner, of Edinburgh.[17] Not further traced.
      v.   Christian Falconer, baptized 16 November 1609.[18]

S2 **Hugh Falconer** of Little Inverlochtie was living 12 May 1619.   He probably died between 20 June 1621, when his father was described as "elder," and 25 April 1622, when Francis Doctor Aparisiis was granted liberty to take the seat in Elgin kirk where Hew Falconer's seat was.[19]

He married, on 18 July 1615 at Elgin,[20] Grisel Douglas, daughter of William Douglas of Erlsmilne at Dyke. She was the spouse of Leonard Leslie of Chapelhill on 3 June 1662, when she lent 1000 marks to Margaret Douglas and her husband Mr. John Ross of Pittendreich, on behalf of her daughter Magdalen.[21]

Their only daughter and heir was:

      i.   Magdalen Falconer, living in 1662. She married James Leslie of Arnellie.[22]

NOTES

[1] Testament, Commissariot of Edinburgh, CC8/37, SRO.

[2] William Cramond, *The Records of Elgin, 1234-1800*, vol. 2, Aberdeen University Studies, no. 35 (Aberdeen: for the University, 1908), p. 113.

[3] Obligation, 2 Apr. 1589, Register of Deeds, RD1/31, f. 326, SRO; *Register of the Privy Council*, 5: 291.

[4] Innes, *Family of Rose of Kilravock*, p. 278.

[5] *Register of the Privy Council*, 5: 708.

[6] Cramond, *Records of Elgin 1234-1800*, vol. 2, pp. 67, 87.

[7] Pitcairn, *Criminal Trials in Scotland*, 3: 435f.

[8] *Register of the Privy Council*, 11: 577.

[9] Pitcairn, *Criminal Trials in Scotland*, 3: 484.

[10] Cramond, *Records of Elgin 1234-1800*, vol. 2, pp. 145, 166, 169.

[11] *Register of the Privy Council*, 13: 349.

[12] Ibid., 13: 513.

[13] Ibid., 2nd ser., 2: 552.

[14] Testament of Margaret Falconer, Commissariot of Edinburgh, CC8/37, which names children Hew, Elspeth, and Jean, SRO.

[15] Particular Register of Sasines for Elgin, Forres, and Nairn, RS28/4, ff. 175v., 232, 416, SRO.

[16] Cramond, *Records of Elgin 1234-1800*, 2: 140.

[17] Francis J. Grant, ed., *The Register of Apprentices of the City of Edinburgh, 1583-1666* (Edinburgh: for the Scottish Record Society by James Skinner, 1906), p. 61.

[18] Elgin Parish Register. Patrick Dunbar, "guidman of Kilboyack" was a witness.

[19] Cramond, *Records of Elgin 1234-1800*, 2: 166, 169.

[20] Ibid., 2: 144.

[21] Register of Deeds, RD2/18, f. 175, SRO.

[22] Ibid.

CHAPTER T

Falconer of Kincorth

T1 **Samuel Falconer** of Kincorth, third son of Alexander Falconer of Halkerton (A4) and Elizabeth Douglas, born probably about 1560, died 15 April 1640 and was buried at Auldearn, Nairnshire.[1]

The name of his son's mother is not known.

His title "Master," which he used as early as 1587, when he witnessed his father's testament, indicates formal training in the law. He was chamberlain to the Earl of Moray in 1608[3] and baillie to him in 1610.[4] He was a Member of Parliament for Forres in 1617; Provost of Forres from 1619 to 1621; and Justice of the Peace for Elgin and Nairn in 1623 and 1634.[5] The Privy Council appointed him and Hucheon Ros of Kilravock on 26 July 1631 to try a number of tanners who had refused to adopt a new process of tanning.[6] On 17 September 1634, he received a commission from the Privy Council to apprehend masterless men and thieves.[7]

He was involved in 1604 in a feud which contested the Countess of Erroll's wardship of the earldom of Moray. Styled "Mr. Samuell Falcouner of Ar," he, James Keith, Archibald Falcouner of Fernichtie (U1), and William Douglas of Erlismylne were cautioned in the amount of £1000; William Falcouner in Lethinbar (X1), Hew Falcouner in Lethinbar, William Tulloch in Lethinbar, and Alexander Falcouner in Newtoun of Tarneway in the amount of £500, not to harm the Countess of Erroll. They were also to answer before the Lords of Secret Council to a complaint by the Countess of Erroll that they had come to the castle of Darnaway with arms, taken it by force, and captured a prisoner.[8]

On 7 May 1607, Hew Falconer (S1) of Little Innerlithe was made cautioner in the amount of £1000 that Mr. Samuel Falconer in Air would not harm Johne Lawrie, merchant of Edinburgh.[9] Styled "of Quhytmyre," he disputed fishing rights on the Findhorn with Thomas Urquhart of Burrisyairds, who went before the Privy Council to petition against him, claiming that on 28 June 1607, Samuel and sixty other persons came to Urquhart's fishers and servants and took away salmon, damaged their nets, and struck them with batons and halberds.[10] On 20 August 1610, Walter Kynnaird of Cowbin was cautioner in the amount of £1000 for Alexander Kynnaird of Cowbin, William Dunbar of Brako, and for others, not to harm Mr. Samuell Falconer of Kyncorth.[11]

Either he or his son was probably responsible for the construction of a burial vault in the choir of the kirk at Auldearn, since a monogram with his initials is carved into its side. The inscription on the tablet at its head reads as follows:[12]

THE SEPULCHRE OF THE HONOURABLE AND ANCIENT THE LAIRD OF HALKERTOWN AND LEATIN AND DUNEARN AND HIS FAMILY. 'BLESED AR THE DEAD WHICH DE IN THE LORD HENSEFURTH IS LAID UP FOR ME A CROWN OF RIGHTEOUSNESS O DEATH WHERE IS THY STING. O GRAVE WHERE IS THY VICTORY.'

Falconer tomb at Auldearn kirk, early seventeenth century.

In sixteenth-century Scotland, even after the break with Rome, it was usual for lawyers and ministers to remain unmarried, although they frequently had natural children. Mr. Samuel's natural son, who received letters of legitimization on 24 July 1629, by an unknown mother, was:[13]

T2   i.   William Falconer of Kincorth, born about 1600.

T2 **William Falconer** of Kincorth, born about 1600, died 18 June 1674 in Dyke, Morayshire.
He married, as his first wife, on 19 April 1625,[14] Margaret Tulloch, eldest

daughter and only child of Thomas Tulloch of Tannachie by his wife Isobel Dunbar.[15]   On 22 March 1626, at Elgin, Mr. Samuel Falconer gave Margaret Tulloch a sasine for land.[16]

He married, as his second wife, Katherine Sutherland, daughter of John Sutherland of Kinstearie by his wife Lilias Hay. She died 24 August 1668. By a bond of provision with precept of sasine to James Sutherland in Kinstearie dated 2 June 1669, William and his eldest son Thomas were obliged to pay to his children John, Hugh, Robert, Jean, Helen, Katharin, and Grisell 9000 merks, 3000 to John, the eldest son of his second marriage, and 1000 each to each of the other children.[17]

Educated at King's College, Aberdeen, receiving the degree of M.A. in 1617, he was appointed minister of Dyke. On 16 May 1625, his father gave him a charter of the lands of Kincorth. He was presented by Charles, Earl of Dunfermline, and his tutor, George, Earl of Winton, in July, and ordained before 25 October 1625. William Falconer was a member of the Assemblies of the Church of Scotland in 1638 and 1639. He subscribed the Marquess of Huntly's Bond, in July 1646, alleging that he was compelled to do so.   He was appointed by Parliament one of the Visitors to the University of Aberdeen in 1649, and gave a donation towards the erection of King's College, in 1658.[18] He was parson of Moy in 1642.[19]

For many years, one of his parishioners in Dyke was Alexander Brodie of Brodie, who kept a diary all his life. What survives of this diary, fair or not, provides most of our knowledge of Falconer's character and beliefs. On 5 November 1655, for example, Brodie met with Ninian Dunbar of Grangehill and William Falconer of Kincorth, and "found much corruption and addictednes to self will" in the issue over which they met.[20] Brodie occasionally took comfort in his preaching, although on 8 June 1656, he remarked "Oh that the Lord would give him the tongue of the learned!"[21] Visiting him on 22 August 1673, during an illness, Falconer "exprest much sence and tendernes on the divisions and breaches in the Church of Scotland" and renounced Episcopacy, "in obedienc to an ecclesiastick ordinanc, not as contrari to the word of God."[22]

Children of William Falconer and Margaret Tulloch:[23]

i.   Alexander Falconer, buried 23 May 1635 at Dyke.

ii. Thomas Falconer of Kincorth, his heir, baptized 27 December 1635 at Dyke.[24] He married, on 10 February 1662 in Edinburgh,[25] Alison Kellie, daughter of James Kellie, portioner of Coldinghame.   He pursued an action on 10 and 11 February 1669 against Alexander Hume of Lanthill and others for stealing, in March 1666, twenty bolls of bear [barley] and oats from his barns of Hallydown and thirty bolls of oats, bear, peas, and wheat, from his barnyard in Coldingham.[26] On 22 June 1680, he was served heir to his mother, Margaret Tulloch.[27] He was commissioner of the assessment for Berwickshire in 1686.[28] On 12 February 1694, he discharged his brothers and sisters Mr. John, Mr. Robert, Katheran, and Grissell or the heirs of Hugh and Helen Falconar, for any intromissions they might have had belonging to the estate of their father.[29] He was served heir-male to his father Mr. William Falconer of Kincorth on 29 August 1694, in the town and lands of Drumriach, in Dyck.[30] There seems to have been no issue.

iii. Samuel Falconer, buried 21 August 1638 at Dyke.

iv. Christian Falconer. She married, by contract dated July 1665,[31] Thomas

Allan, burgess of Forres.

v. Lilias Falconer. She married, at Dyke on 6 November 1665,[32] Thomas Craig, minister of St. Andrews. As an episcopalian, he refused to take oaths to William and Mary. After leaving St. Andrews, they lived in Elgin, and had issue, surname *Craig*:[33] a. *James*, a writer in Elign, married, by license 20 July 1708, Agnes King, sister of Jean King, who married Alexander Falconar (X7); b. *Thomas*, a merchant.

Children of William Falconer and Katherine Sutherland:[34]

vi. John Falconer. Educated at King's College, Aberdeen (M.A., 1670); he was signet and clerk of the parish of Dyke, in 1671, and schoolmaster of Dyke. Alexander Brodie of Brodie complained in his diary that he had "weak gifts" and a "lifeles dead ministri."[35] He was living 12 February 1694.

vii. Hugh Falconer, died before 12 February 1694.

viii. Helen Falconer, died before 12 February 1694.

ix. Grisel Falconer, living 12 February 1694.

x. Robert Falconer, baptized 4 or 6 October 1663,[36] living 12 February 1694, and styled "Mr." He was probably a minister.

xi. Colin Falconer, baptized 1 February 1665,[37] died before 2 June 1669.

xii. Katharine Falconer, baptized 9 September 1666,[38] living 12 February 1694.

SOURCES

[1] Dyke Parish Register.

[2] Particular Register of Sasines for Elgin, Forres, and Nairn, RS29/3, f. 51, SRO. This reference, however, is ambiguous, as it may refer to Margaret Tulloch, wife of William Falconer of Kincorth.

[3] *Book of the Thanes of Cawdor*, p. 223.

[4] *Register of the Privy Council*, 8: 476.

[5] Ibid., 8: 346; 2nd ser., 5: 429.

[6] Ibid., 2nd ser., 4: 295.

[7] Ibid., 2nd ser., 5: 363.

[8] Ibid., 2nd ser., 6: 819.

[9] Ibid., 7: 673.

[10] Ibid., 14: 494.

[11] Ibid., 8: 476.

[12] George Bain, *History of the Parish of Auldearn*, p. 62. The inscription is rather worn today.

[13] *Register of the Great Seal*, vol. 8: *1620-1633*, no. 1465, p. 494.

[14] Hew Scott, *Fasti Ecclesiae Scoticanae: The Succession of Ministers in the Church of Scotland from the Reformation*, new ed. (Edinburgh: Oliver and Boyd, 1926), 8: 642.

[15] Particular Register of Sasines for Elgin, Forres, and Nairn, RS28/4, f. 271, SRO.

[16] Ibid., RS28/3, f. 51, SRO.

[17] Ibid., RS29/2, f. 79, SRO.

[18] Scott, *Fasti Ecclesiae Scoticanae*, new ed., 6: 416.

[19] Particular Register of Sasines for Elgin, Forres, and Nairn,, RS28/4, f. 271, SRO.

[20] *The Diary of Alexander Brodie of Brodie, MDCLII-MDCLXXX, and of His Son James Brodie of Brodie, MDCLXXX-MDCLXXXV* (Aberdeen: for the Spalding Club, 1858), p. 167.

[21] Ibid., p. 182.

[22] Ibid., p. 344.

[23]Dyke Parish Register; Scott, *Fasti Ecclesiae Scoticanae*, 6: 416.

[24]Dyke Parish Register.

[25]Edinburgh Old Parish Register.

CHAPTER U

Falconer of Coltfield

U1 Archibald Falconer, fourth son of Alexander Falconer of Halkerton (A4) and Elizabeth Douglas, portioner of Coltfield, in the parish of Alves, Morayshire, died before 3 February 1631, when his son James was served heir.[1]

His wife was Jean Dunbar, whose parentage is unknown.

One of the barons and gentlemen of Moray who mustered at the Carne of Kilboyak in 1595 in response to a proclamation by the King, he appeared with one jack and one spear.[2] Styled "of Fernichtie," he was involved in the 1604 feud over wardship of the Earldom of Moray between the Falconers and others with the Countess of Erroll, which saw the Falconers take the castle of Darnaway by force. Archibald Falconer in Easter Alves and Jeane Dunbar, his spouse, complained to the Privy Council on 20 December 1610 that William Dunbar of Hemprigis, Patrick Dunbar of Conzie, and Alexander Dunbar of Kilboyaik, remained "unrelaxed" from a horning of 22 August 1610.[3] He was Justice of the Peace for Elgin and Forres in 1623.[4] On 24 June 1624, Archibald Falconer in Easter Alves was cautioned in the amount of 300 merks by Hew Falconer, Commissary of Moray, not to intercommune with John Dunbar, younger, of Hemprigis.[5]

Issue of Archibald Falconer and Jean Dunbar:

U2   i.   James Falconer, portioner of Coltfield.

V1   ii.   John Falconer of Tulloch, later of Phesdo, warden of the Scottish mint.

    iii.   Jean Falconer. She married John Kinnaird of Culbin, son of Walter Kinnaird of Culbin. On 12 April 1655, her daughter's marriage contract was written by John Falconer, warden, and witnessed by James Falconer of Coltfield. Issue, surname *Kinnaird*:[6] a. *Jean*, married George Innes of Caldcoats.

    iv.   Magdalen Falconer. She married, as her first husband, Peter Mortimer in Auldrochtie, and, in 1637 or shortly after, as her second husband, Mark Mawer, portioner of Urquhart.[7]

    v.   Ursula Falconer, youngest daughter. She married, by 30 November 1635, George Innes of Wasthill of Pluscarden.[8]

U2 James Falconer, portioner of Coltfield, born perhaps about 1605, died 21 January 1665 in Alves, Morayshire.[9]

His first wife was Jonet Dougall, probably the natural daughter of John Dougall, merchant burgess of Edinburgh. She received letters of legitimation from him on 14 April 1632,[10] an act which was probably in preparation for her marriage.

He married, as his second wife, Jonet Dunbar. Their contract of marriage provided his heirs to provide her and the heirs of this marriage with the sum of 5000 merks, and a bond of provision, dated 10 November 1651, infefted her and her male heirs in the lands of Coltfield "sumtyme pertainieng to James Spence of Alveskirktoun."[11]

He married, as his third wife, on 2 August 1657 at Alves, Marjorie Dunbar, daughter of Sir Alexander Dunbar.[12]   She married, as her second husband, John Campbell of Achindoune.[13]

He was served heir to his father on 3 February 1631, in two eighths of the town and lands of Coutfould, in the barony of Kinlos.[14] He and John Falconer, presumably his brother, witnessed the disposition, on 1 June 1631, of William Innes of Blackhills to John Dougall, burgess of Edinburgh, of Mill of Meff, called Mill of Langhills, and multures of Over and Nether Mefts.[15]   On 26 September 1633, he and his spouse Jonet Dougall were seised in one-eighth of the lands of Cautfauld.[16]   He was named a Commissioner of War for Elgin and Forres in 1648.[17]

Issue of James Falconer and Jonet Dougall:[18]

U3 i.   Alexander Falconer, portioner of Coltfield, later of Corsbie, born about 1636.

ii. Margaret Falconer. She married, by contract dated 3 September 1654,[19] John Tulloch, baillie of Nairn.

iii. Marjorie Falconer. She married, by contract dated 30 October 1656,[20] Patrick Dunbar, apparent of Eisterbin. On 20 April 1657, according to the provisions of the marriage contract, she was seised in the Westerkirklands of Moy, with precept directed to John Tulloch, baillie of Nairn.[21]

iv. Agnes Falconer. She married, on 10 January 1660 at Alves, by contract dated 4 December 1659,[22] John Dunbar, fiar of Boiggis. As she was alive then, another "Annas," daughter of James Falconer of Coltfield, died 31 January 1664.[23]

Issue of James Falconer and Jonet Dunbar:[24]

v.   Archibald Falconer, baptized August 1649 at Alves,[25] was served heir of provision to his father on 20 October 1671. He studied from 1663 to 1667 at King's College, Aberdeen.[26] Living 21 August 1672,[27] but not further traced.

vi. Jean Falconer, living 6 December 1672.[28]

Issue of James Falconer and Marjorie Dunbar:[29]

vii. Christian Falconer. She, Marjorie, and Beatrix were served as portionary heirs of James Falconer of Coltfield, on 12 April 1678.[30]

viii. Marjorie Falconer, baptized 29 July 1658, died young.[31]

ix. Marjorie Falconer, baptized 29[?] May 1661.[32]

x.   Elizabeth Falconer, baptized 28 July 1662, died young.

xi. Beatrix Falconer, baptized 3 March 1664.

U3 **Sir Alexander Falconer,** portioner of Coltfield, later of Corsbie, born about 1636, died 23 October 1716, aged about 80, was buried at St. Germain-en-Laye, Seine-et-Oise, France.[33] His knighthood was probably granted by the Jacobite claimant, James II, or his heir.

He married, by 1664, Jean Raith, daughter of James Raith of Edmistoun, by Margaret, sister of Sir John Wauchop of Niddrie.[34] Jean was buried 27 March 1685 at Greyfriars, Edinburgh.[35]

He was served heir to his father on 22 May 1666, in four-eighths of the town and lands of Coltfold.[36] By 1672, he was seised of the lands of Corsbie.[37] As "obstinat Papists," he and his wife were summoned to appear before the Presbytery of Alves in 1666, but did not.[38] His religion thus leaves little doubt that he was Sir Alexander Falconer, quartermaster-general to the exiled Stuart pretender, who lived in exile at the Jacobite court in France after 1690. He appears as a witness in the parish register of St. Germain-en-Laye in 1694, 1695, and 1697.[39]

Issue of Alexander Falconer of Corsbie and Jean Raith:[40]

i. James Falconer, eldest son, living 14 July 1664, probably dead by 29 June 1671, as he was not named in a deed in which Andrew Wauchop, fiar of Nidrie, agreed to pay a debt of 4000 merks to Alexander Falconer and Jean Raith, his spouse, and failing them, to their children Andro, George, and Margaret.[41]

ii. Andrew Falconer. It is uncertain whether he or other sons of Sir Alexander survived to adulthood, but it is worth noting here that one *Capitaine* Falconer was among the official list of Jacobite exiles who arrived at Avignon, France, on 2 April 1716.[42]

iii. George Falconer.

iv. Margaret Falconer.

v. Archibald Falconer, born about 1673. Described as son of Alexander, from London, he enrolled at the Scots College at Douai, France, 18 September 1688.[43]

NOTES

[1] *Inquisitiones*, vol. 1, no. 53.

[2] *Register of the Privy Council*, 14: 377.

[3] *Register of the Privy Council*, 9: 105. Hempriggs is next to Coltfield. William Dunbar of Hempriggs was the natural son of Alexander Dunbar of Conzie, who was son of James Dunbar of Conzie, who was son of Alexander Dunbar of Conzie and Kilboyak, the presumed father of Mariot Dunbar who married David Falconer of Halkerton.

[4] Ibid., 13: 349.

[5] Ibid., 13: 513.

[6] Forbes, *Ane Account of the Families of Innes*, p. 243. Her brothers' involvement in this transaction leads to her placement here, although there is no proof that she was Archibald's daughter.

[7] Ibid.; RS28/4, ff. 129, 227, SRO.

[8] Particular Register of Sasines for Sheriffdoms of Elgin, Forres and Nairn, RS28/4, ff. 80, 142, SRO.

[9] Alves Parish Register.

[10] *Register of the Great Seal*, 1620-1633, p. 670.

[11] Register of Deeds, RD2/37, f. 441ff., SRO.

[12] Alves Parish Register.

430   *FALCONER OF COLTFIELD*

[13] Particular Register of Sasines for Sheriffdoms of Elgin, Forres, and Nairn, RS29/3, f. 27, SRO.

[14] *Inquisitiones*, vol. 1, no. 53.

[15] Sir Thomas Innes of Learney, *Inventory of the Principal Progress-Writs of the Barony of Innes 1225-1767*, Scottish Record Society, part 153 (Edinburgh: for the Society by J. Skinner, 1948), p. 55.

[16] Particular Register of Sasines for Sheriffdoms of Elgin, Forres, and Nairn, RS28/4, f. 11ff., SRO.

[17] *Acts of the Parliaments of Scotland*, 6, pt. 2: 33.

[18] *Inquisitiones*, vol. 1: no. 120; vol. 2: nos. 5467, 6071; Alves Parish Register.

[19] Alves Parish Register.

[20] Ibid.

[21] Particular Register of Sasines for Sheriffdoms of Elgin, Forres, and Nairn, RS28/5, f. 269v., SRO.

[22] Alves Parish Register.

[23] Ibid.

[24] Register of Deeds, RD2/37, f. 441ff., SRO.

[25] Alves Parish Register.

[26] P. J. Anderson, *Roll of Alumni in Arts of the University and King's College of Aberdeen, 1596-1860*, Aberdeen University Studies 1 (Aberdeen: for the University, 1900), p. 26.

[27] Register of Deeds, RD 2/37, f. 441ff., SRO.

[28] Ibid., RD2/34, f. 784., SRO.

[29] Particular Register of Sasines for Sheriffdoms of Elgin, Forres, and Nairn, RS29/3, f. 27, SRO.

[30] *Inquisitiones*, vol. 2, no. 6071.

[31] Alves Parish Register.

[32] Ibid.

[33] Etat Civil, Registre des actes de decés, cited in: Thomas Falconer, *The Family of Dalmahoy of Dalmahoy, Ratho, County of Edinburgh* (London: C. W. Reynell, 1870), p. 35.

[34] Register of Deeds, RD3/23, f. 364ff., SRO.

[35] Paton, ed., *Register of Interments in the Greyfriars Burying-Ground, Edinburgh, 1658-1700*, p. 212.

[36] *Inquisitiones*, 1: no. 120.

[37] Register of Deeds, RD2/37, f. 441ff., SRO.

[38] William Cramond, *The Church of Alves* (Elgin: "Courant and Courier" Office, 1900), p. 40.

[39] C. E. Lart, ed., *The Parochial Registers of Saint Germain-en-Laye: Jacobite Extracts of Births, Marriages and Deaths*, vol. 1, *1689-1702* (London: St. Catherine Press, 1910).

[40] Register of Deeds, RD2/37, p. 645, RD3/23, p. 364, SRO. I have been unable to locate notarial records for Alexander, but if any of his children left descendants, they would presumably have lived in France.

[41] Register of Deeds, RD2/37, p. 645, SRO.

[42] R. W. Twigge, "Jacobite Papers at Avignon," *Scottish Historical Review* 10 (1913): 61.

[42] *Records of the Scots Colleges at Douai, Rome, Madrid, Valladolid and Ratisbon*, Vol. 1: *Registers of Students* (Aberdeen: for the New Spalding Club, 1906), p. 60.

CHAPTER V

Falconer of Phesdo

PARATUS AD AETHERA

fon falconer

V1   **John Falconer** of Tulloch and later of Phesdo, second son of Archibald Falconer, portioner of Coltfield, Morayshire (U1), was born perhaps about 1610 and died shortly before 2 October 1682 at Phesdo, in the parish of Fordoun, Kincardineshire.

He married Agnes Spens, daughter of James Spens of Alves Kirktoun, in Alves, Morayshire, by Agnes Tulloch, his wife.

Joining his cousin John Falconer, Master of the Mint, and indicating how important kinship remained in Scottish government, he was appointed Warden of the Scottish Mint in 1643, and he was granted the gift of that office again, on 17 January 1662.[1] This office required its holder to be present at the allaying of the metals; to enter the amounts of bullion brought in to the mint and the amount of money coined; to have custody of the irons and dies; to superintend the sizing, making, and weighing the money; and to keep one of the keys of the chest in which the money was placed until the trials were taken.[2]

The mint was inactive during the Interregnum, and he must have lived on his lands of Tulloch, in Alves, Morayshire, as his children were baptized at Alves between 1649 and 1663 and he was styled "of Tulloch." On 26 May 1649, John and Agnes were seised in two-eighths of the lands of Cautfald, having the alienation of precept of sasine from James Spens of Alves Kirktoun, with consent of Agnes Tulloch his spouse.[3] On 24 June 1650, he renounced his fourth part of the town and lands of Coltfield in favor of James Spens of Alves Kirktoun, and Agnes Spens, his spouse, received 5000 merks.[4] From this we can infer that he was the son of Archibald Falconer, who held a portion of the lands of Coltfield.

He had acquired Phesdo by 13 January 1670, when he was appointed a justice of the peace for Kincardineshire.[5] He was of Phesdo when he matriculated his arms, as follows: Or, a hawk's head issuing from an heart proper betwixt three mollets azure all within a bordure of the second charged with eight pleats.[6] As he was an "old infirm man," the Privy Council appointed, in his place, on 24 February 1681, Mr. James Falconer, "now of Phaesdo," commissioner of excise and justice of the peace in Kincardineshire.[7] He retired from the office of Warden before 26 January 1682, when described as "John Falconer of Tulloch late princ[ll] warden," Alexander Maitland taking his place.[8]

On 2 October, 1682, the King issued a warrant to prosecute the officers of the mint before the Lords of Session.[9] As the oldest officer, John Falconer, the former warden, had been under particular suspicion, since the Privy Council's commission believed he could have taught the other officers methods of embezzlement.[10] Sir John Lauder of Fountainhall noted the rumor in government circles that, upon hearing the news of this action, Falconer died suddenly of "heart-break," although "some averred he hanged himselfe in his stable." On 24 November 1682, the Treasurer put up the gift of his moveable escheat, as *felo de se*, and gave it to Hugh Wallace, writer.[11]

Issue of John Falconer of Tulloch by Agnes Spens:[12]

V2 i. Sir James Falconer of Phesdo, born 16 August 1648.

ii. Archibald Falconar, baptized 23 September 1649,[13] died at the house of Robert Falconar and was buried 28 September 1687 at St. Andrew Undershaft, London.[14] Apprenticed to Robert Mitchell, merchant of Edinburgh, on 30 August 1665,[15] he was a merchant in Edinburgh. On 10 January 1682, a warrant was issued for a gift to him of the office of counterwarden of the Mint,[16] and on 26 January 1682, the office was granted, with a monthly salary of £3,6s.,8d.[17] On 2 October 1682, a warrant was issued to prosecute him and the other officers of the Mint.[18]

iii. daughter, baptized November 1651.[19]

iv. John Falconer, baptized 10 September 1654, died, without issue, 21 January 1679 in St. Clement Eastcheap, London, was buried 23 January 1678/9 at St. Andrew Undershaft, London.[20] He was apprenticed to James Stewart, merchant of Edinburgh, on 18 November 1668.[21] He was admitted to the burgess roll of Edinburgh on 2 February 1676.[22] On 29 May 1677, he was named "ensigneer" of a company of young merchants, to muster on the King's birthday, in order to control a demonstration of weapon showing by merchant youth on that day.[23] In his testament, he appointed his brother Mr. James Falconer, advocate in Edinburgh, executor and administrator and nominated his "cussing" Robert Falconer (G3) the charge of his funeral; he also mentioned George Falconer, merchant burgess of Edinburgh.[24]

W1 v. Patrick Falconar, a merchant who settled in Newark, New Jersey, born about 1658.

vi. Anna Falconer, baptized 16 March 1659.

vii. Alexander Falconer, baptized 4 October 1660, probably died young.

viii. Marjorie Falconer, baptized 10 July 1663.

V3 ix. Charles Falconer, born, say, 1672.

V2 **Sir James Falconer** of Phesdo, born 16 August 1648, probably in Alves, Morayshire, died 9 June 1706 in Edinburgh, was buried at Greyfriars.[25]

He married Elizabeth Trent, daughter of Maurice Trent, a Quaker merchant in Leith, and Margaret Young, baptized 7 January 1655 at South Leith, died July 1748.

He was apprenticed on 16 December 1663 to David Mitchell, merchant in Edinburgh,[26] although he later entered law as a profession. He was granted a charter of the lands of Phesdo, in Kincardineshire, on 1 March 1672.[27] On 10 May 1683, the Lords of Session fined him, as his father's heir, six years' rent of his entire personal and real estate.[28] He paid his father's debts resulting from the charges of malversation against him and other officers of the mint, and, on 4 April 1685, he received a discharge from the Crown.[29]

He was admitted to the Faculty of Advocates on 6 January 1674.[30] Unlike the rest of his family, Sir James strongly supported the cause of William of Orange and rose high in the Scottish government following his succession. He was appointed a Commissioner of Justiciary on 16 January 1690; Auditor of Treasury, in 1690, 1692, 1695, 1696, 1697, 1698, and 1701; Commissioner of Justiciary for the Highlands, 20 December 1693; Privy Councillor, 21 October 1698, 4 February 1703, and 17 November 1704; Auditor of Admiralty Accounts, 20 December 1698; Commissioner for the Union, 25 August 1702; and Commissioner of the Exchequer, 17 November 1704.[31] He served as Senator of the College of Justice, his highest honor, for several years. He was also one of the Lords of the Criminal Court.

He was admitted to the burgess roll of Edinburgh on 18 July 1694.[32] On 28 February 1695, he, his wife, and son John were granted a charter of the lands of Laurenston.[33] He was a Commissioner for Kincardineshire in 1704.[34]

On 24 December 1738, Elizabeth Trent executed a bond of tailzie on the lands of Balmakettle and others, in the parish of Fettercairn, Kincardineshire. The petition was entered on 6 June 1752 by James Falconer of Monkton, who claimed those lands, as her son John, grandson James, and son James had died without issue.[35]

Issue of Sir James Falconer of Phesdo and Elizabeth Trent:[36]

i. John Falconer of Phesdo, baptized 21 October 1674, died, unmarried, 21 November 1764 in South Leith. He was admitted to the Faculty of Advocates, 21 January 1700. He was appointed a Commissioner of Justiciary for the Highlands, 30 May 1701.[37] On 18 February 1702, he was admitted to the burgess roll of Edinburgh.[38] He was Commissioner for Kincardineshire in 1702 and 1704.[39] On 26 April 1711, he was served heir to his father.[40] He then disappears from Scottish politics until 1734, when he began to serve as Member of Parliament for Kincardineshire until 1741.[41] He petitioned the Edinburgh Town Council on 28 June 1742 for a small addition to the burial place in Greyfriars purchased for the late Sir James Falconer, Lord Phesdo.[42] On 29 July 1751, he was served heir-special to his father in the lands of Pitnamoon, Dronachmyre, Mill of Kincardine, Phesdo, Broadland, Auchkernie, etc., in Kincardineshire.[43] According to a 19th-century story, his father disinherited him and he disappeared, possibly serving in the French army, then returning to England, where he worked as a farmer's servant. He returned to Scotland not long before his election as Member of Parliament for Kincardineshire and claimed his fortune. He was an avid golfer and a "very facetious, pleasing" companion.[44] Since John was served heir to his father, he was not disinherited, but at this period we might speculate that, unlike his father, the son supported the Stuart cause and may indeed have gone to France to serve in a Jacobite regiment.

V4   ii.   Alexander Falconer of Kipps and of Hillhead.

iii.   Margaret Falconer, baptized 2 August 1678. She married John Arbuthnot of Fordoun, who died in 1737, and had issue, surname *Arbuthnot*:[45] a. *James*, died, unmarried, 1727; b. *John*, afterwards 6th Viscount Arbuthnott; c. *Thomas*, of Balglassie, died 1767, married Margaret Forbes; d. *Elizabeth*, died 16 April 1775; e. *Margaret*, died 25 December 1779; f. *Jean*, died 19 July 1781; g. *Anne*, died 15 February 1777; h. *Mary*, died 25 May 1783, married John Douglas of Tilwhilly; i. *Catherine*, died 28 January 1775, married James Moir of Invernettie.

iv.   David Falconer. He was alive in 1694.[46]

v.   Elizabeth Falconer, baptized 17 March 1685. She married Thomas Arbuthnot, merchant in Edinburgh, who died in November 1745, and had issue, surname *Arbuthnot*:[47] a. *James*, of Finnart, died 1747; b. *Robert*; c. *Anne*; d. *Elizabeth*; e. *Mary*, died 25 March 1754, married, 22 July 1750, Robert Arbuthnot.

vi.   Mary Falconer, baptized 8 March 1687, died 26 March 1767. She married, 22 April 1711, Patrick Falconer of Monkton (P1), son of John Falconer of Newton, and had issue.

vii.   James Falconer, Lieutenant, Lieutenant-General Kerr's Regiment of Dragoons, baptized 24 September 1689, was killed at the battle of Dettingen, Germany, in June, 1743.[48] He was commissioned a cornet, 11 January 1714, and a lieutenant, 25 October 1731.[49]

viii.   Agnes Falconer, baptized 8 June 1691, probably dead by 1717.

ix.   Helen Falconer, born 23 January 1693, died, unmarried, before 19 July 1786, when Margaret Falconer and Alexander Anderson, her niece and great-nephew, were served heirs portioner general.[50]

x.   Maurice Falconer, baptized 25 June 1696, died young.

xi.   Maurice Falconer, born 21 December 1697, died December 1714.[51]   On 7 November 1717, his brother Alexander Falconer, advocate, was served heir.[52]

xii.   William Falconer, merchant in Edinburgh, died, unmarried, in 1733.[53]

V3 **Charles Falconer**, born, say, 1672, was living in 1708 in London.

He married, on 23 June 1693 in St. George Southwark, Surrey, Sarah Dogood.[54]

He was apprenticed to Hew Brown, chirurgeon-apothecary of Edinburgh, on 1 December 1686.[55] Called "Doctor" in the baptismal records of his children, we can assume he went from Edinburgh to London at the end of his apprenticeship. He witnessed the marriage in 1705 of John Falconar (H2) and Anna Quare.

Issue of Charles and Sarah (Dogood) Falconer:[56]

i.   Henry Falconer, born 26 January 1699/1700 in Basing Lane. Not further traced, unless perhaps he was the "Henry Fawkner a young Gent" buried 25 April 1709 from St. Andrew's parish in St. Dunstans in the West, London.

ii.   Ann Falconer, born 23 November 1701, died, unmarried, shortly before 10 January 1777. The will of Ann Falconer, "spinster," of St. George Hanover Square, gave her estate to her niece Elizabeth Birchall.[57]

iii.   Elizabeth Falconer, born about 1702. She married, 12 February 1725,[58] George

Birchall. At the time of her marriage, she resided in Chelsea, Middlesex.[59] Issue, surname *Birchall*: a. *Elizabeth*.

iv. Charles Falconer, baptized 13 June 1708.[60] Not further traced.

V4 Alexander Falconer of Hillhead, died February 1728 at Kipps, parish of Torphichen, Linlithgowshire.[61]

He married, as his first wife, 12 April 1708, Elizabeth Colquhoun, only daughter of Sir James Colquhoun of Luss, 4th Baronet, by Penuel Cunningham. She died in 1709 in Edinburgh.[62]

He married, as his second wife, 4 October 1716, Elizabeth Sibbald, daughter of Sir Robert Sibbald of Kipps, the noted physician, and Anna Orrock, baptized 10 April 1685 in Edinburgh; Through her he inherited Kipps.

He married, as his third wife, 10 August 1720, Jean Ramsay, daughter of Rev. Alexander Ramsay, one of the ministers of Edinburgh.

Admitted to the Faculty of Advocates, 21 February 1701,[63] Alexander Falconer's legal abilities were held in esteem by Barbara Jaffray, widow of Sir John Falconar (G2), who called him in 1717 a "man of Knowledge and Integrity."[64]

Issue of Alexander Falconer and Elizabeth Colquhoun:[65]

i. Elizabeth Falconer, born 18 January 1709. She married Hugh Anderson, writer in Edinburgh, and had issue, surname *Anderson*: a. *Alexander* of Udole.

Issue of Alexander Falconer and Elizabeth Sibbald:[66]

ii. James Falconer, Ensign, General Sinclair's Regiment, born 24 September 1717, died, without issue, 21 February 1742 in Chelsea.[67] His sister Margaret, spouse of Thomas Tulloch of Bridgetoun was his heir.[68]

iii. Margaret Falconer. She was divorced from Thomas Tulloch, merchant in Edinburgh, by decreets 3 December 1756 and 11 February 1757.[69] She and Alexander Anderson of Udole were served heirs portioner general to her aunt and his grandaunt Helen Falconer, 19 July 1786.[70]

Issue of Alexander Falconer and Jean Ramsay:[71]

iv. Alexander Falconer, baptized 19 July 1721, died young.

v. Maurice Falconer, born 6 November 1722, died young.

NOTES

[1] Register of the Privy Seal, PS3/1, p. 163f., SRO.

[2] Cochran-Patrick, *Records of the Coinage of Scotland*, 1: xxiv.

[3] Particular Register of Sasines for Elgin, Forres, and Nairn, RS28/4/458, SRO.

[4] Ibid., RS28/5/37, SRO.

[5] *Register of the Privy Council*, 3rd ser., 3: 124.

[6] Scotland, Lord Lyon, Public Register of All Arms and Bearings in Scotland, 1: 304.

[7] *Register of the Privy Council*, 2nd series, 7: 44.

[8] Register of the Privy Seal, PS3/3, f. 386, SRO.

[9] *Calendar of State Papers (Domestic Series)*, vol. *1682*, p. 451.

[10] Patrick Ogilvie to Sir John Falconar, 13 Oct. 1682, Moses Bundle 254/7793a, Edinburgh District Archives.

[11] Lauder of Fountainhall, *Historical Notices of Scottish Affairs*, 1: 376.

[12] Baptisms in Alves Parish Register. Proof for the others comes from the Edinburgh apprenticeship rolls (see note 15) and from the fact that James was the heir of John Falconer of Phesdo.

[13] Alves Parish Register. The name of the child is off the fragmentary page, but, as one of the witnesses was Archibald Dunbar, it is likely that the child was named Archibald.

[14] St. Andrew Undershaft Parish Register.

[15] Grant, ed., *The Register of Apprentices of the City of Edinburgh, 1583-1666*, p. 61.

[16] Great Britain, *Calendar of State Papers (Domestic)*, vol. *1682*, p. 21.

[17] Register of the Privy Seal, PS3/3, f. 386, SRO.

[18] Great Britain, *Calendar of State Papers (Domestic)*, vol. *1682*, p. 451.

[19] The name is off the fragmentary page of the register.

[20] Testament, Commissariot of Edinburgh, CC8/3/76, SRO; Register of St. Andrew Undershaft.

[21] Charles B. Boog Watson, ed., *Register of Edinburgh Apprentices, 1666-1700* (Edinburgh: for the Scottish Record Society by J. Skinner, 1929), p. 32. Two sons of John Falconer of Tulloch named John appear on the apprentice register of Edinburgh; the earlier one, apprenticed to David Mitchell in 1663, must either be James or another John.

[22] Watson, *Roll of Edinburgh Burgesses, 1406-1700*, p. 177.

[23] Lauder, *Historical Notices of Scottish Affairs*, 1: 152.

[24] Testament, Commissariot of Edinburgh, CC8/3/76, SRO.

[25] Brown, *Epitaphs and Monumental Inscriptions in Greyfriars Churchyard, Edinburgh*, p. 244.

[26] Grant, ed., *The Register of Apprentices of the City of Edinburgh, 1583-1666*, p. 61. He is named as "John," which must be a clerical error, as there is no apprenticeship indenture for James and the father clearly did not have two sons with the same name.

[27] Register of the Great Seal, C2 /63/59, SRO.

[28] Lauder, *Historical Notices of Scottish Affairs*, 1: 439.

[29] Register of the Privy Seal, PS3/3/642, SRO.

[30] Grant, ed., *The Faculty of Advocates in Scotland*, p. 69.

[31] Register of the Great Seal, C2/13/15, 58; C2/14/1, 63, 123, 185, 214, 233, 240, 241; C2/15/39, 66, 86, 155, 156, SRO.

[32] Watson, *Roll of Edinburgh Burgesses, 1406-1700*, p. 177.

[33] Register of the Greal Seal, C2/73/185, SRO.

[34] *Acts of the Parliaments of Scotland*, 2: 145.

[35] Register of Tailzies, RT1/12, f. 40ff., SRO.

[36] Baptisms in Edinburgh Parish Register.

[37] Register of the Great Seal, C2/15/36, SRO.

[38] Watson, *Roll of Edinburgh Burgesses, 1701-1760*, p. 67.

[39] *Acts of the Parliaments of Scotland*, 2: 23, 149.

[40] *Decennial Indexes to Services of Heirs*, vol. 1 (1710-1719), 7.

[41] Grant, *The Faculty of Advocates in Scotland*, p. 69.

[42] Moses Bundle 161/6225, Edinburgh District Archives.

[43] *Decennial Indexes to Services of Heirs*, vol. 1 (1750-1759), 9.

[44] Alexander Allardyce, ed., *Scotland and Scotsmen in the Eighteenth Century* (Edinburgh: William Blackwood, 1888), 1: 56f.

[45] Arbuthnot, *Memories of the Arbuthnots of Kincardineshire and Aberdeenshire*, p. 73.

[46] *Edinburgh Poll Tax Returns for 1694*, p. 43.

[47] Arbuthnot, *Memories of the Arbuthnots of Kincardineshire and Aberdeenshire*, p. 74.

[48] *Gentleman's Magazine* 13 (1743): 384.

[49] *List of the Colonels, Lieutenant Colonels, Majors, Captains, Lieutenants, and Ensigns of His Majesty's Forces on the British Establishment* (London: for Thomas Cox, Charles Bathurst, John Pemberton, 1740), p. 10.

[50] *Decennial Indexes to the Services of Heirs in Scotland*, 2 (1780-1789): 15.

[51] Testament, Commissariot of Edinburgh, CC8/8/86, SRO.

[52] *Decennial Indexes to the Services of Heirs in Scotland*, 1 (1710-1719), p. 9.

[53] Testament, Commissariot of Edinburgh, CC8/8/101, SRO.

[54] St. George Southwark Parish Register, transcript at Guildhall Library (FHS microfilm 416,731).

[55] Watson, *Register of Edinburgh Apprentices, 1666-1700*, p. 32.

[56] The first two baptisms appear in *The Parish Register of St. Mary Aldermary, London, 1558-1754*, pp. 113, 115.

[57] Will, P.C.C., 1777, Jan., fol. 17, PRO.

[58] St. Bride Fleet Street parish register.

[59] Diocese of London, Marriage Allegations, 6-1-24, f. 49, Guildhall Library.

[60] St. Andrew Hubbard with St. Mary at Hill parish register.

[61] Testament, Commissariot of Edinburgh, CC8/8/110, SRO.

[62] Testament, Commissariot of Edinburgh, CC8/8/95, SRO.

[63] Grant, ed., *The Faculty of Advocates in Scotland,*, p. 68.

[64] Barbara Jaffray to the proprietor of Gallraw, 30 Oct. 1717, Moses Bundle 254/7793a, Edinburgh District Archives.

[65] Testament, Commissariot of Edinburgh, CC8/8/101, SRO.

[66] Edinburgh Parish Register. Margaret's mother is uncertain.

[67] Testament, Commissariot of Edinburgh, CC8/8/110, SRO; *Gentleman's Magazine*, 12 (1742): 107, called "Capt.," "a brave old officer [sic]."

[68] Testament, Commissariot of Edinburgh, CC8/8/101, SRO.

[69] *The Commissariot of Edinburgh. Consistorial Processes and Decreets, 1658-1800*, Scottish Record Society, part 47 (Edinburgh: for the Society by J. Skinner, 1909), p. 36.

[70] *Decennial Indexes to the Services of Heirs in Scotland*, 2 (1780-1789): 15.

[71] Edinburgh Parish Register.

CHAPTER W

Patrick Falconar of New Jersey

W1 **Patrick Falconar**, fourth son of John Falconer of Tulloch and of Phesdo, Warden of the Scottish Mint (V1), born about 1658 in the parish of Alves, Morayshire, Scotland, died 27 January 1691/2, aged 33 years, at Newark, New Jersey,[1] was buried in the old cemetery in Newark.

He married, on 2 October 1689 in New Haven, Connecticut, Hannah Jones, daughter of Rev. William Jones and Hannah (Eaton) Jones,[2] born about 1660 in New Haven, Connecticut, died 29 May 1717 in Stratford, Connecticut. She married, as her second husband, James Clark, who died in 1712 in Stratford, Connecticut; and, as her third husband, on 31 January 1714/5, John Booth.

Described as "son of John Falconer of Tulloch," he was apprenticed, on 24 February 1675, to James Fall, merchant of Edinburgh.[3] On 15 April 1680, Patrick Falconer, merchant in Edinburgh, and George Gordone, merchant in Banff, borrowed £2407 from Robert Donalsone, late baillie of Elgin.[4] John Frier in Mossielie, who was incarcerated in the tolbooth of Melrose for a debt to Patrick Falconer, merchant in Edinburgh, assigned £105 to Maurice Trent, merchant in Leith, and was released by a bond of corroboration dated 8 September 1680.[5] In 1684, he went to New Jersey. From Patrick's letter to Maurice Trent, dated in Elizabeth Town, New Jersey, on 28 October 1684, and published in 1685, we learn that he had been in America a short time, but long enough to have walked one hundred miles in East and West New Jersey, Pennsylvania, and Maryland.[6] He had probably been one of those "Gentlemen and Merchants of very good Repute" who had arrived on a vessel which left Leith in July 1684 with 160 passengers on an eight-week voyage to New Jersey.[6A]

Some descendants have assumed, because Smyth's article mentions his epitaph, written by his friend Rev. Abraham Pierson, which says that he "suffered much for Christ,"[7] that Patrick came to New Jersey to escape some sort of religious persecution. He was not a Quaker, so these words perhaps may indicate that he supported the cause of the Covenant, unlike the rest of his family. There is, nevertheless, compelling evidence to suggest that he probably came to America for economic reasons. His own family's fortunes had been tied up in the mint, as were those of the Quaker David Falconar and the trading network associated with the business of the mint. His father's estate was ruined and Robert Falconar (G3), the London merchant who supported Patrick's brothers Archibald and John, was bankrupt. David Falconar (H1) undoubtedly influenced Patrick to try his luck in New Jersey. The young merchant may have intended to export furs to London and Edinburgh and import manufactured items for the Indian trade.

He resided in Woodbridge, New Jersey, on 17 August 1688, when Israel Thornell of Woodbridge appointed him an overseer of his will, and on 4 January 1688/9, when he was granted the administrations of the estates of Robert Adam and George Atkinson and a bondsman in the granting of administration on the estate of William Haig to Miles Forster.[8]   Patrick lived in Newark on 20 June 1690, when he was granted the administration of the estate of Samuel Kitchel,[9] and on 25 August 1690, made an inventory of the estate of John Ward, of Newark.[10] He witnessed the will of William Sandford, of East New Jersey, on 2 January 1690/1.[11] He was styled "merchant" in the Adam administration; clearly his accounting skills were in demand to settle estates. On 5 January 1690/1, Patrick was chosen to be Collector of the Town of Newark, to receive and make payment of the money for the soldiers.[12]

By his will, dated 23 January 1691/2, he gave to his daughter Hannah £50, when of age; to his wife Hannah he gave his whole estate, both real and personal, "being in any part of Europe, New England, New Jersey, or elsewhere;" to Mr. Abraham Pierson, teacher of the church in Newark (who in 1701 became the first president of Yale College), he bequeathed £3; to Abigail Pierson, daughter of Abraham Pierson, he gave 20 shillings; he appointed his "loving friend" James Smeth to be an overseer in assisting his wife in making up his accounts in "New York, Long Island, New Jersey, or elsewhere on the west side of the Hudson River," his executrix to pay him £4 for his trouble; he appointed his father-in-law Mr. William Jones and brother-in-law Mr. John Jones to be overseers to assist his wife in any concerns of his in New England; and he requested that his brother Mr. James Falconar be his overseer to "take care to preserve and secure what I have in Europe for the use of my wife and child."[13]

Proof of his identity is certain, for the following reasons: 1.) His will mentions his brother "Mr." James, a title used by ministers and lawyers and used at that time by James Falconer of Phesdo, a lawyer; 2.) He was associated with Maurice Trent, the Edinburgh merchant and father-in-law of his brother Sir James, both in New Jersey and Scotland; 3.) The merchant of this name appears in New Jersey in 1684 and afterwards, while the Edinburgh merchant seems to disappear after 1680.

Issue of Patrick and Hannah (Jones) Falconar:[14]

   i.   Hannah Falconar, born 1690. She married, 2 August 1710, Seth Morse, son of Ezra and Joanna (Hoare) Morse, born 1686 in Dedham, Massachusetts, died 12 June 1783 in Guilford, Connecticut, and had issue, surname *Morse*:[15] a. *John*, born 17 August 1711, died 18 August 1791, married Hannah Pierce; b. *Hannah*, born 1713, died 10 July 1794, married Noah Hotchkin; c. *Seth*, born 29 August 1716, died 9 November 1721; d. *Ezra*, born 6 September 1719, died 28 March 1784; e. *Ruth*, born 6 September 1721, died 3 March 1804, married Samuel Lee; f. *Lois*, born 30 May 1723, married Jonathan Munger; g. *Lucy*, born 30 August 1725, died 5 November 1754, married Beriah Bishop; h. *Sarah*, born 6 May 1728, died 27 January 1828, married Timothy Baldwin.

W2   ii.   Patrick Faulkner, born 12 August 1692.[16]

W2 Patrick Faulkner, born 12 August 1692 in New Haven, Connecticut, died July, 1735 in Guilford, Connecticut.

He married, in 1722, Deliverance, daughter of Thomas and Sarah (Mason) Cooke, born 12 January 1694/5 in Guilford, Connecticut, died 12 February 1781 in Guilford, Connecticut. She married, as her second husband, prior to July, 1737, —— Hill.

Issue of Patrick and Deliverance (Cooke) Faulkner, born in Guilford, Connecticut:[17]

    i.   Hannah Faulkner, born 23 August 1723. She married, 6 March 1744/5, in Guilford, Connecticut, Charles Miller, son of Thomas and Mabel Miller, born 1 May 1721 in Middletown, Connecticut, and had issue, surname *Miller*:[18] a. *Lois*, born 12 November 1747; b. *Hannah*, born 30 November 1748; c. *Thomas*, born 9 January 1750.

    ii.   Sarah Faulkner, born 15 March 1726/7, died, unmarried, 24 September 1797 in Guilford, Connecticut.

    iii.   Mary Faulkner, born 11 April 1729. She married, 20 November 1755, Simeon Norton, son of Joseph and Mary (Champion) Norton, born 3 March 1728/9 in Guilford, Connecticut, died 22 December 1772 in Guilford, Connecticut, and had issue, surname *Norton*:[19] a. *Rufus*, born 9 August 1756, died 1812, married Hannah Cook; b. *Adah*, born 27 June 1758, died 11 March 1848, unmarried; c. *Chloe*, born 3 November 1760, died 16 April 1788; d. *Zina*, born 9 May 1767, lived in Vermont; e. *Mary*, born 20 August 1769, died 10 April 1791; f. *Julia*, born 22 April 1772, died 27 March 1862, unmarried.

W3   iv.   Charles Faulkner, born 11 May 1731.

    v.   Rebecca Faulkner, born 13 January 1733/4, died, unmarried, 9 February 1816 in Guilford, Connecticut.

W3 Charles Faulkner, born 11 May 1731 in Guilford, Connecticut, died 18 October 1803 in Guilford, Connecticut.

He married, as his first wife, 6 January 1760, Hannah Morse, daughter of John and Hannah (Pierce) Morse, born 16 November 1742 in Guilford, Connecticut, died 30 April 1765 in Guilford, Connecticut.

He married, as his second wife, on 4 March 1767, Mary Bly, of Middletown, Connecticut, who died 28 February 1810 in Guilford, Connecticut.

He served in the French and Indian War, as his name is found in a muster roll of men detached from the 7th Connecticut Regiment and put under the command of Nathaniel Johnson, captain of the 2nd company in the expedition at Fort William Henry.[20] During the American Revolution, he enlisted, on 10 April 1781, for eight months, twenty days, in Captain Peter Vail's company of guards stationed in Guilford for the defense of the sea coast.[21]

Issue of Charles and Hannah (Morse) Faulkner, born in Guilford, Connecticut:[22]

    i.   Benoni Faulkner, born 1 July 1760, died 16 July 1760.

    ii.   Hannah Faulkner, born 3 September 1761. She was probably the Hannah Faulkner who married Asa Page, son of Asa and Eunice (Page) Page, born 15 August 1761 in Branford, Connecticut. They lived first in Litchfield, Connecticut, and in 1792 settled in Lisle, Broome County, New York. Issue, surname *Page*:[23] a. *Rufus*, born 7 December 1779, died 7 May 1849 in Mansfield, Pennsylvania, married Chloe ——; b. *Lewis*; c. *Sherman*; d. *Lucy*, married —— Thurston; e. *Anna*, born 1796, died 1871 in Lisle, New York, married Thomas Tracy.

   iii. Mary Faulkner, born 10 July 1763, died 10 July 1768.

   iv. Charles Faulkner, born 13 October 1764, died 15 October 1769.

Issue of Charles and Mary (Bly) Faulkner, born in Guilford, Connecticut:[24]

W4   v.   Patrick Faulkner, born 30 November 1767.

      vi. Mary Faulkner, born 26 January 1771, died 8 April 1791.

W5   vii. Charles Faulkner, born 20 March 1773.

W6   viii. Friend Lyman Faulkner, born 15 February 1775.

      ix. Sally Faulkner, born 12 October 1779, died 28 December 1839 in Branford, Connecticut. She married, on 24 June 1835, in Branford, Connecticut,[25] as his second wife, Obed Tyler, son of Joseph and Jerusha Tyler, born 2 April 1768 in Branford, Connecticut, died there 29 March 1840.

W4 Patrick Faulkner, born 30 November 1767 in Guilford, Connecticut, died November 1857 in Middletown, Delaware County, New York, was buried on the knoll in front of the old Dowie homestead in what later was known as the Faulkner and Sanford Cemetery.

He married, at Guilford, Connecticut, Prudence Goldsmith, daughter of John and Deborah (Terry) Goldsmith, born 6 April 1772 in Southold, Long Island, New York, died in 1847 in Middletown, New York.

They moved to Rensselaerville, Albany County, New York, between 1793 and 1798, then lived, after 1800 and before 1813, in Coxsackie, Greene County, New York. They settled in Middletown between 1810 and 1813, where Patrick leased a 67-acre tract from Robert E. Livingston and built a house on the land.

Issue of Patrick and Prudence (Goldsmith) Faulkner:[26]

      i.   Oreit Faulkner, born 30 January 1791, died 13 October 1793 in Guilford, Connecticut.

W7   ii. Harvey Faulkner, born 15 February 1793.

W8   iii. James Faulkner, born 15 February 1793.

      iv. Mary (Polly) Faulkner, born 25 April 1798 in Rensselaerville, Albany County, New York, died 8 April 1873, buried in the Arkville Cemetery. She married, on 22 May 1819, at Middletown, New York, Milow Hubbell, son of Joseph Hubbell, born 17 February 1798 in Connecticut, died 21 February 1880, buried in the Arkville Cemetery. They had issue, surname *Hubbell*:[27] a. *George Washington*, born 2 February 1820, died 28 November 1821; b. *Lyman Burr*, born 3 March 1821, died 28 February 1824; c. *Nancy Goldsmith*, born 25 August 1822, died 29 September 1847 (?), married, 9 September 1841, John H. Potts; d. *Catherine Cook*, born 11 August 1824; e. *Charles Lewis*, born 25 March 1826; f. *Harvey*, born 6 February 1828, married, 5 November 1846, Emeline Hewitt; g. *Patrick Faulkner*, born 4 March 1830, married, 1 January 1851, Frances M. Kilpatrick; h. *Mariam*, born 11 November 1831, married, 3 May 1850, Aaron D. Reed; i. *Fanny Jane*, born 5 November 1833, married, 27 December 1853, Norman Kelley; j. *John Davis*, born 8 July 1836, married, 22

September 1857, Eliza M. Jaquish; k. *David Willard*, born 26 November 1839, married, 7 December 1854, Huldah M. Jaquish.

v. Prudence Faulkner, born 5 November 1800 in Rensselaerville, Albany County, New York, died December 1892 in Arena, New York. She married, on 1 December 1825, in Middletown, New York, Francis O'Connor, then of Bovina, New York, born 18 September 1801 in Bloomville, New York, died 10 June 1880, buried in Sanford Cemetery. Issue, surname *O'Connor*:[28] a. *Mary*, born about 1828; b. *Francis*, born about 1833; c. *James F.*, born 26 January 1835, died 26 October 1912 in Roxbury, New York, married, 15 October 1863, Mary Janet Dickson; d. *Hannah*, born about 1838; e. *Juliann*, born about 1840; f. *Edward*, born about 1843.

W9 vi. Jeremiah Faulkner, born 15 July 1802.

vii. Sally Faulkner, born 5 September 1804 in Coxsackie, Greene County, New York, died 8 March 1848 in Greene Township, Erie County, Pennsylvania, buried in Phillipsville Cemetery. She married John Dumond, born 1802 in Middletown, New York, died 8 September 1865, aged 63 years, 4 months, in Greene Township, Erie County, Pennsylvania, buried in Phillipsville Cemetery. Issue, surname *Dumond*:[29] a. *Roxana Mary*, married —— Mory; b. *Joel H.*, born about 1830, died 4 October 1910 in Greene Township, Erie County, Pennsylvania; c. *Emeline R.*, married —— Owen; d. *Prudence M.*, married —— Griffin; e. *Milo N.*, born about 1843; f. *Miranda J.*, married —— Stitzsenger; g. *Charles W.*, born about 1847.

viii. Mariah Faulkner, born 5 January 1807 in Coxsackie, Greene County, New York. She married, on 20 March 1831,[30] David Akerly, a hotelkeeper of Middletown, born about 1810 in New York. Issue, surname *Akerly*:[31] a. *Jeremiah*, born about 1832; b. *Sabra*, born about 1834; c. *Jane*, born 1838.

ix. Jane Ann Faulkner, born 4 October 1809 in Coxsackie, Greene County, New York, died 15 May 1880, buried in the Margaretville Cemetery. She married, on 18 May 1831, William O'Connor, born 12 February 1805,[32] died 16 May 1877, buried in the Margaretville Cemetery.[33] He built the Riverside Hotel in Margaretville. They had issue, surname *O'Connor*: a. *James H.*, born 29 April 1832; b. *Margaret E.*, born 16 July 1833; c. *Susan A.*, born 11 July 1835; d. *Mary P.*, born 26 May 1837; e. *Fanny J.*, born 17 October 1839; f. *William C.*, born 11 November 1841; g. *Edward L.*, born 15 June 1845; h. *Orrit M.*, born 4 December 1847; i. *William H. N.*, born 11 July 1850.

x. Emaline Faulkner, born 14 November 1813 in Middletown, Delaware County, New York, living in 1860 in Hannibal, Oswego County, New York. She married Henry H. Gardinier, born about 1811 in New York, and had issue, surname *Gardinier*:[34] a. *Wilson H.*, born about 1837; b. *Mary A.*, born about 1841; c. *Burlin*, born about 1846; d. *Edgar L.*, born about 1849; e. *N. L.*, born 1851; f. *Emerick*, born about 1854.

W10 xi. Charles Goldsmith Faulkner, born 3 January 1817.

W5 Charles Faulkner, born 20 March 1773 in Guilford, Connecticut, died in 1835 in Philadelphia, Pennsylvania.

He married, on 1 May 1800, in Guilford, Connecticut, Clarinda Stow, daughter of Isaac and Phebe (Griswold) Stow, born 23 January 1780 in Guilford Connecticut, died 30 August 1868 in Guilford, Connecticut.

Issue of Charles and Clarinda (Stow) Faulkner, born in Guilford, Connecticut:

i. Charles Faulkner, born 28 February 1801, died March 1802.

W11 ii.   Charles Hand Faulkner, born 15 April 1803.

iii. Mary Ann Faulkner, born 3 January 1807, died 17 March 1886 in Guilford, Connecticut. She married, on 4 May 1833, Joel Stone, son of Solomon and Thankful (Bartlett) Stone, born 21 February 1806 in Guilford, Connecticut, died 15 November 1880 in Guilford, Connecticut, and had issue, surname *Stone*:[35] a. *Anna Mary*, born 26 January 1836, married William Andrus; b. *Ellen Pierson*, born 26 May 1839, died 27 September 1841; c. *Henry Joel*, born 12 March 1842, married Nellie F. Rogers.

W12 iv.   William Faulkner, born 27 December 1808.

W6 Friend Lyman Faulkner, born 15 February 1777 in Guilford, Connecticut, died 1 June 1828 in Brookfield, Madison County, New York, was buried in the small family cemetery on his farm.[36]

He married, as his first wife, on 1 January 1802,[37] in Paris, Oneida County, New York, Jerusha Steele, daughter of Rev. Eliphalet and Elizabeth (Strong) Steele, of Paris, New York, baptized in 1780 in Egremont, Massachusetts. They appear not to have had any issue.

He married, as his second wife, on 19 December 1802,[38] Azubah Fisk, daughter of John and Irena (Buck) Fisk, born 29 October 1785 in Union, Connecticut, died 23 March 1869 in Brookfield, New York, buried in the Faulkner Cemetery.[39]

He settled in Brookfield about 1803. On 21 December 1818, Friend L. Faulkner, of Brookfield, sold land in lot number 17 in township 19 (in Brookfield) in three different deeds: he sold 40 acres to Jacob Moore of Brookfield for $250; to Benjamin Palmer of Brookfield for $504; and to David Fisk of Brookfield for $56.[40]

Issue of Friend Lyman and Azubah (Fisk) Faulkner:[41]

i.   George Faulkner, born 19 October 1803. There was a George "Faulker" listed in the 1830 census in Chenango, Broome County, New York, with one male under 5, one male 5 to 10, one male 20 to 30, and one female 20 to 30.[42] I have been unable to determine his identity. As George was the only Faulkner in that county in 1830, a possible son was George Lewis Faulkner, born 17 August 1832 in Broome County, New York, died 3 October 1911 in Cleveland, Klickitat County, Washington, who married, in 1856 in Wisconsin, Albertine Adelia Gruhlke, and had seven children. More information on this George Faulkner is necessary to determine whether George Lewis was his son.

ii. Samantha Faulkner, born 11 May 1805, died 4 March 1882 in Brookfield, New York, buried in the Old Fisk Farm Cemetery. She married Charles Lovett, born about 1801 in Maine, died 25 September 1880 in Brookfield, New York. No issue.

W13 iii. Sherman Faulkner, born 8 April 1807.

W14 iv.   Edward Faulkner, born 26 August 1809.

W15 v.   John Faulkner, born 28 December 1812.

vi. Olive Jane Faulkner, born 30 October 1815, died 15 July 1831, buried in the Faulkner Cemetery.

W16 vii. Friend Lyman Faulkner, born 28 April 1818.

W17 viii. Charles Faulkner, born 6 September 1820.

W18 ix.   Alonzo Faulkner, born 15 February 1823.

W7 Harvey Faulkner, born 15 February 1793 in Guilford, Connecticut, died 11 April 1830 in Middletown, Delaware County, New York.[43]

He married, on 19 March 1818, in Middletown, New York, Rachel Yaple, daughter of Christian and Anna (Dumond) Yaple, born 13 April 1801 in Middletown, New York, died 22 December 1872 in Middletown, New York. She married, as her second husband, Daniel Northrup.[44]

He served as a private in the War of 1812 for three months in Captain John H. Gregory's Company of Detached Militia from Delaware County, being discharged 29 August 1814.[45] He leased a tract neighboring to that of his father and, about 1825, built a house, which at mid-twentieth century belonged to a Faulkner descendant, Earl Sanford.

Issue of Harvey and Rachel (Yaple) Faulkner, born in Middletown, Delaware County, New York (there may have been others):

    i.   Clarissa L. Faulkner, born about 1820, died, unmarried, 31 August 1899, aged 79, in Middletown, New York.

    ii.   Mary Ann Faulkner, born 25 May 1821, died 16 December 1889, buried in Philipsville Cemetery, Venango Township, Erie County, Pennsylvania.[46] She married, on 20 December 1841, Evan Roberts, born 11 September 1813, died 20 April 1866, buried in Philipsville Cemetery. Issue, surname *Roberts*:[47] a. *Harvey*, born 20 June 1844/5, died 11 September 1912, married, firstly, Sarah Roberts; b. *Clara*, married —— Ellithrop; c. *Emma*, married —— Vosburg; d. *Ellen Rachel*, born 8 August 1849 in West Greene, Pennsylvania, died 1 February 1908, married, July 1870, in Waterford, Pennsylvania, William S. Bowman; e. *Lill*; f. *Leroy*.

W19 iii.   Richard Miles Faulkner, born 16 August 1823.

W20 iv.   Edward M. Faulkner, born 18 November 1825 [calculated].

W8 James Faulkner, born 15 February 1793 in Guilford, Connecticut, died 10 February 1863 in Hancock, Delaware County, New York,[48] was buried in the Old Hancock Cemetery.

He married, as his first wife, on 30 November 1820, in Roxbury, Delaware County, New York, Abigail Scudder, said to have died in 1825.[49]

He married, as his second wife, Susan Fry (or Frei), of Pennsylvania Dutch origin, born about 1812 in Pennsylvania, died "at the age of 60 years," buried in the Old Hancock Cemetery.

On 22 January 1824, James Faulkner and Abigail, his wife, of Roxbury, sold land in Roxbury to William Decker, for $650.[50] He sold further land in 1825 and 1826.[51] He seems to have gone to Lancaster, Pennsylvania, by 1830, and possibly then to New Jersey. He was a carpenter and building contractor and was involved with the construction of the Croton Water Works and built the New York and Erie Railroad's first bridge. By 1849, he and his second wife Susan were living in Hancock, Delaware County, New York. In 1851, he was supervisor of the Town of Hancock. He expanded the hotel in Hancock, changing its name to the "Faulkner House" (later known as the "Hancock House"), and operated it for a number of years. He also built numerous houses in Hancock.

Issue of James and Abigail (Scudder) Faulkner:[52]

    i.   Hannah Faulkner, born about 1823, living in 1850 in Hancock, New York.

She married Lewis Wood, born about 1812 in New Jersey. Issue, surname *Wood*:[53] a. *Herbert S.*, born about 1843.

W21 ii. Benjamin Scudder Faulkner, born 11 December 1824.

iii. Ruth Ann Faulkner, born about 1825, living in 1893 in Elmira, New York. She married Asahel B. Chamberlin, born 15 April 1820 in Franklin, Delaware County, New York, died 3 June 1891 in Elmira, New York, station and freight agent at Hancock until 1867, when they moved to Elmira, where he later was land agent for the D. L. & W. Railroad. Issue, surname *Chamberlin*:[54] a. *Charles D.*, of St. Paul, Minnesota; b. *Burton S.*

Issue of James and Susan (Fry) Faulkner:[55]

W22 iv. Hugh White Faulkner, born 25 August 1830.

W23 v. Henry Porter Faulkner, born 13 November 1832.

W9 Jeremiah Faulkner, born 15 July 1802 in Coxsackie, Greene County, New York, died 14 September 1885 in Middletown, Delaware County, New York, was buried in South New Kingston Cemetery.

He married, on 7 December 1828, in Middletown, New York, Jane Catherine Hewitt, daughter of John and Sally (Van Benschoten) Hewitt, born 22 April 1809 in Middletown, New York, died 9 April 1884 in Middletown, New York, buried in the Sanford Cemetery.[56]

He was a farmer who lived near the village of New Kingston, in the Town of Middletown. He took over the lease which his father had originally taken from Robert E. Livingston and eventually expanded the farm to 275 acres. During the anti-rent troubles in Delaware County in the 1840s, he sheltered two of his neighbors, who were actively involved in the struggle, and, as a result, spent about two years in the county jail. After his release, he opened a grocery store in Delhi, but, on his wife's insistance, soon returned to the farm on Bull Run. His farm, with a dairy herd of about 40 cows, produced butter, which he sold to commission houses in New York City and buyers in Kingston and Poughkeepsie, and vinegar, pork, and other articles. He liked to travel. He saw Robert Fulton's first steamboat on the Hudson River, when he was seven, and he and his wife took the first excursion run on the Erie Railroad from Hancock to New York City.[57]

Issue of Jeremiah and Jane Catherine (Hewitt) Faulkner, born in Middletown, Delaware County, New York:[58]

i. Sarah M. Faulkner, born 5 August 1830, died 23 April 1892 in Margaretville, New York, buried in South New Kingston Cemetery. She married, on 15 January 1852, Cornelius D. Sanford, son of William S. and Harriett (Dumond) Sanford, born 17 November 1830, died 1902, and had issue, surname *Sanford*:[59] a. *Herman*; b. *George*, married Martha Streeter; c. *John*, married Florence Sanford; d. *William*; e. *Emory*; f. *Lyman*; g. *Frank*; h. *Hattie*; i. *Evelyn*; j. *Mary*; k. *Emma*.

W24 ii. Lyman Faulkner, born 19 February 1833.

iii. Susan Faulkner, born 20 April 1840, died 17 May 1845, buried in South New Kingston Cemetery.

W25 iv. Silas Faulkner, born 4 July 1842.

W26 v. George Lewis Faulkner, born 27 May 1844.

vi. Mary Catherine Faulkner, born 10 March 1846, died 8 November 1918 in Middletown, New York, buried in Archibald Cemetery. She married, on 22 March 1865, in Middletown, New York, Morris Faulkner, born 4 February 1840 in Greene County, New York, died 15 December 1927 in Middletown, New York, buried in Archibald Cemetery. He belonged to an unrelated family. They had issue, surname *Faulkner:*[60] a. *Bertha J.*, born 16 May 1867, died 3 December 1942, married M. C. Sanford; b. *Anna O.*, born about 1871, married, 29 October 1895, in Middletown, —— Kiff; c. *Nora M.*, born March 1879, married, 11 December 1895, in Middletown, Harry Sanford.

vii. Phoebe J. Faulkner, born 30 August 1847, living in 1929 in Margaretville, New York, unmarried.

viii. Sophronia A. Faulkner, born 8 August 1849, died 17 May 1850, buried in South New Kingston Cemetery.

W10   Charles Goldsmith Faulkner, born 3 January 1817 in Middletown, Delaware County, New York, died 21 September 1899 near Cannonsville, Town of Sanford, Broome County, New York, was buried in Pine Grove Cemetery.

He married, on 29 January 1840,[61] Maria Hilton, daughter of Eliab and Abigail (Davis) Hilton, born 19 July 1823 in Garrettsville, Otsego County, New York.[62]

In 1842, he lived in the town of Hamden, in Delaware County. In 1845, his home was in the vicinity of Pleasant Valley in the town of Middletown. He and his family moved in the spring of 1857 to Shaver Hill, in the town of Sanford, Broome County, New York.

Issue of Charles Goldsmith and Maria (Hilton) Faulkner, born in Middletown, Delaware County, New York:[63]

W27   i.   John D. Faulkner, born 8 November 1842.

W28   ii.   William Harvey Faulkner, born 22 February 1845.

iii.   Priscilla K. Faulkner, born 13 September 1846, died 7 February 1852 in Middletown, New York.

iv.   Maria Faulkner, born 1847, died young.

v.   Eliab Hamilton Faulkner, born July 1851, died 2 October 1908 in Binghamton, New York. He married, on 17 April 1878, in Deposit, New York, Sarah E. White, born October 1850 in New York, living in 1900. In 1900, they lived in Tompkins, Delaware County, New York. They had an adopted son, George S. Faulkner, born 14 January 1885, died April 1970 in Deposit, New York, who married Rachel M. Faulkner, daughter of Nathan Hilton Faulkner (W29).

W29   vi.   Nathan Hilton Faulkner, born 30 May 1856.

W11   Charles Hand Faulkner, born 15 April 1803 in Guilford, Connecticut, died 16 September 1842, probably in Georgetown, South Carolina.

He married, as his first wife, Ann Edwards Roberts, born February 1811, died 1 February 1833.

He married, as his second wife, in February 1840, Martha Folk, of Georgetown, South Carolina.

He lived in Buenos Aires, Argentina, and Georgetown, South Carolina.

Issue of Charles Hand and Ann Edwards (Roberts) Faulkner, born in Guilford, Connecticut:

i.   William Roberts Faulkner, born 20 June 1829, died about 1856. He or his father had two children who died young.

ii. Christiana Plummer Faulkner, born 20 April 1832, died 1912 in Guilford, Connecticut. She married, on 4 July 1855 in Guilford, Connecticut, Harvey Ward Leete, son of Morris A. and Clarinda (Graves) Leete, born 9 November 1832 in Guilford, Connecticut. Issue, surname *Leete*:[64] a. *Henry Walter*, born 17 May 1856; b. *Robert Clyde*, born 14 September 1859.

W12   **William Faulkner**, born 27 December 1808 in Guilford, Connecticut, died 27 March 1878 in Guilford, Connecticut.

He married, as his first wife, on 15 October 1829, in Guilford, Connecticut, Frances Harriet Lord, daughter of Elias and Irene (Carey) Lord, born 5 September 1807 in Norwich, Connecticut, died 20 April 1848 in Norwich, Connecticut.[65]

He married, as his second wife, on 27 March 1850, in Hartford, Connecticut, his first cousin, Mary Griswold Stowe, daughter of Pitman and Lois (Austin) Stowe of Hartford, Connecticut.

They apparently lived in West Virginia about 1853 and later in California. In 1871, he was president of the California Type Foundry Company in San Francisco. He returned to Connecticut before his death.

Issue of William and Frances Harriet (Lord) Faulkner, born in Guilford, Connecticut:

W30   i.   Francis William Faulkner, born 4 August 1830.
W31   ii. George Lord Faulkner, born 27 February 1833.
        iii. Caroline Pierson Faulkner, born 15 May 1836, died 21 June 1851 in Guilford, Connecticut.
        iv. Ella Faulkner, born 10 September 1841, living in 1900 in Oakland, California. She married Henry H. Beach.

Issue of William and Mary Griswold (Stowe) Faulkner:

W32   v.   Charles Pitman Faulkner, born 4 May 1853.

W13   **Sherman Faulkner**, born 8 April 1807 in Brookfield, Madison New York, died 1873 in Lenox, Madison County, New York.[66]

He married, as his first wife, Lucy ——, born 1806, died 12 August 1832, aged 25 years, 11 months, buried in the Faulkner Cemetery in North Brookfield.

He married, as his second wife, Armenia Higgins, born about 1807 in Otsego County, New York, died 29 July 1874 in Lenox, New York, aged 67 years, buried in the Faulkner Cemetery.

On 1 January 1834, then of Brookfield, he sold to Edward Faulkner, of Brookfield, for $800, part of lot number 17 in the 19th township. On 22 April 1836, he and his wife Armenia sold to Azubah Faulkner, Semantha, Lyman, Alonzo, and John Faulkner, for $550, part of lot number 17 in township number 19.[67] He moved to Lenox about 1843.

Issue of Sherman and Lucy Faulkner:[68]

i.   Mary J. Faulkner, born about 1827.

Issue of Sherman and Armenia (Higgins) Faulkner, born in Brookfield, Madison County, New York:[69]

W33   ii.   Ephraim Faulkner, born 21 January 1835.

iii.   William S. Faulkner, born July 1837, died 6 March 1915 in Lenox, Madison County, New York, was buried in Whitelaw Cemetery. He married, as his first wife, Anna M. ——, his wife in 1875 and 1878. He married, as his second wife, Mary Ellen Lee, born July 1850 in New York.

W14   **Edward Faulkner**, born 26 August 1809 in Brookfield, Madison County, New York, died 10 February 1848 in Mansfield, Pennsylvania.[70]

He married, on 28 May 1833, in Mansfield, Pennsylvania, Abigail Doolittle Beach, daughter of Rev. Lyman and Polly (Doolittle) Beach, born 8 July 1815 in Wallingford, Connecticut, died 21 October 1887 in Mansfield, Pennsylvania. She married, as her second husband, on 30 June 1849, John Voorhees,[71] born about 1823 in Pennsylvania, and had children by him.[72]

He moved to Richmond Township, Tioga County, Pennsylvania.

Issue of Edward and Abigail Doolittle (Beach) Faulkner, born in Richmond Township, Tioga County, Pennsylvania:[73]

W34   i.   ·Lyman Beach Faulkner, born 24 November 1836.
W35   ii.   John E. Faulkner, born April 1838.
iii.   Olive Jane (Jennie) Faulkner, born about 1842. She married, on 30 December 1869 in Richmond Township, Tioga County, Pennsylvania, Merit D. Reynolds.[74] She married, as her second husband, Weston D. Lang, and had issue.
W36   iv.   Charles Edward Faulkner, born 12 July 1844.

W15   **John Faulkner**, born 28 December 1812 in Brookfield, Madison County, New York, died 1880 in Brookfield, Madison County, New York, was buried in the Old Fisk Farm Cemetery.

He married Sophia Stevens, daughter of William B. Stevens, born 1823 in Madison County, New York, died 9 March 1894 in Brookfield, Madison County, New York, buried in the Old Fisk Farm Cemetery.

Issue of John and Sophia (Stevens) Faulkner:[75]

W37   i.   Edward Lyman Faulkner, born 19 February 1842.
ii.   Frances Faulkner, died at the age of five.

W16   **Friend Lyman Faulkner**, born 28 April 1818 in Brookfield, Madison County, New York, died 1908 in Venango Township, Erie County, Pennsylvania, was buried in Wattsburg Cemetery. He never used his first name.

He married, as his first wife, Diana R. Whitford, probably the daughter of Ezekiel and Ruth (Rice) Whitford, born 19 July 1820 [calculated], in Columbus, Chenango County, New York, died 4 December 1872 in Venango Township, Erie County, Pennsylvania, buried in Wattsburg Cemetery.

He married, as his second wife, Rebecca ——, born May 1838, living in 1900 in Venango Township, Erie County, Pennsylvania.

Lyman and Diana Faulkner went to Harmony, Chautauqua County, New York, by 1839, but returned to Brookfield. They were of Brookfield, Madison County, New York, when on 29 September 1846, they sold to Azubah Faulkner, for $1200, all their rights to a farm in Brookfield, part of lot number 17 in the 19th township.[76] They moved to Venango Township prior to 1850. In 1860, they lived in Amity Township. His farm amounted to 300 acres in 1873.

Issue of Friend Lyman and Diana R. (Whitford) Faulkner:[77]

W38 i.   Henry (Harry) H. Faulkner, born 29 August 1839.

     ii. Mary Jane Faulkner, born about 1841. She married, on 25 December 1856, Amos F. Tanner, born 9 October 1835 in Greenwich, New York, a farmer in Venango and Amity Townships. Issue, surname *Tanner*:[78] a. *Rose*, married —— Smith; b. *William L.*; c. *Linn*, married —— Rouse; d. *Mary*; e. *Kittie*; f. *Jessie*; g. *Frederick A.*; h. *Gertie*.

     iii. Rhoda (Rose) Faulkner, born about 1843.

     iv. Harriet Faulkner, born about 1845.

W39 v.   Charles D. Faulkner, born March 1848.

     vi. Sarah Faulkner, born 1850, living in 1925 in Findley Lake, New York. She married —— Hubble.

     vii. Amanda Faulkner, born about 1852.

W40 viii. Alonzo D. Faulkner, born November 1856.

W17   **Charles Faulkner**, born 6 September 1820 in Brookfield, Madison County, New York, died 23 August 1891 in Brookfield, Madison County, New York, was buried in the Old Fisk Farm Cemetery.

He married, in 1855, Elnora Welsh, daughter of John Welsh, born October 1837 in Ireland, died 25 February 1909 in Brookfield, Madison County, New York, buried in the Old Fisk Farm Cemetery.

Issue of Charles and Elnora (Welsh) Faulkner, born in Brookfield, Madison County, New York:[79]

     i.   Mary Ann Faulkner, born 1856, died May 1903 in Stockwell, New York, buried in the Old Fisk Farm Cemetery. She married Albert Campbell and had issue, surname *Campbell*: a. *Grace*, married K. Stewart; b. *Charles*.

     ii. Charles P. Faulkner, born March 1860, died, unmarried, 9 September 1939 in Waterville, New York.

     iii. Hattie L. Faulkner, born September 1863, living in 1931 in Sangerfield, Oneida County, New York. She married Charles O. Livermore, but had no issue.

W41 iv. William Scott Faulkner, born July 1865.

W42 v.   Sherman Lyman Faulkner, born 4 August 1868.

     vi. Geneva Faulkner, born March 1871, living in 1931 in Skaneateles, New York. She married, on 20 August 1902, in Syracuse, New York, Holmes P. Case, and had issue, surname *Case*: a. *Holmes*.

W43 vii. Edward I. Faulkner, born March 1873.

W18   **Alonzo Faulkner**, born 15 February 1823[80] in Brookfield, Madison County, New York, died 30 June 1909 in Sangerfield, Oneida County, New

York, was buried in the Old Fisk Farm Cemetery.

He married, on 29 April 1871, Rebecca (Loomis) Mattison, daughter of Elisha and Katie Loomis, born 1847 in Vermont, died 4 January 1886 in Brookfield, Madison County, New York, buried in Old Fisk Farm Cemetery.

He was a dairy farmer and hop grower, owning 600 acres in 1880.[81] They were Baptists.

Issue of Alonzo and Rebecca (Loomis) Faulkner, born in Brookfield, Madison County, New York:[82]

    i.   Adeline (Addie) E. Faulkner, born May 1872. She married, on 5 September 1893, in Sherburne, New York, —— Fitch.

    ii.   Helen Beatrice Faulkner, born August 1873. She married, on 15 February 1902, in Sangerfield, New York, Abram Cushman Fay. They lived in Earlville, New York.

W19   **Richard Miles Faulkner**, born 16 August 1823 in Middletown, Delaware County, New York, died 7 May 1901 in Middletown, New York, was buried in South New Kingston Cemetery.

He married Orret Maria Dumond, born 29 August 1827 in Middletown, New York, died 12 October 1905 in Middletown, New York, buried in South New Kingston Cemetery.

He was a shoemaker.

Issue of Richard Miles and Orret Maria (Dumond) Faulkner, born in Middletown, Delaware County, New York:[83]

    i.   Martha R. Faulkner, born August 1852, died, unmarried, 14 February 1936 in Oneonta, New York, buried in South New Kingston Cemetery.

    ii.   Reuben A. Faulkner, born 30 April 1855, died 12 May 1855, buried in South New Kingston Cemetery.

    iii.   Rosena Faulkner, born April 1867, living, unmarried, in 1900.

W20   **Edward M. Faulkner**, born 18 November 1825 [calculated] in Middletown, New York, died 17 March 1893, aged 67 years, 3 months, and 27 days, in Roxbury, Delaware County, New York, was buried in South New Kingston Cemetery.

He married, as his first wife, Catherine ——, born 9 May 1825 [calculated], died 20 January 1849, buried in South New Kingston Cemetery.

He married, as his second wife, Jane Crosby, born about 1828 in New York, died 22 November 1887, aged 60, buried in South New Kingston Cemetery.

He married, as his third wife, Mrs. Elsie Carroll, a widow, who died 2 June 1909 in Hobart, New York.

In 1850, he lived in Middletown, and, in 1860, in Andes.

Issue of Edward M. and Catherine (——) Faulkner, born in Middletown, Delaware County, New York:[84]

    i.   Harvey S. Faulkner, born February 1849 [date is dubious], was living in 1900 in Newark, New Jersey. He married, about 1882, Emilie Vautier, daughter of Philip and Emma Vautier, born August 1863 in Indiana. They had two children, both dead by 1900.[85] In Newark, he was a partner with James H.

Fletcher in a retail store selling sewing machines, art novelties and materials. He was a drug salesman in 1900.

Issue of Edward M. and Jane (Crosby) Faulkner:[86]

ii. Mary Ann Faulkner, born 29 April 1851, died 8 June 1898 in Franklin, Delaware County, New York. She married Harvey J. Delameter, son of Cornelius Brink and Betsy Ann (Birdsall) Delamater, born 2 July 1845 in Middletown, New York, and had issue, surname *Delamater*: a. *Nora Emma*, born 11 September 1874.[87]

iii. Maransa C. Faulkner, born September 1854, living in 1920 in Trenton, New Jersey.[88] He married Mary J. ——, born July 1854 in New Jersey, living in 1920.

W44 iv. Evan Roberts Faulkner, born June 1866.

v. Asa J. Faulkner, born March 1869, living in 1920 in Newark, New Jersey.[89] He married Annette ——, born February 1867 in Pennsylvania, living in 1920.

W21 **Benjamin Scudder Faulkner**, born 11 December 1824 in Roxbury, Delaware County, New York, died 15 April 1892 at Riverside Home in Scott Township, Wayne County, Pennsylvania,[90] was buried in Hancock Cemetery, Hancock, New York.

He married, on 30 November 1847, in Hancock, New York, Jane Plaskett, daughter of Joseph and Lucretia Plaskett, born 20 October 1828 in Ludlow, Northumberland County, New Brunswick, died 30 April 1901 in Hancock, New York, buried in Hancock Cemetery.

He was a clerk at the New York and Erie Railroad depot in Hancock in 1860. He served as a private in Company F, 144th New York Infantry, from 27 August 1864 to 25 June 1865. In 1869, he and his wife moved to a 600-acre farm four and one-half miles from the village of Hancock, in Scott Township, Wayne County, Pennsylvania, known as "Riverside Home."

Issue of Benjamin Scudder and Jane (Plaskett) Faulkner, born in Hancock, Delaware County, New York, except the last:[91]

W45 i. James LaPierre Faulkner, born 15 September 1848.

ii. Joseph Plaskett Faulkner, born 20 August 1850, died 22 February 1855 in Hancock, New York, buried in Hancock Presbyterian Church Cemetery.

iii. Louis Porter Faulkner, born 10 April 1852, died 19 December 1930 in Hancock, New York, was buried in Hancock Cemetery. He married, on 10 April 1883, in Avon, Livingston County, New York, Sara L. Sonn, born 26 December 1858 in New York, died 21 March 1945, probably in Hancock, New York, buried in Hancock Cemetery. No issue. He was an accountant and a lay preacher.

iv. Asahel Chamberlain Faulkner, born 24 February 1854, died after 1860.

v. Nellie L. Faulkner, born 18 November 1855, died, unmarried, July 1911 in Hancock, New York, buried in Hancock Cemetery.

vi. Amy Faulkner, born 20 April 1858, died young.

vii. Abbie Faulkner, born 24 May 1859, was living in 1911 in Spring City, Pennsylvania. She married, on 18 October 1887, in Scott Township, Wayne County, Pennsylvania, James C. Hogan, born August 1861 in New York, and had issue, surname *Hogan*:[92] a. *James*, born December 1889; b. *Ruth*, born February 1891; c. *Louis*, born May 1892; d. *Benjamin*, born July 1893; e. *William*, born September 1896; f. *Charles*, born May 1899. In 1900, they lived in New York, New York, and in 1901, in East Orange, New Jersey.

viii. Milton Faulkner, died young.

ix. John P. Faulkner, died young.

x. Ruth Faulkner, born 15 April 1866, was living in 1911 in Schenectady, New York. She married, on 10 September 1889, in Hancock, New York, Seth Sonn, born August 1863 in Pennsylvania, and had issue, surname *Sonn*:[93] a. *John I.*, born June 1890; b. *Myrtle*, born November 1891; c. *Nellie F.*, born 15 September 1893, died May 1975 in Scotia, New York, married B. S. Horton.

xi. Edward S. Faulkner, born 4 April 1874 in Scott Township, Wayne County, Pennsylvania, died 1948 in Binghamton, New York, buried in Hancock Cemetery. He married Anna Davison, born 1888, died 1 November 1956 in Albany, California. They lived in Binghamton, New York, where he worked at such occupations as laborer, shipping clerk, and machinist. No issue.

W22 **Hugh White Faulkner**, born 25 August 1830 in Buck, near Lancaster, Pennsylvania, died 4 January 1917 in Fort Collins, Colorado, was buried in Lakeside Cemetery (then Loveland City Cemetery).

He married, on 25 September 1851, in Wayne County, Pennsylvania, Filena Reynolds, daughter of George and Julia (Purdy) Reynolds, born 7 August 1831 in Sherman, Wayne County, Pennsylvania, died 4 August 1901 in Loveland, Colorado, buried in Lakeside Cemetery.

He was a farmer and carpenter. He lived in Scott Township, near Sherman, Wayne County, Pennsylvania, from 1847 to 1869. He enlisted as a private on 11 November 1864, at Philadelphia, in Company C, 67th Pennsylvania Infantry, and was discharged at Washington, D.C., on 16 August 1865, having served in Virginia. In 1869 they moved to Bucklin, Linn County, Missouri, living there until 1901, where he was known as an "orphan-farmer," apparently a farmer who provided a home for orphans from eastern cities. They moved to Loveland, Colorado, where he stayed for two years. He then obtained a homestead claim due him as a former soldier in the Big Thompson Canyon near Loveland. His cottage, called "Moss Glen," (later "Grandpa's Retreat") was close to the Big Thompson River, rich in trout.[94] His last years were spent in Buckhorn Creek and Fort Collins, Colorado.

Issue of Hugh White and Filena (Reynolds) Faulkner, born in Scott Township, Wayne County, Pennsylvania:[95]

i. Susan R. Faulkner, born 3 July 1852, died 9 September 1864, of consumption, buried in the Old Hancock Cemetery. She sang "The Battle Hymn of the Republic" at a church rally at the outset of the Civil War and made a great impression on those who heard her.

W46 ii. Norman Reynolds Faulkner, born 14 May 1854.

iii. Julia F. Faulkner, born 30 June 1856, died February 1865, of scarlet fever.

iv. Emma F. Faulkner, born 24 February 1858, died 21 December 1939 in Iowa City, Iowa, buried in Lone Tree Cemetery, Lone Tree, Iowa. She married, on 24 October 1877, Jacob Chester Loehr, son of Jacob H. and Lovina (Hock) Loehr, born 15 September 1843 in Plainfield, Pennsylvania, died 28 June 1926 in Lone Tree, Iowa. Issue, surname *Loehr*:[96] a. *Lena May*, born 17 February 1879, died 1968, married, 16 November 1898, Fredrick C. Jahnke; b. *Frank Elmer*, born 13 November 1881, died 22 March 1964, married, 23 November 1903, Maude Furniss Siverly; c. *Mertie Ellen*, born 6 August 1883, married, 26 September 1905, Rev. Blanchard Allen Black; d. *Clement Leslie*, born 7 October 1885, died 19 August 1970, married, 20 December 1910, Grace Margaret Davidson; e. *Katherine Lavina*, born 19 March 1887, married, 22 Septmeber 1908, Guy C. Black; f. *Emma Alice*, born 12 January 1891, died 25 February 1976 in Waterloo, Iowa, married, 19 March 1911, William H. Yakish.

v.   Ida May Faulkner, born 28 November 1862, died 18 September 1931 in Denver, Colorado, buried in Grandview Cemetery, Fort Collins. She married, on 2 June 1881, in Linn County, Missouri, as his second wife, William W. Nutter, son of Jacob and Lucy (Coffin) Nutter, born 15 September 1856 in Greenville, Ohio, died 13 November 1922 in San Leandro, California. They were divorced 8 December 1913 in Larimer County, Colorado. They moved to Nebraska, then to Colorado, where he worked as a salesman, and had issue, surname *Nutter*.[97] a. *Elmer Hugh*, born 26 January 1884, died January 1967 in Vista, California, married, January 1910, Ada Pilcher; b. *Mildred Blanche*, born 3 September 1886, died 14 January 1960, married, 20 April 1904, Charles C. Johnson; c. *Susan Leland*, born 4 October 1887, married, 20 July 1905, T. Knox Bell; d. *Hilton Harrison*, born 24 February 1889, died May 1981 in Montebello, California, married, 31 December 1911, Nora Metzger; e. *Elery Delos*, born 26 November 1890, married Lela Bullock; f. *Clarence Everett*, born 30 November 1892, died October 1975 in Bakersfield, California, married Dorothy Six; g. *Edna Mae*, born 30 October 1894, died April 1987 in Port Orchard, Washington, married, 10 December 1913, Denward Belmont Arvine; h. *Leroy Milton*, born 15 April 1898, died January 1966, married Alice Slesser.

W47   vi.   Hilton D. Faulkner, born August 1865.

W23   **Henry Porter Faulkner**, born 13 November 1832 in New Jersey, died 5 June 1897 in Gibson, Town of Corning, Steuben County, New York, was buried in Hope Cemetery.

He married Emily (or Emma) Brewer, born in January 1851[98] in New York, died 1910 in Corning, New York, buried in Hope Cemetery.

He lived in Hancock, New York, in 1860 and 1875, and in Elmira, New York, in 1880. He was employed by the D. L. & W. Railroad as a flagman at the Gibson bridge near Corning.[99]

Issue of Henry Porter and Emily (Brewer) Faulkner, the first three born in Hancock, New York, the last in Elmira, New York:[100]

i.   Susan Faulkner, born about 1871. She married, 16 December 1892, in Addison, New York, Frank Cowan, who died February 1954 in Rochester, New York, aged 80 years, 9 months, and 21 days, and was buried in Grove Cemetery, Bath, New York. Issue, surname *Cowan*: a. *Emily L.*, born about 1893, married, 22 July 1914, in Erwin, New York, —— Metcalf.

ii.   Jennie Faulkner, born 10 August 1873 [calculated], died 13 November 1952, buried in Grove Cemetery, Bath, New York. She married Francis Cephas Platt, born 23 January 1866 [calculated], died 31 May 1952, buried in Grove Cemetery. Issue, surname *Platt*: a. *Gerald E.*, born October 1895, married 19 May 1920, in Erwin, New York, —— Button; b. *Chester F.*, born 21 October 1898, died October 1974 in Camanche, Iowa, married, first, 10 May 1919, in Erwin, New York, —— Brown; and second, 1 January 1925, in Erwin, New York, —— Shea.

iii.   Grace Faulkner, born 1875, died, unmarried, 1937, buried in Hope Cemetery. She supported herself as a maid and cook in Corning. She may have married —— Sours.

iv.   Emma P. Faulkner, born November 1879, died, unmarried, 2 August 1904 in

Corning, New York, buried in Hope Cemetery.

W24 **Lyman Faulkner,** born 19 February 1833 in Middletown, New York, died 15 February 1889 in Somerset, Barbour District, Orange County, Virginia, was buried in the Graham Cemetery, Orange, Virginia.

He married, on 21 December 1876, Sarah Margaret Stokes, daughter of John and Mary (Cool) Stokes, born 27 May 1848 in Bridgewater, Virginia, died 6 January 1927 in West Conesville, New York.

Sarah went to Middletown, New York, with her children by 1892.

Issue of Lyman and Sarah Margaret (Stokes) Faulkner, born in Somerset, Virginia:[101]

W48 i.   Myron Jeremiah Faulkner, born 19 September 1877.
W49 ii. Morris S. Faulkner, born 20 October 1879.
W50 iii. Monroe Hanford Faulkner, born 13 April 1882.
W51 iv. Marvin Cleveland Faulkner, born 8 July 1884.
     v.   infant son, born 20 October 1886, died 12 December 1886.
     vi. Maude Ellen Faulkner, born 16 October 1888, died 25 April 1970, buried in Prattsville, New York. She married, on 9 November 1910, in Gilboa, New York, Raymond Mayhan, born 30 January 1884 in Gilboa, New York, died 14 April 1952 in Mount Kisco, New York. They had no children.

W25 **Silas Faulkner,** born 4 July 1842 in Middletown, New York, living in 1907 in Bovina Center, Delaware County, New York.

He married, on 4 October 1872, Hannah E. Hendrix, born 8 September 1856.

He took over his father's farm near New Kingston.

Issue of Silas and Hannah E. (Hendrix) Faulkner, born in Middletown, Delaware County, New York:[102]

     i.   Anna Jane Faulkner, born about 1874.
     ii. Emma Viola Faulkner, born about 1878.
     iii. Frances R. Faulkner, born about 1880.

W26 **George Lewis Faulkner,** born 27 May 1844 in Middletown, New York, died 25 October 1913 in Fleischmanns, Town of Middletown, New York.

He married, on 7 November 1872, Emily Lawrence, born 17 September 1846 in New York, living in 1913. She was possibly the Emily J. Faulkner who died 11 September 1934 in Erwin, New York.

He built a barn about 1890 on the farm which belonged to his father. In later years he was a merchant.

Issue of George Lewis and Emily (Lawrence) Faulkner, born in Middletown, Delaware County, New York:[103]

     i.   Vernon J. Faulkner, born October 1876, living in 1920 in Kingston, New York. He married, on 27 April 1904, in Kingston, New York, Clara V. ——, born about 1874 in New York.
     ii. Abigail C. Faulkner, born 1881, died 25 September 1899 in Oneonta, New York, buried in Fleischmanns Cemetery. She had just entered Oneonta Nor-

mal School.

iii.   George A. Faulkner, born 1886, died 1890, buried in Fleischmanns Cemetery.

iv.   Edith A. Faulkner, born March 1888.

W27   John D. Faulkner, born 8 November 1842 in Hamden, Delaware County, New York, died 1905 in Ceres Township, McKean County, Pennsylvania, was buried in Evergreen Cemetery.

He married, in November 187-, in Hamden, New York,[104] Mary Lucinda Pratt, daughter of —— and Mary Pratt, born August 1851 in New York, living in 1910 in Ceres Township, McKean County, Pennsylvania.

Issue of John D. and Mary Lucinda (Pratt) Faulkner, born in Ceres Township, McKean County, Pennsylvania:[105]

W52   i.   Gerald S. Faulkner, born 25 May 1877.

ii.   Leslie J. Faulkner, born November 1885, died 4 February 1901, aged 15 years, 3 months, buried in Evergreen Cemetery.

W53   iii.   Guy H. Faulkner, born 7 September 1889.

W28   William Harvey Faulkner, born 22 February 1845 in Middletown, Delaware County, New York, died 1 March 1925 in Olean, New York, was buried in Evergreen Cemetery, Ceres, Pennsylvania.

He married, as his first wife, on 11 January 1868, in Afton, New York, Nancy Beebe Jennings, daughter of George G. and Elmira Jennings, born 1847 in Sanford, Broome County, New York, died 3 November 1891 in Ceres Township, McKean County, Pennsylvania, buried in King's (now Evergreen) Cemetery.

He married, as his second wife, Rachel E. Moon, born 11 November 1858 in Wayland, New York, died 17 January 1896 in Ceres Township, McKean County, Pennsylvania, buried in Evergreen Cemetery.

He married, as his third wife, Sarah L. Williams, who died 24 June 1915 in Delaware.

He married, as his fourth wife, on 13 March 1916, in Portville, New York, Cathrine (Pothe) Cowans, widow of Benjamin F. Cowans and daughter of Henry and Elizabeth (Snyder) Pothe, born 10 April 1856 in Chambersburg, Pennsylvania.

He was a farmer and mason. He enlisted at Deposit, New York, on 31 August 1863, as a private in Company H, 1st New York Veteran Cavalry, and mustered out on 20 July 1865 at Camp Piatt, West Virginia. He lived in Deposit, New York, until 1869, when he moved to Ceres Township, McKean County, Pennsylvania. He lived in Salisbury, Maryland, in 1916, but after his fourth marriage lived in Olean, New York.

Issue of William Harvey and Nancy Beebe (Jennings) Faulkner, the first born in Afton, New York, the rest born in Ceres Township, McKean County, Pennsylvania:[106]

W54   i.   Charles Gordon Faulkner, born 7 April 1871.

ii.   Winifred Faulkner, born 6 June 1876, died 13 December 1960 in Ceres, Pennsylvania, buried in Evergreen Cemetery. She married, on 27 April 1894,

Frederick Bell King, born July 1869 in Pennsylvania, died 1923, buried in Evergreen Cemetery, and had issue, surname *King*: a. *Nellie Martha*, born 8 November 1894, died 9 or 10 February 1972 in Tarpon Springs, Florida; married, 30 April 1911 Raymond W. McCoy; b. *Gertrude H.*, born 11 October 1897, married, in 1920, C. Walter Skipper; c. *Maurice Frederick*, born 16 February 1901, died 29 September 1938 in Ceres, Pennsylvania; married, in 1921, Edith Marie Hickel; d. *Frank William*, born 14 February 1907, died 15 or 16 January 1969 in Buffalo, New York; married, February 1928, Ina A. Ferguson; e. *Lois Winifred*, born 4 August 1909, died 1984, married, 14 June 1941, Ervin E. Gleson; f. *Ruth Elizabeth*, born 18 March 1912, died August 1968 in St. Petersburg, Florida; married, November 1935, Elmer C. Knudson; g. *John Faulkner*, born 2 April 1914, died 16 June 1978 in Olean, New York; married, 21 June 1941, Ruth Reed.

W55   iii.   George Percy Faulkner, born 20 November 1879.

       iv.   Elmira (Mira) Pearl Faulkner, born 19 December 1884, died 24 November 1954 in Harrisburg, Pennsylvania, buried in Evergreen Cemetery. She married, on 21 August 1903, in Portville, New York, Merle V. Dickinson, born 1878, died 1959, and lived in Bingham, Pennsylvania. Issue, surname *Dickinson*: a. *Bernice*, born 13 July 1904, married, 11 June 1925, Fred M. Warner; b. *Irma Rosamond*, born 14 January 1906.

       v.   Inez Katherine Faulkner, born 20 September 1886, died 22 March 1976 in Allegany, New York. She married, on 6 November 1908, Conrad J. Blessing, born about 1862 in New York, living in 1920 in Olean, New York. Issue, surname *Blessing*: a. *Gertrude Hilda*, born 18 January 1910, married, on 11 June 1925, Warner Miles Bramlee; b. *Conrad John*, born 6 October 1914, married Helen Cleaver.

Issue of William Harvey and Rachel E. (Moon) Faulkner:

       vi.   Gretchen Moon Faulkner, born 11 September 1895, died 9 November 1970 in Buffalo, New York. She married, on 10 August 1918, Glenn H. Buckley, born 14 July 1897 in Olean, New York, and lived in Olean, New York. Issue, surname *Buckley*: a. *William Faulkner*, born 26 October 1919; b. *Robert Glenn*, born 9 June 1926; c. *Nancy Ann*, born 26 June 1931, married, 21 November 1954 Dudley Bruce Phillips.

W29   **Nathan Hilton Faulkner**, born 30 May 1856 in Middletown, Delaware County, New York, died 27 September 1939 in Deposit, New York, was buried in Oakwood Cemetery.

He married, on 5 October 1880, Ella L. Haynes, daughter of Luther and Rachel (Curry) Haynes, born 1862 in New York, died 31 July 1938 in Deposit, New York, buried in Oakwood Cemetery.

He attended Deposit Academy, and at 19 taught school in Stilesville, then at McLure, and Gulf Summit. He returned to his family's farm on Shaver Hill, and, in 1881, rented a neighboring farm while a new house was built on the old homestead. Continuing to teach during the winters, he operated a truck farm until 1897. He then bought a farm in Stilesville, New York, but in 1912 sold all but fifty acres to a company proposing hydroelectric power on the Delaware River and built a new house. In 1927 he retired to a house on Brookside, in Deposit. Known locally as a poet, he published a book of poems, *Historical Poems of Delaware Valley*, in 1933.[107]

Issue of Nathan Hilton and Ella L. (Haynes) Faulkner, born in Sanford,

Broome County, New York:[108]

W56   i.   Archie Bryant Faulkner, born 7 February 1882.

ii.   Washington Irving Faulkner, born 30 June 1883, died 1 May 1958 in Deposit, New York, buried in Oakwood Cemetery. He married, as his first wife, on 22 June 1904, in Deposit, New York, Nellie Violetta Kelsey, born 26 May 1884, daughter of John and Emma (Snell) Kelsey,[109] but later divorced. He married, as his second wife, Frances A. Bier. No issue. He was a carpenter and cabinetmaker.

iii.   Herman C. Faulkner, born 9 May 1885, died 1 March 1974 in Deposit, New York. He married, as his first wife, on 20 September 1905, in Deposit, New York, Laura R. Kelsey, born about 1886 in New York, living in 1920. He married, as his second wife, Hazel, widow of Harper H. Kays, born 20 October 1890, died 15 April 1974 in Deposit, New York.

iv.   Rachel M. Faulkner, born 1892, died 13 September 1956 in Deposit, New York, buried in Oakwood Cemetery. She married, on 5 October 1906, in Deposit, New York, George Scofield Faulkner, adopted son of Eliab Hamilton and Sarah E. (White) Faulkner, born 1884, died 1970, buried in Oakwood Cemetery. Issue, surname *Faulkner*: a. *Clifford S.*, born 15 January 1913, died 16 December 1987 in Deposit, New York, married, by license filed 5 September 1934, in Delaware County, New York, Gertrude M. Neale; b. *George N.*, born about 1915, who died in Florida.

v.   Gladys H. Faulkner, born 1901, died 1970, buried in Oakwood Cemetery. She married, on 1 November 1922, in Delaware County, New York, Cyrus S. Beebe, born 29 March 1897, died April 1967 in Sidney, New York. They lived in Mount Upton, New York.

W30   **Francis William Faulkner**, born 4 August 1830 in Norwich, Connecticut, died 18 December 1906 in San Joaquin County, California.

He married, as his first wife, on 24 July 1859, in New Haven, Connecticut, Emily C. D. Stevens. They divorced in 1876 in San Francisco, California.

He married, as his second wife, on 30 October 1879, in Norwich, Connecticut, Sarah B. (Prentice) Williams.

He enlisted first, on 11 May 1861, in Company D, 3rd Connecticut Infantry, and served until 12 August 1861. He re-enlisted, on 12 August 1862, 15th Connecticut Infantry, and served as a corporal and sergeant until his discharge on 27 June 1865. He lived in San Francisco, California, after the war, and worked as a salesman in his father's business until 1878, when he moved to Norwich, Connecticut.

Issue of Francis William and Emily C. D. (Stevens) Faulkner, born in Connecticut:[110]

i.   William B. Faulkner, born 24 January 1860, living, unmarried, in 1920 in Concord, California. In 1900, he lived in San Francisco.[111] He was employed in the freight department of the Southern Pacific Railroad.

ii.   Ella Brainard Faulkner, born 28 February 1862, living in 1920 in Concord, California. She married Fred R. Koening.

W31   **George Lord Faulkner**, born 27 February 1833 in Norwich, Connecticut, died in San Francisco, California.

He married Irene Wildman, born April 1841 in Massachusetts, living in

1900 in San Francisco.

He worked as an agent for his father's type foundry company in the early 1870s and lived in Brooklyn, Alameda County, California.

Issue of George Lord and Irene (Wildman) Faulkner:

    i.   Carrie Pierson Faulkner, born July 1868 in California. She married —— Kennedy.[112]

    ii. George A. Faulkner, born November 1869, died 23 February 1945 in Oakland, California. He married Lena H. Condict, born 2 December 1872 in Missouri, died 13 March 1968 in Lincoln County, California. He sold bicycles and motorcycles in Oakland.[113]

W32   Charles Pitman Faulkner, born 4 May 1853 in West Virginia, died 6 December 1916 in Lake County, California.

He married, as his first wife, Eleanor U. McMorris, daughter of Robert and Annie McMorris, born February 1855 in Canada, living in 1920 in Oakland, California. The couple divorced, as in 1900 she and her son lived in Hot Springs Township, San Luis Obispo County, California.[114]

He married, as his second wife, Harriet A. (——) Sharp, born October 1854 in California, living in 1910.

He lived in San Francisco, California.

Issue of Charles Pitman and Eleanor U. (McMorris) Faulkner:

    i.   Pitman L. Faulkner, born October 1874 in California, living, unmarried, in 1920 in Oakland, California. He was Deputy City Assessor of Oakland.

W33   Ephraim Faulkner, born 21 January 1835 in Brookfield, Madison County, New York, died 29 May 1921 in Lenox, Madison County, New York, was buried in Mount Pleasant Cemetery, Canastota.

He married, in 1863, Julia A. Boyer, born February 1842 in New York, died 19 September 1905 in Lenox, Madison County, New York.

His farm was located at Union Corners, in the Town of Lenox.

Issue of Ephraim and Julia A. (Boyer) Faulkner, born in Lenox, Madison County, New York:[115]

W57   i.   Charles E. Faulkner, born October 1865.

    ii. Lura (Louie) A. Faulkner, born about 1870, died 17 September 1938 in Lenox, New York. She married, on 24 November 1892, Eugene Donnelly, and had issue, surname *Donnelly*: a. *Bertha M.*, married Willard Swartwood; b. *Robert E.*

W58 iii. Edward H. Faulkner, born 29 March 1878.

W34   Lyman Beach Faulkner, born 24 November 1836 in Brookfield, Madison County, New York, died 2 August 1887 in Topeka, Kansas.

He married, as his first wife, on 22 March 1854, in Mansfield, Pennsylvania, Julia Ann Bailey, daughter of Roswell and Julia Bailey, born 23 November 1835 in Charleston Township, Tioga County, Pennsylvania, died 25 May 1875 in Waverly, New York, buried in Prospect Cemetery, Mansfield.

He married, as his second wife, on 23 October 1876, Ursula V. Alger Russell, born 10 August 1847 in Pennsylvania, died 3 August 1913 in Pomona,

California.

He lived in Richmond Township and Mansfield, Tioga County, Pennsylvania; in 1880, he was in Waverly, New York, where his occupation was listed as "drover." In 1883, the family moved to Marionville, Missouri, where he resided at the time of his death.

Issue of Lyman Beach and Julia Ann (Bailey) Faulkner, the first three born in Tioga County, Pennsylvania:[116]

W59 i.   Edward L. Faulkner, born 20 January 1855.

      ii.   Charles Copeland Faulkner, born 2 February 1858, died 14 June 1859, buried in Prospect Cemetery.[117]

W60 iii. Charles E. Faulkner, born 12 November 1860.

      iv. Caroline Olive Faulkner, born 25 June 1867 in Waverly, New York, died 21 October 1953 in Los Angeles, California. She married, on 31 December 1891, in Marionville, Missouri, Rev. Phydelia P. Carroll, born 1861, died 1945, and had issue, surname *Carroll*: a. *Julia E.*, born 2 February 1896 in Cuba, New York, died 9 March 1924 in Los Angeles, California; b. *Philip P.*, born 2 March 1910 in Santa Barbara, California, lives in Vacaville, California.

W61 v.   John Weston Faulkner, born 7 February 1871.

Issue of Lyman Beach and Ursula V. (Alger) Faulkner:

      vi. Corry E. Faulkner [daughter], born 12 December 1878, died 8 July 1880, buried in Poheta Cemetery, Saline County, Kansas.[118]

      vii. Ellen B. Faulkner, born 31 July 1880 in Waverly, New York, was living in 1950 in Arroyo Grande, California. She married, on 6 February 1908, in Pomona, California, Charles R. Ross, born 1875 in Indiana, died 6 May 1934 in Arroyo Grande, California. They had no issue.

W35   **John E. Faulkner**, born April 1838 in Brookfield, Madison County, New York, died 1922 in Waverly, New York, was buried in Glenwood Cemetery.

He married, on 12 January 1860, at Mitchell's Creek, Tioga County, Pennsylvania, Milletta A. Mitchell, daughter of William K. Mitchell,[119] born November 1837 in Tioga County, Pennsylvania, died 11 May 1920 in Waverly, New York, buried in Glenwood Cemetery.

He was a businessman in Waverly, owning a meat market in 1888 and an insurance agency in 1900.

Issue of John E. and Milletta A. (Mitchell) Faulkner (there were two others, neither alive in 1900):[120]

      i.   Caroline Pearl Faulkner. She married, on 24 August 1899, in Waverly, New York, Rev. Hugh Carpenter, and had issue.

W62 ii.   William E. Faulkner, born August 1872.

W36   **Charles Edward Faulkner**, born 12 July 1844 in Earlville, Madison County, New York, died 29 June 1933 in West Palm Beach, Florida, was buried in Arlington National Cemetery.

He married, on 6 September 1871, in Waverly, New York, Clementina A. Coryell, daughter of Rev. Vincent Matthews and Rachel (Lounsberry) Coryell,[121] born 17 April 1846 in Newark, Tioga County, New York, died 19 July 1934 in Lake Worth, Florida.

He enlisted, on 15 May 1861, at Harrisburg, Pennsylvania, in Company K, 5th Pennsylvania Reserve Volunteer Corps, and was discharged 14 June 1864. He served as a private and corporal and was held as a prisoner. After the war, he served as a civilian in the Commissary Department and under General Schofield, under the Reconstruction Acts, in Virginia, until 1866. He was in Williamsport, Pennsylvania, from 1866 to 1869. He moved to Salina, Kansas, in 1869, and served two terms in the Kansas legislature. He was a member of the State Board of Trustees of Charitable Institutions of Kansas for ten years. From 1887 to 1897 he was superintendent of the Soldier's Orphans Home in Atchison, Kansas. He went to Minneapolis, Minnesota, in 1897, where he held the office of superintendent of the Washburn Memorial Orphan Asylum. In 1930 he and his wife retired to Florida.[122]

Issue of Charles Edward and Clementina A. (Coryell) Faulkner, born in Salina, Kansas:[123]

    i.   Coryell Faulkner [daughter], born 8 January 1873 in New York. She served as a hospital steward, in the 20th Kansas Infantry, during the Spanish-American War.

W63 ii.   Charles Edward Faulkner, born 13 September 1874.

W37   **Edward Lyman Faulkner**, born 19 February 1842 in Brookfield, Madison County, New York, died 8 May 1914 in Brookfield, Madison County, New York, was buried in the Old Fisk Farm Cemetery.

He married, 5 November 1866, in Earlville, New York, Sarah E. Carpenter, born 20 August 1846 in Eaton, New York, died 16 August 1928 in Brookfield, Madison County, New York, buried in Old Fisk Farm Cemetery.

Issue of Edward Lyman and Sarah E. (Carpenter) Faulkner, born in Brookfield, Madison County, New York:[124]

    i.   Waldo Emerson Faulkner, born 15 March 1869, died 27 April 1943, was buried in the Graham Cemetery, Hubbardsville, New York. He married, on 10 May 1899, in North Brookfield, New York, Louisa H. York, daughter of Alonzo L. and Arzelia (Heminway) York, born 6 February 1869 in Brookfield, New York, died 1929 in Blue Mountain Lake, New York. She was a graduate of the State Normal School at Oneonta and went to Puerto Rico as a teacher by appointment by the Federal government.[125] They ran a hotel at Blue Mountain Lake, Hamilton County, New York. No issue.

    ii.   Caroline Amelia Faulkner, born 15 December 1871. She married, on 1 July 1891, Fred D. Rogers, born 29 October 1866, died 7 October 1941, and had issue, surname *Rogers*:[126] a. *Pauline Louise*, born 17 August 1894, died 28 December 1924, married, 8 October 1914, Bernard Kelly; b. *Victorine Marie*, born 11 July 1897, married first, 30 April 1920, Daniel Powell, second, 23 February 1929, Alfred Despard; c. *Charles Faulkner*, born 6 September 1898, died 27 February 1936 in Sherburne, New York, married, 16 June 1934, Winifred Moe; d. *Helen Lucille*, born 15 July 1906, married, 6 March 1926, Elbert Arwood.

    iii.   Elnora E. Faulkner, born 10 May 1874, died 3 March 1961 in Norwich, New York, buried in Stockwell Cemetery. She married, on 25 June 1895, in North Brookfield, New York, George H. Agan, but had no issue.

     iv.   Walter Pearl Faulkner, born 18 January 1879, buried in West Hill Cemetery, Sherburne, New York. He married, on 8 February 1905, in Sherburne, New York, Florence J. Newell, daughter of H. J. Newell.

     v.   John Faulkner, born 1883, died 1887.

W64 vi. James Alfred Faulkner, born 27 May 1887.

    vii. Ferroll Marguerite Faulkner, born 22 September 1891, died 29 May 1936 in Trenton, New Jersey, buried in Old Fisk Farm Cemetery. She married —— LaVeck.

W38   **Henry (Harry) H. Faulkner**, born 29 August 1839 in Harmony, Chautauqua County, New York, died 15 September 1924 in Spokane, Washington.[127]

He married, as his first wife, on 28 June 1866, in Venango Township, Erie County, Pennsylvania, Esther Delana Peck, probably daughter of Davis and Delana Peck, born 6 September 1842 in New York, died 1 January 1905 in Deer Park, Washington.

He married, as his second wife, on 28 November 1910, in Spokane, Washington, Amanda (Lemon) Johnson, widow of William Henry Johnson, born about 1854 in Pennsylvania, living in 1924.

He enrolled, on 18 August 1862, at Oil City, Pennsylvania, and mustered in on 6 September 1862 as a private, at Harrisburg, Pennsylvania, in Company A, 16th Pennsylvania Cavalry. He was promoted to corporal, wounded in action at Harrison's Shop, Virginia, on 28 May 1864 (from which he lost the use of his right hand and arm), transferred to Company C in the same regiment, and was discharged on 10 April 1865. He and his family afterwards lived in Venango Township, Erie County, Pennsylvania. They moved to Saline County, Nebraska, after 1880, and he lived in Friend, Nebraska, in 1900.[128] He and his wife came to Washington about 1905.

Issue of Henry H. and Esther Delana (Peck) Faulkner, born in Venango Township, Erie County, Pennsylvania:[129]

     i.   Anna Elizabeth Faulkner, born 12 May 1867, died 21 June 1946 in Thompson Falls, Montana. She married, on 3 March 1887, in Dorchester, Nebraska, Joseph Benjamin Louis Janson Kemmerer, son of Joseph and Elizabeth Mathilda (Johnson) Kemmerer, born 8 May 1849 in Bethlehem, Pennsylvania, died 25 December 1926 in Jordan, Montana, and had issue, surname *Kemmerer*.[130] a. *Esther Lois*, born 22 September 1889, died 28 April 1985 in Libby, Montana, married, 2 July 1907, William Clyde Edwards; b. *Harry F.*, born 5 November 1895, died 1987 in Thompson Falls, Montana, married, firstly, 9 November 1919, Laura Stoller, and, secondly, February 1974, Kathryn Haas; c. *Dewey Lewis*, born about 1900, died about 1902; d. *Lester Alton*, born 16 July 1904, died 16 September 1967 in Thompson Falls, Montana, married, 9 April 1931, Vera Hazel Martin.

    ii. Agnes E. Faulkner, born 12 October 1869, living in 1924 in Spokane, Washington. She married —— Shawgo.

    iii. Etta Faulkner, born 8 April 1872. She married —— Feister.

W65 iv. George Judson Faulkner, born 19 April 1875.

W39   **Charles D. Faulkner**, born March 1848 in Brookfield, Madison County, New York, died 6 June 1925 in Amity Township, Erie County, Pennsylvania, was buried in Wattsburg Cemetery.

He married, as his first wife, Emma A. Tanner, daughter of Morgan B. and Electa (Whitney) Tanner,[131] born December 1845 in Venango Township, Erie County, Pennsylvania, died 7 February 1910, buried in Wattsburg Cemetery.

He married, as his second wife, on 21 November 1914, in Union City, Pennsylvania,[132] Mrs. Harriet F. Hopkins, daughter of Erastus and Phoebe (Jewett) Hopkins, born about 1875 in Amity Township, Erie County, Pennsylvania.

He was a farm agent and farmer in Venango and Amity Townships.

Issue of Charles D. and Emma A. (Tanner) Faulkner, born near Wattsburg, Erie County, Pennsylvania:[133]

      i.   Charles Chester Faulkner, born April 1868, died, unmarried, 26 November 1934 in Amity Township, Erie County, Pennsylvania, buried in Wattsburg Cemetery.

W66 ii.   Lee J. Faulkner, born 1870.

W67 iii. Alonzo J. Faulkner, born 10 October 1876.

     iv.   May Faulkner, born about 1878, living in 1934 in Union City, Pennsylvania. She married C. B. Brown.

     v.   Mary E. Faulkner, born August 1883, died 6 March 1948 in Union City, Pennsylvania, buried in Wattsburg Cemetery. She married —— Chase. Issue, surname *Chase*: a. *Hattie*; b. *Charles F.*, born 1912, died 1983, married Helen J. ——; c. *Lyle F.*, died 4 January 1978; d. *Robert.*

     vi.   Sherman F. Faulkner, born 9 August 1889, died 6 March 1964 in Union Township, Erie County, Pennsylvania. He married, 8 April 1916, in Beaverdam, Pennsylvania,[134] Helena (Lanah) Thiem, daughter of Paul O. and Minnie (Engel) Thiem, born 12 May 1894 in Pennsylvania, died June 1979 in Spartansburg, Pennsylvania. They farmed near Union City from 1918 to 1947, after which he worked at a mill and at a chair factory, and also drove a truck and made maple syrup.[135]

W40   **Alonzo D. Faulkner**, born November 1856 in Amity Township, Erie County, Pennsylvania, died 10 October 1908 in Erie, Pennsylvania, was buried in Wattsburg Cemetery.

He married Sarah A. Whitney, born 22 February 1857 in French Creek, New York, died 1916 in Venango Township, Erie County, Pennsylvania, buried in Wattsburg Cemetery. She married, as her second husband, on 31 August 1912,[136] Lewis L. Randall, born 25 December 1865 in Greenfield Township, Erie County, Pennsylvania.

He was a farmer in Venango Township, Erie County, Pennsylvania. In 1900, the family lived in Elk Lick Township, Somerset County, Pennsylvania, where he had an interest in the Farmers Bank of Meyersdale, Pennsylvania.

Issue of Alonzo D. and Sarah A. (Whitney) Faulkner, born in Venango Township, Erie County, Pennsylvania:[137]

      i.   Stanley Faulkner, born July 1877, living in 1900, but dead without issue by 1908.

     ii.   Stella Faulkner, born about 1879, living in 1920 in Erie County, Pennsylvania. She married Leon D. Reynolds, born about 1874 in Pennsylvania. Issue, surname *Reynolds*:[138] a. *Gladys E.*, born about 1904.

    iii. Cora Betsy Faulkner, born 12 February 1881, died 21 January 1959 in Jamestown, New York, buried in Wattsburg Cemetery. She married, 28 June 1906, in Wattsburg, Pennsylvania,[139] William H. More, born 18 October 1883 in Wattsburg, Pennsylvania. They lived in Maysville, Pennsylvania, in 1908. They had two adopted children, Arnold C. Depp, and Anna R.[140]

    iv. Minnie E. Faulkner, born September 1883, living in 1956 in Fishertown, New York. She married —— Corley.

    v. Helen A. Faulkner, born August 1889, died 13 January 1956 in Erie, Pennsylvania, buried in Wattsburg Cemetery. She married, 26 June 1909, in Wattsburg, Pennsylvania,[141] Glenn D. Wilkinson, born 8 December 1888, died May 1972 in Erie, Pennsylvania. Issue, surname *Wilkinson*:[142] a. *Leona*, born about 1914, married James Cessna; b. *Stanley S.*, born 1917.

W41 **William Scott Faulkner**, born July 1865 in Brookfield, Madison County, New York, died November 1937 in Rochester, New York, was buried in Riverside Cemetery.

He married, as his first wife, on 14 November 1894, in New York Mills, New York, Carrie Johnson. They divorced about 1906.

He married, as his second wife, Elizabeth I. Strader, born November 1876 in Utica, New York, died May 1967, was buried in Riverside Cemetery. She married, as her second husband, —— Kiemle.

They lived in Sangerfield, New York, in 1900; Phelps, New York, in 1910; and in 1920, they lived in Sangerfield, New York. By 1931, he was in Rochester.

Issue of William Scott and Carrie (Johnson) Faulkner, born in Sangerfield, Oneida County, New York:[143]

W68 i. Floyd Johnson Faulkner, born 2 December 1895.

    ii. Elizabeth E. Faulkner, born September 1898, died about 1985. She married —— Kase, and had issue, surname *Kase*: a. *Norman B.*

    iii. Harold Faulkner, lived in Rochester, New York, possibly the one born 19 September 1900, died December 1960.

Issue of William Scott and Elizabeth I. (Strader) Faulkner, born in Phelps, New York:[144]

W69 iv. Donald L. Faulkner, born 14 June 1910.

W42 **Sherman Lyman Faulkner**, born 4 August 1868 in Brookfield, Madison County, New York, died 1947 in Oriskany Falls, Town of Augusta, Oneida County, New York.

He married Anna McCabe, daughter of Nicholas and Catherine McCabe, born January 1869 near North Brookfield, New York,[145] died 3 July 1924 near Oriskany Falls, New York.

Issue of Sherman Lyman and Anna (McCabe) Faulkner, born in Brookfield, Madison County, New York:[146]

    i. Raymond Sherman Faulkner, born 16 October 1900, died 18 May 1972 in Utica, New York. He married Winifred L. Jones, daughter of William P. and Sarah Ann (Williams) Jones, born 20 October 1899, died 20 November 1986 in New Hartford, New York, buried at Crown Hill Memorial Park, Kirkland,

New York, but had no issue.

W70   ii.   Leonard Faulkner, born 10 October 1902.

iii.   Fred Faulkner, born 1903, died after 1924.

iv.   Ruth Faulkner, born 1 March 1905, living in 1947 in Ilion, New York. She married John Stephenson and had issue, surname *Stephenson*: a. *Betty Jane*, born March 1927, married ——— Cross; b. *John F.*, born 15 October 1935.

W71   v.   Charles Philip Faulkner, born 21 May 1907.

vi.   Carrie Elnora Faulkner, born 21 April 1909, died 27 September 1909.

W43   Edward I. Faulkner, born March 1873 in Brookfield, Madison County, New York, died 26 February 1909 in Brookfield, Madison County, New York, buried in Old Fisk Farm Cemetery.

He married W. Minnie Meinkheim, daughter of George Meinkheim, of Syracuse, New York. She died 17 January 1899 in Brookfield, Madison County, New York, aged 25 years. Their child was raised by him.

Issue of Edward I. and W. Minnie (Meinkheim) Faulkner:[147]

i.   Elnora Faulkner, born January 1899, living in Syracuse, New York, in 1909.

W44   Evan Roberts Faulkner, born June 1866 in Middletown, New York, was living in 1910 in Scranton, Pennsylvania.

He married Nora Emery, born December 1865 in Pennsylvania, living in 1910.

Issue of Evan Roberts and Nora (Emery) Faulkner, born in Scranton, Pennsylvania:[148]

i.   Roy E. Faulkner, born 5 July 1894, died 21 April 1975 in Wilkes Barre, Pennsylvania, buried in Abington Hills Cemetery. He served in World War I and worked as a salesman for H. J. Heinz Company and also for the Berwick Ordinance Department, living in Scranton, Pennsylvania. He married Anna Betelak, but had no issue.[149]

W45   James LaPierre Faulkner, born 15 September 1848 in Hancock, New York, died 12 May 1892 in Scott Township, Wayne County, New York, was buried in Hancock Cemetery.

He married, on 15 September 1869, in Deposit, New York, Alice Elizabeth Willis, born 1 May 1851 in Barton, New York, died 23 February 1924 in Barton, New York, buried in Hancock Cemetery.

In 1870, they were in Barton, where he worked as a railroad station agent. In 1880, they lived in Avon, New York, but by 1885 were in North Tonawanda, New York.

Issue of James LaPierre and Alice Elizabeth (Willis) Faulkner:[150]

i.   Olive Jane (Jennie) Faulkner, born May 1870 in Hancock, New York,[151] died 2 January 188- [Saturday], aged 15, in North Tonawanda, New York, buried in Barton, New York.

W72   ii.   William Willis Faulkner, born October 1871.

iii.   Julia L. Faulkner, born December 1881[152] in Avon, New York, died 16 May 1904 in Sayre, Pennsylvania. She married, on 18 June 1902, in Barton, New

York, Truman Vincent, and had issue, surname *Vincent*: a. *Walter L.*

    iv.   James L. Faulkner, born 30 January 1885 in North Tonawanda, New York, died 7 May 1888 in North Tonawanda, New York, buried there.

    v.   Benjamin Sylvester Faulkner, born 15 February 1890, died, unmarried, 15 October 1959, buried in Fort Logan National Cemetery, Denver, Colorado. He lived in Elmira, New York until 1929.

W73 vi.   Frank LaPierre Faulkner, born 6 September 1892.

W46   **Norman Reynolds Faulkner**, born 14 May 1854 in Scott Township, Wayne County, Pennsylvania, died 26 March 1930 in Glendale, California, was buried in Lakeside Cemetery, Loveland, Larimer County, Colorado.

He married, in 1875 in Lone Tree, Iowa, Ellen (Ella) Sophia Richey, daughter of Newton Boone and Catherine (Loehr) Richey,[153] born 26 September 1857 in Van Buren, Ohio, died 12 November 1931 in Glendale, California, buried in Lakeside Cemetery.

He moved to Lone Tree, Iowa, in 1872, where he farmed, until 1882, when they moved to Loveland, Colorado. He pioneered the cultivation of sugar beets in Colorado, now the leading agricultural product of the Loveland area, and was instrumental in introducing a sugar processing plant there in 1908.

Issue of Norman Reynolds and Ellen Sophia (Richey) Faulkner, the first three born in Lone Tree, Iowa, the rest in Loveland, Colorado:[154]

    i.   William R. Faulkner, born 13 May 1876 [calculated], died 21 August 1877, buried in Lone Tree Cemetery.[155]

    ii.   Nellie V. Faulkner, born 2 April 1879 [calculated], died 12 June 1879, buried in Lone Tree Cemetery.

W74 iii.   Harry Reynolds Faulkner, born 30 November 1880.

    iv.   Lena Faulkner, born 25 April 1883, died 19 June 1956 in Loveland, Colorado, buried in Loveland Burial Park. She married, on 28 April 1901, in Loveland, Colorado,[156] Charles W. Lakey, born 1870 in Missouri, died 9 June 1960 in Loveland, Colorado. Issue, surname *Lakey*: a. *Dwight E.*, born 1902, died 1933, married Helen M. ——.

    v.   Guy Faulkner, born 24 September 1885, died 24 August 1903, buried in Lakeside Cemetery.

    vi.   Clinton Faulkner, born May 1891, died 17 December 1893, aged two years, seven months, buried in Lakeside Cemetery.

W75 vii.   Alva Raymond Faulkner, born October 1894.

W47   **Hilton D. Faulkner**, born August 1865 in Sherman, Wayne County, Pennsylvania, died 22 January 1952 in Montclair, New Jersey, was buried in Mt. Hebron Cemetery.[157]

He married, on 10 February 1887, in Linn County, Missouri, Nellie L. Herriman, born December 1869 in Missouri, died in 1943 in Montclair, New Jersey.

They moved to Jersey City, New Jersey, in 1900, where he first worked as a poultry merchant. Until his retirement, about 1932, he worked for A. Silz and Company as a buyer of hotel supplies.

Issue of Hilton D. and Nellie L. (Herriman) Faulkner, born in Missouri:[158]

i. Bernice Faulkner, born August 1888, living in Montclair, New Jersey, in 1952. She married P. Paul Pearse.

W76 ii. Bayard H. Faulkner, born 19 July 1894.

iii. Rex W. Faulkner, born February 1896, a physician, living in Rochester, New York, in 1952.

W48 **Myron Jeremiah Faulkner**, born 19 September 1877 in Barbour District, Orange County, Virginia, died 23 March 1953 in New Kingston, New York, was buried in New Kingston Cemetery.

He married, as his first wife, on 3 September 1902, in Margaretville, New York, Sarah E. Sanford, born 12 June 1880 in Margaretville, New York, died 26 September 1926 in New Kingston, New York,[159] buried in New Kingston Cemetery.

He married, as his second wife, Carrie B. (——) Van Valkenburgh, who died 15 November 1936 in New Kingston, New York.

He married, as his third wife, Nellie Bretz, born 14 June 1889, died 24 October 1974, buried in Andes Cemetery.

He ran a dry goods store in New Kingston.

Issue of Myron Jeremiah and Sarah E. (Sanford) Faulkner, born in Middletown, Delaware County, New York:[160]

W77 i. Lyman George Faulkner, born 22 May 1903.

W78 ii. Curtis Lewis Faulkner, born 16 February 1907.

W49 **Morris S. Faulkner**, born 20 October 1879 in Barbour District, Orange County, Virginia, died 7 September 1926 in West Conesville, New York.

He married, on 21 June 1905, in West Conesville, New York, Nora E. Morse, born about 1886 in New York, living in 1920.

Issue of Morris S. and Nora E. (Morse) Faulkner:[161]

i. Mildred S. Faulkner, born 6 March 1907, died 25 December 1970, and lived in Gilboa, New York. She married, on 23 June 1932, Clayton Jackson.

W50 **Monroe Hanford Faulkner**, born 13 April 1882 in Barbour District, Orange County, Virginia, died 27 January 1951 in Margaretville, New York.

He married, on 2 October 1907, in New Kingston, New York, Mabel Jane McCumber, born 13 December 1884 in Margaretville, New York, died December 1980 in Chicago, Illinois.

He was a farmer.

Issue of Monroe Hanford and Mabel Jane (McCumber) Faulkner, born in Middletown, Delaware County, New York:[162]

i. Virginia Irva Faulkner, born 7 August 1910, living in Chicago, Illinois. She married, on 23 August 1930, in Crown Point, Indiana, Thomas Akira Fujibayashi, born 30 August 1909 in Makawao, Maui, Hawaii. They had issue, surname *Fujibayashi*: a. *Ellen Mitsuye*, born 2 April 1931, married, 4 April 1952, Norman Paul Fors; b. *Wendell Masato*, born 13 July 1932, married, 23 August 1950, Barbara Ann Carter; c. *Tamiye Marcia*, born 14 October 1942, married, 1 September 1962, Rudolph Joseph Trejo; d. *Craig Monden*, born 28 March 1948.

ii.   Lenora Birdella Faulkner, born 13 August 1911, living in Delhi, New York. She married, on 16 April 1932, in Binghamton, New York, Louis Lester Bush, born 19 March 1908 in Fleischmanns, New York, and had issue, surname *Bush*: a. *Marjorie Ann*, born 27 March 1933, married, 11 October 1949, Gordon Richard Mason; b. *Evelyn Marie*, born 16 April 1934, married, 19 July 1953, Harold Durward Owens; c. *Louis Lester*, born 10 July 1945, married, 17 August 1968, Kathy Knox Farnsworth.

W79 iii. Woodrow Telford Faulkner, born 13 February 1923.

W51 **Marvin Cleveland Faulkner**, born 8 July 1884 in Barbour District, Orange County, Virginia, died 24 January 1962 in Stamford, New York, was buried in Manorkill Cemetery.

He married, on 28 May 1911, in Conesville, New York, Birdell Pearsall, daughter of George Washington and Melissa Carolyn (Scovill) Pearsall, born 27 March 1887 in Conesville, New York,[163] died 15 September 1972 in Manorkill, New York, buried in Manorkill Cemetery.

He was a farmer.

Issue of Marvin Cleveland and Birdell (Pearsall) Faulkner:[164]

i.   Pauline Irene Faulkner, born 20 April 1912 in Dunraven, New York. She married, on 25 September 1937, Cleneth Barkman. They divorced in 1940. Issue, surname *Barkman*: a. *Janet Maxine*, born 7 February 1938, married, 26 March 1955, George Medrick Haight; b. *Wayne Selwyn*, born 21 May 1939, married, 14 March 1964, Mary Ann Bennett.

ii.   Elwood Marvin Faulkner, born 27 August 1914 in West Conesville, New York, died 22 September 1978 in Warrensburg, New York, buried in the Bates Cemetery, Johnsburg, New York. He married, in August 1953, Blossom Dunkley. No issue.

W80 iii. Clayton Pearsall Faulkner, born 14 August 1915.

iv.   Marjorie Doris Faulkner, born 24 September 1916, living in Margaretville, New York. She married, on 5 December 1936, William Preston Ackerley, and had issue, surname *Ackerley*: a. *Douglas Lee*, born 16 June 1937, married Diane Dewitt; b. *Donald William*, born 6 April 1941, married, 28 March 1964, Barbara Brockway; c. *Joyce Marie*, born 19 July 1942, married, 24 September 1960 Jon Benson; d. *Iris Elaine*, born 2 March 1947, married, firstly, 12 December 1964, John Franklin Guyette, and, secondly, Milton Wood; e. *Gary Lynn*, born 5 May 1949, married Diane Fancher; f. *Jacquelyn Faye*, born 5 January 1954.

W81 v.   Louis Scoville Faulkner, born 10 July 1918.

vi.   Vera Elizabeth Faulkner, born 7 January 1920, living in Preston Hollow, New York. She married, on 11 August 1940, Dewitt Malcolm Cook, and had issue, surname *Cook*: a. *Milton Stephen*, born 10 April 1941, married, 25 February 1961, Irene Garner; b. *Bonnie Francine*, born 20 Jun 1942, married, 2 April 1960, Philip Norman Bates; c. *Barbara Jean*, born 9 October 1945, married, September 1965, Steven Warren Wood.

vii. Margaret Maxine Faulkner, born 5 December 1920. She married, on 1 November 1939, Guy Wilbur Miller, and had issue, surname *Miller*: a. *Lawrence Edward*, born 8 October 1939, married, 11 June 1962, Marian Jean ——; b. *Walter Marvin*, born 16 January 1941, married, firstly, 21 December 1961, Naomi Ruth ——; c. *Donna Lee*, born 1 January 1943, married, 2 September 1961, Edward Thomas Loy, Jr.

W82   viii. Carl Lincoln Faulkner, born 12 February 1930.

W52   **Gerald S. Faulkner**, born 25 May 1877 in Ceres Township, McKean County, Pennsylvania, died 29 July 1967 in Cuba, New York, was buried in Chestnut Hill Cemetery, Portville, New York.[165]

He married, on 28 January 1904, in Ceres, New York, Clara A. MacDonald, daughter of Randall MacDonald, born 10 September 1885 in Ceres Township, McKean County, Pennsylvania, died 26 February 1959 in Helmuth, New York, buried in Chestnut Hill Cemetery.[166]

Their home was in Franklinville, New York, for a number of years.

Issue of Gerald S. and Clara A. (MacDonald) Faulkner:[167]

W83   i.   John Donald Faulkner, born 28 December 1904.
      ii.   Hugh S. Faulkner, born about 1907, died, unmarried, 8 December 1931 in Wirt, New York.

W53   **Guy H. Faulkner**, born 7 September 1889 in Ceres Township, McKean County, Pennsylvania, died 21 February 1972 in Bradford, Pennsylvania, buried in St. Bernard Cemetery.

He married, on 20 August 1917, in Olean, New York, Margaret Mulcay, daughter of John and Mary (O'Donnell) Mulcay, born 26 July 1894 in Machias, New York, died 10 October 1975 in Bradford, Pennsylvania, buried in St. Bernard Cemetery.

In 1920, they lived in Olean, New York, where he operated a meat market. In Bradford he also owned a meat market and worked for another store as a butcher.[168]

Issue of Guy H. and Margaret (Mulcay) Faulkner:[169]

      i.   Guy R. Faulkner, born 29 June 1918 in Olean, New York, died, unmarried, 4 April 1983 in Buffalo, New York, buried in St. Bernard Cemetery. A graduate of Tri-State College, he was an employee of the Quaker State Oil Refining Company.[170]

W54   **Charles Gordon Faulkner**, born 7 April 1871 in Afton, New York, died 22 January 1917 in Ceres Township, McKean County, Pennsylvania, was buried in Evergreen Cemetery.

He married, on 5 February 1895, in Ceres, Pennsylvania, Irena May Hamilton, daughter of George G. and Mary Esther (Holmes) Hamilton, born 22 June 1876 in Ceres Township, McKean County, Pennsylvania, died 26 February 1965 in Olean, New York, buried in Evergreen Cemetery.

He purchased his father's farm in Ceres in 1900. He was a member of the Grange and the Maccabees.

Issue of Charles Gordon and Irena May (Hamilton) Faulkner, born in Ceres Township, McKean County, Pennsylvania:[171]

      i.   Harry Charles Faulkner, born 2 March 1897, died 9 September 1911 in Ceres Township, McKean County, Pennsylvania, buried in Evergreen Cemetery.
      ii.   Margaret Irene Faulkner, born 4 March 1898, died 18 July 1988 in Tulsa, Oklahoma, buried in Lamphier Cemetery, Eldred, Pennsylvania. She was a graduate of Lock Haven State College and taught school. She married, on 21

October 1926, in Frewsburg, New York, William S. Sullivan, who died 30 December 1974, and had issue, surname *Sullivan*: a. *Richard Faulkner*, born 14 September 1927, of Tulsa, Oklahoma; b. *Charlene Esther*, born 1 April 1935, of Batavia, Ohio, married William Baird.

iii. Mildred Louise Faulkner, born 13 June 1900, died 30 June 1995 in Olean, New York, buried in Mount Prospect Cemetery. She worked as a bookkeeper and accountant and lived in Franklinville, New York.. She married, on 29 November 1928, in Franklinville, New York, Robert Duncan Hatch, who died 29 September 1967. No issue.

W84 iv. Raymond Elbert Faulkner, born 19 October 1901.

v. Laura Elmira Faulkner, born 24 September 1906, died 31 July 1962. She married, on 25 February 1953, Lloyd Smith.

W85 vi. Merritt Gordon Faulkner, born 15 September 1911.

W55 George Percy Faulkner, born 20 November 1879 in Ceres Township, McKean County, Pennsylvania, died 6 December 1926 in Portville, New York, was buried in Chestnut Hill Cemetery.

He married, on 6 May 1900, in Ceres, New York, Alice May Baker, born 24 September 1879 in Wellsville, New York, died 28 June 1959 in Portville, New York, buried in Chestnut Hill Cemetery.

He worked as an engineer and stonemason.

Issue of George Percy and Alice May (Baker) Faulkner:[172]

i. Clifford Ernest Faulkner, born 2 February 1901, died 5 November 1913, buried in Chestnut Hill Cemetery.

W86 ii. Chester William Faulkner, born 19 January 1903.

W87 iii. George Percy Faulkner, born 10 October 1905.

W88 iv. John Reginald Faulkner, born 28 February 1909.

W89 v. Roland Baker Faulkner, born 20 March 1911.

vi. Ruth Louise Faulkner, born 9 May 1916, died 24 June 1916 in Olean, New York, buried in Chestnut Hill Cemetery.

vii. Janet Maxine Faulkner, born 9 December 1918, lives in Florida. She married, as her first husband, Buford Taylor, but divorced. She married, as her second husband, Charles Keller, and had issue, surname *Keller*: a. *Virginia*, married Vern Cummins; b. *John Taylor*.

viii. Alice Joan Faulkner, born 20 September 1920, died 24 July 1982 in Salt Lake City, Utah. She married, on 25 June 1938, in Olean, New York, Cloyd Norton Plummer, and had issue, surname *Plummer*: a. *Sharon*; b. *Cloyd Norton*.

W90 ix. Emmett Dwight Faulkner, born 10 July 1922.

W56 Archie Bryant Faulkner, born 7 February 1882 in Sanford, Broome County, New York, died 24 June 1955 in Hale Eddy, New York, was buried in Hale Eddy Cemetery.

He married, on 19 June 1906, in Deposit, New York, Hazel Aliene Vanakin, daughter of Jacob and Florence (Crisman) Vanakin, born 1887 in New York, died 1969 in Hale Eddy, New York, buried in Hale Eddy Cemetery. She married, as her second husband, Ivan Lobdell.

He worked on his father's farm until 1920, when he and his family moved to a farm in Hale Eddy. He was a Baptist in Deposit and a Methodist in Hale Eddy.

Issue of Archie Bryant and Hazel Aliene (Vanakin) Faulkner, born in Deposit, New York:[173]

    i.   Shirley Irene Faulkner, born 9 August 1908, died 16 August 1963 in Deposit, New York, buried in Hale Eddy Cemetery. She married, on 20 September 1926, in Deposit, New York, Carl William Clark, son of William James and Emeroy (Mayo) Clark, born 23 August 1904 in Deposit, New York, died 1978 in Binghamton, New York. They had two sons.

W91 ii. Jacob Hilton Faulkner, born 4 September 1910.

    iii. Yective Yolia Faulkner, born 22 April 1919, lives in Walton, New York. She married Russell Neale and has two sons and one daughter.

    iv. Elizabeth Jane Faulkner, born 3 March 1925, lives in Athol, Massachusetts. She married Frederick Hillis and has two daughters.

W57   **Charles E. Faulkner**, born October 1865 in Brookfield, Madison County, New York, was living in 1937 in Lenox, Madison County, New York.

He married, on 25 February 1890, in Whitelaw, Madison County, New York, Elnora B. ——, born February 1875 in New York, died 7 July 1937 in Lenox, Madison County, New York, buried in Whitelaw Cemetery.[174]

Issue of Charles E. and Elnora B. Faulkner, born in Lenox, Madison County, New York:[175]

    i.   Nellie M. Faulkner, born December 1891, lived in Canastota, New York, in 1937. She married, on 16 February 1910, in Lenox, New York, Vincent Rogers, born about 1882 in New York, and had issue, surname *Rogers*:[176] a. *Harriet*, born about 1911; b. *Vincent*, born about 1912; c. *Esther*, born about 1914; d. *Ruth*, born 1919.

    ii. Wesley C. Faulkner, born 15 April 1897, living in 1937 in Canastota, New York.

    iii. Dewey Elmer Faulkner, born June 1898, died 24 July 1932 in Lenox, Madison County, New York, was buried in Whitelaw Cemetery. He married, before 1926, Ethel Phillips. No issue.

    iv. Mildred J. Faulkner, born 5 June 1912, lived on Oneida Lake in 1937. She married Edward James.

W58   **Edward H. Faulkner**, born 29 March 1878 in Lenox, Madison County, New York, died September 1962.

He married, 24 February 1902, in Lenox, Madison County, New York, Goldie J. ——, born 24 October 1883 in New York, died 22 August 1966 in Oneida, New York.

Issue of Edward H. and Goldie J. Faulkner:

    i.   Kenneth L. Faulkner, living in Canastota, New York, 1970.

W59   **Edward L. Faulkner**, born 20 January 1855 in Mansfield, Pennsylvania, died 19 February 1889 near Mansfield, Pennsylvania, was buried in Prospect Cemetery.

He married, on 23 March 1883, in Mansfield, Pennsylvania, Mary (Mamie) E. Cook, of Bath, New York,[177] born 1861, died 1947.

He worked as a cattle drover, probably between Mansfield and Waverly,

New York. At the time of his marriage, he resided in Elmira, New York.
Issue of Edward L. Faulkner and Mary E. (Cook) Faulkner:[178]

W92   i.   Louis Edward Faulkner, born 2 November 1883.

    ii.   Ethel Julia Faulkner, born 18 July 1888. She married, on 18 August 1914, in Coudersport, Pennsylvania, Herbert Lawrence Grove, and had issue, surname *Grove*: a. *Carolyn*.

W60   **Charles E. Faulkner**, born 12 November 1860 in Mansfield, Pennsylvania, died 27 June 1929 in Agnew, California.

He married, on 28 December 1898, in Ruth, Stone County, Missouri, Martha E. Mason, born November 1877 in Illinois.

After editing the Marionville *Buz Saw*, he and his family lived in Drexel, Cass County, Missouri, from 1900 to about 1909, when they moved to Corning, California. They were in Hanford, California, in 1914 and 1916, and in San Leandro, California, in 1919.

Issue of Charles E. and Martha E. (Mason) Faulkner:[179]

    i.   Audra Caroline Faulkner, born 13 January 1900 in Marionville, Missouri, died June 1981 in Hanford, California. She married, 1 March 1919, in San Leandro, California, Engelbert A. Prangner, born 8 June 1889, died April 1974 in Hanford, California, and had issue, surname *Prangner*: a. *Martha Marie*, born 6 January 1920 in Hanford, California, married, June 1946, Allen Coutchie.

    ii.   Lydia Helen Faulkner, born 10 August 1904 in Drexel, Missouri, died in 1976. She married, as her first husband, on 25 July 1925, in San Leandro, California, Wesley Oliver Engblom, and had issue, surname *Engblom*: a. *Wesley O.*, born 1936. She married, as her second husband, on 7 December 1940, Albert E. McKean.

W93 iii. Charles Howard Faulkner, born 18 August 1906.

W94 iv. Patrick Henry Faulkner, born 26 April 1908.

    v.   Julia Ann Faulkner, born 22 October 1910 in Corning, California, died 14 June 1985. She married, as her first husband, on 4 June 1932, Hector Dove. She married, as her second husband, on 21 April 1939, Randall H. Smith, and had issue, surname *Smith*: a. *Saralee Ann*, born 1941.

    vi.   Todd Downs Faulkner, born 6 August 1912 in Corning, California, died 19 June 1921 in San Leandro, California.

    vii.   James Mason Faulkner, born 12 September 1914 in Hanford, California, died 8 July 1990 in Pleasanton, California.

    viii.   Robert Edward Faulkner, born 16 January 1916, died 17 August 1983 in Alameda County, California.

W61   **John Weston Faulkner**, born 7 February 1871 in Waverly, New York, died 5 July 1950 in Aurora, Missouri, was buried in Marionville Cemetery.

He married, on 29 October 1890, in Marionville, Missouri, Alice Reid DeFever, daughter of Jesse and Malinda DeFever, born 15 April 1872 in Morton, Missouri, died 14 October 1952 in Marionville, Missouri, buried in Marionville Cemetery.

He attended Marionville College in 1888 and 1889. For several years, he and his brother Charles edited a newspaper in Marionville, *The Buz Saw*, which name they later changed to the Marionville *Free Press*. They later sold out and John and Alice homesteaded a quarter-section of land in Stone County, Missouri. They proved their rights, sold the land, and moved to a farm near Harrisonville, Missouri, from which, after four years, they returned to Marionville, where he farmed.

Issue of John Weston and Alice Reid (DeFever) Faulkner:[180]

	i.	infant, born and died in 1891, buried in Marionville Cemetery.
	ii.	Bernice Olive Faulkner, born 30 January 1896, died 1959 in Marionville, Missouri. She married, in February 1920, Frank A. Moore, and had issue, surname *Moore*: a. *Mildred*, born 22 December 1920.
W95	iii.	John DeFever Faulkner, born 19 August 1901.
W96	iv.	Charles F. Faulkner, born 18 January 1904.
W97	v.	Edward Carroll Faulkner, born 6 July 1906.

W62   William E. Faulkner, born August 1872 in Pennsylvania, died after 1920, when in Canton Township, Bradford County, Pennsylvania.

He married Lena A. ——, born about 1878 in Pennsylvania, living in 1920. He worked as a finisher in a cabinet factory in Canton in 1920.

Issue of William E. and Lena A. Faulkner:[181]

	i.	Egbert E. Faulkner, born 28 November 1904 in Pennsylvania, died August 1980 in Troy, Pennsylvania.
	ii.	John W. Faulkner, born about 1906 in New York.

W63   Charles Edward Faulkner, born 13 September 1874 in Salina, Kansas, died April 1969 in Minneapolis, Minnesota.

He married, on 24 October 1905, in Binghamton, New York, Caroline Mann, born 7 October 1879 in Binghamton, New York, died January 1975 in Minneapolis, Minnesota.

He served as a sergeant and 2nd master sergeant in Company M, 15th Minnesota Infantry, during the Spanish-American War. In 1935, he was a clerk in the Chamber of Commerce Clearing Association in Minneapolis.

Issue of Charles Edward and Caroline (Mann) Faulkner:[182]

	i.	Marion Faulkner [daughter], born about 1906.
	ii.	Edward C. Faulkner, born about 1908, possibly the Edward born 8 February 1908, died March 1988 in Remer, Minnesota.
	iii.	Louise Faulkner, born 1917.

W64   James Alfred Faulkner, born 27 May 1887 in Brookfield, Madison County, New York, died 29 May 1947 in Sherburne, New York, was buried in Brookfield Cemetery.

He married, on 18 November 1912, Reta Ulea Gould, daughter of Frank DeAlton and Donna Inez (Maine) Gould, born 3 November 1892 in New York, died 23 November 1973 in Norwich, New York, buried in Old Fisk Farm Cemetery. She married, as her second husband, Harry Purdy.

Issue of James Alfred and Reta Ulea (Gould) Faulkner:[183]

W98   i.   Fay Edward Faulkner, born 13 February 1915.

W65   George Judson Faulkner, born 19 April 1875 in Venango Township, Erie County, Pennsylvania, died 27 August 1941 in Spokane, Washington.

He married, on 3 January 1900, in Tobias, Nebraska, Hattie Chase, daughter of Luman and Lucy Elizabeth (Pratt) Chase, born 20 November 1884 in Tobias, Nebraska, died 23 December 1968 in Spokane, Washington.

They lived in 1900 in Lincoln Precinct, Saline County, Nebraska. In 1920, he was the manager of a grain farm in Freeman Township, Spokane County, Washington.

Issue of George Judson and Hattie (Chase) Faulkner:[184]

   i.   Ethel Miriam Faulkner, born 5 April 1901 in Friend, Nebraska, lives in Spokane, Washington. She married, on 29 March 1923, Cecil Ellis Womack, born 6 June 1904 in Elkton, Missouri, died 19 January 1983 in Spokane, Washington, and had issue, surname *Womack*: a. *Jessie Cecelia*, born 27 July 1925, died 1 December 1977, married, 5 February 1944, Dale William Conboy; b. *Walter LaVerne*, born 21 February 1929, died 23 September 1992, married, 28 August 1949, Delores Charlene Berg.

   ii.   Millie M. Faulkner, born 30 March 1903, died 19 January 1976. She married Clarence Snodgrass and had issue, surname *Snodgrass*: a. *Harold*; b. *Glen*; c. *Dale*; d. *Alice*, married —— Blattner; e. *Betty*, married —— Savon.

W99   iii. Harry Judson Faulkner, born 21 March 1905.

W100 iv.   George Luman Faulkner, born 5 July 1914.

W101 v.   Ralph Gordon Faulkner, born 14 June 1917.

W102 vi.   Wayne Lester Faulkner, born 28 February 1922.

W66   Lee J. Faulkner, born September 1870 in Venango Township, Erie County, Pennsylvania, died 22 November 1934 in Amity Township, Erie County, Pennsylvania, was buried in Wattsburg Cemetery.

He married Leafy J. Maynard, born January 1875 in Wattsburg, Pennsylvania, died 24 November 1960 in Corry, Pennsylvania, buried in Wattsburg Cemetery.

He was a farmer in Amity Township.

Issue of Lee J. and Leafy J. (Maynard) Faulkner:[185]

W103 i.   Robert Lee Faulkner, born 18 September 1898.

   ii.   Marjorie G. Faulkner, born about 1901, living in Corry, Pennsylvania, in 1969. She married, as her first husband, Burt Hurst, and, as her second husband, Andrew Paulson.

W67   Alonzo J. (Jay) Faulkner, born 10 October 1876 in Venango Township, Erie County, Pennsylvania, died 25 July 1969 in Union City, Pennsylvania, was buried in Evergreen Cemetery.

He married, as his first wife, Flora E. Lord, born 1877 in Pennsylvania, died 10 April 1926 in Union City, Pennsylvania, buried in Evergreen Cemetery.

He married, as his second wife, on 7 September 1926,[186] in Erie, Pennsylvania, Lucia A. (Blakeslee) Peterson, daughter of Sanford and Malinda (Richardson) Blakeslee, born 1883, died 25 December 1967 in Union City,

Pennsylvania, buried in Evergreen Cemetery.

The family lived in Union Township, then in Union City, where he worked as a laborer and night watchman.

Issue of Alonzo J. and Flora E. (Lord) Faulkner:[187]

W104 i.   Carl N. Faulkner, born 18 August 1895.

W105 ii.   Charles Earl Faulkner, born 2 April 1897.

W106 iii.   Oral Kenneth Faulkner, born 31 August 1898.

iv.   Ruth Caroline Faulkner, born 26 July 1903 in Amity Township, Erie County, Pennsylvania, died 20 May 1988 in Erie, Pennsylvania. She married Charles E. Loomis, and had issue, surname *Loomis:*[188] a. *Charles*; b. *Ervin G.*; c. *Paul M.*; d. *Edith*, married Robert Stubenhofer; e. *Bette*, married LeRoy Pircio; f. *Norma Jean*, married Delivan Kitts.

v.   Mabel Ellen Faulkner, born about 1906, living in Centerville, Pennsylvania, in 1976. She married, on 23 January 1924, in Erie, Pennsylvania, Gale Bidwell, son of Leonard and Anna (Barnhart) Bidwell, born about 1897 in Centerville, Pennsylvania.

vi.   Harold Faulkner, born 1908, living in Selinsgrove, Pennsylvania, in 1969.

vii.   Herbert Faulkner, born about 1910, died young.

viii.   Margaret Faulkner, born 1915, living in Oil City, Pennsylvania, in 1988. She married —— Edwards.

W68   **Floyd Johnson Faulkner**, born 2 December 1895 in North Brookfield, New York, died 21 May 1980 in Columbus, Mississippi, was buried in Waterville Cemetery, Waterville, New York.

He married, as his first wife, on 14 June 1922, in Waterville, New York, Laura Marion Snell, born 24 December 1898 in Waterville, New York, died 11 November 1965 in Waterville, New York, buried in Waterville, New York.

He married, as his second wife, in 1969, Margaret (Pugh) Stott. She died in 1971.

He was an electrical contractor in Waterville and Skeneateles, New York..

Issue of Floyd Johnson and Laura Marion (Snell) Faulkner:

i.   Marion Elizabeth Faulkner, born 28 July 1926 in Utica, New York, lives in Starkville, Mississippi. She married, on 13 October 1951, in Waterville, New York, John Henry Honsinger, son of Harvey and Agnes (Svenson) Honsinger, born 11 June 1925 in Earlville, New York, died 4 August 1972 in Artesia, Mississippi, and had issue, surname *Honsinger:* a. *John Henry*, born 9 July 1952, married, 21 October 1978, Jean Carol Ballard; b. *Richard Kyle*, born 25 January 1954, married, 10 December 1982, Mary Elizabeth Beasley; c. *Tad Alan*, born 10 August 1955, married, 21 December 1980, Jan Tisha Brown.

ii.   son, stillborn about 1933.

W69   **Donald L. Faulkner**, born 14 June 1910 in Phelps, New York, lives in Green Valley, Arizona.

He married June M. Greene, born June 1916 in Rochester, New York.

Issue of Donald L. and June M. (Greene) Faulkner:

i.   Donnalee M. Faulkner, born March 1943. She married, as her first husband, —— Atkinson, and had issue, surname *Atkinson:* a. *Scott L.*, born September 1971. She married, as her second husband, —— Butcher.

W107 ii.   William R. Faulkner, born January 1945.

iii.   Marrianne L. Faulkner, born 23 October 1950. She married —— Falconer.

W70   Leonard Faulkner, born 10 October 1902 in Brookfield, Madison County, New York, died 24 July 1968 in Oriskany Falls, New York.

He married, on 26 January 1927, Linnie Roberts, daughter of Clara Roberts, born 10 October 1910.

Issue of Leonard and Linnie (Roberts) Faulkner:[189]

i.   Shirley Ann Faulkner, born 23 April 1931, lives in Oriskany, New York. She married Harold Morris Biederman, and had issue, surname *Biederman*: a. *Steven Keith*, born 25 July 1952.

W108 ii.   Leonard Raymond Faulkner, born 10 August 1932.

W71   Charles Philip Faulkner, born 21 May 1907 in Brookfield, Madison County, New York, died 6 November 1981 in Hamilton, New York.

He married, on 26 October 1929, Edna Cahaw, born 3 May 1908.

He was a farmer near Oriskany Falls, New York.

Issue of Charles Philip and Edna (Cahaw) Faulkner:

i.   Anna C. Faulkner, lives in Minoa, New York. She married George Meyer, and had issue, surname *Meyer*: a. *William*.

ii.   Scott Faulkner, born 1935, died September 1945.

iii.   Joan Faulkner, lives in Sherburne, New York. She married Richard Day, and had issue, surname *Day*: a. *Bonnie Marie*, born 12 August 1958, died 13 August 1958; b. *Becky Ann*, born 12 August 1958, died 14 August 1958; c. *Brenda Lee*, born 12 August 1958; d. *Karen*; e. *Amy*.

iv.   Sally Lou Faulkner, born 1946, living in 1986 in Rome, New York.

W109 v.   Charles Philip Faulkner, born 24 May 1948.

W72   William Willis Faulkner, born October 1871 in Barton, New York, died 6 April 1949 in North Tonawanda, New York.

He married, on 22 September 1897, in North Tonawanda, New York, Catherine Elsie Smith, born 21 October 1872 in North Tonawanda, New York, died 31 December 1947 in North Tonawanda, New York.

Raised in North Tonawanda, he graduated from North Tonawanda High School in 1890. In 1900, he and his wife lived in Leechburg, Pennsylvania.[190] He was associated with the Creo-Dept Company from 1915 to 1948, retiring as secretary-treasurer. He was also a director of the Niagara Savings and Loan Association of Tonawanda.[191]

Issue of William Willis and Catherine Elsie (Smith) Faulkner, the first two born in Leechburg, Pennsylvania:[192]

i.   Catherine Jane Faulkner, born 18 June 1900, died 19 May 1908 in Tonawanda, New York.

ii.   William Willis Faulkner, born 9 October 1903, died, unmarried, 29 August 1978 in Bedford, Virginia. He married, in 1937, Mary Murphy.

W110 iii.   James Levant Faulkner, born 7 May 1908.

W73   Frank LaPierre Faulkner, born 6 September 1892 in Scott Township, Wayne County, Pennsylvania, died 1 February 1972 in Norwich, New York, was buried at Afton, New York.

He married, on 27 December 1919, in Deposit, New York, Margaret Kniskern, daughter of James Mathew and Katherine Jane (Sherman) Kniskern, born 14 November 1897 in Sanford, New York, died 2 April 1963 in Afton, New York.

Raised by his uncle Louis, he graduated from Cornell University in 1916, with the degree of Bachelor of Science in Agriculture. During World War I, he served in the United States Infantry, Second Division, and was awarded a Purple Heart. In the early 1920s, they lived at Southbury and Georgetown, Connecticut, moving to Afton, New York, in 1924, where he operated a dairy farm.

Issue of Frank LaPierre and Margaret (Kniskern) Faulkner:[193]

    i.   James Louis Faulkner, born 15 November 1920, died, unmarried, 14 October 1983 in Yonkers, New York.

W111 ii.   Frank Kniskern Faulkner, born 21 April 1922.

    iii.   Alice Katherine Faulkner, born 24 December 1924, lives in White Plains, New York. She married, on 17 January 1964, in New York, New York, Robert Beryl Heller, son of Abbott and Mollie (Lavitt) Heller, born 29 March 1921, and had issue, surname *Heller*: a. *Steven Daniel*, born 7 November 1965; b. *Marc Ronald*, born 3 January 1968.

W74   Harry Reynolds Faulkner, born 30 November 1880 in Lone Tree, Iowa, died 19 October 1956 in Loveland, Colorado, was buried in Lakeside Cemetery, Loveland, Colorado.

He married, on 15 December 1904, in Loveland, Larimer County, Colorado,[194] Ida Bell Kerr, daughter of John Wesley and Susan N. (Neeley) Kerr, born 31 August 1887 in Lyons, Colorado, died 17 December 1971 in Fort Collins, Colorado, buried in Lakeside Cemetery.

He was a farmer in the Highland Lake district of Weld County, thirteen miles southeast of Loveland.

Issue of Harry Reynolds and Ida Bell (Kerr) Faulkner:[195]

    i.   Kathryn Ruby Faulkner, born 13 March 1905, died 13 March 1965 in Loveland, Colorado. She married Leo Bencomo, born 1896, died 23 January 1964. No issue.

    ii.   Norma Jean Faulkner, born 1906, died 1933 in Lima, Ohio. She married —— Stephenson.

W112 iii.   Estes Leslie Faulkner, born 11 January 1908.

    iv.   Verda Arlene (Billie) Faulkner, born 13 July 1911. She married Al Powell, born 1904, died 1974. No issue.

    v.   Newell R. Faulkner, born 21 September 1913, died 15 May 1915, buried in Lakeside Cemetery.

    vi.   Charlotte Maxine Faulkner, born 2 July 1915, died 10 April 1992 in Denver, Colorado. She married, on 30 July 1934, in Fort Collins, Colorado, Glenn Robert Kirkman, born 18 December 1907 in Fairbury, Nebraska, died 18 June 1985 in Denver, Colorado. Issue, surname *Kirkman*: a. *Patricia Jo*, born 23 March 1941, lives in Colorado Springs, Colorado, married, 17 January 1959, Richard Lee Sullivan.

vii.   Susie Faulkner, born 8 July 1917, lives in Denver, Colorado. She married, as her second husband, Samuel Wilson. No issue.

W113 viii.   Edwin Curtis Faulkner, born 5 September 1919.

W75   Alva Raymond Faulkner, born October 1894 in Loveland, Colorado, died 10 December 1956 in Glendale, California, was buried in Forest Lawn Cemetery.

He married, as his first wife, on 12 March 1915, Ellen Laura Fletcher, daughter of James Monroe and Emma (Lowe) Fletcher, born 28 January 1893 in Sherman, Pennsylvania, died June 1951 in Glendale, California, buried in Forest Lawn Cemetery.

He married, as his second wife, Ingrid ——, born 26 November 1893, died April 1971 in Glendale, California.

Issue of Alva Raymond and Ellen Laura (Fletcher) Faulkner, born in Glendale, California:[196]

i.   Marion Eleanor Faulkner, born 11 December 1915, lives in Newport Beach, California. She married, as her first husband, on 6 June 1941, Gareth Spencer Ortman, and had issue, surname *Ortman:* a. *Nancy Ann*, born 30 April 1944 in Glendale, California; b. *John Fletcher*, born 6 August 1947 in Chattanooga, Tennessee. She married, as her second husband, on 14 July 1976, Charles Ecclestone.

W114 ii.   Alva Raymond Faulkner, born 23 January 1926.

W76   Bayard H. Faulkner, born 19 July 1894 in Bucklin, Missouri, died 13 November 1983 in Montclair, New Jersey.

He married, in 1916, Eleanor Ross Collins, daughter of Samuel Ross and Ada Belle (Post) Collins, born 11 July 1893 in New Jersey, died 12 October 1990 in Montclair, New Jersey. She was a member of the Montclair Dramatic Club and appeared in many of the group's productions.

He graduated from Dickinson High School in Jersey City, New Jersey, in 1911 and then received the degree of Bachelor of Commercial Science from New York University. He first worked as an accountant and then in steel manufacturing, and then in 1927 became active in Wall Street. In 1930, he joined the Seaboard Oil Company as treasurer.

He and his family moved to Montclair in 1919. In 1934, he led a local movement to introduce the city manager form of government to the community. Although the proposal was defeated, he was elected to the Montclair City Commission first in 1936 and served until 1947, in addition to being Director of Revenue and Finance, Director of Public Safety, and mayor at various times. Governor Alfred E. Driscoll appointed him in 1948 chairman of the New Jersey Committee on Municipal Government, a group which wrote the Municipal Optional Charter Law, popularly known as the Faulkner Act. From 1957 to 1968 he was a member of the executive committee of the New Jersey Taxpayers Association. He also served on the Montclair Board of Education, as a trustee and vice-president for administration of planning of Mountainside Hospital, and as a member of the Board of Managers of the Montclair Savings Bank.[197]

Issue of Bayard H. and Eleanor Ross (Collins) Faulkner:[198]

W115 i.   Ross H. Faulkner, born 1917.
    ii.   Dean H. Faulkner, born 1919, a management consultant living in 1990 in Denver, Colorado.
    iii. Kent V. Faulkner, living in 1990 in Montclair, New Jersey, a retired executive of IBM.

W77   **Lyman George Faulkner**, born 22 May 1903 in New Kingston, New York, died 9 September 1946 in New Kingston, New York, was buried in New Kingston Cemetery.

He married, on 25 June 1929 in Cabin Hill, New York, Helen Sutherland, born 25 August 1900 in Cabin Hill, New York, died 3 December 1986 in Schoharie, New York, buried in New Kingston Cemetery.

He worked in his father's store.

Issue of Lyman George and Helen (Sutherland) Faulkner:

W116 i.   George Richard Faulkner, born 23 August 1930.

W78   **Curtis Lewis Faulkner**, born 16 February 1907 in New Kingston, New York, lives in Binghamton, New York.

He married, on 22 November 1936, in Lake Delaware, New York, Gertrude E. Adee, born 9 June 1914 in Arena, New York.

He worked as a machine operator in Binghamton.

Issue of Curtis Lewis and Gertrude E. (Adee) Faulkner:

W117 i.   Donald Lewis Faulkner, born 1 June 1940.
W118 ii. Robert Eugene Faulkner, born 6 November 1943.
    iii. Sara Mae Faulkner, born 25 June 1950, lives in Shelton, Connecticut. She married, on 5 August 1972, in Kattelville, New York, Robert Charles Greenwood, born 28 May 1944 in Williamsport, Pennsylvania.

W79   **Woodrow Telford Faulkner**, born 13 February 1923 in Middletown, New York, lives in Vaucluse, Sydney, New South Wales, Australia.

He married, on 9 March 1946, in Balmain, Australia, Lorna May Brown, born 26 August 1927 in Snails Bay, Balmain, Sydney, New South Wales, Australia.

Issue of Woodrow Telford and Lorna May (Brown) Faulkner:

    i.   Diann May Faulkner, born 15 May 1948 in Chicago, Illinois.
    ii. Gary Wayne Faulkner, born 1 February 1952 in Sydney, New South Wales, Australia. He married, on 3 May 1975, in Sydney, Glenys Cecelia Beard, born 13 November 1954 in Sydney, Australia.

W80   **Clayton Pearsall Faulkner**, born 14 August 1915 in Manorkill, New York, lives in Stamford, New York.

He married, on 22 July 1938, Bernice Gordon Goss.

Issue of Clayton Pearsall and Bernice Gordon (Goss) Faulkner:

    i.   Gordon Cleveland Faulkner, born 1 December 1943.

    ii.   Jean Carroll Faulkner, born 12 September 1949.

W81   **Louis Scoville Faulkner**, born 10 July 1918 in Manorkill, New York, died 7 February 1991 in Stamford, New York, was buried in Manorkill Rural Cemetery.

    He married, on 1 August 1942, Gertrude Adaline Warner.

    Issue of Louis Scoville and Gertrude Adaline (Warner) Faulkner:

    i.   Joan Mildred Faulkner, born 25 March 1943.

    ii.   Garry Louis Faulkner, born 8 October 1946, lives in Stamford, New York.

    iii. Larry Paul Faulkner, born 8 October 1946.

W82   **Carl Lincoln Faulkner**, born 12 February 1930 in Manorkill, New York.

    He married, on 26 April 1953, Patricia Ann Gray. They divorced in 1972.

    Issue of Carl Lincoln and Patricia Ann (Gray) Faulkner:

    i.   Amy Lynn Faulkner, born 16 January 1953.

    ii.   Michael Steven Faulkner, born 16 October 1957.

W83   **John Donald Faulkner**, born 28 December 1904 in Ceres Township, McKean County, Pennsylvania, died 18 October 1992 in Bolivar, New York, was buried in Maple Grove Cemetery, Friendship, New York.

    He married, on 12 March 1929, in Ceres, Pennsylvania, Mary E. Dick, born 15 February 1905, died August 1986 in Bolivar, New York.

    A graduate of Portville High School, following a teachers' training course, he taught at the Main Settlement School. For several years he was a member of the New York State Police at the Batavia Barracks. Later he worked in the Bolivar oil fields as a pumper and worked as a cement finisher for various construction companies. Towards the end of his life, he was the owner of a second-hand store in Friendship.

    Issue of John Donald and Mary E. (Dick) Faulkner:[199]

    i.   Donn Dick Faulkner, born 6 July 1930, lives in Bolivar, New York.

    ii.   John S. Faulkner, lives in Bolivar, New York.

    iii. Duane K. Faulkner, lives in Bolivar, New York.

    iv.   Jerry H. Faulkner, lives in Friendship, New York.

    v.   Molly Faulkner, lives in Bolivar, New York. She married Richard Bishop.

W84   **Raymond Elbert Faulkner**, born 19 October 1901 in Ceres Township, McKean County, Pennsylvania, died 6 September 1978 in Olean, New York, was buried in Evergreen Cemetery, Ceres.

    He married, as his first wife, Marie Dininey. They later divorced.

    He married, as his second wife, on 23 January 1942, in Pittsford, New York, Elizabeth Catherine Currie, daughter of Samuel J. and Agnes (Cogle) Currie, born 23 July 1910 in Pavilion, New York, died 14 May 1992 in Olean, New York, buried in Evergreen Cemetery.

Issue of Raymond Elbert and Marie (Dininey) Faulkner:

W119 i.   Raymond C. Faulkner.
ii.   Jane Marie Faulkner, died 3 March 1981.
iii.   Theodore R. Faulkner, lives in Lockport, New York.

Issue of Raymond Elbert and Elizabeth O. (Currie) Faulkner:

iv.   Sally Irene Faulkner, lives in Randolph, New York. She married Robert Jacky.
v.   Patrick J. Faulkner, lives in Olean, New York.

W85   **Merritt Gordon Faulkner**, born 15 September 1911 in Ceres Township, McKean County, Pennsylvania, lives in Olean, New York.

He married, in 1936 in Olean, New York, Helen Christine Keegan, daughter of Thomas M. and Johanna (Flynn) Keegan, born 16 September 1911 in Coudersport, Pennsylania, living in Olean, New York.

He worked for the Exchange National Bank of Olean, ultimately becoming its president, until his retirement in 1972. Carpentry was his avocation; he was involved in civic activities.

Issue of Merritt Gordon and Helen Christine (Keegan) Faulkner:

W120 i.   Phillip Gordon Faulkner, born 10 October 1936.
W121 ii.   Thomas Keegan Faulkner, born 10 October 1940.
W122 iii.   John David Faulkner, born 26 February 1945.

W86   **Chester William Faulkner**, born 19 January 1903 in Little Genesee, Allegheny County, New York, died 12 October 1974 in Olean, New York.

He married, on 1 July 1929, in Cuba, New York, Evelyn A. Jordan.

Issue of Chester William and Evelyn A. (Jordan) Faulkner:

i.   Chester Clyde Faulkner, born 11 November 1932, lives in Olean, New York. He married Virginia Dawn Hatch.
W123 ii.   Richard L. Faulkner, born 1 June 1934.
iii.   Robert E. Faulkner, lives in Olean, New York. He married Bonita Elliott.
W124 iv.   Donald H. Faulkner, born 9 October 1939.
v.   Diane Faulkner, born 10 February 1946. She married Ted Shaw.

W87   **George Percy Faulkner**, born 10 October 1905 in Ceres Township, McKean County, Pennsylvania, died 12 January 1993 in Snow Hill, North Carolina.

He married, on 1 June 1926, Katherine Senn.

He was a farmer in the Olean, New York, area.

Issue of George Percy and Katherine (Senn) Faulkner:

i.   Margaret Faulkner, born 17 May 1928, lives in Gainesville, Georgia. She married —— Pasford.
ii.   Allen H. Faulkner, lives in Sebastian, Florida.
iii.   George Percy Faulkner, lives in Snow Hill, North Carolina.

    iv.   Jean Faulkner, lives in Dona Ana, New Mexico. She married —— Judd.

    v.   Frederick W. Faulkner, lives in Ceres, New York.

    vi.   John Faulkner, lives in Sebastian, Florida.

    vii.   Suzanne Faulkner, lives in Snow Hill, North Carolina. She married —— Kenniston.

W88   **John Reginald Faulkner**, born 28 February 1909 in Olean, New York, lives in Portville, New York.

    He married, as his first wife, Ann ——. They divorced.

    He married, as his second wife, Janet Mary Yardman.

    Issue of John Reginald and Ann Faulkner:

    i.   Jean Faulkner.

    Issue of John Reginald and Janet Mary (Yardman) Faulkner:

    ii.   Kathy Ann Faulkner, born September.

W125 iii.   James Michael Faulkner, born October.

    iv.   John Reginald Faulkner, born October.

W89   **Roland Baker Faulkner**, born 20 March 1911 in Olean, New York, died 4 March 1982 in Phoenix, Arizona, was buried in Chestnut Hill Cemetery, Portville, New York.

    He married, on 9 September 1932, in Little Genesee, Allegany County, New York, Rhea Edna Chisholm, born 15 June 1914.

    Issue of Roland Baker and Rhea Edna (Chisholm) Faulkner:[200]

    i.   Donna Rae Faulkner, born 19 April 1933, lives in Los Angeles, California. She married, as her first husband, on 4 February 1950, Robert James Gordon, born 11 April 1928, died 1 January 1974, and had issue, surname *Gordon*: a. *Sally Ann*, born 18 August 1950, married, first, Gabriel Castorena; second, Javad Borzonei; b. *Donna Teresa*, born 3 November 1953, married William Reid, born 8 February 1950. She married, as her second husband, Leonard Kesky, and had issue, surname *Kesky*: c. *Leonard Edward*, born 19 February 1961, married, 23 April 1988, Donna Jo Blackburn; d. *LaDawn Marie*, born 19 September 1963, married Jesse Napolis. She married, as her third husband, Arthur Gerhart, but divorced.

W126 ii.   Roland Clifford Faulkner, born 18 September 1934.

W127 iii.   David Lee Faulkner, born 29 March 1938.

W128 iv.   Reginald Roy Faulkner, born 6 June 1941.

W129 v.   Paul Brian Faulkner, born 22 September 1946.

    vi.   Denise Ann Faulkner, born 19 November 1959, lives in Wellsville, New York. She married, on 19 February 1977, Donald Michael Hodgkins, born 15 April 1958, and has issue, surname *Hodgkins*: a. *Jonah Michael*, born 13 May 1977; b. *Amber Rhea*, born 13 May 1979; c. *Asya LeAnn*, born 5 June 1990; d. *Aaron Michael*, born 16 February 1992.

W90   **Emmett Dwight (Zeke) Faulkner**, born 10 July 1922 in Olean, New York, lives in Whittier, California.

    He married, on 6 December 1945, in Corpus Christi, Texas, Carolyn

Eleanor Lloyd, daughter of David Thomas and Edith May (Thomas) Lloyd, born 21 May 1923 in Pittsburgh, Pennsylvania, died February 1996..

He worked as a plant manager.

Issue of Emmett Dwight and Carolyn Eleanor (Lloyd) Faulkner:[201]

W130 i. James Lloyd Faulkner, born 24 February 1948.

ii. Edward Dennis Faulkner, born 8 April 1951 in Olean, New York, living in Signal Hill, in 1982. He married, on 31 August 1991, in Laughlin, Nevada, Patricia Salas.

iii. Kenneth Alvin Faulkner, born 3 March 1953 in Huntington Park, California.

W91 **Jacob Hilton Faulkner,** born 4 September 1910 in Deposit, New York, died 28 August 1960 in Hancock, New York, was buried in Hale Eddy Cemetery.

He married, on 7 July 1932, in Deposit, New York, Lois Lonelle Constable, born 1915, died 1983, buried in Hale Eddy Cemetery.

He lived in Deposit. For many years he worked as a machinist for the Scintilla Aviation plant in Sidney, New York. He moved there two years before his death.

Issue of Jacob Hilton and Lois Lonelle (Constable) Faulkner:

W131 i. Hilton Edward Faulkner, born 21 July 1933.

iii. Annette Lois Faulkner, born 31 August 1935, lives in Deposit, New York. She married, on 7 January 1951, in Deposit, New York, Richard James Stanton, son of Howard and Margaret (Melious) Stanton, born 7 March 1933 in Deposit, New York, and has issue, surname *Stanton*: a. *Kenneth Lee*, born 30 July 1951, lives in Deposit, New York, married first, 30 October 1971, Carolyn Rae Lee (divorced), second, 26 August 1983, Nancy Louise Vaughn Shaver; b. *Gary James*, born 29 March 1953, lives in Abilene, Texas, married first, 30 November 1974, Eve Marie Warner, second, Sally Ann Hart; c. *Richard Hilton*, born 2 October 1959, lives in Bainbridge, New York, married first, August 1980, Denise Ann Paul, and second, 19 May 1983, Ann Baudendistel.

W132 ii. Paul David Faulkner, born 1938.

W92 **Louis Edward Faulkner,** born 2 November 1883 in Mansfield, Pennsylvania, lived in Hattiesburg, Mississippi.

He married, on 9 October 1907, Flora Metcalf, born 30 August 1878 in New York, died July 1965 in Hattiesburg, Mississippi.

He was vice-president of the Mississippi Central Railroad.

Issue of Louis Edward and Flora (Metcalf) Faulkner:[202]

i. Mary Elizabeth Faulkner, born about 1914, of Hattiesburg, Mississippi. She married —— Mapp.

W93 **Charles Howard Faulkner,** born 18 August 1906 in Drexel, Missouri, died 23 March 1971 in Willows, California.

He married, as his first wife, on 12 June 1926, Edith Louise Kernan, who died in January 1937 in Bakersfield, California.

He married, as his second wife, on 31 July 1937, Lucille Agnew.

Issue of Charles Howard and Edith Louise (Kernan) Faulkner:

    i.   Charles H. Faulkner, born 1928, lives in Bellevue, Michigan.

    ii.   Donald M. Faulkner, born 1934, lives in West Sacramento, California.

W94   **Patrick Henry Faulkner**, born 26 April 1908 in Drexel, Missouri, lives in Glendora, California.

He married, on 25 May 1929, in Reno, Nevada, Mary Coogley.

Issue of Patrick Henry and Mary (Coogley) Faulkner:

    i.   Patrick H. Faulkner, born 1934, lives in Olalla, Washington.

    ii.   Ronald Todd Faulkner, born 1938. He married, on 25 June 1960, in Glenn County, California, Avon Katzenberger.

    iii. Robin James Faulkner, born 1943, lives in Dublin, California. He married first, on 9 June 1962, in San Mateo County, California, Deanna A. Thomas. He married, as his second wife, on 22 July 1967, in Monterey County, California, Sharon L. Hardin.

W95   **John DeFever Faulkner**, born 19 August 1901 in Marionville, Missouri, died 23 December 1989 in Bowling Green, Kentucky.

He married, on 1 October 1929, Alice Solari, born 1901.

He lived in many places, including North Dakota, and, in 1952, Rushville, Illinois.

Issue of John DeFever and Alice (Solari) Faulkner:[203]

    i.   Alice Louise Faulkner, born 3 February 1937. She married, on 27 August 1957, Charles G. O'Neil, and had issue, surname *O'Neil*: a. *Jon G.*, born 1959, died 1989; b. *Brenden P.*, born 1969.

    ii.   Joann D. Faulkner, born 1938, lives in Bowling Green, Kentucky. She married, on 27 January 1961, Basil Jones, Jr., born 1936, and had issue, surname *Jones*: a. *Cynthia L.*, born 1963, married, 21 December 1981, Larry W. West; b. *Christopher F.*, born 1966.

W96   **Charles F. Faulkner**, born 18 January 1904 in Marionville, Missouri, died 6 January 1988 in North Kansas City, Missouri.

He married, on 4 March 1933, Josephine Brixey, born 25 May 1909, died 19 June 1987 in Aurora, Missouri.

He lived in Aurora, Missouri, from 1935, where he owned and operated a household appliance dealership.

Issue of Charles F. and Josephine (Brixey) Faulkner:

W133 i.   Charles Brixey Faulkner, born 11 February 1934.

W97   **Edward Carroll Faulkner**, born 6 July 1906 in Marionville, Missouri, lives in Birmingham, Michigan.

He married, on 21 October 1929, Barbara Ann Fite, born 1906, lives in Birmingham, Michigan.

Both graduated from the University of Missouri in 1929, he with a B.S. in civil engineering and she with a B.A. in education. They soon moved to Detroit, Michigan, where he was a construction engineer, owning the Faulkner Construction Company, an industrial contractor now based in Midland, Michigan.

Issue of Edward Carroll and Barbara Ann (Fite) Faulkner:[204]

    i. Ann Elizabeth Faulkner, born 12 August 1931 in Detroit, Michigan, lives in Franklin Lakes, New Jersey. She married, on 15 May 1954, Robert E. Esch, born 1932, and had issue, surname *Esch*: a. *Linda Ann*, born 22 April 1956; b. *Thomas Robert*, born 12 July 1959; c. *Susan Elizabeth*, born 8 January 1963; d. *Jean Constance*, born 25 November 1965; e. *Daniel Edward*, born 31 August 1971.

    ii. Barbara Carol Faulkner, born 20 June 1934 in Detroit, Michigan, lives in Burtonsville, Maryland. She married, 18 December 1954, Lawrence D. Peck, born 1934, and had issue, surname *Peck*: a. *David Edward*, born 12 February 1961, married, 25 August 1983, Carla Eklund; b. *Wendy Carol*, born 4 October 1965, married, 17 October 1987, Marc P. Webster.

W98 **Fay Edward Faulkner**, born 13 February 1915 in Watertown, New York, died 12 April 1967 in Sherburne, New York.

He married, on 22 July 1934, in Schenectady, New York, Hilda Harriet Gaylord, daughter of Joseph Karl and Clara Mae (Baker) Gaylord, born 22 February 1915 in Hamilton, Madison County, New York, living in Sherburne, New York.

Issue of Fay Edward and Hilda Harriet (Gaylord) Faulkner:[205]

W134 i. Frank Karlton Faulkner, born 22 March 1935.

    ii. Shelley Inez Faulkner, born 26 May 1936, lives in Cazenovia, New York. She married, on 15 October 1954, in Sherburne, New York, Lynn John Keator, son of Lynn Avery and Alice Edith (Lindridge) Keator, born 12 March 1934 in Norwich, New York, and has issue, surname *Keator*: a. *Monica Lynn*, born 12 June 1956, married, firstly, John William Colucy, and secondly, Kevin Stone.

W135 iii. James Fay Faulkner, born 9 October 1937.

W136 iv. Ronald Blaine Faulkner, born 17 July 1939.

    v. Lana Joy Faulkner, born 11 May 1943, lives in Vestal, New York. She married, on 30 May 1964, in Ithaca, New York, Paul Harold Roske, son of Fredrick Melvin and Lillian Berniece (Grimes) Roske, born 30 June 1941 in Hackensack, New Jersey, and has issue, surname *Roske*: a. *Timothy Paul*, born 2 December 1964, married, 26 May 1990, Julia Bartlett Hinton; b. *Michael Fay*, born 9 July 1967, married, 16 November 1991, Deborah Ann Giusti; c. *Maegan Lynelle*, born 10 July 1971.

    vi. Sara Anne Faulkner, born 9 June 1944 in Utica, New York.

    vii. John Faulkner, born 14 November 1947, died 15 November 1947.

W137 viii. Fay Edward Faulkner, born 2 February 1952.

W99 **Harry Judson Faulkner**, born 21 March 1905 in Spokane Bridge, Idaho, died 24 February 1979 in Coeur d'Alene, Idaho.

He married, on 26 November 1933 Ina B. Wilson, born 15 April 1902 in Emmett, Idaho, died 13 February 1995 in Coeur d'Alene, Idaho.

He was a staff officer for the U.S. Forest Service.

Issue of Harry Judson and Ina B. (Wilson) Faulkner:[206]

    i. Carol Louise Faulkner, born 12 November 1936.

W138 ii. David Roger Faulkner, born 7 April 1939.

W100   George Luman Faulkner, born 5 July 1914 in Mica, Washington, lives in Castroville, California.

He married, on 7 December 1941, Eva John, born 17 May 1912 in Cambridge, Nebraska.

Issue of George Luman and Eva (John) Faulkner:

W139 i.   Richard Allen Faulkner, born 16 April 1943.

W140 ii.   Donald Lee Faulkner, born 11 April 1945.

W101   Ralph Gordon Faulkner, born 14 June 1917 in Spokane, Washington, died 23 June 1983 in Spokane, Washington.

He married, on 13 July 1946, in Paris, France, Genevieve (Ginette) Lina Clement, born 21 September 1914 in France, died 25 January 1995 in Spokane, Washington.

Issue of Ralph Gordon and Genevieve Lina (Clement) Faulkner:[207]

i.   Diana France Faulkner, born 14 March 1950, living in 1983 in Spokane, Washington. She married James Barry and had two children.

ii.   Phillip Gordon Faulkner, born 8 March 1955 in Abqaiq, Saudi Arabia, died 30 May 1980 in Spokane, Washington.

W102   Wayne Lester Faulkner, born 28 February 1922 in Freeman, Washington, died 13 May 1993 in Chandler, Arizona, was buried in Pine Cemetery, Spokane, Washington.

He married, on 9 August 1946, in San Diego, California, Rosemary Skinnin, daughter of John William and Mary (Weaver) Skinnin, born 1 August 1923 in Crooksville, Ohio, lives in Sun Lakes, Arizona.

He worked as a meter man for the Washington Water Power Company in Spokane, Washington, for many years.

Issue of Wayne Lester and Rosemary (Skinnin) Faulkner:[208]

i.   Karen Faulkner, born 20 May 1947, lives in Mercer Island, Washington. She married, on 18 January 1986, Andy Carlos.

ii.   Maureen Faulkner, born 14 October 1949, lives in Spokane, Washington. She married, on 16 July 1983, Michael Girtz.

W141 iii.   John Judson Faulkner, born 14 February 1951.

iv.   Christine Mary Faulkner, born 26 August 1952, lives in Spokane, Washington. She married, on 19 December 1970, Scott M. Jamison.

v.   Michael Wayne Faulkner, born 11 April 1954, lives in Redondo Beach, Washington. He married, on 3 January 1981, Michelle McNeely.

vi.   Janice Marie Faulkner, born 14 December 1956, lives in Liberty Lake, Washington. She married Jeffrey Hoover.

vii.   Brian Joseph Faulkner, born 28 July 1959, lives in Spokane, Washington. He married, on 16 February 1985, Charline Kelly Stakelin.

viii.   Jeffrey James Faulkner, born 14 January 1963, lives in Spokane, Washington. He married, on 16 July 1994, Kristen Baumert.

W103   Robert Lee Faulkner, born 18 September 1898 in Wattsburg, Pennsylvania, died 23 March 1973 in Eastlake, Ohio, was buried in Evergreen Cemetery, Union City, Pennsylvania.

He married, 15 August 1923, in Union City, Pennsylvania,[209] Margaret Oakes Chapin, daughter of Frank C. and Addie A. (Oakes) Chapin, born 17 October 1896 in Mount Hope, Pennsylvania, died 2 August 1981 in Cleveland, Ohio, buried in Evergreen Cemetery.

He graduated from Allegheny College in 1919 and received his M.D. in 1923 from Johns Hopkins University and worked as a physician in Cleveland, Ohio, specializing in obstetrics-gynecology. He was also, from 1929 to 1966, a member of the faculty of Western Reserve University Medical School.

Issue of Robert Lee and Margaret Oakes (Chapin) Faulkner:[210]

    i.   Anne Faulkner, living in 1981. She married Ronald L. Golden, M.D.

    ii.   Robert Lee Faulkner, living in 1981 in Tucson, Arizona.

W104 Carl N. Faulkner, born 18 August 1895 in Union Township, Erie County, Pennsylvania, died 20 December 1976 in Pinellas Park, Florida.

He married, as his first wife, on 29 May 1920, in Union City, Pennsylvania,[211] Mildred A. Dorais, daughter of M. F. and Minnie (Nelson) Dorais, born about 1901 in Union City, Pennsylvania.

He married, as his second wife, Jeannette Walleze.

He served in the U. S. Army during World War I. He lived in Erie, Pennsylvania, where he worked for the General Electric Company for thirty years.

Issue of Carl N. and Mildred A. (Dorais) Faulkner:[212]

    i.   Jeannine A. Faulkner, lives in Erie, Pennsylvania. She married Richard J. Liebel.

    ii.   Alice Faulkner, lives in Waterford, Pennsylvania. She married Raymond Williams.

    iii. Ronald F. Faulkner, lives in Erie, Pennsylvania.

    iv. Keith M. Faulkner, lives in Erie, Pennsylvania.

    v.   Paul Robert Faulkner, living in Erie, Pennsylvania, in 1976.

    vi. Barry Faulkner, living in California in 1976.

W105 Charles Earl Faulkner, born 2 April 1897 in Union Township, Erie County, Pennsylvania, died 21 June 1983 in Erie, Pennsylvania.

He married, as his first wife, Bertha V. Fuller, who died in October 1966 in Erie, Pennsylvania.

He married, as his second wife, Daisy Peterson, born 18 October 1907, died 5 August 1990 in Erie, Pennsylvania.

He worked as a machinist at General Electric Company in Erie for about 25 years, retiring in 1962. He was a charter member of Bethel Baptist Church.

Issue of Charles Earl and Bertha (Fuller) Faulkner:[213]

    i.   Doris Faulkner, lives in Erie, Pennsylvania. She married —— Nelson.

    ii.   Charles Earl Faulkner, lives in Erie, Pennsylvania.

W142 iii. William A. Faulkner, born 25 November 1926.

    iv. Norman L. Faulkner, lives in White Stone, Virginia.

W106   Oral Kenneth Faulkner, born 31 August 1898 in Union Township, Erie County Pennsylvania, died 3 August 1989 in Erie, Pennsylvania.
He married, as his first wife, Helen ——.
He married, as his second wife, Dorothy M. (——) Young, born 14 July 1912, died February 1994 in Erie, Pennsylvania.
Issue of Oral Kenneth and Helen Faulkner:[214]

    i.   Myron Faulkner, living in McKean, Pennsylvania, in 1989.
    ii.   Howard K. Faulkner, living in Boca Raton, Florida, in 1989.

W107   William R. Faulkner, born January 1945 in Rochester, New York.
He married, as his first wife, Patricia Ennis.
He married, as his second wife, Mary Ann Kuric, born 4 June 1949 in Steubenville, Ohio.
Issue of William R. and Patricia (Ennis) Faulkner, born in Rochester, New York:

    i.   Erick A. Faulkner, born March 1972.

Issue of William R. and Mary Ann (Kuric) Faulkner, born in Rochester, New York:

    ii.   David A. Faulkner, born 4 June 1985.
    iii. Kathleen M. Faulkner, born 4 June 1985.

W108   Leonard Raymond Faulkner, born 10 August 1932 in Oriskany Falls, New York, lives in Vernon Center, New York.
He married, on 6 November 1954, DeLores Ann Dowd, daughter of James and Ellen (Murphy) Dowd, born 23 September 1934.
Issue of Leonard Raymond and DeLores Ann (Dowd) Faulkner:[215]

    i.   Scott Leonard Faulkner, born 15 March 1957.
    ii.   Gerry Ann Faulkner, born 7 May 1959. She married, as her first husband, William Efland, Jr., but divorced. By Lyle Donald Shoen, Jr., she had issue, surname *Shoen*: a. *Erica Ann*, born 27 April 1983. She married, as her second husband, in August 1985, Gregory Clinch, born 7 March 1956, and had issue, surname *Clinch*: a. *Randi Lee*, born 19 January 1988.
W143 iii. Kevin James Faulkner, born 19 January 1963.
    iv. Loren David Faulkner, born 26 October 1969.

W109   Charles Philip Faulkner, born 24 May 1948 in Oriskany Falls, New York, lives in Nicholasville, Kentucky.
He married, in 1967, Phyllis Morgan.
Issue of Charles Philip and Phyllis (Morgan) Faulkner:[216]

    i.   Deborah Lee Faulkner, born 21 March 1968. She married, on 2 September 1989, in Jessamine County, Kentucky, Terry J. Reed.
    ii.   Charles Philip Faulkner, born 13 January 1971. He married, on 16 October

1993, in Jessamine County, Kentucky, Sabrina J. Taulbee.

iii. Raymond Sherman Faulkner, born 6 September 1974.

W110 **James Levant Faulkner**, born 7 May 1908 in Tonawanda, New York, died 10 February 1990 in Farmington, Maine, was buried in Kents Hill Cemetery.

He married, on 8 November 1933, at Pine Mountain, Harlan County, Kentucky, Barbara Page Wilbur, daughter of Willard E. and Florence (Bemis) Wilbur, born 17 July 1911 in Somerville, Massachusetts, lives near Mount Vernon, Maine.

He was a professional engineer. They lived in Ridlonville, Maine, in 1940 and later near Mount Vernon.

Issue of James Levant and Barbara Page (Wilbur) Faulkner:

    i. Hannah Bayley Faulkner, born 5 March 1939, lives in Mount Vernon, Maine.

W144 ii. Timothy Willis Faulkner, born 1 March 1942.

    iii. Martha Peirce Faulkner, born 1 June 1944, lives in Phillips, Maine. She married, on 11 May 1968, Stephen Fenno. They adopted a son, Timothy James, born 16 May 1973.

W111 **Frank Kniskern Faulkner**, born 21 April 1922 in Danbury, Connecticut, lives in Chame, Panama.

He married, on 12 September 1943, in Matawan, New Jersey, Ruth Elizabeth Russell, daughter of Franklin and Mildred (Henry) Russell, born 4 August 1922.

He worked as an electrical engineer, retiring from Ebasco Services, Inc., in 1987. He moved to Panama in 1990.

Issue of Frank Kniskern and Ruth Elizabeth (Russell) Faulkner:

    i. Margaret Ruth Faulkner, born 5 December 1944, lives in Haddonfield, New Jersey. She married Kenneth Hollister and has issue, surname *Hollister*: a. *Kari Lynn*.

W145 ii. Frank Russell Faulkner, born 13 September 1946.

    iii. Katherine Elizabeth Faulkner, born 10 November 1948. She married, on 25 August 1973, Terence Joseph Snipe, and has issue, surname *Snipe*: a. *Matthew*; b. *Andrew*; c. *Joshua*.

    iv. Mildred Anne Faulkner, born 20 November 1950. She married, in 1988, Jens Waale, and had issue, surname *Waale*: a. *Anna Katherine*.

    v. Carolyn Faulkner, born 2 December 1956. She married Ramazon Bulca, and has issue, surname *Bulca*: a. *Ibrahim Mikail*, born 28 January 1988 in Nuremburg, Germany.

W112 **Estes Leslie Faulkner**, born 11 January 1908 in Highland Lake District, Weld County, Colorado, died 2 July 1936 in Colorado, was buried in Lakeside Cemetery, Loveland.

He married, in 1928, Leona Mae Miller, daughter of Burt and Bertha Miller, born 9 June 1908, died February 1962 in Arvada, Colorado.

Issue of Estes Leslie and Leona Mae (Miller) Faulkner (she also had an adopted daughter, Bertha Maxine, born 16 August 1936):

    i.   Sadie Juanita Faulkner, born 30 December 1928 in Lyons County, Colorado, lives in Northglenn, Colorado. She married —— Wilburn, and has issue, surname *Wilburn*: a. *Linda Gale*, born 24 August 1949, married 30 August 1968 Randy Perkins; b. *Willa Arlene*, born 3 August 1950, married Steve Rawley; c. *Rose Marie (Deb)*, married Thomas Stark; d. *David Tracey*, born 11 January 1959, married Julie ——; e. *Quintin William*, born 8 December 1960, married Cindy ——.

W146 ii.   Donald Keith Faulkner, born 20 May 1930.

    iii.   Gertrude Alberta Faulkner, born 16 September 1932.

**W113	Edwin Curtis Faulkner**, born 5 September 1919 in Highland Lake District, Weld County, Colorado, died 29 January 1986 in Fort Lupton, Colorado.

He married, on 14 December 1941, in Kimball, Nebraska, Caroline Katherina Fiechtner, daughter of Jacob Wilhelm and Louisa (Heinrich) Fiechtner, born 16 July 1920 in Java, South Dakota, died 12 August 1989 in Denver, Colorado.

Their children were born in Loveland, Colorado, but they later moved to Fort Lupton.

Issue of Edwin Curtis and Caroline Katherina (Fiechtner) Faulkner:

W147 i.   Larry Edwin Faulkner, born 23 March 1943.

W148 ii.   James Estel Faulkner, born 13 February 1945.

W149 iii.   Samuel Francis Faulkner, born 29 July 1947.

    iv.   Ida Louise Faulkner, born 7 October 1958, lives in Fort Lupton, Colorado. She married, on 5 September 1981, in Fort Lupton, Colorado, Robert William Gordon, born 11 July 1944 in Grand Junction, Colorado, and has issue, surname *Gordon*: a. *Tina Louise*, born 15 May 1983.

    v.   Terry Lynn Faulkner, born 18 May 1962, died 22 December 1982 in Fort Lupton, Colorado.

**W114	Alva Raymond Faulkner, Jr.**, born 23 January 1926 in Glendale, California, lives in Avon, Connecticut.

He married, on 8 July 1949, Margaret Parcher, daughter of Carroll Wilmer and Frances (Morgan) Parcher, born 24 August 1927 in Glendale, California.

He worked as a mechanical engineer.

Issue of Alva Raymond and Margaret (Parcher) Faulkner:[217]

    i.   Mark Jeffrie Faulkner, born 9 January 1951, lives in San Diego, California.

    ii.   Carolyn Frances Faulkner, born 9 January 1951, lives in Vienna, Virginia. She married, on 18 March 1992, Lynn Arthur Dangelmier. By an earlier marriage, she had a daughter: a. *Kelly*.

W150 iii.   David Raymond Faulkner, born 12 April 1954, lives in Medford, New Jersey. He married, on 16 August 1975, Judy Crowley.

W151 iv.   Paul Howard Faulkner, born 2 August 1956, lives in South Boston, Virginia. He married, on 8 May 1981, Debbie Dellen.

    v.   Gareth Morgan Faulkner, born 17 November 1962 in Hartford, Connecticut, is a blacksmith in Woodbine, Maryland. He married, on 27 October 1990, in Colesville, Maryland, Elizabeth Ann Nicholls, born 25 September 1953 in

Washington, D.C.

vi. Ellen Elizabeth Faulkner, born 24 April 1965, lives in Germantown, Maryland. She married, on 29 August 1992, Scott Raines.

W115 Ross H. Faulkner, born 1917 in Montclair, New Jersey, was living in 1967 in Montclair, New Jersey.
He married Diane D. ——.
He was an investment banker.
Presumed child of Ross H. and Diane D. Faulkner:

i. Suzanne R. Faulkner.

W116 George Richard Faulkner, born 23 August 1930 in West Delhi, New York, was living in 1975 in Polk, Pennsylvania.
He married, on 2 February 1952, in New Paltz, New York, Joyce E. Clarkson, born 16 June 1932.
Issue of George Richard and Joyce E. (Clarkson) Faulkner:

i. George Richard Faulkner, born 7 August 1954 in Belleville, Illinois.
ii. Linda Lee Faulkner, born 5 April 1956 in Biloxi, Mississippi, lives in Canton, Ohio. She married, on 16 September 1975, David Foltz, born 3 August 1952 in Orange County, Indiana.
iii. Robert Nelson Faulkner, born 7 January 1963 in Ellenville, New York, lives in Canton, Ohio.
iv. Heather Marie Faulkner, born 6 December 1964 in Oneonta, New York.

W117 Donald Lewis Faulkner, born 1 June 1940 in Binghamton, New York, lives in Binghamton, New York.
He married, on 9 September 1961, in Binghamton, New York, Sharon J. Van Buskirk, born 24 January 1941 in Binghamton, New York.
He works as an accounting clerk.
Issue of Donald Lewis and Sharon J. (Van Buskirk) Faulkner:

i. David Keith Faulkner, born 10 June 1968. He married, on 17 August 1991, Tricia Sue Hutchison, born 19 August 1969.
ii. Michele Eileen Faulkner, born 17 June 1970.

W118 Robert Eugene Faulkner, born 6 November 1943 in Binghamton, New York, was living in 1975 in Afton, New York.
He married, on 5 April 1968, in Binghamton, New York, Caroline Lucille Arquette, born 6 April 19— in Binghamton, New York.
Issue of Robert Eugene and Caroline Lucille (Arquette) Faulkner:

i. Timothy Curtis Faulkner, born 20 June 1969 in Johnston City, New York. He married, on 31 December 198-, Jacki Lyn Becker.
ii. Tammy Lynn Faulkner, born 17 March 1971 in Sidney, New York.

W119 Raymond C. Faulkner, lives in Allegany, New York.
He married Mary C. ——.

He has worked as a lineman and serviceman for a power company.
Issue of Raymond C. Faulkner:

 i. Brian M. Faulkner.

 ii. Bruce R. Faulkner, lives in Allegany, New York.

 iii. Mark K. Faulkner.

W120 **Phillip Gordon Faulkner**, born 10 October 1936 in Olean, New York,
lives in Dallas, Texas.

He married, in 1956, in Olean, New York, Suzanne Marie Ryan, daughter
of Theodore Maker and Ruth Jo (Maxon) Ryan, born 2 November 1938 in
Olean, New York, lives in Dallas, Texas.

He received a B.S. degree in real estate and finance from Ohio State University, and did graduate studies at the University of Colorado and Michigan
State University. He lived in Arvada, Colorado, before moving to Dallas, Texas,
in 1974, where he is president of USLife Real Estate Service Corporation, a
subsidiary of USLife Corporation.

Issue of Phillip Gordon and Suzanne Marie (Ryan) Faulkner:[218]

 i. Deborah Marie Faulkner, born 24 May 1957. She married, on 7 November 1981, in Dallas, Texas, Paul Connery Shea.

 ii. Kathleen Jo Faulkner, born 11 September 1958. She married, in 1979, in Dallas, Texas, Kevin McCormick Nunley.

 iii. Diane Christine Faulkner, born 3 February 1960. She married, on 28 April 1990, in Dallas, Texas, Michael Eudy.

 iv. Margaret Ann Faulkner, born 11 July 1961. She married, on 23 May 1981, in Dallas, Texas, Hershell Malett, but divorced.

W121 **Thomas Keegan Faulkner**, born 10 October 1940 in Olean, New
York, lives in Allegany, New York.

He married, in 1962 in Olean, New York, Mary Ann Woodgie.

He is a banker. She works in retailing.

Issue of Thomas Keegan and Mary Ann (Woodgie) Faulkner:

 i. Tim Gordon Faulkner, born 29 June 1964.

 ii. Pamela Faulkner, born 9 June 1965. She married, on 10 June 1989, in Newport News, Virginia, Francis Malboeuf.

 iii. Michael Faulkner, born 25 June 1967.

W122 **John David Faulkner**, born 26 February 1945 in Olean, New York.

He married, in June 1971 in Buffalo, New York, Pamela Elizabeth Johnson,
born 30 September 1950 in Buffalo, New York.

He is a mechanical engineer.

Issue of John David and Pamela Elizabeth (Johnson) Faulkner:

 i. Jennifer Faulkner, born 16 February 1973.

 ii. Scott Matthew Faulkner, born 21 February 1976.

W123 **Richard L. Faulkner**, lives in Olean, New York.

He married Alberta M. ——.
He is a building contractor.
Issue of Richard L. Faulkner:

   i.   Vickie L. Faulkner, lives in Olean, New York. She married —— Tuttle.
   ii. Randy L. Faulkner, lives in Olean, New York.
   iii. Cindy A. Faulkner.
   iv. Wendy K. Faulkner.

W124 **Donald H. Faulkner**, born 9 October 1939 in Olean, New York, lives near Olean, New York.

He married, on 31 July 1960, in Obi, New York, Sue Brewer, daughter of Robert and Sarah (Foster) Brewer, born 27 January 1942 in Shinglehouse, Pennsylvania.

He is a builder.
Issue of Donald H. and Sue (Brewer) Faulkner:[219]

   i.   Lynne Faulkner, born 2 March 1961, lives in Allegeny, New York.
   ii. Kimberly Faulkner, born 22 July 1964, lives in Richmond, Virginia. She married Brian Merkel.
   iii. Amy Faulkner, born 24 September 1974, lives in Richmond, Virginia.

W125 **James Michael Faulkner**, lives in Portville, New York.
He married Gail Cook McCoy.
Issue of James Michael and Gail (Cook) Faulkner:

   i.   Matthew James Faulkner.

W126 **Roland Clifford Faulkner**, born 18 September 1934 in Portville, New York, lives in Prescott Valley, Arizona.

He married, as his first wife, on 25 August 1959, Dorothea Ann Margeson, born 5 June 1942.

He married, as his second wife, on 12 March 1977, Cynthia Joan Merry.
Issue of Roland Clifford and Dorothea Ann (Margeson) Faulkner (they also had an adopted son, Bryan Eugene, born 8 October 1958):

   i.   Michael Craig Faulkner, born 25 February 1960. He has a daughter, born 1982.
   ii. Renee Dee Faulkner, born 6 January 1962. She married, on 29 March 1985, Gene Perdock, and had issue, surname *Perdock:* a. *Monique Danielle*, born 16 June 1984; b. *Destiny Nicole*, born 25 December 1985; c. *Brandon Eugene*, born 25 March 1989.
   iii. Rory Dean Faulkner, born 6 January 1962, died 20 May 1989.
   iv. Rolinda Leigh Faulkner, born 14 March 1969. She married, on 29 August 1986, Arthur Eugene Gilbert, born 12 August 1965, and has issue, surname *Gilbert:* a. *Anthony Jacob*, born 26 February 1988; b. *Ruby Estelle*, born 16 March 1993.

W127 **David Lee Faulkner**, born 29 March 1938 in Portville, New York, lives in Scio, New York.

He married, as his first wife, on 15 November 1958, Sharon Ann Lounsberry, born 29 October 1942.

He married, as his second wife, on 22 February 1969, Mary Rose (Waters) Carlin, born 17 July 1942.

Issue of David Lee and Sharon Ann (Lounsberry) Faulkner:

W152 i.   David James Faulkner, born 22 March 1959.

W153 ii.   Robin Leigh Faulkner, born 29 November 1961.

W154 iii. Mark Leland Faulkner, born 18 November 1962.

     iv.   Gene Harvey Faulkner, born 18 November 1962.

W128 **Reginald Roy Faulkner**, born 6 June 1941 in Portville, New York, lives near Scio, New York.

He married, on 4 July 1960, Judy Elaine Hackett, born 2 February 1942.

Issue of Reginald Roy and Judy Elaine (Hackett) Faulkner (they also adopted her daughter Judith Eilene, born 23 December 1957):

W155 i.   Reginald Roy Faulkner, born 3 December 1961.

     ii.   Julie Ellen Faulkner, born 14 January 1964. She married, on 2 June 1984, Thomas Roger Giddings, and has issue, surname *Giddings*: a. *Joshua Thomas*, born 16 July 1989; b. *Juliana Eve*, born 11 May 1991.

     iii. June Elizabeth Faulkner, born 14 January 1965, lives in Scio, New York. She had a child, *Jill Elizabeth*, born 17 April 1985, whose father is Andy Mareno. She married, on 25 April 1987, Jeffrey Frederick Culbertson, and has issue, surname *Culbertson*: b. *Jaci Elise*, born 27 January 1988; c. *Jeffrey Kalib*, born 14 January 1989; d. *Joel Benjamin*, born 14 January 1989; e. *Josiah Aaron*, born 25 September 1990.

     iv. July Elaine Faulkner, born 15 March 1966, lives in Scio, New York. She married, on 1 July 1984, Glen Daniel Layfield, and has issue, surname *Layfield*: a. *Glen Derek*, born 20 December 1984; b. *Guy Daniels*, born 9 September 1986; c. *Craig Devon*, born 15 October 1990; d. *Kyle David*, born 11 May 1992.

     v.   Ronald Roy Faulkner, born 16 May 1967. He married, in June 1991, Sandra L. Fanton.

     vi. Jan Estelle Faulkner, born 1 December 1968. She married, on 14 June 1987, Timothy Baker, and has issue, surname *Baker*: a. *Timothy Levi*, born 8 January 1989; b. *Titus Luke*, born 18 August 1990.

     vii. Joleen Evelyn Faulkner, born 7 September 1978.

W129 **Paul Brian Faulkner**, born 22 September 1946 in Portville, New York.

He married, on 3 July 1965, Mary Margaret Reynolds, born 21 January 1946.

Issue of Paul Brian and Mary Margaret (Reynolds) Faulkner:

W156 i.   Paul Bruce Faulkner, born 12 June 1966.

     ii.   Philip Dion Faulkner, born 1 November 1969. He married, on 16 November 1992, Kerry Williamson.

W130 James Lloyd Faulkner, born 24 February 1948 in Lynwood, California, lives in Costa Mesa, California.

He married, on 20 December 1972, in Provo, Utah, Emelyn Castleton, daughter of Ralph Howard and Emelyn (Reading) Castleton, born 23 August 1951 in Provo, Utah.

Issue of James Lloyd and Emelyn (Castleton) Faulkner:

  i.   Emelyn Faulkner, born 11 September 1973 in Inglewood, California.

  ii.   James Castleton Faulkner, born 4 September 1975 in Provo, Utah.

  iii. John Robert Faulkner, born 14 August 1977 in San Gabriel, California.

  iv. Jeffrey Keith Faulkner, born 30 January 1979 in Inglewood, California.

  v.   Megan Faulkner, born 18 June 1980 in Inglewood, California.

W131 Hilton Edward Faulkner, born 21 July 1933 in Deposit, New York, died 26 May 1986 in Roscoe, New York.

He married, as his first wife, Ann Buchanan.

He married, as his second wife, Joan Neer. They divorced, and she married —— Kelsey.

He married, as his third wife, on 15 August 1965, in Roscoe, New York, Betty Davenport, daughter of Faron and Ethel (Finkle) Davenport, born 25 December 1944 in Roscoe, New York. She lives in Roscoe, New York.

He worked as a truck driver.

Issue of Hilton Edward and Joan (Neer) Faulkner:[220]

  i.   Hilton Edward Kelsey, born 15 September 1961. He was adopted by his stepfather.

Issue of Hilton Edward and Betty (Davenport) Faulkner:

  ii.   Deborah Lee Faulkner, born 26 June 1966, lives in Roscoe, New York. She married Wayne Melvin, and has issue, surname *Melvin*: a. *Tyler James*, born 11 January 1994.

  iii. James Edward Faulkner, born 12 May 1968, died 15 July 1984 in Roscoe, New York.

  iv. Connie Lucille Faulkner, born 2 April 1973.

  v.   Daniel Jacob Faulkner, born 14 January 1976.

W132 Paul David Faulkner, born 1938 in Deposit, New York, died July 1960, was buried in Hale Eddy Cemetery.

He married, in August 1959, Carol Ann Smith.

Issue of Paul David and Carol Ann (Smith) Faulkner:

  i.   Dawne Elaine Faulkner, born 22 February 1960, lives in Sidney, New York. She has issue, surname *Newell*: a. *Tonya Judy*, born 7 July 1978.

W133 Charles Brixey Faulkner, born 11 February 1934 in Missouri, lives in Shell Knob, Missouri.

He married, on 29 December 1956, Noralee Phariss, born 27 July 1933 in Monett, Barry County, Missouri.

He is a physician who had a practice in Kansas City, Missouri, for many years.

Issue of Charles Brixey and Noralee (Pharess) Faulkner:[221]

    i.   Charlisa Faulkner, M.D., born 18 October 1959 in Columbia, Missouri. She married, on 25 May 1991, in Kansas City, Missouri, Robert Wayne Allen, M.D., son of Walter Wayne and Judith Ann (Hillier) Allen, born 14 April 1963 in Guymon, Oklahoma, and has issue, surname *Allen*: a. *Joshua Lee*, born 13 September 1993. She is a psychiatrist.

W157 ii.   Charles Byron Faulkner, born 1962.

W134 Frank Karlton Faulkner, born 22 March 1935 in Norwich, New York, lives in Sherburne, New York.

He married, on 11 June 1956, in Oneonta, New York, Frinda Louise Palmer, adopted daughter of Elton Jay and Helen Francis (Reed) Palmer, daughter of Ken Schroer and Helen Yonalaitus, born 14 March 1936.

Issue of Frank Karlton and Frinda Louise (Palmer) Faulkner:

    i.   Rosemary Eileen Faulkner, born 3 May 1956, lives in Sherburne, New York. She married, as her first husband, Castle Creasy McHenry, by whom she had one son, but they divorced. She married, as her second husband, on 26 December 1981, in Sherburne, New York, Larry Henry Barker, born 28 March 1956 in Norwich, New York, and has issue, surname *Barker*: a. *Skipper John*, born 14 November 1975; b. *Krystal Leigh*, born 3 June 1983; c. *Cory Alexander*, born 2 May 1985.

    ii.   Susan Beth Faulkner, born 29 August 1957, lives in Norwich, New York.

W135 James Fay Faulkner, born 9 October 1937 in Sherburne, New York, lives in South New Berlin, New York.

He married on 8 June 1963, in Norwich, New York, Ann Marie (Jensen) Baldwin, daughter of Aage and Sigrid (Nielsen) Jensen, born 7 March 1940 in New Berlin, New York, lives in South New Berlin, New York.

Issue of James Fay and Ann Marie (Jensen) Faulkner:

    i.   Gary Allen Faulkner, born 26 May 1964, lives in Myrtle Beach, South Carolina.

W136 Ronald Blaine Faulkner, born 17 July 1939 in Sherburne, New York, lives in San Diego, California.

He married, on 21 September 1962, in Sherburne, New York, Judy Bierce, daughter of John Oakes and Janette Ruth (Lodor) Bierce, born 15 December 1944 in Lebanon, Madison County, New York.

Issue of Ronald Blaine and Judy (Bierce) Faulkner:

    i.   Ronald Blaine Faulkner, born 18 July 1963. He married, on 19 August 1989, in San Diego, California, Danielle Marie Garcia, born 16 April 1966.

    ii.   Jon Carroll Faulkner, born 9 July 1966.

    iii.   Christopher Yale Faulkner, born 1 December 1967.

W137 Fay Edward Faulkner, born 2 February 1952 in Norwich, New York, lives in San Diego, California.

He married, on 16 December 1972, in Sherburne, New York, Mary Lou Cunningham, daughter of Bernard James and Margaret Elizabeth (Smith) Cunningham, born 11 November 1953 in Norwich, New York, living in San Diego, California.

Issue of Fay Edward and Mary Lou (Cunningham) Faulkner:

    i.   Erin Elizabeth Faulkner, born 23 April 1982.

W138 **David Roger Faulkner**, born 7 April 1939 in Coeur d'Alene, Idaho, lives in Marysville, Washington.

He married, on 22 May 1965, Charlene Delauder, born 26 March 1937.

Issue of David Roger and Charlene (Delauder) Faulkner:

    i.   Amy Beth Faulkner, born 11 February 1967.
    ii. Scott David Faulkner, born 22 October 1969 in Osborn, Idaho.

W139 **Richard Allen Faulkner**, born 16 April 1943 in Abilene, Texas, lives in California.

He married, on 11 February 1968, Judy Ann Goodsell, born 14 October 1942 in New York State.

Issue of Richard Allen and Judy Ann (Goodsell) Faulkner:

    i.   Michael John Faulkner, born 18 August 1971 in Pacific Grove, California.

W140 **Donald Lee Faulkner**, born 11 April 1945 in Abilene, Texas, lives in Beech Creek, Pennsylvania.

He married, on 3 June 1966, Bonnie Poole Dorcy, born 3 February 1945.

Issue of Donald Lee and Bonnie Poole (Dorcy) Faulkner:

    i.   Amanda Faulkner, born 7 August 1972.
    ii. Hillary Faulkner, born 4 May 1974.
    iii. Elliott Charles Faulkner, born 16 May 1976 in Lock Haven, Pennsylvania.

W141 **John Judson Faulkner**, born 14 February 1951 in Spokane, Washington, lives in Spokane, Washington.

He married, on 10 November 1973, Cris Shriner.

Issue of John Judson and Cris (Shriner) Faulkner:

    i.   Tyson John Faulkner, born 30 July 1983.

W142 **William A. Faulkner**, born 25 November 1926 in Erie, Pennsylvania, lives in Lake City, Pennsylvania.

He married, on 21 August 1948, in Erie, Pennsylvania, as his first wife, June M. Sutch, daughter of John and Marie (Bullock) Sutch, born 10 January 1930 in Erie, Pennsylvania, died 18 March 1985 in Buffalo, New York, buried in Laurel Hill Cemetery, Erie, Pennsylvania.

He married, as his second wife, Doris Kane.

He had an insurance agency before his retirement.

Issue of William A. and June M. (Sutch) Faulkner:[222]

   i.   Janet L. Faulkner, born 12 August 1949, lives in Girard, Pennsylvania. She married Edward Blystone and has three children.

   ii.   Gary W. Faulkner, born 15 July 1952, lives in Lake City, Pennsylvania. He married Debra Laughlin and has two children.

   iii.   Beth A. Faulkner, born 28 March 1955, lives in Girard, Pennsylvania. She married David Fox and has one child.

   iv.   John E. Faulkner, born 14 August 1956, lives in Girard, Pennsylvania.

W143 **Kevin James Faulkner**, born 19 January 1963, lives in Vernon Center, New York.

He married, on 14 February 1988, Nancy Kitchen.

Issue of Kevin James Faulkner and Marsha Lopitz:

   i.   Melissa Marie Lopitz, born 14 April 1984.

Issue of Kevin James and Nancy (Kitchen) Faulkner:

   ii.   Dawn Faulkner, born 27 May 1988.

W144 **Timothy Willis Faulkner**, born 1 March 1942 in North Tonawanda, New York, lives in Augusta, Maine.

He married, on 2 September 1967, in Readfield, Maine, Evelyn Sylvester.

Issue of Timothy Willis and Evelyn (Sylvester) Faulkner:

   i.   Susan Mae Faulkner, born 19 July 1968 in Augusta, Maine.

   ii.   Sarah Faulkner, born 15 September 1970 in Charlotte, North Carolina.

W145 **Frank Russell Faulkner**, born 13 September 1946 in New Jersey.

He married, on 6 July 1968, in Wycoff, New Jersey, Margaret Ann Rieder, daughter of Harold and Irene (Lynch) Rieder, born 2 February 1947.

Issue of Frank Russell and Margaret Ann (Rieder) Faulkner:

   i.   Michelle Lynn Faulkner.

   ii.   Adam Michael Faulkner, born 15 August 1974.

W146 **Donald Keith Faulkner**, born 20 May 1930 in Loveland, Colorado, died 1956 in Denver, Colorado.

Issue of Donald Keith Faulkner:

   i.   Donald Keith Faulkner, born 13 May 1950.

   ii.   Douglas Faulkner.

   iii.   Dee Dee Faulkner.

   iv.   Della Darlene Faulkner. She was adopted.

W147 **Larry Edwin Faulkner**, born 23 March 1943 in Nevada, Missouri, lives in Loveland, Colorado.

He married, as his first wife, —— Scoggins.

He married, as his second wife, on 12 April 1974, in Loveland, Colorado, E. LaVerne Brown, born 16 March 1937 in Longmont, Colorado, died 18 June 1993 in Loveland, Colorado.

Issue of Larry Edwin Faulkner by his first marriage:

i.   Terry Dean Scoggins, born 12 June 1965 in Greeley, Colorado. He married, on 12 August 1991 in Greeley, Colorado, Carmen Maria Cooper, born 30 January 1960 in Great Falls, Montana. He adopted her child, Dakota Edwin Scoggins (born Charlie Dakota Cooper, 18 April 1986 in Anchorage, Alaska).

W148   James Estel Faulkner, born 13 February 1945 in Loveland, Colorado, lives in Fort Lupton, Colorado.

He married, on 27 February 1970, in Brighton, Colorado, Phyllis Jane Miller, born 16 July 1951 in Brighton, Colorado.

Issue of James Estel and Phyllis Jane (Miller) Faulkner, born in Loveland, Colorado:

i.   Jamie Kay Faulkner, born 31 October 1970.
ii. Larry Curtis Faulkner, born 5 December 1976.

W149   Samuel Francis Faulkner, born 29 July 1947 in Fort Collins, Colorado.

He married, on 26 February 1973, in Greeley, Colorado, June Ann Pound, born 14 January 1955 in Greeley, Colorado.

Issue of Samuel Francis and June Ann (Pound) Faulkner:

i.   Brandi Carol Faulkner, born 20 December 1973.
ii. Beau Eugene Faulkner, born 22 February 1979.

W150   David Raymond Faulkner, born 12 April 1954 in Glendale, California, lives in Medford, New Jersey.

He married, on 16 August 1975, Judy Crowley.

Issue of David Raymond and Judy (Crowley) Faulkner, born in Pennsauken, New Jersey:

i.   Allison Frances Faulkner, born 2 September 1984.
ii. Emma Caroline Faulkner, born 17 November 1993.

W151   Paul Howard Faulkner, born 2 August 1956 in Glendale, California, lives in South Boston, Virginia.

He married, on 8 May 1981, Debbie Dellen.

Issue of Paul Howard and Debbie (Dellen) Faulkner, born in South Boston, Virginia:

i.   Jonathan Howard Faulkner, born 29 May 1987.
ii. Lauren Faulkner, born 20 February 1990.

W152   David James Faulkner, born 22 March 1959, lives in Wellsville, New York.

He married, as his first wife, on 17 May 1980, Mary Therese D'Agostino. They divorced on 19 October 1985.

He married, as his second wife, on 9 November 1985, Jacquelynn Rene Wonderling, born 10 July 1966.

Issue of David James and Mary Therese (D'Agostino) Faulkner:

    i.   Matthew David Faulkner, born 11 April 1981.

    ii.   Benjamin Lee Faulkner, born 29 April 1983.

Issue of David James and Jacquelynn Rene (Wonderling) Faulkner:

    iii.   Ashley Elizabeth Faulkner, born 28 April 1986.

    iv.   Justin Daniel Faulkner, born 11 March 1988.

W153   Robin Lynn Faulkner, born 29 November 1961.

He married, on 1 November 1980, Nancy Lynn Priday, born 25 April 1962.

Issue of Robin Lynn and Nancy Lynn (Priday) Faulkner:

    i.   Jeremy Lynn Faulkner, born 24 January 1982.

    ii.   Trisha Lynn Faulkner, born 10 June 1983.

    iii.   Bethany Lynn Faulkner, born 3 July 1985.

W154   Mark Leland Faulkner, born 18 November 1962.

He married, on 12 July 1980, Cynthia Evelyne Spinks, born 27 January 1962.

Issue of Mark Leland and Cynthia Evelyne (Spinks) Faulkner:

    i.   Nathan Lee Faulkner, born 2 November 1980.

    ii.   Adam Richard Faulkner, born 23 November 1984.

    iii.   Brandon Scot Faulkner, born 29 June 1987.

W155   Reginald Roy Faulkner, born 3 December 1961, lives near Scio, New York.

He married, on 14 July 1984, Catherine Marie Ryan, born 2 May 1963.

Issue of Reginald Roy and Catherine Marie (Ryan) Faulkner:

    i.   Regis Ryan Faulkner, born 26 March 1989.

W152   Paul Bruce Faulkner, born 12 June 1966.

He married, in 1986, Vivian Daily.

Issue of Paul Bruce Faulkner and Tina Straight:

    i.   Emily Ann Straight, born 23 September 1986.

Issue of Paul Bruce and Vivian (Daily) Faulkner:

    ii.   Brittney Ann Faulkner, born 4 January 1988.

    iii.   Christopher Faulkner, born 27 May 1991.

W156 **Charles Byron Faulkner**, born 12 September 1962 in Aurora, Missouri, lives in Philadelphia, Pennsylvania.

He married, on 10 August 1985, in Kansas City, Missouri, Mary Louise Frische, daughter of Howard J. and Carolyn (Lachele) Frische, born 26 November 1962 in Seattle, Washington.

He is an ophthamologist and eye surgeon.

Issue of Charles Byron and Mary Louise (Frische) Faulkner:

    i.   Laura Elisabeth Faulkner, born 6 July 1990.

    ii.   Victoria Marie Faulkner, born 25 March 1992.

NOTES

[1] Ralph D. Smyth, "Mr. Patrick Falconer of Newark, N.J., and His Descendants," *New England Historical and Genealogical Register* 60 (Jan. 1906): 21-23; and Alvan Talcott, *Families of Early Guilford, Connecticut*, ed. Jacquelyn L. Ricker (Baltimore: Genealogical Pub. Co., 1984), pp. 421-422, are the main sources for the branch of the family which lived in Connecticut.

[2] See Ralph D. Smyth, "Lieutenant Governor William Jones, of New Haven Jurisdiction, and His Descendants," *New England Historical and Genealogical Register* 60 (Apr. 1906): 164-168. Her grandfather was Theophilus Eaton, first governor of New Haven, through whom a descent from Edward I, King of England, can be traced.

[3] Watson, *Register of Edinburgh Apprentices, 1666-1700*, p. 32.

[4] Scotland, Register of Deeds, RD2/54, p. 611, SRO.

[5] Register of Deeds, RD4/51, p. 155, SRO.

[6] George Scott, *The Model of the Government of the Province of East-New-Jersey in America* (Edinburgh: John Reid, 1685), pp. 196-198.

[6A] Ibid., reprinted in *Collections of the New Jersey Historical Society*, vol. 1 (Newark: the Society, 1874), p. 473.

[7] Smyth, "Mr. Patrick Falconer of Newark, N.J., and His Descendants," p. 21.

[8] *Documents Relating to the Colonial History of the State of New Jersey*, vol. 21: *Calendar of Records in the Office of the Secretary of State*, Archives of the State of New Jersey, 1st ser., vol. 21 (Paterson, N.J.: Press Printing and Pub. Co., 1899), pp. 164, 217.

[9] Ibid., p. 175.

[10] *Documents Relating to the Colonial History of the State of New Jersey*, vol. 23: *Calendar of New Jersey Wills, vol. 1, 1670-1730* , Archives of the State of New Jersey, 1st ser., vol. 23 (Paterson, N.J.: Press Printing and Pub. Co., 1901), p. 489.

[11] Ibid., p. 101.

[12] *Records of the Town of Newark, New Jersey* (Newark: for the New Jersey Historical Society, 1864), p. 104.

[13] Photostat of original will, Burton Historical Collection, Detroit Public Library. Will is recorded in East Jersey Deeds, D: 339, New Jersey State Archives.

[14] Smyth, "Mr. Patrick Falconer of Newark, N.J., and His Descendants," 21-23.

[15] Alvan Talcott, *Families of Early Guilford, Connecticut*, p. 831f.

[16] "son of Patrick ffalconar, late of Newark," New Haven Vital Records, 1: 108.

[17] Guilford (Conn.) Vital Records.

[18] Goshen (Conn.) Vital Records, 1: 268.

[19] Alvan Talcott, *Families of Early Guilford, Connecticut*, p. 880.

[20] Bernard Christian Steiner, *A History of the Plantation of Menunkatuck and of the Original Town of Guilford, Connecticut, Comprising the Present Towns of Guilford and Madison* (Baltimore: the author, 1897), p. 424.

[21] *Record of Service of Connecticut Men in the I. War of the Revolution II. War of 1812 III. Mexican War* (Hartford: 1889), p. 584.

[22] Guilford (Conn.) Vital Records.

[23] Sketch by Fred E. Page of Page family in *Whitney Point Reporter*, 27 Jan. 1949, at Broome County Library, Binghamton, N.Y.

[24] Guilford (Conn.) Vital Records.

[25] Branford (Conn.) Vital Records.

[26] Bible record, D.A.R. Collection, B.8: 92, in New York State Library, microfilm ed. This was transcribed in 1929 from the Bible then in possession of Phoebe J. Faulkner, of Margaretville, N.Y.

[27] *Biographical Review: This Volume Contains Biographical Sketches of the Leading Citizens of Delaware County, New York* (Boston: Biographical Review Pub. Co., 1895), p. 121.

[28] 1850 census, Delaware Co., N.Y., p. 491.

[29] Will, Erie Co. (Pa.) Register of Wills, file 1196.

[30] *Delhi Gazette*, 30 Mar. 1831, in Gertrude Barber, "Marriages Taken from the Delhi Gazette," typescript at Library of Michigan.

[31] 1850 census, Delaware Co., N.Y., p. 447.

[32] Gravestone; Bible record says born 12 January 1805.

[33] Ibid., 25 May 1831.

[34] 1850 census, Oswego Co., N.Y., p. 73; 1860 census, Oswego Co., N.Y., p. 617.

[35] Alvan Talcott, *Families of Early Guilford, Connecticut*, p. 1166.

[36] Tombstone inscriptions in Faulkner Cemetery from "Madison County Cemeteries," typescript at Oneida Public Library.

[37] Records of the Paris Religious Society.

[38] Bible record of Friend Lyman Faulkner, in D.A.R. Bible Records, vol. 3, at Guernsey Memorial Library, Norwich. N.Y. This was copied in 1948 from a bible owned by Mrs. George H. Agan of Norwich.

[39] Frederick Clifton Pierce, *Fiske and Fisk Family* (Chicago: W. B. Conkey, 1896), p. 237.

[40] Madison Co. (N.Y.) Deeds, P: 51, 52, 54.

[41] Bible record of Friend Lyman Faulkner, which gives dates of birth for the children; *Biographical Review: This Volume Contains Biographical Sketches of the Leading Citizens of Madison County, New York* (Boston: Biographical Review Publishing Co., 1894), pp. 379, 566.

[42] 1830 census, Broome Co., N.Y., p. 14.

[43] Dates are from the Patrick Faulkner Bible record; however, his widow's application for claims based on his military service says that he died 11 April 1832.

[44] Doris Yaple Geist and Roland W. Yaple, Jr., *The Yaple Family in America: Ancestors and Descendants of 1753 Immigrant Philip Henry Yaple* (Decorah, Ia.: Anundsen Publishing Co., 1990), p. 440.

[45] Claims, no. 12185, Box 48, Folder 2, New York State Archives.

[46] Tombstone inscriptions from Mrs. John F. Kuhns, *Cemetery Records: Erie County, Pennsylvania*, at Erie Public Library.

[47] Geist, *Yaple Family in America*, p. 440ff.

[48] *Delhi Gazette*, 18 Feb. 1863, in Gertrude Barber, "Deaths Taken from the Delhi Gazette," typescript at Library of Michigan. His birth date or age must be in error.

[49] Memorandum of Bayard H. Faulkner, possession of Charles H. Rose.

[50] Delaware Co. (N.Y.) Deeds, F: 393.

[51] Ibid., G: 310, 387; H: 113.

[52] Hugh's and Henry's death certificates name their parents as James Faulkner and Susan Fry; Delaware County deeds indicate James Faulkner was probably the father of Benjamin S., Hugh W., and Henry P.; a genealogy compiled by a grandson of Jeremiah Faulkner, in possession of Phillip G. Faulkner, 4421 Mendenhall Dr., Dallas, TX 75244, mentions James's children as Benjamin, Hannah, and Ruth; Benjamin's pension file includes an affidavit from Ruth A. Chamberlin, identified as his sister; typescript reminiscences of Emma Faulkner Loehr, 1932, sent by Charles Rose.

[53] 1850 census, Delaware Co., N.Y., p. 347. This identification will remain tentative until further confirmation can be made. Hannah Wood was named as a daughter of James in the sketch of Patrick's family by Willard Sanford.

[54] Chemung Co. (N.Y.) Surrogate's Records, file no. 1250.

[55] Death certificates of Hugh W. and Henry P. Faulkner.

[56] William Henry Van Benschoten, *Concerning the Van Bunschoten or Van Benschoten Family in America: A Genealogy and Brief History* (West Park-on-Hudson, N.Y.: the author, 1907), p. 778f.

[57] Willard Sanford, "Seventh Generation May Stretch Span of Bull Run Farm for Two Centuries," news clipping in possession of Curtis L. Faulkner.

[58] Van Benschoten, *Concerning the Van Bunschoten or Van Benschoten Family in America*, p. 779.

[59] Willard Sanford, "Seventh Generation May Stretch Span of Bull Run Farm for Two Centuries."

[60] Delaware Co. (N.Y.) Surrogate's Court, Box 450.

[61] *Delhi Gazette*, 12 Feb. 1840.

[62] Kitty R. (Hilton) Oman, Lillian G. Hughes, and Betty Gay, *The Descendants of Three Hilton Brothers* (Vancouver, Wash.: Kitty R. Oman, 1985), p. 17.

[63] Family record in possession of Phillip G. Faulkner; 1850 census, Delaware Co., N.Y., p. 927; Oman, *Descendants*

of Three Hilton Brothers, p. 17.

[64] Alvan Talcott, *Families of Early Guilford, Connecticut*, p. 802.

[65] Kenneth Lord, *Genealogy of the Descendants of Thomas Lord: An Original Proprietor and Founder of Hartford, Connecticut* (New York, n.p., 1946), p. 340.

[66] Tuttle, *Pioneers of Madison County, New York*, p. 87.

[67] Madison Co. (N.Y.) Deeds, AN: 197, 198.

[68] 1850 census, Madison Co., N.Y., p. 237.

[69] Ibid.

[70] *Tioga Eagle*, 16 Feb. 1848, in *Tioga County, Pennsylvania, Records* (n.p., 1981).

[71] *Mansfield Advertiser*, 26 Oct. 1887, in *Tioga County, Pennsylvania, Records*.

[72] 1860 census, Tioga Co., Pa., p. 546.

[73] Tioga Co. (Pa.) Wills, Registers Docket, A: 250; 1850 census, Tioga Co., Pa., p. 192.

[74] *Tioga County Agitator*, 12 Jan. 1870.

[75] Bible record, D.A.R. collection, B. 123: 48, New York State Library; 1855 census, Madison Co., N.Y.; 1860 census, Madison Co., N.Y. p. 953.

[76] Madison Co. (N.Y.) Deeds, BG: 65.

[77] *Boston Transcript* query, 2 Apr. 1928; 1850 census, Erie Co., Pa., p. 65; 1860 census, Erie Co., Pa., p. 23.

[78] *History: Erie County, Pennsylvania* (Chicago: Warner, Beers, 1884), p. 10.

[79] *Biographical Review: This Volume Contains Biographical Sketches of the Leading Citizens of Madison County, New York*, pp. 379-80; 1880 census, Madison Co., N.Y., 41-47-9-1.

[80] *Biographical Review: This Volume Contains Biographical Sketches of the Leading Citizens of Madison County, New York*, p. 566; but the Friend Lyman Faulkner Bible record says Feb. 13, 1828.

[81] James H. Smith, *History of Chenango and Madison Counties, New York* (Syracuse: D. Mason, 1880), 2: xii.

[82] *Biographical Review: This Volume Contains Biographical Sketches of the Leading Citizens of Madison County, New York*, p. 566.

[83] 1860 census, Delaware Co., N.Y., p. 955; 1875 state census, Delaware Co., N.Y.; 1900 census, Delaware Co., N.Y., 31-23-7-74.

[84] Delaware Co. (N.Y.) Surrogate's Court, Box 97.

[85] 1900 census, Essex Co., N.J., 20-108-1-33.

[86] 1850 census, Delaware Co., N.Y., p. 460; 1860 census, Delaware Co., N.Y. p. 1034; Delaware Co. (N.Y.) Surrogate's Court, Box 97; 1875 state census, Middletown, no. 324.

[87] Individual ordinance submission, L.D.S, by Mary Elizabeth Zufelt, P.O. Box 64, Rough and Ready, CA 95975.

[88] 1900 census, Mercer Co., N.J., 42-61-15-32; 1920 census, Mercer Co., N.J., 77-54-6-3.

[89] 1900 census, Essex Co., N.J., 17-58-5-76; 1920 census, Essex Co., N.J., 40-340-8-2.

[90] Civil War pension (certificate no. 367,198), National Archives.

[91] Bible of Benjamin S. Faulkner, in possession of Barbara W. Faulkner, R.R. 1, Box 2810, Mount Vernon, ME 04352; Delaware Co. (N.Y.) Surrogate's Court, Box 229.

[92] 1900 census, New York Co., N.Y., 131-194-9-78.

[93] 1900 census, Livingston Co., N.Y., 189-25-9-8.

[94] *Loveland Herald*, 15 July 1909; Bayard H. Faulkner memo.

[95] Pension file, National Archives; 1860 census, Wayne Co., Pa., p. 641.

[96] *Pioneer Families and Their Descendants in Fremont, Lincoln, and Pleasant Valley Townships Area, Johnson County, Iowa, 1837-1900* (Marceline, Mo.: Walworth Pub. Co., 1979), pp. 413-416.

[97] Charles H. Rose.

[98] 1900 census, Steuben Co., N.Y., 237-20-11-5, gives the birth year as 1849; her gravestone says 1851.

[99] *Corning Daily Democrat*, 7 June 1897.

[100] 1880 census, Chemung Co., N.Y., 10-79-32-29; 1900 census, Steuben Co., N.Y., 237-20-11-5; indexed marriage and death records in Steuben County Historian's office.

[101] Genealogy of Stokes family by a Mrs. Royer of Ohio, supplied by Curtis L. Faulkner, 94 Kattelville Rd., Binghamton, NY 13901. I would like to acknowledge the compiler of this very complete genealogy, which was done in the mid-1970s. This is the source for all of Lyman's descendants listed here.

[102] 1880 census, Delaware Co., N.Y., 15-77-40-24; 1892 state census, Delaware Co., N.Y.

[103] 1900 census, Delaware Co., N.Y., 31-22-20-51; Delaware Co. (N.Y.) Surrogate's Court, Box 248.

[104] Family record in possession of Phillip G. Faulkner.

[105] 1880 census, McKean Co., Pa., 52-84-19-1; 1900 census, McKean Co., Pa., 132-103-6-54.

[106] Pension file, National Archives; Records in possession of Phillip G. Faulkner; 1880 census, McKean Co., Pa., 52-84-18-44.

[107]"Biography of Nathan Faulkner," at Deposit Historical Society, information from Mark R. Clark.

[108]Most of the information on this branch is from Mark R. Clark, R.D. 1, Box 71W, Hancock, NY 13783.

[109]Edward A. Claypoole and Azalea Clizber, *A Genealogy of the Descendants of William Kelsey*, vol. 3 (n.p., 1947), p. 183.

[110]Pension, cert. 2,549,567, National Archives.

[111]1900 census, San Francisco Co., Cal., 32-158-4-69; 1920 census, Contra Costa Co., Cal., 17-11-7-100.

[112]1900 census, San Francisco Co., Cal., 32-167-9-47.

[113]1900 census, Alameda Co., Cal., 2-353-4-4; 1920 census, Alameda Co., Cal., 3-38-3-43.

[114]1900 census, San Luis Obispo Co., Cal., 38-25-2-94.

[115]Madison Co. (N.Y.) Surrogate's Court, file no. 9356.

[116]Most of the information on this branch comes from Edward C. Faulkner, 1611 Yorkshire Rd., Birmingham, MI 48009; *Mansfield Advertiser*, 10 Aug. 1887, in: *Tioga County, Pennsylvania, Records*; 1880 census, Tioga Co., N.Y., 96-204-55-24.

[117]The dates on his gravestone (born 14 June 1859, died 12 July 1861) are incorrect.

[118]*Deaths and Interments in Saline County, Kansas, 1859-1985* (Saline, Kans.: Smoky Valley Genealogical Society and Library, 1985).

[119]*Tioga County Agitator*, Jan. 1860, in: *Tioga County, Pennsylvania, Records*.

[120]1900 census, Tioga Co., N.Y., 15-120-3-2; Edward C. Faulkner.

[121]Charles L. Albertson, *History of Waverly, New York, and Vicinity* (Waverly, N.Y.: Waverly Sun, 1943), pp. 194-195.

[122]Pension file, National Archives.

[123]1880 census, Kans., 18-301-46-1; Pension file.

[124]Bible record, D.A.R. collection, B. 123: 48, New York State Library; Madison Co. (N.Y.) Surrogate's Court, file no. 5580-C-54; records of Paul H. Roske; 1880 census, Madison Co., N.Y., 41-47-7-28.

[125]Cyrus Henry Brown, *Brown Genealogy* (Boston: Everett Press Co., 1907), 1: 209f.

[126]Bible record, D.A.R. collection, B. 123: 48, New York State Library.

[127]Dates are from his pension file. His given name is uncertain. He appears as Harry H., Harry Henry, and Henry H. Since "Harry" is a nickname for "Henry," and many boys were being named for William Henry Harrison, it is likely that his name was Henry Harrison Faulkner.

[128]1900 census, Saline Co., Neb., 35-112-10-88.

[129]Pension file, cert. no. 75511, National Archives, the source for nearly all the information about him and his family; the birth dates of the children are given ten years too late, as can be shown from the 1880 census.

[130]Information from Jennifer Adams, 18523 Woodland Terrace, Gurnee, IL 60031.

[131]*History: Erie County, Pennsylvania* (Chicago: Warner, Beers, 1884), p. 199.

[132]Erie Co. (Pa.) Marriage License Docket, 21: 113.

[133]1870 census, Erie Co., Pa., p. 449; 1900 census, Erie Co., Pa., 83-61-4-48.

[134]Erie Co. (Pa.) Marriage License Docket, 23: 61.

[135]*Union City Times-Enterprise and Waterford Leader*, 12 Mar. 1964.

[136]Erie Co. (Pa.) Marriage License Docket, 18: 48.

[137]1900 census, Erie Co., Pa., 205-177-1-93; Erie Co. (Pa.) Register of Wills, file no. 3353.

[138]1920 census, Erie Co., Pa., 122-142-5-32.

[139]Erie Co. (Pa.) Marriage License Docket, 14: 491.

[140]1920 census, Erie Co., Pa., 122-143-6-38.

[141]Erie Co. (Pa.) Marriage License Docket, 16: 70.

[142]1920 census, Erie Co., Pa., 117-82-34-59.

[143]1900 census, Oneida Co., N.Y., 191-45-3-30; Marion Honsinger, 1005 Howard Rd., Starkville, MS.

[144]Donald L. Faulkner, 998 S. Labellota, Green Valley, AZ 85614.

[145]1900 census, Madison Co., N.Y., 104-2-1-12.

[146]1920 census, Oneida Co., N.Y., 326-109-6-34; Leonard Faulkner.

[147]1900 census, Onondaga Co., N.Y., 197-93-10-12.

[148]1900 census, Lackawanna Co., Pa., 106-96-12-67.

[149]*Scranton Times*, 22 Apr. 1975.

[150]Records of Barbara (Mrs. James L.) Faulkner; Tioga Co. (N.Y.) Administrations, file no. 336; 1880 census, N.Y., 40-18-6-37.

[151]1870 census, Tioga Co., N.Y., p. 64.

[152]1900 census, Delaware Co., N.Y., 30-17-4-88.

[153] *Pioneer Families and Their Descendants in Fremont, Lincoln, and Pleasant Valley Townships Area, Johnson County, Iowa*, p. 350-351.

[154] 1900 census, Larimer Co., Colo., 1-214-13-33.

[155] *Cemeteries: Fremont Township, Johnson County, Iowa* (Des Moines: Iowa Genealogical Society, 1984), p. 4.

[156] Larimer Co. (Colo.) Marriages, C: 229.

[157] *Montclair Times*, 24 Jan. 1952.

[158] 1900 census, Hudson Co., N.J., 37-131-19-1.

[159] The index to New York vital records says 7 September 1926.

[160] Curtis L. Faulkner; Delaware Co. (N.Y.) Surrogate's Court, Box 22,677.

[161] 1920 census, Schoharie Co., N.Y., 367-83-6-6; Curtis L. Faulkner.

[162] Royer, Genealogy of Stokes family.

[163] Homer Worthington Brainard, *A Survey of the Scovils or Scovills in England and America* (Hartford: 1915), p. 421.

[164] Royer, Genealogy of Stokes family; 1920 census, Schoharie Co., N.Y., 367-83-3-20.

[165] *Olean Times Herald*, 29 July 1967.

[166] *Olean Times Herald*, 27 Feb. 1959.

[167] Cattaraugus Co. (N.Y.) Surrogate's Records, file no. 10625; 1910 census, McKean Co., Pa., 256-128-253; 1920 census, McKean Co., Pa., 187-124-6-88.

[168] *Bradford Era*, 22 Feb. 1972.

[169] 1920 census, Cattaraugus Co., N.Y., 16-79-15-95.

[170] *Bradford Era*, 5 April 1983.

[171] Phillip G. Faulkner; 1900 census, McKean Co., Pa., 14-103-1-97; 1920 census, McKean Co., Pa., 187-124-6-82.

[172] Mary Faulkner, Waugh Rd., Box 363, Scio, NY 14880, provided most of the information on this branch; Emelyn Faulkner, 3206 Michigan Ave., Costa Mesa, CA 92626; 1920 census, Cattaraugus Co., N.Y., 16-86-7-56.

[173] Information from Mark R. Clark; 1920 census, Delaware Co., N.Y., 32-155-8-2.

[174] *Canastota Bee-Journal*, 9 July 1937.

[175] 1900 census, Madison Co., N.Y., 104-17-4-37; 1920 census, Madison Co., N.Y., 77-115-5-2.

[176] 1920 census, Madison Co., N.Y., 77-115-1-83.

[177] *Wellsboro Agitator*, 3 Apr. 1883, in: *Tioga County, Pennsylvania, Records*.

[178] *Mansfield Advertiser*, 18 July 1888, 20 Feb. 1889, in: *Tioga County, Pennsylvania, Records*; records of Edward C. Faulkner.

[179] Records of Edward C. Faulkner; 1900 census, Cass Co., Mo., 18-29-1-51.

[180] 1900 census, Lawrence Co., Mo., 55-32-12-24; 1920 census, Lawrence Co., Mo., 61-104-5-62; *Marionville Free Press*, 13 July 1950, 16 Oct. 1952.

[181] 1920 census, Bradford Co., Pa., 69-1-2-61.

[182] 1920 census, Hennepin Co., Minn., 35-256-3-54.

[183] 1920 census, Otsego Co., N.Y., 27-140-11-32; Paul H. Roske, 217 Greenlawn Rd., Vestal, NY 13850.

[184] 1920 census, Spokane Co., Wash., 41-132-7-2.

[185] Erie Co. (Pa.) Register of Wills, file nos. 37728, 73011.

[186] Erie Co. (Pa.) Marriage License Docket, 46: 69.

[187] Erie Co. (Pa.) Register of Wills, Proof of Death, 30: 96; Erie Co. (Pa.) Record of Births; 1910 census, Erie Co., Pa., 111-132-36.

[188] *Erie Times-News*, 22 May 1988.

[189] Leonard R. Faulkner, 3801 Bleecker Rd., Vernon Center, NY 13477.

[190] 1900 census, Armstrong Co., Pa., 30-21-18-94.

[191] *Buffalo Courier-Express*, 7 Apr. 1949.

[192] Niagara Co. (N.Y.) Surrogate's Records, file no. 12471; 1920 census, Niagara Co., N.Y., 320-140-8-76.

[193] Alice Heller, 49 Ralph Ave., White Plains, NY 10606.

[194] Larimer Co. (Colo.) Marriages, C: 430.

[195] Patricia Jo Kirkman Sullivan, 2618 Alteza Ln., Colorado Springs, CO 80917; records of Lakeside Cemetery.

[196] Gary Faulkner, PO Box 111, Ashton, MD 20861.

[197] *Montclair Times*, 19 Nov. 1983.

[198] Ibid., 18 October 1990; 1920 census, Hudson Co., N.J., 32-82-15-1.

[199] *Olean Times-Herald*, 20 Oct. 1992.

[200] Mary (Mrs. David) Faulkner, Scio, NY.

[201] Emelyn Faulkner.

[202] 1920 census, Forest Co., Miss., 15-10-2-6; Edward C. Faulkner.

[203] Edward C. Faulkner.

[204] Edward C. Faulkner.

[205] Information on all descendents from Paul H. Roske.

[206] *Polk's Coeur d'Alene City Directory* (Detroit: R. K. Polk, 1963).

[207] *Spokane Spokesman-Review*, 24 June 1983.

[208] Rosemary Faulkner, Sun Lakes, AZ.

[209] Erie Co. (Pa.) Marriage License Docket, 38: 296.

[210] *Cleveland Plain Dealer*, 25 Mar. 1973, 4 Aug. 1981.

[211] Erie Co. (Pa.) Marriage License Docket, 31: 26.

[212] *Erie Daily Times*, 23 Dec. 1976.

[213] *Erie Daily Times*, 22 June 1983.

[214] *Erie Daily Times*, 5 Aug. 1989.

[215] Leonard R. Faulkner.

[216] Anna Meyer, 101 Whiskwood Lane, Minoa, NY 13116.

[217] Gary Faulkner.

[218] Phillip G. Faulkner.

[219] Donald H. Faulkner, RD 2 1950 Melody Lane, Olean, NY 14760.

[220] Annette Stanton, Main St., PO Box 162, Deposit, NY 13754.

[221] Noralee Faulkner, P.O. Box 392, Shell Knob, MO 65747.

[222] William A. Faulkner, 8958 W. Lake Rd., Lake City, PA 11642.

CHAPTER X

Bishop Colin Falconer and His Family

X1 William Falconer in Logie and in Dunduff, youngest son of Alexander Falconer of Halkerton (A4) by his wife Elizabeth Douglas, born perhaps about 1570, was living in 1616, but had died by 16 June 1625.

The name of his wife has not been determined.

He received a bequest in the testament of his father, dated 2 November 1587. His designations indicate that at different times he held the family lands of Lethenbar, Logie, and Dounduff, perhaps by wadset. On 30 June 1602, Mark Dunbar of Durris was cautioner for Archibald Falconer in Farnichtie and William Falconer in Lethinbar, not to reset or intercommune with Alexander McRanald of Gargavach and others.[1] William Falconer of Logie witnessed a contract of sale at Elgin on 4 August 1608, whereby Mark Dunbar of Durris, with consent of Ninian, his eldest son, sold the lands of the barony of Durris to Sir John Campbell of Cawdor.[2] Mark Dunbar and Issobelle Falconar, his spouse, were confirmed in a charter, granted 20 February 1612, of the lands of Wester and Eister Dunduff and Kincorthie, with precept of sasine directed to William Falconar in Logie; witnesses, dated 2 November 1608, included Hugh Falconar in Inverlochtie, William Falconar in Logy, and Mr. Samuel Falconar, chamberlain to the Earl of Moray.[3] On 9 January 1616, he and other uncles of Alexander Falconer of Halkerton received a Commission under the Signet to apprehend Mr. John Oschell, a physician, who was accused of murdering David Falconer.[4]

Issue of William Falconer:[5]

X2   i.   William Falconer.

X2 William Falconer in Lethinbar, born perhaps about 1600, died between 13 July 1644 and 30 October 1649.

He married Beatrix Dunbar, daughter of J. Dunbar of Bogsmoray, and widow of Patrick Dunbar of Haldoch. She died in 1681.[6]

On 16 June 1625, he and his future wife, Beatrix Dunbar, took precept of sasine, from Mr. Samuel Falconer of Kincorth, of half of the town and lands of Drumreache.[7] On 13 July 1644, he and his wife had sasine of the lands of Netherplench of Brichmonie, called Gerballis.[8] A tablet with the initials "WF"

Arms and initials of William Falconer (X2), Auldearn Parish Kirk.

and the arms of the Falconers of Halkerton, above the family crypt in the choir of Auldearn kirk, is a memorial to either him or his father.

Issue of William Falconer in Lethinbar and Beatrix Dunbar (others, if any, are unknown):

X3   i.   Colin Falconer, born about 1626.

X3 **Colin Falconer**, born about 1626, died 11 November 1686 at Spynie, Moray, was buried at Elgin Cathedral.

On 24 July 1648, he married Lilias Rose, daughter of William Rose of Clava by a daughter of —— Chisholm of Comer.[9] She died at Elgin 6 May 1688 and was buried at Elgin Cathedral.

He was educated at St. Leonard's College, St. Andrews. Styled "of Gerbelleis," he was cautioner for Andro Innes, merchant burgess of Elgin, in a marriage contract with Marjorie Ferguson, on 30 October 1649.[10] He was ordained minister of Essil on 2 October 1651. He served as minister of Forres from 1658 to 1679. Appointed bishop of Argyll in 1679, he was not able to speak Gaelic, so he was unable to satisfy the needs of that bishopric. He then secured an appointment as bishop of Moray and served from 1679 to 1686. A portrait of him is in the collections of the Scottish Episcopal Church. His body and that of his wife were interred at Elgin Cathedral, whose chapter house contains a tablet with an inscription to their memory.

He wrote his testament at Spynie on 8 April 1685. In it, he requested that he be buried at Forres. Having already secured a liferent in bonds for his wife, he gave to his eldest son William 9000 merks and three roods of land at Forres. He gave to his son Hugh a sum of money and to his son Alexander

Memorial tablet of Bishop Colin Falconar and his wife Lilias Rose, Elgin Cathedral.

he gave 3500 merks "because he has been of Great [service] these divers years." He gave his daughter Isabel 2500 merks, with the provision that, if she did not marry someone he had disliked, but someone whom her mother had approved, she would have an additional 500 merks. Although his daughter Jean was married and he was obliged to give her 800 merks, she was of "so Christian & of beging a Carriage & so affectionat a Child," that he gave her an additional 1300 merks, to amount to 2500 merks. He gave half of the remainder of his moveable estate to his eldest son William and the other half to be divided equally among the rest of his children. He appointed his sons William and Alexander to be executors.[11]

Issue of Colin Falconer and Lilias Rose:[12]

  i. Beatrice Falconar, born 1649.

  ii. Jean Falconar, born February 1651. She married, on 15 August 1678 at Forres, Beroald Innes, A.M., minister at Alves, who died 27 March 1722, aged about 78. He owned the lands of Inchstellie in Alves. They had issue, surname *Innes*:[13] a. *Lilias*, baptized 2 June 1681, died 7 June 1682; b. *James*, baptized 30 January 1683, married Katharine, daughter of his uncle Hugh Falconar; c. *William*, baptized 25 July 1686; d. *John*, baptized 21 October 1690; e. *Robert*, baptized 10 July 1692; f. *Jean*, baptized 3 September 1694; g. *Hugh*, baptized 31 March 1698; h. *William*, baptized in 1701.

X4 iii. William Falconar, born 1652.

  iv. Katherine Falconar, born 24 March 1653, baptized 29 March 1654 at Speymouth, Moray.[14]

  v. Hugh Falconar, born 16 September 1654, probably died young.

  vi. John Falconar, born 24 August 1655, probably died young.

  vii. Isabel Falconar, born 20 August 1656, died young.

X5 viii. Hugh Falconar, born October 1657.[15]

X6 ix. Alexander Falconar, born 23 April 1659.

  x. son [Osbert?] Falconar, born 18 October 1660.

  xi. John Falconar, born 12 April 1662.

  xii. Robert Falconar, born 20 July 1663, died young.

  xiii. Isabel Falconar, born 4 November 1664, living in 1685, unmarried.

  xiv. Margaret Falconar, born 8 March 1666.

xv.   Robert Falconar, born July 1668.

X4 William Falconar, born 1652, died after 1712, when of Forres.[16]
   He married, 29 April 1675, at Dyke,[17] Elizabeth, eldest daughter of
Alexander Tulloch of Tannachie.
   He was educated at King's College, Aberdeen, and received the degree of
M.A. in 1667. From 1668 to 1670, he was schoolmaster of Dyke. Ordained
in England by Henry, bishop of Oxford, he was presented by Alexander, Earl
of Dunfermline, collated on 16 September, and admitted on 23 September
1674. He succeeded his cousin and namesake as minister of Dyke in 1674.[18]
Brodie of Brodie, who had presbyterian beliefs, felt, upon hearing his preaching for the first time on 30 January 1674, that he was "an ignorant and
unsufficient person, and unfit for that work;" that Brodie had "heard of his
high conformiti with prelaci and all the corruptions in England;" and that he
was disaffected "from this that fear God in this land."[19] For neither reading
the Proclamation of the Estates, nor praying for King William and Queen
Mary, he was deprived by decreet of Privy Council, 10 October 1689.[20]
   Issue of William Falconar and Elizabeth Tulloch:[21]

   i.   Jean Falconar, baptized 16 August 1677. She married, as her first husband,
         George Chalmer of Milntoun of Linkwood, town clerk of Elgin, and had issue,
         surname *Chalmer.*[22] a. *George*, baptized 9 February 1701; b. *James*, bap-
         tized 24 August 1702. She married, secondly, by 1707, William Cumming of
         Craigmill.[23]
   ii.   Colin Falconar, baptized 18 December 1679, died young.
X7 iii. Alexander Falconar, baptized 9 July 1682.

X5 Hugh Falconar, born October 1657,[24] died 23 August 1709 at Inverness.[25]
   He married, by contract dated 27 April 1681, on 24 or 25 May 1681, in
Edinburgh,[26] Isobel Innes, daughter of James Innes, writer in Edinburgh.
Her tocher (dowry) was reputedly more than £10,000.[27]
   He had been appointed Commissary Clerk of Inverness by the time of his
marriage.
   Issue of Hugh Falconar and Isobel Innes:[28]

   i.   Isobel Falconar, baptized 28 February 1684.
   ii.   Jean Falconar, baptized 11 February 1688, probably the "child of Hugh
         Falconar" who died 17 December 1688 at Inverness.
X8 iii. Colin Falconar, baptized 16 June 1689.
   iv.   Anna Falconar, baptized 29 September 1692.
   v.   Katharine Falconar, baptized 19 April 1694, living in 1769, married James
         Innes of Inchstellie, son of Beroald Innes and Jean Falconar, and had issue,
         surname *Innes:*[29] a. *Jean*, baptized 3 June 1725; b. *Hugh*, baptized 30 July
         1727; c. *Beroald*, baptized 15 May 1730. She was served heir of provision
         general to Alexander Falconar of Inverness, 5 October 1763.[30]
   vi.   James Falconar, baptized 12 June 1698.
   vii. Alexander Falconar, baptized 16 August 1700, died, without issue, before 5
         October 1763 in Inverness.

X6 **Alexander Falconar** of Blackhills, born 23 April 1659, died shortly before 1 February 1749,[31] probably in the parish of Auldearn, Nairnshire.

He married Anna Tulloch, daughter of William Tulloch, baillie of Nairn. They had become engaged by 11 June 1684, when Thomas Tulloch of Tannachie, his son John, and Lord Doune, son of Lord Moray, after a bout of drinking, drove into Nairn during the night and carried off the young lady. Apparently Tannachie, chief of the Tullochs in Nairnshire, disapproved of the match, as Anna stood to inherit a considerable fortune. The laird of Brodie says there was a great talk in the country about the abduction. The Tullochs of Tannachie were compelled to restore the lady to her father's house.[32]

On 11 February 1674, Alexander Falconar, son of Bishop Colin Falconar, was apprenticed to Bartlemew Home, merchant in Edinburgh.[33] In 1681, the Synod of Moray ordered that a contribution for the Montrose merchants be collected and sent to him.[34] He served as Member of Parliament for Nairn in 1685-1686.[35] Alexander was styled "in Kinstearie" in the early 1690s, but must have acquired the wadset to the lands of Blackhills (or Blackhill), in the parish of Auldearn, Nairnshire, between the time of the baptisms of his children Lilias and William. Alexander Falconer of Blackhills was named a Commissioner for Nairnshire, 1704.[36]

In 1712 Alexander Falconer of Blackhills petitioned the Nairn town council to feu out to him "a piece of useless ground be-east Broadley's corff-house, that he might have the convenience of building some fishers' houses for accommodating some seamen who might labour a boat or yoale for his son's use, whom he designed to settle amongst them for following merchandise, and for building a corff-house for the convenience of washing his fish in the neighbouring fresh water." The council agreed to give off the feu, measuring one hundred feet in breadth, and about one hundred and ten feet in length, at 20 shillings Scots of a yearly feu duty.[37] The National Library of Scotland has two letters of Alexander Falconar of Blackhills, dated 1721.[38]

Issue of Alexander Falconar of Blackhills and Anna Tulloch:[39]

i. Alexander Falconar, born probably about 1687, died, unmarried, before 1736.[40] In 1708, he was admitted a burgess of Elgin.[41] He was a baillie of Nairn. Alexander Falconar, younger of Blackhills, was cautioner, in a process dated 16 October 1710 at Inverness, for Alexander Falconar of Blackhills, his father, and John Jackson, commissary clerk of Inverness, that they should exhibit and deliver up to Katharin Falconar, daughter to Hugh Falconar, late commissary clerk of Inverness, and to James Inness, writer in Elgin, a bond containing the principal sum of 3000 merks, granted by Hugh Ross, elder, and Hugh Ross, younger, of Kilravock, to Hugh Falconar in liferent, etc.[42] Baillie Alexander Falconer was one of several appointed 21 April 1729 to prosecute the settlement of Mr. Lachlan Rose as minister of Nairn.[43]

ii. Jean Falconar, born 5 January 1692.

iii. Lilias Falconar, baptized 18 July 1694.

iv. William Falconar, baptized 23 June 1696,[44] died young.

v. James Falconar of Gerbellies, born 12 January 1699, living in 1735, but had died without issue by 1749.

vi. George Falconar, born 14 August 1701, died young.

X9 vii. David Falconar of Grieshop, born 7 April 1703.

viii. Aemilia Falconar, baptized 12 January 1707.

    ix.   daughter, baptized 28 February 1711.

X7 Alexander Falconar, baptized 9 July 1682 in Dyke, Morayshire, died 4 August 1737 in Elgin, Morayshire.[45]

He married, by contract dated 12 March 1705,[46] Jean, daughter of William King of Newmill.[47]

He was a merchant and one of the baillies of Elgin.

Issue of Alexander Falconar and Jean King:[48]

    i.   William Falconar, bishop of the Scottish Episcopal Church, baptized 3 March 1707,[49] died, unmarried, 15 June 1784 at Edinburgh.[50] Ordained 10 June 1728, he was consecrated bishop coadjutor for Caithness and Orkney in 1741. In 1742 he was elected to Moray and accepted the office in 1743. In 1762 he was made Bishop Primus, and in 1776, Bishop of Scotland.[51] One writer asserted that he guided the Episcopal Church "through her most tying crisis and deserves her undying gratitude."[52] James Boswell dined with him on 31 January 1779, Falconar toasting to Dr. Samuel Johnson and Flora Macdonald, the Jacobite heroine, and regaling him with stories of Thomas Ruddiman, the distinguished philologist, under whom Falconar had served as reader.[53]

    ii.   Samuel Falconar of Falcon Park, writer in Edinburgh, who died 5 February 1798 at Nairn.[54] He married, 29 September 1785 at Nairn,[55] Amelia Stewart, daughter of John Stewart of Cardneys. No issue.

X10 iii.   James Falconar.

    iv.   child.[56]

X8 Colin Falconar, baptized 16 June 1689 at Inverness, was living there in 1715, at the time of the baptism of his child.

He married Anna Stewart.

Admitted a burgess of Elgin in 1708,[57] he was served heir to his father on 10 May 1710.[58] He was a merchant in Inverness in 1714.[59] We can assume that he, like other members of his family, was a supporter of the Stuarts; his apparent disappearance after the baptism of his daughter might have resulted from some role he played in the 1715 Rising.

Issue of Colin Falconar and Anna Stewart:[60]

    i.   child, baptized 24 May 1715.

X9 David Falconar of Grieshop, born 7 April 1703 at Auldearn, Nairnshire, died 19 August 1784 at Nairn, Nairnshire.[61]

He married Isabella Dunbar.

Anna Tulloch, his mother, inherited the lands of Grieshop from her father. David Falconar of Grieshop was served heir to his father Alexander Falconar of Blackhill on 1 February 1749, indicating by that time that his elder brother James had died without heirs. David, according to George Bain, was "a very energetic and somewhat eccentric personage, and was known among his contemporaries as 'The Admiral.' " He owned an eighth part of the salmon fishings of the river Nairn, and according to an entry in the Sheriff Court books in 1766, possessed the property 'lying immediately to the east of Kilravock's great stonehouse in the burgh, and bounded on the east by the tenements belonging to Broadley'——a description answering to Falconer's

Lane." By 1769, he had alienated the lands of Grieshop to Patrick Grant of Rothiemurchus and lived in Nairn.[62]

Only child of David Falconar and Isabella Dunbar:

    i.   Emilia Falconar, who died unmarried. She was a "beautiful and accomplished woman," according to a memorandum written by Robert Falconar (1752-1823), sheriff-substitute of Nairn.[63]

X10   **James Falconar,** M.A., born perhaps about 1718, died 8 June 1769 at Edinburgh.[64]

He married Charlotte Rattray, daughter of Dr. Thomas Rattray, bishop of the Scottish Episcopal Church.[65]

Earning an A.B. at Marischal College, Aberdeen, in 1738, he was a nonjurant Episcopal minister in London and Glasgow. He was a prisoner in London and elsewhere after the '45. He was sent to sea as a prisoner at Aberdeen on 6 April 1746, and on 18 September 1746, he was a prisoner on board the *Elmham*, moored at Leith.[66] Six months later he remained on board a ship, the *James and Mary*, lying off Tilbury Fort.[67] Robert Forbes, historian of the rebellion, heard that he "was scarce ever any way ill in his health, that he bore up better than any one of them, having a great fund of spirits, being always chearful, and never wanting something to say to divert them in [the prisoners'] state of darkness and misery."[68] He witnessed the hanging of Dr. Archibald Cameron, a Jacobite rebel, in 1753 and published an account of Cameron's last words, "Sir, you see a Fellow-Subject just going to pay his last Debt to his King & Country," the "King & Country" having been omitted by contemporary news reporters.[69]

Issue of James Falconar by his wife Charlotte Rattray:[70]

    i.   Mary Clementina Charlotte Falconar. She married, 6 October 1785,[71] as his second wife, James Elphinston, of Elstree, Hertfordshire, born 1721, died 1809, a schoolmaster and classicist. Samuel Johnson remarked of him: "He has a great deal of good about him, but he is also very defective in some respects. His inner part is good, but his outer part is mighty awkward. I would not put a boy to him, whom I intended for a man of learning. But for the sons of citizens, who are to learn a little, get good morals and then go to trade, he may do very well."[72] No issue.

X11 ii.   James Alexander Sobieski Falconar, born about 1764.

    iii.   Jane Frances Stuart Falconar. She married Dr. James Wright, 6th Regiment, who was dead by 1798, and had issue, surname *Wright.*[73] a. *Margaret*; b. *Rachel*; c. *Charlotte*; d. *Janetta.*

    iv.   Anne Falconar. She married John Bethune, an indigo manufacturer who lived in Pirpainty, Bihar, and Rangpur and Mirzapur, Bengal, from 1784 to 1811,[74] and had issue, one daughter.

X11   **James Alexander Sobieski Falconar,** born about 1764, died 10 February 1812, in his 49th year, at Colaba (now part of Bombay), India.[75]

He married, 26 February 1791, at St. Mary le Bone, Middlesex,[76] Margaret Gleadah, daughter of J. Gleadah. She died 28 August 1812 in Colaba.[77]

He was employed in the India House, in London, when he was served heir general to his uncle Samuel Falconar of Falcon Park, 5 June 1798.[78] He was appointed storekeeper at Mangalore in February 1801. In September 1802, he moved to the port of Tellicherry. In April 1805, he became Deputy Marine Paymaster and Storekeeper at Bombay and arrived there in January 1806. He introduced various reforms in the warehouses under his control, saving the East India Company 18,000 rupees.[79]

Issue of James Alexander Sobieski and Margaret (Gleadah) Falconar (there were also three sons and a daughter who died young):[80]

- i.   James William Micheau Falconar, Captain, 1st Native Infantry, born 9 December 1791, baptized 19 March 1792 at St. George Hanover,[81] died 18 October 1827 at Ahmedabad.[82] He married, on 23 February 1824, at Forres, Elizabeth Macdonell, daughter of Rev. John Macdonell, minister of Forres. She died 3 May 1825, aged 20, at Alleppey, Travancore. He was a cadet in 1807; commissioned lieutenant, 8 April 1813; captain, 29 October 1821. They had no issue.[83]

- ii. Samuel John Croft Falconar, Captain, Bombay Regiment of Artillery, baptized 25 December 1794,[84] died 20 August 1835 at Ahmedabad, India, buried in St. Thomas's Cathedral, Bombay.[85] He was commissioned lieutenant on 25 October 1811,[86] and captain on 1 September 1818.

- iii. Charlotte Janetta Falconar, born about September 1801, buried 17 June 1831 in Chelsea New Churchyard, aged 29 years, 9 months. She married, on 31 October 1822, at Kensington,[87] David Rae Newall, Captain, of the Scaleby Castle, H.E.I.C., born 2 June 1789 in Dumfries, and had issue, surname *Newall:*[88] a. *David John Falconer*, of the Bengal Artillery, born 19 February 1825 at Michael Place, died 8 March 1901; b. *James Torrington*, of the Bombay Native Infantry, born 9 July 1827 in London, died 13 March 1911; c. *Adam Gordon*, born 4 May 1829, died 21 May 1853 in India; d. *John Liddell*, born 2 June 1831, buried 17 June 1831 in Chelsea. David Rae Newall married, as his second wife, on 12 August 1833, Mary (Prothero) Blewitt, widow of Edmund Blewitt, by whom he had several more sons.

NOTES

[1] *Register of the Privy Council*, 6: 735.

[2] *Book of the Thanes of Cawdor*, p. 222.

[3] *Register of the Great Seal*, vol. 7: *1609-1620*, no. 623, p. 231.

[4] *Register of the Privy Council*, 10: 490f.

[5] Particular Register of Sasines for Elgin, RS28/3, f. 28, SRO.

[6] *Diary of Alexander Brodie of Brodie*, p. 455.

[7] Particular Register of Sasines for Elgin, RS28/3, f. 28, SRO.

[8] Ibid., RS28/4, f. 352, SRO.

[9] Innes, *Family of Rose of Kilravock*, p. 529.

[10] Register of Deeds, RD2/11, f. 700ff., SRO.

[11] Testament, Commissariot of Moray, CC16/4/1, SRO.

[12] Letter, apparently from Donald Mackinnon, about 1954, in Falconer file, Library of the Society of Genealogists, London.

[13] Alves Parish Register; Cramond, *The Church of Alves*, p. 52f.

[14] Speymouth Parish Register, IGI.

[15] According to the above letter from Donald McKinnon, the name of the child born in October 1657 was not clearly legible in the original source; "Hew" (and "Osbert") were guesses. If these guesses are correct, then the earlier Hugh died before 1657.

[16] Scott, *Fasti Ecclesiae Scoticanae*, 6: 416.

[17] Dyke Parish Register.

[18] Scott, *Fasti Ecclesiae Scoticanae*, 6: 416.

[19] *Diary of Alexander Brodie of Brodie*, p. 349.

[20] *Register of the Privy Council*, 3rd ser., 14: 393-394.

[21] Dyke Parish Register.

[22] Forres Parish Register, IGI.

[23] Scott, *Fasti Ecclesiae Scoticanae*, 6: 416, 8: 643.

[24] According to the above letter from Donald McKinnon, the name of the child born in October 1657 was not clearly legible in the original source; "Hew" (and "Osbert") were guesses. If these guesses are correct, then the earlier Hugh died before 1657.

[25] Inverness Old Parish Register.

[26] Register of Deeds, RD3/50/630, SRO; Patrick Ogilvie to Sir John Falconar, 26 May 1680, Moses Bundle 254/7793a, Edinburgh District Archives.

[27] Patrick Ogilvie to Sir John Falconar, 26 May 1680, Moses Bundle 254/7793a, Edinburgh District Archives.

[28] Inverness Old Parish Register. There may have been other children, as the baptismal register lacks records for the years 1696 and 1702-1707.

[29] Alves Parish Register.

[30] *Decennial Indexes to Services of Heirs*, vol. 2 (1760-1769): 13.

[31] *Decennial Indexes to Services of Heirs*, vol. 1 (1740-1749): 12.

[32] George Bain, *History of Nairnshire*, p. 224.

[33] Watson, *Register of Edinburgh Apprentices*, 1666-1700, p. 31.

[34] William Mackay, ed., *Records of the Presbyters of Inverness and Dingwall 1643-1688* (Edinburgh: University Press by T. & A. Constable for the Scottish History Society, 1896), p. 102f.

[35] Joseph Foster, *Members of Parliament, Scotland...* (London: Hazell, Watson, and Viney, 1882), p. 131.

[36] Scotland, *Acts of the Parliaments of Scotland*, 2: 47.

[37] Bain, *History of Nairnshire*, p. 248.

[38] ADV MSS 29.2.11, ff. 182-185, National Library of Scotland.

[39] Auldearn Parish Register.

[40] Testament, Commissariot of Moray, CC16, SRO.

[41] Cramond, *Records of Elgin*, p. 465.

[42] Court of Session Processes, CS 271/16,548, SRO.

[43] Bain, *History of Nairnshire*, p. 256.

[44] Although the child's name is not legible in the parish register, the names of the witnesses (William Falconer in Forres, William Sutherland, and William Grant in Nairn) indicate it was William.

[45] Testament, Commissariot of Moray, CC16/4/2, SRO.

[46] Dyke Parish Register.

[47] *Memoir of the Family of Kings of Newmill*, p. 17.

[48] John Dowden, *The Bishops of Scotland* (Glasgow: James Maclehose & Sons, 1912), p. 423.

[49] Forres Parish Register, IGI.

[50] *Scots' Magazine*, 46: 335.

[51] Dowden, *The Bishops of Scotland*, p. 423.

[52] J. B. Crowe, *History of the Episcopal Church in the Diocese of Moray* (London: Skeffington and Son, 1889), p. 122.

[53] Joseph W. Reed and Frederick A. Pottle, *Boswell: Laird of Auchinleck, 1778-1782*, pp. 46-47.

[54] *Gentleman's Magazine*, 68: 175.

[55] *Scots' Magazine*, 47: 518.

[56] Testament, Commissariot of Moray, CC16/4/2, SRO.

[57] Cramond, *Records of Elgin, 1234-1800*, 2: 465.

[58] *Decennial Indexes to Services of Heirs*, vol. 1 (1700-1749).

[59] Court of Session Processes, CS271/7645.

[60] Inverness Old Parish Register.

[61] Scots' Magazine, 46: 504.

[62] Bain, History of Nairnshire, p. 386f.

[63] Ibid., p. 386f. This Robert was a grandson of Hugh Falconar in Foynesfield, whose connection to the main branch has not been established.

[64] Scots' Magazine, 31: 279.

[65] Untitled manuscript on the Falconer family, Library of Society of Genealogists, London.

[66] Lord Milton's General Correspondence, MS 16620, f. 161, National Library of Scotland.

[67] Henry Paton, ed., The Lyon in Mourning: or a Collection of Speeches, Letters, Journals, etc., Relative to the Affairs of Prince Charles Edward Stuart by the Rev. Robert Forbes, A.M., Bishop of Ross and Caithness 1746-1775, Scottish History Society 20 (Edinburgh: at the University Press by T. and A. Constable for the Scottish History Society, 1895), 3: 15.

[68] Ibid., 1: 182.

[69] Forbes of Culloden MSS, ADV MSS 32.6.23, f. 81, National Library of Scotland.

[70] Testament of Samuel Falconer of Falcon Park, Commissariot of Moray, CC16.

[71] St. Mary le Bone, Middlesex, Parish Register; Gentleman's Magazine, 55: 834.

[72] J. L. Smith-Dampier, Who's Who in Boswell? (New York: Russell & Russell, 1970), p. 123.

[73] Untitled manuscript on Falconer family, Library of the Society of Genealogists, London. James Wright could not have been the one who was Captain in the 6th Native Infantry, served in India from 1790 to 1803 and died in Edinburgh 25 February 1805.

[74] East India Kalendar, various years, at India Office Library and Records, London.

[75] The Bombay Kalendar and Register, for the Year 1813 (Bombay: for the Proprietors by Samuel Rans, n.d.), p. 186.

[76] St. Mary le Bone, Middlesex, Parish Register.

[77] Bombay Kalendar for 1813, p. 187.

[78] Decennial Indexes to Services of Heirs, 2 (1790-1799): 16.

[79] Personal records, etc., O/6/9, f. 77, India Office Library.

[80] Untitled manuscript on Falconer family, Library of the Society of Genealogists, London.

[81] Card file, citing L/MIL/9/117, f. 191, India Office Library.

[82] The Bombay Calendar and Register for the Year 1828 (Bombay: Courier Press, 1828), p. 140.

[83] Untitled Falconer manuscript, Library of Society of Genealogists.

[84] St. Matthew, Bethnal Green, Middlesex, Parish Register, IGI.

[85] Bombay: List of Tombs and Monuments, India Office Records and Library.

[86] The East-India Register and Directory for 1814 (London: Cox & Baylis, 1814), p. 286.

[87] Gentleman's Magazine, 2nd ser., 92: 464.

[88] Untitled Falconer manuscript, Library of Society of Genealogists.

CHAPTER Y

Falconers of Queensbury, St. Elizabeth Parish, Jamaica

The home of the following branch is located in southwestern Jamaica, in a dry savanna near the coast. Perhaps the poor quality of the soil originally caused white planters to ignore it, resulting in the settlement there of free persons of color, where their descendants remain. Most of the Falconers of this branch were small farmers, known as "settlers" or "planters," and raised vegetables on plots of land ever decreasing in size. In recent years, many have emigrated to Great Britain, the United States, and Canada.

Y1 **John Craskell Falconer**, "reputed"[1] son of Thomas Keith Falconer (C3), was probably born in 1798 and died 12 February 1875, aged 76 years, in Queensbury, St. Elizabeth Parish, Jamaica.[2]

By 1819, he had taken, as his common-law wife, Dorothy Bent, quadroon daughter of Nicholas Bent and Sarah Powell, born 1 July 1802 in St. Elizabeth Parish,[3] buried there 23 March 1864.[4] They were married on 24 December 1836 in St. Elizabeth Parish.[5]

Described as an infant on 3 November 1798, when Thomas Keith Falconer, of St. Elizabeth Parish, Jamaica, planter, gave a parcel of land in the Brownshill Mountains in St. Elizabeth Parish, containing one hundred acres, to him and George Ann Falconer, presumably his sister.[6] Thomas Keith Falconer gave to Sarah Powell, on 9 April 1804, fifty acres of land, bounded by the fifty acres which was John Craskell Falconer's settlement. John Craskell Falconer was the owner of two slaves in 1817.[7] Described as a "person of colour," he sold to Henry Cerf, for an undisclosed sum, a tract of 100 acres in St. Elizabeth Parish, on 15 October 1818.[8] He then purchased, on 15 January 1819, from Henry Cerf, for £350, a tract of 115 acres in St. Elizabeth Parish,[9] in Queensbury, basically a trade for the land given him by his father. John Craskell Falconer, a "free Mestee" (i.e., one-eighth African), was baptized 6 July 1819 at St. Elizabeth.[10] On 14 February 1833, he sold to Dorothy Bent, for £240, the 115-acre tract he owned, apparently to ensure succession to his children in the event of his death.[11]　Descendants say that he owned a signet ring and was buried at Alligator Pond, Manchester Parish.[12]

Children of John Craskell Falconer and Dorothy Bent, baptized in St. Elizabeth Parish:[13]

Y2	i.	Aaron Shickle Falconer, born 25 August 1819.
Y3	ii.	Cornelius Keith Falconer, baptized 9 July 1823, aged about two years.
	iii.	Maria Ann Falconer, baptized 9 July 1823, aged about two years.
	iv.	Susan Eleanor Falconer, baptized 7 November 1830, aged five years, seven months. She married, on 5 February 1875, as his second wife, Thomas Yowell James, born about 1816, of Unity, St. Elizabeth Parish.
	v.	Thomas Keith Falconer, baptized 7 November 1830, aged three years, ten months, buried 17 November 1847 in St. Elizabeth Parish.
	vi.	Catherine Craskell Falconer, baptized 24 October 1830, aged 18 months, died, unmarried, 3 April 1911 in Queensbury, St. Elizabeth Parish.
	vii.	John Benjamin Falconer, baptized 7 October 1832, aged 16 months.
Y4	viii.	Samuel Keith Falconer, baptized 15 December 1833, aged six weeks.
Y5	ix.	Charles Keith Falconer.
Y6	x.	Joshua Keith Falconer, born 30 January 1838.
	xi.	Lydia Craskell Falconer, born 9 May 1840. She married, on 7 June 1867,[14] John David Myers, son of Michael and Amelia Myers, born 28 January 1841 in St. Elizabeth Parish,[15] and had issue, surname *Myers*: a. *Arthur Darling*, born about 1870, married, 31 May 1893, Alice Beryl Falconer, daughter of Alexander Keith Falconer (Y7).
Y7	xii.	Alexander Keith Falconer, born 13 March 1843.
Y8	xiii.	Joseph Keith Falconer, born 20 March 1845.

Y2 Aaron Shickle Falconer, born 25 August 1819 in St. Elizabeth Parish, was living in 1872 in Mandeville, Jamaica.

He married, 29 October 1839, at St. Elizabeth,[16] Priscilla Elliott.

He was a policeman in St. Elizabeth Parish before moving to Mandeville.

Children of Aaron Shickle and Priscilla (Elliott) Falconer:[17]

	i.	Leonora Elizabeth Falconer, baptized 18 July 1841. She married, on 13 December 1871, in Old England, Mandeville District, Manchester Parish, Alexander Bent, born about 1841.[18]
	ii.	Joseph Christopher Falconer, born 25 June 1846.
	iii.	Margaret Adelaide Falconer, born about 1846. She married, on 10 April 1872, in Mandeville, Theophilus Bartholomew Sparks, a carpenter, born about 1851. She had the consent of Aaron Falconer.[19]
	iv.	Dudley Ann Falconer [son], born 17 August 1848.
	v.	Phoebe Falconer.[20]　She married, on 31 January 1877, William Dennis, a planter of Coleytown, Manchester Parish.

Y3 Cornelius Keith Falconer, born about 1821, died 24 November 1912, was buried on his family burying ground in Queensbury.

His wife was Fidelia ——, who died 25 February 1907, aged 85 years, in Queensbury.

He was a planter at Mahogany Hall and Queensbury, St. Elizabeth Parish.

Children of Cornelius Keith and Fidelia Falconer:[21]

    i.   Elizabeth Falconer, born about 1841. She married, on 15 December 1871, William Staple Barrett, born about 1834, a planter of Content, St. Elizabeth Parish. Cornelius Falconer was a witness.[22]

Y9   ii.   Richard H. Falconer, born about 1842.

Y10   iii.   Ebenezer Octavius [baptized as Augustus] Falconer, born 9 April 1845.

    iv.   Mary Maria Falconer, baptized 12 July 1850. She married, on 16 July 1868,[23] Frederick Samuel Bent and had issue, surname *Bent*: a. *Julia Adelaide*, born 24 July 1869; b. daughter, born 22 June 1889; c. *Francilla*, born 3 June 1892.

Y11   v.   David [baptized as Dudley] Craskell Falconer, born 31 March 1852.

    vi.   Emma Euphemia Falconer, born 16 March 1857. She married, on 25 November 1887, in St. Elizabeth Parish,[24] Joseph Adolphus Little, a planter, son of George Little, born about 1858. Issue, surname *Little*: a. *Annette*, born 12 June 1888; b. *Vera*, born 10 May 1892; c. *Sarah Margaret Louise*, born 10 July 1896.

    vii.   Susan Eleanor Falconer, born 24 January 1860, died 10 March 1942, buried in Queensbury. Issue, surname *Clark*: a. *Frederick*, born 5 May 1882, who was in the care of Frederick Bent; b. *William*; c. *Irene*, born 21 October 1888.

Y12   viii.   John Matthew Falconer, born 10 November 1862.

Y4 Samuel Keith Falconer, baptized 15 December 1833 in St. Elizabeth Parish.

He married, on 7 December 1864, at St. Elizabeth,[25] Ann Eliza Myers.

He was an overseer at Berlin, St. Elizabeth Parish, in 1866, and a planter there and in 1876 in Coffee Grove, St. Elizabeth Parish.

Children of Samuel Keith and Ann Eliza (Myers) Falconer:[26]

    i.   Joseph Keith Gunter Falconer, born 8 April 1866.

    ii.   Esther Lalow Falconer, born 10 December 1867.

    iii.   Phoebe Rosella Rebecca Falconer, born 12 June 1876.

Y5 Charles Keith Falconer, born perhaps about 1835, was living in Fairmount, St. Elizabeth Parish, in 1879.

He married, on 16 July 1869, at St. Elizabeth,[27] Catherine Merchant Williamson.

Children of Charles Keith and Catherine Merchant (Williamson) Falconer:

    i.   Anna Susan Louisa Falconer, born 22 August 1871.

Y13   ii.   William Simeon Falconer, born 21 December 1879.

Y6 Joshua Keith Falconer, born 30 January 1838 in Queensbury, St. Elizabeth Parish, died 17 May 1906 in Queensbury, St. Elizabeth Parish.

He married Euphemia Bent.

Children of Joshua Keith and Euphemia (Bent) Falconer:[28]

Y14　i.　Edward Kingtore Falconer, born 4 September 1863.

　　　ii.　Ada Arabella Falconer, born 6 August 1866. She married, on 14 March 1894, in Southfield, St. Elizabeth Parish, Arthur Leon Gordon, son of Arthur Gordon, born about 1863, a planter of Portugal, St. Elizabeth Parish.

　　　iii.　Dorothy Elizabeth Falconer, born 4 March 1869. She married, on 30 January 1901, Frederick William Staple, son of Walter Staple, born about 1872, a planter and fisherman of Top Hill, St. Elizabeth Parish. Issue, surname *Staple*: a. *Ernest Mitwood*, born 15 June 1898; b. son, born 24 March 1901; c. *Arnold*, born 13 September 1907.

　　　iv.　Joshua Josiah Falconer, born 23 October 1871.

　　　v.　Julia Emily Falconer, born 28 March 1874. She had a daughter, Florence Falconer, born 26 August 1896, by Samuel McDonald. She possibly had married —— Stephenson by 1901.

　　　vi.　Samuel K. Falconer, born 28 November 1876.

　　　vii.　John Wentworth Falconer, born 22 September 1882. He married, on 29 December 1915, Edith Matilda Campbell, daughter of Joseph Campbell, born about 1890. He was a planter of Queensbury, St. Elizabeth Parish.

Y7 Alexander Keith Falconer, born 13 March 1843 in Queensbury, St. Elizabeth Parish.

He married, as his first wife, Ann ——.

He married, as his second wife, on 5 August 1874 in St. Elizabeth Parish, Lydia Abigail Bent, born about 1852.

He was a laborer in Keith Hall, Malvern Chase and Queensbury, Southfield District, St. Elizabeth Parish.

Children of Alexander and Ann Falconer:[29]

Y15　i.　William Alexander Falconer, born 16 September 1864.

　　　ii.　Grace Anne Falconer, born 4 October 1866.

　　　iii.　James Vassall Falconer, born 23 March 1869.

Children of Alexander Keith and Lydia Abigail (Bent) Falconer:[30]

　　　iv.　Alice Beryl Falconer, born 17 November 1874. She married, on 31 May 1893, Arthur Darling Myers, son of John David and Lydia Craskell (Falconer) Myers, born about 1870, a planter of Queensbury, St. Elizabeth Parish. Issue, surname *Myers*: a. *Ernest*, born 21 November 1907; b. *Linvall*, born 3 September 1910; c. *Garnet*, born 30 October 1913.

Y16　v.　William Alexander Falconer, born 8 August 1878.

　　　vi.　Daniel Falconer, born 22 January 1881.

Y17　vii.　Henry Shickle Falconer, born 20 April 1883.

Y18　viii.　Aaron Elisha Falconer, born 16 December 1886.

　　　ix.　Nicholas Falconer, born 4 July 1889, died 29 November 194-, buried in Queensbury.

　　　x.　Jabez Falconer, born 3 October 1892, died young.

　　　xi.　Hannah Olivia Falconer, born 12 January 1895.

　　　xii.　Birdie Falconer, born 19 January 1900.

Y8 Joseph Keith Falconer, born 20 March 1845 in St. Elizabeth Parish, was probably the Joseph Falconer, a laborer of Belmont, Westmoreland Parish, who died in 1901, although this identity is uncertain. This person equally may well have been Joseph Christopher Falconer, son of Aaron (Y2).

His wife seems to have been a sister of John Cunningham, whom Joseph Falconer, in his will, called his "brother."

He owned a two-acre parcel in Belmont, called Rocky Hill, which he divided between his son and daughter.

Children of Joseph Keith Falconer:[31]

Y19   i.   Albert Augustus Falconer, born about 1867.

     ii.   Jane Wilhelmina Falconer, died in 1919 in Belmont, Westmoreland parish.

Y9 Richard H. Falconer, born about 1842, died 1 March 1912, aged 69 years, in Queensbury, St. Elizabeth Parish.

His wife was his cousin Amaritta Ann Gordon, daughter of Larckin and Ann Frances (Falconer) Gordon, born 20 February 1843 in St. Elizabeth Parish.[32]

He was a planter and laborer of Plains, Barbary Valley, and Queensbury, St. Elizabeth Parish.

Children of Richard H. and Amaritta Ann (Gordon) Falconer:

     i.   Sandford Falconer.

     ii.   Bridget L. Falconer, baptized 13 July 1871.

Y20   iii.   James Henry Falconer, born 26 May 1873.

     iv.   Hubert Laila Jeremiah Falconer, born 7 January 1875.

     v.   Christiana Catalina Falconer, born 1 February 1877. Issue, surname (at birth) *Falconer*: a. *Vera*, born 24 May 1908.

     vi.   Joshua Josiah Falconer, born 14 December 1878, died, unmarried, 18 June 1911 in Queensbury, St. Elizabeth Parish.

     vii.   Ann Frances Euphemia Falconer, born 16 June 1881. She married William Alexander Falconer (Y16).

     viii.   Edwin Falconer, born 18 June 1884.

     ix.   Richard Falconer, born 20 November 1886.

Y10   Ebenezer Octavius Falconer, born 9 April 1845 in Queensbury, St. Elizabeth Parish, died 1928 in Queensbury, St. Elizabeth Parish.

He married, on 28 September 1881, in St. Elizabeth Parish, Drusilla Isabella Senior, daughter of Charles Gale Senior, born about 1861.

He was a planter in Queensbury. At the time of his death, he owned more than twenty acres, which he distributed to his sons Charles and George and daughter Hilda.[33]

Child, born out of wedlock, of Ebenezer Octavius Falconer and Ruth Ebanks:

     i.   Timothy Alexander Falconer, born 10 March 1881.

Children of Ebenezer Octavius and Drusilla Isabella (Senior) Falconer, born in St. Elizabeth Parish:[34]

    ii.   Cornelius Falconer, born 11 November 1883.

    iii.   Thomas Falconer, went to Panama, where he died.

Y21   iv.   Charles Cameron Falconer, born 9 March 1890.

    v.   Hilda Elena Falconer, born 16 September 1894. She married, on 26 March 1918, in Queensbury, St. Elizabeth Parish, Charles Ralph Bent, born about 1888, son of Ralph Gale Bent, a cultivator of Southfield, St. Elizabeth Parish.

    vi.   Jane Adelaide Falconer, born 20 May 1899, died, unmarried, 16 December 1918 in Queensbury, St. Elizabeth Parish.

    vii. George Falconer, born in 1902.

Y11   **David Craskell Falconer**, born 31 March 1852 in Queensbury, St. Elizabeth Parish.

He married, on 24 May 1878, Amaretta Malvina Ebanks. Prior to his marriage, however, he had relationships with Elizabeth Morsella Ebanks and Roberta Buchanan.

He was a laborer and planter in Mud Hill, Pedro Plains District, St. Elizabeth Parish.

Child of David Craskell Falconer and Elizabeth Marcella Ebanks:[35]

Y22   i.   David Samuel Falconer, born 31 July 1873.

Child of David Craskell Falconer and Roberta Buchanan:

    ii.   Alice Evangeline Falconer, born 8 February 1876. She married, on 12 December 1900, Joseph Powell, born about 1870, of Queensbury. Issue, surname *Powell*: a. *Ann Maria*, born 22 December 1906. She married, as her second husband, Joseph Bent, and had issue, surname *Bent*: b. *Wilfred*, born 27 January 1913.

Children of David Craskell and Amaretta Malvina (Ebanks) Falconer:[36]

Y23   iii.   James Henry Falconer, born 4 March 1875.

    iv.   John Bernard Falconer, born 24 August 1877.

    v.   son, born 20 September 1878.

    vi.   Charles Joshua Falconer, born 12 August 1880.

Y12   **John Matthew Falconer**, born 10 November 1862 in Queensbury, St. Elizabeth Parish.

He married, on 17 August 1893, Mary Sophia Gale, daughter of Richard Gale, born about 1867.

He was a planter in Queensbury, St. Elizabeth Parish.

Child of John Matthew and Mary Sophia (Gale) Falconer:

    i.   Albertina Rosetta Falconer, born about 1888. She married, on 7 March 1912, Charles Lawrence Hill, son of Isaac Hill, born about 1887, a shopkeeper of Pedro Plains, St. Elizabeth Parish. Issue, surname *Hill*: a. *Sidney*, born 28 May 1912; b. *Viola*, born 17 September 1913; c. *Marian*, born 6 August 1915; d. *Silvah Boswell*, born 21 March 1917.

Y13   **William Simeon Falconer**, born 21 December 1879 in St. Elizabeth Parish, living in 1913 in Mount Sinai, Malvern District, St. Elizabeth Parish.

He married, on 12 April 1899, at Bethlehem, St. Elizabeth Parish, Theodora Elizabeth Brown, daughter of Henry Brown, born about 1871.

He was a planter and laborer in Fairmount, Malvern District, St. Elizabeth Parish.

Children of William Simeon and Theodora Elizabeth (Brown) Falconer:

    i.   Gwendoline M. Falconer, born 1904.

    ii.   Ernest Gerald Falconer, born 23 October 1906 in Fairmount, Malvern District.

    iii.   Muriel Maud Falconer, born 9 March 1908 in Fairmount, Malvern District.

    iv.   Kathleen Falconer, born 26 September 1913.

Y14   **Edward Kingtore Falconer**, born 4 September 1863 in Queensbury, St. Elizabeth Parish.

He married, on 27 June 1895, in Queensbury, St. Elizabeth Parish, Adelaide Rebecca Crowe, daughter of Thomas Crowe, born about 1864.

He was a small farmer and shoemaker of Queensbury, St. Elizabeth Parish.

Children of Edward Kingtore and Adelaide Rebecca (Crowe) Falconer, born in Queensbury, Southfield District, St. Elizabeth Parish:

    i.   Noel Barzillai Falconer, born 25 July 1897. He married, as his first wife, in August 1926, Gwendoline Evena Linton, daughter of Enoch Elijah Linton, and had two sons and two daughters. He married, as his second wife, on 1 November 1952, Mildred May Logan. He was a schoolteacher and headmaster in the Windward Road Government School from 1945.[37]

    ii.   Stella Falconer, born 2 January 1900.

    iii.   Cyril Falconer, born 1903.

    iv.   Sidney Falconer, born 22 July 1907.

    v.   Etheline Victoria Falconer, born 4 December 1910.

    vi.   Winston Percival Falconer, born 25 December 1914, lives in Fort Lauderdale, Florida. He married, in December 1947, Carmen Donalda Smith, daughter of Hubert Maxwell Smith. They had two daughters born by 1954. He was Senior Sanitary Inspector of the Malaria Research Department of Jamaica from 1948.[38]

Y15   **William Alexander Falconer**, born 16 September 1864 in Buildings, St. Elizabeth Parish, died 27 January 1905 in Retrieve, Mountainside District, St. Elizabeth Parish.

He married, on 5 January 1881, at New Bethlehem, St. Elizabeth Parish, Rose Ann Elizabeth Swaby, daughter of Francis Swaby, born about 1858.

He was a cooper and lived in Silent Hill and Retrieve, St. Elizabeth Parish.

Children of William Alexander and Rose Ann Elizabeth (Swaby) Falconer:

    i.   James Williams Falconer.

    ii.   Mary Ann Eliza Falconer, born about 1884. She married, on 9 February 1904, Joseph Nathaniel Samuels, son of Joseph Samuels, born about 1881, a laborer of Burnt Savannah, St. Elizabeth Parish.

iii.   Thomas Emmanuel Senior Falconer, born about 1886. He was a laborer of Retrieve, St. Elizabeth Parish. He married, on 28 December 1910, Priscilla Adina Hibbert, daughter of Alexander Hibbert, born about 1888.

iv.   son, born 20 March 1893 in Retrieve, St. Elizabeth Parish.

v.   Margaret Roberta Falconer, born in 1897 in Santa Cruz District, St. Elizabeth Parish.

vi.   son, born 5 January 1901 in Retrieve, Burnt Savannah, Lacovia District, St. Elizabeth Parish.

Y16   **William Alexander Falconer**, born 8 August 1878 in Queensbury, Southfield District, St. Elizabeth Parish, was living there in 1916.

He married Ann Frances Euphemia Falconer (known as Frances), daughter of Richard H. (Y9) and Amaritta Ann (Gordon) Falconer, born 16 June 1881 in Queensbury, Southfield District, St. Elizabeth Parish.

Children of William and Ann Frances Euphemia (Falconer) Falconer, born in Queensbury:

i.   Lovina Falconer, born 14 July 1907.

ii.   Barzillai Falconer, born 17 September 1909.

iii.   Roderick Falconer, born 20 March 1912.

iv.   Magsie Falconer, born 10 September 1914.

v.   Lillian Falconer, born 1916.

Y17   **Henry Shickle Falconer**, born 20 April 1883 in Queensbury, St. Elizabeth Parish, died 15 January 1954, was buried in his family burying ground in Queensbury.

He married, on 31 March 1920, in Queensbury, St. Elizabeth Parish, Irene Emily Roach, daughter of Alfred Roach, born 24 October 1888, died 28 October 1975.

He was a cultivator in Queensbury, St. Elizabeth Parish.

Children of Henry Shickle and Irene Emily (Roach) Falconer:[39]

i.   Cornelius Falconer, born 17 April 1907, died 24 May 1987, buried in Queensbury.

ii.   Alfred Falconer, born 1910, died 6 June 1967, buried in Queensbury. He married Mabel E. ——, who died 4 July 1978.

iii.   Gerald Henry Falconer, born 1912, died 18 October 1945, buried in Queensbury.

iv.   Simeon Falconer.

v.   Mavis Falconer, born 27 May 1916, died 31 March 1989, buried in Queensbury. She married Harold Falconer, son of Julia Falconer, born 29 October 1913, died 25 August 1977, and had issue, surname *Falconer*: a. *Henry*, lives in Winnipeg, Manitoba, Canada; b. *Earl*, lives in Queensbury.

vi.   Henry Falconer, born 2 March 1919, died 13 October 1981, buried in Queensbury.

vii.   Isilda Falconer, lives in London, England.

viii.   Reuben Alexander Falconer, born 25 December 1922, died 4 January 1992, buried in Queensbury.

ix.   Jobert Falconer, born 29 August 1925, died 17 May 1976, buried in

Queensbury.

x. Annette Falconer, lives in Queensbury. She married Claudius Myers, a grand-son of Arthur Darling and Alice Beryl (Falconer) Myers. They formerly lived in Brooklyn, New York.

xi. Leila Falconer.

Y18 **Aaron Elisha Falconer**, born 16 December 1886 in Queensbury, St. Elizabeth Parish.

He married, on 8 January 1919, Roberta Adina Bent, daughter of Norman Bent, born about 1889.

He was a planter of Queensbury.

Child of Aaron Elisha and Roberta Adina (Bent) Falconer:

i. Adelaide Falconer, born about 1922.

Y19 **Albert Augustus Falconer**, born about 1867, was living in 1911 in Round Hill, Mountainside District, St. Elizabeth Parish.

He married, on 13 September 1907, in Mountainside, St. Elizabeth Parish, Mary Ann Elizabeth Braham, daughter of Edmund Braham.

Child of Albert Augustus and Mary Ann Elizabeth (Braham) Falconer:[40]

i. son, born 1 May 1911.

Y20 **James Henry Falconer**, born 26 May 1873 in St. Elizabeth Parish.

He married, on 22 July 1908, Leah Gordon, daughter of Herbert Gordon.

He was a laborer in Queensbury, St. Elizabeth Parish.

Children of James Henry and Leah (Gordon) Falconer:

i. Herbert Falconer, born 20 December 1908.

ii. Clarence Falconer, born 11 October 1911, died 19 November 1911 in Queensbury, St. Elizabeth Parish.

iii. Arthur Theophilus Falconer, born 4 October 1912.

iv. Gerald Falconer, born 17 May 1915.

Y21 **Charles Cameron Falconer**, born 9 March 1890 in Queensbury, Southfield District, St. Elizabeth Parish, died 1957 in Southfield District, St. Elizabeth Parish.

The name of his wife is not known. He owned plots of land in Malvern and Southfield.

Children of Charles Cameron Falconer:[41]

i. Clunis Falconer.

ii. Daniel Falconer.

iii. Evelyn Falconer. She married — Witter.

Y22 **David Samuel Falconer**, born 31 July 1873 in Pedro Plains District, St. Elizabeth Parish, a planter in Flagamond, St. Elizabeth Parish.

He married, on 4 July 1900, Charlotte Eliza Ebanks, daughter of George

Ebanks, born about 1877.
    Children of David Samuel and Charlotte Eliza (Ebanks) Falconer:

    i.   Ismelia Mercella Falconer, born 23 July 1897.
    ii.   Lena Elizabeth Falconer, born 16 September 1900.
    iii. Lydia Falconer, born 16 October 1902.
    iv.   daughter, born in 1905.
    v.   Elsworth Varian Falconer, born 15 August 1906.
    vi.   Mary Ann Falconer, born 20 December 1909.
    vii. Ivy Falconer, born 15 January 1912.
    viii. daughter, born 6 August 1915.
    ix.   Clifton Falconer, born in 1919, died 13 June 1919 in Flagamond, Pedro Plains
          District, St. Elizabeth Parish.

Y23   **James Henry Falconer**, born 4 March 1875 in Pedro Plains District,
St. Elizabeth Parish, a planter of Flagamond, St. Elizabeth Parish.
    He married, on 29 April 1904, Jane Matilda Ebanks, daughter of John
Ebanks, born about 1873.
    Child of James Henry and Jane Matilda (Ebanks) Falconer, born in
Flagamond, Pedro Plains District, St. Elizabeth Parish:

    i.   Thomas Falconer, born 14 August 1907.

NOTES

[1] Jamaica Deeds, 558: 244. "Reputed" was standard terminology to indicate illegitimacy.

[2] Jamaica, Law 6 of 1871, Parish Registers, Burials, 2: 76.

[3] St. Elizabeth Parish Register, 2: 129.

[4] St. Elizabeth Burial Register, 1826-1870.

[5] Ibid., 14: 242.

[6] Jamaica Deeds, 457: 230. From this act, we can assume that Thomas Keith Falconer was the father of the two infants.

[7] Slave Registration Lists, T71/164, p. 422f., PRO.

[8] Jamaica Deeds, 683: 75.

[9] Ibid., 695: 31.

[10] Register of St. Elizabeth, 1: 258.

[11] Jamaica Deeds, 789: 114.

[12] Claudius and Annette Myers, Queensbury, Southfield, St. Elizabeth parish, Jamaica.

[13] Register of St. Elizabeth, 2: 21, 212; 3: 220, 221, 377, 213; 4: no. 361, pp. 38, 78, 154; 5: no. 544; 6: no. 343; 5: 47. The record of the baptisms of Aaron, Maria, and Cornelius do not name their parents, although they are described as free quadroon children. The will of Susannah Eleanor Bent, Jamaica Wills, 118: 60, names the six "reputed" children of John Craskell Falconer by Dorothy Bent living in 1831; Charles Keith was a presumed son.

[14] St. Mary's Marriage Register, 1864-1871, Jamaica Archives.

[15] Register of St. Elizabeth, 3: 77.

[16] Register of St. Elizabeth. Marriages, 3: 355.

[17] Ibid., Births, vol. 6, no. 421; 5: 79, 224.

[18] Jamaica, Law 6 of 1871, Parish Registers, Marriages, 1: 112.

[19] Ibid., 1: 213.

[20] Her identity is uncertain.

[21] Register of St. Elizabeth, Births, 5: 22, 242, 337, 617; 6: 23; St. Elizabeth Baptismal Register, 1863-1871.

[22] Jamaica, Law 6 of 1871, Parish Registers, Marriages, 1: 103.

[23] St. Mary's Marriage Register, 1864-1871.

[24] Jamaica Vital Records, St. Elizabeth Parish, Southfield District. The source for all marriages, births, and deaths between 1880 and 1920 in this chapter is this series of records. Rather than citing this source each time, I do it here with this explanation.

[25] St. Mary's Marriage Register, 1864-1871.

[26] St. Elizabeth Baptismal Register, 1863-1871; Jamaica, Law 6 of 1871, Parish Registers, Baptisms, 5: 394.

[27] St. Mary's Marriage Register, 1864-1871.

[28] Jamaica, Law 6 of 1871, Parish Registers, Baptisms, 2: 21; 4: 174; 6: 118; St. Elizabeth Baptismal Register, 1863-1871.

[29] St. Elizabeth Baptismal Register, 1863-1871.

[30] Parish Registers, Baptisms, 4: 405; Birth Records, St. Elizabeth.

[31] Jamaica Wills, N.S., 7: 476.

[32] Register of St. Elizabeth, 4: 154.

[33] Jamaica Wills, N.S., 19: 171.

[34] Birth records, St. Elizabeth.

[35] Jamaica, Law 6 of 1871, Register of Baptisms, 3:393.

[36] Ibid.

[37] *Who's Who Jamaica 1954*, ed. Clifton Neita (Kingston: Who's Who Jamaica Ltd., 1954), pp. 161-162.

[38] Ibid., p. 162.

[39] Claudius and Annette (Falconer) Myers, Queensbury, are the source for the names of the children; the dates are from their gravestones or from the series of vital records.

[40] The birth record calls the father Albert Adolphus Falconer, so there might be some question of identity.

[41] Jamaica Wills, N.S. 42: 131.

CHAPTER Z

Falconer of Ballandro

Z1 Robert Falconer was the first of the Ballandro line, which was, by tradition, related to the Falconers of Halkerton. Perhaps he belonged to the branch settled in Montrose since the beginning of the fourteenth century (see Appendix 1).

He was a burgess of Montrose, when on 8 November 1465, Robert Mortymair of Balandrow granted him, by charter of sale, the third part of the lands of Balandro, with the sixteenth part of the two parts of the said lands of Balandro, for yearly payment at Whitsunday of 12d. in the name of Blench Farm.[1] Mortymair granted him, on 22 April 1466, one-eighth part of the lands of Ballandro.[2] On 10 March 1472/3, the King confirmed a charter of Mr. Gilbert Tyry, rector of the parish church of Lyne and Master of the Hospital of the Blessed Virgin Mary, near the burgh of Montrose, made to Robert Falconare of Ballandro of lands and crofts around the hospital, called Newhame, in Forfarshire, and of lands of Spettailschelis, Kincardineshire, a single fishing of two parts of one rethis on the Northesk, and with one chalder of oat meal according to the measure of the late William, King of Scots, from the lands of Ovirstane, Nethirstane, Erbirne, and Ballandro, in Kincardineshire.[3]

The line of heritors of Ballandro continued until 1611, starting with his son:

Z2 David Falconer of Ballandro, living in 1508.

He was said to have married a daughter of —— [probably Alexander, A1] Falconer of Halkerton.[4]

He was named son and heir-apparent of Robert Falconare, when John Erskine of Dun resigned the lands of Ballandro by a charter under the Great Seal, on 3 October 1469, reserving life-rent to Robert Falconare.[5] On 29 October 1490, he alienated a tenement, giving Cathedral Church of Brechin an annualrent of ten shillings.[6] Alexander Falconer of Halkerton pursued an action against him on 10 May 1498.[7] On 24 May 1502, he resigned the lands of Ballandro in favor of his son and heir-apparent, Robert.[8] On 1 April 1507, a letter was made to him of the gifts of the non-entries of the lands of

Ballandro.[9]   On 1 February 1507/8, a letter of license for three years and
protection and respite was made to him, taking him under his "ferme" peace
and protection of the lands of Ballandro.[10]

Z3 **Robert Falconer** of Ballandro, son and heir of David Falconer, died about
1520.
    He was said to have married a daughter of —— Moncur of Slain.[11]
    On 10 December 1507, George Falconer of Halkerton discharged his
"kynnisman" Robert Falconer, fiar of the lands of Ballandro.[12]   He witnessed
the resignation of Mungo Hepburn of Wauchton of lands of Brethertoun on 4
April 1514.[13]

Z4 **Thomas Falconer** of Ballandro, born about 1515, died at the battle of
Falside, 10 September 1547.
    He was said to have married a daughter of —— Rait of Halgreen.
    On 20 July 1537, he was seised in the lands of Ballandro.[14]   An instru-
ment of sasine, dated 21 August 1537, in the hands of James Rait, professor
of arts, diocese of St. Andrews, notary public, was granted in favor of Thomas
Falconer, son and heir of Robert Falconer of Balandro, the lands having been
in the king's hands for sixteen years and one term by reason of ward.[15]

Z5 **Robert Falconer** of Ballandro, son and heir of Thomas Falconer of
Ballandro, died about 1585.
    He married Elizabeth, daughter of David Falconer of Halkerton (A3). She
died in September 1592.[16]   On 16 September 1585, Elspet, relict executrix of
Robert Falconer of Ballandro, and Robert Falconer, his son and heir, were to
appear in Kincardine Sheriff Court.[17]   Mr. David Lindsay, minister, pursued
an action against Elizabeth Falconer, lady of Ballandro, and Robert Falconer,
her son, about this time.[18]
    On 30 June 1548, Robert, son of Thomas Falconer of Ballandro, who
died in the battle at Fawsyde, was seised in the lands of Ballandro.[19]   He
resigned the lands of Ballandro in favor of Elizabeth Falconer in her virginity,
for life on 5 November 1552.[20]
    Issue of Robert Falconer of Ballandro and Elizabeth Falconer:

Z6   i.   Robert Falconer.
      ii. William Falconer. He and Robert Falconer of Ballandrow witnessed the testa-
           ment of Isobel Gray, spouse of Alexander Falconer of Halkerton, on 19 Octo-
           ber 1589.[21]

Z6 **Robert Falconer** of Ballandro, living in 1605.
    He married Helen Barclay, as his first wife, and Isobel Guthrie, as his
second wife. Their testaments were confirmed on 5 January 1600.[22]
    On 31 October 1586, he took sasine of the lands of Balandro and
Quhytefeild.[23]   On 2 November 1598, Mr. Alexander Sym, as procurator, registered a bond by Robert Falconer of Ballandro, for Hew Falcouner in
Innerlochtie, for £1000, not to harm Thomas Hepburn of Innerlochtie.[24]   On
10 August 1604, he was bondsman for George Barclay of Mathers and others, not to harm David Barclay, fiar of Mathers and others.[25]   On 9 April
1605, he was bondsman for Mr. James Sibbald, parson of Benholm and oth-

ers. Alexander, his son, was a witness.[26] A sasine to Robert Falconer of Ballandro and Helen Barclay, his spouse, was recorded on 26 June 1606.[27]

Issue of Robert Falconer of Ballandro:

Z7   i.   Robert Falconer.
    ii.   Alexander Falconer.
Z8   iii. William Falconer.

Z7 **Robert Falconer** of Ballandro, living in 1630.

His wife was Margaret Allardes, daughter of John Allardes of that Ilk.

He received, on 15 November 1605, documents from John Allardes of that Ilk relating to the claim of Margaret Allardes, his spouse, to £500 left in legacy by the deceased Robert, Lord Altrie, to Beatrix Keycht.[28] Between 1605 and 1608, he and Margaret Allardes, his spouse, took sasines of the lands of Ballandro.[29] On 16 March 1608, Robert Falconer of Ballandro, younger, was seised in the lands of Ballandro.[30] On 19 December 1611, he confirmed a charter of Ballandrow, by which, with consent of Henry Wischeart of Carnebeg, donator by escheat and life-rent of the said Robert, for perimpletion the contract, it gave to William Rait of Halgrene, in life-rent, the lands of Ballandrow.[31] On 8 December 1618, he witnessed a charter to Elizabeth Allerdes, spouse of Alexander Strathauchin, fiar of Brigtoun, daughter of John Allardes of that Ilk.[32] On 23 May 1630, Mr. Robert Falconer, sometime of Ballandro, received a discharge from Sir Alexander Falconer of Halkerton of the annualrent of 300 merks from Martinmas 1629 and for the future, the latter denuding himself of any title to that annualrent.[33]

Issue of Robert Falconer of Ballandro (order uncertain):

    i.   Alexander Falconer. On 18 January 1628, he assigned his father the sum of 4000 merks.[34] On 14 January 1630, an order was issued to apprehend Mr. Alexander Falconer, a Jesuit, son to Falconer of Ballandro.[35]

    ii.   Patrick Falconer, died by 14 November 1634.

    iii. Isobel Falconer, spouse of John Ogilvie in Turing. On 14 November 1634, she was served heir to her brother Patrick, son of Robert Falconer of Ballandro.[36]

    iv.   John Falconer. On 3 November 1628, Mr. Robert Falconer, sometime of Ballandro, acting for himself and John and Margaret, his children, with consent of Sir Alexander Falconer of Halkerton, discharged to John Allardes of that Ilk an annualrent of 200 merks for the terms Martinmas 1627 to Whitsunday 1628 on a sum of 2000 merks, as part of a sum of 3000 merks owed by Allardes to Robert Falconer.[37]

    v.   Margaret Falconer.

Z8 William Falconer.

A burgess of Montrose, he was made assignee of a sum of money by his brother german Robert Falconer, "somtyme of Ballandrow," on 24 July 1630.[38]

Issue:[39]

    i.   John Falconer.

NOTES

[1] Calendar of Charters, RH6/386, SRO.

[2] Ibid., RH6/392.

[3] *Register of the Great Seal, 1424-1513*, no. 1113, p. 228.

[4] "1578 Manuscript Genealogy," p. 218; this identification is mostly based on chronology.

[5] Calendar of Charters, RH6/420, SRO.

[6] *Registratum Episcopatus Brechinensis* (Edinburgh: for the Bannatyne Club, 1856), p. 135f.

[7] *Acts of the Lords of Council in Civil Causes*, 2: 203f.

[8] *Register of the Great Seal, 1424-1513*, no. 2652.

[9] *Register of the Privy Seal*, 1: 207, no. 1453.

[10] Ibid., 1: 232, no. 1593.

[11] "1578 Manuscript Genealogy," p. 218. This is the source for most of the spouses of the Ballandro line.

[12] *Protocol Book of John Foular, 1503-1513* (Edinburgh: for the Scottish Record Society by J. Skinner, 1940), p. 68.

[13] Donaldson, ed., *Protocol Book of James Young, 1485-1515*, p. 434.

[14] *Exchequer Rolls*, 17: 741.

[15] Calendar of Charters, RH6/1152.

[16] Testament, Commissariot of Edinburgh, CC8/8/37.

[17] Arbuthnott Papers, ADV 20.5.7., f. 117, National Library of Scotland.

[18] Ibid., ADV 20.5.7., ff. 160-161, National Library of Scotland.

[19] *Exchequer Rolls*, 18: 436.

[20] *Register of the Great Seal, 1513-1546*, no. 719, p.159f.

[21] Testament, 23 March 1589/90, Commissariot of Edinburgh, CC8.

[22] Francis J. Grant, ed., *The Commissariot Record of Edinburgh: Register of Testaments*, Part 1: *Volumes 1 to 35—1501-1600* (Edinburgh: for the British Record Society—Scottish Section, 1898), pp. 20, 118.

[23] *Exchequer Rolls*, 22: 531.

[24] *Register of the Privy Council*, 5: 708.

[25] Ibid., 7: 562.

[26] Ibid., 7: 593.

[27] Scotland, Scottish Record Office, *Index to Secretary's and Particular Register of Sasines for Kincardine: 1600-1608: 1617-1657*, Indexes no. 16 (Edinburgh: H. M. Stationery Office, 1929), pp. 47, 48.

[28] Barclay-Allardice Muniments, no. 385, SRO.

[29] *Index to Kincardine Sasines*, pp. 47, 48.

[30] Ibid., p. 48.

[31] *Register of the Great Seal, 1609-1620*, no. 600, p. 225.

[32] Ibid., no. 1940, p. 703f.

[33] Barclay-Allardice Muniments, no. 417, SRO.

[34] Register of Deeds, RD1/457, 2 Dec. 1630.

[35] *Register of the Privy Council*, 3: 408.

[36] *Inquisitiones Generales*, no. 2086.

[37] Barclay-Allardice Muniments, no. 411, SRO.

[38] Register of Deeds, RD1/457, 1 Dec. 1630.

[39] Ibid.

APPENDIX 1

Untraced or Possible Cadet Branches

As we go further back into the history of Scotland, especially before the middle of the fifteenth century, records become scarce, and it thus becomes more difficult to document branches off the main Falconer line. Certainly we know that as late as the seventeenth century, kinship formed the basis of relations in Scottish society, and assumed or fictive kinship allowed the chief of the family to assist a poorer kinsman at odds with a person of superior social status, as in the example of the physician accused of murdering the father of Harie Falkonner in Blakbalk in 1615. It is impossible to document whether all Scottish families with the surname Falconer are descended from the Falconers of Halkerton, even if they assumed a relationship. Nevertheless it is likely that between the thirteenth and sixteenth centuries, branches developed from the senior line, as about nine generations separate Ranulf the Falconer from the earliest ancestor from which descendants can be traced, Alexander Falconer of Halkerton (A1). Younger sons of landed families went into the church or into the towns as merchants, or held land in wadset, a feudal form of tenure. By the seventeenth century, concentrations of Falconers could be found in Nairnshire and Morayshire, in Kincardineshire, in Fifeshire, in Bo'ness, and in the cities of Edinburgh and Glasgow, and certainly some of them descended from the main stem.

Few early records survive to show Falconers in thirteenth- or fourteenth-century Scotland. Peter (Piers) le Faukener was *clericus regis* (King's clerk) during the reign of Alexander II (1214-1249).[1] Muriel, widow of Ranulf le Falconer, had letters under the Great Seal of Edward I restoring to her her dower lands in England, on 29 June 1304.[2] Gervase le Falconer, a Scottish prisoner, was confined in Wisbeach Castle in 1305 and 1307.[3]

A number of Falconers, no doubt cadet members of this family, were prominent in the affairs of Montrose. William Falconer was provost in 1330.[4] Elis (*Eliseus*, in Latin) Falconer, a burgess of Montrose, was a Member of Parliament for Montrose in 1367, and custumar of Montrose in 1372.[5] William Falconer was a baillie in 1377 and 1379.[6] Probably he was the same

William Fauconer who, with Sir William Ramsay of Colluthie and others, were granted safe conduct through England, on their way as pilgrims to France, 27 March 1371.[7] Three succeeded Elis in the office of custumar in Montrose: Alan Falconer, in 1373 and 1379; Robert Falconer, between 1384 and 1410; and John Falconer (dead by 1435) in 1426.[8] Robert may have been the man of his name who received safe conduct to England, in company with David, Earl of Crawford, and others, on 19 October 1398.[9] In 1434, Elis and Thomas Falconer, burgesses of Montrose, established a foundation for the Altar of the Blessed Trinity or Holy Trinity, to be supported by certain lands in the "Murra Strete" of Montrose.[10] Henry Falconer was instituted as vicar of the chapel of the Holy Trinity in the parish church of Montrose in 1450.[11] Perhaps the Falconers of Ballandro descended from this Montrose family, since Robert, the founder of this line, was a burgess of Montrose at the time he bought the lands of Ballandro in 1465.

David Falconer, probably a younger member of the Montrose family or perhaps a son of the laird of Halkerton, born about 1345, died in 1411, a godson of David II, was granted an annual pension of eight pounds by the king on profits of the chamberlain's ayres, 2 April 1366. He received a Bachelor of Arts degree at Paris in February 1364/5, later a Master of Arts degree; was a student and lecturer in law at Orleans and later held various posts in the Church. He was archdeacon in Aberdeen from 1407 to 1411.[12]

Another churchman was Thomas Fauconer, who was confirmed precentor of Ross on 16 August 1417. He still held the position in 1451, but was dead by 16 March 1454.[13]

Thomas Fauconer and John Fauconer were among those who served on an inquisition made at Nairn on 11 April 1431 concerning the succession of the lands of the deceased Hugh le Ros of Kilravock.[14]

John Fauconare of Murtholme in 1468 witnessed a retour of Duncan Grant as heir of Gilbert Grant of Glencharny, his grandfather, in the lands of Connygais. He is probably identical with John Fauconer of Murrestoune, who was mentioned in a precept by Sir Duncan Grant of Freuchie infefting James Douglas of Pettindreich in the fifth part of the half of Surastoun, on 25 September 1475.[15] John Falconer of Mureistoune resigned the lands of Middilhauch or Moreistoun, between the lands of Francoklaw and the lands of Auchterspyne, or Schirefmyll, in the barony of Spynie, Elgin, in favor of his son James, which failing, to his son Thomas, on 22 April 1480.[16] This branch existed in 1539, when Robert Falconer of Murrestoun witnessed a retour of James Grant of Freuchie.[17] John Falconar of Murestoun was dead by 13 May 1563, when a precept of legitimation was made to Andrew Allan, of Elgin, bastard son of the deceased James Allane, chaplain, and his spouse Katherine Falconare, bastard daughter of the deceased John Falconar of Murestoun.[18]

Robert and Duncan Falconer witnessed, together with Alexander Falconer of Lethen, a revocation to the sale of lands of Ester Kyndes by Mariot Sutherland on 13 July 1485.[19]

Henry Falconar was a witness to a charter of the third part of the town of Caym, in Duffous, Elgin, granted to William Hay of Lochloy, on 16 April 1489.[20]

Walter Falconer was Presbyter of Brechin and notary public between 1491 and 1499, when he witnessed and notarized some writs in Aberdeenshire.[21]

Robert Falconare and George Falconare of Halkertoun received a precept of remission, dated 9 July 1510 at Inverness.[22] No relationship was stated.

He may have been the same Robert mentioned above in a writ of 1485, or possibly the one mentioned below in 1533.

In November 1528, the Earl of Angus slew David Falconer, an officer "greatly esteemed by King James,"[23] who was then in command of infantry near Dirleton. Another David Falconer was slain at the siege of Tantallon, prior to 29 July 1542, leaving a daughter Barbara.[24]

A number of Falconers signed a petition for Sir Thomas Erskine of Brechin, dated 25 February 1533. Besides David Falconar of Halkertoun and his brother George, there were Alestar Falconar, Johnne Falconar, Robert Falconar, and Walter Falconar, chaplain of Tantallon.[25]

Witnesses to an instrument of sasine, dated 7 June 1555, of the temple lands of Myddiltoun, in the parish of Conveth, to Alexander Falconar of Halcartoun and Elissabet Douglas, his spouse, included Robert Falconar of Balándrow, George Falconar in Faisdo, David Falconer and Alexander, his brother german.[26] George Falconer in Tannoquhy (apparently Tannachie, Kincardineshire), described as her servant, received a bequest by the testament of Janet Falconer, widow of Sir John Wishart of Pitarrow, dated 5 January 1580.[27] His testament was confirmed 28 February 1591/2.[28]

David Falconer was a notary in Montrose between 1589 and 1607.[29]

Robert Falkonar in Ar was a cautioner in a proceeding dated 25 June 1577 between Hugh Rose of Kilravock and Alexander Falconer of Halkerton over the marches between Kilravock's lands of Farness and Aitnach and Halkerton's lands of Dunern, in which the latter was to place stones to mark the boundary.[30] He can probably be identified with Robert Falconer in Bar, who witnessed the testament of Alexander Falconer of Halkerton in 1587, and with Robert Falconar of Pluscarden, who was one of the barons, gentlemen, and others of Morayshire who appeared with one jack and one spear at a mustering in 1595,[31] and Robert Falconer in Lethinbar, a tenant of Alexander Falconer of Halkerton in 1596.[32] Robert Falconer was placed in possession of the Clune, in Nairnshire, as a tenant shortly before autumn 1598, when the Roses of Kilravock, led by David Rose Macwilliam, drove out the new tenants and their wives, set fire to their houses, and made off with plunder.[33]

At the Morayshire muster of 1595, David Falconar in Arde was also present, with a bow and bag, steel bonnet, and sword.[34] He was probably identical with David Falconer in Auchinan, who witnessed the testament of Alexander Falconer of Halkerton in 1587. David Falconer in "Auchermow" was deceased by 16 December 1602, when his relict Kathrene Innes was listed as a creditor of the estate of Margaret Falconer, spouse of Hew Falconer (S1).[35] Because they were able to bear arms and witnessed Halkerton's testament, it might be suggested that Robert and David were perhaps sons of George Falconer of Are and Findowray, younger son of George Falconer of Halkerton (d. 1511), or of Robert Falconer of Laik (fl. c.1545), although proof is completely lacking.

Similarly, the relationship of other prominent men in Nairn and Moray living in the seventeenth century remains unknown. George Falconer was a messenger in Auldearn and a writer in Nairn in 1616.[36] William Falconer was a merchant in Elgin about 1638, and perhaps was the father of Robert Falconer, a burgess of Elgin about 1670.[37] William Falconer of Raitloan lived in the 1650s.[38]

In Kincardineshire, Alexander Falconer, a prosperous wadsetter in

Carnebeg, died February 1683, leaving a son Alexander.[39]

John Falconar, said to be a cadet of the family of Halkerton,[40] received an M.A. from the University of Edinburgh in 1679 and died 6 July 1723 at Inglismaldie and was buried at Pert, Angus. His epitaph calls him "a good & grave man & very modest, tall, black and stooping." He was minister of Carnbie, then Bishop of Brechin (from 1709) of the Scottish Episcopal Church, married Elizabeth Galloway, and had two sons, James and Thomas. He was the tutor to the 3rd Lord Falconer of Halkerton.

Looking at families in Angus (Forfar), we can consider Colonel William Falconer, in Quhyt-Wall, parish of Tannadyse, whose testament was confirmed 22 August 1640.[41] Presumably it was Colonel William, not Colonel John, named as the first spouse of Catharine Lyall, who married, as her second husband, Captain John Ogilvy, brother of James Ogilvy of Schannallie, who had a charter in 1643 of the lands of Baldavie, in the regality of Aberbrothok, Forfar.[42] John Falconer of Balmashanner, parish of Forfar, was, in the 1680s, factor to David Carnegie, Earl of Northesk, and died in August 1703, leaving a son and heir David Falconer of Balmashanner, whose testament, confirmed in 1752, names daughters Jean and Magdalen.

In Fifeshire, Falconers reached prominence in the 17th and 18th centuries. At the beginning of the seventeenth century, James Falconer in Creich was a portioner of the lands of Craigfuddie. He married Margaret Beaton, possibly the daughter of David Beaton of Creich. Their son and heir was Robert Falconer, portioner of Craigfudie, who married Jean Weymes. On 17 October 1649, David Falconer, his son, was served heir in one-fourth of the towns and lands of Craigfuddie. Further research is necessary to connect this landed family with the Falconer ministers and baillies of St. Andrews. David, a minister, was Regent of St. Leonard's College in 1663, and later principal master of New College, St. Andrew's. He died in January 1682, having married, in 1666, Margaret Brydie. His son and heir was John Falconer. David Falconer, a merchant and baillie of St. Andrew's, died 27 April 1668 at the age of 47.[43] He married, in 1652, Janet Jack, and had sons James, born in 1653; William, born in 1656; and David, born in 1662, died 1691. The baillie's nephew was John Falconer of Allanhill, advocate (1670-1720), who married Margaret, daughter of Lewis Craig of Riccarton, and had a son David Falconer of Allanhill, advocate (1712-1776).

Bo'ness, a seafaring town, was home to a Falconer family, most of whom followed maritime occupations. Richard Falconer in Borrowstounes was served heir to his father Richard on 24 January 1630. A scion of this family, Magnus Falconar (1754-1778), wrote some medical tracts. His father was probably Magnus Falconar, Captain, R.N., master attendant of Chatham dockyard (died 16 September 1785, aged 64), who on 24 July 1766 was served heir to his grandmother Elizabeth Jolly, wife of John Hodge, shipmaster, of Bo'ness. Another son of Capt. Magnus was probably George Falconar, Lieutenant, R.N., who died 24 September 1841, aged 75. George Augustus Hayward Falconer, Lieutenant-Colonel, Madras Native Infantry, son of George and Margaret Falconar (the latter was the niece of David Barclay of Bury Hill), born 16 August 1806, died 26 September 1888, lived at Douglas, Isle of Man, amd left issue.[44]

In the North, a number of branches become prominent in the eighteenth century. Aeneas Falconar, laird of Blackhills, in Nairnshire, was the son of

Mrs. Magdalen Falconar. He married, on 2 May 1805, Margaret Macpherson,[45] and had children baptized in Auldearn. His younger brother, William, went to Jamaica in the 1780s, eventually becoming a major sugar planter in St. Catherine parish. He returned to Scotland and, on 20 December 1805 in Inverness,[46] married Christian Mackintosh, and had issue. His eldest surviving son, James John Falconer of Lentran, Inverness, received a grant of arms in 1868, noting that his family was "believed to be" descended from the Falconers of Halkerton.[47]

Hugh Falconar, a tenant in Auldearn, Nairn, was the progenitor of a family which gained some prominence during the course of the eighteenth century. He married Bessie Kinnaird in 1700 and had several children, among which were John, of Drakies, Inverness, Robert, and Hugh (1713-1784) both merchants in Nairn. John Falconar (died 29 September 1843, aged 75), a descendant of this family, was H.M. Consul at Leghorn.[48]

Colin Falconar, a merchant of Portsoy, Banffshire, in the first half of the eighteenth century, married, on 22 June 1710, at Keith, Banffshire, Marjorie Geddes and had a large family. His son William (baptized 21 March 1721 at Fordyce), of Inveravon, Banffshire, provided his family with "above average property and education."[49] He married, on 7 July 1763 at Auldearn, Nairn, Anna Rose, and had a family which included three sons, William (baptized 31 January 1765 at Inveravon, died 1818), a stationer in New York City and Albany, New York; Patrick (baptized 1 January 1775 at Inveravon, died 1837), a cotton merchant who followed William to America about 1794, but returned to Scotland during the War of 1812 and bought Blythe Park, near Glasgow; and Robert, who joined his brothers in New York.[50] Another son of Colin, John (baptized 22 January 1733 at Fordyce, died 16 June 1788), became a London goldsmith. He married Lydia Turton, bought property in Banff named Durn, and was buried in the kirkyard of Fordyce.

Alexander Falconar, A.M., took his degree at King's College, Aberdeen on 2 May 1706, was schoolmaster of Cromarty, ordained in 1718, served as minister of Ardersier, then minister of Ferrintosh, now Urquhart and Logie Wester, Inverness, from 1727 until his death on 8 April 1756, aged about 70.[51] He married Jean Houston, who died 5 January 1778. He had a son, Major William Falconer, fort-adjutant of Fort George and Fort Augustus, who died in 1787 in Inverness.[52] He married Lydia, daughter of John Davidson of Drumhall near Cromarty and Janet, daughter of Sir Patrick Grant of Dalvey, and had the following: Alexander of Falcon Hall, Edinburgh, First Secretary of the Madras Presidency from 1790 to 1808,[53] born 26 August 1766 at Fort George, Nairn, died 10 December 1847, who married Eliza, daughter of Alexander Davidson; Peter, died in Jamaica, unmarried; Patrick Cook, baptized 23 December 1767 at Nairn, died young; Lewis, baptized 6 December 1769, died in 1790 on passage to Jamaica, unmarried; Thomas, baptized 6 November 1770, died young; Elizabeth, who married Dr. Richard Hall Kerr, senior chaplain to the Presidency of Madras; John, born 6 December 1776 at Fort Ross, a soldier who died 28 October 1804 at Bellary, Bengal, where he was fort-adjutant; Lydia, born 14 December 1776, died 23 May 1849 at Nindmills, Inverness, who married, 27 November 1800, at Inverness, Ian Macdonald of Ness Castle. Jessie, who married Lieutenant Peter McIntyre, R.M.; and Chesborough Grant, Colonel of the 73rd Foot Regiment, died 10 January 1860 at Hazelbank, near Edinburgh,[54] who married, on 13 February 1810 at Inverness, Jean, daughter of Dr. William Kennedy, of Inverness.[55]

Among numerous Scottish Falconers who went to India were Alexander Falconer, a merchant of Calcutta in the 1760s, who had issue by his wife Susanna, including Alexander, baptized 3 April 1764 at Calcutta; and James, born 20 May 1776.[56] Alexander Falconer, an indigo planter in Dacca in the early nineteenth century, also left issue. Several met death in India and only the lucky returned. Colin Falconer returned from India a wealthy man, bought Woodcote Park, and died 24 January 1787.[57] Living in true nabob style in Earlston parish, his servants in 1778 included a footman, Osemin, a Negro.[58] His brother Alexander (died March 1795), a surgeon in the East India Company's service at Madras who returned to Europe in 1785, had a son George Home Falconer.[59]

The index to the Old Parish Registers of the Church of Scotland, compiled by the Genealogical Society of Utah, provides a good source from which one can determine the distribution of surnames in Scotland. Falconers appear to be most numerous in Nairnshire and Morayshire, with less in Kincardineshire and Aberdeenshire. This seems to reflect the primary residence of the chief, which was at Lethen, in Nairnshire, from the 1290s or earlier, to the latter part of the sixteenth century. Unfortunately, we shall never know the extent to which all Scottish Falconers actually descend, legitimately or illegitimately, from the Falconers of Halkerton or from ancestors who perhaps may have assumed the surname as feudal dependents.

NOTES

[1] Paul, *Scots Peerage*, 5: 242, citing *Chartulary of Kelso*, 128, 145, and *Caledonia*, 1: 541.

[2] Ibid., citing *Calendar of Documents*, 2: 1551, 1646.

[3] Ibid., citing *Calendar of Documents*, 2: 1679, 1937.

[4] *Exchequer Rolls of Scotland*, 1: 263.

[5] Joseph Foster, *Members of Parliament: Scotland, 1357-1882* (London: Hazell, Watson, and Viney, 1882), p. 132; *Exchequer Rolls*, 2: 381.

[6] *Exchequer Rolls*, 2: 576; 3: 23.

[7] *Rotuli Scotiae* (n.p.: by H.M. King George III, 1814), 1: 943.

[8] *Exchequer Rolls*, 2: 406; 3: 12, 115, 622; 4: 14, 107, 407, 533, 612.

[9] *Rotuli Scotiae*, 2: 145.

[10] James G. Low, *Memorials of the Church of St. John the Evangelist: Being an Account Biographical, Historical, Antiquarian, and Traditionary, of the Parish Church of Montrose and Clergy Thereof* (Montrose: William Jolly, 1891), p. 23.

[11] Ibid., p. 31.

[12] D. E. R. Watt, *A Biographical Dictionary of Scottish Graduates to A. D. 1410* (Oxford: Clarendon Press, 1977), p. 185f.

[13] Francis McGurk, ed., *Calendar of Papal Letters to Scotland of Benedict XIII of Avignon, 1394-1417* Scottish History Society, 4th ser., vol. 13 (Edinburgh: for the Scottish History Society by T. & A. Constable Ltd., 1976), p. 360; D. E. R. Watt, *Fasti Ecclesiae Scoticanae Medii Aevi*, Scottish Record Society, new ser., vol. 1 (Edinburgh: for the Society by Smith and Ritchie, 1969), p. 275..

[14] Innes, *Genealogical Deduction of the Family of Rose of Kilravock*, p. 127.

[15] Fraser, *The Chiefs of Grant*, 3: 28, 33.

[16] *Register of the Great Seal, 1580-1593*, no. 1008, p. 330.

[17] Fraser, *The Chiefs of Grant*, 3: 82.

[18] *Register of the Privy Seal*, 5, pt. 2: 357.

[19] Cosmo Innes, *Book of the Thanes of Cawdor*, p. 68-69.

[20] *Register of the Great Seal*, 1580-1593, no. 133, p. 42.

[21] *Registrum Episcopatus Aberdonensis*, Publications of the Spalding Club (Aberdeen: for the Spalding Club, 1845-1847), 1: 329; 2: 430; 3: 259.

[22] *Register of the Privy Seal of Scotland*, vol. 1: *1488-1529*, no. 2091, p. 320.

[23] Sir Herb. Maxwell, *A History of the House of Douglas* (London, 1902), 2: 99.

[24] Robert Pitcairn, *Criminal Trials in Scotland*, 1, pt. 1.

[25] *Acts of the Lords of Council, 1501-1554* (Edinburgh: 1932), p. 420.

[26] Calendar of Charters, RH6/1648, SRO.

[27] Commissariot of Edinburgh, CC8, SRO.

[28] Francis J. Grant, ed., *The Commissariot Record of Edinburgh: Register of Testaments*, Part 1: *Volumes 1 to 35—1501-1600* (Edinburgh: for the British Record Society—Scottish Section, 1898), p. 90.

[29] *Register of the Privy Council*, 4 (1585-1592): 533, 703; 8 (1604-1607): 592; 14: 514.

[30] Innes, *Genealogical Deduction of the Family of Rose of Kilravock*, p. 269.

[31] *Register of the Privy Council*, 14: 376.

[32] Ibid., 5: 291.

[33] George Bain, *History of Nairnshire*, p. 184.

[34] *Register of the Privy Council*, 14: 379.

[35] Commissariot of Edinburgh, CC8/37.

[36] *Index to Particular Register of Sasines for Sheriffdoms of Elgin, Forres and Nairn*, 1: 48, citing RS28/1/148; Jean Munro, ed., *The Inventory of Chisholm Writs, 1456-1810*, Scottish Record Society n.s. 18 (Edinburgh: 1992), p. 16.

[37] *Index to Particular Register of Sasines for Sheriffdoms of Elgin, Forres and Nairn*, 1: 49-50, citing RS28/4, RS29/2/237.

[38] Ibid., 1: 47.

[39] Commissariot of St. Andrews, CC20/4/14.

[40] Jervise, *Epitaphs and Inscriptions from Burial Grounds and Old Buildings in the North East of Scotland*, 1: 210. A survey in 1974 did not see this standing.

[41] Francis J. Grant, ed., *The Commissariot Record of St. Andrews: Register of Testaments, 1549-1800* (Edinburgh: for the Scottish Record Society by J. Skinner, 1902), p. 120.

[42] *Register of the Great Seal, 1641-16* , no. 1429.

[43] Charles Rogers, *Monuments and Monumental Inscriptions in Scotland* (London: Charles Griffin & Co., 1872), 2: 131.

[44] Card file, India Office Records and Library.

[45] *Scots' Magazine*, 67: 563.

[46] Ibid., 68: 154.

[47] Lord Lyon, Register of Arms.

[48] See Falconar file, Wyldbore-Smith Collection, Society of Genealogists, for more on this family.

[49] William R. Brock, *Scotus Americanus: A Survey of the Sources for Links between Scotland and America in the 18th Century* (Edinburgh: University Press, 1982), p. 163.

[50] Testament, Commissariot of Inverness, CC11/1/6.

[51] Hew Scott, *Fasti Ecclesiae Scoticanae: the Succession of Ministers in the Parish Churches of Scotland* (Edinburgh: William Paterson, 1870), v. 3, pt. 1, pp. 244, 303.

[52] Testament, Commissariot of Inverness, CC11/1/6.

[53] See *The Chief Secretary: Madras Diaries of Alexander Falconar, 1790-1809*, ed. by N. S. Ramaswami (Madras: New Era, 1983).

[54] *Gentleman's Magazine*, 208: 306.

[55] "Mackintosh of Farr" MS (1833), National Library of Scotland.

[56] N/1/2/ff. 57, 154, India Office Library and Records.

[57] *Scots' Magazine*, 49: 51.

[58] Cecil Sinclair, *Tracing Your Scottish Ancestors: a Guide to Ancestry Research in the Scottish Record Office* (Edinburgh: HMSO, 1990), p. 97.

[59] *Decennial Indexes to the Services of Heirs in Scotland*, 1780-1789, p. 15; 1800-1809, p. 19.

APPENDIX 2

Falconers and Faulkners in America

Several unrelated families with the surnames Faulkner and Falconer—or their variants Falkner, Falkiner, Falknor, Forkner—living in the United States today descend from English, German, Scottish, Irish, and French ancestors. They began arriving in the early 17th century. It is worth presenting a summary of some of the earlier immigrants and their families, noting first those of Scottish origin.

Falconers perhaps had been part of the movement of individual Scots to the Baltic littoral and to Ireland, but the earliest known colonial adventure of any member of the family was the involvement of David Falconar (H1) and his relatives in the East New Jersey colony in the 1680s. The family's entry into India began with Thomas Falconer's sojourn there from 1709 to 1727. As the 18th century progressed, others continued to seek their way in Britain's expanding empire. Most were professionals of some sort. They went to India as soldiers, naval surgeons, administrators, merchants, and planters, and, beginning in the 1730s, to Jamaica as planters, merchants, and overseers.

Scots in the North American Colonies

Reverend Patrick Falconer became minister of Hungar's Parish, Northampton County, Virginia, in 1713 and died there testate in 1718.[1] He may have married the daughter of Henry Newton, of Essex County, Virginia, who mentioned, in his will of 1713, a daughter Mary who married —— Falconer and a grandson David Falconer.

Patrick was probably a brother or other close relative of Reverend James Falconer, a native of Morayshire, who was ordained for Virginia on 19 June 1709 and succeeded Patrick as minister of Hungar's Parish. He was minister of Elizabeth River Parish, Norfolk County, in 1720, of Elizabeth City Parish, Elizabeth City County, from 1720 to 1724, and of Charles Parish, York County, from 1725 until his death on 2 February 1727.[2] His wife's father was George Newton, of Norfolk County, Virginia.

Captain Nathaniel Falconer was a mariner who lived in Philadelphia, and was that port's first collector of customs. He died or was buried 7 November 1803 in the Friends Burial Ground, aged 77.[3] From his use of a bookplate with the arms of Falconer of Halkerton,[4] we can assume that he believed he was descended from the Falconers of Halkerton, and thus he was probably of Scottish origin. By his wife Sarah, he had a daughter Prudence, baptized 12 October 1755 at Holy Trinity (Old Swedes') Church, Wilmington, Delaware, although no issue survived them.

Scots in the New Republic

William Falconer, born in Inveravon, Banffshire, came to Albany, New York, in 1785, then later to New York City, where he enjoyed a prosperous career as a stationer and bookseller (see Appendix 1).[5] His younger brother, Robert Falconer (born 22 December 1780 in Inveravon, Banffshire, died 25 October 1852 in Sugar Grove, Pennsylvania), said to be a graduate of Aberdeen University, joined his brother Patrick in New York in 1801, where they engaged in exporting cotton to Liverpool and Glasgow. Broken by the collapse of trade during the War of 1812, in 1817 he moved to Jamestown, New York, and invested in a tract in Sugar Grove, Pennsylvania.[6] The city of Falconer, New York, is named for his family. Patrick Falconer retired to Scotland, but his son Patrick settled in Warren, Pennsylvania, in 1835.[7]

Archibald Falconer, son of William Falconer and Elspeth Miller, of Geddes Mills, Auldearn, Nairnshire, born 1760, married Elspeth Russell, and settled in Stamford, Dutchess County, New York, where he died in 1842, leaving children.[8]

Alexander Falconer, an attorney, born in St. Andrews, Fifeshire, came to Franklin County, North Carolina, prior to 17 February 1797, when he married Mrs. Polly Harriet Wynne.[9] He died at the Glebe, Franklin County, 17 March 1818.[10]

William Falconer, a native of Inverness, left from Greenock for Baltimore in 1804 and settled in Madison Township, Columbiana County, Ohio. He died 12 May 1809, aged 30, was buried in the Township Line Cemetery, and left issue by his wife Nancy, who died 8 October 1810, aged 30.[11]

Scots in Early Canada

Early sojourners or immigrants to Canada include William Falconer, from Essil, Speymouth, Morayshire, born about 1739, who was in the employ of Hudson's Bay Company at Fort Severn, but returned to Garmouth, Morayshire, and died 16 September 1804. Alexander Falconer, from Lochbroom, Ross and Cromarty, sailed on the *Hector* in 1773 and settled near Hopewell, Pictou County, Nova Scotia. Hector Falconer, with his wife and nine children, came to Pictou, Nova Scotia, on the *Ellen* in 1799.[12]

Scots in the Caribbean

A sugar plantation with slaves could yield a handsome income to an ambitious entrepreneur. Few reached their original goal of establishing a successful plantation and returning to Great Britain to live off the income in comfort. Some died of disease and others fell into debt before reaching their goals. The earliest of the name to settle in the Caribbean to have come to my attention was Colin Falconer, who was buried in St. Elizabeth Parish, Jamaica on 6 December 1732. Others who went to Jamaica include John Falconer (C1), probably in 1746, and James Falconer, from Stonehaven, Kincardineshire, who came to the island by 1743 and died there in 1759.[13]

James Falconer, born about 1758, died 1829 in St. Andrew Parish. He appears to have entered Jamaica in 1780 and was associated with a John Falconer, perhaps a brother, in the 1790s.[14] In 1820, he owned "Mount Friendship" and 54 slaves.[15] He had, by Charlotte Thompson, a free woman of color, two children, Mary, who married Robert Ellis; and John, M.D., born 17 May 1796, died 1857.[16] James also left sisters Janet and Margaret and had a deceased brother Alexander.

William Falconer, brother of Aeneas Falconer of Blackhills, went to Jamaica before 1787. Perhaps a brother Hugh, who died in St. Thomas in the East Parish in 1799 and whose estate was administered by William Falconer,[17] followed. He built up his holdings in St. Catherine Parish and returned to Scotland in 1805, when he married and lived first at his seat of Brightmony and then at Lentran, near Inverness. In 1820, he owned three plantations and 266 slaves.[18] Before he returned to Scotland, he fathered a number of children of color.[19]

John Falconer, brother of William Falconer, a resident of Muirkill, Ayrshire, settled in Jamaica before 1810. He died at his plantation of Grange Hill, Westmoreland Parish, in 1840. He married Elizabeth King, a free woman of color, and had issue.[20]

George Charles Falconer lived in Roseau, Dominica. His wife Margaret died 9 August 1819, aged 29 years.[21] George Charles Falconer, their son, was supposed to have been born in Barbados, but lived on Dominica. He was speaker of the assembly there.[22] Another son, Charles Gordon Falconer, was editor of a newspaper and in the 1850s led a group called the "Mulatto Ascendancy" in the Dominica Assembly.[23]

John Falconer, a merchant from Morayshire, lived in Pensacola, West Florida, until the American Revolution, then followed his trade in Nassau, Bahamas, until his death on 3 November 1793, aged 51.[24] He never married.[25]

William Falconer, son of Sylvester Falconer, of the parish of Logie, Aberdeenshire, was a storekeeper on Cole's Creek, District of Natchez, Province of Louisiana, making a will there and bequeathing his property to his brother Cosmo, writer in Edinburgh, and other brothers and sisters. He died in 1794 in the District of New Feliciana and the will was probated 8 November of that year.[26]

During the 19th century, Scottish Falconers emigrated to Upper Canada, Australia, and other British colonies, as well as to the United States. Those who came to Canada, the United States, and Australia probably tended to be tenant farmers who sought the opportunity to purchase land and permanently emigrated. Young members of the aspiring professional and mercantile class, on the other hand, sojourned abroad in India and the newer colonies as soldiers and planters, although some continued to come to Virginia and Kentucky as tobacco factors. Their descendants are numerous, but beyond the scope of this book.

Possible Scots in the North American Colonies

The origin of other people whose names were spelled "Falconer" is uncertain, but may well be Scottish. A John Falconer, for example, was transported to North Carolina in 1702 and was later in Albemarle County, North Carolina.[27]

John Falconar or Faulkner resided in Little Creek Hundred, Kent County, Delaware, from 1733.[28] The administration of the estate of John Falconar, of Kent County, Delaware, was granted on 2 November 1749 to his widow Elizabeth.[29] He may have been the father of Samuel Faulkner, taxed in Little Creek Hundred between 1756 and 1766, and James Falconer, taxed there from 1770. The administration of the estate of James Falconer, of Little Creek Hundred, Kent County, Delaware, yeoman, was granted on 3 March 1786 to Robert Hirons and his wife Anne, formerly Anne Falconer.[30] John could have been related to Robert Falconer of Kent County, Maryland, whose widow Anne and Joshua Beck and William Ash were bound on 26 February 1753 to administer his estate;[31] Joshua Beck and Edward Beck were named as his next of kin, indicating that he probably was childless.[32] Since both John and Robert lived near the family of Gilbert Falconar (J1), it is conceivable that they might have been related.

William Falconer, of Kent County, Delaware, died prior to 26 May 1786, when the administration of his estate was granted to Alexander Jackson; heirs were his widow Sarah and children Elizabeth, Thomas, Andrew, William, and Sophia Falconer.[33]

A Survey of the Origins of Some Other Faulkner Families in the United States

Starting geographically with New England and going southward, we find Edmund Fawconer or Fawkner, an early settler of Andover, Massachusetts (d. 1687). He was a younger brother of Francis Fawconer, of Kingscleare, Hampshire, gentleman, who left Edmund property in his will of 1662, proved in 1663.[34] Edmund married Dorothy, widow of Joseph Robinson and had two sons, Francis and John, and two daughters, Mary and Hannah. Descendants of this family (spelling their name "Faulkner") lived in New England and further west.

David Faulkner, born about 1620, settled in Boston by 1653. He deposed concerning the inventory of the estate of Thomas Faulkner, taken 25 July 1656 in Boston. David and his wife Mary had children, including Martha, born 30 March 1653; Mary, born 10 November 1654; Thomas, born 26 September 1656; and David, born 7 June 1661. Both David the father and the son served in militia units during King Philip's War in 1676. David Faulkner, Jr., lived in Malden, Massachusetts, and had a family.

Samuel Faulkner, a clothier, born about 1700, settled in Bristol, Rhode Island, by 1725, and died in 1775, leaving a large family, most of whom lived in Connecticut and Rhode Island.

Pierre Fauconnier, born about 1653, was a French merchant who settled in New Jersey. His descendants, who spelled their name "Falconer," lived in New York City and southern New York state.[35]

Two brothers, both sons of Daniel Falckner, a Lutheran pastor in Langen-Reinsdorf, near Crimmitschau, Saxony, were pietist Lutheran ministers. Daniel Falckner (born 25 November 1666, alive 1741 in New Germantown, Hunterdon County, Pennsylvania) came to Germantown in 1693 and the next year published a description of Pennsylvania in Germany. Justus Falckner (born 22 November 1672, died at the age of 51) was the pastor of the Lutheran congregation in New York City. Both left children, although it is uncertain whether the male line persisted.[36] There are families named Falknor, believed to be of Pennsylvania "Dutch" background, in any case, who lived in Ohio and further west.

Thomas Faulkner, born about 1686, perhaps in Ireland, died in 1752 in Bethlehem Township, Northampton County, Pennsylvania. He married, on 30 June 1715, in New Castle County, Delaware, Mary Catharine Ferree, and had children Mary, John, Jacob, Jesse, Eve, and Susannah, and became a Quaker. Jesse's descendants lived in Pennsylvania and Ohio.

John Falconer died in Queen Annes County, Maryland in 1727. Probably born in England, although descendants have pointed to a Welsh origin, he had several children by his wife Sarah Ford: John, Temperance (who married Burton Francis Faulkner), Thomas, Ann (married John Rakes), James, Francis, William, and Emanuel. Francis died in 1794 in Anson County, North Carolina; William died in 1807 in Surry County, North Carolina; and Emanuel died 1798 in Iredell County, North Carolina.[37] William Faulkner, the author, probably descended from this family. Descendants spell the name "Falkner," "Forkner," and "Faulkner," and are concentrated in Tennessee and other Southern states and in states further west.

Francis Faulkner, born about 1644-1646, was living in Queen Annes County, Maryland, as late as 1735.[38] He was likely the father of Thomas Faulkner (or Falconer), born about 1686, who lived in Queen Annes County, Maryland; Benjamin Falkener, a planter of Queen Annes County, who died in 1726, leaving a wife Eleanor and issue; Burton Francis Faulkner, born about 1699, died 1776 in Queen Annes County; Francis, born about 1703, married Ann; and John, born about 1705. Since Burton Francis Faulkner married John Faulkner's daughter Temperance and because of the similarity of given names, it would seem likely that Francis and John were brothers.

Thomas Faulconer came to Virginia by 1623 and left presumed descendants, who spell their name "Faulconer" and "Faulkner." These are treated in two recently published genealogies.[39] In 1810, descendants lived in Orange and Essex Counties, Virginia. A family with the spelling "Faulkner" which lived in Halifax County, Virginia, may also descend from Thomas.

By the time of the first census in 1790, Faulkners (and those with homonymic names) lived in states from Massachusetts to South Carolina. The founders had left different homes, first England, then Scotland, France, Germany, and Ireland, and arrived in different colonies in different circumstances. Their descendants today, content to be Americans, have, for the most part, forgotten the origins of their immigrant ancestors.

NOTES

[1] Ralph T. Whitelaw, *Virginia's Eastern Shore: A History of Northampton and Accomack Counties* (repr., Camden, Me.: Picton Press, 1989), 1: 391; 2: 1397-1398.

[2] Landon C. Bell, *Charles Parish, York County, Virginia: History and Registers* (Richmond, Va.: Virginia State Library Board, 1932), p. 26.

[3] Francis Olcott Allen, "Earliest Records of the Burials in Philadelphia from the Board of Health," *Pennsylvania Genealogical Magazine* 1 (1898): 230.

[4] Charles Knowles Bolton, *Bolton's American Armory* (Boston: F. W. Faxon Co., 1927), p. 57.

[5] His papers are at the New-York Historical Society.

[6] John P. Downs, ed., *History of Chautauqua County, New York, and Its People* (Boston: American Historical Society, Inc., 1921), 3: 374. This family's papers are at the New York Historical Association.

[7] Byron Barnes Horton, *The Ancestors and Descendants of Zachariah Eddy of Warren, Pa.* (Rutland, Vt.: Tuttle, 1930), p. 100.

[8] Eliza Howe Gilbert, *A Record of the Benjamin Gilbert Branch of the Gilbert Family in America* (n.p.: Johnson City Publishing Co., 1920), pp. 59-64.

[9] *Virginia Gazette and Petersburg Intelligencer*, 17 Feb. 1797, in: Robert K. Headley, Jr., *Genealogical Abstracts from 18th-Century Virginia Newspapers* (Baltimore: Genealogical Pub. Co., 1987), p. 119.

[10] David Dobson, *Directory of Scots in the Carolinas: 1680-1830* (Baltimore: Genealogical Pub. Co., 1986), p. 67.

[11] McCord, *History of Columbiana County, Ohio*.

[12] Donald Whyte, *A Dictionary of Scottish Emigrants to Canada before Confederation* (Toronto: Ontario Genealogical Society, 1986), pp. 87-88.

[13] "Eighteenth Century Letters from Jamaica (from Dr. McNaughton's Collection in Aberdeen University Library)," *Scottish Notes and Queries*, 3rd series, 13: 3-5; Jamaica Inventories, 39: 60, 76.

[14] Jamaica Deeds, Indexes.

[15] *Jamaica Almanack for the Year 1820*, p. 61.

[16] Jamaica Wills, 110: 41.

[17] Jamaica Inventories, 102: 130, Jamaica Archives.

[18] *Jamaica Almanack for the Year 1820*, pp. 5, 19, 35.

[19] St. Catherine Parish Register.

[20] Jamaica Wills, 120: 64.

[21] Vere Langford Oliver, *The Monumental Inscriptions of the British West Indies* (Dorchester: Longman, 1927), p. 19.

[22] Joseph A. Boromé, "George Charles Falconer," *Carribean Quarterly* 6 (1959): 11-17.

[23] Patrick L. Baker, *Centring the Periphery: Chaos, Order, and the Ethnohistory of Dominica* (Montreal: McGill-Queen's University Press, 1994), p. 131.

[24] Oliver, *Monumental Inscriptions of the British West Indies*, p. 244.

[25] His career is well documented in the Mrs. L. A. Parrish Collection, Houghton Library, Harvard University, according to William R. Brock, *Scotus Americanus: A Survey of the Sources for Links Between Scotland and America* (Edinburgh: University Press, 1982), p. 142.

[26] May Wilson McBee, *The Natchez Court Records, 1767-1805: Abstracts of Early Records* (Baltimore: Genealogical Pub. Co., 1979), p. 153.

[27] Weynette Parks Haun, *Old Albemarle County, North Carolina, Miscellaneous Records, 1678-1737*.

[28] Kent Co. (Del.) tax lists, 1733-1748.

[29] Kent Co. (Del.) Register of Wills, K: 3.

[30] Delaware Archives, A17: 85, Delaware State Archives.

[31] Kent Co. (Md.) Administrations, 5: 63.

[32] Maryland Inventories, 55: 92.

[33] Delaware Archives, A17: 95-96.

[34] Henry F. Waters, *Genealogical Gleanings in England* (Boston: New England Historic Genealogical Society, 1885), 1: 98f; a pedigree of the family is in the Visitation of Hampshire for 1634.

[35] See Abraham Ernest Helffenstein, *Pierre Fauconnier and His Descendants* (Philadelphia: Press of S. H. Burbank & Co., 1911).

[36] See Julius Friedrich Sachse, *Justus Falckner, Mystic and Scholar* (Philadelphia: for the author, 1903); "A Contribution to Pennsylvania History: Missives to Rev. August Herman Francke from Daniel Falckner, Germantown, April 16, 1702 and Justus Falckner, New York, 1704, Supplemented with a Genealogical Chart of Daniel Falckner," *Pennsylvania-German Society. Proceedings and Addresses* 18 (1909).

[37] John P. Forkner, "William Forkner Senior and the Forkners of Surry County, North Carolina," in Mona Forkner Paulas, *The Forkner Clan: Forkner/Fortner/Faulkner*, vol. 2 (Baltimore: Gateway Press, 1985), p. 228ff. She

published vol. 1 in 1981 and vol. 3 in 1995.

[38]Henry C. Peden, *More Maryland Deponents, 1716-1799* (Westminster, Md.: Family Line, 1992), pp. 36-37.

[39]James G. Faulconer, *The Faulconer Family* (Troy, Ohio: the author, 1980); James G. Faulconer, *Thomas Faulconer and His Descendants* (Baltimore: Gateway Press, 1984); J. William Mann, *Faulconers of Virginia and Related Families of Spotsylvania and Orange Counties, Virginia* (Fredericksburg, Va.: the author, 1989).

APPENDIX 3

Letters

The following letters and other documents were chosen to illustrate aspects of the lives and times of the principals of this genealogy. Most were written by Falconers to their relatives, friends or lawyers, but some were written by tutors and other relatives and describe family members or their activities. At the time of the earliest letters, in the seventeenth century, Falconers were mostly living in Scotland, but with the growth of empire in the following century, descendants lived in New Jersey, Maryland, India, Holland, and Jamaica, as well as England. We read of court intrigue, of local politics, Naval battles, the American Revolution, the Grand Tour, patronage, trade among distant ports, the operations of a Jamaican sugar plantation, frontier migration in America, besides more mundane issues such as the availability of viol strings, family quarrels, a funeral procession, prodigal sons, and the inevitable debts and pleas for money. Arranged chronologically, they begin in 1601 and end with a letter from Arkansas in 1848. Very few have been published. They are found in various manuscript collections, principally that of the Earl of Kintore at Aberdeen University, but also in others in repositories in Britain and the United States. In editing these, I have preserved the original spelling and capitalization but have made occasional changes in punctuation to clarify the meaning of the texts.

Alexander Falconer of Halkerton (A6) to the Laird of Grant

Halcartoun, the 24 December 1601.

RYCHT HONORABILL SCHIR,——I resawit your letter, with the contractis subcrywit be your cationaris and yourself. I hawe delywerit to the berair the just transsumpis or dibillis quhilk ye left with me, and hes subcrywit the accuttance. I mynd, God willing, to be in Murray in Appryll. Quhair ye desayir me to bring yow ane gud grewe hund, I haw not one gud for the present. Quhen I hawe ony ye sall hawe puer to command, or ony vther geir I hawe sall be at your diwotioun. As to nowallis ther is none; bot my lordis of Mar and Berwik ar come in——came to Edinburgh the xxiiij of December. The conspirasie againis his Majestie is prentit, so ye will get it at lenthe. The pleage is ewill in Edinburgh. The Cession is continuit till the xiij of Januar. The feid betuix Edzell, Clony and Pittaro is submittit. This to the nixt occatioun I commitis yow with your leady to God, to quhom let thir present impairt my lowing commendatioun.

Your lowing frind alwayis at commandment,

Alex^r Falconar of Halcartoun

SOURCE: William Fraser, *The Chiefs of Grant*, vol. 2: *Correspondence*, p. 39.

Patrick Falconer of Newton (P1) to John Erskine, 18th Earl of Mar

My Lord

PLeis your Lordship I resavit your Lordship's Letter and according to the desair theroff I have delayit the placeing of my saitt in Mary kirk till now, quhilk is loing efter the tyme your Lordship did apoint the Laird off Dun and the Minister according to your Lordship's desair. Efter the consitation off the kirk and saittis theroff hes found that your Lordship Tennents in Haltoun may be fittly and commodiously placed in ane nether pairt of the kirk. But the Laird off Dune waits not taik upon him to transplant that daisk of the Haltouns. But your Lordship's exspreiss warrand to him to that effect, in respect of the generalyte off your Lordship's last letter direct to him thereanent. For the Reverend respect I kain [?] to your Lordship quihir off broad denatie I am obliest. I have veray long delayit. That makes allready haveing the full Rycht boith off the Presbetre and Archybishoip off Santandrus as your Lordship knowes. Therffor I humbly intreit your Lordship not delay that mater any loinger, bot that your Lordship would be pleised to wryt the expreiss warrand to the Laird off Dune to transplant that daisk to ane nether conwenient place as the Laird of Dun and the minister hes found fitting for your Lordship's tennents at Haltouns and lykways your Lordship waild be plaised to send ane Termination [?] to theis young men In Haltons to obey and obtein pece to your Lordship's will and determination anent thir Bissines. Thus exspectant humbly your Lordship's favor and resolwit answer, I continew

Your Lordship's humbill and
affectionat servand
ready to serve,
Patrik Falconer

Neutoun 28 Jannar 1633

SOURCE: Papers of the Earl of Mar, GD124/15/97, SRO.

NOTES: The location of one's seat in church was an important reflection of status in a community. His distant cousin the Laird of Dun apparently held the lands of Halton (Hatton), and Patrick did not like the position of the Halton tenants' pew.

Alexander Falconer, Master of Halkerton (A8), to James Ogilvy, 2nd Earl of Airlie

Edinburge januarie 2
1666

My Verie Honorable and Noble Lord

My best wishes and deu respects premitted, in obedience to your Lordship's commands I haue acquainted My Lord Craford and My Lord Bannfe that your Lordship will not faille to be hier att Ed[r] the 13 or 15 of this current januarie 1666. Bothe of them uill waitt upon your Lordship hier the forsaid day. As for my self I haue nothing els to doe hier; I am confident your Lordship will prepair busines soe befor the forsaid day that ther may be ane finalle close to that is intended and be noe longer retarded uhiq is my earnest desir and of all weill wissers to your Lordship and me bothe as hes bein since my coming hier impairted to me by seuerales. Soe wissing your Lordship all healthe and happines and longeing for to sie your Lordship hier rests and euer sall remain

My Lord
Your Lordship's most louing Cousing faithfull
frind and humble seruitour to the utmost of my
power
A Falconer Maister of Halcartoune

My Lord

Be pleased to suffer this postscript.

I acquainted my Cousing Maister David Falconer as your Lordship comanded me uhoe hes promised to be Cairfull your Lo will be pleased to present my humble seruice and deu respects to My Lord your faither my laidie your Lordship's Mother Sir David and the rest of the laidies of the familie and pardon me this trouble I put your Lordship to. As for neues ther is mutche talking of ane neu comet[1] greater then anie of the former and of ane ligue betuixt our Kinge the Emperor the Kings of Spaine Denmarke and Suaidin agaynst the King of France and the Irlanders and the King of Denmark hes caused mest all ther schippes.

SOURCE: Airlie Muniments, GD16/34/131, SRO.

NOTES: [1]The comets which occurred in 1664 and 1665 were blamed for the outbreak of the plague in London in the latter year and the Great Fire in the year that followed.

Inventory of Personal Estate of Sir John Falconer (G1)

ITEM THER WES restand auand to the said umq[uhil][ll] defunct the time of his deceaese with his goods and gear following of the availes and pages eftir mentionat pertaineng to his the tyme of his decease forsaid

Imprimis in his oune chamber ane griencloth shewed bed with chyres stooles tables table clothes and v[the]r furnetour relating [there]to and vset [there]in, ane black cabinet ane ordinarie cabinet with some peapers ane clock ane watch and signet rigne and rwoupe [?] with ane small shurt sword xx suit of old stey [?] hirgengs certane clymnes and v[the]r Iron work in the roumes and red cloth restnig shyre sex stuff old shyres ix old lather shyres iij old trunckes [quher]in [there] is some gownes and some v[the]r wearing clothes belongeng to his wyfe with certane leddin napries ane chist with draweres containeng some shewed work and worsettes [where]in ane v[the]r chist containeng the Wearing linenys of his wife with some of his oune iij Wanscott press with certane pewther veschelles certane candelstikes and Iron and [...]cuse in the nether roume kitching and v[the]r places of his hous his wholl bed clothes some sadels and bryddells with some v[the]r ffurnitour in the presses some emptie boxes with some old keyes and lockes some old bookes and peaperes relating to the mint with some old v[the]r peapers in the studie and some v[the]r roomes certane old tables bedstedes chistes with certane timber and Ironwork in the wardrope with some v[the]r small trasi [there]in

estiat all in cuinze to the somne of iiij^c xxx^{lb} scotis

> Summa of the Inv —— iiij^c xxx^{lb}
> sua the debtis exceadeis the goodes xilj^{c}Slb

Sir David Falconer understandnig & s & we decerin q[uhe]^{r}upon Willm Stevnistone merchand in Ed[inbur]gh became as cau[tione]r as ane ait beires.

SOURCE: Testament dative, Commissariot of Edinburgh, CC8, SRO.

Petition of Sir John Falconar (G2) to James, Duke of York

MAY IT PLEASE YOUR ROYAL HIGHNESS

Finding the delivery & passing of the late Mark of his Majesties Favour, Which was procured by Your Royal Highness's Goodness, To Sr John Falconar, & to his son after him, of the Gift of his Office has met with several stops, partly from ye resenting Information of some upon other heads and causes, and the Insinuations of others, appearing for his brother David Falconar, The last of which has been pleased to represent him as one who once had a Title to that Gift, but by his altering his principles in Religion was rendered uncapable thereby to possess & exerce the same, And that he having suffered for his Majesty, and not being in such good condition in his fortune as his brother, Therefore ought to share in a part of Sir John's. And least this insinuation have any impression, Sir John has presumed to adventure to give Your Royal Highness the true state of the case, betwixt himself and his brother as follows.

In the year 1635 Monsieur Nicholas Briot, who was in your Royal Father's service from y[ea]^r 1626 as Graver to the Mint of England & Master of the Meddals, he having justly the reputation of one of the most knowing persons in Mint Affairs & one of ye greatest Artists in his age, And being sent down to Scotland in the year 1633 to prepare and coyne ye Coronation pieces; And therafter George Fowlis (who was Master of the Mint in 1634) dying, The said Mr Briot was sent down again & placed by his Majesty, Master of the Mint here, And did accordingly excerce solely till ye year 1637. At which time Sr John's father being a servitor to, & marrying his Daughter, Mr Briot did procure to himself a new Gift conjoyning his son in law in the Office with himself, And therafter he being called to England by his Majesties Command (whcre he served with great faithfulness & constancy, & in ye time of ye Rebellion ventured to carry ye punches and roller Instruments for Coyning (by his Majesties Mandate) tursed up in sadles and otherways privately, with the hazard of his life, to his Arms. And after the King's murder, he dyed with grief & want. He left and resigned the exercise and benefits of the Office to his Son in Law, taking his promise, that if he intended to join any with him in the Office, It should be one of his Grandchildren. Notwithstanding of which, in the Year 1646 Sir John's father was over-ruled by David's friends, to deal to get him joined with himself in the said Office, And accordingly procured ye same, from his late Majesty at Newcastle. But some mistakes falling out, betwixt David & his father, to a high degree, made him declare many times, his breach of promise to his father in Law, was punished by ye disobedience of his Son, upon whose Education in France & England and outreik in 1648 and otherways, cost him more than all his Children besides. In the year 1660, his present Majesty being happily restored to the exercise of his royal Government, all Gifts of Offices, necessarily being to be renued, Sir John being at London with his father, having not the least design for any such Office, and living in great affection with his Brother, endeavouring to make up David's peace with his father, and prevailed with his Mother to consent, that his name should be continued in the new Gift, did write it with his own hand, Which accordingly did pass his Majesties hand, when in the interim he turning Quaker, his father out of much anger and grief, went to his present Majesty, And after representing the case, gave up the lately renued Gift and humbly begged his Majesty to cancell the same, and to order the Secretary to draw another for himself and his son John, which the King was pleased, out of his wonted bounty to Order. Yet to evidence the affection and Justice, Sr John did shew to his brother, he knowing his fathers design to fill up his name in the Gift, he was so denyed to his own Interest, that he not only gave his brother timeous advertisement therof, but also went to the present Earl of Airly & Sir James Ogilvy, who were the only Mother's friends David had at London, And told them of his father's resolution of Changing the Substitution, and frankly intreated them to deal with his father, that the Gift might be keeped blank in the name for some competent time. Wherein it might be hoped, through endeavours with him, he might be reclamed, & so capacitate to enjoy it himself, which accordingly was done, And for a year was keepd blank, till all means proved ineffectual, and till Sr John found there were designs of a third person to out them both, he was necessitate to carry the Gift to the King, and to desire his Majesty to fill up his son John's name, which accordingly was done, he being off the place & in Scotland at the time. So that anything Sr John possesses was an Office which was vacant by David's incapacitating himself, & which a Stranger would have got, if it had not been thus prevented. And although there were no legal tyes on Sir John, nor commands from his father, and that he sufficiently loaded himself with three of the Children's portions, his father's whole debt, and a yearly aliment of 150 lib sterling to his father, which alone might rationally compense his Substitution (his own portion being allowed) Yet Sr John out of meer Affection to his brother, did voluntarly pay him 600 lib Sterling, & took his Discharge, renuncing and resigning in Sir John's favours all pretensions he could have to the said Office, which he has to show under his hand. All which as it Justifyes Sir John that he has done his Brother no Injury, Nor is he the cause of his brother's mean condition; So he humbly conceives there is as little ground for to have his wants made up by Sir John, till he give greater proofs of his friendship & better requitals than ever Sir John has mett with yet.

And as for Sir John's Estate, which is represented to be so great, as it is not above 200 £ a year, the annual rents of his debts and liferent to his Mother in Law being first deduced, So the fond therof was not the profit of the Mint alone, he having got by his wife, her sister and her Mother 1800 lib Sterling, which with his own Industry might in 17 year's time turn to some account, And if it be objected that Sir John might have had a greater Estate, If he had not lived so highly. To this it may be returned That Hospitality to Strangers, and kind offices to relations and Friends, will hardly amongst Gentlemen be reckoned prodigality. And though Sir John's Fortune were as great, as it is called, He has a wife and seaven Children, who perhaps may deserve as well as others, and who in their due time, may evidence as much true Loyalty, as any in their Station. As for his brother's sufferings & merits, Sir John is far from detracting from them, but wishes he may fall upon another way to repair them, And although, it has never been his lot to serve his Majesty in that manner, Yet in all the capacities, he ever yet was honoured with, he hopes he has not been wanting with as much zeal and sincerity as others, And when further oportunities offer, peradventure, he may be as useful in any Station his Prince shall call him to, as greater pretenders.

SOURCE: Moses Bundle 254, item 7734, Edinburgh District Archives.

NOTES: This petition dates from between 1679 and 1681, when James (the future King) resided at Holyroodhouse.

George Falconer to Sir John Falconar (G2)

Ed[inburgh] Sep[t] 25. 1683.
RYT HONOB[LL]
I receved yours and would heave returned you a new ansver ye nixt day, bot ye Chancolar going from this Place his jurnay tovards ye North & expected you would wait uppone him as him passid bay you, so I should not doubt bot you would gait ane accompt off what head passed, thereffor I thought fitt to wait untill ye nixt post. Ye newes ve received uer veray great That ye Citay off Veenna was relived. Ye battell betuixt ye Germanes and ye Turkes uer ffoughten. Ye Turkes defet, his holl infantray being cutt to pices upone ye place. Ye Cavilray fled leaving ther baggag with 60000 tents 3000 pices off cannones and 2000000 off crounes got in ye Grand Kishias[1] Pavelion. Ye King off Pollend tack his Standart with ye tuo hors-tails which uer ye sayds off War. This was done upone ye Sabbath day. Ye Imperialists stod all that night in ther armes fearing ye enimay would have realied. Ye nixt morning ye Keing off Poll[and] followed ye persoutt. Count Stairnberg[2] guverner off ye Citay did in ye tyme off battell Rallay out u[i]t 5000 men which uer onlay lefft him off 15000. He did cut off all ye Janissaries that head lodged them selves in ye ditches. Ye neves give an accompt off 60000 Turkes killed at ye Seig beside what is nou killed in ye battell. Ye Citay uas not able to hold out above ffour day langar. This dayes neves does confirme ye fformer and that ther hes bein ane second battell, ye Turkes Cavilray heaving met w[i]lt 30000 cumming for ther suffre did ralie, so that ye Keing of Poll[and] w[oul]d retret untill ye dooke off Lor[ra]ine cam up u[i]t ye main boday and then gave batell, did totallay defet them. It is said ye christianes heave 20000 men in this Second Conflicke and in ye first [*margin*] four or fyve hundred ye noumber off ye Christianes armay uer 40000 hors and 40000 Futt.[3] Ye neves heir q[uhe]r on Sabath day ther cam ane letter From ye Keing docked by midltone not sufferscrived to ye Magestrants wherin he recomends Balzie Drummond to be ellected ffor this inshouing years Provist. This heas uray much alaromed them, They heaving intended to heave chosene Provist Dicke, with all orders that ye toun clarks may heave no conjunct with him and was to heave given him on thousand pound sterling for ye half of ye place.

This day Erlstone[4] is to be called in ye bouk by order off ye Keing ther ues ane Proclamatione let say wherin ye Keing grants ane longar tyme For tacking off ye Testt which is until ye firt off March accept ye murderers of ye Prince or ther recetters also ye recetters off Seditious ministers and thos who heave ane hand in ye let conspirisay. Ye heritors who heave tackene ye test are indemnifayed as to ye layve's bot remits them to ye Privi councell For ther arbitrarie Ponnishment & understand my Lord Matland was to tacke his jurnay For London. The Laird off Claverhouss went ye lest weik to Gallavay after ye interment of his sevant Dobay, hou found his Forloff[5] comes from ye Keing doune. He is to tacke his Jurnay for Londone which he expects ueray shortlay though he ues refoused it From ye Privicouncell. As I understand my Lord Lavderdell and he is not leak to agrie, I can lerne nothing about ye mint, & understand by ye President that my Lord Hay

Thrasurer will be med mor your Frind before you meit then he hes being Formerlay & wish you may find ye affects off it. Al your Frinds heir are in good helth and does much long to see you. I shall leave anay Farder at ye tyme onlay heath my service presented to your selff your Lady and all ye childrens caution Sir:

Your Louing cousing and honerbl servant

George Falconer

Your mother in Lav is in good helth and heath hir love
presented to you & ye:
Old mamay hath hir blisshing remembred to you & wholl Famlay
[at side:]
This day the Eearle heath suspended Cleverhous

SOURCE: Moses Bundle 254, Edinburgh District Archives.

NOTES: The writer was the natural son of Sir Alexander Falconer (A6) of Halkerton. [1]Kara Mustafa, the Grand Vizier, led the Turkish attack on Vienna. [2]Rüdiger von Stahremberg. [3]This appears to be a fairly accurate account of the final defense of Vienna on 12 September 1683, which had been under siege for almost two months. The Ottomans had reached the limits of their empire. [4]Sir Alexander Gordon of Earlston, covenanter and rebel, had been tried for conspiracy in the Rye House Plot and was sentenced to die 28 September 1683. [5]Furlough.

Sir John Falconar (G2) to Barbara Jaffray

Ed[inburgh] 11 Jan[ry] 1684

My Dear Heart

Since yours by Will[iam], I have been still waiting to see what favo[r] I could procure from the T[hesaurer],[1] who after wee had a long debate togeather vppon the articles of the discharge, and finding that he was straitned, and that in reason he behoved to allow the 400:[lib] of the a[nnual]rent of the stock & the 600[lib] of remedies both which I haveing paid out once to my Lord Laud[erdale] & the wardens & alse are two of the articles of the lords decreit vppon which I was fyned by which I pay it hoyse, they are perswaded to allow these and 350[lib] of my pension till this Candlemas. But when they found themselves so pressed, they aplyed these articles to the ease they had given me before, which was about 1100[lib], so that if yet owe them no obligation what further they will doe I know not. But the T[hesaurer] & the Th[esaure]r Dep[uty] declares they would faine show favo[r] but they have ruined themselves so farr out against me (which now they regrate) that they cannot retreat exept they should contradict what the cause can be of [thei]r being so industrious in persecuting me. They tell & confess it wes only because I took wrong measures, and in emulation to the Ch[ancellor],[2] who they thought protected me as if I had depended on him. They vsed this rigour when God knowes all the favour I ever can expect from the Chan[cello]r is yet to receave. However my friends are not out of hope but ther furie may be abated. But that which troubles me most & which I resolve to stand out against is the fyne which now is declared to be 3000[lib] betwixt Phesdo[3] & me & devyded betweixt the two secretaryes each 1500[lib]. This made themselves ashamed and considering what assurances they gave me and which they all acknowledge does amaze people, for now the Chancellor did acknowledge to my Lady Erroll that it was most true he did give me assurances & he would owne them & give it vnder his hand whatever My Lords Montrose & Perth would draw vp. And if the King or Duke could be prevailed with to ask so much att him he would tell them that it was so that I should [be] intirely preserved and that they wer in honno[r] concerned to doe so. But seing his appearing for me had done me prejudice already he would not off himself further appear except the Duke should write & ask att him which then he should to My owne satisfaction & my friends amply testifye it and further declares that all those assurances wer given with the advyse & concurrence of the The[saure]r who concurred in giveing these noble persons warrand to make these promises. And this I am now about to gett Perth & Montrose to bestirr and declare that it may be a ground for the Duke to ask the Chan[cello]r. And in order therto about 10 dayes since I writt a letter to My Lord Montrose to awaken him & to be serious for me, I haveing hung on many tymes att his lodgeing but to little purpose. The double of this letter you have heir inclosed which after perused returne to me. I have writt another to Perth much of the same straine but with severall alterations.

And now, least those that be the manadgeing of the dilligence for the fyne should arreist the fermes & inhibitt & by that meanes light vppon My Lord Halcartounes debt & the lyke, I have sent you a disposition which is blank in the persons name for the Victuall that it may be prior to any arrestment the person I could have you (if you thinke fitt to fill vp is Logie⁴), which if you agree to send for him as soone as possible & hold a court vpon some other pretense & cause intimat it to determine to pay the duty [...] to Logie conforme to the assignation & cause make a pryce for every vndelyvered boll at 5ˡⁱᵇ the bear & 4ˡⁱᵇ the meall. The reason I would have you to putt Logies name in is because he hes freindship for vs. And whatever corn he can supply vs when wee want also I think it fitt & am so advysed that some lawfull creditor named may be borrowed to Halcartounes debt to protect it against the forty of the people I have to doe with till I settle with them att the best termes I can. And therfore send back with Will Irving the assignation last granted be Halcartoun to me that I may cause draw the paper accordingly. And whose ever named you fill vp in the disposition of the fermes cause them give a back tickett to hold compt to me for what they shall receave by vertew thereof; and show Glenfarquhar that for his security & Phesdoes I intend to send per ferst a bond bearing infeftment in Claver[h]ous[e's] name vppon which without noyse lett infeftment be taken. My Dear, lett nothing of this surpryse you, foras I would have none to suffer by ane so much less my kynd friends and what we doe now is but to prevent the rigour of vnreasonable men, which as a speatt when ruined out may be better dealt with. It is no small affliction to me that I cannot stirr from this and especially when one anothers presence would mutually encouradge vp, but wee must submitt to the alwise providence of the blessed God that does all for the best of those he loves. My dear, be not discouradged att any thing you or I can meet with, for I doubt not but alle shall turne about for our good. But his tyme wee must patiently waitt. I beseech you take care for yo[u]ʳ owne health and the childrens and sitt loose to all injoyments, for He who made the widows excise increase can make a little with his blessing goe a great length. It is true yo[u]ʳ Mother hes gott but little from me of late, but, God willing, she shall the next week gett what she needs & wee shall part, though it wer but a grott. I intreat you to excuse me to Logie & Glenfarquhar,⁵ to whom I intend to write by tomorrows post, not haveing tyme for the tyde, but my service to all friends & write frequently to me & pray for

Yo[u]ʳ ever indeared husband
Jo: Falconar

SOURCE: Moses Bundle 254, Edinburgh District Archives.

NOTES: ¹William Douglass, Marquess of Qugensberry. ²Sir George Gordon of Haddo, 1st Earl of Aberdeen. ³James Falconer of Phesdo. ⁴James Scott of Logie. ⁵Sir Alexander Falconar of Glenfarquhar, Bart.

Bessie Johnston to Barbara Jaffray

Ed[inburgh] April 5. [16]84

Dear daughter

Yo[u]rs w[ith] yo[u]r man came to my hand the 4 of this instant, q[uher]rof I was verie glad it bearing yo[u]r health and the childrens, quhich I pray the Lord may long continue, but I could not dispatch him this day for I was putting up yo[u]r things quhich I have sent with him. I was thinkeing ye white holland courtens should have been sent, but ye other courtins of that cloath bed I had sent away w[ith] the vessel [tha]t is gone from this before I had this last of yo[u]rs. Sir John went from this on Sondays night as I wrot in my last. I have had no letters from him as yet but as soon as I hear from him I shall communicat it to yow with the first occasion [the]rafter. As for Davids effair I gave yow some account in my last of a delay he had graunted for two moneths before Sir John went hence. I wonder yow should be discontent at my goeing thither seing I was indeavouring to take away ye difference betwixt them and it had no bad effect, for a suspension could not be had nor is it ordinarie to get any in such a case. Such arrestments are unloosable being laid on upon a reg[ist]rat bond. I said in one of mine Davids wife told me if you had written a line to him he had not done q[uha]t he did, so if you think fitt you would write a line to him. As for that bill of 60 pound sterling drawn upon David, it is from Robert upon him to pay Sir John for Robert was payd band to Sir John you know. There are 3 gallons of sack[1] bought and is now in Leith waiting for an occasion. I have sent likewise 12 bottells [tha]t [con]tains a choppin[2] a piece and 12 mutchkin[3] bottles. The stoppells are within the cradle and [the]r is a ham also [the]rwith. The skipper [the]r [wh]o is to fetch the bear is gone up for coals and promised to call for them as he returned and carrie these things for now. I have sent the linnens you wrote for, but I can not find that silver spoon yow desyred nor the pearld apron. Oranges are but newlie come but they seek sexpence for the piece of them so I have not bought any as yet. I have sent your blew satin petticoat and the flowered goun & silver saltfats and 2 silver dishes and that suit of Sir Johns you mention and a pair of stockens. I have inclosed the key of yo[u]r cabinet herein for I made not much search [the]rin. Show Elizabeth I have not as yet met with [tha]t man for ye viall strings. About the face cloath and cleats for to use q[uhe]n the barns[4] arms are lett out write to Marie Acmutie w[ith] the next occasion here. It should be done for I have no sleill [the]rin and it shall be done. As for blankets [the]r are none to spare nor could the lad get them carried. I have sent all the yarn I had and is coming to you by sea. I have taken ye round yarn and made 2 pair of sheets for the house. I have given Georg Watson ye barns measurs. Let me know if you will have scots temmin or o[the]r now may have it, here for 14ss an ell. I have sent Nicolas her gown. Isabels mother is dead and so I behoved to let her go to her old fa[the]r and [the]rfor I take [the]m in to my house to at [wh]o remain, yet you may send some meal for the house in summer for I hope we shall all be together yet. I committ you to the Lords mercie and Care and rests

Dear daughter
Your loving mother
Bessie Johnston

Mr. Byrie presents his best respects to you and Mistres Elizabeth. I have lost the key of the writing box Sir John sent you. I was purposing to have sent it herew[ith] but it is lost there being a hole in my pouch. After I had writtin this I found yo[u]r litle key.

SOURCE: Moses Bundle 254, Edinburgh District Archives.

NOTES: [1] wine [2] approximately one-half pint [3] one pint [4] boy's. Bessie Johnston, widow of George Jaffray, was the mother of Barbara Jaffray, wife of Sir John Falconar (G2). This letter was penned by another person, the elderly woman presumably lacking the skills to do so herself.

Patrick Falconer (W1) to Maurice Trent

Elizabeth Town in East-Jersey,
the 28th. of October, 1684.

Sir,

My last was dated the 22. Current, from Philadelphia, at which time I could give you but a small account of the Countrey; and as yet its but a small account, I can give by reason that I have had but a little time here as yet; I have travelled on Foot more then a 100. miles in East and West Jersey, and Pensilvania; I have also Travelled in Maryland, I cannot but say it is a good Countrey, but its possessed with a Debauched, Idle, Leasie People, all that they Labour for is only as much Bread as serves them for one Season, and als much Tobacco as may furnish them with Cloaths, I believe it is the worst improved countrey in the world; for the Indian wheat is that they trust to, and if that fail them they may expect to starve. I find Pensilvania and the two Jerseys are the places which set themselves out most for Planting of Corn; As for the Jersies I need not insist in commending of them, for David Barclay and Arthur Forbes who had a longer stay here than I have had, will give you a more full account; for I intend to write no more than I am able to make good. I may say, that it is a pleasant Countrey, I did never see more pleasant Meadows, and Grass, then I have seen both the Jersies, I have seen plains of good Hay consisting of about 50. Acres of ground, hardly one Tree to be seen upon the whole spot. And there are several places so; I can say, its a well watered Countrey, and good waters, and if they were desirous, they might have very good Quarrie here both for Stone of any sort, and Lime-stone likewise; but so long as Timber is so plenty, they will not be at the pains to seek after Stone; there are some houses in the Countrey built with stone, but very few. Having fallen in here, the end of the year, I cannot be capable to give an account what may be the product of the Countrey, but I hear that all sorts of Grain hath very good Increase, I see the Countrey abounds with Apples, Quinches, Peatches, Walnuts, and Chasnuts, and Strawberries in great abundance, wild-Wine-Grapes are plentifull, wild-Fowl of all sorts, a great number of Deer, Turckie-Fowls-wild, in great abundance and very bigg, I have seen these things in great plenty: I hope ye will excuse me, because I am not capable to give an ampler account of the Countrey, for I have not been two dayes in one place, I will tell you this is a good Countrey, for men who resolves to be Laborious; any who comes here they must resolve to work hard for the first two or three years, till they get a little Ground cleared, for this must be looked on as a wood Countrey, tho I must confess the woods are not so thick as people expects; and there are several places in the Countrey where there is little or no Wood; People are generally curious to have their land near Navigable Rivers, but when they are better acquaint, they will find that the farther back the better is the Land, there are aboundance of Fish and Oysters here, this is not a Countrey for idle people but such as will be at pains, they need not doubt but to get Bread here in plenty, so I wish it be the Lords will that we may have a happy meeting again, his will be done, I wish you may be protected by the Lord, this from,

Your affectionate Friend, and humble,
Servanis Patrick Falconer.

SOURCE: [George Scott], *The Model of the Government of the Province of East-New-Jersey in America: And Encouragements for such as Designs to be concerned there* (Edinburgh: John Reid, 1685), pp. 196-198.

NOTES: Maurice Trent, merchant of Leith, was a Quaker with associations with David Falconar (H1) and interests in West Jersey. In 1680, the young merchant Patrick transferred a payment for a debt to Trent. Perhaps the closest association with Trent was that Patrick's brother James (later Sir James) had married Elizabeth, daughter of Maurice Trent. His son William Trent founded the city of Trenton, New Jersey.

Sir John Falconar (G2) to Barbara Jaffray

London 7 No^r 1685

My Dear Heart

Since my last, I have yo[u]^{rs.} and without date, but I supose it is the last. What I am to say now is it refreshes me extreamly when I hear from you, being very wearie of the place, especially in being idle, although I pass my tyme in the best of company and the most learned, curious, and famous men this place affords. But now I must tell you wee are in earnest and the King and his ministers intends to open the mint presently and, in order therto, Sir William Bruce hes kissed his Maj[es]^{ties} hands to be Generall, and no sooner he did so, but the Thes[aure]^r ordered him to look out for me and to tell me my bussines should pass also with Sir Williams and be reponed to my owne place according to his promise. And accordingly my gift is to be given in to my Lord Murray with the other papers that are to pass the Kings hand. The Thes[aure]^r calld for me this morning and after I had given him thanks for mynding me, he told me it was but what he had resolued to doe & had promised me and, besydes the obligations he had to my relations, he had a kyndness for my selff. And desryed me to meet with Sir William Bruce and putt things in order a good part of this afternoone. Sir Will hes sworne all the friendship and kyndnes to me that I could expect and truly I beleive him to be ingenuous, and since I am to be concerned and to have a generall, I am very well pleased to have a man of his justice & exactnes and circumspection. He hes promised to doe nothing without me. I am prepareing a note of what is to be done vppon this place. So that I hope in a little tyme, it will please the Lord to give vs a outgait of this great trouble (that I may say hes almost crushed me), and give vs occasion to live togeather. And therfore it will be fitt you be quietly putting things in the countrey, in order that vppon my further advertisment you may with the family come to Ed[inburg]^h. But I will not be positive to bidd you come till the papers past the Kings hands, but of this more by my next. Have a care of yo[u]^r selff & the children and remember me to yo[u]^r mother & such others as hes been kynd to you, and cary equall & be not over raised at this change, but owne all to the tender care and mercies of our blessed God. I am

Yo[u]^r intirely affec[tiona]^t
husband   Jo: Falconar

I have little news only, I have it confirmed from the best kinds that the King & Queene goes to Scotland in May or hinderen of aprill.

SOURCE: Moses Bundle 254, Edinburgh District Archives.

Memorial from the Lyon Office concerning the funeral of Sir David Falconer of Newton (E1)

1°   It is advysed that there be 2 Lozange-armes done out, the one to be affixt on the gate of the Lodging, or on the wall of the high-Church fore gainst it, and the other on the entrie of the Gray-friers yeard.

2°   That the Coffin be adorned with helmet, wreath, Cyffers Tears etc. And that the Defunct's eight branches, 4 on the fathers syde and 4 on the mother be affixt on the Corners and sydes of the Coffin (or vpon the pale or herse in case it shall be thought fitt to Carry the Corps vnder a pale or in ane herse).

3°   That the defuncts gown Covered with mourning be Carryed Imediatly Before the Coffin by a friend bareheaded, preceeded by one or tuo of the Maters with y[r] mates trim'd in mourning in y[r] gowns and bare.

4°   That at the processione the Magistrat's of Edinburgh goe before in [thei]r ordinary post and after [the]m the Clergy, Nobilitie, gentrie and multitude, and last of all [tha]t the Lords of Sessione walk in a body in [thei]r formalities Ushered by [thei]r other Maters, and followed (if they will) by the rest of the members of the College of Justice.

5°   That the Defuncts mourning Cloath fall in imediatly efter the Coffin, The Coachman, Postilion and footmen being bare and in mourning.

     All this is humblie offered to [th]e Considera[tio]ne of the Lords, & it is to be observed that there is no other solemnitie allowed by the late act of parliament. The privy Council haveing found not only the Carrying the honours aloft, and led horses etc. but also the vseing the Trumpets (except for giveing the Jubila[tio]ne) to be comprehended vnder the prohibition, Yet it is to be remembred that both open & close trumpets and a led horse were allowed to General Dalzell, [1] but q[uhe]ther that was indulged to him as a Sojer or not is vncertaine

6°   If the friends please, the Corps mey be in the mean time laid in the High Church.

7°   There mey be a funerall sermon preached in the Gray friers Church imediatly before interment, Dureing q[uhi]ch tyme the Coffin is to be sett doun before the Pulpit.

SOURCE: Kintore Papers, Bundle 106, Aberdeen University Library.

NOTES: [1]General Thomas Dalzell died 23 August 1685. Sir David Falconar of Newton, Lord President of Session, died 15 December 1685.

David, 3rd Lord Falconer of Halkerton (A9), to James Ogilvy, Earl of Airlie

Halcartoun the 19
Feb[r] 1686

My Lord
being dissait of grouhunds and hauing tryed all this countrou for sum and can find non: Strigs of nessitie put none so to your promes of the day uhich your so promessed to met at your [...]huff uith all not forgeting my [...]. I serues to your Lopp lidut and so my Lord [...]

your Lo[rdshi]pp son
your affectionat grand child
HALCARTONE

SOURCE: Airlie Muniments, GD16, Scottish Record Office.

Robert Falconar (G3) to Barbara Jaffray

Lond° 18 March 1685/6

DEAR SISTER MADAM.

Since my last (under Faesdoes[1] cover, as all my preceeding went for security of conveyance to your hands), I am now favored w[i]th you[r] La[dyshi]pps 4th Instant owening the recept of myne 22d passt. Our Losse is great in Loossing so dear a Relation, but yours and his childrens farr exceeds in all parts, and were it propper for Christians to grieve overmuch (as it is not fortheassuredly is happy), It might bee well charged on those; called I: men that loaded hym from tyme to tyme with oppression and at last broak Publick faith of which I could write enough, if anyways Edifieing. But your present matter is to wade through the difficultys of the Estate, to save in tyme without excesse of charges which comonly comes by churlish mens over-diligenced) what may bee saved for your owne and childrens good and perhapps it is good advice (under your circumstances) not to meddle at present [...]. I hope by this tyme the Gift of the Escheat is returned in yo[u]r la[dyshi]pps favour uppon which yo will determine the tyme of yo[u]r parture for this place, which will bee necessary for vs to know that Lodgeings neer the Court may bee Provided and since you incline to come by sea, I wish heartily every thing may suite for your comeing in ye Yaucht, which goes hence this week wth my Lord H[igh] Comissioner and his servants &c.

Dear Sister, You must not bee ouermuch troubled, or surprized at any thing you have or shall meet w[i]th for there's little Charity or Generosity to bee mett wth nowadayes. Therefore must resolue bravly against all disappointments and I doubt not God will graunt successe to your endeavors. I will only say without reservation that if it lay in my power to do anything for you or yours you should longar this have had a tender of it. But alas—It is hard to say whoe raised that report—of my Brothers Estate being worth £500: a year, all debts payd, but here I mett wth it and judged necessary to acquaint you w[i]th it in tyme That you may provide yourselfs w[i]th the Necessary to confront those base, ill natured People that would Defeat you, and the Children of releifs. It is happy the Threasurer's Nayles is cutt and that the Chauncellor appeared so ready and kinde in writeing effectually aboute the Escheat on your first addresse. This may convince hym & Melfoord of in part of the sadd and badd my Brother left you and his children in and that you will bring wth you a further supply of proofs in this matter, is very well.

The King did promise my Brother releife from his hard usadge and would have donne it one way or other, th°[ugh] really not by his office. The Quaker B.[1], as I fear and too much reason to beleive possessed hym when hee was Duke, so much of my Brothers Guilt that the King was even resolved against reestablishing hym in it, th°[ugh] at the same tyme knew hee had bein too severely deallt w[i]th and would have placed hym here, in Ireland, in an equivalent or better thing, th°[ugh] not in his owne for the scandall of it. The King haveing little tyme to spare could not hear my Brothers hard Case fully, vppon which my Brother Intreats Hee would bee pleased to appoint Melfoord to hear it and make report of it, which His Majesty Graunted and sayd would order Melfoord accordingly. My Brother accordingly layes his case before Melfoord (where still it lyes). Hee sayd would do my Brother all the right lay in hym and pretended aboundance of freindshipp, but that the King had given hym no order in it, vppon which my Brother went againe and againe to the King. The King told hym hee had forgott, but that hee would do it. In a day or two after my Brother sickned, and thus it stands as I aduised you before, and fitt for nobody to stirr a boot in it since you intend to come, but yourselfe and perhapps your owne appearing will influence and procure greater dispatch then 20 Men. Matters at Court are more tedious then other buissinesse and the great ones expects to bee minded and the King is to bee minded by them.

Now if Melfoord has the Kings order to peruse my Brother's case and make a report of hym of it, then yo[u]r worke will bee the shorter but if hee has not such an order, then you must Petition for it. It will bee readily graunted, and when Melfoord reports in your favour then [you] must putt in for releifs, the easiest way for the King to graunt and that which will best suit wth your and childrens reddresse, of which if anything in England fitt for you to aske. And the King to Graunt shall have it my thoughts. And your La[dy]s[hi]pp will do well to consult your freinds in Scotland, particularly the Chauncellor,[1] what to propose for your reddresse. I know nothing in Scotland to ready, as a Pension and if possible, to gett an exonnoration of my Brother Bond to Sir Wm Sharp, tho[ugh] the yearly Pension were the lesse would bee happy. If ever a good Office in Scotland of £350: or £400: a year that is in the Kings Graunt and might bee manadged for you and the children would still bee easier obtained, or if my Lord Chancellor and Melfoord would concerne [the]mselves in 12000 stone of copper to be coyned and helpe you to obtaine the Graunt, they might hand £5: £6: to £7000 ster[ling] free of all charge, but onely theyr Countenance and helpe of £1000 or £1500 Credit for carrying it on, but this is to bee mentioned vnder the rose. Indeed my Brother did offerr the King, I meane Melfoord for the Kings vse, and paying his force nar £10000: but in your case cannot; and it's more then any besyds hymselfe durst offerr——th°[ugh] I will hand a draught of a Petition and what else may bee necessary in my thoughts against you come Yet may bring a draught wth you, and make choice of the best —— The firrs of your la[dyshi]spp receave [the]m and that you chaunce in your passadge to touch at Yarmouth, pray lett [the]m bee delivered in to Mr Gyles Wakeman, a Mercer there, to bee sent forth to Jam[*seal hole*]ountaine Esq at Sall in Norfolke. John Jeffreys wants forn. Hee has an Itching desire to bee goeing in this Yaucht, but I perswade hym to bee patient. Mr Lindsay and his Wyfe has a faire owtward expression of Kindenesse and respect to you and the memory of my Brother. I hope it will proove reall and since they live near the Court and lett Lodgeings, I wish it may bee empty at yo[u]r comeing that you may have an appartment there. I will attend you, hee is of my oppinion to come here, and doubts not of your finding Melfoords frindshipp. I hear ther is an expresse expected from Scotland before the Earle of Murrays departure bee determined. Were there any woemen or acquaintance goeing in this Yaucht, you might have been troubled my Wyfes company. In order to have waited on you here I have been a little Indisposed, which prevented my writeing these reports, but I hope have made amend. My Wyfe intreats her humble service to yo[u]r la[dyshi]spp and all freinds he[re], lyke pray accept from mee wth my Love to my Cousins. My Brother, it seems, owe [me] £10: or £20. Now if you take a bill on hym, hee may crave allowance of that some out of it, which may bee your present occasions cannot dispense w[i]th. I remaine always

Madam

Yo[u]r lad[yshi]pp very aff[e]ct[ionate] Brother & Seruant
Robert Falconar

SOURCE: Moses Bundle 254, Edinburgh District Archives.

NOTES: [1]James Falconer of Phesdo. [2]Robert Barclay of Urie, the Quaker Apologist. [3]James Drummond, 4th Earl of Perth.

Barbara (Falconar) Menzies to Esther Falconar

Kindmundy 7 March 1719

Esther

I hir you have ben oddous in both cargess and behaver in this litell tyme I thoght all had ben ended bequext you and me, and yet I hir you was so bold as to go to my houss and to take out my bed that was up the sterss and sell it which was both theft and robrey and ounder strest but you may depend on it I shall not want it and also shall make you publekly knowin both as to your behaver and carges which I hir is very bad for it is not His Bauck nor yet her behaver that I any wayss regared also I know not what outher things I may want which I shall have your both for [...]

Bar: Menezes

SOURCE: Moses Bundle 254, Edinburgh District Archives.
NOTES: These two quarrelling sisters were the daughters of Sir John Falconar (G2).

Thomas Falconer to the President, Governor, and Members of Council of His Majesty's East India Company

Honble. Sir and Sirs

By this years Shipping I have received a Letter from Mr Hugh Barker directed to Mr Thomas White and myself, wherein he advises that he had appointed Messrs. Henry Frankland and John Surman his Attorneys here and empowered them to receive all his books and papers and adjust his accounts. I have therefore delivered over to said Gentlemen all the Books and papers belonging to Mr Barker which I found in the possession of the deceased Mr James Williamson who was his former Attorney.

As Mr Barker has made complaint to our Honble. Masters at hom that he had received great injustice from Mr Stephenson and myself at Patna, I earnestly request your Honour &cs. will please to direct that Messrs. Frankland and Surman make the strictest inquiry into this affair, and give in their report to this board. If it shall appear to those Gentlemen that I have been guilty of doing Mr Barker any injustice, or that I have been a gainer by him, I shall most willingly make any satisfaction as shall be judged reasonable, but on the other hand if it shall appear all his complaints are without grounds, I must then hope for an acquitance from the heavy and unjust charge he has laid against Mr Stephenson and myself.

I hope your Honour &ca. will comply with this my just and reasonable request being with great respect

Honble. Sir and Sirs
Your most Obedient Humble Servant

T. Falconer

Fort William
        October 4th 1722.

SOURCE: David Falconer, *Bengal Merchant* (Trowbridge, Wilts.: the author, 1982).

George Falconar (F1) to David, 4th Lord Falconer of Halkerton (A10)

My Lord
I am honoured with your Lordship of 6th and 13th Inst[ant] by which I hope Mr Ramsay
has imparted the miserable State I am inn, which I had not the confidence to doe myself.
By a continewed tract of misfortune has attended me my Losses will exceed £3000 Ster[ling]
besides the mentin[ence] of my family. I am Owing about Two thousand and one hundred pounds Sterling, and what Ile have to pay it I cannot Justly tell for sometyme, but
belive will be about one fourth part, but whatever it is I shall give my Creditors a true
Acc[omp]^{tt}, of whom Ramsay and Strachan is the greatest, and to whom only yet I have
comunicated and what ever method or course is teaken by them I hope others will agree
to it. I Sopose Woodstown will gett your proposall, for I can make none, but Stripp my
self of every thing. Neither have I one freind here that I can expect 1^{oz} of assistance. And
I have not the confidence to press your Lordship, but leaving it intirly to yourself to doe
or not as pleases, and if any thing done most be speedly for if publick I fear will occasion
loss of my office, and will terminat any expectations of redressing affairs with B[oghall].
I am now with a Wife and four Innocent Children reduced to very great Missire, having
new that I can tuch a few dayes sustinance for my family. Last week Bog[hall] wrott inn
to M^r M^ccloud that he hoped was soon comming to the country being he wanted him
much for a Neighbour and that he had some affairs with him, Upon which M^r M^ccload
came down to S: M: and pressed hir going out immediatly to B[oghall] which she did
upon friday last, he forsed his away the same neight, pretending had not Corn for horses,
and that he would not till goe to a Publick stable, he told hir that had Receaved a letter
from me which he would soon answer, and spoak with much more of selftness annent
me and with Oaths and Ass ever atrens promised the undoing the deeds of late done, but
could not be prevailled upon to wrett with hir to make out new Wretts, but upon all this
not much stress or dependance can be mad. M^r M^ccload is not going to the country for
some moneths so every thing makes Cross for me at present. I shall doe my eutmost to
submitt to what Heaven has permitted to happen to me. I Wish My Ladys recovery and
every thing that is good atten upon you and your family I am

My Lord
Geo: Falconar

your Lordship will excuse the confustness of this of mine connseding the weight. I
have at present upon me

Edin[burgh] 18 May 1724

SOURCE: Kintore Papers, Bundle 195, Aberdeen University Library.

Gilbert Falconar (J1) to Richard Bennett

8ber: 22d 1730

Respected Friend
Since thou art so good as to offer to advance my share of the Ballance due to Coulson
Fallows for Jo: Martyn, John S[...], Lewis Guillumer for Jno Radbourn, & Edwd Fellows
for Sir Jno Fallows Bart Deceased, [which] amounts to three hundred fifty seven pounds
ten shillings & 2d. I thankfully accept of it; and if thou will please to order it to be paid
in London and [...] discharged ... This shall oblige me and my heirs to repay it again to
thy content. But [I] must desire thee to prevail on thy friend Capt Hyde to insist on ye

Gentlemens taking only a third part of ye Sum of each of [...] no more in Justice being our dues to pay as thou will know; therefore [I] shall not repeat the reasons here. However I have left it to my Kinsmen David Barclay and John Falconar of London to judge for me, and if they Judge it more advisable for me to pay a half of ye Sum rather than Contend wth ye Gentlemen I am willing it Should be so. But must beg it as a favour of thee to give Capt Hyde orders to pay a third or half as they shall advise him. They will I make no doubt assist him in ye Matter.

The 260lb Philemon Lloyd I hope will come in now by ye [...] given me to ship his Publick Tobacco towards ye discharge of it. But if [...] should not lye in my way to get in Jams Earle Jun:r Debt of 40[?]. I must beg thy favour to be assisting in that.

I shall not trouble thee farther at present but to return thanks for all favours and that I am,

Thy ready & much obliged friend   Gilbert Falconar

SOURCE: Lloyd Family Papers, Maryland Historical Society.

NOTES: The transaction refers to a shipment of African slaves brought to Maryland by Falconar and Richard Bennett.

George Falconar (A14) to David, 4th Lord Falconer of Halkerton (A10)

My Lord
Since you left this place, nothing of moment hapned worth the troubling your Lordship with a line, till yesterday Geo: Robison came to me from the Earl of Balcaress to desire my wretting to you of the E: of Kelley would be accepted in Marrage to your Lordship daughter. I shunnd as much as possible the Commisson, but having pressed me much, I agreed to wrett your Lordship of it. So I leave it to your Lordship and My L[ady] to determine yourselfs in it without passing my privat Judgment of it, with my sinser best wishes to your Lordship My Lady and all your family Adieu

Edin[burgh] 16 June 1731

SOURCE: Kintore Papers, Bundle 195, Aberdeen University Library.

David, 4th Lord Falconer of Halkerton (A10), to George Falconar (F1)

The Answer to B[rothe]r George

I had on saturday last ane unsubscrived letter delivered me quhich by the writte I judge to be from you Wherin you acquaint me that you had a comission delivered you by George Robertson from the Earle of Balcarras to me with a proposol of Marraige for the Earle of Kelly to my daughter

I sh[ould] expect yow[l] doe me the favour to make my most humble duty acceptable to the Earle of Balcarras and returns him my thanks for the honour he designed for me & family tho it is what I cannot accept of neither is her mother for it But I reckon myself so far bound to his Lordship that he shall ever find me both willing and ready to serve him if ever I have any opportunity & am   Yower most aff[ectiona]t B[rothe]r H[alkerto]n

Ingl[ismaldie] june 23d 1731

SOURCE: Kintore Papers, Bundle 195, Aberdeen University Library.
NOTE: This outgoing copy was written on the same sheet of the previous letter.

Gilbert Falconar (J1) to Thomas Penn

Respected Friend

I am still so very weak that I have hardly strength to do my Duty in Requesting thee with an Extraordinary Occurance that has happened here lately.

Our Justices has took upon them to Appoint a new Prothonotary by Vertue of their own Authority, as it they were Legally possessed of all the Powers of Government. Hugh Durborow is the man who they have qualified to both the Office of Clerk of the Peace and Prothonotary thave taken Bonds of him, and Delivered him the Seal and Records.

Their usage of me was in it self so monstrous that it was hard to believe the Account I gave of it tho reely true, but this Mad Action will I hope make my relation cease to seem Incredible. What is aimed at is hard to gues; it looks as if they had a minde to wrest the Power of Governm[en]ᵗ out of thy hands for it is plain this is a Strugle for it. I shall not pretend to Anticipate what thy own good Sence & Just resentments will Suggest to thee on this Occasion, But shall take leave to Signefie to thee that the People here are farr from approving of the Justices Conduct on the Contrary they have it in a Just Abhorance, and say it is an Audacious Impudent Action, and they hope the Propriet[o]ʳ will by this see what usage their poor Neighbours has met and will meet with from them Since they can flye in thy own face and use thy own Power again thee. The most thinking are Alaramed and uneasie till they see what the Issue will be, for they say, if these men are passed as easily over with this as they have been in other things there will be no liveing in the County with them. They say they have long Oppressed them both Publickly and privetly and if they Dont get rid of them now they never shall. The most Numerous and best of the people are thy friends and remain Dutyfull, So that it is in thy Power at once to Oblige the people and assert thy own Just rights.

I had three affidavits prepared to do me Justice, but could get but one compleated which is that about Clem[en]ᵗ Plumsteds Letters. The others thoul see has been offered. It was Timo[thy] Howson prevented there being finished, and had he known of ye other a like sooner that would not have been done neither.

These vexatious disputes hurts me much every way, but nothing sat so heavy as ye Imputation of falshood. I desire to live no longer than I can speak truth. A Lier is the vilest of Characters. I hope I may be by this time sett to rights in thy good Opinion. Thou knows how I am used. Do with me what thou pleases. No Man liveing shall be more gratefull than

> Thy Already very Much Obliged friend
> Gilbᵗ Falconar

Dover Jan[ua]ʳʸ 19ᵗʰ: 1735

I have troubled Rob[er]ᵗ Charles with yᵉ Affidavits &c.

SOURCE: Penn Papers, Historical Society of Pennsylvania.

NOTES: Although not specifically described as such, this political crisis was caused by the resistance to Quaker proprietary government by the increasing numbers of Presbyterian immigrants from Ulster. The letter was written at Dover, Delaware.

Alexander, Master of Halkerton (A11), to David, 4th Lord Falconer of Halkerton (A10)

My Lord

I had the pleasure of writeing you before I left Petersburgh but do not know if it has come to hand. I have been little in one place ever since. General Kieth being ordered to accompany the Turkish Ambassador from the frontiers of Turky to Perevelochna the first town of his Government in the Ukraine. The exchange was in the following manner both haveing marched to their respective frontiers accompanied both by a numerous suite and the troupes of the two forsaid powers encamped, where after settling the ceremonial part both came to their utmost limits where a tent was erected partly on the Russian and partly in the Turkish Dominion where the two commissaries viz General Kieth and the Serasqurer of Bender[1] were set haveing on their right hand the two Ambassadors and after the removal of the dificulties of the exchange the two foresaid Commissaries delivered ym into each other's hand. I never saw such a set of people as the Turks being altogether a noisy rabble not only begging money of us every day but tearing the dishes of meat out of our servants' hands. Once I dined with some of their Bashaws[2] who do not know the use of forks or knives but tear with their hands like ravenous beasts on the contrary the Russian Officers extremely polite and splendide. I shall be extremely straitned before her money can come to hand so that if you plase to remit it to my brother David at London he will give it to a merchant in London who will order his correspondent in Russia to give it me. Our General has been very bad of a Reumatisme occasioned by cold he got in that expedition but I thank God is pretty well recovered. He offers you my mother and sisters his most humble duty as likewise doth I who am with the greatest sincerity and affection

My Lord
Your Most Affect: Son
& Obed^{nt} Hu^{mble} Ser^t
Alex^r Falconer

If I have the pleasure of hearing from you please send it to my brother David as being the surest way

Gleuhoffe Novr 27th 1740

SOURCE: Kintore Papers, Bundle 198, Aberdeen University Library.
NOTES: [1] i.e., *Serasker*, or commanding officer, of Bender, now Bendery in the Transdnistrian Republic [2] pashas, i.e., nobles. Turkey ended a three-year period of war with Russia and earlier that year made alliances with France and Sweden. General James Keith, to whom Alexander was attached as an aide, was earlier that year appointed governor of the Ukraine.

George Falconer (A14) to David, 4th Lord Falconer of Halkerton (A10)

My Lord

I hope your Lordship has gott quett clear of the Rebells, which must have been very troublesome, and a great burthen to the whole country. I am now going a Voyadge to Guinea, and the west indies and hope your Lordship will excuse me in not aquitting you of it, before I left England, but was dispatched away in a few days after our orders came. I took the liberty of drawing upon Mr James Farquhar, in Edinbourgh for eigteen pounds sterling, and my Brother David, advanced me the rest of what your Lordship is pleased to allow me annualy. I was in such distress that it was impossible to be equipt out in necessaries for so long a Voyadge without it, and hope your Lordship will excuse the liberty I have taken. I must aquent you that my Captain, is a great scoundrel but good pritty Gentlmen to my Brother Officers, so that we all putt it out of his power to injure us, his name is Scully, please to give my duety to Mama and sisters I hope this will find you in good health which is the earnest Prayers of your Lordships

Most Affect[t] Son
and Humble Servant
George Falconer

Madera June the 10th 1746

P:S excuse my hast we are just going to sail for Guinea

SOURCE: Kintore Papers, Bundle 105, Aberdeen University Library.

Rev. James Falconar (X10) to Lord Justice Clerk

My Lord
It may seem very presumptive, that one entirely depriv'd of the Honour of your Lordships Acquaintance, should take upon him to Trouble you in this Manner; But that great Humanity, by all confessd to be your Lordships Characteristick, has encourag'd me to take, and I hope, will encline you to pardon the Freedom especially as it is the Effect of Absolute Necessity the only thing can render it Excusable.

I am a poor Distressd Clergyman Prisoner on Board the Eltham now in Leith Road, but to sail tomorrow morning; I was sent to sea at Ab[er]d[ee]n on the sixth Day of April last, depriv'd not of the Conveniencys only but even of the Necessarys of Life having been hurried away without the least Previous Notice, with not so much as a Change of Linnens in My Company, no Bedding nor even a Great Coat, And am now almost in Rags, the Cloaths I had then on me being very much worn out. I was examined at Aberdeen and M[r] David Bruce Judge Advocate told me the Day after, that I was soon to be set at Liberty; "Because," said he, "by what accounts we can learn about you we have Reason to believe you an honnest Man." These, My Lord, were his Express Words, as he will no Doubt remember; And they seemed to be utterd with so much Sincerity, that I rested quite secure, and while others were applying to their Respective Friends for Bail, I gave mine no Trouble, Still Relying on the Word of M[r] Bruce, who is no doubt a man of Honour, but has certainly forgott me, by Reason of More Weighty Business; But at length, I was carried aboard, nor, till now, have I had an Opportunity of Writting to any one for My Deliverance, except to Mr Bruce himself, to put him in mind of his Promise; but have yet had no Return.

Wherefore, My Lord, I humbly & Earnestly Intreat your Lordship would Pitty My Deplorable Case, & take My Affair before your self, and dispose of me as you shall afterwards Judge Proper; only, for the Love of God, & Compassion to your Fellow Creature, let me remain no longer in this Dismal Situation, which is worse than a Thousand Deaths.

Your Lordships Pardoning My Assurance, & Complying with this My Humble Request, is Expected of Your Lordships Goodness as the Greatest Temporal Favour possible to be Conferred upon

My Lord
Your Lordship's
Most humble Petitioner &
most obedient Servant
while
Ja^s Falconar

Elham in Leith Road
Thursday Septr: 18th 1746

SOURCE: Lord Milton's General Correspondence, MS 16620, f. 161, National Library of Scotland.
NOTES: Rev. Falconer was a Jacobite prisoner.

David Falconar to Charles Norris

London, 1st May 1750

Dear Friend Charles

I believe you will be something surprised to hear of me from hence, whom doubtless you concluded to be still amongst my Mussulman Bretheren of Constantinople; I was there indeed since I saw you & came back again by ye advice of the Ambassador & my other friends there, in order to take up my small ship, which I proposed to purchase, with such good as I know most proper for that place, which is what they generally term Bagatelles, such as Watches, clocks, Cabinetware, cutlery, Jewels of all sorts & on all which there is a handsome & never failing profit. This scheme was so well approved of here that I found friends ready to assist me with the Necessarium, but could not for my heart procure a vessell fit for my purpose without which I could do nothing; in which interim came advice of an exorbitant rise of Cottons at Smyrna, which rendered that commodity quite unfit for this market, & my chief dependance for a loading back being on it. I dreaded ye apprehension of a disappointment which must have been attended with ye most pernicious consequences to one circumstanced as I am; & therefore thought it most prudent to decline an undertaking of so much moment on ye good or bad Success of which depended all my hopes and fortune, & accept of a very handsome & Genteel offer made me by my old acquaintance Mr Glover who is in the Insurance way at present, but in all probability will ere long have things of a very different nature to attend to, in which case as far as I find I am designed to succeed him, in the interim I shall wait with patience, & as I think I am now settled in my own country I should be very glad to hear from you my good friend, as well as from any other of my quondam esteemed acquaintance, & if you or they think me anyways qualified to serve them I shall take their command as favours—-

Apropos—I was reading t'other day in one of ye Gazettes an advertisement in your's & Mr Griffith, concerning Squirrell skins which I suppose was in consequence of ye discourse we had together on that point, for my part I believe ye thing feasible, & did not fail to make proper enquiry at Cons|tantinop]^{le} & as far as I find if ye skins are in season & well taned they will answer, so that if you please to make a tryall of a small cask or chest of them I will send ye same over to a very worthy friend of mine there & see what he can make of them, at worst ye loss will be no great matter

Pray my respects to your Brother, & Sister Debby, & to all our old acquaintances. I should be extreamly glad to entertain a little correspondence with any one who has still any regard for their &

Dear friend Charles
Your assured fr^d & Serv:^t
David Falconar

I once more beg your favourable
recomendation of my frd: Mess:^rs Scroope
& Co. @ Leghorn, to any of your
acquaintances who may have to do that
way

Pray in particular be so good as to
present my kind love to Cousin Sanny
Barclay (I wou'd say Alex:^r Barclay Esq)[1]
I wish him joy on his marriage, & shall
be very glad of a line from him

[*endorsed*]:   Read July 8th 1750

SOURCE: Norris Family Papers, 2: 103, Historical Society of Pennsylvania.

NOTES: [1]Grandson of Robert Barclay of Urie. David Falconar was the second son of John Falconar (H2). He had been in Newfoundland in 1729 and likely also in Philadelphia, where he had probably met Isaac Norris, son of one of the chief merchants there.

Excerpt from David Falconar's *A Journey from Joppa to Jerusalem in May, 1751*

We set out from Joppa about six of the clock in the evening, and arrived at Ramah about nine, where we staid till the same hour the next evening, and then mounted directly for Jerusalem, which is distant from that place about ten hours journey; so that, travelling all night, we computed to arrive there by sun-rise the next morning, the excessive heat of the weather rendering it almost impossible to travel by day; we therefore, very reasonably, as we thought, prefer'd the freshness of the night for that purpose, and more especially as it was moon-shine, and in the month of May. —— Oh charming! in May! methinks I hear any untravel'd Englishman cry: ——What pleasure you must have enjoyed that night! How every sense must have been regaled! The sweet lullings of the nightingale! The odoriferous vernal bloom! The cool refreshing breeze! And the whole face of that delightful country gilt with glittering moon shine! It must certainly have enchanted you! —— Why, ay, I was enchanted; or, if you will, bewitch'd, to take all this trouble to see so wretched a land; for as to your nightingales, —— blossoms, — and breezes, —— you may e'en stay at home in your own country to enjoy Them: —— All the music I heard that charming night, was the shrill shriek of some poor melancholy cricket, that seemed to be cursing it's hard fate amongst those hideous rocks; nor were my olfactory nerves any other ways affected, than by a faint and disagreeable smell of the parch'd earth; —— and, as to your breezes, —— why, yes, 'tis true, we had them; —— cool as the gleam of an oven's mouth! and refreshing as the soft zephirs of a glass-maker's furnace! For 'twas our luck to meet with one of those winds, which, in it's pilgrimage, is pleased to take it's way over the Egyptian desarts, whereby it serves as a vehicle to transport the heat of the burning sands all over this happy country; and, as this wind reigns almost all the summer, I leave the reader to judge, how agreeable it must be to the inhabitant, as well as traveller: As for my part, I protest I was almost suffocated; such puffs would come now and then, pouring down the gullies of the mountains, as perfectly scorch'd the face, and fill'd the lungs with fire; I expected every moment when I should burst out into a flame; but, tho' my smoak and steam did not actually come to a blaze, yet I thaw'd and melted like butter, and sure a more uneasy night I never underwent in my life; for not only the atmosphere was intolerable, but the roads too were so monstrous bad, that we were in danger every moment of breaking a leg, if not a neck; such rocks! such precipices! such ups and downs! and the ten thousand millions of tons of loose stones, that lie scatter'd all over the roads, would make one wonder how it could be possible for the poor beasts ever to pick their way thro' them; and yet, by use, they have got the knack of it so cleverly, that they will carry you down a descent, steeper and more intricate than a belfry stair case, without making one *faux pas*: and well for the poor traveller it is, that they are so sure footed, or otherwise, woe to his bones!

Well; befriended with all these agreeable circumstances, we kept *bunyaning it one* for four or five hours, till at last we came to a long and narrow pass, between two steep mountains, comparable enough to honest John's *Valley of the shadow of death*; but, as he only *dreamt* of meeting with a devil or two in his passage, we, too truly, had our passage cut off by five; and, what seem'd to portend us little satisfaction from the encounter, they did not appear to be any of those immaterial essences, that only act on the mental part, by suggestion and insinuation, but, good nervous, well sinew'd sons of Belial, who, by their looks, and the pretty little switches in their hands, no bigger than one's wrist, seem'd to give us to understand, they proposed to inform our judgments by actual contact, or matter acting upon matter: In short, to speak intelligibly, they were five Arabs, who started from behind the rocks, four arm'd with clubs, and the fifth with a gun; however, they were civil enough not to knock us down before they bid us stand, but fell into a parley with our Arab guide, who, to do the fellow justice, really perform'd his part by us; for he swore, entreated, expostulated, and sometimes almost cried: for, the point was, they insisted we were Greeks, and had not paid the *caphar*, and therefore should pay it to them: Why, says our conducter, money they have none, and, as for their cloaths, they belong to *such a one* at Joppa, their acquaintance it seems; therefore, do me not such an injury, as to misuse *Franks* under my protection: These words were accompanied with the most passioned, suppliant voice, and gesture imaginable; and really there was occasion enough for it, for one of them had got up a huge stone, that he aim'd to discharge, or at least pretended so, at my head, which, I promise you, made me shake it a good deal: I now thought the affair began to grow a little serious; for, at first, I was rather diverted than alarmed, and had began to scrape an acquaintance with one of these rugged gentry, whilst our captains were disputeing the point: I had given him a pipe of tobacco, and, by signs, let him understand, I had nothing else worth his acceptance, unless he would uncase me, which was scarce worth his trouble. —— In short, without saying a word, by the help of some whimsical, out of the way gestures, I made shift to make him laugh, and in a moment or two afterwards he went to the gunster, their chief, and, after a short parley between them, we had the consolation to see them all march off, and leave us to pursue our journey. So on we jog'd till we came to the gates of Jerusalem, thro' a country good for nothing, but that of being too good for the scoundrel race that inhabit it. —— A dreary, wild, and uncomfortable prospect of naked and craggy rocks; a soil as stony and ungrateful as their hearts.

SOURCE: David Falconar, *A Journey from Joppa to Jerusalem in May, 1751* (London: for E. Comyns, 1753), pp. 7-15.

NOTES: The author was the same as the author of the preceding letter. He died in 1752 and perhaps his friends had the journal of his trip published.

John Falconer (C1) to Alexander, 5th Lord Falconer of Halkerton (A11)

Jamaica, 23d February 1752

My Lord

Your most kind and good letter of 12 December 1751 I rece'd Acquainting me of my father's death, of which my brother David had advis'd me of some time before.

I believe what you say in regard to my Mother's Conduct. Tho you do not descend to Particulars, yet I can see, and nothing but what I always suspected her of, that she had been promiseing everything she cou'd come at to your prejudice, and by what David writes, that rascally family the Humes are still her Confidants.

I do not know how far the Scots law Extends in regard to the making mens own Evidence against themselves, but in England a Bill in Chancery, her answers to which she must swear to, in every particular. In that case one must either Perjur themselves or answer to the summons, or confers the sum or sums or value in their Possession, belonging to the Partys, who file this Bill in Chancery. And was it my own Case, I certainly wou'd put her to this test, of Purging herself, by Cash. I do not in the least doubt, but she has wronged the family above £60,000 sterling. You may make a rough Calculation, by saying her twenty five years past there ought to have been saved £1,500 Yearly, of the Annual means which wou'd make £37,500. The £7,500 throw away and remains £30,000. When I married, the heirs of the deceas'd husband filed a Bill in Chancery and made Mrs Falconer give up every Individual trifle, as she rather Chose to keep to the marriage Settlement, being Better than her third of Mr Lindseys Estate, which the Laws of England provide in favour of the Widow, and when there is a marriage Settlement, she may Chuse, which she has a mind, at the death of her husband. I have not heard Lately, in regard to a Propos'd agreement you formerly mention'd, amoungst Ourselves, of Equally dividing the £7,000. She Extracted as a Settlement from your Father, But cou'd not get him to give it from the family, & that she cou'd only obtain the Interest of it during life and to give it to any one, two, three &c. or divide it amoungst the whole, as she thought proper. I shall always be ready to join in everything for the proper good, not out of any selfish view as I hope I shall in no ways have occasion for any share that should come to me at that time of day, But to renounce in favour of someone of the family who will want it most. You need not mention to me that you have Consulted the Interest of your Brothers & Sisters, even to your own Prejudice. I am verie Sensible your Generosity will always Show itself upon every occasion. And indeed for my own part, I look upon the whole Branches of the family, to leg, as the logicians Say, when Speaking of Ideas, to be no more than a Collective Idea, the different Branches Joining together in one body, as a Brazen Wall, and when such unanimity hapen, that family will be great & happy, and the more so, that I imagine your Experience in the World has made it fully appear plain to you that by living Chiefly upon your Estate, you'll regain the Lost Dwindled Interest of the family and Increase it to a higher degree, besides the great Sums which you'll in Course Save of your Annual Income. It gave me great Joy to hear from Mr Stephen, of Edinburgh, that you had Sent for your Brother William, with an intention to make up to him what you really thought his Father once intended to have given him. If he is now with you, Please my best wishes to him, & tell him did I think he was in Scotland, I wou'd have wrote him by the Prince of Wales, Capt Swinton of Leith. You may depend upon having a punch[eo]n good Rum. I will Address it to John Stephen, who I Look upon to be a mighty worthy honest man, & I hope you'll always give him the Preference in every thing that he deals in that you at any time will want. I believe him to be a person you can depend upon. I will be oblig'd to give a Power of Attorney to one Charles Bowles Esqr, a Gentleman in Oxfordshire, for the sum unpaid me by my Fathers Will. When he writes to you concerning that matter, you'll Please answer him, and unless he give you a particular direction, You'll direct for him to the Care of Mr George Chandler Merch[an]t in London. You may well imagine it is only necessity that makes me draw it out of your hands, which I shall fully Explain to you. As I intend to give you a full History of my present situation in this Country and will have before you the Whole Circumstances of my family. You knew by former letters that I married the Heiress of Brigadear John Nairn in the beginning of 1749, then the Widow Lindsey. He died in Septemr 1748, then I thought proper to Acquent Madam. I Idely let her go out of my hands the first time, and I was now Determined to Att[r]act her Early, to prevent any others from Interfeering with me, and Accordinglie we came togather. Mr Lindsay before marriage had settled £600 this money p[er] Annum upon her during life, if he died first, and Bound a Pen or Farm in Parish St Andrew and about 80 Negroes, with a Farm in England, and left or Oblig'd his heirs to make up the difference, providing the Whole did not produce that Sum. But after his death, she chose the Settlement rather than the third Part of his estate and upon Enquiry found the Farm in England Mortgag'd for more that it was Worth and his Debts more than his Estate cou'd pay. Therefore I was oblig'd to take the Farm in St Andrews and what of the Negroes were alive, to the Number of 72, and make the most of them. I now find all do not Amount to the Annual Annuity. Therefor I am oblig'd to file a Bill in Chancery against the heirs for Redress, and as there is yet the Land of an Estate with a few Negroes, I am in hope to get my demand some time or other Satisfied, tho I own Law Charges is Verie Extravagant in this Country. Now this is my present Situation in regard to my wifes Annuity.

I shall next tell you our Circumstances in regard to the fortune left her by Mr Nairn.

When she married Mr Lindsey, she had a Plantation or Sugar Work free from all debt, besides some securitys of money lent upon bond. The whole Value I Reckon about £10,000, and might be greatly Improved. But Mr Lindsey bought land Adjoining to the Estate, which was formerly settled, and as he found he was like to have no Children, took off the Negroes from her Estate to Improove his own, which in Course threw hers intirely back, But died before he brought his own to any light, the Consequence of which hurted both. You must Observe that the Planter is not like the Gentlemen at home, who Farm out their Estates in Parcells to Severalls you call tennants, But keep the whole in their own hands, and if Neglicted one Year cannot be recovered to the former or greater Produce under three Years, which was great disapointment to me. However I Pushed it as much as I cou'd and do not dispair of Success. But what gave me more trouble than any thing else was a Security Mr Nairn Entered into for one Evan Cameron, a Brother of Locheills, who rented a large Farm in this Country at £[5]00 Sterling p[er] Annum in 1739 for 21 Year's, which Expires in 1760, but in 1742 sold off a large Quantity of Cattle at a Pritty high Price and lent that money upon a first Mortgage, or what you call in Scotland an Heritable Security, Prior to every other debt upon that Estate, the Interest of which, with another Sum, paid his Security for the rent of that Pen, Now the Property of Charles Bowles Esquire. But as Mr Nairn died in 1745, his Executors never once gave themselves the trouble to Collect this Interest money, nor pay Mr Bowle's Attorneys any part of the rent. And as the Interest money is now about £3000, the poor man had it not to pay, as it Comes upon him by Such a large sum, Principal & Interest is now about £9000. The Principal he is not indeed oblig'd to pay till 1760, the time the Mortgage Expires. Therefor I am oblig'd to advance Between 3 & £4000 to Mr Bowles for rent, Out of the Savings of the Estate, with what I have otherwise of my own. And I must wait till the Expiration of the Mortgage and then take Possession of the whole, which I intend as a fund for my Younger Children, and is the reason why I must send Mr Bowles a Power of Attorney to receive from you the remainder of what my Father left me, otherwise I wou'd have let have in your hands or settled it upon one of Davids Children. Unless the Pinch had hapened, I never intended to have touched a farthing of anything that was coming to me from that Quarter. I shall, in my Power to Mr Bowles, give him full Authority to Grant in my name a full and Ample discharge to you, which will Enable you to get up your Security from my Mother. It wou'd be a Singular Service done to me if you'd Advance or lend £1300 or £500 to Clear off Mr Bowles, and as I mentioned before, I wou'd be able to let the Mortgage lay by till it Expires, and then have the Whole Estate to myself, which I intend as a Provision for my younger children, and the Produce of my

Wife's Estate go to Reimburse you. Please Observe she has made it Over to me, which still makes you more safe. If you think it prudent to advance me above Sum, Please let me know soon, as it wou'd be of greater service to me than four times the Value a few Years hence.

I have got two fine Boys, One above two Years old, and the second about six months, and I believe Mrs Falconer near four Months yon with a third. Last Septemr we had a Hurry Cane, which did me Considerable damage. By throwing down a loose Hill in the River Course, the Water, not having free Vent or Passage, Damm'd up, came Back upon my Works & Washed away Some Sugar I then had ready to go to Markett and toss'd a few Negroes & two Mules by the fall of the Hill. I have now put things in such a manner, as the like cannot hapen to me again. I am verie glad, my Sisters do not stay with their Mother. If they are to pay Board, let it be to one who will use them well. I am in great hopes to be able to go from here by the time my Eldest son is 5 or 6 Years old and Never be oblig'd to return. But I am determined not to stirr from this till I can receive Yearly £1000 or £1500, clear of all Charges. I shall now end, with my sincere good wishes, and hope to hear from you soon and often, I am,

My Lord
Your Lord[ship]s Most Aff[ectiona]t Brother
John Falconer

SOURCE: Delvine Papers, MS 1265, f. 234ff., National Library of Scotland.
NOTES: John Falconer had come to Jamaica in 1746.

John Falconer (C1) to Alexander, 5th Lord Falconer of Halkerton (A11)

Jamaica 1 Novemr 1752

My Lord
I wrote your Lord[shi]p lately a varie long letter, & a copy of it also, but the Person I sent the letters to put ye Original & Copy on Board same Vessel in a mistake, so that you'll Probably receive both at same time.

By a letter I received from Bro. David, he Acquents me that our Mother has refused to Deliver up to Bro. William, his Bond of Provision and that he was obligd to Employ Mr Lockhart, to force her to it; And as I am afraid she will do the same to me, and if it is so— I must beg you'll be so good, to write Charles Bowles Esqr to the Care of Mr George Chandler Mercht in London; the Case, as it really is. And as he has a verie Ample Power from me, a receive what is due to me, by my Fathers Will. What that he will oblige her to it, by Virtue of that Power of Attorney sent him. And if it shoud so hapen, a little charges be necessary, to be laid out. I further Beg you'll Acquent him, you are ready to advance it, as I woud Chuse he received the Net Sum, and upon your leting one know what it is, I will reimburse you. You may also give him a hint, that Alex Lockhart is a proper Person to be Employ'd, providing she has not already Secured him. As I was so full in my last letter to you, I shall say no more, but after wishing you all happiness & satisfaction, Beg the favour You'll write me soon in folio, and no forget the contents of this letter, being with Mrs Falconer

My Lord
Your Lordps Most Affct Brother
John Falconer

SOURCE: Delvine Papers, MS 1265, f. 238, National Library of Scotland.

Alexander, 5th Lord Falconer of Halkerton (A11), to John Mackenzie of Delvine

Caen Ja^{ry} 16th 1754

D^r S^{ir}

I was favoured with yours a few days and am so sensible of the many obligations I owe on all occasions That I should think my self quite happy if I could have an opportunity of acknowledgeing them as I ought and as they deserve. I have wrote James Farquhar about an affair of the Marques of St Germain's. I need not trouble you with a repetition as I have wrote him fully of it he will communicate mine to you. Pray be so good as to assist him in it. I have the moment yours about John Ramsay. I am sorry for himself and family I dont think it is great loss to us if you think Mr Baillie a proper person I have no objection. I have been always told he was a very proper person and very honest and capable and was discharged because he would act as an honest man and would not do dirty work but I know your sincerity too well to pretend to give directions. I leave it altogether to yourself to act as you please. I shall always be pleased. James Farquhar can notefie you more about Baillie then I can do. I have been obliged to a lidle more expense at my comeing to this country by buyin of winter cloaths and a great many people who claim relation by a branch of my family being settled here so that I shall oblidged to draw for a hundred pounds in about 12 or fifteen days but I will be sure not to exceed my bounds you and I aggreed on. Pray make my compliments to Mr Falconar and tell him I would have wrote him but the going off of the Post does not give me time. My compliments to M^{rs.} McKenzie & all the good family and am with the greatest sincerity wishing you all a great many happy new year's Sir

Sir your most Oblidged & Obede^{nt} Se^{vt}
Haulkertoun

I suspect Briclot knows off our precend proceeds from the mortall antipathy her La[dyshi]p bears to him and John Ramsay of late acting throughly by her direction

SOURCE: Delvine Papers, MS 1264, f. 68, National Library of Scotland.

David Falconer (A13) to Alexander, 5th Lord Falconer of Halkerton (A11)

London Sepr 4th 1756

My Lord

I am honoured with your Lordship's of 10th Augt sent me by M^r McKenzie which I must say surprised me not a Little to find that Fellow James Farquhar will not give but his Old Tricks of Endeavouring to throw Dissentions amongst us. I hope you know him too well to have any Regard to what he says, as his design is to blacken my Character to Cover over the Ingratitude of his family who live their all to their getting Acquainted in Ours. Unhappy hour it was to me in Particular his first Introduction and it is horrible to think he should still continue to Persecute me. I Believe When You was in Town you Coud see that no body could keep closer to their Busyness then I do which can be Witnessed by a great many of Your Acquaintance in this Place.

I have heard nothing further from Brother John So do not Believe he Will send his son home this Year; Brother George is not returned from his Cruise but is expected in 14 days. No news of his Preferment nor do I expect it till Admiral Byngs tryall is Over,1 which I suppose will not be till some Months hence and hope to have the Pleasure of seeing You in Town before that time. We Are in Dayly expectations of hearing of an Other Battle in the Mediteranean betwixt Sir Edward Haukes Fleet & Glassioneer² as the Last Accords from thence are Positive that Glassioneer was tailled from London to give Sir Edward Battle and it is Generally believed it will be a Verry Bloody Affair if they Meet. We have no other news in town as that & Mʳ Byngs Affair is the Whole Conversation of this Metropolis.

My Wife joins with me in our most hearty compliments to you sister Molly & Mʳ Lunen and am most Respectfully

My Lord
Your Lordship's Most Affectionate Brother
& Most Obedient Humble servant
David Falconer

SOURCE: Kintore Papers, Bundle 260, Aberdeen University Library.

NOTES: ¹Admiral Byng was shot for cowardice on 14 March 1757, thought to be the scapegoat for the French seizure of Minorca on 26 June 1756. ²*La Gallisoniere*, a French ship in battle at Minorca.

May Falconer to Alexander, 5th Lord Falconer of Halkerton (A11)

Dear Brother

You will no doubt be surprays'd I dede not Congrattalet You on Youre Mariag bi assaired I dow favor my hart with You both at happiness it was oeing to Mʳˢ McKenzie who told me You was to be doun to Scotland so soun that a Letter had no chance to reach Your hands and as I was advancing with him at sam time about my goeing to Englishmaldie was intayerly derecteted by him being satesfayed he intends well for us at [blank] inconcequence of a Letter I hade from You of deat the 30ᵗʰ of May I cam hear end of Jun in Your cheas offer which tiem I receved two letters from You beding me Caradg to go North with my Sister and You to finich my affear at Your hous but the Person hes forsaken me bieng in daly expectaton of seeng You and now the hiearing it is want of health Occasions the delay is realy a great blo to me

I now only beg of You to geve Your Concent to my goeng to London this Winter to stay with David it is not my incleneng to be at London on any particular pleas but to get me owt of the way of al my aquentences in Scotland for I am not Able to biear the Clatter that goes nor dow I know what effeck my bieng at Edinburgh would have on me so I hop You will concedere my cese and dereck me when I shall com up and what Compane You thenk I may get for I most be alon as it is empasable for me to biear Mallys incolts and if I was out of the way I could easely queat my mind as have Notheng to reproch my self but my Spirit cannot biear to hear wheare I and thengs are so well knoan I have opend my mind to non therfor I intreat You by at the tays that are Sakread to sho thes to non but burn it on reding on the recepe of which I beg You well wret me and mention particularly Your oun health I shall remain at Englishmaldie tell I have Your return which hop will be sown

I ever am Dear Bothere
Your most Affect Sister and
Obedent humbell Servant
May Falconer

Englishmaldie
Sepr 26 [1757]

I trouble You with the inclosed to my Lady

SOURCE: Delvine Papers, MS 1265, ff. 258-259, National Library of Scotland.
NOTES: "Mally" was her sister Mary. May was born Marjorie.

William Falconer (A12) to Alexander, 5th Lord Falconer of Halkerton (A11)

D[ea]^r Brother
I was favoured with yours last post. You know very well D[ea]^r Brother that I never refused nor shall never, to Contribute to your Case & pleasure, please be so kind to send me in form what I ought to sign. Last year I was oblidged to ask you, but you Excused your self as not in a situation at that time. D[ea]^r Brother please know that I'm almost three years behind hand of what I must have from Boileduc. I Expect something at the same time from your hands. You shall never be liable for Principal or interest. A Sign that I'm turning old, My Second Daughter is to be Married to a Considerable Man, all which Entitules me to extraordinary Expences. Therefore, I make no doubt of your speedy Compliance. D[ea]^r Brother if I could find any other method to ridd my self I would be very sorry to ask you. I Engage my self to repay fifty pounds yearly with the Interest of what summ I receive from you or by your Credit, as soon as we are quitt of the French out Cleveland. I wrote you formerly that My Deputy to my Misfortune has the greatest part of his Patrimony in Cleveland. Expecting your speedy Answer am

Dear Brother
Your most Affectionate Brother
& very Humble Servant
Willm Falconer

Gron[ingen] 26th Septr 1761

SOURCE: Delvine Papers, MS 1265, f. 158, National Library of Scotland.

William, 6th Lord Falconer of Halkerton (A12), to John Mackenzie of Delvine

Sir
My last to you has certainly miscarried else I had received an answer before now. Sir I must now open my mind frankly. I sent my son to Leyden with a Governor & every thing in Proportion, but he plaid the devil with me, after Contracting very Considerable debts he went of privately for London, but I have got him at length here & flatter my self that he heartily repents his folly. The Payment of these debts has reduced me to great Straits. Now Sir my demand is, if you would procure me a thousand pounds & give it in

to Mr Mason for James Craufuird's Acc[oun]t^t You was pleased to tell me that it was possible to break the Entail with my sons Consent. Pray be so good to Consult & write me fully your opinion. Dr Sir the thoughts of Leaving my younger Children beggars lies very heavy upon me. I can never go of the Stage with a quiet mind before that is settled. I was some days with Lord Marshal in his way to Berlin he told me of the Jewel you mentioned in your last. Mr Craufurd promised me last Post to send you two of the best smoaked salmons with the first Vessel bound for you of your Havens. Stair Baillie wrote me some posts ago of a fellow breaking down the walls of the Clerk's. He ought to be made sensible of the Affront he hes done me & Stair Baillie. He who does anything against the said Stair Baillie affronts me at the same time (this to your self). I don't want that the poor fellow should be pushed to the utmost. As having had a certain regard for the family from my youth, One who has passed a great part of his life in the Military way of doing ought at least to know what is due to an inferiour as well as to a Superiour. Begging My Compliments to your dear Spouse & farther relations, am

Sir
Your most Hum^ble Servt
Haulkertoun

Gron[ingen] 13 Novr 1764

SOURCE: Delvine Papers, MS 1265, f. 168, National Library of Scotland.

Thomas Falconer to Charles Gray

Chester. May 17, 1766

Dear Sir:

In answer to y^r very obliging Letter I can assure you I was not disappointed at not receiving the Books. I judged they were scarce, & that Vaillant of consequence could not easily procure them. Be under no uneasiness I beg on that account; I have Books enow, had I health to examine them, on most of the usefull topics. My studies are interupted with my disorder; & having few companions, & none adapted to my bent, I cannot improve by conversation. The hours devoted to exercise are irksome, because, being alone, I long to get them over. I have been too long disused to think, to carry on a chain of reflections on any subject. Nat[ura]^l History & particularly Botany are the properest amusements for so disspirited a Genius, but my exercise being on Horseback, I am debarred from either. If I am able, I shall make some excursion at the beginning of this summer, but I am as unsettled in my schemes as the present Ministry.

What think you will become of this Administration, if the D[uke]. of Grafton resigns? Will it not unhinge their system? They are, in short, disqualified for doing any good, & it is of little consequence whether they are in or out. L[or]^d Egmont, who is mentioned for his Successor, is a man of business, & such a one must be wanted under so puerile a Ministry. Pitt behaved nobly in the Militia business, but his speech on the American affairs was paradoxical, declamatory, & impertinent. I own it abounded it fine sounding periods & was not unlike the celebrated letter of Brutus to Cicero, which, however, is thought by the best judges a forgery. You see in both a same elevation of sentiment, the same deficiency of argument, lively turns, bold expressions, immoderate vanity; & the strongest dislike to contradiction while they both declare that a free debate is their principal wish. The parallel might be carried on farther, but you have the letter & I will desist.

If Pitt is to be compared with any Man, it is with Pericles, tho' the latter had more softness of disposition. Each, however, had the glory of opposing singly the greatest Geniuses united, of thwarting all their schemes, & of raising the Glory of their several Countries to an uncommon pitch. I wish I could say the parallel would not hold farther, but as Pericles broke the balance of the Constitution & made it impossible for any other person to manage it, so Pitt I fear, by inflaming the passions of the populace, by ridiculing a Minister who deserved to be answered with decency, & by supporting plausible paradoxes with an eloquence equal to that of Athens at any period, will render every future Minister timid & irresolute.

The times call for a strict economy, for great & comprehensive schemes of commerce, for enlarged ideas of the Constitution on the basis of a well regulated freedom, & the most resolute firmness in the Execution of such Measures. I see no prospect of such steps being taken, & I can ascribe the present timidity to no other cause but Pitt's conduct. It was he who repealed the Stamp Act, & laid a foundation for a revolt in our Colonies. Possibly in future times should his life be read, this alone will tinge his character with the deepest shade, when our own Country sinks for want of trade, & a new Empire in America controlls all Europe. These consequences might be prevented, but Pitt's measures are not concerted for such purposes whatever he may affirm of our present power.

I have no time to write more: accept my hearty thanks for the agreeable entertainment y^r Letters afford me, & believe me to be, dear Sir, with the truest regard, Y^r most ob[lige]^d & most obed[ien]^t humble

Thos Falconer

My Mo[the]^r has a bad Cold. I am but indifferent. Both join in Comp[limen]^ts to dear M^rs. Gray.

If you have any interest in Oxford, my application may not yet be too late to desire you to apply it in favour of a worthy young Friend of mine, who is a candidate for the Law Scholarship. His name is George Bower of Queen's College. If any of y^r Fr[ien]^ds at Baliol are not engaged, or if Mr Kilners could be of any use, the interest of both would not be misplaced on my young acquaintance.

I do not doubt but the East Indies might be as productive of real advantage as you mention, but I see no probability of such success as long as underwriters dispose of Kingdoms. I wish to have the War well wrote, or at least to have Orme's spirited & elegant History finished by as able a Pen.

SOURCE: Round Papers, D/DRg 4/13, Essex Record Office.

NOTES: This and the two other letters of Thomas Falconer included here will be published, with further annotations, in Paul Weller's *History of the Falconer Family in England.*

Capt. George Falconer (A14) to John Mackenzie of Delvine

Sir

I see by a Letter of yours to Mrs Falconer I am accus'd by Mr Bailly of not being his friend, I niver receiv'd any Injury from that quarter, in Course can have no personal prejudice, my reason of troubling you with this is intirly out of respect to you that you may not be mislead by his representations not as of Vindication of myself to him, but sure its hard for Mr Falconer to see his Fathers Interist and Familys wasted by Neglects Abuses &c and to put himself on a footting to answer Insidious questions wch he apears to aim at, what he or any Conections of the Family has said I dare say go's upon facts not whispers, in that case, he is certain of your Assistance to gett his Father clear of him. I dare say

Mrs Falconer has too much Spirit and understanding to Enter into a Detail of Jargon with a servant. I will not take your time up by troubling you in saying more as I hope to have the pleasure of seeing you soon at Edinburgh. M^r & Mrs Falconer Joins in Comp^l[imen]^ts to you and Mrs Mackinzie; belive me to be

Sir
Your Most Obedient
and Very Humb^le Servt
George Falconer

Englishmaldie
October the 27th 1766

SOURCE: Delvine Papers, MS 1265, f. 247, National Library of Scotland.

Anthony Adrian Falconer (A15) to John Mackenzie of Delvine

Englismaldie 20th [December] 1767

Dear Sir

I have been favour'd with two of Your letters. You would accuse me perhaps of Laziness in not answering them sooner, indeed. I put it off till Mrs McKenzies things for my wife would arive, but have been put up in Montrose, for a good while, as neither our nearer tenants nor my own carts could go in, on account of the now raging distemper among the horses, & it comes high to hire a cart in Montrose being 6 sh: each cartload to Northwaterbridge. My wife is greatly pleased with Mr McKenzies execution, & returns her thanks to her by a letter. I have got the 60 pds & paid off my bills—which you'll please to do those in Ed[inburgh] when it suits Your conveniency. The 13 lb 15 sh & 3 d depurst by my self, you know is gone for repairs laid out & paid by me, & thus cash out my hand, which some to me or other of much qch from You, as one can't be without some ready money, in regard to the horses, if Lord Haulkertoun does not chuse to pay them to me, I think we won't plague him about them, if he is but reasonable otherwise, I am sure no body has ever blamed me for being greedy. I am fully convinc'd of your good intention to make us happy & easy in this country, & therfore I leave my affars in regard to Lord Haulkertoun entirely to you, as you have great weight with him & can write in a few lines more than I can do in sheets, am surprised he does not mention about the hundred £ he is to draw on my Wifes account again next March, you see I shall be obliged to get it over in exchange, which is loss to me, & would be an advantage for him to receive a thousand gilders in the same town where he stays, & I could get 50 easily here, besides he was the first who offered it when last here to my Wife, with making it a 100 Ster[ling], instead of a 100 Guilders. He neither mentions the 60 £ he drew this spring for my wife, and never has repaid it, which is shamefull, to keep back any of her money, having done so little for her before. But you'll please to refresh his Lordship's memory upon that subject, and if he will draw it in time coming as he has offered, as I must know it again the Spring. In regard you write me about the Doctor & his quarry, I own to you I never as yet could make any connection upon what footing he proposed that scene. I see no reason why Lord Haulkertoun should not have some benefit of it than the Doctor. I really do think if that quarry could be wrought, suppose without any gain, & not being a great throw out of money it would be a vast advetage to that part of the Country, as there is a great deal of very fine improovable ground, but I shall with all my heart tell you my opinion when I have read the Doctors proposals & communicate to you. I own at the same time that it would be idle that Lord Haulkertoun should be at an equall expence & draw no benefit of it, equal with the Doctor, if it is meant in that way. I have inclosed the shoe makers bill, which the man sent me the other day, which You'll cause to be paid at convenient time. My Wife begs her Comp[limen]ts to you & I always continue with regard

Dear Sir

You most
Humble serv[t]
A Falconer.

NB In your list I find You have paid John Farquhar at Leith 46-8-8, the account he sent me out was only 41-12-8, so he has been in a mistake.

SOURCE: Delvine Papers, MS 1267, f. 45ff., National Library of Scotland.

Anthony Adrian Falconer (A15) to John Mackenzie of Delvine

Dear Sir

I have done myself the pleasure of writing you twice, and as I have not heard from You it gives me uneasiness that You may be not well. I had a letter the other day from Mr Mill of Bonniton where in he writes me the operations in regard to the purchase of the lands of Over Pert. I see the difference is great in regard to Mr Lott's demand. I hope to hear Your opinion about it, that I may make a certain plan. Lord Haulkertoun it seems proposes to send both his sons to Scotland for their education as well as to learn the language, & desir'd me to begg the favour to hear Your opinion what Scool You would think most proper for them. They can read & write French & understand the latin tongue. The one is fourteen the other twelve Years of Age. I hope You have receiv'd Your backwhite as I understand she is come to Montrose, when I dont doubt but Mr Gibb has sent Your share as I directed him. I have hear'd of Mr Lunan's death. I would beg the favour You would not dispose of his house before I return, as I would propose to You to have these houses accommodat'd for ploughman's habitations I have so much need off. Mrs Falconer joins me in best respects to Mrs MacKenzie and You & beg You wont spare us in case You have commissions for us both and I most sinceerly am

D[ea]r Sir
Your most Obed[ien]t Ser[van]t
& Aff[ectionate]: friend
Anthy Falconer.

Groningen 15[th] Nov: 1769

SOURCE: Delvine Papers, MS 1267, f. 80, National Library of Scotland.

Anthony Adrian Falconer (A15) to George Keith, 10th Earl Marischal

My Lord
The Relation wherein I have the honour to stand with your Lordship, The Justice I owe my Father Lord Haulkerton my growing Family and to myself & our Common Connection with the family and Estate of Kintore must plead my Apology for this Trouble. My Father Continuing still in Holland with the Bulk of his Family, Chose on my Marriage, That my

wife and I should Live in Scotland for this among other Reasons That if our Children had been born abroad The Honours and Estate of Kintore might have forfeited to the Crown on Your Demise by their being Aliens. I oby'd my Father and settl'd here and found the family estate in very indifferent Order, far from that Extent in which I had been taught to expect it and my Father loaded with Some debts his Elder Brother the last Lord Haulkerton had Contracted. I do not complain of any of those Circumstances Expecially as I was strongly imprest to believe Your Lo[rdshi]p would do me no hardship in the natural prospect of our Family's Succeeding after you to the entailed Estate as well as the Titles of Kintore.

The Late Earl my Great Uncle made some small purchases in Addition to that Estate for Rendering it more Commodious. He had a particular Regard for you and fearing your Distress before you might be Restored to your own Estate He settled all he had in Trustees for your better Support But still having in his Eye the preservation of his own Family by keeping the Estate convenient for the heirs in his honour, Recommended Specially in Writing to the Trustees & to you That his small purchases should be Offered & Sold to the Lord Haulkerton for £1500.

Your Lo[rdshi]p on your Return to Scotland, by the Repurchase of your own Estate at an easy Rate Came to have a Liberal Fortune, And besides this by the Death of my two Great Uncles the Successive Earls of Kintore came properly to have the possession also of the estate of Kintore. Pardon me to observe what has happened Since these events. You Chose to Sell your Buchan Estate at Such a price as pleas'd yourself to one worthy Gentleman and to give away Dunottar to another at much less than I or any other Could safely give for it. Your house in Aberdeen was Sold to the Town for Less than was offer'd and the Estate of Kintore laid under Leases which prevents its Improvement for many years while every other in the Neighbourhood rise in their Value.

None of these Transactions Severe as they are on the Haulkerton Family, Since it was your Choice, we presum'd to Complain of But forgive me to Observe that to propose to my father (as has been done) that he must either pay £2000 for Redemption of these small parcels which Lord Kintore ordered to be Offered and given him at £1500 is a hardship and Threatning that they will otherwise be sold to Strangers with whom I understand M[r] Keith either is negotiating or has your directions to do it is still more severe. I humbly Submit this to your own Recollection and honour.

My Father's distance makes him less acquainted as well as Your Lordship with his Affairs in this Country, Spare Money for purchases of any kind he has none Which you may easily believe from the Numerous Family he has to educate and provide. Yet if your Lordship will be so good as make over these Subjects to me at the £1500 agreeable to Lord Kintore's directions, I have Some Friends in this Country who from Relation or Sympathy will find that Sum in my behalf and Trust to my Integrity, and the Subject itself that so soon as in my power I will honestly Replace it and thus the heirs of the honours and entailed Estate of Kintore may be in Less hazard of being harrass'd in Marches or Otherwise by emulous Neighbours.

I know you have Several Necessitous Relations the Grand Children of your Sister. With these or any acts of your Generosity or Benevolence you intend them I mean not to interfere. Strangers have already got easy Bargains of Inverugy Dunottar & the houses at Aberdeen. Had these Subjects gone to the best Avail, It would have been more in your power to gratify Blood Relations at your pleasure. But you Certainly have not got matters laid properly before You when Mr Keith to whom you gave Dunottar at a Trifle more than you bought it was desired to ask £2000 from my Father for these small parcells added by the late Earl of Kintore to the entailed Estate.

I Appeal to M[r] Mackenzie formerly your own Agent for the Truth of all I have said. He best knows all your private Transactions here from the purchase of your own Estate till you Sold it & has no Interest in the Matter to mislead Either you or me. Your Lordship who have benefited Strangers so much cannot surely intend to distress me or my growing family who have the honour of so near a Connection both with you and the late Earl of Kintore who preferred you very Justly to us without supposing that either was to be Injured by it. I beg your Lordships Answer for tho my Title to complain may be distant I an others Seem to Doubt if You Yet had a fair Representation of the Case laid before You when £2000 is demanded of my Father in place of £1500 prescribed by Lord Kintore the Benefactor to us both for the Redemption of these small Subjects which he Acquired for the Advantage of his heirs of Entail in their order. I have the honour to be

My Lord

Your most Obedient Servant
& Affectionate Cousine

SOURCE: Delvine Papers, MS 1267, f. 97, National Library of Scotland.
NOTES: This was written in December 1770.

Anthony Adrian Falconer (A15) to John Mackenzie of Delvine

Dear Sir

I am sorry I must trouble you again upon the foolish behaviour of My Brother Willm, as You will find in the enclosed of Prof: Browns, & as it is in vain to keep him there any longer, I have given orders to Joseph Gibb, according to Your former advice, to go to St Andrews & bring him to Inglismaldie, where we must keep him till You hear from Lord Haulkertoun how we are to dispose of him. To keep him with me any time, You will be sensible, is doing him no service, & can not be agreable to Us. I Suspect very much he has fallen in with bad advisers, which I even perceive out of his letter to You, which does not seem to me his diction. It gives both Mrs Falconer & me great uneasiness, as we realy had better expectations from him. In case it should be some time before You hear from L. Haulkertoun, what do You think, we should put him in the mean time with one Mr Borck, a minister at Tannadrie in the west of Angus, who has been in the way for some Years past to keep Young gentlemen to teach them reading writing & mathematicks. At least it would be better than to keep him idle all together. However I shall act as You think proper. The shorter he is here the better, in case his Father should not agree, which by the by I wish he may, to get him a Commission in the Army, I think the only way for Us is to send him over to Holland. What You mention about David Middletons affair in regard to the levy money by a little enquiry I find it may be due, & as it is no great affair at any rate, if You approve of it, I think he should be payed it. With Mrs Falconers best Compts to Mrs Mackenzie

I am
Dear Sir
You most Obedient Servt
Ant^y Falconer

Inglishmaldie Jany 5th 1775

SOURCE: Delvine Papers, MS 1267, f. 142, National Library of Scotland.

Alexander Falconer (B1) to John Mackenzie of Delvine

Perth Jan: 16ᵗʰ [1775]

Dear Sir

I acknowledged myself bound under many obligations, for the past favours, with which you have honoured me, I am affraid, that it will be never in my power to make you a suitable return. The tea pot & the plate came safely to hand, which, when I delivered it to Mʳˢ Hamilton, she almost fainted for joy, the recompense, I hope shall be, that Mʳ Hamilton shall pay closer attention to me as he has done hither to. I am vexed to hear that Mʳ Gibb is at present at St Andrews with a intention to take Willie from thence in a few days. I would wish him only to consider what a disgrace he has inflicted upon himself & a mortification to all his connexions. My best respect at Mʳˢ Mackenzie.

Dʳ Sir

I am your humble
Servant. A: Falconer

SOURCE: Delvine Papers, MS 1268, f. 4, National Library of Scotland.

John Mackenzie of Delvine to Robert Hamilton

I hope you will not think it Officious in me, to ask how Mʳ· [William] Falconer Lord Haulkertouns Son Improvd, under your Eye.

He Appears to me a discreet tractable Young man And tho not remarkably Smart, So as to Catch on every the first kind, Yet like other Dutchmen, he repairs that by labour And Assiduity by Cool & kind instruction which is your province.

I Observe by his Letters his hand writing Very much amended since he came under your Care But how far he has made equall progress in figures Latin or French, Or even in our own Language, You can best inform me For he was pretty much at a loss for the last when I Advised putting him under your Eye. His father wrote me to send him Over last winter. I withstood it Ashamed that one so Illiterate who was brought here in quest of Education should return so little Improved. I still incline to Suspend his journey for some time provided you, who can best judge, think that he can profite by a longer stay for 6 or 8 moneths. I am Miserably disappointed in a Younger Brother of his who is as Sharp as a Needle, But has misbehaved And so lands in the Common Shore of the Army. I think this lad may do well in private or Civil life in Holland where he is Conected with the greatest men in that Country.

Give me your Opinion which will have Considerable Influence on mine And Oblige Sir &c.

Edin[burgh] 9ᵗʰ March 1775.

I will Spare no Cost on the Young Mans
Education if he is thought Capable of it;

To Mʳ Hamilton Master
of the Academy in Perth

SOURCE: Delvine Papers, MS 1268, f. 11, National Library of Scotland.

NOTES: Robert Hamilton was then Master of the Academy at Perth. John Mackenzie of Delvine was Lord Falconer's attorney in Scotland.

Alexander Falconer (B1) to John Mackenzie of Delvine

Perth April 30th 1775

Dear Sir

Being sensible of the many advantages, that I reap from your kind letters, I think I should be very ungrateful, were I to leave of writing to one, who is to me, both as a father, and a friend, I am always happy, when I hear from you, & shall ever esteem it a great honour, to have the liberty of writing you, that I may improve therby. I am still going on in the prosecution of the studies I mentioned last. I am very attentive to the English. I shall not say any thing of the success myself, as I hope you have seen Dr. Hamilton, or may perhaps see him, for he is just now in Edinburgh. I hope & shall be very happy to see you in Perth, in your way to Inglismaldie. My best respects to Mrs Mackenzie.

I am Dear Sir
your most humble servant
Alexander Falconer

SOURCE: Delvine Papers, MS 1268, f. 9, National Library of Scotland.

Thomas Falconer to Charles Gray

My d[ea]^r S[i]^r

So long a time has elapsed since I had the pleasure of hearing from you that I am determined to begin the correspondence anew. Your engagements in Parliam[en]^t having been of more consequence than mine, so I can readily excuse a silence which has been however a little irksome to me. On one account indeed I have particularly wished it. The late accounts of America have been so partially given that one cannot depend much on either side. The true state of the case is seldom to be found in a Newspaper, tho of late they have condescended to admit papers against the rebellious Bostonians. You have I dare say read Tuckers pamphlets on the subject of our Colonies. This scheme of abandoning them to themselves is as I am told the thing they are most afraid of, as conscious of a want of Strength as yet to support themselves. They seem divided in several of the Colonies but how far these divisions will operate to do us service, I want information to ascertain. You have kept in L[or]^d North much longer than I expected. His abilities must be very great to manage so large a body as the corrupt part of the house of Commons, & yet merit the regard & assistance of you independant Members. Y^r Bill for issuing Writs, & Mr Grenvilles have done great service in these times, but I should be glad to know what was the purport of young Mr Grenvilles late motion. It seemed to be an extension of y^r Act to all cases. You forbare extending it for fear of the ministers taking advantage of it during the recess of Parl[iamen]^t by inducing members to vacate their seats. M^r Gr[enville]^s motion in this case would seem to favour the Ministry, yet L[or]^d North opposed it; at least it was not carried. I am concerned to see so little of our national debt is paid. It is now 13 y^{rs} since the peace; & the difference is hardly perceptible. Such is the blessed consequence of L[or]^d Chathams boasted ignorance of our finances. But to wave our national Concerns at present wch I can neither mend by complaining nor offer any thing better than what is done; being equally ignorant of facts & inadequate to the employment of a Statesman, let me now enquire after y^r own health. The town of Colchester had the best reasons to persist in its former choice, & y^r declining the first offer was a happy circumstance to make their selection of you more honourable than any preceding one.

I am now at Bath, just enjoying the pleasures of the place, but in a domestick style, much better for my Constitution. The D[uke] & D[utche]^{ss} of Cumberland are here. The D[utche]^{ss} of Grafton sate near her at a Ball, but took no notice of her. This I suppose is the etiquette of the Court, but it seems hard that a Peers daughter married to a Kings Brother, should be unnoticed by a Baronets daughter married to a Duke. They behave very well here, & I hope in time that his Majesty will be reconciled. To descend to a lower topic I lately came from Oxford where I had stayed 5 weeks, fully engaged most of the time in examining authors & collecting materials for a future publication. The B[isho]^p of Chester & Dr Bagot have now so completely hampered me with writing notes on Strabo, that I cannot for a long time to come release myself. However my confinement is made more easy, (contrary to other imprisonments) by not being limited in time. The Esinal & the Royal Library at Paris have been consulted, & I fancy those at Milan & Venice must be ransacked. I am too insignificant to move all this machine myself. D Anoille will engage for the maps, but we have not settled whether there are to be any plates of city medals. When you return to Colchester you would oblige me very much by looking over y^r catalogue of Colony Coins, & Greek Imperials (Which were all struck by foreign cities) to inform me whether you have any not yet published or very rare.

My Bro[the]^r & Mrs Falconer join in very best wishes to you & Mrs Gray to w[hi]^{ch} I beg

I may join those of d[ea]^r S^{ir}
Y[ou]^r most truly ob[lige]^d and aff[ectiona]^{te} Kinsman
Thos Falconer
May 6 1775
Bath

If you can favour me with a line I must desire you to address it to me at Dr Falconers Gay St Bath

Mrs Dupree enquires much after you & Mrs Gray, & so did a Mrs Barker, who has left this place. Have you read Burys answer to Lindsays apology. It is a very extraordinary performance for a disciple of that antitrinitarian Priestly. His notions in politicks are too republican, but I am glad to find one instance of Christianity, & republican sentiments combined. The Univ of Oxford disappointed me much by not conferring a diploma Degree on the Writer.

SOURCE: Round Papers, D/DRg 4/29, Essex Record Office.

Thomas Falconer to Charles Gray

Bath. June 3, 1775

Dear Sir:

I was much pleased with your kind letter, w[hi]^{ch} while it breathed a true English spirit shewed a firmness & composure under our present disturbances w[hi]^{ch} I heartily wish was more general. The late accounts from America have been more alarming than ever: If the Sword is drawn once, it is seldom sheathed without much mischief. I have seen no authentick account of the late action. It is bad enough to suppose there has been an action, before the additional troops could arrive. I hope the commanding Officer did not exceed his orders. Their intention seems to have been to attack General Gage before the rest could come up. Nothing else could justify our Forces in beginning first; supposing they did begin.

I am always so unlucky at conjectures, that I shall form no supposition what will happen hereafter. The patriotic party must I think divide on this point. The Rockingham faction cannot be so depraved as the Wilksites, who seem to rejoice in the idea of our losing half the British Empire. They will probably join with the Ministry in part, tho' they cannot repair the mischief they have done. The promotion of my old friend Beaumont Hotham has surprised many, but none more than himself, as he has assured me by a letter I rec[eive]ᵈ yesterday. Administration has thus lost one member of the opposition, & gained a friend in Morton. This is but little, but I wish it may be a prelude to a coalition. L[or]ᵈ North has much on his hands & his praise or blame will depend upon the success of our arms.

A state of war is very alarming, & a civil war still more so, & if the land tax must be raised you will have all the Country Gentlemen warm advocates for peace on any terms. I agree with you that Tucker's scheme savoured more of the Commercialist than the spirited Englishman, but neither did I think it undeserving a serious consideration. The grand question about right can never be settled; for the Americans have bandied it about so long that if they could have convinced us, or we them, it must have been effected long ago. The question then is merely political, & so complicated that I shall not pretend to decide upon it; it is now brought to a crisis. Force alone can determine it, for we cannot propose giving them up at this time.

I was in hopes some divisions had arisen amongst them, but we seem to have very few friends there. You will think me too low spirited & condemn me for anticipating evils before any authentick account is arrived. I read Burgoyne's speech with great pleasure, but should be afraid to send a desperate Gamester to play so difficult a Game. It is well he is not Commander in Chief. Men of broken fortunes generally lose every good Principle, & notwithstanding his abilities, he was never much respected as a man, tho' esteemed as an Officer.

B Trecothick is gone, just at the first blaze of the mischief he had excited by various means. He lived long enough to hate Sʳ W Meredith most heartily. Our fr[ien]ᵈ Jack Ford has made a large purchase which I hope will answer fully. He wanted employment, & tho' it lessens his income a little for the next four years, yet even now he will have more than he has ever yet spent. He is a very good oeconomist & must neccessarily have a large addition come to him.

My studies go on very slowly, or rather, indeed, are stopped at Bath w[hi]ᶜʰ is no place for improvement either in reading or conversation. Mʳ Mason of Cambridge has invited me to his house to look over Mʳ Gray's papers, but my health is too precarious to promise either that or a journey to Wexham. This hot Spring weather has not agreed well with my complaint, neither have I found good or harm from the water w[hi]ᶜʰ I have been over persuaded to take. I beg my very best wishes to good Mrs. Gray, & am with respects from my Bro[the]ʳ Y[ou]ʳ most truly ob[lige]ᵈ and affect[iona]ᵗᵉ Kinsman

Thoˢ Falconer

SOURCE: Round Papers, D/Drg 4/28, Essex Record Office. As "May" was overwritten "June 3," the sequence of letters 4/28 and 4/29 has to be reversed to be consecutive by date.

NOTES: He refers to the Battles of Lexington and Concord, Massachusetts,18 April 1775.

William Falconer to John Mackenzie of Delvine

Cork   20 Decbr 1775

Dear Sir,

I make no doubt, youll be a good deal surprised, at my troubling you so soon; but I hope you will excuse me when you have perused the few lines in which I mean to intimate the little affair that vexed me very much when I heard it.

Having the honour to dine with our Lieut: Col: Gabbet a few days ago, among many questions I asked; I asked him to whose company I had the honor to belong. He told me that I was in one of the additional ones, I said I apprehended he must be mistaken because I had paid for my commission & that by General Irvine's order the money had been lodged with Cox & Mair. He opined me I was a mistaken & that I never could pay a single sixpence for a commission in an additional Company; I don't know how General Irvin could desire you to lodge the money in his agents hands when I had nothing to pay.

I thought this of some consequence to myself, and therefore took the liberty to take up your attention for a few minutes, in hopes you will withdraw the money and either supply me with the 400 pounds from time to time or destroy the obligation I signed for what was never laid out on my account.

The 40£ I received from Sir Wm Montgomery being absolutely insufficient for the main things wanted for going abroad. Our Major is exceedingly obliging he won't permit me to purchase anything for myself in case I should be imposed on. I humbly beg you will be good enough to grant me a few Pounds more which you may do now, since my Commission hath not cost my old scrub of a mother one divit.

My most respectfull Compl[imen]ts to Mrs. Mackensie & the other ladies.

I have the honour to be with all respect, Sir

Your most obedient humble servant,
Willm Falconer

P.S. We will embark a boat 10 days hence and depart thereafter.

SOURCE: Delvine Papers, MS 1267, f. 221, National Library of Scotland.
NOTES: William Falconer was the youngest son of William, 6th Lord Falconer of Halkerton.

Ensign William Falconer to John Mackenzie of Delvine

From on Board the Union, Transport, Cove Harbour
Jan y 22d 1776

Dear Sir,

I had the pleasure to receive yours of the 22d Dec. & I am happy to find yours & my Brother's concurrence in advanceing me a few pounds more; had my absolute necessities not forced me to draw for Twenty pounds on Messrs John Lock & Hogg, before the receipt of yours I would have waited, untill you had desired me to draw on some one else, but I could not, for I waited to the last sixpence in my pocket.

My Brother is very well acquainted with Mr Kinloch who I believe corresponds with him & I therefore drew on him finding that I could not get a bill on anyone in Edinb[urgh], nobody in Corke having any transactions with that place. I hope you will be so good as answer the Bill whenever it appears.

We are at present in a very unsettled situation having been aboard for this fortnight past, and won't perhaps sail for as far as we know, these six weeks. No doubt you have heard of the great armament that is to be sent out. There are 120 sail of transports taken for 20 thousand Germans, & 8 regiments out of & in this Kingdom have got orders to get themselves in readiness, so that this country is left in a defenseless state, and will in all probability be altogether overrun with those rascally banditticall white boys,[1] who commit the most unheard of murders almost every day, there however are a great many of them taking within these few days past.

I hope you received my letter in which I referred to the information I received from General Gabbet informed you of my having got my Ensigncy for nothing which will enable one the better to purchase a Lieutenancy, which I hope won't be long hence.

Just while I was writing the last word of the foregoing line I received yours of the 6 of Jan & an answer to which I will return you the first time I can see B. General Gabbet. I would do it immediately, but am not permitted to go on shore, on any business whatsoever, but I am pretty certain he will persist in his former opinion of my not having purchased.

I am

Dear Sir,
Your most obedient
Humble servant

Willm Falconer

SOURCE: Delvine Papers, MS 1267, f. 223, National Library of Scotland.
NOTES: [1]"Whiteboys" was the name given to Irish peasant rebels who were active in the 1760s.

Ensign William Falconer to John Mackenzie of Delvine

Camp Statton Island
15th August 1776

Dear Sir

I am sorry that the first letter I do myself the honor to write you from this paradise, should be partly the bearer of bad news; the unlucky circumstance of not having received my Commission when I left Ireland has already been the occasion of my loosing two steps in the way of promotion, just now made by General Flower. Which is just as bad if not worse than loosing the 400£ which General Irvine demanded for a Commission we the King made me a present of. I have made all the enquiries about it, & nobody can be found from whom I could purchase, but it is clearly proved that I came in upon the Augmentations, & of course got my Ensigncy for nothing, wherefore I beg you will be so obliging as inform General Irvine of his mistake.

To write you the particulars of my life (a scene so totally new to me, would be abusing your patience[)]—Let it suffice then that we left Ireland the 12 of February & arrived at Cape Fear the 1st of May. At this place we remained 'till all the Fleet arriv'd, then we sailed for Charlestown, South Carolina where we landed and encamped upon the deserts of Arabia, lived entirely upon salt pork, bad rum & bad water, nothing to sleep upon but sand, which burn'd your feet as you walk'd upon it in the heat of the day—exposed all the horrors of that climate. The intention was that the ships of war were to have silenced a formidable Battery on Sullevans Island when that was done the Commodore was to make a signal for us to land on the back of the Island in the force of two 8 & two 6 Pounders loaded with Grape; which must undoubtedly blown us out of the water before we could have landed, however, we had not an opportunity of trying it for the ships after fighting for nine hours & a half were obliged to retreat with the loss of the finest frigate in the King's Navy & 290 killed and wounded, the Battery received little or no damage.

The Hessians are all arrived here, & we expect to attack every moment, we have now an army of between 20 & 3000 able to take the field.

I almost had forgot to mention to you that the Bill you order'd me to draw on Sir Wm Montgomery for 20£ was protested by him which in case that the Bill is return'd will proved very disagreeable.

As I have always heard my Brother say that he wish'd to purchase me up as far as possible now suppose I could get the purchase of a lieutenancy, nobody will take Bills nor do I know on whom to draw, therefore I immagine if I could get a Lietter of Credit for the Price of a Lieut[enan]cy — it would be the most ready way of getting what I have lost for want of my Commission.

My most respectfull Complts to Mrs. McKenzie. I am Sir

> Your most Obdt
> humble servt
> Willm Falconer

SOURCE: Delvine Papers, MS 1267, f. 224, National Library of Scotland.

NOTES: On 28 June 1776, the Colonial troops repelled the British attack at Sullivan's Island. Admiral Sir Peter Parker had earlier assembled a fleet in Ireland. The British had hoped to take advantage of the large Tory support in North Carolina, but the Loyalist Highlanders had been defeated at Moore's Creek Bridge, on 27 February 1776, threatening the success of the planned mission. The fleet withdrew to New York.

Anthony Adrian Falconer (A15) to John Mackenzie of Delvine

Dear Sir

You no doubt will be surprised at my long Silence but severall little incidents has prevented me from Acknowledging Your three different favours; the first anent William's Commission, is perfectly satisfactory to me as for as You have been concerned, and from what I have been able to observe from William during his abode with me I may Venture to say he will be as Gratefull for you good endeavours towards him, as I myself have been, & always hope to be. Concerning Mr Hamilton's Account, that you'll find in the list my Wife gave You in When here as part of outstanding Debts, & will be obliged to pay & charge to our Account, as Mrs Falconer is to latly my Manager, I hope You shall have no reason to complain of unneccessary Expences. I had a few Days ago a letter from My Mother full of obliging expressions, but not a Word about the Matrimoniall Scene, but recommending her & Concerns to our Attention & Sending her Grandson a pair of Excellent Globes as a present, telling me at the same time of Our Father being in the Same Debilitated State. She seems to hint that he begs the favour You would write him a few lines how You & Mrs Mackensie are doing directed to himself & seemed to rejoice much in Your from other, which favour I dare say You'll comply with, when at leasure. Her Ladyship seems to give a distant hint that when a little Cash with Convenience can be spared she would not be Averse to a remittance of it. Sandy writes me by the same part, not a syllable about his project. So Suspect this blown one for the present, which we don't regrett. Am glad Mr Cumin gives so good an Account of the Opinion of our Councill in Lawson's case who is an impudent refractory Tenant, & has much need of some restriction, & I shall never regrett we have tryed him, though we should faill in the issue, for as You have often observed to me the issue of Law is doubtfull. Mr Anderson & his Wife are now settled at Mill of Pert, both seem to be Discreet good people. He is busy in collecting, the issue of which Mr Cumin will be soon informed off: one thing I may venture to say it is safer than this time twelve month. Joseph Gibb has got a purser Warrant on board the sloop Sylf Leutenant Davis Commander. I hope he may think of his disconsolate Wife & children, as well as Creditors if Mrs Falconer should have Occasion for some Cash to pay off some debts in Montrose, which are in Your list, I beg You'll give an order to Mr Anderson to give it to her. Our friend Sir Alexr Ramsay has been bad with the Jaundice, but is recovering. I have tired Your patience & therfore shall only add Mrs Falconer's & my wishes that Both Mrs Mackensie & Yourself may have many returns of the season joined with health & prosperity, & believe me to be with Sinceerity,

Dear Sir

Your Obliged
Humble Servant
Anthy Falconer

Inglismaldie
Decemb: 5th 1776

We had a Visit of Sir David Carnegie, his Mother, & Sister the day befor yesterday spending an Evening with us all begged to be remembered when I should write

SOURCE: Delvine Papers, MS 1267, ff. 18-19v., National Library of Scotland.

Lt. William Falconer to Anthony Adrian, 7th Lord Falconer of Halkerton (A15)

New York 20th March 1777

My Dear Brother
It is with the utmost & most sincere satisfaction, I acknowlledge the receipt of both your Letters, that of the 7th Janry coming to hand after days previous to the one dated ye 18th Octbr 76. My joy to find that you were in perfect health, greatly consold me for the loss of our Father, therefore I shall not condole with you. I think the dissolution of so noble & generous a Soul as he possessed, from a distress'd & wornout body, the happiest event that could beffall him.

To attempt making any answer to your very kind assurance of assistance, & attention to my interest & promotion, by so bad a Pen as mine, would only be impoverishing the warmest wish of my heart. Therefore I shall shew by my Behaviour, the high value, I must sett upon your Affections qc I am so well convinc'd of by long & happy experience, Gratitude, & an entire submission to your will, then being the only possible action I can make I never shall be deficient in these. Before I had the honor to receive your Letter, I took the Liberty to draw on you for the price of a Lieutcy, as you will find advice. Lt Col. Bird has since obtain'd a blank Commission for me by which means I shall receive 5 pr Cent: for my money, & if the Ensigncy sold for 5 pence the purchaser is on no pay till the regulated price is made good. I am happy to inform you, that this is not the only instance in qc the Colonel has manifested his good wishes towards me. He has appointed me to the care of a Compy tho: there were older Lieuts than me who would have acccepted of it; it is not a litle owing to my good & worthy Friend Captn Leslie that I am so well in his graces.

I am sorry to find by your Letter that you have lost so valuable a member of Society as Mr Ouchterlonie, no doubt the litle widow felt her loss most severly. I am much hurt that Poor Young & Sister have been betrayed into absolute poverty by that wretch Gibb, it is doubly unlucky for poor Young since he has been render'd unfit for Service. It was a pity he did come out here as it in all likelyhood have warded of the Baby for sometime longer & perhaps procur'd him an easy competency for old age and its attendants. The Navy people have of late taken some valuable prizes, among other Captn Ferguson has made his fortune, Captn Falconer was so good as to recommend me to him, but I have as yet not been fortunate enough to meet with him. We are at present, dormant, except on the foraging parties in New Jersey, on one of these the 17th Reg^t under the command of Lt Col Mawhood, had distinguished themselves most gloriously, they along charg'd 5000 rebels, repulsed & pursued them with prodigious loss.[1] Poor McPherson was severly wounded upon this occasion, however he is recovering fast.

Nothing worth mentioning has happen'd since, except a Brigade of Hessians allowing themselves to be surprised & taken prisoners without resistance.

I hope you will be so obliging as assure my Dear Sister of my unalterable Love & affections & pray for her happy delivery of a Nephew. When you visit Holland I beg you will remember me to my Mother & Sisters, whom I shall ever esteem in spite of their unkind usage, but I defy them while I remain happy in your affections & L: Haulkerton's (not meaning the Dowager)

I should wish to hear from Alex^r & keep up a brotherly correspondence with him. I would write if I knew where to direct to him. I am sorry I can't answer Mr Ritchie's Letter just now as the mail is just closing.

I have nothing further to add

Then— Where'er I roam, whatever realm to see,
My heart untravell'd fondly turns to thee,
Till to my Brother turns with ceaseless pain
And drags at each remove a lengthening chain.
Eternal blessing, crown my earliest Friend
And round his dwelling Guardian Saints attend.

G:T:

Your most aff: Brother
& Humble Servant
Willm Falconer
L^t

SOURCE: Kintore Papers, Bundle 197, Aberdeen University Library.
NOTES: [1] He describes the British victory at Princeton, New Jersey, on 3 January 1777.

Lt. William Falconer to John Mackenzie of Delvine

New Yorke April 10th 1777

Dear Sir,
I have taken the liberty by my Brother's desire to draw on you for £50, & hope you will be so obliging as answer that Bill whenever it appears. I drew for fifty because I did not wish to trouble you or my friends for the year to come.

I am happy to inform you that the Rebellion is dwindling away very fast, desertion is become so frequent among them, that hardly a day passes, that they don't come in from 60 to a 100, & mostly with their arms, this I believe is owing greatly to a most lenient proclamation of Sir Willm Howe's wherein he promises to all a free pardon such as desire to go home he offers ships to transport them to England, or they may list if they will in the Provincial Reg[limen]ts of wc we have a prodigous number. A considerable number of these deluded wretches have embodied & intrenched themselves in ye lower counties of Maryland & keep the Rebels at Bay, thus since the seeds of Dissension have now sprung up among, they must fall to the ground even without our assistance, which will be very vigorous this campaign if they will but give us an opportunity.

Shipping for 4,000 men has just now been order'd to lay in 3 months Provissions and a number of ships for the Heavy Artillery, but where the destination of this fleet is has not yet transpired.

I should be happy if you would honor me with a few lines to assure me of your health, & Friendship which to preserve shall be the everlasting Duty of

Dear Sir
Your most obedient Servant
Willm Falconer

SOURCE: Delvine Papers, MS 1267, f. 226, National Library of Scotland.

William Ritchie to Anthony Adrian, 5th Earl of Kintore (A15)

Edin[burgh] 7th Novr 1778

My Lord
Your Lordship will now have received Lord Inverury's Letter which he wrote on Wednesday. I will say nothing of its Contents, for he was left entirely to himself, but I thought him rather careless about the handwriting. If your Lordship think proper, I am persuaded that a gentle hint about his writing in your first Letter to him would have a good effect. He never was in better health & never felt greater happiness than he does now. The boy Paisley & he are perfect friends. Tho' from his former Solitude he is necessarily inferior to the Boys here in every sort of Play, yet, Much to his honour & my very great satisfaction, he never loses his Temper with his playfellows, but exerts himself most vigorously to equal them in every amusement. This is a piece of Education of very great importance, & it is with pleasure I inform your Lordship that he makes a rapid progress both in acquiring dexterity & in checking the violence of his Passions. I wish his literary Education could be as cheaply carried on. The Teachers here are very high with their Fees. I am not yet able to say whether their attendance & Care will be equal to their demands. The plan for Lord Inverury is what is followed here by people of Fashion, only that I have reserved two Hours for exercise which the other boys want. The general way here is that boys go to School at 9 in the morning & have not a moments relaxation till 3 o'clock which is the hour of dinner. After Dinner they have drawing writing & dancing which employ their whole Evenings. Lord Inverury's French Master comes to them at 9 in the morning & reads with them till 10. From 10 to 11 he is with me preparing his Latin Lesson for Mr Matthieson to whose house he goes at 11 & stays till One. After One he writes a little at home & plays till 3. From 4 to 5 a master attends him for reading English. From 6 to 7 his Music Master attends him, from 7 to 8 he plays, & from 8 to 9 his dancing Master comes. We sup regularly at 9 & his Lordship goes to bed about 10. Tho' he has such a variety of Masters, yet he is perpetually under my Eye, (for I always attend most carefully to the way in which these masters go on) except when he is with Matthieson who teaches only in his own house. In the Latin Class there are about 12

boys besides Lord Inverury, are gentlemen's sons, but I am an entire stranger to their Tempers & dispositions. The reason why I have taken so many of the Teachers in to the house, is Lord Inverury's been wholly unacquainted with the Town, & the danger of his losing the way to & from their houses which are most of them at a very great distance. I go with him to M^r. Matthieson & return for him, but to do so with every one of them is a piece of drudgery which I flatter myself your Lordship will not desire me to undertake. After a month I intend that he shall go to the French School, & in a month or two to the dancing school. Each of his Masters take a Guinea per Month. I grudge none of them so much as his musick master. He teased me almost to death before I consented that he should learn Music, & it was with great reluctance that I at last agreed. It is an elegant amusement but it is the most expensive & laborious he could have undertaken. He did not think so, but now he finds it to be truth, & begins to tire already. His ear is far from being fine, his patience is not remarkably great, & without both of these he can never be a musician. I will not discourage him, but I shall not be displeased to find that he is soon glad to give it up. A Fiddle, the cheapest he could [hole] with decency, has cost him about 2 Guineas. [D]rawing is a less dangerous & as elegant an amusement much more suited to his Rank. Were he ever to make a figure in Music, or even were his Taste for it to increase, he would, like all Musicians, prefer the Company of an Italian Fiddler or an Opera Singer, to the first Company in Britain. Since my coming to Ed[inburgh]· I have found it necessary to take advantage of your Lordships kind offer, & draw from Mr Cumin my half years salary which is to be due only at Martinmass next. Lord Inverury begs his kindest Comp^s to his Papa & Mamma & to each of his Sisters. I call upon M^r. Cumin almost every day. M^r. Erskine of Dun calld for Lord Inverury on Thursday, but unluckily he was abroad. I am, My Lord,

> Your Lordship's most obed^t
> humble Servt
> Will: Ritchie

SOURCE: Kintore Papers, Bundle 197, Aberdeen University Library.

NOTES: Ritchie, like many young clergymen, was employed as tutor of William, Lord Inverury (A16), eldest son and heir of Anthony Adrian, 5th Earl of Kintore.

William Ritchie to Anthony Adrian, 5th Earl of Kintore (A15)

Edin[burgh]· 13th Jan^y· 1779

My Lord,

After the Vacations of Christmass & the new Year, Lord Inverury has again entered to his Classes, & things go on in their ordinary way. After a treat of near three Months, I cannot say that he makes progress in his Education, neither can I lay much blame upon him. We live in perfect friendship, & sit down to our Lessons with the firmest Resolution to apply carefully, but the incessant rattling of Chaises & Carts, the Cries of one wife with Oysters, of another with salt, of a third with yellow sand, &c: catch his Lordship's Attention, & away go his thoughts full gallop after the Chaises & wives, so that it takes some time & trouble to recall them. But the greatest interruption we meet with is within doors. All the boarders, except one Mr Vaughan & myself, are Musicians. From 7 in the Morning to 12 at Night they are perpetually playing in one or other of the Rooms. Amidst the mingled sounds of the Flute, Fiddle, Spinet & Violincello I find it no easy Task to command my own Attention, far less can it be supposed that his Lordship should be master of his. These accidental inconveniences which must be expected in Life will become familiar by Habit, & habits can be produced only by Time. The Swedes indeed, upon a hint that so much Music was rather disagreeable, have almost entirely given up their's, & the other Gentlemen begin to follow their example. His Lordship still continues to have a Music Master. Upon reading the Advice your Lordship gave him, he instantly put the Letter in my hand, & said with deep Regret, Oho! I find Papa grudges the Money. I must give up My Music. This Idea surprised me, & to convince him that this was not the Case, promised to plead with you for some longer time upon condition of his making more progress. But I'm sorry to say that his progress has not been better, not for want of an Ear, but Attention. We have now agreed to dismiss the Master after this week till Summer. And that he may not in the meantime forget what little he has learned, the Master is to attend him one day of the week. It would be hard to disappoint him wholly of the only object on which I ever found him set his heart with so much Keenness, but tho fond of Music, he will not submit to the drudgery of learning it. At that hour I leave him entirely to his own disposal, & find that he coaxes the Master to spend Most of the Time in playing Reels to amuse him. A clear proof that the strongest desire for any Science is no Evidence of a Genius fit to acquire it. During the Vacation, as the weather was so bad, that we could have no Amusements without doors, we indulged ourselves in going again to the playhouse. His Lordship was not half so much entertained as at first. He saw Lady Carnegie there, & at her Request is to wait upon her Ladyship soon. He still continues to have perfect health & spirits, & is indeed the hardiest little fellow I ever knew. Tho' every one in the family have by turns had Colds, he has yet stood it out. He has indeed had sometimes a trifling sort of Cough, but Barley Sugar proves an infallible Cure. The dancing goes on tolerably well. Pringle is a wicked little Body, & from a fear of being affronted, is very attentive. By talking often with Dr Blacklock on the advantages of teaching Boys a high-dance, I have at last prevailed upon him to engage Pringle for Paisley, & as Lord Inverury & he get their Lessons together, the Emulation between them will be of use to both.

I have no opportunities of mingling with Company & cannot send Your Lordship any news. Our society nev[er] meddle with Politics, as there is abundance of Conversation on other Subjects, which is sometimes spun out to a very great Length. The opinions about Admiral Keppel are as various as mens faces. In general it is said that his friends in London much dread the worst.[1] The famous Letter to Sir William How engrosses much Conversation. It is ascribed by some to Sir John Dalrymple, by others to Dr Cowper a Clergyman here, & by others to one Dr Stuart. But it is only guess work at the best. Lord Inverury offers Comp.s to your Lordship, to Lady Kintore, & his sisters. He proposes to write his sisters soon. He has now more time as the English & Music Masters are both given up. But he is not fond of letterwriting as it deprives him of much of his Play. I am, My Lord,

Your Lordship's most obed.t hum.ble Ser.t
Will: Ritchie

SOURCE: Kintore Papers, Bundle 197, Aberdeen University Library.

NOTES: [1]Admiral Keppel, commander-in-chief of the grand fleet, was court-martialed on 7 January 1779, after having failed in an attack on the French at Brest, but was acquitted on 11 February.

William Ritchie to Anthony Adrian, 5th Earl of Kintore (A15)

Scorton 24th Jan.ry 1782.

My Lord,

On Monday last we came hence from York, & are now settled again in our calm retirement at Scorton. Lord Inverury is perfectly well after all our journeys, & has never once had a Cold. He intends to write an Account of our York expedition, so that I dare not say one word about it. But he cannot write this week, as he is at present sadly tormented with the Whitlow in his Thumb, which occasions the most acute pain, as I know from experience. We have had abundance of jaunting during this vacation, & at a far easier

Rate than any of our Scotch expeditions, for we have been always lodged in private houses, & have abundant reason to speak well of English hospitality. Travelling thro' this Country is indeed most extravagantly expensive. Chaise hire, horse hire & tolls would consume the Estate of an Indian Noble. We spent a good deal of Money at York, but none except what could not be decently saved. His Lordship did not throw away sixpence without my knowledge. His Clothes, hat, silk stockings, worsted stockings, & hankerchiefs amounted to upwards of £12, & yet they are all as plain & grave as your Lordship could possibly desire. His expence at the playhouse was but six shillings for two nights. He's never entered a saddlers shop, & never went near a Teyshop except when I was with him, so that in point of Money his behaviour has been as moderate as I would wish. He still has too little regard to the Value of Money, but if he had all the Cautious oeconomy of an old man, I should certainly despise him. He who is too prudent in Youth, will be a wretch in old age. His present hobby horse is hunting. His whole heart & soul is bent upon the Chace, & this is not to be wondered at, for it is scarcely credible how universal the passion for hunting is in this country. It is the only Employment of the Country Gentlemen. I have seen a farmer loose his horse from the plough, & ride away after the hounds, old & young, man, wife & child speak of its pleasures with all the raptures of Enthusiasm. You may easily judge that his Lordship cannot resist this powerful torrent. But how far to indullge him in it, I know not. The young Gentlemen here who hunt either have their own horses, or borrow them from Gentlemen of their acquaintance. That we cannot do. To hire horses is *very* expensive. A forenoon's ride costs us 3 shillings each, a days hunting costs 5. This soon amounts to a great sum. I cannot, without your consent, allow him to go by himself, because, if in my absence, any little accident were to happen, you would, I fear, think it a poor excuse for me, that I wish'd to save your Lordship the expence of five shillings. I shall be glad to know what you think of this Matter. Tho' I do not like hunting myself, as it shakes my bones almost asunder, yet I am so far from blaming his Lordship for loving, that I should regard him as a Lump of lifeless clay, if he was not fond of what other young men are induldged in. Lord Darlington's eldest son, about 16 years of Age, in this Neighbourhood, has a pack of hounds for himself, & he & his tutor are left in the Country to spend the winter in hunting, while the father lives in London. An admirable plan of Education! & worthy of a British Peer. As I have mentioned expence, it may be proper to shew your Lordship how widely I was misinformed about the School fees & other charges at Scorton. Besides the Account inclosd, Mr Holmes got a Guinea & a half of what is called Entrance money, on the first day the School met. The long list of Books may surprise you. We have every Book that is mentioned in this Catalogue, but as they were not the same *Editions* taught here, & as *Mr Holmes supplies the Scholars with Books*, it was found necessary to give his Lordship a new Copy of every Book, & Now they be as lumber upon our hands. The writing master got half a Guinea of entrance Money, & his Account for the last half year is £1.3.4. His account I find it necessary to keep because his honour is not to be trusted. I have also sent inclosed a Copy of our expences for board for the last 7 Months. Some of the Articles may appear strange, but it is easy, if your Lordship require it, fully to account for them. The Article of Coals may seem most extravagant. But they are brought 20 Miles by land Carriage. Our little Room needs very little fire, & in our Bed Room we have never once had a fire, & it we continue in health shall never have one here. I send no accounts of how the rest of the money has been spent. On that my Character & credit depend & I shall, whenever you choose, give a full explanation. Some of the Articles will make you smile & others may cause a frown. But I shall stand a firm advocate for his Lordships expence ever since we came to Scorton. I am, My Lord,

Your Lordship's most obed^t
Ser^t Will: Ritichie

SOURCE: Kintore Papers, Bundle 197, Aberdeen University Library.

William, Lord Inverury (A16) to Adrian Anthony, 5th Earl of Kintore (A15)

Jena 22^d January 1787

My Dear Father
Your last Letter from Keithhall I received some time ago. We have been a good deal distressed about the journey to Vienna which you have been kind enough to propose to us. The Engagements we had made here & the season of the year were such that we could not think of going away immediately. About the beginning of April we propose going to Vienna, because our views are not to throw away money on the diversions of the Carnival but to see a little of the company & the curiosities of that capital of the Empire, which is so much spoken of. The Christmass holidays we spent at Weimar were I find every sort of civility & attention that can possibly be desired. Our Living here is not cheap, but we find more opportunity for improvement & more good society than any place we have seen in Germany. I attend the Professor of Mathematics an hour a day & have also a drawing master & read a little Italian. When I want a little amusement I can always slip over to Weimar which is only about 10 English miles distant. The winter here has not yet been sever but very disagreeable from the inconstancy of the weather. I have not forgot your commission about a Jäger.[1] There are plenty of them to be had, but many of them are too fine. Gentlemen & others are too stupid. I have however no doubt of soon getting a good one, but his wages will be high. The best Rifles are to be had at Ratisbon,[2] through which we pass in going to Vienna. I am much obliged to you for the trouble you taken about a Commission for me, & I hope to hear soon about its being secured. That Your My Mother & Sisters may pass a happy year & that every blessing may attend you is my earnest wish & shall ever be so dum spiritus hos regit artus.

I am
Dear Father

Your affectionate Son
Inverury

SOURCE: Kintore Papers, Bundle 197, Aberdeen University Library.
NOTES: [1]Hunting rifle. [2]Regensburg.

Alexander Falconer (B1) to Adrian Anthony, 5th Earl of Kintore (A15)

(Translation from Dutch by Dr. Jaap Lucassen)

Very Honourable Sir, and Brother.
With due respect I take the liberty, once again, to address your Lordship with a few words, although I hesitate to write, as I have not been honoured with a small letter for nearly 2 years, which sometimes makes me press the tears from my eyes, though I dare say before God and men that as far as I am aware I did in now way offend your Lordship in writing. If it happened that I expressed something incorrectly, then forgive me, much respected and amiable brother; it was unknowingly and unwittingly, but nothing will give me greater pleasure or satisfaction, than if a single little letter, which I wish with heart and soul, will follow this one. Truly it gives me great pleasure that I have been informed by the Lieutenant Colonel's[1] lady that her Ladyship the Countess and her dear children find themselves in perfect health, and she was not a little desirous to receive some letters from your Lordship's spouse. Her Ladyship's[2] two oldest and the youngest daughter will shortly be wed, the oldest, Miss Sybille, with Sir Lieutenant Hardess, now in service of the Republic, a man of fashion and birth, the second, Bartha, with a Cap-

tain, a man of erudition, called Shevikhaaven, the youngest daughter, Francois, with Guyot,[3] a French minister, spirited with French qualities, in one word: *de bon l'esprit.* Thus remains Madam and her Ladyship's third daughter Quirina, whom I can recommend to a man of taste. I have now the pleasure to communicate to your Lordship that my beloved housewife happily and prosperously delivered a well-shaped son, who will be called Jan Herman, after my father-in-law, his grandfather, to whom I haven't spoken since my second son was born, because his Honour was very offended by the fact that I called my son Antoon Adriaan, at your Lordship's request. His Honour withheld by revenge the promised annuity, which is for us not a little painful and burdensome, as I receive so little from my inheritance and my post that I cannot maintain my household, and now, from the higher tree, will have to eat into my capital, which is an unpleasant idea for someone without prospects, because I cannot expect much from my parents-in-law, since I have a thriftless and evil mother-in-law. Moreover a wife who bears a child every year, which is not a small disadvantage for housekeeping. One calls it a blessing and a sign of respectability. But one lives only once. Thus there is nothing left for us but to recommend myself and my family to your Lordship's attention and thought, however little the soutiens or support may be, as I refer to a message from your Lordship that we should not suffer any hardship. We are really and truly poor. Moreover, it is very difficult to obtain anything, considering the troubles which have taken place in the Netherlands, and the animosity which still prevails. And the hatred, envy, and malice which inspires my father-in-law is really not understandable, as he gives no other reason but that it is the general custom here that the second child should be presented to him. In short, your Lordship can see from all this how stubborn and hateful the friend is, that his Honour attempts to oppress us so much. Which, for me, is a sign of little intelligence, and therefore it is correct to call him a fool. I am sorry to address my father-in-law in such a way. But to my consolation, it is better to be in the grace of a wise, well-knowing brother, rather than in the favour of insensitive parents-in-law. He has no idea what it means: Earl of Kintore. If he would comprehend this, reason would prevail.

In human memory, we have not had such a cold and bitter winter than the one we hope has now ended. According to our amateurs, the thermometer has been two degrees below zero. Thus this cold spell surpassed the one of the year 1740. Several people have crossed a part of the Zuiderzee with their goods and skated from one place to the other. One hears every day about sad accidents, as through the breaking up of the ice various ships have disintegrated. One is afraid here for a second campaign with the Emporer and the Turk, because Ockzakov has been conquered by the Russians, which is not disadvantageous for the Emperor and should bring the Turk to reason. For the rest, dark and sombre clouds gather over the North, which, when the storm breaks, will put the whole of Europe in fire and flame. Daily, justice is meted out, here and in other places, to the rebellious, who get what they deserve.[4] The Burgomaster A. A. van Iddekinge gives up blood continuously which is very significant, and the cork is from the bottle, which sounds too sweet for the old gentleman's ears, though immediately forbidden by the medics. We hope the chest with the novels and the other things has arrived, which we sent last Christmas. With the recently arrived new year we wish your Lordship and dear dependents good luck, wishing a long life and a happy death. We send our compliments to her Ladyship the Countess and further relatives, not to forget My Lord Inverurie.

Honourable Sir, and Brother,
A: Falconer.

Gron: 20th January 1789

SOURCE: Kintore Papers, Bundle 251, Aberdeen University Library.

NOTES: [1] Berend van Iddekinge, Lieutenant Colonel, Imhoff's Regiment, was the brother of Alexander's mother and burgomaster of Groningen from 1786 to 1795. [2] These were the children of Tobias Jan van Iddekinge, brother of Alexander's mother, by his wife Sibilla Volkera Sichterman, sister of Lord Kintore's wife. [3] Frans Daniel Guyot, a minister of the French Reformed Church, founded a school for the deaf in Groningen. [4]He refers to the adherents of the republican Patriot movement.

William, Lord Inverury (A16) to Anthony Adrian, Earl of Kintore (A15)

London August 10
1789

My Dear Father

You will be perhaps surprised at my not having wrote you before now but I thought it was well to let it stand till I came to London. Our Travels as far as Perth I suppose you would learn from Sam after the disagreeable business of parting with M[r] Ritchie who certainly during the long period of 14 Years always behaved to me with the greatest attention & *affection* & I hope as soon as is an opportunity offers, you will do something for him. We set out for Edinburg & arrived there on Thursday where I visited Lord Henderland who was out of Town M[rs] Falconer, the Miss Keiths M[r] & M[rs] Wauchop D[r] Blacklock M[r] Cumin with whom I settled matters, & on Friday set out for London along with M[r] Dauney who wished to go to London. M[r] Cuming had looked out for a Companion for me & friend a M[r] Trotter writer to the Signet but he set out the very Day I arrived having gone there to marry a rich wife. I have been here three days & have being running about settling my business. I have dined twice with Lord Adam Gordon who is remarkably civil & has supplied me with plenty of Letters both for the Officers & the Bishop of St Asaph, with regard to a Charger General Johnstone wrote to Lord Adam that there was one at the Regiment ready broke & and if I chose I might have him, as with regard to Saddle horses I must let that stand for some time. I have got my Uniforms & part of the things & as soon as I have got all my accoutrements I shall send all the bills to M[r] Cumin & shall live upon as an economical plan as possible, do my duty, & try to make myself liked both by Officers & men. Lord Adam told me that they are all very good men & very sober. He likewise told me that we are to be reviewd before the King next year. As to all our adventure here I refer you to M[r] Dauney. I set out to morrow for Winchester & after having been two or three days there I will write how matters go on. Be persuaded Dear Father that it shall alway be my very object to behave in such a manner as to make up in some measure for the pains & money that has been bestowed upon me. Lord Adam & the Dutchess join me in kind Compli|men|ts My Dear Mother & Sister &

I am
Dear Father

Your affectionate Son
Inverury

P S Excused my writing as I find myself a little flustered in writing This the next shall be better

SOURCE: Kintore Papers, Bundle 198, Aberdeen University Library.

Alexander Falconer (B1) to Anthony Adrian, 5th Earl of Kintore (A15)

(Translated from Dutch by Dr. Jaap Lucassen)

My Lord
I am extremely happy and satisfied to have been informed by *ubique*[1] that your Lordship and the Countess enjoy a perfect treasure of health, and moreover that your Lordship has the intention to write me before the next post-day, which will give me great joy as such has not happened for six years, and for which I felt very uncomfortable and had the idea that I had perhaps offended your Lordship in my writings. If this has happened, *excuse moi*, and I ask for forgiveness, but due to a long absence the close relationship is not being cultivated, which I hope and wish will not take place, although we have not seen or spoken to each another for sixteen years. Yes, I dare say that if I were convinced that my person would not be disagreeable to your Lordship, I would like to attempt to have verbal communication with your Lordship, as it would be clearly for the last time, and to lay my circumstances at your Lordship's feet; my wife is now pregnant with her seventh child, and therefore because of heavy expenses, we cannot live on our interest any longer, but have to eat into our capital from year to year and the conclusion is: the end tries all. Moreover there are special taxes due to critical circumstances in which the Republic has been, caused by the unjust war imposed upon it by France, or rather by the King's murderers.[2] Thank God they have left the Republic after capitulation, having first inflicted some destruction on various cities through the fire of war, yes, even vacated the whole of Brabant. General Demorier has even put on the white cockade and is marching with his whole army towards France, the common people have sworn an oath of loyalty not to desert their general, who will attempt to restore order and peace there. The Prussians, the Emporer, and the Orangists will concentrate at the frontiers to assist General Demourier if necessary. Rijssel[3] and some other places will now be occupied by the combined powers. Here opinion is divided about the behaviour of Demourier, since His Excellency always has been a proponent of the sons of freedom, namely Liberty and Equality, and now in a moment has changed, and would use the sword of war against those who would carry him on their shoulders. I do not sit in the cabinets. I think more than I would judge proper to write about the future. Thank heaven they did not achieve their plans, because they would have brought the whole of Europe in the hobble and raised Hell. Where can these King's murderers seek refuge? Every virtuous soul disapproves of this deed. The Powers will not make life easy for them; no hiding place should be available for this rabble. I know from reliable sources that the English court has made a proposition to that extent. They are worse than the servants of *jogsoom*.[4] I would write extensively about the riots which took place here and elsewhere, but your Lordship will not be unaware of them.

My Lord I am your humble Serv[an]^t
A: Falconer

Gron[ingen]: 17 April 1793

SOURCE: Kintore Papers, Bundle 251, Aberdeen University Library.

NOTES: [1] Latin for everywhere, omnipresent. [2] The abortive campaign by Dumouriez, February/March 1793. [3] Lille. [4] Meaning uncertain.

Maria Rembertina Keith-Falconer to Anthony Adrian, 5th Earl of Kintore (A15)

Elgin 22^d Oct^r [*no year; 1790s?*]

Though only four days are elapsed since I wrote you my dearest father yet during that short space Catherine & I have been such travellers, have seen so many of the beauties of Murray, there & have already enjoyed so much pleasure in our various excursions, that I cannot help feeling anxious to let you know what we are doing, & I know that your goodness will make you a partaker in the happiness. We are enjoying under this friendly & hospitable roof indeed *we* may ask it so for I do think of the purest benevolence the warmest goodness of heart, & the most endearing friendship can be personified they may be represented by Brodie, whose unremitting attention to us is beyond expression, & when I add that in that respect Mrs Brodie is the counterpart of himself you may imagine to what homely friendship & kindness we are indebted. Though our excursions have been confined to morning rides yet we have seen & admired a great part of Murrayshire. The face of the country is really beautiful—rich cultivated fields & extensive plantations every where meet the eye & the prospect is almost constantly varied wth some old Castle in decay or some neat little villa, of which there are a great many in this neighbourhood. On Monday we went to see the Ruins of Pluscardine Abbey formerly a Bishop's seat & now a venerable ruin. On Teusday we went to Innes where L^{lord} Fife has certainly left nothing undone that can beautify & compleat his policy & pleasure Grounds. The house tho Old is a goose, one & we you may believe partook Brodie's & his Lady's desire to inhabit it, which is very strong but I suppose very unavailing. On Wed^y forenoon we rode to Lake or Loch Moboy which without partiality, I think the most beautiful scene of that kind I ever beheld superior so far as my recollections lead me, to that of Windermere. But I will not detain you longer My Dear Father, at present tho perfectly happy here, often do Catherine & I turn our thoughts towards the fireside at home, & I shall be gratified if but for a few moments this can engage your attention. Catherine writes My Mother to morrow, when I shall write to my Dear Cappy. I sincerely hope that My Mother does not miss the Carriage. Brodie wrote to Mr Cumins & is surpris'd he does not receive an answer. Adieu My Dearest Father, Kindest & cordial wishes from all here to which C— & I add our most affectionate love & Duty, — Sir Hector Manes, & his Daughter din'd here yesterday & set off for Navarre. There has been no Company except two, or three Gentlemen of this place, however we have been very merry & dancing away almost every night. Mr Cross dines here to day, his Brother was married the 15th. Once more Adieu My ever dear & respected Father, & Believe that I ever remain

Your Affectionate Daughter
M[aria] R[embertina] Keith

SOURCE: Kintore Papers, Bundle 198, Aberdeen University Library.

Abraham Falconar (J5) to William Falconer (J9)

George Town, Kent County Dec[embe]^r 15th 1803

D[ea]^r William

Your esteemed favor of the 21st Sep^t is before me: Contents noted, I hope 'ere this you have perfectly recovered your health. You mention that you had wrote me before. I did not receive it: I am much pleased to hear you are situated with an agreeable family, and hope you have on your part acted in like manner, of this I have no doubt. I have received a Letter from John dated 23^d Octr last, informing that you and him are to begin business together in the spring. This I am pleased to hear as business is very good with you: no doubt you'll do better together, besides it will give me great pleasure to hear of your increasing your brotherly ties, thereby you'll not only receive mutual advantages in your business, but make the most favorable impressions on your Acquaintances. Your Sister is very well also the rest of my family; she has quit School and is now waiting Pere's return. He is expected in February by way of Orleans. Oldden & him has opened a wholesale store in Baltimore; the business he is now on is for B. & J. Comegys. The family are all very desirous to see you as soon as you can make it convenient, & desires to be remembered to you. I hope to hear from you 'ere long.

D[ear] Will. Yours Sincerely

Abraham Falconar

SOURCE: Mary Stay Buckner Papers, Tennessee State Library.

NOTES: "Oldden" was David Olden, who married 25 July 1803, at St. Paul's, Baltimore, Susan Levy, sister of Peregrine's wife.

Rowland Williams Fearon to Richard Pennant, 1st Baron Penrhyn

Jamaica Clarendon June 9th 1804

Lord

I am extremely sorry to apprize your Lordship of [the d]eath of M[r] Alexander Falconer; His illness was not of sufficient duration to admit of my communicating to you the prospect there was of this event taking place.

By your Lordships favor I am now placed in the situation which Mr Falconer lately filled [as] Agent here, and the zeal and unwearied assiduity with which he discharged that trust will call forth all my exertions to [make] myself worthy of his recommendation and your Lordships Notice.

My own Estate being entirely committed to the management of my Brother leaves me at liberty to [...] the whole of my time and attention to your Lordships concerns and I beg leave to assure you that what ever commands your Lordship may be pleased to impose upon me, shall be punctually observed.

Mr Falconers death having so recently taken place and the attention which as a very near connection I have been obliged to pay to his family in their present distress; preclude me at this moment from entering into a description of the situation of your Lordships Estates; I shall however loose no time in informing myself accurately on this subject and communicate the result of my information to your Lordship the earliest opportunity.

In the meantime I am to [...] your Lordship that shipments have already been made by the Fleet which is about to sail, of the quantity of Sugar as stated in the Memorandum and for which I shall transmit to Mess[rs] Davidson & Graham Bills of Lading and I shall use every exertion to get the Remainder of the Crop taken off and shipped with the utmost dispatch.

There are already made on Denbigh Estate 170 H[ogs]h[ea]ds & 52 Trs of Sugar and I am given to understand by the overseer that he will make 20 to 30 H[ogs]h[ea]ds more, [...] on the Mountain Estates 302 H[ogs]h[ea]ds and 109 Trs, the overseer [...] make 500 H[ogs]h[ea]ds altogether. I cannot conclude this letter my Lord without repeating to your Lordship, the deep sense I entertain of the favor your Lordship has been pleased to confer upon me, which I shall endeavour to merit by every means in my power. I am with the utmost respect

My Lord

Yr Lordships much obliged Servant
Rowland Williams Fearon

SOURCE: Penrhyn MSS 1327, University of North Wales.

NOTES: Rowland Williams Fearon (bp. 1762), of Clarendon, Jamaica, was the son of Wheeler and Elizabeth (Smith) Fearon. His mother was the daughter of Samuel and Mary (Williams) Smith and the half-sister of Alexander Falconer's mother Frances Nairn. He and his cousin Francis Smith were the executors of Alexander Falconer's estate. Rowland's wife was the sister of Alexander's wife. The condition of this letter is rather poor, apparently having suffered damage from mold.

Rowland Williams Fearon to Richard Pennant, 1st Baron Penrhyn

Clarendon Jamaica July 14th 1804

My Lord

I did myself the honor of writing to your Lordship on the 9th of June last since which I have given your Estates my utmost attention. I am sorry to say Pennants and Kupids have not yet finished their Crops, it is a very late period of the year to be making of Sugar, highly detrimental both to Negroes and Stock; the Canes will not yield and the Produce must be of a very inferior quality.

I have enquired very minutely in the cause of this delay. Forbes the overseer vindicates himself by saying the Weather and the want of fuel has impeded his progress; I suppose he has been indolent during Mr Falconers illness which has certainly been the case. There is a good shew of Canes for the next Crop, but backward which has arisen from the lateness of the last years Crop; These Estates my Lord appear to me to be over planted generally, were they confined to 100 acres and those well put in and highly manured they would be equally Productive as the 140 acres usually planted in the common way; and will afford an opportunity of puting the Estates in better Culture, the Rattoons will have more attention and will amply repay any extraordinary labor bestowed upon them; in pursuing that plan the hilly lands may be thrown out and them planted in Grass for the purpose of making manure.

As I well know My Lord the disadvantages which arise from late Crops your Lordship may rest assured that I shall take great care and pains that the plant for the present Fall (and am now taking steps to forward it) shall be completed by the end of October so that there shall not be any hindrance in taking of the Crop in time and the produce sent early to market.

While on these Estates I served the Negroes with their Cloathing; there were amongst them a Number of Old and infirm people perfectly useless, the rest were healthy and amongst whom were a fine parcel of Girls and Boys and some in their Mothers arms; These Young People I shall have put on a better plan than the present; the overseer shall regularly have boiled a Mess of victuals every day at Noon and all to be assembled and each to have a share, under his Eye and two old Women, will attend to keep them clean; they will be beneficial in keeping the Young Canes in order. The Stock My Lord calld my attention also; I was sorry to say they were in very bad Condition. Forbes has also shewn his neglect here, he has not been watchful over the Cattlemen and Waggoners, the number is sufficient to carry on the operations of the Estates but they have been abused; I drew off 20 that appeared to be old and will not stand another Crop and sent them to Coatess to be put up for fattening; as soon as the Crop is finished which will be two weeks hence the whole must be sent away to pasture as they will not be capable to take down to market the remainder of the Produce, without losses which will be my Study to prevent.

Mr Falconer in his arrangements for these Estates intending building a New Mill House at EP and at EP a New Mill House and Water Wheel, which appear highly necessary and expedient to be done; I shall follow up his intentions and have ordered the Sawyers to go to Bog Hole to saw the Cedar or Mahogany for the Wheel. The Coopers will get the Shingles and the Carpenters the other wood work on the Kenco lands; the Coppers are also to be hung anew on both Estates; in doing these I shall have them on the same plan as they are on my Estate; to make a good weeks work and save feed, which Mr Falconer highly approved of the last time he visited me previous to his death. The Sugar and Rum made to Friday last your Lordship will have in the Memorandum annexed.

Denbigh my Lord has finished Crop as you will see in the Journal forwarded by this opportunity. This Estate had a very fine appearance and shewed a prospect of a large Crop the ensuing year at the time of the death of Mr Falconer, since which we have had 5 Weeks dry Weather attended with severe winds which made the Canes look in some places where the lands were light like thatch, however I am happy to inform your Lordship that very heavy rains have fallen last Week which have revived our hopes.

I served the Negroes with their Cloathing, there were a number of Old and infirm People amongst them yet a very able and sufficient Strength of Negroes to carry on the function of the Estate, and a very promising appearance of young Creoles, I really have never seen so large a number upon any Estate before; I shall certainly have them under the same Management as I mentiond before and to carry it fully into execution I have ordered Williamson to give in a Model of two Stones for the purpose of grinding Corn to be wrought by the Steam Engin which I shall submit to your Lordships approval and directions to be sent out; The Stock were in good condition and in heart to carry on the Tillage of the lands; there will be 84 acres planted in the Fall your Lordship will have the names of the Pieces when put in.

The Steam Engin My Lord attracted my attention. I am well aware that Your Lordship has been at a very heavy expence to erect and expedite the operation of this Machinery and I am fully certain Mr Falconer has cooperated with your Lordship to carry into execution your sanguin Expectations; the Well has been deepen'd 7 feet, Williamson says they can go no farther, in the last diging they came to a quick sand which endangered the lives of the People and were obliged to desist; it was supposed they had got upon the bed of the River; The Guttering has been carried to some extent; in the present Stage of I am given to understand Mr Falconer intended to have given it a fair trial as to the watering System, and to report to your Lordship the result of the experiment, but his illness and death defeated his wishes. I am now to inform your Lordship that I had that Gentlemans intentions put into execution at two different periods, the first in the last Months dry Weather, the Machin drained the well in ten Minutes and suppose it would have taken a day to regain the Water, the second was on Wednesday last after the return of the Rains and the River full of water it was exhausted in half an hour; these two trials My Lord shew the Well is not sufficient to furnish Water to carry on the Watering Plan; As this is a matter of great consideration and any instructions you may be pleased to give shall be implicitly executed.

Mr Mitchell the Proprietor of Moreland Estate in the Parish of Vere has a Steam Engin on a larger Scale than the One at Denbigh, he finds it will not answer for watering (as I am told) but will confine it totally for grinding of Canes; Mr Richards proposes the same on the Bog Estate; these two Gentlemen I intend to call upon and know precisely their Sentiments.

I have now all the Iron Work of the Rotative Mill on the Estate and hope in the course of a few days to have it in complete order, so that the next Crop shall be taken off with it; I have ordered all the Young Men on the Estate to get into the Knowledge of the Machinery; Saxon is the first on the list to take a lesson. This I have done in case of the death of Williamson that no Obstruction may occur during Crop and shall see that my orders are put into execution. I shall send in the Ceres with other Papers the Plan of the Rotative Mill which will give your Lordship an Idea how it is erected. I have had the Old Overseers House on New Denbigh put in repair, where I intend to reside occasionally, to give these properties my utmost attention; it has been attended with no expence.

I spent some days on Coatess, there is a sufficiency of Grass to carry on the Wainage business and the Stock even in good Condition, I was obliged to send from there 12 Steers to Pennants Thos River to assert in taking off the Crop. I had an examination of the Negroes there, there are some Old and infirm People the rest were healthy and some fine Young Creoles coming on; tho I must say the Strength is not adiquate to carry on this property and Penrhyn. I took several rides over Penrhyn that property My Lord appears to be overstocked and I do think so many Breeders ought not to be kept upon it, At this Period of the Year, after the fine Seasons we have had, there should be a fine flush of Grass but it is not the case, it would be more advantagious, to buy in now and then a Meagre or a lot of Spanish Cattle and fatten for the Butcher you will then be enabled to pasture the Stock from the Mountain Estates which has been hitherto obliged to be sent to Grass elsewhere at a very heavy expence.

I am very sorry to find there has been a disease affecting the Stock at that Penn, it began to shew itself again, soon after the death of Mr Falconer; I immediately ordered the whole to be drenched twice a Week with a strong solution [of] Tar water indiscriminately, and some tar put into the trough which they drank Water which Castairs the Overseer informs me had the desired effect; I had one of these animals opened in the presence of a very respectable Medical Gentleman but could discover no part of the vicerals to be the least affected; this disorder has appeared in several Shapes over the Country and great mortalities have ensued from it. In going over your Lordships properties I had an Inventory and List taken of all the Articles of Plantation Supplies that were in the Stores from which circumstance I have it in my Power to curtail very considerably the List of Supplies which has been hitherto accustomed to be sent for; this your Lordship will note on the perusal of the Present List sent per this opportunity.

I have shipped on board the Ceres 120 H[ogs]h[ea]ds and 51 Trs Sugar, also 50 H[ogs]h[ea]ds and 20 Trs on board the Tiger, there are no Sugars shipping on board the West Indian for London some also will be shipped on the Lady Sinclair for Leith

The Loss of the Shipping on the Coast of Portugal has caused a very great scarcity in this quarter for London which has obliged me to catch the opportunity of making the shipments to Liverpool and Leith. The remainder of the Sugars shall be shipped on the first London ship that offers after the sailing of the Convoy to depart the 25th inst

The Sugar and Coffee with the Sweatmeats, oil & plants will be shipped on board the Tiger; Capt Oxten has promised to take great care and deliver them safe to Mr Marrow; from your Letters to Mr Falconer, your Lordship has been [...] to disappointed in the Supply of Coffee sent you in the quality; I have endeavoured to obviate this inconvenience by having the Cask doubly cased, and it will be for your Lordships consideration when it arrives to have it put into 100 Wt bags it will loose any bad smells or Taste it might have acquired on board the Ship.

The loss of the Herrings on board the Neptune is a serious disappointment to the Negroes; I have according to the advice from Messrs Davidson & Graham to Mr Falconer written to Mr Armstrong to loose no opportunity for sending for your Lordships Estates 100 Barrels of Fish and shall purchase 50 more in the Country to give them a temporary supply.

I did not wish to write to Mr Armstrong for a larger quantity as I am certain they will not keep long, and are a perishable comodity. I beg to mention to your Lordship that the salted meats that were furnished the Estates by Mr Armstrong became putrid before the White people could make use of them; I have made mention of this circumstance to that Gentleman that he may look into it, as such losses are of serious moment; I suspect they have been Barrelled off too soon and not sufficiently impregnated with the Salt. I have not put down any Salt in the List of supplies for your Lordships Estates as I well know, that Article is invoiced very high from London, it would be better to come from Liverpool; which, will thank your Lordship to order Mr Marrow to send per the first opportunity; the quantity required will be 10 H[ogs]h[ea]ds.

Your Lordships Letter of the 2^d of May to Mr Falconer has come to hand in which you have limitted price per head and time of payment, in consequence of which I wrote to learn from Messrs Bogle Jopp & Co, as I knew they had a Cargo of Negroes for Sale, the terms and prices that your Lordship may be acquainted with the circumstance. They wrote me the following:

> We have now a Cargo of Windward Coast negroes which we are selling for Cash or Bills of Exchange 85 to 90 pounds Currency payable in 12 Months with Interest after 90 days.

If it is still your Lordships intention to purchase Negroes for your Estates (of which you will inform me) for it is highly necessary in the first instance that provisions of the Country & Houses be first considered; we must fall land and plant at Thomas River at least 20 acres of Ground provisions which must be done by hand labor; that Estate does certainly require additional Strength and will take 35 Negroes, to be purchased at two different periods; Coatess will require 15; Denbigh wants none, it is very sufficiently handed; in the choice of Negroes Eboe Women are to be prefered they breed well and take great care of themselves; Chambas or Whidaws are prefered for Men.

I observed in your Letter to Mr Falconer it is your Lordships wish to sell the brown Sugars in the Country, this I shall comply with, but should an opportunity offer of shipping them to London, I will do it, unless your Lordship instructs Me to the Contrary by an early opportunity, as the Prices of Sugar at present in Kingston are very low and nothing but the fairest quality will go off in the Market.

I shall make a reserve of Rum to be shipped to Mr. Armstrong as your Lordship mentiond to be done in per your Letter to Mr Falconer, that article is very low in price just now in Kingston only 3/4.

The Power to manumise the Several Slaves came after the death of Mr Falconer consequently the Manumission can not be executed by me which I shall return to your Lordship to renew if you think proper per the Ceres; three people are very anxious to have it done, and in the meantime your Lordship may instruct me by Letter not to call upon them for their Services, they paying in the several [...] Mr Falconer had mentiond to your Lordship they were to pay, untill the arrival of the Power.

Your Lordship may rest assured every exertion will be made use of to promote the prosperity of your Estates and managed with Ability and economy. I am happy to inform your Lordship we are in the utmost tranquility here, all fears from St Domingo and its influence have subsided. I have the Honor to be in

> Lordships most faithfull & Obliged serv't
> R W Fearon

My Lord
Since writing the foregoing it is with much pleasure that I inform your Lordship that we have the finest seasons that has ever fallen, at this period of the year unknown to the Oldest inhabitant; from which we have a sight to look for abundant Crops! tho this may be flattering to us yet we have to fear Ministerial taxation.

Kupids's have finished Crop Pennants will in another Week. I have sent your Lordship the Stock and other Acc[oun]ts &c. You will have a Copy also of a Letter from Mr Armstrong lately come to hand to Mr Falconer. As soon as the Vessell arrives alluded to, I shall go on with the troughs and shall give her Rum which is reserved as mentiond in my former Letter, as the market for that article is more flattering than the one of this Country.

Mr Falconer My Lord died of the 5th of June which was occasioned by two large Carbuncles one on his Neck the other on his back, he is much lamented by all his acquaintances. He has left a Widow and two infant Daughters; Mr Francis Smith of Spanish Town and a relation of mine and myself are his Executors.

In conversation with that Gentleman we have agreed what balance may be due on the Commission Account; I am to mention to your Lordship will be made convenient and suitable as to the time of payment; to pay an Interest after the sum known.

The amount I wish to have ascertained and will thank your Lordship to give instructions to have the Account made up, as Executors are bound to return and Inventory of all the effects of the deceased into the Secretaries Office of this Island. The commission Acc[oun]t is made up for the years 1797 98, 99, 1800 in your Lordships Books; I require for the Years 1796, 1801, 1802, 1803 and part of 1804 of the Sugars shipped in the Thete, Aberdeen and Frances & Eliza, which your Lordship will do me the favor of transmitting when it may suit your leisure.

I am now to inform you precisely of the Shipments made of your Lordships Sugars as will appear in the memorandum annexed. The Power of Attorney mentioned in my former Letter to manumise the several Slaves is inclosed to be renewed if it should be your Lordships Will and Pleasure; the name of Alexr Falconer can be erased and mine substituted. Elenor McLean was also considered by your Lordship to be manumitted, there is room enough in the Power to add her name also.

The expence of a New Probit will be saved by your Lordship calling the Evidences to see your go over your Lordships name again with a Penn, and reacknowledge the same before the Mayor at the same time altering the dates.

The People to be manumitted will pay all expences; the Monies to be received from their Manumissions, I observe your Lordship mentiond in a Letter to Mr Falconer are to be vested in New Negroes, but your Lordship did not say on which of the properties they were to be placed; your Lordship will therefore instruct me on that head.

Mrs Fearon offers her respectfull Considerations to My Lord and My Lady with

My Lord

Yr Lordships most faithfull
& Ob^t hu^{ll} St

R W Fearon

SOURCE: Penrhyn MSS 1327, University of North Wales.

NOTES: Rowland Williams Fearon was the second cousin of both Alexander Falconer (C2) and his wife Sarah (Bryan) Falconer.

George Gordon Falconar to Henry Dundas, 1st Viscount Melville

My Lord,

Unauthorised by the honor of an acquaintance or a personal Introduction, and, relying not on strong facts for my justification, after a long liberty I take the liberty again to obtrude myself on Your Lordship's attention. Several years have elapsed since the decease of My Friend and Relation Lord Adam Gordon, who first offered me to your Lordships notice, and being impress'd with the strongest friendship for My Father the Hon^ll Captn Falconer of the Navy, and with a warm zeal for my welfare, recommended me in terms of panegyric far above my merits, to Your Lordship to be provided for in a situation under Government.

Your Lordship, thro' your Secretary Mr Garthshare, was pleas'd to return an answer very flattering to my hopes, on the presumption of which I ventured thro' the medium of Correspondence to read myself to Your Lordships remembrance. My representations owing perhaps to their miscarriage, or to their having met Your Lordships eye at a time when matters of more consequence engrossed your Mind, met with no return. The death of Lord Adam has deprived me of a steady Patron and one who would readilly vouch for my accuracy in this statement; and after an anxious expectation of some years, I thus find myself at least as far from the accomplishment of my views as ever. The Interval, however, has not been misapplied, and by the store of knowledge it has enabled me to lay up has, I hoped, capacitated me to fill with more abillity as employment I have uniformly aimed at, namely an Office under Government suited to my age, now 24, and to My Birth which, I beleive I need scarcely inform your Lordship, is that of a Gentleman. Sanctioned therfore by your Lordships encouragement, by additional competency, and by the circumstances of my never having been vexatiously importunate on the subject, I presume so far as to sollicit your Lordships assistance towards the completion of my wishes. These certainly derive no additional support from personal services, yet I am confident those of my Father which for very many years were faithfully & ably directed to the Service of his Country, and for which he lived not to receive the reward, will more than supply this difficiency in my claims. When last in the North I took the liberty of mentioning the outline of these particulars to M^r & Mrs Drummond of Dorumtruchty, who probably may have laid them before your Lordship. May I flatter myself that you will excuse the probaity of this address, which the very nature of it renders necessary and may I also be so sanguine as to indulge in the hopes that it will entitle me to the consideration due to one who has the Honor to subscribe himself

Respectfully
Your Lordships
Most Ob. Hum^ble Serv
Geo: Gordon: Falconar
Wimpole Street 73
Tuesd^y Eve

To the Right Hon^ll Lord Melville

SOURCE: Melville Muniments, GD51/1511/1, Scottish Record Office.

NOTES: George Gordon Falconar was the son of Capt. George Falconer of Phesdo (A14). This letter was written about 1804.

Anthony Adrian, Lord Inverurie (A17) to William, 6th Earl of Kintore (A16)

Benson Sunday Morning May 21st 1811

I get your letters the fifth Morning and
so will you mine

My Dear Father

I got yours on Saturday last, and was as you may suppose very sory to hear that My Mother still continued to be so dreadfully plagued with her eyes. I hope the delightful warm Weather which we have had here, will come to you and that she will get better. Much am I obliged for your further great indulgence and again repeat my thanks. Mr Judgson was of your opinion, that I should get a strong one. After I received yours on Saturday, Mr Judgson and I went to look at the Galloway, that he, Mr Shipperdson, Sir, I saw when M^r S was here—but the Farmer was not at home. Accordingly we went yesterday afternoon and found him at home. We asked him to show us the Galloway, brought it out, and I looked it all over. Then asked his price he said £30 and We however with a great deal of difficulty, got him down £2 which brought it to £28. As he had been offered that money for it a few weeks ago, would not sell it at that time for he thought he would get more money. Mr Judgson and I was with him almost an hour tried all we could to bring him down to £25 which we thought the real worth of the Pony, but no persuasion would do. And as M^r J thought we might be a long time of getting such a one, and as that sort of animal is so high priced here, we bought him. I am only sorry it is some pounds beyond the high mark you gave me. It shall certainly stimulate me to go on well. I can in reality sing now "I ride as good a Galloway" but now for the description of it. In the first place it is four rising five, stands 13½ hands high, and may grow an inch, a beautiful bay, four black legs, and not a spot of white about him, the only thing against his appearance is he is a *little* too long in his middle pace and thickish in the shoulder but very probable in a year the latter may get finer, he is a *famous* walker trots very well. I did not try his galoping. The Farmer who's name is King from whom he was bought told me he has rode 70 miles in a day and said he eat his dinner, at the end of it, as well, as he did his breakfast. The Innkeeper of the Castle Inn talks of buying little ponatowski and as he is a humane sort of Fellow hope he will buy it. We have had a most heavenly Spring in England, and never did I see a country in greater Verdure than this is a present, and it promises to be a plentiful harvest and great Fruit year, and hope you will have the same. There has been no particular news from Portugal and every lodg waiting for them. The Aberdeen Cronicle which I get regularly, is a great treat to me. I have got a song which Mr Shipperdson was so as [good] as send to me, from Durham, which should you like I dare say Mr Adam would favour me with a frank—the song is Howell Wood or the [Rake of] Yorkshire a very good one, made by Martin Ha[...] [Ship]perdson gave me a very kind invitation, which was if I ever passed through Durham, I should come and see him, and that if it was in the hunting season he would mount me, and if it were in the shorting, he would give me some very good. I told him that if ever he should be at Aberdeen You would be very glad to see him, and more especially you being an old fox hunter. I heard from Ally not very long ago and wrote Mary about a fortnight ago. I hope the Footman is arrived and that his appearance pleases you. I must now conclude As we are just going to begin to our morning's work & now with Love to You and My Mother I Ever Am

Your Most Affectionate Son
Inverury

I shall be anxious to hear about Manes eyes

SOURCE: Kintore Papers, Bundle 226, Aberdeen University Library.

Anthony Adrian, Lord Inverury (A17), to William, 6th Earl of Kintore (A16)

August 17th 1811

My Dear Father

I would have wrote you at Brechin, but as I was in my Mothers debt I thought it better to get her letter answered, and to write you the week after. We spent three *very* pleasant days with Sir Edward Littleton, he is a most Gentlemany old man, quite of the old school, and was exceedinly kind to us. Jeddesley Park is at the bottom of the Hetchford training hill a nice place but bare of trees. Sir Edward has got a Lady who lives with about 45 years old, she is rather of the last horse breed, not at all genteel, and affects to be very learned, talks about her Lovies her ducks &c. which belong to Sir Edward. Her name is Barker she was an Iron Masters daughter in Staffordshire. There were some odd stories about her, and him, but I dont think there is any truth in them. One of the stories was that she was his Mistress, another that she was privately married to him. Sir Edward has left off hunting some time ago. You know he had a famous track. And he told me he used to hunt twice a week, and that one reason they were out 28 days and killed 28 foxes his old Huntsman is stil with him, a famous old fellow and has a voice equall to Will Harrison. Sir E keeps three couples of Buck hounds Fair Maid, Countess, & Riot Woodman. Forrester, and Carver Sam gave me a *hallow* or two real vermin ones *very* like yours. We then on the fourth day after we had been at Sir Edwards, completed our journey and arrived at the Revd William Judgsons where we now have been nearly a month. *This* Mr Judgson is a real *honest very* good manners and *most* hospitable man. In short a man whom I know you would like very much. He has none of those pendantic airs that Clergymen sometimes have. I shall be not a little sorry when I leave Shropshire on *his* account and the Families near who have been most kind to me. Mr Judgson has got a capital house here, keeps 12 Cows, has a good deal of Land two horses, three grey-hounds, and 2 pointers. The horse that he rides himself is 27 years old as fresh as a four year old, and rides him continually fine shapt one vavy [?], & like a Gentleman's horse. He is Clergyman of Adderly in Shropshire, which living he got from Sir Corbet Corbet, whose place is a mile from this and where we have been a great deal since we came to Highfields. We dine there evry Sunday and stay all night besides being there during the week for a couple of days very often, especially this week because Lord Curzon Lady Bromeley and Miss Curzon were there. Sir Corbet and Lady Corbet quite thorough bred, have been a good deal abroad travelled through Switzerland, Germany and Italy. Lady C *a jewel* of a woman her a Lady Bromley ought to run in a curvielle. I mean they are so Gentlewomen like. The Curzons have been at Adderly-hall a week to day and leave it on Tuesday. We have been three days there this week and dine there to morrow again. Lady Corbet took me to Combermere Abbey, the seat of Sir Stapleton Cotton who is with our Army in Portugal. His Brother who is a Parson, and his Mother and Sister live at Combermere. We were there two days last week, and I rode over with Lady Corbet and Lord Curzon this week and asked us to come to day a day or two again before we left the country. Combermere is a beautiful place and has a field of wheat close to the house that covers 30 acres. William Cotton Sir Stapleton's Brother is a *very* fine fellow, endeed, thorough bred, a sporting Parson and does his duty on Church remarcably well. A great farmer has 300 acres in his own Land, a great many thorough bred horses and mares with foales famous sleds for them fenced with gauze in a particular which I dare say you have seen. He took me over to his farmer showed me all his horses, stud mares &c., among whom I had the honor of seeing two very great horses namely Dimond, that ran with Hambletonian and a horse called Castrel both of whom belong to him now. Dimond is a picture Castrel a fine horse but a great deal more lone. He also had a mare in foal which I liked much that he bought from Bell of Thirsk, whom I dare say you know well. I must now conclude as I am not up to Cross handed Germen. *My* Mr Judgson desires his best Respects And with my Love to you and Mamma I ever am My Dear Father

Your Ever Most Affectionate Son
Inverury

PS The Hospitable Land Lord has given the *Irot away* a summers Grass, he has now been out a month and will have another fortnight he is as *fat as a pig*. I like him evry bit as well as at first. He leaps over all the rails about here. We remain here until the middle of September and Mr Judgson senior has promised me a fortnight of good shooting. The harvest is well on here. I am glad to hear your Crops stock &c. are so good Wishing you good Weather to get them in. Poor Jim I am very sorry for him. I allways thought him a nice lad. It would be salt to poor Davison.

SOURCE: Kintore Papers, Bundle 226, Aberdeen University Library.

Peregrine Falconer (J8) to William Falconer (J9)

Baltimore, Oct[obe]^r 1st 1816

Dear William;

I am just in receipt of your esteemed favor of the 19th September, & now hasten to reply to it. The Letter communicating your misfortune I received, and immediately answered it fully; and am astonished to hear, that it never reached you. I will not recommend to you to change your residence because I do not know the advantages attaching your present abode but this far I do most possitively beg you will go this year, and view the Country about Huntsville, and notice it well before you determine [...] any thing. Having once seen that Country & its Wealth & its population, I feel pursuaded you will not remain on your Land in South Carolina longer than you can leave it, notwithstanding the advantages of navigation which South Carolina affords. You are under wrong impression when you say the expenses of sending your produce to market, will nearly absorb your Crop. How is it then that so many people or I may say planters, become rich in that Country, which you propose to Visit this fall? They all have the same mode of sending their produce to Market, which you seem to think costs them nearly all they make to send the balance to a place of disposal. My dear William, be assured you are mistaken in your ideas, as regards the expenses in the as the Western Country. There is no Country in earth in my opinion to have [...] advantages unite to render every industrious planter independent & rich. The tract of land which I bought near Huntsville, a few years ago cost me $3,900 & for which I have been pressed by many to take $12,000—this then is a further proof of the great increase of Wealth in that quarter. Go and see it yourself & I am satisfied you'll go there to live. My place is at your service to live on untill you can suit yourself permanently. You are now Comfortable and easy in life, and I recommend you by all means & every tie of Brotherly affection, not to meddle with a business which from the very nature of your past pursuits in life, you cannot have a knowledge of. Rest assured, there are now more in the merchandising business than can stand the present distress of the times, & there must & will be a great change in 12 Months. Many of my acquaintances wish they had never seen a piece of Goods, but for their own immediate use—depend on it, hundreds more will wish the same, as for myself

I wish I was now pursuing the same; you seem desirous of leaving [...] disgusted & tired with the present state of trade and [...] still worse no stoping place to present distresses can [...] be anticipated. Tell John I have rec[eive]ᵈ his Letter & will send him the articles wanted to Charleston.

> Remember me affectionately to y[ou]r fami[l]y In]
> haste		Your Aff: Bro:

							Pere: Falconer

John Falconar to Abraham Hall Falconar (J7)

						Fork Richland, So Ca: March 26, 1817

Dear Abram:

Your Letters I received this day on my way from Wm Falconars, with the painful newes of the death of our Dear Brother. After all his exertions to provide for his beloved Family, he is taken away & left five small children to travel through Life without a Father to Direct them. I know that it must have gave him great Heartfelt pain to have left them & his dear wife, unprotected, alas it is the will of Providence & we must submit. I contemplated in a few years we should all have got together once more, before we Left this world of trouble. I have been settling up my business this 4 months to go to the westward & am most ready & Wm is going with me & if he liks the cuntry he will moove out theare. Who is to settle up pore Brothers buisiness & see his family writed. Wm & my self will start from hear, about the 8th or 10th of April next for Huntsvill & we will consult Joshua & if our Deceased B[rother] has not willed it otherwise, I think it would be best for Joshua to under take to see to the affares, of our pore Brothers, as he knows more of this buisiness & well convinced he would do the best for the Interests, of our Brothers Family. If Joshua will go to Baltimore & it meets the Approbation of our Brothers Dear wife & family, I will stay & attend to his buisiness while he comes on to Baltimore. Say to our sister be cautious in whome she confids in to take care of the Interest of her Dear Little Family. Be asured none will have there Interest at Heart as much as Brother or a relation of Princeable known.

Wm F. was to start to Charleston to morrow morning & knows not the Death of Brother to sell his crop: to start on his return with me to H[unts]vill. Write us on the receipt this Huntsville Madison County Upper M[ississippi].

Say to Eliza I know not how to offer her any consolation for so repareable Loss.

					I am Dear Abram F. yours truly
						Jno Falconar

Make my best wishes	)
to your Mother & Family)

NOTES: John Falconar, son of William Falconar (J6), is considered one of the founders of Montgomery, Alabama. He refers to the death of his brother Peregrine (J8).

Abraham Hall Falconar (J7) to Jonathan Hall Falconar

Baltimore May 2, 1818

My dear Brother

Yours of the 28 April is this moment at hand. Enclosed you will find the Sum requested 100$. You hope that I will be pleased to see you find from those vices Which first Caused your having borrd [?]. You will know that I would & that it rest entirely with yourself to help me in the support of our mother & Sisters or be an incumbrance to them & myself and a nuisance to society. If you chose the last I do most solemnly avow that every tie of affection shall be broken and you no longer a Brother. I will treat you as one determined to destroy my peace and that of our Mother & Sisters and cut you off forever. I hope to God it will never be the case, but painful as it will be it must be done (& more particularly you) do not suppose that I have written the preceding with a wish to get rid of you. Oh no (if it is as you state) I would divide my last loaf with you and rejoice that it was in my power to administer to your wants in the smallest degree. You need not fear that I will not take you by the hand if you'r [...] I again repeat which I have so often done I will divide with you as long as you think yourself worth of it. I hope this will be last that will be written on the Subject [and] the past be buryed in oblivion. Mother has a cold that has confined her to the House and sometimes to her Bed all winter. She is now better tho' extremely weak. Ann is getting well. Kitty has been confined to her Bed & Room for 3 or 4 weeks. The rest are well. You will be in Balt°·in 5 days from this at last you know how anxiety we will be until we see you.

Yours sincerely
AHF

SOURCE: Falconar Papers, Maryland Historical Society.

Jonathan Hall Falconar to Abraham Hall Falconar (J7)

New Orleans March 23, 1819

Dear Brother,

Before this may reach you I shall perhaps be the bearer of the news of my own return. Nothing but the most cogent causes could induce me to the end. And as I shall return almost as the prodigal son, Brother, yet this is far more laudible than remaining here, neglectid because I am poor avoided because unfortunate. To you who so firmly holds the ties of brotherly affection I appeal. Nothing can be done here on one way or the other. Terror for the fear of absolute want haunts me hourly and only through the Friendship of W D Griffith I could not even now promise myself a passage home. Wretched in deed is the fate of the Captive but equally so is that of the Unfortunate.

I hear that Capt. Dieter is in the river. Should this be the fact I will not again trouble you with the appearance of my unfortunate countenance, but rely on his well established friendship for me make an attempt to go out with him.

Should I safely arrive I will be the bearer of the fact and should I leave here in the Buenos Ayres I will advise my Love to Catherine & the residue of the family & am yours

Jonathan

James Cantwell enjoys good health and is in high spirits. Sewell Reese has not written me since he got up to Alexa but I suppose he wrote by Mr. Ferguson who went on to Philadelphia in the ship Orleans.

SOURCE: Falconar Papers, Maryland Historical Society.

Jonathan Hall Falconar to Abraham Hall Falconar (J7)

New Orleans Mar. 24, 1819

Dr Br.
Yours of the 12th ulto. is at hand. I admit your excuse but the Girls I cannot find one for. I drew the draft on you when first by dire necessity and what will he think when it is returned unpaid. I did write you by the Casket to New York advising you of the affair & which vessel has since returned to this place. You offer me your House as a home but it is almost so far from me even to embrace a Brothers offers to that effect as to almost dispose me not to return but to linger but the summer out here a miserable existence.

Would to God that the Earthquake at LaGuayra[1] or efforts of the British in their attempt on Baltimore had caused my quieties. But he who holds the Rod of controul over the destinies of man may have had a favorable object in view for me. But here I am a desolate and unfortunate Being, surrounded by a multitude of the same cast. As I wrote you before "how the matter will end God only knows." But towards home I will attempt to go. Should I not be able to do so my latest Breath will be poured forth in wishes for my mothers, sisters, yours & your wifes Happiness. To the latter of whom & yourself I beg to subscribe sincerely your Bro

Jona. H. Falconar

PS. Before this reaches you you will have noted by my letters my full misery even with the aid of my draft on you for 150.

SOURCE: Falconar Papers, Maryland Historical Society.
NOTES: [1]La Guaira, now in Venezuela.

Anthony Adrian, 7th Earl of Kintore, (A17) to Capt. William Keith (A18)

Inglismaldie Wed. July 28th 1819

My dear William
Little indeed did I think that I should, so early as this, have to communicate to you the death of my ever to be lamented and much beloved Juliet. Such an awful sudden and severe blow cannot be expressed in writing, for in her my loss is unspeakable. She was every thing that was amiable, that was virtuous, and that was good, as one more sincerely and deeply interested *in my welfare* and not have been much do I know will you (from that you saw of her the little time you was with us) lament and sympathise with me the dreadful and irrepairable loss I have sustain'd, every action she had was from the heart and if she coud have done a Friends thing for anyone, was the first to do it; And as

I have said over and over again I might have gone the road all over and here have got one more after my oun heart. I am bearing up as well as I can under the calamity, but it is hard hard to do so. There indeed is her loss to her poor sisters, and to everyone else that knew her but what is it in comparison to *mine*. She had for some considerable time complained of severe Rheumatism and pains in her head, which the Medical people thought arose from Nothing else but nervousness and stomach complaints and the Medical assistance called in at Edin[burgh] so completely assured us of his firm belief that it arose entirely from the *stomach* and that she woud soon get better, that we treated it as such; we left Broadstone on Friday the 11th of June got to Inglismaldie Monday the 21st, and Friday the 9th of July poor Juliet was a corpse. She died of water in the head which is they say always incurable. This chiefly My Dear William is the Melancholy purport of this letter and much am I aware will both you and Jim Macdonald feel for me. I received your* the very day I believe she died dated St Johns and would have answered it sooner had I been able to do so. I regret much that Lord Melville has not performed his promise But I trust that next Mail or rather that the one that carries this out, will bring directions for your promotion. L[or]d Keith is exceedingly anxious about it and wrote to Sir Tho* Hamilton about you and Sir Cha* returned a very handsome reply to the L[or]d Keith saying he woud do all he could to further your promotion L[or]d Keith inclosed me his letter advising me also to write L[or]d Melville to remind him of his promise and I yesterday wrote much a letter that I think he will give now immediate orders for your promotion the first vacancy that may occur.

My plans at present are very *unfixed* but when they are so I will write you at present this afternoon I am going over to Keith Hall for a week to pay there a sorrowful visit, and after that return here where *Miss Kinny* and Robina have kndly agreed to stay with me until such time as my plans and affairs are settled. Present my sincere thanks and regards to Capt Rowley

As Ever Believe Me
My Dear William
Your Much Afflicted but
Affectionate Brother,

Kintore

SOURCE: Kintore Papers, Bundle 327, Aberdeen University Library.

William Keith (A18) to Anthony Adrian, 7th Earl of Kintore (A17)

H.M.S. Dartmouth
off Navarin
Octr 20th 1827

My dear Kintore
Ere this, you will have heard notwithstanding my first fear to the contrary that all's *right* about my promotion, having within the last week received my Commission & appointment to the Philomel, taking Ingestries place who is in her and removes to the Garnet. We have now assembled the French & Russian Squadrons & in an hours time we are to enter perforce the Port of Navarino where lies the Turkish, & Egyptian Fleet. We have some *work* before us, but I have not a shadow of doubt as to the result. Should anything happen to me, I have left a will, which Edward my servant will should he see the day out take home with my Writing case [etc.] or failing him Ingestrie or my friend Hamilton the Capt who I respect is at the moment absent at Malta & I have only *time* to say may *God bless you, & all.* Take care of Inverurys *education*

Remain - Your Most aff
Brother
WKeith

I hope I live to see every Turkish ship sunk
Nous Verrons

SOURCE: Kintore Papers, Bundle 327, Aberdeen University Library.
NOTES: The allied fleets defeated the Turkish fleet that day.

David Faulkner (M6) to Gilbert Faulkner (M8)

Barren County Ky
January the 15th 1832

Dear Brother
Your letter of the 25th of September came safe to hand the 10th of Last month and was glad to hear that you was well. We are all well as usual I have nothing on impo[r]tance to write to you. I received a letter from brother John Lately and they were all well and their corn were badly frostbitten in that country. You wish to know who Marcus mar[ri]ed. He mar[ri]ed betsy williams and he has moved [to] the Illinois this last fall and he lives close to Brother John.

You wish to know something about James Dale. I forgot when I wrote to you before to let you know Caty is dead. Died about 2 years ago. James Dale is mar[ri]ed again and is doing very well.

You wish to know particular[l]ly about Samuel and Jane. They are living close by his father and are doing Tollerably well, but he is very much in debt. I believe he treats her well. He is very much altered. He quit drinking so much and quit swearing. Uncle[1] and most of the family has joined the Cumberlands. Rest of brother Samuels Children are living with father and mother except the one that brother John had and he took him allong with him to the Illinois.

Your widow you mentioned is single yet but has some offers, William Abot for one. You said you forgot her name. It is Betsy Emery. The Sidox Maid Carmin is yet single but wants to mary.

You wish to know something about John. He has moved to Obine in Tenn. 2 year ago. I received a letter from him last sumer and he let me know he Lived full and fat. So I have give you all the information about all the Relations that I can conveniently so I have nothing more but Remaine your Brother and Friend

David Faulkner

PSB
Father and Mother is about as well as they generaly are. Mother dont see but she is as smart as she was when you was here but Father is very much broke since you was here. He can ride a litle about in the neighborhood but cant walk but very litle, to my house is about his farthest.

I should be glad for you to let us know in your next leter what you are folowing and how you are doin. Rite soon as you receive this. Rite to Glasgow.

DF

SOURCE: Typescript copy at Metcalfe County Library, Edmonton, Kentucky; original in possession of Juanita (Faulkner) Max.
NOTES: [1] Samuel Faulkner (M3).

William Andrew Falconer (J12) to Eliza (Levy) Falconer

Fort Smith May 10th 1848

My Dear Mother

Your letter of the 6th April last is before me and the contents noted. I am pleased to hear of Comegys safe return home with an improved state of health. I shall look for his letter with anxiety to know of him how pleased with the inhabitants celestial empire. Had I the means & circumstances otherwise permitted it is just a voyage as I would like to make. Time is money and the expences of such a pleasure trip would not exactly suit my finances. I should like to be inquisitive to ask how much Com. outfit, etc. was. I regret that he was disappointed in his expectations. He must not suffer himself to give way to dispondency, as the world is large and owes everyone a livelihood by proper exertions.

Bishop Freeman was prevented from visiting us when at Ft. Smith last winter owing to the severity of the weather. His coadjutor, the Rev. Mr. Townsend, calls frequently to see us and by whom I propose having the children christened, at as early a day as the convenience of the case will permit. We are in our new buildings but they are not as far finished as I wish them to be for the reception of a large congregation and Mr. Townsend wishes the Baptism to be a public one at which time a sermon will be delivered applicable to the case, at which time I wish to make a respectable show of manner & habits early inculcated. When I meet with Mr. T. I will shew him the Jewish Chronicle, as he always inquires when I last heard from you.

I will write to George as soon as leisure permits. This is a very busy time with me. I am now ploughing over my corn the 2nd time which is promising and if middle of May if seasonable, then safe from drought. My oats and vegetables are very promising as yet. This is the season, as you will know, with the farmer, of care, anxiety & labour, and may it please a Benificient Providence to crown our labours with Health, peace & plenty.

You wish to know if it is advisable that I should assume to the title of M. D. or the practice of medicine without study or a diploma. I am loth to speak of myself, in the way justice demands, least I might be looked upon in the light of a egotist. As I observed in a former letter that my practice had grown upon me imperceptibly. The little that I have heretofore done in this line, was from a sense of duty and philanthropy and from the success that I have had, I have obtained the right sort of a diploma. The confidence of my fellow citizens unasked for, and least expected in this case, but nevertheless I shall endeavor not to [...]gate to myself the practice is by no means agreeable to me. My past services have been entirely gratuitous and I made it known that I wanted no compensation, if for the future, they would not molest me. They would not hear to my relinquishment, but observed that I must obey their calls and that I should be paid my bill. Time to me is money which I cannot consistently withdraw from my family as heretofore and if they insist, they shall pay for the service rendered. There is no law to prevent me from practising or collecting my fees. Many of my warm friends advise me to quit the plough, turn my whole attention to the practice of medicine which will enable me to hire plough man. This advice I shall not take. My mode of practice so far has been fully sanctioned by the old school, doctors, and from whom I have obtained with their experience and my own judgment, collectively, a tolerable idea of the treatment of some, if not the most, of diseases peculiar to the South. Indeed I have not been an idle observer for near 16 years. I have some works on medicine, which gives me as far as my understanding leads, some information, beyond this I do not presume to go, and I am well aware of the length of time it takes to make one proficient in the study of medicine. The many technicalities, etc. I am not bound to follow all the preceipts of the old school. The books I wrote to Aunt Susan for I thought she might have on hand. If not, by no means do I wish her to purchase or obtain them from others. I know of no one leaving these parts for the cities, as it is past the season for merchants until they go on to make their fall purchases.

In compliance with your request, you will find the record of my family. Mary Ellen Falconer, daughter of John & Rebecca Titchenal, born near Clarksburgh, Harrison Co., Va., on the 23rd Augt. 1815. Hy Irvine Falconer, born near Choctaw Agency West, 2 Nov. 1836. Susan Eliza, born in Crawford Co., Ark., 25th Feb. 1838. Wm. Chas., born in Ditto, 14th Oct. 1839. Geo. Com., born in Ditto, 21st 1843. Jno. Perigrine born in Ditto, 21st May 1845. Susan Eliza, died 11th June 1841, aged 2 yrs. 3 mos. 14 ds.

I have not changed my mind as respects the keeping of a public house. As yet we are not fully prepared, but are progressing consistently with the means afforded. It affords no revenue as yet, but I still live in anticipation of having our plans perfected in a great while when, I flatter myself, that Mary & myself will make the establishment the most reputable, as well as the best furnished on the road, a distance covering over 200 miles. It will depend on us you know to make the stand one of profit. The newspapers are regularly received and welcome visitors.

Dear Mother, we are all falible creatures and I well know that I will never be able to return the one thousandth part of the favours that I and mine have received from you and my kind Aunt. Indeed I feel conscious of my neglect in not writing more frequently and must plead guilty, but I am not without a hope, knowing her generous disposition I believe I have a grateful Heart but the debt of gratitutde is greater than I shall ever be able to pay. You will please look over the many errors this sheet contains as it is written in haste. I have concluded it was better than not writing at all. I have been ploughing all day and the clock has struck 12. I must therefore be thinking how many hours I have to sleep till the clock strikes 4.

Through the mercies of providence we are all permitted to enjoy good health although Mary, as well as myself, have the burden of the season to bear. We will have 17 or 18 young calves this spring. The milking of the cows, butter making, housekeeping, cooking, etc. fall to her lot. With all we are thankful that our pecuniary affairs are not as they once were, but that our prospects are brightening, and as is generally the case our society courted, and coming into notice. When we needed aid, it was not hear to be obtained. Save me from my friends is an old saying, but often to the point. Write on receipt of this. I shall be anxious to hear from you in detail. The children all send their love, with their mother, remember me to old friends, and believe ever Your Affect. Son.

Wm. A. Falconer

I should like to hear that Com. is engaged in some profitable business or some prospect of it. If not, how he would like to spend the time in the South. Board would cost nothing and clothing a trifle.

SOURCE: Typescript copy at Fort Smith Public Library; original in Falconer papers at St. John's Episcopal Church, Fort Smith, Arkansas.

APPENDIX 4

Some Older Traditional Genealogies

[Falconers of Washington County, Pennsylvania]

The Falconers, of Washington Co., Pa. were from Queen Ann County, Maryland. Samuel F. the father of this family removed from Maryland to Virginia in company with his brother David (Berkely County), then he (Samuel) was married to Elizabeth Newkirk. Four children were born to them there, viz: Henry and Keziah, twins, Abram and Susanah. Then they removed to Washington Co., Penn., and settled on Pigeon Creek near Bentleysville, and had in their new residence the following children. Samuel and Betsy, twins, Margaret, Helen, Jane, Isaac, Ann, Reuben. The removal took place in the year of 1772. Samuel F. the elder was in Crawfords defeat together with his brother-in-law Isaac Newkirk and escaped without a wound. The other brother-in-law removed to Lancaster. Samuel F. Sr., died about 1787 of Small Pox, his wife in 1809 - August 15th. (The physician who attended Samuel Falconer was the same Dr. Knight who was tied to be burned with Crawford at Sandusky, but who succeeded in making his escape.)

Henry the eldest Son and Susannah and Samuel who was married to a Mr. Giffard all removed to Madison County, Ohio. They have all left children. Keziah married a VanHorn; she died in August 1830 near Rossville) and removed to Butler Co., Ohio. Betsy married to Moses Knox removed to Butler County, Ohio, and has left a large family. Margaret married a Nichols and their descendants still live in Washington County. Helen married a Ramsey. Jane never married. Ann married Geo. Smedley and they live on The Ohio River. Reuben with a large family lives in Belmont Co., O.

Abram married to Elizabeth Smedley in Washington County, where his widow who furnishes these facts still lives. They had six children, George, Hannah, Samuel, Christian, Lizzie, Rhody. Lizzie married to John Freeman who has rendered much service and kindness to my mother. David Brother the Father of Samuel the elder removed to Kentucky. Nancy Wilkins maternal Grandfather John Smedly came from Baden in Germany as also his wife. He was born in 1732, the same year as Washington, imigrated to Washington

County, Pennsylvania in 1750. They had seven children. The old man died in Flemingsburg, Ky., Mason County. Agnus, the Mother of Nancy Falconer died also in Mason Co. Sussannah married a Mr. Fitch and removed to Pike County, Ohio. Elizabeth who married Abram Falconer is now living. Agnes Smedly married to Samuel Wilkins in 1787. Samuel Wilkins father was named John, came from near London, came to America in easy circumstances. Abram Falconer, a son of my Fathers oldest brother Henry lives in Wauseon, Fulton Co., Ohio, and is an excellent christian gentleman.

PROVENANCE: In possession of Edna Falconer, of Tryon, North Carolina, widow of Robert Crawford Falconer (N25), in 1984. Her original was typed on the letterhead of the First National Bank of Hamilton, Ohio, of which Samuel D. Fitton, son-in-law of Cyrus Falconer (N13), was president, as late as 1919. Photocopies of this were provided by Edward Nicholas, who received copies from Don Fitton. We can infer, from information contained it, that it was written by Elizabeth (Falconer) Freeman (1805-1878) between 1854 and 1860 (probably closer to 1854) and sent to Cyrus Falconer, her first cousin.

Statement of my Family's Ancestry from David Lord Falconer down to present time.

W. H. Barnes.

Lord David Falconer of Monckton Scotland died leaving two heirs.
Lady Jane Falconer of Edinburg, Scotland only daughter and eldest daughter of David Lord Falconer lived an died a maiden lady came to the Colonies to see her brother returned to Scotland and died. Alexander Falconer only son of David Lord Falconer came to the colonies and settled at Williamsport, Maryland.
George W. Falconer
John B. Falconer died on a voyage to Scotland. His widow married a Mr. Knight. She had one child by Mr. John Falconer Mrs. Susan Hoffman, wife of Dr. Hoffman of Baltimore, Maryland.
Susan Falconer married a Mr. Wilson, George Wilson's father, she had Alexander, Geo., Amy and May as children.
Charity Falconer married Elisha Barnes, she had two children, Nancy Barnes and Alexandra Barnes. My fathers father. Elisha Barnes and wife died four days apart of Typhus fever. Uncle Washington took Father and reared him to manhood.
John Falconer, Decatur, Ill.
Ann Falconer,   "   "
Elza Falconer,   "   "
Enoch Falconer   "   "
Mary Falconer   "   "
Susan Hoffman had half brother and sisters. Wm. Snyder of Baltimore, Maryland married one of her half sisters.
Geo. Wilson, Catholic Priest.

PROVENANCE: In possession of Harry W. Falconer II, Rossford, Ohio. Typescript by Harry W. Falconer, accompanying carbon copy of letter, dated 15 Feb. 1917, to Mrs. George LeaSure, of Delphos, Ohio, acknowledging this genealogy. W. H. Barnes was grandson of Elisha and Charity (Falconer) Barnes and was apparently an ancestor of Mrs. Leasure. This appears to have been originally written after 1840 but before 1880.

[Genealogical notes of John M. Faulkner, ca.1896]

John Faulkner, born in Scotland in the year [*blank*] came to America in the year [*blank*] and settled in Virginia, where he died in the year [*blank*] David Faulkner, son of John Faulkner, born in the year [*blank*] in Scotland or Virginia and died in Virginia in the year [*blank*] Mark Faulkner, son of David Faulkner, born in Virginia in the year [*blank*] moved to Kentucky where he died in Madison County in the year [*blank*] Alexandra Faulkner, son of Mark Faulkner, born in Virginia in the year 1756, moved to Kentucky near where Richmond now stands in thence to where Lebanon now stands, thence in 1812 moved to near where Knob Lick in Metcalf Co. now is, and died in 1834.

Our Grand Father Alexandra Faulkner married Margaret Conyers about the year of 1782. That is about all in information I am able to give with certainty. Our Grand Mother Margarett Conyers Faulkner died early in July 1836. She was the first person that I ever Witnessed the death of. It is vivid in my memory yet, though sixty years ago.

David Faulkner

SOURCE: "Bible Records of the Faulkner Family of Marion County, Kentucky," *Kentucky Ancestors* 4 (1966): 60. The second paragraph was written by David Faulkner (1828-1904) (M21) to John M. Faulkner (M29) (1848-1941). The first paragraph was perhaps written by the latter. It was kept in Gilbert Faulkner's (M8) family Bible, owned in 1966 by Marilyn (Faulkner) Burchett, of Louisville, Kentucky.

[Fragment of draft of letter from Nelson Faulkner]

We were chrisened by an oald local methodist preacher by the name of higgins

carried your father & Mrs. Nelson carried me & Mrs. Nelson insisted on having us called Elisha Nelson so we got his full name & your father took his father's name

I think it very strange indeed that my brother never toald their children their father's name well most I suppose You are my brother reubens son Falconer yor grandfathers name was Elisha Falconer. He was the father of 15 children 10 sons & 5 daughters thair names was Reubin, John, Mahlon, Ralph James, Elisha, Nelson Eaden William H Alfred & Joshua the names of the daughters Mariah betsy Sarah Susan & Ellin

PROVENANCE: Fragment of draft of outgoing letter from Nelson Faulkner (1815-1896) (L8) to his nephew, probably Mortimer Falconer, undated, but probably between 1890 and 1896, in possession of Richard Arthur Popp, of Bradenton, Florida, and Chautauqua, New York. Communicated by George E. Spaulding, Jr., of Grand Rapids, Michigan.

APPENDIX 5

Notes on the Succession to the Halkerton Peerage

The title Lord Falconer of Halkerton, in the peerage of Scotland, was granted to Sir Alexander Falconer in 1646, with designation to his heirs-male whatsoever. Since the death in 1966 of Arthur George Keith-Falconer, 10th Earl of Kintore and 12th Lord Falconer of Halkerton, the only arms matriculated in the Lyon Court have been those of Peter Serrell Falconer (Q12) and John Philip Egerton Falconer (Q11). This genealogy, however, has demonstrated that many senior lines exist, all of them American.

The successful claimant to this title must demonstrate, with sufficient evidence, that he is the senior male heir. This means that all male lines senior to him must be proven to be extinct. Sir Crispin Agnew of Lochnaw, Bt., Slains Pursuivant of Arms in the Lyon Court, argues for the jurisdiction of the Lyon Court to determine succession claims to titles.[1] Once the claimant has successfully petitioned the Lyon Court for a matriculation of arms, he may assume the title. He would then need to petition the Committee of Privileges of the House of Lords, as the Lordship Falconer of Halkerton was left off the roll of 1842 by mistake. Should the heir be a citizen of the United States, he might have to become a British citizen in order to fully implement his prerogatives as a peer. Although the United States Constitution forbids its citizens to accept the grant of a title of nobility from another government, it does not deny the right to inherit one.

This genealogy has identified one senior male heir, Henry Irving Falconer, but the quality of evidence documenting the extinction of legitimate senior lines is wanting. Hector M'Kechnie's classic essay on Scottish genealogy points out the need for proof of relationship and proof of identity for each link in the chain.[2] Many kinds are admissible, but evidence close to the event, such as a baptismal or marriage register, is better than an indirect piece of evidence.

The difficulty with this case is the number of male heirs needed to be proven extinct.

For the closer relatives of the 12th Lord, we can reasonably assume the failure of male issue. Adrian Wentworth Keith-Falconer (1888-1959) was identified in his obituary as heir-presumptive to the title, but he died without issue. Going back one generation further to identify heirs, we see that William Keith-Falconer (A18) (1799-1846) had one son, Adrian William Keith-Falconer (1837-1887), who seems to have had no issue, although here the only evidence I have found to indicate that the latter had no issue is that his cousin administered his estate. As William's brother Alexander Keith-Falconer (1798-1821) died unmarried, it is necessary to go back two generations to that of Anthony Adrian, 7th Lord (A15), to find a brother.

Only one of his brothers left issue. Alexander (1754-1826) (B1) lived in Groningen, Holland, and had four sons who reached adulthood. Two of them married, but none had surviving children, according to research compiled and certified in 1970 by the Centraal Bureau voor Genealogie in The Hague. Here it would be desirable to have further legal evidence showing failure of male issue.

Alexander's father, William, 6th Lord (A12), had three younger brothers. David, a London merchant, had three sons, but none survived to adulthood, as can be shown by his will. John went to Jamaica, where he married and had eight sons. George, the youngest brother, had a son and heir, George Gordon Falconar (1780-1856), whose widow left no apparent heirs, according to her East India Company pension.

Of the eight sons born to John in Jamaica, only two (Alexander and Shickle) can be proven by legal evidence, in this case by wills, to have left no surviving legitimate male issue. Another son (Thomas Keith) can be proven to have had illegitimate children. If we are liberal in allowing some evidence, we might be able to account for each of the lives of the remaining brothers, John, David, William, George, and Nairn Lindsay, but whether John, William, and George are the same Falconers who appear in Jamaican probate records is uncertain and, in any case, they fail to reveal heirs. Following a search of all the Church of England parish registers in Jamaica, all relevant deeds, wills, Chancery Court proceedings, and other records, we can feel confident that only illegitimate male lines survived on that island. Searches in the slave registration records of various other colonies in the Caribbean, including Demarara, Trinidad, St. Lucia, Grenada, Dominica, Tobago, Antigua, and St. Kitts, made in the years before 1820,[3] reveal no Falconers. There does not appear to be any trace of them in the United States. In short, it appears possible that the legitimate line of this brother is extinct, even if the quality of proof is less than acceptable. It is doubtful, however, that full proof of extinction of this line can ever be found.

In the next generation back, David, 4th Lord (A10) (1681-1751) had two younger brothers. Alexander Falconer alias Hay of Delgaty (1682-1745) was married to the Countess of Erroll and had no children. George Falconar (1685-1743), however, left a line which ended with Maj. Cyril Falconar-Stewart of Feddal (F6) (1884-1962), whose only son died in World War II. The father of the 4th Lord was the younger of two surviving sons, so it is necessary to go back another generation, to that of the first Lord.

The 1st Lord's next-born brother, Sir John Falconer (G1) (d. 1670), had three surviving sons, the eldest of which was David (H1) (c.1632-1713), the Quaker merchant. David's eldest son John (H2) (1677-1730) had two sons, John (1709-1783) and David (1710-1752), the identity of whom can be proved by a letter and, through his will, to have left no children. John's case is not so clear, however, as there seems to be an unidentified David Falconer mentioned in the wills of John's maternal cousins. The evidence for this branch, consisting mostly of Prerogative Court of Canterbury wills and Quaker records, is not as conclusive as one would like.

The identity of David's second surviving son, Gilbert (J1) (1686-1736) is solidly proved through Quaker records, court cases, and private letters. His two sons, Abraham and John, both left children. Both Abraham's two sons, Gilbert (J4) and Abraham (J5), had children, but Gilbert can be shown to have left no surviving male issue. Abraham's children included two sons, Jonathan Hall Falconar (1790-1865), who never married, and Abraham Hall Falconar (J7) (1793-c.1848), who had three sons. The eldest, John Henry (J11) (1819-1889), had a son by his first wife, Gilbert Henry, born 1852, living 1859, but who was not living with either parent in 1870 and who was not mentioned in his father's will. Abraham H. Falconar's second son, A. Smith Falconar (1829-1886), can be shown not to have had children. The third son, Edward White Falconar (born 1831), is obscure, apparently living in Baltimore up to 1870. Nevertheless, the French Spoliation case that the heirs of Abraham Falconar (J5) pursued for many years indicate that, by 1886, the sole survivor of the family was John Henry Falconar (J11), and John H. Falconar's will mentioned only his second wife. Barring the possibility that Edward White Falconar had children, which seems unlikely, in order to find a surviving male line we must go back to the second son of the immigrant, John Falconar (J3). With relatively little trouble we can document the senior male line of descent from John down to Henry Irving Falconer.

Perhaps it is reasonable to assume that, after almost thirty years of dormancy, if the only descendants of this family to have matriculated arms or appeared in *Debrett's Peerage* are the Falconers of Gloucestershire, descendants of more senior male lines are extinct, at least in Great Britain. However, while one cannot rule out the possibility, for example, that one of the legitimate Jamaican-born Falconers went to some obscure colony or foreign possession and established a family, the conclusion that I must make, after many years of research, is that the line of Gilbert Falconar (J1) is most likely the senior surviving male line of this family.

For the benefit of foreign nationals, the Lyon Court does grant arms to Scottish ancestors, if the applicant is the senior male descendant. Although I have identified senior male descendants of the immigrants Gilbert Falconar (J1), Alexander Falconar (K1), and Patrick Falconar (W1), the evidence for those lines of descent may be problematic. Alexander's eldest son Alexander (K2) had two sons, the elder of whom died without issue, but the only proof for the paternity of those sons is indirect and comes from a private record written many years after the sons had died. For Patrick (W1), the problem is that the senior male line runs down to twin sons of Patrick (W4), Harvey (W7) and James (W8). The line from James descends without any major problems, but that of Harvey presents several. Although I believe that Harvey's male line is extinct, proof would need to be found to document it.

Unfortunately, the lack of satisfactory evidence documenting every step of the complex succession will probably render it virtually impossible for a future claimant to petition for the title successfully. The succession to the Lordship Falconer of Halkerton will remain dormant for many years, possibly forever. One of the purposes of this book has been to attempt to document the succession to the title. In this attempt I have failed. Although I have identified the probable heir, I have not discovered evidence which would incontrovertibly document the extinction of all intervening senior lines. Perhaps the publication of this genealogy will inspire others to continue to search for this proof. It is, after all, a first attempt to untangle a complex web of relationships, relying on sources in archives in five countries.

NOTES

[1] Sir Crispin Agnew of Lochnaw, Bt., "Peerage and Baronetcy Claims in the Lyon Court: Reassertion of Jurisdiction," *Journal of the Law Society of Scotland* 26 (Aug. 1981): 311-315.

[2] Hector M'Kechnie, "The Pursuit of Pedigree," *Juridical Review* 40 (1928): 205-233; 304-340.

[3] Slave Registration Lists, T71/397, T71/505, T71/376, T71/267, T71/347, T71/461, T71/494, T71/244, T71/253, PRO.

APPENDIX 6

Note on Sources

This genealogy has been compiled from a great many sources. Much of it, especially the more recent generations, has been contributed by the descendants themselves. Other information was written or compiled by family members in the past, including genealogical registers of children and marriages kept in Bibles. Some relevant family papers have been deposited at public archives. Other genealogical records of branches of the family have appeared in print, both in monograph and periodical form. Perhaps other papers remain undiscovered, although I have tried to be exhaustive in my search.

The genealogy of the Lords Falconer of Halkerton appeared in print for the first time in George Crawfurd, *The Peerage of Scotland* (Edinburgh: for the author by George Stewart, 1716). This was followed by Sir Robert Douglas, *The Peerage of Scotland* (1767), and John Philip Wood's revision of Douglas, (Edinburgh: G. Ramsay, 1813). William Ruxton Fraser's *History of the Parish and Burgh of Laurencekirk* (Edinburgh: William Blackwood & Sons, 1888) included a vastly improved genealogy. Sir James Balfour Paul, *The Scots Peerage* (Edinburgh: Davis Douglas, 1908-1919) was extensively based on research in original records and remains a model of scholarship. "Copy of a Manuscript Entitled 'A Genealogie of the Barons of the Mearns of Late Memory Descending Lineally unto the Year of God 1578'," in *Miscellany of the Third Spalding Club* (Aberdeen: for the Third Spalding Club, 1950), an old manuscript in the Barclay-Allardice Papers, included a genealogy of the Falconers with new details.

The publications of the Scottish clubs, especially the Scottish Record Society, Spalding Club, Bannatyne Club, and the Scottish History Society, have been extremely useful. But even more valuable are the series of legal and administrative records published by the government: the *Registrum Magni Sigilli Regum Scotorum: The Register of the Great Seal of Scotland*, containing charters; the *Register of the Privy Council*, with legal cases; the *Decennial Indexes to the Services of Heirs in Scotland*; the *Rotuli Scaccarii Regum*

Scotorum: The Exchequer Rolls of Scotland; and other series. The Scottish Record Office has published very useful indexes to the Particular and General Register of Sasines and the the Register of Deeds, which, even as indexes alone, are probably the most valuable source for the genealogies of landowning families in the seventeenth century.

Burke's Landed Gentry (1952 ed.) provided almost all the information on the Falconars of Carlowrie and Falconar-Stewarts. The distinguished line of English Falconers appeared in the 1844 edition of *Burke's*, as well in entries in the *Dictionary of National Biography*, and pamphlets written and published by Thomas Falconer.

The American branches have seen little in print. Harry Wright Newman, *Mareen Duvall of Middle Plantation* (Washington: 1952) includes a good record of Alexander Falconar (K1) and his family. An article by Ralph D. Smyth, "Mr. Patrick Falconer of Newark, N. J., and His Descendants." *New England Historical and Genealogical Register* 60 (Jan. 1906): 21-23, and Alvan Talcott, *Families of Early Guilford, Connecticut*, Jacquelyn L. Ricker, ed. (Baltimore: Genealogical Pub. Co., 1984), cover Patrick Falconar (W1) and some of his descendants.

Any extensive American genealogy will make use of the many local histories and biographical collections published in the late 19th and early 20th centuries, as I have. The genealogies of some branches of the Falconers have appeared more recently, for example, in Elizabeth Dill Hartline, *A Jolliff Family History* (Anna, Ill.: the author, 1982), *History of Adams County, Iowa* (n.p.: Adams County History Book Committee, 1984), *Barry County, Michigan History 1985* (Hastings, Mich.: Barry County Book Committee, 1985), and *History of Stone County, Missouri* (Marionville, Mo.: Stone County Historical Society, 1989). Much recent genealogical source material has been published in recent years, for example, compilations of gravestone inscriptions, newspaper items, and marriage records, which have eased research on people in the twentieth century and the Western states.

Published material facilitates searching, but it is limited, so any serious attempt at a full genealogy must rely on original records. The archives where I spent the most time was the Scottish Record Office (SRO), in Edinburgh, with its marvelous collection of government records as well as deposits of family papers. I made use of the following series of records: the various commissariots (class numbers CC3, CC8, CC16, CC20); the Register of Deeds (RD2, RD3, RD3); the Particular and General Registers of Sasines (RS7, RS28, RS29,); the Register of the Privy Seal (PS3); the Register of the Great Seal (C2); the General Register of Inhibitions (DI57); the Court of Session Processes (CS18, CS138, CS181, CS236, CS271); the Chancery (C22); Register of Tailzies (RT1); and the Calendar of Charters (RH6). The Scottish Record Office holds the Old Parish Registers, although I viewed microfilm of them through the Family History Centers of the Church of Jesus Christ of Latter-Day Saints. I did look at the records of the Aberdeen Monthly Meeting of Friends. Also useful were the Airlie Muniments (GD16); the Barclay-Allardice Muniments; and the John C. Brodie Papers (GD247).

The Kintore Papers at the University of Aberdeen Library were, of course, extremely useful for the families of the fourth and later Lords and for the family in the seventeenth century. I would like to express my thanks here to Lord Kintore for permission to make copies of his papers. We must regret the loss of the family's muniments caused by the 1679 fire in Halkerton Castle, which would have let much light on the early history of the family. The Delvine Papers at the National Library of Scotland contain much correspondence from the fifth and sixth Lords, and other items in its well cataloged collection were of interest Finally, the Edinburgh District Archives holds the fascinating papers of Sir John Falconar (G2), in its Moses Bundles.

London repositories with material on the Falconers include the Public Record Office (PRO) in Chancery Lane, with the series of the Chancery (C10), Prerogative Court of Canterbury Wills (PROB11), Inland Revenue Office (IR1), and State Papers, Domestic Series (SP29); the Public Record Office in Kew, with records of the Admiralty (ADM11, ADM25) and Slave Registration Lists (T71); the India Office Library and Records, where I looked at Haileybury College Petitions (J), Personal records, etc. (O), and Regular and Elders Widows' Funds (L) and Regular Widow's Fund Minutes (L); the Friends Historical Library, with the Devonshire House Monthly Meeting register, Barclay of Bury Hill Papers, Box Meeting Manuscripts, London Two-Weeks Meeting minutes, Peel Monthly Meeting minutes, and the Digest of Births, Marriages, and Deaths, of the Society of Friends Meeting in Scotland. I did further research at the Guildhall Library and the Society of Genealogists, with its many valuable indexes, manuscripts, and books, and at Somerset House.

Research on the Jamaican branch was based on parish registers and vital records, mostly on microfilm held by the Family History Library of the Church of Jesus Christ of Latter-Day Saints, and on records at the Island Record Office (deeds and wills) and Jamaica Archives in Spanish Town (Chancery records, letters of administration, inventories, parish registers). I also found useful material at the Institute of Jamaica in Kingston.

I was able to visit over thirty county court houses in the course of this research, in Maryland, Pennsylvania, New York, Ohio, Indiana, Kentucky, Illinois, Michigan, and Missouri. Research in other local archives was done for me in Alabama, Texas, Arkansas, Nebraska, and California. The National Archives has the Civil War pension files, and the French Spoliation Cases, as well as the manuscript Federal census schedules on microfilm, which was the source for the skeleton on which most of the American genealogy is based. The Maryland State Archives holds many valuable records; other state archives which I visited include those of Pennsylvania, Indiana, and Illinois. Personal papers which include Falconer material are held by the Maryland Historical Society (Falconar Papers); Tennessee State Library (Mary Elizabeth Stay Buckner Papers); and the Historical Society of Pennsylvania.

As well as the libraries of some of the preceding institutions, I visited the following local libraries with collections or rare books useful for my search, although this is not a complete list: Erie, Pa., Public Library, Washington, Pa., Public Library, Medina, Ohio, Public Library, Illinois State Historical Library, Ohio Historical Society, Hamilton, Ohio, Public Library, Kentucky Historical Society, Adair County, Ky., Public Library, Metcalfe County, Ky., Public Library, Green County, Ky., Public Library, Filson Club, Indiana State Library, Centralia, Ill., Public Library, Mt. Vernon, Ill., Public Library, Decatur, Ill., Public Library, Brookfield, Mo., Public Library; Chicago Public Library; Burton Historical Collection, Detroit Public Library; Library of Michigan, New York State Archives. They hold early directories, collections of gravestone inscriptions, newspaper indexes, and genealogies.

Much of the library research was done at the Allen County Public Library in Fort Wayne, Indiana, with its large genealogical collection. Compilations of gravestone inscriptions, county marriage records, and city directories held by this library enabled many lines to be traced past 1920. Through the University of Michigan-Flint Library, I ordered, on inter-library loan, microfilms of local newspapers, which contained obituaries of descendants, without which it would be impossible to locate living descendants.

During the course of this project, new digital sources appeared and proved very useful. It would have been impossible to trace so many lines to the present without the Social Security Death Benefits Index, on CD-ROM, which lists most Americans for whom death benefits were paid who died after 1962. The rapid expanding capabilities of Internet has allowed me to search the Kentucky Death Record Index, for example, and to communicate information over the network. Another new source is a nationwide telephone directory on CD-ROM.

In order to limit the number of endnotes, which would overwhelm the reader if referenced to every fact, I have omitted references to the Social Security Death Benefits Index. Where the death date (primarily 1962-1989) of a person consists of a month and year, and the birth date is known, the source is this database. A birth date consisting of a month and year prior to 1900 can be assumed to be based on information in the 1900 census. Typically a birth date given as "about 1841" means that the date was derived from the age of the person at the first census after his or her birth. Unless otherwise noted, death dates with burial places mentioned indicate that the information comes from the tombstone, either taken by me directly or from published compilations.

The search for descendants of the immigrants to America began with the framework of decennial census schedules, which are now indexed from 1790 to 1860. Partial indexes exists for 1880 and 1910, while the indexes for the 1900 and 1920 censuses are complete. The vital task of tracing the migrations of descendants would have been impossible without these indexes. Once the locations were identified, I consulted publications concerning those areas, and in many cases, the local records themselves and inspected gravestones on site. The final step was to look for likely descendants in local directories and write to them. The compact disc and online telephone directories which began to appear towards the end of the research proved to be the best method for locating living descendants.

Index